DIRECTORY OF TOWN PLANS IN BRITAIN

Southern England	London
Central England and Wales	Northern England and Scotland

Published by the Automobile Association
Fanum House, Basingstoke, Hants RG21 2EA

Produced by the Publications
Division of the Automobile
Association.

Maps in this book can be found in
Thomson Local Directories.

Published by the Automobile
Association, Fanum House,
Basingstoke, Hampshire RG21 2EA.

Printed and bound by Graficromo
SA, Spain.

ISBN 0 86145 278X

TO USE THIS BOOK

This book is divided into four colour-coded sections:

SOUTHERN ENGLAND ■   LONDON ■
CENTRAL ENGLAND AND WALES   ■
NORTHERN ENGLAND AND SCOTLAND   ■

Look for the town or airport you want in the complete
index below. Use the colour coding to find the right
section, then turn to the page number shown.

INDEX OF TOWNS AND AIRPORTS

Contents

Route Planning Maps   IV – XII
Southern England
London
Central England and Wales
Northern England and Scotland

See opposite for how to use this book. For easy reference, a regional list of contents is also given at the start of each section, showing town and airport plans with page numbers and a regional location map.

INDEX OF TOWNS AND AIRPORTS

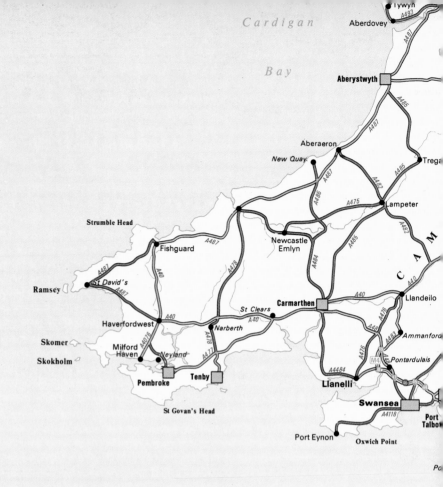

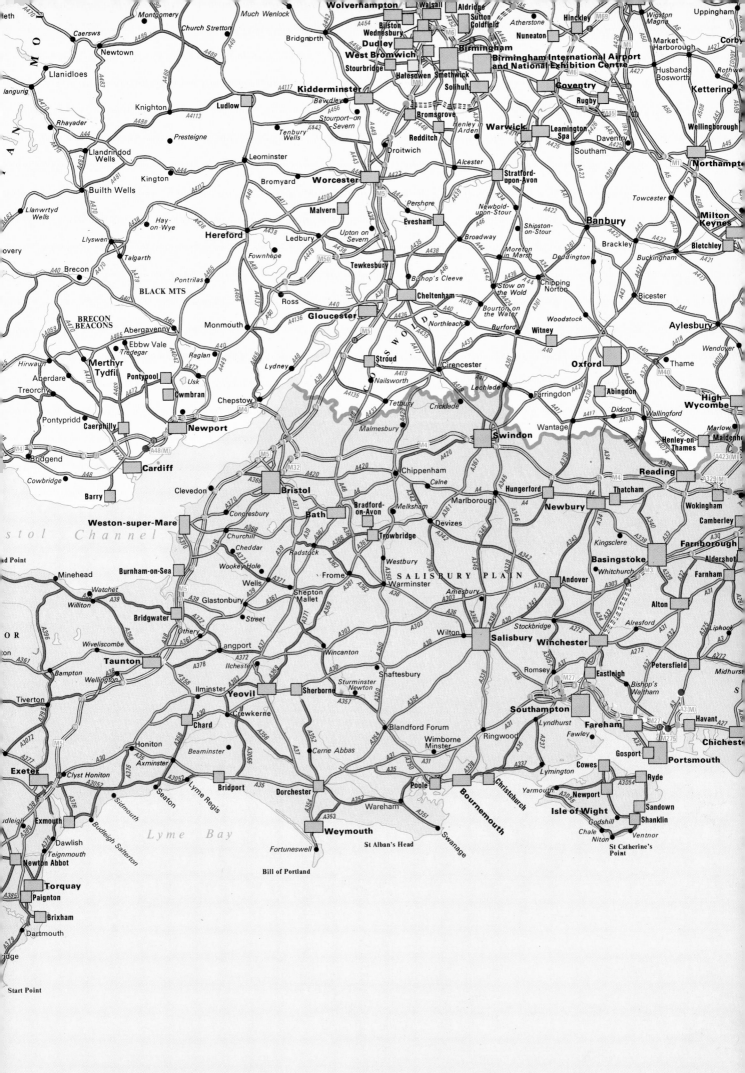

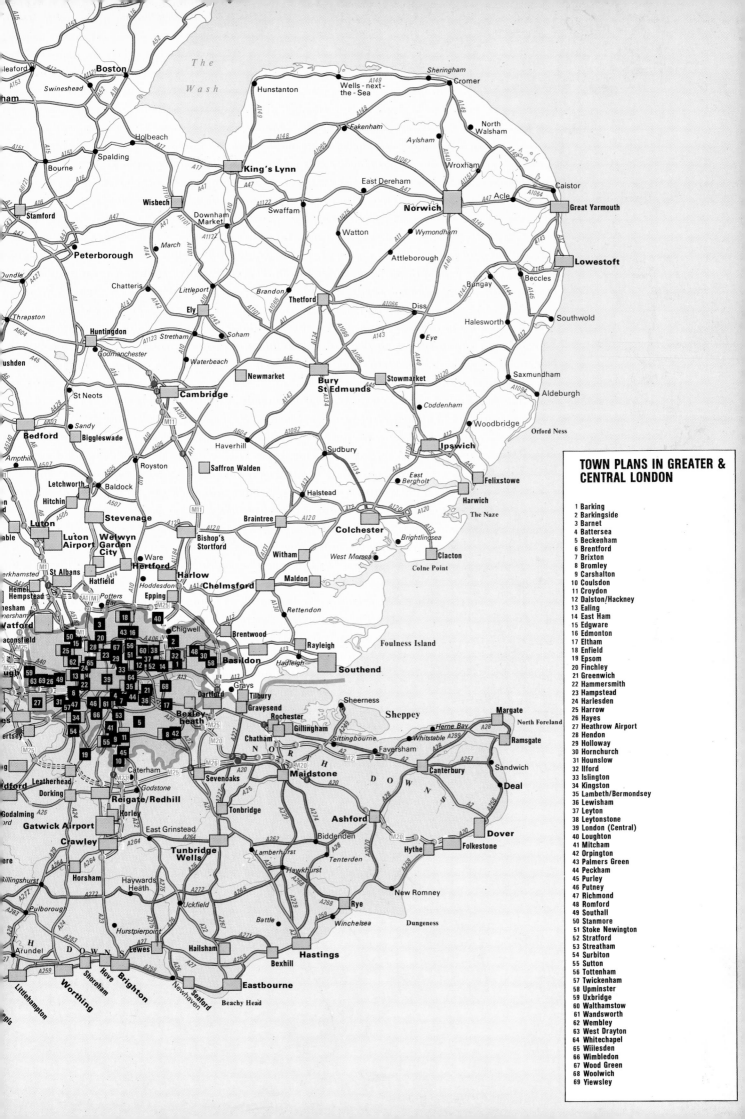

**TOWN PLANS IN GREATER &
CENTRAL LONDON**

1 Barking
2 Barkingside
3 Barnet
4 Battersea
5 Beckenham
6 Brentford
7 Brixton
8 Bromley
9 Carshalton
10 Coulsdon
11 Croydon
12 Dalston/Hackney
13 Ealing
14 East Ham
15 Edgware
16 Edmonton
17 Eltham
18 Enfield
19 Epsom
20 Finchley
21 Greenwich
22 Hammersmith
23 Hampstead
24 Harlesden
25 Harrow
26 Hayes
27 Heathrow Airport
28 Hendon
29 Holloway
30 Hornchurch
31 Hounslow
32 Ilford
33 Islington
34 Kingston
35 Lambeth/Bermondsey
36 Lewisham
37 Leyton
38 Leytonstone
39 London (Central)
40 Loughton
41 Mitcham
42 Orpington
43 Palmers Green
44 Peckham
45 Purley
46 Putney
47 Richmond
48 Romford
49 Southall
50 Stanmore
51 Stoke Newington
52 Stratford
53 Streatham
54 Surbiton
55 Sutton
56 Tottenham
57 Twickenham
58 Upminster
59 Uxbridge
60 Walthamstow
61 Wandsworth
62 Wembley
63 West Drayton
64 Whitechapel
65 Willesden
66 Wimbledon
67 Wood Green
68 Woolwich
69 Yiewsley

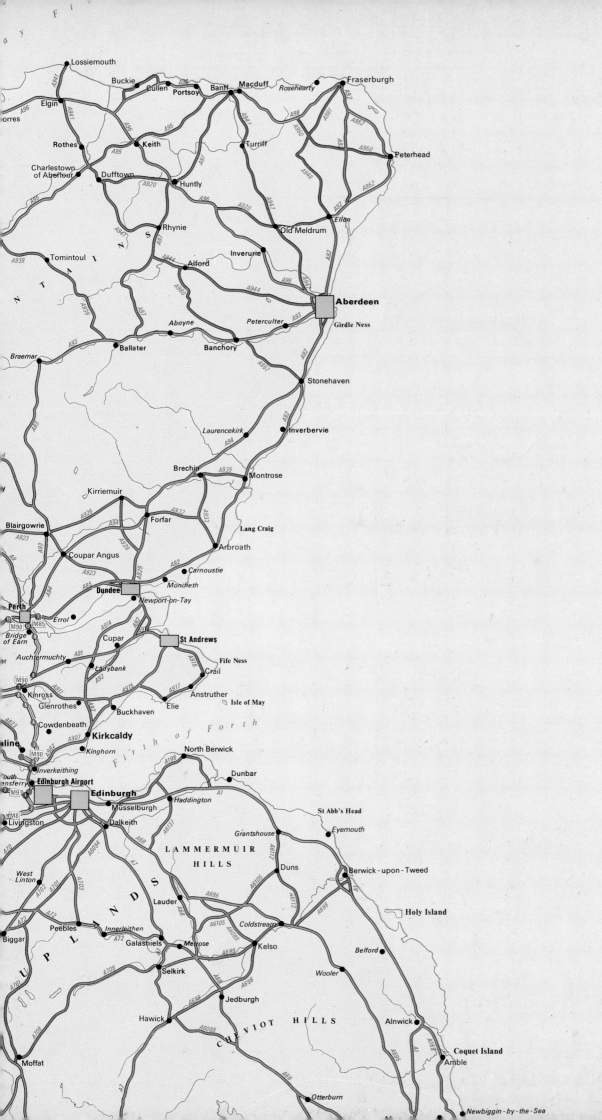

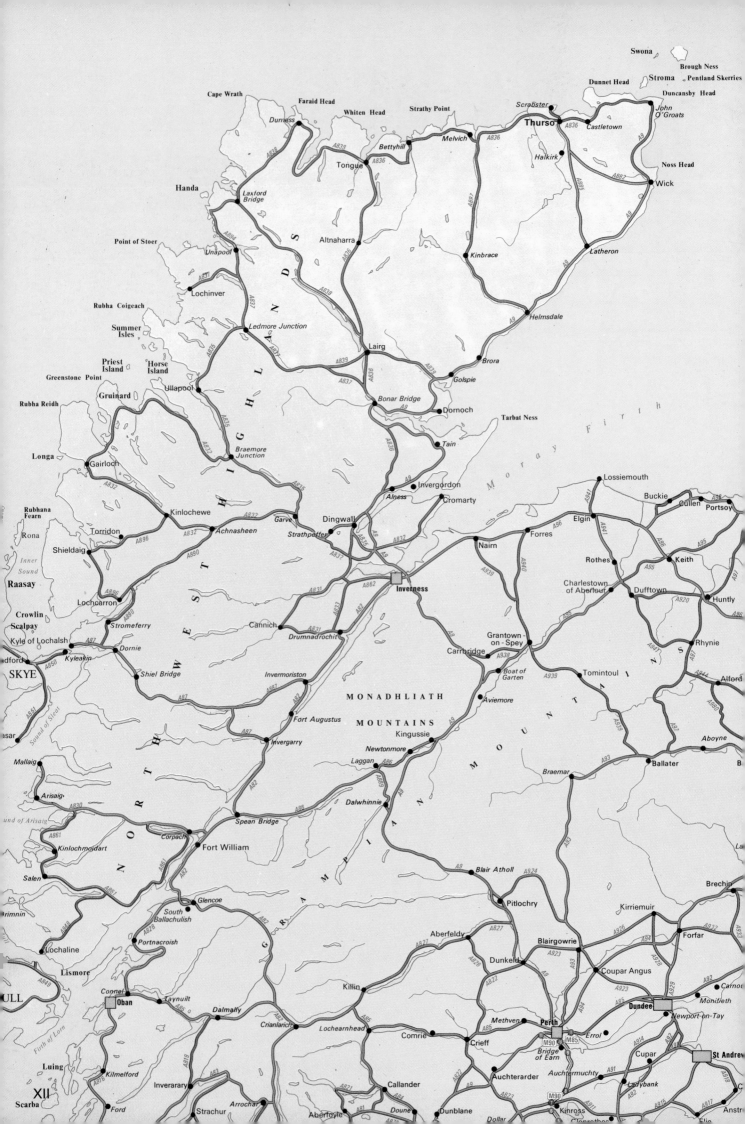

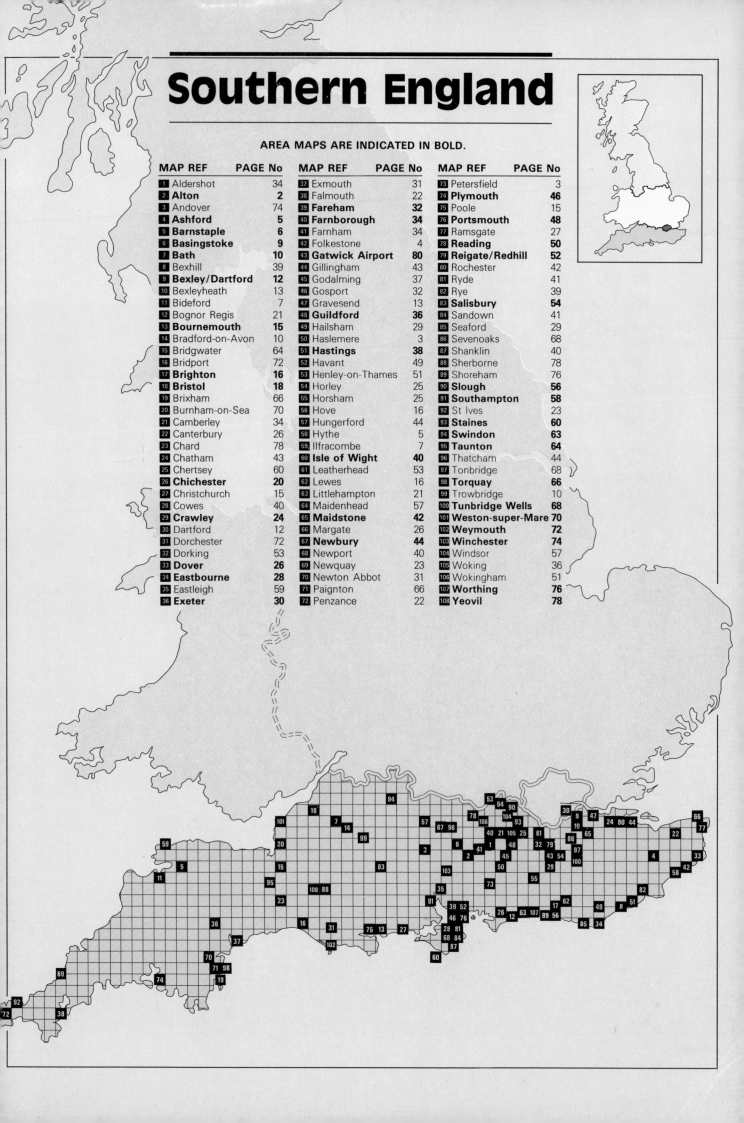

Southern England

AREA MAPS ARE INDICATED IN BOLD.

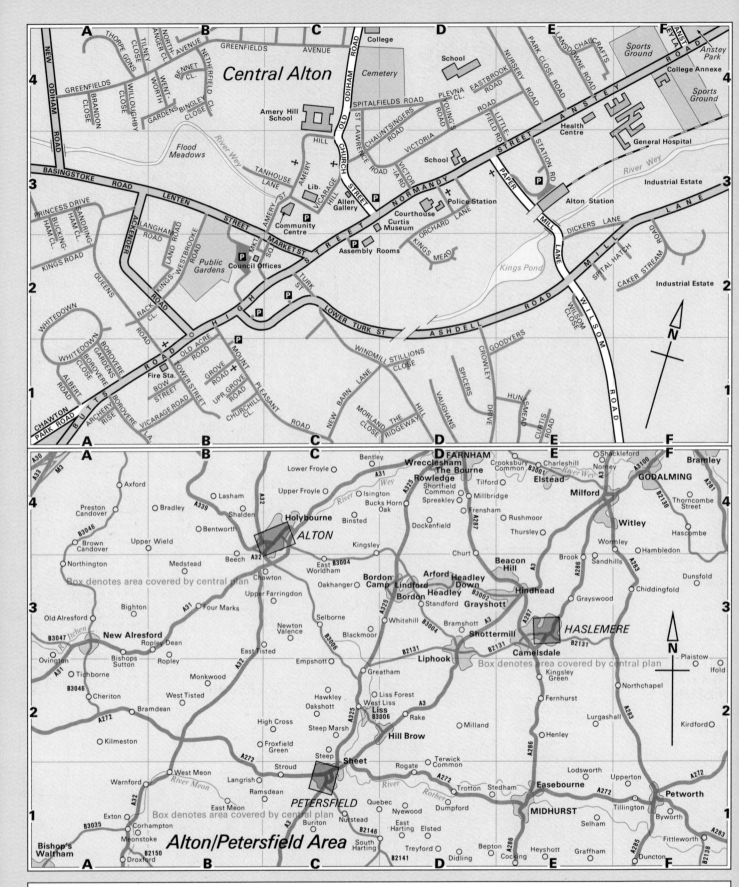

Alton

Locally grown hops and water from the Wey Spring were once the mainstay of the brewers of Alton, a town whose origins stretch back to Roman times. Modern Alton has two attractive parks and a fine modern sports centre which is in great demand from both the locals and those in the surrounding area. The Curtis Museum, founded in 1855, contains local records and natural history.

Petersfield's focal point is The Square, a centuries-old market place, and the town also boasts a number of late 16th-century buildings, dating from before its days as a coaching route staging post. This attractive market town's amenities include the Festival Hall, for opera, concerts and plays, a modern sports centre, and the Heath, which lies to the south and is good for boating, fishing and rambling.

Haslemere in summer re-echoes to the sounds of medieval and Elizabethan music — the speciality of the annual Haslemere Festival, which is one of the oldest in the country. Once dependent on its iron, cloth and leather industries, this is now a popular residential area, and a number of well-preserved old buildings survive, particularly around the High Street. For local organisations, the town's best feature is possibly its Educational Museum, which they use extensively for its archaeology, geology, zoology, and art.

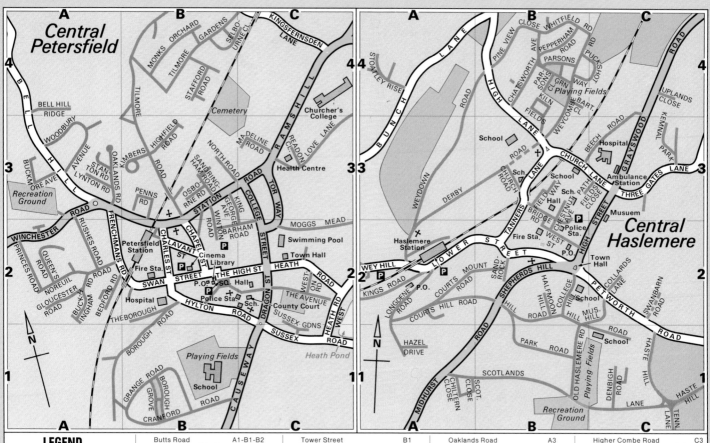

Central Petersfield / **Central Haslemere**

LEGEND

Town Plan
- AA recommended route
- Restricted roads
- Other roads
- Buildings of interest — Court
- Car parks — P
- Parks and open spaces

Area Plan
- A roads
- B roads
- Locations — Froxford ○
- Urban area

Street Index with Grid Reference

Alton

Ackender Road	A3-A2-B2
Albert Road	A1
Amery Hill	C3
Amery Street	C3
Anstey Lane	F4
Anstey Road	E3-E4-F4
Archery Rise	A1
Ashdell Road	D2-E2
Basingstoke Road	A3
Bennet Close	B4
Bingley Close	B4
Borovere Close	A1
Borovere Gardens	A1
Borovere Lane	A1-B1
Bow Street	B1
Brandon Close	A4
Buckingham Close	A3-A2

Butts Road	A1-B1-B2
Caker Stream Road	F2-F3
Chalcrafts	E4
Chauntsingers Road	C3-D3-D4
Chawton Park Road	A1
Church Street	C3
Churchill Close	B1
Crowley Drive	D2-D1
Curtis Road	C1
Dickers Lane	E2-E3-F3
Eastbrook Road	D4-E4
Goodyers	D1-E1-E2
Greenfields Avenue	A4-B4-C4
Grove Road	B1
High Street	B2-C2-C3
Huntsmead	E1
Kings Road	A2
Kingsland Road	B2-B3
Kings Mead	D2
Lansdowne Road	E4
Langham Road	A3-B3-B2
Lenten Street	B3-B2-C3
Littlefield Road	D4-E4-E3
Lower Turk Street	C2-D2
Market Square	B2-C2
Market Street	C3-C2
Mill Lane	E2-F2-F3
Morland Close	C1-D1
Mount Pleasant Road	B2-B1-C1
Netherfield Close	B4
New Barn Lane	C1-D1
New Odiham Road	A4-A3
Normandy Street	C3-D3-E3-E4
Northanger Close	B4
Nursery Road	D4-E4
Old Acre Road	B1-B2
Old Odiham Road	C3-C4
Orchard Lane	D2-D3
Paper Mill Lane	D3-E3-E2
Park Close Road	E4
Plevna Close	D4
Princess Drive	A3
Queens Road	A2-B2-B1
Rack Close	A2-B2
St Lawrence Road	C4-C3-D3
Sandringham Close	A3
Spicers	D1
Spitalfields Road	C4-D4
Spital Hatch	E2-F2
Station Road	E3
Stillions Close	D1
Tanhouse Lane	B3-C3
The Ridgeway	D1
Thorpe Gardens	A4
Tilney Close	A4

Tower Street	B1
Turk Street	C2
Upper Grove Road	B1
Vaughans	D1
Vicarage Hill	C3
Vicarage Road	A1-B1
Victoria Road	D3-D4-E4
Wentworth Gardens	B4-A4
Westbrooke Road	B2-B3
Whitedown	A2-A1
Willoughby Close	A4
Wilsom Close	E2
Wilsom Road	E2-E1-F1
Windmill Hill	C2-C1-D1
Young's Road	D4

Petersfield

Barham Road	B2-C2
Bedford Road	A2
Bell Hill	A4-A3
Bell Hill Ridge	A4
Borough Grove	B1
Borough Road	A1-B1-B2
Buckingham Road	A2
Bucksmore Avenue	A3
Causeway	B1-C1
Chapel Street	B2
Charles Street	B2
College Street	C3-C2
Cranford Road	B1
Dragon Street	C2
Frenchmans Road	A3-A2-B2
Gloucester Road	A2
Grange Road	B1
Heath Road	C2
Heath Road West	C1-C2
Highfield Road	B3
High Street	B2-C2
Hylton Road	B2-C2-C1
Kimbers	B3
King George Avenue	B3-C3-B2-C2
Kingsfernsden Lane	C4
Lavant Street	B2
Love Lane	C3
Lynton Road	A3
Madeline Road	C3
Moggs Mead	C2
Monks Orchard	B4
Noreuil Road	A2
North Road	B3

Oaklands Road	A3
Osborne Road	B3
Penns Road	B3
Princes Road	A2
Queen's Road	A2
Ramshill	C3-C4
Readon Close	C3
Rushes Road	A3-A2
Sandringham Road	B3
Selbourne Close	B4-C4
Stafford Road	B4
Stanton Road	A3
Station Road	B2-B3-C3
Sussex Gardens	C2-C1
Sussex Road	C2-C1
Swan Street	B2
The Avenue	C2
The Borough	B2
The Square	B2
Tilmore Gardens	B4-C4
Tilmore Road	B4-B3
Tor Way	C3-C2
Weston Road	C2
Winchester Road	A2-A3
Winton Road	B3-B2
Woodbury Avenue	A3

Haslemere

Bartholomew Close	B4
Beech Road	B3-C3-C4
Bridge Road	B3
Bunch Lane	A3-A4-B4
Chatsworth Avenue	B4
Chestnut Avenue	B2-B3
Church Lane	B3-C3
Church Road	B3
Chiltern Close	A1
Collards Lane	C2
College Hill	B2
Courts Hill Road	A2-B2
Courts Mount Road	A2-B2
Denbigh Road	C1
Derby Road	A2-A3-B3
Field Way	B3
Grayswood Road	C3-C4
Great Gates Lane	C3
Halfmoon Hill	B2
Haste Hill	C1
Hazel Drive	A1
High Lane	B4-B3
High Street	B2-C2-C3

Higher Combe Road	C3
Hill Road	B2-B1-C1
Kemnal Park	C3
Kiln Fields	B4-B3
Kings Road	A2
Longdene Road	A1-A2
Lower Street	A2-B2
Midhurst Road	A1-B1-B2
Museum Hill	B2-C2
Old Haslemere Road	B1
Park Road	B2-B1
Parsons Close	B4
Parsons Green	B4
Path Fields Close	B3-C3
Pepperham Road	B4
Petworth Road	B2-C2-C3
Pine View Close	B4
Puckshot Way	B4-C4
Sandrock Street	B2
Scotland Close	A1
Scotlands Lane	A1-B1-C1
Shawbarn Road	C2
Shepherds Hill	B2
Stoatley Rise	A4
Tanners Lane	B2-B3
Tennysons Lane	C1
Uplands Close	C4
West Road	B2
Wey Hill	A2
Weycombe Road	B3-B4-C4
Weydown Road	A2-A3-A4-B4
Whitfield Road	B4

PETERSFIELD
Butser Ancient Farm, reconstructed to a prehistoric design, is one of the attractions of Queen Elizabeth Country Park — a serene area of countryside covering over 1,000 acres, which lies just three miles south of Petersfield on the A3.

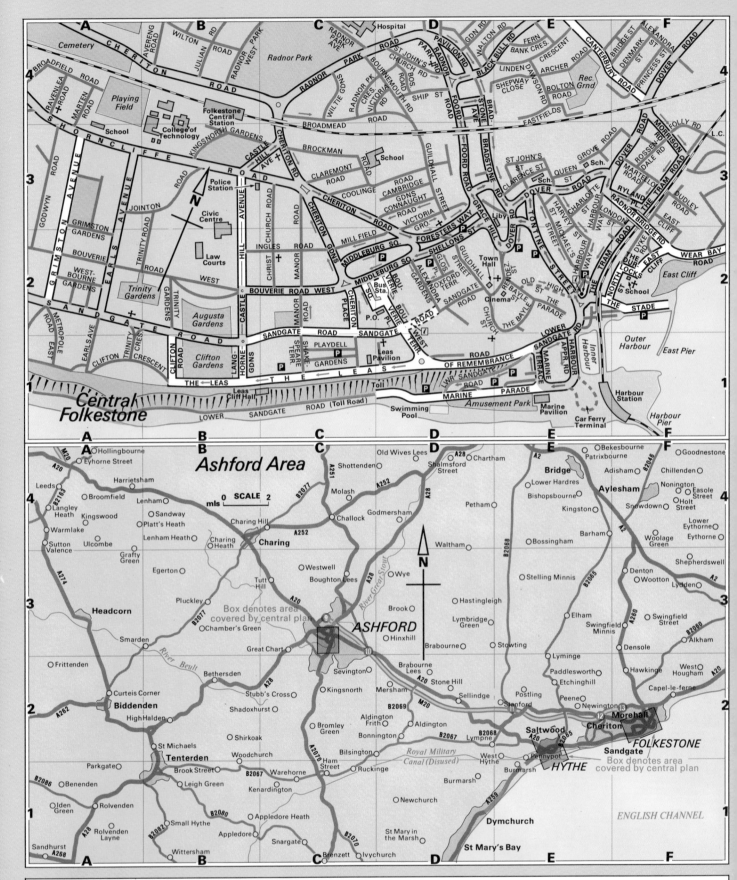

Ashford

One of Britain's more unusual museums is that of the Intelligence Corps at Ashford's Templar Barracks — but those who only wish to investigate the secrets of this thriving market town might prefer to visit the Local History Museum or the Ashford Heritage Centre, which traces its bygones through to Roman times. Now an important industrial and commercial centre with good shops, Ashford also enjoys the facilities of the Stour Sports Centre and the greenery of Victoria Park.

Folkestone is a town of contrasts — between the gleaming modern ferries carrying holidaymakers to France and Belgium, and the narrow cobbled streets and old buildings which lie around its harbour. Flanked by 15th-century Martello towers on the clifftop is the Leas promenade, site of the Leas Cliff Hall (a major entertainment centre), and the New Metropolitan Arts Centre, which stages regular exhibitions. Visitors to the Leas can go by road or by lift — an unusual water-driven model has been in operation here since the 19th century.

Hythe Main terminus for the Romney, Hythe and Dymchurch Light Railway, which runs along the coast from here to Dungeness, Hythe is a peaceful, unspoiled resort. One of the Cinque Ports, its places of interest include the 17th-century Old Manor House and a parish church which has several 13th-century features.

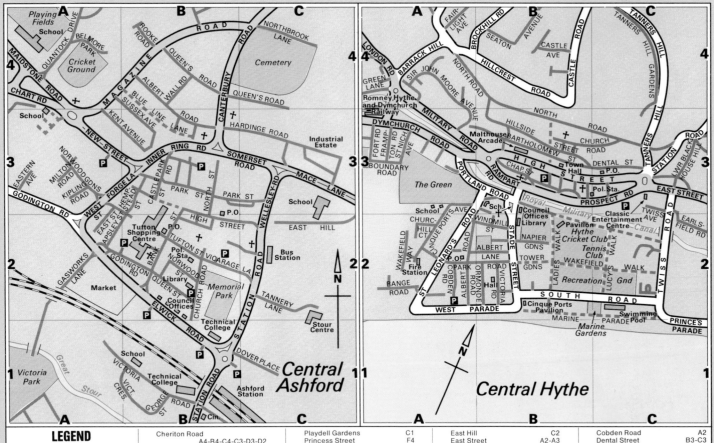

Central Ashford

Central Hythe

LEGEND

Town Plan
- AA recommended route
- Restricted roads
- Other roads
- Buildings of interest — Library
- Car parks — P
- Parks and open spaces
- One way streets

Area Plan
- A roads
- B roads
- Locations — Bawdip ○
- Urban area

Street Index

Folkestone

Alexandra Gardens	D2
Alexandra Street	F4
Archer Road	E4
Avereng Road	B4
Bayle Street	E2
Black Bull Road	D4-E4
Bolton Road	E4
Boscombe Road	D4
Bournemouth Road	C4-D4
Bouverie Place	D2
Bouverie Road West	A2-B2-C2
Bouverie Square	C2-D2
Bradstone Avenue	D3-D4
Bradstone Road	D3-E3
Bridge Street	F4
Broadfield Road	A4
Broadmead Road	C4-D4
Brockman Road	C3
Cambridge Gardens	D3
Canterbury Road	E4-F4
Castle Hill Avenue	B1-B2-B3-C3
Charlotte Street	E3
Cheriton Gardens	C2-C3
Cheriton Place	C2
Cheriton Road	A4-B4-C4-C3-D3-D2
Christ Church Road	C2-C3
Church Street	D2-E2
Claremont Road	C3
Clarence Street	E3
Clifton Crescent	A1-B1
Clifton Road	B1
Connaught Road	D3
Coolinge Road	C3-D3
Dawson Road	E4
Denmark Street	F4
Dover Road	E2-E3-F3-F4
Dudley Road	F3
Dyke Road	F2
Earls Avenue	A1-A2-A3
East Cliff	F2-F3
Eastfields	E4
Fern Bank Crescent	E4
Folly Road	F3
Foord Road	D3-D4
Foresters Way	D2-D3
Garden Road	D4
Gloucester Place	D2
Godwyn Road	A2-A3
Grace Hill	D3-D2-E2-E3
Grimston Avenue	A2-A3
Grimston Gardens	A2-A3
Grove Road	E3-F3
Guildhall Street	D3-D2
Harbour Approach Road	E1
Harbour Way	E2-E3
Harvey Street	E2-E3
Ingles Road	B2-C2
Jointon Road	A3-B3
Julian Road	B4
Kingsnorth Gardens	B3-C3
Langhorne Gardens	B1
Linden Crescent	E4
London Street	E3-F3
Lower Sandgate Road	A1-B1-C1-D1-E1-E2
Manor Road	C1-C3
Marine Parade	D1-E1
Marine Terrace	E1
Martello Road	F3
Marten Road	A3-A4
Metropole Road East	A1-A2
Middleburg Square	C2-D2
Mill Field	C2-D2
Morrison Road	F3-F4
North Street	E2-F2
Old High Street	E2
Oxford Terrace	D2
Pavilion Road	D4

Playdell Gardens	C1
Princess Street	F4
Queen Street	E3
Radnor Bridge Road	E3-F3-F2
Radnor Park Avenue	C4
Radnor Park Crescent	C4-D4
Radnor Park Road	C4-D4
Radnor Park West	B4-C4
Ravenlea Road	A4
Rendezvous Street	D2-E2
Road of Remembrance	D1-E1
Rossendale Road	F3
Ryland Place	F3
St John's Church Road	D4
St Johns Street	E3
St Michael's Street	E2-E3
Sandgate Road	A2-B2-B1-C1-C2-D2-D1
Shakespeare Terrace	D1
Shellons Street	D2-D3
Shepway Close	D4-E4
Ship Street	D4
Shorncliffe Road	A4-A3-B3-C3
The Bayle	E2
The Durlocks	F2
The Leas	B1-C1-D1
The Parade	E2
The Stade	E2-F2
The Tram Road	E2-F2-F3
Tontine Street	E2-E3
Trinity Crescent	A1-A2
Trinity Gardens	B2
Trinity Road	A2-B2-B3
Victoria Grove	D2-D3
Victoria Road	C4-D4
Walton Road	D4-E4
Wear Bay Road	F2
Westbourne Gardens	A2
West Terrace	D1-D2
Wiltie Gardens	C4
Wilton Road	B4

Ashford

Albert Road	B4-B3
Apsley Street	A2-B2
Bank Street	B2-B3
Belmore Park	A4
Blue Line Lane	B4-B3
Canterbury Road	B3-B4-C4
Castle Street	B3
Chart Road	A4
Church Road	B2
Dover Place	B1-C1
Eastern Avenue	A3
East Hill	C2
East Street	A2-A3
Elwick Road	B2-B1
Forge Lane	A3-B3
Gasworks Lane	A2
George Street	B1
Godington Road	A3-A2-B2
Hardinge Road	B3-C3
Hempstead Street	B3
High Street	B3-B2-C2
Inner Ring Road	B2
Kent Avenue	A3-B3
Kipling Road	A3
Mace Lane	C3
Magazine Road	A3-A4-B4-C4
Maidstone Road	A4
Milton Road	A3
New Street	A3-B3
Northbrook Lane	C4
North Street	B2-B3
Norwood Gardens	A3
Norwood Street	B2
Park Road	B3
Park Street	B3-C3
Quantock Drive	A4
Queen's Road	B4-C4
Queen Street	B2
Rooke Road	B4
Somerset Road	B3-C3
Station Road	B1-C1-C2
Sussex Avenue	A4-B4-B3
Tannery Lane	C2
Tufton Street	B2
Vicarage Lane	B2-C2
Victoria Crescent	A1-B1
Victoria Road	A1-B1
Wall Road	B4
Wellesley Road	C2-C3
West Street	A2-A3

Hythe

Albert Lane	A2-B2
Albert Road	A2
Barrack Hill	A4
Bartholomew Street	B3
Boundary Road	A3
Brockhill Road	A4-B4
Castle Avenue	B4
Castle Road	B4
Chapel Street	B3
Churchill Court	A2
Church Road	B3-C3
Cinque Ports Avenue	A2-A3
Cobden Road	A2
Dental Street	B3-C3
Dymchurch Road	A3
Earlsfield Road	C3-C2
East Street	C3
Fairlight Avenue	A4
Fort Road	A3
Frampton Road	A3
Green Lane	A4
High Street	B3-C3
Hillcrest Road	B4
Hillside Street	B3
Ladies Walk (footpath)	B2
London Road	A4
Lower Blackhouse Hill	C3
Lucy's Walk (footpath)	C2
Marine Parade	B2-C2
Military Road	A4-A3-B3
Napier Gardens	B2
North Road	A4-B4-B3-C3
Ormonde Road	B2
Park Road	A2-B2
Portland Road	A3-B3
Prospect Road	B3-C3
Prince's Parade	C2-C1
Rampart Road	B3
Range Road	A2
St Leonard's Road	A2-A3-B3
St Nicholas Avenue	A3
Seaton Avenue	B4
Sir John Moore Avenue	A4-A3
South Road	B2-C2
Stade Street	B2-B3
Station Road	C3
Tanners Hill	C3-C4
Tanners Hill Gardens	C4
Tower Gardens	B2
Twiss Avenue	C3
Twiss Road	C2-C3
Victoria Road	B2
Wakefield Walk (footpath)	B2-C2
Wakefield Way	A2
West Parade	A2-B2
Windmill Street	A2-B2

HYTHE
Running from Hythe to Dungeness Lighthouse, the 15-inch-gauge Romney, Hythe and Dymchurch Railway, with its 11 diminutive steam locomotives and one diesel, proudly claims the title of The Smallest Public Railway in the World.

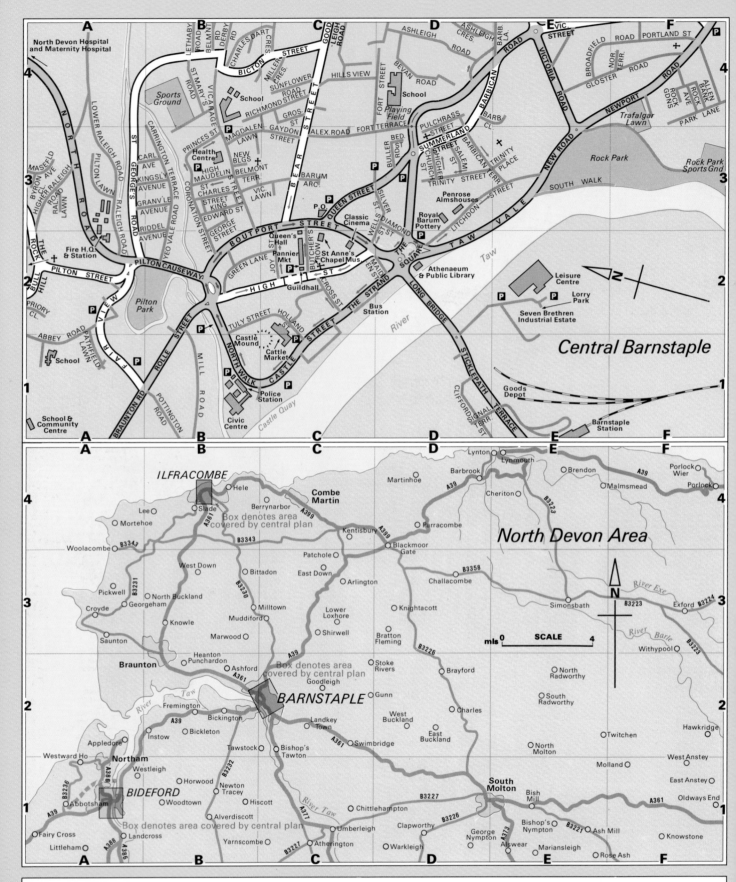

Barnstaple

During the 18th century the wool trade created a prosperity in Barnstaple to which the town's elegant Georgian buildings testify. Queen Anne's Walk, a colonnade where merchants conducted business, is both a fine example of this period and a reminder that Barnstaple has always been a trading centre. This tradition continues as today it is one of the area's busiest market towns. Of the many picturesque shopping streets Butchers Row is particularly attractive.

Ilfracombe This is North Devon's well-established "Queen of the Coast". Originally a fishing harbour, Ilfracombe evolved in the 19th century – when enterprise was all – into one of the typical seaside resorts that mushroomed all over England. Here, terraces of large Victorian hotels and houses follow the contours of the hills down to the harbour and a welter of little coves. The town is also the main departure point for Lundy Island.

Bideford South-west of Barnstaple and Ilfracombe, Bideford too has always made its living by trading and the sea. Sir Richard Grenville, a Bideford man famous for his fight against the Spaniards in the Azores, gained a charter for the town from Elizabeth I and it prospered as a port and shipbuilding centre until the 18th century. A nautical air still pervades Bideford and the long, tree-lined quay is popular.

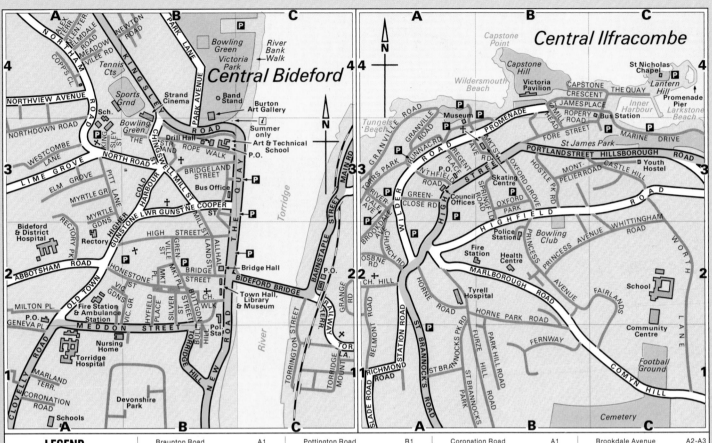

Central Bideford

Central Ilfracombe

LEGEND

Town Plan

AA recommended route
Restricted roads
Other roads
Buildings of interest — Station
Car parks — P
Parks and open spaces
One way streets

Area Plan

A roads
B roads
Locations — Patchole ○
Urban area

Street Index with Grid Reference

Barnstaple

Abbey Road	A1-A2
Alexandra Road	C3
Allen Bank	F4
Ashleigh Crescent	D4-E4
Ashleigh Road	D4
Barbican Close	D4-E4
Barbican Lane	E4
Barbican Road	D4-E4
Barbican Terrace	D3-E3
Barum Arcade	C3
Bear Street	C3-C4
Bedford Street	D3
Belmont Road	B4
Belmont Terrace	B3-C3
Bevan Road	D4
Bicton Street	B4-C4
Boutport Street	B2-B3-C3-C2
Braunton Road	A1
Broadfield Road	E4-F4
Buller Road	D3
Bull Hill	A2
Butcher's Row	C2-C3
Byron Close	A3
Carlyle Avenue	A3-B3
Carrington Terrace	B3-B4
Castle Street	C1-C2
Charles Dart Crescent	B4-C4
Charles Street	B3
Clifford Street	D1
Coronation Street	B2-B3
Cross Street	C2
Derby Road	B4
Diamond Street	D2-D3
Fair View	A1-A2
Fort Street	C3-C4-D4
Fort Terrace	C3-D3
Gaydon Street	C3
George Street	B2-B3
Gloster Road	E4-F4
Goodleigh Road	C4
Granville Avenue	A3-B3
Green Lane	B2-C2
Grosvenor Street	C4
Higher Church Street	D3
Higher Raleigh Road	A3
High Maudelin Street	B3
High Street	B2-C2
Hills View	C4
Holland Street	C1-C2
Joy Street	C2
King Edward Street	B3
Lethaby Road	B4
Litchdon Street	D2-D3-E3
Long Bridge	D2
Lower Raleigh Road	A3-A4
Magdalen Lawn	B3
Maiden Street	D2
Masefield Avenue	A3
Miller Crescent	C4
Mill Road	B1-B2
New Buildings	B3
Newport Road	E3-E4-F4
New Road	E3
Norfolk Terrace	F4
North Road	A2-A3-A4
North Walk	B1-B2
Park Lane	F4
Pathfield Lawn	A1-A2
Pilton Causeway	A2-B2
Pilton Lawn	A3
Pilton Street	A2
Portland Street	F4

Pottington Road	B1
Princes Street	B3
Priory Close	A2
Pulchrass Street	D3-D4
Queen Street	C3-D3
Raleigh Lawn	A3
Raleigh Road	A2-A3
Richmond Street	B4-C4
Riddel Avenue	A2-B2-B3
Rock Avenue	F4
Rock Gardens	F4
Rolle Street	B1-B2
St George's Road	A2-A3-A4
St Mary's Road	B4
Salem Street	D3
Signal Terrace	D1-E1
Silver Street	D3
South Walk	E3-F3
Sticklepath Terrace	D1-E1
Summerland Street	D3-D4
Sunflower Road	C4
Taw Vale	D2-D3-E3
The Rock	A2
The Square	D2
The Strand	C2-D2
Trinity Place	E3
Trinity Street	D3
Tuly Street	B2-C2
Vicarage Lawn	B3-C3
Vicrarage Street	B3-B4
Victoria Road	E4
Victoria Street	E4
Wells Street	C2-D2-D3
Yeo Vale Road	B2-B3

Bideford

Abbotsham Road	A2
Alexandra Terrace	A4
Allhalland Street	B2
Barnstaple Street	C2-C3
Bideford Bridge	B2-C2
Bridgeland Street	B3
Bridge Street	B2
Bull Hill	B1-B2
Buttgarden Street	B2
Chingswell Street	B3
Church Walk	B2
Clovelly Road	A1
Cold Harbour	B3
Cooper Street	B3
Copp's Close	A4

Coronation Road	A1
Elmdale Road	A4
Elm Grove	A3
Geneva Place	A1-A2
Glendale Terrace	A4
Grange Road	C2
Grenville Street	B2
Higher Gunstone	A2-B2-B3
High Street	A2-B2
Honestone Street	A2-B2
Hyfield Place	B2
Kingsley Road	A4-B4-B3
Kingsley Street	A3
Lime Grove	A3
Lower Gunstone	B3
Main Road	C3
Market Place	B2
Marland Terrace	A1
Meadowville Road	A4
Meddon Street	A1-A2-B2-B1
Mill Street	B2-B3
Milton Place	A2
Myrtle Gardens	A2-A3
Myrtle Grove	A3
New Road	B1-B2
Newton Road	A4-B4
Northam Road	A3-A4
Northdown Road	A3-A4
North Road	A3-B3
Northview Avenue	A4
Old Town	A2
Park Avenue	B3-B4
Park Lane	B4
Pitt Lane	A2-A3
Railway Terrace	C1-C2
Rectory Park	A2-A3
Rope Walk	B3
Silver Street	B2
The Quay	B2-B3-C3-C2
The Strand	B3
Torridge Hill	B1
Torridge Mount	C1
Torrington Lane	C1
Torrington Street	C1-C2
Victoria Gardens	A2-B2
Victoria Grove	A2-B2
Westcombe Lane	A3

Ilfracombe

Avenue Road	A3-B3
Belmont Road	A1-A2

Brookdale Avenue	A2-A3
Capstone Crescent	B4-C4
Castle Hill	C3
Church Hill	A2
Church Road	A2-A3
Comyn Hill	B1-C1
Fairlands	B2-C2-C1
Fernway	B1
Fore Street	B3-C3
Furze Hill Road	A2-A1-B1
Granville Road	A3-A4
Green Close Road	A3
Highfield Road	A2-B2-B3-C3
High Street	A2-A3-B3
Hillsborough Road	C3
Horne Park Road	A2-B2-B1
Horne Road	A2
Hostle Park Road	B3
Marine Drive	C3-C4
Market Street	B3
Marlborough Road	A2-B2
Mill Head	B3-B4
Montpellier Road	B3-C3
Northfield Road	B2
Osborne Road	A2
Oxford Grove	B3
Oxford Park	B3
Park Hill Road	B1-B2
Portland Street	B3-C3
Princess Avenue	B3-B2-C2
Promenade	B3-B4
Regent Place	A3
Richmond Road	A1
Riverdale Avenue	A3
Ropery Road	B4-C4
Runnacleave Road	A3
St Brannocks Road	A1
St Brannocks Park Road	A1-A3
St Brannocks Road	A1-A2
St James Place	B4-C4
Slade Road	A1
Springfield Road	B3
Station Road	A1-A2
The Quay	C4
Torrs Park	A3
Whittingham Road	C2-C3
Wilder Road	A2-A3
Worth Lane	C1-C2-C3

BARNSTAPLE
This ancient town stands on the Taw estuary and until the 19th century was an important port. The bridge across the river was originally built in the 1400s but has since been widened and extensively altered.

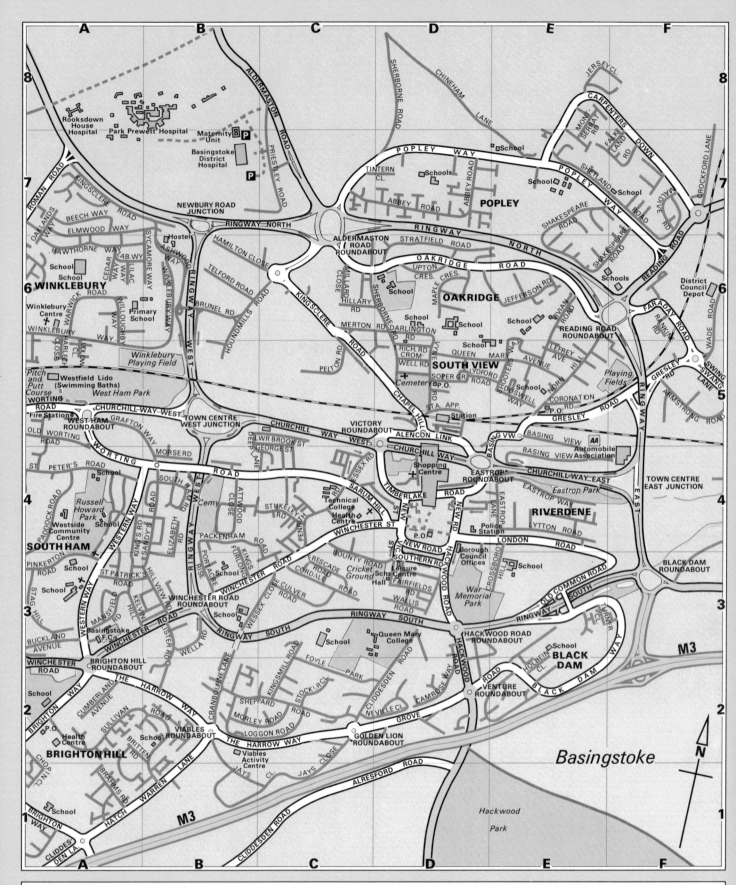

Basingstoke

Ever-expanding Basingstoke has seen a remarkable transformation in the last half-century, from quiet market town to major commercial and industrial centre, with a population of about 90,000. Rehousing for thousands of Londoners in the 1960s began the process, and easy access by road and rail to Heathrow Airport, Southampton Docks and London has made moving here an attractive proposition for large companies.

At the heart of the town is a large pedestrian shopping centre with good parking, a Sports Centre and a thriving theatre. Several specially created sports parks are in easy reach, and Mays Bounty, the local cricket ground, is regularly used by Hampshire for part of its County programme.

Basingstoke still boasts a number of older buildings, notably the 13th-century ruins of the Holy Ghost Chapel, which lie to the north of the railway station on the site of an ancient burial ground. St Michael's Parish Church dates mainly from the 16th century and has traces of Norman influence, although Second World War bombing destroyed most of the stained glass. The church also suffered damage in the Civil War from Cromwell's forces; two miles to the east of Basingstoke lie the ruins of Basing House, destroyed in 1645 by Parliamentary forces after a three-year resistance.

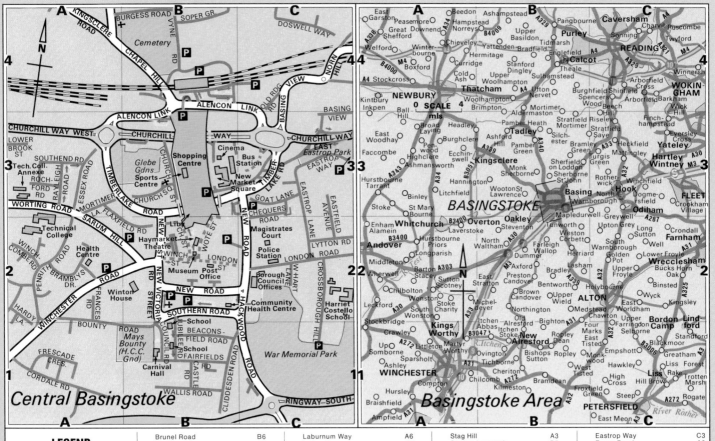

Central Basingstoke

Basingstoke Area

LEGEND

Town Plan

AA recommended route	
Restricted roads	
Other roads	
Buildings of interest	Station
Car parks	P
Parks and open spaces	
One way streets	←

Area Plan

A roads	
B roads	
Locations	Faccombe ○
Urban area	

Street Index with Grid Reference

Basingstoke

Abbey Road	C7-D7
Aldermaston Road	B8-C8-C7
Alencon Link	D4-D5
Alresford Road	C1-D1-D2
Armstrong Road	F5
Ashwood Way	B6
Attwood Close	B4
Basing View	E5-E4-F4
Beech Way	A7
Blackdam Way	E2-F2-F3-E3
Bounty Road	C4-C3-D3
Brahms Road	A1
Brighton Way	A1
Brighton Way	A2
Britten Road	A2-B2
Brunel Road	B6
Buckland Avenue	A3
Camrose Way	D2-D3
Carpenters Down	E7-E8-F8-F7
Cedar Way	B5
Chapel Hill	D5
Chineham Lane	D8-E8-E7
Chopin Close	A1-A2
Chuchill Way	D5-D4
Churchill Way East	E4-F4
Churchill Way West	A5-B5-C5-C4
Cliddesden Lane	A1
Cliddesden Lane	B1-C1-C2-D2-D3
Cordale Road	C3
Coronation Road	E5
Cranbourne Lane	B2-B3
Crockford Lane	F7-F8
Cromwell Road	D5
Crossborough Hill	E3-E4
Culver Road	C3
Cumberland Avenue	A2
Darlington Road	D6
Deepwell Lane	B5-B4-C4
Doswell Way	E5
Eastrop Lane	E4
Elizabeth Road	B3-B4
Elmwood Way	A6-A7-B7
Essex Road	C4
Fairfields Road	D3
Falkland Road	E7-F7-F8
Faraday Road	F5-F6
Foyle Park	C3-C2-D2
Frescade Close	C3
Grafton Way	A5-B5-B4
Gresley Road	F5
Grove Road	C2-D2
Hackwood Road	D4-D3-D2
Hamilton Close	B6-C6
Harlech Close	A5-A6
Hatch Warren Lane	A1-B1-B2
Hawthorne Way	A6
Hillary Road	C6-D6
Hill View Road	B3
Holbein Close	E2-E3
Houndmills Road	B5-B6-C6
Jays Close	B2-B1-C1-C2
Jefferson Road	E6
Jersey Close	E8-F8
Kelvin Road	A3
Kingsclere Road	C6-C5-D5
Kingsclere Road	A7-B7
Kings Furlong	B3-B4
Kingsmill Road	C2-C3
Kings Road	A3-A4
Laburnum Way	A6
Lefrey Avenue	E5
Lilac Way	A6
Lister Road	B2-B3
Loggan Road	B2-C2
London Road	D4-E4-E3-F3
Lower Brook Street	B5-C5
Ludlow Close	A5-A6
Lydford Road	D5-E5
Lytton Road	E4
Maldive Road	F7
Mansfield Road	A3
Maple Crescent	D6
Merton Road	C6-D6
Millard Road	C3
Montserrat Road	E7-F7
Morley Road	B2-C2
Morse Road	B4
Neville Close	C2-D2
New Road	D4-D3
New Street	D4
Norn Hill	E5-E6
Oaklands Way	A6-A7
Oakridge Road	C6-D6-E6
Old Common Road	E3-E6
Old Worting Road	A5
Packenham Road	B4-C4-C3
Paddock Road	A3-A4
Pelton Road	C5
Penrith Road	C3
Pinkerton Road	A3
Popley Way	C7-D7-E7-F7-F6
Portacre Rise	B3-B4
Priestley Road	C7-C8
Queen Mary Avenue	D5-E5
Rankine Road	F6
Reading Road	F6-F7
Richmond Road	D6
Ringway East	F6-F5-F4-F3
Ringway North	B7-C7-D7-D6-E6
Ringway South	B3-C3-D3-E3-F3
Ringway West	B3-B4-B5-B6
Roman Road	A7
St Patrick's Road	A3-B3
St Peter's Road	A4
Sandy's Road	B3-B4
Sarum Hill	C4-D4
Shakespeare Road	E7-E6-F6-F7
Sheppard Road	B2-C2
Sherborne Road	D7-D8
Sherborne Road	C6-D6-D5
Shooters Way	E5-E6
Soper Grove	D5
Southern Road	D3
South Ham Road	B4
Stag Hill	A3
Station Approach	D5
Stocker Close	C2
Stratfield Road	D6-D7
Stukeley Road	B4-C4
Sullivan Road	A2-B2
Swing Swang Lane	F5
Sycamore Way	B6-B7
Telford Road	B6
The Harrow Way	A2-B2-C2
Timerlake Road	D4
Tintern Close	C7-D7
Upton Crescent	D6
Victoria Street	D3-D4
Vivian Road	E6
Vyne Road	D5-D6
Wallis Road	D3
Warwick Road	A6
Wella Road	B3
Wessex Close	B3-C3
Western Way	A3-A4-B4
Willoughby Way	A5-A6
Winchester Road	A2-A3-B3-C3-C4-D4
Winklebury Way	A6-A5-B5-B6
Worting Road	A5-A4-B4-C4

Basingstoke Central

Alencon Link	A3-B3-B4-C4-C3
Basing View	C3-C4
Beaconsfield Road	B1
Bounty Road	A1-B1
Bramblys Drive	A2
Burgess Road	A4-B4
Castle Road	B1
Chapel Hill	A4-B4
Chequers Road	C2-C3
Churchill Way	A3-B3-C3
Churchill Way East	C3
Churchill Way West	A3
Church Square	B3
Church Street	B2-B3
Cliddesden Road	B1
Clifton Terrace	B4
Cordale Road	A1
Council Road	B1
Crossborough Hill	C1-C2
Doswell Way	C4
Eastfield Avenue	C2-C3
Eastrop Lane	C2-C3
Eastrop Way	C3
Essex Road	A3
Fairfields Road	B1
Flaxfield Road	A3-A2-B2
Frances Road	A2
Frescade Crescent	A1
Goat Lane	C3
Hackwood Road	C1-C2
Hardy Lane	A1-A2
Jubilee Road	B1-B2
Kingsclere Road	A4
London Road	C2
London Street	B2-C2
Lower Brook Street	A3
Lytton Road	C2
Mortimer Lane	A3
New Road	B2-C2-C3
New Street	B2
Norn Hill	C4
Old Reading Road	C4
Penrith Road	A1-A2
Rayleigh Road	A3
Ringway South	C1
Rochford Road	A3
Sarum Hill	A3-A2-B2
Soper Grove	B4
Southend Road	A3
Southern Road	B2
Timberlake Road	A3-B3-C3
Victoria Street	B2
Vyne Road	B4
Wallis Road	B1
White Hart Lane	C2
Winchcombe Road	A2
Winchester Road	A1-A2-B2
Winchester Street	B2
Worting Road	A3
Wote Street	B2

BASINGSTOKE
Fanum House, headquarters of the AA, rises out of the Eastrop business area of town, which overlooks tranquil Eastrop Park.

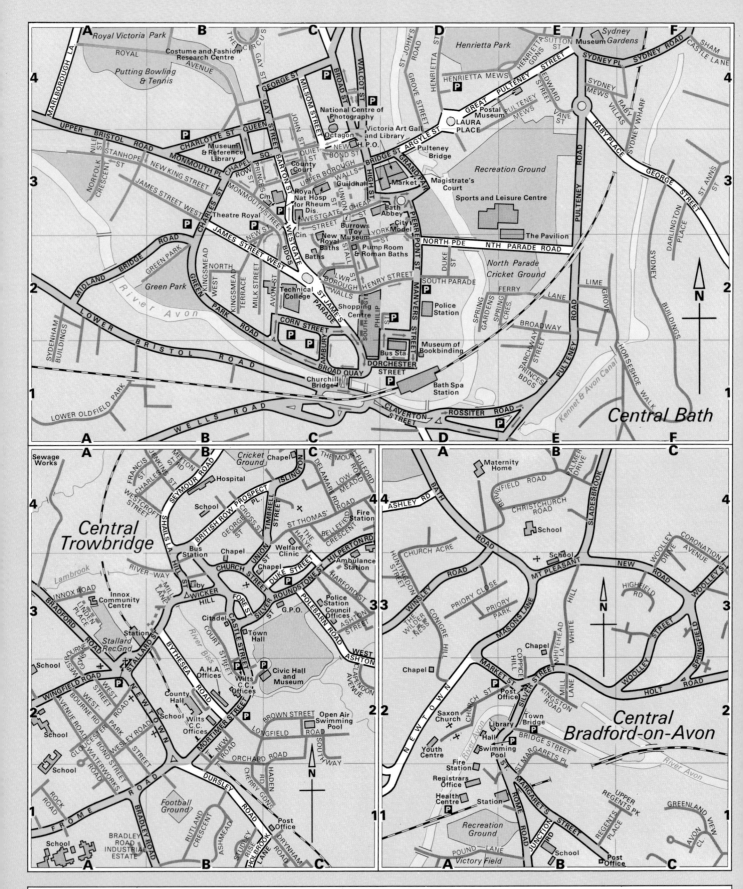

Bath

This unique city combines Britain's most impressive collection of Roman relics with the country's finest Georgian townscape. Its attraction to Romans and fashionable 18th-century society alike was its mineral springs, which are still seen by thousands of tourists who visit the Roman Baths every year. They are now the centre-piece of a Roman museum, where exhibits give a vivid impression of life 2000 years ago. The adjacent Pump Room to which the waters were piped for drinking was a focal point of social life in 18th- and 19th-century Bath.

The Georgian age of elegence also saw the building of Bath's perfectly proportioned streets, terraces and crescents. The finest examples are Queen Square, the Circus, and Royal Crescent, all built of golden local stone. Overlooking the Avon from the west is the great tower of Bath Abbey – sometimes called the "Lantern of the West"

because of its large and numerous windows.

Bath has much to delight the museum-lover. Near the abbey, in York Street, is the Burrows Toy Museum – a treasure-trove of playthings spanning two centuries. The Assembly Rooms in Bennett Street, very much a part of the social scene in Georgian Bath, are now the home of the Museum of Costume, and nearby, in Circus Mews, is the Carriage Museum, which vividly recalls coaching days.

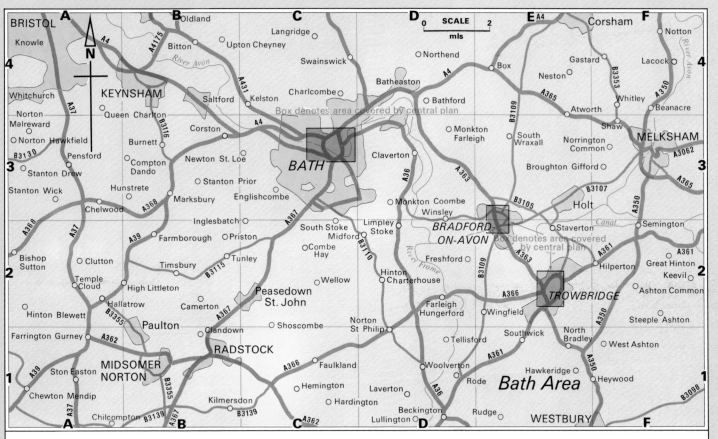

Key to Town Plan and Area Plan

Town Plan

A A Recommended roads
Other roads
Restricted roads
Buildings of interest   Library
Car Parks   P
Parks and open spaces
Churches   +
One Way Streets   ←

Area Plan

A roads
B roads
Locations   Box ○
Urban Area

Street Index with Grid Reference

Central Bath

Ambury	C1-C2
Archway Street	E1-E2
Argyle Street	D3-D4
Avon Street	C2
Barton Street	C3
Bridge Street	C3-D3
Broadway	E2
Broad Street	C3-C4
Broad Quay	C1
Chapel Row	B3
Charles Street	B2-B3
Charlotte Street	B3-B4
Cheap Street	C3
Claverton Street	C1-D1
Corn Street	C2
Darlington Place	F2-F3
Dorchester Street	C1-D1
Duke Street	D2
Edward Street	E4
Ferry Lane	D2-E2
Gay Street	B4-C4-C3
George Street	B4-C4
George Street	F2-F3
Grand Parade	D3
Great Pulteney Street	D4-E4
Green Park	A2-B2
Green Park Road	B1-B2-C2-C1
Grove Street	D3-D4
Henrietta Gardens	E4
Henrietta Mews	D4-E4
Henrietta Street	D4
Henry Street	C2-D2
High Street	C3
Horseshoe Walk	F1
James Street West	A3-B3-B2-C2
John Street	C3-C4
Kingsmead North	B2
Kingsmead Terrace	B2
Kingsmead West	B2
Laura Place	D3-D4
Lime Grove	E2-F2-F1
Lower Bristol Road	A2-A1-B1-C1
Lower Borough Walls	C2
Lower Oldfield Park	A1
Manvers Street	D1-D2
Marlborough Lane	A4
Midland Bridge Road	A2-B2-B3
Milk Street	B2
Milsom Street	C3-C4
Monmouth Place	B3
Monmouth Street	B3-C3
New Street	B2-B3-C3
New Bond Street	C3
New King Street	A3-B3
Nile Street	A3
Norfolk Crescent	A3
North Parade	D2
North Parade Road	D2-E2
Philip Street	C1-C2
Pierrepont Street	D2-D3
Princes Buildings	E1
Princes Street	B3
Pulteney Mews	E4
Pulteney Road	E1-E2-E3-E4
Queen Square	B3-B4-C4-C3
Quiet Street	C3
Raby Place	E4-E3-F3
Raby Villas	E4-F4
Rossiter Road	D1-E1
Royal Avenue	A4-B4
St Ann's Street	F3
St Jame's Parade	C2
St John's Road	D4
Sham Castle Lane	F4
Southgate	C1-C2
South Parade	D2
Spring Crescent	E2
Spring Gardens	D2
Stall Street	C2-C3
Stanhope Street	A3
Sutton Street	E4
Sydenham Buildings	A1-A2
Sydney Buildings	F1-F2-F3
Sydney Mews	E4-F4
Sydney Place	E4-F4
Sydney Road	F4
Sydney Wharf	F3-F4
The Circus	B4
Union Street	C3
Upper Borough Walls	C3
Upper Bristol Road	A4-A3-B3
Vane Street	E4
Walcot Street	C3-C4
Wells Road	A1-B1-C1
Westgate Buildings	C2-C3
Westgate Street	C3
York Street	C2-D2-D3

Trowbridge

Ashmead	B1
Ashton Street	C3
Avenue Road	A2
Bellefield Crescent	C4
Bond Street	A1-A2
Bradford Road	A2-A3
Bradley Road	A1-B1
British Row	B4
Brown Street	B2-C2
Bythesea Road	B2-B3
Castle Street	B2-B3
Charles Street	A4-B4
Cherry Gardens	B1-C1
Church Street	B3-C3
Clapendon Avenue	C2
Court Street	B2-B3
Cross Street	B4-C4
Delamere Road	C4
Drynham Road	C1
Duke Street	C3-C4
Dursley Road	B1-C1
Fore Street	B3
Francis Street	A4-B4
Frome Road	A1-B1
Fulford Road	C4
George Street	B4
Gloucester Road	A2
Haden Road	C1
Harford Street	C3
Hill Street	B3
Hilperton Road	C3-C4
Holbrook Lane	B1-C1
Innox Road	A3
Islington	C4
Jenkins Street	A4-B4
Linden Place	A3
Longfield Road	B2-C2
Lowmead	C4
Melton Road	B4
Mill Lane	B3
Mortimer Street	B2
New Road	B1-B2
Newtown	A2-B2
Orchard Road	B1-B2-C2-C1
Park Street	A2-A1-B1
Polebarn Road	C3
Prospect Place	B4-C4
River Way	A3-B3
Rock Road	A1
Roundstone Street	C3
Rutland Crescent	B1
St Thomas' Road	C4
Seymour Road	B4
Shails Lane	B3-B4
Silver Street	B3-C3
Southway	C2
Stallard Street	A2-A3-B3
Studley Rise	B1
The Hayle	C4
The Mount	C4
Timbrell Street	C4

Union Street	B3-B4-C4-C3
Waterwoks Road	A1-A2
Wesley Road	A2-B2
West Street	A2
West Ashton	C2-C3
Westbourne Gardens	A2-A3
Westbourne Road	A2
Westcroft Street	A4-B4
Wicker Hill	B3
Wingfield Road	A2

Bradford-on-Avon

Ashley Road	A4
Avon Close	C1
Bath Road	A3-A4-B4-B3
Berryfield Road	A4-B4
Bridge Street	B2
Christchurch Road	B4
Church Acre	A4
Church Street	A2-B2
Conigre Hill	A2-A3
Coppice Hill	B2-B3
Coronation Avenue	C3-C4
Greenland View	C1
Highfield Road	C3
Holt Road	B2-C2
Huntingdon Street	A3
Kingston Road	B2
Junction Road	B1
Market Street	A2-B2
Masons Lane	A3-B3
Mill Lane	B2
Mount Pleasant	B3
Newtown	A1-A2-A3
New Road	B3-C3
Palmer Drive	B4
Pound Lane	A1-B1
Priory Close	A3-B3
Priory Park	A3-B3
Regents Place	B1-C1
Rome Road	B1
St Margaret's Place	B1-B2
St Margaret's Street	B2-B1-C1
Silver Street	B2
Sladesbrook	B3-B4
Springfield	C2-C3
The Wilderness	A3
Upper Regents Park	B1-C1
White Hill	B2-B3
Whitehead Lane	B2-B3
Winsley Road	A3-A4
Woolley Drive	C3-C4
Woolley Street	C2-C3

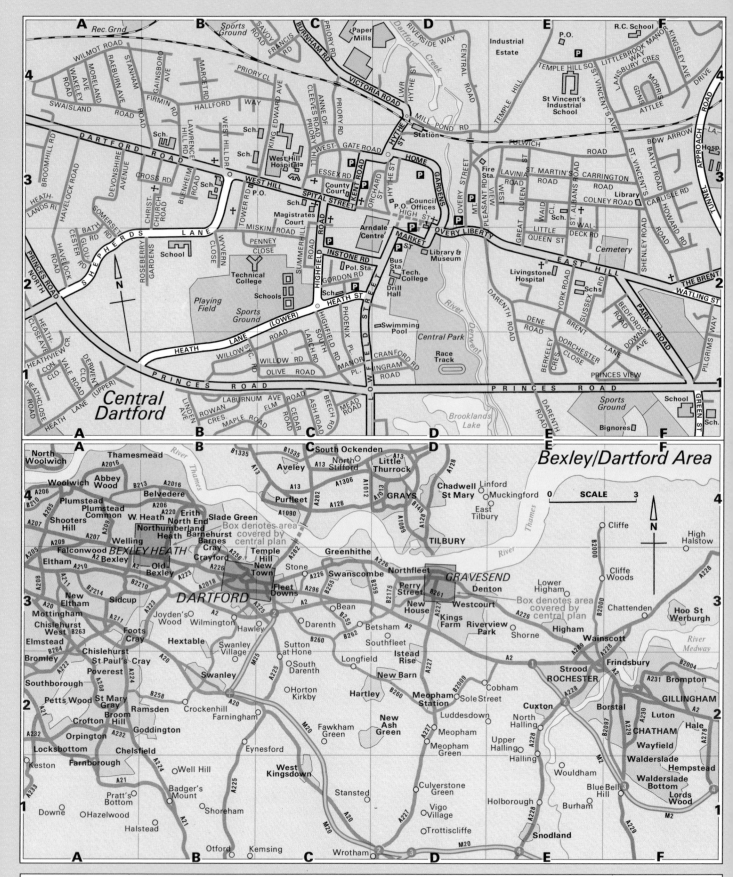

Bexley/Dartford

The rural sights and sounds of Stone Lodge Farm Park and Farm Museum — just east of town off the A226 — make an unexpected contrast with the old River Darent market town of Dartford. Its main concerns for many years have been engineering and papermaking, and Dartford enjoys some excellent modern facilities such as the Arndale Centre and the Orchard theatre complex. A number of old buildings survive in the centre, the oldest being the Norman-towered parish church of Holy Trinity. There is also a local museum.

Bexleyheath was once known simply as Bexley New Town. This is the administrative centre for the Borough of Bexley. Modern development has brought the Broadway Shopping Centre and the swimming pool and solarium of the Crook Log Sports Centre. Out of doors, Danson Park, scene of the July Danson Show, was first designed by Capability Brown.

Gravesend Making a vital link with Essex through the Tilbury ferry service, Gravesend's prime position on the Thames Estuary has always been a major factor in its growth, and the recent restoration of the 1842 Royal Terrace Pier celebrates a long maritime tradition. Much of the town was destroyed by fire in the 18th century, but several older buildings still survive in the Promenade area, including 14th-century Milton Chantry, a former chapel.

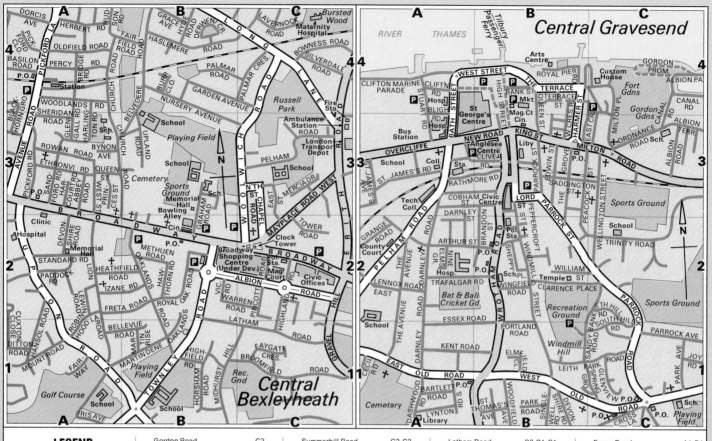

Central Bexleyheath

Central Gravesend

LEGEND

Town Plan

AA recommended route	
Restricted roads	
Other roads	
Buildings of interest	
Car parks	P
Parks and open spaces	

Area Plan

A roads	A210
B roads	B258
Locations	Bean○
Urban area	

Street Index with Grid Reference

Dartford

Anne of Cleaves Road	C3-C4
Ash Road	C1
Attlee Drive	F4
Bath Road	A2-A3
Bayly Road	F3
Beech Road	C1
Bedford Road	F2
Berkeley Crescent	E1
Blenheim Road	B3
Bow Arrow Lane	F3
Brent Lane	E2-E1-F1
Broomhill Road	A3
Burnham Road	C4
Carlisle Road	F3
Carrington Road	E3-F3
Cedar Road	C1
Central Road	D4-D3
Christchurch Road	B3
Colney Road	E3-F3
Coniston Close	A1
Cranford Road	D1
Cross Road	A3-B3
Darenth Road	D2-E2-E1
Dartford Road	A4-A3-B3
Dene Road	E2
Derwent Close	A1
Devonshire Avenue	A3
Dorchester Close	E1
Downs Avenue	F1-F2
East Hill	E2-F2
Elm Road	C1
Essex Road	C3
Firmin Road	B4
Francis Road	C4
Fulwich Road	D3-E3-F3
Gainsboro Avenue	B4
Gloucester Road	A2

Gordon Road	C2
Great Queen Street	E2-E3
Green Street	F1
Hallford Way	B4-C4
Havelock Road	A2-A3
Heathclose Avenue	A1-A2
Heathclose Road	A1
Heathlands Rise	A3
Heath Lane (Lower)	B1-B2-C1-C2
Heath Lane (Upper)	A1
Heath Street	C2
Heathview Crescent	A1
Highfield Road	C2-C3
Highfield Road South	C1-C2
High Street	C3-D3
Home Gardens	D3
Howard Road	F2-F3
Hythe Street	D3-D4
Ingram Road	D1
Instone Road	C2-D2
Kent Road	C3
King Edward Avenue	C3-C4
Kingsley Avenue	F4
Laburnum Avenue	B1-C1
Lansbury Crescent	F4
Larch Road	C1
Lavina Road	E3
Lawrence Hill Road	B3-B4
Littlebrook Manor Way	E4-F4
Little Queen Street	E2
Linden Avenue	B1
Lower Hythe Street	D4
Lowfield Street	C1-C2-D2
Manor Place	C1
Maple Road	B1-C1
Marcet Road	B4
Market Street	D2
Mead Road	C1
Mill Pond Road	D3-D4
Miskin Road	B2-C2
Moreland Avenue	A4
Morris Gardens	F4
Mount Pleasant Road	D3
Olive Road	C1
Orchard Street	C3-D3
Overy Liberty	D3-D2
Overy Street	D3
Park Road	F1-F2
Penney Close	B2-C2
Phoenix Place	C1-C2
Pilgrims Way	F1-F2
Princes Road	
	A2-A1-B1-C1-D1-E1-F1
Princes Road North	A2
Princes View	E1-F1
Priory Close	B4-C4
Priory Hill	C3-C4
Priory Road	C3-C4
Raeburn Avenue	A4
Riverside Way	D4
Roseberry Gardens	F4
Rowan Crescent	B1
St Albans Road	E2-E3
St Martins Road	E3
St Vincent's Avenue	E4-F4-F3
St Vincent's Road	F3-F2
Savoy Road	B4-C4
Shenley Road	F2-F3
Shepherds Lane	A2-B2-B3
Somerset Road	A2-A3
Spital Street	C3
Stanham Road	A4-B4-B3

Summerhill Road	C2-C3
Sussex Road	E2-F2
Swaisland Road	A4
Sycamore Road	B1-C1
The Brent	F2
Temple Hill	D3-E3-E4
Temple Hill Square	E4
Tower Road	B3
Tunnel Approach Road	F3-F4
Vale Road	A1
Victoria Road	C4-D4
Waid Close	E3
Wakeley Road	A4
Waldeck Road	E2
Watling Street	F2
Westgate Road	C3-D3
West Hill	B3-C3
West Hill Drive	B3-B4
West View	E3
Willow Road	B1-C1
Wilmot Road	A4-B4
Wyvern Close	B2
York Road	E2

Bexleyheath

Abbey Road	A3
Albion Road	B2-C2
Avenue Road	A3-A4
Basilon Road	A4
Bellevue Road	A1-B1
Belvedere Road	A3-B3-B4
Blackthorne Grove	A3-A4
Bowness Road	C4
Bridge Road	A4
Broadway	A3-A2-B2-C2
Broomfield Road	B1-C1
Burr Close	B4
Bynon Avenue	A3
Chapel Road	C2-C3
Church Road	A4-A3-B3
Cuxton Close	A1-A2
Derwent Crescent	B4
Devonshire Road	A2
Ditton Road	A1
Dorcis Avenue	A4
East Street	C2-C3
Erith Road	C2-C3-C4
Ethronvi Road	A3
Fairfield Road	A4-B4
Fairway	A1
Faygate Crescent	C1
Freta Road	A2-B2
Garden Avenue	B4-C4
Glengall Road	A3-A4
Grace Avenue	B4
Graham Road	B2-B3
Gravel Hill	C1-C2
Hansol Road	A1-A2
Harcourt Road	A3
Harlington Road	A3-A4
Haslemere Road	B4
Hawthorn Road	B2
Heathfield Road	A2-B2
Herbert Road	A4
Highfield Road	B1
Highland Road	C1-C2
Horsham Road	B1
Hudson Road	A4
Hyde Road	B4
Iris Avenue	A1
Izane Road	A2-B2

Latham Road	B2-B1-C1
Lavernock Road	C4
Lewin Road	A2
Lion Road	A2-A1
Long Lane	B4-C4-C3
Martin Dene	A1-B1
Martin Rise	B1
Mayplace Road West	C2-C3
Mercia Drive	C3
Methuen Road	B2
Midhurst Hill	B1-C1
Mount Road	A1
North Street	C3
Nursery Avenue	B4-B3-C3
Oaklands Close	B1-B2
Oaklands Road	B1-B2
Oldfield Road	A4
Paddock Road	A2
Palmar Crescent	C4
Palmar Road	B4-C4
Pelham Road	C3
Percy Road	A4
Pickford Close	A4
Pickford Lane	A4
Pickford Road	A4
Pincott Road	C2
Princes Street	A3
Queen Street	A3
Robin Hood Lane	A1-A2
Rowan Road	A3
Royal Oak Road	B2
Sandford Road	A3
Sheridan Road	A3
Silverdale Road	C4
Standard Road	A2
Tower Road	C2
Townley Road	B1-B2
Upland Road	B3
Upton	A3-A2-A1-B1
Victoria Road	B2
Warren Road	B2-C2
West Street	A3
Woodlands Road	A4
Woolwich Road	C2-C3-C4

Gravesend

Albion Parade	C4
Albion Road	C3
Albion Terrace	C3
Arthur Street	A2-B2
Bank Street	B4
Bartlett Road	A1
Bath Street	A3-A4
Bligh Road	A4-A3
Brandon Street	B2-B3
Canal Road	C3-C4
Cecil Road	A1
Clarence Place	B2-C2
Clifton Marine Parade	A4
Clifton Road	A4
Clive Road	A3-B3
Cobham Street	A3-B3
Cross Lane	C1
Darnley Road	A1-A2-A3
Darnley Street	A3-B3
Dashwood Road	A1
Devonshire Road	A1
East Crescent	B3-B4-C4
East Old Road	A1-B1
Edwin Street	B3
Elmfield Close	B1

Essex Road	A1-B1
Glenview	C1
Gordon Promenade	C4
Grange Road	A2
Harmer Street	B3-B4
High Street	B4-B3
Joy Road	C1
Kent Road	A1-B1
King Street	B3
Leith Park Road	B1-C1
Lennox Road East	A2
Lord Street	B3
Lynton Road South	A1
Milton Place	C3-C4
Milton Road	B3-C3
New Road	A3-B3
Nine Elms Grove	A2
Ordnance Road	C3
Overcliffe	A3
Park Avenue	C1
Park Road	B1
Parrock Avenue	C1
Parrock Road	C1-C2
Parrock Street	B2-B3
Peacock Street	B2-B3
Pelham Road	A2-A3
Peppercroft Street	B3-B2
Portland Road	B1-B2
Queen Street	B4-B3
Rathmore Road	A3-B3
Royal Pier Road	B4
St James's Avenue	A3
St James's Road	A3
St Thomas's Avenue	B1
Saddington Street	B3-C3
Sandy Bank Road	B1-B2-C2
Sheppy Place	B2
Singlewell Road	B1
South Hill Road	C1-C2
Spring Grove	B1-C1
Stuart Road	A4-A3
The Avenue	A1-A2
The Grove	B2-B3
The Terrace	B4
Terrace Street	B4
Trafalgar Road	A2-B2
Trinity Road	C2
Wellington Street	C2-C3
West Crescent Road	B3-B4
West Old Road	B1-C1
West Street	A4-B4
William Street	B2-C2
Windmill Street	B2-B1
Wingfield Road	B2
Woodfield Avenue	B1
Wrotham Road	A1-B1-B2-B3

13

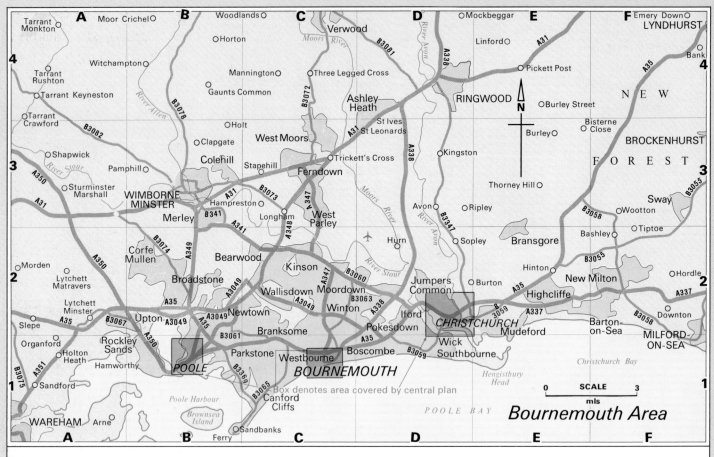

Bournemouth Area

SCALE

0 3

mls

Box denotes area covered by central plan

Street Index with Grid Reference

Bournemouth

Albert Road	C3-D3
Avenue Road	B3-C3
Bath Road	D2-E2-E3-E4-F4
Beacon Road	C1
Bodorgan Road	C4
Bourne Avenue	B3-C3
Braidley Road	B3-B4
Branksome Wood Road	A4
Cambridge Road	A2-A3
Central Drive	B4
Chine Crescent	A1-A2
Chine Crescent Road	A1-A2
Christchurch Road	F4
Cotlands Road	F4
Cranbourne Road	B2-C2
Crescent Road	A3-B3
Dean Park Crescent	C4-D4
Dean Park Road	C4
Durley Chine Road	A1-A2
Durley Gardens	A1-A2
Durley Road	A1-A2-B1
East Overcliff Drive	E2-F2-F3
Exeter Crescent	C2
Exeter Lane	C2-D2
Exeter Park Road	C2-D2
Exeter Road	C2-D2
Fir Vale Road	D3-D4
Gervis Place	C3-D3
Gervis Road	E3-F3
Glenfern Road	D3-E3-E4
Grove Road	E3-F3
Hahnemann Road	A1-B1-B2
Hinton Road	D2-D3-E2
Holdenhurst Road	F4
Lansdowne Road	E4-F4
Lorne Park Road	E4
Madeira Road	D4-E4
Marlborough Road	A2
Meyrick Road	F3-F4
Norwich Avenue	A2-A3-B3
Norwich Avenue West	A3
Old Christchurch Road	D3-D4-E4-F4
Parsonage Road	D3-E3
Poole Hill	A2-B2
Poole Road	A2
Priory Road	C1-C2

Richmond Hill	C3-C4
Russell Cotes Road	E2
St Michael's Road	B2-B1-C1
St Peter's Road	D3-E3
St Stephen's Road	B3-B4-C4-C3
Stafford Road	E4
Suffolk Road	A3-B3
Surrey Road	A3
Terrace Road	B2-C2
The Triangle	B2-B3
Tregonwell Road	B2-C2-C1
Undercliffe Drive	D1-D2-E1-E2-F2
Upper Hinton Road	D2-D3-E2
Upper Norwich Road	A2-B2
Upper Terrace Road	B2-C2
Wessex Way	A3-A4-B4-C4-D4-E4
West Cliff Gardens	B1
West Cliff Promenade	B1-C1-D1-C1
West Cliff Road	A1-B1
Westhill Road	A2-B2-B1-C1
Westover Road	D2-D3
West Promenade	C1-D1
Wimborne Road	C4
Wootton Gardens	E3-E4
Yelverton Road	C3-D3

Christchurch

Albion Road	A4
Arcadia Road	A4
Arthur Road	B3
Avenue Road	A3-B3-B4
Avon Road West	A3-A4-B4
Bargates	B2-B3
Barrack Road	A4-A3-B2-B3
Beaconsfield Road	B2-C3
Bridge Street	C2
Bronte Avenue	B4
Canberra Road	A4
Castle Street	B2-C2
Christchurch By-Pass	B2-C2-C3
Clarendon Road	A3-B3
Douglas Avenue	A2-B2
Endfield Road	A4
Fairfield	A3
Fairmile Road	A4-B4-B3
Flambard Avenue	B4
Gardner Road	A3-A4
Gleadowe Avenue	A2-B2
Grove Road East	A3-B3

Grove Road West	A3
High Street	B2
Iford Lane	A1
Jumpers Avenue	A4
Jumpers Road	A3-A4-B4
Kings Avenue	A2-B2
Manor Road	B2
Millhams Street	B2-C2
Mill Road	B3-B4
Portfield Road	A3-B3
Queens Avenue	B1
Quay Road	B1
St John's Road	A2
St Margarets Avenue	B1
Sopers Lane	B1
South View Road	A1-B1
Stony Lane	C4-C3-C2
Stour Road	B3-B2-A1-A2
The Grove	A4
Tuckton Road	A1
Twynham Avenue	B2-B3
Walcott Avenue	A4-B4
Waterloo Place	C2
Wickfield Avenue	B1-B2
Wick Lane	A1-B1-B2
Willow Drive	A1-B1
Willow Way	A1-B1
Windsor Road	A3

Poole

Ballard Road	B1-C1
Church Street	A1
Dear Hay Lane	A2-B2
Denmark Road	C3
East Quay Road	B1
East Street	B1
Elizabeth Road	C3
Emerson Road	B1-B2
Esplanade	B3
Garland Road	C4
Green Road	B2-B1-C1
Heckford Road	C3-C4
High Street	A1-B1-B2
Hill Street	B2
Johns Road	C3-C4
Jolliffe Road	C4
Kingland Road	B2-C2
Kingston Road	C3-C4
Lagland Street	B1-B2

Longfleet Road	C3
Maple Road	C3-C4
Mount Pleasant Road	C2-C3
Newfoundland Drive	C1
New Orchard	A1-A2
North Street	B2
Old Orchard	B1
Parkstone Road	C3-C2
Perry Gardens	B1
Poole Bridge	A1
St Mary's Road	C3
Seldown Lane	C2-C3
Shaftesbury Road	C3
Skinner Street	B1
South Road	B2
Stanley Road	B1
Sterte Avenue	A4-B4
Sterte Road	B2-B3-B4
Stokes Avenue	B4-C4
Strand Street	A1-B1
Tatnam Road	B4-C4
The Quay	A1-B1
Towngate Bridge	B2-B3
West Quay Road	A1-A2-B2
West Street	A1-A2-B2
Wimborne Road	B3-C3-C4

LEGEND

Town Plan
AA Recommended route
Other roads
Restricted roads
Buildings of interest — Town Hall
AA Centre — AA
Car Parks — P
Parks and open spaces
One way streets

Area Plan
A roads
B roads
Locations — Mudeford O
Urban area

Bournemouth

Until the beginning of the 19th century the landscape on which Bournemouth stands was open heath. Its rise began when a scattering of holiday villas were built by innovative trend-setters at a time when the idea of seaside holidays was very new. Soon a complete village had taken shape. In the next 50 years Bournemouth had become a major resort and its population catapulted to nearly 59,000.

Today's holidaymakers can enjoy Bournemouth's natural advantages – miles of sandy beaches, a mild climate and beautiful setting, along with a tremendous variety of amenities. These include some of the best shopping in the south – with shops ranging from huge departmental stores to tiny specialist places. Entertainments range from variety shows and feature films to opera, and the music of the world-famous Bournemouth Symphony Orchestra.

Poole has virtually been engulfed by the suburbs of Bournemouth, but its enormous natural harbour is still an attraction in its own right. At Poole Quay, some 15th-century cellars have been converted into a Maritime Museum, where the town's association with the sea from prehistoric times until the early 20th century is illustrated, and the famous Poole Pottery nearby offers guided tours of its workshops.

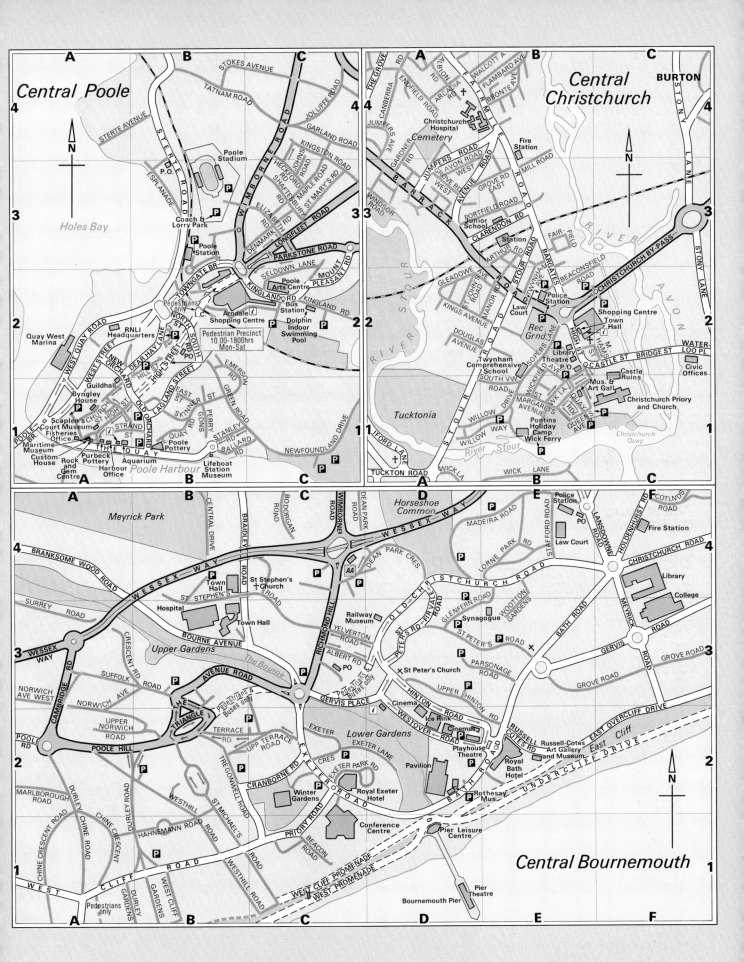

BOURNEMOUTH
The pier, safe sea-bathing, golden sands facing south and sheltered by steep cliffs, and plenty of amenities for the holiday maker make Bournemouth one of the most popular resorts on the south coast of England.

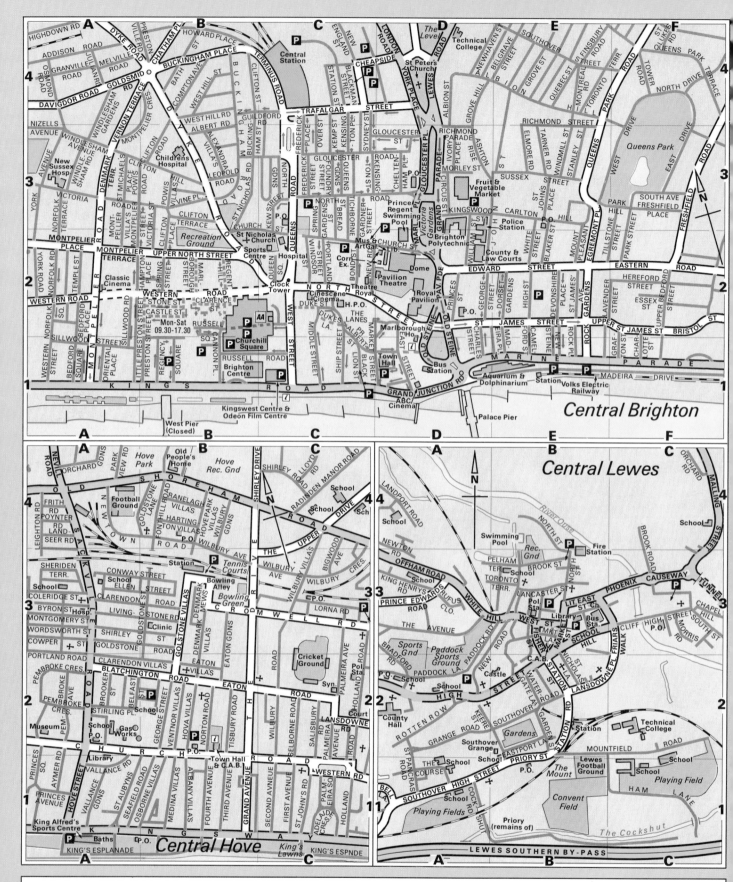

Brighton

Dr Richard Russell, from nearby Lewes, created the resort of Brighton almost singlehandedly. And he did it not by building houses or hotels, but by writing a book. His book, which praised the health-giving properties of sea-bathing and sea air, soon came to the attention of George, then Prince Regent and one day to become King George IV. He stayed at Brighthelmstone – as it was then known – in 1783 and again in 1784. In 1786 the Prince rented a villa on the Steine – a modest house that was eventually transformed into the astonishing Pavilion. By 1800 – its popularity assured by royal patronage – the resort was described in a contemporary directory as 'the most frequented and without exception one of the most fashionable towns in the kingdom'.

Perhaps the description does not quite fit today, but Brighton is a perennially popular seaside resort, as well as a shopping centre, university town and cultural venue. The Pavilion still draws most crowds, of course. Its beginnings as a villa are entirely hidden in a riot of Near Eastern architectural motifs, largely the creation of John Nash. Brighton's great days as a Regency resort *par excellence* are preserved in the sweeping crescents and elegant terraces, buildings which help to make it one of the finest townscapes in the whole of Europe.

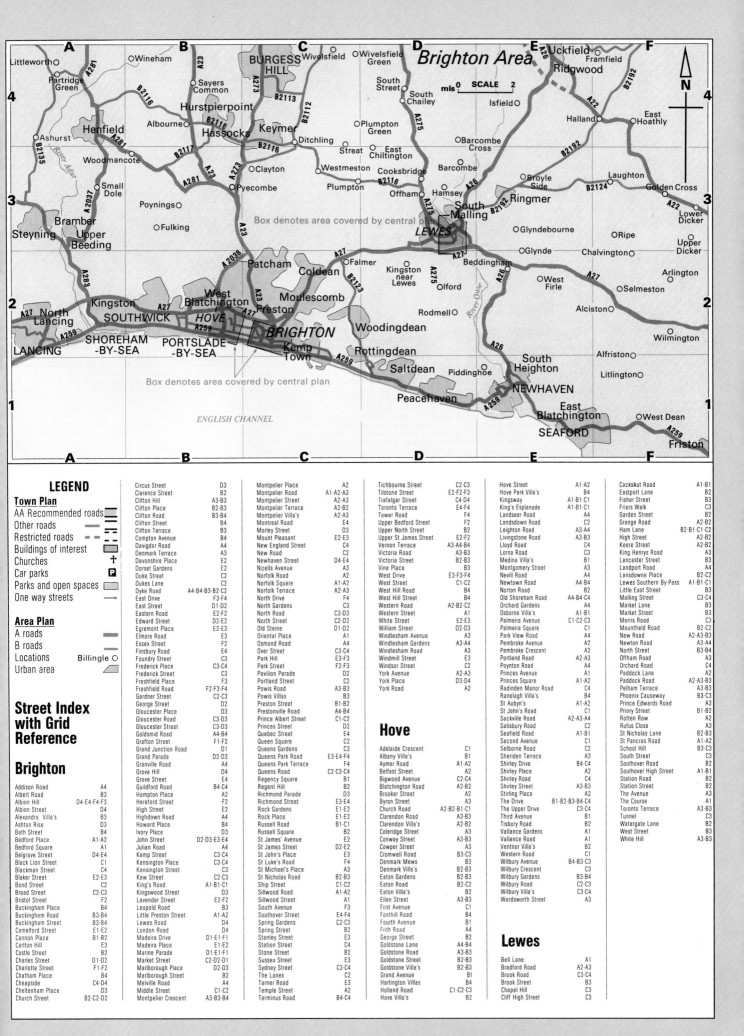

LEGEND

Town Plan
AA Recommended roads
Other roads
Restricted roads
Buildings of interest
Churches   ✝
Car parks   P
Parks and open spaces
One way streets   →

Area Plan
A roads
B roads
Locations   Billingle ○
Urban area

Street Index with Grid Reference

Brighton

Addison Road	A4
Albert Road	B3
Albion Hill	D4·E4·F4·F3
Albion Street	D4
Alexandra Villa's	B3
Ashton Rise	D3
Bath Street	B4
Bedford Place	A1·A2
Bedford Square	A1
Belgrave Street	D4·E4
Black Lion Street	C1
Blackman Street	C4
Blaker Street	E2·E3
Bond Street	C2
Bread Street	C2·C3
Bristol Road	F2
Buckingham Place	B4
Buckingham Road	B3·B4
Buckingham Street	B3·B4
Camelford Street	E1·E2
Cannon Place	B1·B2
Carlton Hill	E3
Castle Street	B2
Charles Street	D1·D2
Charlotte Street	F1·F2
Chatham Place	B4
Cheapside	C4·D4
Cheltenham Place	D3
Church Street	B2·C2·D2
Circus Street	D3
Clarence Street	B2
Clifton Hill	A3·B3
Clifton Place	B2·B3
Clifton Road	B3·B4
Clifton Street	B4
Clifton Terrace	B3
Compton Avenue	B4
Davigdor Road	A4
Denmark Terrace	A3
Devonshire Place	E2
Dorset Gardens	E2
Duke Street	C2
Dukes Lane	C2
Dyke Road	A4·B4·B3·B2·C2
East Drive	F3·F4
East Street	D1·D2
Eastern Road	E2·F2
Edward Street	D2·E2
Egremont Place	E2·E3
Elmore Road	E3
Essex Street	F2
Finsbury Road	E4
Foundry Street	C3
Frederick Place	C3·C4
Frederick Street	C3
Freshfield Place	F3
Freshfield Road	F2·F3·F4
Gardner Street	C2·C3
George Street	D2
Gloucester Place	D3
Gloucester Road	C3·D3
Gloucester Street	C3·D3
Goldsmid Road	A4·B4
Grafton Street	F1·F2
Grand Junction Road	D1
Grand Parade	D2·D3
Granville Road	A4
Grove Hill	D4
Grove Street	E4
Guildford Road	B4·C4
Hampton Place	A2
Hereford Street	F2
High Street	E2
Highdown Road	A4
Howard Place	B4
Ivory Place	D3
John Street	D2·D3·E3·E4
Julian Road	A4
Kemp Street	C3·C4
Kensington Place	C3·C4
Kensington Street	C3
Kew Street	C2·C3
King's Road	A1·B1·C1
Kingswood Street	D3
Lavender Street	E2·F2
Leopold Road	B3
Little Preston Street	A1·A2
Lewes Road	D4
London Road	D4
Madeira Drive	D1·E1·F1
Madeira Place	E1·E2
Marine Parade	D1·E1·F1
Market Street	C2·D2·D1
Marlborough Place	D2·D3
Marlborough Street	B2
Melville Road	A4
Middle Street	C1·C2
Montpelier Crescent	A3·B3·B4

Montpelier Place	A2
Montpelier Road	A1·A2·A3
Montpelier Street	A2·A3
Montpelier Terrace	A2·B2
Montpelier Villa's	A2·A3
Montreal Road	E4
Morley Street	D3
Mount Pleasant	E2·E3
New England Street	C4
New Road	C2
Newhaven Street	D4·E4
Nizells Avenue	A3
Norfolk Road	A2
Norfolk Square	A1·A2
Norfolk Terrace	A2·A3
North Drive	F4
North Gardens	C3
North Road	C3·D3
North Street	C2·D2
Old Steine	D1·D2
Oriental Place	A1
Osmond Road	A4
Over Street	C3·C4
Park Hill	E3·F3
Park Street	F2·F3
Pavilion Parade	D2
Portland Street	C2
Powis Road	A3·B3
Powis Villas	B3
Preston Street	B1·B2
Prestonville Road	A4·B4
Prince Albert Street	C1·C2
Princes Street	D2
Quebec Street	E4
Queen Square	C2
Queens Gardens	C3
Queens Park Road	E3·E4·F4
Queens Park Terrace	F4
Queens Road	C2·C3·C4
Regency Square	B1
Regent Hill	B2
Richmond Parade	D3
Richmond Street	E3·E4
Rock Gardens	E1·E2
Rock Place	E1·E2
Russell Road	B1·C1
Russell Square	B2
St James's Avenue	E2
St James Street	D2·E2
St John's Place	E3
St Luke's Road	F4
St Michael's Place	A3
St Nicholas Road	B2·B3
Ship Street	C1·C2
Sillwood Road	A1·A2
Sillwood Street	A1
South Avenue	F3
Southover Street	E4·F4
Spring Gardens	C2·C3
Spring Street	B2
Stanley Street	E3
Station Street	C4
Stone Street	B2
Sussex Street	E3
Sydney Street	C3·C4
The Lanes	C2
Tarner Road	E3
Temple Street	A2
Terminus Road	B4·C4

Tichbourne Street	C2·C3
Tilstone Street	E2·F2·F3
Trafalgar Street	C4·D4
Toronto Terrace	E4·F4
Tower Road	F4
Upper Bedford Street	F2
Upper North Street	B2
Upper St James Street	E2·F2
Vernon Terrace	A3·A4·B4
Victoria Road	A3·B3
Victoria Street	B2·B3
Vine Place	B3
West Drive	E3·F3·F4
West Street	C1·C2
West Hill Road	B4
West Hill Street	B4
Western Road	A2·B2·C2
Western Street	A1
White Street	E2·E3
William Street	D2·D3
Windlesham Avenue	A3
Windlesham Gardens	A3·A4
Windlesham Road	A3
Windmill Street	E3
Windsor Street	C2
York Avenue	A2·A3
York Place	D3·D4
York Road	A2

Hove

Adelaide Crescent	C1
Albany Villa's	B4
Aymer Road	A1·A2
Belfast Street	A2
Bigwood Avenue	C2·C4
Blatchington Road	A2·B2
Brooker Street	A2
Byron Street	A3
Church Road	A2·B2·B1·C1
Clarendon Road	A3·B3
Clarendon Villa's	A2·B2
Coleridge Street	A3
Conway Street	A3·B3
Cowper Street	A3
Cromwell Road	B3·C3
Denmark Mews	B3
Denmark Villa's	B2·B3
Eaton Gardens	B2·B3
Eaton Road	B2·C2
Eaton Villa's	B2
Ellen Street	A3·B3
First Avenue	C1
Fonthill Road	B4
Fourth Avenue	B1
Frith Road	A4
George Street	B2
Goldstone Lane	A4·B4
Goldstone Road	A3·B3
Goldstone Street	B2·B3
Goldstone Villa's	B2·B3
Grand Avenue	B1
Hartington Villas	B4
Holland Road	C1·C2·C3
Hove Villa's	B2

Hove Street	A1·A2
Hove Park Villa's	B4
Kingsway	A1·B1·C1
King's Esplanade	A1·B1·C1
Landseer Road	A4
Landsdown Road	C2
Leighton Road	A3·A4
Livingstone Road	A3·B3
Lloyd Road	C4
Lorna Road	C3
Medina Villa's	B1
Montgomery Street	A3
Nevill Road	A4
Newtown Road	A4·B4
Norton Road	B2
Old Shoreham Road	A4·B4·C4
Orchard Gardens	A4
Osborne Villa's	A1·B1
Palmeira Avenue	C1·C2·C3
Palmeira Square	C1
Park View Road	A4
Pembroke Avenue	A2
Pembroke Crescent	A2
Portland Road	A2·A3
Poynton Road	A4
Princes Avenue	A1
Princes Square	A1·A2
Radinden Manor Road	A4
Ranelagh Villa's	B4
St Aubyn's	A1·A2
St John's Road	C1
Sackville Road	A2·A3·A4
Salisbury Road	C2
Seafield Road	A1·B1
Second Avenue	C1
Selborne Road	C2
Sheriden Terrace	A3
Shirley Drive	B4·C4
Shirley Place	A2
Shirley Road	C4
Shirley Street	A3·B3
Stirling Place	A2
The Drive	B1·B2·B3·B4·C4
The Upper Drive	C3·C4
Third Avenue	B1
Tisbury Road	B2
Vallance Gardens	A1
Vallance Road	A1
Ventnor Villa's	B2
Western Road	C1
Wilbury Avenue	B4·B3·C3
Wilbury Crescent	C3
Wilbury Gardens	B3·B4
Wilbury Road	C2·C3
Wilbury Villa's	C3·C4
Wordsworth Street	A3

Lewes

Bell Lane	A1
Bradford Road	A2·A3
Brook Road	C3·C4
Brook Street	B3
Chapel Hill	C3
Cliff High Street	C3

Cockshut Road	A1·B1
Eastport Lane	B2
Fisher Street	B3
Friars Walk	C3
Garden Street	B2
Grange Road	A2·B2
Ham Lane	B2·B1·C1·C2
High Street	A2·B2
Keere Street	A2·B2
King Henrys Road	A3
Lancaster Street	B3
Landport Road	A4
Lansdowne Place	B2·C2
Lewes Southern By-Pass	A1·B1·C1
Little East Street	B3
Malling Street	C3·C4
Market Lane	B3
Market Street	B3
Morris Road	C3
Mountfield Road	B2·C2
New Road	A2·A3·B3
Newton Road	A3·A4
North Street	B3·B4
Offham Road	A3
Orchard Road	C4
Paddock Lane	A2
Paddock Road	A2·A3·B3
Pelham Terrace	A3·B3
Phoenix Causeway	B3·C3
Prince Edwards Road	A3
Priory Street	B1·B2
Rotten Row	A2
Rufus Close	A3
St Nicholas Lane	B2·B3
St Pancras Road	A1·A2
School Hill	B3·C3
South Street	C3
Southover Road	B2
Southover High Street	A1·B1
Station Road	B2
Station Street	B2
The Avenue	A3
The Course	A1
Toronto Terrace	A3·B3
Tunnel	C3
Watergate Lane	B2
West Street	B3
White Hill	A3·B3

17

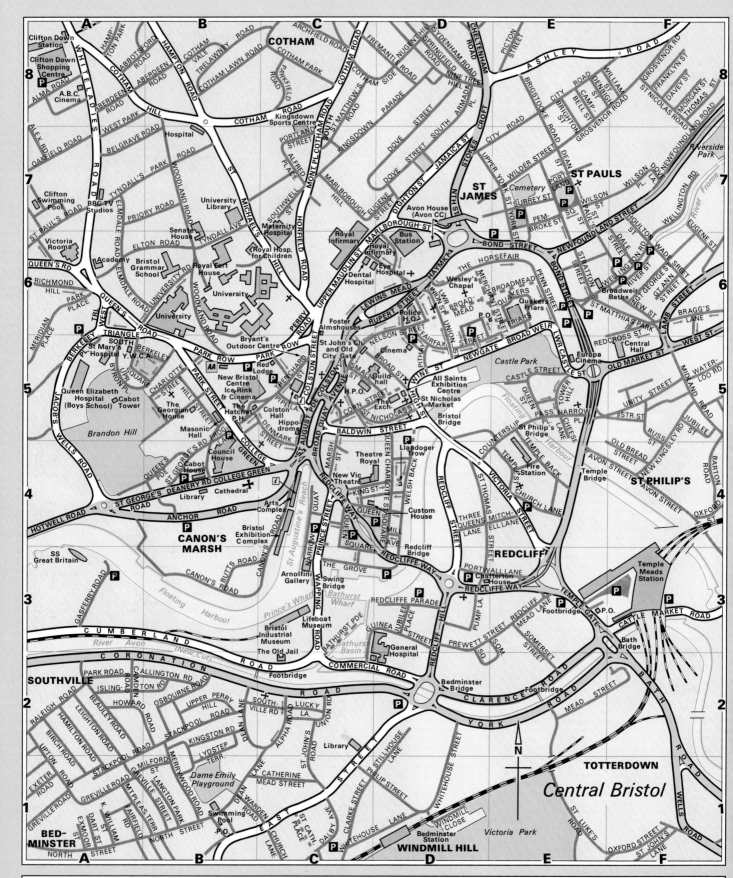

Bristol

One of Britain's most historic seaports, Bristol retains many of its visible links with the past, despite terrible damage inflicted during bombing raids in World War II. Most imposing is the cathedral, founded as an abbey church in 1140. Perhaps even more famous than the cathedral is the Church of St Mary Redcliffe. Ranking among the finest churches in the country, it owes much of

its splendour to 14th- and 15th-century merchants who bestowed huge sums of money on it.

The merchant families brought wealth to the whole of Bristol, and their trading links with the world are continued in today's modern aerospace and technological industries. Much of the best of Bristol can be seen in the area of the Floating Harbour – an arm of the Avon. Several of the old warehouses have been converted into museums, galleries and exhibition centres. Among them are

genuinely picturesque old pubs, the best-known of which is the Llandoger Trow. It is a timbered 17th-century house, the finest of its kind in Bristol. Further up the same street – King Street – is the Theatre Royal, built in 1766 and the oldest theatre in the country. In Corn Street, the heart of the business area, is a magnificent 18th-century corn exchange. In front of it are the four pillars known as the 'nails', on which merchants used to make cash transactions, hence 'to pay on the nail'.

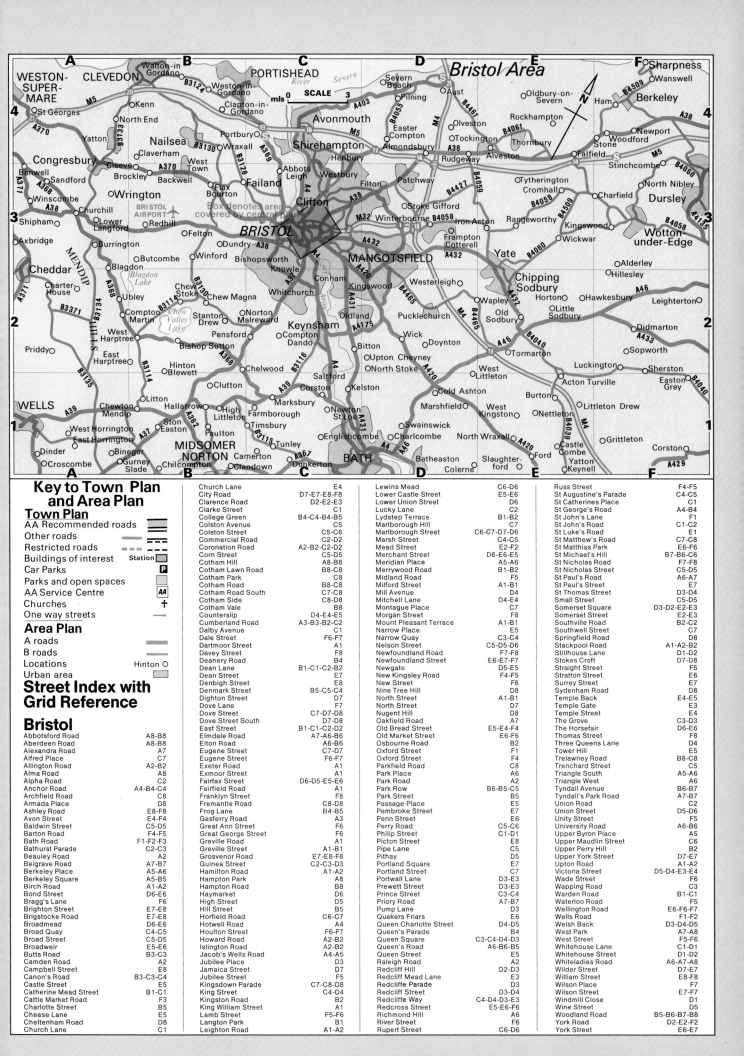

Key to Town Plan and Area Plan

Town Plan

AA Recommended roads	═══
Other roads	━━━
Restricted roads	╌╌╌
Buildings of interest	Station ▢
Car Parks	ⓟ
Parks and open spaces	▢
AA Service Centre	AA
Churches	✝
One way streets	→

Area Plan

A roads	━━━
B roads	━━━
Locations	Hinton O
Urban area	▢

Street Index with Grid Reference

Bristol

Abbotsford Road	A8-B8
Aberdeen Road	A8-B8
Alexandra Road	A7
Alfred Place	C7
Allington Road	A2-B2
Alma Road	A8
Alpha Road	C2
Anchor Road	A4-B4-C4
Archfield Road	C8
Armada Place	D8
Ashley Road	E8-F8
Avon Street	E4-F4
Baldwin Street	C5-D5
Barton Road	F4-F5
Bath Road	F1-F2-F3
Bathurst Parade	C2-C3
Beauley Road	A2
Belgrave Road	A7-B7
Berkeley Place	A5-A6
Berkeley Square	A5-B5
Birch Road	A1-A2
Bond Street	D6-E6
Bragg's Lane	F6
Brighton Street	E7-E8
Brigstocke Road	E7-E8
Broadmead	D6-E6
Broad Quay	C4-C5
Broad Street	C5-D5
Broadweir	E5-E6
Butts Road	B3-C3
Camden Road	A2
Campbell Street	E8
Canon's Road	B3-C3-C4
Castle Street	E5
Catherine Mead Street	B1-C1
Cattle Market Road	F3
Charlotte Street	B5
Cheese Lane	E5
Cheltenham Road	D8
Church Lane	C1
Church Lane	E4
City Road	D7-E7-E8-F8
Clarence Road	D2-E2-E3
Clarke Street	C1
College Green	B4-C4-B4-B5
Colston Avenue	C5
Colston Street	C5-C6
Commercial Road	C2-D2
Coronation Road	A2-B2-C2-D2
Corn Street	C5-D5
Cotham Hill	A8-B8
Cotham Lawn Road	B8-C8
Cotham Park	C8
Cotham Road	B8-C8
Cotham Road South	C7-C8
Cotham Side	C8-D8
Cotham Vale	B8
Counterslip	D4-E4-E5
Cumberland Road	A3-B3-B2-C2
Dalby Avenue	C1
Dale Street	F6-F7
Dartmoor Street	A1
Davey Street	F8
Deanery Road	B4
Dean Lane	B1-C1-C2-B2
Dean Street	E7
Denbigh Street	E8
Denmark Street	B5-C5-C4
Dighton Street	D7
Dove Lane	F7
Dove Street	C7-D7-D8
Dove Street South	D7-D8
East Street	B1-C1-C2-D2
Elmdale Road	A7-A6-B6
Elton Road	A6-B6
Eugene Street	C7-D7
Eugene Street	F6-F7
Exeter Road	A1
Exmoor Street	A1
Fairfax Street	D6-D5-E5-E6
Fairfield Road	A1
Franklyn Street	F8
Fremantle Road	C8-D8
Frog Lane	B4-B5
Gasferry Road	A3
Great Ann Street	F6
Great George Street	F6
Greville Road	A1
Greville Street	A1-B1
Grosvenor Road	E7-E8-F8
Guinea Street	C2-C3-D3
Hamilton Road	A1-A2
Hampton Park	A8
Hampton Road	B8
Haymarket	D6
High Street	D5
Hill Street	B5
Horfield Road	C6-C7
Hotwell Road	A4
Houlton Street	F6-F7
Howard Road	A2-B2
Islington Road	A2-B2
Jacob's Wells Road	A4-A5
Jubilee Place	D3
Jamaica Street	D7
Jubilee Street	F5
Kingsdown Parade	C7-C8-D8
King Street	C4-D4
Kingston Road	B2
King William Street	A1
Lamb Street	F5-F6
Langton Park	B1
Leighton Road	A1-A2
Lewins Mead	C6-D6
Lower Castle Street	E5-E6
Lower Union Street	D6
Lucky Lane	C2
Lydstep Terrace	B1-B2
Marlborough Hill	C7
Marlborough Street	C6-C7-D7-D6
Marsh Street	C4-C5
Mead Street	E2-F2
Merchant Street	D6-E6-E5
Meridian Place	A5-A6
Merrywood Road	B1-B2
Midland Road	F5
Milford Street	A1-B1
Mill Avenue	D4
Mitchell Lane	D4-E4
Montague Place	C7
Morgan Street	F8
Mount Pleasant Terrace	A1-B1
Narrow Place	E5
Narrow Quay	C3-C4
Nelson Street	C5-D5-D6
Newfoundland Road	F7-F8
Newfoundland Street	E6-E7-F7
Newgate	D5-E5
New Kingsley Road	F4-F5
New Street	F6
Nine Tree Hill	D8
North Street	A1-B1
North Street	D7
Nugent Hill	D8
Oakfield Road	A7
Old Bread Street	E5-E4-F4
Old Market Street	E6-F6
Osbourne Road	B2
Oxford Street	F1
Oxford Street	F4
Parkfield Road	C8
Park Place	A6
Park Road	A2
Park Row	B6-B5-C6
Park Street	B5
Passage Place	E5
Pembroke Street	E7
Penn Street	E6
Perry Road	C5-C6
Philip Street	C1-D1
Picton Street	E8
Pipe Lane	C5
Pithay	D5
Portland Square	E7
Portland Street	C7
Portwall Lane	D3-E3
Prewett Street	D3-E3
Prince Street	C3-C4
Priory Road	A7-B7
Pump Lane	D3
Quakers Friars	E6
Queen Charlotte Street	D4-D5
Queen's Parade	B4
Queen Square	C3-C4-D4-D3
Queen's Road	A6-B6-B5
Queen Street	E5
Raleigh Road	A2
Redcliff Hill	D2-D3
Redcliff Mead Lane	E3
Redcliffe Parade	D3
Redcliff Street	D3-D4
Redcliffe Way	C4-D4-D3-E3
Redcross Street	E5-E6-F6
Richmond Hill	A6
River Street	F6
Rupert Street	C6-D6
Russ Street	F4-F5
St Augustine's Parade	C4-C5
St Catherines Place	C1
St George's Road	A4-B4
St John's Lane	F1
St John's Road	C1-C2
St Luke's Road	E1
St Matthew's Road	C7-C8
St Matthias Park	E6-F6
St Michael's Hill	B7-B6-C6
St Nicholas Road	F7-F8
St Nicholas Street	C5-D5
St Paul's Road	A6-A7
St Paul's Street	E7
St Thomas Street	D3-D4
Small Street	C5-D5
Somerset Square	D3-D2-E2-E3
Somerset Street	E2-E3
Southville Road	B2-C2
Southwell Street	C7
Springfield Road	D8
Stackpool Road	A1-A2-B2
Stillhouse Lane	D1-D2
Stokes Croft	D7-D8
Straight Street	F5
Stratton Street	E6
Surrey Street	E7
Sydenham Road	D8
Temple Back	E4-E5
Temple Gate	E3
Temple Street	E4
The Grove	C3-D3
The Horsefair	D6-E6
Thomas Street	F8
Three Queens Lane	D4
Tower Hill	E5
Trelawney Road	B8-C8
Trenchard Street	C5
Triangle South	A5-A6
Triangle West	A6
Tyndall Avenue	B6-B7
Tyndall's Park Road	A7-B7
Union Road	C2
Union Street	D5-D6
Unity Street	F5
University Road	A6-B6
Upper Byron Place	A5
Upper Maudlin Street	C6
Upper Perry Hill	B2
Upper York Street	D7-E7
Upton Road	A1-A2
Victoria Street	D5-D4-E3-E4
Wade Street	F6
Wapping Road	C3
Warden Road	B1-C1
Waterloo Road	F5
Wellington Road	E6-F6-F7
Wells Road	F1-F2
Welsh Back	D3-D4-D5
West Park	A7-A8
West Street	F5-F6
Whitehouse Lane	C1-D1
Whitehouse Street	D1-D2
Whiteladies Road	A6-A7-A8
Wilder Street	D7-E7
William Street	E8-F8
Wilson Place	F7
Wilson Street	E7-F7
Windmill Close	D1
Wine Street	D5
Woodland Road	B5-B6-B7-B8
York Road	D2-E2-F2
York Street	E6-E7

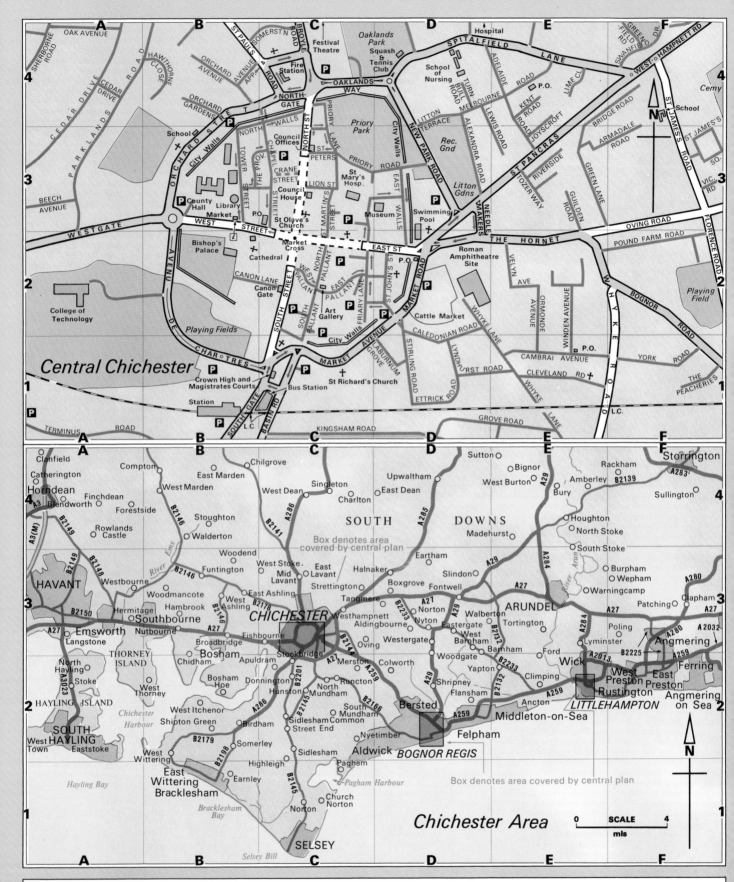

Central Chichester

Chichester Area

SCALE 0 — 4
mls

N

Chichester

The graceful spire of Chichester Cathedral, consecrated in 1184, rises over the rooftops to the west of this city, which dates back to Roman times and is one of Britain's oldest. Notable among its 18th-century streets are the Pallants and the Pallant House, and at Fishbourne Priory nearby, visitors can admire the mosaics, formal garden and other remains of the largest Roman residence found in Britain.

Chichester today gives pleasure to thousands with its Festival Theatre and its harbour — thronged with sailing enthusiasts throughout the summer and with a variety of wild birds during the winter. Other attractions are the Open Air Museum and West Dean Gardens.

Bognor Regis was plain Bognor until 1929 when George V granted the suffix Regis after convalescing there. A former fishing village, it began its transformation into a seaside town in the 1790s, and is now a favourite destination for family holidays. Elegant Hotham Park House is worth a visit.

Littlehampton at the mouth of the River Arun was once a busy port for passengers and cargo going to France; today it is a popular target for holidaymakers, who come here for the good fishing, bathing and sailing. The local museum concentrates on marine subjects.

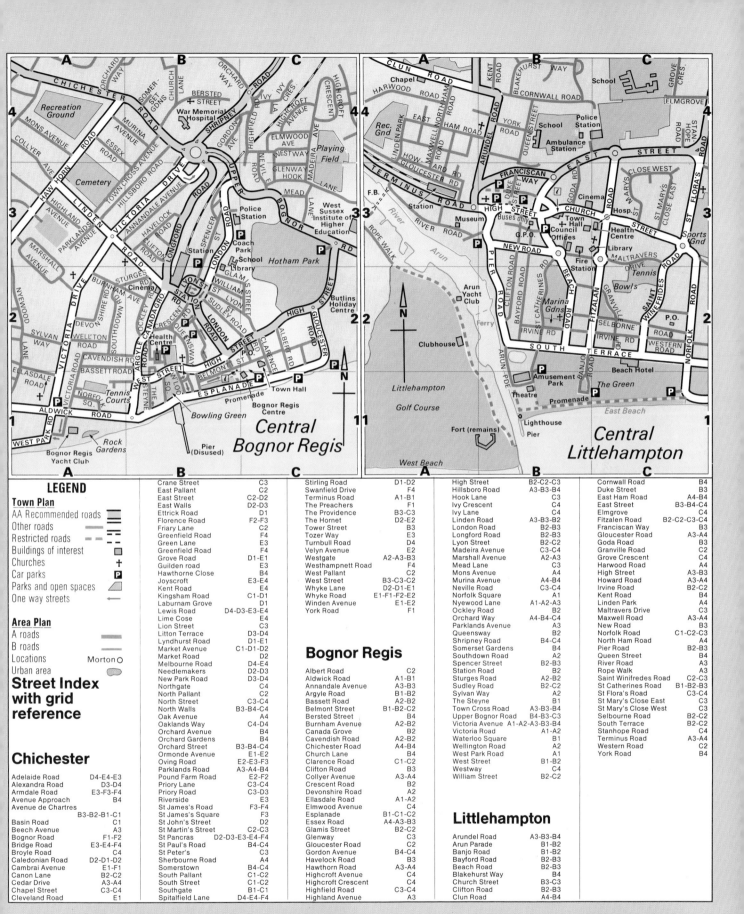

Central Bognor Regis

Central Littlehampton

LEGEND

Town Plan

AA Recommended roads	▬
Other roads	▬
Restricted roads	▬
Buildings of interest	▨
Churches	+
Car parks	P
Parks and open spaces	▱
One way streets	←

Area Plan

A roads	▬
B roads	▬
Locations	Morton ○
Urban area	◯

Street Index with grid reference

Chichester

Adelaide Road	D4-E4-E3
Alexandra Road	D3-D4
Armdale Road	E3-F3-F4
Avenue Approach	B4
Avenue de Chartres	B3-B2-B1-C1
Basin Road	C1
Beech Avenue	A3
Bognor Road	F1-F2
Bridge Road	E3-E4-F4
Broyle Road	C4
Caledonian Road	D2-D1-D2
Cambrai Avenue	E1-F1
Canon Lane	B2-C2
Cedar Drive	A3-A4
Chapel Street	C3-C4
Cleveland Road	E1
Crane Street	C3
East Pallant	C2
East Street	C2-D2
East Walls	D2-D3
Ettrick Road	D1
Florence Road	F2-F3
Friary Lane	C2
Greenfield Road	F4
Green Lane	E3
Greenfield Road	F4
Grove Road	D1-E1
Guilden road	E3
Hawthorne Close	B4
Joyscroft	E3-E4
Kent Road	E4
Kingsham Road	C1-D1
Laburnam Grove	D1
Lewis Road	D4-D3-E3-E4
Lime Cose	E4
Lion Street	C3
Litton Terrace	D3-D4
Lyndhurst Road	D1-E1
Market Avenue	C1-D1-D2
Market Road	D2
Melbourne Road	D4-E4
Needlemakers	D2-D3
New Park Road	D3-D4
Northgate	C4
North Pallant	C2
North Street	C3-C4
North Walls	B3-B4-C4
Oak Avenue	A4
Oaklands Way	C4-D4
Orchard Avenue	B4
Orchard Gardens	B4
Orchard Street	B3-B4-C4
Ormonde Avenue	E1-E2
Oving Road	E2-E3-F3
Parklands Road	A3-A4-B4
Pound Farm Road	E2-F2
Priory Lane	C3-C4
Priory Road	C3-D3
Riverside	E3
St James's Road	F3-F4
St James's Square	F3
St John's Street	D2
St Martin's Street	C2-C3
St Pancras	D2-D3-E3-E4-F4
St Paul's Road	B4-C4
St Peter's	C3
Sherbourne Road	A4
Somerstown	B4-C4
South Pallant	C1-C2
South Street	C1-C2
Southgate	B1-C1
Spitalfield Lane	D4-E4-F4
Stirling Road	D1-D2
Swanfield Drive	F4
Terminus Road	A1-B1
The Preachers	F1
The Providence	B3-C3
The Hornet	D2-E2
Tower Street	B3
Tozer Way	E3
Turnbull Road	D4
Velyn Avenue	E4
Westgate	A2-A3-B3
Westhampnett Road	F4
West Pallant	C2
West Street	B3-C3-C2
Whyke Lane	D2-D1-E1
Whyke Road	E1-F1-F2-E2
Winden Avenue	E1-E2
York Road	F1

Bognor Regis

Albert Road	C2
Aldwick Road	A1-B1
Annandale Avenue	A3-B3
Argyle Road	B1-B2
Bassett Road	A2-B2
Belmont Street	B1-B2-C2
Bersted Street	B4
Burnham Avenue	A2-B2
Canada Grove	B2
Cavendish Road	A2-B2
Chichester Road	A4-B4
Church Lane	B4
Clarence Road	C1-C2
Clifton Road	B3
Collyer Avenue	A3-A4
Crescent Road	B2
Devonshire Road	A2
Ellasdale Road	A1-A2
Elmwood Avenue	C4
Esplanade	B1-C1-C2
Essex Road	A4-A3-B3
Glamis Street	B2-C2
Glenway	C3
Gloucester Road	C2
Gordon Avenue	B4-C4
Havelock Road	B3
Hawthorn Road	A3-A4
Highcroft Avenue	C4
Highcroft Crescent	C4
Highfield Road	C3-C4
Highland Avenue	A3

High Street	B2-C2-C3
Hillsboro Road	A3-B3-B4
Hook Lane	C3
Ivy Crescent	C4
Ivy Lane	C4
Linden Road	A3-B3-B2
London Road	B2-B3
Longford Road	B2-B3
Lyon Street	B2-C2
Madeira Avenue	C3-C4
Marshall Avenue	A2-A3
Mead Lane	C3
Mons Avenue	A4
Murina Avenue	A4-B4
Neville Road	C3-C4
Norfolk Square	A1
Nyewood Lane	A1-A2-A3
Ockley Road	B2
Orchard Way	A4-B4-C4
Parklands Avenue	A3
Queensway	B2
Shripney Road	B4-C4
Somerset Gardens	B4
Southdown Road	A2
Spencer Street	B2-B3
Station Road	B2
Sturges Road	A2-B2
Sudley Road	B2-C2
Sylvan Way	A2
The Steyne	B1
Town Cross Road	A3-B3-B4
Upper Bognor Road	B4-B3-C3
Victoria Avenue	A1-A2-A3-B3-B4
Victoria Road	A1-A2
Waterloo Square	B1
Wellington Road	A2
West Park Road	A1
West Street	B1-B2
Westway	C4
William Street	B2-C2

Littlehampton

Arundel Road	A3-B3-B4
Arun Parade	B1-B2
Banjo Road	B1-B2
Bayford Road	B2-B3
Beach Road	B2-B3
Blakehurst Way	B4
Church Street	B3-C3
Clifton Road	B2-B3
Clun Road	A4-B4
Cornwall Road	B4
Duke Street	B3
East Ham Road	A4-B4
East Street	B3-B4-C4
Elmgrove	C4
Fitzalen Road	B2-C2-C3-C4
Franciscan Way	B3
Gloucester Road	A3-A4
Goda Road	B3
Granville Road	C2
Grove Crescent	C4
Harwood Road	A4
High Street	A3-B3
Howard Road	A3-A4
Irvine Road	B2-C2
Kent Road	B4
Linden Park	A4
Maltravers Drive	C3
Maxwell Road	A3-A4
New Road	B3
Norfolk Road	C1-C2-C3
North Ham Road	A4
Pier Road	B2-B3
Queen Street	B4
River Road	A3
Rope Walk	A3
Saint Winifredes Road	C2-C3
St Catherines Road	B1-B2-B3
St Flora's Road	C3-C4
St Mary's Close East	C3
St Mary's Close West	C3
Selbourne Road	B2-C2
South Terrace	B2-C2
Stanhope Road	C4
Terminus Road	A3-A4
Western Road	C2
York Road	B4

CHICHESTER
Opened in 1962 under the direction of Sir Laurence (later Lord) Olivier, the Festival Theatre draws an annual audience of half a million to its wide range of music and drama, both during the summer festival and throughout the year.

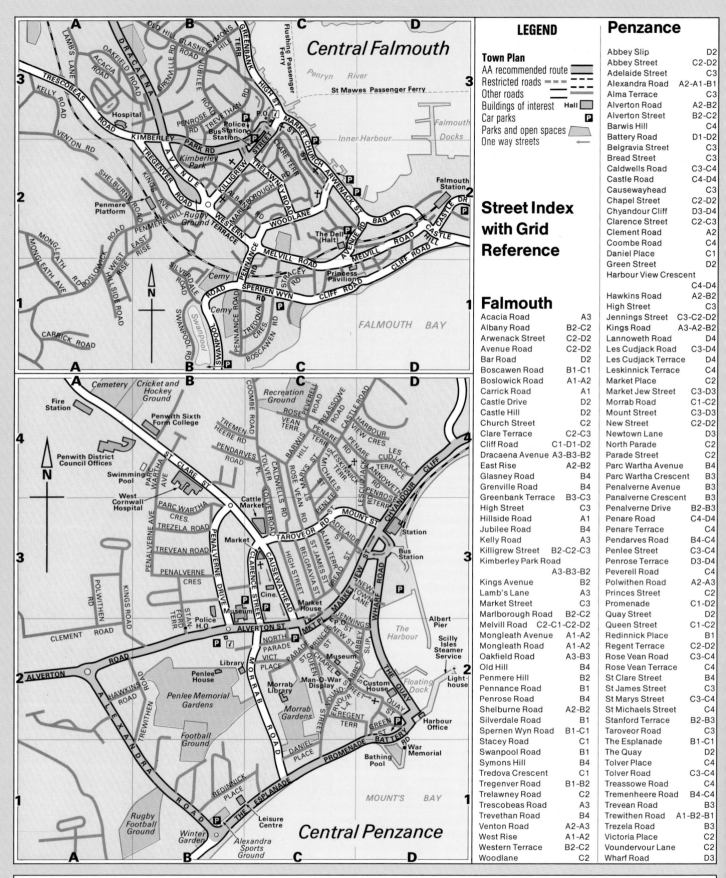

LEGEND

Town Plan

AA recommended route
Restricted roads
Other roads
Buildings of interest   Hall
Car parks   P
Parks and open spaces
One way streets

Street Index with Grid Reference

Falmouth

Acacia Road	A3
Albany Road	B2-C2
Arwenack Street	C2-D2
Avenue Road	C2-D2
Bar Road	D2
Boscawen Road	B1-C1
Boslowick Road	A1-A2
Carrick Road	A1
Castle Drive	D2
Castle Hill	D2
Church Street	C2
Clare Terrace	C2-C3
Cliff Road	C1-D1-D2
Dracaena Avenue	A3-B3-B2
East Rise	A2-B2
Glasney Road	B4
Grenville Road	B4
Greenbank Terrace	B3-C3
High Street	C3
Hillside Road	A1
Jubilee Road	B4
Kelly Road	A3
Killigrew Street	B2-C2-C3
Kimberley Park Road	A3-B3-B2
Kings Avenue	B2
Lamb's Lane	A3
Market Street	C3
Marlborough Road	B2-C2
Melvill Road	C2-C1-C2-D2
Mongleath Avenue	A1-A2
Mongleath Road	A1-A2
Oakfield Road	A3-B3
Old Hill	B4
Penmere Hill	B2
Pennance Road	B1
Penrose Road	B4
Shelburne Road	A2-B2
Silverdale Road	B1
Spernen Wyn Road	B1-C1
Stacey Road	C1
Swanpool Road	B1
Symons Hill	B4
Tredova Crescent	C1
Tregenver Road	B1-B2
Trelawney Road	C2
Trescobeas Road	A3
Trevethan Road	B4
Venton Road	A2-A3
West Rise	A1-A2
Western Terrace	B2-C2
Woodlane	C2

Penzance

Abbey Slip	D2
Abbey Street	C2-D2
Adelaide Street	C3
Alexandra Road	A2-A1-B1
Alma Terrace	C3
Alverton Road	A2-B2
Alverton Street	B2-C2
Barwis Hill	C4
Battery Road	D1-D2
Belgravia Street	C3
Bread Street	C3
Caldwells Road	C3-C4
Castle Road	C4-D4
Causewayhead	C3
Chapel Street	C2-D2
Chyandour Cliff	D3-D4
Clarence Street	C2-C3
Clement Road	A2
Coombe Road	C4
Daniel Place	C1
Green Street	D2
Harbour View Crescent	C4-D4
Hawkins Road	A2-B2
High Street	C3
Jennings Street	C3-C2-D2
Kings Road	A3-A2-B2
Lannoweth Road	D4
Les Cudjack Road	C3-D4
Les Cudjack Terrace	D4
Leskinnick Terrace	C4
Market Place	C2
Market Jew Street	C3-D3
Morrab Road	C1-C2
Mount Street	C3-D3
New Street	C2-D2
Newtown Lane	D3
North Parade	C2
Parade Street	C2
Parc Wartha Avenue	B3
Parc Wartha Crescent	B3
Penalverne Avenue	B3
Panalverne Crescent	B3
Penalverne Drive	B2-B3
Penare Road	C4-D4
Penare Terrace	C4
Pendarves Road	B4-C4
Penlee Street	C3-C4
Penrose Terrace	D3-D4
Peverell Road	C4
Polwithen Road	A2-A3
Princes Street	C2
Promenade	C1-D2
Quay Street	D2
Queen Street	C1-C2
Redinnick Place	B1
Regent Terrace	C2-D2
Rose Vean Road	C3-C4
Rose Vean Terrace	C4
St Clare Street	B4
St James Street	C3
St Marys Street	C3-C4
St Michaels Street	C4
Stanford Terrace	B2-B3
Taroveor Road	C3
The Esplanade	B1-C1
The Quay	D2
Tolver Place	C4
Tolver Road	C3-C4
Treassowe Road	C4
Tremenheere Road	B4-C4
Trevean Road	B3
Trewithen Road	A1-B2-B1
Trezela Road	B3
Victoria Place	C2
Voundervour Lane	C2
Wharf Road	D3

Cornish towns

Falmouth Twin fortresses, St. Mawes and Pendennis, guard the harbour entrance and serve as a reminder of Falmouth's once vital strategic importance. Lying in the sheltered waters of the Carrick Roads and provided with one of the world's largest natural harbours, Falmouth prospered on trade until the 19th century. Today the town is popular with holidaymakers.

St Ives is one of the few British towns with a style of painting named after it, for both artists and holidaymakers are drawn to the port, with its charming old quarter known as Down-Long. Regular exhibitions of local painting, sculpture and pottery are held, and the work of sculptor Barbara Hepworth, who spent much of her creative life here, is displayed in the Hepworth Gallery.

Penzance is the first and last town in Britain — it lies at the western extremity of Mounts Bay and basks in a temperate climate and sub-tropical vegetation. Places of interest include the ornate Egyptian House (now a National Trust shop), and steamers and helicopters go to the Scilly Isles.

Newquay Favourite haunt of surfboarders for its Fistral and Watergate beaches, Newquay has a 'Huer's House' where lookouts once warned fishermen of approaching shoals of pilchards. There are fine beaches for holidaymakers, such as Towan, Lusty Glaze and Great Western.

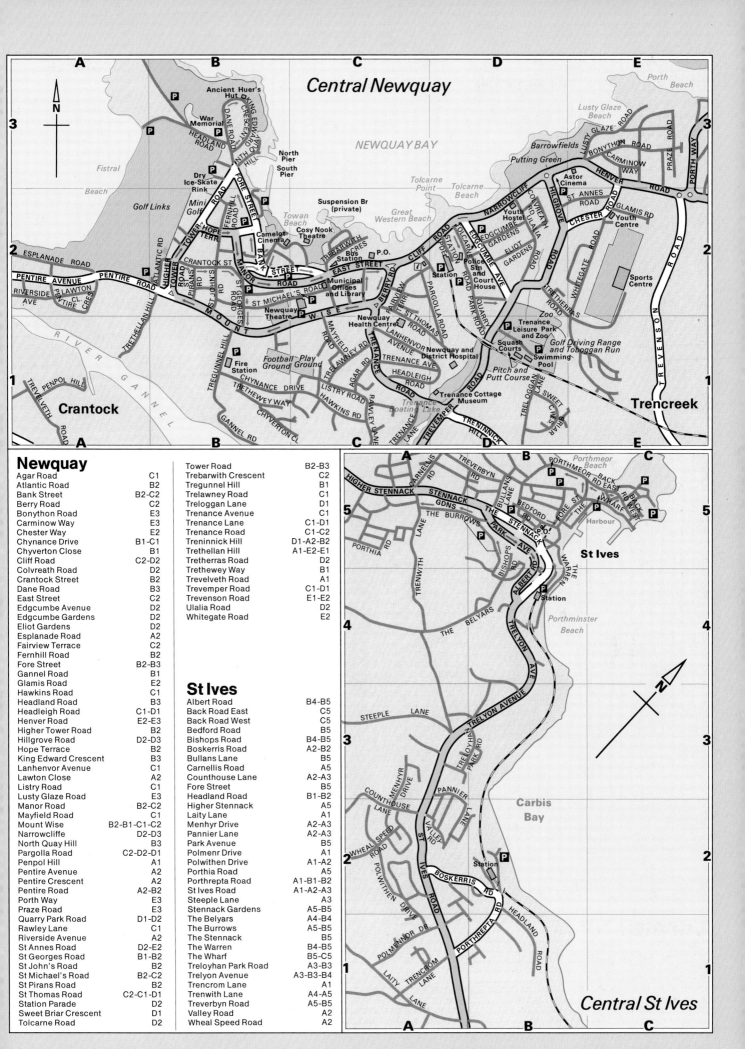

Central Newquay

Newquay

St Ives

Central St Ives

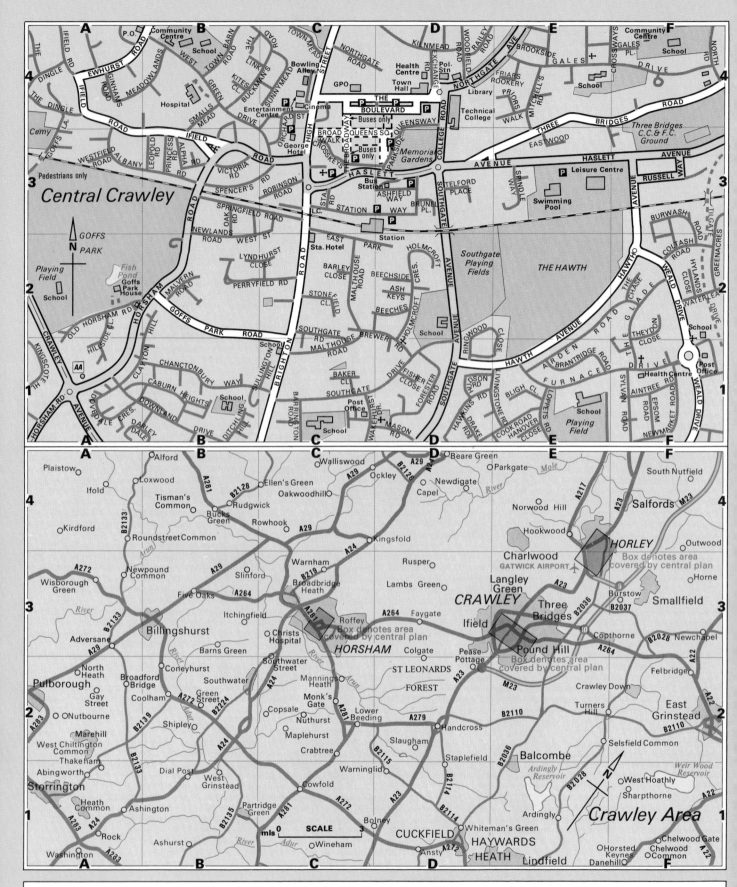

Crawley

Crawley New Town, the only one of that generation of post-war new towns to be built south of London, has been grafted on to the old Crawley where many ancient buildings resolutely survive. However, the new town does have its own examples of good architecture, including the bandstand in Queens Square which came from nearby Gatwick Racecourse – now the site of Gatwick Airport.

This, London's second largest airport, is expected to increase its passenger handling capacity from 16 million to 25 million passengers a year in the 1990s on completion of a second terminal.

Horsham is another town that has suffered from a rash of modern development as a result of being within striking distance of the capital. However, one or two corners of the original centre reveal some interesting old buildings. One of these

is a 16th-century black-and-white timbered house containing the local museum. Here, a period Sussex kitchen, a blacksmith's forge and a wheelwright's shop can be seen.

East Grinstead The well-heeled residential housing of commuter-land radiates from this old market town that has retained a number of Tudor buildings along its High Street. Sackville College, the 17th-century almshouses founded by the 2nd Earl of Dorset, forms an attractive group.

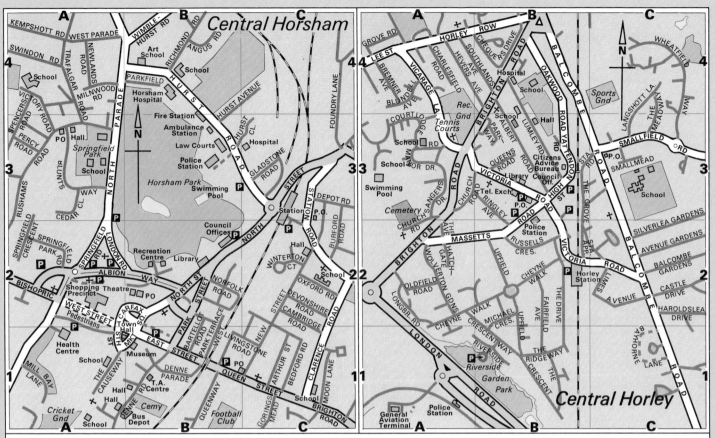

Central Horsham

Central Horley

Key to Town Plan and Area Plan

Town Plan
A A Recommended roads
Other roads
Restricted roads
Buildings of interest — Mill
Car Parks — P
Parks and open spaces
A A Service Centre — AA

Area Plan
A roads
B roads
Locations — Lickey End O
Urban Area

Street Index with Grid Reference

Crawley

Aintree Road	F1
Albany Road	A4-A3-B3
Alpha Road	B3
Arden Road	E1-E2-F2
Ash Keys	D2
Ashfield Way	D3
Baker Road	C1
Barley Close	C2
Barrington Road	C1
Beeches	C2-D2
Beechside	D2
Bligh Close	E1
Brantridge Road	E1
Brewer Road	C2-D2-D1
Brighton Road	B1-C1-C2-C3
Broad Walk	C3
Brookside	E4
Brunel Place	D3
Buckman's Road	B4-C4-B4
Burwash Road	F2-F3
Caburn Heights	A1-B1
Chanctonbury Way	A1-B1-C1
Clayton Hill	A1-B1-B2
College Road	D3-D4
Coltash Road	F2
Cook Road	D1-E1
Crawley Avenue	A1-A2
Crosskeys	C3
Crossways	E4-F4
Darley Dale	A1-B1
Ditchling Hill	B1
Dovedale Crescent	A1
Downland Drive	A1-B1
Drake Road	D1
East Park	C3-C2-D2
Eastwood	E3
Epsom Road	F1
Ewhurst Road	A4-B4
Exchange Road	D4
Fisher Close	D1
Forester Road	D1
Friars Rookery	E4
Furnace Drive	E1-F1
Gales Drive	E4-F4
Gales Place	F4
Ginhams Road	A4
Goffs Lane	A3-A4
Goffs Park Road	B2-C2-C1
Greenacres	F2-F3
Hanover Close	E1
Haslett Avenue	C3-D3-E3-F3
Hawkins Road	D1
Hawth Avenue	D1-E1-E2-F2-F3
High Street	C3-C4
Hillside Close	A1-A2
Holmcroft	D2
Holmcroft Crescent	D2
Horsham Road	A1-A2-B2-B3
Hudson Road	D1
Hylands Close	F2
Ifield Road	A4-A3-B3-C3
Kilnmead	D4
Kingscote Hill	A1
Kites Close	B4
Leopold Road	B3
Livingstone Road	D1-E1
Loppets Road	E1
Lyndhurst Close	B2-C2
Malthouse Road	C1-C2
Malvern Road	B2
Mason Road	C1-D1
Meadowlands	A4-B4
Mitchell's Road	E4
Newlands Road	B2-B3
Newmarket Road	F1
North Road	C3
Northgate Avenue	D4-E4
Northgate Road	C4-D4
Oak Road	B3
Old Horsham Road	A1-A2
Orchard Street	C3-C4
Parkside	D3
Perryfield Road	B2-C2
Princess Road	B3
Priors Walk	E4
Queens Square	C3-D3
Queensway	D3-D4
Railey Road	D4
Ringwood Close	D1-D2-E2-E1
Robinson Road	C3
Russell Way	F3
Smalls Mead	B3-B4
Southgate Avenue	D1-D2-D3
Southgate Drive	C1-D1
Southgate Road	C1-C2
Spencer's Road	B3-C3
Spindle Way	E3
Springfield Road	B3-C3
Station Road	C3
Station Way	C3-D3
Stonefield Close	C2
Sullington Hill	C1
Sunnymead	C4
Sylvan Road	F1
Telford Place	D3
The Boulevard	C4-D4
The Broadway	C3-C4
The Chase	F2
The Dingle	A4
The Glade	F1-F2
The Link	B4-C4
Theydon Close	F2
Three Bridges Road	D3-E3-E4-F4
Tilgate Drive	F1-F2-F3
Town Barn Road	B4
Town Mead	C4
Victoria Road	B3
Wakehurst Drive	C1
Waterlea	F2
Weald Drive	F1-F2
West Street	B2-B3-C3
Westfield Road	A3
West Green Drive	B4-B3-C3
Woodfield Road	D4

Horsham

Albion Way	A2-B2
Angus Road	B4
Arthur Street	C1
Bartellot Road	B1-B2
Bedford Road	C1
Bishopric	A2
Blunts Way	A3
Brighton Road	C1
Burford Road	C2-C3
Cambridge Road	C1-C2
Carfax	A2-B2
Cedar Close	A3
Clarence Road	C1-C2
Denne Parade	B1
Denne Road	A1-B1
Depot Road	C3
Devonshire Road	C2
East Street	B1
Foundry Lane	C3-C4
Gladstone Road	C1
Gorings Mead	C1
Hurst Avenue	B3-B4-C4
Hurst Close	B3-C3
Hurst Road	B4-B3-C3
Kempshott Road	A4
Livingstone Road	B1-C1
London Road	A2-B2
Market Square	A1-B1-B2
Mill Bay Lane	A1
Milnwood Road	A4
Moon Lane	C1
New Street	C1-C2
Newlands Road	A4
Norfolk Road	B2
North Parade	A3-A4-B4
North Street	B2-C2-C3
Oxford Road	C2
Park Street	B1-B2
Park Terrace West	B1-B2
Parkfield	B4
Percy Road	A3
Queen Street	B1-C1
Queenway	B1
Richmond Road	B4
Rushams Road	A2-A3
South Street	A1
Spencers Road	A3-A4
Springfield Crescent	A2-A3
Springfield Road	A2
Springfield Park Road	A2
Station Road	C2-C3
Swindon Road	A4
The Causeway	A1
Trafalgar Road	A3-A4
Victory Road	A3-A4
West Parade	A4
West Street	A2
Wimblehurst Road	B4
Winterton Court	C2

Horley

Albert Road	B3-B4
Avenue Gardens	C2
Balcombe Gardens	C2
Balcombe Road	B4-B3-C3-C2-C1
Bayhorne Lane	C1
Blundell Avenue	A4
Bremner Avenue	A4
Brighton Road	A2-A3-B3-B4
Castle Drive	C2
Charlesfield Road	A4
Chequers Drive	C2
Cheyne Walk	A2-B2
Church Road	A2-A3-B3
Court Lodge Road	A3
Crescent Way	A2-B2-B1
Fairfield Avenue	B1-B2
Grove Road	A4
Haroldslea Drive	A4
Hatchgate	C2
Hevers Avenue	A4-B4
High Street	B3
Horley Row	A4-B4
Langshott Road	C3-C4
Lee Street	A4
Limes Avenue	C2
London Road	A2-A1-B1
Longbridge Road	A2
Lumley Road	B3-B4
Manor Drive	A3
Massetts Road	A2-B2-B3
Michael Crescent	B1-B2
Oakwood Road	B3-B4
Oldfield Road	A2
Parkway	B3
Queens Road	B3
Ringley Avenue	B2-B3
Riverside	A1-B1
Russells Crescent	B2
Sangers Drive	A3
Silverlea Gardens	C2-C3
Smallfield Road	C3
Smallmead	C3
Southlands Avenue	A4-B4
Station Approach	B2
Station Road	B2-B3
The Avenue	A2
The Crescent	B1
The Drive	B1-B2
The Grove	B2-B3
The Meadway	C3-C4
The Ridgeway	B1
Upfield	B1-B2
Vicarage Lane	A3-A4
Victoria Road	A3-B3-B2-C2
Wheatfield Way	C3-C4
Wolverton Gardens	A2
Yattendon Road	B3

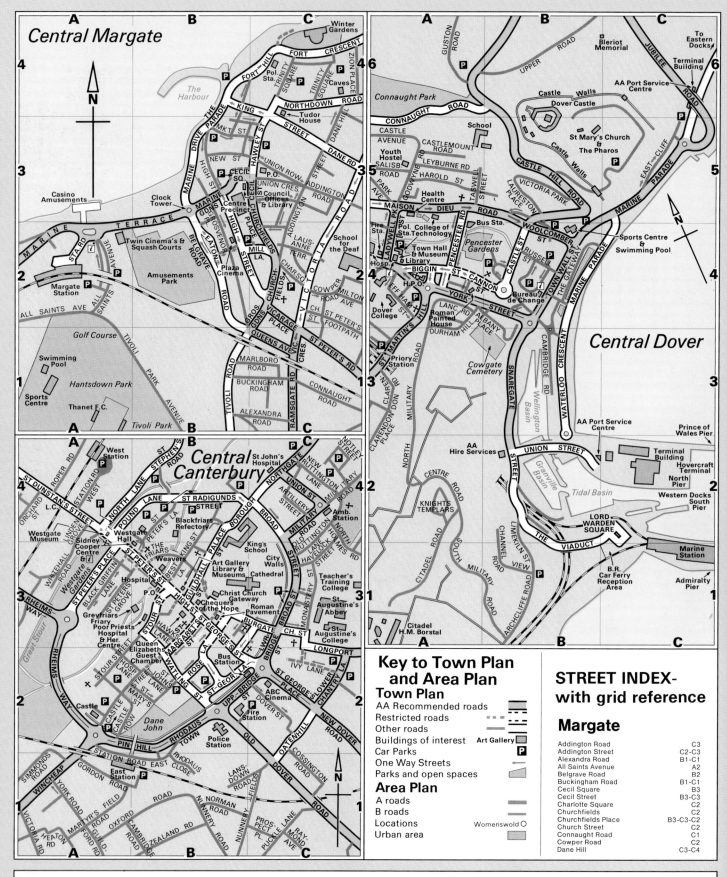

Key to Town Plan and Area Plan

Town Plan

AA Recommended roads	
Restricted roads	
Other roads	
Buildings of interest	Art Gallery
Car Parks	P
One Way Streets	
Parks and open spaces	

Area Plan

A roads	
B roads	
Locations	Womenswold O
Urban area	

STREET INDEX- with grid reference

Margate

Dover

Travellers tend to rush through Dover – it is one of the busiest passenger ports in England – and by so doing miss an exciting town with much of interest. Outstanding is the castle. Its huge fortifications have guarded the town since the 12th century, but within its walls are even older structures – a Saxon church and a Roman lighthouse called the Pharos. In the town itself, the town hall is housed within the walls of a 13th-century guest house called the Maison Dieu. The Roman Painted House in New Street consists of substantial remains of a Roman town house and include the best-preserved Roman wall paintings north of the Alps.

Canterbury is one of Britain's most historic towns. It is the seat of the Church in England, and has been so since St Augustine began his mission here in the 6th century. The cathedral is a priceless work of art containing many other works of art, including superb displays of medieval carving and stained glass. Ancient city walls – partly built on Roman foundations – still circle parts of the city, and a wealth of grand public buildings as well as charming private houses of many periods line the maze of lanes in the shadow of the cathedral.

Margate and **Ramsgate** both grew as commercial ports, but for many years they have specialised in catering for holidaymakers who like safe, sandy beaches and excellent facilities.

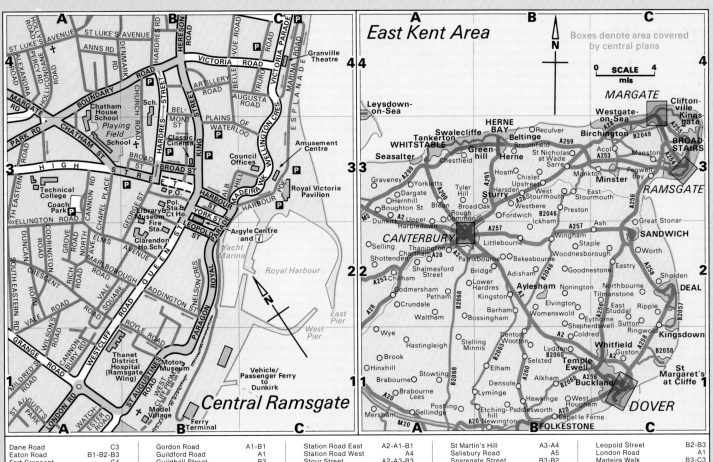

Central Ramsgate

East Kent Area

Boxes denote area covered by central plans

Dane Road	C3	Gordon Road	A1-B1	Station Road East
Eaton Road	B1-B2-B3	Guildford Road	A1	Station Road West
Fort Crescent	C4	Guildhall Street	B3	Stour Street
Fort Hill	B4-C4	Havelock Street	C3-C4	The Friars
Grosvenor Gardens	C1-C2	Hawks Lane	B3	Union Street
Grosvenor Place	B2-B3	Heaton Road	A1	Upper Bridge Street
Hawley Street	C3	High Street	B3	Victoria Road
High Street	B3-B2-C2	Hospital Lane	A2-B2	Watling Street
King Street	B4-C4-C3	Ivy Lane	C2	Whitehall Road
Lausanne Terrace	C2	King Street	B3-B4	Wincheap
Marine Drive	B3	Lansdown Road	B1-C1	York Road
Marine Gardens	B3	Linden Grove	A3-A4	Zealand Road
Marine Terrace	A2-A3-B3-B2	Longport	C3-C2	
Market Street	B3-C3	Lower Chantry Lane	C2	
Marlborough Road	B1-C1	Martyr's Field Road	A1	
Mill Lane	B2-C2	Military Road	C4	
Milton Avenue	C2	Monastery Street	C3	
New Street	B3	New Dover Road	C2	
Northdown Road	C4	New Ruttington Lane	C4	
Queens Avenue	C1	Norman Road	B1	
Ramsgate Road	C1	Northgate	C4	
St Peter's Footpath	C1-C2	North Holmes Road	C4-C3	
St Peter's Road	C1	North Lane	A4-B4	
Station Road	A2	Notley Street	C4	
The Parade	B3-B4	Nunnery Fields	B1-C1	
Tivoli Park Avenue	A1-B1	Nunnery Road	B1	
Tivoli Road	B1	Oatenhill	C1-C2	
Trinity Square	C4	Old Dover Road	B2-C2-C1	
Union Crescent	C3	Old Ruttington Lane	C3-C4	
Union Row	C3	Orchard Street	A4	
Vicarage Crescent	C1	Oxford Road	A1-B1	
Vicarage Place	C1-C2	Palace Street	B3-B4	
Victoria Road	C2-C3	Pin Hill	A2-B2	
Zion Place	C4	Pound Lane	A4-B4	
		Prospect Place	C1	
		Puckle Lane	C1	
		Raymond Avenue	C1	

Canterbury

Artillery Street	C4
Best Lane	B3
Black Griffin Lane	A3
Borough	B4-C4
Broad Street	C4-C3
Burgate	B3-C3
Cambridge Road	A1-B1
Castle Street	A2-B2
Castle Row	A2-B2
Church Street	C3
Cossington Road	C2-C1
Dover Street	C2

Rheims Way	A3-A2
Rhodaus Town	B2
Roper Road	A4
Rose Lane	B2-B3
St Dunstan's Street	A4
St Georges Lane	B2-C2
St George's Place	C2
St George's Street	B3-B2
St John's Lane	B2
St Mary's Street	A2-B2
St Peters Grove	A3-B3
St Peter's Lane	B4
St Peter's Place	A3
St Peter's Street	A3-B3
St Stephen's Road	B4
St Rudigunds Street	B4
Simmonds Road	A1-A2

Station Road East	A2-A1-B1
Station Road West	A4
Stour Street	A2-A3-B3
The Friars	B3
Union Street	C4
Upper Bridge Street	B2-C2
Victoria Road	A1
Watling Street	B2
Whitehall Road	A3
Wincheap	A1-A2
York Road	A1
Zealand Road	B1

Dover

Albany Place	A4-B4-B3
Archcliffe Road	B1
Biggin Street	A4
Cambridge Road	B3
Cannon Street	A4-B4
Castle Avenue	A5
Castle Hill Road	B5
Castlemount Road	A5
Castle Street	B4
Centre Road	A2
Channel View Road	B2-B1
Citadel Road	A1-A2
Clarendon Place	A2-A3
Clarendon Road	A3
Connaught Road	A5-A6
Durham Hill	A4-A3
East Cliff	C5
Effingham Street	A4
Godwyne Road	A5
Guston Road	A6
Harold Street	A5
Jubilee Road	C6
Knights Templars	A2
Ladywell Park Road	A4-A5
Lancaster Road	A4
Laureston Place	B5
Leyburne Road	A5
Limekiln Street	B2-B1
Maison Dieu Road	A5-B5
Marine Parade	B4-C4-C5
North Military Road	A2-A3
Park Avenue	A5
Pencester Road	A4-A5
Russell Street	B4

St Martin's Hill	A3-A4
Salisbury Road	A5
Snaregate Street	B3-B2
South Military Road	A2-A1-B1
The Gateway	B4
The Viaduct	B2-B1
Taswell Street	A5
Town Hall Street	B4
Union Street	B2
Upper Road	A6-B6
Victoria Park	B5
Woolcomber Street	B4
York Street	A4-B4

Ramsgate

Addington Street	B2
Albion Hill	B3
Alexandra Road	A4
Anns Road	A4
Artillery Road	B4
Augusta Road	B4-C4
Belle Vue Road	B4
Belmont Street	B4
Boundary Road	A3-A4-B4
Broad Street	B3
Cannonbury Road	A1
Canon Road	A3
Chapel Place	A2-A3
Chatham Street	A3
Church Road	B3-B4
Codrington Road	A2
Crescent Road	A2
Denmark Road	A4-B4
Duncan Road	B4
Ellington Road	A2-A3
Elms Avenue	A2-B2
Esplanade	C3-C4
George Street	B2-B3
Grange Road	A1
Grove Road	A2
Harbour Parade	B3-C3
Harbour Street	B3
Hardres Street	B3-B4
Hereson Road	B4
High Street	A3-B3
Hollicondane Road	A4
Holly Road	A4
King Street	B3-B4

Leopold Street	B2-B3
London Road	A1
Madeira Walk	B3-C3
Margate Road	A3-A4
Marina Road	C4
Marlborough Road	A2-B2
Mildred's Road	A1
Nelson Crescent	B2
North Avenue	A2
Paragon Royal Parade	B1-B2-B3
Park Road	A3
Percy Road	A4
Plains of Waterloo	B3-C3
Queen Street	B2-B3
Richmond Road	A2
Royle Road	A2-B2-B1
St Augustines Road	A1-B1
St August's Park	A1
St Luke's Avenue	A4-B4
South Eastern Road	A1-A2-A3
Truro Road	C4
Vale Road	A1-A2
Vale Square	A2-B2
Victoria Parade	C4
Victoria Road	B4-C4
Watchester Road	A1
Wellington Crescent	C3-C4
West Cliff Promenade	B1
Westcliff Road	A1-A2-B2
Wilson's Road	A1-A2
York Street	B2-B3

DOVER
The famous White Cliffs of Dover provide exhilarating coastal walks with views out across the Channel. Paths to the north-east lead to Walmer and to the south-east, to Folkestone.

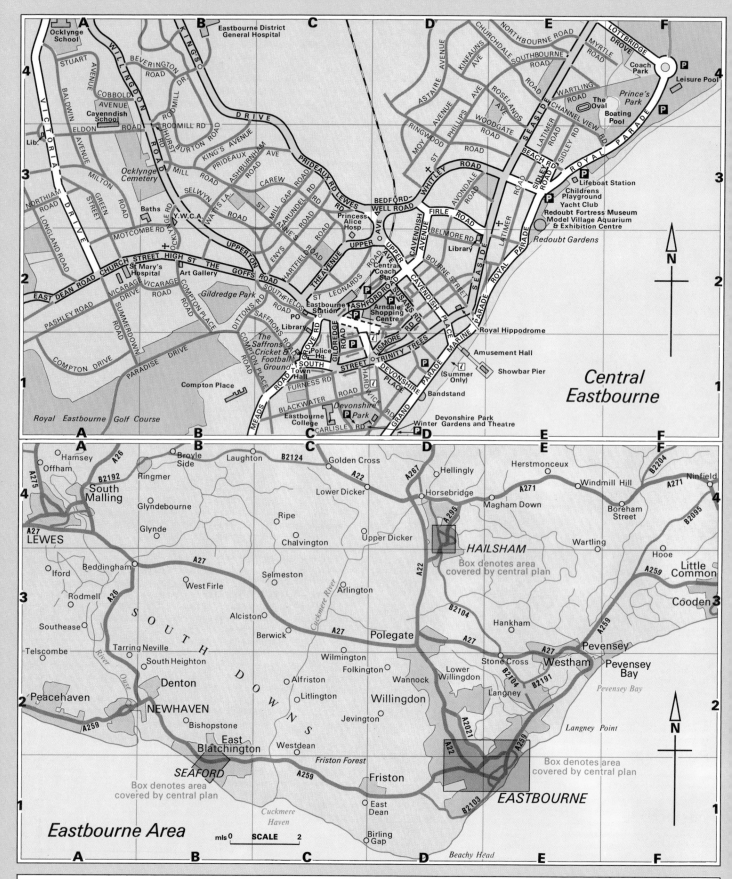

Central Eastbourne

Eastbourne Area

mls 0 SCALE 2

Eastbourne

Magnificent flower displays along the promenade combine with parks and gardens to provide a dazzling spectacle of colour from spring to autumn for this resort, which is one of the largest on the south coast and lies in the shelter of dramatic Beachy Head. Major sporting events take place throughout the year, including International and Championship tennis; on the cultural side, Eastbourne's Towner Art Gallery, Lifeboat Museum and Redoubt Fortress are all worth visiting. The town also offers good shopping and a wide choice of theatres and cinemas. For children, the imaginative Playcentre is designed with paddling pools, slides and big models of jungle animals.

Seaford boasts a three mile long promenade, which leads down to the seashore and to the Martello Tower (at the eastern end of the Esplanade) which houses the local museum. From Seaford Head a breathtaking view can be had of the coastline and the Seven Sisters, a line of cliffs stretching out along the shoreline. Between Cuckmere River and Seaford Head, a nature reserve supports a wide variety of plant and bird life.

Hailsham and ropemaking have gone together since the early 19th century, and another long-standing feature of the town is its cattle market, which has been operating on the same site since 1868.

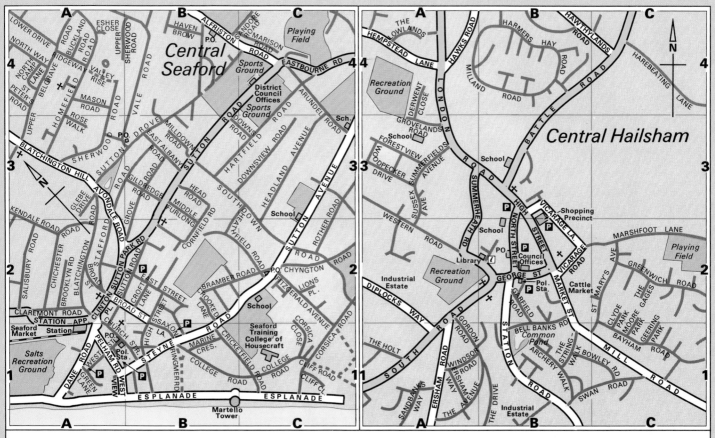

Key to Town Plan and Area Plan

Town Plan

A A Recommended roads
Other roads
Restricted roads
Buildings of interest
Car Parks
Parks and open spaces
One way streets

Area Plan

A roads
B roads
Locations   Ripe O
Urban Area

Street Index with Grid Reference

Eastbourne

Arundel Road	B2-C2-C3
Ashburnham Road	B3-C3
Ashford Road	C2-D2
Astaire Avenue	D4
Avondale Road	D3
Baldwin Avenue	A3-A4
Beach Road	E3
Bedfordwell Road	C3-D3
Belmore Road	D2
Beverington Road	A4-B4
Blackwater Road	C1-D1
Bourne Street	D2
Burton Road	B3-B4
Carew Road	B3-C3
Carlisle Road	C1-D1
Cavendish Avenue	D2-D3
Cavendish Place	D1-D2
Channel View Road	E3-E4
Church Street	A2-B2
Churchdale Road	D4-E4
Cobbold Avenue	A4

Compton Drive	A1
Compton Place Road	B2-B1-C1
Devonshire Place	D1
Dittons Road	B2-C2
East Dean Road	A2
Eldon Road	A3-B3
Enys Road	C2-C3
Firle Road	D2-D3
Furness Road	C1
Gildredge Road	C1-C2
Grand Parade	D1
Green Street	A2-A3
Grove Road	C1-C2
Hardwick Road	C1-D1
Hartfield Road	C2-C3
High Street	B2
Hurst Road	B3-B4
Kinfauns Avenue	D4
King's Avenue	B3-B4
King's Drive	B4-C4-C3
Latimer Road	E2-E3-E4
Lewes Road	C3
Lismore Road	D1-D2
Longland Road	A2-A3
Lottbridge Drive	E4-F4
Meads Road	B1-C1
Mill Gap Road	C2-C3
Mill Road	B3
Milton Road	A3
Marine Parade	D1-D2-E2
Motcombe Road	A2-A3-B3
Moy Avenue	D3-D4
Myrtle Road	E4-F4
Northbourne Road	E4
Northiam Road	A3
Ocklynge Road	B2-B3
Paradise Drive	A1-B1-B2
Pashley Road	A1-A2
Prideaux Avenue	B3-C3
Prideaux Road	C3
Ringwood Road	D4-D3-E3
Rodmill Drive	B4
Rodmill Road	B3-B4
Roselands Avenue	D4-E4-E3
Royal Parade	E2-E3-F3-F4
St Anne's Road	B3-C3-C2
St Leonard's Road	C2-D2
St Phillip's Avenue	D3-D4-E4
Saffrons Road	B2-C2-C1
Seaside	D2-E2-E3-E4
Selwyn Road	B3-B4-B2
Sidley Road	E3-E4
South Street	C1
Southbourne Road	D4-E4
Southfields Road	C2
Stuart Avenue	A4
Summerdown Road	A1-A2
Susan's Road	D2
The Avenue	C2
The Goffs	B2
Trinity Trees	D1-D2
Upper Avenue	C2-D2-D3
Upperton Road	B2-C2
Vicarage Drive	D2
Vicarage Road	A2-B2
Victoria Drive	A2-A3-A4
Wartling Road	E4
Watts Lane	B3
Whitley Road	D3-E3
Willingdon Road	A4-B4-B3
Woodgate Road	D4-D3-E3

Seaford

Alfriston Road	B4-C4
Arundel Road	C3-C4
Avondale Road	A2-B2-A3
Blatchington Hill	A3
Blatchington Road	A2-A3
Bramber Road	B2-C2
Broad Street	A2-B2
Brooklyn Road	A2
Buckland Road	A4
Chichester Road	A2
Church Street	A2-A1-B1
Chyngton Road	C2
Claremont Road	A2
Cliff Close	C1
Cliff Road	C1
Clinton Place	A2
College Road	B1-C1
Cornfield Road	B2-B3
Corsica Close	C1-C2
Corsica Road	C1-C2
Cricketfield Road	B1-C1
Croft Lane	B2
Crooked Lane	B2
Dane Road	A1
Downs Road	B3-C3
Downsview Road	B3-C3
East Street	B2
East Albany Road	B3
Eastbourne Road	C4
Esher Close	A4
Esplanade	A1-B1-C1
Fitzgerald Avenue	C1-C2
Gildredge Road	B3
Glebe Drive	A3
Green Lane	A1
Grove Road	B2-B3
Hartfield Road	B3-C3-C4
Haven Brow	B4
Head Road	B3
Headland Avenue	C2-C3
Heathfield Road	C3-B3-B2-C2
High Street	B1-B2
Homefield Road	A3-A4
Kendale Road	A2-A3
Lions Place	C2
Lower Drive	A4
Marine Crescent	B1
Marison Road	B4-C4
Mason Road	A4
Middle Furlong	B2-B3
Milldown Road	B3
North Camp Lane	A4
North Way	A4
Pelham Road	A1
Ridgeway	A4
Ringmer Road	B1
Rose Walk	A3
Rother Road	C2-C3
St Peter's Road	A2
Salisbury Road	A2
Sandore Road	B4-C4
Saxon Lane	B1
Sherwood Road	A3-A4
Southdown Road	B3-C3-C2
Stafford Road	A2-A3-B3
Station Approach	A1-A2
Steyne Road	B1-B2-C2
Sutton Avenue	C2-C3

Sutton Drove	A3-B3-B4-C4
Sutton Road	A2-B2-B3-B4-C4
Sutton Park Road	A2-B2
Upper Belgrave Road	A3-A4
Upper Sherwood Road	A4-B4
Vale Road	A3-B3-B4
Valley Rise	A4
West Street	A1
West View	A1-B1

Hailsham

Archery Walk	B1
Battle Road	B3-B4-C4
Bayham Road	C1-C2
Bell Banks Road	B1-B2
Bowley Road	B1-C1
Clyde Park	C1-C2
Derwent Close	A3-A4
Diplocks Way	A1-A2
Ersham Road	A1
Ersham Way	A1
Forest View	A3
Garfield Road	B2
Geering Park	C1-C2
George Street	B2
Gordon Road	A1-A2
Greenwich Road	C2
Grovelands Road	A3
Harebeating Lane	C4
Harmers Hay Road	B4
Hawks Road	A4
Hawthylands Road	B4-C4
Hempstead Lane	A4
High Street	B2-B3
London Road	A4-A3-B3
Market Street	B1-B2
Marshfoot Lane	C2
Mill Road	B1-C1
Milland Road	A4-B4
Moore Park	C1-C2
North Street	B2-B3
St Mary's Avenue	C1-C2
Sandbanks Way	A1
South Road	A1-A2-B2
Station Road	B1-B2
Summerfields Avenue	A3
Summerheath Road	A2-A3-B3-B2
Sussex Avenue	A2-A3
Swan Road	B1-C1
The Avenue	A1-B1
The Drive	B1
The Gages	B2
The Lowlands	A4
The Holt	A1
The Stringwalk	B1
Vicarage Lane	B2-B3
Vicarage Road	B2-C2
Western Road	A2-A3
Windsor Road	A1
Woodpecker Drive	A3

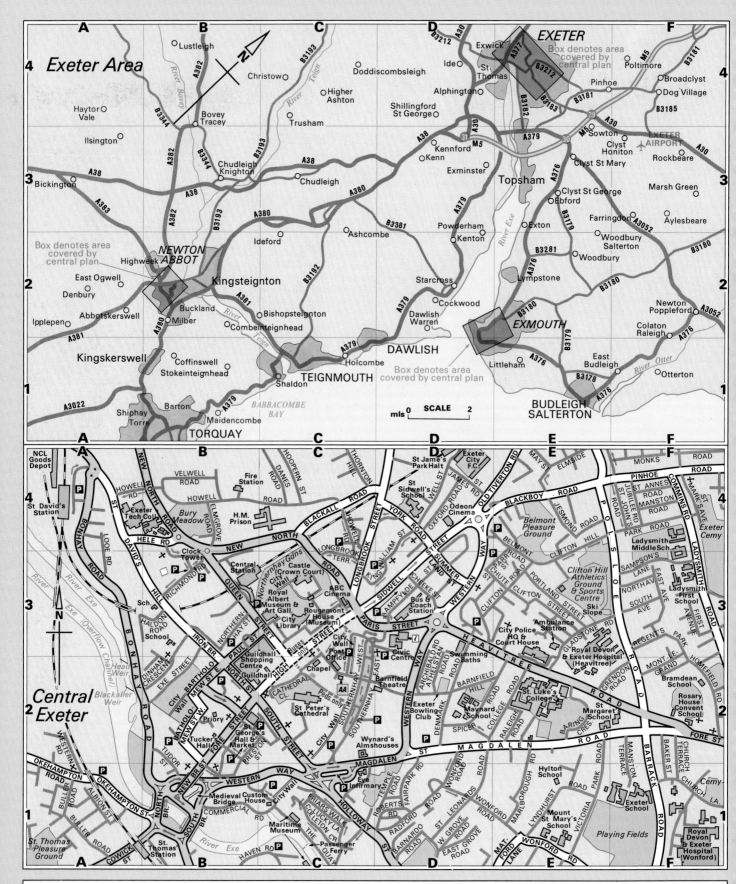

Exeter

The cathedral is Exeter's greatest treasure. Founded in 1050, but rebuilt by the Normans during the 12th century and again at the end of the 13th century, it has many beautiful and outstanding features – especially the exquisite rib-vaulting of the nave. Most remarkable, perhaps, is the fact that it still stood after virtually everything around it was flattened during bombing raids in World War II.

There are still plenty of reminders of Old Exeter, which has been a city since Roman times. Roman and medieval walls encircle parts of the city; 14th-century underground passages can be explored; the Guildhall is 15th-century and one of the oldest municipal buildings in the country; and Sir Francis Drake is said to have met his explorer companions at Mol's Coffee House. Exeter is famous for its extensive Maritime Museum, with over 100 boats from all over the world. Other museums include the Rougemont House and the Royal Albert Memorial Museum and Art Gallery.

Exmouth has a near-perfect position at the mouth of the Exe estuary. On one side it has expanses of sandy beach, on another a wide estuary alive with wildfowl and small boats, while inland is beautiful Devon countryside.

Newton Abbot lies on the River Teign. It is a busy market town and has been an important railway junction since the mid 19th century.

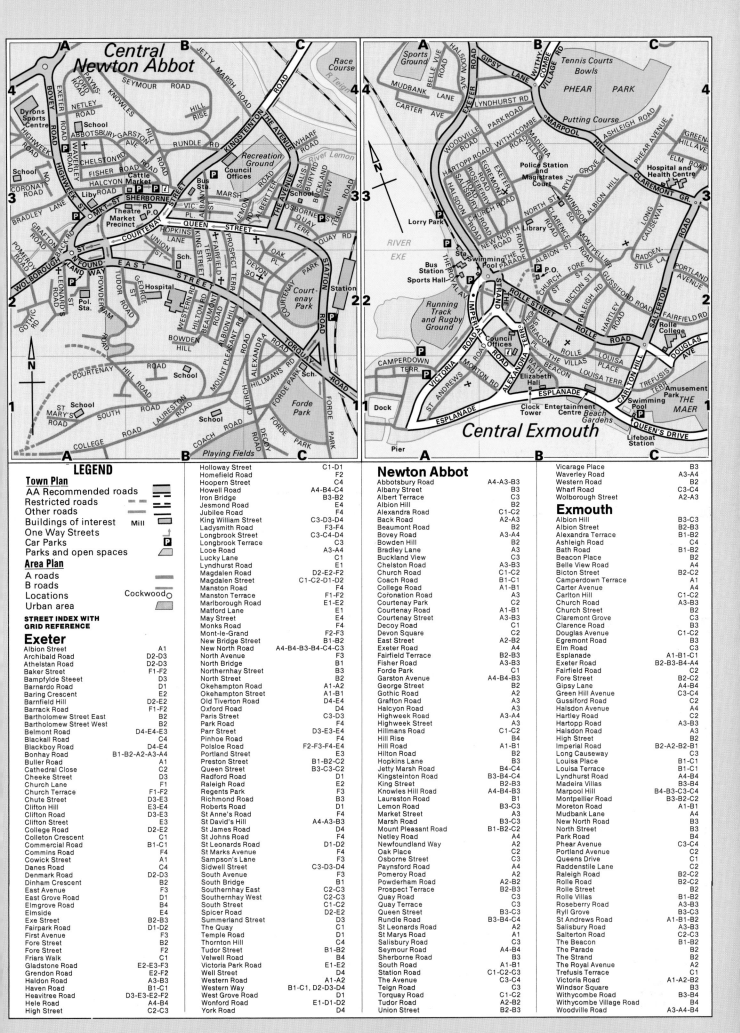

LEGEND

Town Plan

AA Recommended roads	
Restricted roads	
Other roads	
Buildings of interest	Mill
One Way Streets	
Car Parks	P
Parks and open spaces	

Area Plan

A roads	
B roads	
Locations	Cockwood o
Urban area	

STREET INDEX WITH GRID REFERENCE

Exeter

Albion Street	A1
Archibald Road	D2-D3
Athelstan Road	D2-D3
Baker Street	F1-F2
Bampfylde Steeet	D3
Barnardo Road	D1
Baring Crescent	E2
Barnfield Hill	D2-E2
Barrack Road	F1-F2
Bartholomew Street East	B2
Bartholomew Street West	B2
Belmont Road	D4-E4-E3
Blackall Road	C4
Blackboy Road	D4-E4
Bonhay Road	B1-B2-A2-A3-A4
Buller Road	A1
Cathedral Close	C2
Cheeke Street	D3
Church Lane	F1
Church Terrace	F1-F2
Chute Street	D3-E3
Clifton Hill	E3-E4
Clifton Road	D3-E3
Clifton Street	E3
College Road	D2-E2
Colleton Crescent	C1
Commercial Road	B1-C1
Commins Road	F4
Cowick Street	A1
Danes Road	C4
Denmark Road	D2-D3
Dinham Crescent	B2
East Avenue	F3
East Grove Road	D1
Elmgrove Road	B4
Elmside	E4
Exe Street	B2-B3
Fairpark Road	D1-D2
First Avenue	F3
Fore Street	B2
Fore Street	F2
Friars Walk	C1
Gladstone Road	E2-E3-F3
Grendon Road	E2-F2
Haldon Road	A3-B3
Haven Road	B1-C1
Heavitree Road	D3-E3-E2-F2
Hele Road	A4-B4
High Street	C2-C3

Holloway Street	C1-D1
Homefield Road	F2
Hoopern Street	C4
Howell Road	A4-B4-C4
Iron Bridge	B3-B2
Jesmond Road	E4
Jubilee Road	F4
King William Street	C3-D3-D4
Ladysmith Road	F3-F4
Longbrook Street	C3-C4-D4
Longbrook Terrace	C3
Looe Road	A3-A4
Lucky Lane	C1
Lyndhurst Road	E1
Magdalen Road	D2-E2-F2
Magdalen Street	C1-C2-D1-D2
Manston Road	F4
Manston Terrace	F1-F2
Marlborough Road	E1-E2
Matford Lane	E1
May Street	E4
Monks Road	F4
Mont-le-Grand	F2-F3
New Bridge Street	B1-B2
New North Road	A4-B4-B3-B4-C4-C3
North Avenue	F3
North Bridge	B1
Northernhay Street	B3
North Street	B2
Okehampton Road	A1-A2
Okehampton Street	A1-B1
Old Tiverton Road	D4-E4
Oxford Road	D4
Paris Street	C3-D3
Park Road	F4
Parr Street	D3-E3-E4
Pinhoe Road	F4
Polsloe Road	F2-F3-F4-E4
Portland Street	E3
Preston Street	B1-B2-C2
Queen Street	B3-C3-C2
Radford Road	D1
Raleigh Road	E2
Regents Park	F3
Richmond Road	B3
Roberts Road	D1
St Anne's Road	F4
St David's Hill	A4-A3-B3
St James Road	D4
St Johns Road	F4
St Leonards Road	D1-D2
St Marks Avenue	F4
Sampson's Lane	F3
Sidwell Street	C3-D3-D4
South Avenue	F3
South Bridge	B1
Southernhay East	C2-C3
Southernhay West	C2-C3
South Street	C1-C2
Spicer Road	D2-E2
Summerland Street	D3
The Quay	C1
Temple Road	D1
Thornton Hill	C4
Tudor Street	B1-B2
Velwell Road	C3
Victoria Park Road	E1-E2
Well Street	D4
Western Road	A1-A2
Western Way	B1-C1, D2-D3-D4
West Grove Road	D1
Wonford Road	E1-D1-D2
York Road	D4

Newton Abbot

Abbotsbury Road	A4-A3-B3
Albany Street	B3
Albert Terrace	C3
Albion Hill	B2
Alexandra Road	C1-C2
Back Road	A2-A3
Beaumont Road	B2
Bovey Road	A3-A4
Bowden Hill	A3
Bradley Lane	A3
Buckland View	C3
Chelston Road	A3-B3
Church Road	C1-C2
Coach Road	B1-C1
College Road	A1-B1
Coronation Road	A3
Courtenay Park	C2
Courtenay Road	A1-B1
Courtenay Street	A3-B3
Decoy Road	C1
Devon Square	C2
East Street	A2-B2
Exeter Road	A4
Fairfield Terrace	B2-B3
Fisher Road	A3-B3
Forde Park	C1
Garston Avenue	A4-B4-B3
George Street	A2
Gothic Road	A2
Grafton Road	A3
Halcyon Road	A3
Highweek Road	A3-A4
Highweek Street	A3
Hillmans Road	C1-C2
Hill Rise	B4
Hill Road	A1-B1
Hilton Road	B2
Hopkins Lane	B3
Jetty Marsh Road	B4-C4
Kingsteinton Road	B3-B4-C4
King Street	B2-B3
Knowles Hill Road	A4-B4-B3
Laureston Road	B1
Lemon Road	B3-C3
Market Street	A3
Marsh Road	B3-C3
Mount Pleasant Road	B1-B2-C2
Netley Road	A4
Newfoundland Way	A2
Oak Place	C2
Osborne Street	C3
Paynsford Road	A4
Pomeroy Road	A2
Powderham Road	A2-B2
Prospect Terrace	B2-B3
Quay Road	C3
Quay Terrace	C3
Queen Street	B3-C3
Rundle Road	B3-B4-C4
St Leonards Road	A2
St Marys Road	A1
Salisbury Road	C3
Seymour Road	A4-B4
Sherborne Road	B3
South Road	A1-B1
Station Road	C1-C2-C3
The Avenue	C3-C4
Teign Road	C3
Torquay Road	C1-C2
Tudor Road	A2-B2
Union Street	B2-B3

Vicarage Place	B3
Waverley Road	A3-A4
Western Road	B2
Wharf Road	C3-C4
Wolborough Street	A2-A3

Exmouth

Albion Hill	B3-C3
Albion Street	B2-B3
Alexandra Terrace	B1-B2
Ashleigh Road	C4
Bath Road	B1-B2
Beacon Place	B2
Belle View Road	A4
Bicton Street	B2-C2
Camperdown Terrace	A1
Carter Avenue	A4
Carlton Hill	C1-C2
Church Road	A3-B3
Church Street	B2
Claremont Grove	C3
Clarence Road	B3
Douglas Avenue	C1-C2
Egremont Road	B3
Elm Road	C3
Esplanade	A1-B1-C1
Exeter Road	B2-B3-B4-A4
Fairfield Road	C2
Fore Street	B2-C2
Gipsy Lane	A4-B4
Green Hill Avenue	C3-C4
Gussiford Road	C2
Halsdon Avenue	A4
Hartley Road	C2
Hartopp Road	A3-B3
Halsdon Road	A3
High Street	B2
Imperial Road	B2-A2-B2-B1
Long Causeway	C3
Louisa Place	B1-C1
Louisa Terrace	B1-C1
Lyndhurst Road	A4-B4
Madeira Villas	B3-B4
Marpool Hill	B4-B3-C3-C4
Montpellier Road	B3-B2-C2
Moreton Road	A1-B1
Mudbank Lane	A4
New North Road	B3
North Street	B3
Park Road	B4
Phear Avenue	C3-C4
Portland Avenue	C2
Queens Drive	C1
Raddenstile Lane	C2
Raleigh Road	B2-C2
Rolle Road	B2-C2
Rolle Street	B2
Rolle Villas	B1-B2
Roseberry Road	A3-B3
Ryll Grove	B3-C3
St Andrews Road	A1-B1-B2
Salisbury Road	A3-B3
Salterton Road	C2-C3
The Beacon	B1-B2
The Parade	B2
The Strand	B2
The Royal Avenue	A2
Trefusis Terrace	C1
Victoria Road	A1-A2-B2
Windsor Square	B3
Withycombe Road	B3-B4
Withycombe Village Road	B4
Woodville Road	A3-A4-B4

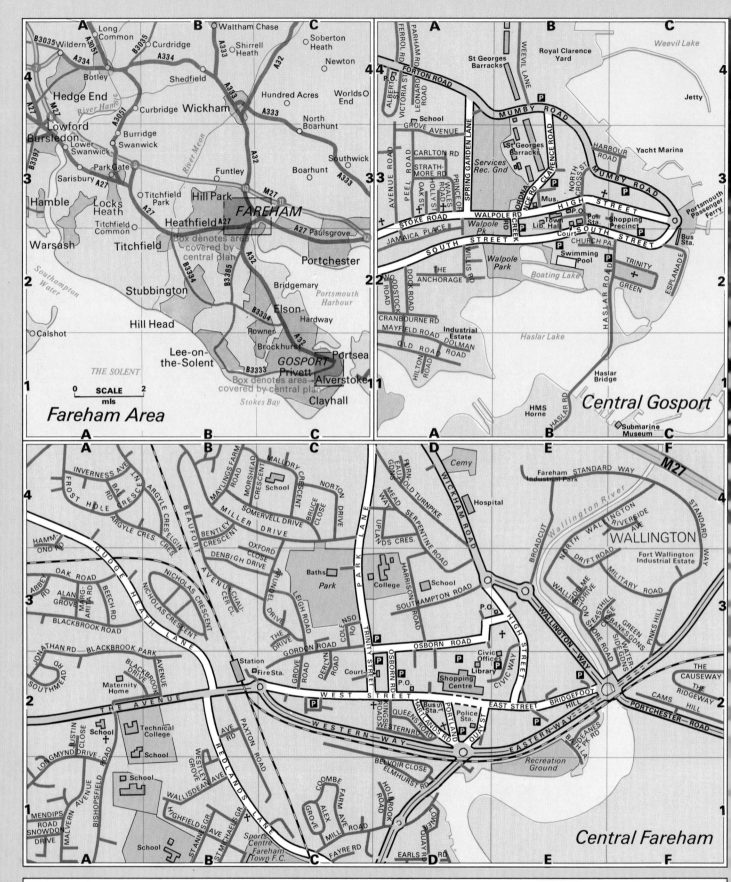

Fareham

Naval connections have long been a feature of this old market town. A large number of its residents work at the Naval Base in Portsmouth, naval training establishment HMS Collingwood stands on the town's outskirts, and its pre-19th century importance as a boat-building centre is being recaptured today with the manufacture of small sailing craft.

The trade is centred mainly around the Lower Quay on Fareham Creek (which flows virtually into the town centre), and buildings used as a hospital for French prisoners during the Napoleonic Wars can also be seen in this part of town. The High Street has retained a distinctly Georgian flavour; neighbouring West Street reflects Fareham's popularity as a shopping centre and has seen a good deal of development.

Gosport is another town whose trade has always been associated with the needs of the navy. Lying on the west side of Portsmouth Harbour and a major naval port since the 17th century, Gosport has probably the most extensive areas of military and naval housing in the country. HM Submarine Alliance, which houses a submarine museum, can be seen in Haslar Creek, and also of interest are Gosport Museum, 19th-century Fort Brockhurst, and the parish church, which dates from the 17th century and has an almost unchanged interior.

HM Submarine Alliance and Submarine Museum

Gosport's history as a submarine base goes back almost as far as submarines themselves, so this is a fitting home for the Royal Navy Submarine Museum and HM Submarine Alliance.

Submarines have come a long way since the days when a disgruntled Controller of the Navy said that "submariners should be hanged as pirates in wartime". In spite of early Admiralty misgivings, these sleek but lethal underwater travellers are the frontrunners of the Royal Navy today.

At the Submarine Museum in Gosport's Haslar Creek, visitors can see just how submarines have developed to become a crucial part of the modern fleet. Centrepiece of the museum is HM Submarine Alliance, which was intended for use in World War II but not ready in time to take part in any engagements. On her 'retirement' from service, she was presented to the Submarine Museum, and has been completely restored and raised up out of the water for easy access. Visitors enter through doors which have been cut in the pressure hull, and can walk right through the vessel. On the way, they are given a feel of the life and work of the submariners of World War II and they can also explore a more modern side to submarining, by looking at the new equipment which has been installed here. Guides are on hand to explain the functions of the various compartments, and to answer questions.

A recent arrival at the museum is HM Submarine Holland I — Britain's first submarine, newly salvaged from the seabed after the unlikely reprieve of sinking on her way to the breaker's yard. Named after her inventor John Philip Holland, she was launched in 1901, but has the porpoise-hull profile of the most up-to-date nuclear versions.

In the main body of the museum, models of all varieties of submarine are on display, coming right up to the advanced nuclear versions of today. Models featured in this section include HM Submarine Conqueror, while representing an earlier period in submarine development is the 1776 Turtle, built for American revolutionaries to launch an (unsuccessful) attack on Admiral Lord Howe's flagship in New York Harbour.

Visitors are advised to give themselves at least an hour and a half in order to do justice to all the museum has to offer, and to allow longer at busy times like the summer.

OPENING TIMES The Museum is open all year round, from 9.30am to 4.30pm, every day except Christmas Eve and Christmas Day.

TO GET THERE See town plan **Gosport**, grid squares B1 and C1. Cross Haslar Bridge and then turn left off Haslar Road. From here follow signs to the Submarine Museum.

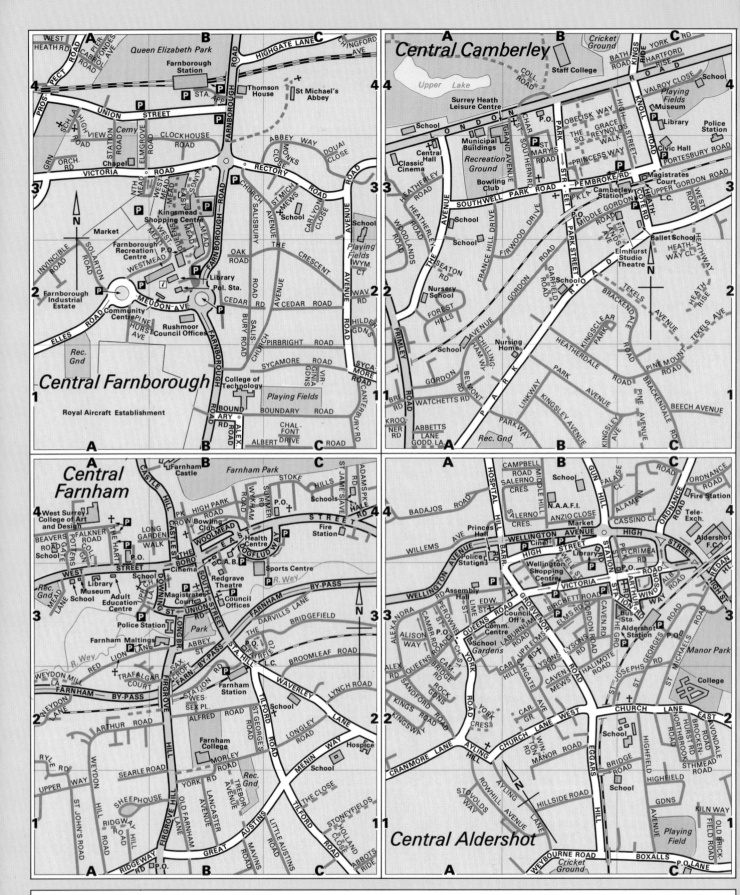

Farnborough

Dick Turpin is said to have been associated with Farnborough's Tumbledown Dick inn and the Ship Inn was once used by patrons of illegal prize fights — but today the town is synonymous with the high technology of aeronautical research, and with the army. This is the scene of the biennial Farnborough Air Show, and the town's growth really began in the mid-19th century, when large numbers of military personnel were moved into the area.

Aldershot is the appropriate home of the Wellington Monument, which was moved here from London's Hyde Park Corner in 1885. It stands near the 19th-century Royal Garrison Church — another symbol of Aldershot's military importance since the Army arrived here in 1885 and instigated the town's expansion. Every two years in June the Army Display is held in the Rushmoor Arena and in 1969, the Army combined with the council to found the Stainforth Ski Centre.

Camberley is mainly a residential town, close to the Royal Staff College and the Royal Military Academy at Sandhurst.

Farnham is the home of the thriving Redgrave Theatre, and its cultural life is also served by the Maltings, an Adult Education and community centre. Much of Farnham's character as an 18th-century market town has been retained, and the castle dates back to the 12th century.

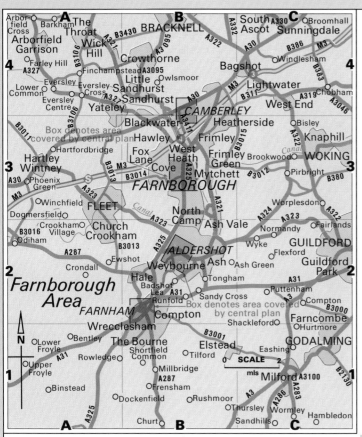

Key to Town Plan and Area Plan

Town Plan

AA Recommended roads	
Other roads	
Restricted roads	
Buildings of interest	Cinema
Car Parks	P
Parks and open spaces	
One Way Streets	←

Area Plan

A roads	
B roads	
Locations	Elstead○
Urban area	

Street Index with Grid Reference

Farnborough

Abbey Way	B3-C3
Albert Road	B1-C1
Alexandra Road	B1
Avenue Road	C1-C2-C3
Boundary Road	B1-C1
Cabrol Road	A4
Canterbury Road	C1
Carlyon Close	C3
Cedar Road	B2-C2
Chalfont Drive	C1
Chingford Avenue	C4
Church Avenue	B1-B2-C2-C3-B3
Clockhouse Road	A3-B3
Eastmead	B2-B3
Elles Road	A1-A2
Elmgrove Road	A3-A4
Farnborough Road	B1-B2-B3-B4
Green School Lane	A3-A4
Highgate Lane	B4-C4
Highview Road	A3-A4

Hilder Gardens	C1-C2
Invincible Road	C2
Kingsmead	B2-B3
Meudon Avenue	A2-B2
Monks Close	C3
Northmead	A3
Oak Road	B2
Orchard Road	A3
Pierfondes Avenue	A4
Pinehurst Avenue	A2-B2
Pirbright Road	B1-C1
Prospect Road	A4
Queensmead	B2-B3
Rectory Road	B3-C3
St Michaels Mews	C3
Salisbury Road	B1-B2-B3
Solatron Road	A2-A3
Station Approach	B4
Station Road	A3-A4
Sycamore Road	B1-C1
The Crescent	B2-C2
Union Street	A4-B4
Victoria Road	A3-B3
Virginia Gardens	C1
Waverley Road	C2
West Heath Road	A4
Westmead	A2-B2-B3-A3-B3
Wymering Court	C2

Camberley

Abbetts Lane	A1
Bath Road	B4-C4
Beech Avenue	C1
Belmont Road	A1
Brackendale Road	B2-C2-C1
Bridge Road	A1
Charles Street	B4
Chillingham Way	A1-A2
College Road	A4-B4
Firlands Avenue	B3-C3-C2
Firwood Drive	A2-B2-B3
Forest Hills	A2
France Hill Drive	A2-A3
Frimley Road	A1-A2
Garfield Road	B2
Goddards Lane	A1
Gordon Avenue	A1-A2
Gordon Road	A2-B2-B3
Grace Reynolds Walk	B3-B4-C4
Grand Avenue	B3-B4
Hartford Rise	C4
Heathcote Road	C3

Farnborough (Heatherdale–York)

Heatherdale Road	B2-B1-C1
Heatherley Road	A2-A3
Heath Rise	C2
Heathway	C2-C3
Heathway Close	C2
High Street	B4-C4-C3
Kingsclear Park	B1-B2
Kingsley Avenue	B1-C1
Kings Ride	C4
Knoll Road	C3-C4
Krooner Road	A1
Linkway	B1
London Road	A3-A4-B4-C4
Middle Gordon Road	B3-C3
Obelisk Way	B4
Park Avenue	B1-C1
Park Lane	B3
Park Road	A1-B1-B2-C2-C3
Park Street	B2-B3-B4
Parkway	A1-B1
Pembroke Road	B3-C3
Pine Avenue	C1
Pine Mount Road	C1
Portesbury Road	C3
Princes Way	B3-C3
St Mary's Road	B3
Seaton Road	A2
Southern Road	B3
Southwell Park Road	A3-B3
Tekels Avenue	B2-C2-C1-C2
Th Avenue	A2-A3
The Square	B3
Upper Gordon Road	C3
Valroy Close	C4
Watchetts Road	A1
West Road	C3
Woodlands Road	A2-A3
York Road	C4

Farnham

Abbey Street	B3
Abbots Ride	C1
Adams Park Road	C4
Alfred Road	B2
Arthur Road	A2-B2
Beavers Road	A4
Bridgefield	C3
Broomleaf Road	C2-C3
Castle Hill	A4-B4
Castle Street	B4
College Garden	A3-A4
Darvills Lane	B3-C3
Dogflud Way	B4-C4
Downing Street	B3
East Street	B4-C4
Falkner Road	A4
Farnham By-pass	A2-B2-B3-C3
Firgrove Hill	B1-B2-B3
Great Austins	B1-C1
Hale Road	C4
High Park Road	B4
Holland Close	C1
Lancaster Avenue	B1
Little Austins Road	C1
Long Bridge	B3
Long Garden Walk	A4-B4
Longley Road	C2
Lynch Road	C2
Mavins Road	B1
Mead Lane	A3
Menin Way	C1-C2
Morley Road	B1-B2-C2
Old Farnham Lane	B1
Park Row	B4
Potters Gate	A3-A4
Red Lion Lane	A2-A3-B3
Ridgway Hill Road	A1
Ridgway Road	A1-B1
Ryle Road	A1-A2
St George's Road	B2
St James's Avenue	C4
St John's Road	A1
Saxon Croft	B2-B3
Searle Road	A1-B1
Sheephouse	A1-B1
South Street	B3-B4
Station Hill	B2-B3
Station Road	B2-B3-B2-B3
Stoke Hills	C4
Stoneyfields	C1
Summer Road	C4
The Borough	B3-B4
The Close	C1
The Fairfield	B3-C3
The Hart	A3-A4
Tilford Road	B2-C2-C1
Trafalgar Court	A2-B2
Trebor Avenue	B1-B2
Union Road	B3
Upper Church Lane	A3-B3
Upper Way	A1
Waverley Lane	B2-C2
Wessex Place	A1
West Street	A3-B3-B4
Weydon Hill Road	A1-A2
Weydon Lane	A2
Weydon Mill Lane	A2
Woolmead	B4

Farnborough (Wykham–York)

Wykham Road	B4
York Road	B1-B2

Aldershot

Alamein Road	B4-C4
Albert Road	C3
Alexandra Road	A2-A3-B3
Alison Way	A3
Anzio Close	B4
Arthur Road	C3
Avondale Road	C2
Ayling Hill	A2
Ayling Lane	A2-A1-B1
Badajos Road	A2
Barrack Road	A4-A3-B3-B4
Birchett Road	B3
Boxalls Lane	B1-C1
Bridge Road	B1-B2-C2
Brockenhurst Road	C2
Cambridge Road	A2-A3
Campbell Road	B4
Cargate Avenue	B2-B3
Cargate Grove	B2
Cargate Hill	A2-B2-B3
Cassino Close	B4-C4
Cavendish Mews	B2
Cavendish Road	B3
Church Lane East	B2-C2
Church Lane West	A2-B2
Church Street	A2-A3
Cranmore Lane	A1-A2
Crimea Road	C4
Edward Street	A3-B3
Eggars Hill	B1-B2
Elms Road	B3
Falaise Close	B4-C4
Gordon Road	B3
Grosvenor Road	B2-B3
Gun Hill	B4
Halimote Road	B2-B3
Highfield Avenue	C1-C2
Highfield Gardens	C2
High Street	B4-C4-C3
Hillside Road	B1
Hospital Hill	A4-B4
Kilnway	C1
Kings Road	A2
Kingsway	A2
Laburnum Road	B3
Lime Street	A3
Lysons Road	B2-B3
Manor Road	B2
Middle Hill	B4
Northbrook Road	C2
Old Brickfield Road	C1
Ordnance Road	C4
Perowne Street	A3
Pickford Street	B4-C4-C3
Queens Road	A2-A3-B3
Redan Hill	C3-C4
Rock Gardens	A2
Rowhill Avenue	A2-A1-B1
St Georges Road	C2-C3
St Josephs Road	B2-C2-C3
St Michaels Road	C2-C3
Salerno Crescent	B4
Sandford Road	A2
Southmead Road	C2
Station Road	B4-B3-C3
Stovolds Way	A1
The Grove	B3
Upper Elms Road	B3
Victoria Road	B3-C3-C4
Wellington Avenue	A3-A4-B4
Wellington Street	B3-B4
Weybourne Road	B1
Willems Avenue	A4
Windsor Way	C3
Winton Road	B2
York Crescent	A2
York Road	A2-A3

FARNHAM
Attractive shops and houses line the broad thoroughfare of Castle Street, which is overlooked by the castle itself. Founded in the 12th century, this was once the seat of the bishops of Winchester and of Guildford.

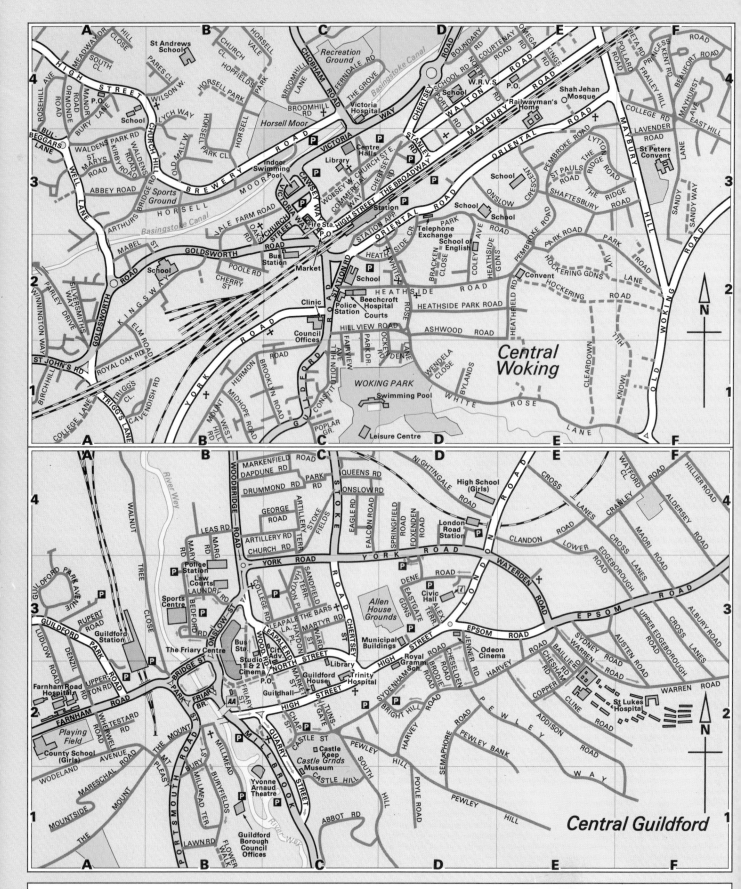

Guildford

Guildford's impressive modern redbrick Anglican cathedral, consecrated in 1961, looks down on the county town of Surrey from its hill-top setting on the outskirts. Nearby are the differently-styled modern buildings of the University of Surrey. Another example of modern architecture is the Yvonne Arnaud Theatre, which opened in 1958 on the banks of the River Wey. Despite being a busy modern shopping centre the town retains many old buildings and its steep, partly-cobbled High Street has an unchanging Georgian character. Most prominent is the Guildhall with its hexagonal bell-turret and gilded clock overhanging the pavement. All that remains of the city's castle, just off the High Street, is the 12th-century keep built by Henry II, but close by the Castle Museum has a comprehensive range of local antiquities.

Godalming An important staging post on the London to Portsmouth road in stagecoach days, this attractive North Downs town still has several old coaching inns as well as a number of other 16th-century buildings. Local artefacts can be found in the Borough Museum.

Woking A residential and commuter town on the disused Basingstoke Canal, Woking developed as a direct result of the arrival of the railway in the 1830s. Its most distinctive feature is its large Mosque, built in 1889.

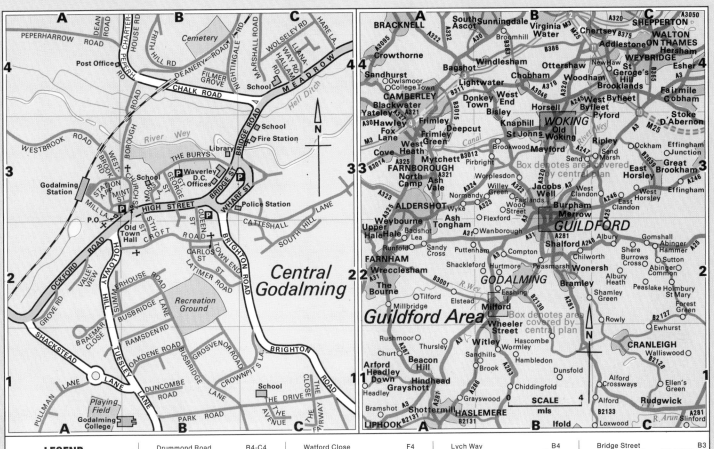

LEGEND

Town Plan

AA recommended route
Restricted roads
Other roads
Buildings of interest Station
Car parks P
Parks and open spaces
One way streets

Area Plan

A roads
B roads
Locations Fairlands ○
Urban area

Street Index with Grid Reference

Guildford

Abbot Road	C1
Addison Road	E2-F2-F1
Albury Road	F2-F3
Aldersey Road	F4-F3
Alexandra Terrace	D3
Artillery Road	B4-C4
Artillery Terrace	C4
Austen Road	E3-F3-F2
Baillie Road	E2-E3
Bedford Road	D2
Bridge Street	B2-B3
Bright Hill	D2
Brodie Road	D2
Buryfields	B1
Bury Street	B1-B2
Castle Hill	C1
Castle Street	C2
Chapel Street	C2
Chertsey Street	C3
Cheselden Road	D2-D3
Chesham Road	E2-E3
Church Road	B3-B4-C4
Clandon Road	D4-E4
Cline Road	E2-F2
College Road	B4-C4
Copper Road	E2
Cranley Road	E4-F4
Cross Lanes	E4-F4-F3-F2
Dapdune Road	B4-C4
Dene Road	D3
Denzil Road	A2-A3

Drummond Road	B4-C4
Eagle Road	C4
Eastgate Gardens	D3
Epsom Road	D3-E3-F3
Falcon Road	C4
Farnham Road	A2-B2
Flower Walk	B1
Foxenden Road	D4
Friary Bridge	A2
Friary Street	B2
George Road	B4-C4
Guildford Park Avenue	A3
Guildford Park Road	A2-A3
Harvey Road	D2-E2-E3
Haydon Place	C3
High Street	B2-C2-D2-D3
Hillier Road	F4
Jenner Road	D2-D3
Laundry Road	B3
Lawn Road	B1
Leapale Lane	C3
Leapale Road	C3
Leas Road	B4
London Road	D3-D4-E4
Lower Edgeborough Road	E4-E3-F3
Ludlow Road	A2-A3
Maori Road	F4-F3
Mareschal Road	A1-A2
Margaret Road	B4-B3
Markenfield Road	B4-C4
Market Street	C2
Martyr Road	C3
Mary Road	B4-B3
Millbrook	B2-C2-C1
Millmead	B1-B2
Millmead Terrace	B1
Mount Pleasant	B1-B2
Mountside	A1
Nightingale Road	D4
North Street	C2-C3
Onslow Road	C4-D4
Onslow Street	B3
Park Road	C4
Park Street	B2
Pewley Bank	D2-E2-E1
Pewley Hill	C2-D2-D1-E1
Pewley Way	D2-E2-E1-F1
Portsmouth Road	B1-B2
Poyle Road	D1
Quarry Street	C2-C3-B3
Queens Road	C4-D4
Rupert Road	A3
Sandfield Terrace	C3
Semaphore Road	D1-D2
South Hill	C2-C1-D1
Springfield Road	D4
Stoke Fields	C3
Stoke Road	C3-C4
Sydenham Road	C2-D2-D3
Sydney Road	E3-F3-E2
Testard Road	A2
The Bars	C3
The Mount	A1-B1-B2
Tunsgate	C2
Upper Edgeborough Road	F3-F2
Upperton Road	A2
Walnut Treet Close	B2-B3-A3-A4
Ward Street	C3
Warren Road	E3-E2-F2
Waterden Road	D2-E3

Watford Close	F4
Wherwell Road	A2
Woodbridge Road	B4-B3-C3-C2
Wodeland Avenue	A1-A2-B2
York Road	B3-C3-C4-D3-D4

Woking

Abbey Road	A3
Arthurs Bridge Road	A2-A3-B4
Ashwood Road	D2-E2
Beaufort Road	F4
Beta Road	F4
Birch Hill	A1
Boundary Road	D4
Bracken Close	D2
Brewery Road	B3-C3-C4
Brooklyn	B1-C1
Broomhill Lane	B4
Broomhill Road	C4
Bulbeggars Lane	A3
Bury Lane	A3-A4
Bylands	D1
Cavendish Road	A1-B1
Cawsey Way	C3
Cherry Street	B2
Chertsey Road	C3-D3-D4
Chobham Road	C4
Church Close	D2
Church Hill	B3-B4
Church Street	C2-C3
Church Street East	C3-D3
Cleardown	E1-E2
Coley Avenue	D2-D3
College Lane	A1
College Road	F4
Commercial Way	C3
Constitution Hill	C1
Courteney Road	D4-E4
Elm Road	A2-A1
East Hill	F3-F4
Fairview Avenue	C1-C2
Ferndale Road	C4
Frailey Hill	F4
Goldsworth Road	A1-A2-B2-C2
Guildford Road	B1-C1-C2
Heathside Crescent	C1-D1-D2
Heathside Gardens	D2
Heathside Park Road	D1-E1
Heathside Road	C1-D1-E1
Heathside Road	E2
High Street	A3-B4
High Street	C3
Hill Close	A4
Hill View Road	C2-D2
Hockering Gardens	E2
Hockering Road	E2-F2
Hopfields	B4
Horsell Moor	A3-B3-C3
Horsell Park	B3-B4-C4
Horsell Park Close	B3-B4
Horsell Vale	B4-C4
Ivy Lane	E2-F2
Kent Road	F4
Kings Road	E4
Kings Way	A1-A2-B2
Kirby Road	A3
Knowl Hill	F1-F2
Lavender Road	F3

Lych Way	B4
Lytton Road	E3-F3
Mabel Street	A2-B2
Manor Road	A4
Maybury Hill	E4-F4-F3-F2
Maybury Road	D3-D4-E4
Mayhurst Avenue	F4
Meadway Drive	A4
Midhope Road	B1
Mount Hermon Road	B1-C1
North Road	D4-E4
Oaks Road	B2-B3
Ockenden Road	D1-D2
Old Malt Way	B3
Old Woking road	F1-F2-F3
Omega Road	E4
Onslow Crescent	D3-E3
Oriental Road	C2-C3-D2-D3-E3-E4
Ormonde Road	A4-A3
Pares Close	A4
Park Drive	C1-C2
Park Road	D3-E3-E2-F2
Parley Drive	A1-A2
Pembroke Road	E2-E3-E4
Pollard Road	F4
Poole Road	B2-C2
Poplar Grove	C1
Port Road	D4
Princes Road	F4
Rosehill Avenue	A4
Royal Oak Road	A1
St Johns Road	A1
St Marys Road	A3
St Pauls Road	E3
Sandy Lane	F2-F3-F4
Sandy Way	F3
School Road	D4
Shaftesbury Road	E3-F3
Silversmiths Way	A2
South Close	A4
Stanley Road	D3
Station Approach	C2-C3-D3
Station Road	C2
The Broadway	D3
The Grove	C4-D4
The Ridge	E3-F3
Trigg's Close	A1
Trigg's Lane	A1
Vale Farm Road	B2-B3-C3
Victoria Way	C2-C3-C4-D4
Waldens Park Road	A3
Waldens Road	A3
Walton Road	D3-D4-E4
Well Lane	A3
Wendella Close	D1
West Hill Road	B1
White Rose Lane	D2-D1-E1-F1
Winnington Way	A1-A2
Wilson Way	B4
Wolsey Way	C3
York Road	B1-B2-C2

Godalming

Borough Road	B3-B4
Braemar Close	A1-A2
Bridge Road	B3-C3-C4

Bridge Street	B3
Brighton Road	B3-B2-C2-C1
Busbridge Lane	A2-B2-B1
Carlos Street	B2
Catteshal Lane	B3-C3-C2
Chalk Road	B4-C4
Charterhouse Road	B4
Church Street	B3
Croft Road	B2
Crownpits Lane	B1-C1
Dean Road	A4
Deanery Road	B4
Duncombe Road	B1
Filmer Grove	B4
Frith Hill Road	B4
Great George Street	B3
Grosvenor Road	B1
Grove Road	A2
Hallam Road	C4
Hare Lane	C4
High Street	B3
Holloway Hill	A2
Latimer Road	B2
Llanaway Road	C4
Marshall Road	C4
Meadrow	C4
Mill Lane	A3
Mint Street	A3-B3
Moss Lane	B3
Nightingale Road	B4-C4
Oakdene Road	A4
Ockford Road	A2-A3-B2-B3
Park Road	B2
Peperharow Road	A4
Pullman Lane	A1
Queen Street	B3-B2
Ramsden Road	A1-B1-B2
Shackstead Lane	A2-A1-B1
South Hill	C2-C3
South Street	B3-B2
Station Approach	A3
Summerhouse Road	A2-B2
The Avenue	C1
The Burys	B3
The Close	C1
The Drive	C1
The Fairway	C1
Town End Street	B2-C3
Tuesley Lane	A2-A1-B1
Valley View	A2
Westbrook Road	A3
Wharf Street	B3-C3
Wolseley Road	C4

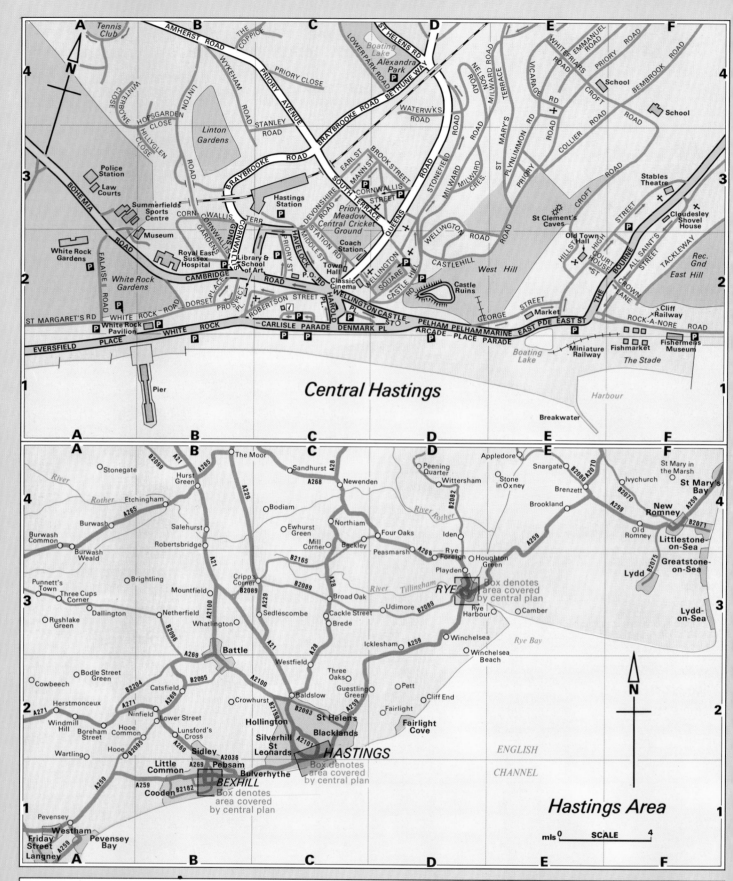

Hastings

Overlooking the beach of this popular resort are the remains of a castle established by William the Conqueror; Battle Abbey, the actual site of the great conflict of 1066, lies to the north of the town on the A2100. The Hastings Embroidery, which was commissioned in 1966 to commemorate the battle's 900th anniversary and depicts 81 memorable events in British history, can be seen at the Town Hall.

Rich in historical associations, Hastings also has a historic Old Town — a pleasant jumble of ancient buildings and narrow streets, and site of the local fish market and Fisherman's Museum. Theatres, pubs and amusement areas fill the main resort, which has all the amenities expected of a major holiday centre.

Bexhill offers the entertainment facilities of the De La Warr Pavilion, which overlooks the sands, and a good range of outdoor activities can be enjoyed in nearby Egerton Park. Manor Gardens, in the older part of the town, contains the Manor Costume Museum and the ruins of the manor house.

Rye is an atmospheric town of cobbled streets and half-timbered houses. A gang of smugglers had its headquarters at the 15th-century Mermaid Inn, and other places of interest include the Baddings Tower Museum, the Rye Town Model and the old harbour, which is now a nature reserve.

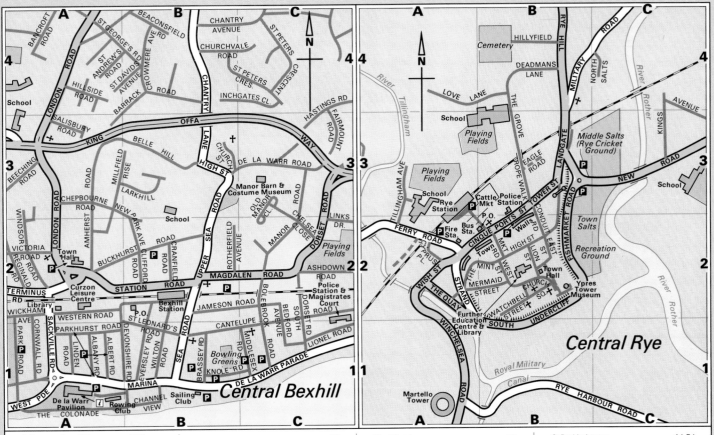

Central Bexhill

Central Rye

Key to Town Plan and Area Plan

Town Plan

AA Recommended roads
Restricted roads
Other roads
Buildings of interest — Castle ▢
Car Parks — P
One way streets — ←
Parks and open spaces — ▢

Area Plan

A roads
B roads
Locations — Kingston ○
Urban area

Street Index with Grid Reference

Hastings

Amherst Road	B4
All Saints Street	F2-F3
Bembrook Road	F4
Bethune Way	D4
Bohemia Road	A3-A2-B2
Braybrooke Road	B3-C3-C4-D4
Brook Street	C3-D3
Cambridge Road	B2-C2
Carlisle Parade	C2
Castle Hill Road	D2-E2-E3
Castle Street	D2
Collier Road	E3-E4-F4
Cornwallis Gardens	B3-B2
Cornwallis Street	C3-D3
Cornwallis Terrace	B3-C3
Courthouse Street	E2
Croft Road	E4-F4-F3-E3
Crown Lane	F2
Denmark Place	C2-D2
Devonshire Road	C3
Dorset Place	B2
Earl Street	C3
East Parade	E2
East Street	E2
Emmanuel Road	E4
Eversfield Place	A1
Falaise Road	A2
George Street	D2-E2
Harold Place	C2
Havelock Road	C2
High Street	E2-F2-F3
Hill Street	E2
Hillyglen Close	B3
Hopsgarden Close	B3-B4
Linton Road	B4-B3
Lower Park Road	C4-D4
Mann Street	C3-D3
Marine Parade	D2-E2
Middle Street	C2
Milward Crescent	D3
Milward Road	D3-D4-E4
Nelson Road	D4
Pelham Arcade	D2
Pelham Place	D2
Plymlimmon Road	E3-E4
Priory Avenue	B4-C4-C3
Priory Close	C4
Priory Road	E3-E4-F4
Priory Street	C2
Prospect Place	B2
Queens Road	C2-D2-D3-D4
Robertson Street	B2-C2
Rock-a-Nore Road	E2-F2
St Helens Road	D4
St Margaret's Road	A2
St Mary's Terrace	E3-E4
South Terrace	C3-D3
Stanley Road	B3-C3-C4
Station Road	C2-C3
Stonefield Road	D3-D4
Tackleway	F2-F3
The Coppice	B4-C4
The Bourne	E2-F2
Vicarage Road	E4
Waterworks Road	D4
Wellington Place	C2-D2
Wellington Road	D3-D2-E2
Wellington Square	D2
White Rock	B1-B2
White Rock Road	A2-B2
Whitefriars Road	E4
Winterbourne Close	A3-A4
Wykeham Road	B4-B3-C3

Bexhill

Albany Road	A1
Albert Road	A1
Amherst Road	A2-A3
Ashdown Road	C2
Bancroft Road	A4
Barrack Road	A3-B4
Beaconsfield Road	B4
Bedford Avenue	C2-C1
Beeching Road	A3
Belle Hill	B3
Bolebrook Road	C2-C1
Brassey Road	B1
Buckhurst Road	A2-B2
Cantelupe Road	B1-C1-C2
Channel View	B1
Chantry Avenue	B4-C4
Chantry Lane	B4-B3
Chelsea Close	C2
Chepbourne Road	A3
Church Street	B3
Churchvale Road	B4-C4
Clifford Road	B2
Cornwall Road	A2-A1
Cranfield Road	B2
Crowmere Avenue	B4
De la Warr Parade	B1-C1
De la Warr Road	C3
Devonshire Road	A1-B1
Dorset Road	C2-C3
Dorset Road South	C2-C1
Eversley Road	B1
Fairmount Road	C3-C4
Hastings Road	C4-C3
High Street	B3
Hillside Road	A4
Inchgates Close	B4-C4
Jameson Road	A3-B3-C3
King Offa Way	A3-B3
Knole Road	B1-C1
Larkhill	A3-B3
Linden Road	A1
Links Drive	C2
Lionel Road	C1
London Road	A4-A3-A2
Magdalene Road	B2-C2
Manor Road	C2-C3
Marina	A1-B1
Middlesex Road	C1
Millfield Rise	A3-B3
New Park Avenue	A3-B3-B2
Old Manor Close	C2-C3
Park Road	A1-A2
Parkhurst Road	A1
Reginald Road	A2
Rotherfield Avenue	B2
St Andrews Road	A4-B4
St Davids Avenue	A4-B4
St George's Road	A4-B4
St Leonard's Road	B2-B1
St Peters Crescent	B4-C4
Sackville Road	A2-A1
Salisbury Road	A3
Sea Road	B1-B2
Station Road	A2-B2
Terminus Road	A2
The Colonade	A1
Upper Sea Road	B2-B3
Victoria Road	A2
West Parade	A1
Western Road	A2
Wickham Avenue	A2
Wilton Road	B1
Windsor Road	A3-A2

Rye

Church Square	B2
Cinque Ports Street	A2-B2-B3
Conduit Road	B3-B2
Cyprus Place	A2
Deadmans Lane	B4
Eagle Road	B3
East Street	B2
Ferry Road	A2
Fishmarket Road	B2-B3
High Street	B2
Hillyfield	B4
Kings Avenue	C3-C4
Landgate	B3
Lion Street	B2
Love Lane	A4-B4
Market Road	B2
Mermaid Street	A2-B2
Military Road	B4-C4
New Road	B3-C3
North Salts	C4
Rope Walk	B3
Rye Harbour Road	B1-C1
Rye Hill	B4
South Undercliff	B1-B2
Strand	A2
The Grove	B4-B3
The Mint	A2-B2
The Quay	A2
Tillingham Avenue	A2-A3
Tower Street	B3
Watchbell Street	B2
West Street	B2
Winchelsea Road	A1-A2
Wish Street	A2

HASTINGS
Although the harbour of this one-time Cinque Port silted up centuries ago, fishing boats are still winched up on the shingle beach, and fishermen's net-drying huts at the foot of the cliff railway are a distinctive feature.

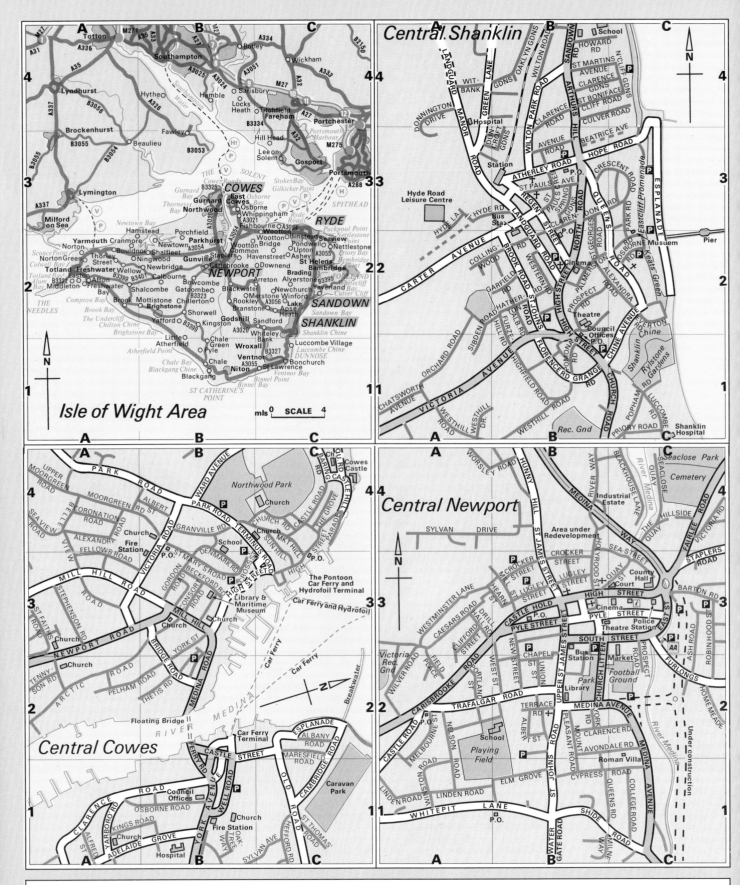

Isle of Wight

Most visitors to the island arrive at Ryde so its streets are always busy throughout the summer months. During the 19th century it was turned from a small village into a fashionable holiday resort which is as popular as ever today; sandy beaches, a pier with an electric railway, a boating lake and pleasant gardens are its main attractions.

Sandown lies at the centre of Sandown Bay on the south-east side of the island and as the largest resort, its holiday facilities are numerous. The Museum of Isle of Wight Geology houses, among other exhibits, over 5000 fossils from the island.

Shanklin Here attractions range from the excitement of the pier to the seclusion of Hope Beach. The old village has thatched cottages festooned with roses, and the natural gorge called Shanklin Chine has lovely gardens and a waterfall.

Newport, capital of the island, occupies a conveniently central position. Just south-west of the town is the 12th-century Carisbrooke Castle where Charles I was imprisoned for a year before his execution in London. Other places of interest include the Roman Villa in Cypress Road.

Cowes is the headquarters of the Royal Yacht Squadron and Cowes Week, held during the first week of August, is the fashionable event of the yachting calendar. The club house stands on the site of a castle built by Henry VIII.

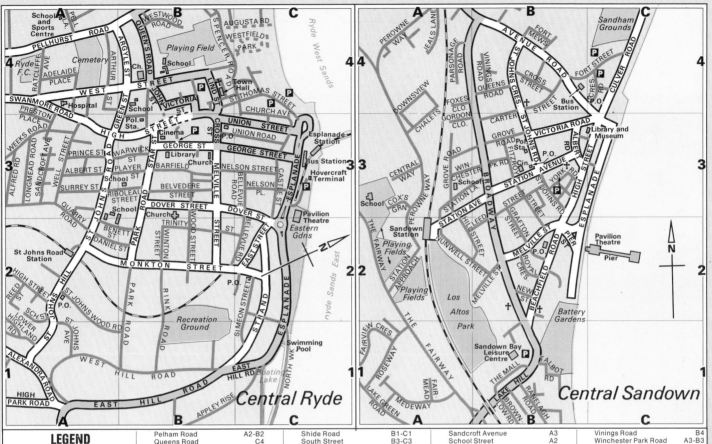

Central Ryde

Central Sandown

LEGEND

Town Plan

AA recommended route
Restricted roads
Other roads
Buildings of interest   Cinema
Car parks
Parks and open spaces

Area Plan

A roads
B roads
Locations   WoottonO
Urban area
Hovercraft   (H)
Hydrofoil   (Hf)
Passenger Ferry   (P)
Vehicle Ferry   (V)

Street Index
Cowes

Adelaide Grove	A1-B1
Albany Road	C2
Albert Street	A4-B4
Alexandra Road	A4
Alfred Street	A1
Arctic Road	A2-A3-B3
Baring Road	C4
Beckford Road	B3
Belleview Road	A3-A4
Bridge Road	B2-B3
Cambridge Road	C1-C2
Castle Hill	C4
Castle Road	C4
Castle Street	B2-B1-B2-C2
Church Road	B4-C4
Clarence Road	A1-B1
Consort Road	B3
Coronation Road	A4
Cross Street	C2
Denmark Road	B3-B4-B3
Esplanade	C2
Fellows Road	A3
Ferry Road	B1-B2
Granville Road	B4
Gordon Road	B3
Hefford Road	C1
High Street	B3-C3-C4
Kings Road	A1-B1
Maresfield Road	C2
Market Hill	C3-C4
Medina Road	B2-B3
Mill Hill	B3
Mill Hill Road	A3-B3
Moorgreen Road	A4-B4
Newport Road	A2-A3-B3
Oaktree Way	B1
Old Road	C1-C2
Osborne Road	A1-B1
Parade	C4
Park Road	A4-B4

Newport

Albert Street	B2
Ash Road	C2-C3
Avondale Road	B2-C2
Barton Road	C3
Blackhouse Lane	C4
Caesars Road	A3
Carisbrooke Road	A2-A3
Castle Hold	B3
Castle Road	A1-A2
Chapel Street	B2-B3
Church Litten	B2-B3
Clarence Road	B2-C2
Clifford Street	A3
College Road	C1
Crocker Street	B3
Cypress Road	B1-C1
Drill Hall Road	A3
East Street	C3
Elm Grove	A1-B1
Fairlee Road	C3-C4
Field Place	A2-A3
Furlongs	C2-C3
Hearn Street	A3-B3
Hillside	C4
High Street	B3-C3
Holyrood Street	B3-B4
Home Meade	C2
Hunny Hill	B4
Linden Road	A1
Lugley Street	B3
Medina Road	B2-C2-C1
Melbourne Street	A1-A2
Mill Street	A3-B3
Milne Way	B1
Mount Pleasant Road	B1-B2
Nelson Road	A1-A2
New Street	B2-B3
Portland Street	A2
Prospect Road	C2-C3
Pyle Street	B3-C3
Quay Street	B3-C3
Queens Road	B1
Riverway	B4
Robin Hood Street	C2-C3
St James Street	B3-B4
St Johns Road	B3
Sea Street	B4-C4-C3
Seaclose Quay	C4

(Cowes continued)

Pelham Road	A2-B2
Queens Road	C4
St Faiths Road	A2-A3
St Mary's Road	B3-B4
St Thomas' Road	C1
Seaview Road	A4
Stephenson Road	A3
Sun Hill	C3-C4
Sylvan Avenue	B1-C1
Tennyson Road	C2
Terminus Road	B4-C4-C3
The Grove	C4
Thetis Road	A2-B2
Upper Moorgreen Road	A4
Victoria Road	A3-B3-B4
Ward Avenue	B4
Well Road	B1-B2
Westhill Road	B3
Yarborough Road	A1
York Avenue	B1
York Street	B2-B3

Shide Road	B1-C1
South Street	B3-C3
Staplers Road	C3-C4
Sylvan Drive	A4-B4
Terrace Road	B2
The Quay	C4
Trafalgar Road	A2-B2
Union Street	B2
Upper St James Street	B2-B3
Victoria Road	B4
Water Gate Road	B1
Westminster Lane	A3
West Street	B2-B3
Whitepit Lane	A1-B1
Wilver Road	A2-A3
Winston Road	A1
Worsley Road	A4-B4
York Road	B2

Ryde

Adelaide Place	A4
Albert Street	A3
Alexandra Road	A1
Alfred Road	A3
Appley Rise	B1-C1
Argyle Street	A4-B4
Arthur Street	A4
Augusta Road	B4-C4
Barfield	B3
Bellvue Road	B2-C2-C3
Belvedere Street	B3
Benett Street	A2-B2
Castle Street	C3
Church Avenue	C3-C4
Cross Street	B3
Daniel Street	A2-B2
Dover Street	B3-C3-C2
East Hill Road	A1-B1-C1
East Street	C2
Esplanade	C1-C2-C3
George Street	B3-C3
Green Street	A3-B3-B4
High Park Road	A1
High Street	A2
High Street	A3-B3-B4
John Street	B4
Lind Street	B4
Longmead Road	A3
Lower Highland Road	A1-A2
Melville Street	B2-B3
Monkton Street	A2-B2-C2
Nelson Place	C3
Nelson Street	B3-C3
North Walk	C1
Park Road	B1-B2-B3
Pell Lane	A4
Pellhurst Road	A4-B4
Player Street	A3-B3
Preston Place	A3-A4
Prince Street	A3
Quarry Road	A2-A3
Queen's Road	B4
Ratcliffe Avenue	A4
Reed Street	A2
Riboleau Street	A3-B3
Rink Road	B1-B2
St Johns Avenue	A1
St Johns Hill	A1-A2
St Johns Road	A2-A3
St Johns Wood Road	A2-A1-B1
St Thomas Street	B4-C4-C3

Sandown

Sandcroft Avenue	A3
School Street	A2
Simeon Street	C1-C2
Spencer Road	B4-C4
Star Street	B3
Strand	B1-C1-C2
Surrey Street	A3
Swanmore Road	A3-A4
Trinity Street	B2-C2
Union Road	B3-C3
Union Street	B3-C3
Victoria Street	B4
Warwick Street	A3-B3
Weeks Road	A3
Well Street	A3
Westfield Park	B4-C4
West Hill Road	A1-B1
West Street	A4-B4
Westwood Road	B4
Winton Street	B2
Wood Street	B2-B3

Albert Road	B3
Avenue Road	A4-B4-C4-C3
Beachfield Road	B1-B2
Broadway	A4-B4-B3-B2-B1
Brownlow Road	B1
Carter Street	B3-B4
Central Way	A3
Cox's Green	A3
Crescent Road	C4
Cross Street	B4
Culver Road	C3-C4
Downsview Chalets	A3-A4
Esplanade	B2-B3-C3
Fairmead	A1
Fairview Crescent	A1
Fitzroy Street	B2-B3
Fort Mews	B4
Fort Street	B4-C4
Foxes Close	A4
Gordon Close	A3
Grafton Street	B26B3
Grove Road	A3-B3
High Street	B2-B3-C3
Hill Street	A2-B2
Jeals Lane	A3-A4
Lake Green Road	A1
Lake Hill	B1
Leed Street	A2-B2-B3
Medeway	A1
Melville Street	B2
New Street	B2
Nunnwell Street	A2-B2
Parsonage Road	A4
Perowne Way	A2-A3-A4
Pier Street	B2
Queens Road	B4
Ranelagh Road	A1
Roseway	A1
Royal Crescent	B2
St Johns Crescent	B4
St Johns Road	B3-B4
Station Avenue	A2-A3-B3
Station Approach	A2
Station Lane	A2-A3-B3
Talbot Road	B1
The Fairway	A3-A2-A1-B1
The Mall	B1
Victoria Road	B3-C3

Vinings Road	B4
Winchester Park Road	A3-B3
York Road	B3

Shanklin

Albert Road	B2
Alexandra Road	B2-C2
Arthurs Hill	B3-B4
Atherley Road	B3
Avenue Road	B3
Beatrice Avenue	B3-C3
Brook Road	B2
Carter Avenue	A2-B2-B3
Chatsworth Avenue	A1
Chine Avenue	B1-C1-C2
Church Road	B1-C1-B1
Clarence Gardens	B4-C4
Clarence Road	B3-B4
Clarendon Road	B3-C3
Collingwood Road	A2-B2
Crescent Road	B3-C3
Culver Road	B4-C4
Donnington Drive	A3-A4
Duncroft Gardens	A3-B3
Esplanade	C2-C3-C2
Everton Road	C2
Florence Road	B1
Furzehill Road	B1-B2
Garfield Road	A2-B2
Grange Road	B1
Green Lane	A3-A4-B4
Hatherton Road	B2
High Street	B1-B2
Highfield Road	B1
Hope Road	B3-C3
Howard Road	B4-C4
Hyde Lane	A2-A3
Hyde Road	A3-B3
Landguard Road	B2-B3
Landguard Manor Road	A4-A3-B3
Luccombe Road	C1
Northcliffe Gardens	C4
North Road	B2-B3
Oaklyn Gardens	B4
Orchard Road	A1-A2
Osborne Road	C2
Palmerston Road	B2-C2
Park Road	C2-C3
Pomona Road	B1
Popham Road	C1
Priory Road	C1
Prospect Road	B2
Queens Road	B3-B2-C2
Regent Street	B2-B3
St Boniface Cliffe Road	B4-C4
St Georges Road	B2-B3
St Johns Road	B2
St Martins Road	B4-C4
St Pauls Avenue	B3
St Pauls Crescent	B3
Sandown Road	B4
Sibden Road	A1-A2-B2
Spring Gardens	B3
Victoria Avenue	A1-B1-B2
Western Road	B2
Westhill Drive	A1
Westhill Road	A1, B1
Wilton Road	B4
Wilton Park Road	B3-B4
Witbank Gardens	A4-B4

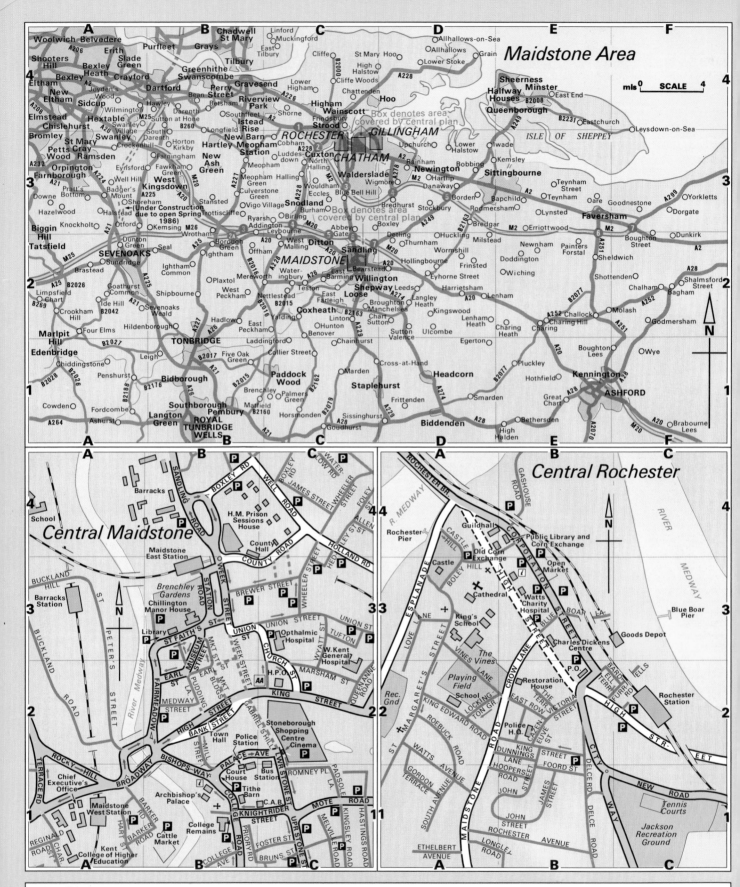

Maidstone

County town of Kent, Maidstone has long been a place of importance. The ruins of the 14th-century Archbishop's Palace overlook the River Medway, and Allington Castle dates from the 13th century. Maidstone Museum and Art Gallery explores the town's extensive history; also of interest is the Tyrwhitt-Drake Museum of Carriages, housed in the Palace stables.

Rochester Medieval walls enclose the Norman castle and cathedral of this attractive and historic town, but its quaint old shops, inns and tea shops give it a distinctly Victorian flavour. Charles Dickens spent much of his life in the area and featured Rochester in his novels: justly proud of its associations with the great man, the town boasts an award-winning Charles Dickens Centre.

Gillingham has been associated with the nearby Royal Naval Dockyard since Tudor times and it

continues the tradition with the Royal Naval Barracks and the Royal School of Military Engineering, both situated in the Brompton area.

Chatham Home of the Royal Naval Dockyard since the 16th century, Chatham today is dominated by the office tower block which crowns the Pentagon Centre, a shopping and entertainments complex. Pleasant riverside gardens have been laid out on the site of the old Gun Wharf, and the Medway Heritage Centre is in Dock Road.

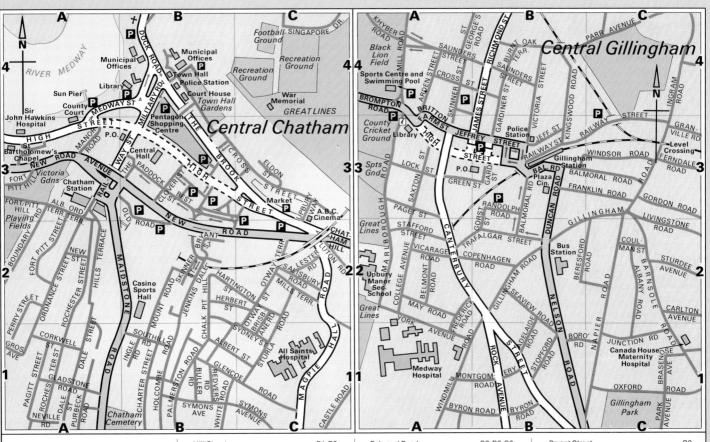

LEGEND

Town Plan
AA Recommended roads
Restricted roads
Other roads
Buildings of interest — Station
Churches — +
Parks and open spaces
Car Parks — P
One Way Streets — L

Area Plan
A roads
B roads
Locations — Muckingford O
Urban area

Street Index with Grid Reference

Maidstone

Allen Street	C4
Bank Street	B2
Barker Road	A1-B1
Bishops Way	B1-B2
Boxley Road	B4-C4
Brewer Street	B3-C3
Broadway	A1-B1-B2
Brunswick Street	C1
Buckland Hill	A3
Buckland Road	A2-A3
Charles Street	A1
Church Street	C2-C3
College Avenue	B1
College Road	B1
County Road	B4-B3-C3-C4
Earl Street	B2-B3
Fairmeadow	B2-B3
Foley Street	C4
Foster Street	B1-C1
Gabriel's Hill	B2-C2
Hart Street	A1
Hastings Road	C1
Hedley Street	C3-C4
High Street	B2
Holland Road	C3-C4
James Street	C4
Kingsley Road	C1
King Street	B2-C2
Knightrider Street	B1-C1
Lower Stone Street	C1-C2
Market Buildings	B2
Market Street	B2-B3
Marsham Street	C2
Medway Street	B2
Melville Road	C1

Mill Street	B1-B2
Mote Road	C1
Museum Street	B2-B3
Padsole Lane	C1
Palace Avenue	B1-B2-C2
Priory Road	B1
Pudding Lane	B2
Queen Anne Road	C2
Reginald Road	A1
Rocky Hill	A1-A2
Romney Place	C1
St Faith's Street	B3
St Peter's Street	A2-A3
Sandling Road	B4
Station Road	B3
Terrace Road	A1-A2
Tufton Street	C3
Union Street	B3-C3
Upper Stone Street	C1
Waterlow Road	C4
Week Street	B2-B3
Well Road	B4-C4
Wheeler Street	C3-C4
Wyatt Street	C2-C3

Rochester

Bardell Terrace	B2-C2
Blue Boar Lane	B3
Boley Hill	A3
Castle Hill	A3-A4
Cazeneuve Street	B2
City Way	B2-B1-C1
Corporation Street	A4-B4-B3-B2
Crow Lane	B2-B3
Delce Road	B1-B2
Dunnings Lane	A2-B2
East Row	B2
Esplanade	A2-A3-A4
Ethelbert Avenue	A1
Foord Street	B1
Furrells Road	B2-C2
Gashouse Road	B4
Gordon Terrace	A1-A2
High Street	A4-A3-B3-B2-C2
Hoopers Road	A1-B1
James Street	B1
John Street	B2-B1-A1-B1
King Edward Road	A2
King Street	B2
Lockington Grove	A2-B2
Longley Road	A1-B1
Love Lane	A2-A3
Maidstone Road	A1-A2-B2
New Road	B1-C1
Rochester Avenue	A1-B1
Rochester Bridge	A4
Roebuck Road	A1-A2
St Margaret's Street	A1-A2-A3
South Avenue	A1
The Terrace	B2
Victoria Street	B2
Vines Lane	A3-A2-B2
Watts Avenue	A1-A2

Gillingham

Adelaide Road	B1-B2
Albany Road	C1-C2
Arden Street	A4
Balmoral Road	B2-B3-C3
Barnsole Road	C1-C2-C3
Belmont Road	A2
Beresford Road	C2-B2-C2
Borough Road	B1-C1
Brasenose Avenue	C1
Britton Farm Street	A3-A4
Brompton Road	A4
Burnt Oak Terrace	B4
Byron Road	A1-B1
Canterbury Street	A3-A2-B2-B1
Carlton Avenue	C2
College Avenue	A2
Copenhagen Road	A2-B2
Coulman Street	C2
Cross Street	A4-B4
Duncan Road	B2-B3
Ferndale Road	C3
Franklin Road	B3-C3
Frederick Road	A1-A2
Gardiner Street	B3-B4
Gillingham Road	B2-B3-C3
Gordon Road	C3
Gorst Street	B2-B3
Granville Road	C3
Green Street	A3-B3
High Street	A3-B3
Ingram Road	C3-C4
James Street	A3-B3-B4
Jeffrey Street	A3-B3
Junction Road	C1
Kingswood Road	B3-B4
Khyber Road	A4
Livingstone Road	C2-C3
Lock Street	A3
Marlborough Road	A2-A3-A4
May Road	A2
Mill Road	A4
Montgomery Road	A1-B1
Napier Road	B1-C1-C2-C3
Nelson Road	B2-B1-C1
Oxford Road	C1
Paget Street	A3
Park Avenue	C1
Parr Avenue	B4-C4
Railway Street	B3-C3
Randolph Road	B3
Richmond Street	B4
Rock Avenue	B1-B2
St George's Road	A4-B4
Saunders Street	A4-B4
Saxton Street	A2-A3
Seaview Road	B1-B2
Skinner Street	A3-A4
Stafford Street	A2
Stopford Road	B1
Sturdee Road	C2
Trafalgar Street	A2-B2
Vicarage Road	A2
Victoria Street	B3-B4
Windmill Road	A1-B1-B2
Windsor Road	B3-C3
York Avenue	A1-A2

Chatham

Albany Terrace	A3
Albert Street	B1-C1
Best Street	B3
Boundary Road	A2-A3
Brisbane Road	C1-C2

Bryant Street	B2
Buller Road	B1
Castle Road	C1
Chalk Pit Hill	B1-B2
Charter Street	B1
Chatham Hill	C2
Clover Street	B3
Corkwell Street	A1
Cross Street	B3-C3
Dale Street	A1-A2
Dock Road	B4
Eldon Street	C3
Fort Pitt Hill	A3
Fort Pitt Street	A2-A3
Gladstone Road	A1
Glencoe Road	B1-C1
Grosvenor Avenue	A1
Hartington Street	B2-C2
Herbert Street	B2-C2
High Street	A3-B3-C3
Hills Terrace	A2
Holcombe Road	B1-B2
Ingle Road	B1
Jenkins Dale	B2
Lester Road	C2
Luton Road	C2
Magpie Hall Road	C1-C2
Maidstone Road	A3-A2-B2-B1-A1
Manor Road	A3
Medway Street	A3-A4-B4
Military Road	B3-B4
Mills Terrace	C2
Mount Road	B1-B2
Neville Road	A1
New Road	B3-B2-C2
New Road Avenue	A3-B3
New Street	A2
Old Road	A3-B3-B2
Ordnance Street	A1-A2-A3
Ordnance Terrace	A3
Otway Street	C1-C2
Otway Terrace	C2
Pagitt Street	A1
Palmerston Road	B1
Perry Street	A1-A2
Purbeck Road	A1
Railway Street	A3-B3
Redvers Road	B1
Rochester Street	A1-A2
Salisbury Road	C2
Singapore Drive	C4
Skinner Street	B2
Southill Road	B1
Sturla Road	C1-C2
Sydney Street	B2-C2-C1
Symons Avenue	B1-C1
The Brook	B4-B3-C3
The Paddock	B3
Upbury Way	C2-C3
White Road	B1

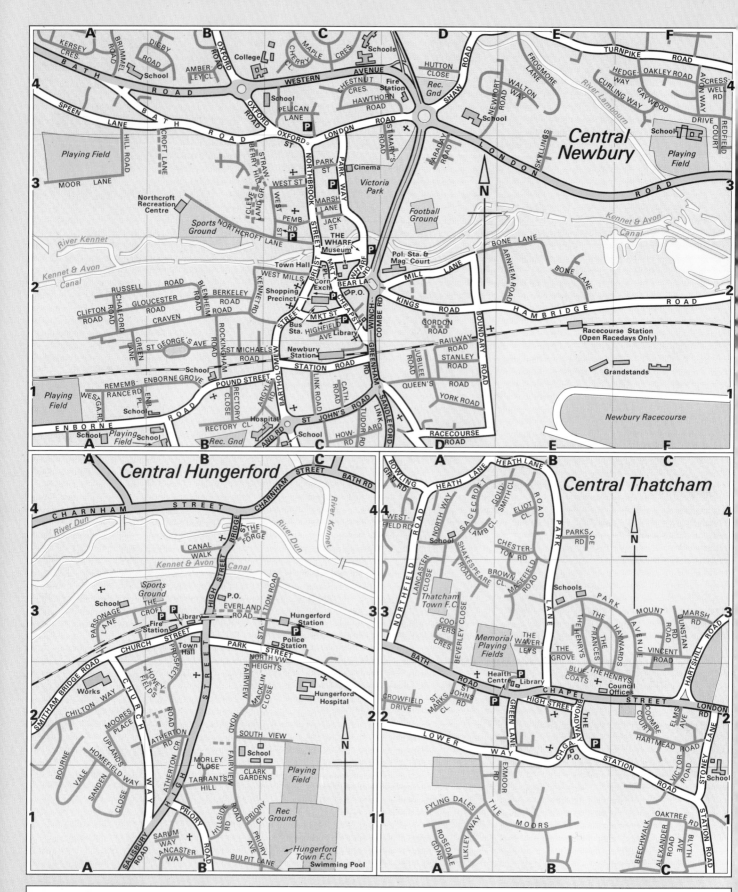

Newbury

Racegoers flock to Newbury's racecourse all the year round, but in the 15th century this principal town of West Berkshire was better known for broadcloth than for betting. The cloth manufacturing era is recalled in the Newbury District Museum, which is appropriately housed in the former Cloth Hall and lies near to the area known as the Wharf. A number of well preserved

17th- and 18th-century buildings can be seen here, including the 18th-century Granary.

Other places of interest include St. Nicholas' Church, built in the 16th century in the Perpendicular style.

Hungerford still retains a flavour of its years as a staging point on the Bath Road, notably in the Bear Inn and in the 17th- and 18th-century shops and houses of the High Street.

Two miles to the north west lies Littlecote

House, a charming Tudor manor which features 'Frontier City' (an authentic Wild West town), and excavations of a Roman villa in its grounds.

Thatcham has also kept several buildings from the 17th and 18th centuries in the midst of its industrial and residential expansion. Notable are two interesting old coaching inns, the King's Head and the White Hart. An early 14th-century chapel at the eastern end of town has been converted into an antiques shop.

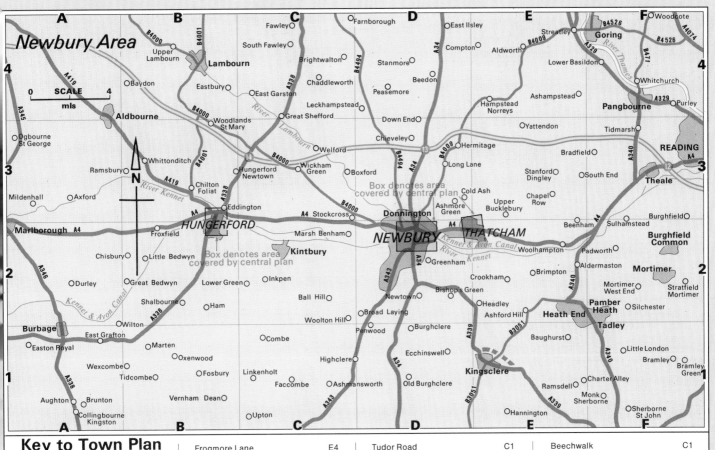

Newbury Area

SCALE
0   4
mls

Box denotes area covered by central plan

Box denotes area covered by central plan

Key to Town Plan and Area Plan

Town Plan
AA Recommended roads
Restricted roads
Other roads
Buildings of interest   Station
Car Parks
Parks and open spaces
Churches

Area Plan
A roads
B roads
Locations   BradfieldO
Urban area

Street Index with Grid Reference

Newbury

Amberley Close	B4
Andover Road	B1-C1
Argyle Road	B1-C1
Arnhem Road	E2
Avon Way	F4
Bartholomew Street	C1-C2
Bath Road	A4-B4-B3-C3
Bear Lane	C2
Berkeley Road	B2
Blenheim Road	B2
Bone Lane	D2-E2
Boundary Road	D1-D2
Bridge Street	C2
Brummell Road	A4
Catherine Road	C1
Chalford Road	A2
Cheap Street	C2
Cherry Close	C4
Chestnut Crescent	C4-D4
Cleveland Grove	B3
Clifton Road	A2
Craven Road	A2-B2-C2
Cresswell Road	F4
Croft Lane	B3-B4
Curling Way	E4-F4
Digby Road	A4-B4
Enborne Grove	A1-B1
Enborne Place	A1
Enborne Road	A1-B1
Faraday Road	D3-D4
Frogmore Lane	E4
Gaywood Drive	F4
Gloucester Road	A2-B2
Gordon Road	D2
Green Lane	A1-A2
Greenham Road	C2-C1-D1
Hambridge Road	D2-E2-F2
Hawthorn Road	C4-D4
Hedgeway	E4-F4
Highfield Avenue	C2
Hill Road	A3-A4
Howard Road	C1-D1
Hutton Close	D4
Jack Street	C3
Jubilee Road	D1
Kennet Road	B2
Kersey Crescent	A4
Kings Road	D2
Link Road	C1
London Road	C3-C4-D4-D3-E3-F3
Maple Crescent	C4
Market Place	C2
Market Street	C2
Marsh Lane	C3
Mill Lane	D2
Moor Lane	A3
Newport Road	D3-D4-E4
Northbrook Street	C2-C3
Northcroft Lane	B3-C3-C2
Oakley Road	F4
Oxford Road	B4-C4
Oxford Street	C3-C4
Park Street	C3
Park Way	C3
Pelican Lane	C4
Pembroke Road	C3
Pound Street	B1-C1
Queen's Road	D1
Racecourse Road	D1
Railway Road	D1-D2
Rectory Close	B1
Redfield Court	F3-F4
Remembrance Road	A1
Rockingham Road	B1-B2
Russell Road	A2-B2
St George's Avenue	A1-B1
St John's Road	C1
St Mary's Road	D3-D4
St Michael's Road	B1-C1
Sandleford Link	C1-D1
Shaw Road	D4
Skyllings	E3-E4
Speen Lane	A4-B4
Stanley Road	D1
Station Road	C1
Strawberry Hill	B3-C3
The Wharf	C2
Tudor Road	C1
Turnpike Road	E4-F4
Walton Way	E4
Western Avenue	B4-C4-D4
Westgate Road	A1
West Mills	B2-C2
West Street	C3
Wharf Road	C2
Winchcombe Road	C2
York Road	D1

Hungerford

Atherton Crescent	B1-B2
Atherton Road	B2
Bath Road	C4
Bourne Vale	A1-A2
Bridge Street	B4
Bulpit Lane	B1-C1
Canal Walk	B4
Charnham Street	A4-B4-C4
Chilton Way	A2
Church Street	A3-B3
Church Way	A3-A2-B2-B1
Clark Gardens	B1-C1
Everland Road	B3-C3
Fairview Road	B1-B2-B3
High Street	B1-B2-B3-B4
Hillside Road	B1
Homefield Way	A1-A2
Honeyfields	A2-B2
Lancaster Way	B1
Macklin Close	B2-C2
Moores Place	A2
Morley Close	B1-B2
North View Heights	B3-C3-C2
Park Street	B3-C3
Parsonage Lane	A3
Priory Avenue	B1-C1
Priory Close	B1
Priory Road	B1
Prospect Road	B2-B3
Salisbury Road	A1-B1
Sanden Close	A1
Sarum Way	B1
Smitham Bridge Road	A2-A3
South View	B2-C2
Station Road	C3
Tarrant's Hill	B1
The Croft	A3-B3
The Forge	B4-C4
Uplands	A2

Thatcham

Alexander Road	C1
Bath Road	A3-A2-B2
Beechwalk	C1
Beverley Close	A2-A3
Bluecoats	B2
Blyth Avenue	C1
Bowling Green Road	A4
Brown Close	A3-B3
Chapel Street	B2-C2
Chesterton Road	B4
Church Gate	B2
Coombe Court	C2
Coopers Crescent	A3
Crowfield Drive	A2
Dunstan Road	C3
Eliot Close	B4
Elms Avenue	C2
Exmoor Road	A1-B1-B2
Fyling Dales	A1
Goldsmith Close	B4
Green Lane	B2
Hartmead Road	C2
Hartshill Road	C2-C3
Heath Lane	A4-B4
High Street	B2
Ilkley Way	A1
Lamb Close	A4
Lancaster Close	A3-A4
London Road	C2
Lower Way	A2-B2
Masefield Road	B3-B4
Marsh Road	C3
Mount Road	C3
Northfield Road	A3-A4
North Way	A4
Oaktree Road	C1
Park Avenue	B3-C3-C2
Park Lane	B2-B3-B4
Parkside Road	B4
Rosedale Gardens	A1
St Johns Road	A2
St Marks Close	A2
Sagecroft Road	A4-B4-B3
Shakespeare Road	A3-A4
Station Road	B2-C2-C1
Stoney Lane	C1-C2
The Broadway	B2
The Frances	B2-B3
The Grove	B3
The Haywards	B3-C3-C2
The Henrys	B3-B2-C2
The Moors	A2-A1-B1
The Waverleys	B3
Victor Road	C1-C2
Vincent Road	C3
Westfield Road	A4

45

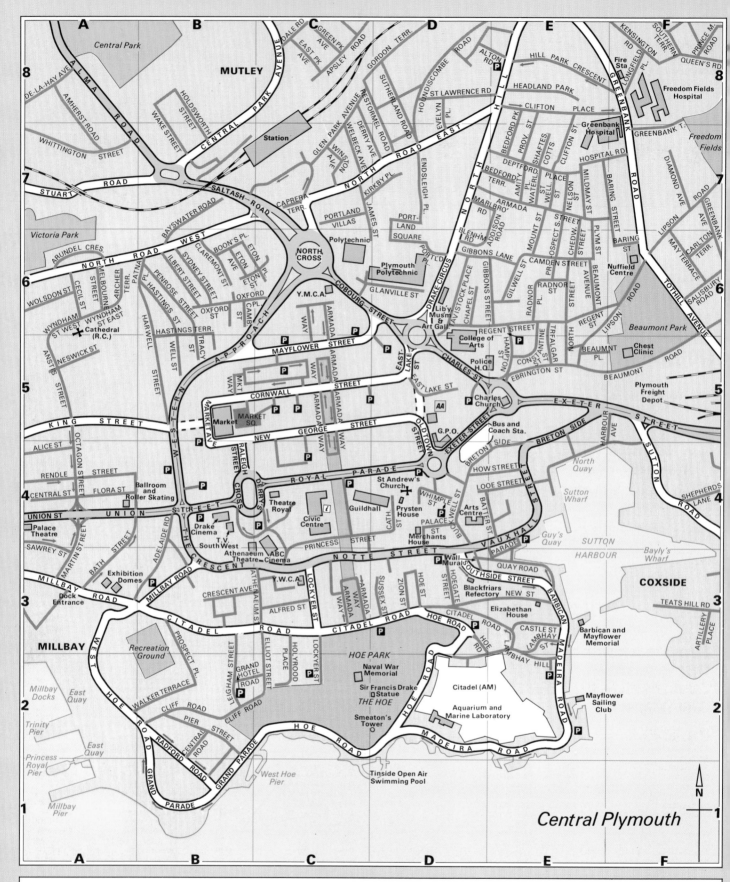

Plymouth

Ships, sailors and the sea permeate every aspect of Plymouth's life and history. Its superb natural harbour – Plymouth Sound – has ensured its importance as a port, yachting centre and naval base (latterly at Devonport) over many centuries. Sir Francis Drake is undoubtedly the city's most famous sailor. His statue stands on the Hoe – where he really did play bowls before tackling the Spanish Armada. Also on the Hoe are Smeaton's Tower, which once formed the upper part of the third Eddystone Lighthouse, and the impressive Royal Naval War Memorial. Just east of the Hoe is the Royal Citadel, an imposing fortress built in 1666 by order of Charles II. North is Sutton Harbour, perhaps the most atmospheric part of Plymouth. Here fishing boats bob up and down in a harbour whose quays are lined with attractive old houses, inns and warehouses. One of the memorials on Mayflower Quay just outside the harbour commemorates the sailing of the *Mayflower* from here in 1620. Plymouth's shopping centre is one of the finest of its kind, and was built after the old centre was badly damaged in World War II. Nearby is the 200ft-high tower of the impressive modern Civic Centre. Some buildings escaped destruction, including the Elizabethan House and the 500-year-old Prysten House. Next door is St Andrew's Church, with stained glass by John Piper.

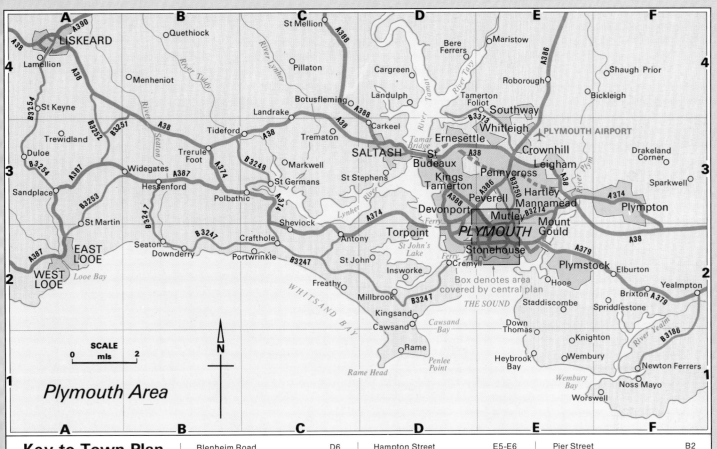

Key to Town Plan and Area Plan

Town Plan

AA Recommended roads
Other roads
Restricted roads
Buildings of interest
Car Parks
Parks and open spaces
One way streets

Area Plan

A roads
B roads
Locations　　　　Sandplace ○
Urban area

Street Index with Grid Reference

Plymouth

Addison Road	D6-D7-E7
Adelaide Road	B3-B4
Alfred Street	C3
Alice Street	A4
Alma Road	A8-A7-B7
Alton Road	D8-E8
Amherst Road	A7-A8
Amity Place	E7
Anstis Street	A5-A6
Apsley Road	C8
Archer Terrace	A6
Armada Street	D7-E7-F7
Armada Way	C3-C4-C5-C6
Artillery Place	F3
Arundel Crescent	A6
Athenaeum Street	C3
Barbican	E3
Baring Street	E7-F7-F6
Bath Street	A3-A4
Batter Street	D4-E4
Bayswater Road	B6-B7
Bedford Park	E7-E8
Bedford Terrace	D7-E7
Beaumont Avenue	E6
Beaumont Place	E5-F5
Beaumont Road	E5-F5-F6

Blenheim Road	D6
Boon's Place	B6
Breton Side	D4-E4-E5
Buckwell Street	D4
Cambridge Street	B6
Camden Street	E6
Caprera Terrace	C7
Carlton Terrace	F6
Castle Street	E3
Catherine Street	D4
Cecil Street	A6
Central Road	B2
Central Street	A4
Central Park Avenue	B7-B8-C8
Chapel Street	D6
Charles Street	D5
Chedworth Street	E6-E7
Citadel Road	B3-C3-D3-E3
Claremont Street	B6
Cliff Road	B2-C2
Clifton Place	E8-F8
Clifton Street	E7-E8
Cobourg Street	C6-D6
Constantine Street	E5-E6
Cornwall Street	B5-C5-D5
Crescent Avenue	B3-C3
Dale Road	C8
De-la-Hay-Avenue	A8
Deptford Place	D7-E7
Derry Avenue	C8-C7-D7
Derry's Cross	B4-C4
Diamond Avenue	F7
Drake Circus	D6
East Park Avenue	C8
Eastlake Street	D5
Ebrington Street	E5
Elliot Street	C2-C3
Endsleigh Place	D7
Eton Avenue	B6
Eton Place	B6-C6
Eton Street	B6-C6
Evelyn Place	D7-D8
Exeter Street	D4-D5-E5-F5
Flora Street	A4
Gibbons Lane	D6-E6
Gibbons Street	E6
Gilwell Street	E6
Glanville Street	C6-D6
Glen Park Avenue	C7-C8
Gordon Terrace	C8-D8
Grand Hotel Road	B2-C2
Grand Parade	B1-B2-C2
Great Western Road	B1-B2
Green Park Avenue	C8
Greenbank Avenue	F6-F7
Greenbank Road	F6-F7-F8-E8
Greenbank Terrace	F7-F8

Hampton Street	E5-E6
Harbour Avenue	E5-F5
Harwell Street	B5-B6
Hastings Street	B6
Hastings Terrace	B5-B6
Headland Park	E8
Hill Park Crescent	E8-F8
Hoe Road	C2-D2-D3
Hoe Street	D3
Hoegate Street	D3
Holdsworth Street	B7-B8
Holyrood Place	C2-C3
How Street	D4-E4
Hospital Road	E7-F7
Houndiscombe Road	D7-D8
Ilbert Street	B6
James Street	C6-C7
Kensington Road	F8
King Street	A5-B5
Kirkby Place	C7-D7
Lambhay Hill	E2-E3
Lambhay Street	E3
Leigham Street	B2-B3
Lipson Road	E5-E6-F6-F7
Lockyer Street	C2-C3
Longfield Place	F8
Looe Street	D4-E4
Madeira Road	D2-E2-E3
Marlborough Road	D7-E7
Market Avenue	B4-B5
Market Square	B5-C5
Market Way	B5
Martin Street	A3-A4
May Terrace	F6
Mayflower Street	B5-C5-C6-D5-D6
Melbourne Street	A6
Mildmay Street	E7
Millbay Road	A3-B3
Mount Street	E6-E7
Nelson Street	E7
Neswick Street	A5
New Street	D3-E3
New George Street	B4-B5-C5-D5
North Cross	C6
North Hill	D6-D7-E7-E8
North Road East	C7-D7-D8-E8
North Road West	A6-B6-B7-C7
North Street	E5-E6
Notte Street	C3-D3-D4
Octagon Street	A4-A5
Old Town Street	D4-D5
Oxford Place	B6-C6
Oxford Street	B6
Palace Street	D4
Parade	E3-E4
Patna Place	B6
Penrose Street	B6

Pier Street	B2
Portland Place	D6
Portland Square	D6-D7
Portland Villas	C7
Plym Street	E6-E7
Prince Maurice Road	F8
Princess Street	C3-C4-D4
Prospect Place	B2-B3
Prospect Street	E6-E7
Providence Street	E7-E8
Quay Road	D3-E3
Queen's Road	F8
Radford Road	B1-B2
Radnor Place	E6
Radnor Street	E6
Raleigh Street	B4
Regent Street	D6-E6-F6
Rendle Street	A4
Restormel Road	C8-D8-D7
Royal Parade	C4-D4
St Lawrence Road	D8-E8
Salisbury Road	F6
Saltash Road	B7-C7-C6
Sawrey Street	A3-A4
Shaftesbury Cottages	E7
Shepherds Lane	F4
Southern Terrace	F8
Southside Street	D3-E3
Stuart Road	A7-B7
Sussex Street	D3
Sutherland Road	D7-D8
Sutton Road	F4-F5
Syney Street	B6
Tavistock Place	D6
Teats Hill Road	F3
The Crescent	B4-B3-C3
Tothill Avenue	F5-F6
Tracy Street	B5
Trafalgar Street	E5-E6
Union Street	A4-B4
Vauxhall Street	D3-D4-E4
Wake Street	B7-B8
Walker Terrace	A2-B2
Waterloo Street	E7
Welbeck Avenue	C7
Well Street	B5
Well Street	E7
West Hoe Road	A3-A2-B2
Western Approach	B4-B5-B6-C6
Whimple Street	D4
Whittington Street	A7
Winston Lane	C7
Wolsdon Street	A6
Wyndham Street East	A6
Wyndham Street West	A6
Zion Street	D3

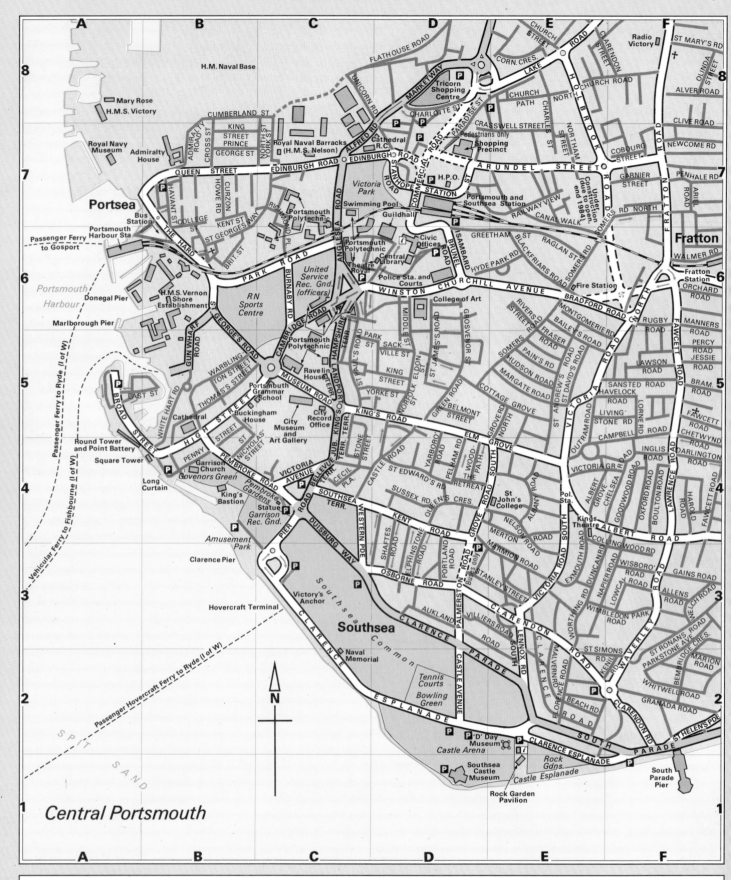

Portsmouth

Richard the Lionheart first recognised the strategic importance of Portsea Island and subsequently ordered the first docks, and later the town of Portsmouth, to be built. Over the centuries, succeeding monarchs improved the defences and extended the docks which now cover some 300 acres – as befits Britain's premier naval base. Of the defensive fortifications, Fort Widley and the

Round Tower are the best preserved remains. Two famous ships rest in Portsmouth; HMS Victory and the Mary Rose. The former, Lord Nelson's flagship, has been fully restored and the adjacent Royal Naval museum houses numerous relics of Trafalgar. The Mary Rose, built by Henry VIII, lay on the sea bed off Southsea until she was spectacularly raised in 1982. She has now been put on display and there is an exhibition in Southsea Castle of artefacts that have been recovered from

her. Portsmouth suffered greatly from bombing in World War II and the centre has been almost completely rebuilt. However, the old town, clustered around the harbour mouth, escaped severe damage and, now restored, forms an attractive and fashionable area of the city.

Southsea, Portsmouth's near neighbour, developed in the 19th century as an elegant seaside resort with fine houses and terraces, an esplanade and an extensive seafront common.

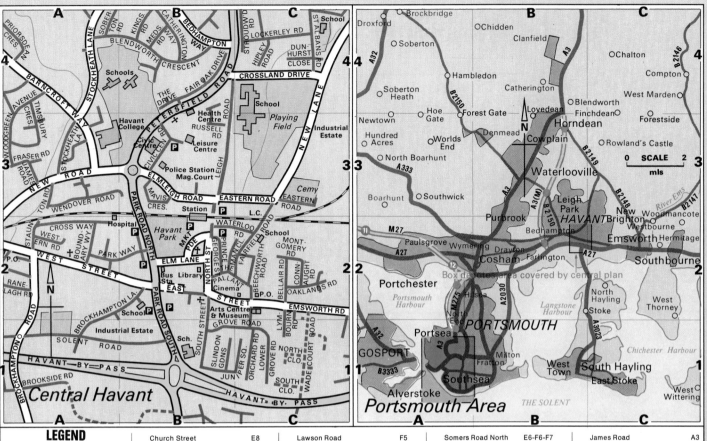

Central Havant

Portsmouth Area

LEGEND

Town Plan

AA recommended route	
Restricted roads	
Other roads	
Buildings of interest	Station ▢
Car parks	Ⓟ
Parks and open spaces	
One way streets	←

Area Plan

A roads	
B roads	
Locations	○ Lovedean
Urban area	

Street Index with grid reference

Portsmouth

Admiralty Road	B7-B8
Albany Road	E4
Albert Grove	E4-F4
Albert Road	E4-F4
Alfred Road	C7-D7-D8
Allens Road	F3
Alver Road	F8
Anglesea Road	C6-C7
Ariel Road	F7
Arundel Street	D7-E7-F7
Aukland Road	D3-E3-E2
Bailey's Road	E5-E6
Beach Road	E2
Bellvue Terrace	C4
Belmont Street	D5
Bembridge Crescent	F2-F3
Blackfriars Road	E6
Boulton Road	F4
Bradford Road	E6-F6
Bramble Road	F5
Britain Street	B6
Broad Street	A5-A4-B4
Burnaby Road	C6
Cambridge Road	C5-C6
Campbell Road	E4-F4-F5
Canal Walk	E6-E7
Castle Avenue	D2-D3
Castle Road	C4-D4-D5
Cecil Place	C4
Charles Street	E7-D8
Charlotte Street	D8
Chelsea Road	F4
Chetwynd Road	F4-F5
Church Path	E8
Church Street	E8
Clarence Esplanade	C3-C2-D2-E2-E1-F1
Clarence Parade	C3-D3-D2-E2
Clarence Road	E2-E3
Clarendon Road	D3-E3-E2-F2
Clarendon Street	E8-F8
Clive Road	F7-F8
Cobourg Street	F7
College Street	B6-B7
Collingwood Road	E4-E3-F3
Commercial Road	D6-D7-D8
Cornwallis Crescent	E8
Cottage Grove	D5-E5
Crasswell Road	D7-E7
Cross Street	B7-B8
Cumberland Street	B8-C8
Curzon Howe Road	B7
Darlington Road	F4
Duisburg Way	C3-C4
Duncan Road	E3-F3-F4
East Street	A5-B5
Edinburgh Road	C7-D7
Eldon Street	D5
Elm Grove	D5-D4-E4
Exmouth Road	E3-E4
Fawcett Road	F4-F5-F6
Elphinstone Road	D3-D4
Flathouse Road	C8-D8
Florence Road	E2
Fraser Road	E5-E6
Fratton Road	F6-F7-F8
Gains Road	F3
Garnier Street	F7
Goodwood Road	F4
Granada Road	F2
Green Road	D5
Greetham Street	D6-E6
Grosvenor Street	D5-D6
Grove Road North	E5
Grove Road South	D4-E4
Gun Wharf Road	B5-B6
Hampshire Terrace	C5-C6
Harold Road	F4
Havant Street	B7
Havelock Road	E5-F5
High Street	B4-B5-C5
Holbrook Road	E7-F7-F8
Hudson Road	F5
Hyde Park Road	D6-E6
Inglis Road	F4
Isambard Brunel Road	D6-D7
Jessie Road	F5
Jubilee Terrace	C4-C5
Kenilworth Road	C5
Kent Road	C4-D4
Kent Street	B7
King Street	B7-C7
King Street	C5-D5
King's Road	C5-D5
King's Terrace	C5
Lake Road	D8-E8
Landport Terrace	C5
Lawrence Road	F4-F5

Lawson Road	F5
Lennox Road South	E2-E3
Livingstone Road	E5-F5
Lorne Road	F5
Lowcay Road	F3
Malvern Road	E2-E3
Manners Road	F5-F6
Margate Road	E5
Marion Road	F2
Market Way	D8
Marmion Road	D4-D3-E3
Merton Road	D4-E4
Middle Street	D5-D6
Montgomerie Road	E6-E5-F5
Museum Road	C5
Napier Road	E3-F3-F4
Nelson Road	D4-E4-E3
Newcombe Road	F7
Norfolk Street	D5
North Street	C7-C8
Northam Street	E7
North Church Road	E8-F8
Olinda Street	F8
Orchard Road	F6
Osborne Road	C3-D3
Outram Road	E4-E5
Oxford Road	F4
Pain's Road	E5
Palmerston Road	D3
Paradise Street	D7-D8
Park Road	B6-C6
Park Street	C5-D5
Parkstone Avenue	F2-F3
Pelham Road	D4-D5
Pembroke Road	B4-C4
Penhale Road	F7
Penny Street	B4-B5
Percy Road	F5
Pier Road	C3-C4
Portland Road	D3-D4
Prince George Street	B7-C7
Queen's Crescent	D4
Queen Street	B7
Raglan Street	E6
Railway View	D7-E7
Richmond Place	C6-C7
Rivers Street	E6
Rugby Road	F6
St Andrew's Road	E4-E5-E6
St David's Road	E5
St Edward's Road	D4
St George's Road	B6-B5-C5
St Georges Way	B6-B7-C7
St Helen's Parade	F2
St James's Road	D5-D6
St Mary's Road	F8
St Nicholas' Street	B4-B5
St Paul's Road	C5-C6
St Ronans Road	F2-F3
St Simons Road	E2-F2
Sackville Street	D5
Sansted Road	E5-F5
Shaftesbury Road	D3-D4
Somers Road	D5-E5-E6

Somers Road North	E6-F6-F7
South Parade	E2-F2
Southsea Terrace	C4
Stanhope Road	D7
Stanley Street	D3-E3
Station Street	D7
Stone Street	C4-C5
Sussex Road	D4
The Hard	B6-B7
The Retreat	D4
Thomas's Street	B4-B5-C5
Unicorn Road	C8-D8
Victoria Avenue	C4
Victoria Grove	E4-F4
Victoria Road North	E4-E5-F5-F6
Victoria Road South	E3-E4
Villiers Road	D3-E3
Walmer Road	F6
Warblington Street	B5
Waverley Road	F2-F3-F4
Welch Road	F3
Western Parade	C3-C4
White Hart Road	B4-B5
Whitwell Road	F2
Wimbledon Park Road	E3-F3
Winston Churchill Avenue	C6-D6-E6
Wisborough Road	F3
Woodpath	D4
Worthing Road	E2
Yarborough Road	D4-D5
York Street	C7-C8
Yorke Street	C5-D5

Havant

Barncroft Way	A3-A4
Bedhampton Way	B4
Beechworth Road	C2
Bellair Road	C2
Blendworth Crescent	A4-B4
Brockhampton Lane	A1-A2-B2
Brockhampton Road	A1-A2
Brookside Road	A1
Boundary Way	A2
Catherington Way	B4
Civic Centre Road	B3
Connaught Road	C2
Cross Way	A2
Crossland Drive	C4
Dunhurst Close	C4
East Street	B2-C2
Eastern Road	B3-C3
Elm Lane	B2
Elmleigh Road	B3
Emsworth Road	C2
Fairfield Road	B2-C2-C3
Fair Oak Drive	B4
Fraser Road	A3
Grove Road	B1-C1
Havant By-Pass	A1-B1-C1
Hipley Road	C4

James Road	A3
Juniper Square	B1-C1
Kingsworthy Road	B4
Leigh Road	B3-B4-C4
Lockerley Road	C4
Lower Grove Road	C1
Lymbourn Road	C1-C2
Manor Close	B2-C2
Market Parade	B2
Mavis Crescent	B3
Medstead Road	B4
Montgomery Road	C2
New Lane	C3-C4
New Road	A3-B3
North Close	C1
North Street	B2
Oaklands Road	C2
Orchard Road	C1
Park Road North	B2-B3
Park Road South	B1-B2
Park Way	A2-B2
Petersfield Road	B3-B4
Prince George Street	B2
Priorsdean Crescent	A4
Ranelagh Road	A2
Russell Road	B3
St Albans Road	C4
Slindon Gardens	B1
Solent Road	A1-B1
Soberton Road	A4
South Close	C1
South Street	B1-B2
Staunton Road	A2-A3
Stockheath Lane	A3-A4
Stroudwood Road	C4
The Drive	B4
The Pallant	B2-C2
Timsbury Crescent	A3-A4
Wade Court Road	C1-C2
Waterloo Road	B2-C2
Wendover Road	A3-B3
West Street	A2-B2
Western Road	A2
Woolgreen Avenue	A3-A4

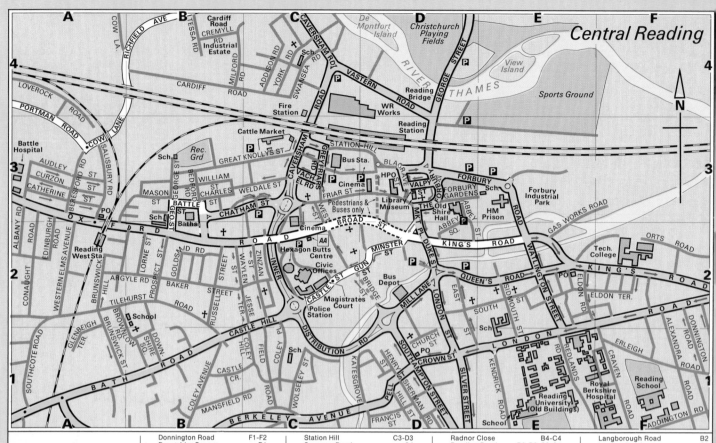

Central Reading

Street Index with Grid Reference

Reading

Abbey Square	D2-D3
Abbey Street	D2-D3
Addington Road	F1
Addison Road	C4
Alexandra Road	F1-F2
Argyle Road	A2-B2
Audley Street	A3
Baker Street	A2
Bath Road	A1-B1
Battle Street	B3
Bedford Road	B3
Beresford Road	A3
Berkeley Avenue	B1-C1-D1
Blagrave Street	D3
Bridge Street	C2-D2
Broad Street	C2-C3-D3-D2
Brownlow Road	A2-B2-B1
Brunswick Hill	A2
Brunswick Street	A1-A2
Cardiff Road	B4-C4
Castle Crescent	B1-C1
Castle Hill	B1-B2-C2
Castle Street	C2
Catherine Street	A3
Caversham Road	C3-C4
Charles Street	B3
Chatham Street	B3-C3
Church Street	D1
Coley Avenue	B1
Coley Hill	C1
Coley Place	C1-C2
Conaught Road	A2-A3
Cow Lane	A3-A4
Craven Road	F1-F2
Cremyll Road	B4
Crown Street	D1
Curzon Street	A3

Donnington Road	F1-F2
Downshire Square	B1
Duke Street	D2
East Street	D1-D2
Edinburgh Road	A2-A3
Eldon Road	E2
Eldon Terrace	E2-F2
Elm Park Road	A2-A3
Erleigh Road	F1
Field Road	C1
Forbury Gardens	D3-E3
Forbury Road	D3-E3-E2
Francis Street	D1
Friar Street	C3-D3
Gas Works Road	E2-E3-F3
George Street	B2-B3
George Street	D3-D4
Glenbeigh Terrace	A1-A2
Goldsmid Road	B2
Great Knollys Street	B3-C3
Greyfriars Road	C3
Gun Street	C2-D2
Henry Street	D1
Hill Street	D1
Inner Distribution Road	
	C3-C2-C1-D1-D2
Jesse Terrace	B2-C2
Katesgrove	C1-D1
Kendrick Road	E1
King's Road	D2-E2-F2
London Road	D1-E1-E2-F2
London Street	D1-D2
Lorne Street	B2
Loverock Road	A3-A4
Mansfield Road	B1-C1
Market Place	D2-D3
Mason Street	B3
Milford Road	B4
Mill Lane	D2
Minster Street	D2
Orts Road	E2-F2
Oxford Road	A3-A2-B2-C2
Pell Street	D1
Portman Road	A3-A4
Prospect Street	B2
Queen's Road	D2-E2
Redlands Road	E1
Richfield Avenue	A4-B4
Russell Street	B2
Salisbury Road	A3
Sidmouth Street	E1-E2
Silver Street	D1
Sherman Road	D1
Southampton Street	D1
Southcote Road	A1-A2
South Street	D2-E2

Station Hill	C3-D3
Swansea Road	C4
Tessa Road	B4
The Forbury	D3
Tilehurst Road	A2-B2-B1
Vachel Road	C3
Valpy Street	D3
Vastern Road	C4-D4
Watlington Street	E2
Waylen Street	B2
Weldale Street	B3-C3
Western Elms Avenue	A2
West Street	C2-C3
William Street	B3
Wolseley Street	C1
York Road	C4
Zinzan Street	C2

Henley

Albert Road	B2
Ancastle Green	A2-A3
Badgemore Lane	A4-B4
Bell Street	B3-B4
Crisp Road	A4
Deanfield Avenue	A2-B2
Deanfield Road	A1-A2
Duke Street	B3
Friday Street	B3-C3
Gainsborough Hill	A1
Grange Road	C1
Gravel Hill	A3-B3
Greys Hill	B3
Greys Road	A1-A2-B2-B3
Grove Road	C1
Hamilton Avenue	B1-B2-C2
Hart Street	B3-C3
Hop Gardens	A3-A4
King's Close	A3-B3
King's Road	B3-B4
Luker Avenue	A4
Market Place	B3
Meadow Road	C2
Milton Close	A1
Mount View	A4-B4
New Street	B4-C4-C3
Norman Avenue	B2
Queen Street	B3-B2-C2
Paradise Road	A2-A3
Park Road	C1

Radnor Close	B4-C4
Reading Road	B3-B2-C2-C1
Remenham Lane	C3-C4
Riverside	C3
River Terrace	C2-C3
Rupert Close	B4
St Andrew's Road	B1-C1
St Mark's Road	B1-C1
Simmons Road	A4
Station Road	C2
Thames Side	C3
The Close	A1
Upton Close	C1-C2
Vicarage Road	B1
Walton Avenue	C1
West Street	A3-B3
White Hill	C3
York Road	A3-B3

Wokingham

Arthur Drive	A2-A3
Ashridge Road	C3-C4
Barkham Road	A1-A2
Barrett Crescent	C2-C3
Bell Foundry Lane	B4
Benning Way	C4
Broad Street	B2
Budges Road	C3
Cantley Crescent	A4
Carey Road	B1
Clare Avenue	B3
Clifton Road	A3-A4
Copse Drive	A3
Crutchley Road	C3
Denmark Street	B2
Easthampstead Road	B2-C2-C1
Eastheath Avenue	A1
Elisabeth Road	C2-C3
Elms Road	B2
Finchampstead Road	A1-B1-B2
Fish Ponds Road	A1
Gipsy Lane	B2-B1-C1-C2
Glebelands Road	B3
Holmes Crescent	A1
Holt Lane	A3-B3
Howard Road	B2
Hughes Road	C3
Jubilee Avenue	A4-A3-B3
Keephatch Road	C3-C4

Langborough Road	B2
London Road	C2
Marks Road	A4
Martins Drive	A3-A4
Mathewsgreen Road	A4-B4
Meadow Road	A2
Milton Road	B2-B3-B4
Molly Millars Road	A2-A1-B1
Murdoch Road	B2-C2
Murray Road	A2
Norreys Avenue	C3
Oaklands Drive	A1
Oxford Road	A2-A3
Park Road	A2-B2
Peach Street	B2-C2
Reading Road	A3-B3
Rectory Road	B2-B3-C3
Rose Street	B2-C2
Sarum Crescent	C3
Sewell Avenue	A4
Shute End	B2-B3
South Drive	B2-B1-C1
Southlands Road	C1
Station Road	A2-B2
Sturges Road	B2-C2
Twyford Road	A4-B4
Warren House Road	B4-C4
Wellington Road	A2-B2
Westcott Road	B2
Wiltshire Road	B4-B3-C3

LEGEND

Town Plan

AA recommended route

Restricted roads

Other roads

Buildings of interest School

Car parks P

Parks and open spaces

One way streets

Area Plan

A roads

B roads

Locations Wilsden o

Urban area

Reading

Shopping and light industry first spring to mind when thinking of Reading, but the town actually has a long and important history. Its rise to significance began in 1121 when Henry I founded an abbey here which became the third most important in England. However, after the Dissolution of the Monasteries, only a few ruins were left. Reading also used to be one of the major centres of the medieval cloth trade, but, already declining in the early 17th century, this source of income was reduced still further as a result of Civil War disturbances.

A fascinating collection of all types of farm implements and domestic equipment can be found in the extremely comprehensive Museum of English Rural Life, situated in the University Campus at Whiteknights Park. The town's own museum has major displays about nearby Silchester – the powerful Roman town of *Calleva*.

Henley-on-Thames, famous for its annual rowing regatta, is a lovely old town, well-provided with old coaching inns, Georgian façades and numerous listed buildings.

Wokingham has been a market town for centuries and over the years has been known for its silk industry and its bell-foundry. Half-timbered gabled houses can be seen in the town centre, although modern development surrounds it.

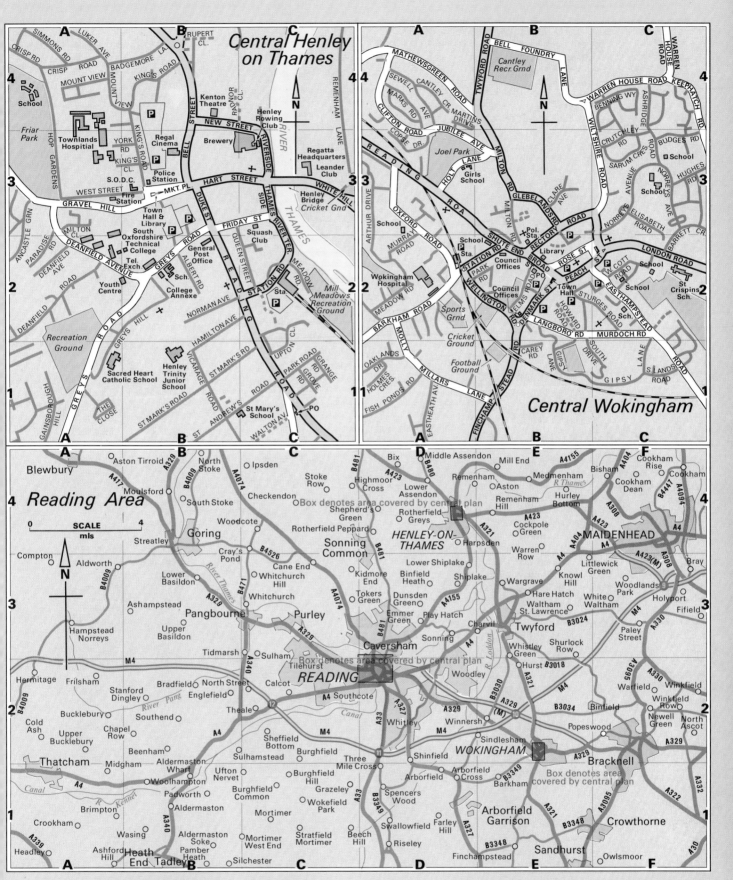

Central Henley on Thames

Central Wokingham

Reading Area

SCALE
0   mls   4

Box denotes area covered by central plan

READING
Whiteknights, which consists of 300 acres of landscaped parkland, provides Reading's modern university with an incomparable campus setting and includes a conservation area and a biological reserve for research purposes.

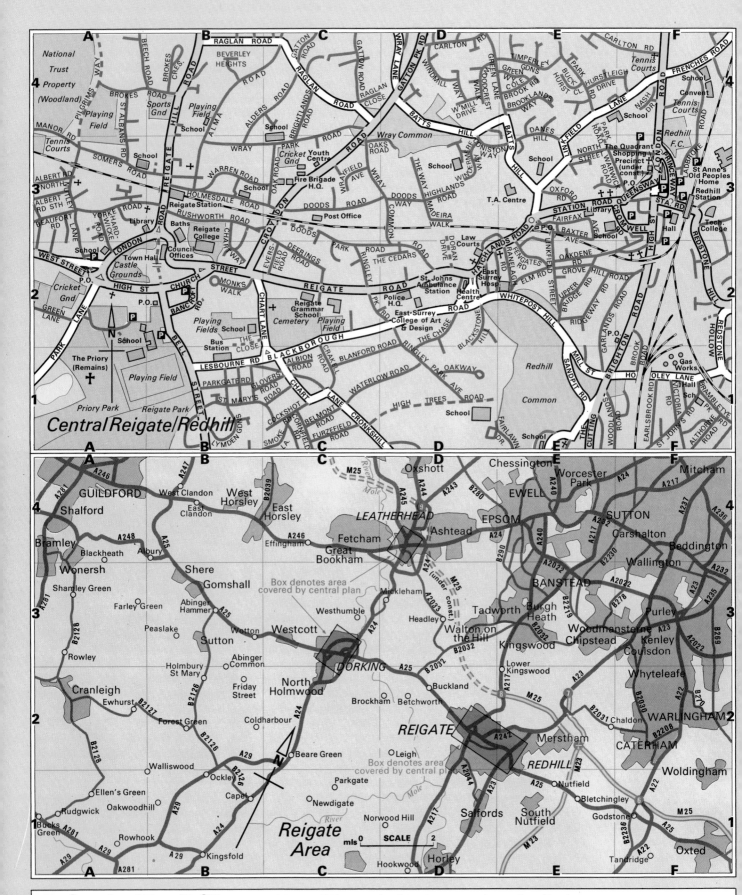

Reigate/Redhill

One of the earliest public libraries in the country can be found in Reigate's parish church of St. Mary Magdalen. The library dates from 1701; the church goes back as far as the 12th century. Industry and commerce are changing the face of the area, especially in Redhill, but Reigate has kept a number of open spaces, such as Reigate Park (the site of a former priory), Reigate Heath (where an 18th-century windmill has been converted into a church) and Earlswood Common.

Dorking lies at the foot of Box Hill, a popular beauty spot today and at least as far back as the early 1800s, when Jane Austen featured it in her novel *Emma*.

Modernisation has done little to erode the charm of the town, where weeping willows surround the attractive Mill Pond. Overlooking the High Street is the gabled White Horse Inn, reminiscent of coaching days.

Leatherhead's Thorndyke Theatre has been entertaining the area since the 1960s, and the town is also known for its Royal School for the Blind, which was founded here in the late 18th century. With a museum that traces the history of the region, and a parish church which dates mainly from the 12th to the 15th centuries, Leatherhead today is the home of several industrial research establishments.

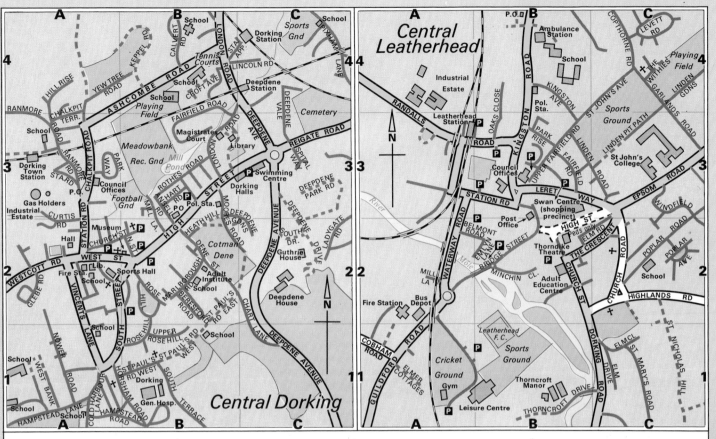

Central Leatherhead

Central Dorking

Key to Town Plan and Area Plan

Town Plan

A A Recommended roads
Other roads
Restricted roads
Buildings of interest — Theatre
Car Parks — P
Parks and open spaces
Churches

Area Plan

A roads
B roads
Locations — Leigh ○
Urban Area

Street Index with Grid Reference

Redhill/Reigate

Albert Road North	A3
Albert Road South	A3
Albion Road	C1
Alders Road	B3-B4-C4
Alma Road	B3-B4-C4
Althorne Road	F1
Bancroft Road	B2
Batts Hill	D4-E4-E3
Baxter Avenue	E3
Beaufort Road	A3
Beech Road	A4
Bell Street	B1-B2
Belmont Road	C1
Beverley Heights	B4
Blackborough Road	C1-C2-D2
Blackstone Hill	D2
Blanford Road	C1-D1-D2
Brambletye Park Road	F1
Brightlands Road	C3-C4
Brighton Road	E1-F1-F2
Brokes Crescent	B4
Brokes Road	A4-B4
Brook Road	F1-F2
Brooklands Way	E4
Buckhurst Close	E4
Carlton Road	D4, E4-F4
Chart Lane	B2-C2-C1
Chartway	B2-B3
Church Street	B2
Cockshot Road	C1
Colebrook Road	E4
Coniston Way	D3-E3
Cornfield Road	C1
Crakell Road	C1

Cromwell Road	E3-F3
Cronkshill	C1-D1
Croydon Road	B2-B3-C3-C4
Danes Hill	E3-E4
Deerings Road	C2-C3
Doods Road	C2-D3
Doods Way	D3
Doods Park Road	C3-C2-D2
Doran Drive	D2-D3
Earlsbrook Road	F1
Elm Road	E2
Eversfield Road	C2
Fairfax Avenue	E3
Fairlawn Drive	D1-E1
Fengates Road	E2
Frenches Road	F4
Furzefield Road	C1
Garlands Road	E1-E2-F2
Gatton Road	C4
Gatton Park Road	D4
Glovers Road	B1-C1
Green Lane	A2
Green Lane	D4-E4
Green Way	D4-E4
Grove Hill Road	E2-F2
Hardwicke Road	A2-A3
Hatchlands Road	D2-E2-E3
High Street	A2-B2
High Street	F2-F3
Highlands Road	D3
High Trees Road	C1-D1
Holmesdale Road	B3-C3
Hooley Lane	E1-F1
Hurstleigh Drive	E4-F4
Ladbroke Road	F3-F4
Lesbourne Road	B1
Linkfield Lane	E3-E4-F4
Linkfield Street	E2-E3
London Road	A2-A3-B3
London Road	F3-F4
Lymden Gardens	B1
Madeira Walk	D3
Manor Road	A3-A4
Mill Street	E1
Monks Walk	B2
Nash Drive	F4
North Street	E3
Nutley Lane	A2-A3
Oak Road	C3
Oakdene Road	E2
Oaks Road	C3-D3
Oakway	D1
Oxford Road	E3
Park Lane	A1-A2
Park Road	E3-E4
Parkgate Road	B1
Pilgrims Way	A3-A4
Prince Way	E3
Queensway	F3
Raglan Close	C4
Raglan Road	B4-C4
Ranelagh Road	E2
Redstone Hill	F2-F3
Redstone Hollow	F1-F2
Reigate Road	B2-C2-D2
Reigate Hill Road	B3-B4
Ridgeway Road	E2
Ringley Park Avenue	D1-D2
Ringley Park Road	C2-D2
Rushworth Road	B3
St Albans Road	A3-A4

St John's Road	F1
St Mary's Road	B1-C1
Sandpit Road	E1
Smoke Lane	C1
Somers Road	A3-B3
Station Road	E3-F3
The Cedars	C2-D2
The Chase	D1-D2
The Close	B2
The Cutting	E1
The Way	D3
Timperley Gardens	D4-E4
Upper Bridge Road	E2
Victoria Road	F1
Warren Road	B3-C3
Warwick Road	E3-F3
Waterlow Road	C1-D1
West Street	A2
Whitepost Hill	D2-E2
Windermere Way	D3
Windmill Drive	D4
Windmill Way	D4
Woodcrest Walk	D4
Woodlands Road	E1
Wray Lane	D4
Wray Common Road	C3-D3-D2
Wrayfield Avenue	C3
Wray Park Road	B3-C3-C4
Yorke Road	A3-B3

Dorking

Ansell Road	B2-B3
Ashcombe Road	A3-A4-B4
Beresford Road	B2
Calvert Road	B4
Chalkpit Road	A3
Chalkpit Terrace	A3-A4
Chart Lane	C1-C2
Church Street	A2-B2
Cold Harbour Lane	A1
Croft Avenue	B4
Curtis Road	A2-A3
Deepdene Avenue	C1-C2-C3-C4
Deepdene Drive	C2-C3
Deepdene Gardens	B3-C3-C2
Deepdene Park Road	C3
Deepdene Vale	C3-C4
Dene Street	B2
Fairfield Road	B3-B4
Glebe Road	A2
Hampstead Lane	A1
Hampstead Road	A1-B1
Hart Road	B3
Heath Hill	B2-B3
High Street	B2-B3-C3
Hill Rise	A4
Horsham Road	A1-B1
Keppel Road	A4-B4
Ladygate Road	C2-C3
Lincoln Road	B4-C4
London Road	B3-B4-C4-B4
Marlborough Road	B2
Mill Lane	B2-B3
Moores Road	B3-B2-C2
North Street	B2
Nower Road	A1-A2
Park Way	A3
Pixham Lane	C4

Ranmore Road	A3-A4
Reigate Road	C3
Rose Hill	B1-B2
Rothes Road	B3
St Paul's Road East	B2
St Paul's Road West	A1-B1
South Drive	C2
South Street	A1-B1-B2-A2-B2
South Terrace	B1
Spital Way	C3
Station Approach	B4-C4
Station Road	A2-A3
Upper Rose Hill	B1
Vincents Lane	A1-A2
West Street	A2-B2
West Bank	A1
Westcott Road	A2
Yew Tree Road	A4-B4

Leatherhead

Belmont Road	A2-B2
Bridge Street	A2-B2
Church Road	C2-C3
Church Street	B2
Cobham Road	A1
Copthorne Road	C4
Dorking Road	B2-B1-C1
Elm Close	C1
Elm Drive	C1
Elm Road	B2-C2
Elmer Cottages	A1
Emlyn Lane	B2
Epsom Road	C3
Fairfield Road	B3
Garlands Road	C3-C4
Guildford Road	A1-A2
High Street	B2-B3-C3
Highlands Road	C2
Kingston Avenue	B3-B4
Kingston Road	B3-B4
Leret Way	B3-C3
Levett Road	C4
Linden Gardens	C4
Linden Pit Path	C3-C4
Linden Road	B3-C3
Mill Lane	A2
Minchin Close	B2
Oaks Close	B3-B4
Park Rise	B3
Poplar Avenue	C2
Poplar Road	C2-C3
Randalls Road	A4-A3-B3
St John's Avenue	B3-B4-C4
St Mary's Road	C1
St Nicholas Hill	C1-C2
Station Road	A3-B3
The Crescent	B2-C2
The Withies	C4
Thorncroft Drive	B1-C1
Upper Fairfield Road	B3
Waterway Road	A2-A3
Windfield	C3

53

Salisbury

Its attractive site where the waters of the Avon and Nadder meet, its beautiful cathedral and its unspoilt centre put Salisbury among England's finest cities. In 1220 the people of the original settlement at Old Sarum, two miles to the north, moved down to the plain and laid the first stone of the cathedral. Within 38 years its was completed and the result is a superb example of Early English architecture.

The cloisters are the largest in England and the spire the tallest in Britain. All the houses within the Cathedral Close were built for cathedral functionaries, and although many have Georgian façades, most date back to the 13th century. Mompesson House is one of the handsome mansions here and as it belongs to the National Trust, its equally fine interior can be seen. Another building houses the Museum of the Duke of Edinburgh's Royal Regiment. At one time, relations

between the clergy and the citizens of Salisbury were not always harmonious, so the former built a protective wall around the Close.

The streets of the modern city follow the medieval grid pattern of squares, or 'chequers', and the tightly-packed houses provide a very pleasing townscape. Salisbury was granted its first charter in 1227 and flourished as a market and wool centre; there is still a twice-weekly market in the spacious square.

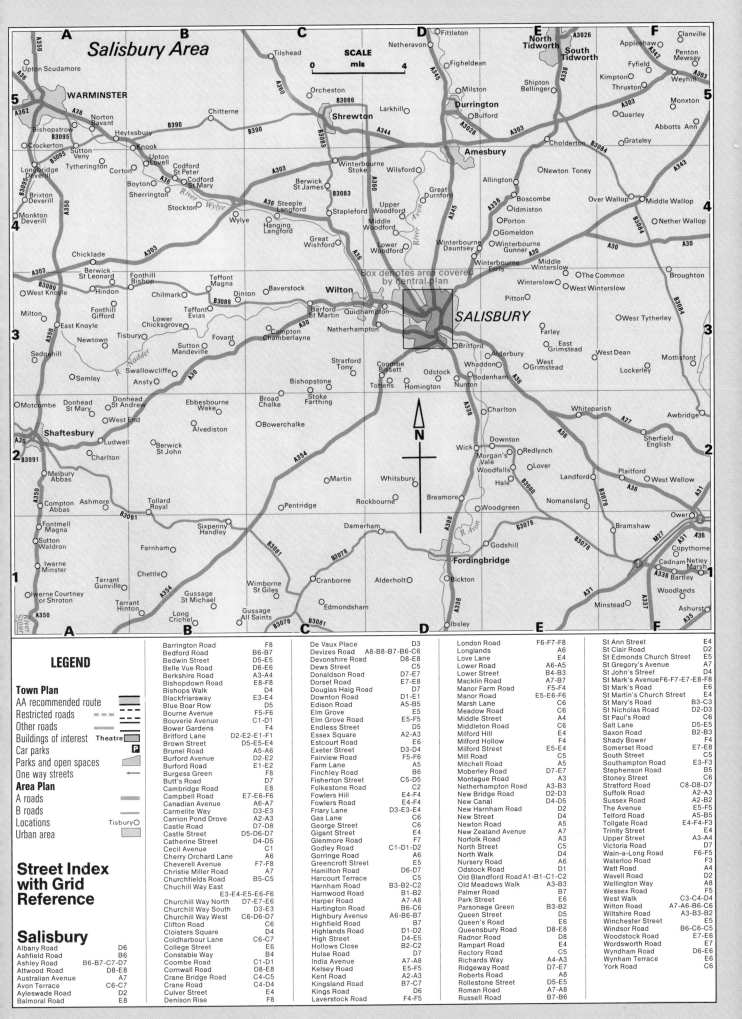

Salisbury Area

Box denotes area covered by central plan

N

LEGEND

Town Plan
AA recommended route
Restricted roads
Other roads
Buildings of interest   Theatre
Car parks   P
Parks and open spaces
One way streets

Area Plan
A roads
B roads
Locations   Tisbury ○
Urban area

Street Index with Grid Reference

Salisbury

Albany Road	D6
Ashfield Road	B6
Ashley Road	B6-B7-C7-D7
Attwood Road	D8-E8
Australian Avenue	A7
Avon Terrace	C6-C7
Aylewade Road	D2
Balmoral Road	E8

Barrington Road	F8
Bedford Road	B6-B7
Bedwin Street	D5-E5
Belle Vue Road	D6-E6
Berkshire Road	A3-A4
Bishopdown Road	E8-F8
Bishops Walk	D4
Blackfriarsway	E3-E4
Blue Boar Row	D5
Bourne Avenue	F5-F6
Bouverie Avenue	C1-D1
Bower Gardens	F4
Britford Lane	D2-E2-E1-F1
Brown Street	D5-E5-E4
Brunel Road	A5-A6
Burford Avenue	D2-E2
Burford Road	E1-E2
Burgess Green	F8
Butt's Road	D7
Cambridge Road	E8
Campbell Road	E7-E6-F6
Canadian Avenue	A6-A7
Carmelite Way	D3-E3
Carrion Pond Drove	A2-A3
Castle Road	D7-D8
Castle Street	D5-D6-D7
Catherine Street	D4-D5
Cecil Avenue	C1
Cherry Orchard Lane	A6
Cheverell Avenue	F7-F8
Christie Miller Road	A7
Churchfields Road	B5-C5
Chuchill Way East	
	E3-E4-E5-E6-F6
Churchill Way North	D7-E7-E6
Churchill Way South	D3-E3
Churchill Way West	C6-D6-D7
Clifton Road	C6
Cloisters Square	D4
Coldharbour Lane	C6-C7
College Street	E6
Constable Way	B4
Coombe Road	C1-D1
Cornwall Road	D8-E8
Crane Bridge Road	C4-C5
Crane Road	C4-D4
Culver Street	E4
Denison Rise	F8

De Vaux Place	D3
Devizes Road	A8-B8-B7-B6-C6
Devonshire Road	D8-E8
Dews Street	C5
Donaldson Road	D7-E7
Dorset Road	E7-E8
Douglas Haig Road	D7
Downton Road	D1-E1
Edison Road	A5-B5
Elm Grove	E5
Elm Grove Road	E5-F5
Endless Street	D5
Essex Square	A2-A3
Estcourt Road	E6
Exeter Street	D3-D4
Fairview Road	F5-F6
Farm Lane	A5
Finchley Road	B6
Fisherton Street	C5-D5
Folkestone Road	C2
Fowlers Hill	E4-F4
Fowlers Road	E4-F4
Friary Lane	D3-E3-E4
Gas Lane	C6
George Street	E4
Gigant Street	E4
Glenmore Road	F7
Godley Road	C1-D1-D2
Gorringe Road	A6
Greencroft Street	E5
Hamilton Road	D6-D7
Harcourt Terrace	C5
Harnham Road	B3-B2-C2
Harnwood Road	B1-B2
Harper Road	A7-A8
Hartington Road	B6-C6
Highbury Avenue	A6-B6-B7
Highfield Road	B7
Highlands Road	D1-D2
High Street	D4-E5
Hollows Close	B2-C2
Hulse Road	D7
India Avenue	A7-A8
Kelsey Road	E5-F5
Kent Road	A2-A3
Kingsland Road	B7-C7
Kings Road	D6
Laverstock Road	F4-F5

London Road	F6-F7-F8
Longlands	A6
Love Lane	E4
Lower Road	A6-A5
Lower Street	B4-B3
Macklin Road	A7-B7
Manor Farm Road	F5-F4
Manor Road	E5-E6-F6
Marsh Lane	C6
Meadow Road	C6
Middle Street	A4
Middleton Road	C6
Milford Hill	E4
Milford Hollow	F4
Milford Street	E5-E4
Mill Road	C5
Mitchell Road	A5
Moberley Road	D7-E7
Montague Road	A3
Netherhampton Road	A3-B3
New Bridge Road	D2-D3
New Canal	D4-D5
New Harnham Road	D2
New Street	D4
Newton Road	A5
New Zealand Avenue	A7
Norfolk Road	A3
North Street	C5
North Walk	D4
Nursery Road	A6
Odstock Road	D1
Old Blandford Road	A1-B1-C1-C2
Old Meadows Walk	A3-B3
Palmer Road	B7
Park Street	E6
Parsonage Green	B3-B2
Queen Street	D5
Queen's Road	E6
Queensbury Road	D8-E8
Radnor Road	D8
Rampart Road	E4
Rectory Road	C5
Richards Way	A4-A3
Ridgeway Road	D7-E7
Roberts Road	A8
Rollestone Street	D5-E5
Roman Road	A7-A8
Russell Road	B7-B6

St Ann Street	E4
St Clair Road	D2
St Edmonds Church Street	E5
St Gregory's Avenue	A7
St John's Street	D4
St Mark's Avenue	F6-F7-E7-E8-F8
St Mark's Road	E6
St Martin's Church Street	E4
St Mary's Road	B3-C3
St Nicholas Road	D2-D3
St Paul's Road	C6
Salt Lane	D5-E5
Saxon Road	B2-B3
Shady Bower	E4
Somerset Road	E7-E8
South Street	C5
Southampton Road	E3-F3
Stephenson Road	B5
Stoney Street	C6
Stratford Road	C8-D8-D7
Suffolk Road	A2-A3
Sussex Road	A2-B2
The Avenue	E5-F5
Telford Road	A5-B5
Tollgate Road	E4-F4-F3
Trinity Street	E4
Upper Street	A3-A4
Victoria Road	D7
Wain-a-Long Road	F6-F5
Waterloo Road	F3
Watt Road	A4
Wavell Road	D2
Wellington Way	A8
Wessex Road	F5
West Walk	C3-C4-D4
Wilton Road	A7-A6-B6-C6
Wiltshire Road	A3-B3-B2
Winchester Street	E5
Windsor Road	B6-C6-C5
Woodstock Road	E7-E6
Wordsworth Road	E6
Wyndham Road	D6-E6
Wynham Terrace	E6
York Road	C6

55

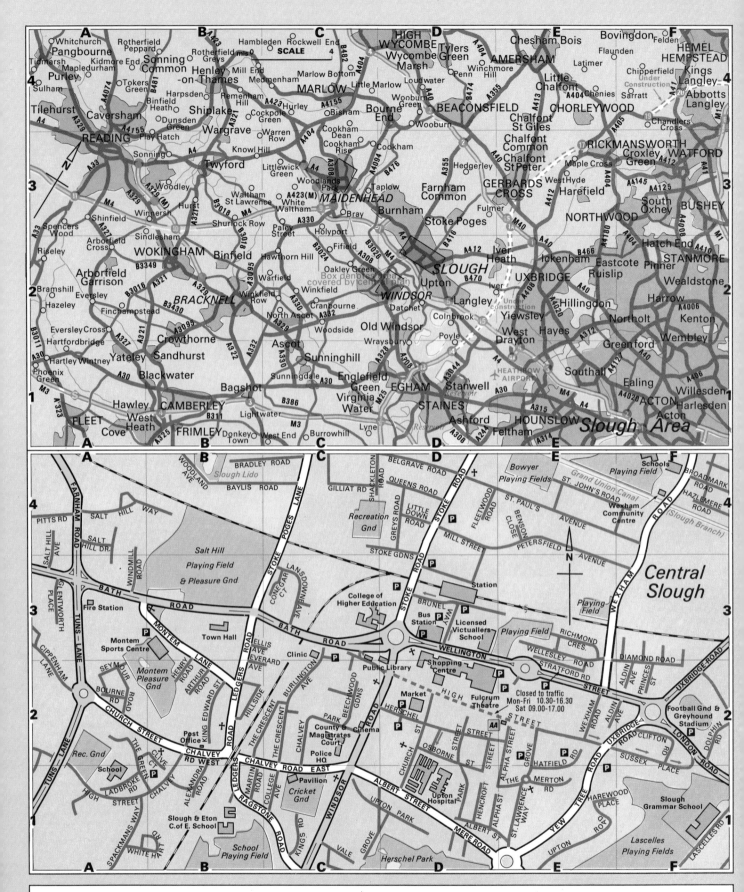

Slough

The town is something of a non-starter as far as architectural beauty or historical interest is concerned. However, it is a good shopping centre and has plenty of sports and leisure facilities.

Windsor The distinctive outline of the castle's towers and battlements above the Thames completely dominates the town. First built by the Normans to guard the approaches to London, it has been altered and added to at different times by various kings, but Henry III and Edward III contributed most to its present haphazard shape. The State Apartments are magnificent, as is St George's Chapel, with its superb fan-vaulted ceiling. Queen Mary's Dolls' House is an exquisite model house of the 1920s, complete down to the last detail. The town itself, squeezed between the castle walls and the river, has several attractive streets graced with fine buildings. One 17th-century colonnaded building by Sir Christopher Wren contains a small museum of local interest, and a recent new attraction is the Madame Tussaud's Royalty and Railways Exhibition.

Maidenhead used to be an important stage-post on the London to Bath road and is now a prosperous Thameside residential town. Oldfield House, near the ancient bridge designed by Brunel, contains the Henry Reitlinger Bequest Museum, specialising in glass and ceramics.

56

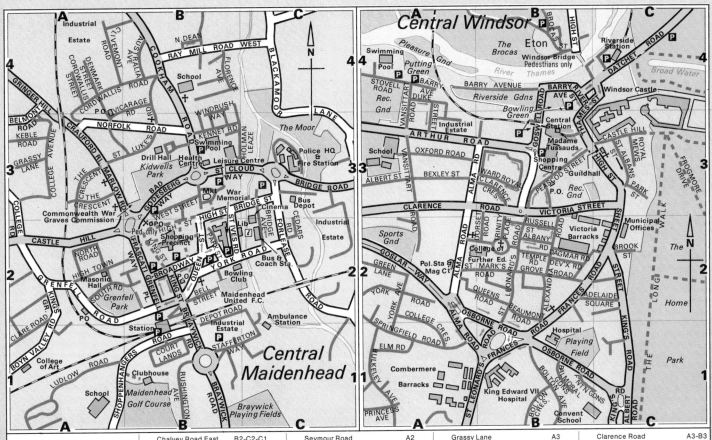

LEGEND

Town Plan

AA recommended route	
Restricted roads	
Other roads	
Buildings of interest	
Car parks	Station **P**
Parks and open spaces	
One way streets	→

Area Plan

A roads	
B roads	
Locations	Hightown○
Urban area	

Street Index with Grid Reference

Slough

Albert Street	C1-D1-E1
Aldin Avenue	E2-F2
Alexandra Road	B1-B2
Alpha Street	D1-E1-E2
Arthur Road	B2
Bath Road	A3-B3-C3
Baylis Road	B4-C4
Beechwood Gardens	C2
Belgrave Road	D4
Benson Close	E4
Bourne Road	A2
Bradley Road	B4-C4
Broadmark Road	B4
Brunel Way	D3
Burlington Avenue	C2-C3
Chalvey Park	C2

Chalvey Road East	B2-C2-C1
Chalvey Road West	B2
Church Street	A2-B2
Church Street	D1-D2
Cippenham Lane	A2-A3
Clifton Road	F2
Clive Court	A2-B2-B1
College Avenue	C1
Conegar Court	C3
Diamond Road	E3-F3-F2
Dolphin Road	F2
Ellis Avenue	B3-C3
Everard Avenue	B3-B2-C2
Farnham Road	A3-A4
Fleetwood Road	D4
Gilliat Road	C4
Glentworth Place	A3
Greys Road	D4
Harewood Place	E1
Hatfield Road	E1-E2
Hazlemere Road	F4
Hencroft Street	D1-D2
Henry Road	B2-B3
Herschel Street	D2-E2
High Street	D2-E2
High Street Chalvey	A2-A1-B1-B2
Hillside	B2
King Edward Street	B2
Kings Road	C1
Ladbroke Road	A1
Landsdowne Avenue	C3
Lascelles Road	F1
Ledgers Road	B1-B2-B3
Little Down Road	D4
London Road	F1-F2
Martin Road	B1
Mere Road	D1
Merton Road	E1
Mill Street	D4
Montem Lane	A3-B3-B2
Osborne Street	D1-D2
Park Street	D1-D2
Petersfield Avenue	E4-E3-F3
Pitts Road	A4
Princes Street	F2
Queens Road	D4
Ragstone Road	B1-C1
Richmond Crescent	E3
St John's Road	E4-F4
St Lawrence Way	E1
St Paul's Avenue	D4-E4-F4
Salt Hill Avenue	A3-A4
Salt Hill Drive	A4
Salt Hill Way	A4-B4
Shackleton Road	C4

Seymour Road	A2
Spackmans Way	A1
Stoke Gardens	C4-D4
Stoke Road	D3-D4
Stoke Poges Lane	B3-C3-C4
Stratford Road	E2-E3
Sussex Place	E2-F2-F1
The Crescent	B2-C2
The Green	A2-A1-B1
The Grove	E1-E2
Tuns Lane	A1-A2-A3
Upton Park	C1-D1
Upton Road	E1
Uxbridge Road	E2-F2-F3
Vale Grove	C1-D1
Wellesley Road	E3
Wellington Street	D3-E3-E2-F2
Wexham Road	E2-E3-F3-F4
White Hart Road	A1-B1
Windmill Road	A3-A4
Windsor Road	C1-C2-D2-D3
Woodland Avenue	B4
Yew Tree Road	E1-E2-F2

Maidenhead

Australia Avenue	B4
Bad Godesberg Way	B3
Bell Street	B2
Belmont Road	A3-A4
Blackamoor Lane	C3-C4
Boyn Valley Road	A1-A2
Braywick Road	B1-B2
Bridge Avenue	C2-C3
Bridge Road	C3
Bridge Street	B3-C3
Broadway	B2
Castle Hill	A2
Cedars Road	C2-C3
Clare Road	A1-A2
Clivemont Road	A4-B4
College Avenue	A3
College Road	A2-A3
Cookham Road	B3-B4
Cordwallis Road	A3-A4-B4
Cordwallis Street	A4
Court Lands	B1
Crauford Rise	A3
Denmark Street	A4
Depot Road	B1-B2-C2
Forlease Road	C2-C3
Frascati Way	B2

Grassy Lane	A3
Grenfell Place	B2
Grenfell Road	A2-B2
Gringer Hill	A4
High Street	B2-B3
High Town	A2-B2
Holman Leaze	B3-C3
Keble Road	A3
Kennet Road	B3
King's Grove	A2
King Street	B2
Ludlow Road	A1
Marlow Road	A3-B3
Norfolk Road	A3-B3
North Dean	B4
North Road	A2
Park Street	B2
Queen Street	B2-B3
Ray Mill Road West	B4-C4
Rushington Avenue	B1
St Cloud Way	B3-C3
St Ives Road	B2-B3
St Luke's Road	A3-B3-B4
Shoppenhangers Road	A1-B1
South Road	A2-B2
Stafferton Way	B1-C1
The Crescent	A3
Vicarage Road	A3-A4-B3
West Street	B3
Windrush Way	B3-B4
York Road	B2-C2

Windsor

Adelaide Square	B2-C2
Albany Road	B2
Albert Road	C1
Albert Street	A3
Alexandra Road	B2-B3
Alma Road	B3-A3-A2-A1-B1
Arthur Road	A3-B3
Balmoral Gardens	B1
Barry Avenue	A4-B4
Beaumont Road	B2
Bexley Street	A3
Bolton Avenue	B1
Bolton Crescent	B1
Brocas Street	B4
Brook Street	C2
Bulkeley Avenue	A1
Castle Hill	C3
Clarence Crescent	B3

Clarence Road	A3-B3
College Crescent	A1-A2
Dagmar Road	B2
Datchet Road	B4-C4
Devereux Road	B2
Dorset Road	B2-B3
Duke Street	A3-A4
Elm Road	A1
Fountain Gardens	B1-C1
Florence Avenue	B4
Frances Road	B1-B2-C2
Frogmore Drive	C3
Goslar Way	A2
Goswell Road	B3-B4
Green Lane	A2
Grove Road	B2
High Street	B4
High Street	B3-C3
King's Road	C1-C2-C2
Osborne Road	A2-B2-B1-C1
Oxford Road	A3
Park Street	C3
Peascod Street	B3
Princess Avenue	A1
Queens Road	A2-B2
River Street	B4
Royal Mews	C3
Russell Street	B2
St Albans Street	C3
St Leonard's Road	A1-B1-B2
St Mark's Road	A2-B2
Sheet Street	C2-C3
Springfield Road	A1-A2
Stovell Road	A4
Temple Road	B2
Thames Street	B3-B4-C4
The Long Walk	C1-C2-C3
Trinity Place	B2-B3
Vansittart Road	A2-A3-A4
Victoria Street	B3-C3
Ward Royal	B3
York Avenue	A1-A2
York Road	A2

SLOUGH

Salt Hill Park in the centre of Slough features a bowling green, tennis courts and a children's play area, as well as pleasant walks through landscaped gardens. This is one of several recreational areas scattered throughout the town.

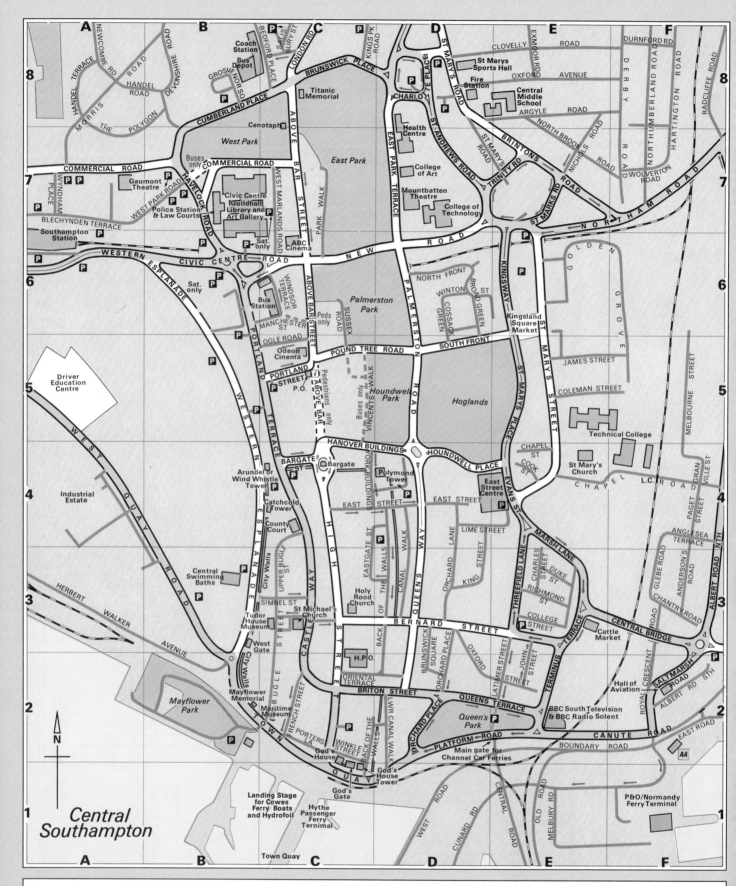

Southampton

In the days of the great ocean-going liners, Southampton was Britain's premier passenger port. Today container traffic is more important, but cruise liners still berth there. A unique double tide caused by the Solent waters, and protection from the open sea by the Isle of Wight, has meant that Southampton has always been a superb and important port. Like many great cities it was devastated by bombing raids during World War II. However, enough survives to make the city a fascinating place to explore. Outstanding are the town walls, which stand to their original height in some places, especially along Western Esplanade. The main landward entrance to the walled town was the Bargate – a superb medieval gateway with a Guildhall (now a museum) on its upper floor. The best place to appreciate old Southampton is in and around St Michael's Square. Here is St Michael's Church, oldest in the city and founded in 1070. Opposite is Tudor House Museum, a lovely gabled building housing much of interest. Down Bugle Street are old houses, with the town walls, pierced by the 13th-century West Gate, away to the right. At the corner of Bugle Street is the Wool House Maritime Museum, contained in a 14th-century warehouse. On the quayside is God's House Tower, part of the town's defences and now an archaeological museum.

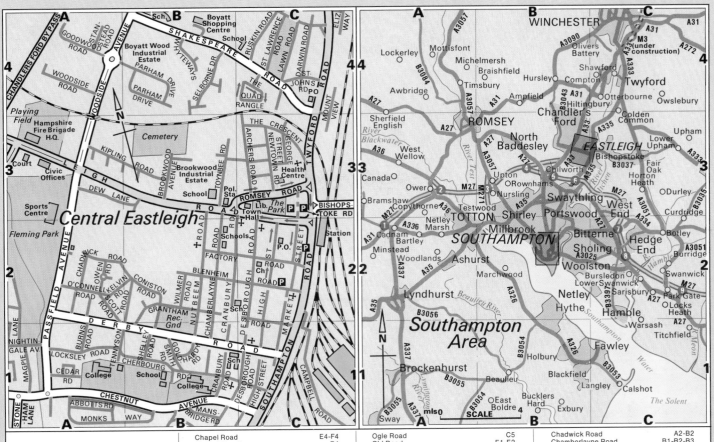

Key to Town Plan and Area Plan

Town Plan

A.A. Recommended roads	
Other roads	
Restricted roads	
Buildings of interest	Cinema
A A Service Centre	AA
Car Parks	P
Parks and open spaces	
One way streets	→

Area Plan

A roads	
B roads	
Locations	Ower ○
Urban Area	

SOUTHAMPTON

Above Bar	C5
Above Bar Street	C5-C6-C7-C8
Albert Road North	F3-F4
Albert Road South	F2
Anderson's Road	F3-F4
Anglesea Terrace	F4
Argyle Road	E8-F8
Back of the Walls	C1-C2-D2-D3-D4
Bargate Street	C4
Bedford Place	B8-C8
Bernard Street	C3-D3-E3
Blechynden Terrace	A7
Boundary Road	E2-F2
Briton Street	C2-D2
Britons Road	D8-E8-E7
Broad Green	D6
Brunswick Place	C8-D8
Brunswick Square	D2-D3
Bugle Street	C2-C3
Canal Walk	D3-D4
Canute Road	E2-F2
Castle Way	C2-C3-C4
Central Bridge	E3-F3
Central Road	E1-E2
Chantry Road	F3
Chapel Road	E4-F4
Chapel Street	E4
Charles Street	E3
Charlotte Place	D8
Civic Centre Road	B6-C6
Clovelly Road	D8-E8-F8
Coleman Street	E5-F5
College Street	E3
Commercial Road	A7-B7-C7
Cook Street	E4
Cossack Green	D5-D6
Cumberland Place	B7-B8-C8
Cunard Road	D1-E1
Derby Road	F7-F8
Devonshire Road	B8
Duke Street	E3
Durnford Road	F8
East Road	F2
East Street	E4
East Park Terrace	D6-D7-D8
Eastgate Street	D3-C3-C4-D4
Evans Street	E4
Exmoor Road	E8
French Street	C2
Glebe Road	F3-F4
Golden Grove	E6-F6-F5
Granville Street	F4
Grosvenor Square	B8
Handel Road	A8-B8
Handel Terrace	A8
Hanover Buildings	C5-C4-D4
Hartington Road	F7-F8
Havelock Road	B6-B7
Herbert Walker Avenue	A3-B3-B2
High Street	C1-C2-C3-C4
Houndwell Place	D4-E4
James Street	E5-F5
John Street	E2-E3
Kingsway	E6-E7
King Street	D3-D4
Kings Park Road	C8
Latimer Street	E2-E3
Lime Street	D4-E4
London Road	C8
Lower Canal Walk	D1-D2
Manchester Street	B6-C6
Marsh Lane	E3-E4
Melbourne Street	F4-F5-F6
Melbury Road	E1
Morris Road	A7-A8-B8
New Road	E6-D6-D7
Newcombe Road	A8
Nichols Road	E7-E8
North Brook Road	E8-E7-F7
North Front	D6
Northam Road	E6-E7-F7
Northumberland Road	F7-F8
Ogle Road	C5
Old Road	E1-E2
Orchard Lane	D3-D4
Orchard Place	D2-D3
Oriental Terrace	C2-D2
Oxford Avenue	D8-E8-F8
Oxford Street	D3-D2-E2
Paget Street	F4
Palmerston Road	D5-D6
Park Walk	C6-C7
Platform Road	D2-E2
Porters Lane	C2
Portland Street	C5
Portland Terrace	B6-B5-C5-C4
Pound Tree Road	C5-D5
Queens Terrace	D2-E2
Queen's Way	D2-D3-D4
Radcliffe Road	F7-F8
Richmond Street	E3
Royal Crescent Road	F2-F3
St Andrews Road	D7-D8
St Mary's Place	E4-E5
St Mary's Road	D8-D7-E7
St Mary's Street	E4-E5-E6
Salisbury Street	C8
Saltmarsh Road	F2-F3
Simnel Street	C3
South Front	D5-E5-E6-D6
Sussex Road	C5-C6
The Polygon	A8-A7-B7-B8
Terminus Terrace	E2-E3
Threefield Lane	E3-E4
Town Quay	B2-C2-C1-D1
Trinity Road	D7-E7
Upper Bugle Street	C3-C4
Vincents Walk	C5
West Marlands Road	C6-C7
West Road	D1-D2-E2
West Park Road	A7-B7
West Quay Road	A5-A4-B4-B3
Western Esplanade	B2-B3-B4-B5-B6-A6
Windsor Terrace	C6
Winkle Street	C1-C2
Winton Street	D6-E6
Wolverton Road	F7
Wyndham Place	A7
York Buildings	C4-D4

EASTLEIGH

Abbots Road	A1
Archers Road	C3
Blenheim Road	B2-C2
Brookwood Avenue	B3
Burns Road	A1
Campbell Road	C1
Cedar Road	A1
Chadwick Road	A2-B2
Chamberlayne Road	B1-B2-B3
Chandlers Ford By-pass	A4
Cherbourg Road	A1-B1-C1
Chestnut Avenue	A1-B1-C1
Coniston Road	B2
Cranbury Road	C1-C2-C3
Darwin Road	B2
Cranbury Road	C1-C2-C3
Darwin Road	B2
Derby Road	A2-A1-B1-C1
Desborough Road	B1-C1-C2
Dew Lane	A3-B3
Elizabeth Way	C4
Factory Road	B2-C2
George Street	C3
Goldsmith Road	B1
Goodwood Road	A4
Grantham Road	B1-B2-C2-C1
High Street	C1-C2
Kelvin Road	A2-B2
Kipling Road	A3-B3
Lawn Road	B2
Leigh Road	A3-B3-C3-C2
Locksley Road	A1
Magpie Lane	A1-A2
Mansbridge Road	B1
Market Street	C1-C2-C3
Monks Way	A1-B1
Mount View	C3-C4
Newtown Road	C3
Nightingale Avenue	B1-B2-B3
Nutbeem Road	B1-B2-B3
O'Connell Road	A2
Owen Road	A2
Parnham Drive	A4-B4
Passfield Avenue	A1-A2-A3
Romsey Road	B3-C3
Ruskin Road	A4
Stanstead Road	A4
Stoneham Lane	A1
St John's Road	C4
St Lawrence Road	C4
Scott Road	A2
Selborne Drive	B4
Shakespeare Road	B4-C4
Shelley Road	B1
Southampton Road	C1-C2
The Crescent	C3
The Quadrangle	C4
Tennyson Road	A1-A2-B2
Toynbee Road	B3
Twyford Road	C3-C4
Whyteways	B4
Wilmer Road	B2
Woodside Avenue	A3-A4
Woodside Road	A4

SOUTHAMPTON
Although liners still use Southampton's docks which handled all the great ocean-going passenger ships before the age of air travel replaced sea travel, the port is chiefly used by commercial traffic today.

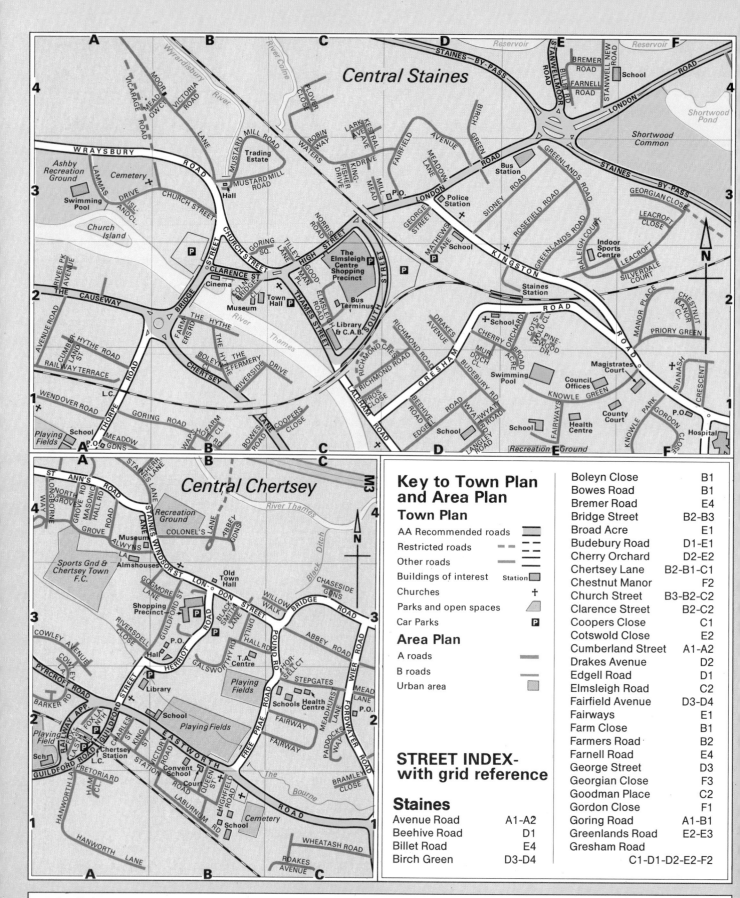

Key to Town Plan and Area Plan

Town Plan

AA Recommended roads	
Restricted roads	
Other roads	
Buildings of interest	Station
Churches	+
Parks and open spaces	
Car Parks	P

Area Plan

A roads	
B roads	
Urban area	

STREET INDEX- with grid reference

Staines

Avenue Road	A1-A2
Beehive Road	D1
Billet Road	E4
Birch Green	D3-D4
Boleyn Close	B1
Bowes Road	B1
Bremer Road	E4
Bridge Street	B2-B3
Broad Acre	E1
Budebury Road	D1-E1
Cherry Orchard	D2-E2
Chertsey Lane	B2-B1-C1
Chestnut Manor	F2
Church Street	B3-B2-C2
Clarence Street	B2-C2
Coopers Close	C1
Cotswold Close	E2
Cumberland Street	A1-A2
Drakes Avenue	D2
Edgell Road	D1
Elmsleigh Road	C2
Fairfield Avenue	D3-D4
Fairways	E1
Farm Close	B1
Farmers Road	B2
Farnell Road	E4
George Street	D3
Georgian Close	F3
Goodman Place	C2
Gordon Close	F1
Goring Road	A1-B1
Greenlands Road	E2-E3
Gresham Road	C1-D1-D2-E2-F2

Staines

The old and the new exist surprisingly happily together in Staines, a flourishing township which pre-dates the Domesday Survey of 1086.

Set in the Surrey countryside, Staines has attracted many new industries. But as well as signs of prosperity like the popular modern shopping centre, the town has a good number of churches and other features to mark its long history, including graceful Staines Bridge, opened in 1832. The London Stone nearby was put in place in 1285 and now marks the Surrey-Berkshire border.

Chertsey has been a boatbuilding centre for many years, and its attractive position on the River Thames appeals both to boating enthusiasts and to commuters working in London and nearby towns. Central to all river activity is handsome Chertsey Bridge. Alongside the water lies the 150-acre open space of Chertsey Meads and Orchard Gardens (site of the ancient Abbey fishponds), while just upstream, Salter river steamers ply their trade.

The local museum has good collections of costumes and porcelain, along with interesting examples of tiles uncovered during the excavation of the original Abbey site. Various sports and recreation facilities are to be found in the town, and visitors can survey a fine view of the surrounding countryside from the top of St Anne's Hill. Lying to the north, it rises to 240ft (73m).

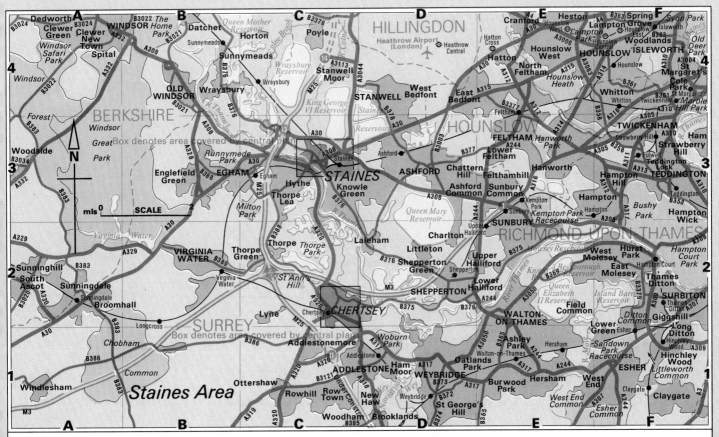

Staines Area

High Street	C2-C3	Priory Green	F2	Wraysbury Road	A3-B3	
Hythe Road	A1-A2	Prospect Close	C1-D1	Wyatt Road	D1-E1	
Island Close	A3	Railway Terrace	A1			

<table>
<tr><td>High Street</td><td>C2-C3</td></tr>
<tr><td>Hythe Road</td><td>A1-A2</td></tr>
<tr><td>Island Close</td><td>A3</td></tr>
<tr><td>Kestral Avenue</td><td>C3-C4</td></tr>
<tr><td>Kingfisher Drive</td><td>C3</td></tr>
<tr><td>Kingston Road</td><td>D3-D2-E2-F2-F1</td></tr>
<tr><td>Knowle Green</td><td>E1-F1</td></tr>
<tr><td>Knowle Park</td><td>F1</td></tr>
<tr><td>Laleham Road</td><td>C1-D1</td></tr>
<tr><td>Lammas Drive</td><td>A3-B3</td></tr>
<tr><td>Langley Road</td><td>D1</td></tr>
<tr><td>Lark Avenue</td><td>C4</td></tr>
<tr><td>Leacroft</td><td>E2-F2-F3</td></tr>
<tr><td>Leacroft Close</td><td>F3</td></tr>
<tr><td>London Road</td><td>C3-D3-E3-E4-F4</td></tr>
<tr><td>Manor Place</td><td>F2</td></tr>
<tr><td>Mathews Lane</td><td>D2-D3</td></tr>
<tr><td>Meadow Court</td><td>A4-B4</td></tr>
<tr><td>Meadow Gardens</td><td>A1</td></tr>
<tr><td>Meadow Lane</td><td>D3</td></tr>
<tr><td>Mill Mead</td><td>C3</td></tr>
<tr><td>Moor Lane</td><td>A4-B4-B3</td></tr>
<tr><td>Murdoch Close</td><td>D1</td></tr>
<tr><td>Mustard Mill Road</td><td>B4-B3-C3</td></tr>
<tr><td>Norris Road</td><td>C3</td></tr>
<tr><td>Pinewood Drive</td><td>E2</td></tr>
<tr><td>Plover Close</td><td>C4</td></tr>
</table>

<table>
<tr><td>Priory Green</td><td>F2</td></tr>
<tr><td>Prospect Close</td><td>C1-D1</td></tr>
<tr><td>Railway Terrace</td><td>A1</td></tr>
<tr><td>Raleigh Court</td><td>E2-E3</td></tr>
<tr><td>Richmond Crescent</td><td>C1-C2-D2-D1</td></tr>
<tr><td>Richmond Road</td><td>C1-D1-D2</td></tr>
<tr><td>River Park Avenue</td><td>A2</td></tr>
<tr><td>Riverside Drive</td><td>B1-C1</td></tr>
<tr><td>Robin Way</td><td>C3-C4</td></tr>
<tr><td>Rosefield Road</td><td>E2-E3</td></tr>
<tr><td>Sianash Crescent</td><td>F1</td></tr>
<tr><td>Sidney Road</td><td>D3-E3</td></tr>
<tr><td>Silverdale Court</td><td>F2</td></tr>
<tr><td>South Street</td><td>C1-C2-D2-C3</td></tr>
<tr><td>Staines By-Pass</td><td>C4-D4-E4-E3-F3</td></tr>
<tr><td>Stanwell Moor Road</td><td>E4</td></tr>
<tr><td>Stanwell New Road</td><td>E4</td></tr>
<tr><td>Thames Street</td><td>C1-C2</td></tr>
<tr><td>The Causeway</td><td>A2</td></tr>
<tr><td>The Fermery</td><td>B1</td></tr>
<tr><td>The Hythe</td><td>B1-B2</td></tr>
<tr><td>Thorpe Road</td><td>A1-A2</td></tr>
<tr><td>Tilley Lane</td><td>C2</td></tr>
<tr><td>Vicarage Road</td><td>A4-A3-B3</td></tr>
<tr><td>Victoria Road</td><td>B4</td></tr>
<tr><td>Wapshott Road</td><td>B1</td></tr>
<tr><td>Waters Drive</td><td>C4-C3-D3</td></tr>
<tr><td>Wendover Road</td><td>A1</td></tr>
</table>

<table>
<tr><td>Wraysbury Road</td><td>A3-B3</td></tr>
<tr><td>Wyatt Road</td><td>D1-E1</td></tr>
</table>

Chertsey

<table>
<tr><td>Abbey Gardens</td><td>B4</td></tr>
<tr><td>Abbey Road</td><td>C2-C3</td></tr>
<tr><td>Alwyns Lane</td><td>A4-B4</td></tr>
<tr><td>Barker Road</td><td>A2</td></tr>
<tr><td>Black Smith Lane</td><td>B3</td></tr>
<tr><td>Bramley Close</td><td>C1</td></tr>
<tr><td>Bridge Road</td><td>C3</td></tr>
<tr><td>Chaeside Gardens</td><td>C3</td></tr>
<tr><td>Charles Street</td><td>A2</td></tr>
<tr><td>Colonel's Lane</td><td>B4</td></tr>
<tr><td>Cowley Avenue</td><td>A2-A3</td></tr>
<tr><td>Cowley Lane</td><td>A2-A3</td></tr>
<tr><td>Drill Hall Road</td><td>B3-C3</td></tr>
<tr><td>Eastworth Road</td><td>A2-B2-B1-C1</td></tr>
<tr><td>Fairway</td><td>B2-C2</td></tr>
<tr><td>Fordwater Road</td><td>C1-C2</td></tr>
<tr><td>Fox Lane North</td><td>A2</td></tr>
<tr><td>Fox Lane South</td><td>A2</td></tr>
<tr><td>Free Prae Road</td><td>B2-C2</td></tr>
<tr><td>Galsworthy Road</td><td>B3</td></tr>
<tr><td>Gogmore Lane</td><td>A4-B4</td></tr>
<tr><td>Grove Road</td><td>A4</td></tr>
<tr><td>Guildford Road</td><td>A1-A3-B3</td></tr>
<tr><td>Guildford Street</td><td>A2-A3</td></tr>
<tr><td>Hamilton Close</td><td>A1</td></tr>
</table>

<table>
<tr><td>Hanworth Lane</td><td>A1-A2</td></tr>
<tr><td>Herrings Lane</td><td>A4-B4</td></tr>
<tr><td>Herriot Road</td><td>A3-A2-B2-B3</td></tr>
<tr><td>Highfield Road</td><td>B1</td></tr>
<tr><td>Horsell Court</td><td>C2-C3</td></tr>
<tr><td>King Street</td><td>A2-B2</td></tr>
<tr><td>Laburnum Road</td><td>B1</td></tr>
<tr><td>London Road</td><td>B3-C3</td></tr>
<tr><td>Longbourne Way</td><td>A4</td></tr>
<tr><td>Masonic Hall Road</td><td>A4</td></tr>
<tr><td>Meadhurst Lane</td><td>C2</td></tr>
<tr><td>Mead Lane</td><td>C2</td></tr>
<tr><td>North Grove</td><td>A4</td></tr>
<tr><td>Paddocks Way</td><td>C2</td></tr>
<tr><td>Pound Road</td><td>C2-C3</td></tr>
<tr><td>Pretoria Road</td><td>A1-A2</td></tr>
<tr><td>Pyrcroft Road</td><td>A2-A3</td></tr>
<tr><td>Queen Street</td><td>B1-B2</td></tr>
<tr><td>Railway Approach</td><td>A2</td></tr>
<tr><td>Riversdell Close</td><td>A3</td></tr>
<tr><td>Roakes Avenue</td><td>C1</td></tr>
<tr><td>St Ann's Road</td><td>A4</td></tr>
<tr><td>Staines Lane</td><td>A4-B4</td></tr>
<tr><td>Station Road</td><td>A2-B2-B1</td></tr>
<tr><td>Stepgates</td><td>C2</td></tr>
<tr><td>Victory Road</td><td>B2</td></tr>
<tr><td>Wheatash Road</td><td>C1</td></tr>
<tr><td>Wier Road</td><td>C2-C3</td></tr>
<tr><td>Willow Walk</td><td>B3-C3</td></tr>
<tr><td>Windsor Street</td><td>B3-B4</td></tr>
</table>

CHERTSEY
Designed by James Paine and completed in 1785, the graceful arches and ashlar stonework of the Bridge overlook the serenity of Chertsey meads and a bustle of activity from boatyards, riverside pubs and river traffic.

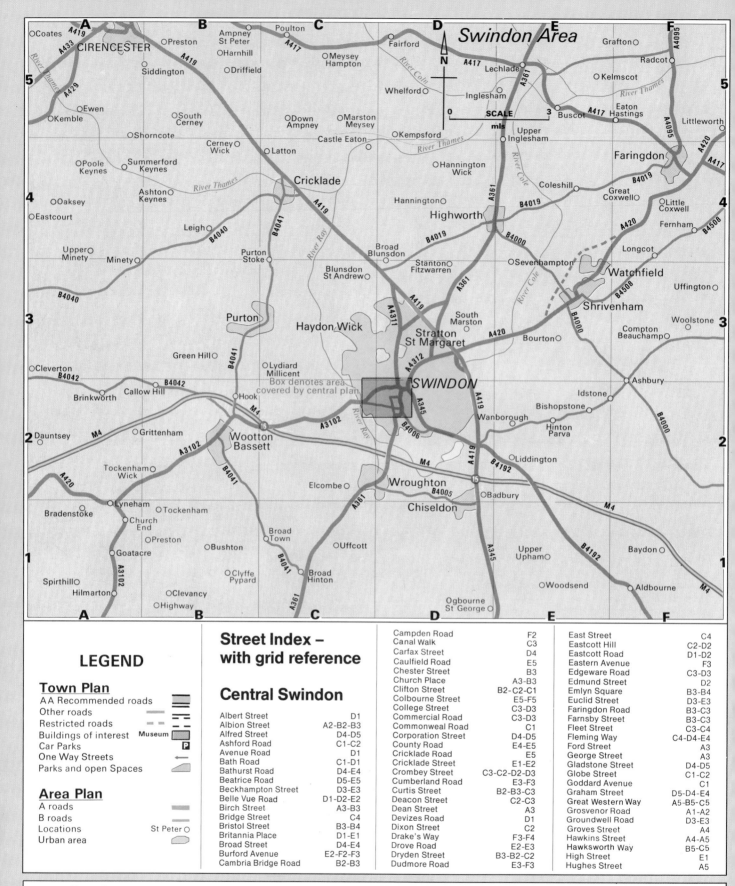

LEGEND

Town Plan

A A Recommended roads
Other roads
Restricted roads
Buildings of interest — Museum
Car Parks — P
One Way Streets
Parks and open Spaces

Area Plan

A roads
B roads
Locations — St Peter ○
Urban area

Swindon

Brunel's decision in 1841 to build the Great Western Railway's workshops here transformed Swindon from an agricultural village into a major industrial centre. The surviving buildings of the original railway village have been restored.

Regrettably the fortunes of the BR Engineering Ltd locomotive and other workshops (the heart of the Great Western system and renowned for locomotives such as the King George V) have declined considerably and even face complete closure — but modern Swindon has seen a remarkable revival. Plans were made in the 1950s to reduce the town's dependence on one industry, and with the combination of development aid and improved road access via the M4, Swindon has seen the arrival of a wide range of manufacturing industries and a near doubling of its population, to 150,000. Aptly chosen for the relocation of the British Rail's Western Region Headquarters from Paddington, the town now boasts a modern shopping complex, a regional theatre and the impressive Oasis Leisure Centre, while an illustrious past is recalled in the Great Western Railway Museum.

Outside Swindon are 19th-century Lydiard Mansion, standing in 150 acres of parkland, the leisure facilities of Coate Water, and a museum on naturalist and writer Richard Jeffries.

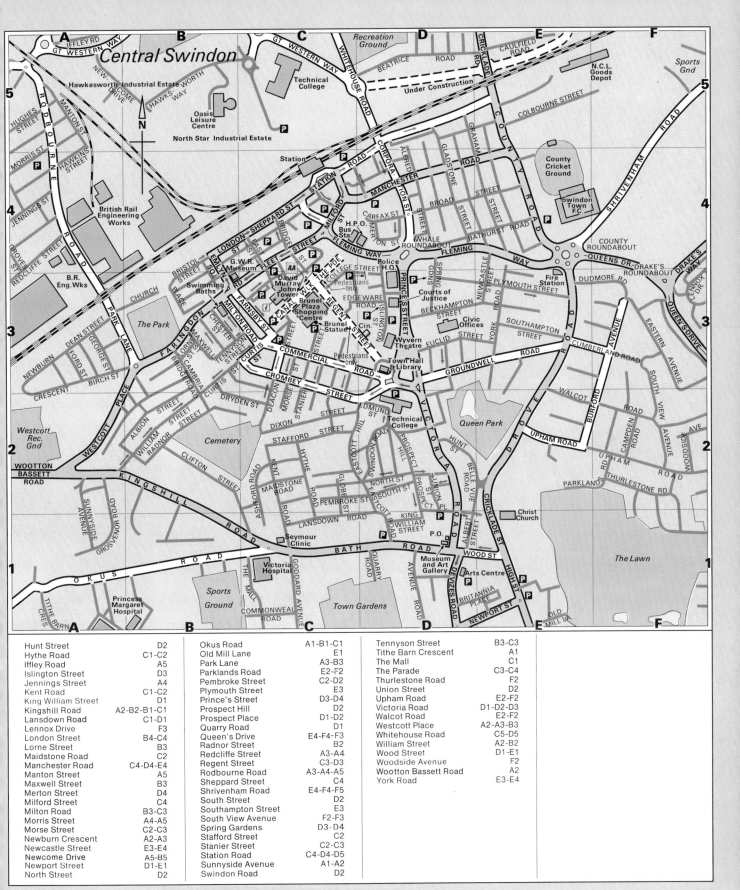

Central Swindon

SWINDON
Making waves at the Oasis Leisure Centre 'free-shaped' pool — under the biggest glazed dome in Britain, the water drops away gradually from inches-deep for paddling to a portholed diving area, and is fringed with tropical shrubs.

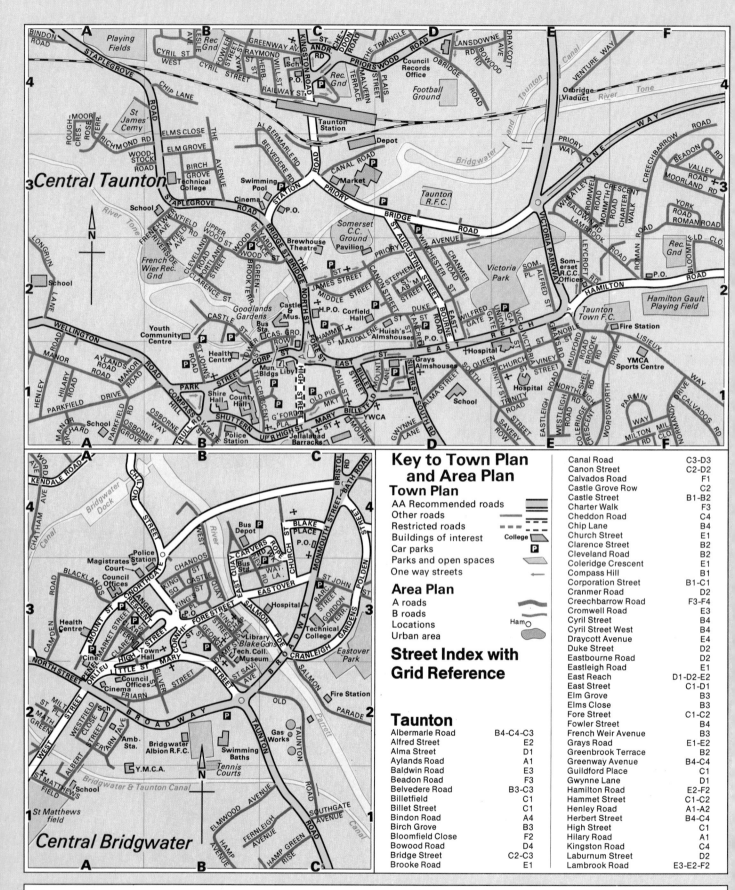

Key to Town Plan and Area Plan

Town Plan

AA Recommended roads	
Other roads	
Restricted roads	
Buildings of interest	College
Car parks	P
Parks and open spaces	
One way streets	←

Area Plan

A roads	
B roads	
Locations	Ham o
Urban area	

Street Index with Grid Reference

Taunton

Albermarle Road	B4-C4-C3
Alfred Street	E2
Alma Street	D1
Aylands Road	A1
Baldwin Road	E3
Beadon Road	F3
Belvedere Road	B3-C3
Billetfield	C1
Billet Street	C1
Bindon Road	A4
Birch Grove	B3
Bloomfield Close	F2
Bowood Road	D4
Bridge Street	C2-C3
Brooke Road	E1
Canal Road	C3-D3
Canon Street	C2-D2
Calvados Road	F1
Castle Grove Row	C2
Castle Street	B1-B2
Charter Walk	F3
Cheddon Road	C4
Chip Lane	B4
Church Street	E1
Clarence Street	B2
Cleveland Road	B2
Coleridge Crescent	E1
Compass Hill	B1
Corporation Street	B1-C1
Cranmer Road	D2
Creechbarrow Road	F3-F4
Cromwell Road	E3
Cyril Street	B4
Cyril Street West	B4
Draycott Avenue	E4
Duke Street	D2
Eastbourne Road	D2
Eastleigh Road	E1
East Reach	D1-D2-E2
East Street	C1-D1
Elm Grove	B3
Elms Close	B3
Fore Street	C1-C2
Fowler Street	B4
French Weir Avenue	B3
Grays Road	E1-E2
Greenbrook Terrace	B2
Greenway Avenue	B4-C4
Guildford Place	C1
Gwynne Lane	D1
Hamilton Road	E2-F2
Hammet Street	C1-C2
Henley Road	A1-A2
Herbert Street	B4-C4
High Street	C1
Hilary Road	A1
Kingston Road	C4
Laburnum Street	D2
Lambrook Road	E3-E2-F2

Taunton

The hub of Somerset, surrounded by the rolling, wooded Quantocks and the Blackdown Hills, Taunton lies on the River Tone in the fertile Vale of Taunton Dene. Famous for its thriving local cider industry, the town is also a lively commercial and agricultural centre whose livestock market rivals Exeter's as the most important in the West Country. In the past it was a major centre of the wool trade.

As befits a county town, Taunton is the headquarters of Somerset's entertaining and successful cricket team. It also offers National Hunt racing, has no fewer than three public schools and, somewhat improbably, the British Telecom Museum where antique telephone equipment is kept. There has been a castle in the town since Norman times: now it is home for the Somerset County and Military Museums.

Bridgwater, an industrial centre, was a busy port until Bristol overshadowed it. Twice a day a bore – a great tidal wave – surges up the River Parrett from Bridgwater Bay; the times are posted on the bridge in the town centre for those who want to see it.

In 1695 the rebel Duke of Monmouth is reputed to have surveyed the field before the Battle of Sedgemoor from the town's church tower. Dating from the 14th century, the Church of St Mary has some particularly fine Jacobean screenwork.

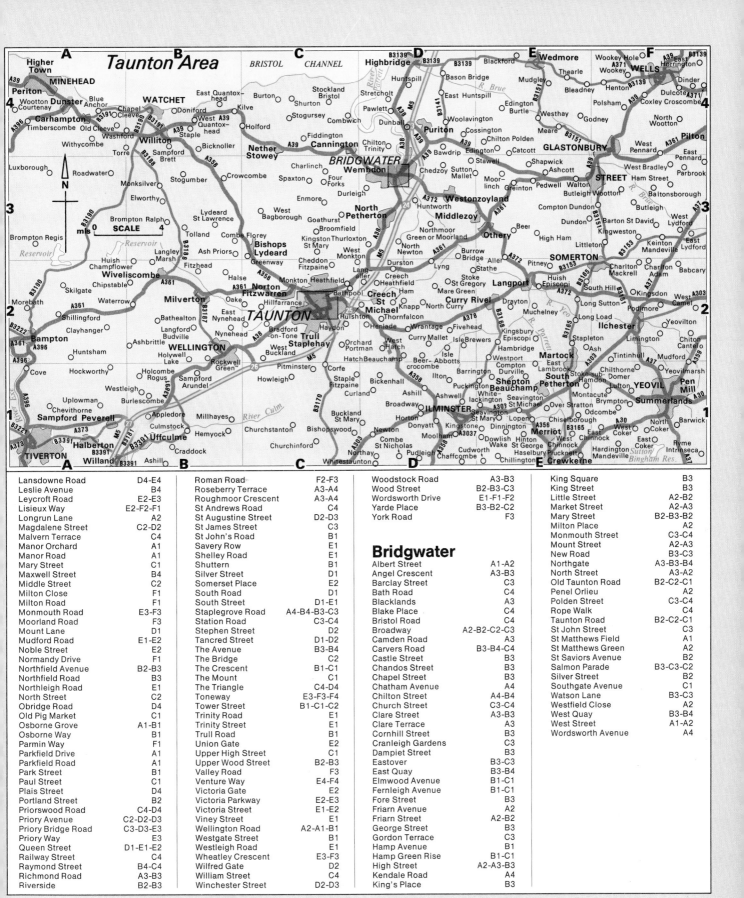

Lansdowne Road	D4-E4	Roman Road	F2-F3	Woodstock Road	A3-B3
Leslie Avenue	B4	Roseberry Terrace	A3-A4	Wood Street	B2-B3-C3
Leycroft Road	E2-E3	Roughmoor Crescent	A3-A4	Wordsworth Drive	E1-F1-F2
Lisieux Way	E2-F2-F1	St Andrews Road	C4	Yarde Place	B3-B2-C2
Longrun Lane	A2	St Augustine Street	D2-D3	York Road	F3
Magdalene Street	C2-D2	St James Street	C3		
Malvern Terrace	C4	St John's Road	B1		
Manor Orchard	A1	Savery Row	E1	**Bridgwater**	
Manor Road	A1	Shelley Road	E1	Albert Street	A1-A2
Mary Street	C1	Shuttern	B1	Angel Crescent	A3-B3
Maxwell Street	B4	Silver Street	D1	Barclay Street	C3
Middle Street	C2	Somerset Place	E2	Bath Road	C4
Milton Close	F1	South Road	D1	Blacklands	A3
Milton Road	F1	South Street	D1-E1	Blake Place	C4
Monmouth Road	E3-F3	Staplegrove Road	A4-B4-B3-C3	Bristol Road	C4
Moorland Road	F3	Station Road	C3-C4	Broadway	A2-B2-C2-C3
Mount Lane	D1	Stephen Street	D2	Camden Road	A3
Mudford Road	E1-E2	Tancred Street	D1-D2	Carvers Road	B3-B4-C4
Noble Street	E2	The Avenue	B3-B4	Castle Street	B3
Normandy Drive	F1	The Bridge	C2	Chandos Street	B3
Northfield Avenue	B2-B3	The Crescent	B1-C1	Chapel Street	B3
Northfield Road	B3	The Mount	C1	Chatham Avenue	A4
Northleigh Road	E1	The Triangle	C4-D4	Chilton Street	A4-B4
North Street	C2	Toneway	E3-F3-F4	Church Street	C3-C4
Obridge Road	D4	Tower Street	B1-C1-C2	Clare Street	A3-B3
Old Pig Market	C1	Trinity Road	E1	Clare Terrace	A3
Osborne Grove	A1-B1	Trinity Street	E1	Cornhill Street	B3
Osborne Way	B1	Trull Road	B1	Cranleigh Gardens	C3
Parmin Way	F1	Union Gate	E2	Dampiet Street	B3
Parkfield Drive	A1	Upper High Street	C1	Eastover	B3-C3
Parkfield Road	A1	Upper Wood Street	B2-B3	East Quay	B3-B4
Park Street	B1	Valley Road	F3	Elmwood Avenue	B1-C1
Paul Street	C1	Venture Way	E4-F4	Fernleigh Avenue	B1-C1
Plais Street	D4	Victoria Gate	E2	Fore Street	B3
Portland Street	B2	Victoria Parkway	E2-E3	Friarn Avenue	A2
Priorswood Road	C4-D4	Victoria Street	E1-E2	Friarn Street	A2-B2
Priory Avenue	C2-D2-D3	Viney Street	E1	George Street	B3
Priory Bridge Road	C3-D3-E3	Wellington Road	A2-A1-B1	Gordon Terrace	C3
Priory Way	E3	Westgate Street	B1	Hamp Avenue	B1
Queen Street	D1-E1-E2	Westleigh Road	E1	Hamp Green Rise	B1-C1
Railway Street	C4	Wheatley Crescent	E3-F3	High Street	A2-A3-B3
Raymond Street	B4-C4	Wilfred Gate	D2	Kendale Road	A4
Richmond Road	A3-B3	William Street	C4	King's Place	B3
Riverside	B2-B3	Winchester Street	D2-D3		

King Square	B3
King Street	B3
Little Street	A2-B2
Market Street	A2-A3
Mary Street	B2-B3-B2
Milton Place	A2
Monmouth Street	C3-C4
Mount Street	A2-A3
New Road	B3-C3
Northgate	A3-B3-B4
North Street	A3-A2
Old Taunton Road	B2-C2-C1
Penel Orlieu	A2
Polden Street	C3-C4
Rope Walk	C4
Taunton Road	B2-C2-C1
St John Street	C3
St Matthews Field	A1
St Matthews Green	A2
St Saviors Avenue	B2
Salmon Parade	B3-C3-C2
Silver Street	B2
Southgate Avenue	C1
Watson Lane	B3-C3
Westfield Close	A2
West Quay	B3-B4
West Street	A1-A2
Wordsworth Avenue	A4

TAUNTON
Taunton School, an attractive rambling building in Staplegrove Road, is one of the town's three public schools for boys. This is the largest of the three in terms of numbers of pupils and is inter-denominational.

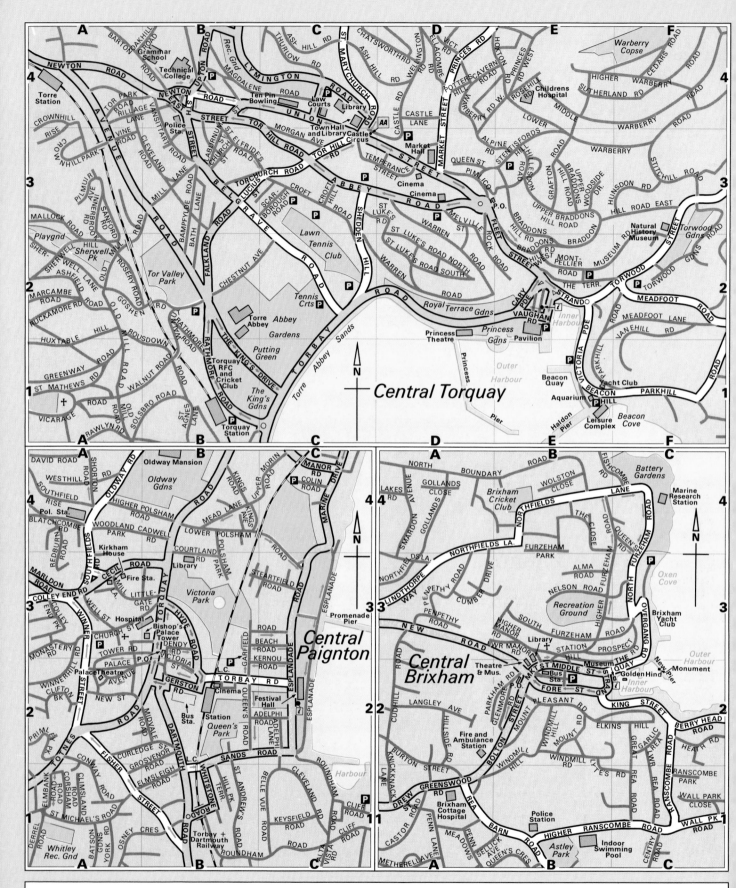

Torquay

With its sparkling houses, colourful gardens and sub-tropical plants set among the limestone crags of the steep hillside, Torquay has the air of a resort on the French Riviera – an impression strengthened by the superb views of sea and coast from Marine Drive, the 'corniche' road that sweeps around the rocky headland. Torquay is undoubtedly the Queen of the Devon coast, a resort carefully planned in

the early 19th century to cater for the wealthy and discriminating visitor. It had begun to be popular with naval officers' families during the Napoleonic wars when no one could travel to the continent, and this burgeoning popularity was exploited by the Palk family through two generations. Sir Robert Palk, who had made his fortune in India, inherited from a friend an estate which included Torquay, and he and his descendants set about transforming it into the spacious, well-planned

town we see today. Among the numerous amenities, Aqualand is particularly interesting.

Paignton, set on the huge sweep of Tor Bay south of Torquay, continues the range of holiday amenities and has good, sandy beaches.

Brixham, which lies a little further down the coast, falls into two parts – the old village on the hill slopes – and the fishing village half a mile below. Less commercialised than its neighbours, it is popular with holidaymakers.

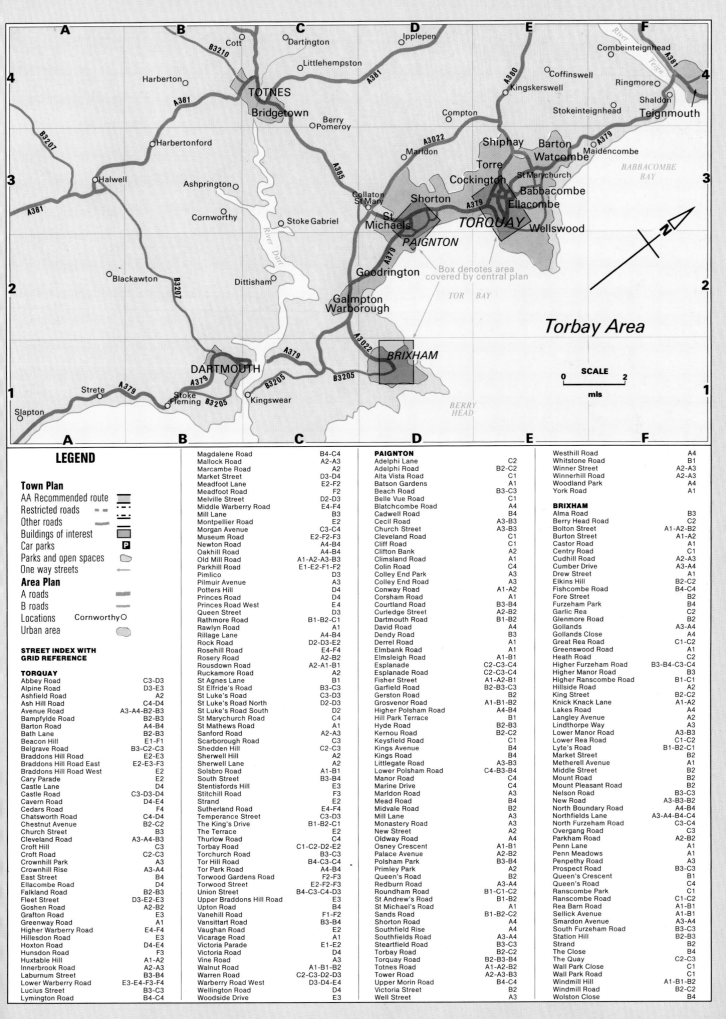

LEGEND

Town Plan

AA Recommended route	
Restricted roads	
Other roads	
Buildings of interest	
Car parks	P
Parks and open spaces	
One way streets	←

Area Plan

A roads	
B roads	
Locations	CornworthyO
Urban area	

STREET INDEX WITH GRID REFERENCE

TORQUAY

Abbey Road	C3-D3
Alpine Road	D3-E3
Ashfield Road	A2
Ash Hill Road	C4-D4
Avenue Road	A3-A4-B2-B3
Bampfylde Road	B2-B3
Barton Road	A4-B4
Bath Lane	B2-B3
Beacon Hill	E1-F1
Belgrave Road	B3-C2-C3
Braddons Hill Road	E2-E3
Braddons Hill Road East	E2-E3-F3
Braddons Hill Road West	E2
Cary Parade	E2
Castle Lane	D4
Castle Road	C3-D3-D4
Cavern Road	D4-E4
Cedars Road	F4
Chatsworth Road	C4-D4
Chestnut Avenue	B2-C2
Church Street	B3
Cleveland Road	A3-A4-B3
Croft Hill	C3
Croft Road	C2-C3
Crownhill Park	A3
Crownhill Rise	A3-A4
East Street	B4
Ellacombe Road	D4
Falkland Road	B2-B3
Fleet Street	D3-E2-E3
Goshen Road	A2-B2
Grafton Road	E3
Greenway Road	A1
Higher Warberry Road	E4-F4
Hillesdon Road	E3
Hoxton Road	D4-E4
Hunsdon Road	F3
Huxtable Hill	A1-A2
Innerbrook Road	A2-A3
Laburnum Street	B3-B4
Lower Warberry Road	E3-E4-F3-F4
Lucius Street	B3-C3
Lymington Road	B4-C4

Magdalene Road	B4-C4
Mallock Road	A2-A3
Marcambe Road	A2
Market Street	D3-D4
Meadfoot Lane	E2-F2
Meadfoot Road	F2
Melville Street	D2-D3
Middle Warberry Road	E4-F4
Mill Lane	B3
Montpellier Road	E2
Morgan Avenue	C3-C4
Museum Road	E2-F2-F3
Newton Road	A4-B4
Oakhill Road	A4-B4
Old Mill Road	A1-A2-A3-B3
Parkhill Road	E1-E2-F1-F2
Pimlico	D3
Pilmuir Avenue	A3
Potters Hill	D4
Princes Road	D4
Princes Road West	E4
Queen Street	D3
Rathmore Road	B1-B2-C1
Rawlyn Road	A1
Rillage Lane	A4-B4
Rock Road	D2-D3-E2
Rosehill Road	E4-F4
Rosery Road	A2-B2
Rousdown Road	A2-A1-B1
Ruckamore Road	A2
St Agnes Lane	B1
St Elfride's Road	B3-C3
St Luke's Road	C3-D3
St Luke's Road North	D2-D3
St Luke's Road South	D2
St Marychurch Road	C4
St Mathews Road	A1
Sanford Road	A2-A3
Scarborough Road	C3
Shedden Hill	C2-C3
Sherwell Hill	A2
Sherwell Lane	A2
Solsbro Road	A1-B1
South Street	B3-B4
Stentisfords Hill	E3
Stitchill Road	F3
Strand	E2
Sutherland Road	E4-F4
Temperance Street	C3-D3
The King's Drive	B1-B2-C1
The Terrace	E2
Thurlow Road	C4
Torbay Road	C1-C2-D2-E2
Torchurch Road	B3-C3
Tor Hill Road	B4-C3-C4
Tor Park Road	A4-B4
Torwood Gardens Road	F2-F3
Torwood Street	E2-F2-F3
Union Street	B4-C3-C4-D3
Upper Braddons Hill Road	D3
Upton Road	B4
Vanehill Road	F1-F2
Vansittart Road	B3-B4
Vaughan Road	E2
Vicarage Road	A1
Victoria Parade	E1-E2
Victoria Road	D4
Vine Road	A3
Walnut Road	A1-B1-B2
Warren Road	C2-C3-D2-D3
Warberry Road West	D3-D4-E4
Wellington Road	D4
Woodside Drive	E3

PAIGNTON

Adelphi Lane	C2
Adelphi Road	B2-C2
Alta Vista Road	C1
Batson Gardens	A1
Beach Road	B3-C3
Belle Vue Road	C1
Blatchcombe Road	A4
Cadwell Road	B4
Cecil Road	A3-B3
Church Street	A3-B3
Cleveland Road	C1
Cliff Road	C1
Clifton Bank	A2
Climsland Road	A1
Colin Road	C4
Colley End Park	A3
Colley End Road	A3
Conway Road	A1-A2
Corsham Road	A1
Courtland Road	B3-B4
Curledge Street	A2-B2
Dartmouth Road	B1-B2
David Road	A4
Dendy Road	B3
Derrel Road	A1
Elmbank Road	A1
Elmsleigh Road	A1-B1
Esplanade	C2-C3-C4
Esplanade Road	C2-C3-C4
Fisher Street	A1-A2-B1
Garfield Road	B2-B3-C3
Gerston Road	B2
Grosvenor Road	A1-B1-B2
Higher Polsham Road	A4-B4
Hill Park Terrace	B1
Hyde Road	B2-B3
Kernou Road	B2-C2
Keysfield Road	C1
Kings Avenue	B4
Kings Road	B4
Littlegate Road	A3-B3
Lower Polsham Road	C4-B3-B4
Manor Road	C4
Marine Drive	C4
Marldon Road	A3
Mead Road	B4
Midvale Road	B2
Mill Lane	A3
Monastery Road	A3
New Street	A2
Oldway Road	A4
Osney Crescent	A1-B1
Palace Avenue	A2-B2
Polsham Park	B3-B4
Primley Park	A2
Queen's Road	B2
Redburn Road	A3-A4
Roundham Road	B1-C1-C2
St Andrew's Road	B1-B2
St Michael's Road	A1
Sands Road	B1-B2-C2
Shorton Road	A4
Southfield Rise	A4
Southfields Road	A3-A4
Steartfield Road	B3-C3
Torbay Road	B2-C2
Totnes Road	A1-A2-B2
Tower Road	A2-A3-B3
Upper Morin Road	B4-C4
Victoria Street	B2
Well Street	A3

Westhill Road	A4
Whitstone Road	B1
Winner Street	A2-A3
Winnerhill Road	A2-A3
Woodland Park	A4
York Road	A1

BRIXHAM

Alma Road	B3
Berry Head Road	C2
Bolton Street	A1-A2-B2
Burton Street	A1-A2
Castor Road	A1
Centry Road	C1
Cudhill Road	A2-A3
Cumber Drive	A3-A4
Drew Street	A1
Elkins Hill	B2-C2
Fishcombe Road	B4-C4
Fore Street	B2
Furzeham Park	B4
Garlic Rea	C2
Glenmore Road	B2
Gollands	A3-A4
Gollands Close	A4
Great Rea Road	C1-C2
Greenswood Road	A1
Heath Road	C2
Higher Furzeham Road	B3-B4-C3-C4
Higher Manor Road	B3
Higher Ranscombe Road	B1-C1
Hillside Road	C1
King Street	B2-C2
Knick Knack Lane	A1-A2
Lakes Road	A4
Langley Avenue	A2
Lindthorpe Way	A3
Lower Manor Road	A3-B3
Lower Rea Road	C1-C2
Lyte's Road	B1-B2-C1
Market Street	B2
Metherell Avenue	A1
Middle Street	B2
Mount Road	B2
Mount Pleasant Road	B2
Nelson Road	B3-C3
New Road	A3-B3-B2
North Boundary Road	A4-B4
Northfields Lane	A3-A4-B4-C4
North Furzeham Road	C3-C4
Overgang Road	C3
Parkham Road	A2-B2
Penn Lane	A1
Penn Meadows	A1
Penpethy Road	A3
Prospect Road	B3-C3
Queen's Crescent	B1
Queen's Road	C4
Ranscombe Park	C1
Ranscombe Road	C1-C2
Rea Barn Road	A1-B1
Sellick Avenue	A1-B1
Smardon Avenue	A3-A4
South Furzeham Road	B3-C3
Station Hill	B2-B3
Strand	B2
The Close	B4
The Quay	C2-C3
Wall Park Close	C1
Wall Park Road	C1
Windmill Hill	A1-B1-B2
Windmill Road	B2-C2
Wolston Close	B4

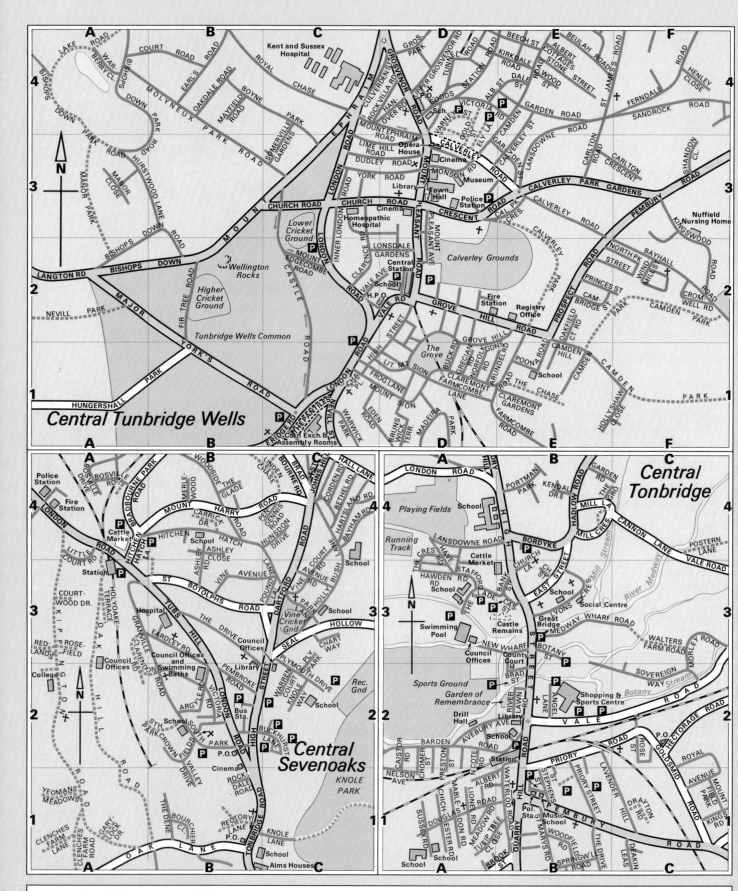

Tunbridge Wells

Dudley, Lord North, set this spa town on the road to fame in the 17th century, when he pronounced on the restorative properties of its Chalybeate Spring. Tunbridge Wells became a fashionable resort under the patronage of Queen Henrietta Maria, wife of Charles I, and later under that of Queen Victoria. It was awarded the title of 'Royal' Tunbridge Wells in 1909.

Today the Chalybeate Spring can still be sampled in the delightful setting of the Pantiles, an elegant precinct started in 1700 and lined with picturesque shops and inns. Fine examples of 19th-century architecture can also be seen in the Mount Pleasant and Mount Ephraim areas, where exclusive Victorian housing estates were built. The Museum and Art Gallery features examples of the wooden souvenir ware which has been produced by the town for over 200 years.

Sevenoaks is a residential town with an old-established Grammar School. Nearby Knole, a fine manor house set in an extensive deer park, was the birthplace of Vita Sackville-West.

Tonbridge has the remains of the Norman castle built here to guard the crossing of the River Medway. Part of the 11th-century wall and the gatehouse, added in the 13th century, are still intact, and stand in attractive gardens. The Angel Centre offers sports, music and drama.

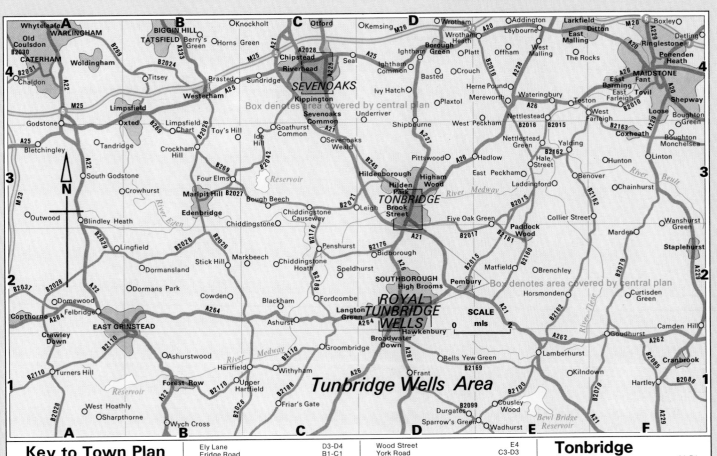

Key to Town Plan and Area Plan

Town Plan

AA Recommended roads	
Restricted roads	
Other roads	
Buildings of interest	Museum
Car Parks	P
Parks and open spaces	
One way streets	←

Area Plan

A roads	
B roads	
Locations	Godstone ○
Urban area	

Street Index with Grid Reference

Tunbridge Wells

Albert Cottages	E4
Albert Street	D4-E4
Arundel Road	D1-E1
Bayhall Road	F2
Beech Street	E4
Beulah Road	E4
Bishops Down	A2-B2
Bishops Down Park Road	A4-A3-B3-B4-A4
Bishops Down Road	A2-A3-B3-B2
Boyne Park	B4-C4-C3
Brunswick Terrace	D1
Buckingham Road	D1-D2
Calverley Park	D3-E3-E2
Calverley Park Crescent	D3-E3
Calverley Park Gardens	E3-F3
Calverley Road	D3-E3
Calverley Street	D3-E3-E4
Cambridge Street	E2
Camden Hill	E1-E2
Camden Park	F1-E1-E2-F2
Camden Road	D3-D4-E4
Carlton Crescent	E3-F3
Carlton Road	E3-E4
Castle Road	C1-C2-C3
Chapel Place	C1
Church Road	C3-D3
Claremont Gardens	E1
Claremont Road	D1-E1-E2
Clarence Road	C2-C3
Court Road	A4-B4
Crescent Road	D3-E3
Cromwell Road	F2
Culverden Street	C4-D4
Dale Street	E4
Dudley Road	C3-D3
Earl's Road	B4
Eden Road	C1-D1
Ely Lane	D3-D4
Eridge Road	B1-C1
Farmcombe Lane	D1
Farmcombe Road	D1-E1
Ferndale Road	E4-F4
Fir Tree Road	B2
Frog Lane	C1-D1
Garden Road	E4
Garden Street	D3-E3
Golding Street	D3-D4
Goods Station Road	D4-E4
Grecian Road	D1
Grosvenor Park	D4
Grosvenor Road	D3-D4
Grove Hill Gardens	D1-D2-E2
Grove Hill Road	D2-E2
Hanover Road	C4-D4
Henley Close	F4
High Street	C1-D1-D2
Hollyshaw Close	E1-F1
Hungershall Park	A1-B1
Hurstwood Lane	A3-B3
Inner London Road	C2-C3
Kingswood Road	F2-F3
Kirkdale Road	D4-E4
Lake Road	A4
Langton Road	A2
Lansdowne Road	E3-E4
Lime Hill Road	C3-D3
Little Mount Sion	C1-D1
London Road	C1-C2-C3-C4
Lonsdale Gardens	C2-D2
Madeira Park	D1
Major York's Road	A2-B2-B1-C1
Manor Close	A3
Manor Park	A2-A3
Mayfield Road	D1
Molyneux Park Road	A4-B4-B3-C3
Monson Road	D3
Mount Edgecombe Road	C2
Mount Ephraim	B2-B3-C3-C4
Mount Ephraim Road	C4-D4-D3
Mount Pleasant Avenue	D2-D3
Mount Pleasant Road	D2-D3
Mount Sion	C1-D1
Nevill Park	A2
Nevill Street	C1
Norfolk Road	D1
North Park Street	E2-F2
Oakdale Road	B4
Oakfield Court Road	E2
Pembury Road	E3-F3
Poona Road	E1-E2
Princes Street	E2-F2
Prospect Road	E2-E3
Rock Villa Road	C4-D4
Royal Chase	B4-C4
St James's Road	E4-F4
Sandrock Road	E4-F4
Shandon Close	F3
Somerville Gardens	C3-C4
Stone Street	E4
The Chase	E1
The Pantiles	C1
Tunnel Road	D4
Upper Grosvenor Road	D4
Vale Avenue	C2-D2
Vale Road	C2-D2
Varney Street	D3-D4
Victoria Road	D4-E4
Warberry Close	A4
Warwick Park	C1
Windmill Street	F2
Wood Street	E4
York Road	C3-D3

Sevenoaks

Argyle Road	B2
Ashley Close	B4
Ashley Road	B3-B4
Avenue Road	C3
Bayham Road	C4
Bethel Road	C4
Bosville Drive	A4
Bosville Road	A4
Bourchier Close	B1
Bradbourne Park Road	A4-B4
Bradbourne Road	C4
Buckhurst Lane	B2-C2
Carrick Drive	B4
Chart Way	C3
Clarendon Road	A3-A2-B2
Clenches Farm Lane	A1
Clenches Farm Road	A1
Corden Road	C4
Courtwood Drive	A3
Crownfields	B2
Dartford Road	C3-C4
Eardley Road	A3-B3-B2
Garylock Drive	A1
Granville Road	A3-B3-B2
Hartsland Road	C4
Hall Lane	C4
High Street	B2-C2-C3
Hitchen Hatch Lane	A3-A4-B4-C4-C3
Holly Bush Lane	C3-C4
Holyoake Terrace	A3
Hunsdon Drive	C4
Kippington Road	A1-A2-A3-A4
Knole Lane	B1-C1
Knole Way	C2
Linden Chase	B4-C4
Little Court Road	A3-A4
London Road	A3-A4, B1-B2
Merlewood	B4
Mount Harry Road	A4-B4
Oak Hill Road	A4-A3-A2-A1-B1
Oak Lane	A1-B1
Park Lane	C3
Pembroke Road	B2
Pendennis Road	C4
Plymouth Drive	C2-C3
Plymouth Park	C2-C3
Pound Lane	C3
Rectory Lane	B1
Redlands	A3
Rockdale Road	B1
Rosefields	A3
St Botolphs Road	A3-B3-C3
St Johns Hill	C4
Seal Hollow	C3
South Park	A2-B2
The Dene	B1
The Drive	B2-B3
The Glade	B4
Tonbridge Road	B1-C1-B2-B1
Tubs Hill	B2-B3
Valley Drive	B1-B2
Victoria Road	B2
Vine Avenue	C3-C4
Vine Court Road	C3-C4
Warren Court	C2
Woodside Road	B4
Yoemans Meadow	A1

Tonbridge

Albert Road	A1-B1
Angel Lane	B2
Avebury Avenue	A2-B2
Bank Street	B3
Barden Road	A2-B2
Bordyke	B4
Botany Street	B3
Bradford Street	B2
Brook Street	A1-B1
Caistor Road	A1-A2
Cannon Lane	C4
Castle Street	B3
Chichester Road	A1
Church Lane	B3
Church Street	B3
Cromer Street	A1-A2
Deakin Leas	C1
Douglas Road	A1-B1
Drayton Road	C1
Dry Hill	A4-B4
East Street	B3-B4
Garden Road	B4-C4
Goldsmid Road	C1-C2
Hadlow Road	B4
Havelock Road	A3-A4
Hawden Road	A3
Hectorage Road	C2
High Street	B2-B3-B4
Kendall Drive	B4
Kings Road	C1
Lansdowne Road	A4-B4
Lavender Hill	B2-B1-C1
Lionel Road	A1
London Road	A4-B4
Lyons Crescent	B3
Mabledon Road	A1
Meadow Road	A1
Medway Wharf Road	B3-C3
Mill Crescent	B4
Mill Lane	B4-C4
Morley Road	C2-C3
Mountfield Park	C1
Nelson Avenue	A1-A2
New Wharf	A3-B3
Northcote Road	A2
Pembury Road	B1-C1
Portman Park	B4
Postern Lane	C4
Preston Street	A1-A2
Priory Road	B1-B2-C2
Priory Street	B1-B2
Quarry Hill Road	B1-B2
River Lawn Road	B2
Rose Street	C2
Royal Avenue	C1-C2
St Marys Road	B1
St Stephens Street	B1
Sovereign Way	C2
Springwell Road	B1
Stafford Road	A3
Sussex Road	A1
The Crescent	A3-A4
The Drive	B1
The Grove	B4-C4
The Slade	A3-B3
Tulip Tree Close	A1-B1
Vale Road	B2-C2-C3, C3-C4
Walters Farm Road	C3
Waterloo Road	B1-B2
Woodfield Road	B1

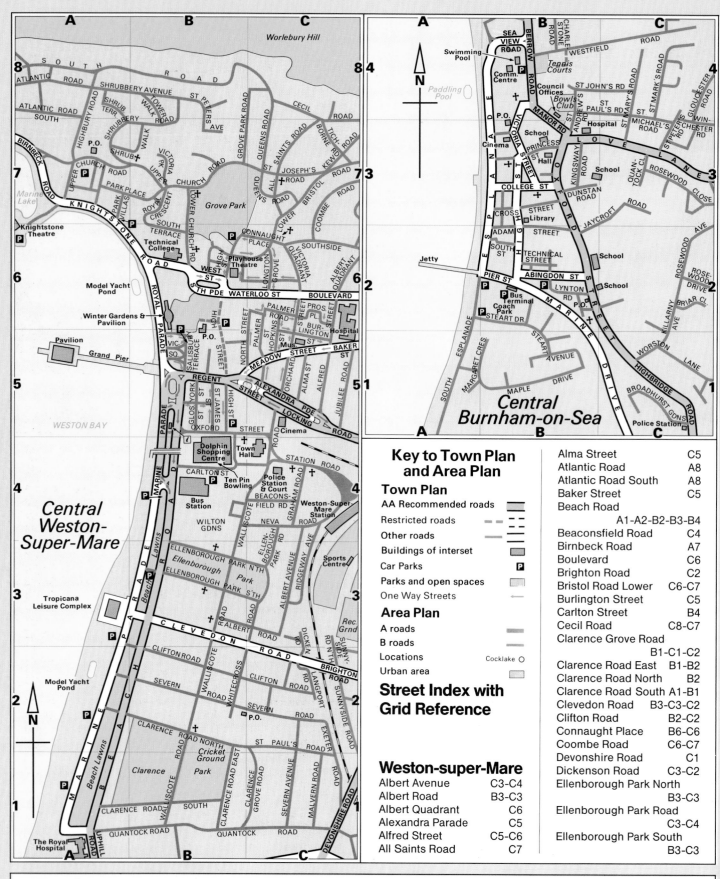

Worlebury Hill

Central Weston-Super-Mare

WESTON BAY

Central Burnham-on-Sea

Key to Town Plan and Area Plan

Town Plan

AA Recommended roads	
Restricted roads	
Other roads	
Buildings of interset	
Car Parks	P
Parks and open spaces	
One Way Streets	←

Area Plan

A roads	
B roads	
Locations	Cocklake O
Urban area	

Street Index with Grid Reference

Weston-super-Mare

Albert Avenue	C3-C4
Albert Road	B3-C3
Albert Quadrant	C6
Alexandra Parade	C5
Alfred Street	C5-C6
All Saints Road	C7
Alma Street	C5
Atlantic Road	A8
Atlantic Road South	A8
Baker Street	C5
Beach Road	A1-A2-B2-B3-B4
Beaconsfield Road	C4
Birnbeck Road	A7
Boulevard	C6
Brighton Road	C2
Bristol Road Lower	C6-C7
Burlington Street	C5
Carlton Street	B4
Cecil Road	C8-C7
Clarence Grove Road	B1-C1-C2
Clarence Road East	B1-B2
Clarence Road North	B2
Clarence Road South	A1-B1
Clevedon Road	B3-C3-C2
Clifton Road	B2-C2
Connaught Place	B6-C6
Coombe Road	C6-C7
Devonshire Road	C1
Dickenson Road	C3-C2
Ellenborough Park North	B3-C3
Ellenborough Park Road	C3-C4
Ellenborough Park South	B3-C3

Weston-Super-Mare

Elegant piers, promenades and hotels mark Weston-Super-Mare's 19th-century transformation into a flourishing seaside resort. At one time nothing more than a small fishing village, the town now boasts several attractive parks and gardens, and near the beach are numerous entertainment and leisure centres.

Havens for children are the Winter Garden Complex and Tropicana, both equipped with water slides, swimming pools and solaria. Madeira Cove attracts visitors to its Marine Lake, aquarium and model village, and Knightstone Island nearby provides further entertainments.

The High Street has been turned into a pedestrian area for easy shopping, and tucked away down a cobbled street is the Woodspring Museum — full of nostalgic memories of a town which still retains its character and charm.

Burnham-on-Sea enjoys two local breweries, responsible for supplying the real ales which are exclusive to the pubs in this area. Developed into a resort as early as the 18th century, Burnham-on-Sea also offers many other amenities, including a mild Somerset climate, acres of sandy beaches, a Leisure Park and a pier which was built in 1856 as a terminal for passing steamers and the railway. Live entertainment can be seen at Princess Hall.

Weston-Super-Mare Area

Exeter Road	C2-C1	Royal Crescent	B7
Gloucester Street	B5	Royal Parade	B6-B5
Graham Road	C4	St James Street	B5
Grove Park Road	B7-B8-C8	St Joseph's Road	C7
Highbury Road	A7-A8	St Paul's Road	C2-C1
High Street	B6-B5	St Peter's Avenue	B8-B7
Hopkin Street	C5-C6	Salisbury Terrace	B5
Jubilee Road	C5	Severn Avenue	C1-C2
Kew Road	C7	Severn Road	B2-C2
Knightstone Road	A7-A6-B6	Shrubbery Avenue	A8-B8
Langport Road	C2	Shrubbery Road	A7-B7-B8
Locking Road	C5-C4	Shrubbery Terrace	A8
Longton Grove	C6	Shrubbery Walk	A7-B7
Lower Church Road	B7-B6	South Parade	B6
Malvern Road	C1	South Road	A8-B8
Marine Parade	A1-A2-A3-B3-B4-B5	Southside	C6
		South Terrace	B7-B6
Meadow Street	B5-C5	Station Road	C4
Neva Road	B4-C4	Sunnyside Road	C2
North Street	B5-C5-C6	Sunnyside Road North	C3-C2
Orchard Street	C5-C6	Tichbourne Road	C7
Oxford Street	B5-C5	Tower Walk	B8
Palmer Road	C6	Upper Church Road	A7-B7
Palmer Street	C5-C6	Victoria Park	B7
Park Place	A7-B7	Victoria Square	B5
Park Villas	A7	Victoria Quadrant	C6
Prospect Place	C6	Walliscote Road	B1-B2-B3-B4-C4-C5
Quantock Road	A1-B1-C1	Waterloo Street	B6-C6
Queens Road	C7-C8	West Street	B6
Regent Street	B5-C5		
Ridgeway Avenue	C3-C4		

Whitecross Road	B2-C2-C3
Wilton Gardens	B4
York Street	B5

Burnham-on-Sea

Abingdon Street	B2
Adam Street	B2-B3
Berrow Road	B4
Briar Close	C2
Broadhurst Gardens	C1
Charlestone Road	B4
College Street	B3
Cross Street	B3
Dunstan Road	B3
Esplanade	A2-B2-B3-B4
Gloucester Road	C4
Highbridge Road	C1
High Street	B2-B3
Jaycroft Road	B2-B3-C3
Kilarny Avenue	C1-C2
Kingsway Road	B3
Love Lane	B3-C3
Lynton Road	B2
Manor Road	B4-B3
Maple Drive	B1
Margaret Crescent	A1-B1
Marine Drive	B2-B1-C1
Oxford Street	B3-B2-C2-C1

Pier Street	B2
Princess Street	B3
Quantock Close	C3
Rosewood Avenue	C2-C3
Rosewood Close	C3
Rosewood Drive	C2
St Andrew's Road	B3-B4
St John's Road	B4-C4
St Marks Road	C4
St Mary's Road	C3-C4
St Michael's Road	C4-C3
St Paul's Road	B4-C4
St Peter's Road	C3-C4
Sea View Road	B4
South Esplanade	A1-A2
South Street	B2
Steart Avenue	B2-B1
Steart Drive	A2-B2
Technical Street	B2
Victoria Street	B4-B3
Westfield Road	B4-C4
Winchester Road	C4-C3
Worston Lane	C1

WESTON-SUPER-MARE
The piers and good beaches of Weston-Super-Mare attract over three million visitors a year, and town spectaculars such as the aircraft displays of Great Weston Air Day and the summer carnival are another powerful draw.

Key to Town Plan and Area Plan

Town Plan

AA Recommended roads	
Restricted roads	
Other roads	
Buildings of interest	
Churches	+
Car Parks	P
Parks and open spaces	
One Way Streets	←

Area Plan

A roads	
B roads	
Locations	Piddletown ○
Urban area	

Street Index with Grid Reference

Weymouth

Weymouth

King George III favoured the ancient port of Weymouth and as a result the town aquired a certain fashionable status as a resort in the late 18th century. Still popular with holidaymakers, it offers good bathing, fishing and golf, and it is also a busy Channel Islands ferry port. Georgian houses – many of which have been turned into guest houses – overlook the broad esplanade, but near the harbour older buildings line narrow, picturesque streets and alleyways. One of the 17th-century houses in Trinity Street has been restored and refurnished in contemporary style, and another place of interest is the museum in Westham Road.

Dorchester is essentially still the busy market town Thomas Hardy featured in many of his novels. He was born at nearby Higher Bockhampton and several of his personal possessions are displayed in the Dorset County Museum in Dorchester. A series of fires in the 17th and 18th centuries left the town rather short of historic buildings, although St Peter's Church, which dates back to the 1400s, survived, as did the Old Shire Hall – scene of the trial of the Tolpuddle Martyrs in 1834.

Bridport's wide pavements used to be called 'ropewalks' because new ropes were laid out on them for twisting and drying. The 750-year-old industry continues to this day, and relics of the old trade are kept in the museum in South Street.

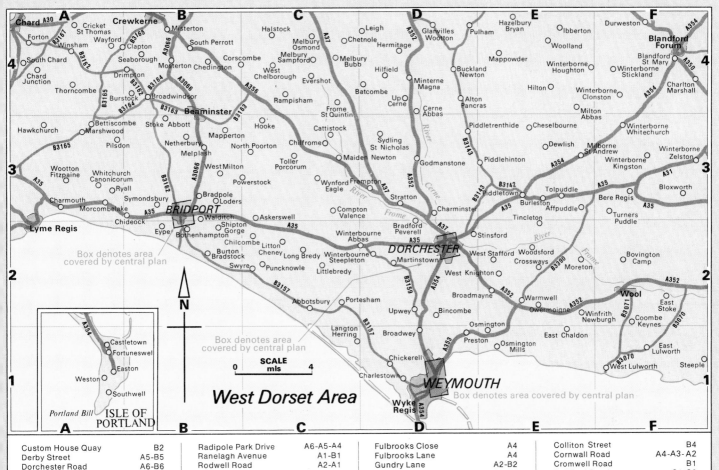

West Dorset Area

ISLE OF PORTLAND

Portland Bill

Box denotes area covered by central plan

SCALE mls 0 4

Custom House Quay	B2	Radipole Park Drive	A6-A5-A4
Derby Street	A5-B5	Ranelagh Avenue	A1-B1
Dorchester Road	A6-B6	Rodwell Road	A2-A1
East Street	B3-B2	Royal Terrace	B3-B4
Embankment Bridge	A3	St Alban Street	B2
Esplanade	B5-B4-B3-B2-C2-C3	St Leonard's Road	A1-B1
Esplanade	C6	St Mary Street	B2-B3
Franchise Street	A1-B1-B2	St Thomas Street	A2-B2-B3
Glendinning Road	A6	Spring Avenue	B1
Gloucester Mews	B4	Spring Gardens	A1
Grange Road	B6-B5	Spring Road	B1
Great George Street	A3-B3-B4	Stavordale Road	A3
Greenhill	B6-C6	Town Bridge	A2-B2
Hanover Road	A6	Trinity Road	B2
Hardwick Street	A5-B5	Trinity Terrace	A2-B2
High Street	A2	Victoria Street	B5
Hope Street	B1-B2	Walpole Street	A5-B5
Horsford Street	B1-B2	Waterloo Place	B5-B6
Kempston Road	A1-B1	Wesley Street	A4
King Street	A4-B4	Westerhall Road	B6
Kirkleton Avenue	A6-B6	Westham Road	A3-B3
Lennox Street	A5-B5	Westway Road	A2-A3
Love Lane	A1-A2	William Street	B5-B6
Lower Bond Street	A3-B3	Wyke Road	A1
Lower St Alban Street	A2-B2		
Maiden Street	B2-B3		
Market Street	B2	**Bridport**	
Marlow Road	B1	Alexandra Road	A2-A1
Maycroft	A1	Barrack Street	B2-B3-C3
Melcombe Road	B6	Beaumont Avenue	C4
Newberry Road	B1	Broadmead Avenue	A4
Newtons Road	B1	Chardsmead Road	B3
Nicholas Street	A2-A3-B3	Church Street	B2
North Parade	B2-C2	Claremont Road	C4
North Quay	A2	Coneygar Lane	C4
Nothe Walk	C2	Coneygar Road	B4-C4
Oakley Place	B1	Crock Lane	C1-C2
Orion Road	A1	Delapre Gardens	C3
Park Drive	A4-A3	Downes Street	B2-B3
Park Street	A3-A4-B4	East Road	C2
Penny Street	A5	East Street	B2-C2
Portway Close	B4-A5	Elizabeth Avenue	A1
Queen Street	B4-B5	Folly Mill Lane	B2

Fulbrooks Close	A4	Colliton Street	B4
Fulbrooks Lane	A4	Cornwall Road	A4-A3-A2
Gundry Lane	A2-B2	Cromwell Road	B1
Hardy Road	C3-C4	Culliford Road	C1-C2
Kenwyn Road	C3	Damers Road	A3-A2
King Street	B2	Durngate Street	B3-C3
Nordons	C1	Edward Road	A2-A1
North Allington	A4-A3	Fairfield Road	A2-B2
North Street	B3	Friary Hill	C4
North Mills Road	B4	Friary Lane	C4
Osborne Road	B4	Frome Terrace	C4
Parsonage Road	A4	Glyde Path Road	B4
Pasture Way	C1	Great Western Road	A2-B2
Princess Road	A1-A2	High Street	C4-C3
Priory Lane	A2	High East Street	B4-C4
Rax Lane	B3-B2	High West Street	A4-B4
Rope Walks	A2	Icen Way	C4-C3-C2
St Andrews Road	C3	Lancaster Road	C2
St Michael's Lane	A3-A2	Linden Avenue	C3
St Swithin's Avenue	A4	London Road	C4
St Swithin's Road	A3-A4-B4	Maumbury Road	A1-A2
Sea Road	B1-C1-C2	Monmouth Road	A1-B1-C1
Sea Road North	C2-C3	North Square	B4
Slades Grove	C1	Orchard Street	C4
South Street	B1-B2	Poundbury Road	A4
Sparacre Gardens	B3-C3	Princes Street	A3-B3-B4
Tannery Road	A3-A2	Prince of Wales Road	B2-C2-C1
Victoria Grove	A3-B3-B4	Queens Avenue	A1
West Allington	A3	Rothesay Road	B1
West Street	A3-A2-B3-B2	St Helens Road	A3
		South Street	B2-B3-B4
		South Court Avenue	B1-C1
Dorchester		South Walks Road	B2-C2-C3
Acland Road	C3-C4	The Grove	A4
Albert Road	A3-A4	Trinity Street	B2-B3-B4
Alexandra Road	A2	Victoria Road	A3-A2
Alfred Road	B1	West Walks	A3
All Saints Road	C3	West Mills Road	A4
Ashley Road	B1	Weymouth Avenue	A1-A2-B2
Bridport Road	A4	Weymouth Road	A1
Charles Street	B2-B3-C3	Wollaston Road	C3
Coburg Road	A1	York Road	C2

WEYMOUTH
Little has changed along the town's seafront since George III first came to the resort in the late 18th century to try out a new-fangled contraption called a bathing machine. A statue of the King stands on the esplanade.

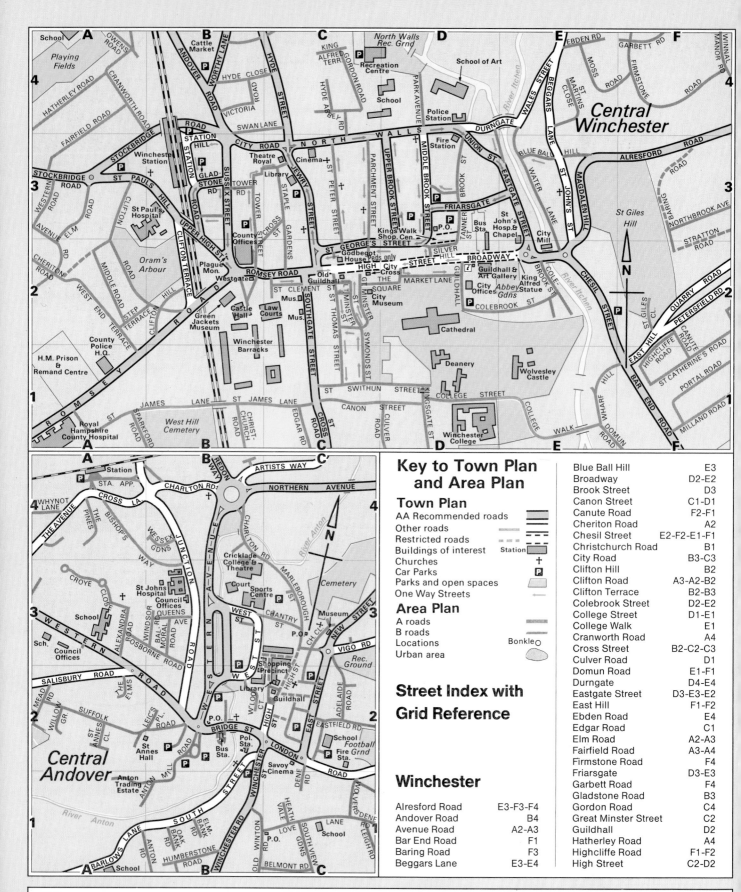

Key to Town Plan and Area Plan

Town Plan
AA Recommended roads
Other roads
Restricted roads
Buildings of interest — Station
Churches
Car Parks
Parks and open spaces
One Way Streets

Area Plan
A roads
B roads
Locations — Bonkle○
Urban area

Street Index with Grid Reference

Winchester

Alresford Road	E3-F3-F4
Andover Road	B4
Avenue Road	A2-A3
Bar End Road	F1
Baring Road	F3
Beggars Lane	E3-E4
Blue Ball Hill	E3
Broadway	D2-E2
Brook Street	D3
Canon Street	C1-D1
Canute Road	F2-F1
Cheriton Road	A2
Chesil Street	E2-F2-E1-F1
Christchurch Road	B1
City Road	B3-C3
Clifton Hill	B2
Clifton Road	A3-A2-B2
Clifton Terrace	B2-B3
Colebrook Street	D2-E2
College Street	D1-E1
College Walk	E1
Cranworth Road	A4
Cross Street	B2-C2-C3
Culver Road	D1
Domun Road	E1-F1
Durngate	D4-E4
Eastgate Street	D3-E3-E2
East Hill	F1-F2
Ebden Road	E4
Edgar Road	C1
Elm Road	A2-A3
Fairfield Road	A3-A4
Firmstone Road	F4
Friarsgate	D3-E3
Garbett Road	F4
Gladstone Road	B3
Gordon Road	C4
Great Minster Street	C2
Guildhall	D2
Hatherley Road	A4
Highcliffe Road	F1-F2
High Street	C2-D2

Winchester

King Alfred designated Winchester capital of England, a status it retained until after the Norman Conquest. Although gradually eclipsed by London, the city maintained close links with the Crown until the reign of Charles II.

Tucked away unobtrusively in the heart of Winchester is the impressive cathedral which encompasses Norman, and all the later Gothic styles of architecture. William of Wykeham was a bishop here in the 14th century and it was he who founded Winchester College, one of the oldest and most famous public schools in England. The buildings lie just outside the peaceful, shady Close where Pilgrims' Hall can be visited. Nearby are the Bishop's Palace and remains of Wolvesley Castle, one of Winchester's two Norman castles. Of the other, only the Great Hall, just outside the Westgate, survives. Here hangs the massive circle of oak claimed to be King Arthur's Round Table.

The streets of the city, which cover a remarkably small area, are lined with many charming old buildings of different periods. A walk along the pedestrianised High Street takes you past the former Guildhall – now a bank – and the old Butter Cross, into the Broadway where a statue of King Alfred stands near the River Itchen. A delightful path follows the river alongside the remnants of the old city walls.

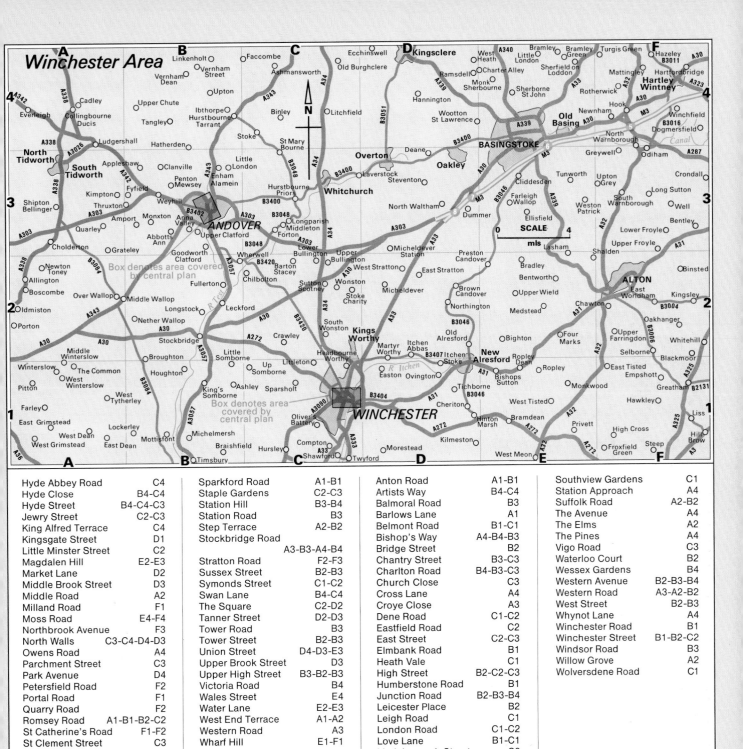

Winchester Area

Hyde Abbey Road	C4
Hyde Close	B4-C4
Hyde Street	B4-C4-C3
Jewry Street	C2-C3
King Alfred Terrace	C4
Kingsgate Street	D1
Little Minster Street	C2
Magdalen Hill	E2-E3
Market Lane	D2
Middle Brook Street	D3
Middle Road	A2
Milland Road	F1
Moss Road	E4-F4
Northbrook Avenue	F3
North Walls	C3-C4-D4-D3
Owens Road	A4
Parchment Street	C3
Park Avenue	D4
Petersfield Road	F2
Portal Road	F1
Quarry Road	F2
Romsey Road	A1-B1-B2-C2
St Catherine's Road	F1-F2
St Clement Street	C3
St Cross Road	C1
St George's Street	C2-D2-D3
St Giles Close	F2
St James Lane	A1-B1-C1
St John's Street	E3
St Martins Close	E4
St Pauls Hill	A3-B3
St Peter Street	C2-C3
St Thomas Street	C1-C2
St Swithun Street	C1-D1
Silver Hill	D2
Southgate Street	C1-C2

Sparkford Road	A1-B1
Staple Gardens	C2-C3
Station Hill	B3-B4
Station Road	B3
Step Terrace	A2-B2
Stockbridge Road	A3-B3-A4-B4
Stratton Road	F2-F3
Sussex Street	B2-B3
Symonds Street	C1-C2
Swan Lane	B4-C4
The Square	C2-D2
Tanner Street	D2-D3
Tower Road	B3
Tower Street	B2-B3
Union Street	D4-D3-E3
Upper Brook Street	D3
Upper High Street	B3-B2-B3
Victoria Road	B4
Wales Street	E4
Water Lane	E2-E3
West End Terrace	A1-A2
Western Road	A3
Wharf Hill	E1-F1
Winnal Manor Road	F4
Worthy Lane	B4

Andover

Adelaide Road	C2
Alexandra Road	A3
Anton Mill Road	A1-B1-B2

Anton Road	A1-B1
Artists Way	B4-C4
Balmoral Road	B3
Barlows Lane	A1
Belmont Road	B1-C1
Bishop's Way	A4-B4-B3
Bridge Street	B2
Chantry Street	B3-C3
Charlton Road	B4-B3-C3
Church Close	C3
Cross Lane	A4
Croye Close	A3
Dene Road	C1-C2
Eastfield Road	C2
East Street	C2-C3
Elmbank Road	B1
Heath Vale	C1
High Street	B2-C2-C3
Humberstone Road	B1
Junction Road	B2-B3-B4
Leicester Place	B2
Leigh Road	C1
London Road	C1-C2
Love Lane	B1-C1
Marleborough Street	C3
Mead Road	A2
New Street	C3
Northern Avenue	B4-C4
Oak Bank Road	B1
Old Winton Road	B1-C1
Osborne Road	A3-B3
Queens Avenue	B3
Redon Way	B4
St Annes Close	A2
Salisbury Road	A2
South Street	B1-B2

Southview Gardens	C1
Station Approach	A4
Suffolk Road	A2-B2
The Avenue	A4
The Elms	A2
The Pines	A4
Vigo Road	C3
Waterloo Court	B2
Wessex Gardens	B4
Western Avenue	B2-B3-B4
Western Road	A3-A2-B2
West Street	B2-B3
Whynot Lane	A4
Winchester Road	B1
Winchester Street	B1-B2-C2
Windsor Road	B3
Willow Grove	A2
Wolversdene Road	C1

WINCHESTER
Standing on the site of the old Hall of Court in the Broadway is the city's Guildhall. Built in 1873, its style was influenced by Northampton Town Hall. It is now a centre for culture and the arts.

75

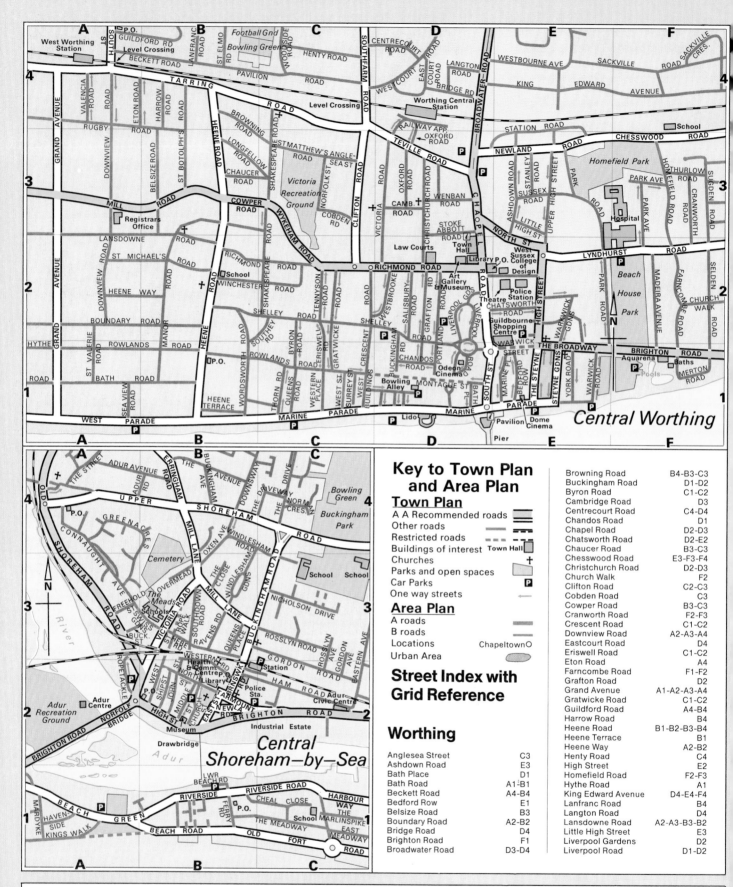

Key to Town Plan and Area Plan

Town Plan

A A Recommended roads	
Other roads	
Restricted roads	
Buildings of interest	Town Hall
Churches	+
Parks and open spaces	
Car Parks	P
One way streets	←

Area Plan

A roads	
B roads	
Locations	Chapeltown O
Urban Area	

Street Index with Grid Reference

Worthing

Anglesea Street	C3
Ashdown Road	E3
Bath Place	D1
Bath Road	A1-B1
Beckett Road	A4-B4
Bedford Row	E1
Belsize Road	B3
Boundary Road	A2-B2
Bridge Road	D4
Brighton Road	F1
Broadwater Road	D3-D4

Browning Road	B4-B3-C3
Buckingham Road	D1-D2
Byron Road	C1-C2
Cambridge Road	D3
Centrecourt Road	C4-D4
Chandos Road	D1
Chapel Road	D2-D3
Chatsworth Road	D2-E2
Chaucer Road	B3-C3
Chesswood Road	E3-F3-F4
Christchurch Road	D2-D3
Church Walk	F2
Clifton Road	C2-C3
Cobden Road	C3
Cowper Road	B3-C3
Cranworth Road	F2-F3
Crescent Road	C1-C2
Downview Road	A2-A3-A4
Eastcourt Road	D4
Eriswell Road	C1-C2
Eton Road	A4
Farncombe Road	F1-F2
Grafton Road	D2
Grand Avenue	A1-A2-A3-A4
Gratwicke Road	C1-C2
Guildford Road	A4-B4
Harrow Road	B4
Heene Road	B1-B2-B3-B4
Heene Terrace	B1
Heene Way	A2-B2
Henty Road	C4
High Street	E2
Homefield Road	F2-F3
Hythe Road	A1
King Edward Avenue	D4-E4-F4
Lanfranc Road	B4
Langton Road	D4
Lansdowne Road	A2-A3-B3-B2
Little High Street	E3
Liverpool Gardens	D2
Liverpool Road	D1-D2

Worthing

A mecca for bowls devotees, Worthing hosts both national and international competitions on the excellent greens at Beach House Park. Golf and sailing are popular pastimes, and more than adequate facilities exist for other sports.

Worthing became a fashionable resort in the 18th century and today it offers the visitor a pleasant mixture of Victorian buildings and areas

of modern development: this is one of the major shopping centres of West Sussex, and several pleasant precincts and covered centres have been built. Brooklands Pleasure Park and a good range of shows in the summer season are another draw for visitors. Worthing Museum and Art Gallery has collections of costumes and toys as well as items of local interest, and exhibitions of arts and crafts are held here regularly. At Tarring, one mile from the town centre, a group of 15th-century

cottages has been restored and now houses the Sussex Folklore Museum.

Shoreham has been the site of a port since Roman times, and by the early 14th century it had become a major shipbuilding town. Lying at the mouth of the River Adur, it still keeps up a thriving maritime life in the shape of a busy harbour and several yachting and sailing clubs. The Marlipins Museum, which explores the history of the area, concentrates on Shoreham's nautical connections.

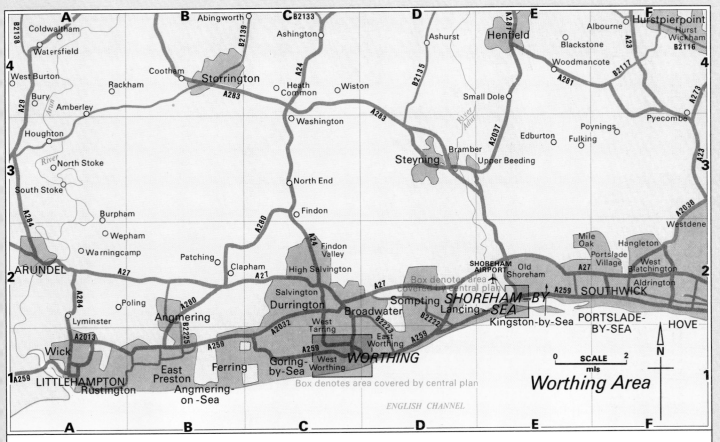

Worthing Area

Scale: 0 — 2 mls

Box denotes area covered by central plan

Longfellow Road	B3-C3		
Lyndhurst Road	E2-F2		
Madeira Avenue	F1-F2		
Manor Road	B1-B2		
Marine Parade	B1-C1-D1-E1		
Marine Place	E1		
Merton Road	F1		
Mill Road	A3-B3		
Montague Street	C1-D1		
Newland Road	D3-E3		
Norfolk Street	C3		
North Street	D3-E3-E2		
Oxford Road	D3-D4		
Park Avenue	F2-F3		
Park Road	E1-E2-E3		
Pavilion Road	B4-C4		
Portland Road	D1-D2		
Queens Road	C1		
Railway Approach	D3-D4		
Richmond Road	B2-C2-D2		
Rowlands Road	A1-B1-C1		
Rugby Road	A4-B4-B3		
St Boltolph's Road	B3-B4		
St Elmo Road	B4		
St Mathew's Road	C3		
St Michael's Road	A2-B2		
St Valerie Road	A1-A2		
Sackville Crescent	F4		
Sackville Road	E4-F4		
Salisbury Road	D2		
Sea View Road	A1		
Seldon Road	F1-F2		
Shakespeare Road	C2-C3-C4		
Shelley Road	B2-C2-D2-D1		
South Street	A4		
South Street	D1-E1		
Southey Road	B2-C2		
Southfarm Road	C4		
Stanley Road	E3		
Station Road	D3-E3-E4-E3		
Steyne Gardens	E1		

Stoke Abbott Road	D3		
Sugden Road	F2-F3		
Surrey Street	C1		
Sussex Road	E3		
Tarring Road	A4-B4-C4-C3		
Tennyson Road	C2		
Teville Road	C4-D4-D3		
The Broadway	E1		
The Steyne	E1		
Thorn Road	C1		
Thurlow Road	F3		
Upper High Street	E2-E3		
Valencia Road	A4		
Victoria Road	D2-D3		
Warwick Gardens	E2		
Warwick Road	E1		
Warwick Street	E1		
Wenban Road	D3		
West Buildings	C1		
West Parade	A1-B1		
West Street	C1		
Westbourne Avenue	D4-E4		
Westbrooke	C2-D2		
Westcourt Road	C4-D4		
Western Place	C1		
Winchester Road	B2-C2		
Woodside Road	C4		
Wordsworth Road	B1-B2		
Wykeham Road	C2-C3		
York Road	E1		

Shoreham

Adur Avenue	A4-B4
Adur Road	A4-B4
Beach Green	A1-B1

Beach Road	A1-B1
Brighton Road	A1-A2, B2-C2
Brunswick Road	B2
Buckingham Avenue	B4
Buckingham Road	B3-C3-C4
Buckingham Street	A3-B3
Cheal Close	B1-C1
Church Street	B2
Connaught Avenue	A3-A4
Downsway	B4-C4
East Meadway	C1
East Street	B2
Eastern Avenue	C2-C3
Erringham Road	B4
Ferry Road	B1
Freehold Street	A3
Gordon Avenue	B3-C3-C2
Gordon Road	B3-C3-C2
Greenacres	A4-B4-A4-A3
Ham Road	B2-C2
Harbour Way	C1
Havenside	A1
Hebe Road	B3
High Street	B2
John Street	B2
Kings Walk	A1
Lower Beach Road	B1
Mardyke	A1
Middle Street	B2
Mill Lane	B3-B4
New Road	B2
Nicholas Drive	C3
Norfolk Bridge	A2
Norman Crescent	C4
North Street	B2
Old Fort Road	B1-C1
Old Shoreham Road	A4-A3-A2-B2
Overmead	B3
Oxen Avenue	B3-B4
Queens Place	B3
Ravens Road	B3

Riverside	B1
Riverside Road	B1-C1
Ropetackle	A2-A3
Rope Walk	B3
Rosslyn Avenue	C2-C3
Rosslyn Road	C3
Ship Street	B2
Southdown Road	B3
Swiss Gardens	A3-B3
Tarmount Lane	B2
The Avenue	B4
The Close	B3
The Drive	C4
The Driveway	C4
The Marlinspike	C1
The Meadway	B1-C1
The Street	A4
Upper Shoreham Road	A4-B4-C4
Victoria Road	A2-B2-B3
West Street	B2-B3
Western Road	B2-B3
Windlesham Gardens	B3-B4
Windlesham Road	B4-C4-C3

WORTHING
The Marine Parade and West Pier — now the largest town in West Sussex, Worthing was a small fishing village until Princess Amelia, youngest daughter of George III, set a new trend by holidaying here in 1798.

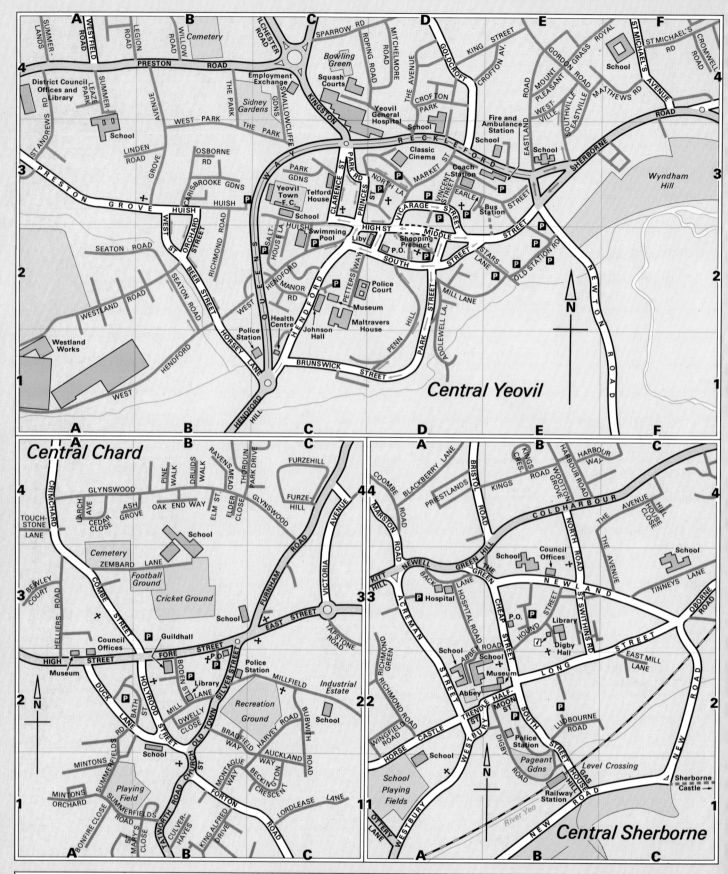

Yeovil

Home of the Westland helicopter and aircraft factory — as a result of which it suffered bomb damage in the Second World War — and six miles south of the Fleet Air Museum at Yeovilton, the market town of Yeovil is also known for its more homely glovemaking. There is a fine 14th-century church, and a collection of firearms and local interest items at Hendford Manor.

Sherborne Full of medieval buildings built in the golden Ham Hill stone, Sherborne has a magnificent, mainly 15th-century, abbey church. Of the town's two public schools, the 1550 boys' school occupies some of the abbey buildings, and the abbey gatehouse has a museum.

East of the town are two castles: a Norman structure which was partly destroyed after the Civil War, and the 'new' castle, a fine Elizabethan house built and occupied by Sir Walter Raleigh, and full of treasures.

Chard was the scene of one of Judge Jeffreys' Bloody Assizes, held in the courthouse (built 1590) here after the Monmouth Rebellion of 1685. The town's grammar school was founded in 1671, the Choughs Hotel is Elizabethan and the porticoed Town Hall dates back to 1834. All stand in the main street, from which streams flow north to the Bristol Channel and south to the English Channel — at 400ft (122m), this is the county's highest town.

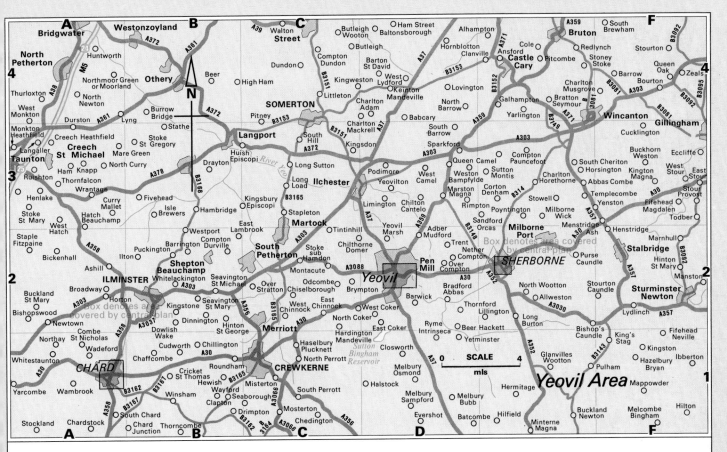

Yeovil Area

Map showing towns including Bridgwater, Taunton, Somerton, Langport, Ilchester, Yeovil, Sherborne, Wincanton, Gillingham, Ilminster, Chard, Crewkerne, Castle Cary, Bruton

SCALE
0 4
mls

Key to Town Plan and Area Plan

Town Plan
AA Recommended roads
Restricted roads
Other roads
Buildings of interest — Library
Car Parks — P
Parks and open spaces
One Way Streets

Area Plan
A roads
B roads
Locations — Terry's Green ○
Urban area

Street Index with Grid Reference

Yeovil

Addlewell Lane	D1-D2
Beer Street	B2
Brunswick Street	C1-D1
Carisbrooke Gardens	B3
Clarence Street	C3
Crofton Avenue	D4-E4
Crofton Park	D4
Cromwell Road	F4
Earle Street	D3-E3
Eastland Road	E3-E4
Eastville	E3-E4
Goldcroft	D3-D4
Gordon Road	E4
Grass Royal	E4-F4
Grove Avenue	B3-B4
Hendford	C1-C2
Hendford Hill	B1-C1
High Street	C2-D2
Horsey Lane	B2-B1-C1
Huish	B3-C3
Ilchester Road	C4
King Street	D4-E4
Kingston	C3-C4
Legion Road	A4
Linden Road	A3-B3
Manor Road	C2
Market Street	D3
Matthews Road	E4-F4
Middle Street	D2-E2-E3
Mill Lane	D2
Mitchelmore Road	D4
Mount Pleasant	E4
Newton Road	E3-E2-F2-F1
North Lane	C3-D3
Old Station Road	E2
Orchard Street	B2-B3
Osborne Road	B3
Queens Way	C1-C2-C3
Park Gardens	C3
Park Road	C3
Park Street	D1-D2
Penn Hill	D1-D2
Petters Way	C2
Preston Grove	A3-B3
Preston Road	A4-B4-C4
Princes Street	C3
Reckleford	C3-D3-E3
Richmond Road	B2-B3
Roping Road	C4-D4
St Andrews Road	A3-A4
St Michael's Avenue	F4
St Michael's Road	F4
Salthouse Lane	C2-C3
Seaton Road	A2-B2-B1
Sherborne Road	E3-F3-F4
South Street	C2-D2
Southville	E3-E4
Sparrow Road	C4-D4
Stars Lane	D2-E2
Summerlands	A4
Summerleaze Park	A4
Swallowcliffe Gardens	C3-C4
The Avenue	D3-D4
The Park	B4-B3-C3
Vicarage Street	D2-D3
Vincent Street	D3
West Hendford	A1-B1-B2-C2
West Park	B2-B3
West Street	B2-B3
Westfield Road	A4
Westland Road	A1-A2-B2
Westville	E4
Willow Road	B4

Chard

Ash Grove	A4-B4
Auckland Way	C1
Bath Street	A2-B2
Beckington Crescent	B1-C1
Bewley Court	A3
Boden Street	B2
Bonfire Close	A1
Bradfield Way	B2-C2-C1
Bubwith Road	C1-C2
Cedar Close	A4
Church Street	B1-B2
Combe Street	A3-B3-B2
Crimchard	A3-A4
Culverhayes	B1
Druids Walk	B4
Duck Lane	A2-B2
Dwelly Close	B2
East Street	C3
Elder Close	B4
Elm Street	B4
Fore Street	B2-B3
Forton Road	B1-C1
Furnham Road	C3-C4
Furzehill	C4
Glynswood	A4-B4-C4
Harvey Road	C1-C2
High Street	A2-B2
Helliers Road	A2-A3
Holyrood Street	B2
King Alfred Drive	B1
Larch Avenue	A4
Lordlease Lane	C1
Mill Lane	B2
Millfield	B2-C2
Mintons	A1
Mintons Orchard	A1
Montague Way	B1
Oak End Way	B4
Old Town	B2
Pine Walk	B4
Ravensmead	B4
St Mary's Close	A1-B1
Silver Street	B2-B3
Summerfields Road	A2-A1-B1
Tapstone Road	C3
Tatworth Road	B1
Thordun Park Drive	B4-C4
Touchstone Lane	A4
Victoria Avenue	C3-C4
Zembard Lane	A3-B3

Sherborne

Abbey Road	A2-B2-B3
Acreman Street	A2-A3
Back Lane	A3
Blackberry Lane	A4
Bristol Road	A4-B4
Cheap Street	B2-B3
Coldharbour	B4-C4
Coombe Road	A4
Digby Road	B1-B2
East Mill Lane	C2
Gas House Hill	B1
Green Hill	A3-B3-B4
Halfmoon Street	B2
Harbour Road	B4
Harbour Way	B4-C4
Hill House Close	C4
Horse Castle	A1-A2
Hospital Road	A3
Hound Street	B3
Kings Crescent	B4
Kings Road	A4-B4
Kitt Hill	A3
Long Street	B2-C2-C3
Ludbourne Road	B2-C2
Marston Road	A3-A4
New Road	B1-C1-C2-C3
Newell	A3
Newland	B3-C3
North Road	B3-B4
Oborne Road	C3
Ottery Lane	A1
Priestlands	A4
Richmond Green	A2-A3
Richmond Road	A2
St Swithins Road	B2-B3
South Street	B1-B2
The Avenue	C3-C4-B4-C4
The Green	A3-B3
Tinneys Lane	C3
Trendle Street	A2-B2
Westbury	A1-A2-B2
Wingfield Road	A1-A2
Wootton Grove	B4

SHERBORNE
The 'new' castle was built by Sir Walter Raleigh in 1594, and is said to be the place where a servant, horrified at the sight of smoke rising from his newfangled tobacco pipe, promptly doused him with ale to 'put out the fire'.

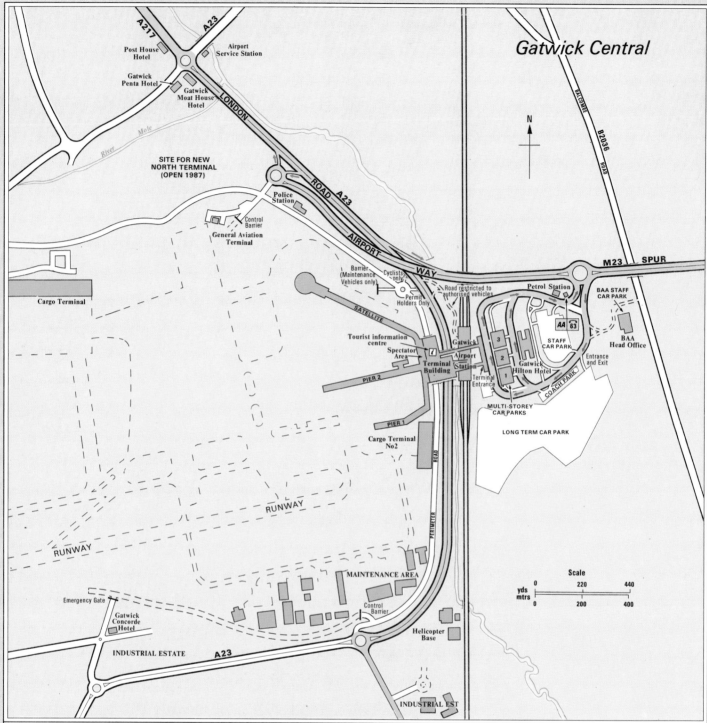

N

Post House
Hotel

Airport
Service Station

A217

A23

Gatwick
Penta Hotel

Gatwick
Moat House
Hotel

LONDON

River Mole

SITE FOR NEW
NORTH TERMINAL
(OPEN 1987)

Police
Station

ROAD

AIRPORT

A23

BALCOMBE ROAD

B2036

M23 SPUR

Control
Barrier

General Aviation
Terminal

WAY

Barrier
(Maintenance
Vehicles only)

Cyclists
only

Road restricted to
authorised vehicles

Petrol Station

BAA STAFF
CAR PARK

Cargo Terminal

Permit
Holders Only

SATELLITE

Tourist information
centre

Spectator
Area

PIER 2

Terminal
Building

Gatwick
Airport
Station

3

2

1

AA 63

STAFF
CAR PARK

Gatwick
Hilton Hotel

BAA
Head Office

Entrance
and Exit

Terminal
Entrance

COACH PARK

MULTI-STOREY
CAR PARKS

PIER 1

Cargo Terminal
No2

ROAD

LONG TERM CAR PARK

RUNWAY

RUNWAY

PERIMETER

Emergency Gate

Gatwick
Concorde
Hotel

MAINTENANCE AREA

Control
Barrier

Helicopter
Base

Scale

yds mtrs	0	220	440
	0	200	400

INDUSTRIAL ESTATE

A23

INDUSTRIAL EST

Rusper

Hookwood

A217

A23

Charlwood

HORLEY

GATWICK AIRPORT

M23

Lambs
Green

Langley
Green

A23

Burstow

CRAWLEY

Three
Bridges

B2036

B2037

Ifield

Copthorne

A264

Pease
Pottage

Pound Hill

A264

Crawley Down

A23

M23

Turners
Hill

B2110

B2110

Handcross

B2114

Staplefield

B2036

B2028

Selsfield
Common

Balcombe

Gatwick Airport

Gatwick is London's second busiest airport,
coming second only to Heathrow. Well situated near
the new town of Crawley, West Sussex, for easy
access via the A23 and M23 London to Brighton
motorway, it also has its own adjoining British
Rail mainline railway station. Fast 15-minute
frequency trains make a link 24 hours a day
between Victoria Station and Gatwick, and a link
is also provided to the capital by a Green Line
Coach service. Coach connections to Heathrow and
Luton, are available.

Lying on the edge of the North Downs, this has
been the site of an airport since 1936. It was
taken over by the Air Ministry, which established
a training school for RAF pilots on the site in
1937. Wartime saw Gatwick's expansion into an RAF
station of major importance, so much so that it
had to be extended to take in the nearby
racecourse. After the war, it went over to
commercial use, but was only opened as an
international airport in 1958, after extensive
modernisation. At that time, it was hailed as the
most advanced airport in Europe, with its linking
of road, rail and air facilities.

Today this busy air traffic centre is used by
most major airlines and by charter services of
other airline companies, as well as being open in
case of need to aircraft diverted from Heathrow.
Passengers travelling between the two airports of
Gatwick and Heathrow can also enjoy the service of
rapid helicopter flights from one to the other.
This helicopter airlink is run daily and takes only
about quarter of an hour.

A spectators' viewing area, signposted through
the International Arrivals section, allows
visitors to watch the ever-changing panorama of an
important international airport in action. A small
fee is charged for this. The viewing area is open
daily until dusk, and includes car parking
facilities. Three linked multi-storey car parks
and an open air car park are also provided for
travellers and other visitors to the airport.

Several bars and eating places catering for
different tastes have been established within the
airport, and can be found on the 'catering level'
above the international arrivals hall.

London

AREA MAPS ARE INDICATED IN BOLD.

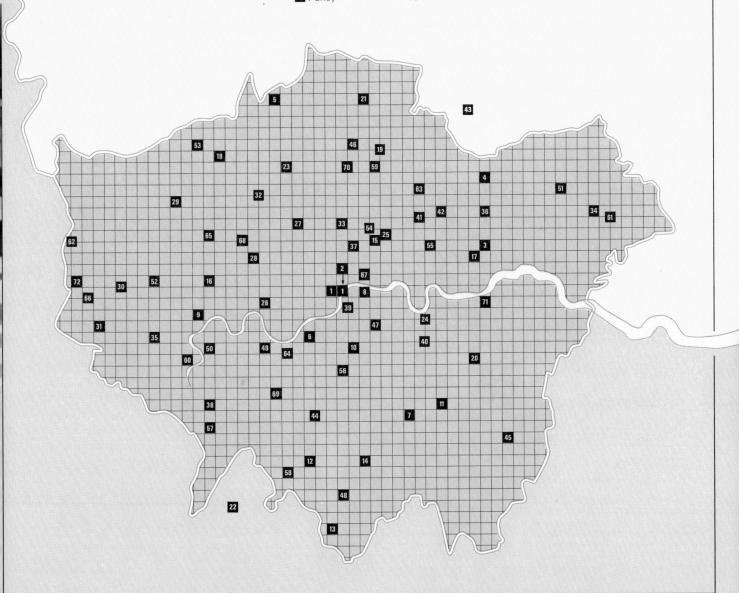

Barking

A flourishing fishing industry operating from the Town Quay was the mainstay of Barking until well into the 19th century, when the coming of the railways and easy access to the east coast ports brought about its decline. The area has since undergone a good deal of industrial development but Barking still has a number of pleasant parks, notably Barking Park, which has a miniature railway and a large open air swimming pool. Still to be seen are the remains of Barking Abbey (founded in the 7th century and focus of the original settlement), Eastbury House, which dates from the 16th century, and the 13th-century Parish Church of St Margaret, where Captain Cook, the explorer, was married in 1762.

East Ham's Central Park is the scene of the colourful Town Show staged by the Borough of Newham each year. Dating back to Roman times, this ancient parish saw heavy development during the late 19th century, when most of the local industry was centred around the nearby docks.

Stratford Controversial new productions are the speciality of the Victorian Theatre Royal, a local landmark near the modern shopping centre. Site of a Roman fording of the River Lea, Stratford also has the Passmore Edwards Museum, which was built to house the collections of the Essex Field Club and now deals with local history and archaeology.

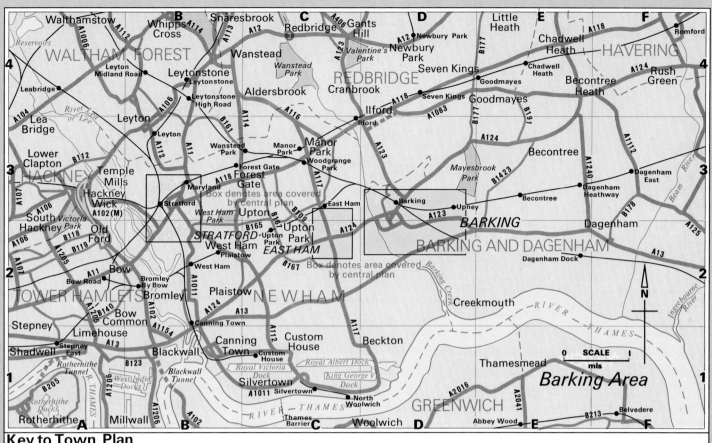

Key to Town Plan and Area Plan

Town Plan

AA Recommended roads	▬
Other roads	▬
Restricted roads	▬ ▬ ▬
Buildings of interest	School ▢
Churches	✝
Car Parks	P
Parks and open spaces	▢
BR and Underground Stations	⊖
One way streets	←

Area Plan

A roads	▬
B roads	▬
Stations	Woodside ⊖
Borough boundary	▬ ▬ ▬

Street Index with Grid Reference

Barking

Abbey Road	A3-A2-B2-B1
Aldersey Gardens	C4-D4
Alfreds Gardens	D1-E1
Bamford Road	B4
Barking By-Pass	D1-E1-F1-F2
Beccles Drive	E4
Blake Avenue	E2-F2
Boundary Road	B1-C1
Broadway	B2
Buller Road	D3-D4
Cecil Avenue	C3-C4
Charlton Crescent	E1-F1
Church Road	B4
Clare Gardens	F4
Cowbridge Lane	A3-B3
Cranbourne Road	C2-D2
Cranleigh Gardens	C4
Dawson Avenue	E3-F3
Denham Way	E2
Devon Road	D2-E2
Digby Road	E3
Eastbury Square	E2
East Street	B2-B3-C3
Edgefield Avenue	F3-F4
Eldred Road	D2
Essex Road	C3-D3-D2
Faircross Avenue	B4-C4
Fanshawe Avenue	B4-C4
Felton Road	D1-E1
Fresh Wharf Road	A1-B1
Gascoigne Road	B2-B1-C1
George Street	B3
Glenny Road	B4-C4
Gordon Road	D2
Greatfields Road	D1-D2
Harpour Road	B4
Harrow Road	D2-E2
Harts Lane	A4-B4-B3
Hertford Road	A2-A3
Highbridge Road	A1-A2
Howard Road	C1-C2-D2
Hulse Avenue	D4-E4-E3
Hurstbourne Gardens	D4-E4
Jackson Road	D1-D2
James Street	B3
Keith Road	D1
Kennedy Road	D1-D2
Keir Hardie Way	F3
King Edwards Road	C2-C1-D1
Lambourne Road	E2-E3
Lancaster Avenue	D2-D3
Levett Road	D4
Linton Road	B3
London Road	A2-A3-B3
Longbridge Road	C3-C4-D4
Loxford Road	A4-B4
Lyndhurst Gardens	D4-E4
Manor Road	E4-F4
Maybury Road	F1
Meadow Road	F3
Melford Avenue	E4
Melish Court	E1-E2
Morley Road	C2-D2
Movers Lane	D1-D2
Netherfield Gardens	C4-D4-D3
Norfolk Road	D3
North Street	B2-B3
Oakley Avenue	F4
Park Avenue	B4-C4
Perth Road	C1-D1
Priory Road	C3
Queens Road	B3-B4
Ripple Road	B3-C3-C2-D2-E2-F2
River Road	D1-E1
Rosslyn Road	C3-C4-D4
St Annes	B2-C2-C1
St Awdrys Road	C3-C2-D2
St Erkenwald Road	C2-C3
St Johns Road	D1-E1
St Margarets	C2
St Marys	C1
St Pauls Road	B2-C2
Sandringham Drive	A4
Salisbury Avenue	C3-D3-D4-E4
Sherwood Gardens	C4-C3-D3
Shirley Gardens	D4-E4
Sisley Road	E2-F2
Somerby Road	C3-C4
Sparsholt Road	D2-E2-E1
Strathfield Gardens	C4-D4
Stratton Drive	E4-F4
Sterry Road	E2
Suffolk Road	C3-D3-D2
Sunningdale Avenue	C2-C3
Surrey Road	D2-D3
Sutton Road	D1-E1
Tanner Street	B4
The Drive	E4-F4
The Shaftesburys	B1-C1
Thornhill Gardens	E3
Thorpe Road	C3
Town Quay	A2-B2
Tresham Road	E3
Upney Lane	E4-E3-F3-F2
Victoria Road	A4-B4
Wakering Road	B4-B3-C3
Wedderburn Road	D2
West Bank	A2
Westbury Road	C2
Westrow Drive	E4-F4
Wheelers Cross	C1
Whiting Avenue	A3-B3
Wilmington Gardens	C4-D4-D3-E3-E4

Stratford

Abbey Lane	A1
Abbey Road	B1
Aileen Walk	C2
Albert Square	C4
Aldworth Road	B2
Alma Street	A4-B4
Angel Lane	B3
Ash Road	C4
Atherton Road	C3-C4
Bridge Road	A2-B2-B1
Bridge Terrace	A2-B2
Broadway	B2-B3
Burford Road	A2-B2-B1
Buxton Road	B4-C4
Caistor Park Road	C1
Carnarvon Road	C3-C4
Carpenters Road	A1-A2
Cedars Road	C3
Chandos Road	A4-B4
Chant Street	B2
Chobham Road	A4-B4
Church Street	B1-C1
Cruickshank Road	C4
David Street	B4
Densham Road	B1-B2-C2
Devenay Road	C4
Earlham Grove	C4
Evesham Road	C2
Fairland Road	C3
Farringford Road	B2-C2
Forest Lane	B4-C4
Francis Street	B4
Geere Road	C1-C2
Glenavon Road	B3-C3-C2
Gibbins Road	A2
Great Eastern Road	A2-A3-B3
Grove Crescent Road	B3
Gurney Road	B4-C4
Ham Park Road	C2-C3
Harberson Road	C1
Hartland Road	C2
Heaton Place	A4
Henniker Road	A4-B4
High Street	A1-A2
Idmiston Road	C4
John Street	C1
Jupp Road	A2
Jupp Road West	A2
Keogh Road	B3-C3-C4
Leyton Road	A4-A3-B3
Leytonstone Road	B4

East Ham

Aintree Avenue	A2-A3
Altmore Avenue	C2-C3-C4
Arthur Road	C1
Barking Road	A2-B2-C2
Bartle Avenue	B1-B2
Basil Avenue	A1
Bedford Road	B2
Bendish Road	B4
Bridge Road	C2
Burgess Road	B4-C4
Caledon Road	B3-C3
Campbell Road	B2-B3
Caulfield Road	B3-C3
Central Park Road	A1-B1-B2
Cheltenham Gardens	A1
Clements Road	B4-C4
Colvin Road	A4-B4-B3
Cotswold Gardens	A1
Ernald Avenue	A2-A1-B1
Eversleigh Road	A4
Flanders Road	B1-C1
Friars Road	A2-A3
Geoffrey Gardens	A1

Livingstone Road	A1
Louise Road	C3-C4
McGrath Road	C3-C4
Major Road	A4
Maneby Grove	B3
Maneby Street	B3-C3
Manor Road	C1
Maryland Park	B4
Maryland Road	B4
Maryland Street	B4
Meath Road	C1
Mortham Street	B1
New Plaistow Road	B1-C1
Paul Street	B1-B2
Pitchford Street	B2
Plaistow Road	C1
Portway	C2
Richford Road	C1-C2
Rokeby Street	B1-B2
Romford Road	B3-C3
St James Road	C4
Sandal Street	B1
Skiers Street	B1
Stephen's Road	B1-C1
Tavistock Road	C3
Temple Mill Lane	A4
Tennyson Road	B2-B3
The Green	C3
The Grove	B3
Union Street	A1
Vaughan Road	C3
Vicarage Lane	C2-C3
Victoria Street	B2
Waddington Road	B3-B4
Waddington Street	B3-B4
Warton Road	A1
Water Lane	B4-B3-C3
West Ham Lane	B1-B2
Willis Road	C1
Windmill Lane	C1
Wise Road	A1

Gillett Avenue	A1-A2
Grangewood Street	A3
Grosvenor Road	A3
Haldane Road	A1
Hall Road	C2-C3
Harrow Road	B3-B4
Hartley Avenue	A2-A3
Heigham Road	A4-B4
Henniker Gardens	A1
Henry Road	B2
High Street North	B2-B3-B4
High Street South	B1-B2
Hockley Avenue	A1-A2
Holme Road	B3
Howard Road	C1
Katherine Road	A2-A3-A4
Kempton Road	B3-C3
Keppel Road	B4-B3-C3-C2
Kimberley Avenue	A1-A2
Ladysmith Avenue	A1-A2
Lathom Road	B4-C4
Latimer Avenue	C2-C3
Lawrence Road	A4-B4
Lloyd Road	B2-C2
Mafeking Avenue	A1-A2
Malvern Road	A3
Market Street	B1-C1
Melbourne Road	C1-C2
Milton Avenue	A4-B4
Montpelier Gardens	A1
Napier Road	C1-C2
Navarre Road	B2
Nelson Street	B2-C2
Norfolk Road	C2-C3
Oakfield Road	A3-B3
Outram Road	A2-A4-B4
Phashet Grove	A4
Poulett Road	B2-C2
Pulleyns Avenue	A1-B1
Rancliffe Road	A1-B1
St Barts Road	B2
St Bernards Road	A2-A3
St Johns Road	A2-B2
Shoebury Road	C4
Sibley Grove	B4
Skeffington Road	B3-C3
Southend Road	B4-C4
Southchurch Road	B1-C1
Spencer Road	A3-A4
Stamford Road	A3-B3
Streatfield Avenue	C2-C3
Talbot Road	C1-C2
Thorpe Road	B3-C3
Tilbury Road	B1-C1
Victoria Avenue	A4
Wakefield Street	A3-B3
Wellington Road	C1-C2
Winter Avenue	B2-B3

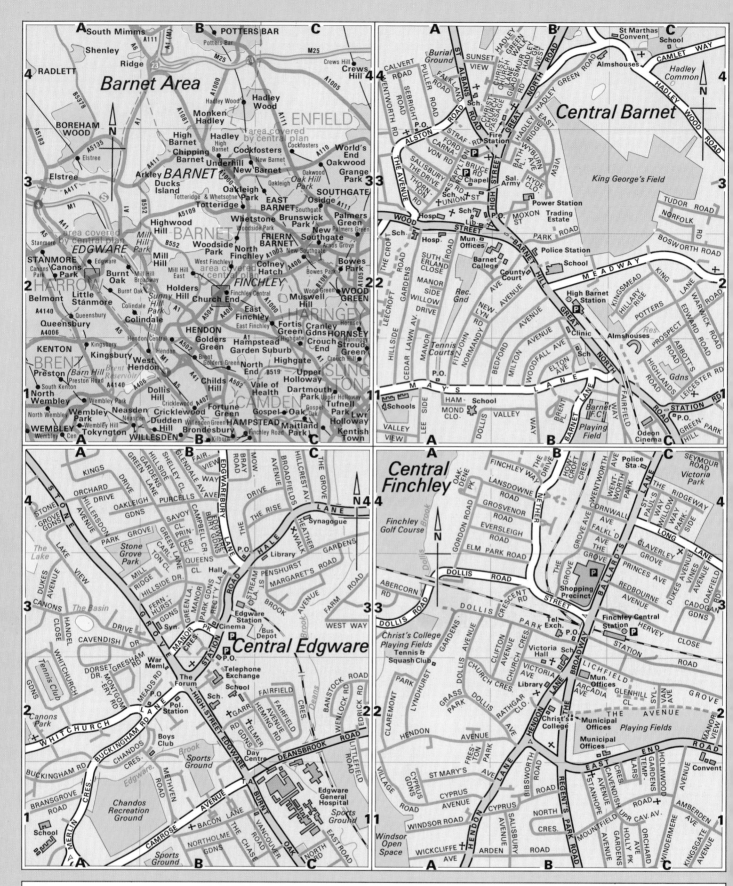

Barnet

Immortalised as the Cockney rhyming slang for 'hair', Barnet Fair started in the Middle Ages and is still held every year in September at Brent Lodge Farm, Mays Lane.

This was a fashionable residential area as early as the 18th century, and after the extension of the main line and underground railways in the late 19th and early 20th centuries, it developed

into an important London borough. Long before this, its position on the Great North Road had made Barnet a popular staging post for coaches, and the High Street probably dates back to the 15th century. The Barnet Museum in Wood Street has an interesting local history collection.

Edgware lies on the line of Watling Street, the major Roman road which is roughly paralleled by the M1. Now mostly residential, Edgware was also at one time an important staging post. Several old

buildings in the High Street date from that period, notably the White Hart, a 17th-century inn which has retained its covered wagon-way.

Finchley kept its country air until the late 19th century when it was heavily built on. The Bishop of London owned an extensive estate in this area during the 14th century, and despite intensive modernisation, Finchley still has several interesting quarters. The old parish church is in the Church End area.

Key to Town Plan and Area Plan

Town Plan

AA Recommended roads
Restricted roads
Other roads
Buildings of interest   Station ▣
Churches   ✝
Car Parks   Ⓟ
Parks and open spaces

Area Plan

A roads
B roads
Stations
Urban area
London Borough Boundary – –

Street Index with Grid Reference

Barnet

Edgeware

(continued)

Finchley

(continued)

BARNET
The Parish Church of St James, Friern Barnet, on the eastern side of the borough. Although part of London, Barnet reaches out into open country and still has distinct village communities.

5

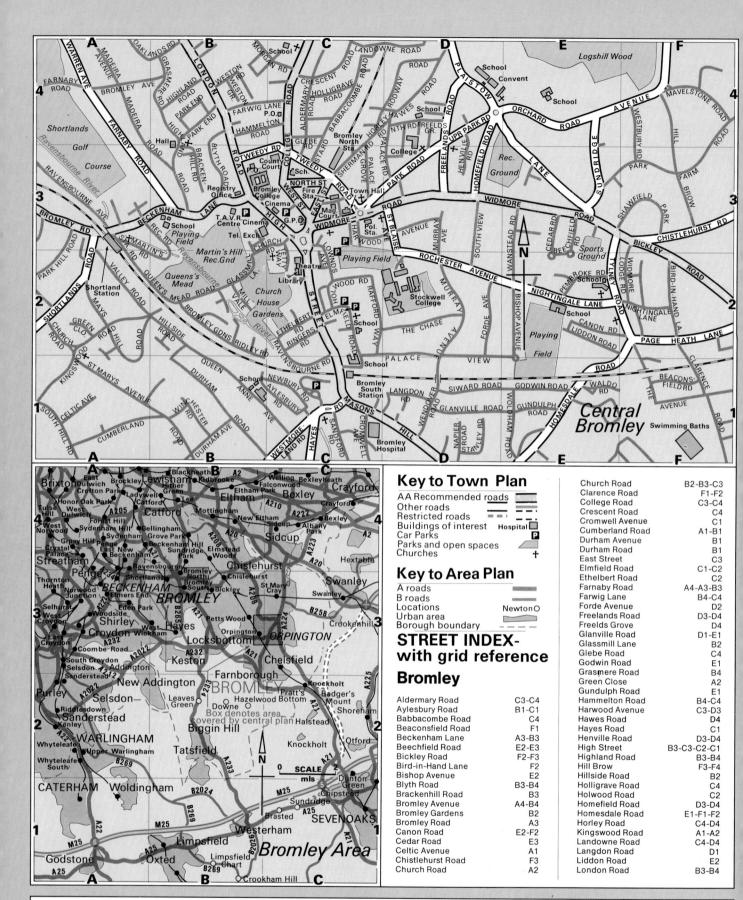

Key to Town Plan

AA Recommended roads
Other roads
Restricted roads
Buildings of interest   Hospital ▫
Car Parks   P
Parks and open spaces
Churches   ✝

Key to Area Plan

A roads
B roads
Locations   Newton ○
Urban area
Borough boundary

STREET INDEX- with grid reference

Bromley

Bromley

Birthplace of H G Wells, Bromley is thought by some to be one of the most favoured residential areas to the south of London. It has an abundance of trees and parks, and even in the centre, Queens Garden and Church House Gardens form quiet oases. In spite of development this century, Bromley has kept many of its older buildings, Bromley Palace and Bromley College among them. The house in which H G Wells was born no longer stands, but a plaque marks its site in the High Street. At Norman Park, Bromley also boasts an excellent all-weather running track.

Beckenham Development in the 1920s and 1930s left few of the older buildings standing except in a small area near the High Street, but Beckenham's tree-lined roads and numerous parks are compensation for this. Kelsey Park, in the town centre, is a beautiful expanse of woods, lawns, flowers and a stream.

Orpington's history can be traced back to the Stone Age, but ironically it was the last of the major areas of the borough to be developed. When it came, in the 1930s and later, development included such innovations as The Walnuts, a town centre shopping precinct, Civic Centre and sports hall. Reminders of the town's past still survive, and the London Borough of Bromley Priory Museum, in Church Hill, has interesting exhibits.

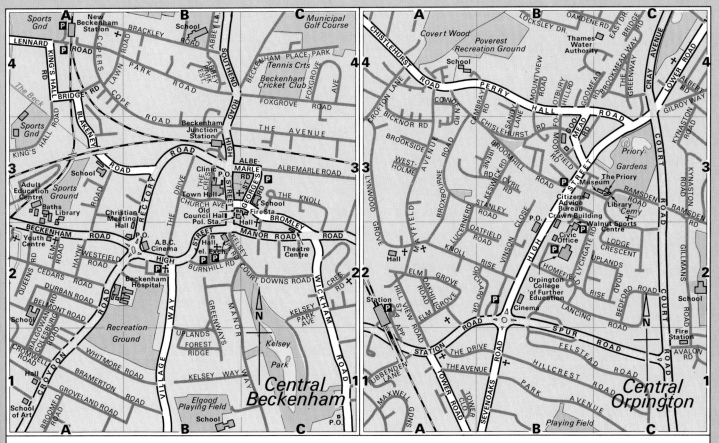

Central Beckenham

Central Orpington

Lownds Avenue	C2-C3	Valley Road	A2
Madeira Avenue	A4	Waldo Road	E1
Madeira Road	A4-A3-B3	Wanstead Road	E2-E3
Martins Road	A3-A2-B2	Warren Avenue	A4
Masons Hill	C1-D1	Wendover Road	D1
Mavelstone Road	F4	West Street	C3
Mays Hill Road	A1-A2	Westbury Road	F3-F4
Mill Vale	B2	Westmoreland Road	C1
Morgan Road	B4-C4	Weston Grove	B4
Murray Avenue	D1-D2-D3	Weston Road	B4
Napier Road	D1	Widmore Road	C3-D3-E3
Newbury Road	B1-C1	Widmore Lodge Road	F2-F3
Nightingale Lane	E2-F2	Winchester Road	B1
North Road	D4	Woldham Road	E1
North Street	C3		
Oaklands Road	A4-B4		
Orchard Road	D4-E4		
Page Heath Lane	F2	**Beckenham**	
Palace Grove	C3		
		Abbey Lane	B4
Palace View	C2-D2-E2	Abbey Park Estate	B4
Park End	B4	Albermarle Road	B3-C3
Park Road	C3-D3	Balgowan Road	A1-A2
Park Farm Road	E3-F3-F4	Beckenham Road	A3-A2-B2
Park Hill Road	A2-A3	Beckenham Place Park	B4-C4
Pembroke Road	E2	Belmont Road	A2
Plaistow Lane	D4-E4-E3	Blakeney Road	A4-A3-B3
Queen Anne Avenue	B2-B1-C1	Brackley Road	A4-B4
Queen's Mead Road	A2-B2	Bramerton Road	A1-B1
Rafford Way	C2	Bridge Road	A4
Ravensbourne Avenue	A3	Bromley Road	C2-C3
Ravensbourne Road	C1-C2	Broomfield Road	A1
Recreation Road	A3-B3	Burnhill Road	B2
Ridley Road	B1-B2	Cedars Road	A2
Ringers Road	C2	Church Avenue	B3
Rochester Avenue	D3-D2-E2	Colesburg Road	A1-A2
Rodway Road	C4-D4	Copers Cope Road	A4-B4-B3
St Blaise Avenue	D2-D3	Court Downs Road	C2
St Marys Avenue	A1-B1	Crescent Road	C2
Sandford Road	C1	Cromwell Road	A1
Shawfield Park	E3-F3	Croydon Road	A1-A2-B2
Sherman Road	C3-C4	Durban Road	A2
Shortlands Road	A2-A3	Elm Road	A2
Siward Road	D1-E1	Forest Ridge	B1
South View	D2-D3	Foxgrove Avenue	C4
South Hill Road	A1	Foxgrove Road	C4
Stanley Road	D1	Greenways	B1-B2
Station Road	A2-A3	Groveland Road	A1-B1
Station Road	C3-C4	Hayne Road	A2-A3
Sundridge Avenue	E3-E4-F4	High Street	B2-B3
Tetty Way	C2-C3	Kelsey Way	B1-C1
The Avenue	F1	Kelsey Park Avenue	C1-C2
The Chase	D2	Kelsey Park Road	B2
Tweedy Road	B3-C3	King's Hall Road	A3-A4
Tylney Road	E3-E2-F2	Lawn Road	A4-B4
Upper Park Road	D4	Lennard Road	A4

Manor Road	B2-C2	Lychgate Road	B2-B3
Manor Way	C2-B2-C2-C1	Lynwood Grove	A2-A3
Park Road	A4-B4	Maxwell Gardens	A1
Queens Road	A2	Mayfield Avenue	A2-A3-A4
Rectory Road	B2-B3	Moorfield Road	B3
St George's Road	C3	Mountview Road	B4
Southend Road	B3-B4	Oakdene Road	B4-C4
The Avenue	B3-C3	Oakhill Road	A2
The Crescent	B3	Oatfield Road	A2-B2
The Drive	B2-B3	Orchard Grove	B2
The Knoll	C2-C3	Park Avenue	B1-C1
Uplands	B1	Perry Hall Road	A4-B4-C4-C3
Village Way	B1-B2	Ramsden Road	C2-C3
Westfield Road	A2	Sandy Lane	B3-B4
Whitmore Road	A1-B1	Sevenoaks Road	B1
Wickham Road	C1-C2	Spur Road	B2-B1-C1
		Stanley Road	A3-B3
		Station Approach	A1-A2
Orpington		Station Road	A1-A2-B2
		The Avenue	A1-B1
Albert Road	C4	The Drive	A1-B1
Avalon Road	C1	The Greenway	C4
Bedford Road	C2	Tower Close	A1
Bicknor Road	A3-A4	Tower Road	A1
Bridge Road	C4	Tubbenden Lane	A1
Brookmead Way	C4	Uplands Road	B2-C2
Brookside	A3	Vinson Close	B2-B3
Broomhill Road	B3	Westholme	A3
Broxbourne Road	A2-A3		
Cambray Road	B3-B4		
Chistlehurst Road	A4-A3-B3		
Court Road	C1-C2-C3		
Cowden Road	A3-A4		
Cray Avenue	C4		
Crofton Lane	A3-A4		
Cyril Road	B3		
East Drive	C4		
Elm Grove	A2		
Felstead Road	B1-C1		
Footbury Hill Road	B3-B4		
Gillmans Road	C1-C2-C3		
Gilroy Way	C4		
Goomead Road	B3-B4-C4		
High Street	B2-B3-C3		
Hillcrest Road	B1-C1		
Hill View Road	A1-A2		
Homefield Rise	B2-C2		
Irene Road	B3		
Keswick Road	B3		
Knoll Rise	A2-B2		
Kynaston Road	C3-C4		
Lancing Road	B2-C2		
Locksley Drive	B4		
Lodge Crescent	C2		
Lower Road	C4		
Lucerne Road	A2-A3		

Central London

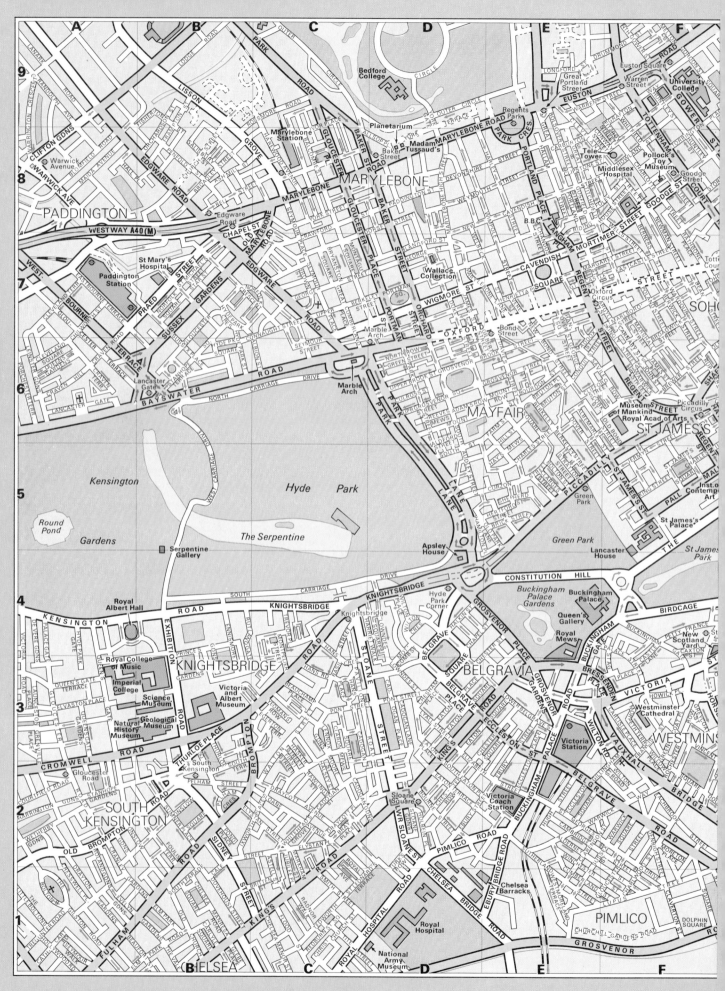

Key to Town Plan

Town Plan

- AA Recommended roads
- Restricted roads
- Other roads
- Buildings of interest — Cinema
- Car Parks — P
- Churches — +
- Parks and open spaces
- Underground Stations
- One Way Streets

Street Index with Grid Reference

Central London

Abingdon Street G3-G4
Adams Row D6-E6
Albany Road K1-L1
Albert Embankment H1-H2-H3
Albermarle Street E6-E5-F5-F6
Alberta Street J2
Albion Street C6
Aldridge Street L2
Alderney Street E2-F2-F1
Aldergate Street J7-K7-K6
Aldford Street D5-D6
Aldwych H6-H7-I7
Allsop Place C8-D8
Alsey Street C2
Amelia Street J2-K2
Appold Street L8-L9
Argyll Street E7-F7
Ashmill Street B8-C8
Astell Street C1-C2
Atterbury Street G2
Aylesford Street G1
Baker Street C8-D8-D7
Balcombe Street C8
Baldwins Gardens I8
Balfour Street K2-K3
Bankside J6-K6
Banner Street K9
Barbican J8
Basil Street C3-C4
Basinghall Street K7-K8
Bath Terrace K3-K4
Baylis Road I4
Bayswater Road A6-B6-C6
Beauchamp Place C3
Beak Street F6
Bear Lane J5
Beaufort Street A1-B1
Bedford Avenue G8
Bedford Place G8
Bedford Square F8-G8
Bedford Walk G9
Beech Street J8-K8
Belgrave Place D3
Belgrave Road E3-E2-F2
Belgrave Square D3-D4
Bell Street B8-C8
Bell Yard I7
Belvedere Street H4-H5
Berkeley Square E6
Berkeley Street C7-D7
Berkeley Street E5-E6
Bermondsey Street L4-L5
Berners Street F7-F8
Berwick Street F6-F7
Birdcage Walk F4-G4
Bishopsgate L7-L8
Blackfriars Bridge J6
Blackfriars Road J4-J5
Black Prince Road H2-I2
Blandford Street D7
Blomfield Road A8
Bloomsbury Street G7-G8
Bloomsbury Way G8-H8
Bolsover Street E8-E9
Bolton Street E5
Borough High Street K4-K5-J5
Borough Road J4-K4
Boswell Street H8
Bourdon Street E6
Bourne Street D2
Bouverie Street I7
Bowling Green Lane I9
Bow Street H7
Braganza Street J1-J2
Brandon Street K2-K3
Bray Place C2
Bressenden Place E3-F3
Brewer Street F6
Brick Street E5
Bridge Street G4-H4
Britten Street B1-C1
Broadley Street B8
Broadwick Street F6-F7
Brompton Road C2-B2-B3-C3-C4
Brook Drive I3-J3
Brook Street D6-E6-E7
Browning Street K2
Brown Street C7
Brunswick Square G9-H9
Bruton Place E6
Bruton Street E6
Bryanston Square C7
Buckingham Gate E3-E4-F4-F3
Buckingham Palace Road E2-E3
Bunhill Row K8-K9
Cadiz Street K1-K2
Cadogan Gardens C2-D2
Cadogan Lane D3
Cadogan Place D3
Cadogan Street C2
Cadogan Square C2-C3
Cale Street B1-B2-C2
Calthorpe Street H9-I9
Cambridge Street E2-F2-F1
Cannon Street J7-K7-K6-L6
Cardigan Street I1-I2
Carey Street H7-I7
Carlisle Lane I3-I4
Carlisle Place F3
Carlyle Square B1
Carnaby Street F6-F7
Carter Lane J7-K7
Carter Road J1-K1
Castle Lane F3-F4
Cathcart Road A1
Cavendish Square E7
Caxton Street F4
Chancery Lane I7-I8
Chandos Place G6
Chandos Street E7-E8
Chapel Street D4-E4
Chapel Street B7-B8-C8
Charing Cross Road G6-G7
Charles Street E5-E6
Charles II Street F5-F6-G6
Charlotte Street F8
Charlwood Street F1-F2
Charterhouse Street J8
Charter Road J1
Chatham Street K3-L3
Cheapside K7
Chelsea Bridge Road D2-D1-E1
Chelsea Manor Street C1
Chelsea Square B1
Chesham Place D3
Chester Row D2
Chester Square D3-E3-E2
Chester Street D3-D4-E4-E3
Chilworth Street A6-A7
Chiswell Street K8-L8
Christchurch Street C1
Church Street B8
Churchill Gardens Road E1-F1
City Road K9-L9-L8
Clabon Mews C2-C3
Clarendon Street E2-F2
Clarges Street E5
Claverton Street F1
Clayton Street I1
Clerkenwell Road I8-I9-J9
Cleveland Square A6
Cleveland Street E9-E8-F8
Cleveland Terrace A7
Clifford Street E6-F6
Clifton Gardens A8
Clifton Street L8-L9
Clink Street K5-K6
Clipstone Street E8-F8
Cock Lane J8
Coin Street I5
Coleman Street K7-K8
Cole Street K4
Compton Street J8
Conduit Street E6-E7
Congreve Street L2-L3
Connaught Street B6-B7-C7-C6
Constitution Hill E4-F4
Conway Street E8-F8
Cook's Road J1
Copperfield Street J5-K5
Cork Street E6-F6
Cornhill K7-L7
Cornwall Road I4-I5
Cosser Street I3
County Street K3
Courtenay Street I1-I2
Courtfield Road A2
Covent Garden G6-H6-H7
Coventry Street F6-G6
Cowan Street L1
Cowcross Street J8
Crampton Street J2-K2
Cranley Gardens A2-A1-B1
Craven Hill A6
Craven Terrace A6
Crawford Street C7-C8-D8
Cresswell Place A1-A2
Cromwell Road A2-A3-B3
Cullcross Street D6
Cumberland Street E2-E1-F1
Curtain Road L9
Curzon Street D5-E5-E6
Dante Road J2-J3
Darwin Street L3
Date Street K2
Davies Street E6-E7
Dawes Street L2
Deacon Way K3
Dean Street F7-G7
Decima Street L4
Delaune Street J1-J2
Denbigh Street F1-F2
Devere Gardens A3-A4
Deverell Street K3-L3
Devonshire Street D8-E8
Doddington Grove J1
Dolben Street J5
Dolphin Square F1
Dorset Street C7-C8-D8
Doughty Street H9
Douglas Street F2-G2
Dovehouse Street B1
Dover Street E5-E6
Downing Street G5
Draycott Avenue C2
Draycott Place C2
Drayton Gardens A1-A2
Drummond Street E9-F9
Dufferin Street K9
Duke Street D7
Durham Street H1
Dury Lane G7-H7
Eastbourne Terrace A7
East Castle Street F7
Eastcheap L6
East Street K2-L2
Eaton Place D3
Eaton Square D3-E3
Eaton Terrace D2
Eccleston Place E2-E3
Eccleston Square E2
Eccleston Street E3
Ebury Bridge Road D1-E1-E2
Ebury Street D2-E2-E3
Edgware Road A8-B8-B7-C7-C6
Egerton Terrace C3
Eldon Street L8
Elizabeth Street D3-D2-E2
Elliots Row J3
Elm Park Gardens B1
Elm Park Road A1-B1
Elsted Street L2
Elvaston Place A3
Elystan Place C2
Elystan Street B2-C2
Emerson Street K5-K6
Endell Street G7-H7
Ennismore Gardens B3-B4
Epworth Street L9
Erasmus Street G2
Euston Road E9-F9
Evelyn Gardens A1-B1
Ewer Street J5
Exhibition Road B3-B4
Exmouth Market I9
Falmouth Road K3-K4
Fann Street J8-J9-K9-K8
Faringdon Road I9
Farm Street D6-E6
Farringdon Road I8-J8
Farringdon Street J7-J8
Fenchurch Street L6-L7
Fielding Street K1
Finsbury Circus L8
Finsbury Square L8-L9
First Street C2-C3
Fisherton Street A9-B9-B8
Fitzalen Street I8
Fitzroy Street F8-F9
Fleet Street I7-J7
Fleming Road J1
Flint Street L2
Flood Street C1
Floral Street G6-G7-H7
Foley Street E8-F8
Fore Street K8
Foulis Terrace B2
Frampton Street B8-B9
Frazer Street I4
Frith Street G7
Fulham Road A1-B1-B2
Gee Street J9
George Street C7-D7
Gerrard Street G6
Gilbert Road I2-I3-J3
Gilbert Street D7-D6-E6
Gillingham Street E2-F2-F3
Gilston Road A1
Giltspur Street J7-J8
Glasshouse Walk H2
Glebe Place B1
Gloucester Place C9-C8-C7-D7
Gloucester Road A2-A3
Gloucester Square B6-B7
Gloucester Street E1-F1-F2
Gloucester Terrace A6-A7
Goodge Street F8
Golden Lane K8-K9
Gordon Square F9-G9
Gordon Street F9
Gossfield Street E8
Goswell Road J8-J9
Gough Street H9-I9
Gower Street F9-F8-G8
Gracechurch Street L6-L7
Grafton Way F9
Gray's Inn Road H9-I9-I8
Great Castle Street E7-F7
Great Cumberland Place C6-C7
Great Dover Street K4-K3-L3
Great George Street G4
Great Guildford Street J5-K5
Great Marlborough Street F7
Great Ormond Street H8-H9
Great Peter Street F3-G3
Great Portland Street E7-E8-E9
Great Russel Street F7-F8-G8
Great Smith Street G3-G4
Great Suffolk Street J4-J5
Great Titchfield Street E8-E7-F7
Greek Street G7
Greencoat Place F3
Green Street D6
Gresham Street K7
Greville Street I8
Greycoat Street F3
Grosvenor Gardens E3
Grosvenor Place D4-E4-E3
Grosvenor Road E1-F1-G1
Grosvenor Square D6
Grosvenor Street D6-E6
Guilford Street G9-H9
Guy Street L4
Halkin Street D4
Hallam Street E8
Hall Place A8-B8
Hamilton Place D4-D5-E5-E4
Hanover Square E7
Hans Crescent C3-C4
Hans Place C3
Hans Road C3
Harewood Avenue C8-C9
Harley Ford Road H1
Harley Street D8-E8-E7
Harper Road K3-K4
Harriet Walk C4-D4-D3
Harrington Gardens A2
Hasker Street C2-C3
Hatfields I5-J5
Hatton Garden I8
Hayle Street J3
Haymarket F6-G6-G5
Hay's Mews E5-E6
Henrietta Place E7
Hercules Road I3-I4
Hertford Street D5-E5
Heygate Street K2-K3
High Holborn G7-H7-H8-I8
Hill Street E5-E6
Holbein Place D2
Holborn H8-I8
Holborn Circus I8
Holborn Viaduct I8-J8-J7
Holland Street J5-J6
Hollywood Road A1
Holyoake Road J2-J3
Hopton Street J5-J6
Horseferry Road F3-G3
Horse Guards Road G4-G5
House Street E8-F8
Howick Place F3
Howland Street F8
Hugh Street E2
Huntley Street F8-F9
Hyde Park Crescent B7
Hyde Park Gate A3-A4
Hyde Park Square B6
Hyde Park Street B6-B7
Innfields H7-I7
Ivor Place C8-C9
Ixworth Place B2-C2
James Street D7
James Street F6
Jermyn Street F5-F6
Jockey's Fields H8
John Adams Street G6-H6
Johnathan Street H2
John Islip Street G2-G3
John Street F6
John Street J9
Jubilee Place C1-C2
Kempsford Road I2-J2
Kennington Lane I2-J2
Kennington Park I1-J1
Kennington Park Road I1-J1-J2
Kennington Road I1-I2-I3
Kensington Road A4-B4
King Charles Street G4
King James Street J4
Kingslake Street L1-L2
Kingly Street F6-F7
King's Road B1-C1-C2-D2-D3-E3
King Street F5
Kingsway H7-H8
King William Street K7-L7-L6
Kipling Street L4-L5
Knightsbridge B4-C4-D4
Lambeth Bridge G3-H3
Lambeth High Street H2-H3
Lambeth Palace Road H3-H4
Lambeth Road H3-I3-I4-J4
Lambeth Walk I3
Lanark Gate A9
Lancaster Gate A6
Langham Place E7-E8
Langle Lane H1
Lant Street K4
Larcom Street K2
Launceston Place A3
Lavington Street J5
Lawn Lane H1
Law Street L3-L4
Leadenhall Street L7
Leather Lane I8-I9
Leather Market Street L4
Leicester Square G6
Leinster Gardens A6-A7
Lennox Gardens C3
Leonard Street L9
Lincoln's H7-H8
Lisle Street G6
Lisson Grove B8-C8
Liverpool Grove K1-K2
Lodge Road B9
Lollard Street H3-I3-I2
Lombard Street K7-L7
London Bridge L5-L6
London Road J2-J3
London Wall K8-L8-L7
Long Acre G6-G7-H7
Longford Street E9
Long Lane J8
Long Lane K4-L4
Lorrimore Road J1
Lower Belgrave Street E3
Lower Marsh I4
Lower Sloane Street D2
Lower Thames Street L6
Lowndes Square D4
Lowndes Street D3
Ludgate Hill J7
Luke Street L9
Lupus Street E1-F1
Lyall Street D3
Maddox Street E6-E7
Maida Avenue A8
Maiden Lane G6-H6
Malet Street F9-G9-G8
Manciple Street K4-L4
Manresa Road B1
Manor Place J1-J2-K2
Marchmont Street G9
Marcia Road L2
Margaret Street E7-F7
Markham Street C1-C2
Marshall Street F6-F7
Marshalsea Road K4-K5
Marsham Street G2-G3
Marylebone High Street D7-D8
Marylebone Lane D7-E7
Marylebone Road B8-C8-D8-D9-E9
Mecklenburgh Square H9
Medway Street G3
Melton Street F9
Merrow Street K1-L1-L2
Methley Street I1-I2
Milk Street K7
Millbank G2-G3
Millman Street H9
Mint Street J4
Monk Street G3
Monmouth Street G6-G7
Montague Place G8
Montford Place I1
Montague Street G8
Montagu Square C7
Montpelier Street C3-C4
Moorfields K8
Moore Street C2-C3
Moorgate K7-K8-L8
Morecambe Street K2
Moreton Place F2
Mortimer Street E7-F7-F8
Morley Street I4
Morpeth Terrace F3
Motcomb Street D3-D4
Mount Row E6
Munton Road K3
Museum Street G7-G8
Neal Street G7
New Bond Street E6-E7
New Bridge Street J6-J7
New Cavendish Street D8-E8-F8
New Change K7
Newcomen Street K5-L5
New Compton Street G7
Newgate Street J7
Newington Butts J2-J3
Newington Causeway J3-J4-K4
New Kent Road J3-K3-L3
Newman Street F7-F8
New Oxford Street G7-G8
Newton Street H7-H8
Nine Elms Lane G1
Norfolk Crescent B7-C7
Norfolk Square B7
North Carriage Drive B6-C6
North Gower Street F9
Northington Street H9-I9
Northumberland Avenue G5-H5
North Row D6
Old Bailey J7
Old Bond Street E6-F6-F5
Old Broad Street L7-L8
Old Brompton Road A1-A2-B2
Old Compton Street F6-G6-G7
Old Marylebone Road B7-C7-C8
Old Park Lane D5-E5
Old Pye Street F3-G3
Old Street J9-K9-L9
Olney Road J1-K1
Onslow Gardens A2-B2
Onslow Square B2
Oswin Street G3
Ontario Street J3-J4
Orb Street K2
Orchardson Street B8-B9
Orchard Street D7
Outer Circle C9-D9-D8-D9-E9
Oval Way H1-I1
Oxford Street D6-D7-E7-F7
Paddington Street D8
Page Street G3
Pages Walk L3
Palace Gate A3-A4
Palace Street E4-F4-F3
Pall Mall F5-G5
Pardoner Street L4
Paris Garden J5
Park Crescent E8-E9
Park Lane C6-D6-D5-D4
Park Road B9-C9
Park Street J5-J6
Parry Street G1-H1
Paul Street L9
Pavilion Road C4-C3-D3-D2
Pearman Street I4
Pelham Crescent B2
Pelham Street B2
Penfold Street B8
Penrose Street K1-J1-K1-K2
Penton Place J2-K2
Piccadilly E4-E5-F5-F6
Pilgrimage Street K4
Pimlico Road D2-E2
Pocock Street J4-J5
Poland Street F7
Pond Place B2
Ponsonby Place G2
Pont Street C3-D3
Porchester Terrace A6
Portland Place E8
Portland Street K2-K1-L1
Portman Square D7
Portman Street D6-D7
Portugal Street H7
Poultry K7
Praed Street A7-B7
Prince's Gardens B3-B4
Queens Gardens A6
Queen's Gate A3-A4
Queens Gate Gardens A3
Queen's Gate Terrace A3
Queen Square G8-G9-H9-H8
Queen Street K6-K7
Queen Victoria Street J7-J6-K6-K7
Radnor Walk C1
Randolph Avenue A8-A9
Rathbone Place F7-F8
Rawlings Street C2
Redburn Street C1
Redcross Way K5
Red Lion Street H8
Reeves Mews D6
Regency Street G2-G3
Regent Street E7-F7-F6-F5-G5
Renfrew Road J2-J3
Rivington Street L9
Rothsay Street L3-L4
Rochester Row F2-F3
Rockingham Street J3-K3
Rodney Road K3-K2-L2
Roland Gardens A1-A2
Romilly Street G6-G7
Rossmore Road B8-B9-C9
Roupell Street I5-J5
Royal Avenue C1-C2
Royal Hospital Road C1-D1-D2
Royal Street H4-I4
Rupert Street F6-G6
Russell Square G8-G9
Rutland Gate B4-B3-C3
St George's Drive E2-F2-F1
St Georges Road I4-I3-J3
St George's Square F1-G1
St George Street E6-E7
St Giles High Street G7
St James Square F5
St James's Street F5
St John Street J8-J9
St Leonard's Terrace C1-D1-D2
St Martin's Lane G6
St Mary Axe L7
St Michael's Street B7
St Thomas Street K5-L5
Saffron Hill I8-I9
Salisbury Street B8
Sancroft Street H2-I2
Savile Row E6-F6
Savoy Place H6
Scritton Street L9
Sekforde Street J9
Seymour Place C7-C8
Seymour Street C6-C7
Seymour Walk A1
Shaftesbury Avenue F6-G6-G7
Shelton Street G7
Shepherd Street E5
Shoe Lane I7-J7
Sidney Street B2-B1-C1
Silk Street K8
Skinner Street I9-J9
Sloane Avenue C2
Sloane Gardens D2
Sloane Street C4-C3-D3-D2
Smith Square G3
Smith Street C1
Snows Fields L5
Soho Square F7
Southampton Row G8
South Audley Street D5-D6
South Carriage Drive B4-C4-D4
South Eaton Place D2-D3
South Parade B1-B2
South Terrace B2-B3
Southwark Bridge K6
Southwark Bridge Road J3-J4-K4-K5
Southwark Street J5-K5
Stag Place F3-F4
Stamford Street I5-J5
Stanhope Gardens A2
Stanhope Terrace B6
Stannary Street I1
Star Street B7
Stead Street K2
Store Street F8-G8
Strand G5-G6-H6-H7
Stratton Street E5
Sturgeon Road J1
Sumner Place B2
Sumner Street J5-K5
Sun Street L8
Surrey Square L2
Sussex Gardens A6-B6-B7
Sussex Place B6-B7
Sussex Street E2-F2
Sutherland Street E1-E2
Sutherland Walk K1
Tabard Street K4-L4-L3
Tabernacle Street L9
Tachbrook Street F2
Tavistock Square G9
Tavistock Street H6-H7
Tedworth Square C1
Temple Avenue I6-I7
The Boltons A1-A2
The Cut I4-I5-J5
Theed Street I5
The Little Boltons A1
The Mall F4-F5-G5
Theobald's Road H8-I8
The Vale B1
Threadneedle Street K7-L7
Throgmorton Street K7-L7
Thurloe Place B2-B3
Thurloe Square B2-B3
Thurloe Street L1-L2
Tite Street C1-D1
Tooley Street L5
Torrington Place F8-F9-G9
Tottenham Court Road F9-F8-G8-G7
Trafalgar Square G5-G6
Tregunter Road A1
Trevor Place C4
Tufton Street G3
Tudor Street I7-J7
Trinity Street J4-K4
Turks Row D1-D2
Turnmill Street I9-I8-J8
Tyers Street H2
Ufford Street I4-J4
Union Street J5-K5
Upper Brook Street D6
Upper Grosvenor Street D6
Upper Ground I5-I6-J6
Upper Thames Street J6-K6-L6
Vauxhall Bridge G1-H1
Vauxhall Bridge Road E3-F3-F2-G2
Vauxhall Street H2-H1-I1
Vauxhall Walk H2
Vere Street E7
Victoria Embankment H5-H6-I6-J6
Victoria Road A3-A4
Victoria Street E3-F3-F4-G4
Vincent Square F2-F3
Vincent Street F2-G2
Walnut Tree Walk I3
Walton Street C2-C3
Walworth Road J3-K3-K2-K1
Wardour Street F6-F7
Warren Street E9-F9
Warrington Crescent A8-A9
Warwick Avenue A8
Warwick Square F2
Warwick Street F6
Warwick Way E2-F2
Waterloo Bridge H6-H5-I5
Waterloo Road I5-I4-J4
Watling Street K7
Webber Street I4-J4
Welbeck Street D8-D7-E7
Wells Street F7-F8
Westbourne Terrace A7-A6-B6
Westcott Road J1
Westminster Bridge H4
Westminster Bridge Road H4-I4-J4
Westmoreland Road K1-L1
Westmoreland Terrace E1
Weston Street F4-F5
West Square J3
Westway A7-A8-B8
Wetherby Gardens A2
Weymouth Street D8-E8
Whitcomb Street G6
Whitecross Street K8-K9
Whitefriars Street I7
Whitehall G4-G5-H5
Whitehall Place G5
Whiteheads Grove C2
Whitfield Street F8-F9
Wigmore Street D7-E7
Wild Street H7
Willow Place F2-F3
Wilson Street L8
Wilton Crescent D4
Wilton Place D4
Wilton Road E3-F3-F2
Wimpole Street D8-E8-E7
Winchester Street E2-E1-F1
Wincott Street I2
Woburn Place G9
Wood Street K7-K8
Woolers Street K2-L2-L1-K1
Worship Street L9
Yeomans Row C3
York Gate D9
York Road H4-H5-I5
York Street C8
York Terrace D8-D9

London

History, tradition, culture, commerce, grandeur and beauty are just a few of the ingredients that make up England's magical capital. London's history begins in the 1st century when the Romans bridged the Thames in order to reach Colchester. An important city rapidly developed and right up until the 16th century London stayed more or less within the limits of the original Roman walls. However, from the 1600s onwards the city grew at an amazing rate, and even the Great Fire of 1666 – to which we owe the creation of the present St Paul's Cathedral and many other churches designed by Wren – did not halt expansion. The Thames winds through the heart of London and along its banks stand some of the city's most famous landmarks. Just by Westminster Bridge are the

Houses of Parliament, easily distinguished by the clock-tower affectionately known the world over as Big Ben. Originally Westminster Palace, Charles Barry designed the present Gothic building, and much of its lavish decoration is the work of Augustus Pugin. Downstream, past the new complex of buildings including the Festival Hall and the National Theatre, is St Paul's Cathedral. Despite surrounding office blocks, the majesty of its enormous dome is not diminished. Next comes Tower Bridge and the Tower of London which, in its time, has been royal residence, prison, stronghold and place of execution.

However, London is not by any means all grand and famous buildings. Another of its many facets is its variety of shops. These range from the luxurious, prestigious Knightsbridge stores, led by Harrods, to the dozens of street markets, each with their own unique character. Covent Garden, Billingsgate, Smithfield and Petticoat Lane have

become household names, but traders sell their wares throughout the city, and specialist shops steeped in tradition cater for individual tastes.

Yet another contrasting aspect of London is its parks and gardens. Best-known of these are the Royal parks. St James's, Green Park, Regent's Park – home of the London Zoo – and Hyde Park are all welcome havens from the busy streets. Past kings and queens were responsible for these green spaces and, in turn, their palaces add grace and splendour to the city. Buckingham Palace with its daily Changing of the Guard – just one of the ceremonies that flourish in London – takes pride of place, but St James's Palace and Kensington Palace deserve no less attention.

No account of London is complete without mentioning its superb theatres, concert halls, galleries and museums. As a cultural centre the capital plays host to the world's greatest performers and gives space to some of its greatest treasures.

Theatres, Concert Halls and Cinemas
A Guide to Entertainments in the Centre of London

THEATRES AND CONCERT HALLS

1 **Adelphi**, The Strand, WC2. Tel: 836 7611
2 **Albery**, St Martin's Lane, WC2. Tel: 836 3878
3 **Aldwych**, Aldwych, WC2. Tel: 836 6404
4 **Ambassadors**, West Street, WC2. Tel: 836 1171
5 **Apollo**, Shaftesbury Avenue, W1. Tel: 437 2663
6 **Apollo** (Victoria), Wilton Road, SW1. Tel: 828 8665 (Not on plan)
7 **Arts** (Theatre Club), Gt Newport Street, WC2 Tel: 836 3334
8 **Astoria**, Charing Cross Road, WC2. Tel: 734 4291
9 **Barbican Centre**, Silk Street, EC2. Tel: 628 8795 (Not on plan)
10 **Cambridge**, Earlham Street, WC2. Tel: 836 6056
11 **Coliseum**, St Martin's Lane, WC2. Tel: 836 3161
12 **Comedy**, Panton Street, SW1. Tel: 830 2578
13 **Criterion**, Piccadilly, W1. Tel: 9303216
14 **Drury Lane**, Theatre Royal, Catherine Street, WC2. Tel: 836 8108
15 **Duchess**, Catherine Street, WC2. Tel: 836 8243
16 **Duke of York's**, St Martin's Lane, WC2. Tel: 836 5122
17 **Fortune**, Russell Street, WC2. Tel: 836 2238
18 **Garrick**, Charing Cross Road, WC2. Tel: 836 4601
19 **Globe**, Shaftesbury Avenue, W1. Tel: 437 1592
20 **Haymarket**, Theatre Royal, Haymarket, SW1. Tel: 930 9832
21 **Her Majesty's**, Haymarket, SW1. Tel: 930 6606
22 **Jeanetta Cochrane**, Theobalds Road, WC1. Tel: 242 7040.
23 **Lyric**, Shaftesbury Avenue, W1. Tel: 437 3686
24 **Mayfair**, Berkeley Street, W1. Tel: 629 3036

25 **Mermaid**, Puddle Dock, EC4. Tel: 236 5568 (Not on plan)
26 **National Theatre**, South Bank, SE1. Tel: 928 2252
27 **New London**, Parker Street, WC2. Tel: 405 0072
28 **Old Vic**, Waterloo Road, SE1. Tel: 928 7616
29 **Palace**, Shaftesbury Avenue, W1. Tel: 437 6834
30 **Palladium**, Argyll Street, W1. Tel: 437 7373.
31 **Phoenix**, Charing Cross Road, WC2. Tel: 836 2294
32 **Piccadilly**, Denman Street, W1. Tel: 437 4506
33 **Prince Edward**, Old Compton Street, W1. Tel: 930 6877
34 **Prince of Wales**, Coventry Street, W1. Tel: 930 8681
35 **Queen Elizabeth Hall**, South Bank, SE1. Tel: 928 3191
36 **Queen's**, Shaftesbury Avenue, W1. Tel: 734 1166
37 **Royal Court**, Sloane Square, SW1. Tel: 730 1745 (Not on plan)
38 **Royal Festival Hall**, South Bank, SE1. Tel: 928 3191
39 **Royal Opera House**, Covent Garden, WC2. Tel: 240 1066
40 **Royalty**, Portugal Street, WC2. Tel: 405 8004
41 **St Martin's**, West Street, WC2. Tel: 836 1443
42 **Sadler's Wells**, Roseberry Avenue, EC1. Tel: 278 8916 (Not on plan)
43 **Savoy**, Strand, WC2. Tel: 836 8888
44 **Shaftesbury**, Shaftesbury Avenue, WC2. Tel: 836 6596
45 **Strand**, Aldwych, WC2. Tel: 836 2660
46 **Vanbrugh**, Malet Street, WC1. Tel: 580 7982 (Not on plan)
47 **Vaudeville**, Strand, WC2. Tel: 836 9988
48 **Victoria Palace**, Victoria Street, SW1. Tel: 834 1317 (Not on plan)

49 **Warehouse**, (Donmar), Earlham Street, WC2. Tel: 836 1071
50 **Westminster**, Palace Street, SW1. Tel: 834 0283 (Not on plan)
51 **Whitehall**, Whitehall, SW1. Tel: 930 7765
52 **Wigmore Hall**, Wigmore Street, W1. Tel: 935 2141
53 **Wyndhams**, Charing Cross Road, WC2. Tel: 836 3028.
54 **Young Vic**, The Cut, SE1. Tel: 928 6363

CINEMAS

1 **ABC 1 & 2**, Shaftesbury Avenue, WC2. Tel: 836 8861
2 **Acadamy 1, 2 & 3**, Oxford Street, W1. Tel: 437 2981
3 **Biograph**, Wilton Road, SW1. Tel: 834 1624 (Not on plan)
4 **Cinecenta**, Panton Street, SW1. Tel: 930 0631
5 **Cinecenta**, Piccadilly, W1. Tel: 437 3561
6 **Classic**, Charing Cross Road, WC2. Tel: 930 6915
7 **Classic Complex**, Haymarket, SW1. Tel: 839 1527
8 **Classic, 1, 2, 3, 4 & 5**, Oxford Street, W1 Tel: 636 0310
9 **Classic**, Shaftesbury Avenue, W1. Tel: 734 5414
10 **Classic Complex**, Tottenham Court Road, W1 Tel: 636 6148
11 **Curzon**, Curzon Street, W1. Tel: 499 3737
12 **Dominion**, Tottenham Court Road, W1. Tel: 580 9562
13 **Empire**, Leicester Square, WC2. Tel: 437 1234
14 **Eros**, Piccadilly Circus, W1. Tel: 437 3839
15 **Filmcenta**, Charing Cross Road, WC2. Tel: 437 4815
16 **Gate 2**, Brunswick Square, WC1. Tel: 837 8402 (Not on plan)
17 **Gate, Mayfair**, Mayfair Hotel, Stratton Street, W1 Tel: 493 2031

18 **Institution of Contemporary Arts**, Carlton House Terrace, SW1. Tel: 930 6393
19 **Leicester Square Theatre**, Leicester Square, WC2 Tel: 930 5252
20 **Lumiere**, St Martin's Lane, WC2. Tel: 836 0691
21 **Minema**, Knightsbridge, SW. Tel: 235 6225 (Not on plan)
22 **Moulin Cinema Complex**, Gt Windmill Street, W1 Tel: 437 1653
23 **National Film Theatre**, South Bank, SE1. Tel: 928 3232
24 **Odeon**, Haymarket, SW1. Tel: 930 2738
25 **Odeon**, Leicester Square. WC2. Tel: 930 6111
26 **Odeon**, Marble Arch, W2. Tel: 723 2011 (Not on plan)
27 **Plaza, 1, 2, 3 & 4**, Regent Street, W1. Tel: 437 1234
28 **Prince Charles**, Leicester Place, WC2. Tel: 437 8181
29 **Scene, 1, 2, 3 & 4**, Swiss Centre, Leicester Square, WC2 Tel: 439 4470
30 **Sherlock Holmes Centa**, Baker Street, W1 Tel: 935 2772
31 **Studio 1, 2, 3 & 4**, Oxford Street, W1. Tel: 437 3300
32 **Times Centa 1 & 2**, Chiltern Court, Baker Street, NW1. Tel: 935 9772
33 **Warner West End, 1, 2, 3 & 4**, Cranbourn Street, WC2 Tel: 439 0791

Key

Parking	P
One Way Street	
Cinema	●
Theatre	●
Underground	⊖

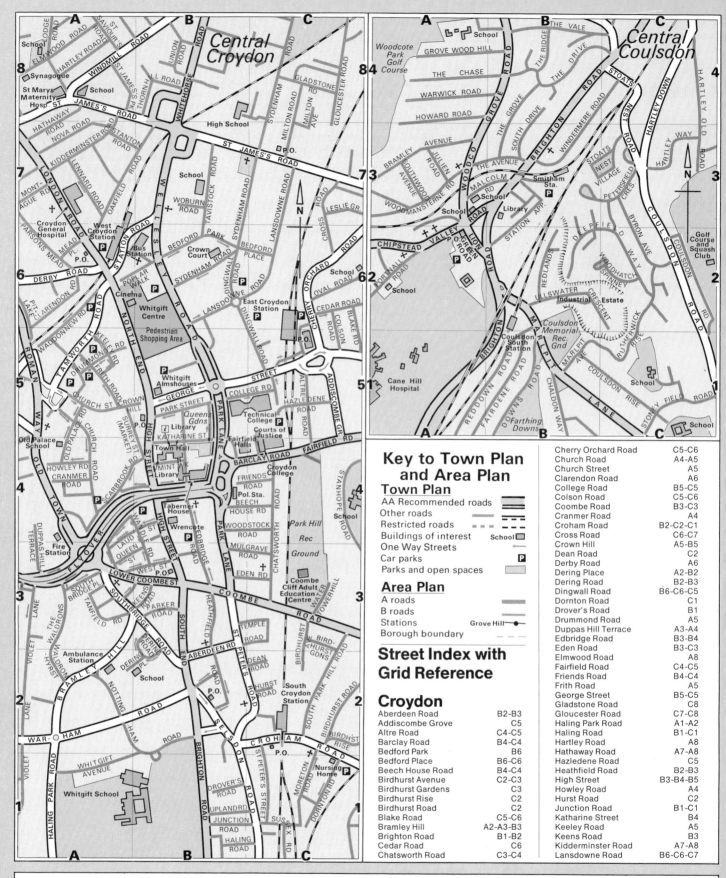

Key to Town Plan and Area Plan

Town Plan

AA Recommended roads	▬▬▬
Other roads	═══
Restricted roads	▬ ▬ ▬
Buildings of interest	School
One Way Streets	←
Car parks	P
Parks and open spaces	▨

Area Plan

A roads	▬▬
B roads	▬▬
Stations	Grove Hill ●━
Borough boundary	▬ ▬ ▬

Street Index with Grid Reference

Croydon

Aberdeen Road	B2-B3
Addiscombe Grove	C5
Altre Road	C4-C5
Barclay Road	B4-C4
Bedford Park	B6
Bedford Place	B6-C6
Beech House Road	B4-C4
Birdhurst Avenue	C2-C3
Birdhurst Gardens	C3
Birdhurst Rise	C2
Birdhurst Road	C2
Blake Road	C5-C6
Bramley Hill	A2-A3-B3
Brighton Road	B1-B2
Cedar Road	C6
Chatsworth Road	C3-C4
Cherry Orchard Road	C5-C6
Church Road	A4-A5
Church Street	A5
Clarendon Road	A6
College Road	B5-C5
Colson Road	C5-C6
Coombe Road	B3-C3
Cranmer Road	A4
Croham Road	B2-C2-C1
Cross Road	C6-C7
Crown Hill	A5-B5
Dean Road	C2
Derby Road	A6
Dering Place	A2-B2
Dering Road	B2-B3
Dingwall Road	B6-C6-C5
Dornton Road	C1
Drover's Road	B1
Drummond Road	A5
Duppas Hill Terrace	A3-A4
Edbridge Road	B3-B4
Eden Road	B3-C3
Elmwood Road	A8
Fairfield Road	C4-C5
Friends Road	B4-C4
Frith Road	A5
George Street	B5-C5
Gladstone Road	C8
Gloucester Road	C7-C8
Haling Park Road	A1-A2
Haling Road	B1-C1
Hartley Road	A8
Hathaway Road	A7-A8
Hazledene Road	C5
Heathfield Road	B2-B3
High Street	B3-B4-B5
Howley Road	A4
Hurst Road	C2
Junction Road	B1-C1
Katharine Street	B4
Keeley Road	A5
Keens Road	B3
Kidderminster Road	A7-A8
Lansdowne Road	B6-C6-C7

Croydon

Lofty office blocks piercing the south London skyline, one of the largest shopping centres in south-east England and modern developments like the Whitgift Centre and Fairfields Hall (an arts and exhibitions complex containing the Ashcroft Theatre) characterise modern Croydon — but it still has numerous features recalling its prosperity in earlier times. The Archbishops'
Palace (now a girls' school) was occupied by the Archbishops of Canterbury until the 18th century. The oldest shop in the town can be seen in South End, a 16th- to 17th-century building with an overhanging upper storey. Wrencote, in the High Street, is a fine example of an 18th-century town house. Other places of interest include the 16th-century Whitgift Hospital (an almshouse) the Flemish style 19th-century Town Hall, and the Parish Church of St John the Baptist, rebuilt in
1867 — after a fire — by Sir Gilbert Scott, in the original 15th-century style.

Purley grew rapidly after the end of the 18th century. There are good shopping facilities and the Village Green on the Webb Estate has been designated a conservation area.

Coulsdon Beautiful Farthing Downs and Happy Valley (where nature trails can be followed) lie close by. The Church of St John the Evangelist is a fine example of 13th-century architecture.

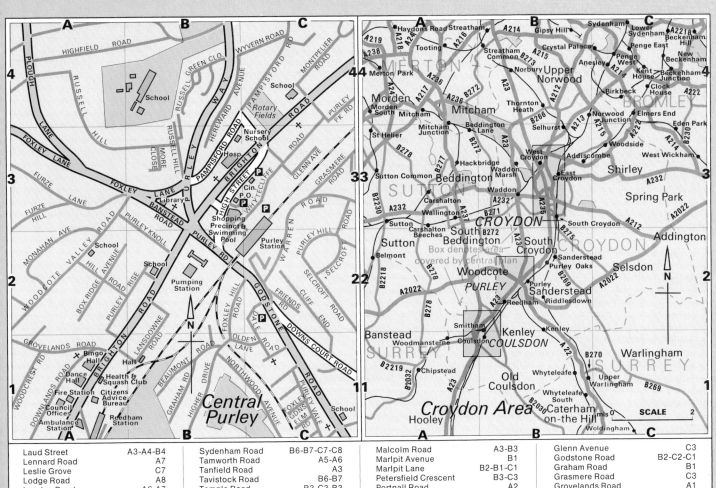

Laud Street	A3-A4-B4	Sydenham Road	B6-B7-C7-C8
Lennard Road	A7	Tamworth Road	A5-A6
Leslie Grove	C7	Tanfield Road	A3
Lodge Road	A8	Tavistock Road	B6-B7
London Road	A6-A7	Temple Road	B3-C3-B3
Lower Coombe Street	A3-B3	The Waldrons	A3
Mead Place	A6	Thornhill Road	B8
Milton Avenue	C7-C8	Union Road	B8
Milton Road	C7-C8	Upland Road	B1-C1
Mint Walk	B4	Violet Lane	A1-A2-A3
Montague Road	A7	Waddon New Road	A5-A6
Moreton Road	C1-C2	Waldronhyst	A2
Mulgrave Road	B3-C3	Wandle Road	A4-B4-B3
North End	A6-A5-B5	Warham Road	A2-B2
Nottingham Road	A2-B2	Water Tower Hill	C3
Nova Road	A7	Wellesley Road	B5-B6-B7
Oakfield Road	A6-A7-B7	West Street	A3-B3
Old Palace Road	A4-A5	Windmill Road	A8-B8-B3
Old Town	A3-A4	Whitehorse Road	B7-B8
Oval Road	C6	Whitgift Avenue	A1-B1-B2
Park Lane	B3-B4-B5	Woburn Road	B7
Park Street	B5	Woodstock Road	B4-C4
Parker Road	B3		
Parsons Mead	A6-A7	**Coulsdon**	
Pitlake	A6	Bramley Avenue	A3
Poplar Walk	A6-B6	Brighton Road	
Queen Street	A3-B3		A1-B1-B2-A2-A3-B3-B4-C4
Roman Way	A5-A6	Byron Avenue	C2-C3
St James's Park	A8	Chaldon Way	A3
St James's Walk	A7-A8-B8-B7-C7	Chipstead Valley Road	A2-A3-B3
St Peter's Road	B3-B2-C2-B2	Coulsdon Court Road	C1-C2
St Peter's Street	C1-C2	Coulsdon Rise	B1-C1
St Saviour's Road	A8	Coulsdon Road	C1-C2-C3
Selsdon Road	B2-B1-C1	Deepfield Way	B2-C2
Scarbrook Road	A4-B4	Downs Road	B1
South Bridge Place	A3	Fairdene Road	A1-B1
South Bridge Road	A3-B3-B2	Grove Wood Hill	A4-B4
South End	B2-B3	Hartley Down	C3-C4
South Park Hill Road	C2-C3	Hartley Old Road	C3-C4
Stanhope Road	C3-C4	Hartley Way	C3
Stanton Road	A7-B7	Howard Road	A3-A4
Station Road	A6-B6-B7	Julien Road	A3
Surrey Street	A5-B5-B4	Lion Green Road	A2
Sussex Road	C1		

Malcolm Road	A3-B3	Glenn Avenue	C3
Marlpit Avenue	B1	Godstone Road	B2-C2-C1
Marlpit Lane	B2-B1-C1	Graham Road	B1
Petersfield Crescent	B3-C3	Grasmere Road	C3
Portnall Road	A2	Grovelands Road	A1
Reddown Road	A1-B1-B2	Hereward Avenue	B3-B4
Redlands	B2	High Street	B2-B3-C3
Rutherwick Rise	C1-C2	Higher Drive	B1
South Drive	B3-B4	Highfield Road	A4-B4
Southwood Avenue	A3	Hill Road	A2
Station Approach	B2-B3	Lansdowne Road	A1-B1-B2
Stoats Nest Road	C3-C4	Monahan Avenue	A2-A3-A2
Stoats Nest Village	B3-C3	Montpelier Road	C4
Stoney Field Road	C1	More Close	B3
The Avenue	A3-B3	Northwood Avenue	B1-C1
The Chase	A4-B4	Olden Lane	B1-C1
The Drive	B4-C4	Pampisford Road	B3-B4-C4
The Grove	B3-B4	Plough Lane	A3-A4
The Ridge	B4	Purley Hill	C2
The Vale	B4-C4	Purley Knoll	A3-B3-B2
Ullswater Crescent	B2-C2	Purley Park Road	C4
Warwick Road	A4-B4	Purley Rise	A1-A2-B2
Windermere Road	B3-B4-C4	Purley Road	B2
Woodcote Grove Road	A3-A4-B4	Purley Vale	C1
Woodhatch Spinney	B2-C2	Purley Way	B3-B4
Woodmansterne Road	A3	Russell Green Close	B4
		Russell Hill	A4-A3-B3-B4
Purley		Selcroft Road	C2-C3
Banstead Road	B3	Warren Road	C2-C3
Beaumont Road	B1	Whytecliffe Road	B2-B3-C3-C4
Box Ridge Avenue	A2	Woodcote Valley Road	A2-A3-B3
Brighton Road	A1-A2-B2-B3-C3-C4	Woodcrest Road	A1
Cliff End	C1-C2	Wyvern Road	B4-C4
Dale Road	C1-C2		
Downlands Road	A1		
Downs Court Road	C1-C2		
Elm Road	C1		
Foxley Gardens	C1		
Foxley Hill Road	B1-B2-C2		
Foxley Lane	A3-B3		
Friends Road	C2		
Furze Hill	A3		
Furze Lane	A3		

CROYDON
Beyond the gleaming blue glass of St Crispins House, the extensive Fairfield Halls complex offers concerts for music-lovers, with drama at the Ashcroft Theatre and exhibitions at the Arnhem Gallery.

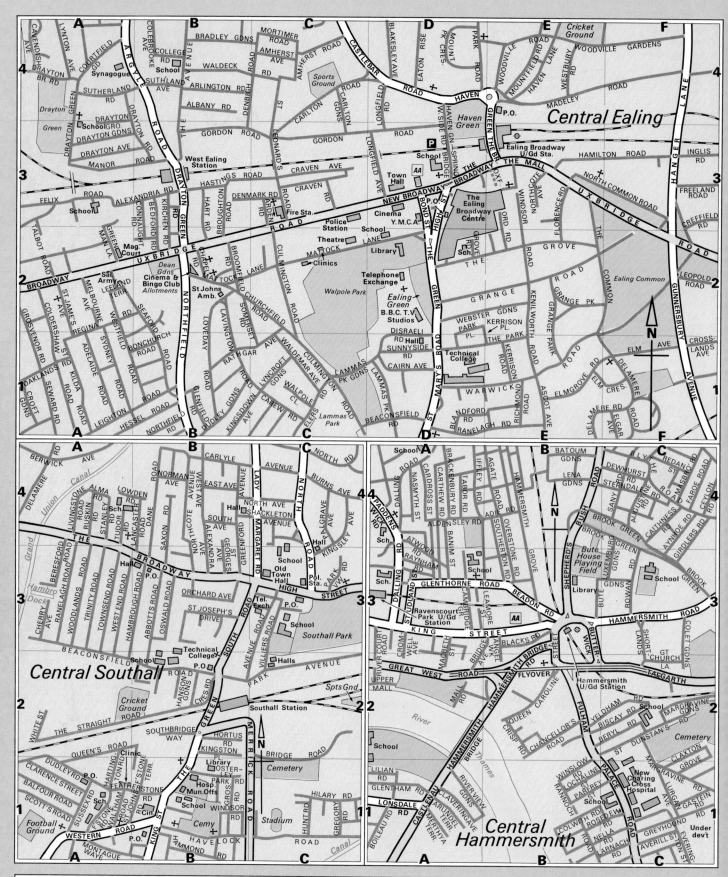

Ealing

The Ealing Comedies, cinema classics of the 1940s and 1950s were made in studios overlooking Ealing Green — studios which have now been taken over by the BBC for the production of television films. Ealing is a pleasantly leafy London suburb. Fine shopping facilities can be found in the Broadway area and buildings of interest include the fine Victorian Town Hall, and the former Pitshanger Manor, in Walpole Park, which has become the central library.

Southall has been known for its cattle market since the late 17th century, and this still takes place every Wednesday, close to the High Street. In recent years the Southall area has become the home of numerous Commonwealth immigrants, and it now has a distinctive Asian character of its own, particularly in the main Broadway shopping area. Southall Manor, standing on the Green, dates originally from the 16th century.

Hammersmith is seen by most of those who pass through as a vista of roof tops — the view from the flyover built to ease congestion where traffic from the Great West Road and Hammersmith Bridge meet with the many vehicles entering and leaving Central London. Hammersmith is also the site of the Lyric Theatre, known for its pre-West End productions; the BBC TV Studios lie a short distance to the north.

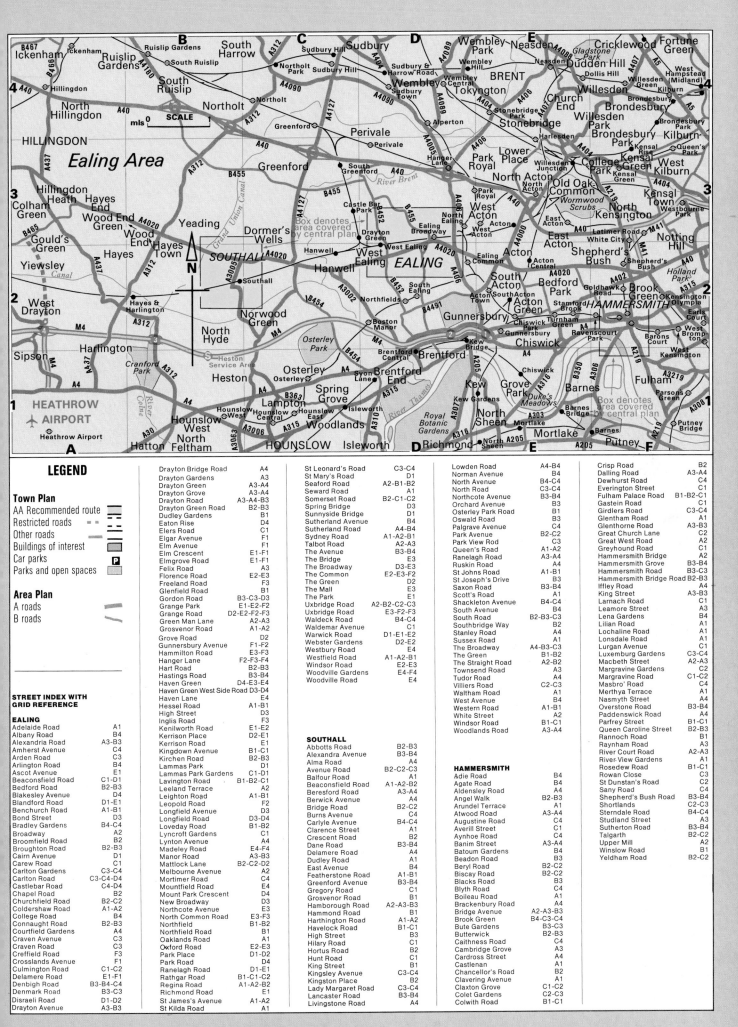

LEGEND

Town Plan

AA Recommended route
Restricted roads
Other roads
Buildings of interest
Car parks
Parks and open spaces

Area Plan

A roads
B roads

STREET INDEX WITH GRID REFERENCE

EALING

Adelaide Road	A1
Albany Road	B4
Alexandria Road	A3-B3
Amherst Avenue	C4
Arden Road	C3
Arlington Road	B4
Ascot Avenue	E1
Beaconsfield Road	C1-D1
Bedford Road	B2-B3
Blakesley Avenue	D4
Blandford Road	D1-E1
Benchurch Road	A1-B1
Bond Street	D3
Bradley Gardens	B4-C4
Broadway	A2
Broomfield Road	B2
Broughton Road	B2-B3
Cairn Avenue	D1
Carew Road	C1
Carlton Gardens	C3-C4
Carlton Road	C3-C4-D4
Castlebar Road	C4-D4
Chapel Road	B2
Churchfield Road	B2-C2
Coldershaw Road	A1-A2
College Road	B4
Connaught Road	B2-B3
Courtfield Gardens	A4
Craven Avenue	C3
Craven Road	C3
Creffield Road	F3
Crosslands Avenue	F1
Culmington Road	C1-C2
Delamere Road	E1-F1
Denbigh Road	B3-B4-C4
Denmark Road	B3-C3
Disraeli Road	D1-D2
Drayton Avenue	A3-B3

Drayton Bridge Road	A4
Drayton Gardens	A3
Drayton Green	A3-A4
Drayton Grove	A3-A4
Drayton Road	A3-A4-B3
Drayton Green Road	B2-B3
Dudley Gardens	B1
Eaton Rise	D4
Elers Road	C1
Elgar Avenue	F1
Elm Avenue	F1
Elm Crescent	E1-F1
Elmgrove Road	E1-F1
Felix Road	A3
Florence Road	E2-E3
Freeland Road	F3
Glenfield Road	B1
Gordon Road	B3-C3-D3
Grange Park	E1-E2-F2
Grange Road	D2-E2-F2-F3
Green Man Lane	A2-A3
Grosvenor Road	A1-A2
Grove Road	D2
Gunnersbury Avenue	F1-F2
Hammilton Road	E3-F3
Hanger Lane	F2-F3-F4
Hart Road	B2-B3
Hastings Road	B3-B4
Haven Green	D4-E3-E4
Haven Green West Side Road	D3-D4
Haven Lane	E4
Hessel Road	A1-B1
High Street	D3
Inglis Road	F3
Kenilworth Road	E1-E2
Kerrison Place	D2-E1
Kerrison Road	E1
Kingdown Avenue	B1-C1
Kirchen Road	B2-B3
Lammas Park	D1
Lammas Park Gardens	C1-D1
Lavington Road	B1-B2-C1
Leeland Terrace	A2
Leighton Road	A1-B1
Leopold Road	F2
Longfield Avenue	D3
Longfield Road	D3-D4
Loveday Road	B1-B2
Lyncroft Gardens	C1
Lynton Avenue	A4
Madeley Road	E4-F4
Manor Road	A3-B3
Mattlock Lane	B2-C2-D2
Melbourne Avenue	A2
Mortimer Road	C4
Mountfield Road	E4
Mount Park Crescent	D4
New Broadway	D3
Northcote Avenue	E3
North Common Road	E3-F3
Northfield	B1-B2
Northfield Road	B1
Oaklands Road	A1
Oxford Road	E2-E3
Park Place	D1-D2
Park Road	D4
Ranelagh Road	D1-E1
Rathgar Road	B1-C1-C2
Regina Road	A1-A2-B2
Richmond Road	E1
St James's Avenue	A1-A2
St Kilda Road	A1

St Leonard's Road	C3-C4
St Mary's Road	D1
Seaford Road	A2-B1-B2
Seward Road	A1
Somerset Road	B2-C1-C2
Spring Bridge	D3
Sunnyside Bridge	D1
Sutherland Avenue	B4
Sutherland Road	A4-B4
Sydney Road	A1-A2-B1
Talbot Road	A2-A3
The Avenue	B3-B4
The Bridge	E3
The Broadway	D3-E3
The Common	E2-E3-F2
The Green	D2
The Mall	E3
The Park	E1
Uxbridge Road	A2-B2-C2-C3
Uxbridge Road	E3-F2-F3
Waldeck Road	B4-C4
Waldemar Avenue	C1
Warwick Road	D1-E1-E2
Webster Gardens	D2-E2
Westbury Road	E4
Westfield Road	A1-A2-B1
Windsor Road	E2-E3
Woodville Gardens	E4-F4
Woodville Road	E4

SOUTHALL

Abbotts Road	B2-B3
Alexandra Avenue	B3-B4
Alma Road	A4
Avenue Road	B2-C2-C3
Balfour Road	A1
Beaconsfield Road	A1-A2-B2
Beresford Road	A3-A4
Berwick Avenue	A4
Bridge Road	B2-C2
Burns Avenue	C4
Carlyle Avenue	B4-C4
Clarence Street	A1
Crescent Road	B2
Dane Road	B3-B4
Delamere Road	A4
Dudley Road	A1
East Avenue	B4
Featherstone Road	A1-B1
Greenford Avenue	B3-B4
Gregory Road	C1
Grosvenor Road	B1
Hamborough Road	A2-A3-B3
Hammond Road	B1
Harthington Road	A1-A2
Havelock Road	B1-C1
High Street	B3
Hilary Road	C1
Hortus Road	B2
Hunt Road	C1
King Street	B1
Kingsley Avenue	C3-C4
Kingston Place	B2
Lady Margaret Road	C3-C4
Lancaster Road	B3-B4
Livingstone Road	A4

Lowden Road	A4-B4
Norman Avenue	B4
North Avenue	B4-C4
North Road	C3-C4
Northcote Avenue	B3-B4
Orchard Avenue	B3
Osterley Park Road	B1
Oswald Road	B3
Palgrave Avenue	C4
Park Avenue	B2-C2
Park View Rod	C3
Queen's Road	A1-A2
Ranelagh Road	A3-A4
Ruskin Road	A4
St Johns Road	A1-B1
St Joseph's Drive	B3
Saxon Road	B3-B4
Scott's Road	A1
Shackleton Avenue	B4-C4
South Avenue	C4
South Road	B2-B3-C3
Southbridge Way	A4
Stanley Road	A4
Sussex Road	A1
The Broadway	A4-B3-C3
The Green	B1-B2
The Straight Road	A2-B2
Townsend Road	A3
Tudor Road	A4
Villiers Road	C2-C3
Waltham Road	A1
West Avenue	B4
Western Road	A1-B1
White Street	A2
Windsor Road	B1-C1
Woodlands Road	A3-A4

HAMMERSMITH

Adie Road	B4
Agate Road	B4
Aldensley Road	B4
Angel Walk	B2-B3
Arundel Terrace	A1
Atwood Road	A3-A4
Augustine Road	C1
Aynhoe Road	A4
Averill Street	C1
Banim Street	A3-A4
Batoum Gardens	B4
Beadon Road	B3
Beryl Road	B2-C2
Biscay Road	B2-C2
Blacks Road	B3
Blyth Road	C4
Boileau Road	A1
Brackenbury Road	A4
Bridge Avenue	A2-A3-B3
Brook Green	B4-C3-C4
Bute Gardens	B3-C3
Butterwick	B2-B3
Caithness Road	C4
Cambridge Grove	A3
Cardross Street	A4
Castlenan	A1
Chancellor's Road	B2
Clavering Avenue	A1
Claxton Grove	C1-C2
Colet Gardens	C2-C3
Colwith Road	B1-C1

Crisp Road	B2
Dalling Road	A3-A4
Dewhurst Road	C1
Everington Street	C1
Fulham Palace Road	B1-B2-C1
Gastein Road	C1
Girdlers Road	C3-C4
Glentham Road	A1
Glenthorne Road	A3-B3
Great Church Lane	C2
Great West Road	C1
Greyhound Road	C1
Hammersmith Bridge	A2
Hammersmith Grove	B3-B4
Hammersmith Road	B3-C3
Hammersmith Bridge Road	B2-B3
Iffley Road	A4
King Street	A3-B3
Larnach Road	C1
Leamore Street	A3
Lena Gardens	B4
Lilian Road	A1
Lochaline Road	A1
Lonsdale Road	A1
Lurgan Avenue	C1
Luxemburg Gardens	C3-C4
Macbeth Street	A2-A3
Margravine Gardens	C4
Margravine Road	C1-C2
Masbro' Road	C4
Merthya Terrace	A1
Nasmyth Street	A4
Overstone Road	B3-B4
Paddenswick Road	A4
Parfrey Street	B1-C1
Queen Caroline Street	B2-B3
Rannoch Road	B1
Raynham Road	A3
River Court Road	A2-A3
River.View Gardens	A1
Rosedew Road	B1-C1
Rowan Close	C3
St Dunstan's Road	C2
Sany Road	C4
Shepherd's Bush Road	B3-B4
Shortlands	C2-C3
Sterndale Road	B4-C4
Studland Street	A3
Sutherton Road	B3-B4
Talgarth	B2-C2
Upper Mill	A2
Winslow Road	B1
Yeldham Road	B2-C2

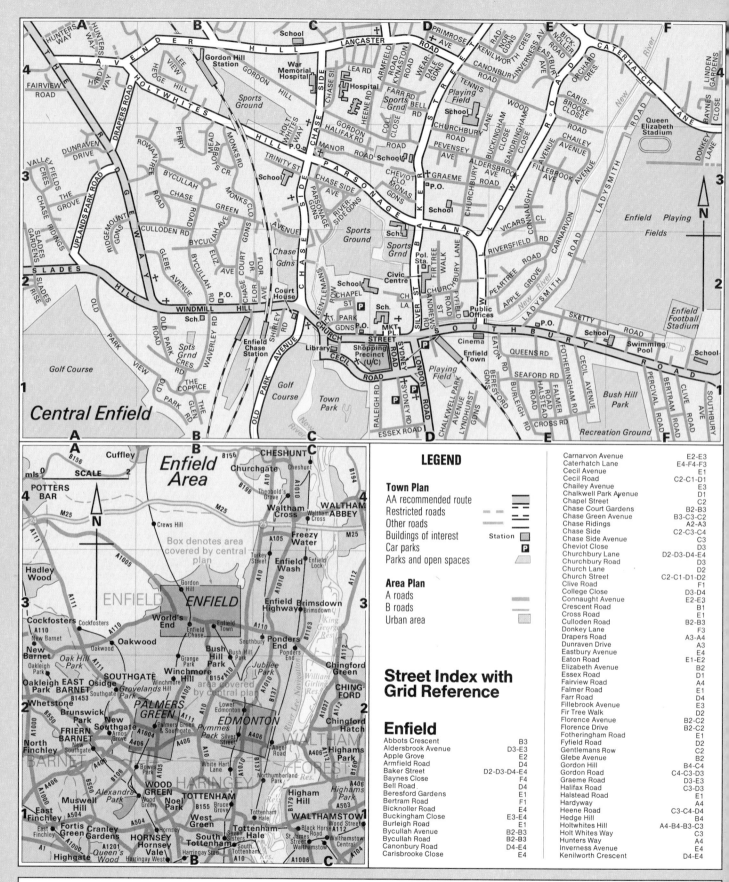

Central Enfield

Enfield Area

LEGEND

Town Plan

AA recommended route	
Restricted roads	
Other roads	
Buildings of interest	Station ▦
Car parks	🅿
Parks and open spaces	

Area Plan

A roads	
B roads	
Urban area	

Street Index with Grid Reference

Enfield

Abbots Crescent	B3
Aldersbrook Avenue	D3-E3
Apple Grove	E2
Armfield Road	D4
Baker Street	D2-D3-D4-E4
Baynes Close	F4
Bell Road	D4
Beresford Gardens	E1
Bertram Road	F1
Bicknoller Road	E4
Buckingham Close	E3-E4
Burleigh Road	E1
Bycullah Avenue	B2-B3
Bycullah Road	B2-B3
Canonbury Road	D4-E4
Carisbrooke Close	E4

Carnarvon Avenue	E2-E3
Caterhatch Lane	E4-F4-F3
Cecil Avenue	E1
Cecil Road	C2-C1-D1
Chailey Avenue	E3
Chalkwell Park Avenue	D1
Chapel Street	C2
Chase Court Gardens	B2-B3
Chase Green Avenue	B3-C3-C2
Chase Ridings	A2-A3
Chase Side	C2-C3-C4
Chase Side Avenue	C3
Cheviot Close	D3
Churchbury Lane	D2-D3-D4-E4
Churchbury Road	D3
Church Lane	D2
Church Street	C2-C1-D1-D2
Clive Road	F1
College Close	D3-D4
Connaught Avenue	E2-E3
Crescent Road	B1
Cross Road	E1
Culloden Road	B2-B3
Donkey Lane	F3
Drapers Road	A3-A4
Dunraven Drive	A3
Eastbury Avenue	E4
Eaton Road	E1-E2
Elizabeth Avenue	B2
Essex Road	D1
Fairview Road	A4
Falmer Road	E1
Farr Road	D4
Fillebrook Avenue	E3
Fir Tree Walk	D2
Florence Avenue	B2-C2
Florence Drive	B2-C2
Fotheringham Road	E1
Fyfield Road	D2
Gentlemans Row	C2
Glebe Avenue	B2
Gordon Hill	B4-C4
Gordon Road	C4-C3-D3
Graeme Road	D3-E3
Halifax Road	C3-D3
Halstead Road	E1
Hardyway	A4
Heene Road	C3-C4-D4
Hedge Hill	B4
Holtwhites Hill	A4-B4-B3-C3
Holt Whites Way	C3
Hunters Way	A4
Inverness Avenue	E4
Kenilworth Crescent	D4-E4

Enfield

Built in the 17th century to bring fresh water from Hertford to London, the attractive New River waterway still winds through the centre of Enfield, separating the Town Park from the Golf Course. Although this residential town on the edge of the Green Belt saw a good deal of expansion when the railways arrived in the 19th century, much of the older part has survived.

Near the 12th- to 14th-century parish church are Holly Walk and Gentleman's Row, which has a number of picturesque old cottages, including one where 19th-century essayist Charles Lamb would often stay with his sister Mary. They later rented a house close by in Chase Side.

Forty Hall, at nearby Forty Hill, dates from the 17th century and has a local history museum.

Edmonton's parish church has some Norman features, and Charles Lamb is buried in the churchyard. Edmonton itself is a residential area with modern shopping facilities centred around the open air market and pedestrian precinct at Edmonton Green.

Palmers Green became a fashionable residential suburb during the early part of the present century, and is the home of the Intimate Theatre, which stages many pre-West End productions. The attractive Broomfield Park (being restored) contains a museum of local history.

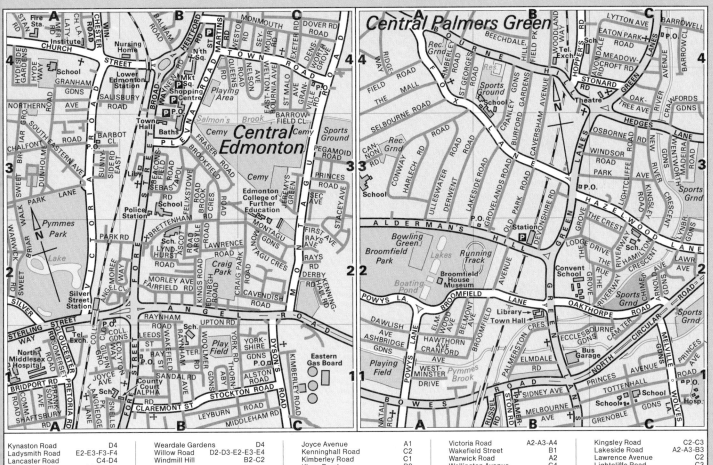

Central Edmonton

Central Palmers Green

Kynaston Road	D4
Ladysmith Road	E2-E3-F3-F4
Lancaster Road	C4-D4
Lavender Hill	A4-B4-C4
Lea Road	C4-D4
Lee View	B4
Linden Gardens	F4
Little Park Gardens	C2
London Road	D1
Lyndhurst Gardens	D1
Manor Road	C3-D3
Monastry Gardens	D3
Monks Close	B3-C3
Monks Road	B3
Old Park Avenue	B1-C1-C2
Old Park Road	B2-B1
Old Park View	A2-A1-B1
Orchard Crescent	E4
Parsonage Gardens	C2-C3
Parsonage Lane	C3-D3-D2
Peartree Road	D2-E2
Percival Road	F1
Perry Mead	B3-B4
Pevensey Avenue	D3
Primrose Avenue	D4
Queens Road	E1
Radnor Gardens	E4
Raleigh Road	D1
Ridgemount Gardens	A2-A3
Riversfield Road	D2-E2
Riverside Gardens	C3
Rowantree Road	A3-B3
St Andrews Road	D2
Sandringham Close	E3
Seaford Road	E1
Shirley Road	C1-C2
Silver Street	B3
Sketty Road	E2-F2-F1
Slades Gardens	A2-A3
Slades Hill	A2-B2
Slades Rise	A2
Southbury Avenue	F1
Southbury Road	D1-D2-E2-E1-F1
Sydney Road	D1
The Coppice	B1
The Glen	B1
The Grove	A3
The Ridgeway	A4-A3-A2-B2
Tennis Wood Road	D4-E4-E3
Trinity Street	C3
Uplands Park Road	A2-A3
Valley Fields Crescent	A3
Vicars Close	E2-E3
Waverley Road	B1-B2
Weardale Gardens	D4
Willow Road	D2-D3-E2-E3-E4
Windmill Hill	B2-C2

Edmonton

Alpha Road	B1
Alston Road	C1
Angel Close	A2-B2
Angel Road	B2-C2-C1
Argyle Road	B2
Ascot Road	B2
Balham Road	B4
Barbot Close	A3
Barrowfield Close	C3-C4
Beconsfield Road	B3
Branksome Avenue	A1
Brettenham Road	B2
Bridport Road	A1
Broadway	B4
Brook Crescent	B3
Brookfield Road	B3
Cavendish Road	C2
Chalfont Road	A3
Church Lane	A4-B4
Church Street	A4-B4
Claremont Street	B1
College Close	A1-A2
College Gardens	A1-B1
Colyton Way	B1
Commercial Road	A1
Craig Park Road	C2
Densworth Grove	C4
Derby Road	C2
Dover Road	C4
Dunholme Road	A3-A4
Dyson's Road	C1-C2
Eastbournia Avenue	C4
Edinburgh Road	B2
Exeter Road	C4
Fairfield Road	B2
Felixstowe Road	B3
First Avenue	C2
Fore Street	A1-B1-B2-B3-B4
Fraser Road	B2
Gilpin Grove	A1
Gloucester Road	A1
Graham Gardens	A4
Grenville Road	C4
Hartford Road	B4
Hydeside Gardens	A4
Hyde Way	A4
Jeremys Green	C3

Joyce Avenue	A1
Kenninghall Road	C2
Kimberley Road	C1
Kings Road	B2
Langhedge Lane	A1
Latymer Road	A4
Lawrence Road	B2-C2
Leeds Street	B1
Leyburn Road	B1-C1
Lyndhurst Road	B2
Middleham Road	B1-C1
Monmouth Road	B4-C4
Montagu Crescent	C2
Montagu Gardens	C2
Montagu Road	C2-C3-C4
Moree Way	A2-B2
Morley Avenue	B2
Nelson Road	C4
New Road	B4
Northern Avenue	A4
Park Lane	A3
Park Road	A2-B2
Pegamoid Road	C3
Plevena Road	B3-B4
Pretoria Road	A1
Princes Road	C3
Queens Road	B4
Raynham Avenue	B1-B2
Raynham Road	B2
Raynham Terrace	B1
Rays Avenue	C2
Rays Road	C2
St Malo Avenue	C4
St Martins Road	B4
S bastapol Road	B3
Salisbury Road	A4-B4
Sandal Road	B1
Second Avenue	C3
Seymour Road	C4
Shaftesbury Road	A1
Silver Street	A1-A2
Snells Park	A1-B1
Somerset Road	A1
South Eastern Avenue	A3
Stacey Avenue	C2-C3
Stanley Road	A4
Sterling Street	A1-A2
Stockton Road	B1-C1
Sunnyside Road East	A3
Sweet Briar Grove	A3-A4
Sweet Briar Walk	A2-A3
Thornaby Gardens	B1
Town Road	B4-C4
Upton Road	B1

Victoria Road	A2-A3-A4
Wakefield Street	B1
Warwick Road	A2
Wellington Avenue	C4
Westoe Road	C4
Winchester Road	A4
Woolmer Road	B1
York Road	B1-B2-C1-C2
Yorkshire Gardens	C1

Palmers Green

Alderman's Hill	A2-B2
Amberley Road	A4
Arnold Gardens	C2
Ashbridge Gardens	A1
Avondale Road	B4-C4
Barrow Close	C4
Barrowell	C4
Beechdale	B4
Belmont Avenue	A1-A2
Bourne Hill	A4-B4
Bowes Road	A1-B1
Broomfield Avenue	A1-B1-B2
Broomfield Lane	A2-B2
Burford Gardens	B3-B4
Cambridge Terrace	C1-C2
Cannon Road	A3
Caversham Avenue	B3-B4
Chimes Avenue	C2
Conway Road	A3-A4
Cranford Avenue	A1
Cranley Gardens	B3-B4
Crawfords Gardens	C3-C4
Dawlish Avenue	A1-A2
Derwent Road	A2-A3-B3
Devonshire Road	B2-B3
Eaton Park Road	C4
Ecclesbourne Gardens	B1-C1
Elmdale Road	B1
Elmwood Avenue	A1-A2
Field Road	A4
Fox Lane	A4-B4-B3
Green Lanes	B1-B2-B3-C3-C4
Grenoble Gardens	B1-C1
Grovelands Road	B2-B3
Hamilton Crescent	C2
Harlech Road	A3
Hawthorn Avenue	A1
Hazelwood Lane	B3-C3-C2
Hedges Lane	C3-C4
Hillfield Park	B4
Hopper's Road	B4

Kingsley Road	C2-C3
Lakeside Road	A2-A3-B3
Lawrence Avenue	C2
Lightcliffe Road	C3
Lodge Drive	B2-C2
Lynbridge Gardens	C2
Lytton Avenue	C4
Madeira Road	C3
Meadowcroft Road	C4
Nelbourne Avenue	B1
Melville Gardens	C1-C2
Matal Road	A1
New River Crescent	C2-C3
North Circular Road	B1-C1-C2
Oakthorpe Road	B2-C2
Oaktree Avenue	C4
Old Park Road	B2-B3
Osbourne Road	C3
Palmerston Crescent	B1
Palmerston Road	B1
Park Avenue	B3-C3
Powys Lane	A1-A2
Princes Avenue	B1-C1
Ridgeway	A4
River Avenue	C3-C4
Riverway	C2
Russel Road	B1
St George's Road	A4-B4
Selbourne Road	A3-A4
Sidney Avenue	B1
Stonard Road	B4-C4
The Crest	B2-C2
The Grove	B3-B2-C2
The Mall	A3-A4
The Rue	C2
Tottenhall Road	B1-C1
Ulleswater Road	A2-A3
Wentworth Gardens	C3
Westminster Drive	A1
Windsor Road	B3-C3
Wolves Lane	C1
Woodland Way	B4

ENFIELD
Lamb's Cottage in Gentleman's Row — Charles Lamb
and his sister Mary came to Enfield to stay with friends
in 1825 and liked it so much that they made repeated
visits back and eventually decided to settle here.

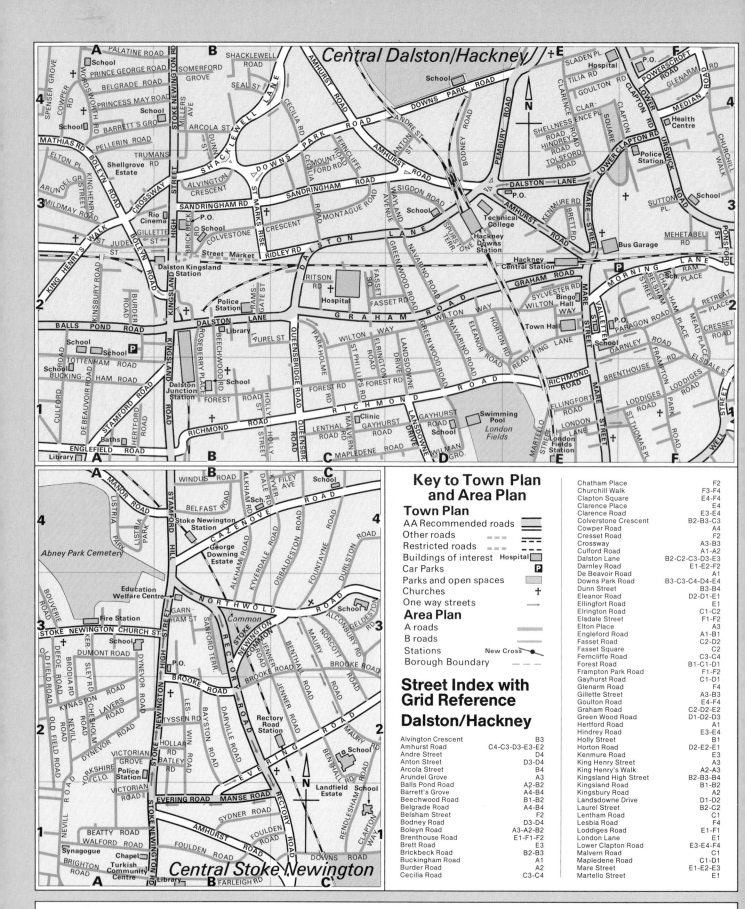

Central Dalston/Hackney

Central Stoke Newington

Key to Town Plan and Area Plan

Town Plan

AA Recommended roads	
Other roads	
Restricted roads	
Buildings of interest	Hospital
Car Parks	P
Parks and open spaces	
Churches	†
One way streets	→

Area Plan

A roads	
B roads	
Stations	New Cross ●—
Borough Boundary	

Street Index with Grid Reference

Dalston/Hackney

Alvington Crescent	B3
Amhurst Road	C4-C3-D3-E3-E2
Andre Street	D4
Anton Street	D3-D4
Arcola Street	B4
Arundel Grove	A3
Balls Pond Road	A2-B2
Barrett's Grove	A4-B4
Beechwood Road	B1-B2
Belgrade Road	A4-B4
Belsham Street	F2
Bodney Road	D3-D4
Boleyn Road	A3-A2-B2
Brenthouse Road	E1-F1-F2
Brett Road	E3
Brickbeck Road	B2-B3
Buckingham Road	A1
Burder Road	A2
Cecilia Road	C3-C4

Chatham Place	F2
Churchill Walk	F3-F4
Clapton Square	E4-F4
Clarence Place	E4
Clarence Road	E3-E4
Colverstone Crescent	B2-B3-C3
Cowper Road	A4
Cresset Road	F2
Crossway	A3-B3
Culford Road	A1-A2
Dalston Lane	B2-C2-C3-D3-E3
Darnley Road	E1-E2-F2
De Beavoir Road	A1
Downs Park Road	B3-C3-C4-D4-E4
Dunn Street	B3-B4
Eleanor Road	D2-D1-E1
Ellingfort Road	E1
Elrington Road	C1-C2
Elsdale Street	F1-F2
Elton Place	A3
Engleford Road	A1-B1
Fasset Road	C2-D2
Fasset Square	C2
Ferncliffe Road	C3-C4
Forest Road	B1-C1-D1
Frampton Park Road	F1-F2
Gayhurst Road	C1-D1
Glenarm Road	F4
Gillette Street	A3-B3
Goulton Road	E4-F4
Graham Road	C2-D2-E2
Green Wood Road	D1-D2-D3
Hertford Road	A1
Hindrey Road	E3-E4
Holly Street	B1
Horton Road	D2-E2-E1
Kenmure Road	E3
King Henry Street	A3
King Henry's Walk	A2-A3
Kingsland High Street	B2-B3-B4
Kingsland Road	B1-B2
Kingsbury Road	A2
Landsdowne Drive	D1-D2
Laurel Street	B2-C2
Lentham Road	C1
Lesbia Road	F4
Loddiges Road	E1-F1
London Lane	E1
Lower Clapton Road	E3-E4-F4
Malvern Road	C1
Mapledene Road	C1-D1
Mare Street	E1-E2-E3
Martello Street	E1

Hackney/Dalston

Not so long ago this was a rural area on the west bank of the River Lea. Although most of its open land was swallowed up by development in the 19th century, pleasant spaces still remain in Hackney Downs, in the north, and London Fields, in the south, and attractive parks have been created.

The only old building of note is the ancient tower of St Augustine's Church, probably dating from the 13th century. This is a good area for street markets, one of the largest being on Saturdays, along busy Kingsland Road.

Stoke Newington was once the home of *Robinson Crusoe* author Daniel Defoe, and his house can still be seen in Stoke Newington Church Street — one of a number of reminders of the past to be found in this area. This old Saxon settlement became a fashionable residential area during the 19th century, but was extensively rebuilt following bomb damage in World War II. The Old Church of St Mary makes a picturesque scene at one corner of pleasantly landscaped Clissold Park.

Whitechapel was the scene of the notoriously grisly Jack the Ripper murders in the late 19th century. Famous also for its markets, which include Petticoat Lane (Middlesex Street), it has been a stopping point for immigrants since the 18th century. The National Museum of Labour History can be seen at nearby Limehouse Town Hall.

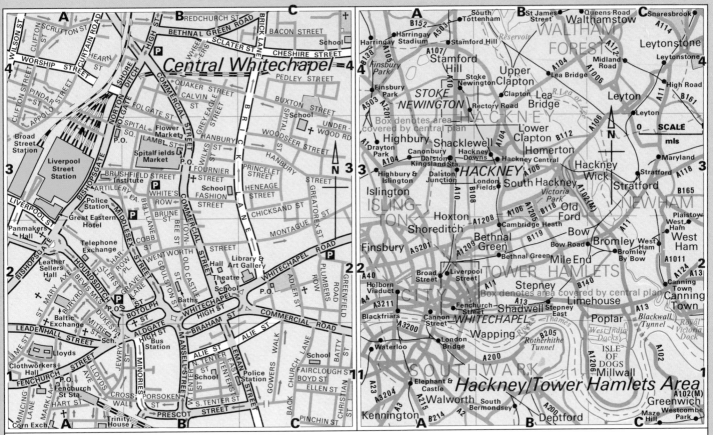

Mathias Road	A4	Brighton Road	A1	Brushfield Street	A3-B3	Wentworth Street	B2-C2

Stoke Newington

Whitechapel

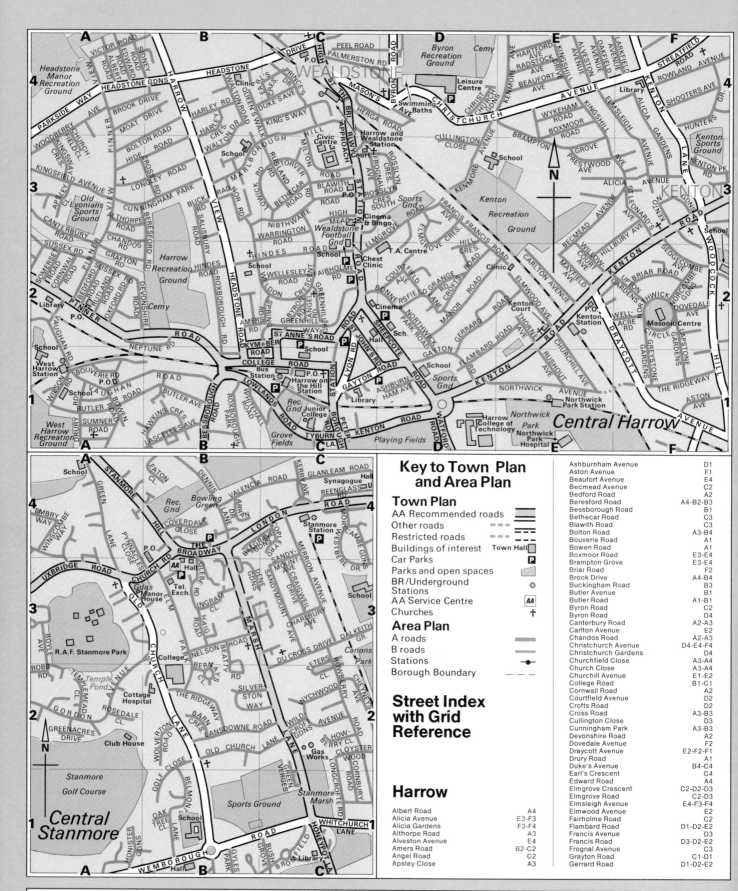

Key to Town Plan and Area Plan

Town Plan

AA Recommended roads	
Other roads	
Restricted roads	
Buildings of interest	Town Hall ▣
Car Parks	P
Parks and open spaces	
BR/Underground Stations	⊖
AA Service Centre	AA
Churches	†

Area Plan

A roads	
B roads	
Stations	●—
Borough Boundary	

Street Index with Grid Reference

Harrow

Harrow

Sheridan, Byron, Anthony Trollope and Sir Winston Churchill all spent time in Harrow — as pupils at the historic public school, which was founded in 1572. During term time, the present-day pupils are recognisable by their distinctive uniform, and tail coats are still worn by members of the Upper School. The school itself has been modernised to some extent over the years, but a number of

ancient buildings still remain, notably the 17th-century schoolroom.

Expanded and developed between the two World Wars, modern Harrow is home of a number of industrial concerns, including the Kodak film and photographic paper factory and the Northern European Office of Hitachi Electronics.

St Mary's Church is of Norman origin but was greatly restored by Sir George Gilbert Scott during the mid-19th century. Headstone Manor,

which dates back to the 14th century, has an impressive restored Tithe Barn which is open to the public.

Stanmore Marconi Space and Defence Systems is one of the occupants of Stanmore's main industrial estate, and as well as such modern innovations, the area still has some older buildings, including fine 18th-century houses on Stanmore Hill. St Lawrence's Church, also 18th-century, is noted for its painted walls and ceiling.

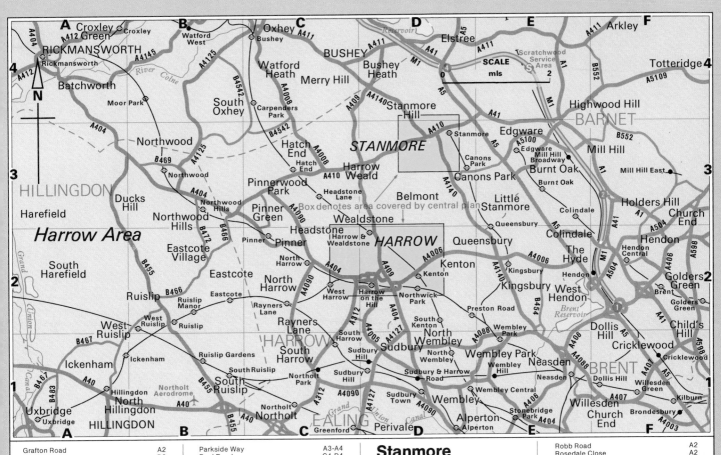

Grafton Road	A2	Parkside Way	A3-A4	**Stanmore**		Robb Road	A2
Grange Road	D2	Peel Road	C4-D4			Rosedale Close	A2
Greenhill Road	C2	Peterborough Road	C1	Arron Drive	B4	Sandymount Avenue	C3-C4
Greenhill Way	C2	Pinner Road	A2-B1-B2	Barn Crescent	B2	Silverston Way	B2-C2
Greystone Gardens	F1-F2	Pinner View	A2-A3-A4	Beatty Road	B2-C3	Stanmore Hill	A4-B4
Harley Crescent	B3-B4	Prestwood Avenue	E3	Belgrave Gardens	B4-C4	Templemead Close	A2
Harley Road	B4	Prince's Drive	B4-C4	Belmont Lane	B1-B2	The Broadway	B4
Harrow View	B2-B3-B4	Queen's Walk	B4-C4-C3	Bernays Close	B2	The Ridgeway	B2
Hartford Avenue	E4	Radnor Road	B3	Boyle Avenue	A2-A3	Uxbridge Road	A3
Hawkins Crescent	B1	Radstock Avenue	E4	Bromfield	C1	Valencia Road	B4-C4
Headstone Drive	B4-C4	Rail Approach	C3-C4	Bush Grove	C1	Wemborough Road	A1-B1-C1
Headstone Gardens	A4-B4	Rosslyn Crescent	D3	Charlbury Avenue	C3	Westbere Drive	C3-C4
Headstone Road	B1-B2	Rosslyn Crescent South	C3-D3	Cheyney's Avenue	C2	Whitchurch Lane	C1
Herga Road	C4-D4	Rowland Avenue	F4	Church Road	A3-B3-B4	Wildcroft Gardens	C2
Hide Road	A3-B3	Roxborough Park	C3	Cloyster Wood	C2	Winscombe Way	A4
High Mead	C3	Roxborough Road	B1-B2	Copley Road	C4	Wolverton Road	B2
High Street	C4	Rushout Avenue	E1	Cornbury Road	C1-C2	Wychwood Avenue	C2
Hill Crescent	D2-D3	Rusland Road	C3	Coverdale Close	B4		
Hillbury Avenue	E2-E3-F3	Rutland Road	A2	Craigweil Drive	C3		
Hindes Road	B2-C2	St Anne's Road	C2	Dalkeith Grove	C3		
Hunters Grove	F4	St John's Road	C2-C1-D1	Dene Gardens	B3-C3		
Kenmore Avenue	D3-D4-E4	St Leonard's Avenue	F3	Dennis Lane	B4		
Kenton Gardens	F3	Salisbury Road	B2-B3	Du Cross Drive	C2-C3		
Kenton Lane	F3-F4	Sedgecombe Avenue	F2-F3	Eaton Close	B4		
Kenton Road	C1-D1-E1-E2-F2-F3	Sheepcote Road	D1-C2-D2	Elm Park	B2-B3		
Kenton Park Road	F3	Shooters Avenue	F4	Embry Way	A4		
King's Way	C4	Sidney Road	A4	Glanleam Road	C4		
Kingsfield Avenue	A3	Somerset Road	A2	Glebe Road	B3-B4		
Kingshill Avenue	E4-E3-F3	Spring Road	F4	Golf Close	B1-B2		
Kingshill Drive	E4	Streatfield Road	F4	Gordon Avenue	A2-A3-B3		
Kingsway Crescent	A3	Station Road	C1-C2-C3	Green Lane	A3-A4		
Kymber Road	B1-B2-C2	Summer Road	A1	Green Verges	C1-C2		
Lascelles Avenue	B1	Sussex Road	A2-A3	Greenacres Drive	A2		
Lapstone Gardens	F1-F2	The Bridge	C4	Gyles Park	B1		
Larkfield Avenue	E4-F4	The Ridgeway	F1	Haig Road	B3		
Longley Road	A3-B3	Thorne Avenue	E2	Honeypot Lane	C1		
Lowick Road	B3-C3	Torver Road	C3	Honister Gardens	A1		
Lowlands Road	B1-C1	Tyburn Lane	C1	Howberry Close	C2		
Lyon Road	C1-C2	Upton Gardens	F2	Howberry Road	C1-C2-C3		
Manor Road	D2-E2	Vaughan Road	A1-A2-B1	Ingram Close	B3		
Marlborough Hill	B3-C3-C4	Victory Road	A4	Kerry Avenue	C4		
Mason's Avenue	C4-D4	Walton Drive	B3-B4	Lansdowne Road	B2-C2		
Mayfield Avenue	E2	Walton Road	B4	London Road	B4-C4		
Milton Road	C3-C4	Warrington Road	B3-C3	Longcrofte Road	C1-C2		
Moat Drive	A4-B4	Watford Road	D1	Marsh Lane	B4-B3-C3-C2-C1		
Neptune Road	A2-B2	Weldon Crescent	B2-C2	Merrion Avenue	C3-C4		
Nibthwaite Road	B3-C3	Wellacre Road	F2	Morecambe Gardens	C3-C4		
Norcombe Gardens	F2	Wellesley Road	C2	Nelson Road	B3		
Northwick Avenue	D1-E1	Whitehall Road	B1-C1	Oak Tree Close	B1		
Northwick Circle	F2	Willow Court Avenue	E2	Old Church Lane	A3-B3-B2-C2		
Northwick Park Road	D1-D2	Wilson Road	A1	Peters Close	C2-C3		
Oakfield Avenue	E4	Woodberry Avenue	A3-A4	Pynnacles Close	A4-A3-B3		
Oxford Road	A2	Woodcock Hill	F1-F2-F3	Reenglass Road	C4		
Palmerston Road	C4-D4	Wykeham Road	E4				

HARROW
The Old School building, Harrow School, whose 1572 founder John Lyon drew up an elaborate pupils' reading list of Latin and Greek — but no English — books, and stipulated that no girls be received into the school.

21

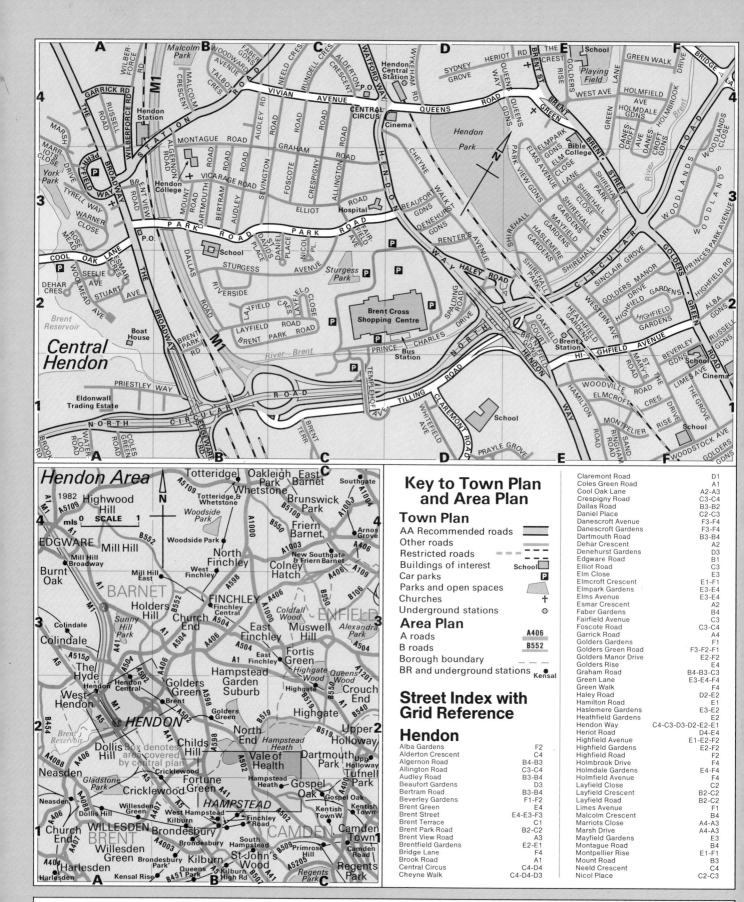

Central Hendon

(Town Plan map of Central Hendon)

Hendon Area

1982

SCALE

Key to Town Plan and Area Plan

Town Plan

AA Recommended roads	
Other roads	
Restricted roads	
Buildings of interest	School
Car parks	P
Parks and open spaces	
Churches	†
Underground stations	

Area Plan

A roads	A406
B roads	B552
Borough boundary	
BR and underground stations	Kensal

Street Index with Grid Reference

Hendon

Alba Gardens	F2
Alderton Crescent	C4
Algernon Road	B4-B3
Allington Road	C3-C4
Audley Road	B3-B4
Beaufort Gardens	D3
Bertram Road	B3-B4
Beverley Gardens	F1-F2
Brent Green	E4
Brent Street	E4-E3-F3
Brent Terrace	C1
Brent Park Road	B2-C2
Brent View Road	A3
Brentfield Gardens	E2-E1
Bridge Lane	F4
Brook Road	A1
Central Circus	C4-D4
Cheyne Walk	C4-D4-D3
Claremont Road	D1
Coles Green Road	A1
Cool Oak Lane	A2-A3
Crespigny Road	C3-C4
Dallas Road	B3-B2
Daniel Place	C2-C3
Danescroft Avenue	F3-F4
Danescroft Gardens	F3-F4
Dartmouth Road	B3-B4
Dehar Crescent	A2
Denehurst Gardens	D3
Edgware Road	B1
Elliot Road	C3
Elm Close	C3
Elmcroft Crescent	E1-F1
Elmpark Gardens	E3-E4
Elms Avenue	E3-E4
Esmar Crescent	A2
Faber Gardens	B4
Fairfield Avenue	C3
Foscote Road	C3-C4
Garrick Road	A4
Golders Gardens	F1
Golders Green Road	F3-F2-F1
Golders Manor Drive	E2-F2
Golders Rise	E4
Graham Road	B4-B3-C3
Green Lane	E3-E4-F4
Green Walk	F4
Haley Road	D2-E2
Hamilton Road	E1
Haslemere Gardens	E3-E2
Heathfield Gardens	E2
Hendon Way	C4-C3-D3-D2-E2-E1
Heriot Road	D4-E4
Highfield Avenue	E1-E2-F2
Highfield Gardens	E2-F2
Highfield Road	F2
Holmbrook Drive	F4
Holmdale Gardens	E4-F4
Holmfield Avenue	F4
Layfield Close	C2
Layfield Crescent	B2-C2
Layfield Road	B2-C2
Limes Avenue	F1
Malcolm Crescent	B4
Marriots Close	A4-A3
Marsh Drive	A4-A3
Mayfield Gardens	E3
Montague Road	B4
Montpellier Rise	E1-F1
Mount Road	B3
Neeld Crescent	C4
Nicol Place	C2-C3

Hendon

The magnificent RAF Museum is situated here, next to Hendon Aerodrome (once famous for its air displays) which is also the site of the Battle of Britain and Bomber Command Museum. People flock to Hendon for these — and for the vast regional shopping centre at Brent Cross. Other local landmarks are the Metropolitan Police Training College and the Church Farm House Museum.

But Hendon is probably best known to the world for its closeness to the M1 Motorway, which has its southern terminal close by, near the Staples Corner Junction on the North Circular road.

Hampstead Artists, poets and politicians have made their homes in Hampstead, where the celebrated Heath stretches for 800 acres of grass and woodland. Fine 17th- to 19th-century houses can be found in the 'village', and the stylish shops of Heath Street and Hampstead High Street add to the colourful atmosphere.

Outstanding buildings open to the public are Keats House (1815), home of the poet John Keats, Fenton House, which is a fine late 17th-century building, and Kenwood House, remodelled in about 1765 by Robert Adam and visited for its paintings and open-air concerts. Noted pubs of Hampstead include the Old Bull and Bush (the original for the music-hall song), the Flask, the Spaniards and Jack Straw's Castle.

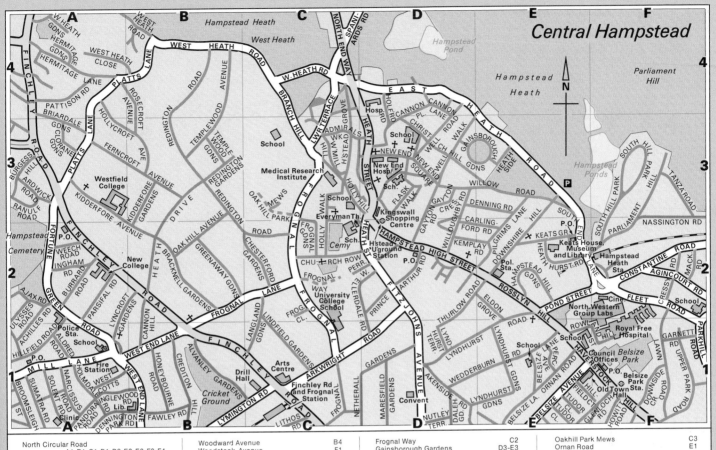

Central Hampstead

HAMPSTEAD

John Keats wrote *Ode to a Nightingale* while living at Wentworth Place (now Keats House) from 1818 to 1820. Books, letters and other mementoes of the poet and his fianceé, Fanny Brawne, can be seen here.

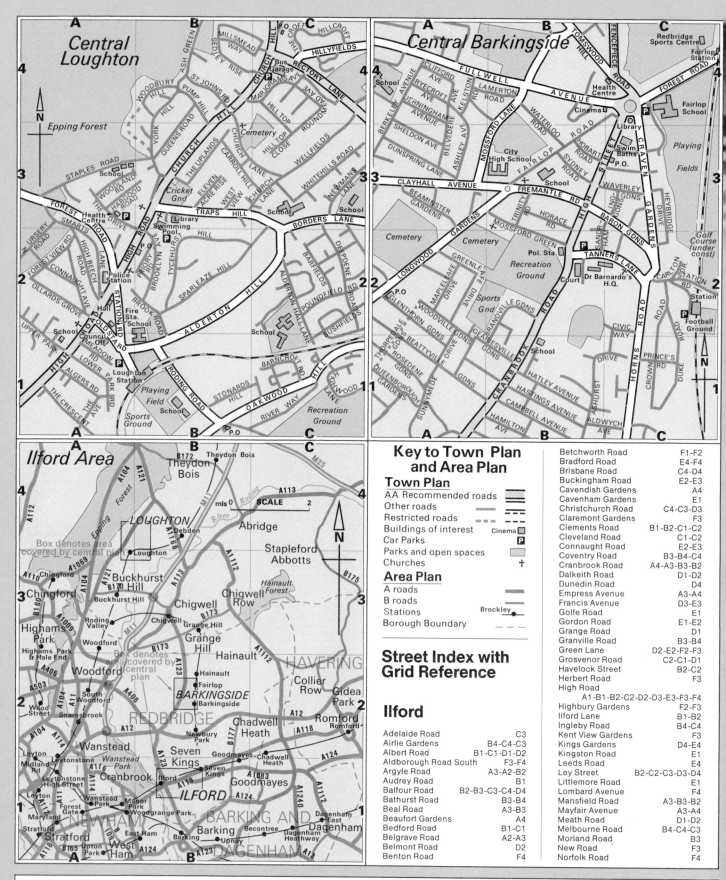

Key to Town Plan and Area Plan

Town Plan

AA Recommended roads	
Other roads	
Restricted roads	- - -
Buildings of interest	Cinema ▩
Car Parks	℗
Parks and open spaces	
Churches	+

Area Plan

A roads	
B roads	
Stations	Brockley ●
Borough Boundary	- - -

Street Index with Grid Reference

Ilford

Adelaide Road	C3
Airlie Gardens	B4-C4-C3
Albert Road	B1-C1-D1-D2
Aldborough Road South	F3-F4
Argyle Road	A3-A2-B2
Audrey Road	B1
Balfour Road	B2-B3-C3-C4-D4
Bathurst Road	B3-B4
Beal Road	A3-B3
Beaufort Gardens	A4
Bedford Road	B1-C1
Belgrave Road	A2-A3
Belmont Road	D2
Benton Road	F4
Betchworth Road	F1-F2
Bradford Road	E4-F4
Brisbane Road	C4-D4
Buckingham Road	E2-E3
Cavendish Gardens	A4
Cavenham Gardens	E1
Christchurch Road	C4-C3-D3
Claremont Gardens	F3
Clements Road	B1-B2-C1-C2
Cleveland Road	C1-C2
Connaught Road	E2-E3
Coventry Road	B3-B4-C4
Cranbrook Road	A4-A3-B3-B2
Dalkeith Road	D1-D2
Dunedin Road	D4
Empress Avenue	A3-A4
Francis Avenue	D3-E3
Golfe Road	E1
Gordon Road	E1-E2
Grange Road	D1
Granville Road	B3-B4
Green Lane	D2-E2-F2-F3
Grosvenor Road	C2-C1-D1
Havelock Street	B2-C2
Herbert Road	F3
High Road	A1-B1-B2-C2-D2-D3-E3-F3-F4
Highbury Gardens	F2-F3
Ilford Lane	B1-B2
Ingleby Road	B4-C4
Kent View Gardens	F3
Kings Gardens	D4-E4
Kingston Road	E1
Leeds Road	E4
Ley Street	B2-C2-C3-D3-D4
Littlemore Road	E1
Lombard Avenue	F4
Mansfield Road	A3-B3-B2
Mayfair Avenue	A3-A4
Meath Road	D1-D2
Melbourne Road	B4-C4-C3
Morland Road	B3
New Road	F3
Norfolk Road	F4

Ilford

Situated seven miles from London, Ilford is developing into a light industrial town with expanding industrial estates and a development programme to pedestrianise several important shopping streets. Valentines Park provides 130˚ acres of recreation area and includes peaceful havens such as the Old English Garden, the Rosary Terrace and Bishops Walk, as well as an ornamental pond and a lake. Set within the grounds of the park is one of the oldest buildings in the borough, Valentines House, which was built at the end of the 17th century.

Loughton's prominent Lopping Hall was built in 1884 by the City of London, after protests by local woodsmen about the lopping rights of the townspeople, and is now used for various community functions. Even today, the woodlands of Epping Forest dominate the town: Loughton stretches along its south-easterly side, and is bordered by the Rover Roding to the east. Interesting older buildings in the area include Loughton Hall and partly 16th-century Alderton Hall.

Barkingside is growing steadily due to recent business and housing developments and has a pleasant shopping area, various recreation grounds and the Redbridge Sports Centre. Fairlop Plain, just north of the town, is used for football, sailing and flying model aeroplanes.

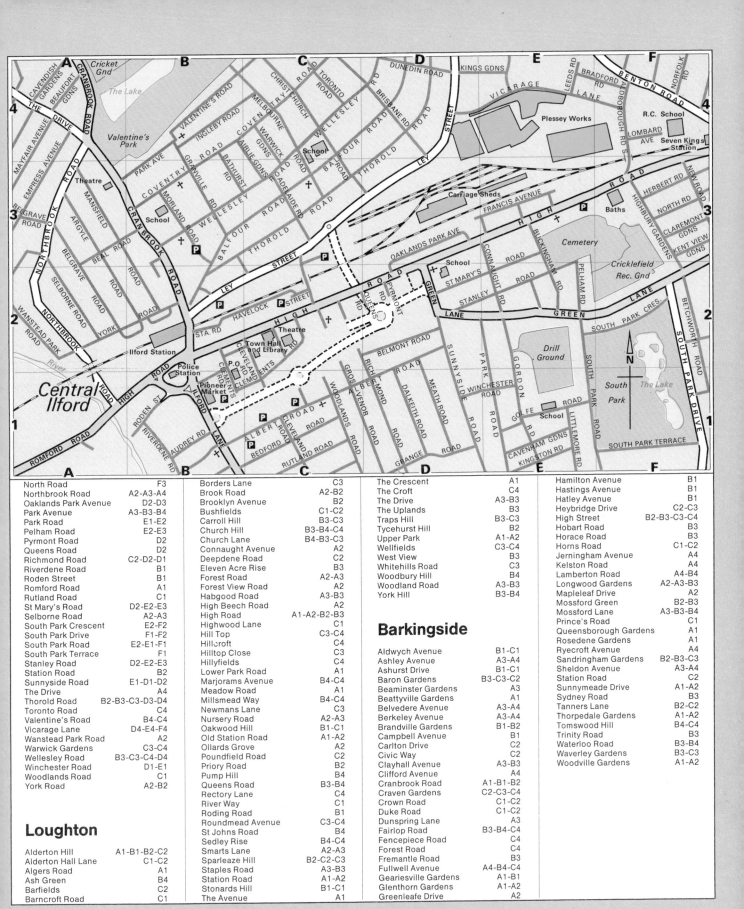

Central Ilford (map)

North Road	F3	Borders Lane	C3	The Crescent	A1
Northbrook Road	A2-A3-A4	Brook Road	A2-B2	The Croft	C4
Oaklands Park Avenue	D2-D3	Brooklyn Avenue	B2	The Drive	A3-B3
Park Avenue	A3-B3-B4	Bushfields	C1-C2	The Uplands	B3
Park Road	E1-E2	Carroll Hill	B3-C3	Traps Hill	B3-C3
Pelham Road	E2-E3	Church Hill	B3-B4-C4	Tycehurst Hill	B2
Pyrmont Road	D2	Church Lane	B4-B3-C3	Upper Park	A1-A2
Queens Road	D2	Connaught Avenue	A2	Wellfields	C3-C4
Richmond Road	C2-D2-D1	Deepdene Road	C2	West View	B3
Riverdene Road	B1	Eleven Acre Rise	B3	Whitehills Road	C3
Roden Street	B1	Forest Road	A2-A3	Woodbury Hill	B4
Romford Road	A1	Forest View Road	A2	Woodland Road	A3-B3
Rutland Road	C1	Habgood Road	A3-B3	York Hill	B3-B4
St Mary's Road	D2-E2-E3	High Beech Road	A2		
Selborne Road	A2-A3	High Road	A1-A2-B2-B3		
South Park Crescent	E2-F2	Highwood Lane	C1	**Barkingside**	
South Park Drive	F1-F2	Hill Top	C3-C4		
South Park Road	E2-E1-F1	Hillcroft	C4	Aldwych Avenue	B1-C1
South Park Terrace	F1	Hilltop Close	C3	Ashley Avenue	A3-A4
Stanley Road	D2-E2-E3	Hillyfields	C4	Ashurst Drive	B1-C1
Station Road	B2	Lower Park Road	A1	Baron Gardens	B3-C3-C2
Sunnyside Road	E1-D1-D2	Marjorams Avenue	B4-C4	Beaminster Gardens	A3
The Drive	A4	Meadow Road	A1	Beattyville Gardens	A1
Thorold Road	B2-B3-C3-D3-D4	Millsmead Way	B4-C4	Belvedere Avenue	A3-A4
Toronto Road	C4	Newmans Lane	C3	Berkeley Avenue	A3-A4
Valentine's Road	B4-C4	Nursery Road	A2-A3	Brandville Gardens	B1-B2
Vicarage Lane	D4-E4-F4	Oakwood Hill	B1-C1	Campbell Avenue	B1
Wanstead Park Road	A2	Old Station Road	A1-A2	Carlton Drive	C2
Warwick Gardens	C3-C4	Ollards Grove	A2	Civic Way	C2
Wellesley Road	B3-C3-C4-D4	Poundfield Road	C2	Clayhall Avenue	A3-B3
Winchester Road	D1-E1	Priory Road	B2	Clifford Avenue	A4
Woodlands Road	C1	Pump Hill	B4	Cranbrook Road	A1-B1-B2
York Road	A2-B2	Queens Road	B3-B4	Craven Gardens	C2-C3-C4
		Rectory Lane	C4	Crown Road	C1-C2
		River Way	C1	Duke Road	C1-C2
Loughton		Roding Road	B1	Dunspring Lane	A3
		Roundmead Avenue	C3-C4	Fairlop Road	B3-B4-C4
Alderton Hill	A1-B1-B2-C2	St Johns Road	B4	Fencepiece Road	C4
Alderton Hall Lane	C1-C2	Sedley Rise	B4-C4	Forest Road	C4
Algers Road	A1	Smarts Lane	A2-A3	Fremantle Road	B3
Ash Green	B4	Sparleaze Hill	B2-C2-C3	Fullwell Avenue	A4-B4-C4
Barfields	C2	Staples Road	A3-B3	Geariesville Gardens	A1-B1
Barncroft Road	C1	Station Road	A1-A2	Glenthorn Gardens	A1-A2
		Stonards Hill	B1-C1	Greenleafe Drive	A2
		The Avenue	A1		

Hamilton Avenue	B1
Hastings Avenue	B1
Hatley Avenue	B1
Heybridge Drive	C2-C3
High Street	B2-B3-C3-C4
Hobart Road	B3
Horace Road	B3
Horns Road	C1-C2
Jerningham Avenue	A4
Kelston Road	A4
Lamberton Road	A4-B4
Longwood Gardens	A2-A3-B3
Mapleleaf Drive	B3
Mossford Green	B2-B3
Mossford Lane	A3-B3-B4
Prince's Road	C1
Queensborough Gardens	A1
Rosedene Gardens	A1
Ryecroft Avenue	A1
Sandringham Gardens	B2-B3-C3
Sheldon Avenue	A3-A4
Station Road	C2
Sunnymeade Drive	A1-A2
Sydney Road	B3
Tanners Lane	B2-C2
Thorpedale Gardens	A1-A2
Tomswood Hill	B4-C4
Trinity Road	B3
Waterloo Road	B3
Waverley Gardens	B3-C3
Woodville Gardens	A1-A2

ILFORD
A resplendent turn-of-the-century Town Hall epitomises the confidence felt by those who fostered Ilford's expansion — one of them guaranteed season ticket sales worth £10,000 when a station opened here in 1889.

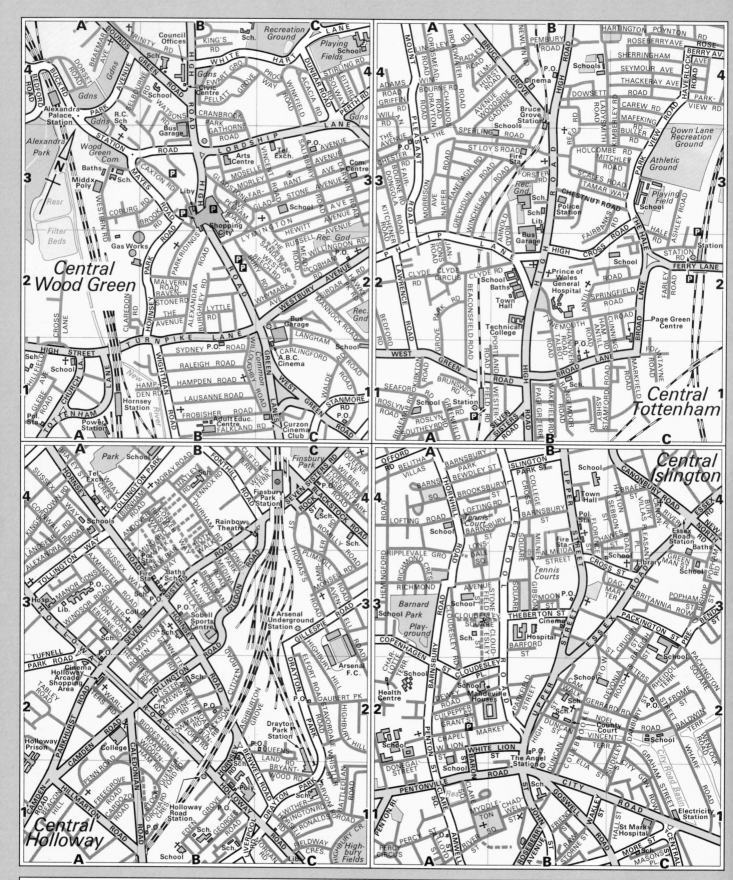

Islington

Taverns and amusements made Islington a fashionable residential area and place of entertainment during the 18th century. Its theatrical traditions are carried on today by Sadler's Wells Theatre, dating from the 17th century and now home of the Sadler's Wells Royal Ballet Company. Cannonbury Tower is a much restored former manor house which is now in use as a theatre, and also worth a visit are the antique shops and market stalls of Camden Passage.

Wood Green has become synonymous in North London with Shopping City, an extensive complex which was officially opened in 1981, and also houses the New River Sports Centre. Once a rural hamlet, Wood Green is now the administrative centre for the London Borough of Haringey.

Holloway is noted for the Sobell Sports Centre, said to be the largest in the country. The Arsenal Football Club is another feature of the local landscape.

Tottenham Rivalling its nearby neighbours Tottenham Hotspur Football Club has its ground here — probably the most widely known aspect of this part-industrial, mainly residential area, which was once an agricultural community on the River Lea. There are several pleasant parks, and Bruce Castle Park has a local museum in a partly-Elizabethan building.

LEGEND

Town Plan

AA Recommended roads	
Other roads	
Restricted roads	
Buildings of interest	College
Car Parks	P
Parks and open spaces	
Churches	†
BR and Underground Stations	⊖

Area Plan

A roads	
B roads	
Stations	Stamford Hill ●
Borough Boundary	

STREET INDEX WITH GRID REFERENCE

WOOD GREEN

Street	Grid
Acacia Road	C4
Alexandra Road	B2
Bedford Road	A4
Bounds Green Road	A4-B4
Braemar Avenue	B3
Brook Road	A4
Buck Road	A4
Burghley Road	B2
Bury Road	B2-C2
Carlington Road	C1
Caxton Road	B3
Church Lane	A1
Clarendon Road	A2-B2
Cobham Road	C2
Coburg Road	A3-B3
Cranbrook Road	B4
Cross Lane	A1-A2
Darwin Road	C3
Dorset Road	A4
Dunbar Road	C4
Ewart Grove	B4
Falkland Road	B1-C1
Farrant Avenue	B3-C3
Frobisher Road	B1-C1
Gathorne Road	B3
Gladstone Avenue	B3-C3
Glebe Road	A1
Green Lanes	C1-C2
Hampden Road	A1-B1
Hawke Park Road	C2
Hewitt Avenue	C2-C3
High Road	B4-B3-B2-C2
High Street	A1
Hillfield Avenue	A1
Hornsey Park Road	B2-B3
King's Road	B4
Langham Road	C1-C2
Lausanne Road	B1
Leith Road	C4
Lordship Lane	B3-C3-C4-B4
Lymington Avenue	B2-B3-C3
Lyttle Road	B2
Malvern Road	B2

TOTTENHAM (continued) / other

Street	Grid
Mannock Road	C2
Mayes Road	A3-B3
Meads Road	C2
Morley Avenue	B3-C3
Moselle Avenue	B3-C3
Park Avenue	A4
Park Ridings	B2-B3
Pelham Road	B3
Pellatt Grove	B4-C4
Perth Road	C4
Progress Way	C4
Raleigh Road	B1
Ravenstone Road	B2
Russell Avenue	C2-C3
Salisbury Road	C3
Selbourne Road	A4-B4
Sirdar Road	C2
Solway Road	C4
Stanmore Road	C1
Stirling Road	C4
Station Road	A4-A3-B3
Sydney Road	B1
The Avenue	B2
The Sandlings	B3-B2-C2
Tottenham Lane	A1
Trinity Road	A4-B4
Turnpike Lane	A1-B1-B2
Vincent Road	C3
Waldeck Road	C1
Watsons Road	B4
West Beech Road	B2-C2
Westbury Avenue	C2
Western Road	A2-A3
West Green Road	C1
White Hart Lane	B4-C4
Whymark Avenue	B2-C2
Wightman Road	B1
Willingdon Road	C2
Willoughby Road	B2-B1-C1
Winkfield Road	C3-C4

TOTTENHAM

Adams Road	A4
Antill Road	B1-B2-C2
Arnold Road	B2-B3
Ashby Road	B1
Ashley Road	C2-C3
Beaconsfield Road	A1-A2
Bedford Road	A1-A2
Braemar Road	A1
Broad Lane	B1-C1-C2
Broadwater Road	A4
Bruce Grove	A4-B4
Brunswick Road	A1
Buller Road	C3
Carew Road	C4
Chandos Road	A4
Chester Road	A3
Chestnut Road	B3-C3
Clyde Circus	A2
Clyde Road	A2-B2
Cunningham Road	B2-C2-C1
Dongola Road	A2-A3
Dowsett Road	B4-C4
Drayton Road	A3-A4
Elmhurst Road	A4-B4
Fairbanks Road	B2-B3
Fairbourne Road	A3
Farley Road	C2
Ferry Lane	C2
Forster Road	B3
Fountayne Road	C1
Greenfield Road	A1
Greyhound Road	A2-A3-B3

Street	Grid
Griffin Road	A4
Grove Park Road	A1-A2
Hale Road	C2-C3
Hanover Road	B1-B2
Hartington Road	B4-C4
Havelock Road	C4
High Road	B1-B2-B3-B4
High Cross Road	B2-C2
Holcombe Road	B3-C3
Jansons Road	A2
Kimberley Road	C3-C4
Kirton Road	A1
Kitchener Road	A2-A3
Ladysmith Road	B3-B4
Lawrence Road	A1-A2
Linley Road	A4
Lordsmead Road	A4
Mafeking Road	C4
Markfield Road	C1
Mitchley Road	B3-C3
Morrison Avenue	A3
Mount Pleasant Road	A2-A3-A4
Napier Road	A3
Newlyn Road	B4
Page Green Terrace	B1
Park View Road	C3-C4
Pembury Road	B4
Phillip Lane	A2-B2
Portland Road	B1
Poynton Road	C4
Radley Road	A4
Ranelagh Road	A3
Rangemoor Road	B1
Reed Road	C4
Roseberry Avenue	A1
Roslyn Road	A3
St Loy's Road	A3-B3
Scales Road	B3-C3
Seaford Road	A1
Seven Sisters Road	A1-B1
Seymour Avenue	B4-C4
Sherringham Avenue	B4-C4
Southey Road	A1
Sperling Road	A4-A3-B3
Stamford Road	C1
Station Road	C2
Talbot Road	B1-B2
Tamar Way	B3-C3
Thackeray Avenue	C4
The Avenue	A3-A4-B4
The Hale	C2-C3
Tynemouth Road	B2-C2
Wakefield Road	B1
Westerfield Road	B1
West Green Road	A1-B1
Willan Road	A3-A4
Wimborne Road	A4
Winchelsea Road	A2-A3-B3
Woodside Gardens	A3-A4-B4

HOLLOWAY

Alexandra Road	A3-A4
Ambler Road	C3-C4
Andover Road	A4-B4
Annette Road	B2
Arvon Road	C1
Ashburton Grove	B2-C2
Aubert Road	C2
Avenell Road	C2-C3
Axminster Road	A3-B3
Battledean Road	C1
Beacon Hill	A1
Benwell Road	B2-B1-C1
Berriman Road	B3
Biddestone Road	A2-B2
Birnham Road	A4-B4
Blackstock Road	C4
Bracey Street	A4
Briset Way	B4
Bryantwood Road	C1
Caledonian Road	A2-A1-B1
Camden Road	A1-A2
Cardozo Road	A1
Citizen Road	B2-B3
Clifton Terrace	B4
Corker Way	B3-B4
Cornwall Road	A3-A4
Drayton Park	C1-C2-C3
Dunford Raod	B2
Durham Road	B4
Eburne Road	A3
Eden Grove	B1
Elford Road	C2-C3
Fieldway Crescent	C1
Finsbury Park Road	C4
Fonthill Road	B4-C4
Freegrove Road	A1
Georges Road	B1
Gillespie Road	C3
Hatley Road	B4
Hertslet Road	A3-A2-B2
Highbury Crescent	C1
Highbury Hill	C2-C3
Hillmarton Road	A1-B1
Holloway Road	A3-A2-B2-B1-C1
Hornsey Road	A4-A3-B3-B2-B1
Horsell Road	C1
Isledon Road	B3-C3-C4
Jackson Road	B2
Kingsdown Road	A4
Landseer Road	A3-A4
Lennox Road	B4
Lister Mews	B2
Liverpool Road	B1-C1
Loraine Road	B2
Lowman Road	B2
Manor Gardens	A3
Mayton Street	A3-B3
Medina Road	B3
Mingard Walk	A3-B3-B4
Moray Road	B4
Morgan Road	C1
Monsell Road	C3
Newington Barrow Way	B3-B4
Parkhurst Road	A1-A2
Penn Road	A1-A2
Plimsoll Road	C3-C4
Queens Avenue	C4
Queensland Road	B2-C2
Quemerford Road	B1-B2

Rock Street	C4
Roden Street	A2-B2-B3
Romilly Road	C3-C4
Ronalds Road	C1
Roth Walk	B4
St Thomas's Road	C3-C4
Salterton Road	A3
Seven Sisters Road	A2-A3-B3-B4-C4
Stavordale Road	C2
Stock Orchard Crescent	B1
Sussex Way	A4-A3-B3
Tabley Road	A2
Thame Villas	B3
Tollington Way	A3-A4
Tufnell Park Road	A2-A3
Warlters Road	A2
Wells Terrace	B4-C4
Whistler Street	C1-C2
Widdenham Road	A2-B2-B1
Wilberforce Road	C4
Windsor Road	A3
Witherington Road	C1
Wray Crescent	A4
Yonge Park	B3

ISLINGTON

Street	Grid
Almeida Street	B3
Amwell Street	A1
Baldwin Terrace	C2
Barford Street	B3
Barnsbury Park	A4-B4
Barnsbury Road	A2-A3
Barnsbury Square	A4
Barnsbury Street	A4-A3
Belitha Villas	A4
Baron Street	A1-A2
Bewdley Street	A4-B4
Bishop Street	C3
Braes Street	C4
Britannia Row	C3
Brooksbury Street	A4-B4
Camden Walk	B2
Canonbury Villas	C4
Central Street	C1
Chadwell Street	B1
Chapel Market	A2-B2
Charlotte Terrace	A2-A3
City Garden Row	C1-C2
City Road	B1-C1
Clare Square	A1
Cloudesley Place	A2-B2
Cloudesley Road	A2-A3
Cloudesley Square	A3-B3
Cloudesley Street	A2-A3
Colebrooke Row	B1-B2-B3
College Cross	B4
Copenhagen Street	A2-A3
Cross Street	B3-C3
Cruden Street	C2-C3
Culpepper Street	A2
Dagmar Terrace	B3-C3
Danbury Street	C2
Devonia Street	B2-C2
Dewey Road	A2
Donegal Street	A1-A2
Duncan Street	B2
Duncan Terrace	B1-B2
Elia Street	B2-B1-C1
Essex Road	B2-B3-C3-C4
Florence Street	B3-B4
Friend Street	B1
Frome Street	C2
Gerrard Road	B2-C2
Gibson Square	B3
Goswell Road	B1-C1
Graham Street	C1-C2
Grant Street	A2
Green Man Street	C3-C4
Hall Street	C1
Halton Road	C3-C4
Hawes Street	B4-C4
Hemingford Road	A3-A4
High Street	B2
Islington Park Street	B4
Liverpool Road	B2-B3-B4
Lloyd Street	A1
Lofting Road	A4-B4
Lonsdale Square	A3-A4
Masons Place	C1
Milner Square	B3-B4
Moon Street	B3
More Street	C1
Myddleton Square	A1-B1
New North Road	C4
Noel Road	B2-C2
Offord Road	A4
Packington Square	C2-C3
Packington Street	C3
Parkfield Street	B2
Penton Rise	A1
Penton Street	A1-A2
Pentonville Road	A1-B1
Percy Circus	A1
Percy Street	A1
Pleasant Place	C3-C4
Popham Road	C3-C4
Popham Street	C3
Prebend Street	C3
Raleigh Street	C2-C3
Rawsthorne Street	B1
Rheidol Terrace	C2
Richmond Avenue	A3-B3
Richmond Crescent	A3
Ripplevale Grove	A3-A4
River Place	C4
River Street	A1
Roseberry Avenue	B1
St John Street	B1
St Peters Street	B3-C3-C2
Sebbon Street	B4-C4
Stonefield Street	A3
Sudeley Street	B1-C1-C2
Theberton Street	B3
Thornhill Road	A3-A4
Upper Street	B2-B3-B4
Vincent Terrace	B2-C2
Wakley Street	B1
Wenlock Road	C1-C2
Wharf Road	C1-C2
White Lion Street	A2-B2

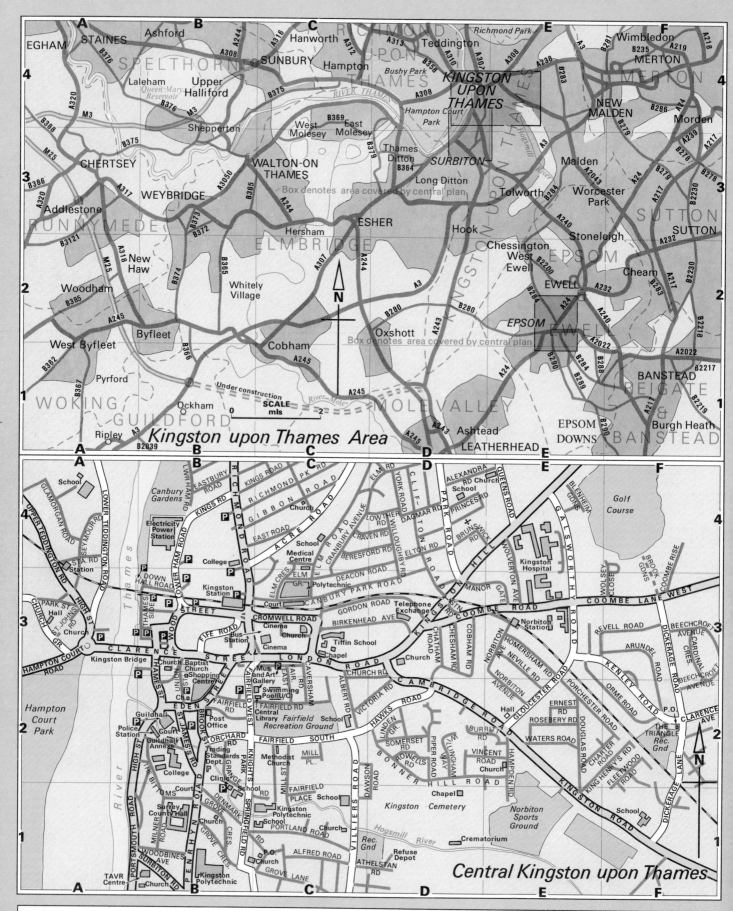

Kingston

Seven Saxon kings — at least — were crowned where the coronation stone now stands, near the Guildhall in the centre of town. Kingston kept up its connections with royalty, and they reached a peak in 1927 when George V confirmed its status as a Royal Borough.

Hampton Court, Kew Gardens and Richmond Park are all nearby. A number of ancient buildings can be seen in the High Street, and the Kingston Heritage Centre in Fairfield West is well worth a visit. A pleasant Thames-side setting, an extensive open-air market, the recently completed Eden Walk shopping precinct and a variety of old-established shops ensure Kingston's continued popularity.

Surbiton was chosen in preference to Kingston for the first local railway station in the 19th century, and rapidly grew in importance. A pleasant residential suburb, it has good entertainment facilities at the Assembly Rooms and the popular Surrey Grass Court Tennis Championships are held at Surbiton Lawn Tennis Club each year.

Epsom was already popular as a 'dormitory' town in the 18th century. Towards the end of that century, horse racing became popular on Epsom Downs, and the first Oaks was run here in 1779, followed by the first Derby in 1780. Modern Epsom is still mainly residential.

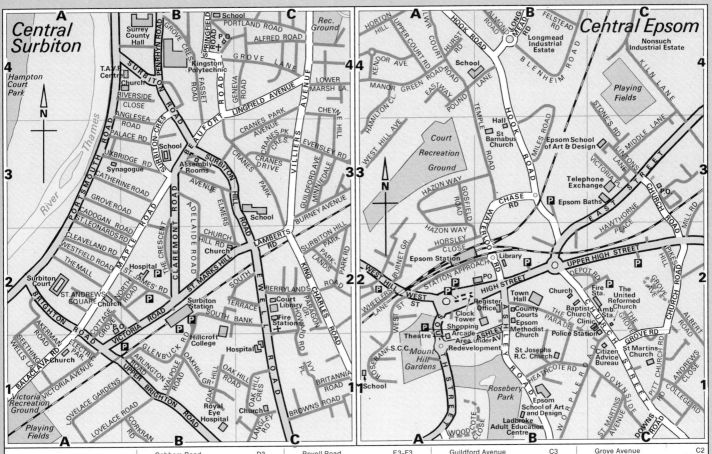

Central Surbiton

(map: Central Surbiton — labels include)
Surrey County Hall, School, PORTLAND ROAD, SPRINGFIELD ROAD, ALFRED ROAD, Rec. Ground, PENRHYN ROAD, GROVE CRES, GROVE LANE, Kingston Polytechnic, T.A.V.R. Centre, Church, RIVERSIDE CLOSE, ANGLESEA ROAD, PALACE RD, CRANES PARK AVENUE, CRANES PK CRES, LOWER MARSH LA., CHEYNE HILL, VILLIERS AVENUE, GUILDFORD AVE, MINNIEDALE, EVERSLEY RD, School, UXBRIDGE RD, Synagogue, CATHERINE ROAD, SURBITON HILL RD, School, Assembly Rooms, CRANES DRIVE, CRANES PARK, BURNEY AVENUE, GROVE ROAD, CADOGAN ROAD, ST.LEONARDS RD, CLEAVELAND RD, WESTFIELD ROAD, THE MALL, Hospital, ST.JAMES' RD, CHURCH HILL RD, Church, ST MARKS HILL, LAMBERTS RD, SOUTH TERRACE, SURBITON HILL PARK, KING CHARLES ROAD, PARK RD, Surbiton Court, ST ANDREWS SQUARE, Church, Surbiton Station, SOUTH BANK, Court Library, Fire Station, BERRYLANDS ROAD, PARAGON, HOWARD RD PK, Hillcroft College, Hospital, GLENBUCK RD, WALPOLE RD, OAKHILL RD, OAK HILL GR., OAK HILL CRES, BRITANNIA ROAD, IVY PL, ARLINGTON ROAD, UPPER BRIGHTON ROAD, LOVELACE GARDENS, LOVELACE ROAD, CORKRAN RD, Royal Eye Hospital, Church, LANGLEY RD, BROWNS ROAD, SEETHING WELLS LA, BALACLAVA RD, Church, AKERMAN RD, ELECTRIC, COTTAGE GROVE, VICTORIA, BRIGHTON ROAD, Victoria Recreation Ground, Playing Fields, Hampton Court Park, River Thames, N

Central Epsom

(map: Central Epsom — labels include)
HORTON HILL, HURST RD, UPPER COURT RD, LWR COURT RD, HOOK ROAD, ALMOND RD, LONG MEAD RD, FELSTEAD RD, Nonsuch Industrial Estate, KENDOR AVE, MANOR GREEN ROAD, EASTWAY, POUND LANE, TEMPLE ROAD, Longmead Industrial Estate, BLENHEIM ROAD, KILN LANE, STONE'S RD, MIDDLE LANE, LINTONS LANE, Playing Fields, School, Hall, St Barnabus Church, MILES ROAD, Epsom School of Art & Design, VICTORIA PL, EAST STREET, CHURCH ROAD, MILL RD, Court Recreation Ground, HAZON WAY, GOSFIELD ROAD, CHASE RD, Telephone Exchange, Epsom Baths, PO, HAWTHORNE PLACE, HAZON WAY, HORSLEY CLOSE, WATERLOO RD, UPPER HIGH STREET, DEPOT RD, Fire Sta., GROVE AVE, The United Reformed Church, WEST HILL, BURNET GR, Epsom Station, Library, STATION APPROACH, HIGH STREET, PO, Town Hall, Church, Baptist Church, Amb. Sta., Clinic, GROVE RD, ST MARTINS, ALBERT RD, WHEELERS LANE, WEST ST, Clock Tower, Shopping Arcade, Register Office, County Courts, Epsom Methodist Church, THE PARADE, Police Station, Citizen Advice Bureau, St Martins Church, Theatre, Rosebank S.C.C., Mount Hill Gardens, Area under Redevelopment, St Josephs R.C. Church, Epsom School of Art and Design, Ladbroke Adult Education Centre, ASHLEY RD, HEATHCOTE RD, DOWNSIDE, ST MARTINS AVENUE, DOWNS ROAD, PITT ROAD, COLLEGE RD, ANDREWS CLOSE, WOODCOTE CLOSE, Rosebery Park, School, N

LEGEND

Town Plan
- AA recommended route
- Restricted roads
- Other roads
- Buildings of interest
- Car parks   **P**
- Parks and open spaces

Area Plan
- A roads
- B roads
- Locations   Ockham○
- Urban area

Street Index with Grid Reference

Kingston Upon Thames

Acre Road	B4-C4
Albert Road	C2-C3
Alexandra Road	D4-E4
Alfred Road	C1
Arundel Road	F2-F3
Athelstan Road	C1-D1
Beechcroft Avenue	F2-F3
Beresford Road	C4-D4
Birkenhead Avenue	C3-D3
Blenheim Gardens	E4
Bonner Hill Road	D2-E2
Brook Gardens	F3-F4
Brook Street	B2
Brunswick Road	D4-E4
Burritt Road	D2-E2
Cambridge Road	D3-D2-E2
Canbury Park Road	C3-D3-D4
Cardinal Crescent	F3
Caversham Road	C2-F2
Charter Road	E2-F2
Chatham Road	D3
Chesham Road	D3
Church Grove	A3
Church Road	C2-C3-D3
Clarence Avenue	F2
Clarence Street	A3-B3
Clifton Road	D3-D4
Cobham Road	D3
Coombe Lane West	E3-F3
Coombe Rise	F3-F4
Coombe Road	D3-E3
Cranbury Avenue	C3-C4-D4
Craven Road	C4-D4
Cromwell Road	B3-C3
Dagmar Road	D4
Dawson Road	C1-D1-D2-C2
Deacon Road	C3-C4-D4
Denmark Road	B1-C1
Dickerage Lane	F1-F2
Dickerage Road	F2-F3
Douglas Road	E1-E2
Down Hall Road	B3
Ernest Road	E2
Eastbury Road	B4
East Road	B4-C4
Eden Street	B2-B3
Elm Crescent	C3-C4
Elm Grove	C3
Elm Road	C3-C4-D4
Elton Road	D4
Fairfield East	C2-C3
Fairfield Place	C1
Fairfield Road	B2-C2
Fairfield South	C2
Fairfield West	B2-B3-C3
Fife Road	B3
Fleetwood Road	F1-F2
Galsworthy Road	E3-E4
Gibbon Road	B4-C4
Glamorgan Road	A4
Gloucester Road	E2-E3
Gordon Road	C3-D3
Grange Road	B2-B1-C1
Grove Crescent	B1
Grove Lane	B1-C1
Hampden Road	E1-E2
Hampton Court Road	A3
Hawks Road	C2-D2
High Street	A3
High Street	A1-A2-B2
Homersham Road	E3
Kenley Road	E3-F3-F2
King Henry's Road	E1-E2-F2
Kings Road	B4-C4
Kingston Hill	D3-D4-E4
Kingston Road	E2-E1-F1
Knights Park	B1-B2
Linden Grove	D2
London Road	B3-C3-D3
Lower Ham Road	B3-B4
Lower Teddington Road	A3-A4
Lowther Road	F2
Manor Gate	D3-E3
Mill Place	C2
Mill Street	C1-C2
Milner Road	B1
Neville Road	E2-E3
Norbiton Avenue	E2-E3
Orchard Road	B2
Orme Road	E3-E2-F2
Park Road	D3-D4
Park Street	A3
Penrhyn Road	B1-B2
Piper Road	D2
Porchester Road	E2-F2
Portland Road	B1-C1
Portsmouth Road	A1-B1
Princes Road	D4
Queens Road	E4
Revell Road	E3-F3
Richmond Park Road	B4-C4
Richmond Road	B3-B4
Rosebery Road	E2
Rowells Road	B2
St James's Road	A3
St Johns Road	A3-A4
Seymour Road	D2
Somerset Road	B1
Springfield Road	A4
Station Road	A4
Station Road	D3
Surbiton Road	B1
Thames Side	B3
Thames Street	B2-B3
The Bittoms	B1-B2
The Triangle	F2
Union Street	B2-B3
Upper Teddington Road	A3-A4
Victoria Road	C2-D2
Villiers Road	C1-C2
Vincent Road	D2-E2
Waters Road	E2
Willingham Way	D2
Willoughby Road	D3-D4
Wolsey Close	F3-F4
Wolverton Avenue	E3-E4
Woodbines Avenue	B1
Wood Street	B3
York Road	D4

Surbiton

Adelaide Road	B2-B3
Akerman Road	A1-A2
Alfred Road	C4
Anglesea Road	A4-B4-B3
Arlington Road	B1
Avenue Elmers	C2-B2-B3
Balaclava Road	A1
Beaufort Road	B3-B4
Berrylands Road	C2
Brighton Road	A1-A2
Britannia Road	C1
Browns Road	C1
Burney Avenue	C3
Cadogan Road	A3-A2-B2
Catherine Road	A3-B3
Cheyne Hill	C3-C4
Church Hill Road	B2
Claremont Road	B2-B3
Cleaveland Road	A2
Corkran Road	B1
Cottage Grove	A1-A2
Cranes Drive	C3
Cranes Park	B3-C3-B2
Cranes Park Avenue	B3-C3-C4
Cranes Park Crescent	C3
Electric Parade	A1
Eversley Road	C3
Ewell Road	C1-C2
Fasset Road	B3-B4
Geneva Road	C4
Glenbuck Road	B1-B2
Grove Crescent	B4
Grove Lane	B4-C4
Grove Road	A3-B3-B2
Guildford Avenue	C3
Howard Road	C1-C2
Ivy Place	C1
King Charles Road	C1-C2
Lamberts Road	C2
Langley Road	C1
Lingfield Avenue	B4-C4
Lovelace Gardens	A1-B1
Lovelace Road	A1-B1
Lower Marsh Lane	C4
Maple Road	A2-B2-B3
Minniedale	C3
North Road	A2-B2
Oakhill	B1
Oakhill Crescent	C1
Oakhill Grove	B1
Oakhill Road	B1-C1
Palace Road	A3-B3
Paragon Grove	C2
Parklands	C2
Park Road	C2
Penrhyn Road	B4
Portland Road	B4-C4
Portsmouth Road	A2-A3-A4
Riverside Close	A4-B4
St Andrews Square	A2
St James' Road	A2-B2
St Leonards Road	A3-A2-B2
St Marks Hill	B2-C2
Seething Wells Lane	A1-A2
South Bank	B2-C2
South Terrace	B2-C2
Springfield Road	B4
Surbiton Crescent	B3-B4
Surbiton Hill Park	C2
Surbiton Hill Road	B3-C3-C2
Surbiton Road	B3-B4
The Crescent	B2-B3
The Mall	A2
Upper Brighton Road	A1-B1
Uxbridge Road	A3-B3
Victoria Avenue	A1
Victoria Road	A1-B1-B2
Villiers Avenue	C2-C3-C4
Walpole Road	B1
Westfield Road	A2

Epsom

Albert Road	C1-C2
Almond Road	B4
Andrews Close	C1
Ashley Avenue	A1-B1
Ashley Road	B1-B2
Blenheim Road	B4
Burnet Grove	A2
Chase Road	B3
Church Road	C1-C2-C3
Church Street	B2-C2-C1
College Road	C1
Depot Road	B2-C2
Downside	C1
Downs Road	C1
East Street	B2-B3-C3
East Way	A4
Felstead Road	B4
Gosfield Road	A2-A3
Grove Avenue	C2
Grove Road	C1-C2
Hamilton Close	A3-A4
Hawthorne Place	C2-C3
Hazon Way	B2-A2-A3-B3
Heathcote Road	B1
High Street	A2-B2
Hook Road	A4-B4-B3-B2
Horsley Close	A3-B2
Horton Hill	A4
Hurst Road	A4
Kendor Avenue	A4
Kiln Lane	C3-C4
Lintons Lane	C3
Long Mead Road	B4
Lower Court Road	A4
Manor Green Road	A4
Middle Lane	C3-C4
Miles Road	B3-B4-B3
Mill Road	C2-C3
Pikes Hill	C2
Pitt Road	C1
Pound Lane	A4-B4
Rosebank	A1
St Martins Avenue	C1
South Street	A1-A2
Station Approach	A2-B2
Stone's Road	C3-C4
Temple Road	A4-B4-A3-B3
The Grove	C1
The Parade	B2-B1-C1
Upper Court Road	A4
Upper High Street	B2-C2
Victoria Place	C3
Waterloo Road	B2-B3
West Hill	A2
West Hill Avenue	A3
West Street	A1-A2
Wheelers Lane	A2
Woodcote Close	A1-B1-A1
Worple Road	B1-C1

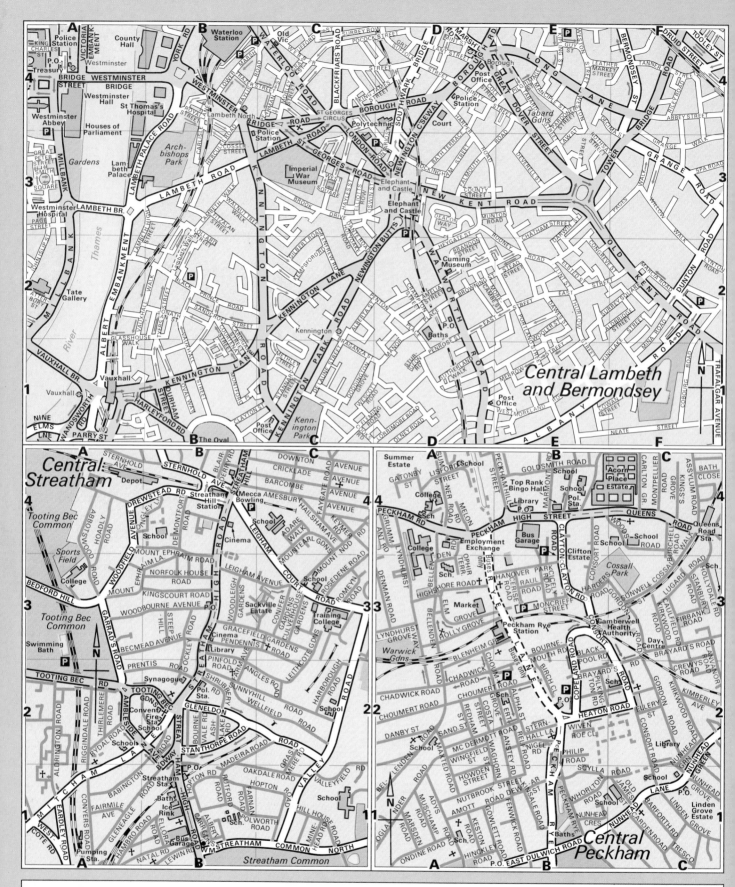

Lambeth

Lambeth/Bermondsey A memory of other times for Lambeth can be found in Cherry Gardens Pier, which juts into the Thames at Bermondsey Wall East and recalls the days when this was a resort area (spa waters were found here in the 18th century). Some 13 Victorian churches can be found in the borough, and two places of interest are the Imperial War Museum and the Cuming Museum, which displays local archaeological finds. The Oval is the home of Surrey County Cricket Club.

Streatham Cinemas, dance halls, theatres, a bowling alley, an ice-rink and a swimming pool made Streatham a major entertainment centre for south London after the Second World War, and to some extent it still has that role. It first became popular with city merchants after the Great Fire because of its pleasant rural setting, and later on, spa waters were discovered on Streatham Common, which still has 36 acres of land.

Brixton The present site was a wasteland until suburban development reached it in the early 19th century. The large Italianate houses of St Johns Crescent are typical of the period.

Peckham was covered with market gardens and pasture until the 19th century. It still enjoys the 64 acres of Peckham Rye Common and the sports facilities of Peckham Rye Park. The house at No 2 Woods Road, Peckham, dates back to about 1690.

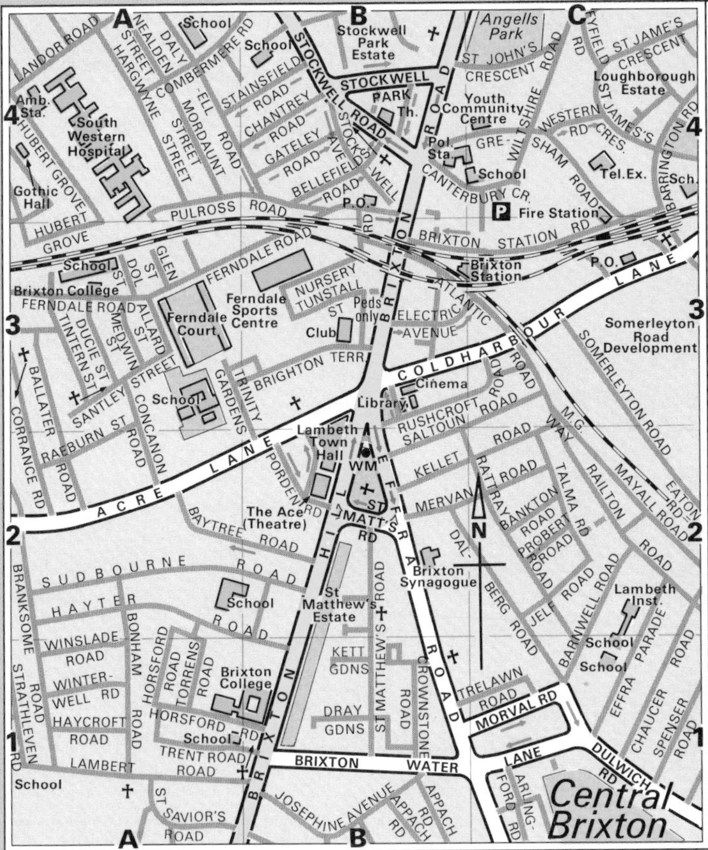

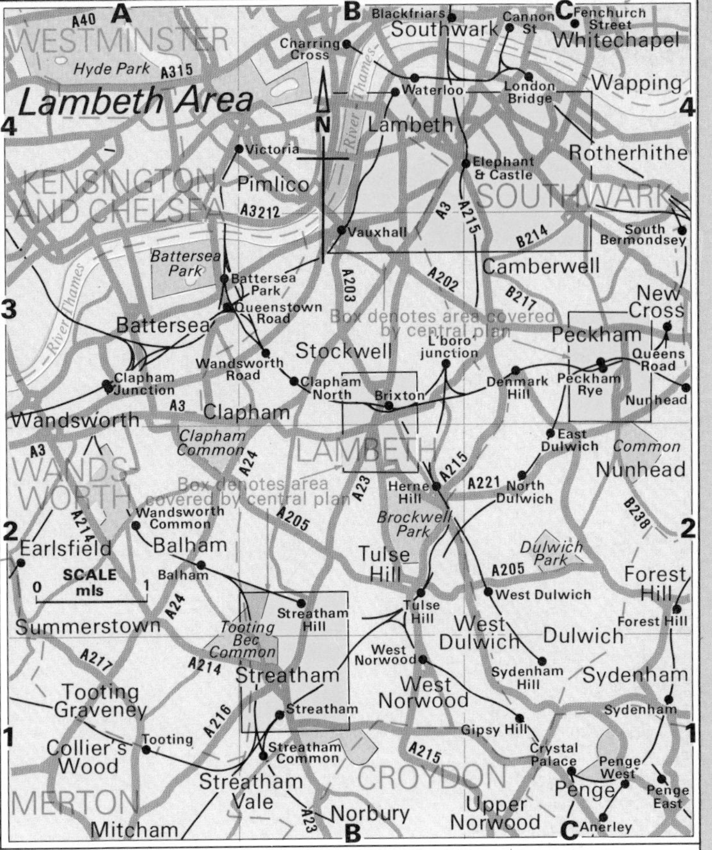

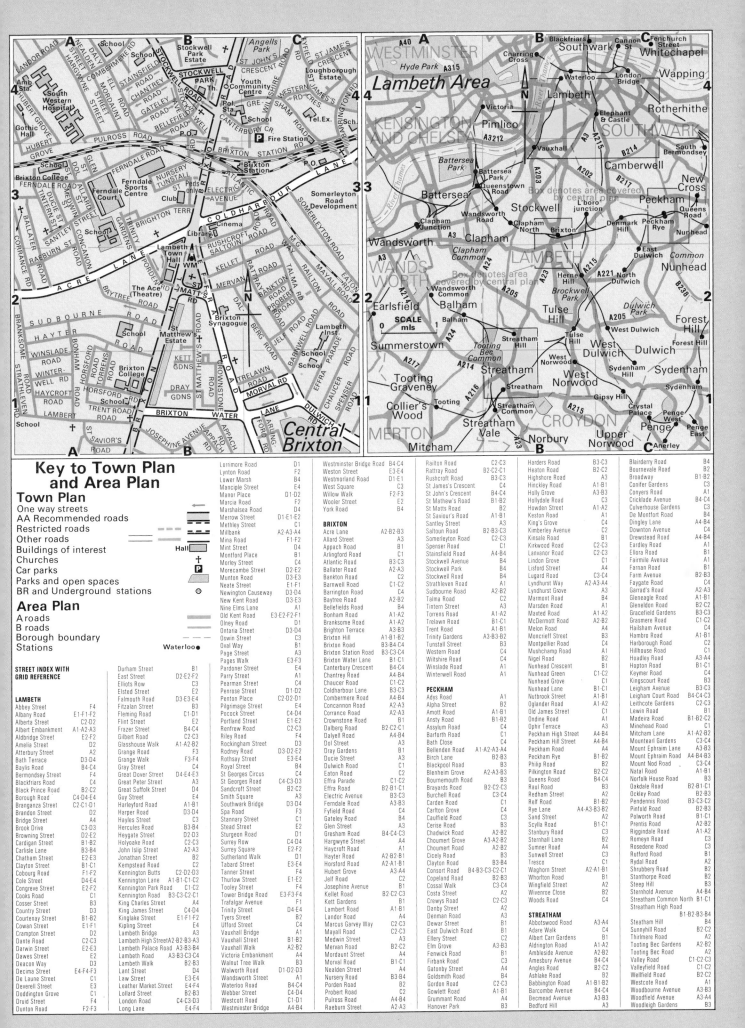

Key to Town Plan and Area Plan

Town Plan

- One way streets
- AA Recommended roads
- Restricted roads
- Other roads
- Buildings of interest — Hall
- Churches
- Car parks
- Parks and open spaces
- BR and Underground stations

Area Plan

- A roads
- B roads
- Borough boundary
- Stations — Waterloo

STREET INDEX WITH GRID REFERENCE

LAMBETH

Abbey Street	F4
Albany Road	E1-F1-F2
Alberta Street	C2-D2
Albert Embankment	A1-A2-A3
Aldbridge Street	E2-F2
Amelia Street	D2
Atterbury Street	A2
Bath Terrace	D3-D4
Baylis Road	B4-C4
Bermondsey Street	F4
Blackfriars Road	C4
Black Prince Road	B2-C2
Borough Road	C4-D4-E4
Branganza Street	C2-C1-D1
Brandon Street	D2
Bridge Street	A4
Brook Drive	C3-D3
Browning Street	D2-E2
Cardigan Street	B1-B2
Carlisle Lane	B3-B4
Chatham Street	E2-E3
Clayton Street	B1-C1
Cobourg Road	F1-F2
Cole Street	D4-E4
Congreve Street	E2-F2
Cooks Road	C1
Cosser Street	B3
Country Street	D3
Courtenay Street	B1-B2
Cowan Street	E1-F1
Crampton Street	D2
Dante Road	C2-C3
Darwin Street	E2-E3
Dawes Street	E2
Deacon Way	D3
Decima Street	E4-F4-F3
De Laune Street	C1
Deverell Street	E3
Doddington Grove	C1
Druid Street	F4
Dunton Road	F2-F3
Durham Street	B1
East Street	D2-E2-F2
Elliots Row	C3
Elsted Street	E2
Falmouth Road	D3-E3-E4
Fitzalan Street	B3
Fleming Road	C1-D1
Flint Street	E2
Frazer Street	B4-C4
Gilbert Road	C2-C3
Glasshouse Walk	A1-A2-B2
Grange Road	F3
Grange Walk	F3-F4
Gray Street	C4
Great Dover Street	D4-E4-E3
Great Peter Street	A3
Great Suffolk Street	D4
Guy Street	E4
Harleyford Road	A1-B1
Harper Road	D3-D4
Hayles Street	C3
Hercules Road	B3-B4
Heygate Street	D2-D3
Holyoake Road	C2-C3
John Islip Street	A2-A3
Jonathan Street	B2
Kempstead Road	C2
Kennington Butts	C2-D2-D3
Kennington Lane	A1-B1-C1-C2
Kennington Park Road	C1-C2
Kennington Road	B3-C3-C2-C1
King Charles Street	A4
King James Street	C4-D4
Kinglake Street	E1-F1-F2
Kipling Street	E4
Lambeth Bridge	A3
Lambeth High Street	A2-B2-B3-A3
Lambeth Palace Road	A3-B3-B4
Lambeth Road	A3-B3-C3-C4
Lambeth Walk	B2-B3
Lant Street	D4
Law Street	E3-E4
Leather Market Street	E4-F4
Lollard Street	B2-B3
London Road	C4-C3-D3
Long Lane	E4-F4
Lorrimore Road	D1
Lynton Road	F2
Lower Marsh	B4
Manciple Street	E4
Manor Place	D1-D2
Marcia Road	F2
Marshalsea Road	D4
Merrow Street	D1-E1-E2
Methley Street	C1
Millbank	A2-A3-A4
Mina Road	F1-F2
Mint Street	D4
Montford Place	B1
Morley Street	C4
Morecambe Street	D2-E2
Munton Road	D3-E3
Neate Street	E1-F1
Newington Causeway	D3-D4
New Kent Road	D3-E3
Nine Elms Lane	A1
Old Kent Road	E3-E2-F2-F1
Olney Road	D1
Ontaria Street	D3-D4
Oswin Street	C3
Oval Way	B1
Page Street	A3
Pages Walk	E3-F3
Pardoner Street	E4
Parry Street	A1
Pearman Street	C4
Penrose Street	D1-D2
Penton Place	C2-D2-D1
Pilgrimage Street	E4
Pocock Street	C4-D4
Portland Street	E1-E2
Renfrew Road	C2-C3
Riley Road	F4
Rockingham Street	D3
Rodney Road	D3-D2-E2
Rothsay Street	E3-E4
Royal Street	B4
St Georges Circus	C4
St Georges Road	C4-C3-D3
Sandcroft Street	B2-C2
Smith Square	A3
Southwark Bridge	D3-D4
Spa Road	F3
Stannary Street	C1
Stead Street	E2
Sturgeon Road	D1
Surrey Row	C4-D4
Surrey Square	E2-F2
Sutherland Walk	D1
Tabard Street	E3-E4
Tanner Street	F4
Thurlow Street	E1-E2
Tooley Street	F4
Tower Bridge Road	E3-F3-F4
Trafalgar Avenue	F1
Trinity Street	D4-E4
Tyers Street	B2
Ufford Street	C4
Vauxhall Bridge	A1
Vauxhall Street	B1-B2
Vauxhall Walk	A2-B2
Victoria Embankment	A4
Walnut Tree Walk	B3
Walworth Road	D1-D2-D3
Wandsworth Street	A1
Waterloo Road	B4-C4
Webber Street	C4-D4
Westcott Road	C1-D1
Westminster Bridge	A4-B4
Westminster Bridge Road	B4-C4
Weston Street	E3-E4
Westmorland Road	D1-E1
West Square	C3
Willow Walk	F2-F3
Wooler Street	E2
York Road	B4

BRIXTON

Acre Lane	A2-B2-B3
Allard Street	A3
Appach Road	B1
Arlingford Road	C1
Atlantic Road	B3-C3
Ballater Road	A2-A3
Bankton Road	C2
Barnwell Road	C1-C2
Barrington Road	C4
Baytree Road	A2-B2
Bellefields Road	B4
Bonham Road	A1-A2
Branksome Road	A1-A2
Brighton Terrace	A3-B3
Brixton Hill	A1-B1-B2
Brixton Road	B3-B4-C4
Brixton Station Road	B3-C3-C4
Brixton Water Lane	B1-C1
Canterbury Crescent	B4-C4
Chantrey Road	A4-B4
Chaucer Road	C1-C2
Coldharbour Lane	B3-C3
Combermere Road	A4-B4
Concannon Road	A2-A3
Corrance Road	A2-A3
Crownstone Road	B1
Dalberg Road	B2-C2-C1
Dalyell Road	A4-B4
Dol Street	A3
Dray Gardens	B1
Ducie Street	A3
Dulwich Road	C1
Eaton Road	C2
Effra Parade	C1-C2
Effra Road	B2-B1-C1
Electric Avenue	B3-C3
Ferndale Road	A3-B3
Fyfield Road	C4
Gateley Road	B4
Glen Street	A3
Gresham Road	B4-C4-C3
Hargwyne Street	A4
Haycroft Road	A1
Hayter Road	A2-B2-B1
Horsford Road	A2-A1-B1
Hubert Grove	A3-A4
Jelf Road	C2
Josephine Avenue	B1
Kellet Road	B2-C2-C3
Kett Gardens	B1
Lambert Road	A1-B1
Landor Road	A4
Marcus Garvey Way	C2-C3
Mayall Road	C2-C3
Medwin Street	A3
Mervan Road	B2-C2
Mordaunt Street	A4
Morval Road	B1-C1
Nealden Street	A4
Nursery Road	B3-B4
Porden Road	B2
Probert Road	C2
Pulross Road	A4-B4
Raeburn Street	A2-A3
Railton Road	C2-C3
Rattray Road	B2-C2-C1
Rushcroft Road	B3-C3
St James's Crescent	C4
St John's Crescent	B4-C4
St Mathew's Road	B1-B2
St Matts Road	B2
St Saviour's Road	A1-B1
Santley Street	A3
Saltoun Road	B2-B3-C3
Somerleyton Road	C2-C3
Spenser Road	C1
Stainsfield Road	A4-B4
Stockwell Avenue	B4
Stockwell Park	B4
Stockwell Road	B4
Strathleven Road	A1
Sudbourne Road	A2-B2
Talma Road	C2
Tintern Street	A3
Torrens Road	A1-A2
Trelawn Road	B1-C1
Trent Road	A1-B1
Trinity Gardens	A3-B3-B2
Tunstall Street	B3
Western Road	C4
Wiltshire Road	C4
Winslade Road	A1
Winterwell Road	A1

PECKHAM

Adys Road	A1
Alpha Street	B2
Amott Road	A1-B1
Ansty Road	B1-B2
Assylum Road	C4
Barforth Road	C1
Bath Close	C4
Bellenden Road	A1-A2-A3-A4
Birch Lane	B2-B3
Blackpool Road	B3
Blenheim Grove	A2-A3-B3
Bournemouth Road	B3
Brayards Road	B2-C2-C3
Burchell Road	C3-C4
Carden Road	C1
Carlton Grove	C4
Caulfield Road	C3
Cerise Road	B3
Chadwick Road	A2-B2
Choumert Grove	A3-A2-B2
Choumert Road	A2-B2
Cicely Road	B3
Clayton Road	B3-B4
Consort Road	B4-B3-C3-C2-C1
Copeland Road	B2-B3
Cossal Walk	C3-C4
Costa Street	A2
Crewys Road	C2-C3
Danby Street	A2
Denman Road	A3
Dewar Street	B1
East Dulwich Road	B1
Ellery Street	C2
Elm Grove	A3-B3
Fenwick Road	B1
Firbank Road	C3
Gatonby Street	A4
Goldsmith Road	B4
Gordon Road	C2-C3
Gowlett Road	A1-B1
Grummant Road	A4
Hanover Park	B3
Harders Road	B3-C3
Heaton Road	B2-C2
Highshore Road	A3
Hinckley Road	A1-B1
Holly Grove	A3-B3
Hollydale Road	C3
Howden Street	A1-A2
Keston Road	A1
King's Grove	C4
Kimberley Avenue	C2
Kinsale Road	B1
Kirkwood Road	C2-C3
Lanvanor Road	C2-C3
Lindon Grove	C1
Lisford Street	A4
Lugard Road	C3-C4
Lyndhurst Way	A2-A3-A4
Lyndhurst Grove	A3
Marmont Road	B4
Marsden Road	A1
Maxted Road	A1-A2
McDermott Road	A2-B2
Melon Road	A4
Moncrieff Street	B3
Montpellier Road	C4
Mushchamp Road	A1
Nigel Road	B2
Nunhead Crescent	B1
Nunhead Green	C1-C2
Nunhead Grove	C1
Nunhead Lane	B1-C1
Nutbrook Street	A1-B1
Oglander Road	A1-A2
Old James Street	C1
Ondine Road	A1
Ophir Terrace	A3
Peckham High Street	A4-B4
Peckham Hill Street	A4-B4
Peckham Road	A4
Peckham Rye	B1-B2
Philip Road	B2
Pilkington Road	B2-C2
Queens Road	B4-C4
Raul Road	B3
Redham Street	A2
Relf Road	B1-B2
Rye Lane	A4-A3-B3-B2
Sand Street	A2
Scylla Road	B1-C1
Stanbury Road	C3
Sternhall Lane	B2
Sumner Road	A4
Sunwell Street	C3
Tresco	C1
Waghorn Street	A2-A1-B1
Whorlton Road	B1
Wingfield Street	A2
Wivenroe Close	B2
Woods Road	C4

STREATHAM

Abbotswood Road	A3-A4
Adare Walk	C4
Albert Carr Gardens	B1
Aldrington Road	A1-A2
Ambleside Avenue	A2-B2
Amesbury Avenue	B4-C4
Angles Road	B2-C2
Ashlake Road	B2
Babbington Road	A1-B1-B2
Barcombe Avenue	B4-C4
Becmead Avenue	A3-B3
Bedford Hill	A3
Blairderry Road	B4
Bournevale Road	B2
Broadway	B1-B2
Conifer Gardens	C3
Conyers Road	A1
Cricklade Avenue	B4-C4
Culverhouse Gardens	C3
De Montfort Road	B4
Dingley Lane	A4-B4
Downton Avenue	C4
Drewstead Road	A4-B4
Eardley Road	A1
Ellora Road	B1
Fairmile Avenue	A1
Farnan Road	B1
Farm Avenue	B2-B3
Faygate Road	C4
Garrad's Road	A2-A3
Gleneagle Road	A1-B1
Gleneldon Road	B2-C2
Gracefield Gardens	B3-C3
Grasmere Road	C1-C2
Hailsham Avenue	C4
Hambro Road	A1-B1
Harborough Road	C2
Hillhouse Road	C1
Hoadley Road	A3-A4
Hopton Road	B1-C1
Keymer Road	C4
Kingscourt Road	B3
Leigham Avenue	B3-C3
Leigham Court Road	B4-C4-C3
Leithcote Gardens	C2-C3
Lewin Road	B1
Madeira Road	B1-B2-C2
Minehead Road	C1
Mitcham Lane	A1-A2-B2
Mountearl Gardens	C3-C4
Mount Ephraim Lane	A3-B3
Mount Ephraim Road	A4-B4-B3
Mount Nod Road	C3-C4
Natal Road	A1-B1
Norfolk House Road	B3
Oakdale Road	B2-B1-C1
Ockley Road	B2-B3
Pendennis Road	B3-C3-C2
Pinfold Road	B2-B3
Polworth Road	B1-C1
Prentis Road	A2-B2
Riggindale Road	A1-A2
Romeyn Road	C3
Rosedene Road	C3
Rutford Road	B1
Rydal Road	A2
Shrubbery Road	B2
Stanthorpe Road	B2
Steep Hill	B3
Sternhold Avenue	A4-B4
Streatham Common North	B1-C1
Streatham High Road	B1-B2-B3-B4
Steatham Hill	B4
Sunnyhill Road	B2-C2
Thirlmere Road	A2
Tooting Bec Gardens	A2-B2
Tooting Bec Road	A2
Valley Road	C1-C2-C3
Valleyfield Road	C1-C2
Wellfield Road	B2-C2
Westcote Road	A1
Woodbourne Avenue	A3-B3
Woodfield Avenue	A3-A4
Woodleigh Gardens	B3

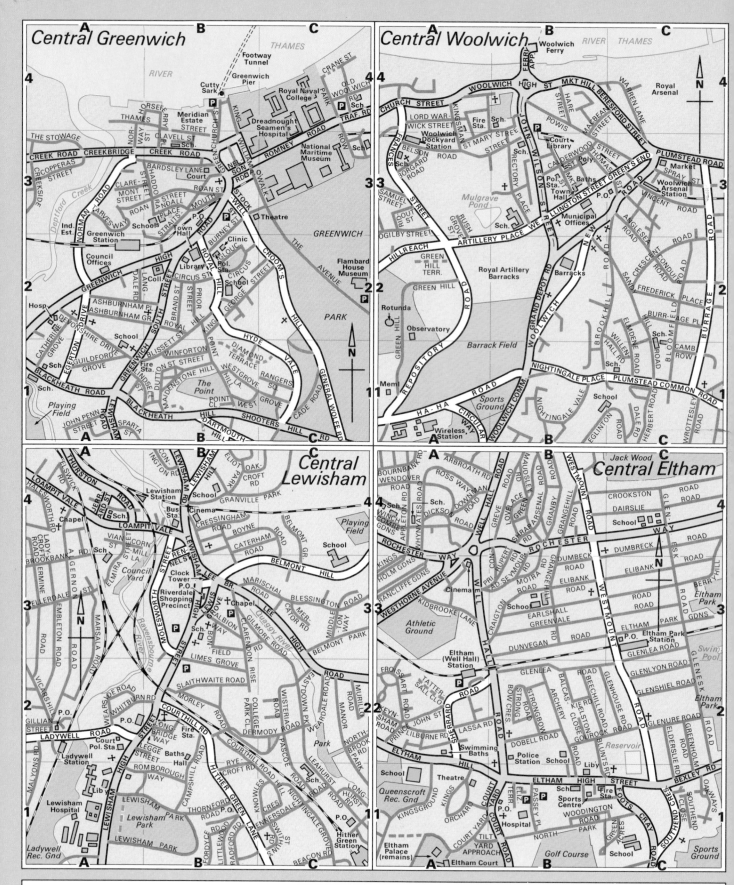

Lewisham

This is a popular destination for south-east Londoners, who come for the good shopping and leisure facilities. Most of these can be found in the Riverside Centre, which also offers the sports facilities of the Lewisham Leisure Centre, and, for social functions, the Riverdale Hall.

Greenwich lies at the heart of Britain's maritime traditions. The Royal Naval College and the National Maritime Museum provide a fascinating insight into the seafaring past. Open to visitors on Greenwich pier is Gypsy Moth IV, the boat in which Sir Francis Chichester sailed singlehanded round the world in 1966. Cutty Sark, a 19th-century clipper, is in dry dock nearby.

The Greenwich Meridian, source of Greenwich Mean Time, can be seen outside the Old Royal Observatory (now a museum) which stands in the extensive and beautiful grounds of Greenwich Park.

The Greenwich Festival takes place each June at various venues throughout the Borough, and offers some 200 events featuring international artists.

Woolwich The South-East London Aquatic Centre, in the Dockyard, offers facilities for most water sports. The Rotunda houses the Museum of Artillery.

Eltham is notable as the birthplace of Bob Hope — and for the restored 14th-century Eltham Palace. The Great Hall was built originally by Edward IV, during the 15th century.

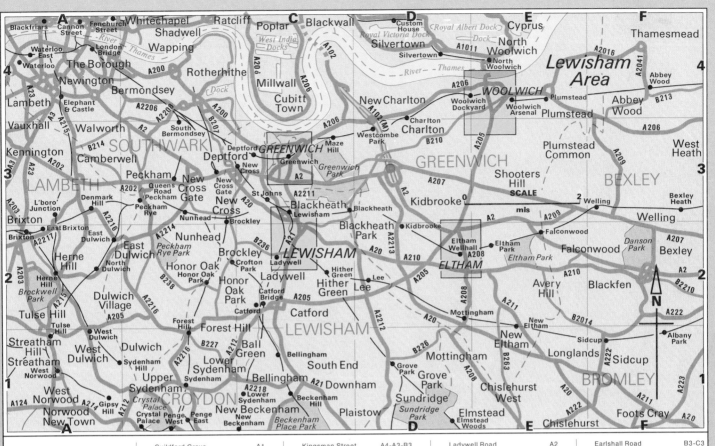

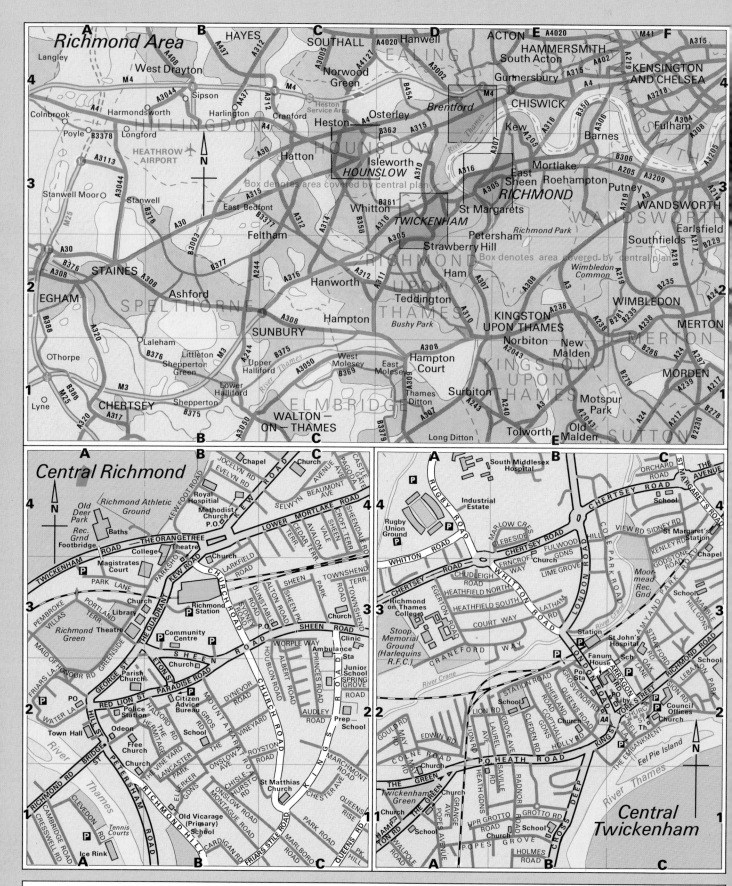

Richmond

Red deer and fallow deer roam Richmond Park's 2,500 acres of woodland and common, and Richmond itself has kept a village-like atmosphere in spite of a great deal of development over the last two centuries. Around the Green, antique and curio shops can be found nestling among the narrow lanes and alleyways of a bygone age. Richmond's other great attraction is the river: this has been a fashionable residential area for several hundred years, due to its pleasant Thames-side location and its proximity to Hampton Court Palace.

Twickenham Regular international matches are played during the season at this home of Rugby Union Football. Places of interest include Marble Hill House, a Palladian villa set in pleasant parkland, the Orleans House Gallery, which has paintings of local scenes, and the nearby Royal Botanic Gardens at Kew.

Hounslow Gunpowder and swords were the pride of Hounslow in the 17th century; three hundred years later, the area is mainly residential, with good shopping and leisure facilities.

Brentford's modern urban appearance belies its numerous places of interest. Gunnersbury Park has a local history museum, and St George's Church, in the High Street, houses a collection of musical instruments. A museum of steam engines can be seen at Kew Bridge Pumping Station.

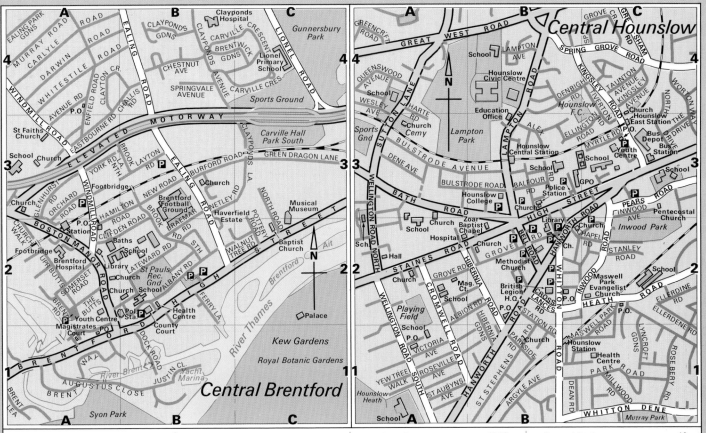

Central Brentford

Central Hounslow

Key to Town Plan and Area Plan

Town Plan

AA Recommended roads
Other roads
Restricted roads
Buildings of interest
Churches   Church
Car Parks   P
Parks and open spaces
AA Service Centre   AA

Area Plan

A roads
B roads
Locations   Honley O
Urban area

Richmond

Albert Road	C2-C3
Alton Road	C3
Audley Road	C2
Avalon Terrace	C3-C4
Beaumont Avenue	C4
Bridge Street	A1-A2
Cambridge Road	A1
Cardigan Road	B1
Castle Gate	C4
Cedar Terrace	C4
Chester Road	C1
Chislehurst Road	B1
Church Road	B3-B2-C2-C1
Clevedon Road	A1
Cresswell Road	A1
Crofton Terrace	C4
Dunstable Road	B3-C3
Dynevor Road	B2
Ellerker Gardens	B1
Eton Street	B2-B3
Evelyn Road	B4
Friars Lane	A2
Friars Stile Road	B1-C1
George Street	A2-A3
Greenside	A2-A3
Grosvenor Road	B2
Halford Road	B2
Hill Street	A2
Houblon Road	C2-C3
Jocelyn Road	B4-C4
Kew Foot Road	B4
Kew Road	B3-B4-C4
Kings Road	C1-C2-C3
Lancaster Park	B1-B2
Larkfield Road	B3-C3
Lower Mortlake Road	B4-C4
Maid of Honour Road	A3-A2
Marchmont Road	C1-C2
Marlborough Road	C1
Montague Road	B1
Mount Ararat Road	B2-B1-C1
Onslow Avenue	B1-B2
Onslow Road	B1-C1

Pagoda Avenue	C4
Paradise Road	B2
Park Hill	C1
Park Lane	A3-B3
Park Road	C1
Parkshot	A3-B3-B4
Pembroke Villas	A3
Petersham Road	A2-A1-B1
Portland Terrace	A3
Princes Road	C2-C3
Queens Rise	C1
Queens Road	C1
Red Lion Street	A2-B2
Richmond Hill	A1-B1
Richmond Road	A1
Royston Road	B2-C2
Selwyn Avenue	C4
Sheendale Road	C4
Sheen Park	C4
Sheen Road	B3-B2-B3-C3
Sheen Vale	C4
Spring Grove Road	C2
Sydney Road	B3
The Hermitage	A2-B2
The Orange Tree	A4-B4
The Quadrant	A3-B3
The Vineyard	A1-B1-B2
Townshend Road	C3
Townshend Terrace	C3
Twickenham Road	A3-A4
Water Lane	A2
Worple Way	C3

Twickenham

Amyand Park Road	C3-C4
Arragon Road	C2
Bell Lane	C2
Chertsey Road	A3-A4-B3-B4-C4
Chudleigh Road	A3-B3
Chuch Street	C2
Clifden Road	B2
Cole Park Road	B3-C3-B3-B4
Colne Road	A1-A2
Copthall Gardens	B2
Court Way	A3-B3
Craneford Way	A2-A3-B3
Cross Deep	B1-B2
Edwin Road	A2
Egerton Road	A3
Erncroft Way	B3-B4
Fulwood Gardens	B4
Glebeside	B4
Godstone Road	C3-C4
Gould Road	A2
Grange Avenue	A1
Grosvenor Road	B2
Grotto Road	B1
Grove Avenue	B2
Hampton Road	A1
Heathfield North	A3-B3
Heathfield South	A3-B3
Heath Gardens	A1-B1
Heath Road	A1-A2-B2
Hill View Road	B4-C4
Holly Road	B2
Holmes Road	B1
Kenley Road	C4
King Street	B2-C2
Latham Road	B3
Laurel Avenue	A2-B2
Lebanon Park	C2
Lime Grove	B3

Brentford

Albany Road	B2
Augustus Close	A1-B1
Avenue Road	A3-A4
Boston Manor Road	A1-A2-A3
Braemar Road	B2-B3
Brentford High Street	A1-B1-B2-C2-C3
Brent Lea	A1
Brent Road	A2
Brent Way	A1
Brentwick Gardens	B4-C4
Brook Lane North	A3-B3
Brook Road South	B2-B3
Burford Road	B3-C3
Carlyle Road	A4
Carville Crescent	B4-C4-B4
Challis Road	A4-B4
Chestnut Avenue	B4
Church Walk	A2
Clayponds Avenue	B4
Clayponds Gardens	B4
Clayponds Lane	B4
Clayton Crescent	A4-B4
Clifden Road	A2-B2-B3
Darwin Road	A4-B4
Dock Road	B1
Ealing Park Gardens	A4
Ealing Road	B4-B3-B2
Eastbourne Road	A3-A4
Enfield Road	A3-A4
Ferry Lane	B2
Glenhurst Road	A2-A3
Green Dragon Lane	C3
Hamilton Road	A2-A3-B3
Justin Close	B1
Lateward Road	B2
Layton Road	B3
Lionel Road	A4
Murray Road	A4
Netley Road	B3-C3
New Road	B3
North Road	C2-C3
Orchard Road	A2-A3
Pottery Road	C2-C3

Lion Road	A2-B2
London Road	B4-B3-B2-C2
Marble Hill Gardens	C3
Marlow Crescent	B4
May Road	A1-A2
Oak Lane	C2-C3
Orchard Road	C4
Popes Avenue	A1
Popes Grove	A1-B1
Queens Road	B2
Radnor Road	B1-B2
Richmond Road	C2-C3
Rugby Road	A4
St Margaret's Road	C4
Saville Road	B1
Sherland Road	B2
Sidney Road	C4
Sion Road	C2
Station Road	B2
Strafford Road	C2-C3
The Avenue	C4
The Embankment	C1-C2
The Green	A1
Upper Grotto Road	A1-B1
Walpole Road	A1
Whitton Road	A3-A4-A3-B3
York Street	C2

Hounslow

Albion Road	A1-A2-B2
Alexandra Road	B3
Argyle Avenue	B1
Balfour Road	B3
Bath Road	A3-B3-B2
Bell Road	B2
Bulstrode Avenue	A3-B3
Bulstrode Road	A3-B3
Chapel Road	B2-C2
Cromwell Road	A2-A1-B1
Cross Lances Road	B2
Dean Road	B1
Denbigh Road	B4-C4
Dene Avenue	A3
Ellerdine Road	C1-C2
Ellington Road	B3-C3
Great West Road	A4-B4
Greencroft Road	A4
Gresham Road	C4
Grove Road	A2-B2
Hanworth Road	A1-B1-B2-B3-C2-C3
Harte Road	A3-A4
Heath Road	B2-C2
Hibernia Gardens	B1-B2
Hibernia Road	A2-B2-B1
High Street	B2-B3-C3
Inwood Avenue	C2-C3
Inwood Road	B2-C2-C3
Kingsley Avenue	C4
Kingsley Road	B4-C4-C3
Lampton Avenue	B4
Lampton Road	B3-B4
Lyncroft Gardens	C1-C2
Maswell Park Road	B1-C1-C2
Millwood Road	C1
Myrtle Road	C3
North Drive	C3-C4
Park Road	B1-C1
Parkside Road	B1
Pears Road	C3
Queenswood Avenue	A4
Rosebery Road	C1
Roseville Avenue	A1
St Aubyns Avenue	A1
St Stephens Road	B1
Spring Grove Crescent	C4
Spring Grove Road	B4-C4
Staines Road	A2-B2
Stanley Road	C2
Station Road	B1-B2
Sutton Lane	A3-A4
Taunton Avenue	C4
The Drive	C3
Tiverton Road	C3-C4
Victoria Avenue	A2-A3
Wellington Road North	A2-A3
Wellington Road South	A1-A2
Wesley Avenue	A3-A4
Whitton Dene	B1-C1
Whitton Road	B1-B2
Worton Way	C3-C4
Yew Tree Walk	A1

Somerset Road	A2
Springvale Avenue	B4
The Butts	A2
Upper Butts	A2
Walnut Tree Road	B2-C2
Windmill Road	A2-A3-A4
Whitstile Road	A4-B4
York Road	A3

35

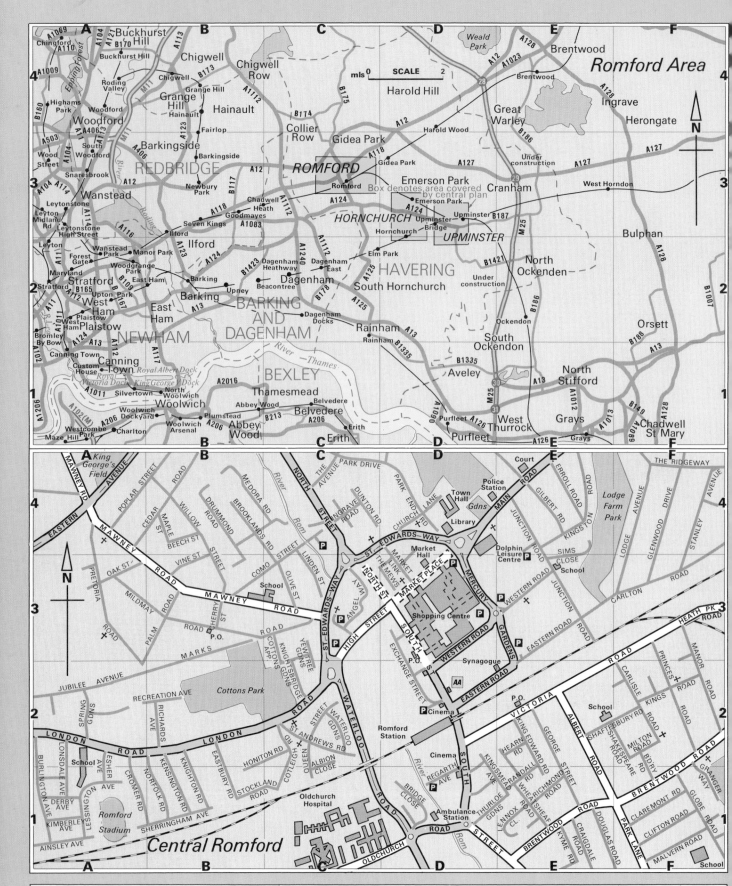

Romford

Reputed to have some of the finest shopping facilities on the east side of London, Romford mixes the ancient with the modern in its high streets and traffic areas. Centrepiece of all shopping is Romford Market, where traders have been setting up stall three times a week for the past 700 years.

The oldest-founded building still standing in Romford is thought to be St Edward's Church, which was rebuilt in 1850 and has some interesting monuments. The Golden Lion survives as a fine example of an old coaching inn.

Hornchurch A bull's head and horns hung over the east window of St Andrew's Church gave Hornchurch its name — thought to be the only example in the country to be used instead of the traditional east end cross. Also unique to the church is the tomb of Thomas Witherings,

17th-century organiser of the postal system.

Modern shops line the High Street, which was once known as Pelt Street: Hornchurch was famous for its leather goods in the 13th century. The Queens Theatre stages concerts and professional repertory performances of a high standard.

Upminster's windmill was constructed in 1803 and has remained in excellent condition. Other buildings of interest include Upminster Hall and 15th-century Upminster Tithe Barn.

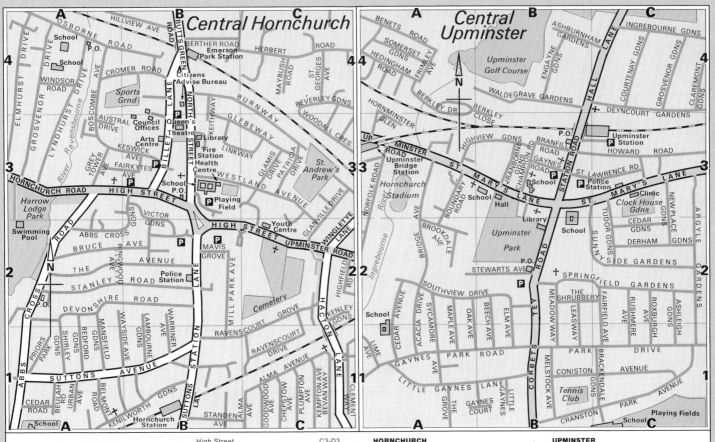

LEGEND

Town Plan

AA Recommended roads
Other roads
Restricted roads
Buildings of interest — Cinema
Car Parks — P
Parks and open spaces

Area Plan

A roads
B roads
Stations — Forest Bridge
Borough Boundary

STREET INDEX WITH GRID REFERENCE

ROMFORD

Ainsley Avenue	A1
Albert Road	E1-E2
Albion Close	C1-C2
Angel Way	C3
Beech Street	B4
Boundary Road	F1-F2
Brentwood Road	E1-F1-F2
Bridge Close	D1
Brooklands Road	B4-C4-C3
Burlington Avenue	A1-A2
Carlisle Road	F2
Carlton Road	E3-F3-F4
Cedar Road	A4-B4
Cherry Street	B3
Church Lane	D4
Claremont Road	F1
Clifton Road	F1
Como Street	B3-C3-C4
Cotleigh Road	C1-C2
Cottons Approach	C2-C3
Craigdale Road	E1
Cromer Road	A2-A1-B1
Derby Avenue	A1
Douglas Road	E1-F1
Drummond Road	B3-B4
Dunton Road	C4
Eastbury Road	B1-B2
Eastern Avenue	A4
Eastern Road	D2-E2-E3
Erroll Road	E4
Esher Avenue	A1-A2
Exchange Street	D2-D3
George Street	E1-E2
Gilbert Road	E4
Glenwood Drive	F3-F4
Globe Road	F1
Granger Way	F1-F2
Hearn Road	E2
Heath Park Road	F3

High Street	C3-D3
Honiton Road	B1-B2-C2
Ingrave Road	C4
Jubilee Avenue	A2
Junction Road	E3-E4
Kensington Road	B1-B2
Kimberley Avenue	A1
King Edward Road	E1-E2
Kings Road	F2
Kingsmead Avenue	D2-D1-E1
Kingston Road	E4
Knighton Road	B1-B2
Knightsbridge Gardens	C2-C3
Kyme Road	E1
Lennox Close	E1
Lessington Avenue	A1
Linden Street	C3-C4
Lodge Avenue	F3-F4
London Road	A2-B2-C2
Lonsdale Avenue	A1-A2
Main Road	D4-E4
Malvern Road	F1
Manor Road	F2-F3
Maple Street	B4
Market Link	D3-D4
Market Place	D3
Marks Road	B2-B3-C3
Mawney Road	A4-A3-B3-C3
Medora Road	B4-C4
Mercury Gardens	D3-E3
Mildmay Road	A3-B3
Milton Road	F2
Norfolk Road	B1-B2
North Street	C4-C3-D3
Oak Street	A3
Oldchurch Road	C1-D1
Olive Street	C3
Palm Road	A3-B3
Park Drive	C4-D4
Park Lane	F1
Park End Road	D4
Pretoria Road	A2-A3-A4
Princes Road	F2-F3
Poplar Street	A4-B4
Queen Street	C1-C2
Randall Road	E1-E2
Recreation Avenue	A2-B2
Regarth Avenue	D1
Richards Avenue	B2
Richmond Road	E1
St Andrews Road	C2
St Edwards Way	C2-C3-C4-D4
Shaftesbury Road	E2-F2
Shakespeare Road	E2-F2
Sherringham Avenue	A1-B1
Sims Close	E3-E4
South Street	D3-D2-D1-E1
Spring Gardens	A2
Stanley Avenue	F3-F4
Stockland Road	B1-C1
The Avenue	C4
The Mews	D3
The Ridgeway	F4
Thurloe Gardens	D1-E1
Victoria Road	D2-E2-E3-F3
Vine Street	B3
Waterloo Gardens	C2-C1-D1
Waterloo Road	C2-C1-D1
Western Road	D2-D3-E3
Wheatsheaf Road	E1
Willow Street	B3-B4
Yew Tree Gardens	C2-C3

HORNCHURCH

Abbs Cross Gardens	A2-B2-C2
Abbs Cross Road	A1-A2-A3
Alma Avenue	C1
Austral Drive	A3
Bedford Gardens	A1-A2
Belmont Road	A4
Berther Road	B4
Beulah Road	A1
Bevan Way	C1
Beverley Gardens	C4
Billet Lane	B3-B4
Boscombe Avenue	A3-A4
Bruce Avenue	A2-B2
Burnway	B4-C4-C3
Butts Green Road	B4
Cedar Road	A1
Chepstow Avenue	C1
Clement Way	C1
Cromer Road	A4-B4
Devonshire Road	A2-B2
Elmhurst Drive	A3-A4
Fairkytes Avenue	A3-B3
Glamis Drive	C3
Glanville Drive	C2-C3
Glebeway	B4-B3-C3
Grey Tower Avenue	A3
Goodwood Avenue	C1
Grosvenor Drive	A3-A4
Hacton Lane	C1-C2
Herbert Road	C4
High Street	A3-B3-B2-C2
Highfield Road	C2
Hillview Avenue	A4-B4
Hornchurch Road	A3
Keithway	B3-B4
Kempton Avenue	C1
Kenilworth Gardens	A1-B1
Kenley Gardens	C2
Keswick Avenue	A3-B3
Lambourne Gardens	B1-B2
Linkway	B3-C3
Lyndhurst Drive	A3-A4
Mansfield Gardens	A1-A2
Mavis Grove	B2
Maybush Road	C4
Mill Park Avenue	B1-B2
North Street	B3-B4
Osborne Road	A4-B4
Patricia Drive	C3
Plumpton Avenue	C1
Priors Park	A1
Ravenscourt Drive	C1
Ravenscourt Grove	B1-C1-C2
Ringwood Avenue	A2
St Georges Avenue	C4
Shirley Gardens	A1-A2
Standen Avenue	B1-C1
Stanley Road	A2-B2
Station Lane	B1-B2
Suttons Avenue	A1-B1
Suttons Lane	B1
The Avenue	C4
Upminster Road	C2
Urban Avenue	A1
Victor Gardens	B2-B3
Warriner Avenue	B1-B2
Wayside Avenue	A1-A2-B1
Westland Avenue	B3-C3-C2
Windsor Road	A4
Wingletye Lane	C2-C3
Woodall Crescent	C3

UPMINSTER

Acacia Drive	A1-A2
Argyle Gardens	C1-C2-C3
Ashburnham Gardens	B4-C4
Ashleigh Gardens	C1-C2
Beech Avenue	B1-B2
Benets Road	A4
Berkley Close	A4-B4-B5
Berkley Drive	A4-A3
Boundary Road	A2-A3
Brackendale Gardens	C1
Branfill Road	B3
Bridge Avenue	A2-A3
Brookdale Avenue	A2
Cedar Avenue	A1-A2
Cedar Gardens	C2
Champion Road	B3
Claremont Gardens	C4
Coniston Avenue	B1-C1
Corbets Tey Road	B1-B2-B3
Courtenay Gardens	C4
Cranborne Gardens	B3
Cranston Park Avenue	B1-C1
Derham Gardens	C2
Deyncourt Gardens	C4
Elm Avenue	B1-B2
Engayne Gardens	B4
Fairfield Avenue	C1-C2
Frimley Avenue	A4
Gaynes Court	A1-B1
Gaynes Road	B3
Gaynes Park Road	A1-B1
Grosvenor Gardens	C4
Hall Lane	B4-C4
Hedingham Road	A4
Highview Gardens	A3-B3
Hornminster Glen	A3-A4
Howard Road	B3-C3
Ingrebourne Gardens	C4
Leasway	B1-B2
Little Gaynes	B1
Little Gaynes Lane	A1-B1
Lime Avenue	A1
Maple Avenue	A1-A2
Meadow Way	B1-B2
Melstock Avenue	B1
New Place Gardens	C2-C3
Norfolk Road	A2-A3
Oak Avenue	A2-A1-B1
Park Drive	B1-C1
Roxburgh Avenue	C1-C2
Rushmere Avenue	C1-C2
St Lawrence Road	B3-C3
St Mary's Lane	A3-B3-C3
Somerset Gardens	A4
Southview Drive	A2-B2
Springfield Gardens	B2-C2
Station Road	B3
Stewarts Avenue	A2-B2
Sunnyside Gardens	B2-C2
Sycamore Avenue	A1-A2
The Grove	A1
The Shrubbery	B2-C2
Tudor Gardens	C2-C3
Upminster Road	A3
Waldegrave Gardens	B4

37

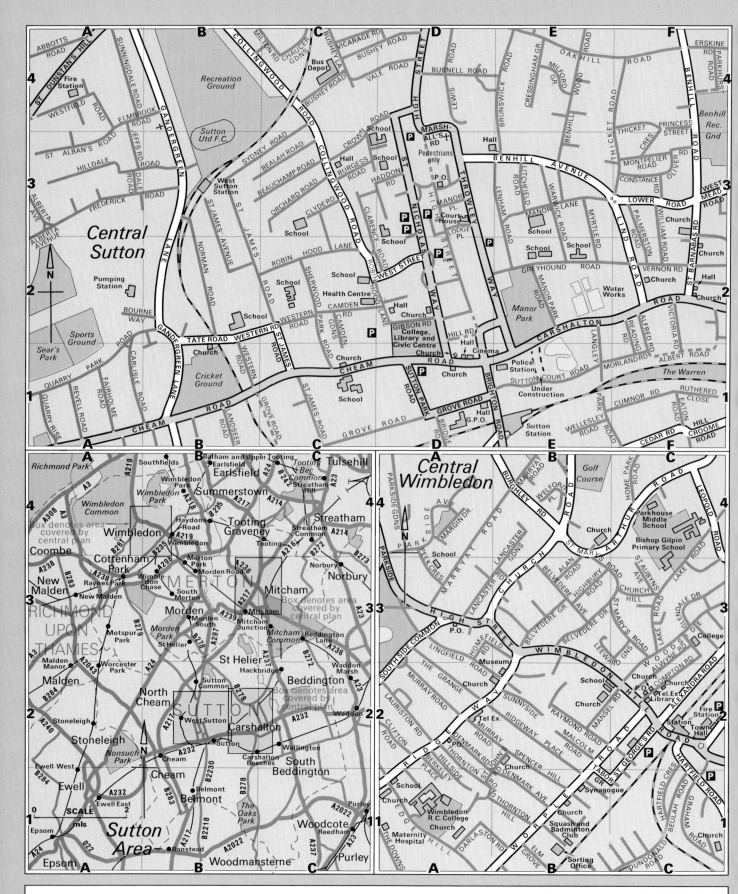

Sutton

Pleasant parks and modern shopping facilities are the chief attractions of Sutton, a residential area which was extensively developed in the 19th century. Recreation is catered for by the Westcroft Sports and Leisure Centre.

Wimbledon was a popular place for duelling in the 19th century, and it is still the site of hard fought contests — between the cream of the world's tennis players, who come here annually for the Lawn Tennis Championships, held at the end of June. The Lawn Tennis Museum can be visited in the grounds of the All England Tennis Club.

Wimbledon grew up around 16th-century Wimbledon House and has now become a pleasant residential area. The Wimbledon Theatre, in the Broadway, is popular for its Christmas pantomime, and the Polka Children's Theatre is based nearby. Wimbledon Common (scene of the duels) lies to the west and covers some 1,100 acres. An interesting restored windmill can be seen here.

Mitcham's cricket green is one of England's oldest pitches, in constant use since 1707.

Carshalton's attractive open spaces are enhanced by the River Wandle, which flows through the town and forms a pond near the centre. All Saints Church has 12th- and 13th-century features, and Little Holland, at Carshalton Beeches, has work by local craftsman Frank Dickenson.

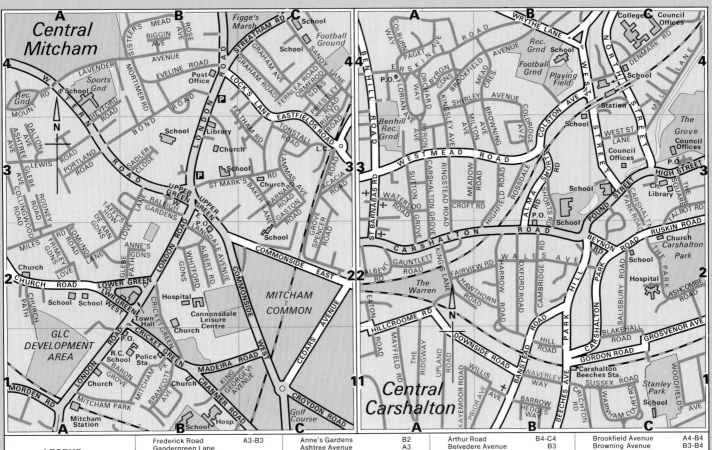

Central Mitcham

Central Carshalton

LEGEND

Town Plan
AA recommended route
Restricted roads
Other roads
Buildings of interest — Hall☐
Car parks — P
Parks and open spaces

Area Plan
A roads
B roads

Street Index with Grid Reference

Sutton

Abbots Road	A4
Albert Road	F1-F2
Alberta Avenue	A2-A3
Alfred Road	F1-F2
Bealah Road	B3-C3
Beauchamp Road	B3-C3
Benhill Avenue	D3-E3-F3
Benhill Road	F3-F4
Benhill Wood Road	E3-E4
Bourne Way	A2-B2
Bridge Road	D1
Brighton Road	D1-E1
Brunswick Road	E3-E4
Burgess Road	C3
Burnell Road	D4-E4
Bushey Lane	C4
Bushey Road	C4 D4
Camden Gardens	C1-C2
Camden Road	C2-D2
Carlisle Road	A2-A1-B1
Carshalton Road	D1-E1-E2-F2
Cedar Road	F1
Chaucer Gardens	C4
Cheam Road	A1-B1-C1-D1
Clarence Road	C3-C2-D2
Clyde Road	C3
Collingwood Road	B4-C4-C3-C2
Constance Road	F3
Cressingham Grove	E4
Crown Road	C3-C4-D4
Cumnor Road	E1-F1
Dale Road	A3
Eaton Road	F1
Elmbrook Road	A4-B4
Erskine Road	F4
Fairholme Road	A1
Frederick Road	A3-B3
Gandergreen Lane	A4-B4-B3-B2-B1
Gibson Road	D2
Greyhound Road	E2-F2
Grove Road	C1-D1
Haddon Road	C3-D3
High Street	D4-D3-D2
Hill Road	D2
Hillcroome Road	F1
Hilldale Road	A3-B3
Jeffs Road	A3-A4
Landseer Road	B1
Langley Park Road	E2-E1-F1
Lenham Road	D3-E3-E2
Lewis Road	D4
Lind Road	F2-F3
Litchfield Road	E3
Lodge Place	D3
Lower Road	F3
Manor Lane	E3
Manor Place	D3
Manor Park Road	E2
Marshall's Road	D3-D4
Milford Grove	E4
Milton Road	B4-C4
Montpelier Road	F3
Morland Road	E1-F1
Myrtle Road	E2-E3
Norman Road	B2-B3
Oakhill Road	E4-F4
Oliver Road	F3
Orchard Road	C3
Palmerston Road	F2-F3
Parkhurst Road	F4
Princess Street	F4
Quarry Rise	A1
Quarry Park Road	A1-A2
Reading Road	F1-F2
Revell Road	A1
Robin Hood Lane	B2-C2-D2
Ruthered Close	F1
St Albans Road	A3-A4
St Barnabas Road	F2-F3
St Dunstan's Hill	A4
St James' Avenue	B2-B3
St James' Road	B3-B2-C2-C1
St Nicholas Way	D1-D2-D3-D4
Sherwood Park Road	C1-C2
Sunningdale Road	A4
Sutton Court Road	E1
Sutton Park Road	D1
Sydney Road	B3-C3-C4
Tate Road	B2
Thicket Crescent	F3-F4
Thicket Road	F3-F4
Throwley Way	D4-D3-D2-E2-E1
Vale Road	C4-D4
Vernon Road	F2
Vicarage Road	F1
Victoria Road	F1-F2
Warwick Road	E2-E3
Wellesley Road	E1
West Street	D2
Western Road	B1-B2-C2
Westfield Road	A4
West Mead Road	F3
William Road	F2-F3

Mitcham

Acacia Road	C3
Albert Road	B2
Anne's Gardens	B2
Ashtree Avenue	A3
Baker Lane	C2-C3
Barnard Road	C3
Baron Grove	A1-B1
Biggin Avenue	A3
Bond Road	A3-B3-B4
Bramcote Avenue	B1
Cedars Avenue	C1-C2
Church Path	A2
Church Road	A2
Collingwood Road	A3-A2
Commonside East	B2-C2
Commonside West	B2-C2-C1
Cranmer Road	B1-C1
Cricket Green	B1-B2
Croydon Road	C1
Dalton Avenue	A3
De'Arn Gardens	A2-A3
Eastfield Road	C3-C4
Edmund Road	A2
Eveline Road	B4
Feltham Road	B4-B3-C3
Fernlea Road	A2
Frimley Gardens	A2
Galston Road	C2-C3
Glebe Avenue	A3
Glebe Path	B2
Graham Avenue	C4
Graham Road	C4
Grove Road	C2-C3
Heyford Road	A3-A4
King George VI Avenue	B1-C1
Lammas Avenue	C3
Langdale Avenue	B2
Lavender Avenue	A4-B4
Lewis Road	A3
Lock's Lane	B4-C4-C3
London Road	A1-B1-B2-B3-B4
Love Lane	A2-B2-B3
Lower Green	A2-B2
Lower Green West	A2-B2
Madeira Road	B1-C1
Miles Road	A2
Mitcham Park	A1-B1
Morden Road	A1
Mortimer Road	B4
Mount Road	A4
Ormerod Gardens	C4
Portland Road	A3
Priestley Road	C3-C4
Raleigh Gardens	B3
Rialto Road	C3-C4
Rodney Road	A2-A3
Rose Avenue	B4
St Mark's Road	B3-C3
Sadler Close	B3
Sandy Lane	C4
Sister's Mead	B4
Spencer Road	C2-C3
Streatham Road	B4-C4
Taffy's How	A3-B3
Tonstall Road	B3
Upper Green East	B3
Upper Green West	B3
Western Road	A4-A3-B3
Whitford Gardens	B2

Wimbledon

Alan Road	B3-B4
Alexandra Road	C2-C3
Alwyne Road	C2-C3

Carshalton

Arthur Road	B4-C4
Belvedere Avenue	B3
Belvedere Drive	B3
Belvedere Grove	B3
Berkeley Place	A1-A2
Beulah Road	C1
Burghley Road	A4-B4
Church Hill	C2
Church Road	A3-B3-B4
Clifton Road	A2
Compton Road	C2-C3
Darlaston Road	A1-B1
Denmark Avenue	B1
Denmark Road	A1-A2
Dundonald Road	C1
Edge Hill	A1
Elm Grove	B1
Glendale Drive	C3
Graham Road	C1
Hartfield Crescent	C1-C2
Hartfield Road	C1-C2
High Street	A3-B3
Highbury Road	B3
Hillside	A1-A2
Homefield Road	A3-B3
Home Park Road	C4
Lake Road	C3-C4
Lancaster Gardens	B3-B4
Lancaster Road	A3-B3
Lauriston Road	A2
Leeward Gardens	B3-C3
Leopold Road	C3-C4
Lingfield Road	A3-A2-B2
Malcolm Road	B2
Mansel Road	B2-C2
Margin Drive	A4
Marryat Road	A3-A4-B4
Murray Road	A2-B2
Parkside	A4
Parkside Avenue	A4
Parkside Gardens	A4
Peek Crescent	A3-A4
Raymond Road	B2
Ridge Way	A1-A2-B2-B3
Ridgeway Place	A2-B2-B1
St Aubyns Avenue	C3
St George's Road	C1-C2
St John's Road	A1-B1-B2
St Mary's Road	B4-B3-C3
South Side Common	A2-A3
Spencer Hill	B1-B2
Sunnyside	B2
Tabor Grove	B1-B2
The Downs	A1
The Grange	A2-A3
Thornton Hill	A1-B1
Thornton Road	A1-A2
Welford Road	A1
Wimbledon Hill Road	B3-B2-C2
Woodside	A2
Worple Road	A1-B1-B2-C2

Carshalton

Albert Road	A2
Alma Road	B2-B3
Ashcombe Road	C2
Banstead Road	B1-B2
Barrow Hedges Way	B1
Beeches Avenue	B1
Benhill Road	A3-A4
Beynon Road	B2-C2
Blakehall Road	C1
Brookfield Avenue	A4-B4
Browning Avenue	B3-B4
Byron Avenue	A3
Byron Gardens	A4
Cambridge Road	B2
Carshalton Grove	A2-A3
Carshalton Road	A2-B2
Carshalton Park Road	B1-C1-C2-C3
Calburn Way	A4
Coldridge Avenue	B3-B4
Colston Avenue	B3-B4
Crichton Road	B1-C1
Croft Road	A3-B3
Denmark Road	C4
Downside Road	A2-A1-B1
Eaton Road	A1-A2
Erskine Road	A4-B4
Fairview Road	A2-B2
Florian Avenue	A3-A4
Gauntlett Road	A2
Gordon Road	B1-C1
Grosvenor Avenue	C1-C2
Harrow Road	B1-B2
Hawthorn Road	B2-C2
High Street	C3
Highfield Road	B2-B3
Hill Road	B1
Hillcroome Road	A1-A2
Kayemoor Road	A1
King's Lane	A2
Kingsley Avenue	A3-A4
Mayfield Road	A1
Mead Crescent	B4
Meadow Road	A3-B3
Mill Lane	C3-C4
Milton Avenue	A4-A3-B3
North Street	C3-C4
Orchard Way	A3-A4
Oxford Road	B1-B2
Paget Avenue	A4
Park Hill	B1-B2
Pound Street	B2-B3-C3
Prior Avenue	A1-B1
Ringstead Road	A2-A3
Rossdale	B3
Ruskin Road	C2-C3
St Barnabas Road	A2-A3
Salisbury Road	C1-C2
Shirley Avenue	A4-B4
Shorts Road	B2-B3
Sussex Road	B1-C1
Sutton Grove	A2-A3
Talbot Road	C2-C3
The Park	C2
The Ridgway	A1-A2
The Square	C3
Upland Road	A1
Wales Avenue	B2
Warnham Court Road	C1
Waterloo Road	A3
Waverley Road	B1
West Street	B4-C4-C3
West Street Lane	C3
Westmead Road	A3-B3
Willis Avenue	A1-B1
Woodfields Avenue	C1
Wrythe Lane	B4

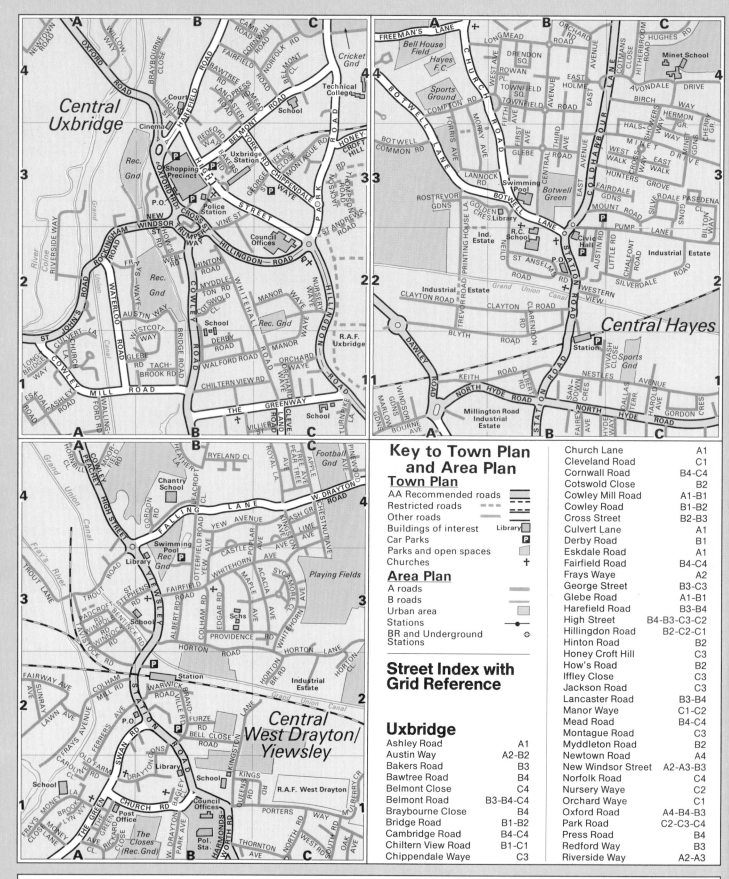

Key to Town Plan and Area Plan

Town Plan

AA Recommended roads	
Restricted roads	
Other roads	
Buildings of interest	Library
Car Parks	P
Parks and open spaces	
Churches	✝

Area Plan

A roads	
B roads	
Urban area	
Stations	•—•
BR and Underground Stations	⊖

Street Index with Grid Reference

Uxbridge

Ashley Road	A1
Austin Way	A2-B2
Bakers Road	B3
Bawtree Road	B4
Belmont Close	C4
Belmont Road	B3-B4-C4
Braybourne Close	B4
Bridge Road	B1-B2
Cambridge Road	B4-C4
Chiltern View Road	B1-C1
Chippendale Waye	C3
Church Lane	A1
Cleveland Road	C1
Cornwall Road	B4-C4
Cotswold Close	B2
Cowley Mill Road	A1-B1
Cowley Road	B1-B2
Cross Street	B2-B3
Culvert Lane	A1
Derby Road	B1
Eskdale Road	A1
Fairfield Road	B4-C4
Frays Waye	A2
George Street	B3-C3
Glebe Road	A1-B1
Harefield Road	B3-B4
High Street	B4-B3-C3-C2
Hillingdon Road	B2-C2-C1
Hinton Road	B2
Honey Croft Hill	C3
How's Road	B2
Iffley Close	C3
Jackson Road	C3
Lancaster Road	B3-B4
Manor Waye	C1-C2
Mead Road	B4-C4
Montague Road	C3
Myddleton Road	B2
Newtown Road	A4
New Windsor Street	A2-A3-B3
Norfolk Road	C4
Nursery Waye	C2
Orchard Waye	C1
Oxford Road	A4-B4-B3
Park Road	C2-C3-C4
Press Road	B4
Redford Way	B3
Riverside Way	A2-A3

Uxbridge

The defence of London and south-east England was planned in an Uxbridge underground control room in World War II, and the headquarters of No 11 Corps Fighter Command was located here. RAF associations go back to 1917, when the Armament and Gunnery School of the Royal Flying Corps was established, although today the RAF Station is mainly concerned with administration.

Shortly before the arrival of the RAF, the opening of the Metropolitan and Great Western Railways had sparked off the expansion of this former market centre and staging post into a thriving suburb. It now has modern shopping precincts and sports facilities, including an artificial ski slope and a big open air swimming pool in Park Road.

Hayes has good shopping and also enjoys the leisure facilities of the modern Alfred Beck

Centre, where concerts and drama can be staged.

West Drayton is a busy suburb lying close to the M4 Motorway and Heathrow Airport. But the West Drayton Green area has been preserved and recalls the town's peaceful origins. The Grand Union Canal runs through it and is popular with boating and fishing enthusiasts.

Yiewsley was once a brick-making town, but has become a London suburb. Few buildings remain from before the 19th century.

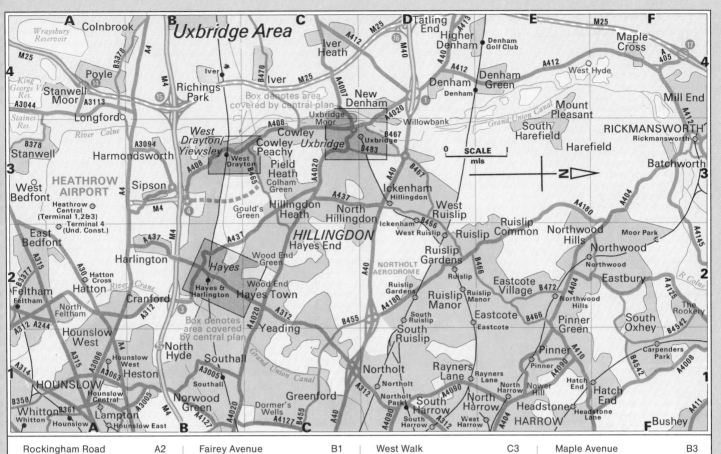

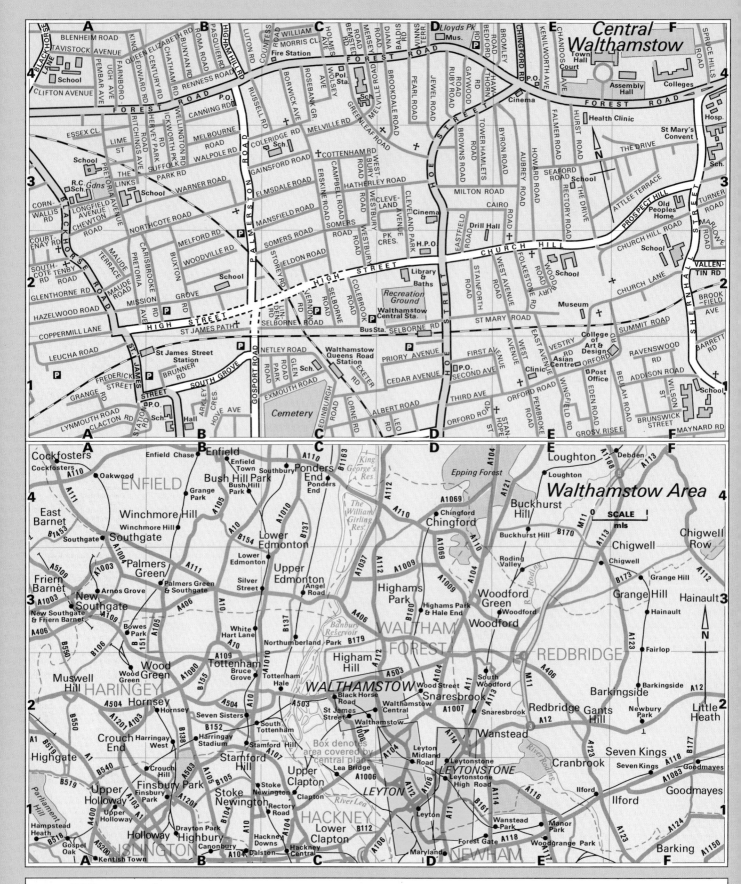

Walthamstow

Greyhound racing at Walthamstow Stadium and a seemingly endless street market — said to be the longest in Britain — are two of the top attractions of Walthamstow, an area of dramatic transformations. Covered in forest before the 15th century, it prospered as a country retreat for London's rich in the 18th and saw even greater prosperity with the industrialisation of the 19th, culminating in the development of Britain's first internal combustion engine car, the Bremer Car, on display at Walthamstow Museum. Little of the old town has survived but Walthamstow Village has many noteworthy buildings and is now a conservation area. Among the few remaining 18th-century houses are the Clockhouse, in Wood Street, and the Water House, home of the William Morris Gallery.

Leyton was a rural retreat for wealthy London merchants, who built their mansions here in the 18th century. Few reminders of this prosperous past withstood severe wartime bombing.

Leytonstone grew up on the Roman route from Epping Forest to London, and became a 'dormitory' town with the development of the railway system. Its growth continued with extensive development and also extensive demolition, so that little of the past remains. The early 19th-century terraced houses in Browning Street are the best examples of the old town.

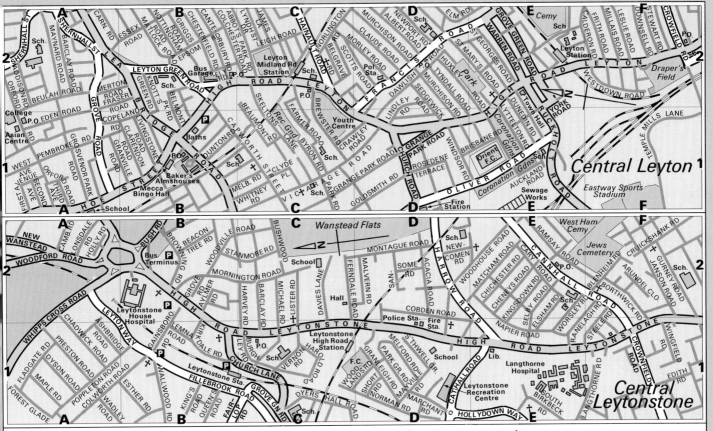

LEGEND

Town Plan

AA Recommended roads
Restricted roads
Other roads
Car Parks   P
Buildings of interest   Station
Parks and open spaces
Churches   +

Area Plan

A roads
B roads
Stations
Borough Boundary

STREET INDEX WITH GRID REFERENCE

WALTHAMSTOW

Addison Road	F1
Albert Road	C1-D1
Arkley Crescent	B1
Attlee Terrace	E3-F3
Aubrey Road	E2-E3-E4
Baldis Road	D4
Barrett Road	F1-F2
Bedford Road	C4
Bemsted Road	D4
Beulah Road	E1-F1
Blackhorse Lane	A4
Blackhorse Road	A2-A3
Blenheim Road	A4
Borwick Avenue	C4
Bromley Road	E4
Brookdale Road	D2-D3
Brookfield Road	E4
Browns Road	D3
Brunner Road	B1
Brunswick Street	F1
Bunyan Road	B4
Buxton Road	B2-B3
Byron Road	E3-E4
Cairo Road	D3-E3-E2
Campbell Road	C3
Canning Road	B4
Carisbrooke Road	A2-B2
Cedar Avenue	D1
Century Road	A4-B4
Chandos Avenue	B4
Chatham Road	B4
Chewton Road	A2-A3
Chingford Road	E4
Church Hill	D2-E2
Church Hill Road	E2-F2-F3
Church Lane	E2-F2
Clacton Road	A1
Cleveland Park Avenue	D2-D3
Cleveland Park Crescent	D2-D3
Clifton Avenue	A4
Colebrook Road	C2
Coleridge Road	B3-C3-C4
Coppermill Lane	A1-A2
Cornwallis Road	A3
Cottenham Road	C3
Countess Road	C4
Diana Road	D4
East Avenue	E1-E2
Eastfield Road	D2-D3
Eden Road	E1
Edinburgh Road	C1
Eldon Road	C2
Elmsdale Road	B3-C3
Erskine Road	C2-C3
Essex Close	A3
Exeter Road	C1
Exmouth Road	B1-C1
Falmer Road	E3-E4
Farnborough Avenue	A4
Folkestone Road	E2
Forest Road	A4-B4-C4-D4-E4-F4
First Avenue	D1-E1
Frederick Street	A1
Gainsford Road	B3-C3
Gaywood Road	B4
Glen Road	C1
Glenthorne Road	A2
Gosport Road	B1-B2
Grange Road	A1
Greenleaf Road	C4-C3-D3
Grosvenor Rise East	E1-F1
Hatherley Road	C3-D3
Hawthorn Road	D4
Hazlewood Road	A4
Hervey Park Road	B3-B4
Higham Hill Road	E2
High Street	A2-B2-C2-D2
Hoe Street	D1-D2-D3-D4-E4-F4
Holmes Avenue	C4
Hove Avenue	B1
Howard Road	E2-E3-E4
Hurst Road	E3-E4
Ickworth Park Road	B4
Jewel Road	D3-D4
Kenilworth Avenue	E4

King Edward Road	A4
Leo Road	D1
Leucha Road	A1
Linden Road	C2
Lime Street	A3
Longfield Avenue	A3
Lorne Road	C1
Luton Road	B4
Lynmouth Road	A1
Mansfield Road	B2-B3-C3
Marlowe Road	F2-F3
Maude Road	A2
Maude Terrace	A2
Maynard Road	F1
Melbourne Road	B3
Melford Road	B2
Melville Road	C3-C4
Mersey Road	C4
Milton Road	D3-E3
Mission Grove	A2-B2
Netley Road	B1-C1
Northcote Road	A2-B2-B3
Orford Road	D1-E1-F1-F2
Palmerston Road	B2-B3-B4
Park Road	C1
Pasquier Road	B4
Pearl Road	D4
Pembar Avenue	A4
Pembroke Road	E1
Pretoria Avenue	A2
Priory Avenue	D1
Prospect Hill	E2-F2-F3
Queen Elizabeth Road	A4-B4
Ravenswood Road	F1
Rectory Road	E2-E3
Renness Road	B4
Ritchings Avenue	A3-A4
Roma Road	B4
Rosebank Grove	C4
Ruby Road	D4
Russell Road	B4-C4-C3
St James Path	B2
St James Street	A1-B1
St Mary Road	D2-E2
Seaford Road	E3
Second Avenue	D1-E1
Selborne Road	B2-C2-D2
Shernhall Street	F1-F2-F3-F4
Somers Road	B2-C2-C3
Southcote Road	A2
South Grove	B1
Spruce Hills Road	F4
Stainforth Road	D2
Station Road	A1
Storey Road	C2
Suffolk Park Road	A3-B3
Summit Road	F2
Tavistock Avenue	A4
Tenby Road	A2
The Drive	E2-E3-E3
The Links	A3
Third Avenue	D1-E1
Tower Hamlets Road	D3-D4
Turner Road	F3
Valentin Road	F2
Vernon Road	C2
Vestry Road	E1-E2
Walpole Road	B3
Warner Road	A3-B3

Wellington Road	B3-B4
West Avenue	E1-E2
West Avenue Road	E2
Westbury Road	C2-C3
William Morris Close	C4
Wingfield Road	E1
Winns Terrace	D4
Wolsey Avenue	C4
Woodbury Road	E2
Woodville Road	B2

LEYTON

Abbot's Park Road	B2-C2
Addison Road	A2
Albert Road	D2
Auckland Road	E1
Barclay Road	A2
Beaumont Road	C2-C1
Belgrave Road	C2
Belmont Park Road	B1-B2
Beulah Road	A2
Brewster Road	C1-C2
Brisbane Road	D1-E1
Byron Road	C1
Calderon Road	E2-F2
Canterbury Road	B2
Carnarvon Road	A2
Capworth Street	B2-B1-C1
Chesterfield Road	B2
Church Road	D1
Clarendon Road	B2
Claude Road	C2-D2
Clyde Place	A2
Colchester Road	B2-C2
Copeland Road	A1-B1
Crowfield Road	F1-F2
Dawlish Road	D1-D2
Downsell Road	D2
Dunedin Road	E1-E2
Dunton Road	B1
Eden Road	A1-A2
Elm Road	D2-E2
Ely Road	B2
Epsom Road	B2
Essex Road	A2-B2
Farmer Road	C1-C2
First Avenue	A1
Francis Road	D1-D2-E2
Fraser Road	A2-B2
Frith Road	F2
Goldsmith Road	C1-D1
Grange Park Road	C1-D1
Granville Road	A1-B1
Griggs Road	B2
Grosvenor Park Road	A1
Grove Green Road	E2
Grove Road	A1-A2
Hainault Road	A2
High Road Leyton	B1-B2-C2-C1-D1-E1-E2-F2
Hoe Street	A1-B1
Huxley Road	D2-E2-E1
James Lane	C2
Knott's Green Road	B1-B2
Lea Bridge Road	A2-B2-B1
Leigh Road	C2
Leslie Road	F2
Leyton Green Road	B2
Lindley Road	D1-D2
Livingstone Road	B1

Lyndhurst Drive	C2
Lyttelton Road	E1-E2
Matlock Road	B2
Maynard Road	A2
Melbourne Road	B1-C1
Merton Road	A2-B2
Millais Road	F2
Morley Road	C2-D2
Murchison Road	C2-D2-D1
Newport Road	D2
Norlington Road	C2
Nottingham Road	B2
Oliver Road	D1-E1
Orford Road	A1-A2
Park Road	C1
Pembroke Road	A1
Rawley Road	C1-D1
Rosedene Terrace	D1
Ruckholt Road	E2-E1-F1
Second Avenue	A1
Shernhall Street	A2
St Georges Road	E2
St Mary's Road	D2-E2
Scotts Road	C2-D2
Sedgewick Road	D1-D2
Shernall Street	A2
Skeltons Lane	C1-C2
Stewart Road	F2
Temple Mills Lane	F1
Third Avenue	A1
Tyndall Road	D1-D2
Vicarage Road	C1-D1
Warren Road	E2
West Avenue	A1
Westdown Road	F2
Windsor Road	D1-E1
Whitney Road	B1-C1
York Road	E1-E2

LEYTONSTONE

Acacia Road	D2
Arundel Close	F2
Ashbridge Road	A1
Aylmer Road	B2
Barclay Road	C1-C2
Beacontree Road	B2
Blenheim Road	F2
Borthwick Road	F1-F2
Browning Road	B2
Burghley Road	C1
Bush Road	B2
Bushwood	C2
Cambridge Road	A2
Cannhall Road	E2-F2-F1
Cary Road	E2
Cathall Road	D1-E1
Chadwick Road	A1-A2
Cheneys Road	E2
Chichester Road	E2
Church Lane	B1-C1
Cobden Road	D2-D1-E1
Colworth Road	A1-B1
Crownfield Road	F1
Cruickshank Road	F2
Davies Lane	C2
Dyers Hall Road	C1
Dyson Road	A1
Edith Road	F1
Elsham Road	E1-E2
Esther Road	A1-B1

Fairlop Road	B1-C1
Ferndale Road	C2
Fillebrook Road	B1-C1
Fladgate Road	A1
Forest Glade	A1
Gainsborough Road	B1-B2
Grove Green Road	C1
Grove Road	B2
Gurney Road	F2
Granleigh Road	B2
Harold Road	C1
Harrow Road	D2-E2-E1
Harvey Road	C1-C2
High Road Leytonstone	B2-B1-C1-D1-E1-F1-F2
Holly Road	A2
Hollydown Way	D1-E1
Janson Road	F2
King's Road	B1
Kingsdown Road	E1-E2
Kirkdale Road	B1
Langthorne Road	E1-F1
Lemna Road	B1
Leyton Way	A2-A1-B1
Lister Road	C1-C2
Lonsdale Road	A2
Malvern Road	D2
Maple Road	A1
Marchant Road	B2
Matcham Road	D2-E2
Mayville Road	D1
Melford Road	D1
Michael Road	C1-C2
Montague Road	C2-D2
Mornington Road	B2-C2
Napier Road	E1-E2
Newcomen Road	D2
New Wanstead	A2
Norman Road	C1-D1
Poppleton Road	A1-B1
Preston Road	A1
Queen's Road	B1
Ramsay Road	E2-F2
Ranelagh Road	E1-E2-F2
Sansome Road	D2
Selby Road	E1-E2
Short Road	C1-D1
South Birkbeck Road	E1
Southwell Grove	D1
Stanmore Road	B2-C2
Steele Road	E1-F1-F2
Vernon Road	C1
Wadley Road	A1
Wallwood Road	B1
Whipps Cross Road	A1-A2
Wingfield Road	F1
Woodlands Road	C1-D1
Woodford Road	A2
Woodhouse Road	D2-E2
Woodville Road	B2-C2
Worsley Road	E1-E2

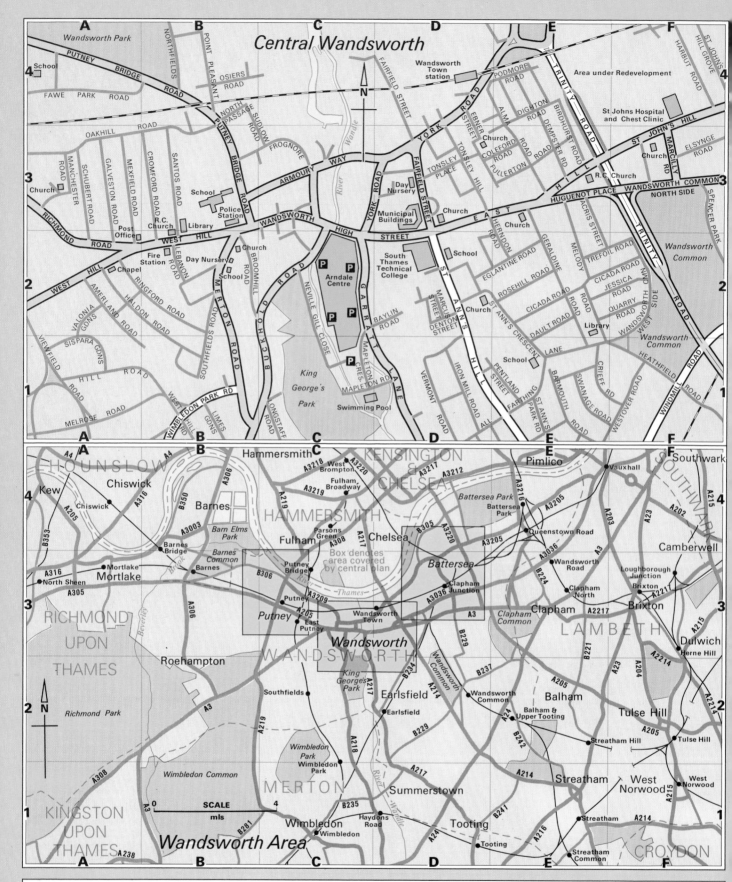

Wandsworth

Oscar Wilde and Great Train Robber Ronald Biggs both spent time in Wandsworth, as inmates of the prison which is one of its best-known features. This is an industrialised area which grew when the railways arrived in the 19th century.

Battersea boasts two great landmarks for Londoners: its park and its power station. Battersea Park was opened in 1853 under royal command, and has since undergone a number of improvements and innovations, including the Festival of Britain Gardens, designed by Sir Osbert Lanchester and John Piper, and established in 1951. The power station dominates the London skyline with its four distinctive chimneys. Designed by Sir Giles Scot and first used in 1937, it is no longer operating but may become the centrepiece of a proposed leisure park. Battersea's Old Town Hall has been converted into an Arts Centre and many theatrical and musical productions are staged there.

Putney gives an overall impression of being distinctly Victorian and Edwardian. It grew into a fashionable London suburb during the 18th century, and continued to undergo a good deal of development right up until the 1920s, but since then has seen relatively little change. Putney Bridge has been the starting point for the University Boat Race since 1845.

44

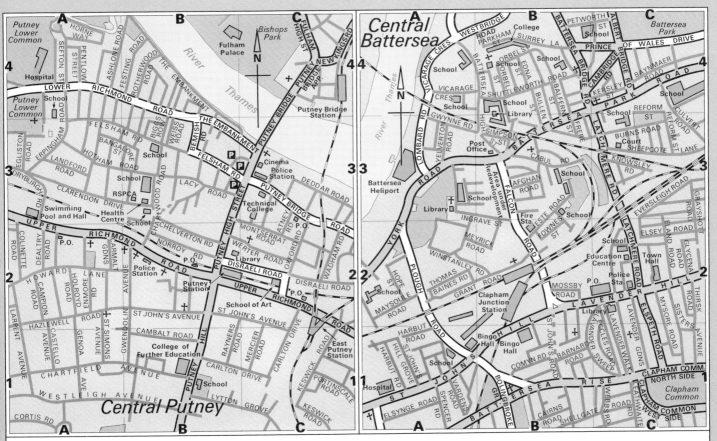

Street Index with with grid reference

Wandsworth

Acris Street	E2-E3
All Farthing Lane	D1-E1
Alma Road	D4-E4-E3
Amerland Road	A2-A1-B1
Armoury Way	B3-C3-D3
Barmouth Road	E1
Baylin Road	C2-D2
Birdhurst Road	E3-E4
Broomhill Road	B2
Buckhold Road	B1-C1-C2-C3
Cicada Road	E2-F2
Coleford Road	D3-E3
Crieff Road	E1-F1
Cromford Road	B2-B3
Dault Road	E1-E2
Dempster Road	E3-E4
Dighton Road	D3-E3-E4
East Hill	D2-D3-E3
Ebner Street	D3-D4
Eglantine Road	D2-E2
Elsynge Road	F3
Fairfield Street	C4-D4-D3
Fawe Park Road	A4-B4
Frognore	B3-C3
Fullerton Road	D3-E3
Galveston Road	A2-A3
Garratt Lane	C2-C1-D1
Geraldine Road	E1-E2-E3
Haldon Road	A2-B2-B1
Harbut Road	F4
Heathfield Road	E1-F1
Herndon Road	D3-E3-E2
Hill Road	A1-B1
Huguenot Place	E3-F3
Iron Mill Road	D1
Jessica Road	E2-F2
Lebanon Road	B2
Limes Gardens	B1
Longstaff Road	C1
Manchester Road	A3
Mapleton Crescent	C1-C2
Mapleton Road	C1-D1
Marcilly Road	F3
Melody Road	E1-E2-E3
Melrose Road	A1-B1
Merton Road	B1-B2
Mexfield Road	A2-A3
Neville Gill Close	C1-C2
Northfields	B4
North Passage	B4
Oakhill Road	A3-B3
Osiers Road	B4-C4
Pentland Street	D1-E1
Podmore Road	D4-E4
Point Pleasant	A4-B4-B3
Putney Bridge Road	E2-F2
Quarry Road	A2-A3
Richmond Road	A2-A3
Ringford Road	E2
Rosehill Road	D2-E2-E1
St Ann's Crescent	

St Ann's Hill	D2-D1-E1
St Ann's Park Road	E1
St John's Hill	E3-F3-F4
St John's Hill Grove	F4
Santos Road	B2-B3
Schubert Road	A2-A3
Sispara Gardens	A1
Southfields Road	B1-B2
Spencer Park	F2-F3
Sudlow Road	B4-B3-C3
Swanage Road	E1-F1
Tonsley Hill	D3
Tonsley Place	D3
Trefoil Road	E2-F2
Trinity Road	E4-E3-F3-F2-F1
Valonia Gardens	A2
Vermont Road	D1
Viewfield Road	F3
Wandsworth Common North Side	F1-F2
Wandsworth Common West Side	F1-F2
Wandsworth High Street	B2-B3-C3-C2-D2
West Hill	A2-B2-B3
West Hill Road	B1
Westover Road	E1-F1
Wimbledon Park Road	B1
Windmill Road	F1-F2
York Road	C3-D3-D4-E4

Putney

Ashlone Road	A4-B4
Atney Road	C2-C3
Bangalore Street	A3-B3
Bemish Road	B3
Biggs Row	B3-B4
Cambalt Road	B1
Campion Road	A2
Carlton Drive	B1-C1-C2
Carmalt Gardens	A2
Castello Avenue	A1-A2
Charlwood Road	B2-B3
Chartfield Avenue	A1-B1
Chelverton Road	B2-B3
Clarendon Drive	A3-B3
Colinette Road	A2-A3
Cortis Road	A1
Dealtry Road	A2
Deddar Road	C3
Disraeli Road	B2-C2
Dryburgh Road	A3
Egliston Road	A3
Enmore Road	A2
Erpingham Road	A3-A4
Felsham Road	A3-B3-C3
Festing Road	B4
Fulham High Street	C4
Genoa Avenue	A1-A2
Gwendolin Road	B1-B2
Hazlewell Road	A2-B2
Holroyd Road	A2
Horne Way	A4
Hotham Road	A3-B3
Howard Lane	A2-B2
Keswick Road	C1
Lacy Road	B3
Landford Road	A3
Larpent Avenue	A1-A2
Lower Richmond Road	A4-B4-B3

Lytton Grove	B1-C1
Mercier Road	C1-C2
Montserratt Road	B3-C3-C2
New Kings Road	C4
Norroy Road	B2
Oxford Road	C2
Pentlow Street	A4
Portinscale Road	C1
Putney Bridge	C3-C4
Putney Bridge Approach	C4
Putney Bridge Approach	A1-A2
Putney Bridge Road	C2-C3
Putney High Street	B2-B3-C3
Putney Hill	B1-B2
Rayners Road	B1-B2
Rotherwood Road	B4
St John's Avenue	B2-C2-C1
St Simons Avenue	A1-A2
Sefton Street	A4
The Embankment	B4-B3-C3
Upper Richmond Road	A3-A2-B2-C2-C1
Wadham Road	C2
Weiss Road	B3
Werter Road	B2-C2
Westleigh Avenue	A1-B1

Battersea

Afghan Street	B3
Albert Bridge Road	C4
Balfern Street	B3-B4
Barnard Road	B1
Battersea Bridge Road	B4-C4
Battersea High Street	A4-B4-B3
Battersea Park Road	B3-B4-C4
Battersea Rise	A1-B1-C1
Baynmaer Road	C4
Bolingbroke Grove	B1
Bullen Street	B3-B4
Burns Road	C3
Cabul Road	B3
Cairns Road	B1
Cambridge Road	B4-C4
Clapham Common North Side	C1
Clapham Common West Side	C1
Comyn Road	B1
Culvert Road	C3-C4
Eccles Road	C1-C2
Edna Street	B4
Eland Road	C2-C3
Elsey Road	C2
Elspeth Road	C1-C2
Elsynge Road	A1
Este Road	B2-B3
Eversleigh Road	C2-C3
Falcon Road	B2-B3
Fownes Street	B3
Frere Street	B3
Glycena Road	C2
Grant Road	A2-B2
Grayshott Road	C2-C3
Gwynne Road	A3-B3
Harbut Road	A1
Hope Street	A2
Ingrave Street	A3-B3-B2
Kersley Street	C4
Knowsley Road	C3
Latchmere Road	C2-C3-C4

Lavender Gardens	C1-C2
Lavender Hill	B2-C2
Lavender Sweep	C1-B1-B2-C2
Lavender Walk	C1-C2
Leathwaite Road	C1
Lombard Road	A3-A4
Maysoule Road	A2
Meyrick Road	A2-B2
Mossby Road	B2
Mysore Road	C1-C2
Orbel Street	B4
Parkham Street	B4
Petworth Street	B4-C4
Plough Road	A1-A2
Prince of Wales Drive	B4-C4
Reform Street	C3-C4
St John's Hill	A1-B1-B2
St John's Hill Grove	A1
St John's Road	B1-B2
Sheepcote Lane	C3
Shellgate Road	B1-C1
Shuttleworth Road	B4
Simpson Street	B3
Sisters Avenue	C1-C2
Spencer Road	A1
Surrey Lane	B4
Thirsk Road	C1-C2
Thomas Baines Road	A2
Vardens Road	A1
Vicarage Crescent	A4-B4-B3
Webbs Road	C1
Westbridge Road	A4-B4
Winstanley Road	A2-B2
Yelverton Road	A3
York Road	A2-B2-B3

LEGEND

Town Plan

AA Recommended roads

Other roads

Restricted roads

Buildings of interest   Cinema ■

Churches   ✝

Car Parks   P

Parks and open spaces

Area Plan

A roads

B roads

Stations   Mitcham ●

Borough Boundary

45

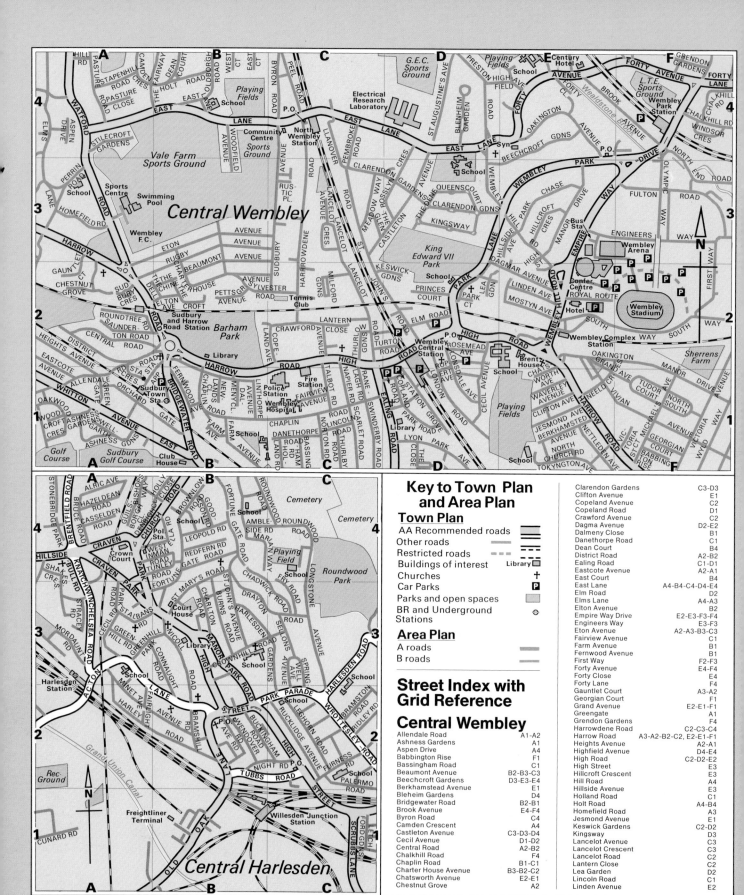

Key to Town Plan and Area Plan

Town Plan

AA Recommended roads	
Other roads	
Restricted roads	
Buildings of interest	Library ▢
Churches	+
Car Parks	▣
Parks and open spaces	
BR and Underground Stations	◉

Area Plan

A roads	
B roads	

Street Index with Grid Reference

Central Wembley

Allendale Road	A1-A2
Ashness Gardens	A1
Aspen Drive	A4
Babbington Rise	F1
Bassingham Road	C1
Beaumont Avenue	B2-B3-C3
Beechcroft Gardens	D3-E3-E4
Berkhamstead Avenue	E1
Bleheim Gardens	D4
Bridgewater Road	B2-B1
Brook Avenue	E4-F4
Byron Road	C4
Camden Crescent	A4
Castleton Avenue	C3-D3-D4
Cecil Avenue	D1-D2
Central Road	A2-B2
Chalkhill Road	F4
Chaplin Road	B1-C1
Charter House Avenue	B3-B2-C2
Chatsworth Avenue	E2-E1
Chestnut Grove	A2

Clarendon Gardens	C3-D3
Clifton Avenue	E1
Copeland Avenue	C2
Copeland Road	D1
Crawford Avenue	C2
Dagma Avenue	D2-E2
Dalmeny Close	B1
Danethorpe Road	C1
Dean Court	B4
District Road	A2-B2
Ealing Road	C1-D1
Eastcote Avenue	A2-A1
East Court	B4
East Lane	A4-B4-C4-D4-E4
Elm Road	D2
Elms Lane	A4-A3
Elton Avenue	B2
Empire Way Drive	E2-E3-F3-F4
Engineers Way	E3-F3
Eton Avenue	A2-A3-B3-C3
Fairview Avenue	C1
Farm Avenue	B1
Fernwood Avenue	B1
First Way	F2-F3
Forty Avenue	E4-F4
Forty Close	E4
Forty Lane	F4
Gauntlet Court	A3-A2
Georgian Court	F1
Grand Avenue	E2-E1-F1
Greengate	A1
Grendon Gardens	C2-C3-C4
Harrowdene Road	C2-C3-C4
Harrow Road	A3-A2-B2-C2, E2-E1-F1
Heights Avenue	A2-A1
Highfield Avenue	D4-E4
High Road	C2-D2-E2
High Street	E3
Hillcroft Crescent	E3
Hill Road	A4
Hillside Avenue	E3
Holland Road	C1
Holt Road	A4-B4
Homefield Road	A3
Jesmond Avenue	E1
Keswick Gardens	C2-D2
Kingsway	D3
Lancelot Avenue	C3
Lancelot Crescent	C3
Lancelot Road	C2
Lantern Close	C2
Lea Garden	D2
Lincoln Road	C1
Linden Avenue	E2

Wembley

Scene of FA and Rugby League Cup Finals, the 1948 Olympic Games, the 1966 World Cup Finals, countless concerts, public appearances and events such as the open air Mass during the 1982 Papal visit, Wembley Stadium is the chief claim to fame for this residential and industrial area.

Originally designed as a centrepiece for the British Empire Exhibition of 1924, the stadium complex includes Wembley Arena, used for horse shows and ice spectaculars, a national squash centre and a modern hotel. Nearby stands the Wembley Conference Centre, opened in 1976, which also provides facilities for exhibitions and concerts. Wembley itself began as a rural district centred around Wembley Park, but saw extensive development after the opening of the London to Birmingham railway in the mid-19th century.

Harlesden Animal shows, handicrafts, music and drama take over Roundwood Park in the north every year, for the annual Brent show. A village until the late 19th century, Harlesden grew when railway yards and sidings were established here and several major industrial companies arrived.

Willesden is another area which has undergone a good deal of housing and industrial development since the mid-19th century, when Willesden Junction was built. Places of interest include St Mary's Church, which is of Norman origin.

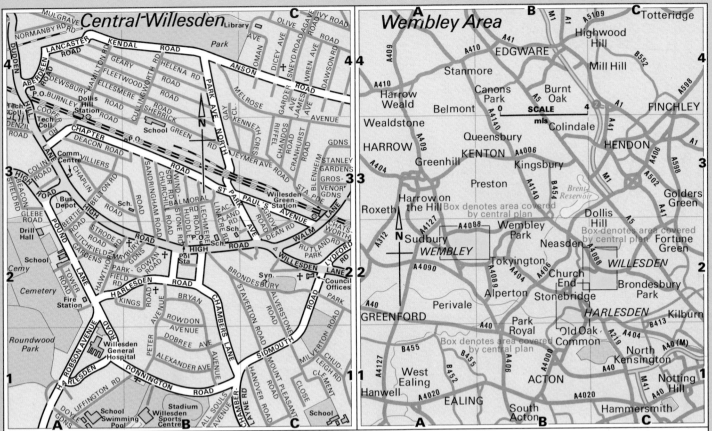

Central Willesden / Wembley Area

Linthorpe Avenue	B1	Victoria Avenue	F1-F2
Llandover Road	C4-C3	Victoria Court	F1
London Road	D2-D1	Vivian Avenue	E2-E1-F1
Lonsdale Avenue	D1-D2	Watford Road	A4-A3-A2
Lyon Park Avenue	D1	Waverley Avenue	E1
Monor Drive	E3	Wellgarth	A1
Meadow Way	C3	Wembley Hill Road	D4-D3-E3-E2
Milford Gardens	C2	Wembley Park	E3-E4
Mostyn Avenue	E2	West Court	B4
Napier Road	C2-C1	Whitton Avenue East	A1-B1
Neeld Crescent	E1-E2-F2	Windsor Crescent	F4
Nettleden Avenue	E1	Woodcroft	A1
Newlands Close	B1	Woodfield Avenue	B4-B3
North Church Road	E1	Wyld Way	F1
North End Road	F4-F3		
North South	F1		
Norton Road	C1		
Oakington Avenue	E4		
Oakington Manor Drive	E2-F2-F1	**Willesden**	
Oakwood Crescent	A1		
Oldborough Road	B4	Aberdeen Road	A4
Olympic Way	F4-F3	Acland Road	B3
Orchard Gate	A1-B1	Agave Road	C4
Park Chase	E3	Alexandra Avenue	B1
Park Court	D2	All Souls Avenue	B1
Park Lane	D2-D3-E3	Alverstone Road	C1-C2
Park Road	D1	Anson Road	B4-C4
Pasture Close	A4	Beaconsfield Road	A3
Pasture Road	A4	Belton Road	A3
Peel Road	C4	Bertie Road	A2-A3
Pembroke Road	C3-C4	Bleneheim Gardens	
Perrin Road	A3	Brondesbury Park	B2-C2
Petts Grove Avenue	B2	Bryan Avenue	B1-B2
Preston Road	D4	Burnley Road	A4-A3-B3
Princes Court	D2	Chamberlayne Road	C1-D1
Queenscourt	D3	Chambers Lane	B1-B2
Ranelagh Road	C1	Chandos Road	C3
Rosemead Avenue	D2	Chaplin Road	A3-B3
Rosslyn Crescent	D3-D4	Chapter Road	A3-B3
Rountree Road	A2	Chatsworth Road	C2
Royal Route	E2	Churchill Road	B2-B3
Rugby Avenue	A2-B2-B3-C3	Clement Close	C1
Rupert Avenue	D1-D2	Colin Road	C3
Rustic Place	C3	Cooper Road	A3-A4
St Augustines Avenue	D4	Cranhurst Road	C3
St John's Road	C3-C2-D2	Cullingworth Road	B3-B4
St Michael's Avenue	F1	Dawson Road	C4
Saunderton Road	A2-B2	Dean Road	C2
Scarle Road	C1	Denzil Road	A3
South Way	E2-F2	Dewsbury Road	A4-B4
Stapenhill Road	A4	Dicey Avenue	C4
Station Approach	B2-B1-A1	Dobree Avenue	B1
Station Crescent	A2-A1	Donnington Road	A1-B1
Station Grove	D1-D2	Doyle Gardens	A1
Stilecroft Gardens	A4	Dudden Hill Lane	A3-A4
Sudbury Avenue	C2-C3-C4	Ellesmere Road	A4-B4
Sudbury Crescent	B4	Fleetwood Road	A4-B4
Swinderby Road	C1	Gardener Avenue	C4
Sylvester Road	B2-C2	Gary Close	B3-B4
Talbot Road	C1	Geary Road	A4-B4
The Chine	B2	Glebe Road	A3
The Close	D1	Gowan Road	B2
The Croft	B2	Grosvenor Gardens	C3
The Dell	B2-A2	Grove Road	C2-C3
The Dene	D3	Hamilton Road	A4
The Fairway	B4-A4-B4	Hanover Road	C1
The Glen	C3	Harlesden Road	A1-A2-B2
Thurlby Road	C1	Hawthorn Road	A2-B2
Thurlow Gardens	C2	Helena Road	B4
Tokyngton Avenue	E1	High Road	A3-A2-B2-C2
Tudor Court	F1	Huddlestone Road	B2-B3
Turton Road	C2-D2	Ivy Road	C4
		James Avenue	C4

Jeymer Avenue	B3-C3	Fry Road	C3-C4
Kendal Road	A4-B4	Furness Road	C2
Kenneth Crescent	B3-C3	Goodson Road	B4
Kings Road	A2-B2	Greenhill Park	A3-B3
Lancaster Road	A4	Greenhill Road	A3
Lechmere Road	B2-B3	Guilsborough Close	A4
Linacre Road	B2-B3	Harlesden Gardens	B3-C3-C2
Litchfield Gardens	A2	Harlesden Road	C2-C3
Lydford Road	C2	Harley Road	A3-A2-B2
Maybury Gardens	A2-B2	Hazeldean Road	A4
Melrose Avenue	B4-C4-C3	High Street	B3-B2-C2-C1
Milverton Road	C1-C2	Hillside	A4
Mount Pleasant Road	C4	Holly Close	B4
Mulgrave Road	A4	Knatchbull Road	A3-A4
Normandy Road	A4	Leghorn Road	B2
North Park Avenue	B3-C3-C2	Leopold Road	B4
Olive Road	C4	Letchford Gardens	C1
Oman Avenue	C4	Longstone Avenue	C3-C4
Park Avenue	B3-B4	Manor Park Road	B2-B3
Parkfield Road	A2-B2	Marian Way	B4
Peter Avenue	B1-B2	Minet Avenue	A2-A2-B2
Pound Lane	A2-A3	Mordaunt Road	A3
Riffel Road	C3-C4	Nicoll Road	B2-B3
Robson Avenue	A1-A2	Night Road	B2-C2
Rowdon Avenue	B1-B2	Old Park Lane	A1-B1-B2
Rutland Park	C2	Palermo Road	C2
St Paul's Avenue	B3-C3-C2	Park Parade	B2-C2
Sandringham Road	B2-B3	Park Road	A3
Sherrick Green Road	B3-B4	Redfern Road	B4
Sidmouth Road	B1-C1-C2	Ridley Road	C2
Sneyd Road	C4	Roundwood Road	B4-C4
Stanley Gardens	C3	Rucklidge Avenue	C2
Station Parade	C3	St Albans Road	A3
Staverton Road	C1-C2-B2	St Mary's Rod	B3-B4
Strode Road	A2-A3	St Johns Avenue	B3-B4
Tower Road	A2	Scrubbs Lane	C1
Uffington Road	A1-B1	Sellons Avenue	C2-C3
Villiers Road	B2-B3-A3	Shakespeare Crescent	A3-A4
Walm Lane	C2-C3	Springwell Avenue	C2-C3
Willesden Lane	C2	Stonebridge Park	A4
Windsor Road	B3	Stracey Road	A3
Wren Avenue	C4	Tubbs Road	B2-C2
		Tunley Road	A4-B4
		Wendover Road	B2
Harlesden		West Ella Road	A4-B4
		West Inman Road	A4-B4
Acton Lane	A2-A3-A2-B2	Winchelsea Road	A3
Alric Avenue	A4	Wrottesley Road	C2
Ambleside Road	B4-C4		
Avenue Road	B2		
Bishops Way	A4		
Bramston Road	C2		
Branshill Road	B2		
Brentfield Road	A4		
Brownlow Road	B4		
Bruce Road	A4		
Buckingham Road	B2-C2		
Burns Road	B3-B4		
Casselden Road	A4		
Cecil Road	A3		
Chadwick Road	B4-C4-C3		
Charlton Road	B3		
Church Road	A4-B4		
Connaught Road	A3-B3-B2		
Craven Park	A3-A4		
Crownhill Road	B3-C3		
Cunard Road	A1		
Denbigh Close	A4		
Drayton Road	B4-B3-C3		
Fairlight Avenue	A2		
Fortune Gate	B3-B4		

Heathrow Airport

Biggest and busiest airport in the United Kingdom, handling more international traffic than any other airport in the world, Heathrow broke its own records on 31 August 1980, when 112,880 passengers passed through. 1983 saw a total of 26,749,200 travellers, assisted by the 45,000-strong staff of the British Airports Authority and the 74 airline companies from 68 countries which operate scheduled services from the airport. Aircraft go to over 90 countries, and Heathrow's No 1 runway, 2.42 miles (3.9km) in length, is the longest used by civilian aircraft in the United Kingdom.

It all began when the site was transferred from the Air Ministry to the Ministry of Civil Aviation on 1 January 1946. On 31 May 1946, it opened as London (Heathrow) Airport, superseding the Airport of London at Croydon, established in 1928. This resulted in the operation of direct services between the United Kingdom and the United States of America. On 16 December 1955, the first three permanent buildings were opened by the Queen, and all three passenger terminals are now interlinked by pedestrian subways with moving walkways. The terminals are situated in the central area of the airport, and are also linked to the M4. A fourth terminal is under construction on the south-eastern side of the airport.

Terminal 1 is used by United Kingdom and Irish airlines for domestic and European flights, and for British Airways flights to and from certain destinations in North America. Terminal 2 is used by other European airlines except for the Irish airlines. Terminal 3 is the one used by intercontinental airlines going to Africa, America, Asia and Australia.

In 1966, the newly appointed British Airways Authority took over the responsibility for both Heathrow and the second airport at Gatwick (the two are linked by a frequent daily helicopter service). Direct rail access came in 1977 when the Underground's Piccadilly Line was extended and in the same year, Heathrow Central Station opened.

Today the Queens Building Roof Gardens and viewing gallery allow visitors to admire the aircraft and to watch the aircraft at work. There is a small admission charge for this.

Visitors who have come to the Queens Building Roof Gardens can also take refreshments there, at one of the many restaurants to be found throughout the airport. All three passenger terminals have licensed restaurants where full meals are served, and there are also grill bars providing hot meals. Light refreshments can also be bought.

Multi-storey car parks are sited at each of the passenger terminals for short term car parking. Heathrow also has long term car parks, situated on the northern perimeter road. A free coach carries passengers between the long term car parks and the terminals. During the night (from midnight to 6am), passengers wanting this service can contact the coach base on the special direct line telephones which are in use at the pick-up points.

Central England and Wales

AREA MAPS ARE INDICATED IN BOLD.

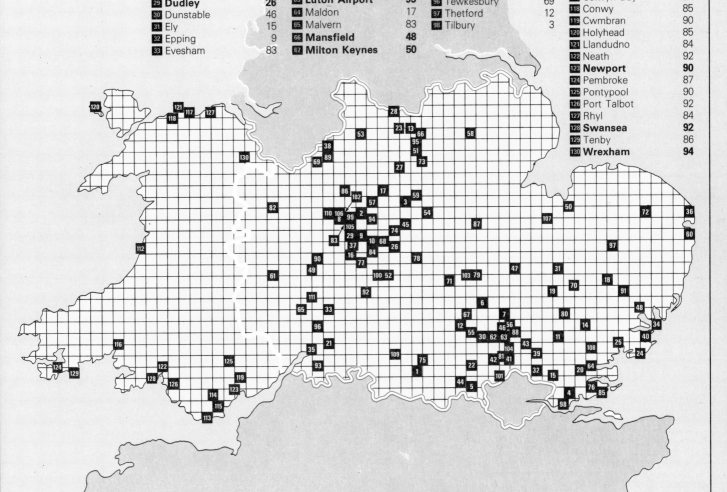

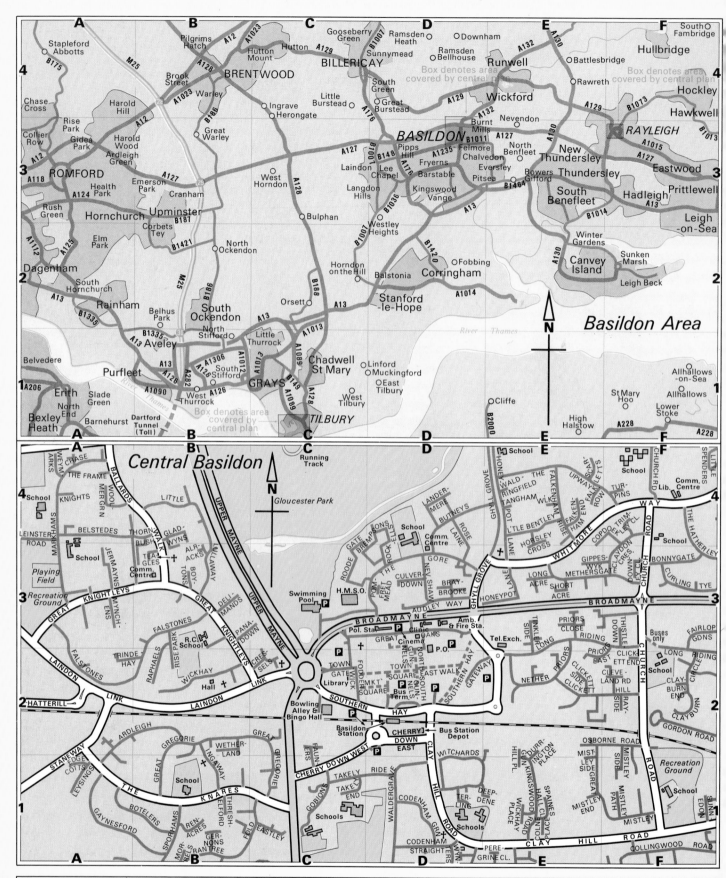

Basildon

'Pussiewillow's Clock' bursting into life at 15-minute intervals and the bronze 'Mother and Child' statue are two of the attractions of bustling Basildon, a town which has developed considerably over the last 50 years. Major companies are attracted to its expanding industrial estates, and as well as the vast Eastgate shopping precinct, it still has several interesting old buildings dotted about.

Rayleigh has kept much of its old world charm, even though some development has taken place within the town. Several of the original buildings still stand in the town centre, alongside bright modern shops, while evidence of a long and interesting history can be seen in Crown Hill's 17th-century Dutch Cottage and the Old Windmill — complete with fan tails and sails this is now used as an exhibition centre.

Tilbury saw the beginning of great changes in 1886, when the now extensive Docks were opened. A massive grain terminal and mill were also constructed on the site, which has become one of the largest container ports in Europe and serves major shipping companies. The pretty parish church at East Tilbury overlooks Coalhouse Fort, whose gun emplacements and granite walls provide the background for the Borough Park. Tilbury Fort stands not far from West Tilbury.

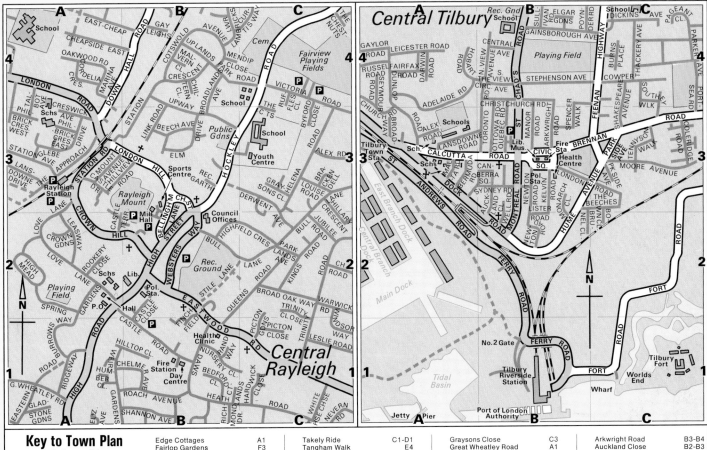

Key to Town Plan and Area Plan

Town Plan

AA Recommended roads
Other roads
Restricted roads
Buildings of interest   Station ▣
Churches   ✝
Car Parks   P
Parks and open spaces

Area Plan

A roads
B roads
Locations   Nevendon O
Urban area

Street Index

Basildon

Alracks	B3
Ardleigh	A1-A2-B2
Audley Way	D3
Ballards Walk	A4-B4-B3
Belstedes	A4
Bonnygate	F3
Boteliers	A1-B1
Boytons	B3
Braybrooke	D3
Brempsons	C3-D3-D4
Broadmayne	C2-C3-D3-E3-F3
Butneys	D3-D4-E4
Cherry Down East	D2
Cherry Down West	C1-C2-D2
Church Road	F1-F2-F3-F4
Clayburn Circle	F2
Clayburn End	F2
Claydon Crescent	F2
Clay Hill Road	D2-D1-E1-F1
Cleveland Road	F2
Clickett End	F2
Clickett Hill	E2-F2
Clickett Side	E2
Codenham Green	D1
Codenham Straight	D1
Collingwood Road	F1
Colne Place	E1
Copdoek	E4-F4
Cressels	C2-C3
Colverdown	D3
Curling Tye	F3
Deepdene	D1-E1
Delimands	B3
Downey Close	F3
Durrington Place	E1-E2
Eastley	C1
East Walk	D2

Edge Cottages	A1
Fairlop Gardens	F3
Falkenham End	E4
Falkenham Rise	E4
Falkenham Row	E4
Falstones	A3-A2-B2-B3
Fauners	C1-C2
Fodderwick	C2
Gateway	D2-E2
Gaynesford	A1-B1
Gernons	B1
Ghyll Grove	D3-E3-E4
Gippeswyk	E3-F3
Gladwyns	B3-B4
Gobions	C1
Gordon Road	F2
Great Gregorie	B1-B2-C2-C1
Great Knightleys	A3-B3-B2-C2
Great Mistley	E2-E1-F1
Great Oaks	C3-D3
Gun Hill Place	E1-E2
Hatterhill	A2
Honeypot Lane	D3-E3-E4
Horsley Cross	E3-E4
Ingaway	B1-B2
Jermayns	A3
Kingswood Road	E1
Knights	A4
Laindon Link	A3-A2-B2-C2
Landermere	D4
Leinster Road	A4
Leysings	A1
Little Bentley	E4
Little Lullaway	B3-B4
Little Spenders	F4
Long Acre	E4
Long Riding	E2-E3-E3-F2
Market Square	C2-D2
Markhams Chase	A3-A4
Methersgate	E3-F3
Mistley Side	E1
Mistley Path	F1
Mistley Side	E1-E2
Mistley Side	F1-F2
Morrels	B1
Mynchens	A3
Nether Priors	E2-E3
Neville Shaw	D3
North Gunnels	D2-D3
Osborne Road	E2-F2
Panadown	B3-C3
Peregrine Close	E1
Pomfret Mead	E2
Priors East	E2-F2-F3
Priors Close	E3
Rantree Fold	B1-C1
Raphaels	B2-B3
Rayside	F2
Renacres	B1
Rise Park	B2-B3
Rockells	D3-D4
Roode Gate	C3-C4-C3-D3
Rose Laine	D3-D4
Scarletts	E4
Short Acre	E3
Southern Hay	C2-D2-D3
South Gunnels	D2
Spaines Hall Close	E1
Sporhams	E1
Staneway	A1-A2
Sunnedon	F1
Takely End	C1

Takely Ride	C1-D1
Tangham Walk	E4
Teagles	B3
Terling	D1
The Frame	A4
The Gore	D3
The Hatherley	F3-F4
The Knares	A2-A1-B1-C1
The Upway	E4-F4
Thistledown	F3
Thornbush	A4-B4
Threshelford	B1
Tinkler Side	E2-E3
Town Gate	C2
Town Square	D2
Trimley Close	F4
Trindehay	A2-B2
Turpins	F4
Upper Mayne	B4-B3-C3-C2
Waldergrave	D1
Waldringfield	E4
Wetherland	B2
Weymarks	A4
Whitmore Way	E3-E4-F4
Wickhay	B2
Wickhay Place	E1
Witchards	D1-D2
Woolmer Green	A4
Wynters	D1

Rayleigh

Alexandra Road	C3
Beech Avenue	B3
Bedford Close	B1
Bellingham Lane	B2-B3
Bracken Dell	C3
Broadlands Avenue	B3-B4
Broad Oak Way	C2
Bull Lane	B2-C2-C3
Burrows Way	A1-A2
Byford Close	C3-C4
Castle Close	B1-B2
Castle Drive	A3
Castle Road	A2-B2-B1
Castle Terrrace	A2
Cheapside East	A4-B4
Chelmer Avenue	A1-B1
Chiltern Close	B4
Church Road	C2
Church Street	B3
Cordelia Crescent	A4
Cotswold Avenue	B4
Courtlands	B1
Creswick Avenue	A3
Crown Gardens	A4
Crown Hill	A3-A2-B2
Curtis Way	B4-C4
Daws	B1
Derwent Avenue	B3-C3-C2
Down Hall Road	A3-A4-B4
East Cheap	A4-B4
Eastern Road	A1
Eastwood Road	B2-B1-C1
Elizabeth Avenue	A1
Elm Drive	B3
Finchfield	B1-B2
Gay Leighs	B4
Gladstone Gardens	A1
Glebe Drive	A3

Graysons Close	C3
Great Wheatley Road	A1
Hardwick Close	C1
Heath Road	B1-C1
Helana Road	C2-C3
Highfield Crescent	B2-C2
High Mead	A2
High Road	A1-A2-B2
High Street	B2
Hillary Crescent	C2-C3
Hilltop Close	A1-B1
Hillview Road	A3-B3
Hockley Road	B3-C3-C4
Humber Close	A1
Jubilee Road	C2
Kings Road	C2
Lansdowne Drive	A3
Leasway	A2
Leslie Road	C1
Link Road	B3-B4
London Hill	A3-B3
London Road	A3-A4
Louise Road	C3
Love Lane	A2-A3
Lower Lambricks	B4
Malvern Close	B4
Marina Avenue	A4
Mendip Close	B4
Mount Avenue	A3
Nevern Road	C1
Nursery Close	B1-C1
Oakwood Road	A4
Parklands Avenue	C2
Philbrick Crescent East	A3
Philbrick Crescent West	A3
Picton Close	C1
Picton Gardens	C1-C2
Queens Road	B1-B2-C2
Randway	B1
Rectory Garth	B3
Richmond Drive	B1
Ridgeway	A3
Roach Avenue	A1-B1
Rookery Close	A2
Ruffles Close	C4
Shannon Avenue	A1-B1
Spring Gardens	A2
Station Avenue	A3
Station Crescent	A3-B3-B4
Station Road	A3
Stile Lane	B2-C2
Talbot Avenue	A3-A4
The Approach	A3
The Chestnuts	C4
The Courts	C3
Trinity Close	C1-C2
Trinity Road	C1-C2
Uplands Park Road	B4-C4
Upway	B3-B4
Victoria Road	C3-C4
Warwick Road	C2
Websters Way	B2
Weir Gardens	A1
White House Chase	C1
Windsor Way	C1-C2

Tilbury

Adelaide Road	A4-A3-A4
Alexandra Road	A3

Arkwright Road	B3-B4
Auckland Close	B2-B3
Bermuda Road	A3
Bown Close	C2-C3
Brennan Road	B3-C3
Broadway	A3
Brunel Close	B4
Burns Place	C4
Calcutta Road	A3-B3
Canberra Square	B3
Central Avenue	B4
Christchurch Road	B4
Church Road	A4-A3-A4
Civic Square	B3
Coleridge Road	C3
Cowper	C4
Darwin Road	A4
Dickins Avenue	C4
Dock Road	A3-B3-C3
Dunlop Road	A3-A4
Elgar Gardens	B4
Fairfax Road	A4
Feenan Highway	C3-C4
Ferry Road	B1-B2
Fort Road	B1-C1-C2-C3
Gainsborough Avenue	B4-C4
Gaylor Road	A4
Hobart Road	A4-B4
Hume Avenue	B2-B3-C3
Kelvin Road	B3
Landsdowne Road	A3-B3
Leicester Road	A4
Lister Road	B2-B3
London Road	B3-C3
Malta Road	A3
Manor Road	B3-B4
Monarch Close	B2-B3
Montreal Road	B2-B3
Moore Avenue	C3
Newton Road	B2-B3
North View Avenue	B4
Ottowa Road	B3-B4
Pageant Close	C4
Parker Avenue	C4
Park Side Avenue	C3
Portsea Road	C3-C4
Poynder Road	B4
Quebec Road	B3-B4
Russel Road	B4
St Andrews Road	A3-A2-B2
St Chad's Road	B3-B4
Seymour Road	A4
Shakespeare Avenue	C3-C4
Southey Walk	C3-C4
South View Avenue	B4
Spencer Walk	B3-B4
Stephenson Avenue	B4-C4
Sullivan Road	B4
Sydney Road	A3-B3
Tennyson Walk	C3
Thackery Avenue	C4
The Beeches	B3-C3
The Circle	B4
Toronto Road	B3-B4
Wellington Road	B2-B3

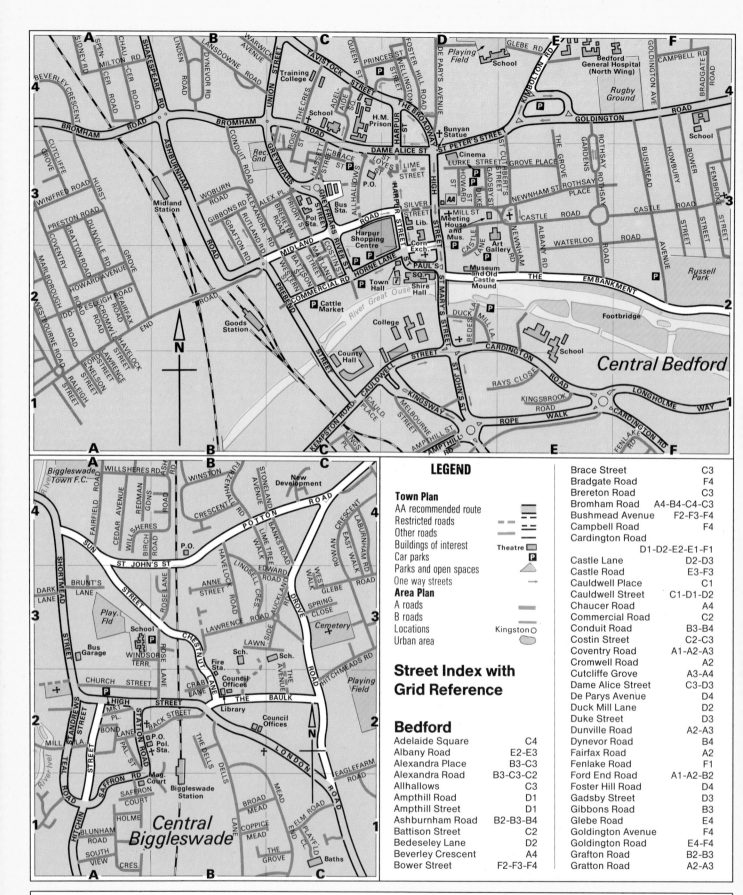

LEGEND

Town Plan

AA recommended route	
Restricted roads	
Other roads	
Buildings of interest	Theatre ▣
Car parks	▣
Parks and open spaces	▲
One way streets	→

Area Plan

A roads	
B roads	
Locations	Kingston ○
Urban area	⬭

Street Index with Grid Reference

Bedford

Adelaide Square	C4
Albany Road	E2-E3
Alexandra Place	B3-C3
Alexandra Road	B3-C3-C2
Allhallows	C3
Ampthill Road	D1
Ampthill Street	D1
Ashburnham Road	B2-B3-B4
Battison Street	C2
Bedeseley Lane	D2
Beverley Crescent	A4
Bower Street	F2-F3-F4
Brace Street	C3
Bradgate Road	F4
Brereton Road	C3
Bromham Road	A4-B4-C4-C3
Bushmead Avenue	F2-F3-F4
Campbell Road	F4
Cardington Road	D1-D2-E2-E1-F1
Castle Lane	D2-D3
Castle Road	E3-F3
Cauldwell Place	C1
Cauldwell Street	C1-D1-D2
Chaucer Road	A4
Commercial Road	C2
Conduit Road	B3-B4
Costin Street	C2-C3
Coventry Road	A1-A2-A3
Cromwell Road	A2
Cutcliffe Grove	A3-A4
Dame Alice Street	C3-D3
De Parys Avenue	D4
Duck Mill Lane	D2
Duke Street	D3
Dunville Road	A2-A3
Dynevor Road	B4
Fairfax Road	A2
Fenlake Road	F1
Ford End Road	A1-A2-B2
Foster Hill Road	D4
Gadsby Street	D3
Gibbons Road	B3
Glebe Road	E4
Goldington Avenue	F4
Goldington Road	E4-F4
Grafton Road	B2-B3
Gratton Road	A2-A3

Bedford

John Bunyan's *Pilgrim's Progress* was written in the unlikely setting of the County Gaol, where he spent 12 years on a charge of holding illegal religious meetings. Most of his life was spent in this area, and the town remembers him by a museum in his former Meeting House and by his statue on St Peter's Green. The Bunyan Centre, opened in 1974, is a popular venue for sports and also has a small theatre and a concert hall. Other places to visit in this county town of Bedfordshire are the Bedford Museum and the Cecil Higgins Art Gallery, which stands on the spot once occupied by Bedford Castle and has a collection of ceramics and glass. The parks and gardens which line the banks of the Great Ouse are a powerful attraction, as is the modern Harpur Shopping Centre, which stands on the site of a former school and has the original Victorian facade incorporated into the new design.

Biggleswade Barges on the River Ivel once carried local produce to London's markets, and Biggleswade itself has been a busy market town since the 16th century. A former staging post for coaches on the Great North Road, it is now chiefly concerned with light industry. A fine classical Town Hall and some charming half-timbered houses can be seen in the Market Square area. The Shuttleworth Collection of cars and cycles is one mile north-west, at Old Warden Aerodrome.

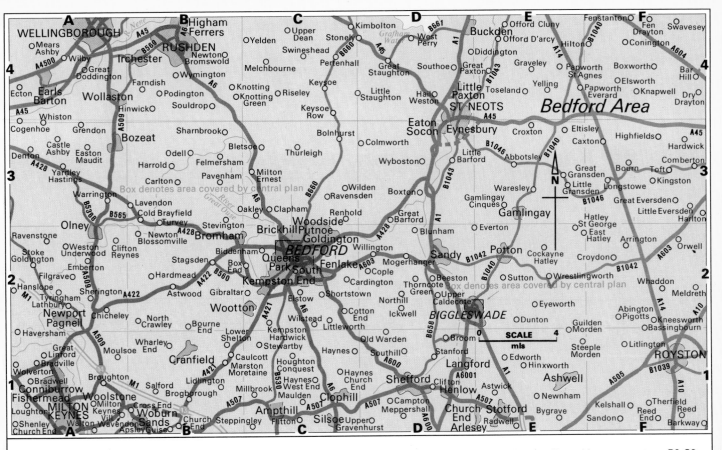

Greyfriars	B4-C4-C3	Preston Road	A3	Woburn Road	B3
Greyfriars Street	C3	Princes Street	C4-D4		
Grove Place	E3	Priory Street	C3	**Biggleswade**	
Hassett Street	C3	Queen Street	C4		
Harpur Street	D2-D3-D4	Raleigh Street	A1	Anne Street	B3
Havelock Street	A1-A2	Rays Close	D1-E1	Ash Road	B4
High Street	D2-D3	River Street	C2-C3	Auckland Road	C3
Horne Lane	C2-D2	Roise Street	C3-C4	Back Street	A2-B2
Howard Avenue	A2	Rope Walk	D1-E1	Banks Road	C4
Howard Street	D3	Rothsay Gardens	E3-E4	Birch Road	A4-B4
Howbury Street	F2-F3-F4	Rothsay Place	E3	Blunham Road	A1
Hurst Grove	A2-A3-A4	Rothsay Road	E2-E3	Bond Lane	A2
Iddesleigh Road	A2	Rutland Road	B2-B3	Broad Mead	B1-C1
Kempston Road	C1	St Cuthbert's Street	E3-E4	Brunt's Lane	A3
Kimbolton Road	E4	St John's Street	D1	Cedar Avenue	A4
Kingsbrook Road	E1	St Loyes Street	C3-D3	Chestnut Lane	B2-B3
Kings Place	C1	St Mary's Street	D2	Church Street	A2-B2
Kingsway	D1	St Paul's Square	D2	Coppice Mead	B1-C1
Landsdowne Road	B4	St Peter's Street	D3-D4-E4	Crab Lane	B2
Lawrence Street	A1	Shakespeare Road	A4-B4	Dark Lane	A3
Lime Street	D3	Sidney Road	A4	Dells Lane	B1-B2
Linden Road	B4	Silver Street	D3	Drove Road	C1-C2-C3-C4
Longholme Way	E1-F1	Spencer Road	A4	Eaglefarm Road	C1-C2
Lurke Street	D3-E3	Tavistock Street	C4-D4	East Walk	C3-C4
Maitland Street	C2	The Broadway	D3-D4	Edward Road	B3-C3
Marlborough Road	A1-A2	The Crescent	C4	Elm Road	C1
Melbourne Street	D1	The Embankment	D2-E2-F2	Fairfield Road	A4
Midland Road	B2-C2-C3-D3	The Grove	E3-E4	Furzenhall Road	B4
Mill Street	D3-E3	Union Street	B4-C4	Glebe Road	C3
Milton Road	A4	Warwick Avenue	B4-C4	Havelock Road	B3-B4
Nelson Street	A1	Waterloo Road	E2-E3-F3	High Street	A2-B2
Newnham Road	E2-E3	Wellington Street	D4	Hitchin Street	A1-A2
Newnham Street	E3	Westbourne Road	A1-A2	Hitchmeads Road	C2-C3
Pembroke Street	F2-F3	Western Street	C2	Holme Crescent	A1
Prebend Street	B2-C2-C1	Winifred Road	A3	Laburnham Road	C3-C4

Lawnside	B3-C3
Lawrence Road	B3-C3
Lime Tree Walk	B4-C4-C3
Lindsell Crescent	B3-B4
London Road	B2-C2-C1
Market Place	A2
Mead End	B2-B1-C1
Mill Lane	A2
Palace Street	A2
Playfield Close	C1
Potton Road	B4-C4
Redman Gardens	A4
Rose Lane	B2-B3
Rowan Crescent	C3-C4
St Andrews Street	A2
St John's Street	A3-A4-B4-B3
Saffron Court	A1-B1
Saffron Road	A1-A2
Shortmead Street	A2-A3-A4
South View	A1
Spring Close	C3
Station Road	A2
Stoneland Avenue	B4-C4
Sun Street	A4-A3-B3
Teal Road	A1-A2
The Avenue	C2-C3
The Baulk	B2-C2
The Dells	B2
The Grove	B1-C1
West Walk	C3
Willsheres Road	A4-B4
Windsor Terrace	A3-B3
Winston Crescent	B4

BEDFORD
Overlooking the River Great Ouse, the 1813 Town Bridge replaced an older version which incorporated the Town Gaol into its structure. A model of the gaol is on display in the Bunyan Museum in Mill Street.

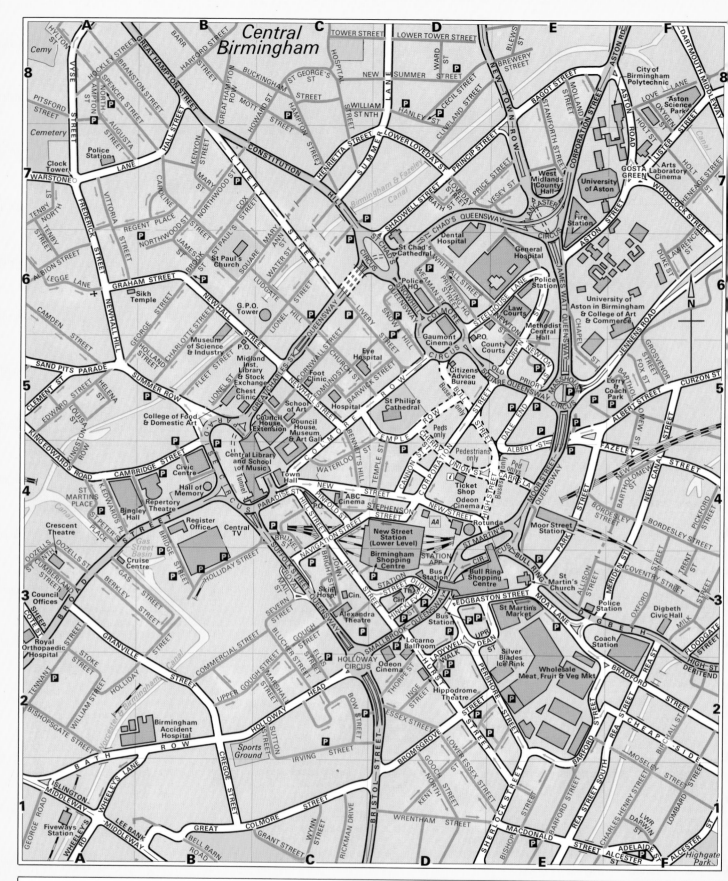

Birmingham

It is very difficult to visualise Birmingham as it was before it began the growth which eventually made it the second-largest city in England. When the Romans were in Britain it was little more than a staging post on Icknield Street. Throughout medieval times it was a sleepy agricultural centre in the middle of a heavily-forested region. Timbered houses clustered together round a green that was

eventually to be called the Bull Ring. But by the 16th century, although still a tiny and unimportant village by today's standards, it had begun to gain a reputation as a manufacturing centre. Tens of thousands of sword blades were made here during the Civil War. Throughout the 18th century more and more land was built on. In 1770 the Birmingham Canal was completed, making trade very much easier and increasing the town's development dramatically. All of that pales into near

insignificance compared with what happened in the 19th century. Birmingham was not represented in Parliament until 1832 and had no town council until 1838. Yet by 1889 it had already been made a city, and after only another 20 years it had become the second largest city in England. Many of Birmingham's most imposing public buildings date from the 19th century, when the city was growing so rapidly. Surprisingly, the city has more miles of waterway than Venice.

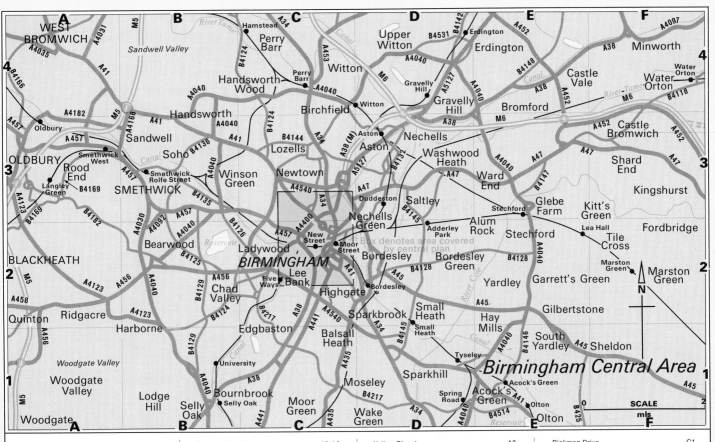

Key to Town Plan and Area Plan

Town Plan

AA Recommended roads	
Restricted roads	
Other roads	
Buildings of interest	Station 🏢
AA Service Centre	AA
Car Parks	P
Parks and open spaces	
One Way Streets	→

Area Plan

A roads	
B roads	
Locations	Meer End ○

Street Index with Grid Reference

Birmingham

Adelaide Street	F1
Albert Street	E4-E5-F5
Albion Street	A6
Alcester Street	F1
Allison Street	E3
Aston Road	E8-F8-F1
Aston Street	E6-E7-F7
Augusta Street	A7-A8
Bagot Street	E8
Barford Street	E1-E2-F2
Barr Street	B8
Bartholomew Street	F4-F5
Barwick Street	C5-D5
Bath Row	A1-A2-B2
Bath Street	D7
Bell Barn Road	C4-C5
Bennett's Hill	C4-C5
Berkley Street	A3-B3
Birchall Street	F1-F2
Bishop Street	E1
Bishopsgate Street	A2
Blews Street	E8
Blucher Street	C2-C3
Bordesley Street	E4-F4-F3
Bow Street	C3
Bradford Street	E3-E2-F2
Branston Street	A8-B8-B7
Brewery Street	E8
Bridge Street	B3-B4
Bristol Street	C1-D1-D2-C2
Broad Street	A2-A3-A4-B4
Bromsgrove Street	D1-D2-E2
Brook Street	B6
Brunel Street	C3-C4
Buckingham Street	B8-C8
Bull Ring	E3
Bull Street	D5-E5-E4
Cambridge Street	A4-B4-B5

Camden Street	A5-A6
Cannon Street	D4
Caroline Street	B6-B7
Carrs Street	E4
Cecil Street	D8
Chapel Street	E5-E6
Charles Henry Street	F1
Charlotte Street	B5-B6
Cheapside	F1-F2
Cherry Street	D4-D5
Church Street	C6-C5-D5
Clement Street	A5
Cliveland Street	D7-D8-E8
Colmore Circus	D5-D6
Colmore Row	C4-C5-D5
Commercial Street	B2-B3-C3
Constitution Hill	B7-C7
Cornwall Street	C5-C6
Corporation Street	D4-D5-E5-E6-E7-E8
Coventry Street	E3-F3
Cox Street	B7
Cregoe Street	B1-B2
Cumberland Street	A3
Curzon Street	F5
Dale End	E4-E5
Dartmouth Middleway	F7-F8
Digbeth	E3-F3
Dudley Street	D3
Duke Street	F6
Edgbaston Street	D3-E3
Edmund Street	C5-D5
Edward Street	A5
Ellis Street	C2-C3
Essex Street	D2
Fazeley Street	E5-E4-F4
Fleet Street	B5
Floodgate Street	F3
Fox Street	F5
Frederick Street	A6-A7
Gas Street	A3-A2-B3
George Road	A1
George Street	A5-B5-B6
Gooch Street North	D1-D2
Gosta Green	F7
Gough Street	C3
Graham Street	A6-B6
Grant Street	C1
Granville Street	A3-A2-B2
Great Charles St Queensway	B5-C5-C6
Great Colmore Street	B1-C1-D1
Great Hampton Row	B8
Great Hampton Street	A8-B8
Grosvenor Street	F5-F6
Hall Street	B7-B8
Hampton Street	C7-C8
Hanley Street	D7-D8
Helena Street	A5
Heneage Street	F7
Henrietta Street	C7-D7
High Street	D4-E4
High Street Deritend	F2-F3
Hill Street	C4-C3-D3
Hinckley Street	D3
Hockley Street	A8-B8
Holland Street	B5
Holliday Street	A2-B2-B3-C3-C4
Holloway Circus	C2-C3-D3-D2
Holloway Head	B2-C2
Holt Street	F7-F8
Hospital Street	C7-C8
Howard Street	B7-C7-C8
Hurst Street	D3-D2-E2-E1

Hylton Street	A8
Inge Street	D2
Irving Street	C2-D2
Islington Middleway	A1
James Street	B6
James Watt Queensway	E5-E6
Jennens Road	E5-F5-F6
John Bright Street	C3-C4
Kent Street	D1-D2
Kenyon Street	B7
King Edward's Place	A4
King Edward's Road	A4-A5
Kingston Row	A4
Ladywell Walk	D2-D3
Lancaster Circus	E6-E7
Lawrence Street	F6-F7
Lee Bank Middleway	A1-B1
Legge Lane	A6
Lionel Street	B5-C5-C6
Lister Street	F7-F8
Livery Street	B7-C7-C6-D6-D5
Lombard Street	F1-F2
Louisa Street	A5
Love Lane	F8
Loveday Street	D7
Lower Darwin Street	F1
Lower Essex Street	D2-D1-E1
Lower Loveday Street	D7
Lower Tower Street	D8
Ludgate Hill	B6-C6
Macdonald Street	E1-F1
Marshall Street	C2
Mary Street	B7
Mary Ann Street	C6-C7
Masshouse Circus	E5
Meriden Street	E3-F3
Milk Street	F3
Moat Lane	E3
Molland Street	E8
Moor Street Queensway	E4-E5
Moseley Street	E2-F2-F1
Mott Street	B8-C8-C7
Navigation Street	C3-C4
New Street	C4-D4
New Bartholomew Street	F4
New Canal Street	F4-F5
Newhall Hill	A5-A6
Newhall Street	B6-B5-C5
New Summer Street	C8-D8
Newton Street	E5
New Town Row	D8-E8-E7
Northampton Street	A8
Northwood Street	B6-B7
Old Square	D5-E5
Oozells Street	A3-A4
Oozells Street North	A3-A4
Oxford Street	F3-F4
Oxygen Street	F7-F8
Paradise Circus	B4-B5
Paradise Street	C4
Park Street	E3-E4
Pershore Street	D3-D2-E2
Pickford Street	F4
Pinfold Street	C4
Pitsford Street	A8
Price Street	D7-E7
Princip Street	D7-E7-E8
Printing House Street	D6
Priory Queensway	E5
Rea Street	E2-F2-F3
Rea Street South	E1-F1-F2
Regent Place	A7-B7

Rickman Drive	C1
Royal Mail Street	C3
St Chad's Circus	C7-C6-D6
St Chad's Queensway	D6-D7-E7
St George's Street	C8
St Martin's Circus	D3-D4-E4-E3
St Martin's Place	A4
St Paul's Square	B7-B6-C6
St Peter's Place	A4
Sand Pits Parade	A5
Severn Street	C3
Shadwell Street	D6-D7
Sheepcote Street	A3
Sherlock Street	D1-E1-E2
Smallbrook Queensway	C3-D3
Snow Hill	D5-D6
Snow Hill Queensway	D6
Spencer Street	A8-A7-B7
Staniforth Street	E7-E8
Station Approach	D3
Station Street	D3
Steelhouse Lane	D6-E6
Stephenson Street	C4-D4
Stoke Street	A2-A3
Suffolk Street Queensway	B4-C4-C3
Summer Row	A5-B5
Summer Lane	C7-D7-D8
Sutton Street	C2
Temple Row	C5-D5
Temple Street	D4-D5-D5
Tenby Street	A6-A7
Tenby Street North	A7
Tennant Street	A2-A3
Thorpe Street	D2-D3
Tower Street	C8-D8
Trent Street	F3-F4
Union Street	D4
Upper Dean Street	D3-E3
Upper Gough Street	B2-C2-C3
Vesey Street	D7-E7
Vittoria Street	A6-A7
Vyse Street	A7-A8
Ward Street	D8
Warford Street	B8
Warstone Lane	A7-B7
Water Street	C6
Waterloo Street	C4-C5-D5
Weaman Street	D6
Wheeley's Lane	A1-B1-B2
Wheeley's Road	A1
Whittall Street	D6-E6
William Street	A2
William Street North	C8-D8
Woodcock Street	F6-F7
Wrentham Street	D1-E1
Wynn Street	C1

7

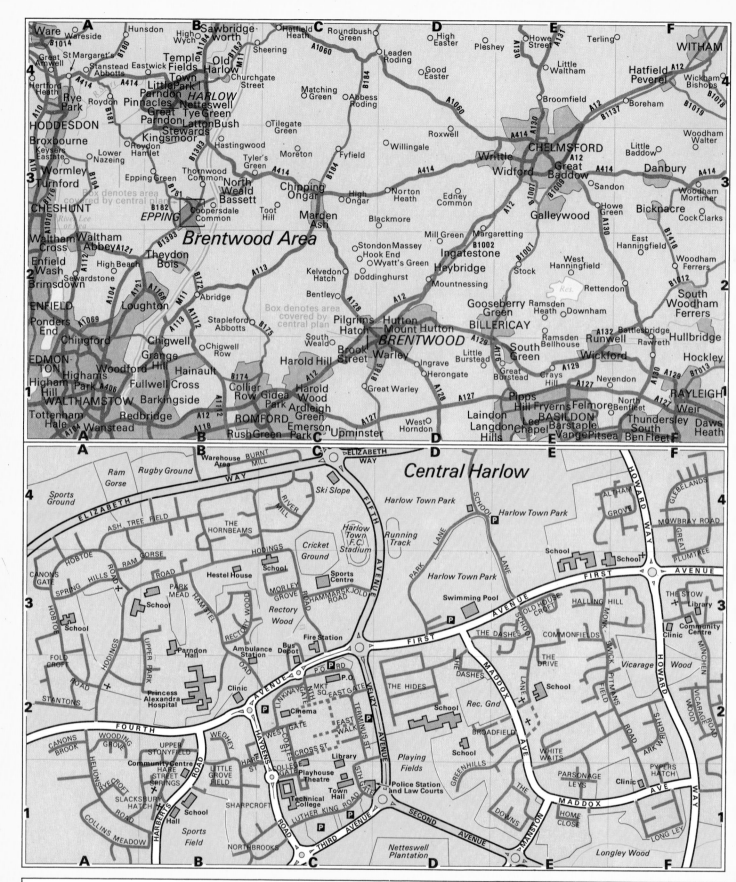

Brentwood area

Harlow Home of the country's first pedestrianised shopping centre and first all-purpose Sportcentre (embracing athletic and football clubs and a dry ski-slope), Harlow is the site of one of Britain's earliest 'New Towns'. Careful planning has produced a tasteful integration of housing, industrial estates and parks around the centre, and the Playhouse has a popular theatre. The ancient settlement of Old Harlow stands side by side with the new, and the Harlow Museum, set in a fine Georgian house with pleasantly landscaped grounds, has exhibits connected with the history of the area.

Brentwood Thermos Ltd and the Ford Motor Co are two of the major companies attracted to this former market town in recent years. It also enjoys modern shopping facilities and has a number of parks and stretches of woodland, while lying within easy reach of two country parks (Weald to the north-west and Thorndon to the south-east). The 'Old House' Arts and Community Centre provides a home for local societies and clubs, in premises dating back to Tudor times.

Epping is linked to London by main line and underground railways, but still enjoys the magnificent 600-acre expanse of Epping Forest which stretches south from the town and makes a peaceful haven from the area's busy main roads.

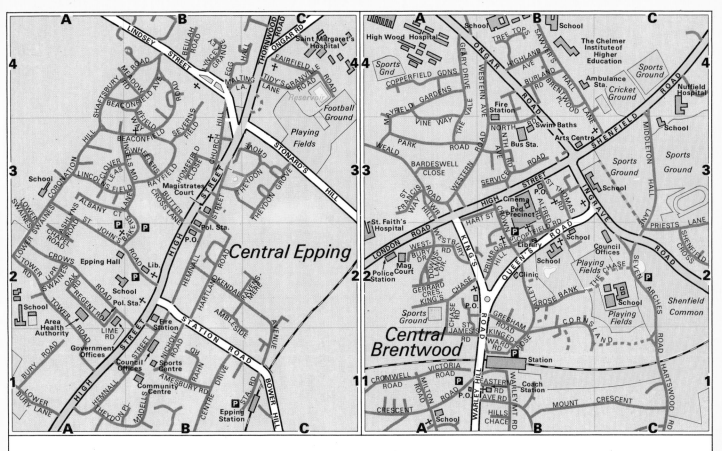

Central Epping

Central Brentwood

BRENTWOOD
The Essex Regimental Chapel at Warley is a reminder of longstanding military links — Warley Barracks was once the Depot of the Essex Regiment, and the Essex HQ of the Royal Anglian Regiment is still in the area.

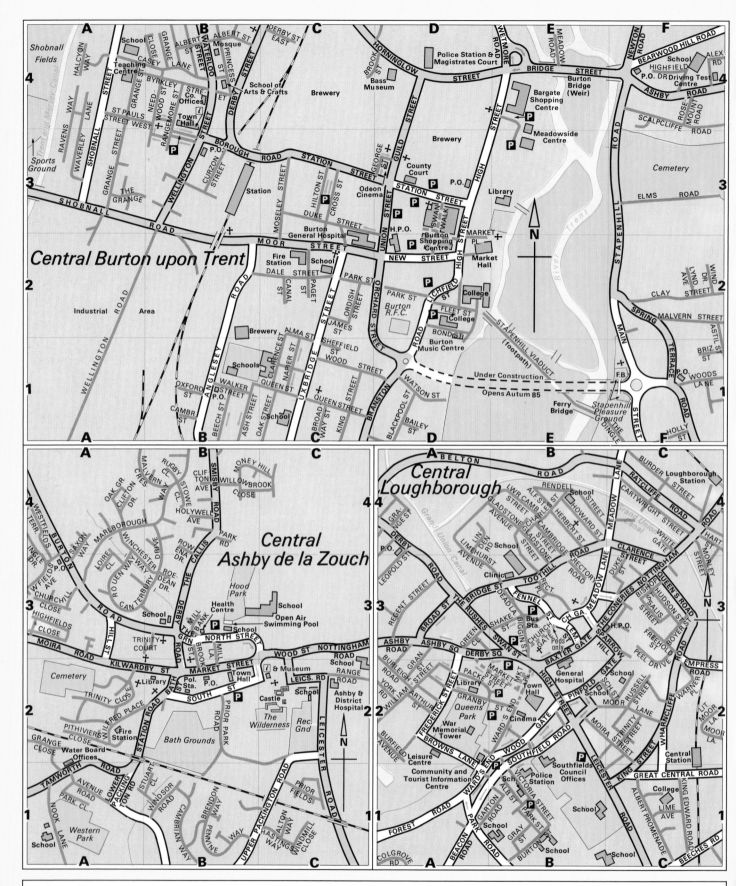

Burton upon Trent

Beer has been brewed here since medieval times and is still prevalent in the town, even though the number of breweries has diminished. The Bass Museum traces the history of the local brewing industry, and other places of interest include the Meadowside Centre, with its fine facilities for sports and the arts. Interesting old buildings can be seen, especially around Horninglow Street, and the Market Hall (now the new shopping centre) dates from the 19th century.

Loughborough Forty-seven locally-made bells ring out from the Queens Park Carillon Tower every Sunday during the summer, and many of Britain's churches have bells from Loughborough's John Taylor Foundry. A busy market and university town situated on the River Stour, Loughborough is also known for its colleges of technology and physical education. Its facilities include a modern Leisure Centre, and amongst local places of interest are the Parish Church of All Saints, dating from the 14th century, the much-restored Old Rectory, and Loughborough Central Station, where steam trains operate most weekends.

Ashby-de-la-Zouch Soap, crisp and biscuit making are the chief present-day concerns of this pleasant market town. The remains of the 15th-century castle are preserved near the centre of the town.

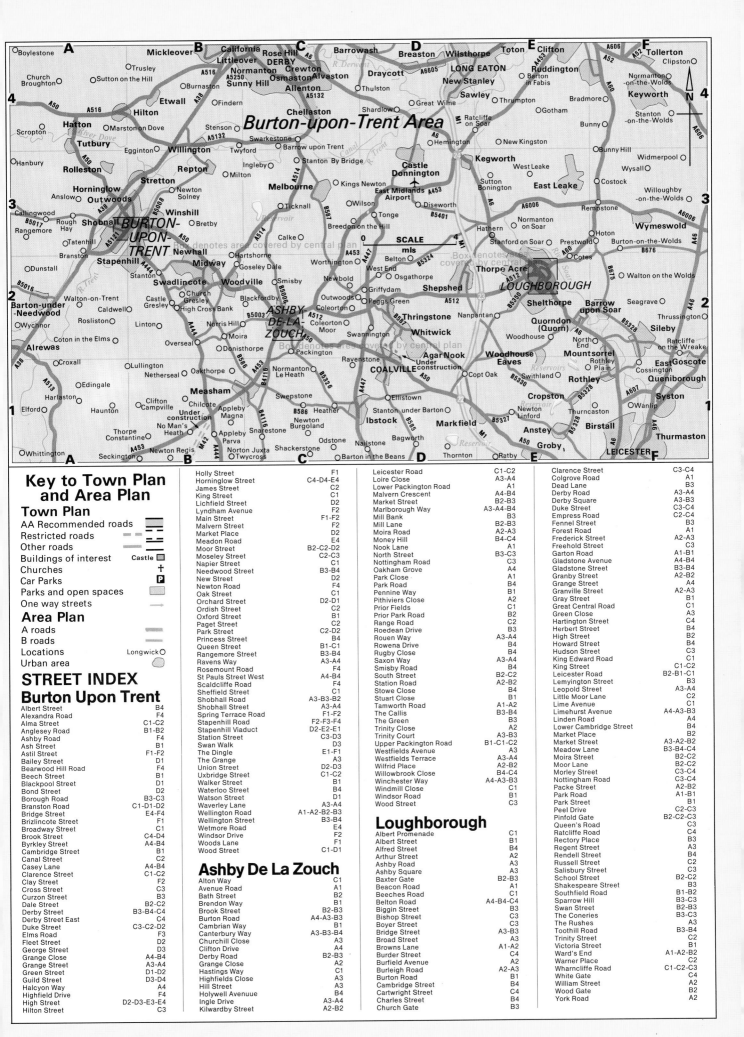

Key to Town Plan and Area Plan

Town Plan

AA Recommended roads
Restricted roads
Other roads
Buildings of interest — Castle ▣
Churches — †
Car Parks — P
Parks and open spaces
One way streets

Area Plan

A roads
B roads
Locations — Longwick ○
Urban area

STREET INDEX

Burton Upon Trent

Albert Street	B4
Alexandra Road	F4
Alma Street	C1-C2
Anglesey Road	B1-B2
Ashby Road	F4
Ash Street	B1
Astil Street	F1-F2
Bailey Street	D1
Bearwood Hill Road	F4
Beech Street	B1
Blackpool Street	D1
Bond Street	D2
Borough Road	B3-C3
Branston Road	C1-D1-D2
Bridge Street	E4-F4
Brizlincote Street	F1
Broadway Street	C1
Brook Street	C4-D4
Byrkley Street	A4-B4
Cambridge Street	B1
Canal Street	C2
Casey Lane	A4-B4
Clarence Street	C1-C2
Clay Street	F2
Cross Street	C3
Curzon Street	B3
Dale Street	B2-C2
Derby Street	B3-B4-C4-D2
Derby Street East	C4
Duke Street	C3-C2-D2
Elms Road	F3
Fleet Street	D2
George Street	D3
Grange Close	A4-B4
Grange Street	A3-A4
Green Street	D1-D2
Guild Street	D3-D4
Halcyon Way	A4
Highfield Drive	A4
High Street	D2-D3-E3-E4
Hilton Street	C3
Holly Street	F1
Horninglow Street	C4-D4-E4
James Street	C2
King Street	C1
Lichfield Street	D2
Lyndham Avenue	F2
Main Street	F1-F2
Malvern Street	F2
Market Place	D2
Meadon Road	E4
Moor Street	B2-C2-D2
Moseley Street	C2-C3
Napier Street	C1
Needwood Street	B3-B4
New Street	D2
Newton Road	F4
Oak Street	C1
Orchard Street	D2-D1
Ordish Street	C2
Oxford Street	B1
Paget Street	C2
Park Street	C2-D2
Princess Street	B4
Queen Street	B1-C1
Rangemore Street	B3-B4
Ravens Way	A3-A4
Rosemount Road	F4
St Pauls Street West	A4-B4
Scaldcliffe Road	F4
Sheffield Street	C1
Shobhall Road	A3-B3-B2
Shobhall Street	A3-A4
Spring Terrace Road	F1-F2
Stapenhill Road	F2-F3-F4
Stapenhill Viaduct	D2-E2-E1
Station Street	C3-D3
Swan Walk	D3
The Dingle	E1-F1
The Grange	A3
Union Street	D2-D3
Uxbridge Street	C1-C2
Walker Street	B1
Waterloo Street	B4
Watson Street	D1
Waverley Lane	A3-A4
Wellington Road	A1-A2-B2-B3
Wellington Street	B3-B4
Wetmore Road	E4
Windsor Drive	F2
Woods Lane	F1
Wood Street	C1-D1

Ashby De La Zouch

Alton Way	C1
Avenue Road	A1
Bath Street	B2
Brendon Way	B1
Brook Street	B2-B3
Burton Road	A4-A3-B3
Cambrian Way	B1
Canterbury Way	A3-B3-B4
Churchill Close	B1
Clifton Drive	A4
Derby Road	B2-B3
Grange Close	A2
Hastings Way	C1
Highfields Close	A3
Hill Street	A3
Holywell Avenue	B4
Ingle Drive	A3-A4
Kilwardby Street	A2-B2

Leicester Road	C1-C2
Loire Close	A3-A4
Lower Packington Road	A1
Malvern Crescent	A4-B4
Market Street	B2-B3
Marlborough Way	A3-A4-B4
Mill Bank	B3
Mill Lane	B2-B3
Moira Road	A2-A3
Money Hill	B4-C4
Nook Lane	A1
North Street	B3-C3
Nottingham Road	C3
Oakham Grove	A4
Park Close	A1
Park Road	B4
Pennine Way	B1
Pithiviers Close	A2
Prior Fields	C1
Prior Park Road	B2
Range Road	C2
Roedean Drive	B3
Rouen Way	A3-A4
Rowena Drive	B4
Rugby Close	B4
Saxon Way	A3-A4
Smisby Road	B4
South Street	B2-C2
Station Road	A2-B2
Stowe Close	B4
Stuart Close	B1
Tamworth Road	A1-A2
The Callis	B3-B4
The Green	B3
Trinity Close	A2
Trinity Court	A3-B3
Upper Packington Road	B1-C1-C2
Westfields Avenue	A3
Westfields Terrace	A3-A4
Wilfrid Place	A2-B2
Willowbrook Close	B4-C4
Winchester Way	A4-A3-B3
Windmill Close	C1
Windsor Road	B1
Wood Street	C3

Loughborough

Albert Promenade	C1
Albert Street	B1
Alfred Street	B4
Arthur Street	A2
Ashby Road	A3
Ashby Square	A3
Baxter Gate	B2-B3
Beacon Road	A1
Beeches Road	C1
Belton Road	A4-B4-C4
Biggin Street	B3
Bishop Street	C3
Boyer Street	C3
Bridge Street	A3-B3
Broad Street	A3
Browns Lane	A1-A2
Burder Street	C4
Burfield Avenue	A2
Burleigh Road	A2-A3
Burton Road	B1
Cambridge Street	B4
Cartwright Street	C4
Charles Street	B4
Church Gate	B3
Clarence Street	C3-C4
Colgrove Road	A1
Dead Lane	B3
Derby Road	A3-A4
Derby Square	A3-B3
Duke Street	C3-C4
Empress Road	C2-C4
Fennel Street	B3
Forest Road	A1
Frederick Street	A2-A3
Freehold Street	C3
Garton Road	A1-B1
Gladstone Avenue	A4-B4
Gladstone Street	B3-B4
Granby Street	A2-B2
Grange Street	A4
Granville Street	A2-A3
Gray Street	B1
Great Central Road	C1
Green Close	A3
Hartington Street	C4
Herbert Street	B4
High Street	B2
Howard Street	B4
Hudson Street	C3
King Edward Road	C1
King Street	C1-C2
Leicester Road	B2-B1-C1
Lemyington Street	B3
Leopold Street	A3-A4
Little Moor Lane	C2
Lime Avenue	C1
Limehurst Avenue	A4-A3-B3
Linden Road	A4
Lower Cambridge Street	B4
Market Place	A3-A2-B2
Market Street	B3-B4-C4
Meadow Lane	B2-C2
Moira Street	B2-C2
Moor Lane	C3-C4
Morley Street	C4
Nottingham Road	C3-C4
Packe Street	A2-B2
Park Road	A1-B1
Park Street	B1
Peel Drive	C2-C3
Pinfold Gate	B2-C2-C3
Queen's Road	C3
Ratcliffe Road	C4
Rectory Place	B3
Regent Street	A3
Rendell Street	B4
Russell Street	C2
Salisbury Street	C2
School Street	B2-C2
Shakespeare Street	B3
Southfield Road	B1-B2
Sparrow Hill	B3-C3
Swan Street	B2-B3
The Coneries	B3-C3
The Rushes	A3
Toothill Road	B3-B4
Trinity Street	B1
Victoria Street	B2
Ward's End	A1-A2-B2
Warner Place	C2
Wharncliffe Road	C1-C2-C3
White Gate	C4
William Street	A2
Wood Gate	B2
York Road	A2

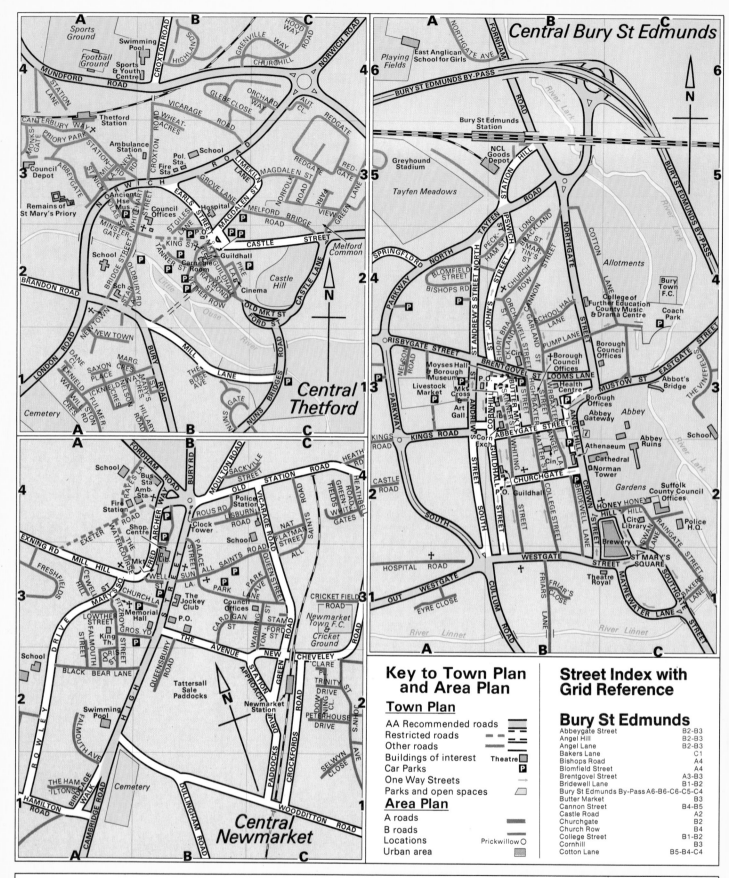

Key to Town Plan and Area Plan

Town Plan

AA Recommended roads	▬▬
Restricted roads	▬ ▬
Other roads	▬
Buildings of interest	Theatre
Car Parks	P
One Way Streets	→
Parks and open spaces	◿

Area Plan

A roads	▬
B roads	▬
Locations	Prickwillow ○
Urban area	▨

Street Index with Grid Reference

Bury St Edmunds

Abbeygate Street	B2-B3
Angel Hill	B2-B3
Angel Lane	B2-B3
Bakers Lane	C1
Bishops Road	A4
Blomfield Street	A4
Brentgovel Street	A3-B3
Bridewell Lane	B1-B2
Bury St Edmunds By-Pass	A6-B6-C6-C5-C4
Butter Market	B3
Cannon Street	B4-B5
Castle Road	A2
Churchgate	B2
Church Row	B4
College Street	B1-B2
Cornhill	B3
Cotton Lane	B5-B4-C4

Bury St Edmunds

This is one of the architectural gems of East Anglia with its streets of Georgian and earlier houses on the Norman grid pattern. The Norman Abbey ruins are set in attractive grounds with a magnificent gateway, and the cathedral church of St Edmunds-bury is adjacent to a massive Norman tower. Also worth seeing are the Guildhall (13th-century and later), the Athenaeum, the colonnaded Corn Exchange (1862) and the 1711 Pentecostal Church. Moyses Hall and Borough Museum goes back to the 12th century and the rebuilt Market Cross and Art Gallery to the 17th. Angel Corner has a fine display of clocks and watches, and St Mary's Church holds Mary Tudor's tomb.

Newmarket Headquarters of British horse racing, breeding and training for nearly 400 years, this is the home of the Jockey Club (founded 1750), the National Stud and the National Horseracing Museum.

The racecourse has the world's longest 'straight'.

Thetford was once a Saxon cathedral city and seat of early kings. London overspill sparked off expansion in the 1960s, but Georgian and medieval buildings can still be seen in the town, as well as a Norman castle mound, 12th-century priory remains and Iron Age earthworks. *Rights of Man* author Thomas Paine was born here in 1737. The 15th-century Ancient House offers local history exhibits and the Museum of Childhood Treasures.

12

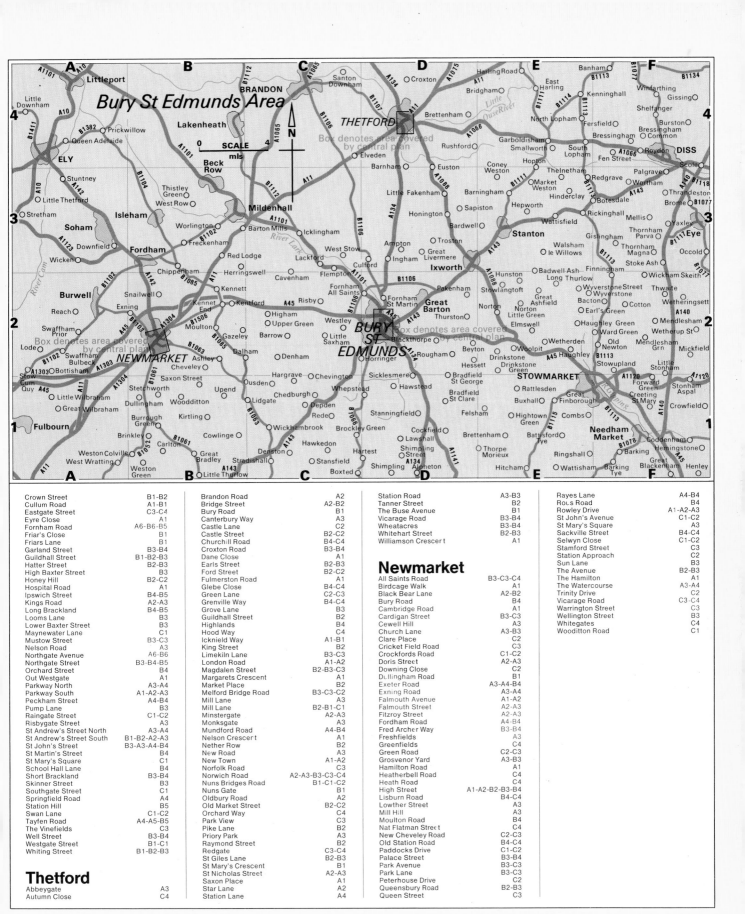

Crown Street B1-B2
Cullum Road A1-B1
Eastgate Street C3-C4
Eyre Close A1
Fornham Road A6-B6-B5
Friar's Close B1
Friars Lane B1
Garland Street B3-B4
Guildhall Street B1-B2-B3
Hatter Street B2-B3
High Baxter Street B3
Honey Hill B2-C2
Hospital Road A1
Ipswich Street B4-B5
Kings Road A2-A3
Long Brackland B4-B5
Looms Lane B3
Lower Baxter Street B3
Maynewater Lane C1
Mustow Street B3-C3
Nelson Road A3
Northgate Avenue A6-B6
Northgate Street B3-B4-B5
Orchard Street B4
Out Westgate A1
Parkway North A3-A4
Parkway South A1-A2-A3
Peckham Street A4-B4
Pump Lane B3
Raingate Street C1-C2
Risbygate Street A3
St Andrew's Street North A3-A4
St Andrew's Street South B1-B2-A2-A3
St John's Street B3-A3-A4-B4
St Martin's Street B4
St Mary's Square C1
School Hall Lane B4
Short Brackland B3-B4
Skinner Street B3
Southgate Street C1
Springfield Road A4
Station Hill B5
Swan Lane C1-C2
Tayfen Road A4-A5-B5
The Vinefields C3
Well Street B3-B4
Westgate Street B1-C1
Whiting Street B1-B2-B3

Thetford

Abbeygate A3
Autumn Close C4

Brandon Road A2
Bridge Street A2-B2
Bury Road B1
Canterbury Way A3
Castle Lane C2
Castle Street B2-C2
Churchill Road B4-C4
Croxton Road B3-B4
Dane Close A1
Earls Street B2-B3
Ford Street B2-C2
Fulmerston Road A1
Glebe Close B4-C4
Green Lane C2-C3
Grenville Way B4-C4
Grove Lane B3
Guildhall Street B2
Highlands B4
Hood Way C4
Icknield Way A1-B1
King Street B2
Limekiln Lane B3-C3
London Road A1-A2
Magdalen Street B2-B3-C3
Margarets Crescent A1
Market Place B2
Melford Bridge Road B3-C3-C2
Mill Lane A3
Mill Lane B2-B1-C1
Minstergate A2-A3
Monksgate A3
Mundford Road A4-B4
Nelson Crescent A1
Nether Row B2
New Road A3
New Town A1-A2
Norfolk Road C3
Norwich Road A2-A3-B3-C3-C4
Nuns Bridges Road B1-C1-C2
Nuns Gate B1
Oldbury Road A2
Old Market Street B2-C2
Orchard Way C4
Park View C3
Pike Lane B2
Priory Park A3
Raymond Street B2
Redgate C3-C4
St Giles Lane B2-B3
St Mary's Crescent B1
St Nicholas Street A2-A3
Saxon Place A1
Star Lane A2
Station Lane A4

Station Road A3-B3
Tanner Street B2
The Buse Avenue B1
Vicarage Road B3-B4
Wheatacres B3-B4
Whitehart Street B2-B3
Williamson Crescent A1

Newmarket

All Saints Road B3-C3-C4
Birdcage Walk A1
Black Bear Lane A2-B2
Bury Road B4
Cambridge Road A1
Cardigan Street B3-C3
Cewell Hill A3
Church Lane A3-B3
Clare Place C2
Cricket Field Road C3
Crockfords Road C1-C2
Doris Street A2-A3
Downing Close C2
Dullingham Road B1
Exeter Road A3-A4-B4
Exning Road A3-A4
Falmouth Avenue A1-A2
Falmouth Street A2-A3
Fitzroy Street A2-A3
Fordham Road A4-B4
Fred Archer Way B3-B4
Freshfields A3
Greenfields C4
Green Road C2-C3
Grosvenor Yard A3-B3
Hamilton Road A1
Heatherbell Road C4
Heath Road C4
High Street A1-A2-B2-B3-B4
Lisburn Road B4-C4
Lowther Street A3
Mill Hill A3
Moulton Road B4
Nat Flatman Street C4
New Cheveley Road C2-C3
Old Station Road B4-C4
Paddocks Drive C1-C2
Palace Street B3-B4
Park Avenue B3-C3
Park Lane B3-C3
Peterhouse Drive C2
Queensbury Road B2-B3
Queen Street C3

Rayes Lane A4-B4
Rous Road B4
Rowley Drive A1-A2-A3
St John's Avenue C1-C2
St Mary's Square A3
Sackville Street B4-C4
Selwyn Close C1-C2
Stamford Street C3
Station Approach C2
Sun Lane B3
The Avenue B2-B3
The Hamilton A1
The Watercourse A3-A4
Trinity Drive C2
Vicarage Road C3-C4
Warrington Street C3
Wellington Street B3
Whitegates C4
Wooditton Road C1

BURY ST EDMUNDS
Overlooked by Moyses Hall, market stalls still crowd
the Cornhill and Buttermarket twice a week, and have
been a feature of the town for several centuries.

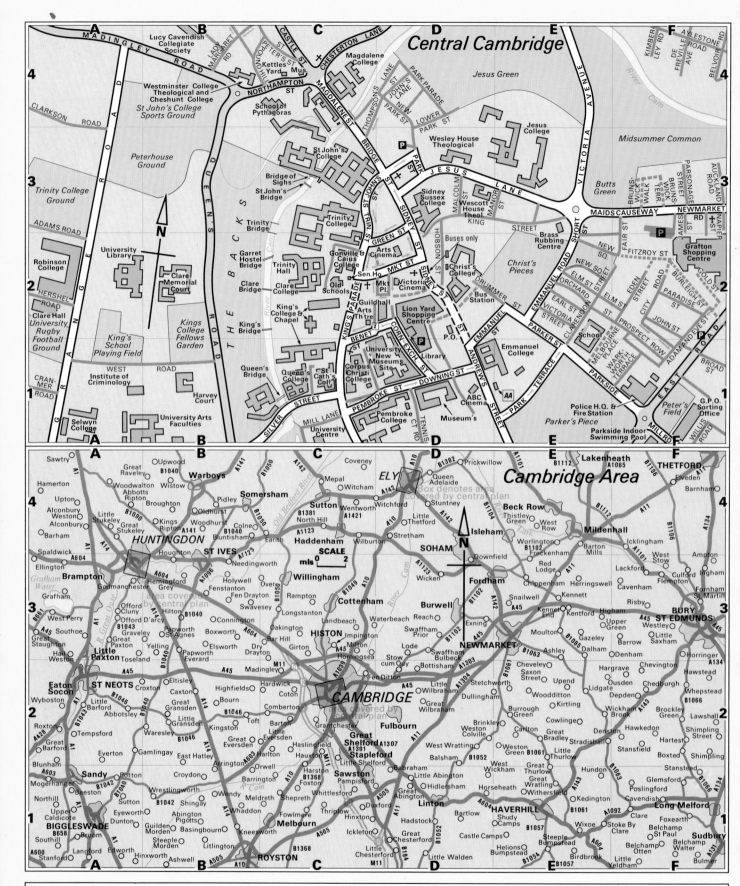

Cambridge

Few views in England, perhaps even in Europe, are as memorable as that from Cambridge's Backs towards the colleges. Dominating the scene, in every sense, is King's College Chapel. One of the finest Gothic buildings anywhere, it was built in three stages from 1446 to 1515.

No one would dispute that the chapel is Cambridge's masterpiece, but there are dozens of

buildings here that would be the finest in any other town or city. Most are colleges, or are attached to colleges, and it is the university which permeates every aspect of Cambridge's landscape and life. In all there are 33 university colleges in the city, and nearly all have buildings and features of great interest. Cambridge's oldest church is St Bene't's, with a Saxon tower; its most famous is the Church of the Holy Sepulchre, one of only four round churches of its kind.

Huntingdon and *Ely* are both within easy driving distance of Cambridge. Oliver Cromwell and Samuel Pepys were pupils at Huntingdon Grammar School. The building is now a Cromwell museum. Ely also has strong Cromwellian connections – he and his family lived here for ten years. Ely's outstanding feature is the cathedral, a Norman foundation crowned by a stately octagonal lantern tower which contains the Stained Glass Museum.

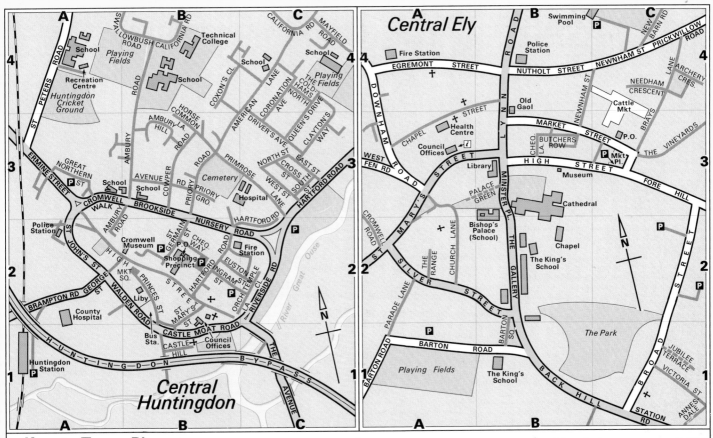

Central Huntingdon

Central Ely

CAMBRIDGE
Behind the gracious university college buildings beautiful lawns and gardens known as the Backs sweep down to the River Cam which, spanned by little bridges and shaded by willows, provides an idyllic setting for punting.

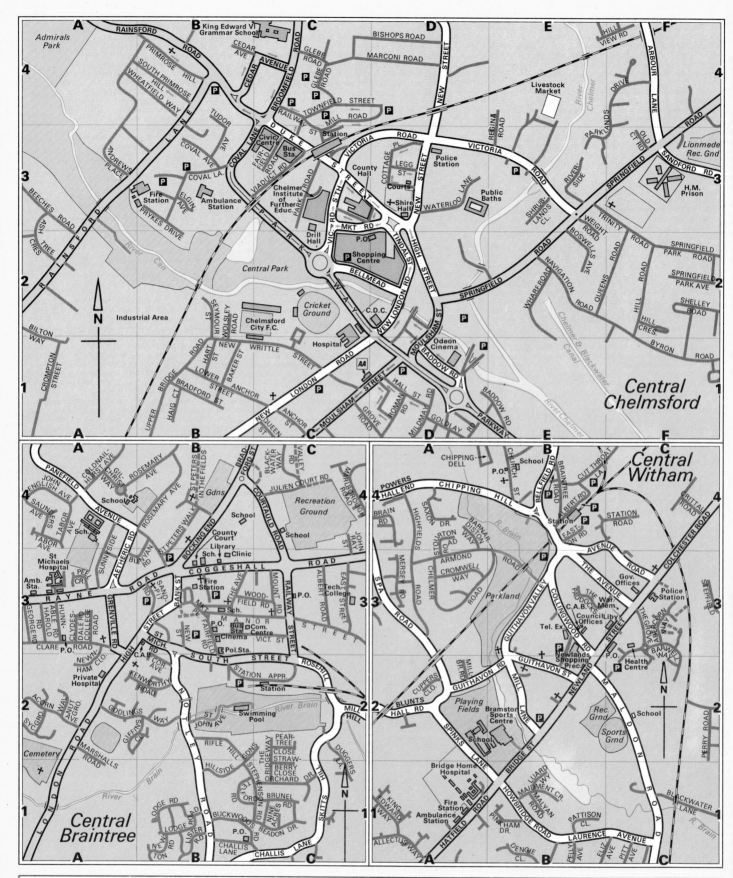

Chelmsford

Important since Roman times, this county town of Essex has undergone a good deal of expansion and development in recent years, providing it with good shopping and leisure facilities. Older buildings are concentrated in the Tindal Street area, notably the Shire Hall and the Cathedral, which dates from the 15th century. The cattle market (now on a modern site) has been going since Elizabethan days, and other places of interest include the Chelmsford and Essex Museum, which also houses the Museum of the Essex Regiment.

Braintree has been concerned with textile making since the early Middle Ages, and still keeps up the connection with the Courtaulds Group, associated with the area since the 19th century.

Maldon has retained a fascinating old quarter around All Saints Church, at the top of the High Street. A river port which has seen some industrialisation, it remains popular with holidaymakers for its position at the junction of the Blackwater and Chelmer rivers, and offers good facilities for boating along the river banks.

Witham's recent Town Development Scheme has brought expansion, incorporating housing estates, offices and factories for this ancient town on the River Brain. It has nevertheless retained some fine Georgian buildings, and several old coaching inns can be seen in the main street.

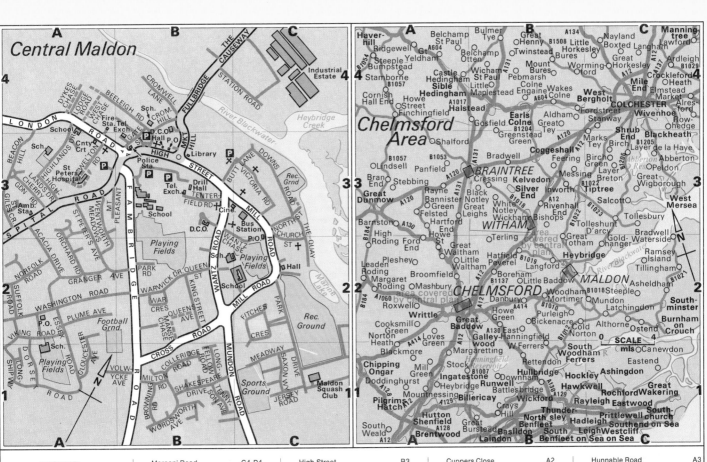

Central Maldon

Chelmsford Area

LEGEND

Town Plan

- AA recommended route
- Restricted roads
- Other roads
- Buildings of interest Theatre
- Car parks P
- Parks and open spaces
- One way streets

Area Plan

- A roads
- B roads
- Locations Notley
- Urban area

Street Index with Grid Reference

Chelmsford

Anchor Street	C1
Andrews Place	A3
Arbour Lane	F4-F3
Ash Tree Crescent	A3-A2
Baddow Road	D1-E1
Baker Street	B1
Beeches Road	A3-A2
Bellmead	C2-D2
Bilton Way	A2-A1
Bishops Road	C4-D4
Boswells Avenue	E3-E2
Bradford Street	B1
Broomfield Road	C4
Byron Road	F2-F1
Cedar Avenue	B4-C4
Cottage Place	D3
Coval Avenue	B3
Coval Lane	B3-C3
Crompton Street	A1
Duke Street	C4-C3-D3
Elgin Avenue	B3
Fairfield Road	C3
Glebe Road	C4
Goldlay Road	D1
Grove Road	C1-D1
Haig Court	B1
Hall Street	D1
Hart Street	B1
High Street	D3-D2
Hill Crescent	F2
Hill Road	F2
Hill View Road	E4-F4
Legg Street	D3
Lower Anchor Street	B1-C1

Marconi Road	C4-D4
Market Road	C3-D3
Mildmay Road	D1
Mill Road	C3-C4-D4
Moulsham Street	C1-D1-D2
Navigation Road	E2
New London Road	B1-C1-D1-D2
New Street	D3-D4
New Writtle Street	B1-C1
Old Court Road	C1
Parklands Drive	E3-F3-F4
Park Road	C3
Parkway	B3-C3-C2-D2-D1-E1
Primrose Hill	B4
Prykes Drive	B3-B2
Queen Street	C1
Queens Road	E2-F2-F3
Railway Street	C4-C3
Rainsford Lane	A2-A3-B3-B4
Rainsford Road	A4-B4
Regina Road	E3-E4
Riverside	E3
Roman Road	D1
Sandford Road	F3
Seymour Street	B2-B1
Shelley Road	F2
Shrublands Close	E3
South Primrose Hill	A4-B4
Springfield Park Avenue	F2
Springfield Park Road	F2
Springfield Road	D2-E2-E3-F3-F4
Tindal Street	D3-D2
Townfield Street	C4-D4
Trinity Road	E3-F3-F2
Tudor Avenue	B4-B3
Upper Bridge Road	B1
Viaduct Road	B3-C3
Victoria Road	C3-D3-E3
Victoria Road South	C2-C3
Waterloo Lane	D3
Weight Road	E3-E2
Wharf Road	E2
Wheatfield Way	A4-B4
Wolsey Road	B1-B2

Maldon

Acacia Drive	A3-A2
Beacon Hill	A3-A4
Beeleigh Road	A4-B4
Browning Road	B1
Butt Lane	B3-C3
Cherry Garden Road	A3
Church Street	C2-C3
Colleridge Road	B1
Cromwell Hill	B4
Cromwell Lane	B4
Cross Road	B1-B2
Dorset Road	A2-A1
Downs Road	C3
Dykes Chase	A4
Essex Road	A2-A1
Fambridge Road	B3-B2-B1
Fitches Crescent	C2
Fullbridge	B4
Gate Street	B3-B4
Gloucester Avenue	A1-A2
Granger Avenue	A2-B2
Highlands Drive	A3-A4

High Street	B3
Jersey Road	C1
King Street	B2
Lodge Road	A4
London Road	A4-A3-B3
Longfellow Road	B1
Longship Way	A1
Manse Chase	B2
Market Hill	B3-B4
Meadway	C1
Mill Road	B2-C2-C3-B3
Milton Road	B1
Mount Pleasant	A3
Mundon Road	B2-B1-C1
Norfolk Road	A2
North Street	C3
Orchard Road	A3-A2
Park Drive	C2-C1
Park Road	B2
Plume Avenue	A2
Queens Avenue	B2
Queen Street	B2
St Giles Crescent	A3
St Peter's Avenue	A2-A3
Saxon Way	C1
Shakespeare Drive	B1
Spital Road	A2-A3-B3
Station Road	B4-C4
Suffolk Road	A2
The Causeway	B4-C4
The Quay	C3-C2
Tennyson Avenue	B1
Tenterfield Road	B3
Victoria Road	C3
Viking Road	A1-A2
Volwycke Avenue	A1-B1
Wantz Chase	B3-C3-C2
Wantz Road	B2-B3
Warwick Crescent	B2
Warwick Drive	B2
Washington Road	A2-B2
Wellington Road	A3
Wentworth Meadows	A3-A2
West Chase	A4
Wordsworth Avenue	B1

Witham

Abercorn Way	C3
Albert Road	B4
Allectus Way	A1
Armond Road	A3-B3
Avenue Road	B4-B3-C4-C3
Barnardiston Way	A4
Barwell Way	C3-C2
Bellfield Road	B4
Blackwater Lane	C1
Blunts Hall Road	A2
Brain Road	A4
Braintree Road	A4
Bridge Street	B1-B2
Chelmer Road	A3-B3
Chippingdell	A4-B4
Chipping Hill	A4-B4
Church Street	B4
Colchester Road	C3-C4
Collingwood Road	B3
Crittal Road	C4
Cromwell Way	A3

Cuppers Close	A2
Cut Throat Lane	B4-C4
Dengie Close	B1
Easton Road	B4
Elizabeth Avenue	B1-C1
Guithavon Road	A2-B2
Guithavon Street	B3-B2
Guithavon Valley	B3
Hatfield Road	A1-B1
Highfields Road	A4-A3
Howbridge Road	B1
King Edward Way	A1
Laurence Avenue	B1-C1
Luard Way	B1
Maidment Crescent	B1
Maldon Road	B2-C2-C1
Malyan Road	B1
Mersey Road	A3
Millbridge Road	A2
Mill Lane	B2
Newland Street	B2-B3-C3
Pattison Close	B1
Pelly Avenue	B1
Perry Road	C2
Pinkham Drive	B1
Pitt Avenue	C1
Powers Hall End	A4
Saxon Drive	A4
Spa Road	A4-A3-A2
Spinks Lane	A2-A1-B1
Station Road	B4-C4
Stepfield	C3
Stourton Road	A3-A4
The Avenue	B3-C3
The Grove	C3
The Paddocks	B3-C3

Braintree

Acorn Avenue	A2
Albert Road	C3
Aetheric Road	A3-A4
Bank Street	B3
Beadon Drive	C1
Blackwater Way	C4
Bocking End	B3-B4
Bradford Street	B4-C4
Brunel Road	C1
Buckwoods Road	B1
Bunyan Road	A3-B3-B4
Challis Lane	B1-C1
Clare Road	A3
Clydesdale Road	A3
Coggeshall Road	B3-C3
Coldnailhurst Avenue	A4
College Road	A3
Coronation Avenue	B2
Courtauld Road	B4-C4-C3
Duggers Lane	C2-C1
East Street	C3
Fairfield Road	B3
George Road	A3
Giffins Close	A2-B2
Gilchrist Way	A4
Godlings Way	A2-B2
Grenville Road	A3
Harold Road	A3
High Street	A2-A3-B3
Hillside Gardens	B1-B2-C2

Hunnable Road	A3
John English Avenue	A4
John Ray Street	C4-C3
Julien Court Road	C4
Kenworthy Road	A2-B2
Lister Road	B1
Lodge Road	B1
London Road	A1-A2
Manor Street	B3-C3
Market Place	B3
Marlborough Road	C4
Marshalls Road	A2-A1
Mill Hill	C2
Mount Road	C3
Newnham Close	A2-A3
New Street	B3
Newton Road	B1
Nine Acres	C1
Notley Road	B2-B1
Orchard Drive	C1
Panfield Avenue	A4
Peartree Close	C2
Peel Crescent	A3
Railway Street	C3
Rayne Road	A3-B3
Rifle Hill	B2
Rosehill	C2
Rosemary Avenue	A4-B4
St John Avenue	B2
St Michaels Road	B3
St Peters in the Fields	B4
St Peters Walk	B3-B4
Sandpit Road	B3
Saunders Avenue	A4
Skitts Hill	C1-C2
South Street	B3-B2-C2
Station Approach	B2-C2
Stephenson Road	B1-C1
Strawberry Close	C1
Sunnyside	A3-A4
Sycamore Grove	A2
The Avenue	B3
The Ridgeway	C1-C2
Tabor Avenue	A4
Telford Road	B1
Valley Road	C4
Victoria Street	B3-C3
Walnut Grove	A2
Woodfield Road	B3-C3

17

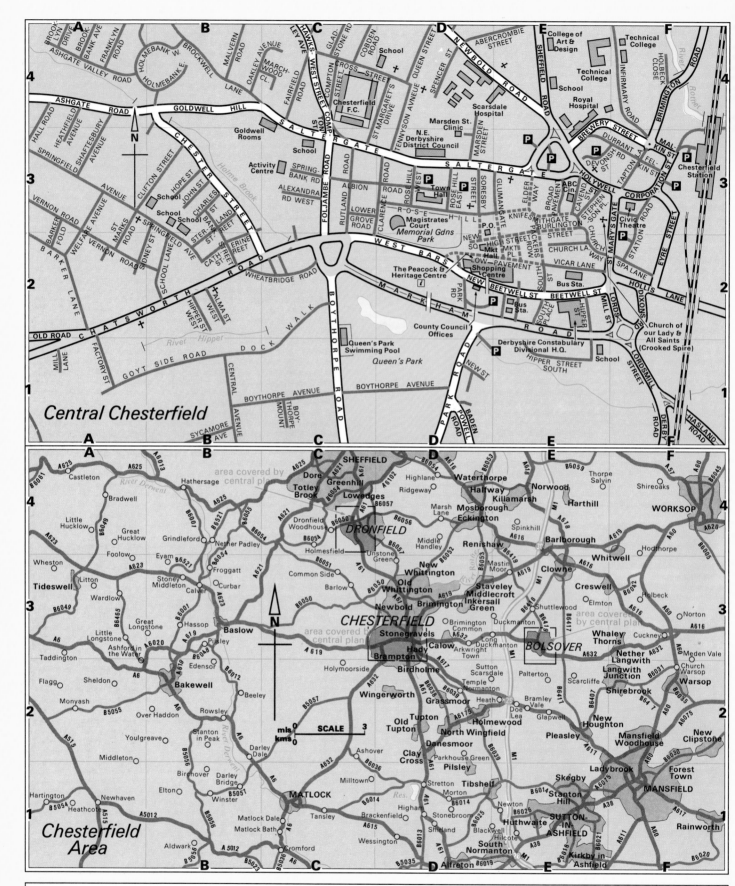

Chesterfield

Known as the Gateway to the Peak because of its proximity to the Derbyshire Peak District, Chesterfield became industrialised in the 18th and 19th centuries and attracted the interest of locomotive designer George Stephenson, who became involved in local industry before his death in 1848. Modern Chesterfield's new buildings have been carefully integrated with the picturesque half-timbered shops and houses to be found near the middle of town. Old shop fronts have been preserved in the 'Pavements' shopping centre, (where the Peacock Information and Heritage Centre is housed in a 16th-century building), but quaintest feature of the town must be the crooked spire of the 14th-century Church of Our Lady and All Saints. This strange phenomenon has never been satisfactorily explained, but may be due to the use of unseasoned timber, and the effect of the sun on the lead cladding.

Dronfield is a residential market town lying on the eastern slopes of the Pennines. Its oldest quarter has been designated a Conservation Area, and includes the 14th-century Parish Church of St John the Baptist and the 18th-century Manor House, which is now the County Library.

Bolsover Set in a district of coalmining and farming, Bolsover boasts a hilltop castle with Norman features, restored in the 17th century.

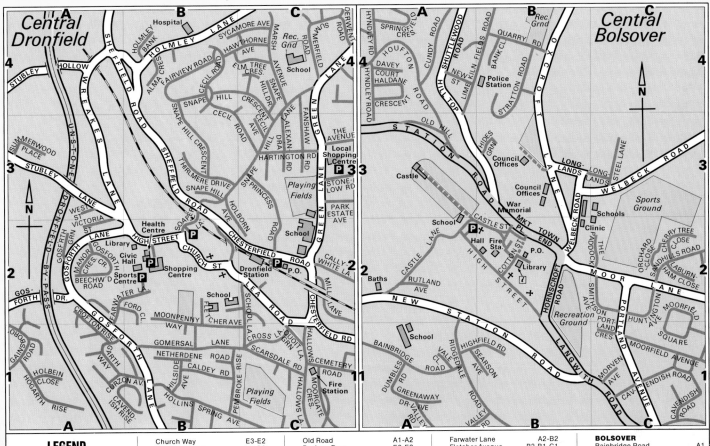

Central Dronfield

Hospital

Central Bolsover

LEGEND

Town Plan
AA recommended route
Restricted roads
Other roads
Buildings of interest — Castle
Car parks — P
Parks and open spaces

Area Plan
A roads
B roads
Locations — Foolow ○
Urban area — Bramp

STREET INDEX

CHESTERFIELD

Abercrombie Street	D4-E4
Albion Road	C3-D3
Alexandra Road West	C3
Alma Street West	B2
Ashgate Road	A4
Ashgate Valley Road	A4
Baden Powell Road	D1
Bank Street	B3-B2
Barker Fold	A2-A3
Barker Lane	A2
Beetwell Street	E2
Boythorpe Avenue	B1-C1-D1
Boythorpe Mount	C1
Boythorpe Road	C1-C2
Brewery Street	E3-E4-F4-F3
Brimington Road	F4
Broad Pavement	E3
Brockwell Lane	B4
Brookbank Avenue	A4
Brooklyn Drive	A4
Burlington Street	E3
Catherine Street	B2
Cavendish Street	E3
Central Avenue	B1
Charles Street	B3
Chatsworth Road	A1-A2-B2-C2
Chester Street	B4-B3-B2
Church Lane	E2
Church Way	E3-E2
Clarence Road	D3
Clifton Street	A3-B3
Cobden Road	C4
Compton Street	C4-C3
Corporation Street	F3
Cross Street	C4-D4
Derby Road	F1
Devonshire Street	E3-F3
Dixons Road	F2
Dock Walk	B1-C1-C2
Durrant Road	E3-F3
Elder Way	E3
Eyre Street	F2-F3
Factory Street	A1
Fairfield Road	C4
Felkin Street	F3
Foljambe Road	C3
Franklyn Road	A4
Goldwell Hill	B4
Goyt Side Road	A1-B1
Gladstone Road	C4
Glumangate	E3
Hall Road	A3-A4
Hasland Road	F1
Hawkesley Avenue	C4
Heathfield Avenue	A3-A4
High Street	D2-E2-E3
Hipper Street	E1
Hipper Street South	E1
Hipper Street West	B2
Holbeck Close	F4
Hollis Lane	F2
Holmebank East	A4-B4
Holmebank West	A4-B4
Holywell Street	E3
Hope Street	B3
Infirmary Road	F4
John Street	B3
Knifesmithgate	E3
Lordsmill Street	E2-F2-F1
Lower Grove Road	C3
Low Pavement	D2-E2
Malkin Street	F3
Malvern Road	B4
Marchwood Close	C4
Market Place	B2
Markham Road	C2-D2-E2
Marsden Street	D3-D4
Mill Lane	A1
New Beetwell Street	D2-E2
Newbold Road	D4-E4
New Square	D2
New Street	D1
Oakley Avenue	B4-C4
Old Road	A1-A2
Packers Row	E3-E2
Park Road	D1-D2
Queen Street	D4
Rose Hill	D3
Rose Hill East	D3
Rose Hill West	D3
Rutland Road	C3
Saltergate	C4-C3-D3-E3
School Lane	B2
Shaftesbury Avenue	A3-A4
Sheffield Road	E2
Sidney Street	A2-B2-B3
Soresby Street	D3
South Place	E2
South Street	E2
Spa Lane	F2
Spencer Street	D4
Springbank Road	C3
Springbank Avenue	A3-B3-B2
St Margarets Drive	C3-C4-D4
St Marks Road	A2-A3
St Mary's Gate	E2-F2-F3
Station Road	F2-F3
Stephenson Place	E3
Sterland Street	B2-B3
Sycamore Avenue	B1
Tapton Lane	F3
Tennyson Avenue	D3-D4
Vernon Road	A3-A2-B2
Vicar Lane	E2
Welfare Avenue	A2-A3
Wheatbridge Road	B2-C2
West Bars	C2-D2
West Street	C4

DRONFIELD

Alma Crescent	B4
Alexandra Road	C3
Beechwood Road	A2
Caldey Road	B1
Callywhite Lane	C2
Cavendish Rise	A1-B1
Cecil Avenue	C3
Cecil Road	B4-C3
Cemetery Road	C1
Chesterfield Road	B2-C2-C1
Church Street	B2
Crofton Rise	A2-A1
Cross Lane	C1
Curzon Avenue	A1-B1
Derwent Road	C4
Elm Tree Crescent	B4-C4
Fairview Road	B4
Fanshaw Road	C3-C4
Farwater Lane	A2-B2
Fletcher Avenue	B2-B1-C1
Ford Close	A2-B2
Gainsborough Road	A1
Garth Way	A1
Green Lane	C2-C3-C4
Gomersal Lane	B1
Gosforth Crescent	A2
Gosforth Drive	A2
Gosforth Green	A2
Gosforth Lane	A2-A1-B1
Hallows Lane	C1
Hartington Road	C3
Hawthorne Avenue	B4-C4
High Street	B2
Hillside Avenue	B1
Hogarth Rise	A1
Holbein Close	A1
Holborn Avenue	B3-B2-C2
Hollins Spring Avenue	B1-C1
Holmley Bank	B4
Holmley Lane	B4-C4
Lea Road	B2-C2
Manor Crescent	A2
Marsh Avenue	C4
Mill Lane	B2
Moonpenny Way	B2-B1
Moorgate Crescent	C1
Netherdene Road	B1
Park Estate Avenue	C3
Pembroke Rise	B1
Princess Road	C3-C2
Quoit Green	C1
Scarsdale Road	C1
School Lane	C2-C1
Sheffield Road	A4-B4-B3
Snape Hill	B3
Snape Hill Crescent	B3-B4-C4-C3
Snape Hill Drive	C4
Snape Hill Lane	B3-C3-C4
Soaper Lane	B2-B3
Stonelow Road	C3
Stubley Hollow	A4
Stubley Lane	A3
Summerfield Road	C4
Summerwood Place	A3
Sycamore Avenue	B4-C4
The Avenue	C3
Thirlmere Drive	C3
Unstone-Dronfield By-pass	A4-A3-A2-A1
Victoria Street	A2-A3
West Street	A3
Wreakes Lane	A4-A3-A2-B2

BOLSOVER

Bainbridge Road	A1
Bank Close	B4
Castle Lane	A2
Castle Street	B2
Cavendish Road	C1
Cherry Tree Close	C2
Cotton Street	B2
Cundy Road	A4
Davey Court	A4
Dumbles Road	A1
Greenaway Drive	A1
Haldane Crescent	A4
Hides Green	B3
High Street	A2-B2
Highfield Road	A1-B1
Hill Top	A4
Hornscroft Road	B2
Houfton Road	A4-A3
Huntington Avenue	C2
Hyndley Road	A4-A3
Laburnam Close	C2
Langwith Road	B1-C1
Lime Kiln Fields Road	A4-B4
Longlands	B3-C3
Market Place	B2
Moor Lane	B2-C2
Moorfield Avenue	C1
Moorfield Square	C2-C1
Morven Avenue	C1
New Street	A4
New Station Road	A2-B1
Old Hill	A3
Orchard Close	C2
Oxcroft Lane	B4-B3-B2
Portland Avenue	C2-C1
Portland Crescent	C1
Quarry Road	B4
Ridgedale Road	A1-B1
Rutland Avenue	A2
Sandhills Road	C2
Searson Avenue	A1-B1
Shuttlewood Road	A4
Smithson Avenue	C2
Springfield Crescent	A4
Station Road	A3-B3
Steel Lane	C3
Stratton Road	B3-B4
The Paddock	C2
Town End	B2
Vale Close	A1
Valley Road	A1-B1
Welbeck Road	B2-B3

CHESTERFIELD
Octagonal in plan, the crooked spire of the Church of Our Lady and All Saints stands 228ft high. Its original position in relation to the building has been marked by brass studs in the church floor.

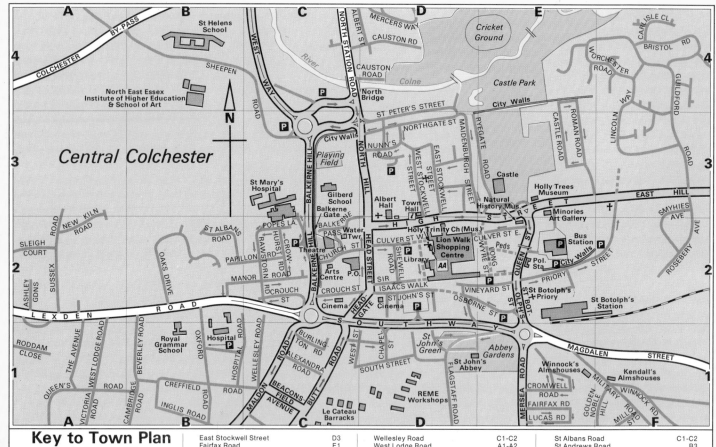

Key to Town Plan and Area Plan

Town Plan

AA Recommended roads	
Restricted roads	
Other roads	
Buildings of interest	Theatre ▉
One Way Streets	←
Car Parks	P
Parks and open spaces	▉
Churches	†

Area Plan

A roads	
B roads	
Locations	Rowhedge O
Urban area	▉

STREET INDEX WITH GRID REFERENCE

COLCHESTER

Albert Street	C4-D4
Alexandra Road	C1
Ashley Gardens	A2
Balkerne Hill	C3
Balkerne Lane	C2-D2
Balkerne Pass	C2
Beaconsfield Avenue	C1
Beverley Road	B1-B2
Bristol Road	F4
Burlington Road	C1
Butt Road	C1
Cambridge Road	B1
Carlisle Road	F4
Castle Road	E3-E4
Causton Road	C4-D4
Chapel Street	D1
Church Street	C2-D2
Colchester By-Pass	A4-B4
Creffield Road	B1-C1
Cromwell Road	E1
Crouch Street	C2
Crowhurst Road	C2
Culver Street East	D2-E2
Culver Street West	D2
East Hill	F4

East Stockwell Street	D3
Fairfax Road	E1
Flagstaff Road	D1
Golden Noble Hill	F1
Guildford Road	F3-F4
Headgate	C2-D2
Head Street	D2
High Street	D3-D2-E2-E3-F3
Hospital Road	B1-B2-C1
Inglis Road	B1
Lexden Road	A2-B2
Lincoln Way	F3-F4
Long Wyre Street	E2
Lucas Road	E1
Magdalen Street	E1-F1
Maidenburgh Street	D3-D3
Maldon Road	B1-C1
Manor Road	B2-C2
Mercers Way	D4
Mersea Road	E1
Military Road	E1-F1
Mill Street	F1
New Kiln Road	A2-A3
Northgate Street	D3
North Hill	C3-D3
North Station Road	C4
Nunn's Road	D3
Oaks Drive	B2
Osborne Street	D2-E2
Oxford Road	B1-B2
Pappillon Road	B2-C2
Priory Street	E2-F2-F3
Queens Road	A1-B1
Queen Street	E2
Rawston Road	C2
Roddam Close	A1
Roman Road	E3-E4
Rosebery Avenue	F2-F3
Ryegate Road	D3-E3
St Albans Road	B2
St Botolph's Street	E2
St John's Street	D2
St Peter's Street	D3-D4
Sheepen Road	C3-B4-C4
Sherwell Road	D2
Sir Isaacs Walk	D2
Sleigh Court	A2
Smythies Avenue	F2-F3
South Street	D2
Southway	C1-C2-D2-D1-E1
Sussex Road	A2-A3
The Avenue	A1
Victoria Road	A1
Vineyard Street	D2-E2
Water Lane	A4

Wellesley Road	C1-C2
West Lodge Road	A1-A2
West Stockwell Street	D3
West Street	C1-D1
West Way	C3-C4
Winnock Road	F1
Worcester Road	E4-F4

CLACTON

Agate Road	A1-A2
Agincourt Road	A4
Alton Park Road	C3
Alton Road	A1-A2
Anchor Road	A3
Astley Road	A4
Beach Road	B1-B2
Beaumont Avenue	A4
Berkeley Road	C4
Cambridge Road	B3-B4
Carnarvon Road	B1-B2-B3
Carrs Road	A4
Chapman Road	B2
Church Road	B1-C1
College Road	C2
Coppins Road	A4-B4
Croft Road	A4-B4
Crossfield Road	B3
Dudley Road	A4-B4
Edith Road	A1-A2
Ellis Road	A2
Ford Road	A3-A4
Granville Road	B2-C2
Harold Road	B1-B2
Harrow Road	B3-C3
Hayes Road	A2-A3
High Street	B2
Holland Road	B2-C2
Jackson Road	A2
Key Road	B3-B4
London Road	B4-C4
Marine Parade East	B1-C1
Marine Parade West	A1
Melbourne Road	B4
Meredith Road	B3
Old Road	A2-A3-B3-B4-C4
Olivers Road	B4
Orwell Road	B1-B2
Oxford Crescent	C3-C4
Oxford Road	B3-C3-C4
Page Road	B3
Pallister Road	B1-B2
Park Road	A3
Penfold Road	A1-A2
Pier Avenue	A2-A3
Rosemary Road	A2-B2

St Albans Road	C1-C2
St Andrews Road	B3
St Anne's Road	B4
St Osyth Road	A3-A4
Severn Road	C3-C4
Skelmersdale Road	B2-B3-C2
Station Road	A2-B2-B3
Tewkesbury Road	C3-C4
The Grove	B2
Thomas Road	B4
Thornbury Road	C3-C4
Thoroughgood Road	C1-C2-C3
Tower Road	A1-A2
Vicarage Gardens	A2
Victoria Road	C1-C2
Victory Road	A4
Vista Road	C1-C2-C3
Walton Road	A4
Warwick Road	A3-A4-B4
Wash Lane	A2
Wellesley Road	A2-B2-B3-C3-C4
West Avenue	A2-A3

HARWICH

Albemarle Street	B3-B4
Albert Street	B3
Ashley Road	A2
Barrack Lane	B3-C3
Church Street	B4
Cliff Road	B2
Fern Lea Road	B3
Fronks Road	A1-A2
George Street	B3-B4
Gordon Road	A1
Grafton Road	B3
Harbour Crescent	B3-C3
Highfield Avenue	A1-A2
High Street	B2
Hill Road	B2
Ingestre Street	B3
King Georges Avenue	A2
King's Quay Street	B4-C4
King's Way	B2
Lee Road	A2-B2
Lime Avenue	A1-A2
Main Road	A2-B2-B3
Marine Parade	A1-A2-B2
Pattricks Lane	A2-B2
Portland Avenue	A2-B2
Seafield Road	A1
Shaftesbury Avenue	A2
Stour Road	B3
The Drive	A1
West Street	B4
Wick Lane	A1

Colchester

The oldest recorded town in England, Colchester was also a Roman capital and the great walls built by the invaders stand to this day. Remains of one of their massive gateways, Balkerne Gate, have also survived. Colchester's Norman castle keep, the largest in Britain, retains an air of dark medieval menace, although it now houses nothing more sinister than the Colchester and Essex Museum where many Roman antiquities can be seen. Colchester's proximity to the continent led to the arrival of Flemish refugees during the 16th century, and they revived the cloth trade that had flourished here in the Middle Ages. Many of their attractive gabled and colour-washed houses line West Stockwell Street, known as the Dutch Quarter. In contrast, much of the town centre has been turned into a modern shopping precinct.

Clacton On Sea was suddenly transformed from a quiet little village into 'the seaside' with the arrival of the railway during the 1870s. The pier, an essential ingredient for such resorts, was erected in 1873, although since rebuilt several times, and seven years later the Pavilion was added.

Harwich, departure point for continental ferries and busy yachting centre, has been a port since medieval times. The 180ft-diameter fort known as the Redoubt was built in 1808 as a defence against Napoleonic invasion.

Colchester Area

Central Clacton

Central Harwich

COLCHESTER

The castle keep, all that remains of Colchester's great fortress that once stretched from the High Street to the north wall of the town, was built round the masonry platform of the Roman Temple of Claudius.

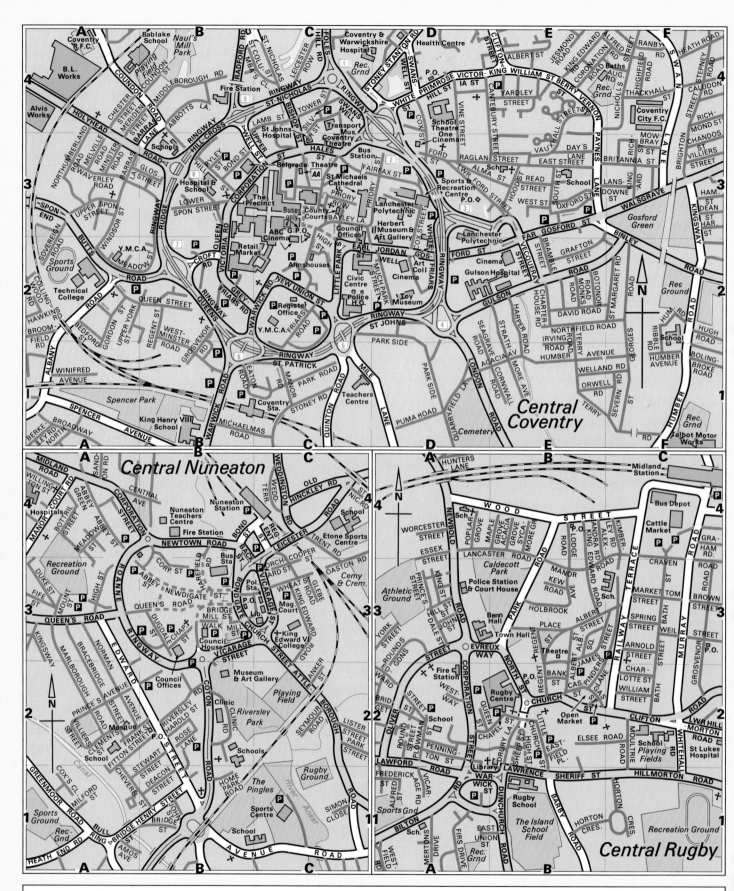

Coventry

Few British towns were as battered by the Blitz as Coventry. A raid in November 1940 flattened most of the city and left the lovely cathedral church a gaunt shell with only the tower and spire still standing. Rebuilding started almost immediately. Symbolising the creation of the new from the ashes of the old is Sir Basil Spence's cathedral, completed in 1962 beside the bombed ruins.

A few medieval buildings have survived intact in the city. St Mary's Guildhall is a finely restored 14th-century building with an attractive minstrels' gallery. Whitefriars Monastery now serves as a local museum. The Herbert Art Gallery and Museum has several collections. Coventry is an important manufacturing centre – most notably for cars – and it is also a university city with the fine campus of the University of Warwick some four miles from the centre.

Nuneaton is an industrial town to the north of Coventry with two distinguished old churches – St Nicholas' and St Mary's. Like Coventry it was badly damaged in the war and its centre has been rebuilt.

Rugby was no more than a sleepy market town until the arrival of the railway. Of course it did have the famous Rugby School, founded in 1567 and one of the country's foremost educational establishments. The railway brought industry – still the town's mainstay.

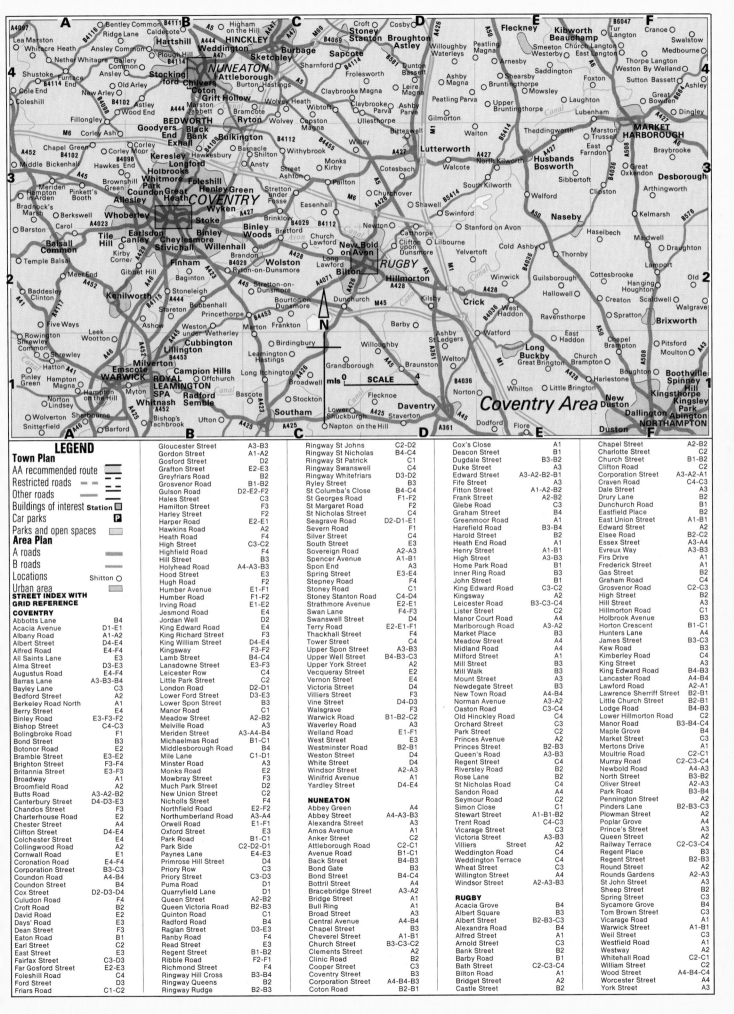

LEGEND

Town Plan

AA recommended route
Restricted roads
Other roads
Buildings of interest — Station
Car parks — P
Parks and open spaces

Area Plan

A roads
B roads
Locations — Shitton O
Urban area

STREET INDEX WITH GRID REFERENCE

COVENTRY

Abbotts Lane	B4
Acacia Avenue	D1-E1
Albany Road	A1-A2
Albert Street	D4-E4
Alfred Road	E4-F4
All Saints Lane	E3
Alma Street	D3-E3
Augustus Road	E4-F4
Barras Lane	A3-B3-B4
Bayley Lane	C3
Bedford Street	A2
Berkeley Road North	A1
Berry Street	E4
Binley Road	E3-F3-F2
Bishop Street	C4-C3
Bolingbroke Road	F1
Bond Street	B3
Botonor Road	E2
Bramble Street	E3-E2
Brighton Street	F3-F4
Britannia Street	E3-F3
Broadway	A1
Broomfield Road	A2
Butts Road	A3-A2-B2
Canterbury Street	D4-D3-E3
Chandos Street	F3
Charterhouse Road	E2
Chester Street	A4
Clifton Street	D4-E4
Colchester Street	E4
Collingwood Road	A2
Cornwall Road	E1
Coronation Road	E4-F4
Corporation Street	B3-C3
Coundon Road	A4-B4
Coundon Street	B4
Cox Street	D2-D3-D4
Culudon Road	F4
Croft Road	B2
David Road	E2
Days' Road	E3
Dean Street	F3
Eaton Road	B1
Earl Street	C2
East Street	E3
Fairfax Street	C3-D3
Far Gosford Street	E2-E3
Foleshill Road	C4
Ford Street	D3
Friars Road	C1-C2
Gloucester Street	A3-B3
Gordon Street	A1-A2
Gosford Street	D2
Grafton Street	E2-E3
Greyfriars Road	B2
Grosvenor Road	B1-B2
Gulson Road	D2-E2-F2
Hales Street	C3
Hamilton Street	F3
Harley Street	F2
Harper Road	E2-E1
Hawkins Road	A2
Heath Road	F4
High Street	C3-C2
Highfield Road	F4
Hill Street	B3
Holyhead Road	A4-A3-B3
Hood Street	E3
Hugh Road	F2
Humber Avenue	E1-F1
Humber Road	F1-F2
Irving Road	E1-E2
Jesmond Road	E4
Jordan Well	D2
King Edward Road	E4
King Richard Street	F3
King William Street	D4-E4
Kingsway	F3-F2
Lamb Street	B4-C4
Lansdowne Street	E3-F3
Leicester Row	C4
Little Park Street	C2
London Road	D2-D1
Lower Ford Street	D3-E3
Lower Spon Street	B3
Manor Road	C1
Meadow Street	A2-B2
Melville Road	A3
Meriden Street	A3-A4-B4
Michaelmas Road	B1-C1
Middlesborough Road	B4
Mile Lane	C1-D1
Minster Road	A3
Monks Road	E2
Mowbray Street	F3
Much Park Street	D2
New Union Street	C2
Nicholls Street	F4
Northfield Road	E2-F2
Northumberland Road	A3-A4
Orwell Road	E1-F1
Oxford Street	E3
Park Road	B1-C1
Park Side	C2-D2-D1
Paynes Lane	E4-E3
Primrose Hill Street	D4
Priory Row	C3
Priory Street	C3-D3
Puma Road	D1
Quarryfield Lane	D1
Queen Street	A2-B2
Queen Victoria Road	B2-B3
Quinton Road	C1
Radford Road	B4
Raglan Street	D3-E3
Ranby Road	F4
Read Street	D4
Regent Street	B1-B2
Ribble Road	F2-F1
Richmond Street	F4
Ringway Hill Cross	B3-B4
Ringway Queens	B2-B3
Ringway Rudge	B2-B3

Ringway St Johns	C2-D2
Ringway St Nicholas	B4-C4
Ringway St Patrick	C1
Ringway Swanswell	C4
Ringway Whitefriars	D3-D2
Ryley Street	B3
St Columba's Close	B4-C4
St Georges Road	F1-F2
St Margaret Road	F3
St Nicholas Street	C4
Seagrave Road	D2-D1-E1
Severn Road	F1
Silver Street	C4
South Street	E3
Sovereign Road	A2-A3
Spencer Avenue	A1-B1
Spon End	A3
Spring Street	E3-E4
Stepney Road	F4
Stoney Road	C1
Stoney Stanton Road	C4-D4
Strathmore Avenue	E2-E1
Swan Lane	F4-F3
Swanswell Street	D4
Terry Road	E2-E1-F1
Thackhall Street	F4
Tower Street	C4
Upper Spon Street	A3-B3
Upper Well Street	B4-B3-C3
Upper York Street	A2
Vecqueray Street	E2
Vernon Street	E4
Victoria Street	D4
Villiers Street	F3
Vine Street	D4-D3
Walsgrave	F3
Warwick Road	B1-B2-C2
Waverley Road	A3
Welland Road	E1-F1
West Street	E3
Westminster Road	B2-B1
Weston Street	D4
White Street	D4
Windsor Street	A2-A3
Winifrid Avenue	A1
Yardley Street	D4-E4

NUNEATON

Abbey Green	A4
Abbey Street	A4-A3-B3
Alexandra Street	A3
Amos Avenue	A1
Anker Street	C2
Attleborough Road	C2-C1
Avenue Road	B1-C1
Back Street	B4-B3
Bond Gate	B3
Bond Street	B4-C4
Bottril Street	B4
Bracebridge Street	A3-A2
Bridge Street	A1
Bull Ring	A1
Broad Street	A3
Chapel Street	B3
Cheverel Street	A1-B1
Church Street	B3-C3-C2
Clements Street	A2
Clinic Road	B2
Cooper Street	C3
Coventry Street	A4-B4-B3
Corporation Street	A4-B4-B3
Coton Road	B2-B1

RUGBY

Acacia Grove	B4
Albert Square	B3
Albert Street	B2-B3-C3
Alexandra Road	B4
Alfred Street	A1
Arnold Street	C3
Bank Street	B2
Barby Road	A1
Bath Street	C2-C3-C4
Bilton Road	A1
Bridget Street	A2
Castle Street	B2

Cox's Close	A1
Deacon Street	B1
Dugdale Street	B3-B2
Duke Street	B3
Edward Street	A3-A2-B2-B1
Fife Street	A3
Fitton Street	A1-A2-B2
Frank Street	A2-B2
Glebe Road	C3
Graham Street	B4
Greenmoor Road	A1
Harefield Road	B3-B4
Harold Street	B2
Heath End Road	A1
Henry Street	A1-B1
High Street	A3-B3
Home Park Road	B1
Inner Ring Road	B3
John Street	B1
King Edward Road	C3-C2
Kingsway	A2
Leicester Road	B3-C3-C4
Lister Street	C2
Manor Court Road	A2
Marlborough Road	A3-A2
Market Place	B3
Meadow Street	A4
Midland Road	A4
Milford Street	A1
Mill Street	B3
Mill Walk	B3
Mount Street	A3
Newdegate Street	B3
New Town Road	A4-B4
Norman Avenue	A3-A2
Oaston Road	C3-C4
Old Hinckley Road	C4
Orchard Street	C3
Park Street	C2
Princes Avenue	A2
Princes Street	B2-B3
Queen's Road	A3-B3
Regent Street	C4
Riversley Road	B2
Rose Lane	B2
St Nicholas Road	C4
Sandon Road	A4
Seymour Road	C2
Simon Close	C1
Stewart Street	A1-B1-B2
Trent Road	C4-C3
Vicarage Road	C3
Victoria Street	A3-B3
Villiers Street	A2
Weddington Road	C4
Weddington Terrace	C4
Wheat Street	C3
Willington Street	A4
Windsor Street	A2-A3-B3

Chapel Street	A2-B2
Charlotte Street	C2
Church Street	B1-B2
Clifton Road	C2
Corporation Street	A3-A2-A1
Craven Road	C4-C3
Dale Street	A3
Drury Lane	B2
Dunchurch Road	B1
Eastfield Place	A1
East Union Street	A1-B1
Edward Street	A2
Elsee Road	B2-C2
Essex Street	A3-A4
Evreux Way	A3-B3
Firs Drive	A1
Frederick Street	A1
Gas Street	B2
Graham Road	C4
Grosvenor Road	C2-C3
High Street	B2
Hill Street	A3
Hillmorton Road	C1
Holbrook Avenue	B3
Horton Crescent	B1-C1
Hunters Lane	A4
James Street	B3-C3
Kew Road	B3
Kimberley Road	C4
King Street	A3
King Edward Road	B4-B3
Lancaster Road	A4-B4
Lawford Road	A2-A1
Lawrence Sherriff Street	B2-B1
Little Church Street	B2-B1
Lodge Road	B4-B3
Lower Hillmorton Road	C2
Manor Road	B3-B4-C4
Maple Grove	B4
Market Street	C3
Mertons Drive	A1
Moultrie Road	C2-C1
Murray Road	C2-C3-C4
Newbold Road	A4-A3
North Street	B3-B2
Oliver Street	A2-A3
Park Road	B3-B4
Pennington Street	B2
Pinders Lane	B2-B3-C3
Plowman Street	A2
Poplar Grove	A4
Prince's Street	A3
Queen Street	A2
Railway Terrace	C2-C3-C2
Regent Place	B3
Regent Street	B2-B3
Round Street	A2
Rounds Gardens	A3
St John Street	B2
Sheep Street	B2
Spring Street	C3
Sycamore Grove	B4
Tom Brown Street	C3
Vicarage Road	A1
Warwick Street	A1-B1
Weil Street	C3
Westfield Road	A1
Westway	A2
Whitehall Road	C2-C1
William Street	C2
Wood Street	A4-B4-C4
Worcester Street	A4
York Street	A3

23

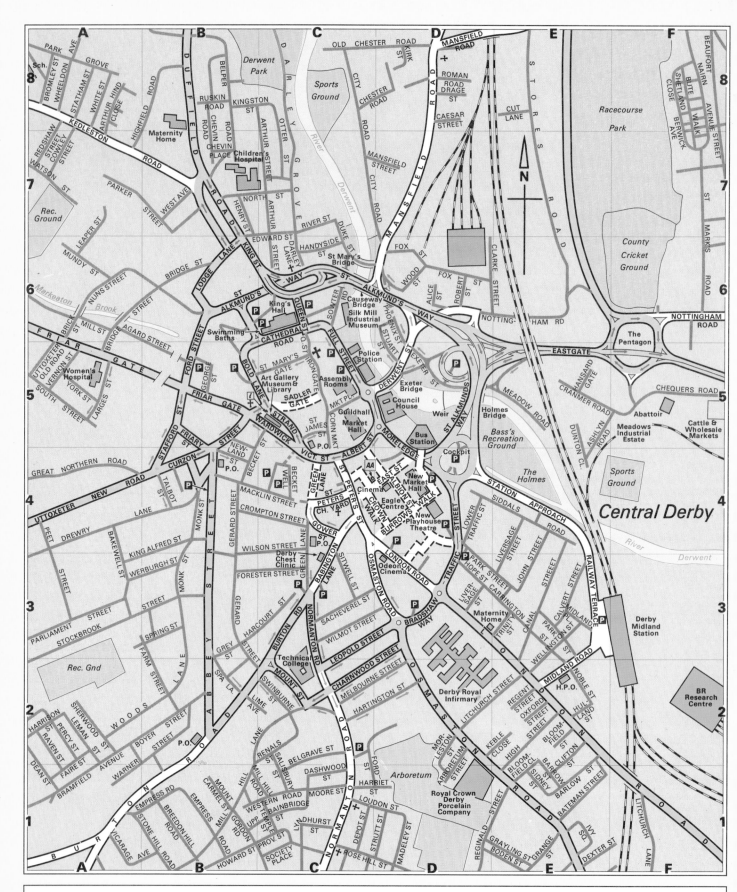

Derby

Present-day Derby, designated a city in 1977, is a
product of the Industrial Revolution. During the
19th century the Midland Railway made its
headquarters in the ancient country town, bringing
with it prosperity and considerable new building.
Around the old Market Place stand the Guildhall,
which is now used as a concert hall, the Market
Hall, and the façade of the old Assembly Rooms

which burnt down in 1963. Later Rolls-Royce
established its car manufacturing works here and
one of the company's founders, Sir Henry Royce, is
commemorated in the Arboretum, laid out by
Joseph Loudon. Rolls-Royce aero engines can be
seen in the Industrial Museum, appropriately
housed in England's first silk mill, set up in 1717 on
the banks of the Derwent.

Despite this strong industrial influence, for
many people Derby means only one thing –

porcelain. The Royal Crown Derby Porcelain
Company produced work of such excellence that
George III granted it the right to use the Crown
insignia. A museum on the premises houses a
treasure-trove of Crown Derby.

Derby's cathedral, All Saint's, was built during
Henry VIII's reign but, except for its 178ft-high
pinnacled tower, was rebuilt in 1725 by James
Gibb. The tomb of Bess of Hardwick, who died in
1607, can be seen inside.

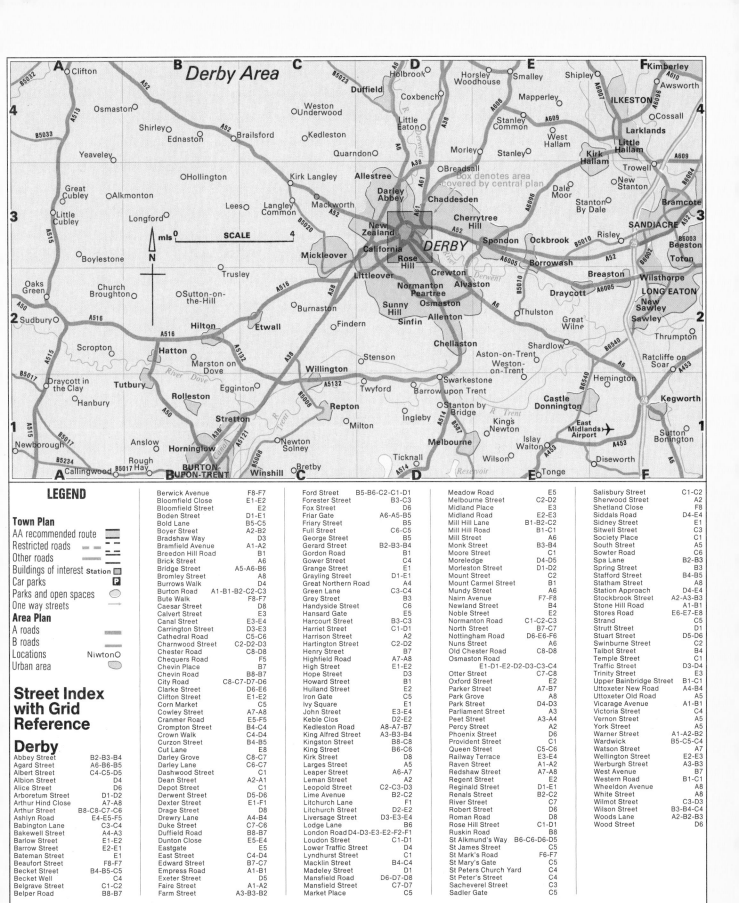

Derby Area

Street Index with Grid Reference

Derby

DERBY

The 1907 Silver Ghost, one of Rolls Royce's first cars, was produced just before the company moved its factory to Derby. Cars were their sole product until World War I when the first aero engine was designed.

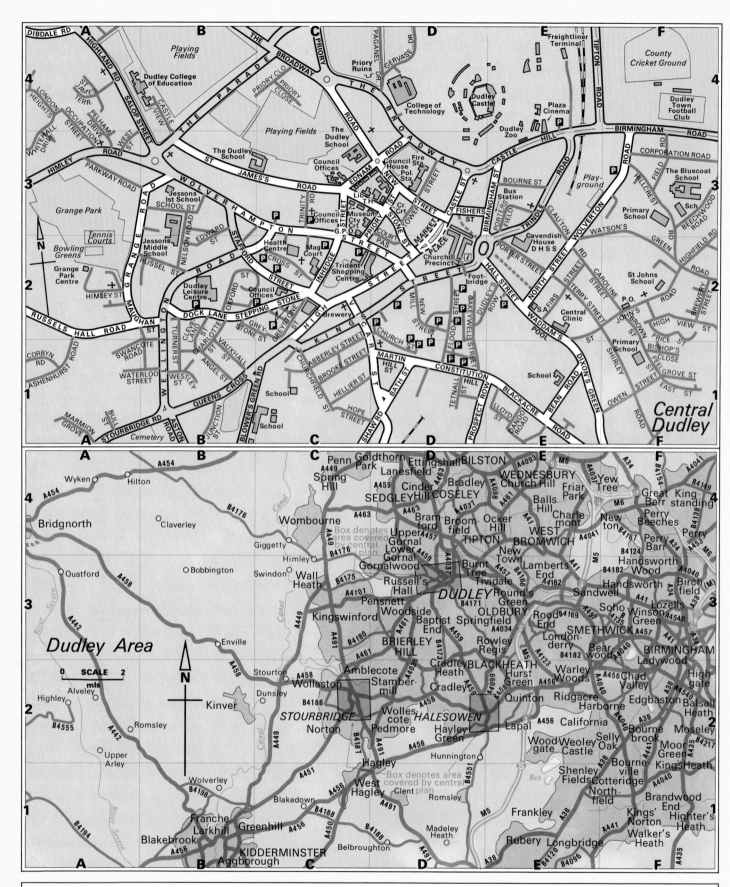

Dudley

The imposing remains of the castle which dominates the skyline bear witness to Dudley's importance as far back as medieval times, and later on it was again important as the capital of the 'Black Country' industrial region. Dudley is now the site of the open-air Black Country Museum, where numerous old buildings have been re-assembled to create a typical Black Country village, complete with examples of working industries and period transport. Other places of interest include Dudley Zoo, situated below the castle, where a fine selection of wild animals and reptiles are displayed in the unusual setting of the old limestone workings and the castle moat.

Halesowen's Leasowes Estate was once the home of 18th-century poet William Shenstone. The finely landscaped grounds were allowed to fall into disuse after his death, but are being restored to their former glory.

Stourbridge Crystal glass is the glittering attraction of this modernised market town, which has a number of glass factories open to visitors. The Broadfield House Glass Museum at nearby Kingswinford traces the evolution of the industry, and looks in particular at local firms such as Richardson's, Stevens and Williams, and Thomas Webb. Techniques of glassmaking and glassblowing are also featured here.

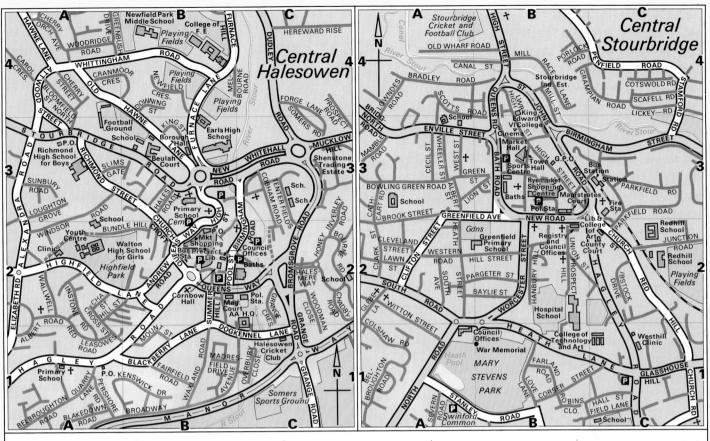

LEGEND

Town Plan

AA Recommended roads	
Other roads	
Restricted roads	
Buildings of interest	Library
Churches	+
Car parks	P
Parks and open spaces	
One way streets	

Area Plan

A roads	
B roads	
Locations	Longford ○
Urban area	

Street Index with Grid Reference

Dudley

Abberley Street	C1-C2
Angel Street	B1
Ashenhurst Road	A1-A2
Aston Road	B1
Bath Street	D1
Bean Road	E1
Beechwood Road	F3
Birmingham Road	F3-F4
Birmingham Street	D3-E3
Bishop's Close	F1
Blackacre Road	E1
Blower's Green Road	B1-C1
Bourne Street	E3
Brewery Street	F2
Brooke Street	C1
Brown Street	F1-F2
Bull Street	A1
Caroline Street	E2-F2
Castle Hill	D3-E3
Castle Street	D3
Castle View	B3-B4
Charlotte Street	B1-B2
Churchfield Street	C1
Church Street	D1-D2
Claughton Road	E2-E3
Cleveland Street	B1-B2
Constitution Hill	D1
Corbyn Road	A1

Corporation Road	F3
Court Passage	D2-D3
Cross Street	C2
Dando Road	E1
Dibdale Road	A4
Dixon's Green	E1-F1
Dock Lane	B2
Dudley's Row	D2-E2
East Street	F1
Ednam Road	C3-D3
Edward Street	B2-B3
Field Road	F3
Firs Street	E2
Fishers Street	D3
Flood Street	D1-D2
Gervase Drive	D4
Grange Road	A2-A3-B3
Greystone Street	B2-C2
Grove Street	F1
Hall Street	D2-E2
Hellier Street	C1
Highfield Road	F2-F3
Highland Road	A4
High Street	C2-D2
High View Street	F2
Hillcrest Road	F2-F3
Himley Road	A3-B3
Himley Street	A2
Hope Street	C1
Inhedge Street	C2-C3
Junction Street	B1
Kings Street	C1-C2-D2
Lloyd Street	E1
London Heights	A4
Market Place	D2-D3
Marmion Grove	A1
Martin Hill Street	D1
Maughan Street	A2-B2
Nelson Road	B2-B3
New Mill Street	D2
New Street	D3
North Street	E2
Oakeywell Street	D1-D2
Occupation Street	A3-A4
Owen Street	F1
Oxford Street	B2
Paganel Drive	D4
Parkway Road	A3
Peel Street	F1
Pelham Drive	A3-A4
Porters Field	E3
Porter Street	F2
Price Street	F1-C2
Priory Close	B4-C4
Priory Road	C4-C3-D3
Priory Street	C2-C3-D3
Prospect Row	D1-E1
Queens Cross	B1
Russsels Hall Road	A2
Russel Street	A2-B2
St James's Road	B3-C3
St James's Terrace	A4
St John's Road	E2-F2
Salop Street	A4-B4-B3
School Street	B3
Shaw Road	C1-D1
Shirley Road	F1-F2
Stafford Street	B3-B2-C2
Stepping Stone	B2-C2
Stone Street	D2-D3
Stourbridge Road	A1-B1

Swancote Road	A1-B1
The Broadway	B4-C4-D4-D3
The Parade	B3-B4-C4
Terry Street	E2
Tetnall Street	D1
Tipton Road	E4-F4
Tower Street	D3
Trindle Road	E2-E3
Trinity Road	C3
Turner Street	B1-B2
Vauxhall Street	B1
Vicar Street	C2-D2-C1-D1
Waddam's Pool	E2-E1
Waterloo Street	A1-B1
Watson's Green Road	E2-E3-F3-F2
Wellington Road	B1-B2
Westley Street	B1
West Street	A3
Whitehall Drive	A3-A4
Wolverhampton Street	B3-C3-C2-D2
Wolverton Road	E2-E3-F3

Halesowen

Albert Road	A1-A2
Alexandra Road	A2-A3
Andrew Road	B2
Attwood Street	A3-A4
Belbroughton Road	A1
Birmingham Road	B2-C2-B3-C3
Blackberry Lane	A1-B1-B2
Blakedown Road	A1
Bloomfield Street North	A3-A4
Broadway Avenue	A1-B1-C1
Bromsgrove Road	C2-C3
Bundle Hill	A2-B2
Carol Crescent	A4
Chadbury Road	C2
Chaple Street	A2
Cherry Orchard Avenue	A4
Cherry Street	A4
Church Croft	B2-B3
Cobham Road	C2-C3
Cranmoor Crescent	A4-B4
Cross Street	A1-A2
Dogkennel Lane	B2-B1-C1
Downing Street	B4
Dudley Road	C3-C4
Elizabeth Road	A1-A2
Fairfield Road	B1
Forge Lane	C3-C4
Furnace Hill	B4-C4
Furnace Lane	B3-B4
Grange Crescent	C2
Grange Road	C1-C2
Greenbush Drive	A4
Hagley Road	A1-B1-B2
Halesmere Way	C2
Hales Road	B3
Hawne Lane	A4
Hereward Rise	C4
Highfield Lane	A2-B2
High Street	B2-B3
Hill Street	A2

Horley Bourne Road	C2
Instone Road	A1-A2
Inverley Road	C2-C3
Kenswick Drive	A1-B1
Loughton Grove	A3
Madresfield Drive	B1
Manor Way	A1-B1-C1-C2
Melbourne Road	B4
Mount Street	B1
Mucklow Hill	C3
Newfield Crescent	B4
New Road	B3-C3
Old Hawne Lane	A4-B4-B3
Overbury Close	C1
Pershore Road	A1
Pool Street	B2
Prospect Road	C3-C4
Quarry Lane	A1
Queens Way	B2-C2
Red Leasowes Road	A1-A2
Richmond Street	A3-B3
Slims Gate	A3-B3
Somors Road	C3-C4
Stourbridge Road	A3-B3
Summer Hill	B2
Sunbury Road	A3
Tenter Fields	C2-C3
Wallwell	A2
Waxland Road	B1
Whitehall Road	C3
Whittingham Road	A4-B4
Windsor Road	A2-A3
Woodman Close	C1-C2
Woodridge Road	A4

Stourbridge

Albert Street	A3
Bath Road	B3
Baylie Street	A2-B2
Belbroughton Road	A1
Birmingham Street	B3-C3
Bowling Green Road	A3
Bradley Road	A4-B4
Bridgnorth Road	A3-A4
Brook Street	A2-A3
Canal Street	A4-B4
Cathcart Road	A2-A3
Cecil Street	A3
Church Road	C1
Church Street	C2
Clark Street	A2
Cleveland Street	A2
Clifton Street	A2-A3
Colshaw Road	A1
Corser Road	B1-C1
Cotswold Road	C4
Enville Street	A3-B3
Farland Road	B1
Field Lane	B1-C1
Glasshouse Hill	C1
Glebe Lane	A2
Grampian Road	B4-C4
Green Street	A3-B3
Hagley Road	B2-C2-C1

Hall Street	B1-C1
Hanbury Hill	B2
Heath Lane	B2-B1-C1
Heath Street	A2
High Street	B3-B4
Hill Street Street	A2-B2
Ibstock Drive	C2
Junction Road	C2
Lawn Street	A2
Lickey Road	C4
Lion Street	A3-B3
Love Lane	B1
Lower High Street	B4-B3
Lowndes Road	A3-A4
Mamble Road	A3
Mill Race Lane	B4
Mill Street	B3-B4
New Road	B2-B3
North Road	A1
Old Wharf Road	A4-B4
Pargeter Street	A2-B2
Parkfield Road	C2-C3
Penfield Road	B4-C4-B4
Porlock Road	B4
Prospect Hill	B2
Queens Road	B3-B4
Red Hill	C1-C2
Robins Close	B1
St Johns Road	B4-B3-C3
Severn Road	A1
Scafell Road	C4
Scotts Road	A4-A3-B3
Stamford Road	C3-C4
Stanley Road	A1-B1
South Road	A2
Union Street	B2-C2
Western Road	A2
West Street	A3
Wheeler Street	A3
Witton Street	A1-A2
Worcester Street	B2

27

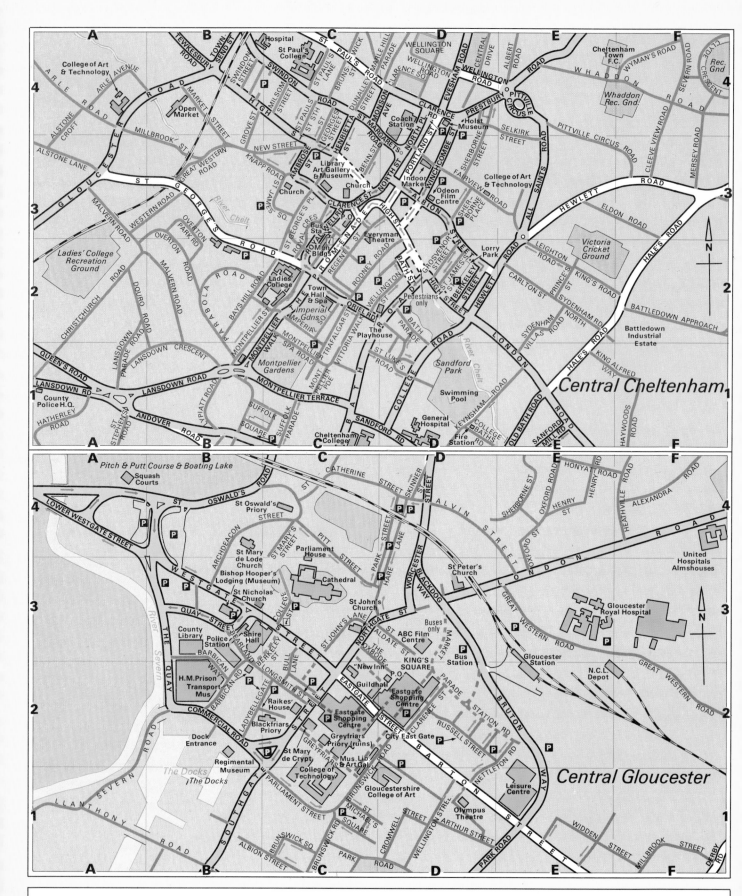

Gloucester

Gloucester's chief asset is its beautiful Norman cathedral. Originally an abbey, the building did not become a cathedral until the reign of Henry VIII and the lovely cloisters enclosing a delightful garden epitomise the tranquil beauty of medieval monastic architecture. The city's four main thoroughfares still follow the cruciform pattern of the original Roman roads built when *Glevum* guarded the lowest Severn crossing. Since those days Gloucester has been an important inland port and today it is one of the country's major commercial and engineering centres.

Tewkesbury Black-and-white timbered buildings and ancient pubs with crooked roofs and curious names, such as *The Ancient Grudge*, lean haphazardly against each other in Tewkesbury's narrow streets. Rising above them all is the vast and beautiful abbey church, saved from destruction in the Dissolution of the Monastries by the townsfolk who bought it from Henry VIII.

Cheltenham Elegant Regency architecture arranged in squares, avenues and crescents is Cheltenham's hallmark. The whole town was purpose-built around the medicinal springs discovered in the 18th century and, under Royal patronage, it became one of the country's most fashionable spas. The composer Gustav Holst was born here and his home is now a museum.

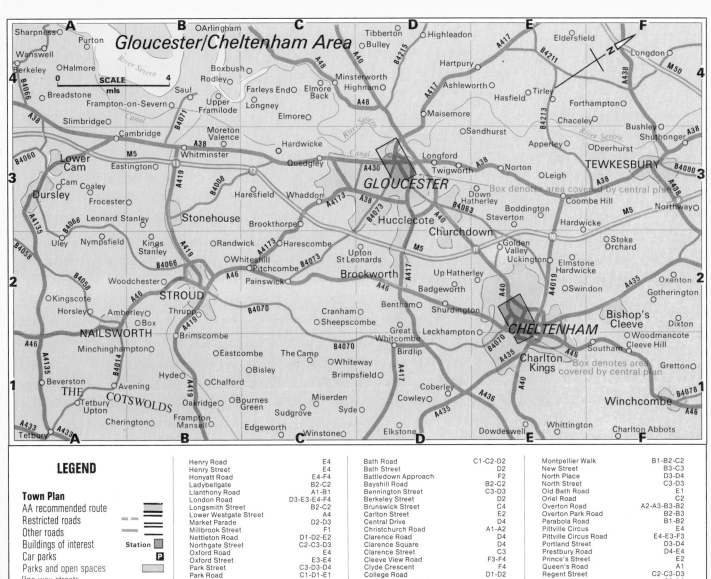

Gloucester/Cheltenham Area

(Map showing the Gloucester/Cheltenham area with towns including Sharpness, Berkeley, Dursley, Stroud, Nailsworth, Stonehouse, Gloucester, Cheltenham, Tewkesbury, Winchcombe and surrounding villages, with A and B roads and motorways M5/M50.)

LEGEND

Town Plan
AA recommended route	
Restricted roads	
Other roads	
Buildings of interest	Station 🔲
Car parks	🅿
Parks and open spaces	
One way streets	←

Area Plan
A roads	
B roads	
Locations	Beedon ○
Urban area	

Street Index with Grid Reference

Gloucester

Albion Street	B1-C1
Alexandra Road	F4
Alvin Street	D4-E4-E3
Archdeacon Street	B3-B4-C4
Arthur Street	D1
Barton Street	D2-D1-E1
Black Dog Way	D3
Brunswick Road	C1-C2-D2
Brunswick Square	C1
Bruton Way	D3-D2-E2-E1
Bull Lane	C2-C3
Clarence Street	D2
Commercial Road	B2
Cromwell Street	D1
Derby Road	F1
Eastgate Street	C2-D2
Great Western Road	E3-F3-F2
Hare Lane	C3-D3-D4
Heathville Road	F4
Henry Road	E4
Henry Street	E4
Honyatt Road	E4-F4
Ladybellgate	B2-C2
Llanthony Road	A1-B1
London Road	D3-E3-E4-F4
Longsmith Street	B2-C2
Lower Westgate Street	A4
Market Parade	D2-D3
Millbrook Street	F1
Nettleton Road	D1-D2-E2
Northgate Street	C2-C3-D3
Oxford Road	E4
Oxford Street	E3-E4
Park Street	C3-D3-D4
Park Road	C1-D1-E1
Parliament Street	C1
Pitt Street	C3-C4
Quay Street	B3
Russell Street	D2
St Catherine Street	C4-D4
St John's Lane	C3
St Mary's Street	C4
St Michael's Square	C1
St Oswald's Road	B4-C4
Severn Road	A1-A2-B2
Sherborne Street	D4-E4
Skinner Street	D4
Station Road	D2-E2
Southgate Street	B1-C1-C2
The Quay	B2-B3
Wellington Street	D1
Westgate Street	B3-C3-C2
Widden Street	E1-F1
Worcester Street	D3-D4

Cheltenham

Albert Road	E4
Albion Street	D2-D3
All Saints Road	E3-E4
Alstone Croft	A3-A4
Alstone Lane	A3
Ambrose Street	C3
Andover Road	A1-B1
Arle Avenue	A4-B4
Arle Road	A4
Bath Parade	D1-D2
Bath Road	C1-C2-D2
Bath Street	D2
Battledown Approach	F2
Bayshill Road	B2-C2
Bennington Street	C3-D3
Berkeley Street	D4
Brunswick Street	C4
Carlton Street	E2
Central Drive	D4
Christchurch Road	A1-A2
Clarence Road	D4
Clarence Square	D4
Clarence Street	C3
Cleeve View Road	F3-F4
Clyde Crescent	F4
College Road	D1-D2
College Baths Road	D1
Douro Road	A2-B2-B1
Dunalley Street	C4
Eldon Road	E3-F3
Evesham Road	D4
Fairview Road	D3-E3
Gloucester Road	A3-A4-B4
Great Western Road	B3
Grosvenor Street	D2
Grove Street	B3-B4
Hale's Road	E1-E2-F2-F3
Hatherley Road	A1
Haywoods Road	F1
Henrietta Street	C3-C4
Hewlett Road	D2-E2-E3-F3
High Street	B4-C4-C3, D2-D3
Imperial Square	C2
Keynsham Road	D1-E1
King's Road	E2-F2
King Alfred Way	E1-F1
Knapp Road	B3-C3
Landsdown Crescent	A1-B1
Landsown Road	A1-B1
Lansdown Parade Road	A1-A2
Leighton Road	E2
London Road	D2-E2-E1
Lypiatt Road	B1
Malvern Road	A3-A2-B2
Market Street	B3-B4
Marle Hill Parade	C4-D4
Mersey Road	F3-F4
Millbrook Street	A4-A3-B3
Milsom Street	C4
Monson Avenue	C4-D4
Montpellier Parade	C1
Montpellier Spa Road	C1-C2
Montpellier Street	B1-B2-C2
Montpellier Terrace	B1-C1
Montpellier Walk	B1-B2-C2
New Street	B3-C3
North Place	D3-D4
North Street	C3-D3
Old Bath Road	E1
Oriel Road	C2
Overton Road	A2-A3-B3-B2
Overton Park Road	B2-B3
Parabola Road	B1-B2
Pittville Circus	E4
Pittville Circus Road	E4-E3-F3
Portland Street	D3-D4
Prestbury Road	D4-E4-E4
Prince's Street	E2
Queen's Road	A1
Regent Street	C2-C3-D3
Rodney Road	C2-D2
Royal Crescent	C2-C3
Royal Well Road	C2-C3
St George's Place	C2-C3
St George's Road	A3-B3-B2-C2
St Georges Street	C3-C4
St James's Square	C3
St James's Street	D2
St Luke's Road	C1-D1
St Margarets Road	C4-D4-D3
St Paul's Lane	C4
St Paul's Road	C4-D4
St Pauls Street South	C4
St Stephen's Road	A1
Sandford Road	C1-D1
Sandford Mill Road	E1
Selkirk Street	D4-E4-E3
Severn Road	D3
Sherborne Place	D3
Sherborne Street	D3-D4
Suffolk Parade	C1
Suffolk Square	B1-C1
Swindon Road	B4-C4
Swindon Street	B4
Sydenham Road North	E2
Sydenham Villas Road	E1-E2
Tewkesbury Road	B4
The Promenade	C2-C3
Trafalgar Street	C1-C2
Townsend Street	B4
Vittoria Walk	C1-C2
Wellington Road	D4-E4
Wellington Square	D4
Wellington Street	C2-D2
Western Road	A3-B3
Whaddon Road	E4-F4
Winchcombe Street	D3-D4
Wymans Road	F4

GLOUCESTER
Gloucester Cathedral, one of the Britain's finest buildings, is a splendid example of Norman architecture. The beautiful stained-glass east window is a memorial to local men who fought at Crécy in 1346.

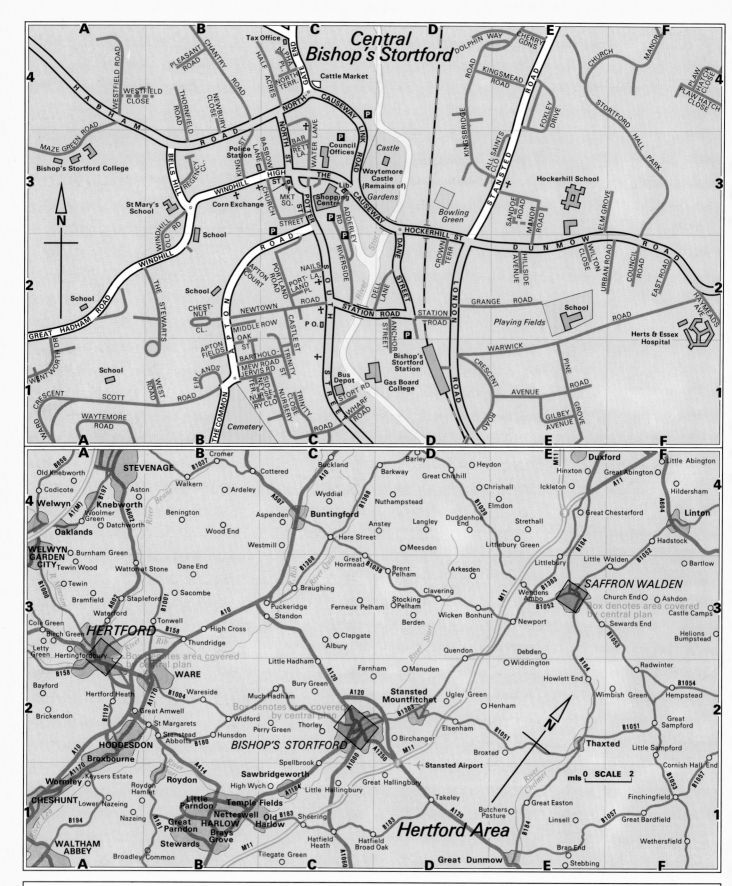

Hertford area

Bishop's Stortford still has a medieval street pattern. A crossing point of the River Lea in Roman times, its centre is dominated by modern buildings and pedestrianised shopping, but the town's oldest monument stands only a few hundred yards away — the remains of Waytemore Castle, which dates back to the 11th century.

Hertford A skilful blend of old and new distinguishes

Hertford, which is set in some of Hertfordshire's most attractive countryside. The Quaker Meeting House is the oldest of its type still in use in the world, and stands alongside newer developments like the Castle Hall exhibition and entertainments complex. Even the modern shopping precinct, sited by the picturesque River Lea, complements the character of the town and indeed has given it a new lease of life.

Saffron Walden takes its name from saffron, an

extract from the crocus which was once grown commercially here and is the celebrated symbol of the town, representing its prosperity over the centuries. This prosperity left numerous fine old buildings of unusual style and completeness: Myddylton Place and the Sun Inn are good 15th-century buildings, and the mile-long brick-built maze on the Common is the oldest of its type in the country. Today's town is built up on a well-preserved medieval street plan.

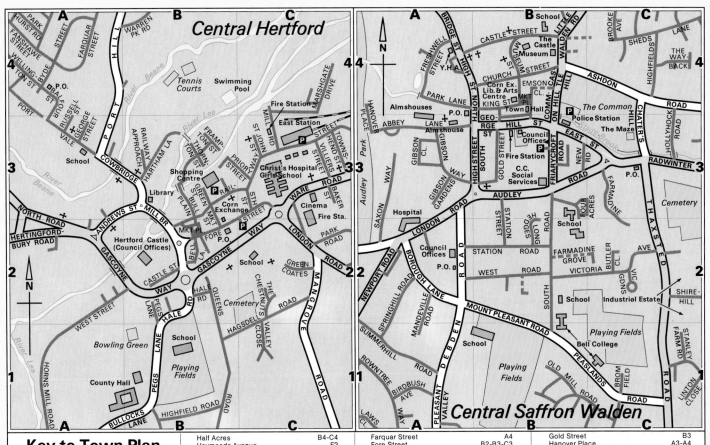

Central Hertford

Central Saffron Walden

Key to Town Plan and Area Plan.

Town Plan

AA Recommended roads	≡
Other roads	
Restricted roads	- - -
Buildings of interest	Theatre
Churches	+
Car Parks	P
Parks and open spaces	

Area Plan

A roads	
B roads	
Locations	Broomfield ○
Urban area	

Street Index with Grid Reference

Bishop's Stortford

Adderley Road	C2-C3
All Saints Close	E3
Alpha Place	C4
Anchor Street	D1-D2
Apton Court	B2
Apton Fields	B1
Apton Road	B1-B2-C2-C3
Avenue Road	E1
Barrett Lane	C3
Bartholomew Road	B1-C1
Basbow Lane	B2
Bells Hill	B3
Castle Street	C1-C2
Causeway Link Road	C3-C4
Chantry Road	E4
Cherry Gardens	B2
Chestnut Close	E4-F4
Church Manor	C3
Church Street	F2
Council Road	D1-E1-D1
Crescent Road	D2
Crown Terrace	C2-D2
Dane Street	D2-D3
Dell Lane	E4
Dolphin Way	D2-E2-E3-F3-F2
Dunmow Road	F2
East Road	E3-F3
Elm Grove	B1
Firlands	E3-E4
Foxley Drive	E1
Gilbey Avenue	D2-E2
Grange Road	A1-A2
Great Hadham Road	A4-B4-B3-B4-C4
Hadham Road	B4-C4

Half Acres	B4-C4
Haymeads Avenue	F2
High Street	C3
Hillside Avenue	E2
Hockerhill Street	D2-D3
Jervis Road	B1-C1
King Street	B3-B4
Kingsbridge Road	E3-D3-D4-E4
Kingsmead Road	D4-E4
London Road	D1-D2
Manor Road	E2-E3
Market Square	C3
Maze Green Road	A3-A4
Middle Row	B2
Nails Lane	C2
Newbury Close	B3-B4
Newtown Road	B2-C2
North Street	C3-C4
North Terrace	C4
Northgate End	C4
Nursery Close	B1-C1
Nursery Road	C1
Oak Street	B1
Pine Grove	E1
Plaw Hatch Close	F4
Pleasant Road	B4
Portland Place	C2
Portland Road	C2
Potter Street	C3
Regency Close	B3
Riverside	C2-C3
Sandoe Road	E3
Scott Road	A1-B1
Sidney Terrace	B1-C1
South Street	C1-C2-C3
Stanstead Road	D2-D3-E3-E4
Station Road	C2-D2
Stort Road	C1
Stortford Hall Park	E4-F4-F3-F2
The Causeway	C3-D3
The Common	B1
The Stewarts	A2-B2-B1
Thornfield Road	B3-B4
Trinity Close	C1
Trinity Street	C1
Urban Road	F2
Ward Crescent	A1
Warwick Road	D1-E1-E2-F2
Water Lane	C3-C4
Waytemore Road	A1
Wentworth Drive	A1-A2
West Road	B1
Westfield Close	A4-B4
Westfield Road	A4
Wharf Road	C1
Wilton Close	E2
Windhill	A2-B2-B3-C3
Windhill Old Road	B2-B3

Hertford

Andrews Street	A2-A3-B3
Baker Street	C3
Balfour Street	A3-A4
Bell Lane	B2
Bull Plain	B3
Bullocks Lane	A1-B1
Byde Street	A4
Castle Street	B2
Cowbridge	A3-B3
Fanshawe Street	A4

Farquar Street	A4
Fore Street	B2-B3-C3
Frampton Street	B3
Gascoyne Way	A2-B2-C2-C3
George Street	A3
Green Coates	C2
Green Street	B3
Hagsdell Road	B1-C1-C2
Hale Road	B2
Hartham Lane	B3
Hertingfordbury Road	A2
Highfield Road	B1
Horns Mill Road	A1
London Road	C2-C3
Mangrove Road	C1-C2
Market Place	B2
Market Street	B2-B3
Marshgate Drive	C4
Mill Bridge	B2-B3
Mill Road	C3-C4
North Road	A2-A3
Park Road	C2
Parkhurst Road	A4
Pegs Lane	B1-B2
Port Hill	A3-A4
Port Vale	A3-A4
Priory Street	B3-C3
Queens Road	B1-B2
Railway Approach	B3
Railway Street	B3-C3
Russell Street	A3-A4
St John Street	C3
South Street	C3
The Chestnuts	C2
Thornton Street	B3
Townshend Street	C3
Valley Close	C1-C2
Villiers Street	C3
Ware Road	C3
Warren Park Road	A4-B4
Wellington Street	A4
West Street	A1-A2-B2

Saffron Walden

Abbey Lane	A3
Ashdon Road	B4-C4
Audley Road	B3-C3
Birdbush Avenue	A1
Borough Lane	A2
Bridge Street	A4
Bromfield	C1
Brooke Avenue	C4
Butler Close	C2
Castle Hill	B4
Castle Street	A4-B4
Chater's Hill	C3-C4
Church Street	B4
Common Hill	B3-B4
Debden Road	A1-A2-A3
East Street	B3-C3
Emson Close	B4
Farmadine	C2-C3
Farmadine Grove	B2-C2
Four Acres	B3-C3
Freshwell Street	A4
Friarycroft Road	B3
George Street	B3
Gibson Close	A3
Gibson Gardens	A3
Gibson Way	A3

Gold Street	B3
Hanover Place	A3-A4
Highfields	C4
High Street North	A3-A4-B4-B3
High Street South	A3-B3
Hill Street	B3
Hollyhock Road	C3-C4
King Street	B4
Laws Close	A1
Linton Close	C1
Little Walden Road	B4
London Road	A2-A3
Long Hedges	B2
Market Place	B4
Mandeville Road	A1-A2
Mount Pleasant Road	A2-B2-B1
Museum Street	B4
New Road	B3
Newport Road	A2
Old Mill Road	B1-C1
Park Lane	A4
Peaslands Road	B1-C1
Pleasant Valley	A1
Radwinter	C3
Rowntree Way	A1
Saxon Way	A2-A3
Sheds Lane	C4
Shirehill	C2
South Road	B1-B2-B3
Springhill Road	A1-A2
Stanley Farm Road	C1
Station Road	A2-B2
Station Road	B2-B3
Summerhill Road	A1-A2
Thaxsted Road	C1-C2-C3
The Wayback	C4
Victoria Avenue	B2-C2
Victoria Gardens	C2
West Road	A2-B2

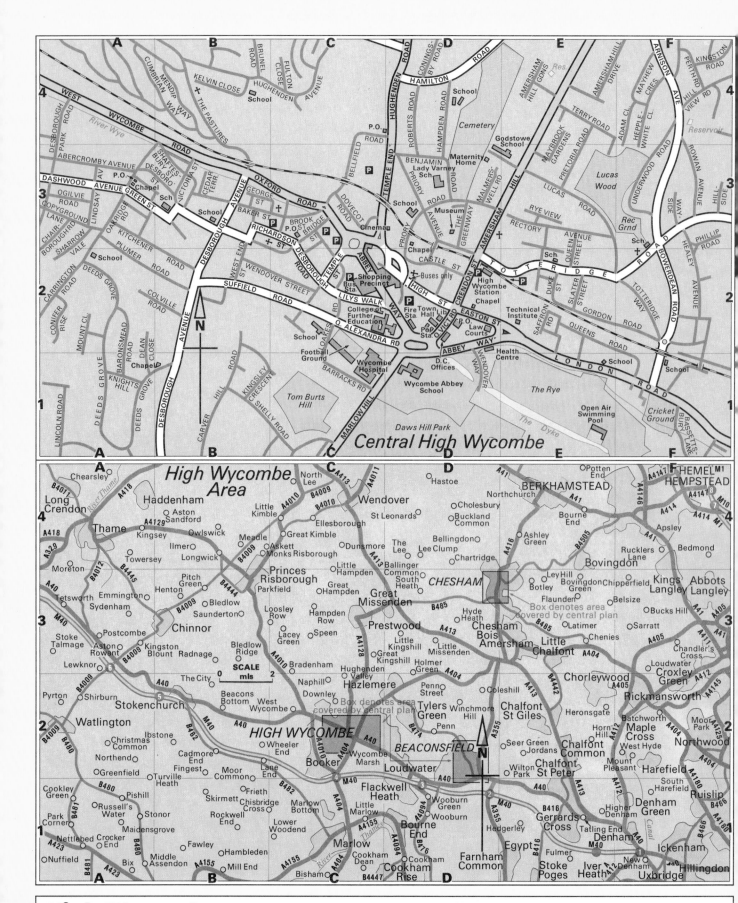

Central High Wycombe

High Wycombe Area

SCALE
mls
0   2

HIGH WYCOMBE

BEACONSFIELD

Box denotes area covered by central plan

High Wycombe

Each year in spring, the newly elected mayor and town officials of High Wycombe are weighed outside the town's Guildhall wearing their traditional vestments, as part of an old-established 'weighing in' ceremony. Interesting old buildings as well as ceremonies have been preserved in the town, particularly around the High Street, and the Market House, known as the Pepperpot, dates from

the mid-18th century. The history of the town is traced in the Guildhall Heritage Exhibition, while the Wycombe Chair and Local History Museum deals mainly with furniture manufacture — probably the best known feature of this important industrial centre today. Two miles to the west lies West Wycombe, site of the caves said to have been the meeting place for Sir Francis Dashwood's Hellfire Club during the 18th century.

Beaconsfield is the home of the Bekonscot Model

Village, said to be one of the oldest in the world, and of a partly 15th-century parish church. A number of old coaching inns still stand here.

Chesham has made a name for itself with the manufacture of wooden articles such as fruit bowls, and is concerned with the leather industry. The oldest buildings in the town are mainly concentrated in the Church Street and Germain Street areas, where 16th- and 18th-century half-timbered gabled houses have been preserved.

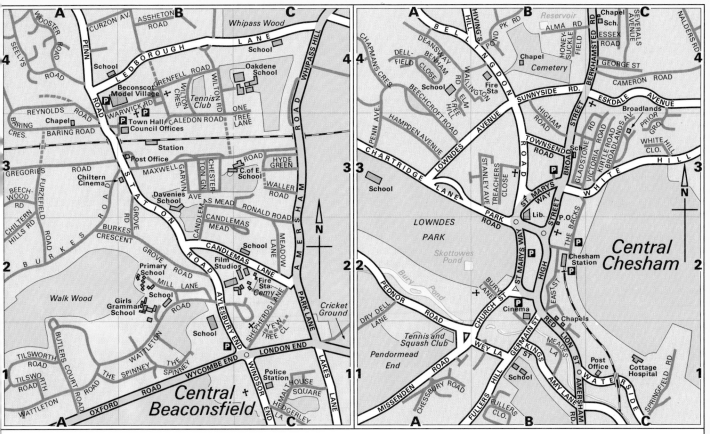

Central Beaconsfield

Central Chesham

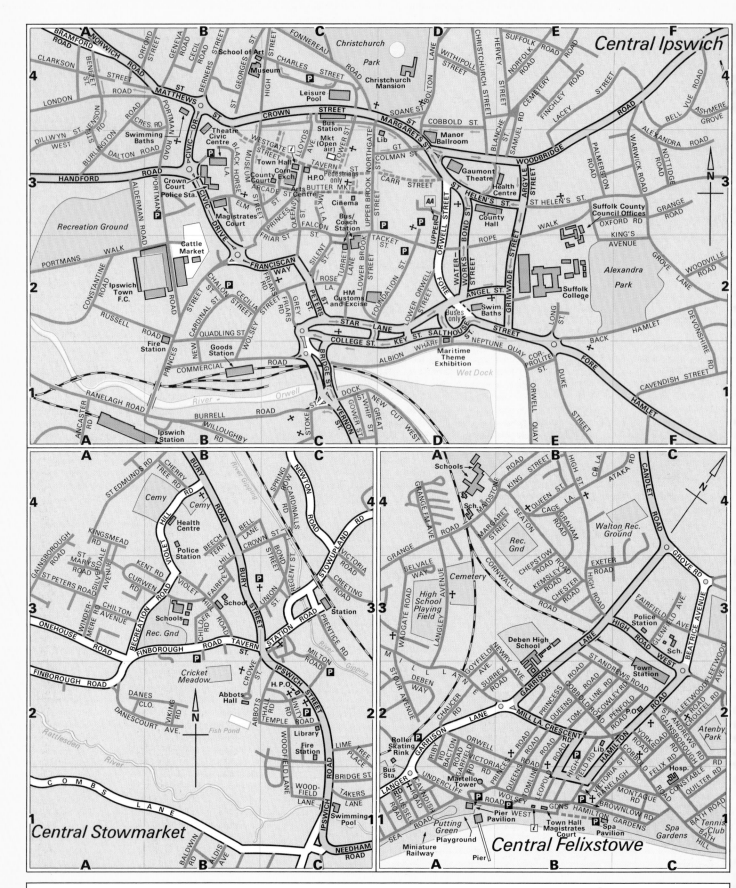

Ipswich

In the Middle Ages England became rich from wool, and East Anglia in particular prospered. Ipswich shared in the wealth, being the port from which wool was exported to Europe. Twelve medieval churches survive in Ipswich, a remarkable number for a town of its size, and all of them have features of beauty and interest. Of the town's nonconformist chapels, the 17th-century Unitarian is outstanding. Unfortunately, many of Ipswich's ancient secular buildings were swept away during the 1960s fever for clearances, precincts and redevelopment; however, some of the finest survive. Best is Ancient House, dating back to 1567 and embellished on the outside with complex decorative plasterwork. Other fine buildings can be seen in Lower Brook Street and Fore Street. Christchurch Mansion dates from 1548 and now houses a museum.

Felixstowe is a seaside resort with Edwardian characteristics, a commercial centre, and a container port. Its handsome promenade is nearly two miles long.

Stowmarket has an excellent country life museum – the Museum of East Anglian Life. Among its exhibits are reconstructed buildings, agricultural machinery and domestic items. The town itself is a shopping and market centre for the rich arable farmlands of Central Suffolk.

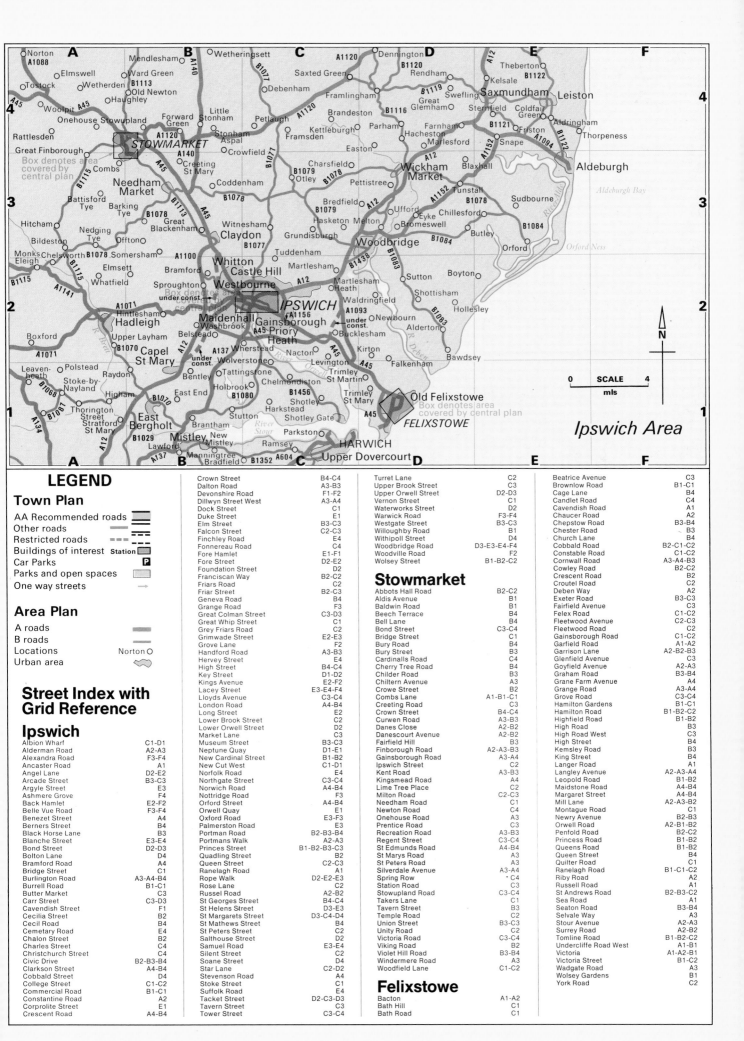

Ipswich Area

SCALE
0 — 4
mls

N

LEGEND

Town Plan

- AA Recommended roads
- Other roads
- Restricted roads
- Buildings of interest — Station
- Car Parks — P
- Parks and open spaces
- One way streets

Area Plan

- A roads
- B roads
- Locations — Norton
- Urban area

Street Index with Grid Reference

Ipswich

Albion Wharf	C1-D1
Alderman Road	A2-A3
Alexandra Road	F3-F4
Ancaster Road	A1
Angel Lane	D2-E2
Arcade Street	B3-C3
Argyle Street	E3
Ashmere Grove	F4
Back Hamlet	E2-F2
Belle Vue Road	F3-F4
Benezet Street	A4
Berners Street	B4
Black Horse Lane	B3
Blanche Street	E3-E4
Bond Street	D2-D3
Bolton Lane	D4
Bramford Road	A4
Bridge Street	C1
Burlington Road	A3-A4-B4
Burrell Road	B1-C1
Butter Market	C3
Carr Street	C3-D3
Cavendish Street	F1
Cecilia Street	B2
Cecil Road	B4
Cemetary Road	E4
Chalon Street	B2
Charles Street	C4
Christchurch Street	C4
Civic Drive	B2-B3-B4
Clarkson Street	A4-B4
Cobbald Street	D4
College Street	C1-C2
Commercial Road	B1-C1
Constantine Road	A2
Corprolite Street	E1
Crescent Road	A4-B4
Crown Street	B4-C4
Dalton Road	A3-B3
Devonshire Road	F1-F2
Dillwyn Street West	A3-A4
Dock Street	C1
Duke Street	E1
Elm Street	B3-C3
Falcon Street	C2-C3
Finchley Road	C4
Fonnereau Road	C4
Fore Hamlet	E1-F1
Fore Street	D2-E2
Foundation Street	D2
Franciscan Way	B2-C2
Friars Road	C2
Friar Street	B2-C3
Geneva Road	B4
Grange Road	F3
Great Colman Street	C3-D3
Great Whip Street	C1
Grey Friars Road	C2
Grimwade Street	E2-E3
Grove Lane	F2
Handford Road	A3-B3
Hervey Street	E4
High Street	B4-C4
Key Street	D1-D2
Kings Avenue	E2-F2
Lacey Street	E3-E4-F4
Lloyds Avenue	C3-C4
London Road	A4-B4
Long Street	E2
Lower Brook Street	C2
Lower Orwell Street	D2
Market Lane	C3
Museum Street	B3-C3
Neptune Quay	D1-E1
New Cardinal Street	B1-B2
New Cut West	C1-D1
Norfolk Road	E4
Northgate Street	C3-C4
Norwich Road	A4-B4
Nottridge Road	F3
Orford Street	A4-B4
Orwell Quay	E1
Oxford Road	E3-F3
Palmerston Road	E3
Portman Road	B2-B3-B4
Portmans Walk	A2-A3
Princes Street	B1-B2-B3-C3
Quadling Street	B2
Queen Street	C2-C3
Ranelagh Road	A1
Rope Walk	D2-E2-E3
Rose Lane	C2
Russel Road	A2-B2
St Georges Street	B4-C4
St Helens Street	D3-E3
St Margarets Street	D3-C4-D4
St Mathews Street	B4
St Peters Street	C2
Salthouse Street	D2
Samuel Road	E3-E4
Silent Street	C2
Soane Street	D4
Star Lane	C2-D2
Stevenson Road	A4
Stoke Street	C1
Suffolk Road	F1
Tacket Street	D2-C3-D3
Tavern Street	C3
Tower Street	C3-C4
Turret Lane	C2
Upper Brook Street	C3
Upper Orwell Street	D2-D3
Vernon Street	C1
Waterworks Street	D2
Warwick Road	F3-F4
Westgate Street	B3-C3
Willoughby Road	B1
Withipoll Street	D4
Woodbridge Road	D3-E3-E4-F4
Woodville Road	F2
Wolsey Street	B1-B2-C2

Stowmarket

Abbots Hall Road	B2-C2
Aldis Avenue	B1
Baldwin Road	B1
Beech Terrace	B4
Bell Lane	B4
Bond Street	C3-C4
Bridge Street	C1
Bury Road	B4
Bury Street	B3
Cardinalls Road	C4
Cherry Tree Road	B4
Childer Road	B3
Chiltern Avenue	A3
Crowe Street	B2
Combs Lane	A1-B1-C1
Creeting Road	C3
Crown Street	B4-C4
Curwen Road	A3-B3
Danes Close	A2-B2
Danescourt Avenue	A2-B2
Fairfield Hill	B3
Finborough Road	A2-A3-B3
Gainsborough Road	A3-A4
Ipswich Street	C2
Kent Road	A3-B3
Kingsmead Road	A4
Lime Tree Place	C2
Milton Road	C2-C3
Needham Road	C1
Newton Road	C4
Onehouse Road	A3
Prentice Road	C3
Recreation Road	A3-B3
Regent Street	C3-C4
St Edmunds Road	A4-B4
St Marys Road	A3
St Peters Road	A3
Silverdale Avenue	A3-A4
Spring Row	C4
Station Road	C3
Stowupland Road	C3-C4
Takers Lane	C1
Tavern Street	B3
Temple Road	C2
Union Street	B3-C3
Unity Road	C2
Victoria Road	C3-C4
Viking Road	B2
Violet Hill Road	B3-B4
Windermere Road	A3
Woodfield Lane	C1-C2

Felixstowe

Bacton	A1-A2
Bath Hill	C1
Bath Road	C1
Beatrice Avenue	C3
Brownlow Road	B1-C1
Cage Lane	B4
Candlet Road	C4
Cavendish Road	A1
Chaucer Road	A2
Chepstow Road	B3-B4
Chester Road	B3
Church Lane	B4
Cobbald Road	B2-C1-C2
Constable Road	C1-C2
Cornwall Road	A3-A4-B3
Cowley Road	B2-C2
Crescent Road	B2
Croutel Road	C2
Deben Way	A2
Exeter Road	B3-C3
Fairfield Avenue	C3
Felex Road	C1-C2
Fleetwood Avenue	C2-C3
Fleetwood Road	C2
Gainsborough Road	C1-C2
Garfield Road	A1-A2
Garrison Lane	A2-B2-B3
Glenfield Avenue	C3
Goyfield Avenue	A2-A3
Graham Road	B3-B4
Grane Farm Avenue	A4
Grange Road	A3-A4
Grove Road	C3-C4
Hamilton Gardens	B1-C1
Hamilton Road	B1-B2-C2
Highfield Road	B1-B2
High Road	B3
High Road West	C3
High Street	B4
Kemsley Road	B3
King Street	B4
Langer Road	A1
Langley Avenue	A2-A3-A4
Leopold Road	B1-B2
Maidstone Road	A4-B4
Margaret Street	A4-B4
Mill Lane	A2-A3-B2
Montague Road	C1
Newry Avenue	B2-B3
Orwell Road	A2-B1-B2
Penfold Road	B2-C2
Princess Road	B1-B2
Queens Road	B1-B2
Queen Street	B4
Quilter Road	C1
Ranelagh Road	B1-C1-C2
Riby Road	A2
Russell Road	A1
St Andrews Road	B2-B3-C2
Sea Road	A1
Seaton Road	B3-B4
Selvale Way	A3
Stour Avenue	A2-A3
Surrey Road	A2-B2
Tomline Road	B1-B2-C2
Undercliffe Road West	A1-B1
Victoria	A1-A2-B1
Victoria Street	B1-C2
Wadgate Road	A3
Wolsey Gardens	B1
York Road	C2

35

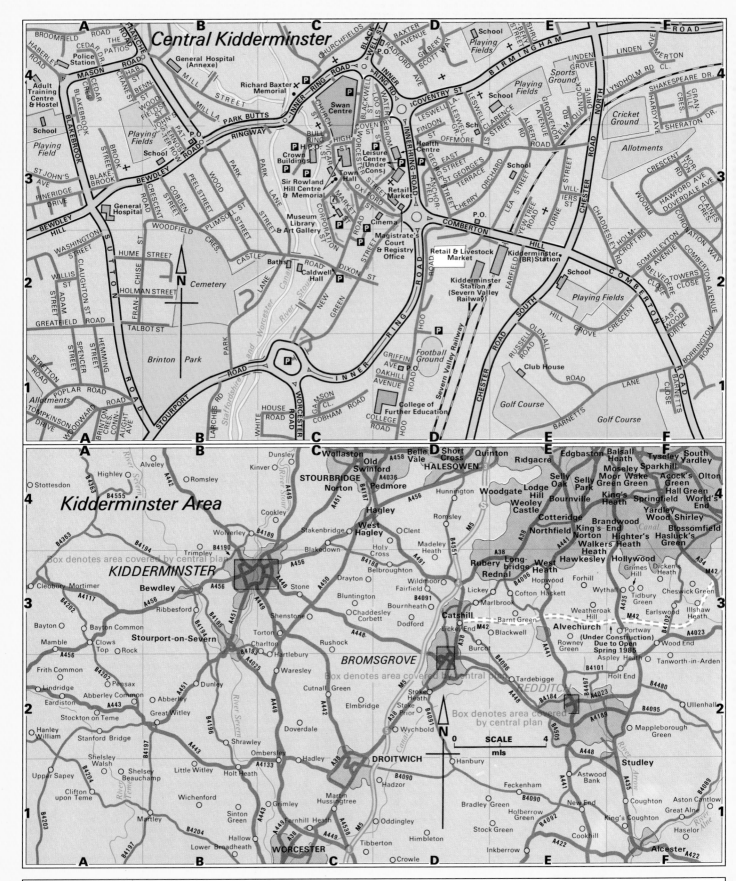

Kidderminster

Carpets and Kidderminster have gone together since at least the 17th century, and this ancient town is also notable as the birthplace of Penny Post founder Sir Rowland Hill. A variety of historic buildings has survived here, and railway enthusiasts can now enjoy the attractions of the Severn Valley Steam Railway — it has recently been extended to Kidderminster and generally operates during the summer and on Bank Holidays. The West Midland Safari Park lies between Kidderminster and Bewdley, covering some 197 acres.

Bromsgrove prospered on nail-making before the arrival of machines in the 19th century, and today this thriving modern town attracts a variety of trades to its recently built industrial estates. But a past which can be traced to pre-Norman times is recalled each year, when Bromsgrove holds its annual Fair at which traditional and ancient customs are displayed. Year round outdoor recreation can be found at Sanders Park.

Redditch has grown up on a rich mix of fishing tackle, cycles and springs — three of the products which have replaced its staple trade of needle-making after the mid-19th century. Set in the heart of England, Redditch today excels in the making of metal and engineering goods and boasts three sports centres, the outdoor Abbey Stadium, and 900-acre Arrow Valley Park, with its 30-acre lake.

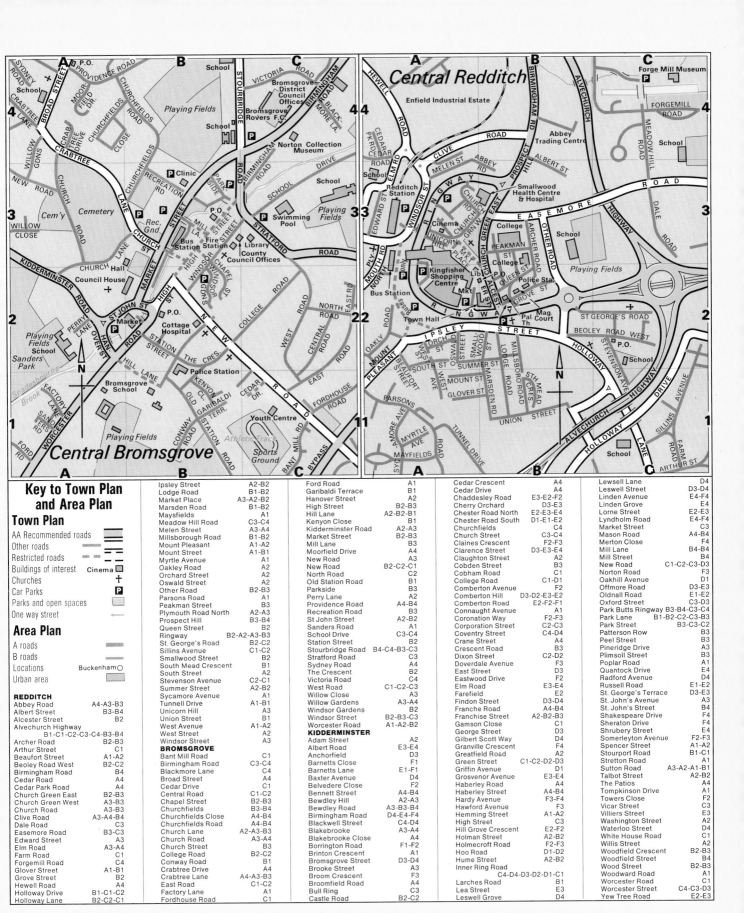

Central Bromsgrove

Central Redditch

Key to Town Plan and Area Plan

Town Plan

AA Recommended roads
Other roads
Restricted roads
Buildings of interest   Cinema ▣
Churches   ✝
Car Parks   ℙ
Parks and open spaces
One way street

Area Plan

A roads
B roads
Locations   Buckenham ○
Urban area

REDDITCH

Abbey Road	A4-A3-B3
Albert Street	B3-B4
Alcester Street	B2
Alvechurch Highway	B1-C1-C2-C3-C4-B3-B4
Archer Road	B2-B3
Arthur Street	C1
Beaufort Street	A1-A2
Beoley Road West	B2-C2
Birmingham Road	B4
Cedar Road	A4
Cedar Park Road	A4
Church Green East	B2-B3
Church Green West	A3-B3
Church Road	A3-B3
Clive Road	A3-A4-B4
Dale Road	C3
Easemore Road	B3-C3
Edward Street	A3
Elm Road	A3-A4
Farm Road	C1
Forgemill Road	C4
Glover Street	A1-B1
Grove Street	B2
Hewell Road	A4
Holloway Drive	B1-C1-C2
Holloway Lane	B2-C2-C1
Ipsley Street	A2-B2
Lodge Road	B1-B2
Market Place	A3-A2-B2
Marsden Road	B1-B2
Maysfields	A1
Meadow Hill Road	C3-C4
Melen Street	A3-A4
Millsborough Road	B1-B2
Mount Pleasant	A1-A2
Mount Street	A1-B1
Myrtle Avenue	A1
Oakley Road	A2
Orchard Street	A2
Oswald Street	A2
Other Road	B2-B3
Parsons Road	A1
Peakman Street	B3
Plymouth Road North	A2-A3
Prospect Hill	A2-B2
Queen Street	B2
Ringway	B2-A2-A3-B3
St. George's Road	B2-C2
Sillins Avenue	C1-C2
Smallwood Street	B2
South Mead Crescent	B1
South Street	A2
Stevenson Avenue	C2-C1
Summer Street	A2-B2
Sycamore Avenue	A1
Tunnell Drive	A1-B1
Unicorn Hill	A3
Union Street	B1
West Avenue	A1-A2
West Street	A2
Windsor Street	A3

BROMSGROVE

Bant Mill Road	C1
Birmingham Road	C3-C4
Blackmore Lane	C4
Broad Street	A4
Cedar Drive	C1
Central Road	C1-C2
Chapel Street	B2-B3
Churchfields	B3-B4
Churchfields Close	A4-B4
Churchfields Road	A4-B4
Church Lane	A2-A3-B3
Church Road	A3-A4
Church Street	B3
College Road	B2-C2
Conway Road	B1
Crabtree Drive	A4
Crabtree Lane	A4-A3-B3
East Road	C1-C2
Factory Lane	A1
Fordhouse Road	C1
Ford Road	A1
Garibaldi Terrace	B1
Hanover Street	A2
High Street	B2-B3
Hill Lane	A2-B2-B1
Kenyon Close	B1
Kidderminster Road	A2-A3
Market Street	B2-B3
Mill Lane	B3
Moorfield Drive	A4
New Road	A3
New Road	B2-C2-C1
North Road	C2
Old Station Road	B1
Parkside	B3
Perry Lane	A2
Providence Road	A4-B4
Recreation Road	B3
St John Street	A2-B2
Sanders Road	A1
School Drive	C3-C4
Station Street	B2
Stourbridge Road	B4-C4-B3-C3
Stratford Road	C3
Sydney Road	A4
The Crescent	B2
Victoria Road	C4
West Road	C1-C2-C3
Willow Close	A3
Willow Gardens	A3-A4
Windsor Gardens	B2
Windsor Street	B2-B3-C3
Worcester Road	A1-A2-B2

KIDDERMINSTER

Adam Street	A2
Albert Road	E3-E4
Anchorfield	D3
Barnetts Close	F1
Barnetts Lane	E1-F1
Baxter Avenue	D4
Belvedere Close	F2
Bennett Street	A4-B4
Bewdley Hill	A2-A3
Bewdley Road	A3-B3-B4
Birmingham Road	D4-E4-F4
Blackwell Street	C4-D4
Blakebrooke	A3-A4
Blakebrooke Close	A4
Borrington Road	F1-F2
Brinton Crescent	A1
Bromsgrove Street	D3-D4
Brooke Street	A3
Broom Crescent	F3
Broomfield Road	A4
Bull Ring	C3
Castle Road	B2-C2
Cedar Crescent	A4
Cedar Drive	A4
Chaddesley Road	E3-E2-F2
Cherry Orchard	D3-E3
Chester Road North	E2-E3-E4
Chester Road South	D1-E1-E2
Churchfields	C4
Church Street	C3-C4
Claines Crescent	F2-F3
Clarence Street	D3-E3-E4
Claughton Street	A2
Cobden Street	B3
Cobham Road	C1
College Road	C1-D1
Comberton Avenue	F2
Comberton Hill	D3-D2-E3-E2
Comberton Road	E2-F2-F1
Connaught Avenue	A1
Coronation Way	F2-F3
Corporation Street	C2-C3
Coventry Street	C4-D4
Crane Street	A4
Crescent Road	B3
Dixon Street	C2-D2
Doverdale Avenue	F3
East Street	D3
Eastwood Drive	F2
Elm Road	E3-E4
Farefield	E2
Findon Street	D3-D4
Franche Road	A4-B4
Franchise Street	A2-B2-B3
Gamson Close	C1
George Street	D3
Gilbert Scott Way	D4
Granville Crescent	F4
Greatfield Road	A2
Green Street	C1-C2-D2-D3
Griffin Avenue	D1
Grosvenor Avenue	E3-E4
Haberley Road	A4
Haberley Street	A4-B4
Hardy Avenue	F3-F4
Hawford Avenue	F3
Hemming Street	A1-A2
High Street	C3
Hill Grove Crescent	E2-F2
Holman Street	A2-B2
Holmcroft Road	F2-F3
Hoo Road	D1-D2
Hume Street	A2-B2
Inner Ring Road	C4-D4-D3-D2-D1-C1
Larches Road	B1
Lea Street	E3
Leswell Grove	D4
Lewsell Lane	D4
Leswell Street	D3-D4
Linden Avenue	E4-F4
Linden Grove	E4
Lorne Street	E2-E3
Lyndholm Road	E4-F4
Market Street	C3
Mason Road	A4-B4
Merton Close	F4
Mill Lane	B4-B4
Mill Street	B4
New Road	C1-C2-C3-D3
Norton Road	F3
Oakhill Avenue	D1
Offmore Road	D3-E3
Oldnall Road	E1-E2
Oxford Street	C3-D3
Park Butts Ringway	B3-B4-C3-C4
Park Lane	B1-B2-C2-C3-B3
Park Street	B3-C3-C2
Patterson Row	B3
Peel Street	B3
Pineridge Drive	A3
Plimsoll Street	B3
Poplar Road	A1
Quantock Drive	E4
Radford Avenue	D4
Russell Road	E1-E2
St. George's Terrace	D3-E3
St. John's Avenue	A3
St. John's Street	B4
Shakespeare Drive	F4
Sheraton Drive	F4
Shrubery Street	C4
Somerleyton Avenue	F2-F3
Spencer Street	A1-A2
Stourport Road	B1-C1
Stretton Road	A1
Sutton Road	A3-A2-A1-B1
Talbot Street	A2-B2
The Patios	A4
Tompkinson Drive	A1
Towers Close	F2
Vicar Street	C3
Villiers Street	E3
Washington Street	A2
Waterloo Street	D4
White House Road	C1
Willis Street	A2
Woodfield Crescent	B2-B3
Woodfield Street	B4
Wood Street	B2-B3
Woodward Road	A1
Worcester Road	C1
Worcester Street	C4-C3-D3
Yew Tree Road	E2-E3

BROMSGROVE
The 'String of Horses' at the Avoncroft Museum of Buildings is one of the many historic buildings dismantled and brought here for reconstruction, when their existence was threatened by development.

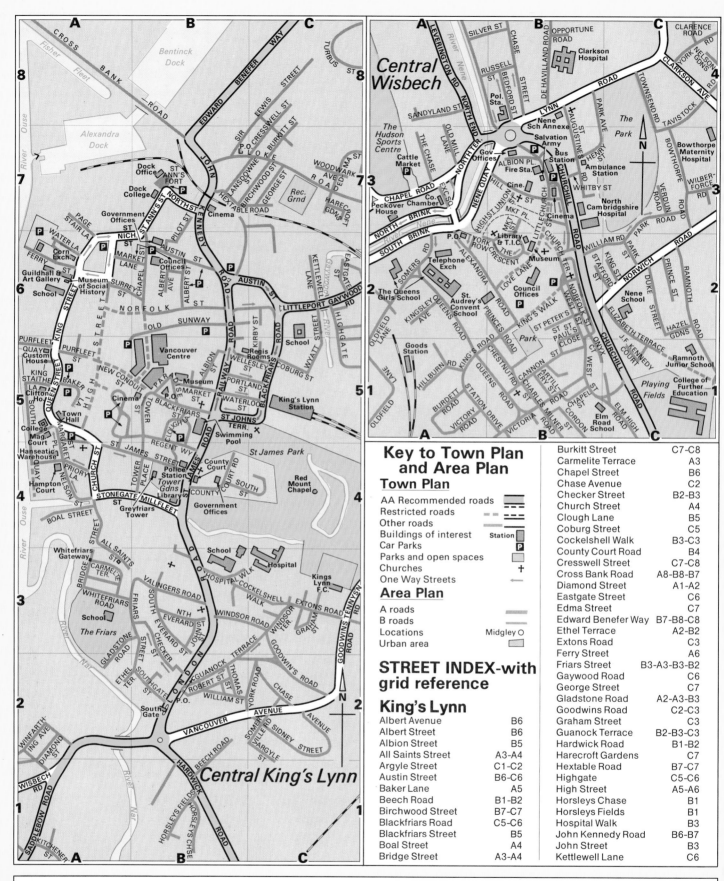

Key to Town Plan and Area Plan

Town Plan

AA Recommended roads	▬▬▬
Restricted roads	▬ ▬ ▬
Other roads	▬▬▬
Buildings of interest	Station ▮
Car Parks	P
Parks and open spaces	▮
Churches	+
One Way Streets	←

Area Plan

A roads	▬▬▬
B roads	▬▬▬
Locations	Midgley ○
Urban area	▮

STREET INDEX-with grid reference

King's Lynn

Albert Avenue	B6
Albert Street	B6
Albion Street	B5
All Saints Street	A3-A4
Argyle Street	C1-C2
Austin Street	B6-C6
Baker Lane	A5
Beech Road	B1-B2
Birchwood Street	B7-C7
Blackfriars Road	C5-C6
Blackfriars Street	B5
Boal Street	A4
Bridge Street	A3-A4

Burkitt Street	C7-C8
Carmelite Terrace	A3
Chapel Street	B6
Chase Avenue	C2
Checker Street	B2-B3
Church Street	A4
Clough Lane	B5
Coburg Street	C5
Cockelshell Walk	B3-C3
County Court Road	B4
Cresswell Street	C7-C8
Cross Bank Road	A8-B8-B7
Diamond Street	A1-A2
Eastgate Street	C6
Edma Street	C7
Edward Benefer Way	B7-B8-C8
Ethel Terrace	A2-B2
Extons Road	C3
Ferry Street	A6
Friars Street	B3-A3-B3-B2
Gaywood Road	C6
George Street	C7
Gladstone Road	A2-A3-B3
Goodwins Road	C2-C3
Graham Street	C3
Guanock Terrace	B2-B3-C3
Hardwick Road	B1-B2
Harecroft Gardens	C7
Hextable Road	B7-C7
Highgate	C5-C6
High Street	A5-A6
Horsleys Chase	B1
Horsleys Fields	B1
Hospital Walk	B3
John Kennedy Road	B6-B7
John Street	B3
Kettlewell Lane	C6

King's Lynn

Pilgrims on their way to Walsingham would stop at the 15th-century Red Mount Chapel in the Walks at King's Lynn, and commercial prominence really began here as far back as the 13th century, when this Great Ouse port had connections with the German trading towns of the Hanseatic League. Prosperity continued until well into the 18th century, and although modern expansion has brought new shopping, sports and entertainment facilities to the town centre, a number of medieval buildings survive, including the Guild Hall of St George (now a theatre) and the Guild Hall of Holy Trinity. St Margaret's Church still has portions of its Norman tower. The Lynn Museum in Old Market Street looks at the history of the area, and is complemented by the Museum of Social History in King Street.

Wisbech is at the heartland of soft fruit cultivation, and is especially known for its strawberries. Set in the low-lying fens and linked to the Wash by the River Nene, it has some fine examples of Georgian architecture in the North and South Brinks which line the river on either side. Eighteenth-century Peckover House now belongs to the National Trust; also of interest is the Clarkson Memorial in Bridge Street, erected in memory of Thomas Clarkson, who campaigned for the abolition of slavery.

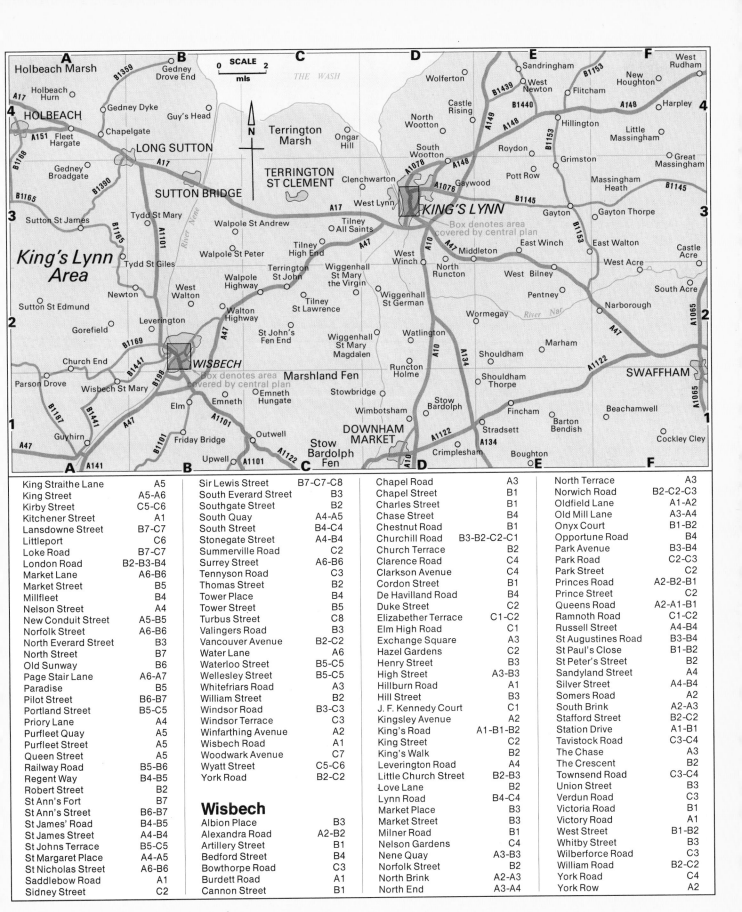

King's Lynn Area map (Holbeach, Long Sutton, Sutton Bridge, Wisbech, King's Lynn, Swaffham, Downham Market)

King Straithe Lane	A5		Sir Lewis Street	B7-C7-C8
King Street	A5-A6		South Everard Street	B3
Kirby Street	C5-C6		Southgate Street	B2
Kitchener Street	A1		South Quay	A4-A5
Lansdowne Street	B7-C7		South Street	B4-C4
Littleport	C6		Stonegate Street	A4-B4
Loke Road	B7-C7		Summerville Road	C2
London Road	B2-B3-B4		Surrey Street	A6-B6
Market Lane	A6-B6		Tennyson Road	C3
Market Street	B5		Thomas Street	B2
Millfleet	B4		Tower Place	B4
Nelson Street	A4		Tower Street	B5
New Conduit Street	A5-B5		Turbus Street	C8
Norfolk Street	A6-B6		Valingers Road	B3
North Everard Street	B3		Vancouver Avenue	B2-C2
North Street	B7		Water Lane	A6
Old Sunway	B6		Waterloo Street	B5-C5
Page Stair Lane	A6-A7		Wellesley Street	B5-C5
Paradise	B5		Whitefriars Road	A3
Pilot Street	B6-B7		William Street	B2
Portland Street	B5-C5		Windsor Road	B3-C3
Priory Lane	A4		Windsor Terrace	C3
Purfleet Quay	A5		Winfarthing Avenue	A2
Purfleet Street	A5		Wisbech Road	A1
Queen Street	A5		Woodwark Avenue	C7
Railway Road	B5-B6		Wyatt Street	C5-C6
Regent Way	B4-B5		York Road	B2-C2
Robert Street	B2			
St Ann's Fort	B7			
St Ann's Street	B6-B7			
St James' Road	B4-B5			
St James Street	A4-B4			
St Johns Terrace	B5-C5			
St Margaret Place	A4-A5			
St Nicholas Street	A6-B6			
Saddlebow Road	A1			
Sidney Street	C2			

Wisbech

Albion Place	B3		Chapel Road	A3		North Terrace	A3
Alexandra Road	A2-B2		Chapel Street	B1		Norwich Road	B2-C2-C3
Artillery Street	B1		Charles Street	B1		Oldfield Lane	A1-A2
Bedford Street	B4		Chase Street	B4		Old Mill Lane	A3-A4
Bowthorpe Road	C3		Chestnut Road	B1		Onyx Court	B1-B2
Burdett Road	A1		Churchill Road	B3-B2-C2-C1		Opportune Road	B4
Cannon Street	B1		Church Terrace	B2		Park Avenue	B3-B4
			Clarence Road	C4		Park Road	C2-C3
			Clarkson Avenue	C4		Park Street	C2
			Cordon Street	B1		Princes Road	A2-B2-B1
			De Havilland Road	B4		Prince Street	C2
			Duke Street	C2		Queens Road	A2-A1-B1
			Elizabether Terrace	C1-C2		Ramnoth Road	C1-C2
			Elm High Road	C1		Russell Street	A4-B4
			Exchange Square	A3		St Augustines Road	B3-B4
			Hazel Gardens	C2		St Paul's Close	B1-B2
			Henry Street	B3		St Peter's Street	B2
			High Street	A3-B3		Sandyland Street	A4
			Hillburn Road	A1		Silver Street	A4-B4
			Hill Street	B3		Somers Road	A2
			J. F. Kennedy Court	C1		South Brink	A2-A3
			Kingsley Avenue	A2		Stafford Street	B2-C2
			King's Road	A1-B1-B2		Station Drive	A1-B1
			King Street	C2		Tavistock Road	C3-C4
			King's Walk	B2		The Chase	A3
			Leverington Road	A4		The Crescent	B2
			Little Church Street	B2-B3		Townsend Road	C3-C4
			Love Lane	B2		Union Street	B3
			Lynn Road	B4-C4		Verdun Road	C3
			Market Place	B3		Victoria Road	B1
			Market Street	B3		Victory Road	A1
			Milner Road	B1		West Street	B1-B2
			Nelson Gardens	C4		Whitby Street	B3
			Nene Quay	A3-B3		Wilberforce Road	C3
			Norfolk Street	B2		William Road	B2-C2
			North Brink	A2-A3		York Road	C4
			North End	A3-A4		York Row	A2

KINGS LYNN
Designed by local architect Henry Bell and dating back to 1683, the elegant Old Customs House bears witness to a longstanding importance as a trading centre serving both the Midlands (via inland waterways) and Europe.

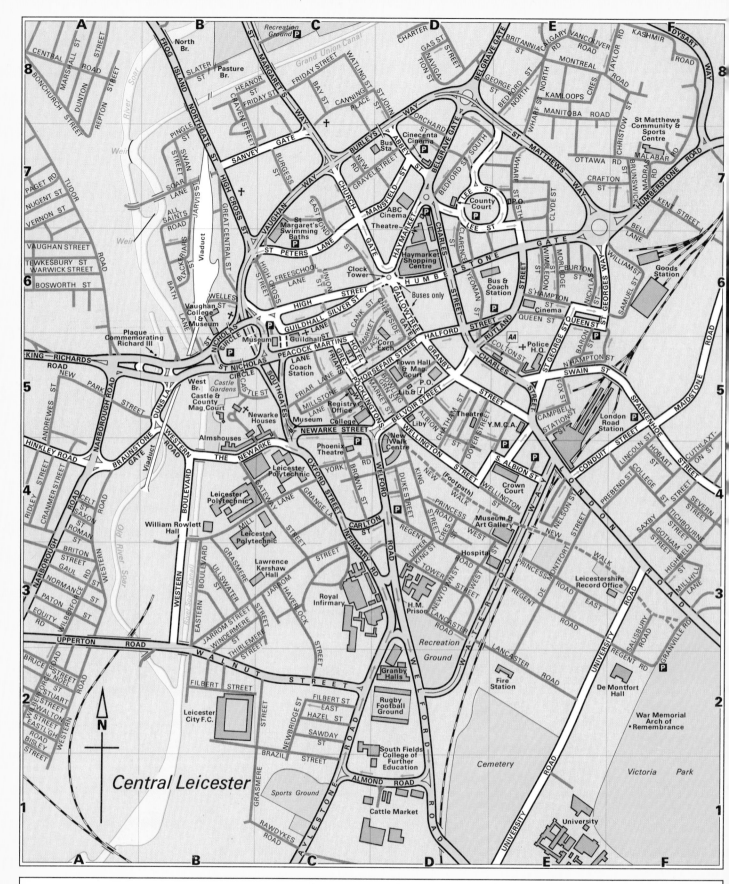

Leicester

A regional capital in Roman times, Leicester has retained many buildings from its eventful and distinguished past. Today the city is a thriving modern place, a centre for industry and commerce, serving much of the Midlands. Among the most outstanding monuments from the past is the Jewry Wall, a great bastion of Roman masonry. Close by are remains of the Roman baths and

several other contemporary buildings. Attached is a museum covering all periods from prehistoric times to 1500. Numerous other museums include the Wygston's House Museum of Costume, with displays covering the period 1769 to 1924; Newarke House, with collections showing changing social conditions in Leicester through four hundred years; and Leicestershire Museum and Art Gallery, with collections of drawings, paintings, ceramics, geology and natural history.

The medieval Guildhall has many features of interest, including a great hall, library and police cells. Leicester's castle, although remodelled in the 17th century, retains a 12th-century great hall. The Church of St Mary de Castro, across the road from the castle, has features going back at least as far as Norman times; while St Nicholas's Church is even older, with Roman and Saxon foundations. St Martin's Cathedral dates mainly from the 13th to 15th centuries and has a notable Bishop's throne.

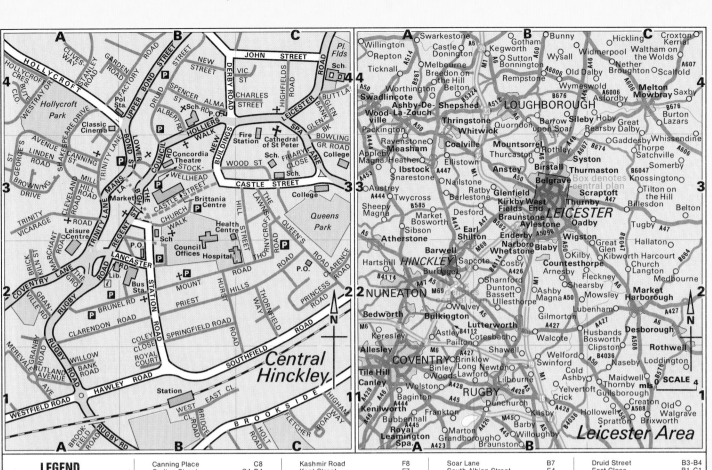

Central Hinckley

Leicester Area

LEGEND

Town Plan

AA Recommended route	
Restricted roads	
Other roads	
Buildings of interest	
Car parks	**P**
Parks and open spaces	
One way streets	→

Area Plan

A roads	
B roads	
Locations	Creaton ○
Urban area	

Street Index with Grid Reference

Leicester

Abbey Street	D7
Albion Street	D4-D5
All Saints Road	B7
Almond Road	C1-D1
Andrewes Street	A4-A5
Aylestone Road	C1-C2
Baron Street	E5-E6
Bath Lane	B5-B6
Bay Street	E8
Bedford Street North	E8
Bedford Street South	D7
Belgrave Gate	D7-D8-E8
Bell Lane	F6-F7
Belvoir Street	D5
Bisley Street	A1-A2
Blackfriars Street	B6
Bonchurch Street	A7-A8
Bosworth Street	A6
Bowling Green Street	D5
Braunstone Gate	A4-B4-B5
Brazil Street	C1-C2
Britannia Street	E8
Briton Street	A3
Brown Street	C4
Bruce Street	A2
Brunswick Street	F7
Burgess Street	C7
Burleys Way	C7-D7-D8
Burton Street	E6
Calgary Road	E8
Campbell Street	E5
Cank Street	C6-D6

Canning Place	C8
Carlton Street	C4-D4
Castle Street	B5-C5
Celt Street	A4
Central Road	A8
Charles Street	D7-D6-D5-E5
Charter Street	D8
Chatham Street	D4-D5
Cheapside	D5-D6
Christow Street	F7-F8
Church Gate	C7-C6-D6
Clarence Street	D6-D7
Clyde Street	E6-E7
College Street	F4
Colton Street	D5-E5
Conduit Street	E4-F4-F5
Crafton Street	E7-F7
Cranmer Street	A4
Craven Street	B7-B8
Crescent Street	D4
Cuthlaxton Street	F4-F5
De Montfort Street	E3-E4
Dover Street	D4-D5
Duke Street	D5
Dunns Lane	B5
Dunton Street	A8
Dysart Way	F8
East Bond Street	C6-C7
Eastern Boulevard	B3-B4
Eastleigh Road	A2
Equity Road	A3
Filbert Street	B2-C2
Filbert Street East	C2
Fox Street	E5
Freeschool Lane	C6
Friar Lane	C5
Friday Street	B8-C8
Frog Island	B8
Gallowtree Gate	D6
Gas Street	D8
Gateway Street	B4-C4-C3
Gaul Street	A3
George Street	D8-E8
Gotham Street	F3-F4
Granby Street	D5-E5
Grange Lane	C4
Granville Road	F2-F3
Grasmere Street	B4-B3-C3-C2-C1-B1
Gravel Street	C7-D7
Great Central Street	B6-B7
Greyfriars	C5
Guildhall Lane	C6
Halford Street	D5-D6-E6
Haverlock Street	C2-C3
Haymarket	D6-D7
Hazel Street	C2
Heanor Street	B8-C8
High Cross Street	B7-B6-C6
Highfield Street	F3
High Street	C6-D6
Hinkley Road	A4
Hobart Street	F4
Horsefair Street	C5-D5
Hotel Street	C5
Humberstone Gate	D6-E6
Humberstone Road	F7
Infirmary Road	C4-C3-D3
Jarrom Street	B3-C3
Jarvis Street	B7
Kamloops Crescent	E8

Kashmir Road	F8
Kent Street	F7
King Richards Road	A5
King Street	D4
Lancaster Road	D3-E3-E2
Lee Street	D6-D7-E7
Lincoln Street	F4-F5
London Road	E5-E4-F4-F3
Madras Road	F7
Maidstone Road	F5-F6
Malabar Road	F7
Manitoba Road	E8
Mansfield Street	C7-D7
Market Place	C5-C6-D6
Market Street	D5
Marshall Street	A8
Morledge Street	E6
Montreal Road	E8-F8
Mill Hill Lane	F3
Mill Lane	B4-C4
Millstone Lane	C5
Narborough Road	A3-A4-A5
Navigation Street	D8
Nelson Street	E4
Newarke Street	C5
New Bridge Street	C2
New Park Street	A5-B5
New Road	C7
Newtown Street	D3
New Walk	D4-E4-E3-F3
Nicholas Street	E6
Noel Street	A2
Northampton Street	E5
Northgate Street	B7-B8
Norman Street	A3
Nugent Street	A7
Orchard Street	D7-D8
Ottawa Road	E7-F7
Oxford Street	C4
Paget Road	A7
Paton Street	A3
Peacock Lane	C5
Pingle Street	B7
Pocklingtons Walk	C5-D5
Prebend Street	E4-F4
Princess Road East	E3-F3
Princess Road West	D4
Queen Street	E6
Rawdykes Road	B1-C1
Regent Road	D4-D3-E3-F3-F2
Repton Street	A7-A8
Ridley Street	A4
Roman Street	A4
Rutland Street	D5-E5-E6
St George Street	E5-E6
St Georges Way	E6-F6
St John Street	D3
St Margaret's Way	B8-C8-C7
St Martins	C5
St Mathews Way	E6-E7
St Nicholas Circle	B6-B5-C5
St Peters Lane	C6
Salisbury Road	F2-F3
Samuel Stuart	F6
Sanvey Gate	B7-C7
Sawday Street	C2
Saxby Street	F4
Saxon Street	A4
Severn Street	F4
Silver Street	C6
Slater Street	B8

Soar Lane	B7
South Albion Street	E4
Southampton Street	E6
Southgates	C5
Sparkenhoe Street	F4-F5
Station Street	E5
Stuart Street	A2
Swain Street	E5-F5
Swan Street	B7
The Newarke	B4-C4
Taylor Road	E8-F8
Tewkesbury Street	A6
Thirlemere Street	B2-B3-C3
Tichbourne Street	F3-F4
Tower Street	D5
Tudor Road	A6-A7-A8
Ullswater Street	B3
Union Street	C6
University Road	E1-E2-E3-F3
Upper King Street	D3-D4
Upperton Road	A3-B3-B2
Vancouver Road	E8
Vaughan Way	C6-C7
Vaughan Street	A6
Vernon Street	A6-A7
Walnut Street	B3-B2-C2
Walton Street	A2
Warwick Street	A6
Waterloo Way	D2-D3-E3-E4
Watling Street	C8
Welford Road	D1-D2-D3-D4
Welles Street	B6
Wellington Street	D4-E4-D5
Western Boulevard	B3-B4
Western Road	A1-A2-A3-A4-B4-B5
West Street	D3-E3-E4
Wharf Street North	E7-E8
Wharf Street South	E7
Wilberforce Road	A2-A3
William Street	F6
Wimbledon Street	E6
Windermere Street	B2-B3-C3
Yeoman Street	D6
York Road	C4

Hinkley

Albert Road	B4
Alma Road	B4
Bowling Green Road	C3
Brick Kiln Street	A2
Bridge Road	B1
Brookfield Road	A1
Brookside	B1-C1
Browning Drive	A3
Brunel Road	A2-B2
Bute Close	A4
Butt Lane	C4
Canning Street	A3
Castle Street	B3-C3
Charles Street	C4
Church Walk	B3
Clarence Road	C2
Clarendon Road	A2-B2
Cleveland Road	A3
Clivesway	A4
Coley Close	B2
Council Road	B3
Coventry Lane	A2
Derby Road	B4

Druid Street	B3-B4
East Close	B1-C1
Factory Road	A4-B4
Fletcher Road	C1
Friary Close	C3
Garden Road	A4-B4
Glen Bank	C4
Granby Road	A1-A2
Granville Road	A2
Hawley Road	A1-B1
Higham Way	C1
Highfields Road	C4
Hill Street	C2-C3
Holliers Walk	B3-B4
Hollycroft	A4
Hollycroft Crescent	A4
Holt Road	C1
Hurst Road	B2-C2
John Street	C4
Lancaster Road	A2-B2
Leicester Road	C4
Linden Road	A3
Lower Bond Street	B3-B4
Mansion Lane	A3-B3
Marchant Road	A2-A3
Merevale Avenue	A1
Mill Hill Road	A3
Mount Road	B2-C2
New Buildings	B3-B4
New Street	B4
Priest Hills Road	B2-C2
Princess Road	C2
Queens Road	C2-C3
Regent Street	A2-A3-B3
Royal Court	B1
Rugby Road	A2-A1-B1
Rutland Avenue	A1
St George's Avenue	A3-A4
Shakespeare Drive	A4
Southfield Road	B1-C1-C2
Spa Lane	C3-C4
Spencer Street	C4
Springfield Road	B2
Stanley Road	B2
Station Road	B1-B2
Stockwellhead	B3
The Borough	B3
The Grove	A2
The Lawns	C3
Thornfield Way	C2
Thornycroft Road	C2-C3
Trinity Lane	A2-A3-A4-B4
Trinity Vicarage Road	A3
Upper Bond Street	B4
Victoria Street	C4
West Close	B1
Westday Drive	A4
Westfield Road	A1
Willow Bank Road	A1
Wood Street	B3-C3

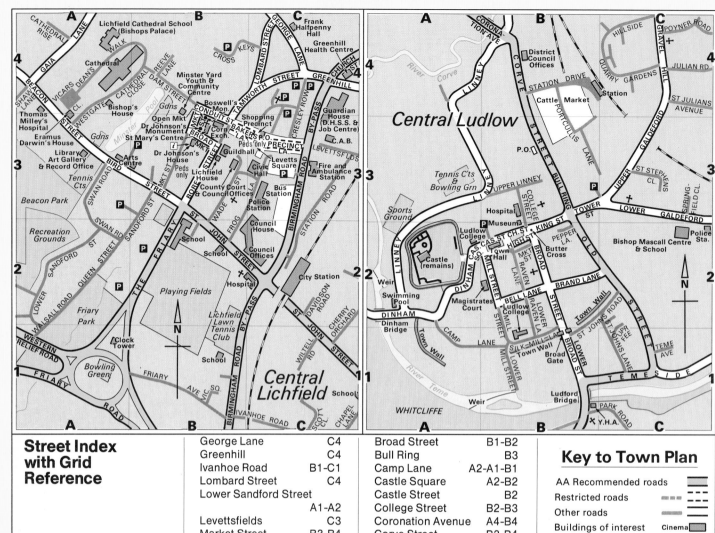

Central Lichfield

Central Ludlow

Street Index with Grid Reference

Lichfield

Bakers Lane	B3-C3
Beacon Street	A3-A4
Bird Street	A3-B3
Birmingham Road By-Pass	B1-B2-C2-C3-C4
Bore Street	B3
Broad Market	B3
Cathedral Close	A4-B4
Cathedral Rise	A4
Chapel Lane	C1
Cherry Orchard	C1-C2
Church Street	C4
Conduit Street	B3-B4
Cresley Row	C3-C4
Crosskeys	B4-C4
Dam Street	B4
Davidson Road	C2
Dean's Walk	A4-B4
Friary Avenue	B1
Friary Road	A1-B1
Frog Lane	B2-B3-C3
Gaia Lane	A4

George Lane	C4
Greenhill	C4
Ivanhoe Road	B1-C1
Lombard Street	C4
Lower Sandford Street	A1-A2
Levettsfields	C3
Market Street	B3-B4
Precinct Lane	C3
Queen Street	A2
Reeve Lane	B4
St John Street	B3-B2-C2-C1
Sandford Street	A2-B2-B3
Scott Close	C1
Shaw Lane	A4
Station Road	C2-C3
Swan Road	A2-A3
Tamworth Street	B3-B4-C4
The Friary	A2-B2-B3
Vicars Close	A4
Victoria Square	B1
Wade Street	B2-B3
Walsall Road	A1-A2
Western Relief Road	A1
Westgate	A3-A4
Wittell Road	C1

Ludlow

Bell Lane	B2
Brand Lane	B2-C2

Broad Street	B1-B2
Bull Ring	B3
Camp Lane	A2-A1-B1
Castle Square	A2-B2
Castle Street	B2
College Street	B2-B3
Coronation Avenue	A4-B4
Corve Street	B3-B4
Dinham	A2
Gravel Hill	C4
High Street	B2
Hillside	C4
Julian Road	C4
King Street	B2-B3
Linney	A2-A3-B3-A3-A4-B4
Lower Broad Street	B1
Lower Galdeford	C2-C3
Lower Mill Street	B1
Lower Raven Lane	B1-B2
Market Street	B2
Mill Street	B1-B2
Old Street	B3-B2-C2-C1
Park Road	B1-C1
Pepper Lane	B2
Portcullis Lane	B4-B3-C3
Poyner Road	C4
Quarry Gardens	C4
Raven Lane	B2
St Johns Lane	C1-C2
St Johns Road	B1-B2-C2
St Julians Avenue	C4
St Stephens Close	C3

Key to Town Plan

AA Recommended roads	
Restricted roads	
Other roads	
Buildings of interest	Cinema
Parks and open spaces	
Car Parks	P
Churches	+

Silk Mill Lane	B1
Springfield Close	C3
Station Drive	B4
Teme Avenue	C1
Temeside	B1-C1
Tower Street	B3-C3
Upper Fee	C1-C2
Upper Galdeford	C3-C4
Upper Linney	B3

Lichfield Three graceful spires known as the 'Ladies of the Vale' soar up from Lichfield's Cathedral of St Mary and St Chad. Constructed in the 13th century and combining early English and decorated Gothic styles, the Cathedral is the most outstanding feature of this attractive city, which has retained a distinctly rural appearance despite a good deal of industrial expansion.

Most distinguished son of Lichfield is Dr Samuel Johnson and his father's 18th-century house in Market Square (which served the family as a dwelling and a bookshop) has been restored and converted into a museum. Johnson's birthday (18 September) is commemorated on the nearest Saturday by a procession from the Guild Hall.

Ludlow, built on a steep hill washed on two sides by the Rivers Corve and Teme, has, since earliest times, been recognised as a strategic site, and the Normans were quick to take advantage of this. Their castle, now an impressive ruin crowning the hilltop, looks out over the Welsh Marches. The town beneath is a charming mixture of wide Georgian streets and narrow medieval alleyways where 18th-century brick and stucco rubs shoulders with half-timbered Tudor buildings with leaning walls and steeply-pitched roofs. The most famous of all the timbered buildings is the Feathers Hotel, although it has plenty of competitors, and the dignified stone Butter Cross houses the town's museum.

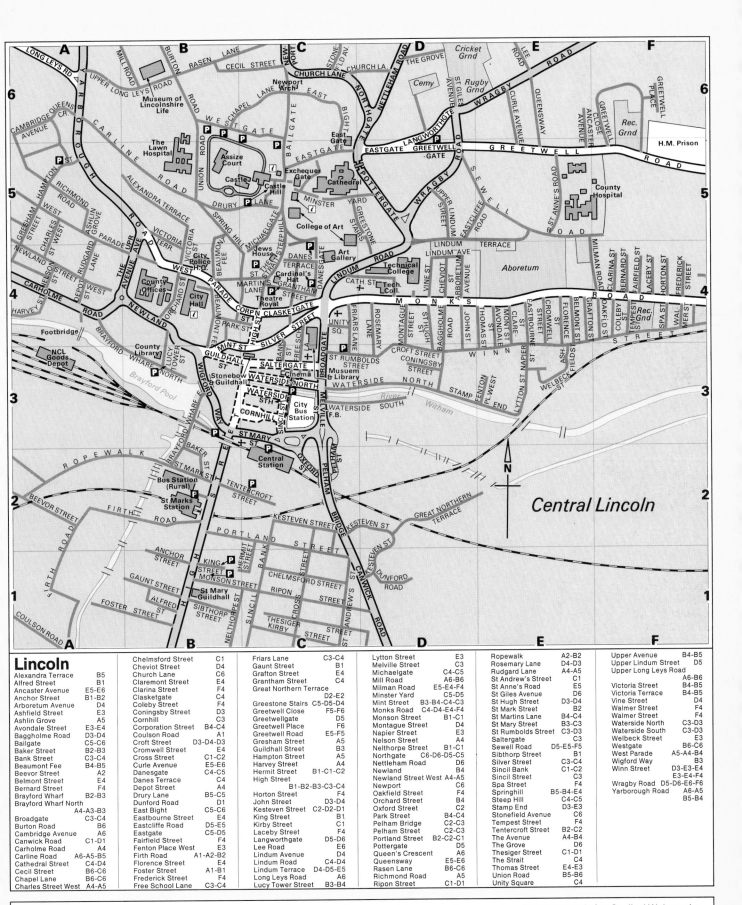

Lincoln

Alexandra Terrace	B5	Chelmsford Street	C1	Friars Lane	C3-C4	Lytton Street	E3	Ropewalk	A2-B2	Upper Avenue	B4-B5
Alfred Street	B1	Cheviot Street	D4	Gaunt Street	B1	Melville Street	C3	Rosemary Lane	D4-D3	Upper Lindum Street	D5
Ancaster Avenue	E5-E6	Church Lane	C6	Grafton Street	E4	Michaelgate	C4-C5	Rudgard Lane	A4-A5	Upper Long Leys Road	
Anchor Street	B1-B2	Claremont Street	E4	Grantham Street	C4	Mill Road	A6-B6	St Andrew's Street	C1		A6-B6
Arboretum Avenue	D4	Clarina Street	F4	Great Northern Terrace		Milman Road	E5-E4-F4	St Anne's Road	E5	Victoria Street	B4-B5
Ashfield Street	E3	Clasketgate	C4		D2-E2	Minster Yard	C5-D5	St Giles Avenue	D6	Victoria Terrace	B4-B5
Ashlin Grove	A5	Coleby Street	F4	Greestone Stairs	C5-D5-D4	Mint Street	B3-B4-C4-C3	St Hugh Street	D3-D4	Vine Street	D4
Avondale Street	E3-E4	Coningsby Street	D3	Greetwell Close	F5-F6	Monks Road	C4-D4-E4-F4	St Mark Street	B2	Walmer Street	F4
Bagholme Road	D3-D4	Cornhill	C3	Greetwellgate	D5	Monson Street	B1-C1	St Martins Lane	B4-C4	Walmer Street	F4
Bailgate	C5-C6	Corporation Street	B4-C4	Greetwell Place	F6	Montague Street	D4	St Mary Street	B3-C3	Waterside North	C3-D3
Baker Street	B2-B3	Coulson Road	A1	Greetwell Road	E5-F5	Montague Street	D4	St Rumbolds Street	C3-D3	Waterside South	C3-D3
Bank Street	C3-C4	Croft Street	D3-D4-D3	Gresham Street	A5	Napier Street	E3	Saltergate	C3	Welbeck Street	E3
Beaumont Fee	B4-B5	Cromwell Street	E4	Guildhall Street	B3	Nelson Street	A4	Sewell Road	D5-E5-F5	Westgate	B6-C6
Beevor Street	A2	Cross Street	C1-C2	Hampton Street	A5	Nelthorpe Street	B1-C1	Sibthorp Street	B1	West Parade	A5-A4-B4
Belmont Street	E4	Curle Avenue	E5-E6	Harvey Street	A4	Newland	B4	Silver Street	C3-C4	Wigford Way	B3
Bernard Street	F4	Danesgate	C4-C5	Hermit Street	B1-C1-C2	Newland Street West	A4-A5	Sincil Bank	C1-C2	Winn Street	D3-E3-E4
Brayford Wharf	B2-B3	Danes Terrace	C4	High Street		Newport	C6	Sincil Street	C3		E3-E4-F4
Brayford Wharf North		Depot Street	A4		B1-B2-B3-C3-C4	Oakfield Street	B4	Spa Street	F4	Wragby Road	D5-D6-E6-F6
	A4-A3-B3	Drury Lane	B5-C5	Horton Street	F4	Orchard Street	B4	Springhill	B5-B4-E4	Yarborough Road	A6-A5
Broadgate	C3-C4	Dunford Road	D1	John Street	D3-D4	Oxford Street	C2	Steep Hill	C4-C5		B5-B4
Burton Road	B6	East Bight	C5-C6	Kesteven Street	C2-D2-D1	Park Street	B4-C4	Stonefield Avenue	C6		
Cambridge Avenue	A6	Eastbourne Street	E4	King Street	B1	Pelham Bridge	C2-C3	Tempest Street	F4		
Canwick Road	C1-D1	Eastcliffe Road	D5-E5	Kirby Street	C1	Pelham Street	C2-C3	Tentercroft Street	B2-C2		
Carholme Road	A4	Eastgate	C5-D5	Laceby Street	F4	Portland Street	B2-C2-C1	The Avenue	A4-B4		
Carline Road	A6-A5-B5	Fairfield Street	F4	Langworthgate	D5-D6	Pottergate	D5	The Grove	D6		
Cathedral Street	C4-D4	Fenton Place West	E3	Lee Road	E6	Queen's Crescent	A6	Thesiger Street	C1-D1		
Cecil Street	B6-C6	Firth Road	A1-A2-B2	Lindum Avenue	D4	Queensway	E5-E6	The Strait	C4		
Chapel Lane	B6-C6	Florence Street	E4	Lindum Road	C4-D4	Rasen Lane	B6-C6	Thomas Street	E4-E3		
Charles Street West	A4-A5	Foster Street	A1-B1	Lindum Terrace	D4-D5-E5	Richmond Road	A5	Union Road	B5-B6		
		Frederick Street	F4	Long Leys Road	A6	Ripon Street	C1-D1	Unity Square	C4		
		Free School Lane	C3-C4	Lucy Tower Street	B3-B4						

Lincoln

The striking triple-spired cathedral of Lincoln, the third largest in England, dominates the countryside for miles. Its impressive west front, decorated with many statues, is all that remains of the first cathedral the Normans built, and most of the rest dates from the 13th century. Among its treasures is one of the four extant original copies of Magna Carta.

Built on a rugged limestone plateau above the River Witham, the cobbled streets of the medieval city straggle down the sides of the hill past old houses built from the same local honey-coloured limestone as the cathedral. Modern Lincoln owes much to engineering industries, but few tentacles of change have crept into the heart of the city where the oldest inhabited house in England, Aaron's House, can be found. Other places of interest include the quaintly-named Cardinal's Hat

– thought to be named after Cardinal Wolsey who was Bishop of Lincoln for one year. Newport Arch, at the end of the picturesque street called Bailgate, is a relic from the Roman city of Lincoln – *Lindum Colonia*. It is the only Roman gateway in the country still open to traffic. Complementing the cathedral in size if not in majesty is the Norman castle. It is possible to walk along the battlements and the old prison chapel provides a grim insight into the punishment meted out in less enlightened times.

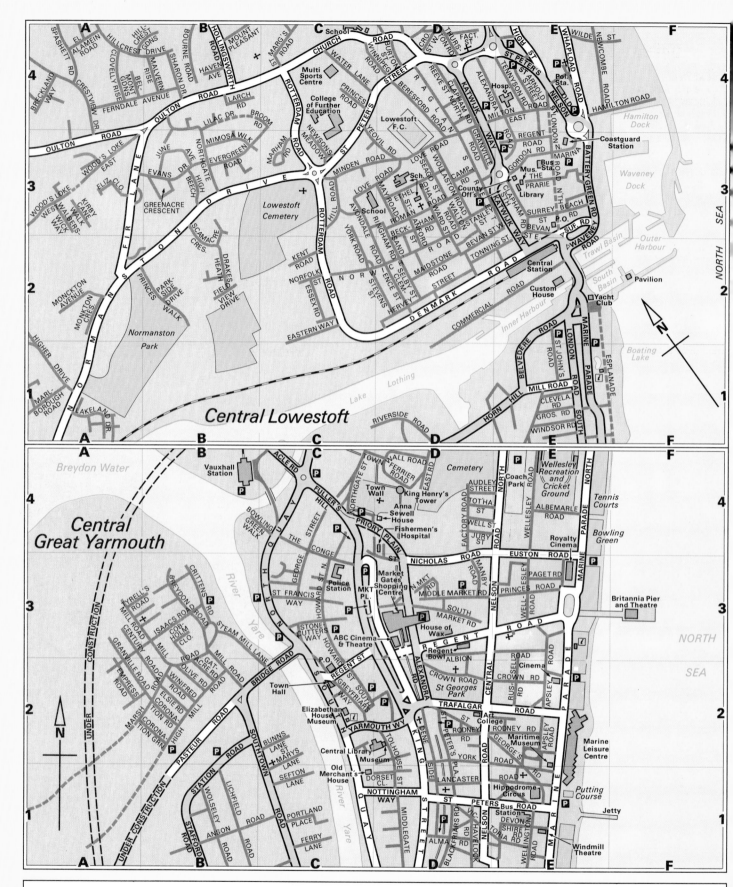

Lowestoft

Freshwater and sea fishing are a major attraction in this resort. Popular with families for over 100 years, it actually owes much of its prosperity to its busy port, which is the home of a major fishing fleet but is also well used today by vessels servicing the oil and gas industries.

Development has taken place within the town to improve its road system and shops, but the Maritime Museum at Sparrows Nest and Europa room collection of the Royal Naval Patrol Service Association give an insight into days gone by.

Great Yarmouth Miles of golden sand, gentle tides and the waterways of the Norfolk Broads make this a favoured holiday resort. Entertainment to suit every taste is on offer from morning till night, and children can choose from a vast selection of amenities like Pleasure Beach and Joyland. Amongst the older buildings and monuments to be seen in the town is the Nelson Column, and there are no less than eight museums, including the Maritime Museum of East Anglia. The Port (originally used by fishermen) dates at least as far back as the 16th century, and is now used by assorted vessels from Rotterdam and other European ports, and by traffic concerned with North Sea oil and gas exploration. The town's lifeboat station started in 1801, and the Royal National Lifeboat Institution base is at this point on the coast.

LEGEND

Town Plan

AA recommended route
Restricted roads
Other roads
Buildings of interest — Station
Car parks — P
Parks and open spaces

Area Plan

A roads
B roads
Locations — Westhead O
Urban area

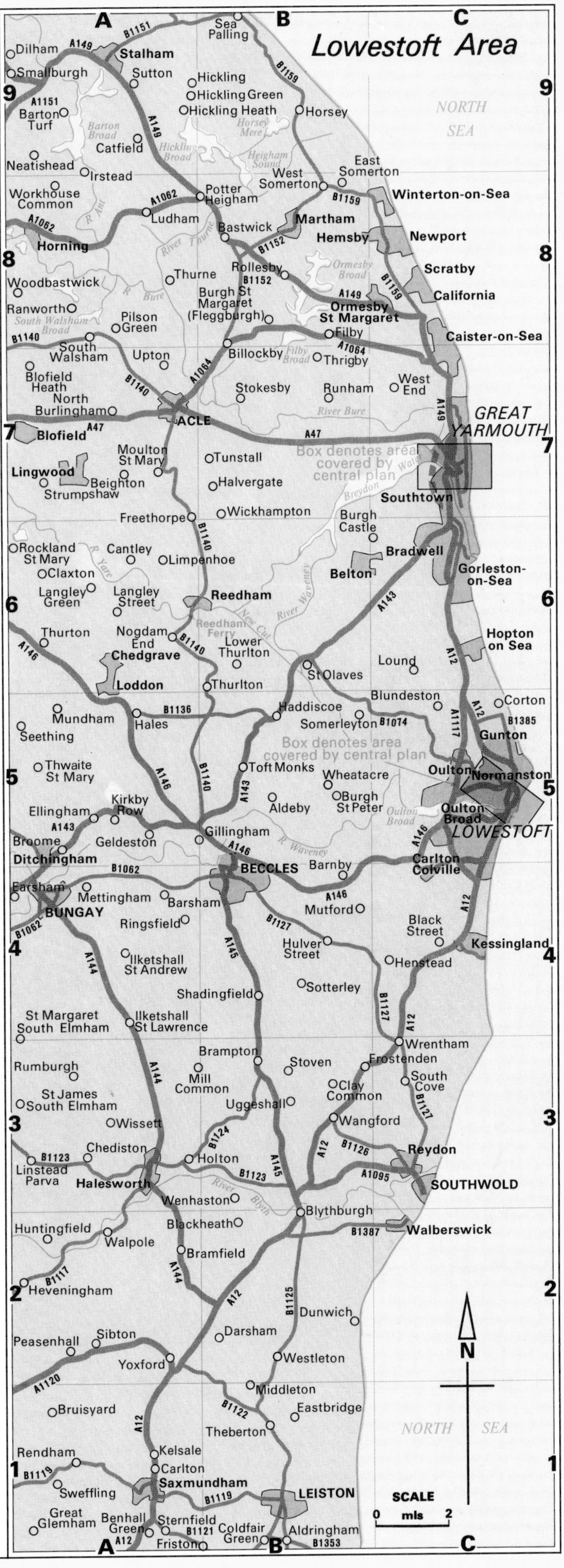

Lowestoft Area
A
B
C
9
8
7
6
5
4
3
2
1
NORTH SEA
Dilham
Stalham
Sea Palling
Smallburgh
Sutton
Hickling
Hickling Green
Hickling Heath
Horsey
Barton Turf
Barton Broad
Catfield
Hickling Broad
Horsey Mere
Heigham Sound
Neatishead
Irstead
West Somerton
East Somerton
Workhouse Common
Potter Heigham
Winterton-on-Sea
Ludham
Bastwick
Martham
Hemsby
Newport
Horning
River Thurne
Rollesby
Ormesby Broad
Scratby
Woodbastwick
Thurne
Burgh St Margaret (Fleggburgh)
California
Ormesby St Margaret
Ranworth
Pilson Green
South Walsham Broad
Filby
Caister-on-Sea
South Walsham
Upton
Billockby
Filby Broad
Thrigby
Blofield Heath
Stokesby
Runham
West End
North Burlingham
River Bure
GREAT YARMOUTH
Blofield
ACLE
Lingwood
Moulton St Mary
Tunstall
Box denotes area covered by central plan
Beighton
Strumpshaw
Halvergate
Southtown
Breydon Water
Freethorpe
Wickhampton
Burgh Castle
Rockland St Mary
Cantley
Limpenhoe
Bradwell
Claxton
Gorleston-on-Sea
Langley Green
Langley Street
Reedham
Belton
River Yare
Reedham Ferry
River Waveney
New Cut
Thurton
Nogdam End
Lower Thurlton
Hopton on Sea
Chedgrave
St Olaves
Lound
Loddon
Thurlton
Blundeston
Corton
Mundham
Hales
Haddiscoe
Somerleyton
Gunton
Seething
Box denotes area covered by central plan
Thwaite St Mary
Toft Monks
Wheatacre
Oulton
Normanston
Kirkby Row
Burgh St Peter
Oulton Broad
Ellingham
Aldeby
LOWESTOFT
Broome
Geldeston
Gillingham
River Waveney
Ditchingham
BECCLES
Barnby
Carlton Colville
Earsham
Mettingham
Barsham
BUNGAY
Mutford
Ringsfield
Black Street
Kessingland
Hulver Street
Ilketshall St Andrew
Henstead
Sotterley
Shadingfield
St Margaret South Elmham
Ilketshall St Lawrence
Wrentham
Brampton
Rumburgh
Stoven
Frostenden
Mill Common
South Cove
St James South Elmham
Clay Common
Uggeshall
Wissett
Wangford
Chediston
Reydon
Linstead Parva
Holton
Halesworth
SOUTHWOLD
River Blyth
Wenhaston
Blythburgh
Huntingfield
Blackheath
Walberswick
Walpole
Bramfield
Heveningham
Dunwich
Peasenhall
Sibton
Darsham
Westleton
Yoxford
Middleton
Bruisyard
Eastbridge
Theberton
NORTH SEA
Rendham
Kelsale
Carlton
Sweffling
Saxmundham
LEISTON
Great Glemham
Benhall Green
Sternfield
Coldfair Green
Aldringham
Friston
N
SCALE
0 mls 2
A149
B1151
B1159
A1151
A149
A1062
A1062
B1159
B1152
B1152
A149
B1159
A1064
B1140
A1064
B1140
A47
A47
A149
B1140
A143
A12
A146
B1140
B1136
B1074
A1117
A12
B1385
A146
A143
A146
B1140
A143
A146
B1062
B1062
A144
A145
B1127
A146
A12
B1127
A12
A144
B1124
A145
A12
B1126
B1127
B1123
B1123
A1095
B1387
B1117
A144
A12
B1125
A1120
B1122
A12
B1119
B1119
B1121
B1353
A12

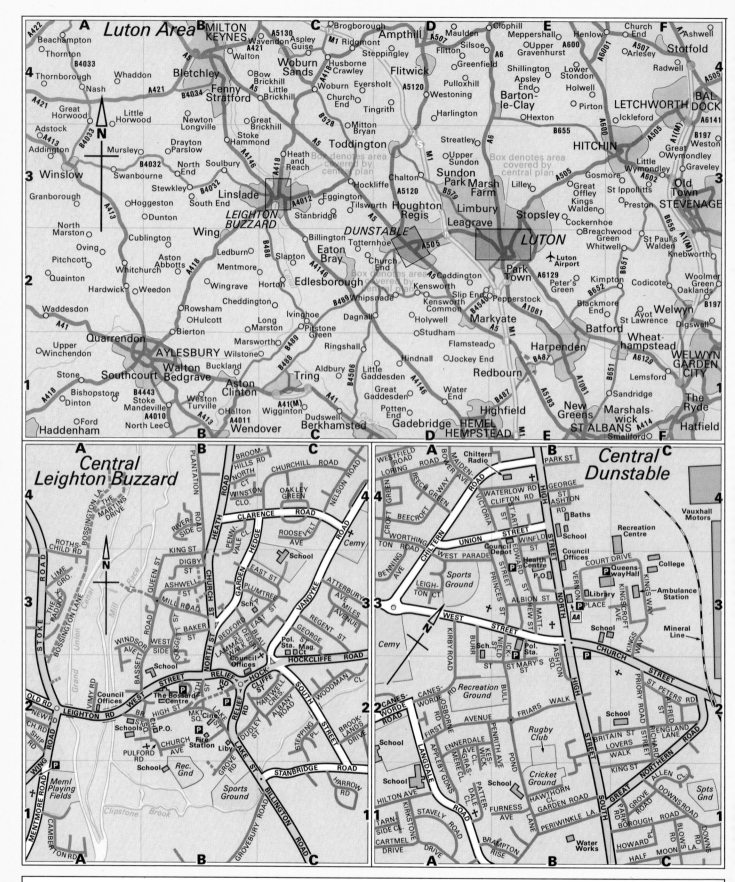

Luton

Huge numbers of people go to Luton each year; for most the stay is very brief since it is the starting-off point for holidays on the Mediterranean and all over Europe. The airport has become Luton's best-known feature, but the town prospered for a long time before the advent of aeroplanes. Straw plaiting and straw hat making were the mainstays of its fortunes from the 19th century onwards, and even

today hats are still made here. In the town's museum and art gallery, at Wardown Park, are exhibits of the hat trade, and of the pillow lace trade, another of the town's traditional industries. Also in the museum are exhibits devoted to natural history and local life, including a 'Luton Life' gallery complete with reconstructed street scene. St Mary's is the parish church. It is a huge building – one of the largest churches in England – containing much of interest. It dates principally

from the 13th to 15th centuries, and has a spectacular font of Purbeck marble, along with many monuments and excellent carving in stone and wood. Just to the south of the town is Luton Hoo, a palatial mansion built to the designs of Robert Adam. It contains a notable collection of pictures and tapestries and sumptuous Fabergé jewellery. The mansion is surrounded by a magnificently landscaped 1,500-acre park laid out by Capability Brown in the 18th century.

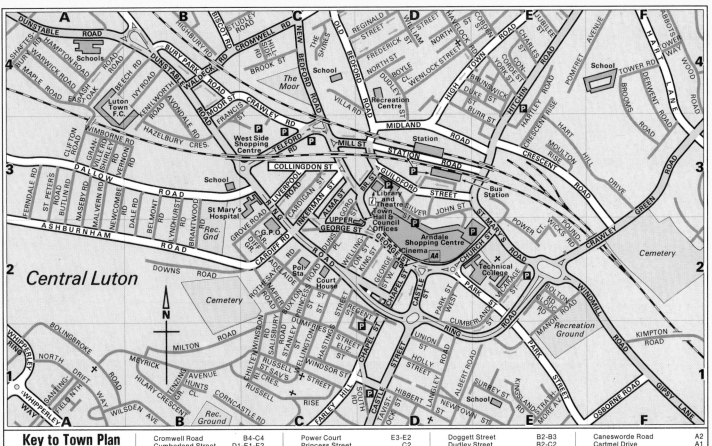

Key to Town Plan and Area Plan

Town Plan

AA Recommended roads	
Other roads	
Restricted roads	
Buildings of interest	Library
Churches	+
Car Parks	P
Parks and open spaces	
AA Service Centre	AA

Area Plan

A roads	
B roads	
Locations	Kensworth○
Urban area	

Street Index

Luton

Abbots Wood Road	F4
Adelaide Street	C2
Albert Road	D1-E1
Alma Street	C2-C3
Ashburnham Road	A3-A2-B2-C2
Ash Road	A4
Avondale Road	B4-B3
Beech Road	A4-B4
Belmont Road	B2-B3
Biscot Road	B4
Bolingbroke Road	A1
Bolton Road	E2
Boyle Close	D4
Brantwood Road	B2-B3
Bridge Street	D3
Brook Street	C4
Brooms Road	F3-F4
Brunswick Street	D4-E4
Burr Street	D4-D3-E4
Bury Park Road	B4
Butlin Road	A2-A3
Buxton Road	C2
Cardiff Grove	C2
Cardiff Road	C2
Cardigan Street	C3
Castle Street	D1-D2
Charles Street	E4
Chapel Street	D1-D2
Chilton Road	C1
Church Street	D2-E2
Clifton Road	A3
Cobden Street	E4
Collingdon Street	C3
Concorde Street	E4
Corncastle Road	B1-C1
Crawley Green Road	E2-F2-F3
Crawley Road	C3-C4
Crescent Rise	E3-E4
Crescent Road	E3-F3-F2

Cromwell Road	B4-C4
Cumberland Street	D1-E1-E2
Dale Road	B2-B3
Dallow Road	A3-B3-C3
Derwent Road	F4-F3
Downs Road	B2-C2
Dudley Street	D4-D3
Duke Street	C1
Dumfries Street	C2-C1-D1
Dunstable Place	C2
Dunstable Road	A4-B4-B3
Elizabeth Street	C1-D1
Farley Hill	C1
Ferndale Road	A3
Francis Street	B3-B4-C4
Frederick Street	D4
George Street	D2
George Street West	D2
Gipsey Lane	F1
Gloucester Road	E2
Gordon Street	C2-C3-D3
Granville Road	A3
Grove Road	B2-C2-C3
Guildford Street	D3
Hampton Road	A4
Hart Hill Drive	E3-F3
Hart Lane	F4-F3
Hartley Road	E3-E4
Hastings Street	C1-C2
Havelock Road	D4-E4
Hazelbury Crescent	B3
Hibbert Street	D1
Highbury Road	B4
Hightown Road	D3-D4-E4
Hilary Crescent	B1
Hillside Road	C4
Hitchin Road	E3-E4
Holly Street	D1
Hunts Close	B1
Inkerman Street	C2-C3
Ivy Road	B4
John Street	D3
Jubilee Street	E4
Kenilworth Road	B3-B4
Kimpton Road	F1
Kingsland Road	E1
King Street	D2
Langley Road	D1
Liverpool Road	C3
Lyndhurst Road	B2-B3
Malvern Road	A2-A3
Manor Road	E1-E2
Maple Road East	A4
Meyrick Avenue	A1-B1-C1
Midland Road	D3-E3
Mill Street	C3-D3
Milton Road	B1-C1
Moor Street	B3-B4-C4
Moulton Rise	E3
Napier Road	C2
Naseby Road	A2-A3
New Bedford Road	C3-C4
Newcombe Road	A2-A3-B3
Newtown Street	D1-E1
North Drift Way	A1
North Street	D4-E4
Oak Road	A4-B4
Old Bedford Road	C4-D4-D3
Osborne Road	E1-F1
Park Street	D2-E2-E1
Park Street West	D2
Pomfret Avenue	E4-F4
Poundwicks Road	E3-E2

Power Court	E3-E2
Princess Street	C2
Regent Street	C2-D2
Reginald Street	C4-D4
Ring Road	C3-C2-D2-D1-E1-E2
Rothesay Road	C2
Russel Rise	C1
Russel Street	C1
St Mary's Road	E2-E3
St Peter's Road	A2-A3
St Saviours Crescent	C1
Salisbury Road	C1-C2
Santingfield North	A1
Shaftesbury Road	A4
Shirley Road	A3
Silver Street	D3-D2
South Road	D1
Stanley Street	C1-C2
Station Road	D3-E3
Strathmore Avenue	E1
Studley Road	B4-C4
Surrey Street	E1
Tavistock Street	D1
Telford Road	C3
Tenzing Grove	B1
The Shires	C4
Tower Road	F4
Tower Way	F4
Union Street	D1
Upper George Street	C2-D2
Vernon Road	A3-B3
Vicarage Street	E2
Villa Road	C4-D4
Waldeck Road	B4
Warwick Road	A4
Wellington Street	C1-C2-D2
Wenlock Street	D4
Whipperley Ring	A1
Whipperley Way	A1
William Street	D4
Wilsden Avenue	A1-B1
Wimborne Road	A3-B3
Windmill Road	E2-F2-F1
Windsor Street	C1
Winsdon Road	C1-C2
York Street	E4

Leighton Buzzard

Albany Road	C2
Ashwell Street	B3
Atterbury Avenue	C3
Baker Street	B3
Bassett Road	A2-B2-B3
Bedford Street	B3
Billington Road	C1
Blau Desert	B3-C3
Bossington Lane	A2-A3-A4
Bridge Street	A2-B2
Brooklands Drive	C2
Broomhills Road	B4-C4
Camberton Road	A1
Church Avenue	B2
Church Road	A2
Churchill Road	C4
Church Square	B2
Church Street	B3
Clarence Road	B4-C4
Digby Street	B3

Doggett Street	B2-B3
Dudley Street	B2-C2
East Street	B3-C3
Garden Hedge	B3-B4-C4
George Street	C3
Grovebury Road	B1-C1
Grove Road	B1-B2
Harrow Road	C1
Hartwell Crescent	B2-C2
Heath Road	B3-B4
High Street	B2
Hockcliffe Road	C2-C3
Hockcliffe Street	B2-C2
King Street	B3
Lake Street	B2-B1-C1
Lammas Walk	B2-B3
Leighton Road	A2
Lime Grove	A3
Market Square	B2
Mentmore Road	A1
Miles Avenue	C3
Mill Road	B3
Nelson Road	C4
New Road	A2
North Court	B4
North Street	B2-B3
Oakley Green	C4
Old Road	A2
Pennivale Close	B3-B4
Plantation Road	B3-B4
Plumtree Lane	B3-C3
Pulford Road	B2
Queen Street	B3
Regent Street	C3
Relief Road	B2
Riverside	B4
Rothschild Road	A3
Roosevelt Avenue	C4
Ship Road	A2
South Street	C1-C2
Stanbridge Road	C1
Stepping Place	C2
Stoke Road	A2-A3-A4
The Martins Drive	A4
The Paddock	A3
Vandyke Road	C2-C3-C4
Vimy Road	A3
West Side	B3
West Street	A2-B2
Windsor Avenue	A3-B3
Wing Road	A1-A2
Winston Close	B4-C4
Woodman Close	C2

Dunstable

Albion Street	B3
Alfred Street	C2
Allen Close	C1
Appleby Gardens	A1-A2
Ashton Road	B4
Ashton Square	B2-B3
Beech Green	A4
Beechcroft Way	A4
Benning Avenue	A3-A4
Blows Road	C1
Borough Road	C1
Brampton Rise	A1-B1
Britain Street	B2-C2
Bull Pond Lane	B1-B2
Burr Street	A3-A2-B2

Canesworde Road	A2
Cartmel Drive	A1
Chiltern Road	A3-A4-B4
Church Street	B3-C3-C2
Clifton Road	A4-B4
Court Drive	B3-C3
Croft Green	A4
Downs Road	C1
Edward Street	B3-B4
England Lane	C2
Ennerdale Avenue	A2
First Avenue	A2-B2
Friars Walk	B2
Furness Avenue	B1
Garden Road	B1
George Street	B4
Grasmere Close	A1-A2
Great Northern Road	B1-C1-C2
Grove Road	C1
Half Moon Lane	C1
Hawthorn Close	B1
High Street North	B3-B4
High Street South	B3-B2-B1-C1
Hilton Avenue	A1
Howard Place	C1
Icknield Street	B2-B3
Keswick Close	A1-A2
Kingscroft Avenue	C3
Kingsway	C3
King Street	B1-C1-C2
Kirby Road	A2-A3
Kirkstone Drive	A1
Langdale Road	A1-A2
Leighton Court	A3
Loring Road	A4
Lovers Walk	B2-C2
Maidenbower Avenue	A4
Matthew Street	B3
Osborne Road	A2
Park Road	C1
Park Street	B4
Patterdale Close	A1
Penrith Avenue	A2-B2-B1
Periwinkle Lane	B1
Princes Street	A4-A3-B3
Priory Road	C2
Richard Street	C2
St Mary's Street	B2
St Peter's Road	C2
Stavely Road	A1
Stuart Street	B4
Tarnside Close	A1
Union Street	A4-B4
Vernon Place	C2
Victoria Street	A4-B4-B3
Waterlow Road	A4-B4
Westfield Road	A4
West Parade	A3
West Street	A3-B3
Winfield Street	B4
Worthington Road	A4

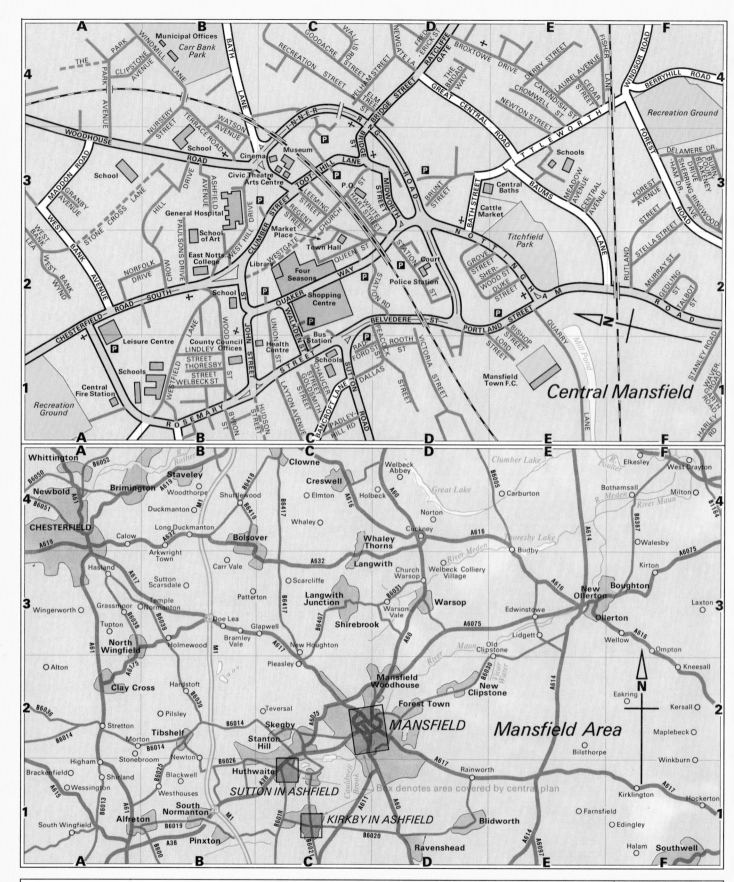

Mansfield

Arching high over the centre of the town, Mansfield's 19th-century railway viaduct epitomises the town's involvement in industry since it developed from agricultural area to industrial centre a century ago. Crucial to the town's growth has been the productive North Nottinghamshire coalfield, but its importance as a commercial and leisure centre should not be underestimated: this is the home of one of the largest open-air markets in the country, while in contrast, the Four Seasons shopping centre offers a modern, totally enclosed and air-conditioned complex. Football League soccer can be seen at Field Mill, and the Mansfield Leisure Centre is purpose-built to seat 1,200 spectators. Places of interest include the 11th-century Parish Church of St Peter and St Paul, the Forest Stone in Sherwood Forest where swains once met to settle their debts, and Mansfield Museum and Art Gallery.

Kirkby-in-Ashfield's expansion was sparked off by the discovery of coal in Kirkby Colliery — now closed, the colliery's place is being taken by modern industrial development.

Sutton-in-Ashfield enjoys a theatre and an ice rink in the Sutton Centre, built to combine community, educational and leisure facilities for this one-time village, which grew with the textile industry from the 17th century onwards.

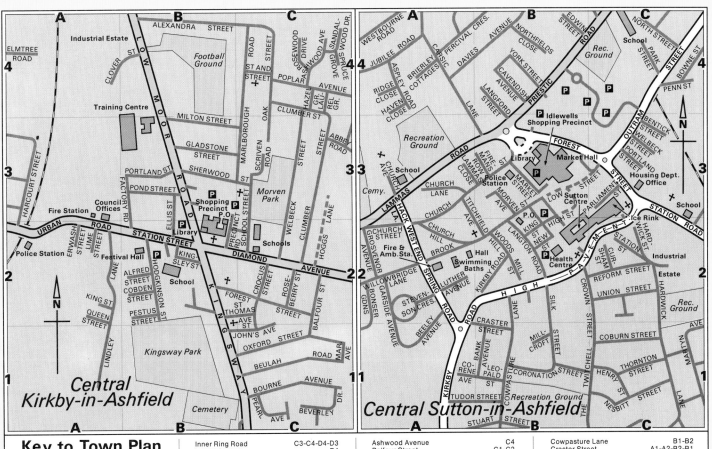

Central Kirkby-in-Ashfield

Central Sutton-in-Ashfield

Key to Town Plan and Area Plan

Town Plan
AA Recommended roads
Other roads
Restricted roads
Buildings of interest   Library
Car Parks   P
Parks and open spaces
Churches   +

Area Plan
A roads
B roads
Locations   Morton ◯
Urban area

STREET INDEX WITH GRID REFERENCE

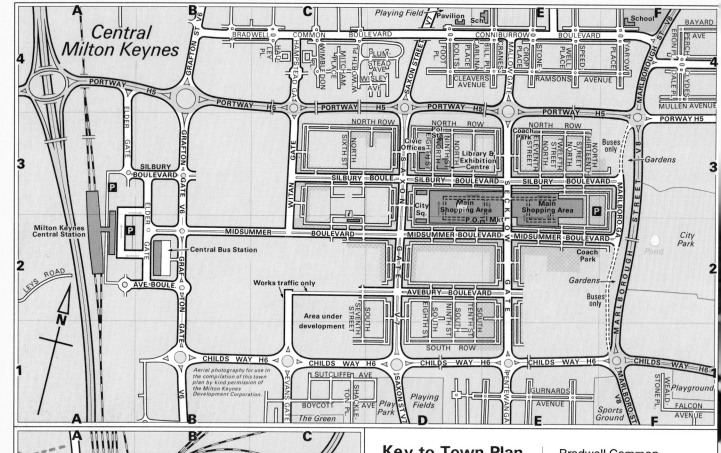

Central Milton Keynes

(Town plan — grid A–F, 1–4)

Playing Field · Pavilion · Sch · School · BAYARD AVE · BERCH · CLYDES · DALE PL · MULLEN AVENUE · PERON PL · YARROW · CONNIBURROW BOULEVARD · BRADWELL COMMON · LEY PL · HALL · WIMBLE · HAMPSTEAD PLACE · MITCHAM · HIGH GATE · WISLEY AVE · PLUMSTEAD · BILL PL · CRANES · COLTS · CARLINA · MALLOW GATE · CROP · STONE · WELL PLACE · SPEED · PLACE · SCHOOL · CLEAVERS AVENUE · RAMSONS · AVENUE · PORTWAY H5 · PORTWAY H5 · PORTWAY H5 · PORWAY H5

ELDER GATE · SILBURY BOULEVARD · GRAFTON GATE V6 · NORTH ROW · NORTH ROW · NORTH ROW · NORTH ROW · Pol Sta · SIXTH ST · NORTH · Civic Offices · NINTH ST · NORTH · Library & Exhibition Centre · Coach Park · ELEVENTH · NORTH · TWELFTH · NORTH · THIRTEENTH · NORTH · Buses only · Gardens

Milton Keynes Central Station · P · P · SILBURY · BOULE · SILBURY · BOULEVARD · SECKLOW GATE V7 · SILBURY · BOULEVARD · City Sq. · Main Shopping Area · P.O. · Mkt · Main Shopping Area · P · City Park · Pond

Central Bus Station · AVE·BOULE · MIDSUMMER · BOULEVARD · MIDSUMMER · BOULEVARD · MIDSUMMER · BOULEVARD · Coach Park · Gardens · Buses only

LEYS ROAD · N · Works traffic only · AVEBURY · BOULEVARD · SEVENTH STREET · SOUTH · EIGHTH ST · SOUTH · NINTH ST · SOUTH · TENTH ST · SOUTH · SOUTH ROW

Area under development · CHILDS WAY H6 · CHILDS WAY H6 · CHILDS WAY H6 · CHILDS WAY H6 · CHILDS WAY H6 · STONE PL · WEALD · Playground · FALCON AVENUE

Aerial photography for use in the compilation of this town plan by kind permission of the Milton Keynes Development Corporation. · EVANS GATE V6 · SUTCLIFFE AVE · SHACKLE · TON PL · SAXON ST V7 · Play Park · BOYCOTT · The Green · Playing Fields · PENTEWAN GA · GURNARDS · AVENUE · MARLBORO ST · Sports Ground · FALCON · AVENUE

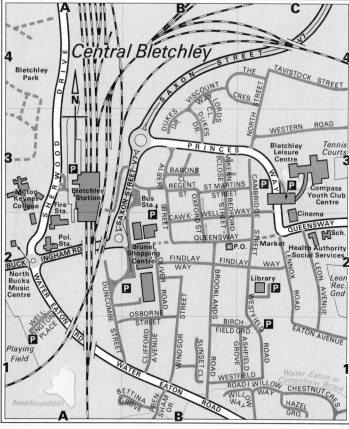

Central Bletchley

(Town plan — grid A–C, 1–4)

Bletchley Park · SHERWOOD DRIVE · SAXON STREET · TAVISTOCK STREET · N · CRES · NORTH STREET · THE · VISCOUNT · WAY · LORDS · CL · DUKES · DUKES DR · WESTERN ROAD · Bletchley Leisure Centre · Tennis Courts

Milton Keynes College · Bletchley Station · P · P · PRINCES · WAY · CAMBRIDGE STREET · BARONS CL · REGENT ST · ALBERT ST · ST MARTINS · STREET · Compass Youth Club Centre · Fire Sta. · Bus Sta. · CAWK · OXFORD ST · WELL · ST · BEDFORD STREET · Cinema · QUEENSWAY · Sch.

Pol. Sta. · INGHAM RD · Brunel Shopping Centre · STREET · QUEENSWAY · P.O. · Market · Health Authority Social Services · North Bucks Music Centre · WELLINGTON PLACE · WATER EATON RD · DUNCOMBE STREET · OLIVER ROAD · STREET · FINDLAY WAY · FINDLAY · WAY · Library · LENNOX · LEON AVENUE · Leon Rec. Gnd

Playing Field · OSBORNE STREET · WINDSOR ROAD · CLIFFORD AVENUE · SUNSET CL · BROOKLANDS ROAD · BIRCH FIELD GRO · ASHFIELD GROVE · WESTFIELD ROAD · EATON AVENUE · Water Eaton or Cottenham Brook

Newfoundout · BETTINA GROVE · FREN · SHAM DR · WATER EATON ROAD · WESTFIELD ROAD · WILLOW WALK · WILLOW WAY · CHESTNUT CRES · HAZEL GRO

Key to Town Plan and Area Plan

Town Plan
AA Recommended roads
Other roads
Restricted roads
Buildings of interest — Library
Parks and open spaces
Car parks and car parking areas — P
One Way Streets

Area Plan
A roads
B roads
Locations — Stanford ○
Urban area

STREET INDEX — with grid reference

Milton Keynes

Avebury Boulevard	A2-B2, C2-D2-E2
Bayard Avenue	F4
Boycott Avenue	C1-D1
Bradwell Common Boulevard	B4-C4-D4
Carlina Place	D4
Childs Way	B1-C1-D1-E1-F1
Cleavers Avenue	D4-E4
Clydesdale Place	F4
Coltsfoot Place	D4
Conniburrow Boulevard	D4-E4-F4
Cranesbill Place	E4
Elder Gate	A4-A3, B3-B2
Evans Gate	C1
Falcon Avenue	F1
Grafton Gate	B1-B2-B3
Grafton Street	B4
Gurnards Avenue	E1
Hadley Place	C4
Hampstead Gate	C4
Leys Road	A2
Mallow Gate	E4
Marlborough Gate	F2-F3
Marlborough Street	F1-F2-F3-F4
Midsummer Boulevard	B2-C2-D2-E2-F2

Milton-Keynes

The most famous of Britain's New Towns, Milton Keynes was officially opened in 1973. The new city was carefully and considerately planned to integrate with the existing towns and villages and countryside, and yet provide a self-sufficient community where industry, business and housing could develop.

Milton Keynes borough covers some 22,000 acres of North Buckinghamshire, including the towns of Bletchley, Stony Stratford and Wolverton, but the hub of the region is Central Milton Keynes. Here, one of the largest and most attractive shopping areas in Britain can be found. All the shops are under cover and are reached from tall glass-walled arcades paved with marble and lined with exotic trees and shrubs.

The variety of modern housing in Milton Keynes is another of the city's exciting attractions.

Purpose-built homes have been imaginatively planned to suit all ages, and the residential areas have generous areas of green open spaces.

Recreational facilities are also an integral part of the city's concept. Bletchley — one of three leisure centres — has a huge multi-purpose sports hall where international events are held, and an exotic free-form swimming pool. Here, beneath the tinted glass of the pyramidal building, real palm trees create a Mediterranean atmosphere.

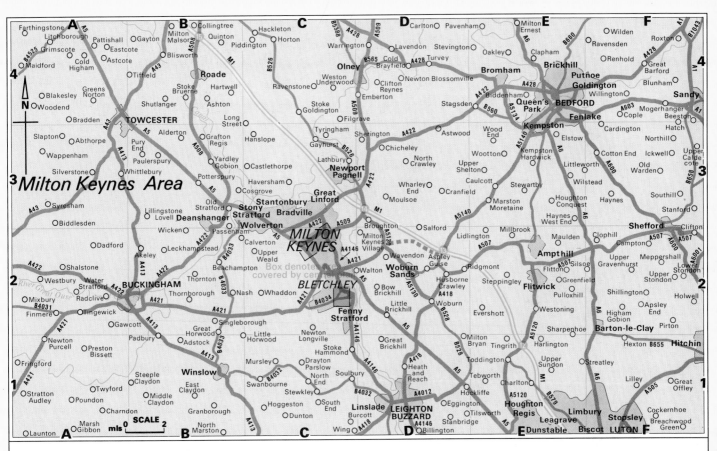

MILTON KEYNES
Huge industrial estates and modern factories were built in Milton Keynes during the 1970s to provide employment for the people who moved to the New Town from London as a result of the capital's housing problems.

51

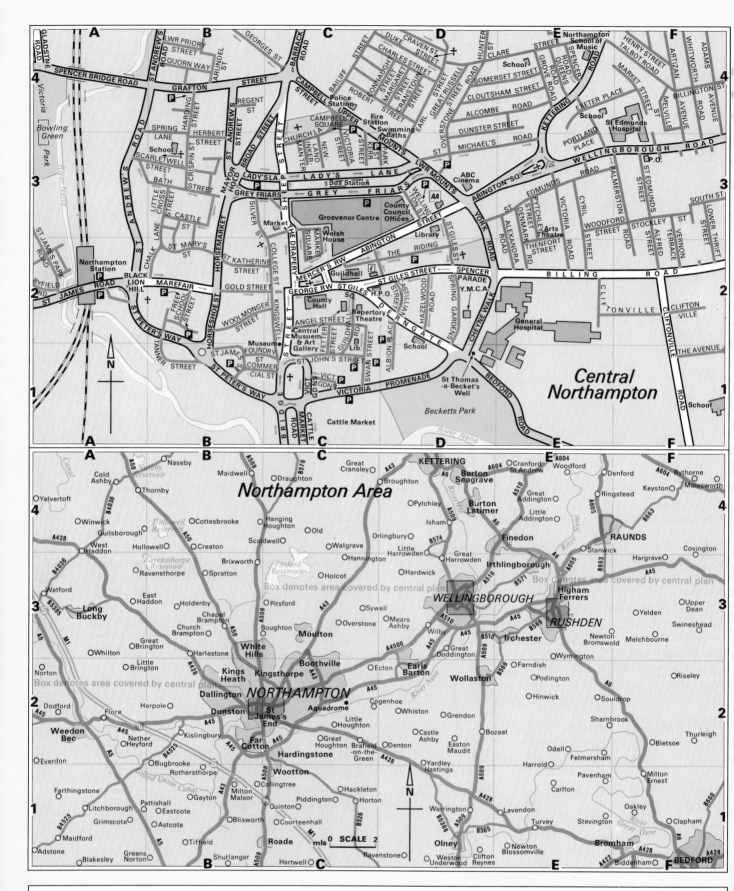

Northampton

The town's long connection with the boot and shoe trade started during the Civil War when Northampton made footwear for Cromwell's army. Now, although still internationally famous for this commodity, it is also an important light industry and distribution centre. Predictably, both the town's museums contain shoes, and include Queen Victoria's wedding shoes and Nijinsky's ballet shoes among their exhibits.

Northampton has a long and important history and its castle became a resting place for every English king from Henry I to Edward III. However, due to Charles II's destruction of the castle and the town walls, and a devastating fire in 1675, little remains of the medieval town. The vast market square – one of the largest in the country – dates from the days of the cattle drovers when Northampton was an important market centre, and many of the street names – such as Horsemarket and Mercer's Row – reflect the town's history.

Wellingborough stands in the valley of the River Nene; like Northampton, the manufacture of footwear is a well-established industry. The two churches of the town form an interesting contrast; All-Hallows retains traces of medieval workmanship and has a 17th-century house as well as a church hall, whilst St Mary's is a modern building designed by Sir Ninian Comper.

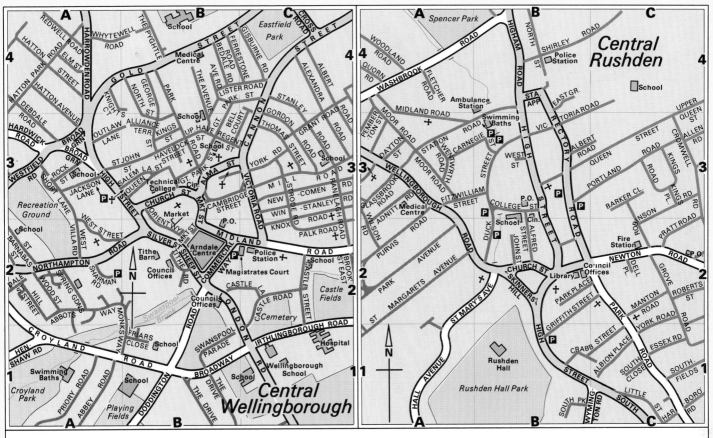

Central Wellingborough

Central Rushden

LEGEND

Town Plan
AA recommended route
Restricted roads
Other roads
Buildings of interest   Library ▢
Car parks   P
Parks and open spaces ▢
One way streets →

Area Plan
A roads
B roads
Locations   Winfarth ○
Urban area ▢

Street Index with Grid Reference

Northampton

Abington Square	D3-E3
Abington Street	C2-D2-D3
Adams Avenue	F3-F4
Albion Place	D1-D2
Alcombe Road	D4-E4
Alexandra Road	E2-E3
Alfred Street	F2-F3
Angel Street	C2
Artizan Avenue	F3-F4
Arundel Street	B4
Bailiff Street	C4
Barrack Road	C4
Bath Street	A3-B3
Bedford Road	D1-E1
Billing Road	E2-F2
Billington Street	F4
Black Lion Hill	A2
Bridge Street	C1-C2
Broad Street	B3-B4-C4-C3
Byfield Road	A2
Campbell Square	C4
Campbell Street	C4
Castle Street	B3
Castillian Street	D2
Cattle Market Road	C1
Chalk Lane	B2-B3
Charles Street	C4-D4
Cheyne Walk	D1-D2-E2
Church Lane	C3-C4
Clare Street	D4-E4
Cliftonville	E2-F2
Cliftonville Road	F1-F2
Cloutsham Street	D4-E4
College Street	C2
Commercial Street	B1-C1

Connaught Street	C4-D4
Cranstoun Street	D4
Craven Street	D4
Crispin Street	B3
Cyril Street	E2-E3
Denmark Road	E2-E3
Derngate	C2-D2-D1
Duke Street	C4-D4
Dunster Street	D3-D4-E4
Earl Street	D3-D4
Exeter Place	E4-F4
Fetter Street	C1-C2
Free School Street	B2
Foundry Street	B1-C1
George Row	C2
George Street	B4-C4
Gold Street	B2-C2
Grafton Street	B4-C4
Great Russell Street	D4
Greyfriars	B3-C3-D3
Grove Road	E4
Guildhall Road	C1-C2
Harding Street	B4
Hazelwood Road	D2
Henry Street	F4
Herbert Street	B3
Horsemarket	B2-B3
Horseshoe Street	B1-B2
Hunter Street	C4
Inkerman Terrace	C3
Kerr Street	C3-C4
Kettering Road	E3-E4
Kingswell	C1-C2
Lady's Lane	B3-C3-D3
Little Cross Street	B3
Lower Mounts	D3
Lower Priory Street	B4
Lower Thrift Street	F2-F3
Marefair	A2-B2
Margaret Street	D4
Market Square	C2-C3
Market Street	E4-F4
Mayor Hold	B3
Melville Street	F4
Mercers Row	C2
Newland	C3
Overstone Road	D3-D4
Palmerston Road	E3-F3-F2
Park Street	C3-D3
Portland Place	E3-E4
Pytchley Street	E3
Queens Road	E4
Quorn Way	B4
Regent Street	B4
Robert Street	C4-D4
St Andrews Road	A2-A3-A4-B4
St Andrews Street	B3-B4
St Edmunds Road	D3-E3-F3
St Edmunds Street	F3
St Giles Square	C2
St Giles Street	C2-D2-D3
St James Road	A2
St James Park Road	A2-A3
St James Street	B1
St John's Street	C1
St Katherine Street	B2-C2
St Mary's Street	B2
St Michael's Road	D3-E3
St Peter's Way	A2-B2-B1-C1
Scarletwell Street	A3-B3
Sheep Street	C3-C4

Silver Street	B3-C3
Somerset Street	D4-E4
South Street	F3
Spencer Road	E4
Spencer Bridge Road	A4
Spencer Parade	D2
Spring Gardens	D2
Spring Lane	A4-B4-B3
Stockley Street	F3
Swan Street	C1-C2
The Avenue	F1
The Drapery	C2-C3
The Riding	C2-D2
Tanner Street	B1-B2
Talbot Road	E4-F4
Thenfort Street	E2-E3
Upper Mounts	C4-C3-D3
Vernon Terrace	F2-F3
Victoria Gardens	C1
Victoria Promenade	C1-D1
Victoria Road	E2-E3
Victoria Street	C3-C4
Wellington Road	E3-F3
Wellington Street	D3
Whitworth Road	F3-F4
Woodford Street	E3-F3
Woolmonger Street	B2-C2
York Road	D3-D2-E2

Wellingborough

Abbey Road	A1
Abbotts Way	A2
Albert Road	C3-C4
Alexandra Road	C3-C4
Alliance Terrace	B3
Alma Street	B3
Avenue Road	B4
Bedale Road	B4
Bell Court	B3-C3-C4
Broad Green	A3
Broadway	B1-C1
Brook Street East	C2
Cambridge Street	B3-C3
Cannon Street	C3-C4
Castle Lane	B2-C2
Castle Road	C1-C2
Castle Street	C2
Church Street	B3
Commercial Way	B2
Cross Road	C4
Croyland Road	A2-A1-B1
Dale Street	A2
Debdale Road	A3-A4
Doddington Road	B1-B2
Ferrestone Road	B4-C4
Friars Close	B1
George Street	B3-B4
Gisburne Road	B4-C4
Gold Street	A4-B4-C4
Gordon Road	C3-C4
Grant Road	C3-C4
Great Park Street	B3-B4-C4
Hardwick Road	A3
Harrowden Road	A3-A4
Hatton Avenue	A3-A4
Hatton Street	A4
Hatton Park Road	A4
Havelock Street	B3

Henshaw Road	A1
High Street	A3-B3-B2
Hill Street	A2
Irthlingborough Road	C1-C2
Jackson Lane	A3
Kings Street	B3
Knights Court	A4-B4
Lister Road	B4-C4
London Road	B1-B2-C2-C1
Market Street	B2-B3
Midland Road	B2-C2
Mill Road	C3
Monks Way	A1-B1-B2
Newcomen Road	C3
North Street	B3-B4
Northampton Road	A2-B2
Outlaw Lane	A3-B3
Palk Road	C2
Park Road	B3-B4
Priory Road	A1
Queen Street	B3
Ranelagh Road	C2-C3
Redwell Street	A4
Regent Street	B3-C3
Rock Street	A3
St Barnabas Street	A2
St John Street	A3-B3
Salem Lane	A3-B3
Sharman Road	A2
Sheep Street	B2
Short Lane	A3
Silver Street	B2
Spring Gardens	A2
Stanley Road	C3-C4
Strode Road	C2-C3
Swanspool Parade	B1
The Avenue	B3-B4
The Drive	B1
The Pyghtle	B4
Thomas Street	C3
Tithebarn Road	B2
Upper Havelock Street	B3
Victoria Road	C2-C3
West Street	A3-A2-B2
Westfield Road	A3
West Villa Road	A2
Whytewell Road	A4-B4
Winstanley Road	C3
Wood Street	A2
York Road	C3

Rushden

Adnitt Road	A2-A3
Albert Road	B3-C3
Albion Place	C1
Alfred Street	B2-B3
Allen Road	C3
Barker Close	C3
Carnegie Street	A3-B3
Church Street	B2
College Street	B3
Crabb Street	B1-C1
Cromwell Road	C2-C3
Dayton Street	A3
Dell Place	C2
Duck Street	B2-B3
East Grove	B4
Essex Road	C1

Fitzwilliam Street	A3-B3
Fletcher Road	A4
Glassbrook Road	A3
Griffith Street	B1-B2-C2
Grove Road	C1-C2
Hall Avenue	A1
Harborough Road	A3
High Street	B2-B3-B4
High Street South	B2-B1-C1
Higham Road	B4
John Street	B2
Kings Road	C3
Kings Place	C3
Little Street	C1
Manton Road	C2
Midland Road	A3-A4
Moor Road	A3-A4
Newton Road	C2
North Street	B4
Park Avenue	A2
Park Place	B2-C2
Park Road	B2-C2-C1
Pemberton Street	A3-A4
Portland Road	B3-C3
Pratt Road	C2-C3
Purvis Road	A2-A3
Queen Street	B3-C3
Quorn Road	A4
Rectory Road	B2-B3-B4
Roberts Street	C2
Robinson Road	C2-C3
St Margarets Avenue	A1-A2
St Mary's Avenue	A1-A2-B2
Shirley Road	B4-C4
Skinners Hill	B2
South Close	C1
South Park	B1
Southfields	C1
Station Approach	B4
Station Road	A3-B3-B4
Upper Queen Street	C3-C4
Victoria Road	B3-B4-C4
Washbrook Road	A4-B4
Wellingborough Road	A3-A2-B2
Wentworth Road	A3
West Street	B3
Wilson Road	A2-A3
Woodland Road	A4
Wymington Road	B1-C1
York Road	C1-C2

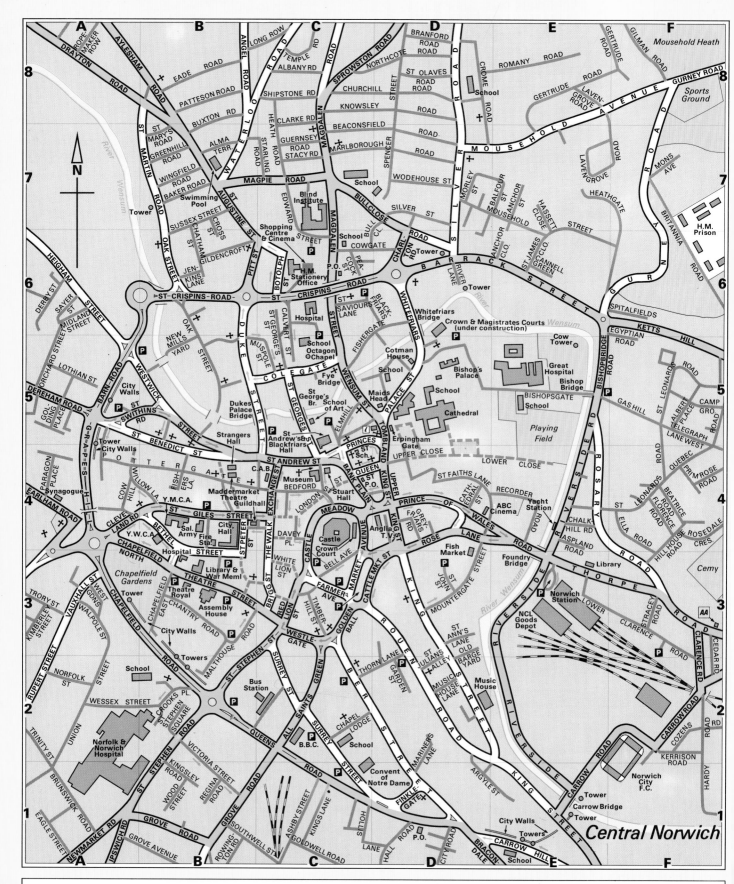

Norwich

Fortunately the heart has not been ripped out of Norwich to make way for some bland precinct, so its ancient character has been preserved. Narrow alleys run between the streets – sometimes opening out into quiet courtyards, sometimes into thoroughfares packed with people, sometimes into lanes which seem quite deserted. It is a unique place, with something of interest on every corner.

The cathedral was founded in 1096 by the city's first bishop, Herbert de Losinga. Among its most notable features are the nave, with its huge pillars, the bishop's throne (a Saxon survival unique in Europe) and the cloisters with their matchless collection of roof bosses. Across the city is the great stone keep of the castle, set on a mound and dominating all around it. It dates from Norman times, but was refaced in 1834. The keep now forms part of Norwich Castle Museum –

an extensive and fascinating collection. Other museums are Bridewell Museum – collections relating to local crafts and industries within a 14th-century building – and Strangers' Hall, a genuinely 'old world' house, rambling and full of surprises, both in its tumble of rooms and in the things which they contain. Especially picturesque parts of the city are Elm Hill – a street of ancient houses; Tombland – with two gateways into the Cathedral Close; and Pull's Ferry – a watergate by the river.

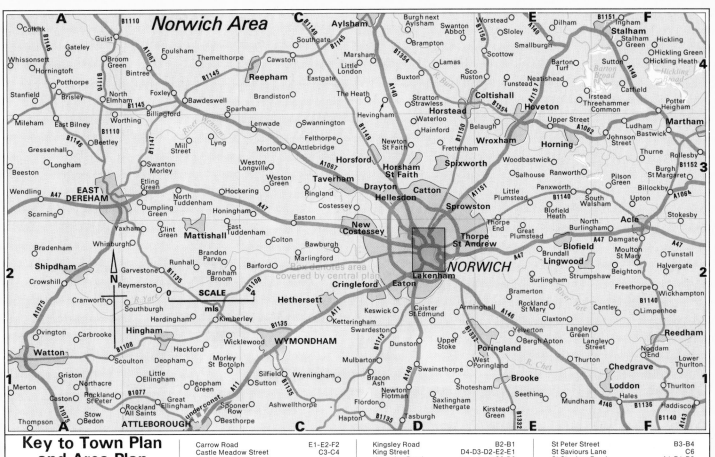

Key to Town Plan and Area Plan

Town Plan

AA Recommended roads	▬▬
Restricted roads	---
Other roads	▬
Buildings of interest	School
AA Service Centre	AA
Car Parks	P
Parks and open spaces	
One Way Streets	→

Area Plan

A roads	▬
B roads	▬
Locations	East Rushton○
Urban area	

Street Index with Grid Reference

Norwich

Albany Road	C8
Albert Place	F5
All Saints Green	C2-C3
Alma Terrace	B7
Anchor Close	E6
Anchor Street	E7
Angel Road	B8
Argyle Street	D2-D1-E1
Ashby Street	C1
Aspland Road	E4
Aylesham Road	A8-B8
Baker Road	B7
Balfour Street	E7
Bank Plain	C4
Barn Road	A5
Barrack Street	D6-E6
Beaconsfield Road	C7-D7
Beatrice Road	F4
Bedford Street	C4
Bell Avenue	C3
Ber Street	C3-C2-D2-D1
Bethel Street	B4-B3
Bishopbridge Road	E5-E6
Bishopsgate	D5-E5
Blackfriars	C6-D6
Botolph Street	C6
Bracondale	D1-E1
Branford Road	D8
Brigg Street	C3
Britannia Road	F7-F6
Brunswick Road	A1
Bull Close	C6-C7-D7
Bull Close Road	C7-D7-D6
Buxton Road	B7-B8
Calvert Street	C6-C5
Camp Grove	F5
Cannell Green	E6
Carrow Hill	D1-E1
Carrow Road	E1-E2-F2
Castle Meadow Street	C3-C4
Cathedral Street	D4
Cattle Market	C3-D3
Cedar Road	F3-F2
Chalkhill Road	E4
Chantry Road	B3
Chapelfield East	B3
Chapelfield North	A4-A3-B4-B3
Chapelfield Road	A3-B3-B2
Chapel Lodge	C2
Churchill Road	C8-D8
Charlton Road	D6
Chatham Street	B7-B6
City Road	D1
Clarence Road	F3-F2
Clarke Street	C7-C8
Cleveland Road	A4-B4
Colegate	B5-C5
Cowgate	C6-D6
Cow Hill	A4
Cozens Road	F2
Crome Road	D8-D7
Crooks Place	B2
Cross Street	B7-B6
Davey Place	C4
Derby Street	A6
Dereham Road	A5
Drayton Road	A8-B8
Duke Street	B6-B5-C5-C4
Eade Road	B8
Earlham Road	A4
Esdelle Street	B7-C7
Edward Street	C7-C6
Egyptian Road	E6-F6-F5
Ella Road	F4-F3
Elmhill	C5
Exchange Street	C4
Farmer Avenue	C3
Finklegate	D1
Fishergate	C5-C6-D6
Fishers Lane	B4
Florence Road	F4
Garden Street	D2
Gas Hill	E5-F5
Gertrude Road	E7-E8-F8
Gildencroft	B6
Gilman Road	F8
Golden Ball	C3
Golding Place	A5
Goldwell Road	C1
Grapes Hill	A5-A4
Greenhill Road	B7
Greyfriars Road	D4
Grove Avenue	A1-B1
Grove Road	A1-B1-C1-C2
Gurney Road	E6-F6-F7-F8
Guernsey Road	C7
Hall Road	D1
Hardy Road	F1-F2
Hassett Close	E7
Heathgate	E7-F7
Heath Road	C8-C7
Heigham Street	A6-A5
Hill House Road	F3-F4
Hollis Lane	C1-D1
Ipswich Road	A1
Jenkins Lane	B6
Kerrison Road	F2
Ketts Hill	E6-F6-F5
Kimberley Street	A3
Kings Lane	C1
Kingsley Road	B2-B1
King Street	D4-D3-D2-E2-E1
Knowsley Road	C8-D8
Lavengrove Road	E8-E7-F7
London Street	C4
Long Row	B8-C8
Lothian Street	A5
Lower Clarence Road	E3-F3-F2
Lower Close	D4-E4
Magdalen Road	C7-C8
Magdalen Street	C7-C6-C5
Magpie Road	B7-C7
Malthouse Road	B2-B3
Mariners Lane	D1-D2
Market Avenue	C3-C4
Marlborough Road	C7-D7
Midland Street	A5-A6
Mons Avenue	F7
Morley Street	D7
Mountergate Street	D3-D4
Mousehold Avenue	D7-E7-E8-F8
Mousehold Street	D7-E7-E6-F6
Music House Lane	D2
Muspole Street	B5-C5
Newmarket Road	A1
New Mills Yard	B5
Norfolk Street	A2
Northcote Road	C8-D8
Oak Street	B6-B5
Old Barge Yard	D2-D3
Orchard Street	A5-A6
Palace Street	D5
Paragon Place	A4
Patteson Road	B8
Peacock Street	C6
Pitt Street	B6-C6
Pottergate	A4-B4
Prince of Wales Road	D4-E4-E3
Primrose Road	F4
Princes Street	C4-C5-D5
Quebec Road	F4-F5
Queens Road	B2-C2-C1
Queen Street	C4-D4
Recorder Road	E4
Red Lion Street	C3
Regina Road	B1
River Lane	D6
Riverside	E3-E2-E1
Riverside Road	E3-E4-E5
Romany Road	D8-E8
Ropemaker Row	A8
Rosary Road	E5-E4-F4-F3
Rosedale Crescent	F4
Rose Lane	D3-D4-E4
Rouen Road	C3-D3-D2
Rowington Road	B1
Rupert Street	A2-A3
St Andrew Street	C4
St Ann's Lane	D3
St Augustine Street	B7-B6
St Benedict Street	A5-B5-B4
St Crispins Road	B6-C6-D6
St Faiths Lane	D4
St George's Street	C6-C5-C4
St Giles Street	B4-C4
St James Close	E6
St John Street	D3
St Juliens Alley	D2-D3
St Leonards Road	E4-F4-F5
St Martin Road	A8-B8-A7-B7
St Mary's Road	B7
St Olaves Road	D8
St Peter Street	B3-B4
St Saviours Lane	C6
St Stephen Road	A1-B1-B2
St Stephen Street	B2-B3-C3
St Stephen Square	B2
St Swithins Road	A5-B5
Sayer Street	A6
Shipstone Road	C8
Silver Road	D6-D7-D8
Silver Street	D7
Southwell Road	B1-C1
Spencer Street	D7-D8
Spitalfields	E6-F6
Sprowston Road	C8-D8
Stacy Road	C7
Starling Road	B7-C7
Stracey Road	F3
Surrey Street	C3-C2-C1-D1
Sussex Street	B6-B7
The Walk	C3-C4
Telegraph Lane West	F5-F4
Temple Road	C8
Theatre Street	B3-C3
Thorne Lane	C2-D2-D3
Thorpe Road	E3-F3
Timberhill Street	C3
Tombland	D5-D4
Trinity Street	A2-A1
Trory Street	A3
Union Street	A1-A2-A3
Upper Close	D4
Upper King Street	D4
Vauxhall Street	A3
Victoria Street	B2-B1
Walpole Street	A3
Waterloo Road	B7-B8-C8
Whitefriars	D6-D5
White Lion Street	C3
Willow Lane	A4-B4
Wingfield Road	B7
Wensum Street	C5-D5
Wessex Street	A2-B2
West Gardens	A3
Westle Gate	C3
Westwick Street	A5-B5-B4
Wodehouse Street	D7
Wood Street	B1

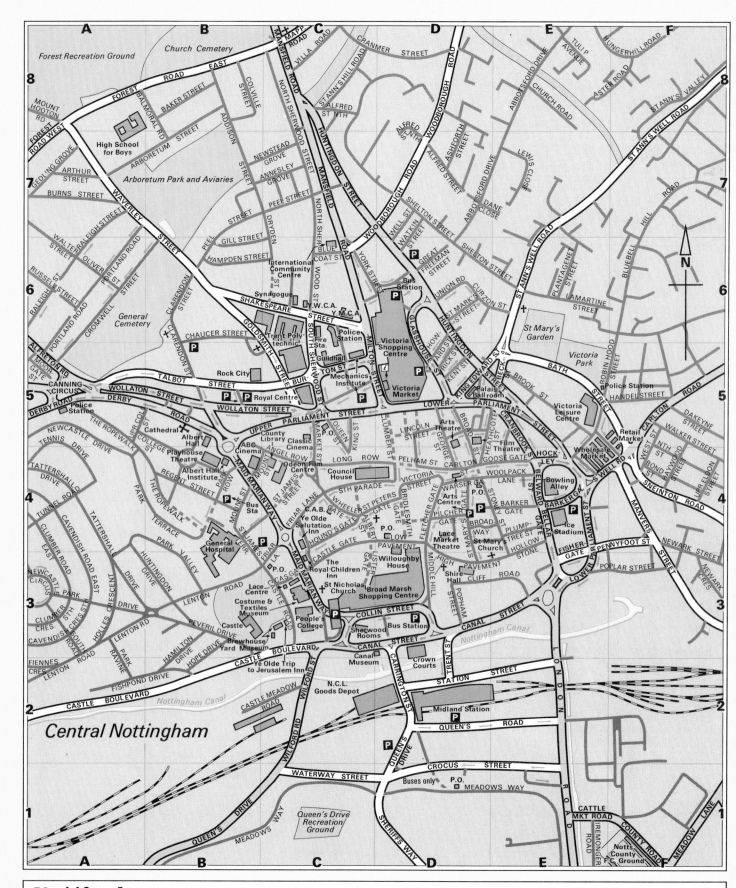

Nottingham

Hosiery and lace were the foundations upon which Nottingham's prosperity was built. The stockings came first – a knitting machine for these had been invented by a Nottinghamshire man as early as 1589 – but a machine called a 'tickler', which enabled simple patterns to be created in the stocking fabric, prompted the development of machine-made lace. The earliest fabric was produced in 1768, and an example from not much later than that is kept in the city's Castlegate Costume and Textile Museum. In fact, the entire history of lacemaking is beautifully explained in this converted row of Georgian terraces. The Industrial Museum at Wollaton Park has many other machines and exhibits tracing the development of the knitting industry, as well as displays on the other industries which have brought wealth to the city – tobacco, pharmaceuticals, engineering and printing. At Wollaton Hall is a natural history museum, while nearer the centre are the Canal Museum and the Brewhouse Yard Museum, a marvellous collection which shows items from daily life in the city up to the present day. Nottingham is not complete without mention of Robin Hood, the partly mythical figure whose statue is in the castle grounds. Although the castle itself has Norman foundations, the present structure is largely Victorian. It is now a museum.

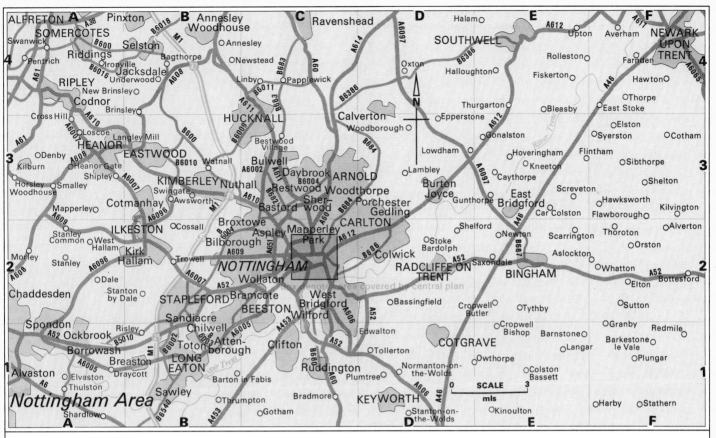

Key to Town Plan and Area Plan

Town Plan

AA Recommended roads	▅▅▅
Restricted roads	═══
Other roads	═══
Buildings of interest	Theatre ■
Car Parks	P
Parks and open spaces	▨
Churches	†
One Way Streets	→

Area Plan

A roads	▅▅▅
B roads	═══
Locations	Bagthorpe○
Urban area	▨

Street Index with Grid Reference

Nottingham

Abbotsford Drive	D7-D7-E7-E8
Addison Street	B7-B8
Albert Street	C4
Alfred Street	D7
Alfred Street North	C8, D7-D8
Alfreton Road	A5-A6
Angel Row	B5-B4-C4
Annesley Grove	B7-C7
Arboretum Street	A7-B7-B8
Arthur Street	A7
Aster Road	E8-F8
Ashford Street	D7-D8
Baker Street	B8
Balmoral Road	A8-B8-B7
Barker Gate	E4
Bath Gate	E5-F5
Beck Street	E5
Bellar Gate	E4
Belward Street	E4
Bluebell Hill Road	F6-F7
Bluecoat Street	C6
Bond Street	F4
Bridlesmith Gate	D4
Broad Street	D4-D5
Broadway	D4-E4
Brook Street	E5
Burns Street	A7
Burton Street	C5
Canal Street	C3-D3-E3
Canning Circus	A5
Carlton Road	F5
Carlton Street	D4
Carrington Street	D2-D3
Castle Boulevard	A2-B2-B3-C3
Castle Gate	C3-C4
Castle Market Road	E1-F1
Castle Meadow Road	B2-C2
Castle Road	C3
Cavendish Crescent South	A3
Cavendish Road East	A3-A4
Chaucer Street	B5-B6
Church Road	E8
Clarendon Street	B5-B6
Cliff Road	D3-E3
Clumber Crescent South	A3
Clumber Road East	A3-A4
Clumber Street	D4-D5
College Street	A5-B5-B4
Collin Street	C3-D3
Colville Street	B8
County Road	F1
Cranbrook Street	E4-E5
Cranmer Street	C8-D8
Crocus Street	D1-E1
Cromwell Street	A5-B6-C6
Curzon Street	D6-E6
Dane Close	D7-E7
Dakeyne Street	F5
Derby Road	A5-B5
Dryden Street	C6-C7
Fieness Crescent	A2
Fishergate	E3-E4
Fishpond Drive	A2-B2
Fletcher Gate	D4
Forest Road East	A8-B8-C8
Forest Road West	A7-A8
Friar Lane	C3-C4
Gedling Grove	A7
George Street	D4-D5
Glasshouse Street	D5-D6
Gill Street	B6-C6
Goldsmith Street	B6-C6-C5
Goose Gate	D4-E4
Great Freeman Street	D6
Hamilton Drive	B2-B3
Hampden Street	B6-C6
Handel Street	E5-F5
Haywood Street	F4-F5
High Pavement	D4-D3-E3
Hockley	E4
Holles Crescent	A3
Hollowstone	E3-E4
Hope Drive	B2-B3
Hound's Gate	C4
Howard Street	D5-D6
Hungerhill Road	E8-F8
Huntingdon Drive	A4-A3-B3
Huntingdon Drive	C8-C7-D7-D6-D5-E5
Huskisson Street	C6
Iremonger Road	E1
Kent Street	D5
King Edward Street	D5-E5
King Street	C4-C5
Lamartine Street	E6-F6
Lenton Road	A2-A3-B3
Lewis Close	E7
Lincoln Street	D5
Lister Gate	C3-C4
London Road	E1-E2-E3
Long Row	C4-D4
Lower Parliament Street	D5-E5-E4-E3
Low Pavement	C4-D4
Maid Marion Way	B4-C4-C3
Mansfield Street	C6-C7-C8
Manvers Street	F3-F4
Mapperley Road	C8
Market Street	C4-C5
Meadow Lane	F1
Meadows Road	B1-C1-D1-E1
Middle Hill	D3-D4
Milton Street	C6-C5-D5
Moorgate Street	A5
Mount Hooton Road	A8
Mount Street	B4-C4
Newark Crescent	F3
Newark Street	F3-F4
Newcastle Circus	A3
Newcastle Drive	A4-A5
Newstead Grove	B7-C7
North Street	F4-F5
North Sherwood Street	C6-C7-C8
Oliver Street	A6
Park Drive	A3-B3
Park Ravine	A2-A3
Park Row	B4
Park Terrace	A4-B4
Park Valley	A4-B4-B3
Peel Street	B6-B7-C7
Pelham Street	D4
Pennyfoot Street	E4-F4
Peveril Drive	B3
Pilcher Gate	D4
Plantagenet Street	E6
Plumptree Street	E4
Popham Street	D3
Poplar Street	E3-F3
Portland Road	A5-A6-A7
Queen's Drive	B1-C1, D1-D2
Queen's Road	D2-E2
Queen Street	C4-C5
Releigh Street	A6-A7
Regent Street	B4
Rick Street	D5
Robin Hood Street	E5-F5-F6
Russell Street	A6
St Ann's Hill Road	C8
St Ann's Valley	F7-F8
St Ann's Well Road	E5-E6-E7-F7-F8
St James Street	C4
St James Terrace	B4-B3-C3
St Mark's Street	D6
St Peters Gate	C4-D4
Shakespeare Street	B6-C6
Shelton Street	D7-D6-E6
Sheriffs Way	D1
Sneinton Road	F4
South Parade	C4-D4
South Road	A3
South Sherwood Street	C5-C6
Southwell Road	E4-F4
Station Street	D2-E2
Stony Street	D4-E4
Talbot Street	A5-B5-C5
Tattershall Drive	A4-A3-B3
Tennis Drive	A4-A5-A4
The Robewalk	A5-A4-B4
Trent Street	D2-D3
Tulip Avenue	A8
Tunnel Road	A4
Union Road	D6
Upper College Street	A5-B5
Upper Eldon Street	F4
Upper Parliament Street	B5-C5-D5
Victoria Street	D4
Villa Road	C8
Walker Street	F4-F5
Walter Street	A6-A7
Warser Gate	D4
Waterway Street	C1-D1
Watkin Street	D6-D7
Waverely Street	A8-A7-B7-B6
Wellington Street	D6-D7
West Street	F4-F5
Wheeler Gate	C4
Wilford Road	C1-C2
Wilford Street	C2-C3
Wollaton Street	A5-B5-C5
Woodborough Road	C6-C7-D7-D8
Woolpack Lane	D4-E4
York Street	C6-D6

57

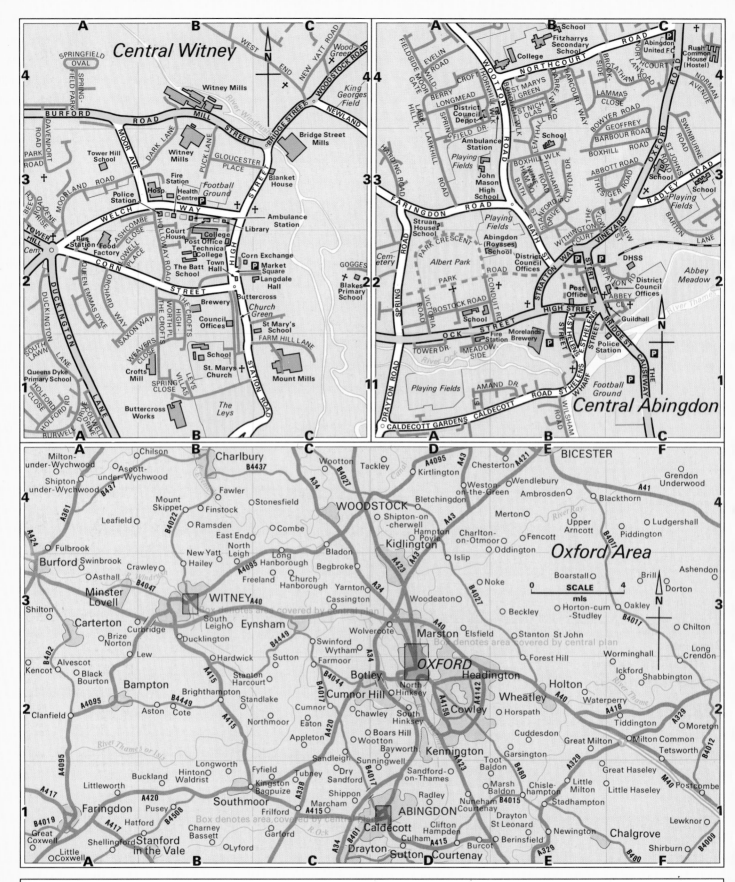

Oxford

From Carfax (at the centre of the city) round to Magdalen Bridge stretches High Street, one of England's best and most interesting thoroughfares. Shops rub shoulders with churches and colleges, alleyways lead to ancient inns and to a large covered market, and little streets lead to views of some of the finest architecture to be seen anywhere. Catte Street, beside St Mary's Church (whose lovely tower gives a panoramic view of Oxford), opens out into Radcliffe Square, dominated by the Radcliffe Camera, a great round structure built in 1749. Close by is the Bodleian Library, one of the finest collections of books and manuscripts in the world. All around are ancient college buildings. Close to Magdalen Bridge is Magdalen College, founded in 1448 and certainly not to be missed. Across the High Street are the Botanical Gardens, founded in 1621 and the oldest such foundation in England. Footpaths lead through Christ Church Meadow to Christ Church College and the cathedral. Tom Tower is the college's most notable feature; the cathedral is actually its chapel and is the smallest cathedral in England. Among much else not to be missed in Oxford is the Ashmolean Museum, whose vast collections of precious and beautiful objects from all over the world repay many hours of study; perhaps the loveliest treasure is the 9th-century Alfred Jewel.

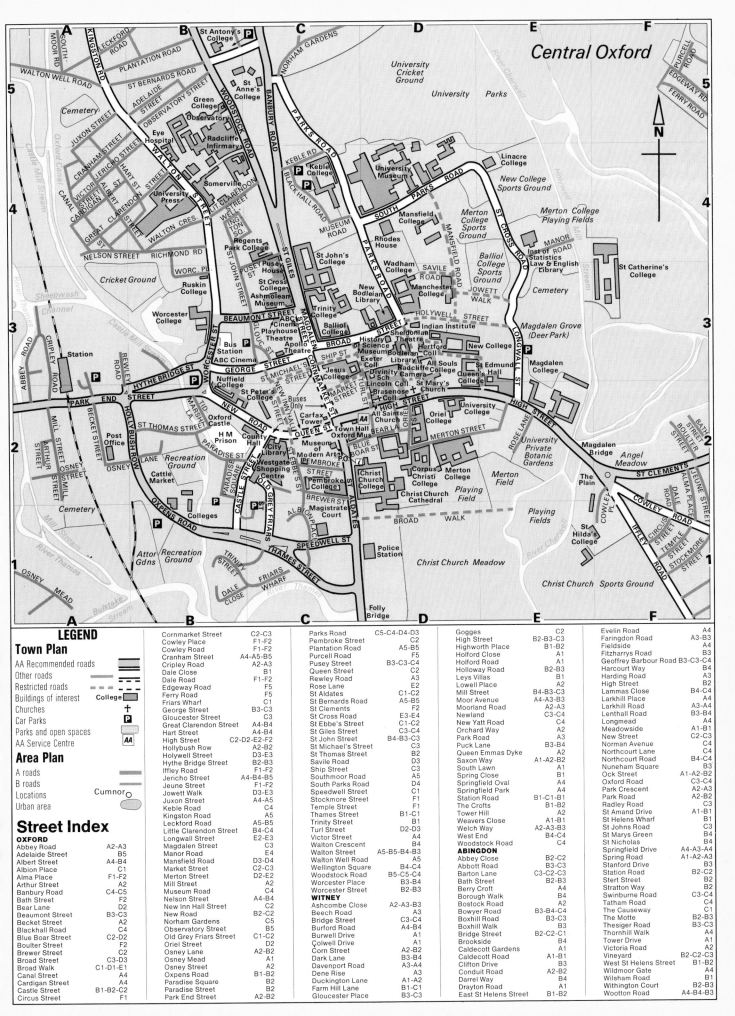

Central Oxford

LEGEND

Town Plan

- AA Recommended roads
- Other roads
- Restricted roads
- Buildings of interest — College
- Churches — †
- Car Parks — P
- Parks and open spaces
- AA Service Centre — AA

Area Plan

- A roads
- B roads
- Locations — Cumnor ○
- Urban area

Street Index

OXFORD

Abbey Road	A2-A3
Adelaide Street	B5
Albert Street	A4-B4
Albion Place	C1
Alma Place	F1-F2
Arthur Street	A2
Banbury Road	C4-C5
Bath Street	F2
Bear Lane	D2
Beaumont Street	B3-C3
Becket Street	A2
Blackhall Road	C4
Blue Boar Street	C2-D2
Boulter Street	F2
Brewer Street	C2
Broad Street	C3-D3
Broad Walk	C1-D1-E1
Canal Street	A4
Cardigan Street	A4
Castle Street	B1-B2-C2
Circus Street	F1
Cornmarket Street	C2-C3
Cowley Place	F1-F2
Cowley Road	F1-F2
Cranham Street	A4-A5-B5
Cripley Road	A2-A3
Dale Close	B1
Dale Road	F1-F2
Edgeway Road	F5
Ferry Road	F5
Friars Wharf	C1
George Street	B3-C3
Gloucester Street	C3
Great Clarendon Street	A4-B4
Hart Street	A4-B4
High Street	C2-D2-E2-F2
Hollybush Row	A2-B2
Holywell Street	D3-E3
Hythe Bridge Street	B2-B3
Iffley Road	F1-F2
Jericho Street	A4-B4-B5
Jeune Street	F2
Jowett Walk	D3-E3
Juxon Street	A4-A5
Keble Road	A5
Kingston Road	A5
Leckford Road	A5-B5
Little Clarendon Street	B4-C4
Longwall Street	E2-E3
Magdalen Street	C3
Manor Road	E4
Mansfield Road	D3-D4
Market Street	C2-C3
Merton Street	D2-E2
Mill Street	A2
Museum Road	C4
Nelson Street	A4-B4
New Inn Hall Street	C2
New Road	B2-C2
Norham Gardens	C5
Observatory Street	B5
Old Grey Friars Street	C1-C2
Oriel Street	D2
Osney Lane	A2-B2
Osney Mead	A1
Osney Street	A2
Oxpens Road	B1-B2
Paradise Square	B2
Paradise Street	B2
Park End Street	A2-B2

Parks Road	C5-C4-D4-D3
Pembroke Street	C2
Plantation Road	A5-B5
Purcell Road	F5
Pusey Street	B3-C3-C4
Queen Street	C2
Rewley Road	A3
Rose Lane	E2
St Aldates	C1-C2
St Bernards Road	A5-B5
St Clements	F2
St Cross Road	E3-E4
St Ebbe's Street	C1-C2
St Giles Street	C3-C4
St John Street	B4-B3-C3
St Michael's Street	C3
St Thomas Street	B2
Savile Road	D3
Ship Street	C3
Southmoor Road	A5
South Parks Road	D4
Speedwell Street	C1
Stockmore Street	F1
Temple Street	F1
Thames Street	B1-C1
Trinity Street	B1
Turl Street	D2-D3
Victor Street	A4
Walton Crescent	B4
Walton Street	A5-B5-B4-B3
Walton Well Road	A5
Wellington Square	B4
Woodstock Road	B5-C5-C4
Worcester Place	B3-B4
Worcester Street	B2-B3

WITNEY

Ashcombe Close	A2-A3-B3
Beech Road	A3
Bridge Street	C3-C4
Burford Road	A4-B4
Burwell Drive	A1
Colwell Drive	A1
Corn Street	A2-B2
Dark Lane	B3-B4
Davenport Road	A3-A4
Dene Rise	A3
Duckington Lane	A1-A2
Farm Hill Lane	B1-C1
Gloucester Place	B3-C3

Gogges	C2
High Street	B2-B3-C3
Highworth Place	B1-B2
Holford Close	A1
Holford Road	A1
Holloway Road	B2-B3
Leys Villas	B1
Lowell Place	A2
Mill Street	B4-B3-C3
Moor Avenue	A4-A3-B3
Moorland Road	A2-A3
Newland	C3-C4
New Yatt Road	C4
Orchard Way	A2
Park Road	A3
Puck Lane	B3-B4
Queen Emmas Dyke	A2
Saxon Way	A1-A2-B2
South Lawn	A1
Spring Close	B1
Springfield Oval	A4
Springfield Park	A4
Station Road	B1-C1-B1
The Crofts	B1-B2
Tower Hill	A2
Weavers Close	A1-B1
Welch Way	A2-A3-B3
West End	B4-C4
Woodstock Road	C4

ABINGDON

Abbey Close	B2-C2
Abbott Road	B3-C3
Barton Lane	C3-C2-C3
Bath Street	B2-B3
Berry Croft	A4
Borough Walk	B4
Bostock Road	A2
Bowyer Road	B3-B4-C4
Boxhill Road	B3-C3
Boxhill Walk	B3
Bridge Street	B2-C2-C1
Brookside	B4
Caldecott Gardens	A1
Caldecott Road	A1-B1
Clifton Drive	B3
Conduit Road	A2-B2
Darrel Way	B4
Drayton Road	A1
East St Helens Street	B1-B2

Evelin Road	A4
Faringdon Road	A3-B3
Fieldside	A4
Fitzharrys Road	B3
Geoffrey Barbour Road	B3-C3-C4
Harcourt Way	B4
Harding Road	A3
High Street	B2
Lammas Close	B4-C4
Larkhill Place	A4
Larkhill Road	A3-A4
Lenthall Road	B3-B4
Longmead	A4
Meadowside	A1-B1
New Street	C2-C3
Norman Avenue	C4
Northcourt Lane	C4
Northcourt Road	B4-C4
Nuneham Square	B3
Ock Street	A1-A2-B2
Oxford Road	C3-C4
Park Crescent	A2-A3
Park Road	A2-B2
Radley Road	C3
St Amand Drive	A1-B1
St Helens Wharf	B1
St Johns Road	C3
St Marys Green	B4
St Nicholas	B4
Springfield Drive	A4-A3-A4
Spring Road	A1-A2-A3
Stanford Drive	B3
Station Road	B2-C2
Stert Street	B2
Stratton Way	B2
Swinburne Road	C3-C2-C3
Tatham Road	C4
The Causeway	C1
The Motte	B2-B3
Thesiger Road	B3-C3
Thornhill Walk	A4
Tower Drive	A1
Victoria Road	A2
Vineyard	B2-C2-C3
West St Helens Street	B1-B2
Wildmoor Gate	A4
Wilsham Road	B1
Withington Court	B2-B3
Wootton Road	A4-B4-B3

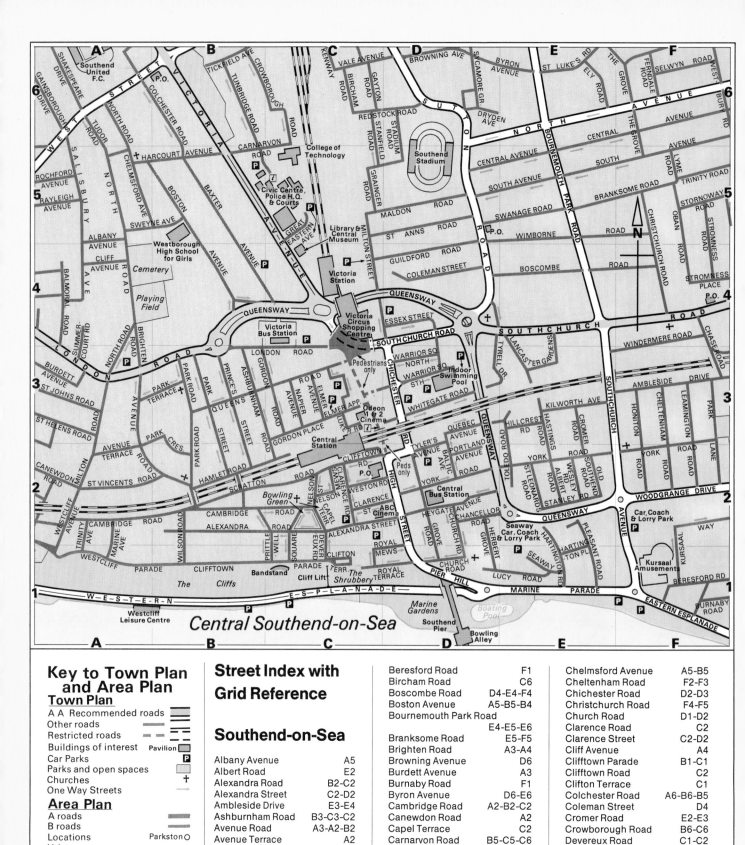

Central Southend-on-Sea

Key to Town Plan and Area Plan

Town Plan

A A Recommended roads	
Other roads	
Restricted roads	
Buildings of interest	Pavilion ▉
Car Parks	P
Parks and open spaces	▨
Churches	†
One Way Streets	→

Area Plan

A roads	
B roads	
Locations	Parkston ○
Urban area	▨

Street Index with Grid Reference

Southend-on-Sea

Southend

The longest pleasure pier in the world and brilliant illuminations along the seafront in autumn are just two of the attractions of this thriving, immensely popular seaside resort, which offers the visitor every facet of the traditional holiday. Dance halls, theatres, amusement arcades and funfairs fill the Marine Parade area, with Peter Pan's Playground next to the pier and the

Kursall Amusement Park at the eastern end of the seafront both attracting crowds of visitors. The Pier itself offers entertainments (not least a wax museum housed in the replica of Sir Francis Drake's *Golden Hind* which lies alongside) and its 1¼ mile length is usually liberally dotted with fishermen. The most popular beaches are at Westcliffe and Thorpe Bay, while Leigh-on-Sea, linked to Southend by a lengthy promenade, makes a peaceful contrast to the main seafront area.

Places of interest include the village of Prittlewell, on the northern edge of town, with its 12th-century Priory and 13th-century church, 13th- to 14th-century Southchurch Hall (a timber-framed manor house with period furniture and beautiful grounds) and the Central Museum, which traces the history of south-east Essex back to the Romans. Good shopping and sports facilities, pleasant parks, professional cricket and football, and greyhound racing are other features of the town.

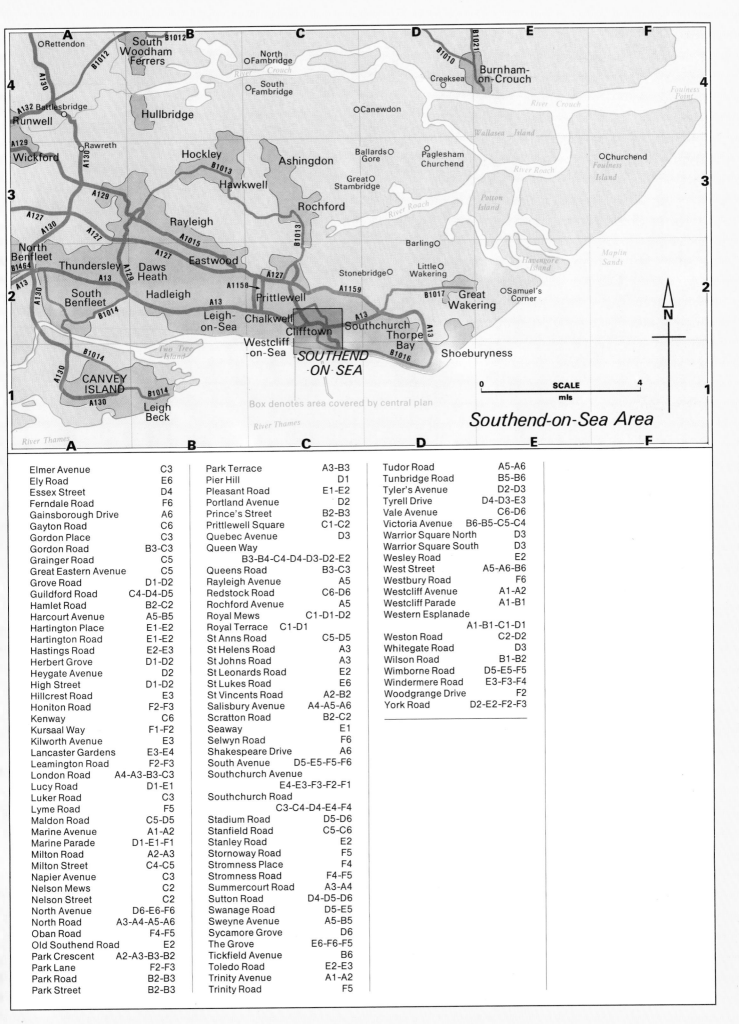

Southend-on-Sea Area

Box denotes area covered by central plan

SCALE 0 — 4 mls

Elmer Avenue		C3
Ely Road		E6
Essex Street		D4
Ferndale Road		F6
Gainsborough Drive		A6
Gayton Road		C6
Gordon Place		C3
Gordon Road		B3-C3
Grainger Road		C5
Great Eastern Avenue		C5
Grove Road		D1-D2
Guildford Road		C4-D4-D5
Hamlet Road		B2-C2
Harcourt Avenue		A5-B5
Hartington Place		E1-E2
Hartington Road		E1-E2
Hastings Road		E2-E3
Herbert Grove		D1-D2
Heygate Avenue		D2
High Street		D1-D2
Hillcrest Road		E3
Honiton Road		F2-F3
Kenway		C6
Kursaal Way		F1-F2
Kilworth Avenue		E3
Lancaster Gardens		E3-E4
Leamington Road		F2-F3
London Road		A4-A3-B3-C3
Lucy Road		D1-E1
Luker Road		C3
Lyme Road		F5
Maldon Road		C5-D5
Marine Avenue		A1-A2
Marine Parade		D1-E1-F1
Milton Road		A2-A3
Milton Street		C4-C5
Napier Avenue		C3
Nelson Mews		C2
Nelson Street		C2
North Avenue		D6-E6-F6
North Road		A3-A4-A5-A6
Oban Road		F4-F5
Old Southend Road		E2
Park Crescent		A2-A3-B3-B2
Park Lane		F2-F3
Park Road		B2-B3
Park Street		B2-B3

Park Terrace		A3-B3
Pier Hill		D1
Pleasant Road		E1-E2
Portland Avenue		D2
Prince's Street		B2-B3
Prittlewell Square		C1-C2
Quebec Avenue		D3
Queen Way		B3-B4-C4-D4-D3-D2-E2
Queens Road		B3-C3
Rayleigh Avenue		A5
Redstock Road		C6-D6
Rochford Avenue		A5
Royal Mews		C1-D1-D2
Royal Terrace		C1-D1
St Anns Road		C5-D5
St Helens Road		A3
St Johns Road		A3
St Leonards Road		E2
St Lukes Road		E6
St Vincents Road		A2-B2
Salisbury Avenue		A4-A5-A6
Scratton Road		B2-C2
Seaway		E1
Selwyn Road		F6
Shakespeare Drive		A6
South Avenue		D5-E5-F5-F6
Southchurch Avenue		E4-E3-F3-F2-F1
Southchurch Road		C3-C4-D4-E4-F4
Stadium Road		D5-D6
Stanfield Road		C5-C6
Stanley Road		E2
Stornoway Road		F5
Stromness Place		F4
Stromness Road		F4-F5
Summercourt Road		A3-A4
Sutton Road		D4-D5-D6
Swanage Road		D5-E5
Sweyne Avenue		A5-B5
Sycamore Grove		D6
The Grove		E6-F6-F5
Tickfield Avenue		B6
Toledo Road		E2-E3
Trinity Avenue		A1-A2
Trinity Road		F5

Tudor Road		A5-A6
Tunbridge Road		B5-B6
Tyler's Avenue		D2-D3
Tyrell Drive		D4-D3-E3
Vale Avenue		C6-D6
Victoria Avenue		B6-B5-C5-C4
Warrior Square North		D3
Warrior Square South		D3
Wesley Road		E2
West Street		A5-A6-B6
Westbury Road		F6
Westcliff Avenue		A1-A2
Westcliff Parade		A1-B1
Western Esplanade		A1-B1-C1-D1
Weston Road		C2-D2
Whitegate Road		D3
Wilson Road		B1-B2
Wimborne Road		D5-E5-F5
Windermere Road		E3-F3-F4
Woodgrange Drive		F2
York Road		D2-E2-F2-F3

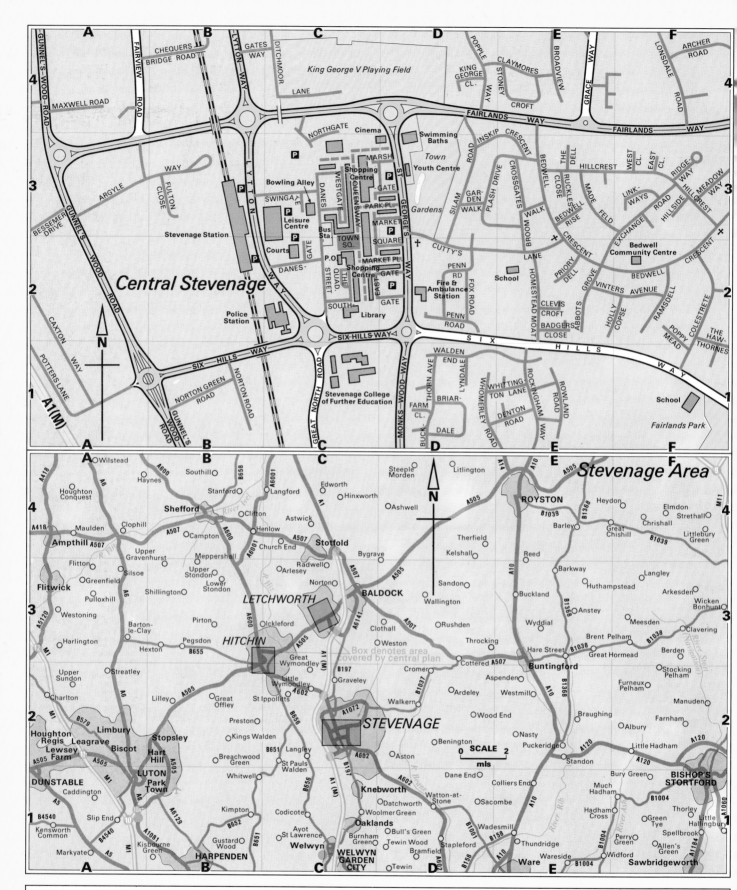

Stevenage

This is one of the New Towns, designed shortly after World War II to provide a pleasant integration of housing, industrial estates and shopping and entertainment facilities, with an attractively landscaped park. A number of older buildings from the original town can still be seen in and around the High Street, including Alleyn's Grammar School, dating from the 16th century, and the Yorkshire Grey, an old coaching inn. The Stevenage Museum, in the undercroft of St George's Church, has an interesting collection of archaeological and historic items.

Hitchin stands on the quaintly named River Hiz, and despite a great deal of redevelopment has retained much of its medieval street plan together with a number of picturesque, half-timbered buildings. The Corn Exchange is a fine example of Italianate architecture, and the parish church offers a delightful mixture of styles, from a 12th-century tower to 17th-century wall paintings.

Letchworth The first Garden City was developed around the village of Letchworth early in the present century, and today the town is a pleasant mixture of unobtrusive industrial estates and attractive, tree-lined avenues. Places of interest include the Museum and Art Gallery and the First Garden City Museum. Norton Common, in the north, provides 63 acres of unspoilt grass and woodland.

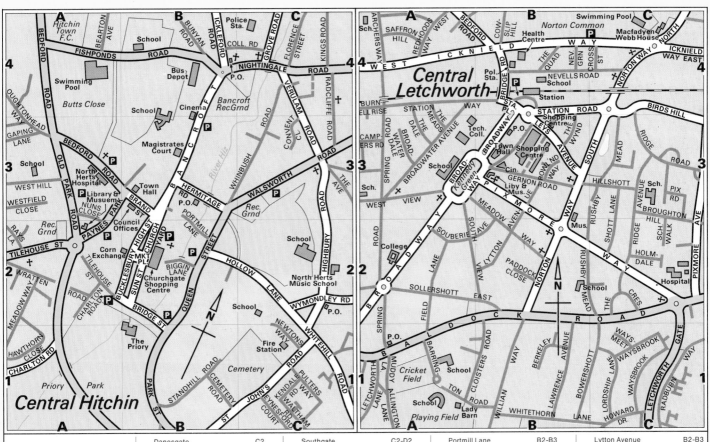

Central Hitchin

Central Letchworth

STEVENAGE

East of the town centre, St George's Way provides a dramatic modern townscape, including the slender 90ft campanile of St George's Church — second largest Anglican church built in Britain since World War II.

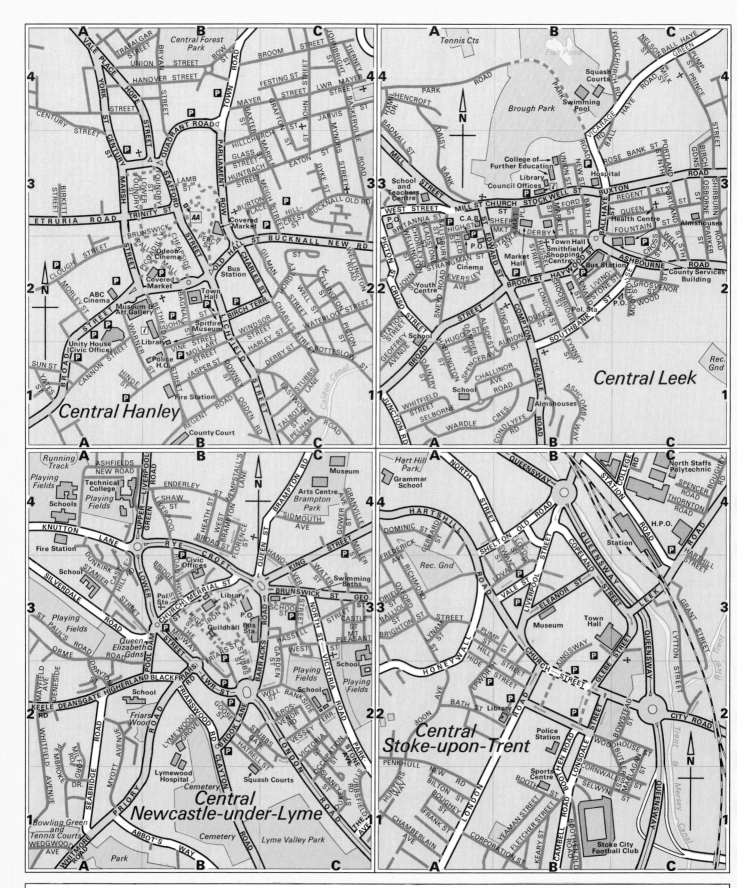

Stoke-on-Trent

Wedgwood, Spode and Royal Doulton are among the names that spring to mind with the mention of Stoke-on-Trent. Renowned for many years as the capital of the pottery industry, the town has numerous museums dealing with the industry's history as well as with leading figures involved in it, and tours of pottery factories can be arranged. On the sporting side, Stoke City, the local football team, which plays in the Canon League, boasts Sir Stanley Matthews amongst its former players.

Hanley is the birthplace of Arnold Bennet, who immortalised the Potteries in his stories about the 'Five Towns'. Born here too was Spitfire designer Reginald Mitchell, and the town has a museum devoted to his life and work. Another great attraction of Hanley for many is the fine woodland expanse of 90-acre Central Forest Park.

Leek was once renowned for silk and dye, but now attracts visitors to its antique shops. Amongst its interesting older buildings, Brindley Mill and Museum specialises in the work of 18th-century canal builder James Brindley.

Newcastle-under-Lyme boasts a fine old Guildhall and several inns dating from the 17th and 18th centuries. Keele University, to the south-west, has contributed to the town's cultural activities in recent years.

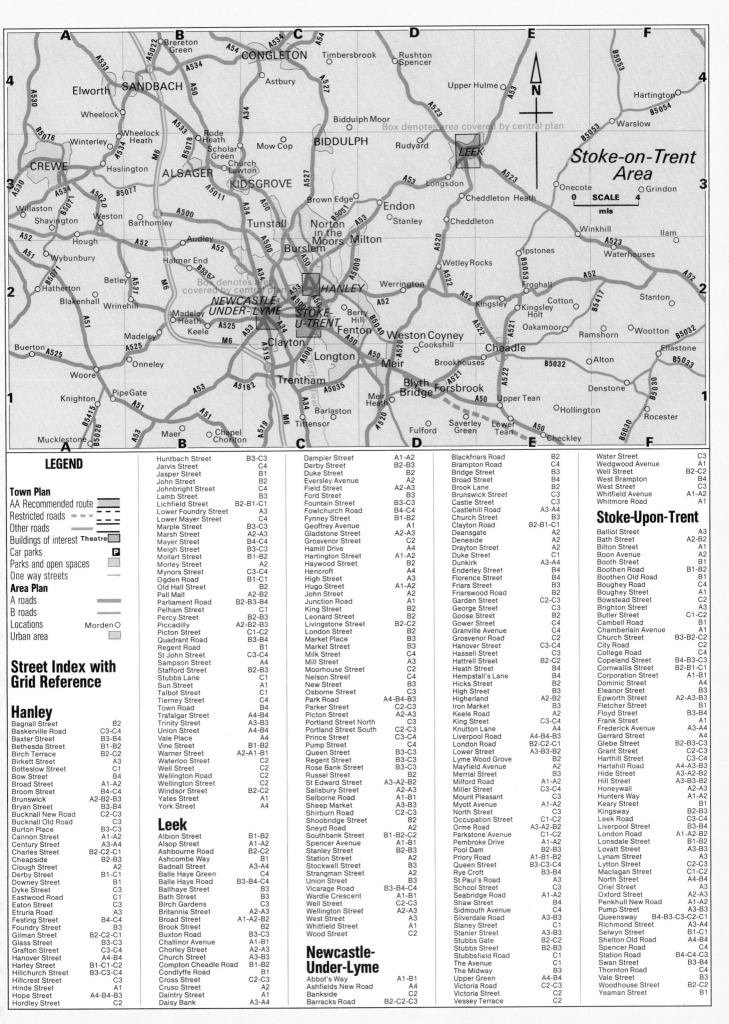

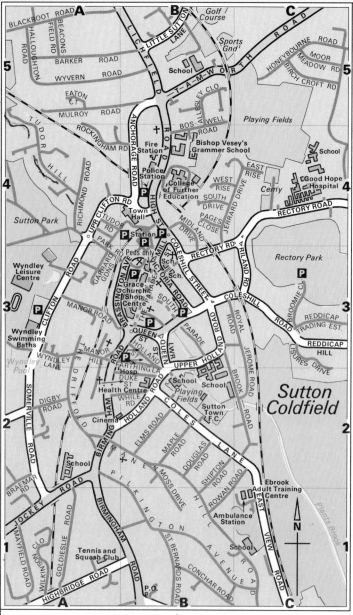
Sutton Coldfield

Jerome Road	C2-C3
Jockey Road	A1-A2
Lichfield Road	A5-B5-B4
Little Sutton Lane	B5
Lisures Drive	C2-C3
Lower Queen Street	B3
Maney Hill Road	A2-B2-B1-C1
Manor Hill	A3
Manor Road	A3-B3
Maple Road	B2
Mayfield Road	A1
Midland Drive	B3-B4
Mill Street	B3-B4
Moor Meadow Road	C5
Moss Drive	B1-B2
Mulroy Road	A5-B5
Pages Close	B4
Park Road	A3-A4
Pilkington Avenue	A2-B2-B1-C1
Queen Street	B3
Rectory Road	B3-B4-C4
Reddicap Hill	C3
Reddicap Trading Estate	C3
Richmond Road	A4
Riland Road	C3-C4
Rockingham Road	A5-A4-B4
Rowan Road	B1-B2-C2
Royal Road	B3-C3
St Bernards Road	B1
Shipton Road	B1-B2
Somerville Road	A1-A2-A3
South Drive	B4
South Parade	B3
The Parade	A3
Tamworth Road	B5-C5
The Driffold	A2-A3
Tudor Hill	A4-A5
Tudor Road	A4
Upper Clifton Road	A4-B4
Upper Holland Road	B2-B3
Victoria Road	B3
West Rise	B4-C4
While Road	A2-B2
Wilkinson Close	A1
Wyndley Lane	A3
Wyvern Road	A5-B5

Shrewsbury

Abbey Foregate	F2-F3
Albert Street	E5-F5
Alma Street	C5
Ashton Road	A1-B1
Barker Street	C3-C4
Beacall's Lane	E5
Beeches Lane	D2
Bellstone	C3
Belmont Bank	C2-D2
Betton Street	F1
Breidden View	A5
Bridge Street	C4
Butchers Row	D3
Canonbury	B1
Castle Foregate	E5
Castlegates	D4-D5
Castle Street	D4
Chester Street	D5
Claremont Bank	B3-B4-C4
Claremont Hill	B3-C3
Claremont Street	C3
Coleham Head	E2-F2
College Hill	C3-C2-D2
Copthorne Road	A5-B5
Coton Crescent	B5
Crescent Lane	C1-C2
Cross Hill	C2-C3
Dogpole	D2-D3
English Bridge	E2-F2
Fish Street	D3
Frankwell	B5
Greyfriars	E1
Grope Lane	D3
High Street	C3-D3-D2
Hills Lane	C4
Holywell Street	F2-F3
Howard Street	E5
Kingsland Bridge	B1-B2-C2
Kingsland Bridge Approach Road	B1
Lessar Avenue	A5
Londen Coleham	D1-E1-F1
Longner Street	C5
Mardol	C3-C4
Market Street	C3
Meadow Place	D5
Milk Street	D2
Moreton Crescent	E1-F1
Mount Street	C5
Muirvance	B2-C2
Nestles Lane	B5-C5
New Street	A4-A5-B5
Old Coleham	F1
Park Avenue	A4
Pengwern Road	A4
Pride Hill	C3-D3-D4
Princess Street	C3-D3-D2
Priory Street	B4
Quarry Place	B2
Raven Meadows	C4-D4-D5
Roushill	C4

Roushill Street	C3-C4
St Austins Friars	B4
St Austins Street	B4-C4
St Chads Terrace	B2-B3
St John's Hill	B2-C2-C3
St Julian's Friars	D2-E2
St Mary's Place	D3-D4
St Mary's Street	D3
Severn Street	F5
Shoplatch	C3
Smithfield Road	C4-D4-D5
Swan Hill	C2-C3
Swan Hill Court	C2
The Dana	E5
The Mount	B5
The Square	C3-D3
Town Walls	C2-D2
Victoria Avenue	C4-B4-A4-A3-A2-B2-B1-C1-D1-D2
Victoria Street	E5-F5
Water Lane	D4-E4
Water Street	F5
Welsh Bridge	B5-C5-C4
Wyle Cop	D2

Solihull

Albany Gardens	F2
Alderbrook Road	A1-A2-B2
Alderpark Road	A1
Arley Road	B2
Ashleigh Road	B3-C3
Beaminster Road	A2-B2-B3
Beauchamp Road	C3-C4
Beaumont Grove	A3-A4
Beechnut Lane	F3-F4
Blossomfield Road	A1-B1-B2-C2
Blyth Avenue	F1
Broad Oaks Road	A4-B4-B3
Broomfields Close	E4
Brueton Avenue	F1-F2
Bryanston Road	A4
Caldwell Grove	D4-E4
Church Hill Road	D1
Cornyx Lane	E4-F4
Damson Lane	F4
Damson Parkway	F3-F4
Dorchester Road	A3-B3-B2
Dury Lane	D2
Elms Close	E4-F4
Ferndown Road	C4-D4
George Road	D2-E2
Glebe Road	E4-F4
Grove Road	D4-D3-E3
Hainfield Drive	F3-F4
Hampton Lane	E2-F2-F3
Herbert Road	C2
Hermitage Road	D4-E4
Heronfield Way	F3
High Street	D1-D2
Homer Road	C2-C2-D1
Ladbrook Road	D1
Lode Lane	C2-D2-D3-D4
Malvern Park Avenue	E1
Manor Road	C3-D3-D4
Marsh Lane	F1-F2-F3
Mells Square	D2
Milcote Road	C3
Mill Lane	D2
Muswell Close	E3
Naseby Road	C4
New Road	E1-E2
Oaken Drive	A3
Oakley Wood Drive	F2
Park Avenue	E1-E1
Park Road	D1-E1
Poolfield Drive	A1
Poplar Road	D2
Princes Way	C2-C1-D2
Radford Rise	F3
Rectory Gardens	E1
Rectory Road	D1-E1
Redlands Close	E4
Redlands Road	D4-E4-F4
Rollswood Drive	A2-B2
Sandal Rise	F2
School Lane	E3-F3-F2
Seven Star Road	B4-C4-D4
Sharmans Cross Road	A2-A3
Shustoke Road	C3
Silhill Hall Road	B4-B3-C3
Silverbirch Road	F2
Solihull By-pass	D4-E4-E3-F3
Station Approach	B3-B2-C2
Station Road	C2-C2
Stonor Park Road	A3-A4
Streetsbrook Road	A3-B3-C3-C2
The Crescent	C2-C3
Thornby Avenue	C4-D4-D3
Touchwood Hall Close	D3
Union Road	D2-E2-E3
Warwick Road	B4-C4-C3-D3-D2-E2-F2-F1
Welcombe Grove	A1-A2
Wherretts Well Lane	F4
White House Green	A1
White House Way	A1-B1
Winterbourne Road	A2-A3
Woodfield Road	C4
Yew Tree Lane	F3-F4

LEGEND

AA Recommended roads	▬▬
Restricted roads	- - -
Other roads	▬▬
Buildings of interest	College ⬛
Car Parks	P
Parks and open spaces	⬛
Churches	✝
One Way Streets	→

Street Index with Grid Reference

Sutton Coldfield

Allesley Close	B5
Anchorage Road	B4-B5
Barker Road	A5-B5

Beaconsfield Road	A5
Birchcroft Road	A5
Birmingham Road	B3-A3-A2-A1-B1
Blackroot Road	A5
Boswell Road	B4-B5
Braemar Road	A1-A2
Brassington Avenue	A3-B3
Brook Road	B3-B2-C2
Broomie Close	C3
Clifton Road	A3-A4
Coles Lane	B2-C2
Coleshill Road	B3-C3
Coleshill Street	B3-B4
Conchar Road	B1-C1
Digby Road	A2
Douglas Road	B2
Duke Street	A2-B2
East Rise	C4
East View Road	C1-C2
Eaton Court	A5
Elms Road	B2
Farthing Lane	A3-B3-B2
Garrard Gardens	A3
Goldieslie Road	A1
Halloughton Road	A5
High Street	A3
Highbridge Road	A1-B1
Holland Road	A2-B2
Holland Street	B2-B3
Honeybourne Road	C5
Jerrard Drive	B4-C4

Sutton Coldfield is one of the most popular residential areas in the Birmingham region — not least because of Sutton Park, which was a royal hunting ground in the 16th century and offers 2,400 acres of heathland, lakes and woodland.

Shrewsbury is celebrated for the wealth of half-timbered black and white buildings which line its narrow streets, many of which are 16th century. Known also as the 'Town of Flowers' because of its parks and gardens, and because of the profusion of window boxes and hanging baskets to be seen in its streets, this historic market town is attractively situated in a horseshoe bend of the River Severn, and has no less than seven bridges. Charles Darwin was born and educated here, and Lord Robert Clive (Clive of India) was its Member of Parliament during the latter part of the 18th century. The Norman castle still has 12th-century features, and St Mary's Church, also 12th-century, has particularly good stained glass.

Amongst the town's many museums, 16th-century Rowley's House deals mainly with archaeology.

Solihull's fine sports facilities include an ice rink, an open air lido in Malvern Park and an athletics track and swimming pool in Tudor Grange Park. A pleasant, part-industrialised suburb lying close to Birmingham's National Exhibition Centre, it also boasts modern conference facilities and has a pedestrianised shopping precinct tucked away behind the High Street.

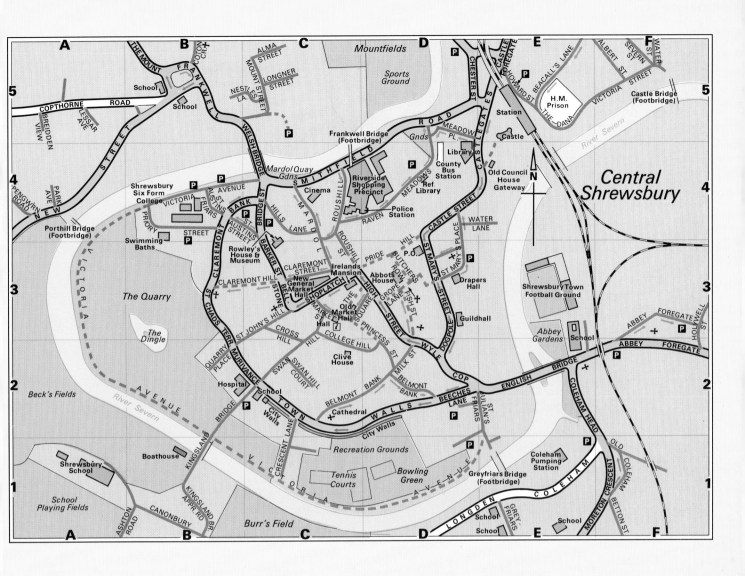

Central Shrewsbury

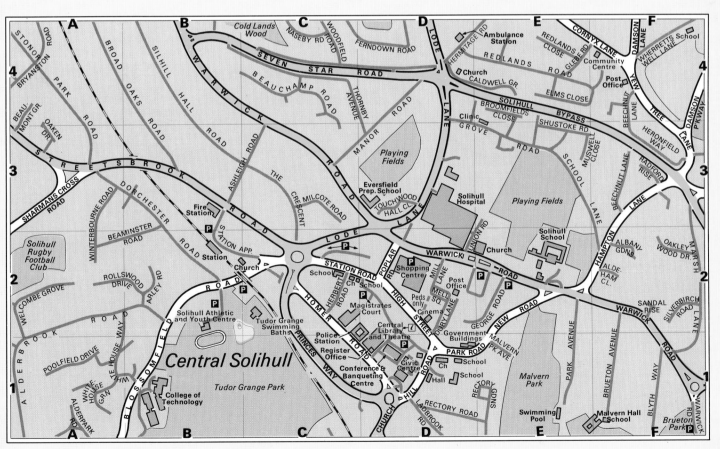

Central Solihull

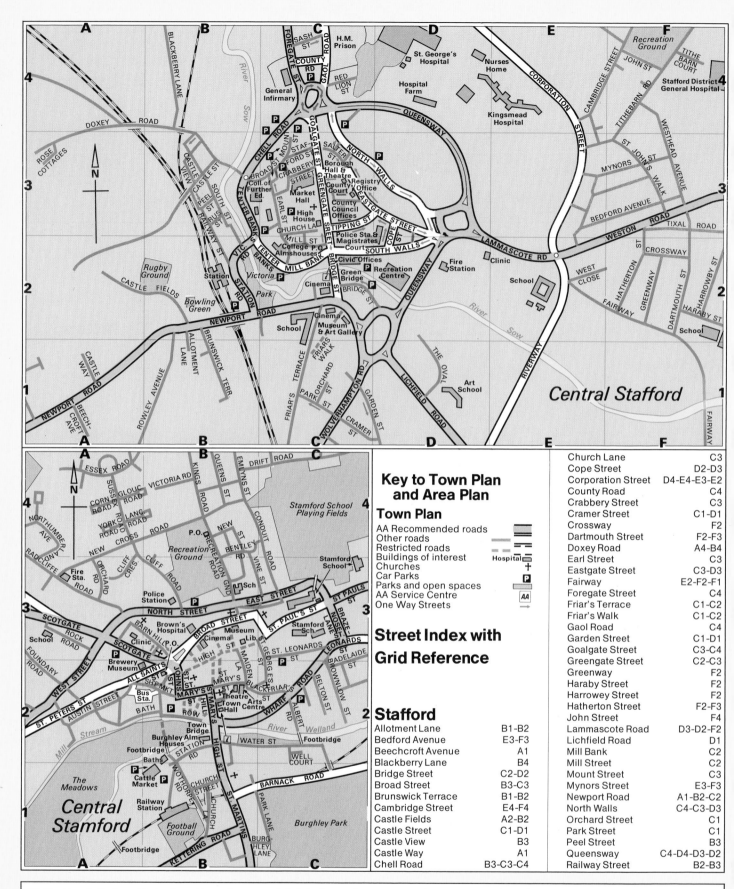

Key to Town Plan and Area Plan

Town Plan

AA Recommended roads	
Other roads	
Restricted roads	
Buildings of interest	Hospital
Churches	+
Car Parks	P
Parks and open spaces	
AA Service Centre	AA
One Way Streets	→

Street Index with Grid Reference

Stafford

Central Stafford

N

Central Stamford

Stafford boasts the largest timber-framed house in England in High House, and has numerous other historic buildings. Prosperous through its wool trade long before the Industrial Revolution, Stafford became an established industrial centre through the manufacture of footwear. Today the town has fine leisure facilities in the Riverside Recreation Centre.

Stamford is thought by many to be one of England's most beautiful towns. Former Danish capital of the Fens and now a conservation area, it stands on a hilly site with fine views of three counties, and offers an admirable blend of the old with the new. Oldest building in the town is the 7th-century ruined chapel of St Leonard's Priory.

Stroud Standing on a steep hill site at the convergence of five valleys, Stroud has a distinctly country 'feel'. Running along its valleys are several early industrial buildings: this was once the most important area for broadcloth manufacture, and more recently has won world renown for its production of billiard table cloth and scarlet dye.

Tewkesbury grew up around Tewkesbury Abbey, and is one of the country's most complete medieval towns, with a wealth of ancient houses and timbered inns. Among them the Black Bear Inn is quite unique: said to date from 1308, it incorporates part of 13th-century King John's Bridge in its structure.

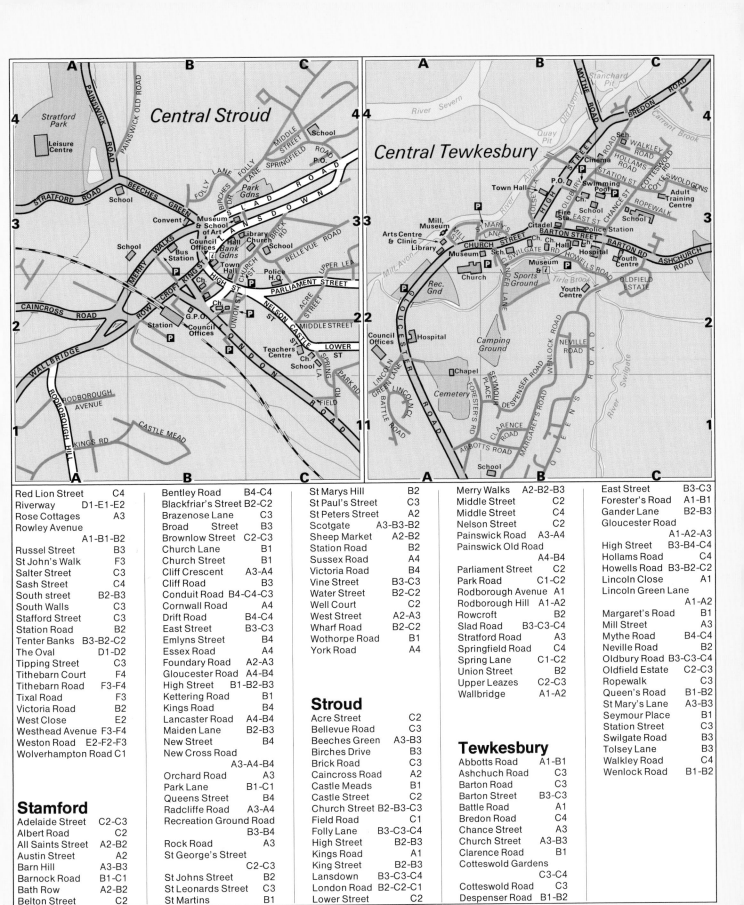

Central Stroud

Central Tewkesbury

Red Lion Street	C4	Bentley Road	B4-C4	St Marys Hill	B2
Riverway	D1-E1-E2	Blackfriar's Street	B2-C2	St Paul's Street	C3
Rose Cottages	A3	Brazenose Lane	C3	St Peters Street	A2
Rowley Avenue		Broad Street	B3	Scotgate	A3-B3-B2
	A1-B1-B2	Brownlow Street	C2-C3	Sheep Market	A2-B2
Russel Street	B3	Church Lane	B1	Station Road	B2
St John's Walk	F3	Church Street	B1	Sussex Road	A4
Salter Street	C3	Cliff Crescent	A3-A4	Victoria Road	B4
Sash Street	C4	Cliff Road	B3	Vine Street	B3-C3
South street	B2-B3	Conduit Road	B4-C4-C3	Water Street	B2-C2
South Walls	C3	Cornwall Road	A4	Well Court	C2
Stafford Street	C3	Drift Road	B4-C4	West Street	A2-A3
Station Road	B2	East Street	B3-C3	Wharf Road	B2-C2
Tenter Banks	B3-B2-C2	Emlyns Street	B4	Wothorpe Road	B1
The Oval	D1-D2	Essex Road	A4	York Road	A4
Tipping Street	C3	Foundary Road	A2-A3		
Tithebarn Court	F4	Gloucester Road	A4-B4		
Tithebarn Road	F3-F4	High Street	B1-B2-B3		
Tixal Road	F3	Kettering Road	B1		
Victoria Road	B2	Kings Road	B4	**Stroud**	
West Close	E2	Lancaster Road	A4-B4	Acre Street	C2
Westhead Avenue	F3-F4	Maiden Lane	B2-B3	Bellevue Road	C3
Weston Road	E2-F2-F3	New Street	B4	Beeches Green	A3-B3
Wolverhampton Road	C1	New Cross Road		Birches Drive	B3
			A3-A4-B4	Brick Road	C3
		Orchard Road	A3	Caincross Road	A2
		Park Lane	B1-C1	Castle Meads	B1
Stamford		Queens Street	B4	Castle Street	C2
Adelaide Street	C2-C3	Radcliffe Road	A3-A4	Church Street	B2-B3-C3
Albert Road	C2	Recreation Ground Road		Field Road	C1
All Saints Street	A2-B2		B3-B4	Folly Lane	B3-C3-C4
Austin Street	A2	Rock Road	A3	High Street	B2-B3
Barn Hill	A3-B3	St George's Street		Kings Road	A1
Barnock Road	B1-C1		C2-C3	King Street	B2-B3
Bath Row	A2-B2	St Johns Street	B2	Lansdown	B3-C3-C4
Belton Street	C2	St Leonards Street	C3	London Road	B2-C2-C1
		St Martins	B1	Lower Street	C2

Merry Walks	A2-B2-B3	East Street	B3-C3
Middle Street	C2	Forester's Road	A1-B1
Middle Street	C4	Gander Lane	B2-B3
Nelson Street	C2	Gloucester Road	
Painswick Road	A3-A4		A1-A2-A3
Painswick Old Road		High Street	B3-B4-C4
	A4-B4	Hollams Road	C4
Parliament Street	C2	Howells Road	B3-B2-C2
Park Road	C1-C2	Lincoln Close	A1
Rodborough Avenue	A1	Lincoln Green Lane	
Rodborough Hill	A1-A2		A1-A2
Rowcroft	B2	Margaret's Road	B1
Slad Road	B3-C3-C4	Mill Street	A3
Stratford Road	A3	Mythe Road	B4-C4
Springfield Road		Neville Road	B2
Spring Lane	C1-C2	Oldbury Road	B3-C3-C4
Union Street	B2	Oldfield Estate	C2-C3
Upper Leazes	C2-C3	Ropewalk	C3
Wallbridge	A1-A2	Queen's Road	B1-B2
		St Mary's Lane	A3-B3
		Seymour Place	B1
Tewkesbury		Station Street	C3
Abbotts Road	A1-B1	Swilgate Road	B3
Ashchuch Road	C3	Tolsey Lane	B3
Barton Road	C3	Walkley Road	C4
Barton Street	B3-C3	Wenlock Road	B1-B2
Battle Road	A1		
Bredon Road	C4		
Chance Street	A3		
Church Street	A3-B3		
Clarence Road	B1		
Cotteswold Gardens			
	C3-C4		
Cotteswold Road	C3		
Despenser Road	B1-B2		

TEWKESBURY
The fine abbey church of St Mary was saved by the local townspeople from possible destruction during the Dissolution of the Monasteries — they found the money to buy it from Henry VIII and so kept it intact.

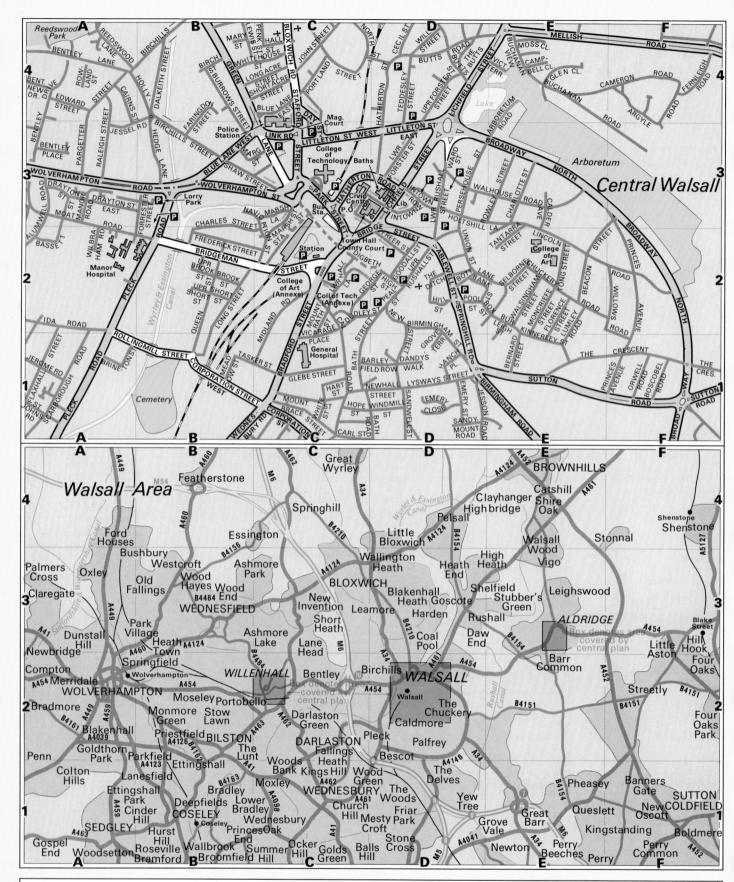

Walsall

Affectionately known as the 'Town of 100 Trades' because of its diversity of industries, Walsall is nevertheless a specialist in one area — leather manufacture. Saddles have been produced here since the 19th century, and all the British Army's saddles in World War I were Walsall-made.

A conservation area has been established at Church Hill, covering the Parish Church of St Matthew (which dates back to the 12th century), and part of the town centre where Italian Renaissance style Taylor's Music Shop is just one of several fine Victorian buildings to be seen. Other places of interest are the Central Library's Local History Gallery, Belsize House, the birthplace of Jerome K. Jerome (now a museum dealing with his life and work) and the Garman Ryan Collection which has art donated by Lady Kathleen Epstein, widow of sculptor Sir Jacob. The Walsall Illuminations appear each September.

Aldridge enjoys the contrasts of an industrial town set in pleasant rural surroundings. The oldest part of town, around the Parish Church, has been declared a conservation area.

Willenhall has kept its old 'Black Country' character, and the market place area is being restored in 19th-century style. A reputation for lock and key making is recalled in the local library's Lock Museum.

70

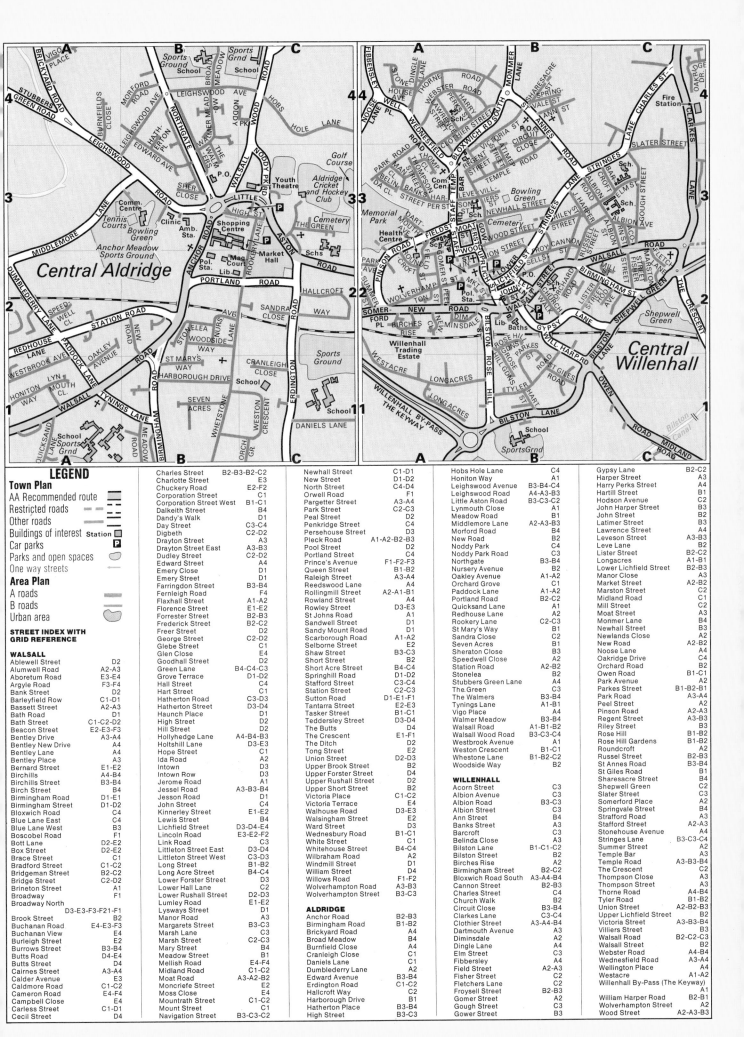

LEGEND

Town Plan

AA Recommended route
Restricted roads
Other roads
Buildings of interest   Station
Car parks   P
Parks and open spaces
One way streets

Area Plan

A roads
B roads
Urban area

STREET INDEX WITH GRID REFERENCE

WALSALL

Ablewell Street	D2
Alumwell Road	A2-A3
Aboretum Road	E3-E4
Argyle Road	F3-F4
Bank Street	D2
Barleyfield Row	C1-D1
Bassett Street	A2-A3
Bath Road	D1
Bath Street	C1-C2-D2
Beacon Street	E2-E3-E3
Bentley Drive	A3-A4
Bentley New Drive	A4
Bentley Lane	A4
Bentley Place	A3
Bernard Street	E1-E2
Birchills	A4-B4
Birchills Street	B3-B4
Birch Street	B4
Birmingham Road	D1-E1
Birmingham Street	D1-D2
Bloxwich Road	C4
Blue Lane East	C4
Blue Lane West	B3
Boscobel Road	F1
Bott Lane	D2-E2
Box Street	D2-E2
Brace Street	C1
Bradford Street	C1-C2
Bridgeman Street	B2-C2
Bridge Street	C2-D2
Brineton Street	A1
Broadway	F1
Broadway North	D3-E3-F3-F21-F1
Brook Street	B2
Buchanan Road	E4-E3-F3
Buchanan View	E4
Burleigh Street	E2
Burrows Street	B3-B4
Butts Road	D4-E4
Butts Street	D4
Cairnes Street	A3-A4
Calder Avenue	E3
Caldmore Road	C1-C2
Cameron Road	E4-E4
Campbell Close	E4
Carless Street	C1-D1
Cecil Street	D4

Charles Street	B2-B3-B2-C2
Charlotte Street	E3
Chuckery Road	E2-F2
Corporation Street	C1
Corporation Street West	B1-C1
Dalkeith Street	B4
Dandy's Walk	D1
Day Street	C3-C4
Digbeth	C2-D2
Drayton Street	A3
Drayton Street East	A3-B3
Dudley Street	C2-D2
Edward Street	A4
Emery Close	D1
Emery Street	D1
Farringdon Street	B3-B4
Fernleigh Road	F4
Flaxhall Street	A1-A2
Florence Street	E1-E2
Forrester Street	B2-B3
Frederick Street	B2-C2
Freer Street	D2
George Street	C2-D2
Glebe Street	C1
Glen Close	E4
Goodhall Street	D2
Green Lane	B4-C4-C3
Grove Terrace	D1-D2
Hall Street	C4
Hart Street	C1
Hatherton Road	C3-D3
Hatherton Street	D3-D4
Haunch Place	D1
High Street	D2
Hill Street	D2
Hollyhedge Lane	A4-B4-B3
Holtshill Lane	D3-E3
Hope Street	C1
Ida Road	A2
Intown	D3
Intown Row	D3
Jerome Road	A1
Jessel Road	A3-B3-B4
Jesson Road	D1
John Street	C4
Kinnerley Street	E1-E2
Lewis Street	B4
Lichfield Street	D3-D4-E4
Lincoln Road	E3-E2-F2
Link Road	C3
Littleton Street East	D3-D4
Littleton Street West	C3-D3
Long Street	B1-B2
Long Acre Street	B4-C4
Lower Forster Street	D3
Lower Hall Lane	C4
Lower Rushall Street	D2-D3
Lumley Road	E1-E2
Lysways Street	D1
Manor Road	A3
Margarets Street	B3-C3
Marsh Lane	C3
Marsh Street	C2-C3
Mary Street	B4
Meadow Street	B1
Mellish Road	E4-F4
Midland Road	C1-C2
Moat Road	A3-A2-B2
Moncriefe Street	E2
Moss Close	E4
Mountrath Street	C1-C2
Mount Street	C1
Navigation Street	B3-C3-C2

Newhall Street	C1-D1
New Street	D1-D2
North Street	C4-D4
Orwell Road	F1
Pargetter Street	A3-A4
Park Street	C2-C3
Peal Street	D2
Penkridge Street	C4
Persehouse Street	D3
Pleck Road	A1-A2-B2-B3
Pool Street	D2
Portland Street	C4
Prince's Avenue	F1-F2-F3
Queen Street	B1-B2
Raleigh Street	A3-A4
Reedswood Lane	A4
Rollingmill Street	A2-A1-B1
Rowland Street	A4
Rowley Street	D3-E3
St Johns Road	A1
Sandwell Street	D1
Sandy Mount Road	D1
Scarborough Road	A1-A2
Selborne Street	E2
Shaw Street	B3-C3
Short Street	B2
Short Acre Street	B4-C4
Springhill Road	D1-D2
Stafford Street	C3-C4
Station Street	C2-C3
Sutton Road	D1-E1-F1
Tantarra Street	E2-E3
Tasker Street	B1-C1
Teddersley Street	D3-D4
The Butts	D4
The Crescent	E1-F1
The Ditch	D2
Tong Street	E2
Union Street	D2-D3
Upper Brook Street	B2
Upper Forster Street	D4
Upper Rushall Street	D2
Upper Short Street	B2
Victoria Place	C1-C2
Victoria Terrace	E4
Walhouse Road	D3-E3
Walsingham Street	E2
Ward Street	D3
Wednesbury Road	B1-C1
White Street	C1
Whitehouse Street	B4-C4
Wilbraham Road	A2
Windmill Street	D1
William Street	D4
Willows Road	F1-F2
Wolverhampton Road	A3-B3
Wolverhampton Street	B3-C3

ALDRIDGE

Anchor Road	B2-B3
Birmingham Road	B1-B2
Brickyard Road	A4
Broad Meadow	B4
Burnfield Close	A4
Cranleigh Close	C1
Daniels Lane	C1
Dumbledery Lane	A2
Edward Avenue	B3-B4
Erdington Road	C1-C2
Hallcroft Way	C2
Harborough Drive	B1
Hatherton Place	B3-B4
High Street	B3-C3

Hobs Hole Lane	C4
Honiton Way	A1
Leighswood Avenue	B3-B4-C4
Leighswood Road	A4-A3-B3
Little Aston Road	B3-C3-C2
Lynmouth Close	A1
Meadow Road	B1
Middlemore Lane	A2-A3-B3
Morford Road	B4
New Road	B2
Noddy Park	C4
Noddy Park Road	C3
Northgate	B3-B4
Nursery Avenue	B2
Oakley Avenue	A1-A2
Orchard Grove	C1
Paddock Lane	A1-A2
Portland Road	B2-C2
Quicksand Lane	A1
Redhouse Lane	A2
Rookery Lane	C2-C3
St Mary's Way	B1
Sandra Close	C2
Seven Acres	B1
Sheraton Close	B3
Speedwell Close	A2
Station Road	A2-B2
Stonelea	B2
Stubbers Green Lane	A4
The Green	C3
The Walmers	B3-B4
Tynings Lane	A1-B1
Vigo Place	A4
Walmer Meadow	B3-B4
Walsall Road	A1-B1-B2
Walsall Wood Road	B3-C3-C4
Westbrook Avenue	A1
Weston Crescent	B1-C1
Whetstone Lane	B1-B2-C2
Woodside Way	B2

WILLENHALL

Acorn Street	C3
Albion Avenue	C3
Albion Road	B3-C3
Albion Street	C3
Ann Street	B4
Banks Street	A3
Barcroft	C3
Belinda Close	A3
Bilston Lane	B1-C1-C2
Bilston Street	B2
Birches Rise	A2
Birmingham Street	B3-B4
Bloxwich Road South	A3-A4-B4
Cannon Street	B2-B3
Charles Street	C4
Church Walk	B2
Circuit Close	B3-B4
Clarkes Lane	C3-C4
Clothier Street	A3-A4-B4
Dartmouth Avenue	A3
Diminsdale	A2
Dingle Lane	A4
Elm Street	C3
Fibbersley	A4
Field Street	A2-A3
Fisher Street	C2
Fletchers Lane	C2
Froysell Street	B2-B3
Gomer Street	C2
Gough Street	C3
Gower Street	B3

Gypsy Lane	B2-C2
Harper Street	A3
Harry Perks Street	A4
Hartill Street	B1
Hodson Avenue	C2
John Harper Street	B3
John Street	B2
Latimer Street	B3
Lawrence Street	A4
Leveson Street	A3-B3
Leve Lane	B2
Lister Street	B2-C2
Longacres	A1-B1
Lower Lichfield Street	B2-B3
Manor Close	A3
Market Street	A2-B2
Marston Street	C2
Midland Road	C1
Mill Street	C2
Moat Street	A3
Monmer Lane	B4
Newhall Street	B3
Newlands Close	A2
New Road	A2-B2
Noose Lane	A4
Oakridge Drive	C4
Orchard Road	B2
Owen Road	B1-C1
Park Avenue	A2
Parkes Street	B1-B2-B1
Park Road	A3-A4
Peel Street	A2
Pinson Road	A2-A3
Regent Street	A3-B3
Riley Street	B3
Rose Hill	B1-B2
Rose Hill Gardens	B1-B2
Roundcroft	A2
Russel Street	B2-B3
St Annes Road	B3-B4
St Giles Road	B1
Sharesacre Street	B4
Shepwell Green	C3
Slater Street	C3
Somerford Place	B2
Springvale Street	B4
Strafford Road	A3
Stafford Street	A2-A3
Stonehouse Avenue	A2
Stringes Lane	B3-C3-C4
Summer Street	A2
Temple Bar	B2
Temple Road	A3-B3-B4
The Crescent	C2
Thompson Close	A3
Thompson Street	A3
Thorne Road	A4-B4
Tyler Road	B1-B2
Union Street	A2-B2-B3
Upper Lichfield Street	B3
Victoria Street	A3-B3-B4
Villiers Street	B3
Walsall Road	B2-C2-C3
Walsall Street	B2
Webster Road	A4-B4
Wednesfield Road	A3-A4
Wellington Place	B1-B2
Westacre	A1-A2
Willenhall By-Pass (The Keyway)	A1
William Harper Road	B2-B1
Wolverhampton Street	A2
Wood Street	A2-A3-B3

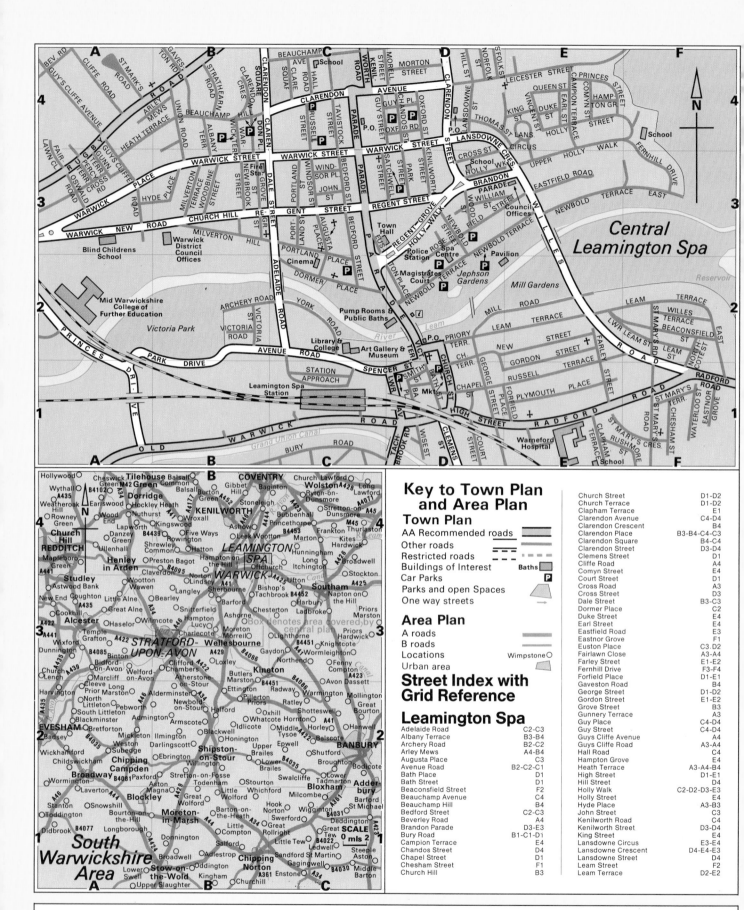

Key to Town Plan and Area Plan

Town Plan

AA Recommended roads	▬▬▬
Other roads	▬▬
Restricted roads	▬ ▬ ▬
Buildings of Interest	Baths ▢
Car Parks	P
Parks and open Spaces	◢
One way streets	→

Area Plan

A roads	▬▬
B roads	▬▬
Locations	Wimpstone ○
Urban area	◢

Street Index with Grid Reference

Leamington Spa

Adelaide Road	C2-C3
Albany Terrace	B3-B4
Archery Road	B2-C2
Arley Mews	A4-B4
Augusta Place	C3
Avenue Road	B2-C2-C1
Bath Place	D1
Bath Street	D1
Beaconsfield Street	F2
Beauchamp Avenue	C4
Beauchamp Hill	B4
Bedford Street	C2-C3
Beverley Road	A4
Brandon Parade	D3-E3
Bury Road	B1-C1-D1
Campion Terrace	E4
Chandos Street	D4
Chapel Street	D1
Chesham Street	F1
Church Hill	B3

Church Street	D1-D2
Church Terrace	D1-D2
Clapham Terrace	E1
Clarendon Avenue	C4-D4
Clarendon Crescent	B4
Clarendon Place	B3-B4-C4-C3
Clarendon Square	B4-C4
Clarendon Street	D3-D4
Clemens Street	D1
Cliffe Road	A4
Comyn Street	E4
Court Street	D1
Cross Road	A3
Cross Street	D3
Dale Street	B3-C3
Dormer Place	C2
Duke Street	E4
Earl Street	E4
Eastfield Road	E3
Eastnor Grove	F1
Euston Place	C3-D2
Fairlawn Close	A3-A4
Farley Street	E1-E2
Fernhill Drive	F3-F4
Forfield Place	D1-E1
Gaveston Road	B4
George Street	D1-D2
Gordon Street	E1-E2
Grove Street	B3
Gunnery Terrace	A3
Guy Place	C4-D4
Guy Street	C4-D4
Guys Cliffe Avenue	A4
Guys Cliffe Road	A3-A4
Hall Road	C4
Hampton Grove	E4
Heath Terrace	A3-A4-B4
High Street	D1-E1
Hill Street	D4
Holly Walk	C2-D2-D3-E3
Holly Street	E4
Hyde Place	A3-B3
John Street	C3
Kenilworth Road	C4
Kenilworth Street	D3-D4
King Street	D4
Lansdowne Circus	E3-E4
Lansdowne Crescent	D4-E4-E3
Lansdowne Street	D4
Leam Street	F2
Leam Terrace	D2-E2

Warwick

The old county town of the shire, Warwick lies in the shadow of its massive, historic castle which occupies the rocky ridge above the River Avon. Thomas Beauchamp and his son built the huge towers and curtain walls in the 14th century, but it was the Jacobean holders of the earldom, the Grevilles, who transformed the medieval stronghold into a nobleman's residence. In 1694,

the heart of the town was almost completely destroyed by fire and the few medieval buildings that survived lie on the outskirts of the present 18th-century centre. Of these Oken House, now a doll museum, and Lord Leycester's Hospital, almshouses dating back to the 14th century, are particularly striking.

Stratford-upon-Avon, as the birthplace of William Shakespeare, England's most famous poet and playwright, is second only to London as a

tourist attraction. This charming old market town is a living memorial to him; his plays are performed in the Royal Shakespeare Theatre which dominates the river bank, a waxwork museum specialises in scenes from his works, and his childhood home in Henley Street is a museum.

Leamington Spa, an inland spa on the River Leam, gained the prefix 'Royal' after Queen Victoria had visited it in 1838, and the town has been a fashionable health resort ever since.

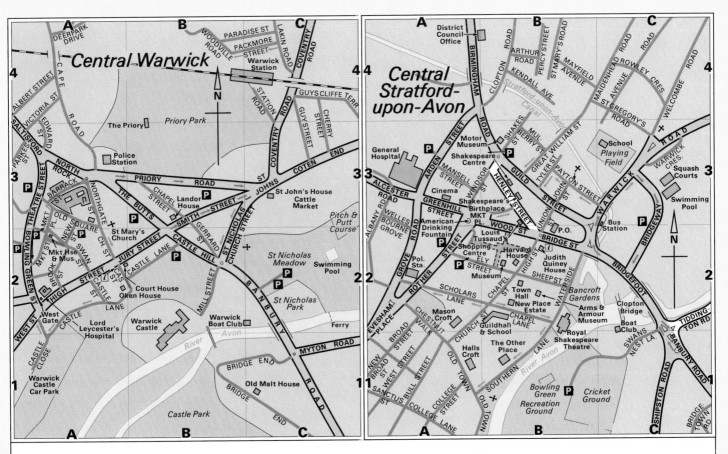

Central Warwick

Central Stratford-upon-Avon

Leam Terrace East	E2-F2-F1	Thomas Street	D4-E4	Mill Street	B2	Henley Street	B2-B3

WARWICK
These pretty brick and timbered cottages standing in the shadow of the great medieval towers of Warwick Castle are among the few buildings in the town that survived a devastating fire in the late 17th century.

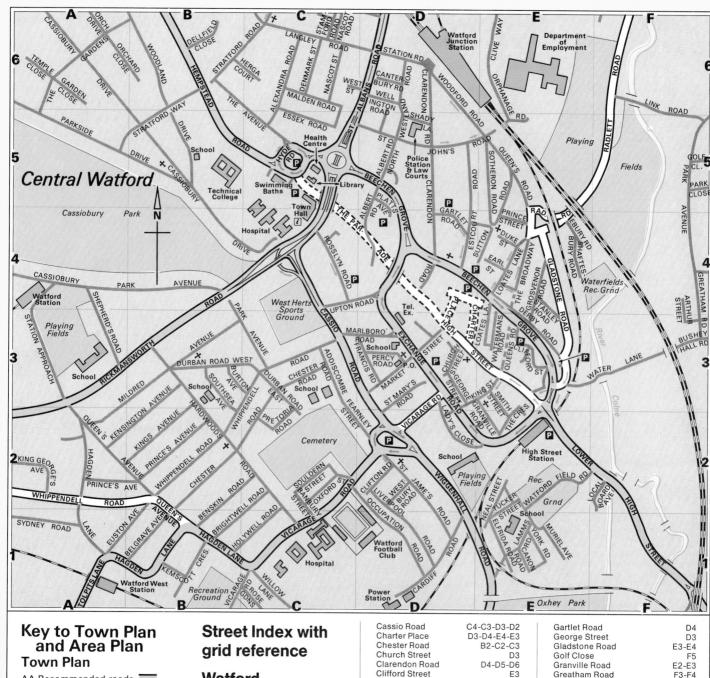

Key to Town Plan and Area Plan
Town Plan

AA Recommended roads
Restricted roads
Other roads
Buildings of interset   Theatre
Car Parks   P
Parks and open spaces
One Way Streets

Area Plan

A roads
B roads
Locations   Wooburn ○
Urban area

Street Index with grid reference

Watford

Watford

Not the least of Watford's successes is its football club, which has reached Division One of the Canon League under the chairmanship of singer Elton John and contributed to some extent to the prosperity of the town. But Watford's present-day expansion really began with the opening of Watford Junction Railway Station in 1838, as an increasing number of commercial and industrial firms set up premises here. Benskins Brewery had its headquarters in Watford until it was taken over in 1957, and the Mothercare chain began life in the town, where it still has a large factory. Watford has modern shopping facilities, and sports are catered for by the extensive Watford Leisure Centre and Cassiobury Park. The Watford Museum is housed in the former Benskins Brewery and has a fascinating collection of local history items.

Hemel Hempstead is a town of two faces: the New Town, with its shopping precincts, Civic Centre and extensive Dacorum Sports Centre, and the carefully preserved older quarter, which stands on a hill to the north of its modern counterpart. A number of ancient inns can be seen in the main street of the old town, and the Old Town Hall is a fine example of Jacobean-style architecture. A collection of medieval wall paintings has been found on the walls of a 15th-century cottage at Piccotts End, on the northern outskirts.

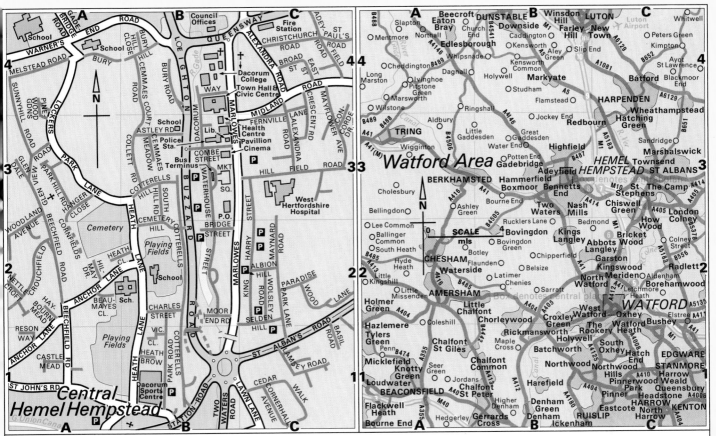

Loates Lane	E3-E4	Souldern Street	C2	Alexandra Road	C3-C4	Lamsey Road	C1
Local Board Avenue	F2	Southsea Avenue	B2-B3	Anchor Lane	A1-A2-B2	Lawn Lane	B1-C1
Lower High Street	E2-F2-F1	Stamford Road	C6	Astley Road	B3	Leighton Buzzard Road B1-B2-B3-B4
Malden Road	C6	Stanley Road	E3-E4	Basil Road	C1-C2	Lockers Park Lane	A4-A3-B3
Market Street	D3	Station Approach	A3-A4	Beaumayes Close	A2	Market Square	B3
Marlborough Road	C3-D3	Station Road	D6	Beechfield Road	A1-A2-A3	Marlowes	B1-B2-C2-C3-B3-B4
Mildred Avenue	A2-A3-B3	Stratford Road	B6-C6	Bridge Street	B2	Mayflower Avenue	C3-C4
Muriel Avenue	E1	Stratford Way	A5-B5-B6	Broad Street	C4	Maynard Road	C2-C3
Nascot Road	C6	Sutton Road	E4-E5	Bury Hill	A4-B4	Melstead Road	A4
Nascot Street	C6	Sydney Road	A1	Bury Hill Close	B4	Midland Road	C3-C4
Neal Street	E1-E2	Temple Close	A6	Bury Road	B4	Moor End Road	B2
Occupation Road	C2-D2-D1	The Avenue	B6-C6-C5	Castle Mead	A1	Nettlecroft	A2
Orchard Close	A6-B6	The Broadway	E4	Cedar Walk	C1	Paradise Wood Lane	C2
Orchard Drive	A6	The Crescent	E2-E3	Cemetery Hill	B2	Parkhill Road	A3
Orphanage Road	E5-E6	The Gardens	A5-A6-B6	Cemmaes Court Road	B3-B4	Park Lane	C1-C2
Oxford Street	C2	The Parade	C5-C4-D4	Cemmaes Meadow	B3	Park Road	B1-B2
Park Avenue	B4-B3-C3	Tolpits Lane	A1	Charles Street	B2	Pinewood Gardens	A3-A4
Park Avenue	F4-F5	Tucker Street	E1-E2	Christchurch Road	C4	Queensway	B4-C4
Park Close	F5	Upton Road	C4-D4	Collett Road	B3	Reson Way	A1
Parkside Drive	A5-B5	Vicarage Road	B1-C1-C2-D2-D3	Combe Street	B3	St Albans Road	C1-C2
Percy Road	D3	Water Lane	E3-F3	Concorde Drive	C3-C4	St Johns Road	A1-B1
Platts Avenue	D4-D5	Watermans Road	E3	Cornerhall Avenue	C1	St Pauls Road	C4
Pretoria Road	C2	Watford Field Road	E2-F2	Cornfields	A2-A3	Selden Hill	C2
Prince's Avenue	A2-B2	Wellington Road	D6	Cotterells	B1-B2-B3	South Hill Road	B3
Prince Street	E4	Westbury Road	D2	Cotterells Hill	B3	Station Road	B1
Queen's Avenue	A3-A2-B2-B1	Westland Road	D5-D6	Crescent Road	C3-C4	Sunnyhill Road	A3-A4
Queens Road	E3-E5	West Street	C6-D6	Crouchfield	A2	Two Waters Road	B1
Radlett Road	E4-E5-F5-F6	Whippendell Road	A2-B2-B3-C3	Dacorum Way	B3-B4	Vicarage Close	B1
Rickmansworth Road		Wigganhall Road	D2-D1-E1	East Street	C4	Warner's End Road	A4-B4
	A2-A3-B3-B4-C4-C5	Willow Lane	C1	Fernville Lane	C3-C4	Waterhouse Street	B2-B3
Rose Gardens	C1	Woodford Road	D6-D5-E5	Gadebridge Road	A4	Wolsley Road	C2
Rosslyn Road	C4	Woodland Drive	A6-B6-B5	Glen Dale	A3	Woodland Avenue	A2-A3
St Albans Road	D5-C5-C6	York Road	E1	Glen View Road	A3	
St Jame's Road	D1-D2			Hanger Close	A3	
St John's Road	D5-E5			Haybourn Mead	A2	
St Mary's Road	D2-D3	**Hemel Hempstead**		Heath Brow	B1	
Shady Lane	D5			Heath Close	A2-B2	
Shaftesbury Road	E4	Adeyfield Road	C4	Heath Lane	B1-B2-B3	
Shepherd's Road	A3-A4	Albion Hill	C2	Hill Field Road	C3	
Smith Street	E2-E3			Hillmay Drive	A2	
Sotheron Road	E4-E5			King Harry Street	C2-C3	

WATFORD
Green leaves and cool water in the High Street precinct are part of a scheme to transform a traffic-congested centre into a safe and pleasant place for pedestrians.

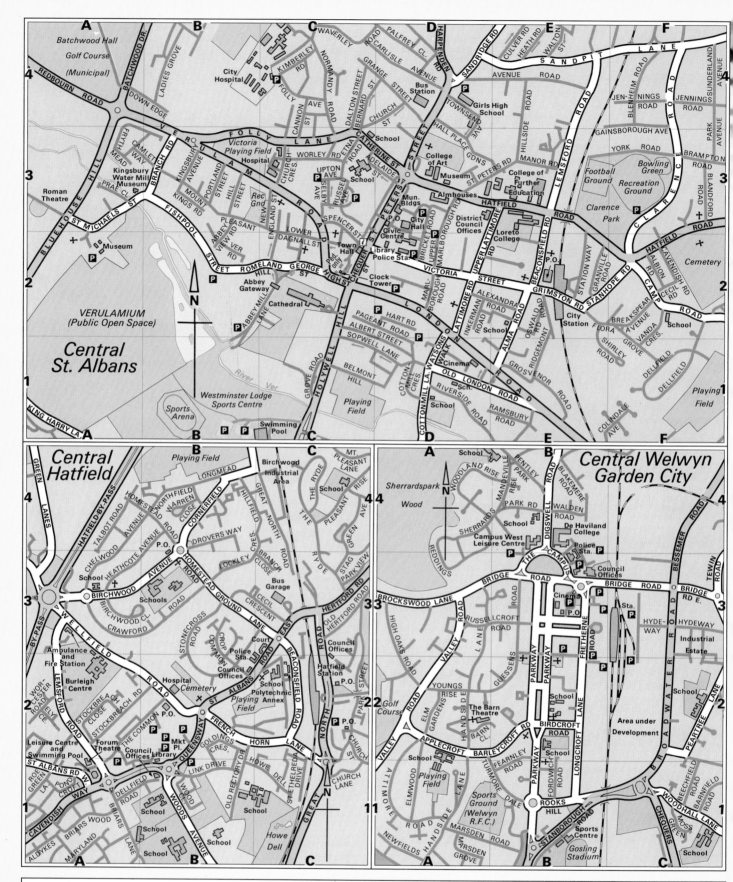

Welwyn area

St Albans is named after the first British Christian martyr. It evolved from the Roman town of Verulamium, and, lying on Watling Street, has always been an important link with the north. The impressive Cathedral dates from the 11th century and overlooks Verulamium Park, where Roman remains and a museum can be seen. Other features are the Roman Theatre on the Gorhambury Estate, the Organ Museum and the Fighting Cocks, said to be the country's oldest licensed establishment.

Hatfield is dominated by Hatfield House, the magnificent Jacobean mansion built by Robert Cecil, Earl of Salisbury, in the early 17th century. It stands in an extensive park close to the remains of the late 15th-century Bishop's Palace, where Queen Elizabeth I is said to have held her first council. Hatfield itself grew up around the nucleus of an ancient village, and has modern shopping, sports and leisure facilities.

Welwyn Garden City was established shortly after World War I, and Welwyn remains a fine example of landscaped town planning. The overall appearance is neo-Georgian, although modern buildings have been added, such as the Campus West leisure complex and the sports centre at Gosling Stadium. Perhaps the most outstanding feature of the town is 126-acre Stansborough Park, with its swimming pool and a lake for sailing.

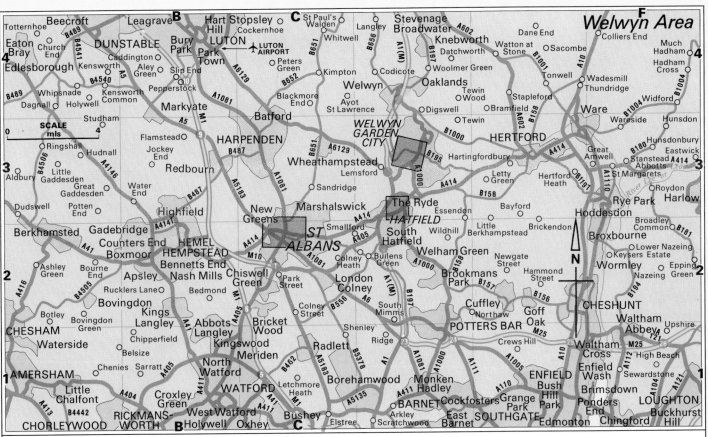

Key to Town Plan and Area Plan

Town Plan
A A Recommended roads
Other roads
Restricted roads
Buildings of interest — Gallery
Parks and open spaces
Car Parks — P
Churches — †
One Way Streets — ←

Area Plan
A roads
B roads
Locations — Clapton○
Urban Area

Street Index with Grid Reference

St. Albans

Abbey Mill Lane	B1-B2-C2
Abbey View Road	B2-B3
Adelaide Street	C3-D3
Albert Street	C2-D2-D1
Albion Road	F2
Alexandra Road	D2-E2
Alma Road	E1-E2
Avenue Road	D4-E4
Batchwood Drive	A4-B4
Beaconsfield Road	E2-E3
Belmont Hill	C1-D1
Bernard Street	C3-C4-D4
Blandford Road	F3
Blenheim Road	F4
Bluehouse Hill	A2-A3-A4
Brampton Road	F3
Branch Road	B3
Breakspear Avenue	F2
Bricket Road	D2-D3
Camlet Way	A3-B3
Camp Road	F2
Cannon Street	C3-C4
Carlisle Avenue	C4-D4
Catherine Street	C3-D3
Cavendish Road	F2
Cecil Road	F2
Chequer Street	C2
Church Crescent	C3
Church Street	C3-C4-D4
Clarence Road	F2-F3-F4
Colindale Avenue	E1-F1
Cottonmill Crescent	D1
Cottonmill Lane	D1
Culver Road	E4
Dalton Street	C3-C4
Dellfield	F1
Down Edge	A4-B4
Etna Road	C3
Fishpool Street	B2-B3
Flora Grove	E2-F2-F1
Folly Avenue	C4
Folly Lane	B3-C3
Fryth Mead	A3-A4
Gainsborough Avenue	E4-F4
George Street	C2
Grange Street	C4-D2
Granville Road	E2
Grimston Road	E2
Grosvenor Road	E1
Grove Road	C1
Hall Place Gardens	D4-D3-E3
Harpenden Road	D4
Hart Road	D2
Hatfield Road	D3-E3-E2-F2-F3
Heath Road	E4
High Street	C2
Hill Street	B3
Hillside Road	E3-E4
Holywell Hill	C1-D2
Inkerman Road	D2
Jennings Road	F4
Kimberley Road	C4
King Harry Lane	A1
Kings Road	B3
Kingsbury Avenue	B3
Ladies Grove	B4
Lattimore Road	D2
Lemsford Road	E3-E4
London Road	C2-D2-D1-E1
Lower Dagnall Street	C2-C3
Manor Road	E3
Marlborough Road	D2
Mount Pleasant	B3-C3
New England Street	C3
Normandy Road	C3-C4
Old London Road	D1-E1
Oswald Road	E2
Pageant Road	C2-D2-D1
Palfrey Close	B1
Park Avenue	F3-F4
Portland Street	B3
Prae Close	A3
Ramsbury Road	D1-E1
Redbourn Road	A4
Ridgemont Road	E1-E2
Riverside Road	D1-E1
Romeland Hill	B2-C2
Russel Avenue	C3
St Michaels Street	A3-B3
St Peters Road	D3-E3
St Peters Street	C2-D2-D3-D4
Sandpit Lane	D4-E4-F4
Sandridge Road	D4-E4
Selby Avenue	C3
Shirley Road	E2-E1-F1
Sopwell Lane	C2-C1-D1
Spencer Street	C2-C3
Stanhope Road	E2-F2
Station Way	E2
Sunderland Avenue	F4
Townsend Avenue	D3-D4
Upper Lattimore Road	D2-D3-E3
Upper Marlborough Road	D2-D3
Upton Avenue	C3
Vanda Crescent	F1-F2
Ver Road	B2
Verulam Road	A4-B4-B3-C3-C2
Victoria Street	C2-D2-E2
Walton Street	E4
Watsons Walk	D1-D2
Waverley Road	C4
Worley Road	C3
York Road	E3-F3

Hatfield

Aldykes	A1
Beaconsfield Road	C2-C3
Birchwood Avenue	A3-B3
Birchwood Close	A3-B3
Branch Close	C3
Briars Lane	A1
Briars Wood	A1
Cavendish Way	A1
Cecil Crescent	B3-C3
Chelwood Avenue	A3-A4-B4
Church Lane	C1
Church Street	C1-C2
Cornerfield	B4
Crawford Road	A3-B3
Crop Common	B2-B3
Dellfield Road	A1-B1
Drovers Way	B4
Ely Close	A2
French Horn Lane	B2-C2-C1
Goldings Crescent	B1-B2
Great North Road	B4-C4-C3-C2-C1
Green Lanes	A3-A4
Ground Lane	B3-C3
Hatfield By-pass	A2-A3-A4
Heathcote Avenue	A3-B3-B4
Hertford Road	B4-C4
Hillfield	A4-B4-B3
Homestead Road	A4-B4-B3
Howe Dell	B1-C1
Lemsford Road	A1-A2-A3
Link Drive	B1
Lockley Crescent	B3-C3-C4
Longmead	B4
Maryland	A1
Mount Pleasant Lane	C4
Northfield	B4
Old Hertford Road	C3
Old Rectory Drive	B1-B2
Park Street	C2-C3
Park View	C3
Pleasant Rise	C4
Pond Croft	A1
Queensway	A1-B1-B2
Roe Green Lane	A1
St Albans Road East	B2-C2-C3
St Albans Road West	A1
St Ethelreda Drive	C1
Stag Green Avenue	C3-C4
Stockbreach Close	A2
Stockbreach Road	A2-B2
Stonecross Road	B2-B3
Talbot Road	A3-A4
The Common	A2-B2
The Ryde	C3-C4

Warren Close	B4
Wellfield Road	A3-A2-B2
Wood Close	B1
Woods Avenue	B1
Worcester Road	A2

Welwyn Garden City

Applecroft	A2
Attimore Road	A1-A2
Barleycroft Road	A2-B2
Barn Close	A2-B2
Barnfield Road	C1
Beechfield Road	C1
Bessemer Road	C3-C4
Birdcroft Road	B2
Blakemore Road	B4
Bridge Road	A3-B3-C3
Bridge Road East	B3
Broadwater Road	C1-C2-C3
Brockswood Lane	A3
Chequers	C1
Digswell Road	B4
Elm Gardens	A2
Elmwood	A1-A2
Fearnley Road	B1-B2
Fordwich Road	B1-B2
Fretherne Road	B2-B3
Guessens Road	A2-B2-B3
Handside Lane	A1-A2-A3
High Oaks Road	A2-A3
Hydeway	C3
Longcroft Lane	B1-B2
Mandeville Rise	B4
Marsden Grove	A1
Marsden Road	A1-B1
Moss Green	C1
Newfields	A1
Parkway	B1-B2-B3
Peartree Lane	C2
Pentley Park	B4
Reddings	A3-A4
Rooks Hill	B1
Russellcroft Road	A3-B3
Sherrard Park Road	A4-B4
Stanborough Road	B1
Tewin Road	C3-C4
The Campus	B3-B4-B3
Turmore Dale	A2-A1-B1
Valley Road	A1-A2-A3
Walden Road	B4
Woodhall Lane	C1
Woodland Rise	A4-B4
Youngs Rise	A2

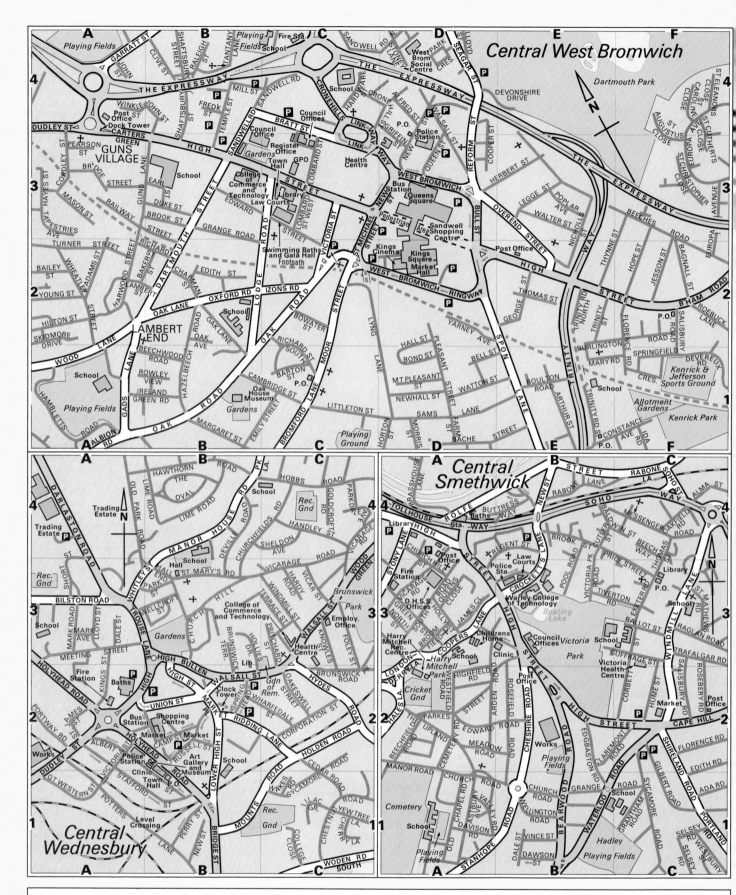

West Bromwich

This was a small hamlet set amid a heath of broom (hence the name) until the discovery of coal and a central position in the national transport system led to the industrial development of the area. A few remaining buildings speak of the town's older history, for example the Manor House, a copybook example of a medieval timber-framed house, and Oak House, which is Tudor, and furnished in period style. Today this is a town well equipped to meet the needs of the 20th century: the Sandwell Centre is a modern, purpose-built shopping centre, the Gala Suite hosts sports events and entertainments, and top league soccer action is provided by local club West Bromwich Albion.

Wednesbury was an important fort in the Anglo-Saxon kingdom of Mercia, but the digging of coal as long ago as the 14th century developed it into a thriving industrial community. The market square is a conservation area, and dominating the town from its hill-top site is the 12th-century Parish Church of St Bartholomew, one of the Midlands' most beautiful perpendicular churches.

Smethwick means 'little village on the plain', but Smethwick itself underwent a major change when the canal system was developed in the 18th century. It is now an established industrial community, and boasts an Olympic standard running track at the Hadley Stadium.

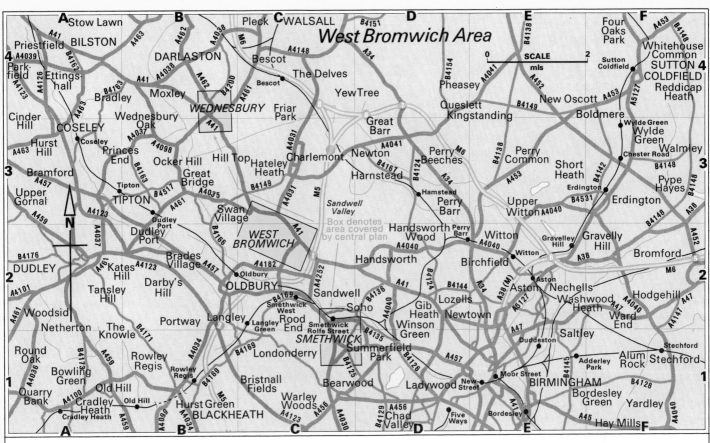

LEGEND

Town Plan

AA Recommended route

Restricted roads

Other roads

Buildings of interest Library

Car parks P

Parks and open spaces

One way streets

Area Plan

A roads

B roads

Street Index with Grid Reference

West Bromwich

Adams Street	A2
Albion Street	A1
Alfred Street	D4
Arthur Street	E1
Bache Street	D1-E1
Bagnall Street	F2
Bailey Street	A2
Baker Street	A2-B2
Barton Street	C1
Beeches Road	E3-F3-F2
Beechwood Road	A1-B1
Bell Street	D1-E1
Birmingham Road	F2
Bond Street	D1
Boulton Road	E1
Bowater Street	C2
Bratt Street	B4-C4-C3
Bridge Street	A3
Bromford Lane	C1
Brook Street	A3-B3
Bull Street	D2-D3
Burlington Road	E2-F2
Cambridge Street	B1-C1
Carters Green	A3-A4
Chapman Street	B2
Clive Street	B4
Constance Avenue	E1-F1
Cooper Street	D3-D4
Cordley Street	A3-A4
Cronehill Street	C4-D4-C4
Cronehills Linkway	C4-C3-D3
Dartmouth Street	A2-B2-B3
Devereux Road	F1
Devonshire Drive	D4-E4
Dudley Street	A4
Duke Street	B3
Earl Street	B3
Edith Street	B2
Edward Street	B3-C3-C2
Emily Street	B1-C1
Europa Avenue	F2-F3-F4
Farm Street	D1
Florence Road	F1-F2
Frederick Street	B4
Gads Lane	A1-A2
Garratt Street	A4-B4
George Street	E2
Grange Road	B2-B3
Griffin Street	C4-D4-D3
Guns Lane	A3-B3
Hall Street	D1-D2
Hambletts Road	A1
Hardware Street	C4
Harwood Street	A2-A3
Hayes Street	A3
Hazelbeech Road	B1-B2
Herbert Street	D3-E3
High Street	B3-C3-D3-D2-E2-F2
Hilton Street	A2
Hope Street	F2-F3
Horton Street	D1
Ida Road	F1
Ireland Green Road	A1-B1
Izons Road	C2
Jesson Street	F2-F3
John Street	A4-B4
Lambert Street	A2-B2
Legge Street	E3
Littleton Street	C1-D1
Lloyd Street	D1
Lodge Road	B1-B2-C2-C3
Lombard Street	C3
Lombard Street West	C3
Lyng Lane	C2-D2-D1
Margaret Street	B1
Mary Road	E1-F1
Mason Street	A3
Mill Street	B4-C4
Moor Street	C1-C2
Morris Street	D1
Mount Pleasant Street	D1
New Street	C3-D3-D4
Newhall Street	D1
Nicholls Street	E2-E3
Oak Avenue	B2
Oak Lane	B1-B2
Oak Road	A1-B1-B2-C2
Overend Street	D3-E3-E2
Oxford Road	B2
Park Crescent	D4
Pearson Street	A3
Pleasant Street	D1-D2
Poplar Avenue	E3
Queen Street	D3
Raleigh Street	B4
Railway Street	A3-B3-B2
Reform Street	D3-D4
Richard Street	A2-B2
Richard Street South	C1-C2
Roebuck Lane	F2
Rowley View	A1-B1

St Augustus Close	F3-F4
St Caroline Close	F4
St Christopher Close	F3
St Cuthberts Close	F3-F4
St Eleanors Close	F4
St Michael Street	C2-C3
Salisbury Road	F1-F2
Sams Lane	D1-E1
Sandwell Road	B3-B4-C4
Sandwell Road North	C4-D4
Seagar Street	D4
Shaftsbury Street	B3-B4
Skidmore Drive	A2
Spon Lane	D2-E2-E1
Springfield Crescent	F1
Stoney Lane	D4
Tantany Lane	B4
Tapestries Avenue	A3
Temple Street	B3-B4
The Expressway	A4-B4-C4-D4-E4-E3-F3
Thomas Street	E2
Thynne Street	E2-F2-F3
Trinity Road North	E2
Trinity Road South	E1
Trinity Street	E2
Trinity Way	E1-E2-E3
Turner Street	A2
Victoria Street	C2-C3
Walsall Street	D3-D4
Walter Street	E3
Watton Street	D1-E1
West Bromwich Ringway	C2-C3
Wheatley Street	A2
Winkle Street	A4
Wood Lane	A1-A2
Yarney Avenue	D2
Young Street	A2

Wednesbury

Albert Street	A2-B2-B1
Bilston Road	A3
Bridge Street	B1
Brunswick Park Road	C2
Brunswick Terrace	B2-B3
Camp Street	B2
Cedar Road	C1-C2
Cherry Lane	C1
Chestnut Road	C1
Church Hill	B3
Churchfields Road	B3-B4-C1
College Close	C2
Corporation Street	C2
Dale Street	A3
Darlaston Road	A3-A4
Deville Road	B3-B4
Dudley Street	A1-A2
Foley Street	C2-C3
Goldcroft Road	C4
Great Western Street	A1
Hall End	B3
Handley Street	C4
Hardy Road	C3
Hawthorne Road	A4-B4
High Street	B2-B3
High Bullen	A2-B2-B3-B2
Hobbs Road	B4-C4

Holden Road	C2
Hollies Drive	B2-B3
Holyhead Road	A3-A2-B2-B1
Hydes Road	C2
Kings Street	A2-A3
Knowles Street	C2-C3
Lilac Grove	C1
Lime Road	B4
Lloyd Street	A3
Lower High Street	B1-B2
Manor House Road	B3-B4
Mark Avenue	A3
Mark Road	A3
Market Place	B2
Meeting Street	A3
Mounts Road	B1-C1-C2
New Street	B1
Oakeswell Street	C2
Old Park Road	A3-A4
Park Lane	B4-C4
Park Street	A3-B3
Parkdale Avenue	C4
Perry Street	B1
Portway Road	A2
Potters Lane	A1-B1
Pritchard Street	C2-C3
Ridding Lane	B2-C2
Russell Street	B2
St James Street	A2
St Mary's Road	B3
Sheldon Avenue	B4-C4
Short Street	A3-A4
Spring Head	B2
Stafford Street	A2-A1-B1
Sycamore Road	C1-C2
Terrace Street	B3-C3
The Oval	B4
Trouse Lane	A3-B3
Union Street	A2-B2
Vicar Street	C3
Vicarage Road	B3-C3-C4
Victoria Street	A1-A2
Wakes Road	C3
Walsall Street	B2-C2-C3
Wellcroft Street	A3-B3
Wharfedale Street	B2-C2
Whitley Street	A3-B3
Windmill Street	C3
Wood Green	C3-C4
Woden Road South	C1
Yew Tree Lane	C1

Smethwick

Ada Road	C1
Alma Street	C4
Arden Road	A2-A3
Astbury Avenue	A1
Baldwin Street	B4-C4
Ballot Street	C3
Bearwood Road	B1-B2
Beech Way	A2
Beechfield Road	A2
Brasshouse Lane	A4
Brook Street	B4
Broom Field	A3
Buttress Way	A4-B4
Cape Hill	C2
Cemetery Road	A2

Cheshire Road	B1-B2
Church Road	A1-B1
Church Hill Street	A3-A4
Claremont Road	B2-C2
Coopers Lane	A3-B3
Corbett Street	C2-C3
Crockett's Lane	B3-B4
Cutler Street	B4
Dale Street	B1
Davison Road	A1
Dawson Street	B1
Edgbaston Road	B1-B2
Edith Road	C1-C2
Edward Road	A2-B2
Exeter Road	C3
Florence Road	C2
Gilbert Road	C1-C2
Grange Road	B1-C1
Grantham Road	C1
Green Street	A3
Hales Lane	A3
High Street	A4-A3-B3-B2-C2
Highfield Road	A2
Holly Street	A3
Hume Street	C2-C3
James Close	A3
Londonderry Lane	A2-A3
Manor Road	A2
Meadow Road	A2-B2
Messenger Road	B4-C4
New Street	B4
North Street	A3
Oakfield Road	C4
Old Chapel Road	A1
Parkes Street	A2
Pool Road	B3-B4
Portland Road	C1
Price Street	B4-C4-C3
Queens Close	A3
Rabone Lane	B4-C4
Raglan Road	C3
Regent Street	A3-A4-B4
Rolfe Street	A4-B4-C4
Roseberry Road	C2-C3
Rosefield Road	B1-B2-B3
St Mathews Road	C3
Salisbury Road	C2-C3
Selsey Road	C1
Shireland Road	C1-C2
Soho Street	C4
Soho Way	B4-C4
South Road	A3-A4
Stanhope Road	A1-B1
Stony Lane	A3-A4
Suffrage Lane	B3-C3
Sycamore Road	C1-C2
The Upland	A2
Thomas Street	C3-C4
Tiverton Road	B3-C3
Tollhouse Way	A4-B4
Trafalgar Road	C3
Valley Road	A1
Vicarage Road	A3
Victoria Park Road	B3-B4
Vince Street	B1
Waterloo Road	B1-C1-C2
Wellington Road	B1
Westbury Street	C1
Westfield Road	A2
Windmill Lane	C2-C3-C4

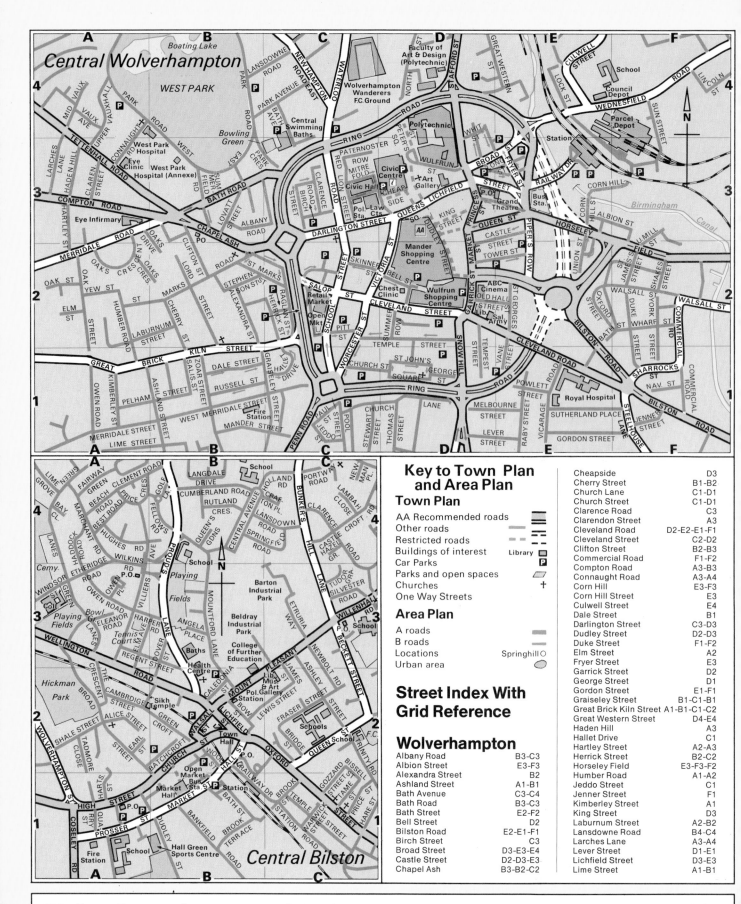

Key to Town Plan and Area Plan

Town Plan

AA Recommended roads	
Other roads	
Restricted roads	
Buildings of interest	Library 🔲
Car Parks	🅿
Parks and open spaces	
Churches	+
One Way Streets	

Area Plan

A roads	
B roads	
Locations	Springhill ○
Urban area	

Street Index With Grid Reference

Wolverhampton

Wolverhampton

Present-day Wolverhampton, capital of the Black Country, is a large and efficient town that belies its ancient origins. It was referred to as 'Heantun' in a 10th-century Royal charter, and the town coat of arms includes a cross ascribed to the Anglo-Saxon King Edgar.

In Victorian times Wolverhampton was widely known for its manufacture of chains, locks and nails, although the workshops were often tiny sheds in people's back yards. Today, many kinds of brass and iron products, as well as aircraft components, leave Wolverhampton's factories. Some different, but no less traditional, products of Midland craftsmen are displayed in the museum inside 19th-century Bantock House. These include japanned tin and papier-maché articles and painted enamels, as well as early Worcester porcelain.

Pre-dating Wolverhampton's industrial history by several hundred years is the carved shaft of Dane's Cross in St Peter's churchyard. Standing 14ft high, near a holed Bargain Stone, it was supposed to commemorate the defeat of the Danes in a local battle. The church mostly dates from the 15th century, and has a panelled tower and fine stone pulpit. There was an earlier monastery on the site, refounded in 994 by Lady Wulfruna, whose charter can now be seen in the vestry.

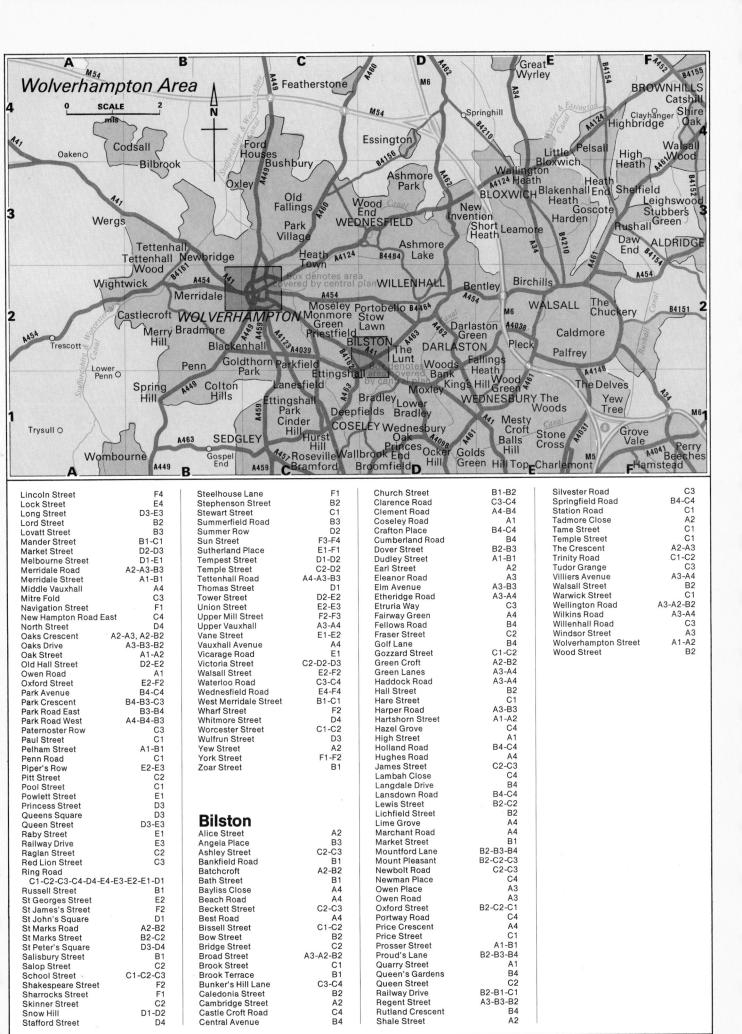

Lincoln Street	F4	Steelhouse Lane	F1
Lock Street	E4	Stephenson Street	B2
Long Street	D3-E3	Stewart Street	C1
Lord Street	B2	Summerfield Road	B3
Lovatt Street	B3	Summer Row	D2
Mander Street	B1-C1	Sun Street	F3-F4
Market Street	D2-D3	Sutherland Place	E1-F1
Melbourne Street	D1-E1	Tempest Street	D1-D2
Merridale Road	A2-A3-B3	Temple Street	C2-D2
Merridale Street	A1-B1	Tettenhall Road	A4-A3-B3
Middle Vauxhall	A4	Thomas Street	D1
Mitre Fold	C3	Tower Street	D2-E2
Navigation Street	F1	Union Street	E2-E3
New Hampton Road East	C4	Upper Mill Street	F2-F3
North Street	D4	Upper Vauxhall	A3-A4
Oaks Crescent	A2-A3, A2-B2	Vane Street	E1-E2
Oaks Drive	A3-B3-B2	Vauxhall Avenue	A4
Oak Street	A1-A2	Vicarage Road	E1
Old Hall Street	D2-E2	Victoria Street	C2-D2-D3
Owen Road	A1	Walsall Street	E2-F2
Oxford Street	E2-F2	Waterloo Road	C3-C4
Park Avenue	B4-C4	Wednesfield Road	E4-F4
Park Crescent	B4-B3-C3	West Merridale Street	B1-C1
Park Road East	B3-B4	Wharf Street	F2
Park Road West	A4-B4-B3	Whitmore Street	D4
Paternoster Row	C3	Worcester Street	C1-C2
Paul Street	C1	Wulfrun Street	D3
Pelham Street	A1-B1	Yew Street	A2
Penn Road	C1	York Street	F1-F2
Piper's Row	E2-E3	Zoar Street	B1
Pitt Street	C2		
Pool Street	C1		
Powlett Street	E1		
Princess Street	D3		
Queens Square	D3		
Queen Street	D3-E3		
Raby Street	E1		
Railway Drive	E3		
Raglan Street	C2		
Red Lion Street	C3		
Ring Road			
C1-C2-C3-C4-D4-E4-E3-E2-E1-D1		**Bilston**	
Russell Street	B1	Alice Street	A2
St Georges Street	E2	Angela Place	B3
St James's Street	F2	Ashley Street	C2-C3
St John's Square	D1	Bankfield Road	B1
St Marks Road	A2-B2	Batchcroft	A2-B2
St Marks Street	B2-C2	Bath Street	B1
St Peter's Square	D3-D4	Bayliss Close	A4
Salisbury Street	B1	Beach Road	A4
Salop Street	C2	Beckett Street	C2-C3
School Street	C1-C2-C3	Best Road	A4
Shakespeare Street	F2	Bissell Street	C1-C2
Sharrocks Street	F1	Bow Street	B2
Skinner Street	C2	Bridge Street	C2
Snow Hill	D1-D2	Broad Street	A3-A2-B2
Stafford Street	D4	Brook Street	C1
		Brook Terrace	B1
		Bunker's Hill Lane	C3-C4
		Caledonia Street	B2
		Cambridge Street	A2
		Castle Croft Road	C4
		Central Avenue	B4

Church Street	B1-B2	Silvester Road	C3
Clarence Road	C3-C4	Springfield Road	B4-C4
Clement Road	A4-B4	Station Road	C1
Coseley Road	A1	Tadmore Close	A2
Crafton Place	B4-C4	Tame Street	C1
Cumberland Road	B4	Temple Street	C1
Dover Street	B2-B3	The Crescent	A2-A3
Dudley Street	A1-B1	Trinity Road	C1-C2
Earl Street	A2	Tudor Grange	C3
Eleanor Road	A3	Villiers Avenue	A3-A4
Elm Avenue	A3-B3	Walsall Street	B2
Etheridge Road	A3-A4	Warwick Street	C1
Etruria Way	C3	Wellington Road	A3-A2-B2
Fairway Green	A4	Wilkins Road	A3-A4
Fellows Road	B4	Willenhall Road	C3
Fraser Street	C2	Windsor Street	A3
Golf Lane	B4	Wolverhampton Street	A1-A2
Gozzard Street	C1-C2	Wood Street	B2
Green Croft	A2-B2		
Green Lanes	A3-A4		
Haddock Road	A3-A4		
Hall Street	B2		
Hare Street	C1		
Harper Road	A3-B3		
Hartshorn Street	A1-A2		
Hazel Grove	C4		
High Street	A1		
Holland Road	B4-C4		
Hughes Road	A4		
James Street	C2-C3		
Lambah Close	C4		
Langdale Drive	B4		
Lansdown Road	B4-C4		
Lewis Street	B2-C2		
Lichfield Street	B2		
Lime Grove	A4		
Marchant Road	A4		
Market Street	B1		
Mountford Lane	B2-B3-B4		
Mount Pleasant	B2-C2-C3		
Newbolt Road	C2-C3		
Newman Place	C4		
Owen Place	A3		
Owen Road	A3		
Oxford Street	B2-C2-C1		
Portway Road	C4		
Price Crescent	A4		
Price Street	C1		
Prosser Street	A1-B1		
Proud's Lane	B2-B3-B4		
Quarry Street	A1		
Queen's Gardens	B4		
Queen Street	C2		
Railway Drive	B2-B1-C1		
Regent Street	A3-B3-B2		
Rutland Crescent	B4		
Shale Street	A2		

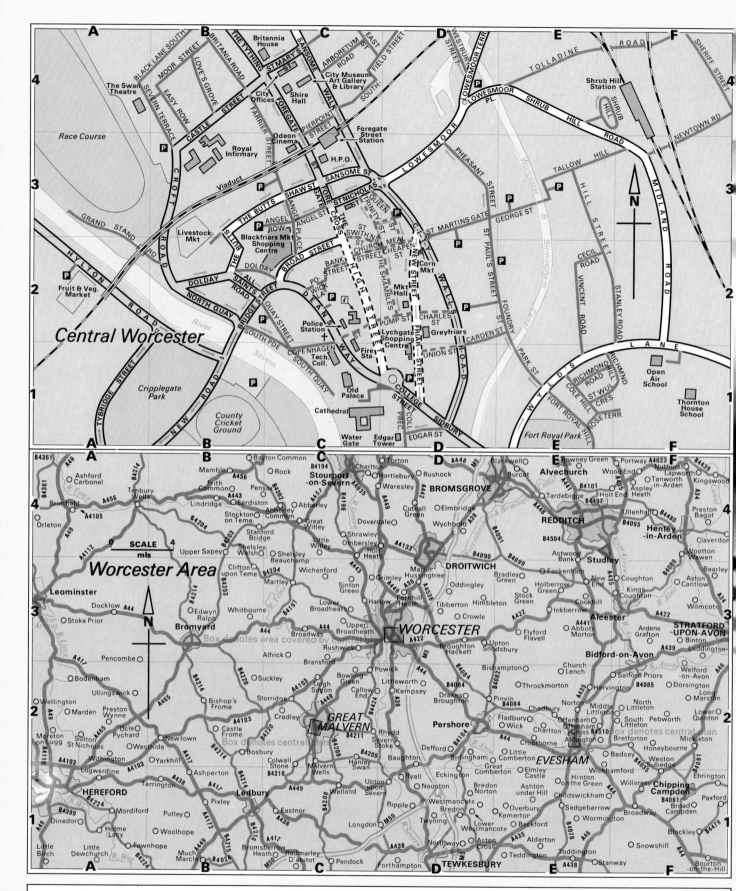

Worcester

County town and cathedral city, Worcester stands on the banks of the Severn in an area of rich agricultural land. Sadly, during the 1960s, the city suffered somewhat from ruthless redevelopment, but there is still much to interest the visitor, including The Commandery and the Tudor House, 15th-century buildings which both house museums. The cathedral, Worcester's oldest building, overlooks the river and the county cricket ground. It is one of the venues of the Three Choirs Festival, alternating with Gloucester and Hereford Cathedrals.

Worcester has become famous for its porcelain industry which was founded during the 18th century as an alternative to the ailing cloth trade. An exquisite collection of 'Royal Worcester' can be seen in the Dyson Perrins Museum.

Evesham is surrounded by the orchards that flourish in the fertile Vale of Evesham. It is an ancient market and light industrial town with two churches, a 16th-century bell-tower and the ruins of a Norman abbey all sharing the same grounds.

Malvern, famous for its mineral water, nestles at the foot of the Malvern Hills which are designated an Area of Outstanding Natural Beauty. Visitors have been drawn to this attractive town since Victorian times, and it retains much of the genteel elegance associated with bygone days.

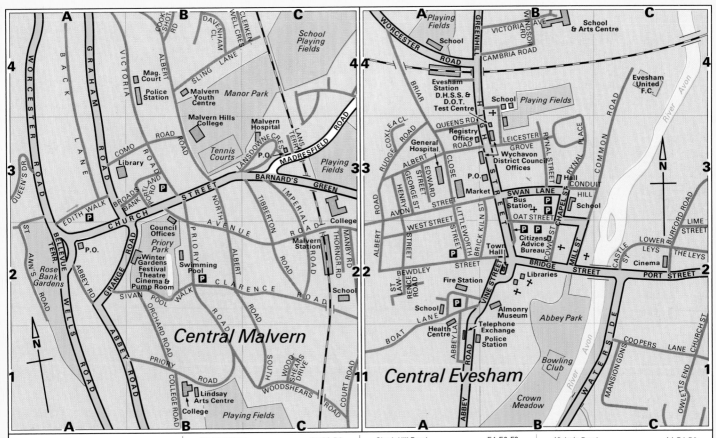

LEGEND

Town Plan

AA Recommended roads	
Restricted roads	
Other roads	
Buildings of interest	Cinema ▣
Car Parks	P
Parks and open spaces	
One Way Streets	→

Area Plan

A roads	
B roads	
Locations	Suckley ○
Urban area	

Street Index with Grid Reference

Worcester

All Saints Road	B2
Angel Place	C2-C3
Angel Row	B3-C3
Angel Street	C3
Arboretum Road	C4
Bank Street	C2
Black Lane South	A4-B4
Bridge Street	B2-C2
Britania Road	B4
Broad Street	C2-C3
Carden Street	D2-E2
Castle Street	B3-B4
Cecil Road	E2
Charles Street	D2
Church Street	C2

City Wall Road	D1-D2-D3
Cole Hill	E1
College Precinct	D1
College Street	D1
Copenhagen Street	C1-C2
Croft Road	B3-B2
Deans Way	C1-C2
Dolday	B2-C2
East Street	C4
Easy Row	B4
Edgar Street	D1
Farrier Street	B4-C4-C3
Foregate	C3
Foregate Street	C4-C3
Fort Royal Hill	E1
Foundry Street	E2
Friar Street	D1-D2
George Street	D3-E3
Grand Stand Road	A3-A2-B2
High Street	C2-C1-D1
Hill Street	E2-E3
Hylton Road	A3-A2-B2-B1
Love's Grove	B4
Lowesmoor	D3-D4
Lowesmoor Place	D4-E4
Lowesmoor Terrace	D4
Meal Cheapen Street	D2
Midland Road	F2-F3
Moor Street	D2-D3
New Road	B1
New Street	D2-D3
Newton Road	F3-F4
North Quay	B2
Park Street	E1-E2
Pheasant Street	D3
Pierpoint Street	C4
Powick Lane	C2
Pump Street	C2-D2
Quay Street	B2-C2-C1
Queen Street	C3-D3
Richmond Hill	E1-F1
Richmond Road	E1
Rose Terrace	E1-F1
St Martin's Gate	D3
St Mary's Street	B4-C4
St Nicholas Street	C3
St Paul's Street	D3-D2-E2
St Swithuns Street	C2-C3
St Wulstans Crescent	E1-F1
Sansome Street	C3
Sansome Walk	C4
Severn Terrace	A4-B4-B3
Shaw Street	C3
Sheriff Street	F4
Shrub Hill	E4-F4

Shrub Hill Road	E4-E3-F3
Sidbury	D1
South Field Street	C4-D4
South Parade	B2-C2-C1
South Quay	C1
Stanley Road	E2-F2
Tallow Hill	E3-F3
The Butts	B2-B3-C3
The Cross	C3
The Shambles	D2
The Tything	B4
Tolladine Road	E4-F4
Trinity Street	C3-C2
Tybridge Street	A1-A2-B2-B1
Union Street	D1
Vincent Road	E1-E2
Westbury Street	D4
Wyld's Lane	E1-F1-F2

Malvern

Abbey Road	A2-A1-B1
Albert Road South	B2-C2-C1
Albert Road North	B4-B3-B2
Avenue Road	B3-B2-C2
Back Lane	A4-A3
Barnard's Green	C3
Bellevue Terrace	A2
Broads Bank	A3-A4
Church Street	A3-A2-B2-B3
Clarence Road	B2-C2
Clerkenwell Crescent	B4-C4
College Road	B1
Como Road	A3-B3
Cookshot Road	B4
Court Road	C1
Davenham Close	B4
Edith Walk	A2-A3
Graham Road	A4-A3
Grange Road	A2-B2
Imperial Road	C2-C3
Lansdowne Crescent	C3
Lansdowne Terrace	C3
Madresfield Road	C3-C4
Orchard Road	B1-B2
Portland Road	B3
Priory Road	B3-B2-B1
Queen's Drive	A3
St Ann's Road	A2-A3
Sivan Pool Walk	A3-B3
Thorn Grove Road	C2
Tibberton Road	C3-C2

Victoria Road	A4-B4-B3
Wells Road	A2-A1
Woodshears Drive	C1
Woodshears Road	C1
Worcester Road	A4-A3-A2

Evesham

Abbey Road	A1-A2
Albert Road	A2-A3-B3
Avon Street	A2-A3-B3
Bewdley Street	A2-B2
Boat Lane	A1-A2-B2
Briar Close	A4-A3
Brick Kiln Street	B2-B3
Bridge Street	B2-C2
Burford Road	C2-C3
Cambria Road	B4
Castle Street	C2
Chapel Street	B2-B3
Church Street	C1-C2
Coopers Lane	C1
Common Road	B3-C3-C4
Conduit Hill	B3-C3
Cowl Street	A3
Coxlea Close	A3
Edward Street	A3
George Street	A3
Greenhill	A3-A4
Henry Street	A2-A3
Leicester Grove	B3
Lime Street	C2
Littleworth Street	A2-A3
Lower Leys	C2
Mansion Gardens	C1
Mill Street	B2-B3
Oat Street	B2
Owletts End	C1
Port Street	C2
Queens Road	A3
Rudge Road	A3
Rynal Place	B3
Rynal Street	B3
St Lawrence Road	A2
Swan Lane	B3
The Leys	C2
Victoria Avenue	B4
Vine Street	A2-B2
Waterside	B1-C1-C2
West Street	A2
Windsor Road	B4
Worcester Road	A4

WORCESTER
Worcester Cathedral, set high on the banks of the Severn with views across the Malvern Hills, has dominated the city for centuries. The chapter house, with its massive central column, is considered one of the finest in Britain.

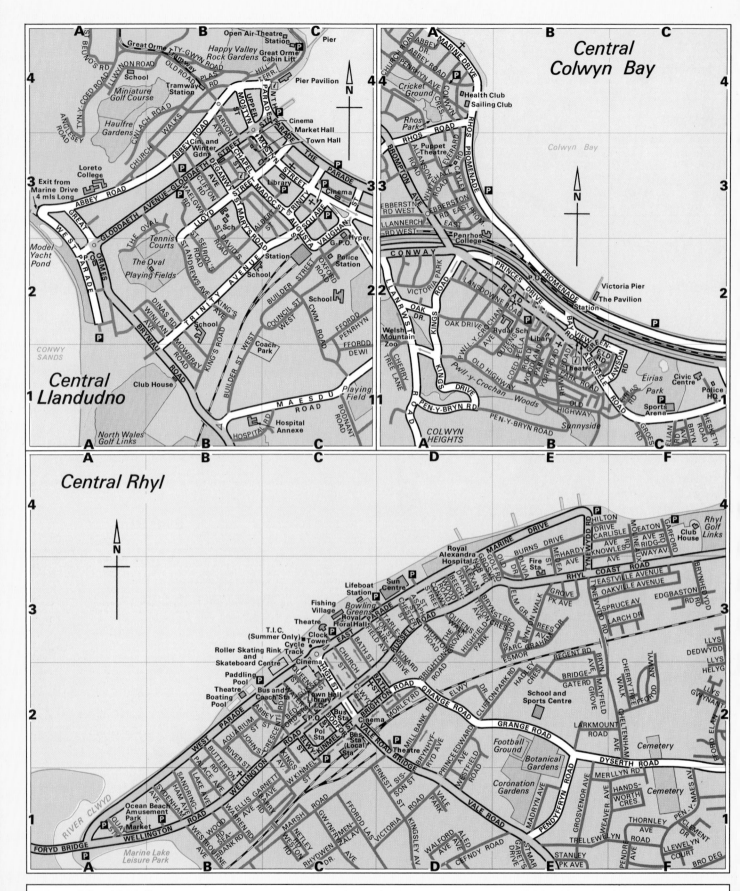

North Wales

Llandudno combines Victorian charm and elegance with the modern amenities of a popular holiday destination. Lying at the foot of Great Orme and Little Orme, its varied attractions include miles of sandy beaches, the Doll Museum, the Mostyn Art Gallery, and the Cabinlift (Britain's longest cable car run). St Tudno's Church is 6th-century.

Colwyn Bay Three miles of golden sand stretch between Rhos-on-Sea and Old Colwyn at Colwyn Bay. Notable in a host of activities for visitors are the Harlequin Puppet Theatre and the extensive facilities of 50-acre Eirias Park.

Rhyl has been a resort for over a century and now attracts more visitors than ever to the glittering attractions of Suncentre, Fishing Village, Skateworld, Cyclorama and Marine Lake. Part of the shoreline is bordered by an elegant promenade edged by flower beds and lawns.

Holyhead The ruins of an ancient settlement at the summit of Holyhead mountain provide a beautiful backdrop to Holyhead, which has become a busy port for car ferry traffic to Laoghaire. The Parish Church of St Cybi is medieval. Close by Trearddur Bay is excellent for watersports.

Conwy boasts Edward I's fine 13th-century castle and Telford's magnificent suspension bridge, built over 150 years ago. The smallest house in Britain stands on the Quay.

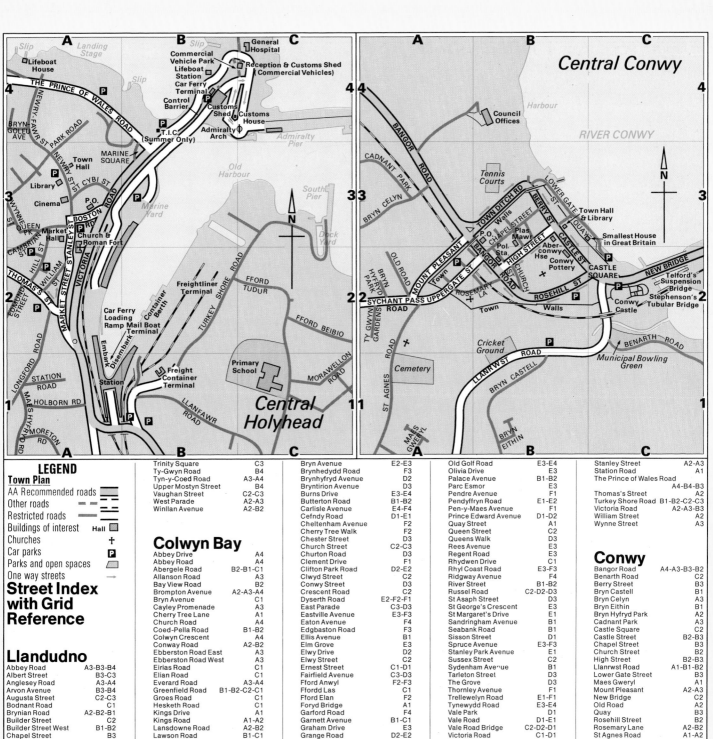

Central Holyhead

(map labels: General Hospital, Commercial Vehicle Park, Lifeboat Station, Car Ferry Terminal, Reception & Customs Shed (Commercial Vehicles), Control Barrier, Customs Shed, Customs House, Admiralty Arch, Admiralty Pier, T.I.C. (Summer Only), Lifeboat House, Landing Stage, Slip, THE PRINCE OF WALES ROAD, NEWRY ST PARK ROAD, NEWRY ST, CYBI ST, BRYN GOLEU AVE, Town Hall, MARINE SQUARE, Library, Cinema, P.O., Market Hall, Church & Roman Fort, BOSTON RD, VICTORIA ROAD, STANLEY ST, MARKET STREET, QUEEN PK, SWYNNE PK, WILLIAM ST, HILL ST, CAMBRIAN ST, THOMAS'S ST, EDMUND STREET, Marine Yard, Old Harbour, South Pier, Dock Yard, Marine Square, Freightliner Terminal, FFORD TUDUR, Container Berth, Car Ferry Loading Ramp Mail Boat Terminal, Embark, Disembark, Station, Freight Container Terminal, Primary School, TURKEY SHORE ROAD, FFORD BEIBIO, MORAWELLON ROAD, LLANFAWR ROAD, LONGFORD ROAD, STATION ROAD, HOLBORN RD, MAES HYFRYD RD, MORETON RD, Central Holyhead)

Central Conwy

(map labels: Council Offices, Harbour, RIVER CONWY, Tennis Courts, BANGOR ROAD, CADNANT PARK, BRYN CELYN, TOWN DITCH RD, LOWER GATE ST, Town Hall & Library, Smallest House in Great Britain, CHAPEL STREET, BERRY ST, HIGH STREET, CASTLE ST, QUAY, Plas Mawr, P.O., Pol. Sta., Aberconwy Hse, Conwy Pottery, MOUNT PLEASANT, BANGOR ROAD, Town Walls, UPPERGATE ST, ROSEMARY LA, CHURCH, ROSEHILL ST, CASTLE SQUARE, Telford's Suspension Bridge, Stephenson's Tubular Bridge, Conwy Castle, NEW BRIDGE, BRYN HYFRYD PARK, SYCHANT PASS ROAD, TY GWYN GARDENS, ST AGNES ROAD, Cemetery, Cricket Ground, Town Walls, LLANRWST ROAD, BRYN CASTELL, BENARTH ROAD, Municipal Bowling Green, BRYN EITHIN, MAES GWERYL, N)

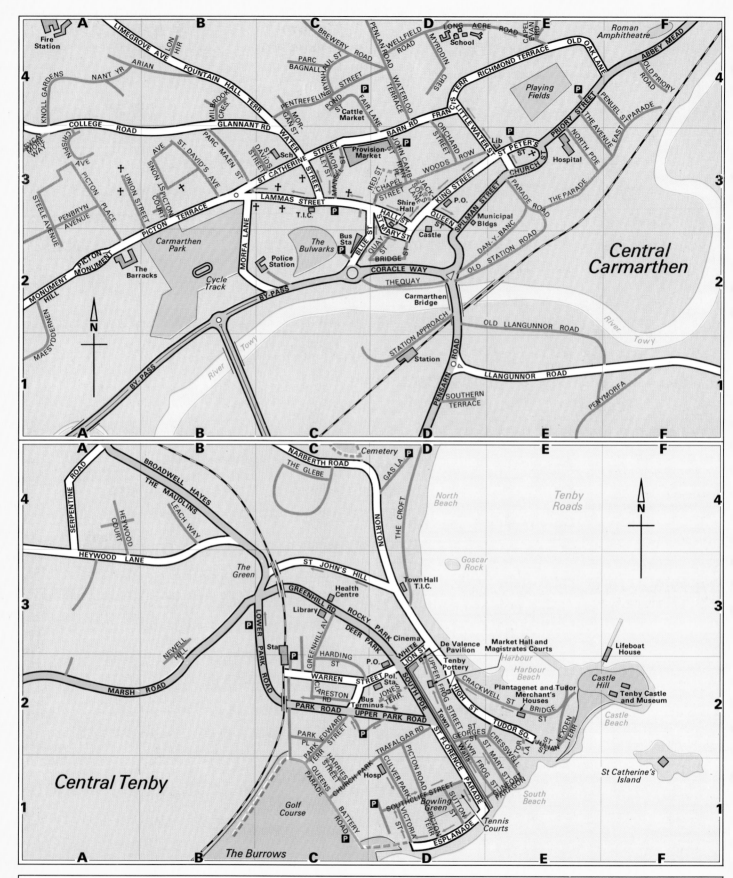

South Wales

Aberystwyth is both a picturesque seaside town and an important centre of learning. The National Library of Wales and several colleges and museums, are here, and by way of contrast, freshwater and sea fishing are also popular. Overlooking the southern seafront are the 1277 castle ruins; the Vale of Rheidol Steam Railway is nearby.

Carmarthen is a hive of activity of industries, colleges and schools. The River Towey offers boating and fishing; the Leisure Centre offers other sports, and St Peter's Church and the County Museum are full of interest. A Redevelopment Scheme has kept the town's old markets.

Tenby Surrounded by 13th-century walls and overlooked by medieval St Mary's church, this major resort boasts four beaches, a pretty harbour and interesting shops and streets. The Tudor Merchant's House and the Tenby Museum are worth seeing; across from Castle Beach stands St Catherine's Rock with its disused fort (closed to visitors). Three miles off the coast are the bird colonies and seals of Caldey Island, which is run by Cistercian monks skilled in producing goods such as perfume from wild flowers.

Pembroke is dominated by a magnificent Norman castle, and other attractions are Monkton Priory and the Mill Pond Walk. The town is a perfect touring centre for South Pembrokeshire.

86

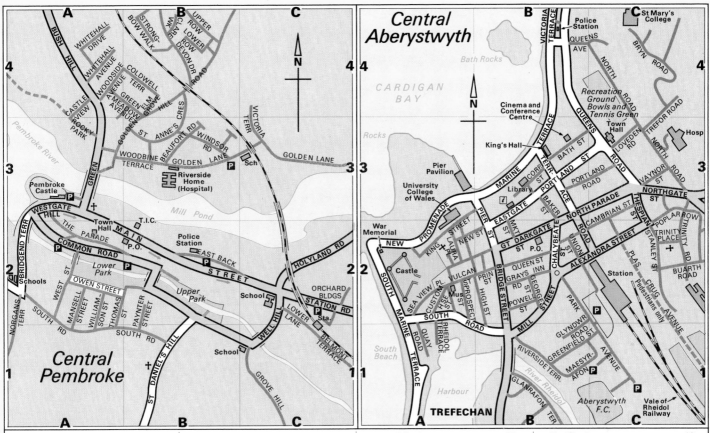

LEGEND

A A Recommended roads	
Other roads	
Restricted roads	
Buildings of interest	Cinema ▧
Parks and open spaces	▢
Churches	†
One Way Streets	←
Car Parks	Ⓟ

Street Index with Grid Reference

Carmarthen

Abbey Mead	F4
Barn Road	D3-D4
Blue Street	C2-C3
Brewery Road	C4-D4
Bridge Street	D2
Brynhaul Street	C4
By-Pass	A1-B1-B2-C2
Cambrian Place	D3
Capel Evan Road	E4
Chapel Street	D3
Church Street	E3
College Road	A4-A3-B3-B4
Coracle Way	C2-D2
Crispin Avenue	A3
Dan-y-Banc	D2-D3-E3
East Parade	F3-F4
Fair Lane	C4-D3-E3
Fountain Hall Terrace	B4-C4
Francis Terrace	D4
Glannant Road	B3-B4-C4-C3
Hall Street	D3
Jackson's Lane	D3
John Street	D3
King Street	D2-D3-E3
Knoll Gardens	A4
Lammas Street	B3-C3
Limegrove Avenue	A4-B4
Little Water Street	D4-D3-E3
Llangunnor Road	D1-E1
Long Acre Road	D4-E4
Lon Hir	B4
Maesyddernen	A1-A2
Mansell Street	C3
Millbrook Crescent	B4
Monument Hill	D4
Morfa Lane	B3-B2-C2
Morgan Street	C4
Morley Street	C3
Myrddin Crescent	D4
Nant Yr Arian	A4-B4
North Parade	E3
Old Llangunnor Road	D2-E2-E1-F1
Old Oak Lane	E4-F4

Old Priory Road	F4
Old Station Road	D2-E2-E3
Orchard Street	D3-D4
Parade Road	E3
Parc Bagnell	C4
Parc Maen Street	B3
Penbryn Avenue	A3
Penlan Road	C4-D4
Pensarn Road	D1-D2
Pentrefelin Street	C4-D4
Penuel Street	E4-F4-F3
Penymorfa	E1-F1
Picton Court	B3
Picton Monument	A2
Picton Place	A2-A3
Picton Terrace	A2-B2-B3
Pond Street	C2
Priory Street	E3-E4
Quay Street	C2-D2
Queen Street	D3
Red Street	D3
Richmond Terrace	D4-E4
St Catherine Street	B3-C3
St David's Avenue	B3
St David's Street	B3-C3
St Mary Street	D2-D3
St Nons Avenue	B3
St Peter's Street	E3
Southern Terrace	D1
Spilman Street	D2-D3-E3
Station Approach	C1-D1-D2
Steele Avenue	A2-A3
Sycamore Way	A3
The Avenue	E4-E3-F3
The Parade	E3
The Quay	C2-D2
Union Street	A2-B2
Waterloo Terrace	D4
Water Street	C3
Wellfield Road	D4
Woods Row	D3

Tenby

Battery Road	C1
Bridge Street	E2
Broadwell Hayes	A4-B4
Church Park	C1-D1
Clareston Road	C2
Crackwell Street	D2-E2
Cresswell	E1-E2
Culver Park	D1
Deer Park	C3-D3-D2
Edward Street	C2
Esplanade	D1
Gas Lane	D4
Greenhill Avenue	C2-C3
Greenhill Road	C3
Gunfort Paragon	E1
Harding Street	C2
Harries Street	C1
Heywood Court	D2
Heywood Lane	A4-A3-B3-B4
High Street	D2
Jones Terrace	D2
Leach Way	B4
Lexden Terrace	E2
Lower Frog Street	D2-D1-E1
Lower Park Road	C2-C3
Marsh Road	A2-B2-B3

Narberth Road	C4
Newell Hill	B2-B3
Norton	C4-D4-D3
Park Place	C2
Park Road	C2
Park Terrace	C1-C2
Picton Road	D1-D2
Picton Terrace	D1
Queens Parade	C1
Rocky Park	C3-D3-D2
St Florence Parade	D1-D2
St Georges Street	D2-E2
St John's Hill	C3-D3
St Julian Street	E2
St Mary Street	D2-E2-E1
Serpentine Road	A4
Southcliffe Street	D1
South Parade	D2
Sutton Street	D1
The Croft	D3-D4
The Glebe	C4
The Maudlins	A4-B4
Tor Lane	E1-E2
Trafalgar Road	D2
Tudor Square	E2
Upper Frog Street	D2-D3
Upper Park Road	C2-D2
Victoria Street	D1
Warren Street	C2-D2
White Lion Street	D2-D3

Pembroke

Beaufort Road	B3
Belmont Terrace	C1
Bridgend Terrace	A2-A3
Bush Hill	A4
Castle View	A4
Clare Walk	B4
Coldwell Terrace	B4
Common Road	A3-A2-B2
Devon Drive	B4
East Back	B2
Elm Grove	B4
Golden Hill Road	A3-B3-B4
Golden Lane	B3-C3
Green	A3
Green Meadow Avenue	A4-B4
Grove Hill	C1
Holyland Road	C2
Lower Lane	C1-C2
Lower Row	B4
Main Street	A3-A2-B2-C2
Mansell Street	A1-A2
Norgans Terrace	A1-A2
Orchard Buildings	C2
Owen Street	A2
Paynter Street	B1-B2
Rocky Park	A3
St Anne's Crescent	B3-B4
St Daniel's Hill	B1-B2
South Road	A2-A1-B1
Station Road	C2
Strongbow Walk	B4
The Parade	A3-A2-B2
Thomas Street	A1-A2-B2
Upper Row	B4
Victoria Lane	C3-C4
Well Hill	C1-C2
Westgate Hill	A3

West Street	A2
Whitehall Avenue	A4
Whitehall Drive	A4
Williamson Street	A1-A2
Windsor Road	B3
Woodbine Terrace	A3-B3
Woodside Avenue	A4

Aberystwyth

Alexandra Street	B2-C2
Baker Street	B3
Bath Street	B3
Bridge Street	B1-B2
Bryn Road	C4
Buarth Road	C2
Cambrian Street	B2-C2-C3
Chalybeate Street	B2
Corporation Street	B3
Custom House Street	A2
Eastgate	B2
George Street	B2
Glanrafon Terrace	B1
Glyndwr Road	B1-B2-C2
Grays Inn Road	B2
Great Darkgate Street	B2
Greenfield Street	B1-C1
High Street	A2-A3-B3
Loveden Road	C3
Maesyrafon	B1-C1
Marine Terrace	B3-B4
Market Street	B2
Mill Street	B1-B2
New Promenade	A2-A3
New Street	A2-B2
Northgate Street	C3
North Parade	B3-C3
North Road	C3-C4
Park Avenue	B2-C2-C1
Pier Street	B2-B3
Plas Crag Avenue	C1-C2
Poplar Row	C2-C3
Portland Road	C2-C3
Portland Street	B3-C3
Powell Street	B2
Prince's Street	B2
Prospect Street	A2
Quay Road	A1
Queens Avenue	B4-C4
Queens Road	B4-B3-C3
Queen Street	B2
Rheidol Terrace	A1-A2
Riverside Terrace	B1
Sea View Place	A2
South Marine Terrace	A1-A2
South Road	A2-A1-B1
Stanley Street	C2
Terrace Road	B3-B2-C2
Thespian Street	C2-C3
Trefor Road	C3-C4
Trinity Place	C2
Trinity Road	C2-C3
Union Street	B2
Vaynor Street	C3
Vulcan Street	A2
Victoria Terrace	B4

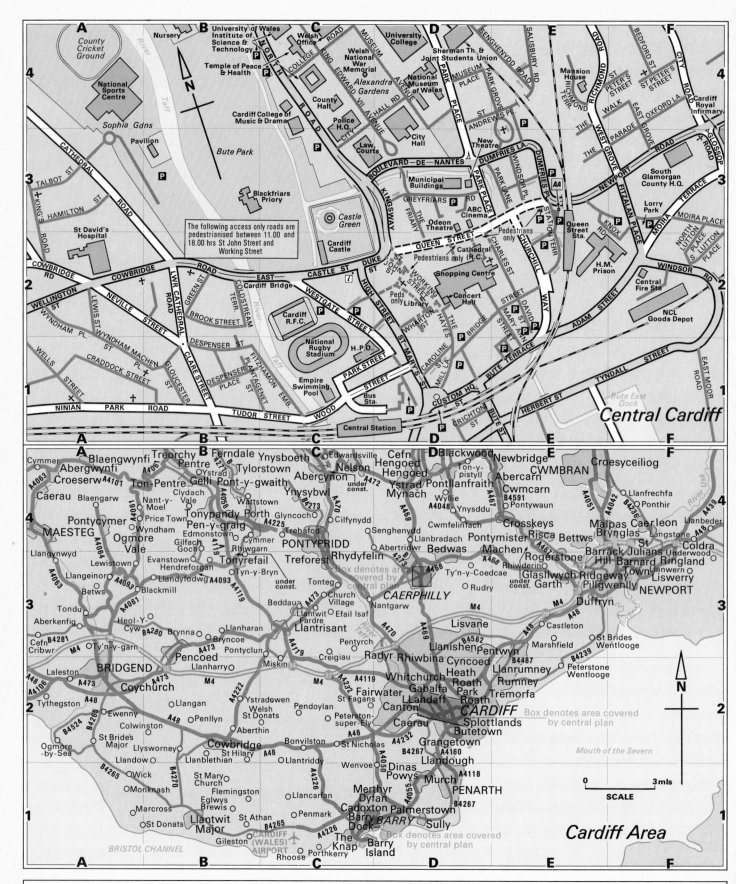

Central Cardiff

Cardiff Area

Cardiff

Strategically important to both the Romans and the Normans, Cardiff slipped from prominence in medieval times and remained a quiet market town in a remote area until it was transformed – almost overnight – by the effects of the Industrial Revolution. The valleys of South Wales were a principal source of iron and coal – raw materials which helped to change the shape and course of

the 19th-century world. Cardiff became a teeming export centre; by the end of the 19th century it was the largest coal-exporting city in the world.

Close to the castle – an exciting place with features from Roman times to the 19th century – is the city's civic centre – a fine concourse of buildings dating largely from the early part of the 20th century. Among them is the National Museum of Wales – a superb collection of art and antiquities from Wales and around the world.

Barry has sandy beaches, landscaped gardens and parks, entertainment arcades and funfairs. Like Cardiff it grew as a result of the demand for coal and steel, but now its dock complex is involved in the petrochemical and oil industries.

Caerphilly is famous for two things – a castle and cheese. The cheese is no longer made here, but the 13th-century castle, slighted by Cromwell, still looms above its moat. No castle in Britain – except Windsor – is larger.

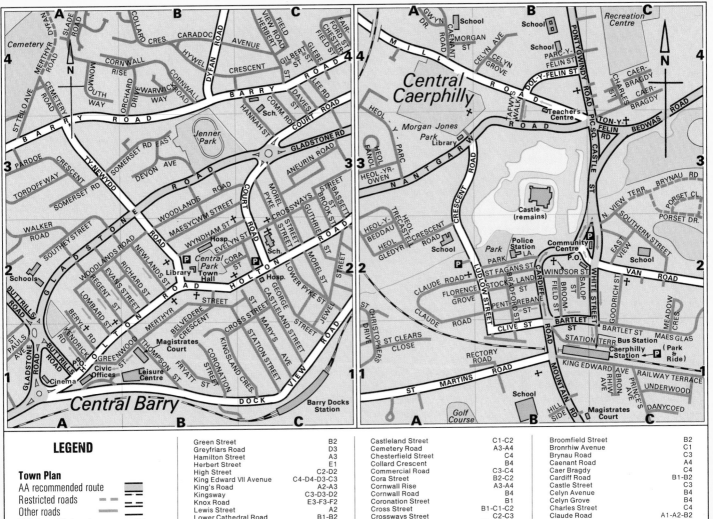

LEGEND

Town Plan

AA recommended route	▭
Restricted roads	- - -
Other roads	▬
Buildings of interest	Cinema ▣
Car parks	P
Parks and open spaces	▲
One way streets	⌐

Area Plan

A roads	▬
B roads	▬
Locations	Glyncoch ○
Urban area	⬭

Street Index with Grid Reference

Cardiff

Adam Street	E1-E2-F2
Bedford Street	F4
Boulevard de Nantes	C3-D3
Bridge Street	D1-D2-E2
Brook Street	B2
Bute Street	D1-E1
Bute Terrace	D1-E1
Caroline Street	D1
Castle Street	C2
Cathedral Street	A4-A3-B3-B2-A2
Charles Street	D2-E2
Churchill Way	E2-E3
City Hall Road	C3-C4-D4
City Road	F4
Clare Street	B1
Coldstream Terrace	B2
College Road	C4
Cowbridge Road	A2
Cowbridge Road East	A2-B2-C2
Craddock Street	A1-B1
Crichton Street	D1
Custom House Street	D1
David Street	E2
Despenser Place	B1
Despenser Street	B1
Duke Street	C2-D2
Dumfries Lane	D3-E3
Dumfries Place	E3
East Grove	F4-F3
East Moor Road	F1
Fitzalan Place	F3-F2
Fitzhamon Embankment	B1-C1
Glossop Road	F3
Gloucester Street	B1
Green Street	B2
Greyfriars Road	D3
Hamilton Street	A3
Herbert Street	E1
High Street	C2-D2
King Edward VII Avenue	C4-D4-D3-C3
King's Road	A2-A3
Kingsway	C3-D3-D2
Knox Road	E3-E2-F3
Lewis Street	A2
Lower Cathedral Road	B1-B2
Machen Place	A1-B1
Mary Ann Street	E1-E2
Mill Lane	D1
Moira Place	F3
Moira Terrace	F2-F3
Museum Avenue	C4-D4
Museum Place	D4
Neville Street	A2-B2-B1
Newport Road	E3-F3-F4
Ninian Park Road	A1-B1
North Luton Place	F2-F3
North Road	B4-C4-C3
Oxford Lane	F4
Park Grove	D4-E4
Park Lane	D3-E3
Park Place	D4-D3-E3
Park Street	C1-D1
Plantagenet Street	B1-C1
Queen Street	D2-D3
Richmond Road	E4
Richmond Terrace	E4
St Andrew's Place	D4-E4
St John Street	D2
St Mary's Street	D1-D2
St Peter's Street	E4-F4
Salisbury Road	E4
Senghenydd Road	D4-E4
South Lutton Place	F2-F3
Station Terrace	E2-E3
The Friary	D2-D3
The Hayes	D1-D2
The Parade	E3-F3-F4
The Walk	E3-E4-F4
Talbot Street	A3
Tudor Street	B1-C1
Tyndall Street	E1-F1
Wellington Street	A2
Wells Street	A1
Westgate Street	C2-D2-D1
West Grove	E4-E3-F3
Wharton Street	D2
Windsor Place	E3
Windsor Road	F2
Wood Street	C1-D1
Working Street	D2
Wyndham Place	A2
Wyndham Street	A1-A2

Barry

Aneurin Road	C3
Barry Road	A3-A4-B3-B4-C4
Bassett Street	C2-C3
Belvedere Crescent	B1-B2
Beryl Road	A1-A2
Brook Street	C2-C3
Buttrills Road	A1-A2
Caradoc Avenue	B4-C4
Castleland Street	C1-C2
Cemetery Road	A3-A4
Chesterfield Street	C4
Collard Crescent	B4
Commercial Road	C3-C4
Cora Street	B2-C2
Cornwall Rise	A3-A4
Cornwall Road	B4
Coronation Street	B1
Cross Street	B1-C1-C2
Crossways Street	C2-C3
Court Road	C2-C3-C4
Davies Street	C3-C4
Devon Avenue	B3
Dock View Road	B1-C1-C2
Dyfan Road	B4
Evans Street	A2-B2
Evelyn Street	B2-C2
Fairford Street	C4
Field View Road	C4
Fryatt Street	B1
George Street	C1-C2
Gilbert Street	C4
Gladstone Road	A1-A2-B2-B3-C3
Glebe Street	C4
Greenwood Street	A1-B1
Guthrie Street	C3-C2
Hannah Street	C4-C3
Herbert Street	C4
Holton Road	A1-B1-B2-C2
Hywell Crescent	B4-C4
Jewel Street	C1-C2
Kendrick Road	A1
Kingsland Crescent	B1-C1
Lee Road	C4
Lombard Street	A1-A2
Lower Pyke Street	C2
Maesycwm Street	B2-B3-C3
Merthyr Dyfan Road	A4
Merthyr Street	B1-B2-C2
Monmouth Way	A4
Morel Street	C2-C3
Newlands Street	B2
Orchard Drive	B3-B4
Pardoe Crescent	A3
Pyke Street	C3-C2
Regent Street	A2-B2
Richard Street	A2-B2
St Mary's Avenue	C1-C2
St Pauls Avenue	A1
St Teilo Avenue	A3-A4
Slade Road	A4
Somerset Road	A3
Somerset Road East	A3-B3
Southey Street	A2-A3
Station Street	C1
Thomson Street	B1
Tordoff Way	A3
Ty-Newydd Road	A3-B3-B2
Walker Road	A2
Warwick Way	B4
Woodlands Road	A2-B2-B3-C3
Wyndham Street	B2-C2

Caerphilly

Bartlet Street	B2-B1-C1
Bedwas Road	C3-C4
Bradford Street	B1-B2
Broomfield Street	B2
Bronrhiw Avenue	C1
Brynau Road	C3
Caenant Road	A4
Caer Bragdy	C4
Cardiff Road	B1-B2
Castle Street	C3
Celyn Avenue	B4
Celyn Grove	B4
Charles Street	C4
Claude Road	A1-A2-B2
Clive Street	B1-B2
Crescent Rod	A2-A3-B3
Danycoed	C1
Dol-y-Felen Street	B4
East View	C2
Florence Grove	A2-B2
Goodrich Street	C1-C2
Gwyn Drive	A4
Heol Fanal	A3
Heol Gledyr	A2
Heol Trecastell	A2-A3
Hillside	B1
Heol-y-Beddau	A2
Heol-yr-Owen	A3
King Edward Avenue	B1-C1
Ludlow Street	A2-B2-B1
Maes Glas	C1
Meadow Crescent	C1-C2
Mill Road	A4-B4-B3
Morgan Street	A4-B4
Mountain Road	B1
Nantgarw Road	A3-B3
North View Terrace	C2-C3
Parc-y-Felin Street	B4
Park Lane	B2
Pentrebone Street	B2
Piccadilly Square	C3
Pontygwindy Road	B4-C4
Porset Close	C3
Porset Drive	C2-C3
Prince's Avenue	C1
Railway Terrace	C1
Rectory Road	A1-B1
St Christopher's Drive	A1-A2
St Clears Close	A1
St Fagans Street	B2
St Martins Road	A1-B1
Salop Street	B2
Southern Street	C2-C3
Station Terrace	B1-C1
Stockland Street	B2
Tafwy Walk	B3-B4
Ton-y-Felin Road	B2
Underwood	C1
Van Road	C2
White Street	C2
Windsor Street	B2

89

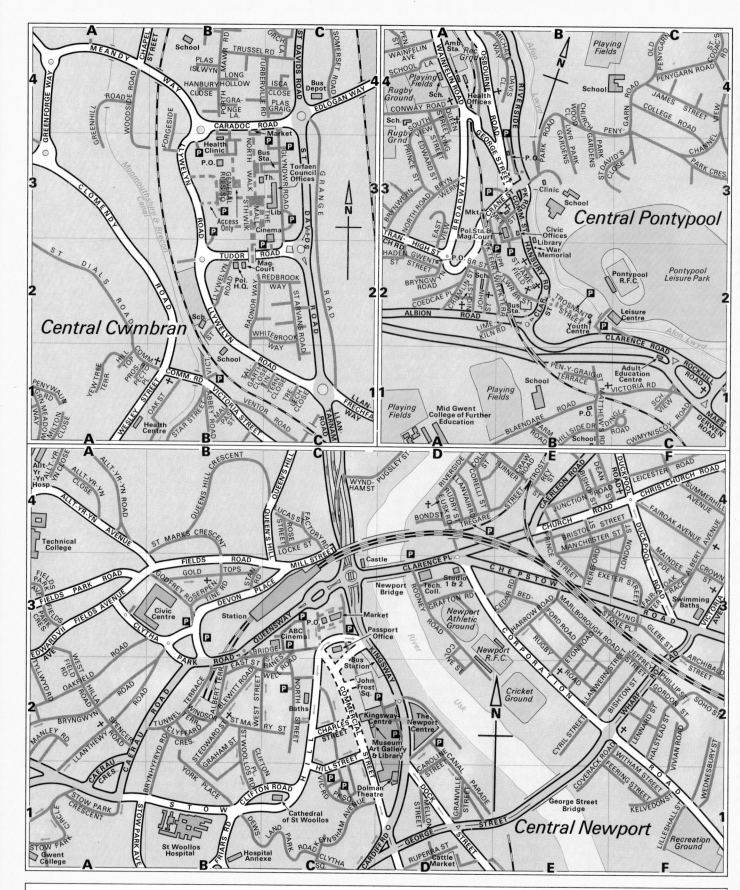

Newport

When the Industrial Revolution hit South Wales Newport, on the River Usk, came into its own as a harbour for the export of the coal and iron products manufactured in the valleys. At the zenith of Newport's activity in the mid 19th century there were six miles of quays. Today it is still an important port but the range of industries using it has expanded as light industry has taken over.

The Civic Centre just to the west of the town centre is a rather striking development which is particularly well-known for a series of modern murals that illustrate the history of Monmouthshire (now part of Gwent). Further background to Newport, including the Chartist Riots of 1839, and the iron industry can be found in the town museum in John Frost Square. There is also an interesting section on the Roman history of the area, particularly concerning the nearby forts of Caerleon

and Caerwent. The city is relatively short of historic buildings, but St Woolos' Cathedral, crowning Stow Hill, dates back to Norman times. Its unusual name is believed to be a corruption of Gwynllyw, a local baron who built the first church on this site.

Perhaps Newport's most remarkable structure is the Transporter Bridge which is one of just two left in Britain – the other is at Middlesbrough. The bridge consists of a suspended moveable platform which carries cars and pedestrians across the river.

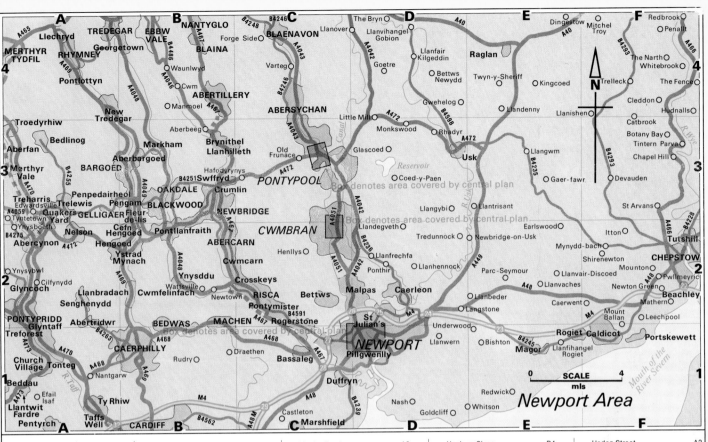

Newport Area

SCALE 0 — 4 mls

Box denotes area covered by central plan

LEGEND

Town Plan

AA recommended route	━━━
Restricted roads	╌╌
Other roads	▬▬
Buildings of interest	Hall ▨
Car parks	🅿
Parks and open spaces	◢
One way streets	→

Area Plan

A roads	▬▬
B roads	▬▬
Locations	Redwick ○
Urban area	▭

Street Index with Grid Reference

Newport

Albert Avenue	F3-F4
Albert Terrace	B2
Allt-yr-yn Avenue	A4-A3-B3-B4
Allt-yr-yn Close	A4
Allt-yr-yn Road	A4
Archibald Street	F2-F3
Barneswell Road	C2-C3
Bedford Road	E3
Bishop Street	E4
Bishton Street	E2-F2
Blewitt Road	B2
Bond Street	D4
Bridge Street	B3-C3
Bristol Street	E4-F4
Bryngwyn Road	A2-B2
Brynhyfryd Road	B1-B2
Caerau Crescent	A1-A2
Caerau Road	A1-A2-B2
Caerleon Road	E4
Canal Parade	D1-D2
Cardiff Road	C1-D1
Caroline Street	D1-D2
Cedar Road	E3
Charles Street	C2
Chepstow Road	D3-E3-F3
Christchurch Road	F4
Church Road	E4-F4
Clarence Place	C3-D3-D4
Clifton Place	B2-B1-C1
Clifton Road	B1-C1
Clyffard Crescent	B2
Clytha Park Road	A3-B2-B1
Clytha Square	C1
Collier Street	D4
Colne Street	D2-D3
Commercial Street	C3-C2-C1-D1
Corelli Street	D4
Corporation Road	D3-E3-E2-F2-F1
Coverack Road	E1-E2-F2
Crawford Road	E4
Crown Street	F3
Cyril Street	E2
Dean Street	E4-F4
Dewsland Park Road	B1-C1
Devon Place	B3-C3
Dock Street	D2-D1-E1
Dos Road	C4
Duckpool Road	F3-F4
East Street	B2
East Usk Road	D4
Edward VII Avenue	A2-A3
Elizabeth Terrace	D1-D2
Eton Road	E2-E3
Exeter Street	E3-F3
Factory Road	C4
Fairoak Avenue	F4
Fairoak Terrace	F3
Feering Street	E2-E1-F1
Fields Avenue	A3
Fields Park Avenue	A3
Fields Park Crescent	A3
Fields Park Road	A3
Fields Road	B3-C3
Friars Road	B1
George Street	C1-D1-E1
Glebe Street	F3
Godfrey Road	B3
Gold Tops	B3
Gordon Street	F2
Grafton Road	D3
Graham Street	B1-B2
Granville Street	D1
Halstead Street	F2
Harrow Road	E3
Henry Street	C4
Hereford Street	E3-E4
Hilla Road	A2
Hill Street	C1-C2
Jeffrey Street	E2-E3
Junction Road	E4-F4
Kelvedon Street	F1
Keynsham Avenue	C1
Kingsway	C3-D3-D2
Leicester Road	F4
Lennard Street	F2
Lilleshall Street	F1
Livingstone Place	E3-F3
Llanthewy Road	A1-A2-B2
Llanvair Road	D4
Llanwern Street	E2-F2-F3
Locke Street	C4
London Street	F3-F4
Lucas Street	C4
Maindee Parade	F3-F4
Manchester Street	E4-F4
Manley Road	A2
Marlborough Road	E3-F3
Mellon Street	D1
Mill Street	C3-C4
North Street	C2
Oakfield Road	A2-A3
Park Square	C1
Phillip Street	F2
Prince Street	E3-E4
Pugsley Street	C4-D4
Riverside	D4
Rodney Road	D3
Rose Street	C4
Rudry Street	D4
Rugby Road	E2-E3
Ruperra Street	D1
St Edward Street	B1-B2
St Marks Crescent	B3-B4
St Mary Street	B2-C2
St Woollos Road	B1-B2
Serpentine Road	B3
Soho Street	F2
Spencer Road	A2
Stanley Road	B3
Stow Hill	A1-B1-C1-C2-C3
Stow Park Avenue	A1
Stow Park Circle	A1
Stow Park Crescent	A1
Summerhill Avenue	F4
Tregare Street	D4-E4
Trostrey Street	E4
Tunnel Terrace	B2
Turner Street	D4-E4
Tyllwyd Road	A2
Queens Hill Crescent	B4-C4-C3
Queensway	B3-C3
Victoria Avenue	F3
Victoria Road	C1
Vivian Road	F1-F2
Wednesbury Street	F1-F2
Westfield Road	A2-A3
West Street	B2-C2-C3
Wharf Road	F2-F3
Windsor Terrace	B2
Witham Street	F1-F2
Wyndham Street	C4
York Place	B1-B2

Cwmbran

Abbey Road	B1
Caradoc Road	B4-C4
Chapel Street	A4-B4
Clomendy Road	A3-A2-B2-B1
Commercial Road	A1-B1
Edlogan Way	C4
Forgeside	B3-B4
General Rees Square	B3
Glyndwr Road	C2-C3-C4
Grange Lane	B4
Grange Road	C1-C2-C3-C4
Greenforge Way	A3-A4
Greenhill Road	A3-A4
Green Meadow Way	A1

Hanbury Close	B4
Hill Top	A1
Isca Close	C4
Llanfrechfa Way	C1
Llantarnam Road	C1
Llywelyn Road	B3-B2-B1-C1
Long Hollow	B4
Malpas Street	B1
Meandy Way	A4-B4
Milton Close	A1
North Walk	B3
Oak Street	B1
Orchard Lane	C4
Penywaun Road	A1
Plas Graig	C4
Plas Islwyn	B4
Porth Mawr Road	B4
Prospect Place	A1
Radnor Way	B1-B2
Redbrook Way	B2-C2
St Arvans Road	C1-C2
St Davids Road	C1-C2-C3-C4
St Dials Road	A2-A1-B1
Somerset Road	C4
South Walk	B2-B3
Star Street	B1
Talgarth Close	B1
The Mall	B3
Tintern Close	B1-C1
Trelech Close	C1
Trussel Road	B4-C4
Tudor Road	B2-C2
Turberville Road	C4
Ventor Road	B1-C1
Victoria Street	B2-B1-C1
Wesley Street	A1-B1
Whitebrook Way	B2-C2
Woodside Road	A3-A4
Yew Tree Terrace	A1

Pontypool

Albion Road	A2-B2
Blaendare Road	A1-B1
Bridge Street	A2
Broadway	A2-A3-A4
Bryngwyn Road	A2
Brynwern	A3
Channel View	C3-C4
Churchwood Close	B4
Clarence Road	B2-B1-C2-C1
Clarence Street	B2
Coedcae Place	A2
College Road	C3-C4
Commercial Street	B3
Conway Road	A4
Crumlin Street	A2
Cwmyniscoy Road	C1
Davis Close	B4
Dingle Road	B1-C1
East View	A2-A3
Edward Street	A3-A4
Farm Road	B1
George Street	A4-A3-B3
Gwent Street	A2

Haden Street	A2
Hanbury Road	B2-B3
High Street	A2-A3
Hillside Drive	B1
James Street	C4
John Street	A2
King Street	A3-A4
Lime Kiln Road	A2-B2
Lower Bridge Street	A2
Lower Park Gardens	B3-B4
Maesderwen Road	C1
Market Street	A3-B3
Michael Way	A4-B4
Nicholas Street	A2
North Road	A3
Old Penygarn	C4
Osbourne Road	A4-A3-B3-B4
Park Crescent	A3
Park Gardens	B3-B4
Park Road	B3-B4
Penygarn Road	B4-C4
Pen-y-Graig Terrace	B1
Penywain Street	A4
Prince Street	A3
Queen Street	A4
Riverside	B3-B4
Rockhill Road	C1
St Codac's Road	C4
St David's Close	B3-C3
St Jame's Field	B2
St Matthew's Road	B1
School Lane	A4
School View	C1
South View	A3-A4
Tranch Road	A2-A3
Trosnant Street	B2
Upper Park Terrace	A2-B2
Victoria Road	B1-C1
Wainfelin Avenue	A4
Wainfelin Road	A4

91

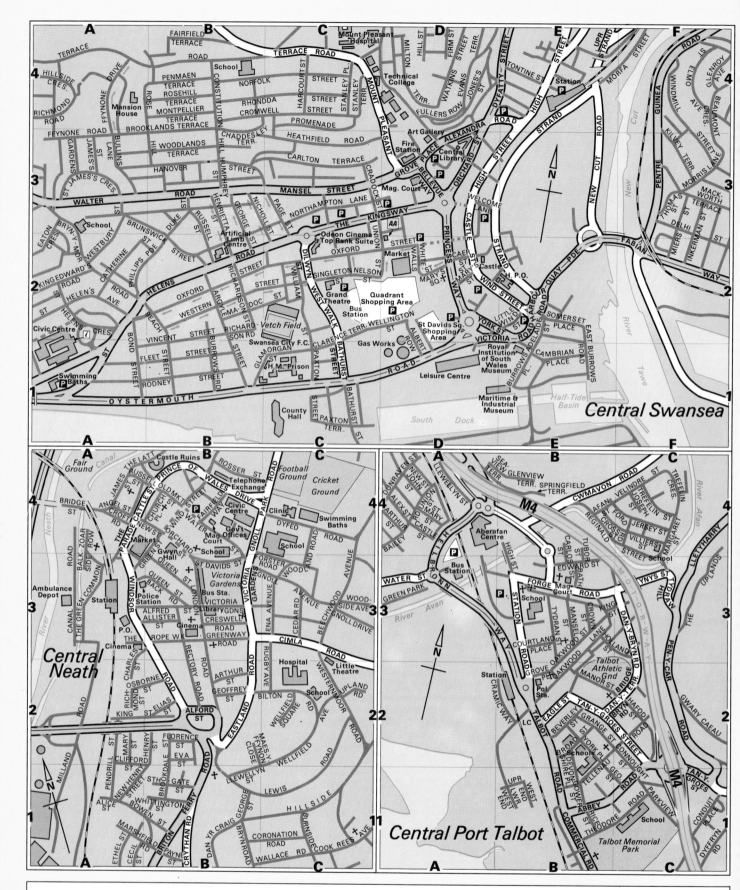

Central Swansea

Central Neath

Central Port Talbot

Swansea

Like nearly all the towns in the valleys and along the coast of Glamorgan, Swansea grew at an amazing speed during the Industrial Revolution. Ironworks, non-ferrous metal smelting works and mills and factories of every kind were built to produce the goods which were exported from the city's docks. There had been a settlement here from very early times – the city's name is derived

from Sweyn's Ea – Ea means island, and Sweyn was a Viking pirate who had a base here. Heavy industry is still pre-eminent in the area, but commerce is of increasing importance and the university exerts a strong influence. Hundreds of acres of parkland and open space lie in and around the city, and just to the west is the Gower, one of the most beautiful areas of Wales. The history of Swansea is traced in the Maritime, Industrial and Royal Institution of South Wales Museums, while

the Glynn Vivian Art Gallery contains notable paintings and porcelain.

Neath and **Port Talbot** are, like Swansea, dominated by heavy industry. Neath was once a Roman station, and later had a castle and an abbey, ruins of which can still be seen. Port Talbot has been an industrial centre since 1770, when a copper-smelting works was built. Steelworks and petrochemical works stretch for miles around Swansea Bay.

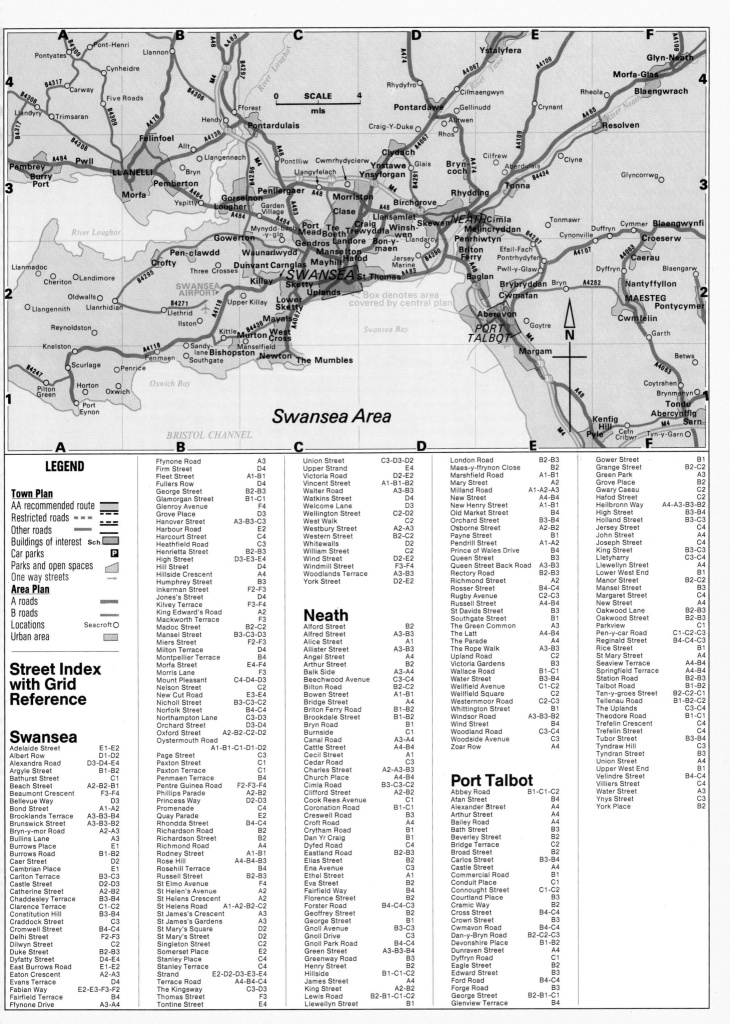

Swansea Area

BRISTOL CHANNEL

LEGEND

Town Plan
- AA recommended route
- Restricted roads
- Other roads
- Buildings of interest — Sch.
- Car parks — P
- Parks and open spaces
- One way streets

Area Plan
- A roads
- B roads
- Locations — Seacroft ○
- Urban area

Street Index with Grid Reference

Swansea

Adelaide Street	E1-E2
Albert Row	D1-D2
Alexandra Road	D3-D4-E4
Argyle Street	B1-B2
Bathurst Street	C1
Beach Street	A2-B2-B1
Beaumont Crescent	F3-F4
Bellevue Way	D3
Bond Street	A1-A2
Brooklands Terrace	A3-B3-B4
Brunswick Street	A3-B3-B2
Bryn-y-mor Road	A2-A3
Bullins Lane	A3
Burrows Place	E1
Burrows Road	B1-B2
Caer Street	D2
Cambrian Place	E1
Carlton Terrace	B3-C3
Castle Street	D2-D3
Catherine Street	A2-B2
Chaddesley Terrace	B3-B4
Clarence Terrace	C1-C2
Constitution Hill	B3-B4
Craddock Street	C3
Cromwell Street	B4-C4
Delhi Street	F2-F3
Dilwyn Street	C2
Duke Street	B2-B3
Dyfatty Street	D4-E4
East Burrows Road	E1-E2
Eaton Crescent	A2-A3
Evans Terrace	D4
Fabian Way	E2-E3-F3-F2
Fairfield Terrace	B4
Ffynone Drive	A3-A4

Ffynone Road	A3
Firm Street	D4
Fleet Street	A1-B1
Fullers Row	D4
George Street	B2-B3
Glamorgan Street	B1-C1
Glenroy Avenue	F4
Grove Place	D3
Hanover Street	A3-B3-C3
Harbour Road	E2
Harcourt Street	C4
Heathfield Road	C3
Henrietta Street	B2-B3
High Street	D3-E3-E4
Hill Street	D4
Hillside Crescent	A4
Humphrey Street	B3
Inkerman Street	F2-F3
Jones's Street	D4
Kilvey Terrace	F3-F4
King Edward's Road	A2
Mackworth Terrace	F3
Madoc Street	B2-C2
Mansel Street	B3-C3-D3
Miers Street	F2-F3
Milton Terrace	D4
Montpellier Terrace	B4
Morfa Street	E4-F4
Morris Lane	F3
Mount Pleasant	C4-D4-D3
Nelson Street	C2
New Cut Road	E3-E4
Nicholl Street	B3-C3-C2
Norfolk Street	B4-C4
Northampton Lane	C3-D3
Orchard Street	D3-D4
Oxford Street	A2-B2-C2-D2
Oystermouth Road	A1-B1-C1-D1-D2
Page Street	C3
Paxton Street	C1
Paxton Terrace	C1
Penmaen Terrace	B4
Pentre Guinea Road	F2-F3-F4
Phillips Parade	A2-B2
Princess Way	D2-D3
Promenade	C4
Quay Parade	E2
Rhondda Street	B4-C4
Richardson Road	B2
Richardson Street	B2
Richmond Road	A4
Rodney Street	A1-B1
Rose Hill	A4-B4-B3
Rosehill Terrace	A4
Russell Street	B2-B3
St Elmo Avenue	F4
St Helen's Avenue	A2
St Helens Crescent	A2
St Helens Road	A1-A2-B2-C2
St James's Crescent	A3
St James's Gardens	A3
St Mary's Square	D2
St Mary's Street	D2
Singleton Street	C2
Somerset Place	E2
Stanley Place	C4
Stanley Terrace	C4
Strand	E2-D2-D3-E3-E4
Terrace Road	A4-B4-C4
The Kingsway	C3-D3
Thomas Street	F3
Tontine Street	E4

Union Street	C3-D3-D2
Upper Strand	E4
Victoria Road	D2-E2
Vincent Street	A1-B1-B2
Walter Road	A3-B3
Watkins Street	D4
Welcome Lane	D3
Wellington Street	C2-D2
West Walk	C2
Westbury Street	A2-A3
Western Street	B2-C2
Whitewalls	D2
William Street	C2
Wind Street	D2-E2
Windmill Street	F3-F4
Woodlands Terrace	A3-B3
York Street	D2-E2

Neath

Alford Street	B2
Alfred Street	A3-B3
Alice Street	A1
Allister Street	A3-B3
Angel Street	A4
Arthur Street	B2
Balk Side	A3-A4
Beechwood Avenue	C3-C4
Bilton Road	B2-C2
Bowen Street	A1-B1
Bridge Street	A4
Briton Ferry Road	B1-B2
Brookdale Street	B1-B2
Bryn Road	B1
Burnside	C1
Canal Road	A3-A4
Cattle Street	A4-B4
Cecil Street	A1
Cedar Road	C3
Charles Street	A2-A3-B3
Cimla Road	B3-C3-C2
Clifford Street	A2-B2
Cook Rees Avenue	C1
Coronation Road	B1-C1
Creswell Road	B3
Croft Road	A4
Crytham Road	B1
Dan Yr Craig	B1
Dyfed Road	C4
Eastland Road	B2-B3
Elias Street	B2
Ena Avenue	C3
Ethel Street	A1
Eva Street	B2
Fairfield Way	B4
Florence Street	B2
Forster Road	B4-C4-C3
Geoffrey Street	B2
George Street	B1
Gnoll Avenue	B3-C3
Gnoll Drive	C3
Gnoll Park Road	B4-C4
Green Street	A3-B3-B4
Greenway Road	B3
Henry Street	B2
Hillside	B1-C1-C2
James Street	A4
King Street	A2-B2
Lewis Road	B2-B1-C1-C2
Llewellyn Street	B1

London Road	B2-B3
Maes-y-ffrynon Close	B2
Marshfield Road	A1-B1
Mary Street	A2
Milland Road	A1-A2-A3
New Street	A4-B4
New Henry Street	A1-B1
Old Market Street	A1-B1
Orchard Street	B3-B4
Osborne Street	A2-B2
Payne Street	B1
Pendrill Street	A1-A2
Prince of Wales Drive	B4
Queen Street	B3
Queen Street Back Road	A3-B3
Rectory Road	B2-B3
Richmond Street	A2
Rosser Street	B4-C4
Rugby Avenue	C2-C3
Russell Street	A4-B4
St Davids Street	B3
Southgate Street	B1
The Green Common	A3
The Latt	A4-B4
The Parade	A4
The Rope Walk	A3-B3
Upland Road	C2
Victoria Gardens	B3
Wallace Road	B1-C1
Water Street	B3-B4
Wellfield Avenue	C1-C2
Wellfield Square	C2
Westernmoor Road	C2-C3
Whittington Street	B1
Windsor Road	A3-B3-B2
Wind Street	B4
Woodland Road	C3-C4
Woodside Avenue	C3
Zoar Row	A4

Port Talbot

Abbey Road	B1-C1-C2
Afan Street	B4
Alexander Street	A4
Arthur Street	A4
Bailey Road	A4
Bath Street	B3
Beverley Street	B2
Bridge Terrace	C2
Broad Street	B2
Carlos Street	B3-B4
Castle Street	A4
Commercial Road	B1
Conduit Place	C1
Connought Street	C1-C2
Courtland Place	B3
Cramic Way	B2
Cross Street	B4-C4
Crown Street	B3
Cwmavon Road	B4-C4
Dan-y-Bryn Road	B2-C2-C3
Devonshire Place	B1-B2
Dunraven Street	A4
Dyffryn Road	C1
Eagle Street	B2
Edward Street	B3
Ford Road	B4-C4
Forge Road	B3
George Street	B2-B1-C1
Glenview Terrace	B4

Gower Street	B1
Grange Street	B2-C2
Green Park	A3
Grove Place	B2
Gwary Caeau	C2
Hafod Street	C2
Heilbronn Way	A4-A3-B3-B2
High Street	B3-B4
Holland Street	B3-C3
Jersey Street	C4
John Street	A4
Joseph Street	C4
King Street	B3-C3
Lletyharry	C3-C4
Llewellyn Street	A4
Lower West End	B1
Manor Street	B2-C2
Mansel Street	B3
Margaret Street	C4
New Street	A4
Oakwood Lane	B2-B3
Oakwood Street	B2-B3
Parkview	C1
Pen-y-car Road	C1-C2-C3
Reginald Street	B4-C4-C3
Rice Street	B1
St Mary Street	A4
Seaview Terrace	A4-B4
Springfield Terrace	A4-B4
Station Road	B2-B3
Talbot Road	B1-B2
Tan-y-groes Street	B2-C2-C1
Tellenau Road	B1-B2-C2
The Uplands	C3-C4
Theodore Road	B1-C1
Trefelin Crescent	C4
Trefelin Street	C4
Tubor Street	B3-B4
Tyndraw Hill	C3
Tyndran Street	B3
Union Street	A4
Upper West End	B1
Velindre Street	B4-C4
Villiers Street	C4
Water Street	A3
Ynys Street	C3
York Place	B2

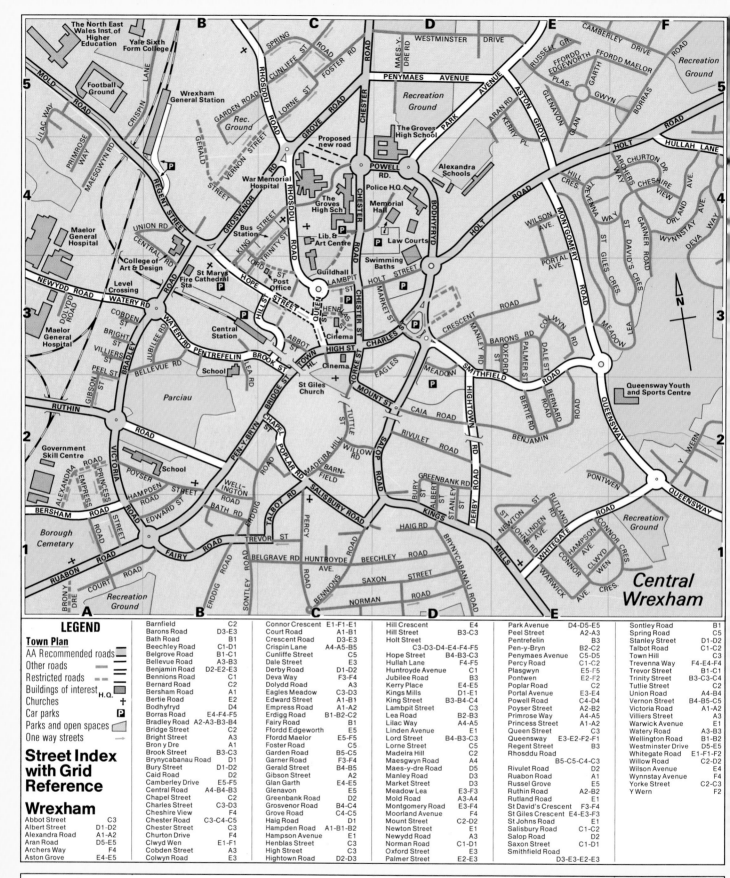

Wrexham

Gateway to North Wales, Wrexham has emerged from a turbulent past of medieval resistance to English rule and action during the Civil War to become a more peaceable — but still active — industrial and residential centre. Kelloggs and GKN (which owns the Brymbo Steel Works) are two of the large industrial concerns which have arrived to replace the coalmining and tanning industries which were previously prevalent, and modernisation has provided pedestrian shopping areas. The development in Regent Street includes a Methodist Church at first floor level above the shops; more traditional is the Parish Church of St Giles, with its 136ft 16th-century tower, a local landmark. The main body of the church dates from the 15th century, and its churchyard contains the grave of Elihn Yale, the local boy who founded Yale University in the USA.

Places of interest within the area include Bersham Industrial Heritage, dealing with the local iron industry, and Erdigg, a late 17th-century house containing most of its original furniture. On the sporting side, Wrexham has long been the home of Association Football in Wales: the Welsh FA has its headquarters here and the Racecourse ground is regularly used for international matches, as well as by Wrexham in the Canon League.

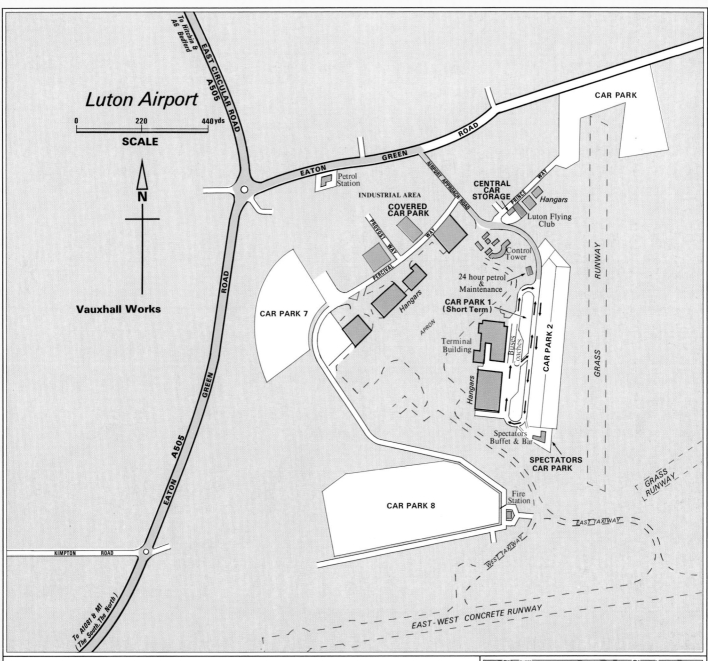

Luton Airport

Opened shortly before World War II when it was used mainly by the local flying club, Luton Airport has now become one of the country's most popular take-off points for holidays in the sunshine resorts of Europe and North Africa. It is used mainly by package holiday operators, and although its heaviest period for passenger traffic is during the summer months, winter breaks are becoming increasingly popular. Catering efficiently for this special demand, Luton has sophisticated snow clearing equipment to ensure that the airport is operational in all but the most severe weather conditions. Aircraft noise is also monitored so that it can be kept to an absolute minimum.

Owned and operated by the Borough of Luton, the airport lies two miles south-east of the centre of Luton and is only 3½ miles from Junction 10 on the M1. The passenger terminal is currently undergoing reconstruction and extension, which will provide extra lounge space, refreshment services and Customs facilities in addition to those which already exist in the main concourse. These include restaurant, buffet, and bar facilities for refreshments, foreign exchange points, banking and postal services.

Space for car parking is available in a number of surface car parks: drivers are advised to go to the Terminal Building to leave passengers and luggage, and to check the car park in use for the day, before driving to the appropriate one to park. Payment is in advance, and a free mini-bus service is available to carry car drivers from the car parks to the Terminal Building. This service is also available to take drivers of cars from the Terminal Building to the appropriate car parks when they return from their flights.

In addition, a car park with spaces for 350 vehicles has been provided next to the taxiway, and gives spectators a good view of the aircraft. A small charge is made for use of this facility.

For those travelling by public transport, Luton is also well-served by express trains, as it lies on the main line from St Pancras to the Midlands and the north of England. The journey from St Pancras takes only 28 minutes by fast train, and frequent bus services operate during the day between the airport and railway station. Express bus services are operated by the National Bus Company between Luton and surrounding towns and with the London area. Regular Green Line services run between the airport and central London, and a Green Line service is also available between Luton Airport and the airports at Heathrow and Gatwick.

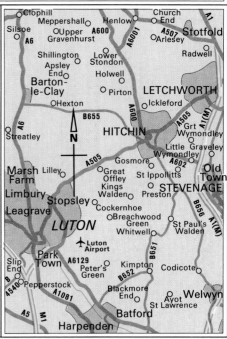

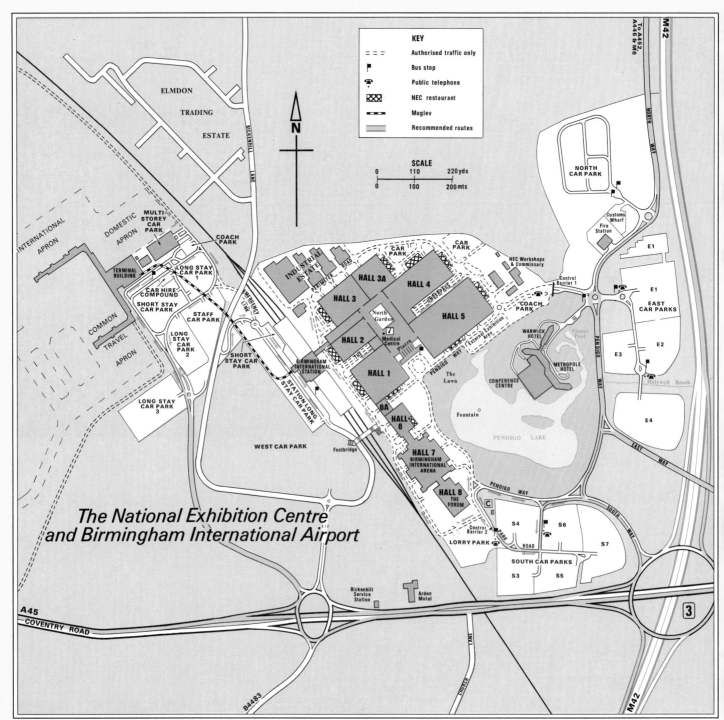

The National Exhibition Centre
and Birmingham International Airport

SCALE

0   110   220 yds
0   100   200 mts

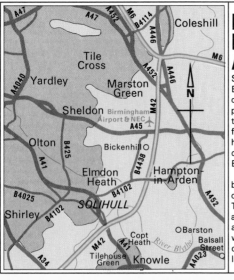

Birmingham International Airport and NEC

Situated just nine miles east of the city, Birmingham International Airport is a short distance from the M6 and M42 motorways, and provides quick and easy access from most parts of the country. This is a popular embarkation point for charter flights to a wide range of European holiday destinations, and it also provides a comprehensive network of scheduled flights to many British and European destinations.

A special viewing area with its own shop and buffet is situated on the third level, with its own access at the front of the terminal building. The airport's choice of buffets and licensed bars also includes the 150-seater Landside Restaurant, and all of them are open to the general public as well as to passengers. Multi-storey and surface car parking is available, while Birmingham International Station offers an 80-minute rail link with London (Euston), and connections to other British cities. The airport is also the site of the Maglev transit system, which sweeps travellers in 90 seconds from the three-storey airport terminal to the Birmingham International Railway Station, and to the National Exhibition Centre. The Maglev has three unmanned cars (each taking up to 32 passengers with their luggage), suspended by magnetic levitation 15mm above guidance tracks and driven without friction by linear induction motors, along a 600 metre elevated track.

National Exhibition Centre The new centre was opened by HM the Queen in February 1976 and lies about eight miles east of Birmingham city centre. The 10 exhibition halls have an interior area of 105,085 square metres and the landscaped setting covers 310 acres. The central feature of the complex — the Piazza — has shops, banks, medical and visitor services, including the Birmingham Convention and Visitor Bureau. The International Area is a multi-purpose hall for conventions, concerts and sporting events, with seating for up to 12,000, and the Forum is designed specifically for presentations and product launches.

Northern England and Scotland

AREA MAPS ARE INDICATED IN BOLD.

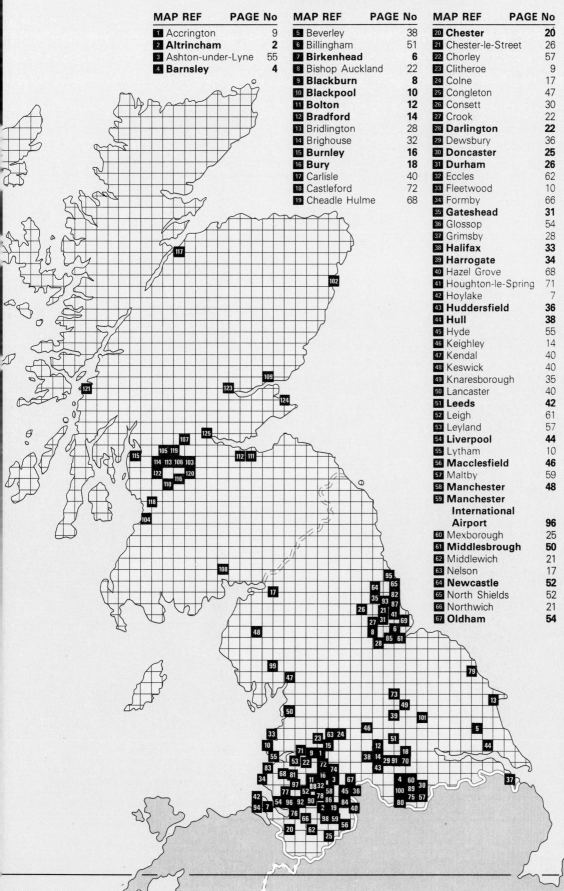

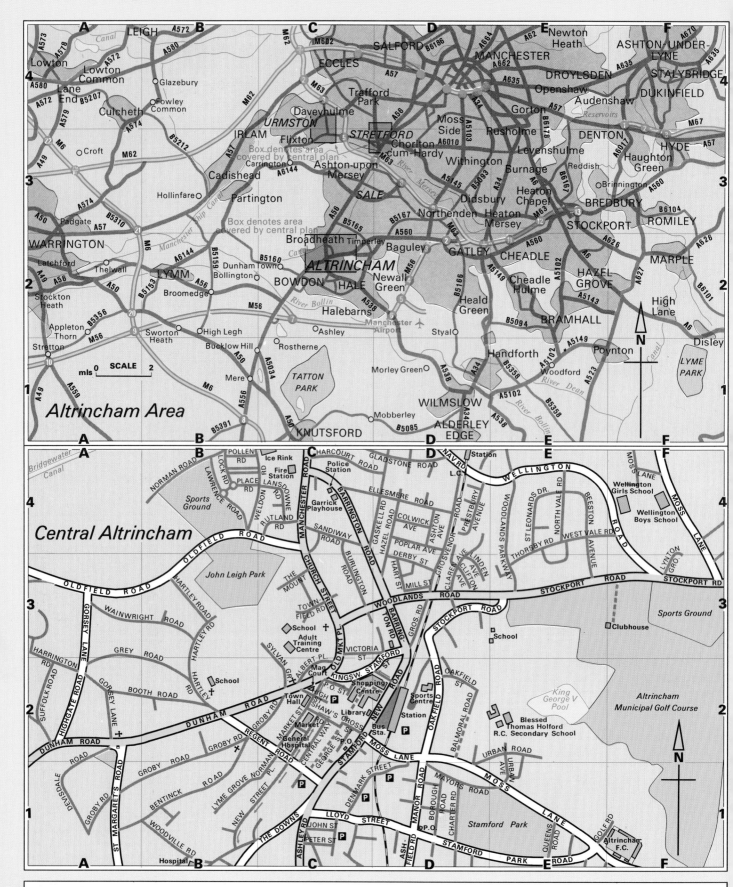

Altrincham Area

Central Altrincham

Altrincham

Bonnie Prince Charlie's troops gathered in Altrincham's Old Market Place during the '45 rebellion, to demand lodgings — and Altrincham is still much in demand today as a residential area. Conveniently close to Manchester, it also has good shops, a modern sports centre, a golf course and an ice rink. Not so very long ago it stood in an agricultural district, but the coming of the railways sparked off the town's development, and it first became a cotton producing town, and later a centre for light industry.

Urmston's Davyhulme Park is one of the most attractive in the area. The town grew with the opening of the Manchester Ship Canal, and the establishment of the Trafford Park industrial estate has brought further development.

Stretford has a chilling reminder of the past in the 'Great Stone' or 'plague stone' which stands at the entrance to Gorse Hill Park. The two holes in its surface were once filled with disinfectant to purify coins which had been handled by plague victims. Stretford itself used to be a centre for the making of woollen goods, but the opening up of a way to the sea by the linking of the Bridgwater Canal and the Manchester Ship Canal began its years of greatest growth. Today it has one of the biggest shopping centres in the borough, and a modern sports centre.

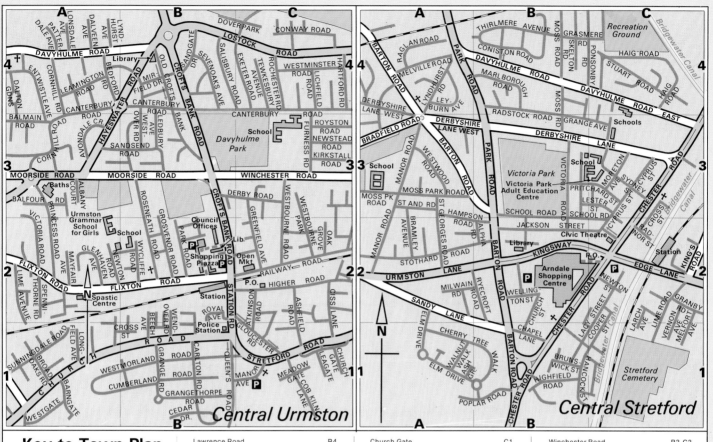

Central Urmston

Central Stretford

Key to Town Plan and Area Plan

Town Plan
AA Recommended roads	
Other roads	
Restricted roads	
Buildings of interest	Cinema
Churches	+
Car Parks	P
Parks and open spaces	
One way streets	←

Area Plan
A roads	
B roads	
Locations	Ibsley○
Urban area	

STREET INDEX

Altrincham

Albert Place	C2
Ashfield Road	D1
Ashley Road	C1
Ashton Avenue	D4
Balmoral Road	D2
Barrington Road	C4-C3-D3
Beeston Avenue	E3-E4
Bentinck Road	A1-B1-B2
Booth Road	A2-B2
Borough Road	D1
Burlington Road	C3-C4
Central Way	C1-C2
Charter Road	D1
Church Street	C3-C4
Clarendon Avenue	D3
Clifton Avenue	D3
Colwick Avenue	D4
Cross Street	C2
Denmark Street	C1-D1
Derby Street	D3
Devisdale Road	A1-A2
Dunham Road	A1-A2-B2-C2
Ellesmere Road	C4-D4
Gaskell Road	C4-D4
George Street	C1-C2
Gladstone Road	C4-D4
Golf Road	E1-F1
Gorsey Lane	A2-A3
Grey Road	A2-A3-A2-B2
Groby Road	A1-B1-B2-C2
Grosvenor Road	D3-D4
Harcourt Road	C4-D4
Harrington Road	A2-A3
Hartley Road	B2-B3
Hart Street	D3
Hazel Road	D3-D4
Highgate Road	A2
High Street	C2
John Street	C1
Kingsway	C2
Landsdowne Road	C4
Lawrence Road	B4
Linden Avenue	D3
Lloyd Street	C1-D1
Lock Road	B4
Lyme Grove	B1
Lynton Grove	F3-F4
Manchester Road	C4
Manor Road	D1
Market Street	C2
Mayors Road	D1-E1
Mill Street	D3
Moss Lane	C2-D2-D1-E1-F1
Moss Lane	F3-F4
Navigation Road	D4
New Street	B1-C1-C2
Norman Place	B1-C1-C2
Norman Road	B4
North Vale Road	E4
Oakfield Road	D2-D3
Oakfield Street	D2
Oldfield Road	A3-B3-B4-C4
Old Market Place	C2-C3
Peter Street	C1
Place Road	B4
Pollen Road	B4
Poplar Avenue	D4
Post Office Street	C2
Prestbury Avenue	D4
Queens Road	E1
Regent Road	E1
Rutland Road	C4
St Leonards Drive	E4
St Margaret's Road	A1-A2
Sandiway Road	C4
Shaw's Road	C2
Stockport Road	D3-E3-F3
Stamford Park Road	D1-E1
Stamford New Road	C1-C2-D2-D3
Stamford Street	C2-D2-D3
Suffolk Road	A2
Sylvan Grove	C2-C3
The Downs	B1-C1
The Mount	C3
Thorsby Road	E3-E4
Townfield Road	C3
Urban Avenue	E1-E2
Urban Road	D1-D2-E2
Victoria Street	C3-D3
Wainwright Road	A3-B3
Weldon Road	B4-C4
Wellington Road	D4-E4-F4-F3
West Vale Road	E4-F4
Woodlands Parkway	E3-E4
Woodlands Road	C3-D3-E3
Woodville Road	B1

Urmston

Albany Court	A3
Ashfield Road	C1-C2
Atkinson Road	C1-C2
Avondale Crescent	A3
Balfour Road	A3
Balmain Road	A3
Barngate	A1
Bedford Road	A4
Beech Avenue	B1-B2
Broadoaks Road	A1
Canterbury Road	A3-A4-B4-C4
Carlton Road	B1
Cedar Drive	B1
Church Gate	C1
Church Road	A1-B1
Ciss Lane	C1-C2
Cob Kiln Lane	C1
Conway Road	C4
Cornhill Road	A3-A4
Crofts Bank Road	B2-B3-B4
Cross Street	A1-B1
Cumberland Road	A1-B1
Dalton Gardens	A3-A4
Dalveen Avenue	A4
Davyhulme Road	A4-B4
Derby Road	B3-C3
Dover Park	B4-C4
Entwistle Avenue	A3-A4
Exeter Road	B4-C4
Flixton Road	A2-B2
Furness Road	C3
Glenhaven Avenue	A2
Gloucester Road	C1-C2
Grange Road	B1
Grangethorpe Road	B1
Grosvenor Road	B2-B3
Greenfield Avenue	C2-C3
Hartford Road	C4
Hayeswater Road	A3-A4-B4
Higher Road	B2-C2
Kirkstall Road	C3
Leagate	C1
Leamington Road	A4
Ledbury Avenue	B3-B4
Lichfield Road	C4
Lime Avenue	A1-A2
Longfield Avenue	A1
Lonsdale Avenue	A4
Lostock Road	B4-C4
Lyndhurst Avenue	A4
Manor Avenue	B1-C1
Mayfair Avenue	A2
Meadow Gate	C1
Mirfield Drive	B4
Moorside Road	A3-B3
Newstead Road	C3
Newton Road	A2
Oak Grove	C2
Old Crofts Bank	B3-B4
Park Road	B2
Patterdale Avenue	A4
Princess Road	A2-A3
Queen's Road	B1
Railway Road	B2-C2
Rochester Road	C4
Roseneath Road	B2-B3
Royal Avenue	B2
Royston Road	C3
Salisbury Road	B4-C4
Sandgate Drive	B4
Sandsend Road	A3-B3
Sevenoaks Avenue	B4
Spennithorne Road	A2
Station Road	B1-B2
Stretford Road	B1-C1
Sunningdale Road	A1
Tewkesbury Avenue	C4
Victoria Road	A2-A3
Wendover Road	B1-B2
Westbourne Park	C2-C3
Westbourne Road	C2-C3
Westgate	A1
Westminster Road	C4
Westmorland Road	A1-B1-C1
Westover Road	B3-B4
Winchester Road	B3-C3

Stretford

Alpha Road	B2
Ash Grove	A1
Barton Road	A4-A3-B3-B2-B1
Bradfield Road	A3
Bramley Avenue	A2-A3
Brunswick Street	B1
Chapel Lane	B1
Cherry Tree Walk	A1-B1
Chester Road	B1-B2-C2-C3-C4
Church Street	B1-B2
Coniston Road	B4
Cooper Street	C1-C2
Cross Street	C2-C3
Cyprus Street	C2-C3
Davyhulme Road	A4-B4
Davyhulme Road East	B4-C4-B2
Derbyshire Lane	B3-C3
Derbyshire Lane West	A4-A3-B3
Edge Lane	C2
Elm Drive	A1-A2
Granby Road	C2
Grange Avenue	B3-C3
Grasmere Road	B4-C4
Haig Road	C4
Hampson Road	A3-A2-B2
Hancock Street	B1-C2
Highfield Road	B1
Jackson Street	B2-C2
King's Road	C2
Kingsway	B2-C2
Lacy Street	B1-C1-C2
Larch Avenue	C1-C2
Lester Street	B3-C3
Leyburn Avenue	A4
Lime Road	C1-C2
Lyndhurst Road	A4
Manor Road	A2-A3
Marlborough Road	B4
Melfort Avenue	C1-C2
Melville Road	A4
Milwain Road	A2-B2
Moreton Avenue	C3
Moss Road	B3-B4
Moss Park Road	A3
Newton Street	C2
Park Road	A4-B4-B2
Ponsonby Road	B4-C4
Poplar Road	A1-B1
Pritchard Street	B3-C3
Rador Street	C2
Radstock Road	B3-B4
Raglan Road	A4
Ryecroft Road	A2-B2
St Andrew's Road	A3
St Georges Road	A2-A3
Sandy Lane	A2-B2-B1
School Road	B3-B2-C2
Skelton Road	B4
Stothard Road	A2-B2
Stuart Road	C4
Sydney Street	C3
Thirlmere Avenue	B4
Urmston Lane	A2-B2
Vernon Avenue	C1-C2
Victoria Road	B2-B3
Walnut Walk	A1
Wellington Street	B2
Westwood Road	A3

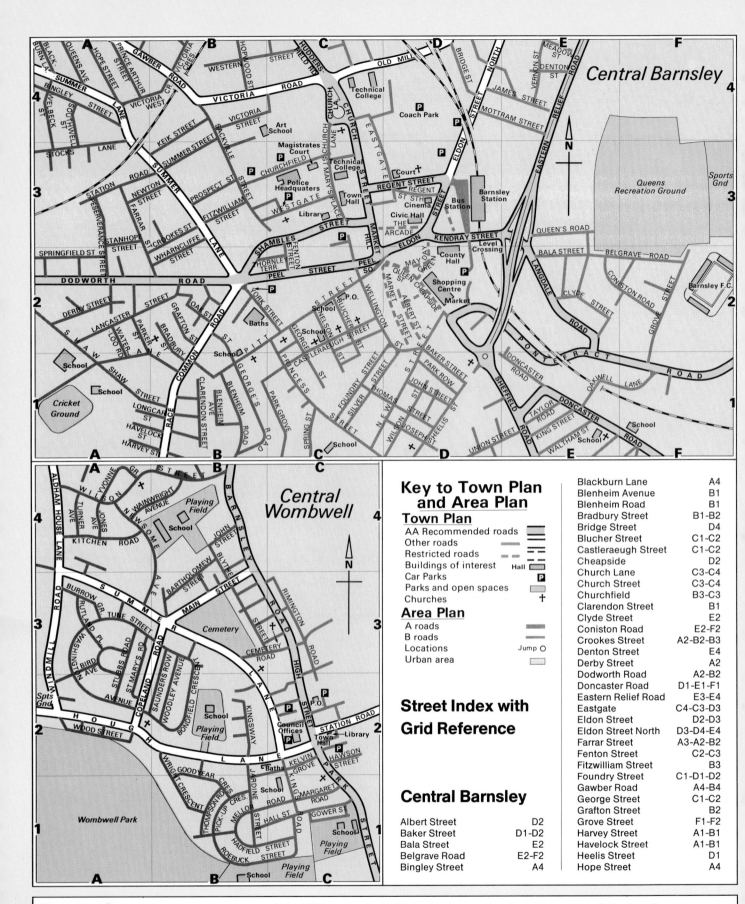

Key to Town Plan and Area Plan

Town Plan
AA Recommended roads	
Other roads	
Restricted roads	
Buildings of interest	Hall
Car Parks	P
Parks and open spaces	
Churches	†

Area Plan
A roads	
B roads	
Locations	Jump O
Urban area	

Street Index with Grid Reference

Central Barnsley

Albert Street	D2
Baker Street	D1-D2
Bala Street	E2
Belgrave Road	E2-F2
Bingley Street	A4

Blackburn Lane	A4
Blenheim Avenue	B1
Blenheim Road	B1
Bradbury Street	B1-B2
Bridge Street	D4
Blucher Street	C1-C2
Castleraeugh Street	C1-C2
Cheapside	D2
Church Lane	C3-C4
Church Street	C3-C4
Churchfield	B3-C3
Clarendon Street	B1
Clyde Street	E2
Coniston Road	E2-F2
Crookes Street	A2-B2-B3
Denton Street	E4
Derby Street	A2
Dodworth Road	A2-B2
Doncaster Road	D1-E1-F1
Eastern Relief Road	E3-E4
Eastgate	C4-C3-D3
Eldon Street	D2-D3
Eldon Street North	D3-D4-E4
Farrar Street	A3-A2-B2
Fenton Street	C2-C3
Fitzwilliam Street	B3
Foundry Street	C1-D1-D2
Gawber Road	A4-B4
George Street	C1-C2
Grafton Street	B2
Grove Street	F1-F2
Harvey Street	A1-B1
Havelock Street	A1-B1
Heelis Street	D1
Hope Street	A4

Barnsley

Amongst the claims to fame of Barnsley must be numbered the local football club — at present in the Second Division of the Canon League. Started in 1887, it achieved fame in the early part of the present century by reaching the FA Cup Final twice, and by winning the trophy in 1911/1912. Barnsley lies in the midst of a coalmining district, and the Yorkshire area of the National Union of Mineworkers has its headquarters in a Victorian building which is one of the many impressive features of the town. Other landmarks are the modern development of the Metropolitan Centre with its new market hall, and the tower which stands in Locke Park (on the south-eastern edge of town) which has a public viewing gallery. Leisure is catered for in the town's four sports centres, and in Worsbrough Country Park. This lies to the south and has a reservoir — popular with both fishermen and wildlife. A working 17th-century watermill which is now a museum can also be seen here, and just north of the town centre are the remains of Monk Bretton Priory, founded in the 12th century.

Wombwell is an area of new industries, which have arrived to replace its declining local collieries. A popular place to live, it has good shops and extensive open spaces in Wombwell Park, to the south-west of the town centre.

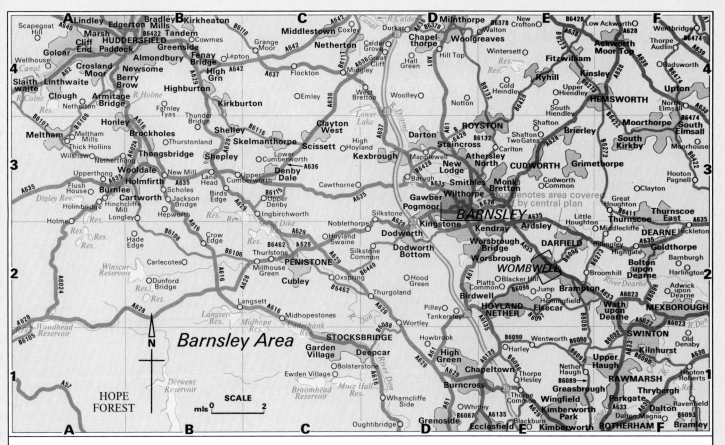

Barnsley Area

N

HOPE FOREST

SCALE
mls 0 — 2

Hopwood Street	B4	Queens Avenue	A4	Westgate	B3-C3	Margaret Road	C1
Huddersfield Road	C4	Race Common Road	B1-B2	Wharncliffe Street	B2-B3	Mellor Road	B1-C1
James Street	D4-E4	Regent Street	C3-D3	Wilson Street	D1	Newsome Avenue	A3-A4-B4-B3
John Street	D1	Regent Street South	D3	York Street	B2-C2	Park Street	C1-C2
Joseph Street	D1	St George's Road	B1-B2			Pick-Up Crescent	B1
Keik Street	B3-B4	St Mary's Place	C3			Rimington Road	C2-C3
Kendray Street	D3-E3	Sackville Street	B4-B3-C3			Roebuck Street	B1-C1
King Street	E1	Shambles Street	B2-B3-C3	**Central Wombwell**		Rutland Place	A3
Lancaster Street	A2-B2	Shaw Lane	A2-A1-B1			St Mary's Road	A2-A3
Langdale Road	E2	Shaw Street	A1-B1	Aldham House Lane	A4	Saunders Row	A2-B2-B3
Longcar Street	A1-B1	Sheffield Road	D1-E1	Bartholomew Street	B3-B4	Station Road	C2
Market Hill	C2-C3	Silver Street	C1-D1-D2	Barnsley Road	B4-B3-C3	Stubbs Road	A2-A3
Market Street	C2-D2	Southwell Street	A3-A4	Bird Avenue	A3	Summer Lane	A4-A3-B3-B2-C2
May Day Green	D2-D3	Spring Street	C1	Blythe Street	B3-B4	Thompson Road	B1
Meadow Street	E4	Springfield Street	A2	Bondfield Crescent	B2-B3	Tune Street	A3-B3
Mottram Street	D4-E4	Stanhope Street	A3	Burrow Grove	A3	Turner Avenue	A4
Nelson Street	C1-C2	Station Road	A3-B3	Cemetery Road	B3-C3	Wainwright Avenue	A4-B4
New Street	C1-D1-D2	Stocks Lane	A3-A4	Copeland Road	A2-A3-B3-B2	Washington Avenue	A2-A3
Newton Street	A3-B3	Summer Lane	A4-A3-B3-B2	Goodyear Crescent	B1-B2	Wilson Street	A4-B4
Oak Street	B2	Summer Street	B3-B4	Gower Street	C1	Windmill Road	A2-A3
Oakwell Lane	E1-F1	The Arcade	C3-D3	Hadfield Street	B1-C1	Wood Street	A2
Old Mill	C4-D4	Taylor Road	E1	Hall Street	B1-C1	Woodley Avenue	B2-B3
Park Grove	B1-C1	Thomas Street	C1-D1	Hawson Street	C2	Wright Crescent	B1-B2
Park Row	D1	Thornley Terrace	B2-C2	High Street	C2-C3	Yvonne Grove	A4
Parker Street	A2	Union Street	D1-E1	Hough Lane	A2-B2-C2		
Peel Square	C2	Vernon Street	E4	Jardine Street	B1-B2		
Peel Street	B2-C2	Victoria Crescent	B4	John Street	B4		
Pitt Street	B1-B2-C2	Victoria Crescent West	A4-B4	Jones Avenue	A4		
Pontefract Road	E2-E1-F1	Victoria Road	B4-C4	Kelvin Grove	C2		
Perserverance Street	A2-A3	Victoria Street	B4-C4	Kings Road	C1-C2		
Prince Arthur Street	A4	Walterloo Road	A1-A2	Kingsway	B2		
Princess Street	C1-C2	Waltham Street	E1	Kitchen Road	A4		
Prospect Street	B3	Welbeck Street	A3-A4	Main Street	B3-B4		
Queen Street	D2	Wellington Street	C2-D2				
Queen's Road	E3	Western Street	B4-C4				

BARNSLEY
Opened by HRH the Prince of Wales on 14 December 1933 and built at a cost of £188,000, the magnificent four-storey Town Hall has a 145ft tower of Portland stone, and is one of the town's most impressive sights.

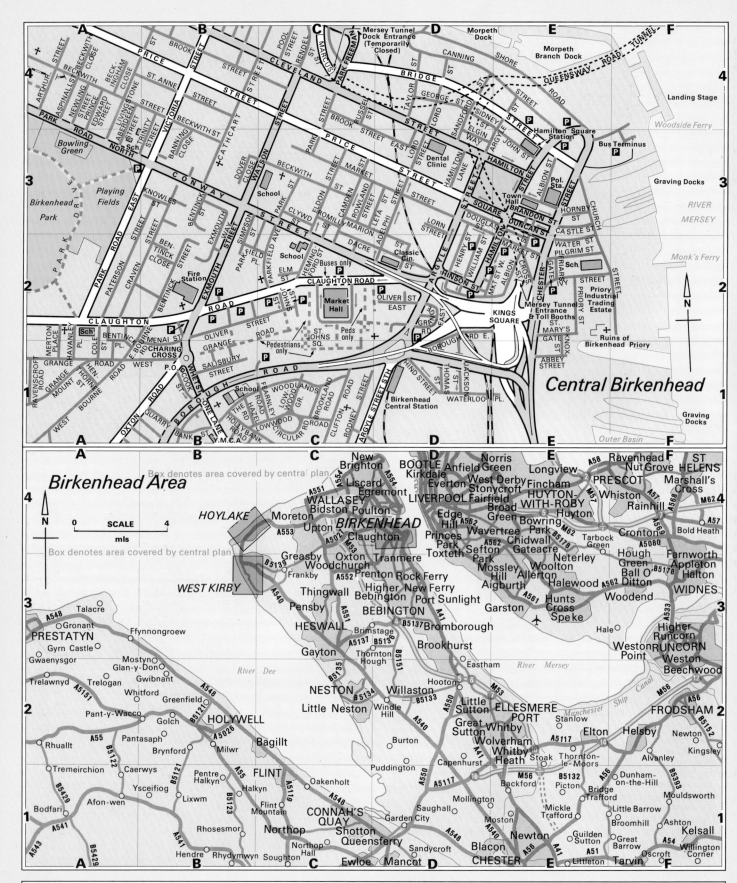

Birkenhead

You can take the famous 'ferry across the Mersey' to reach this largest town on the Wirral Peninsula, but it also connected to Liverpool by bridges and the Mersey Tunnel. The town grew up around the Merseyside docks to become an important ship-building centre, and a number of engineering firms are still located here. Amongst Birkenhead's places of history are the remains of

a 12th-century Benedictine Priory at Monks Ferry, and the Williamson Art Gallery and Museum, which stages regular art exhibitions and also houses the Wirral Maritime Museum.

West Kirby is a place for walking and water. Lying on the estuary of the River Dee, it is well known for its Marine Lake, where boating and sailing can be enjoyed, while just offshore is the wildlife of the Hilbre Islands (accessible only to permit holders). Several pleasant parks can be

found in the town, and to the south, the Wirral Way Country Park incorporates the 12 miles of the Wirral Way footpath.

Hoylake's Windswept and world famous, the Royal Liverpool Golf Course stretches its length along the coast between Hoylake and West Kirby. Numerous parks and gardens are another attraction of this former fishing village, which lies at the north-west corner of the Wirral Peninsula and enjoys an extensive seafront.

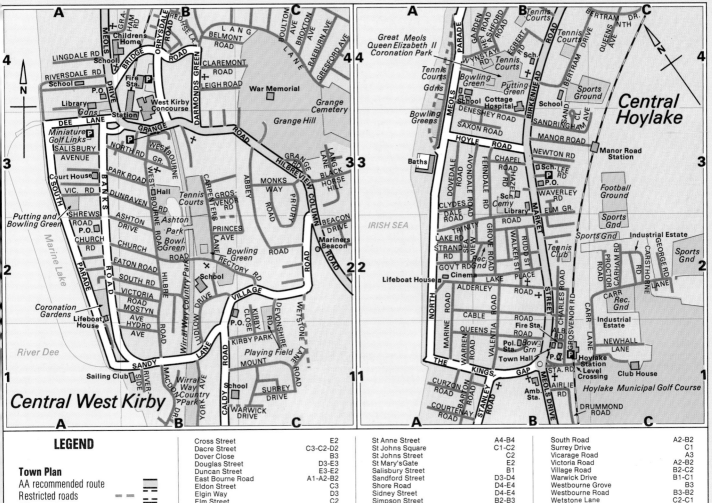

Central West Kirby

Central Hoylake

LEGEND

Town Plan
- AA recommended route
- Restricted roads
- Other roads
- Buildings of interest — Theatre ▪
- Car parks — P
- Parks and open spaces
- One way streets

Area Plan
- A roads
- B roads
- Locations — Littleney ○
- Urban area

Street Index with Grid Reference

Birkenhead

Abbey Street	E1
Aberdeen Street	A3-A4
Adelphi Street	D2-D3
Albion Street	E2-E3
Argyle Street	D2-D3-E3-E4
Argyle Street South	C1-D1
Arthur Street	A4
Aspinall Street	A4
Banning Close	A4
Beckingham Close	B3
Beckwith Close	A4
Beckwith Street	A4-B4-B3, C3
Bentinck Close	B2
Bentinck Place	A1-A2
Bentinck Street	B2-B3
Borough Road	B1-C1-D1
Borough Road East	D1-D2
Brandon Street	E3
Bridge Street	C4-D4-E4-E3
Brook Street	B4-C4
Brook Street East	C4-C3-D3
Brookland Road	C1
Camden Street	C3
Canning Street	D4-E4
Castle Street	E3
Cathcart Street	B3-B4
Charing Cross	B1
Chester Street	E2-E3-E4
Church Street	E3-E2-F2
Circular Road	B1
Claughton Road	A2-B2-C2-D2
Cleveland Street	B4-C4-D4-D3
Clifton Road	C1
Clwyd Street	C3
Cook Street	B1
Cole Street	A1-A2
Conway Street	B3-C3-C2
Craven Street	A2-B2-B3

Cross Street	E2
Dacre Street	C3-C2-D2
Dover Close	B3
Douglas Street	D3-E3
Duncan Street	E3-E2
East Bourne Road	A1-A2-B2
Eldon Street	C3
Elgin Way	D3
Elm Street	C2
Exmouth Street	B2-B3
Exmouth Way	B2-B3
Fearnley Road	C1
Friars Gate	E2
George Street	D4
Grange Mount	A1
Grange Road	B1-B2-C2
Grange Road East	D2
Grange Road West	A1-B1
Hamilton Lane	D3
Hamilton Square	D3-E3
Hamilton Street	D2-E2-E3
Havanley Place	A1-A2
Hazel Road	B1
Hemingford Street	C2
Henry Street	D2-D3
Henthorne Street	A1
Hind Street	D1
Hinson Street	D2
Hollybank Road	B1-C1
Hornby Street	E3
Ivy Street	E2
Jackson Street	D1
John Street	E3
Knowles Street	B3
Knox Street	E1-E2
Leta Street	C3-D3
Livingstone Street	A3-A4-B4
Lord Street	D3-D4
Lorn Street	D3
Lowwood Green	C1
Lowwood Road	B1-C1
Marcus Street	C4
Marion Street	C3-D3-D2
Market Street	C3-D3-E3-E2
Market Street West	D2-E2
Menai Street	B1
Merton Place	A1-A2
Newling Street	A4
Oliver Street	B2-C2
Oliver Street East	D2
Oxton Road	A1-B1
Park Freeman	C4
Park Road East	A2-A3-B3
Park Road North	A4-A3-B3
Park Street	C3-C4
Parkfield Avenue	C2-C3
Parkfield Place	B2-C2
Paterson Street	A2-A3-B3
Pilgrim Street	E2
Pool Street	C4
Price Street	A4-B4-C4-C3-D3
Priory Street	E2
Prince Edward Street	A4
Quarry Bank Street	B1
Queensway Road Tunnel	C4-D4-E4-F4, E2-E3, D3-D4
Ravenscroft Road	A1
Rendel Street	C4
Rodney Street	C1
Romilly Street	C3
Rowland Street	C3
Russel Street	C4

St Anne Street	A4-B4
St Johns Square	C1-C2
St Johns Street	C2
St Mary'sGate	E2
Salisbury Street	B1
Sandford Street	D3-D4
Shore Road	D4-E4
Sidney Street	D4-E4
Simpson Street	B2-B3
Taylor Street	D4
The Woodlands	B1-C1
Thomas Street	D1
Trinity Street	A3-B3-B4
Victoria Street	B3-B4
Waterloo Place	D1-E1
Water Street	E2
Watson Street	B3-C3-C4
West Bourne Road	A1
Whetstone Lane	B1
William Street	D2

West Kirby

Abbey Road	C3-C2
Ashton Drive	A3-A2-B2
Banks Road	A3-A2-A1-B1
Beacon Drive	C2
Belmont Road	B4-C4
Black Horse Hill	C3
Boulton Avenue	C4
Bridge Road	A4-B4
Broxton Avenue	C4
Caldy Road	B1
Carpenters Lane	B3-B2
Church Road	A2-B2
Claremont Road	B4-C4
Darmonds Green	B3-B4
Dee Lane	A3
Devonshire Road	C1-C2
Dunraven Road	A3-B3
Eaton Road	A2-B2
Graham Road	A4-B4
Grange Road	B3-C3
Gresford Avenue	C4
Grosvenor Road	B3
Hilbre Road	B2-B1
Hilbreview Column Road	C3-C2
Hydro Avenue	B1
Kirby Close	C1-C2
Kirby Park	B1-C1
Lang Lane	B4-C4-C3
Leigh Road	B4-C4
Lingdale Road	A4
Ludlow Drive	B1-B2
Macdona Drive	B1
Meols Drive	A4
Monks Way	C3
Mostyn Avenue	B2
Mount Road	B1-C1
North Road	A3-B3
Orrysdale Road	B4
Park Road	A3-B3
Princes Avenue	B2-C2
Priory Road	C2-C3
Raeburn Avenue	C4
Rectory Road	B2-C2
Red House Lane	C1
Riversdale Road	A4
Riverside	B1
Salisbury Avenue	A3
Sandy Lane	A1-B1
Shrewsbury Road	A2-A3
South Parade	A1-A2-A3

South Road	A2-B2
Surrey Drive	C1
Vicarage Road	A3
Victoria Road	A2-B2
Village Road	B2-C2
Warwick Drive	B1-C1
Westbourne Grove	B3
Westbourne Road	B3-B2
Wetstone Lane	C2-C1
York Avenue	B1

Hoylake

Airlie Road	B1
Albion Road	B1
Alderley Road	A2-B2
Ashford Road	B4
Avondale Road	B3-B2
Barton Road	A1
Bertram Drive	B4-C4
Bertram Drive North	C4
Birkenhead Road	B3-B4
Cable Road	A2-B2
Carham Road	C2
Carr Lane	C2-C1
Carsthorne Road	C2
Chapel Road	B3
Charles Road	B1-B2
Clydesdale Road	A3
Courtenay Road	A1
Curzon Road	A1
Deneshey Road	A4-B4-B3
Dovedale Road	A3
Drummond Road	B1
Egbert Road	B4
Elm Grove	B3
Ferndale Road	B3
Garden Hey Road	B4
George Road	C2
Government Road	A2
Grove Road	B2
Grosvenor Road	B1-B2
Hazel Road	B3
Hoyle Road	A3-B3
Lake Place	B2
Lake Road	A2
Lee Road	B3
Manor Road	B3
Marine Road	A1-A2
Market Street	B1-B2-B3
Meols Drive	A3-A4
Newton Road	B2
North Parade	A1-A2-A3
Proctor Road	C2
Queens Avenue	C4
Queens Road	A1-B1
Rudd Street	B2
Sandringham Avenue	B3-B3
Sandringham Close	B3
Saxon Road	A3-B3
Sea View	A2
Stanley Road	B1
Station Road	B1
Strand Road	A2
The Kings Gap	A1-B1
Trinity Road	A2-B2-B3
Valentia Road	B1-B2
Walker Street	B2
Warren Road	A1
Waverley Road	B3
Wynstay Road	A4-B4

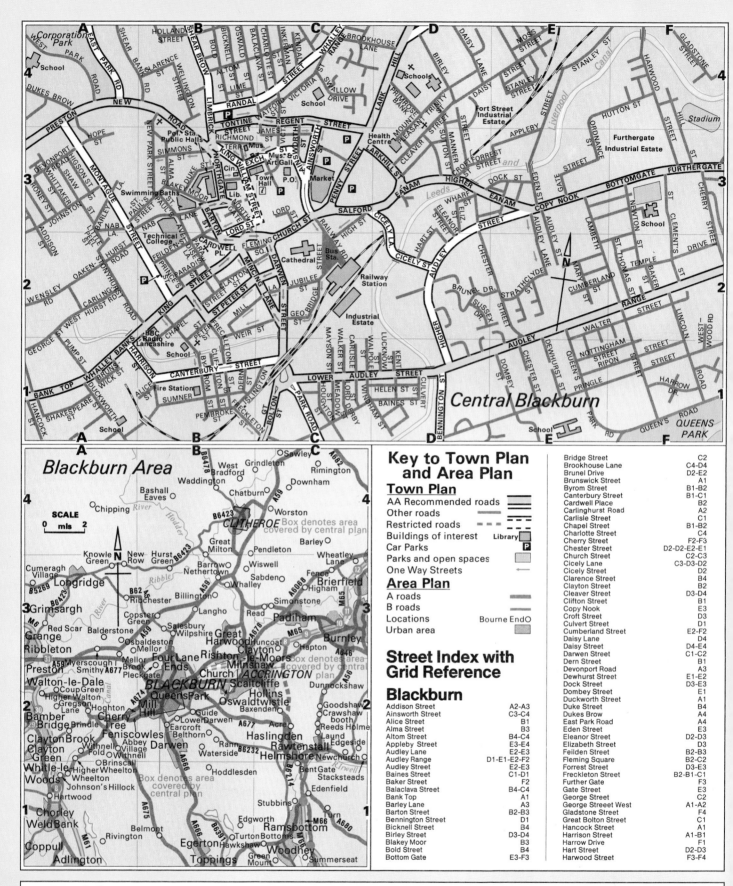

Key to Town Plan and Area Plan

Town Plan

AA Recommended roads	
Other roads	
Restricted roads	
Buildings of interest	Library
Car Parks	P
Parks and open spaces	
One Way Streets	←

Area Plan

A roads	
B roads	
Locations	Bourne End O
Urban area	

Street Index with Grid Reference

Blackburn

Addison Street	A2-A3
Ainsworth Street	C3-C4
Alice Street	B1
Alma Street	B3
Altom Street	B4-C4
Appleby Street	E3-E4
Audley Lane	E2-E3
Audley Range	D1-E1-E2-F2
Audley Street	E2-E3
Baines Street	C1-D1
Baker Street	F2
Balaclava Street	B4-C4
Bank Top	A1
Barley Lane	A3
Barton Street	B2-B3
Bennington Street	D1
Bicknell Street	B4
Birley Street	D3-D4
Blakey Moor	B3
Bold Street	B4
Bottom Gate	E3-F3

Bridge Street	C2
Brookhouse Lane	C4-D4
Brunel Drive	D2-E2
Brunswick Street	A1
Byrom Street	B1-B2
Canterbury Street	B1-C1
Cardwell Place	B2
Carlinghurst Road	A2
Carlisle Street	C1
Chapel Street	B1-B2
Charlotte Street	C4
Cherry Street	F2-F3
Chester Street	D2-D2-E2-E1
Church Street	C2-C3
Cicely Lane	C3-D3-D2
Cicely Street	D2
Clarence Street	B4
Clayton Street	B2
Cleaver Street	D3-D4
Clifton Street	B1
Copy Nook	E3
Croft Street	D3
Culvert Street	D1
Cumberland Street	E2-F2
Daisy Lane	D4
Daisy Street	D4-E4
Darwen Street	C1-C2
Dern Street	B1
Devonport Road	A3
Dewhurst Street	E1-E2
Dock Street	D3-E3
Dombey Street	E1
Duckworth Street	A1
Duke Street	B4
Dukes Brow	A4
East Park Road	A4
Eden Street	E3
Eleanor Street	D2-D3
Elizabeth Street	D3
Feilden Street	B2-B3
Fleming Square	B2-C2
Forrest Street	D3-E3
Freckleton Street	B2-B1-C1
Further Gate	F3
Gate Street	E3
George Street	C2
George Streeet West	A1-A2
Gladstone Street	F4
Great Bolton Street	C1
Hancock Street	A1
Harrison Street	A1-B1
Harrow Drive	F1
Hart Street	D2-D3
Harwood Street	F3-F4

Blackburn

The glittering heights of championship rollerskating at the Starskate roller rink are a far cry from Blackburn's 'workshop of England' image — an image it is doing its best to change. Once the weaving centre of the world but no longer even predominantly a textile town, it has seen the redevelopment of its old industrial areas while the entire town centre is being converted into a

traffic-free shopping precinct. But memories of an older Blackburn can still be seen outside the centre, and some of the stone-built terraces have been declared conservation areas. Blackburn Cathedral is an interesting mixture of old and new: it was built up around the 19th-century church which is now its nave.

Clitheroe is overlooked by a record-breaking castle keep — not only is it the smallest keep in England but it is also one of Lancashire's oldest

stone structures. Little else remains of the castle, which dates back to the 12th century and was a Royalist stronghold in the Civil War. This is a very old industrial town, but one with a pleasantly rural atmosphere. St Mary Magdalene's Church is noted for its twisted spire.

Accrington's fame was built on cotton and bricks: noted for their hardness, the smooth red bricks produced in the town spread its name throughout Victorian Britain.

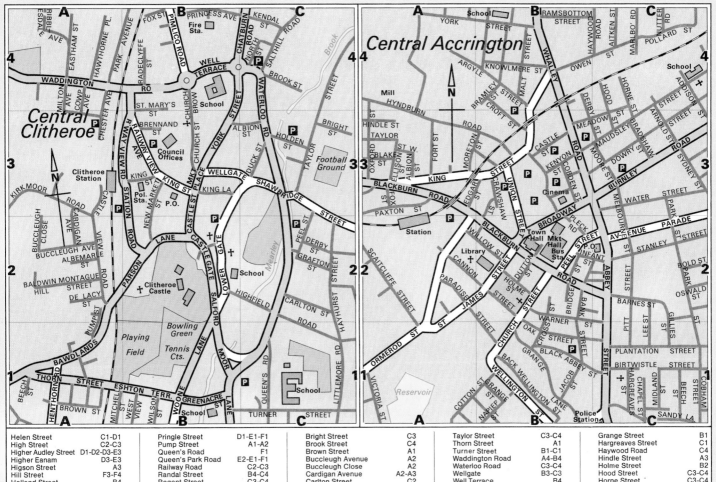

Helen Street	C1-D1	Pringle Street	D1-E1-F1
High Street	C2-C3	Pump Street	A1-A2
Higher Audley Street	D1-D2-D3-E3	Queen's Road	F1
Higher Eanam	D3-E3	Queen's Park Road	E2-E1-F1
Higson Street	A3	Railway Road	C2-C3
Hill Street	F3-F4	Randal Street	B4-C4
Holland Street	B4	Regent Street	C3-C4
Hope Street	A3	Richmond Terrace	B3-C3
Houghton Street	C1	Ripon Street	E1-F1
Hutton Street	E4-F4	Roney Street	A3
Inkerman Street	C4	St Clement's Street	F2-F3
Islington	B1-C1	St Paul's Avenue	B2-B3
James Street	C3	St Paul's Street	B1-B3
Johnston Street	A3	St Peter Street	B1-B2
Jubilee Street	C2	St Thomas Street	F2
Kendal Street	C4	Salford Eanam	C3-D3
Kent Street	D1	Shakespeare Street	A1
King Street	B2	Shaw Street	A3
King William Street	B3-C3	Shear Bank Road	A4-B4
Lambeth Street	E3-E2-F2-F1	Shear Brow	B4
Lark Hill	C4-D4	Simmon Street	B3
Larkhill Street	C3-D3	Stanley Street	E4-F4
Limbrick	B3-B4	Stonyhurst Road	A2-B2
Lime Street	B4	Strathclyde Street	E2
Lincoln Road	F1-F2	Sumner Street	B1
Little Peel Street	A2-A3	Sussex Drive	D2-E2
Lord Street	B2-B3, C1	Swallow Drive	C4
Lord Derby Street	C1	Temple Drive	F2
Lower Audley Street	C1-D1	Tontine Street	B3-B4
Lucknow Street	D1	Trinity Street	D4
Manner Sutton Street	D3-D4	Victoria Street	C3-C4
Mary Street	E2	Walker Street	C1
Mayson Street	C1	Walpole Street	C1
Meadow Street	C1	Walter Street	E2-F2
Mill Lane	B2-C2	Watford Street	C4
Mincing Lane	B2-C2	Weir Street	B2-C2
Montague Street	A4-A3-A2-B2	Wellington Street	B4
Mount Pleasant	D3-D4	Wensley Road	A2
Moss Street	E4	West Park Road	A4
Nab Lane	A3-B3	Westwood Road	F1-F2
Newton Street	F2-F3	Whalley Banks	A1-A2-B2
New Park Street	B3-B4	Whalley Range	A3
Northgate	B3	Wharf Street	D3
Nottingham Street	E1-F1-F2	Whittaker Street	A3
Oakenhurst Road	A2	Windham Street	C1-D1
Ordnance Street	E3-E4		
Oswald Street	B4		
Paradise Lane	B2		
Paradise Street	B2		
Pembroke Street	B1		
Penny Street	C3	**Clitheroe**	
Park Road	C1	Albemarle Street	A2
Preston New Road	A3-A4-B4-B3	Albion Street	B3-C3
Primrose Bank	D4	Baldwin Hill	A2
Prince's Street	B2	Bawdlands	A1-A2
		Beech Street	A1
		Brennand Street	B3

Bright Street	C3	Taylor Street	C3-C4
Brook Street	C4	Thorn Street	A1
Brown Street	A1	Turner Street	B1-C1
Buccleugh Avenue	A2	Waddington Road	A4-B4
Buccleugh Close	A2	Waterloo Road	C3-C4
Cardigan Avenue	A2-A3	Wellgate	B3-C3
Carlton Street	C2	Well Terrace	B4
Castle Gate	B2	West View	B1
Castle Street	B2-B3	Wilson Street	B1
Castle View Road	A2-A3	Woone Lane	B1
Chatburn Road	B4-C4	York Road	B3-B4-C4
Chester Avenue	A3-A4		
Church Brow	B3-B4		
Church Street	B3	**Accrington**	
Cowper Avenue	A3-A4	Abbey Street	C1-C2-C3
De Lacy Street	A2	Addison Street	C3-C4
Derby Street	C2	Aitken Street	C4
Duck Street	C3	Albion Street	A3
Eastham Street	A4	Argyle Street	A4-B4
Eshton Terrace	A1-B1	Arnold Street	C3-C4
Fox Street	C2	Avenue Parade	C2-C3
Grafton Street	C2	Back Wellington Street	B1
Greenacre Street	B1	Bank Street	B1-B2
Hawthorne Place	A4	Barnes Street	C2
Hayhurst Street	C1-C2	Beech Street	C1
Henthorn Road	A1	Birtwistle Street	C1
Highfield Road	B2-C2-C1	Black Abbey Street	B1-C1
Kendal Street	C4	Blackburn Road	A3-A2-B2-C2
King Lane	B3	Blake Street	A3
King Street	B3	Bradshaw Street	C3
Kirkmoor Road	A3	Bramley Street	B4
Littlemore Road	C1	Bridge Street	B2
Lower Gate	B2-B3	Broadway	B2-B3
Market Place	B3	Bold Street	C2
Milton Avenue	A3-A4	Burnley Road	C3
Mitchell Street	A1	Cannon Street	A2-B2
Montague Street	A2	Castle Street	B3
New Market Street	B2-B3	Chapel Street	C1
North Street	C4	Church Street	B1-B2
Peel Street	C2-C3	Cobden Street	B3
Park Avenue	A4-B4	Cobham Street	C1
Parson Lane	A2-B2	Cotton Street	A1-B1
Pimlico Road	B4	Crawshaw Street	B2-B3
Princess Avenue	B4-C4	Croft Street	B3-B4
Pump Street	A1-A2	Cross Street	B1-B2
Queen's Road	. C1	Derby Street	B4-B3-C3
Radcliffe Street	B4	Dowry Street	B3-C3-C4
Railway View Avenue	B3	Dutton Street	B2
Railway View Road	A3-B3	Edgar Street	A3-B3
Ribblesdale Avenue	A4	Ellison Street	A2-A3
St Mary's Street	B3-B4	Fort Street	A3
Salford Moor Lane	B1-B2	Fox Street	A3
Salthill Road	C4	Gillies Street	C1-C2
Shawbridge Street	C2-C3	Grange Lane	B1
Station Road	B2-B3		

Grange Street	B1
Hargreaves Street	C1
Haywood Road	C4
Hindle Street	A3
Holme Street	C3-C4
Hood Street	C3-C4
Horne Street	C3-C4
Hyndburn Road	A4-A3-B3
Infant Street	B2-C2
Jacob Street	B1
Kenyon Street	B3
King Street	A3-B3
Knowlmere Street	B4
Lee Street	C1-C2
Malt Street	B4
Marlborough Road	C4
Maudsley Street	B3-C3-C4
Meadow Street	B3-C3-C4
Melbourne Street	C2-C3
Midland Street	C1
Moore Street	C3
Napier Street	B1
Nutter Road	C4
Oak Street	B2-B1-C1
Ormerod Street	A1
Oswald Street	C2
Owen Street	B4-C4
Oxford Street	A3-A4
Paradise Street	A2-B2-B1
Park Street	C1-C2-C3
Paxton Street	A3
Peel Street	B2-C2
Pitt Street	C1-C2
Plantation Street	C1
Pleck Road	B2
Pollard Street	C4
St James Street	A1-A2-B2
Sandy Lane	C1
Scaitcliffe Street	A1-A2
Stanley Street	C2
Sydney Street	C3
Taylor Street West	A3
Union Street	B2-B3
Victoria Street	A1
Warner Street	B2-C2-C1
Water Street	C3
Wellington Street	B1
Whalley Road	B4-B3-C3
Willow Street	A2-B2
York Street	A4-B4

BLACKBURN
A central sanctuary and altar allow everyone to see the service at the Cathedral, which has a Gothic revival church of Longridge stone for its nave. A church has stood on this site since at least the 10th century.

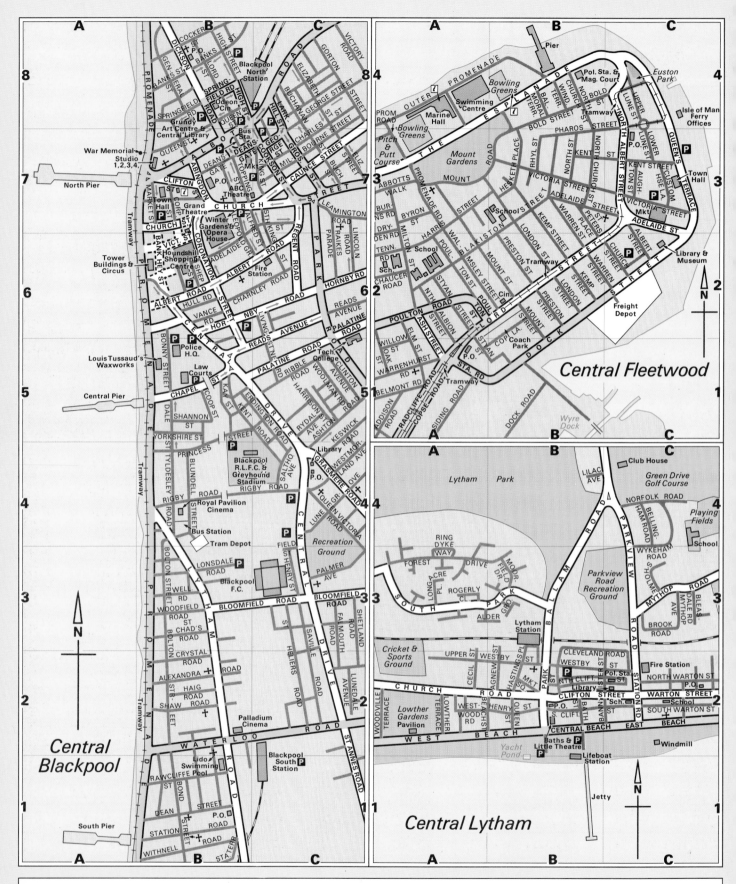

Blackpool

No seaside resort is regarded with greater affection than Blackpool. It is still the place where millions of North Country folk spend their holidays; its famous illuminations draw visitors from all over the world. It provides every conceivable kind of traditional holiday entertainment, and in greater abundance than any other seaside resort in Britain. The famous tower – built in the 1890s as a replica of the Eiffel Tower – the three piers, seven miles of promenade, five miles of illuminations, countless guesthouses, huge numbers of pubs, shops, restaurants and cafes play host to eight million visitors a year.

At the base of the tower is a huge entertainment complex that includes a ballroom, a circus and an aquarium. Other 19th-century landmarks are North Pier and Central Pier, the great Winter Gardens and Opera House and the famous trams that still run along the promenade – the only electric trams still operating in Britain. The most glittering part of modern Blackpool is the famous Golden Mile, packed with amusements, novelty shops and snack stalls. Every autumn it becomes part of the country's most extravagant light show – the illuminations – when the promenade is ablaze with neon representations of anything and everything from moon rockets to the Muppets. Autumn is also the time when Blackpool is a traditional venue for political party conferences.

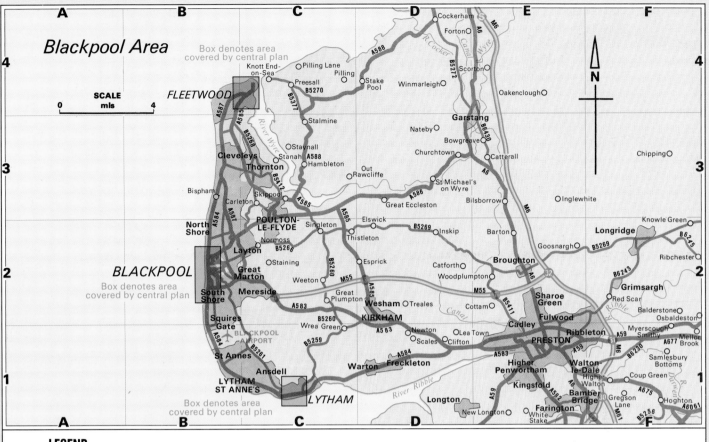

Blackpool Area

SCALE
mls
0 — 4

Box denotes area covered by central plan

FLEETWOOD

BLACKPOOL

LYTHAM ST ANNE'S

Box denotes area covered by central plan

Box denotes area covered by central plan

LYTHAM

LEGEND

Town Plan

AA recommended route	
Restricted roads	
Other roads	
Buildings of interest	School
Car parks	P
Parks and open spaces	
One way streets	

Area Plan

A roads	
B roads	
Locations	Wrea Green O
Urban area	

Street Index with Grid Reference

Blackpool

Abingdon Street	B7
Adelaide Street	B6-B7-C7
Albert Road	B6-C6
Alexandra Road	B2
Alfred Street	B7-C7-C6
Ashton Road	C4-C5
Bank Hey Street	B6-B7
Banks Street	B8
Bloomfield Road	B3-C3
Blundell Street	B4
Bolton Street	B2-B3-B4
Bond Street	B1-B2
Bonny Street	B5-B6
Buchanan Street	C7-C8
Caunce Street	C7-C8
Central Drive	B6-B5-C5-C4-C3-C2
Chapel Street	B5
Charles Street	C7-C8
Charnley Road	B6-C6
Church Street	B7-C7
Clifton Street	B7
Clinton Avenue	C5
Cocker Street	B8
Cookson Street	B8-B7-C7
Coop Street	B5
Coronation Street	B5-B6-B7
Corporation Street	B7
Crystal Road	B2
Dale Street	B4-B5
Deansgate	B7-C7
Dean Street	B1
Dickson Road	B7-B8
Erdington Road	B5-C5-C4
Elizabeth Street	C7-C8
Falmouth Road	C2-C3
Field Street	C3
General Street	B8
George Street	C7-C8
Gorton Street	C8
Grasmere Road	C4
Grosvenor Street	C7
Haig Road	B2
Harrison Street	C5
Henry Street	C3
High Street	B8
Hornby Road	B6-C6
Hull Road	B6
Kay Street	B5
Kent Road	B5-C5-C4
Keswick Road	C4-C5
King Street	C7
Larkhill Street	C8
Leamington Road	C7
Leopold Grove	B7-B6-C6
Lincoln Road	C6-C7
Livingstone Road	C5-C6
Lonsdale Road	B3
Lord Street	B8
Lunedale Avenue	C2
Lune Grove	C4
Lytham Road	B1-B2-B3-B4
Market Street	B7
Milbourne Street	C7-C8
Osborne Road	B1
Palatine Road	B5-C5-C6
Palmer Avenue	C3
Park Road	C5-C6-C7
Princess Parade	A7-A8-B8-B7
Princess Street	B4-B5-C5
Promenade	B1-B2-B3-B4-B5-B6-A6-A7-B7-B8
Queen Street	B7-B8
Queen Victoria Road	C3-C4
Raikes Parade	C6-C7
Rawcliffe Street	B1
Reads Avenue	B5-C5-C6
Regent Road	C6-C7
Ribble Road	C5
Rigby Road	B4-C4
Rydal Avenue	C5
St Annes Road	C1-C2
St Chad's Road	B3
St Heliers Road	C2-C3
Salthouse Avenue	C4
Saville Road	C2-C3
Shannon Street	B5
Shaw Road	B2
Sheppard Street	B6
Shetland Road	C2-C3
South King Street	C6-C7
Springfield Road	B8
Station Road	B1
Station Terrace	B1
Talbot Road	B7-B8-C8
Topping Street	B7
Tyldesley Road	B4
Vance Road	B6
Victoria Street	B6
Victory Road	C8
Waterloo Road	B2-C2
Wellington Road	B3
Westmorland Avenue	C4
Woodfield Road	B3
Woolman Road	C5
Yorkshire Street	B5

Fleetwood

Abbotts Walk	A3
Adelaide Street	B3-C3-C2
Addison Road	A1
Albert Street	C2-C3
Ash Street	A1-A2
Aughton Street	C3
Balmoral Terrace	B4
Belmont Road	A1
Blakiston Street	A2-B2-B3
Bold Street	B4-C4
Burns Road	A3
Byron Street	A3
Chaucer Road	A2
Church Street	C2
Cop Lane	A1-B1-B2
Copse Road	A1
Custom House Lane	C3
Dock Road	B1
Dock Street	B1-B2-C2
Dryder Road	A2-A3
Elm Street	A1-A2
Harris Street	A2-A3-B3
Hesketh Place	B3
Kemp Street	B2-B3
Kent Street	B3-C3
London Street	B2-B3
Lord Street	A1-A2-B2-C2-C3
Lower Lune Street	C3
Milton Street	A2-A3
Mount Road	A3-B3
Mount Street	A2-B2
North Albert Street	C3-C4
North Albion Street	A1-A2
North Church Street	B3-B4
North Street	B3
Oak Street	A1-A2
Outer Promenade	A4-B4
Pharos Street	B3-C3-C4
Poulton Road	A2
Poulton Street	A2
Preston Street	B2
Promenade Road	A3-A4
Queen's Terrace	C3-C4
Radcliffe Road	A1
Rhyl Street	B3
St Peters Place	B2-B3
Siding Road	A1
Station Road	A1
Styan Street	A2-A1-B1
Tennyson Road	A2
The Esplanade	A3-A4-B4
Upper Lune Street	C4
Victoria Street	B3-C3
Walmsley Street	A3-A2-B2
Warrenhurst Road	A1
Warren Street	B3-B2-C2
Willow Road	A1
Windsor Terrace	B4

Lytham

Agnew Street	B2-B3
Alder Grove	A3-B3
Ballam Road	B2-B3-B4-C4
Bannister Street	C2
Bath Street	B2
Beach Street	B2
Bellingham Road	C4
Bleasdale Road	C3
Brook Road	C3
Cecil Street	A2-A3
Central Beach	B2-C2
Church Road	A2-B2
Cleveland Road	B3-C3
Clifton Street	B2-C2
East Beach	C2
Forest Drive	A3-B3
Hastings Place	B2-B3
Henry Street	B2
Lilac Avenue	B4
Longacre Place	A3
Lowther Terrace	A2
Market Square	B2
Moorfield Drive	B3
Mythop Avenue	C3
Mythop Road	C3
Norfolk Road	C4
North Clifton Street	B2-C2
North Warton Street	C2
Park Street	B2
Parkview Road	C2-C3-C4
Queen Street	B2
Ring Dyke Way	A3
Rogerly Close	A3
South Clifton Street	B2-C2
Southolme	C3
South Park	A3-B3
South Warton Street	C2
Station Road	C2
Upper Westby Street	A2-B2
Warton Street	C2
West Beach	A2-B2
Westby Street	B2-C2
Westwood Road	A2
Woodville Terrace	A2
Wykeham Road	C3-C4

BLACKPOOL
Three piers, seven miles of promenade packed with entertainments galore and seemingly endless sandy beaches spread out beneath Blackpool's unmistakable tower which stands 518ft high in Britain's busiest and biggest holiday resort.

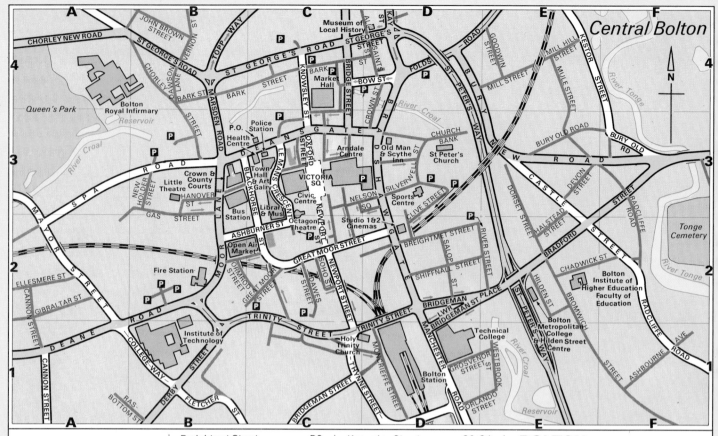

Central Bolton

Key to Town Plan and Area Plan

Town Plan
A.A. Recommended roads
Other roads
Restricted roads
Buildings of interest — Theatre
Car Parks — P
Parks and open spaces
One way streets

Area Plan
A roads
B roads
Locations — Summers O
Urban area

Street Index with Grid Reference

Central Bolton

BOLTON

public buildings and places of interest

Civic Centre (Town Hall and Tourist Information Centre) — C3
Institute of Technology — B1
Library and Museum — C2-C3
Market Hall — C4
New Octagon Theatre — C3
Old Man and Scythe Inn — D3
An historic old inn, where Lord Derby, executed in 1651, is said to have spent his last night
Technical College — D1

Situated in Tonge Moor Road, 1m north-east of the town centre, is the Textile Machinery Museum containing Arkwright's water frame of 1768, Crompton's spinning mule (1799) and Hargreave's original spinning jenny.

2m north, is Hall i'the'Wood, a picturesque, 16th-century, half-timbered house, now a museum. It is associated with William Crompton, 2m north-west is Smithils Hall, a half-timbered 15th-century and later house, noted for its old hall. It is now a museum.

Bolton

This was one of Lancashire's great cotton centres, and a fitting birthplace for revolutioniser of the textile industry Samuel Crompton, whose invention the 'spinning mule' is on display at the Tonge Moor Textile Machinery Museum. Born in 1753, Crompton lived in the picturesque 15th-century house Hall I' Th' Wood, which lies to the north of the town at Firwood Fold.

The town boasts another celebrated son in William Hesketh Lever, born in 1851, who not only founded Lever Brothers (later the giant Unilever Group), but also invented Sunlight Soap. Lever, who became Lord Leverhulme, gave Bolton a school, a church and a park.

Bolton today has become more concerned with engineering than with the textiles for which it was famous, but reminders of the past live on in the town's older monuments. The Victorian Town Hall and Civic Centre stand prominently amidst the 20th-century development in the middle of town, and nearby is The Old Man and Scythe, a medieval inn. Lord Derby spent his last night here before he was executed by Cromwell in retaliation for a massacre by the Royalists in the Civil War. Popular with both locals and outsiders is Bolton's Octagon Theatre, and another attraction for some is Bolton Wanderers Football Club, providing league football at Burnden Park.

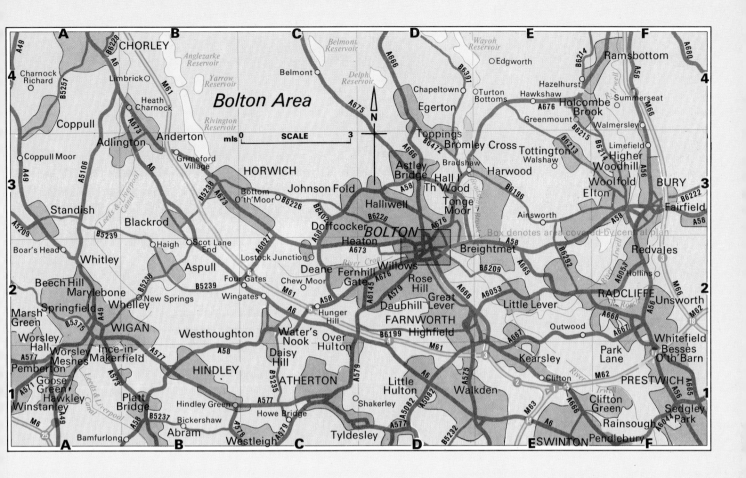

Spinning gold — the machines that made a landscape

It was called a mule because it was a hybrid of two existing machines — and together with a handful of other inventions, it transformed forever the face of northern England. Not overnight and not singlehanded: without the workers and a huge, insatiable demand for cotton, the spinning mule and other 18th-century innovations would have sunk without trace. But coming as they did, when they did, they shaped irrevocably the towns of the industrial north — and most of were the inspiration of local men.

In 1733, **Bury's** John Kay thought up the flying shuttle for faster handloom weaving. Meeting the demand it created for faster spinning of yarn, James Hargreaves of **Blackburn** brought out the 1763 spinning jenny, named after his wife and able to spin six threads at once. Mechanisation came in 1769 with **Preston**-born Richard Arkwright's water-powered spinning frame, and improving on both frame and jenny came the 1770s spinning mule, which could spin fine, strong threads 400 at a time. The frame and the mule took spinning out of the home and into mills — often sited in remote parts of the Pennines to be near water power and probably to keep out radical influences.

For the handloom weavers this was a golden age — but two developments were to make them some of the most pitiable victims of industrialisation. Steam power became the great driving force of the factories when James Watt of **Greenock** added a separate condenser to the steam engine in the 1770s and turned it for the first time into a really effective tool. And in the 1780's the power loom was invented, by Melton Mowbray clergyman Edmund Cartwright who had never even seen the hand driven variety.

Steam needed coal; the new factories needed space, and they moved down from the Pennine streams to the canals and coalfields. And so began the explosive growth of towns like **Manchester,** king of them all, **Burnley, Bolton, Wigan, Rochdale, Oldham** and **Blackburn** — the once-mighty textile centres of the world.

Samuel Crompton's spinning mule made a fortune for the mill owners of Manchester and Bolton — but the inventor gained only a meagre £60, and died a poor and embittered man.

13

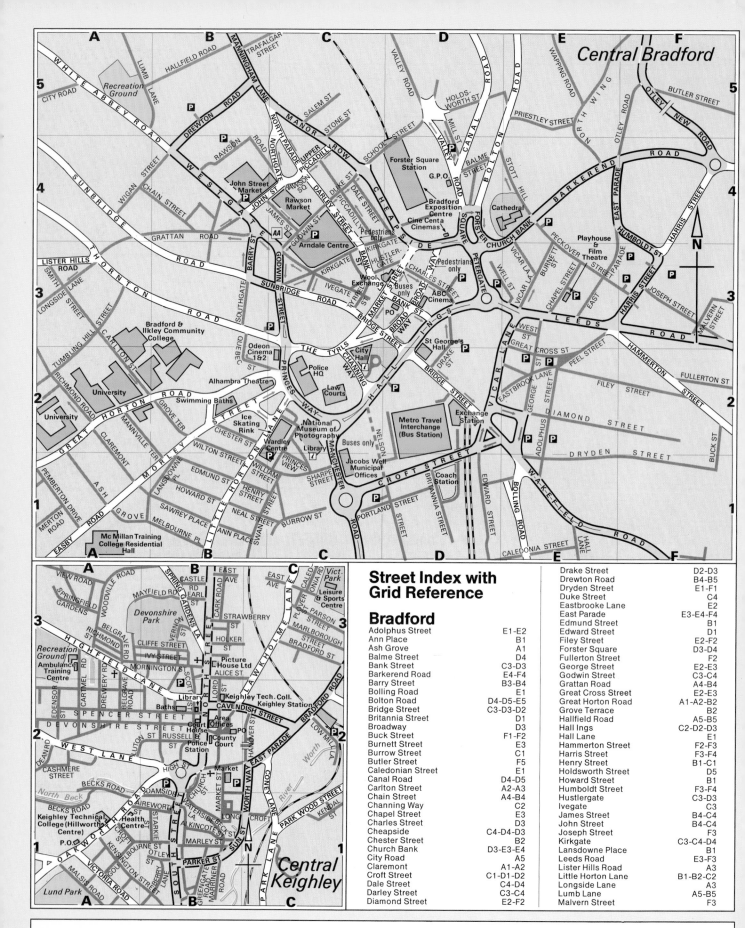

Street Index with Grid Reference

Bradford

Adolphus Street	E1-E2
Ann Place	B1
Ash Grove	A1
Balme Street	D4
Bank Street	C3-D3
Barkerend Road	E4-F4
Barry Street	B3-B4
Bolling Road	E1
Bolton Road	D4-D5-E5
Bridge Street	C3-D3-D2
Britannia Street	D1
Broadway	D3
Buck Street	F1-F2
Burnett Street	E3
Burrow Street	C1
Butler Street	F5
Caledonian Street	E1
Canal Road	D4-D5
Carlton Street	A2-A3
Chain Street	A4-B4
Channing Way	C2
Chapel Street	E3
Charles Street	D3
Cheapside	C4-D4-D3
Chester Street	B2
Church Bank	D3-E3-E4
City Road	A5
Claremont	A1-A2
Croft Street	C1-D1-D2
Dale Street	C4-D4
Darley Street	C3-C4
Diamond Street	E2-F2
Drake Street	D2-D3
Drewton Road	B4-B5
Dryden Street	E1-F1
Duke Street	C4
Eastbrooke Lane	E2
East Parade	E3-E4-F4
Edmund Street	B1
Edward Street	D1
Filey Street	E2-F2
Forster Square	D3-D4
Fullerton Street	F2
George Street	E2-E3
Godwin Street	C3-C4
Grattan Road	A4-B4
Great Cross Street	E2-E3
Great Horton Road	A1-A2-B2
Grove Terrace	B2
Hallfield Road	A5-B5
Hall Ings	C2-D2-D3
Hall Lane	E1
Hammerton Street	F2-F3
Harris Street	F3-F4
Henry Street	B1-C1
Holdsworth Street	D5
Howard Street	B1
Humboldt Street	F3-F4
Hustlergate	C3-D3
Ivegate	C3
James Street	B4-C4
John Street	B4-C4
Joseph Street	F3
Kirkgate	C3-C4-D4
Lansdowne Place	B1
Leeds Road	E3-F3
Lister Hills Road	A3
Little Horton Lane	B1-B2-C2
Longside Lane	A3
Lumb Lane	A5-B5
Malvern Street	F3

Bradford

Wool and Bradford are almost synonymous, such was its importance in the 19th century as a central market after the Industrial Revolution brought steam power to the trade. Like many small market towns that exploded into industrial cities almost overnight, Bradford's architecture is a mish-mash of grand civic buildings, factories and crowded housing. Among the former, the Wool Exchange is

impressive, with its ornate tower adorned with stone busts of 13 famous men, and the massive town hall, also topped by a tower, 200ft high. Few traces remain of the town's past but one obvious exception is the cathedral. Set on a rise, its detailed carvings – particularly the 20 angels that support the nave roof – catch the eye.

Bradford boasts several parks – notably Lister Park where there is a boating lake, an open-air swimming pool, a botanical garden and a scented

garden for the blind – and Bowling Park, on the other side of town. Cartwright Hall, named after the inventor of the power loom, stands in Lister Park. It now houses Bradford's permanent art collection.

Keighley The Brontë sisters used to walk from Haworth to this pleasant 19th-century town for their shopping sprees. Nowadays, the restored Keighley and Worth Valley Railway is a great attraction and passengers can travel to Oxenhope.

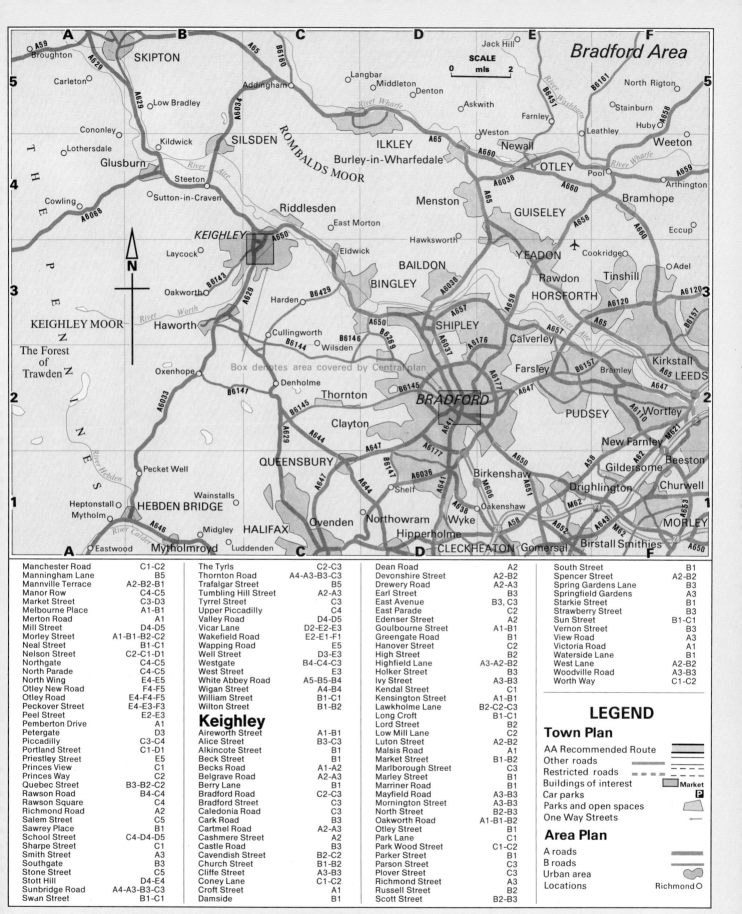

Manchester Road	C1-C2	The Tyrls	C2-C3	Dean Road	A2	South Street	B1
Manningham Lane	B5	Thornton Road	A4-A3-B3-C3	Devonshire Street	A2-B2	Spencer Street	A2-B2
Mannville Terrace	A2-B2-B1	Trafalgar Street	B5	Drewery Road	A2-A3	Spring Gardens Lane	B3
Manor Row	C4-C5	Tumbling Hill Street	A2-A3	Earl Street	B3	Springfield Gardens	A3
Market Street	C3-D3	Tyrrel Street	C3	East Avenue	B3, C3	Starkie Street	B1
Melbourne Place	A1-B1	Upper Piccadilly	C4	East Parade	C2	Strawberry Street	B3
Merton Road	A1	Valley Road	D4-D5	Edenser Street	A2	Sun Street	B1-C1
Mill Street	D4-D5	Vicar Lane	D2-E2-E3	Goulbourne Street	A1-B1	Vernon Street	B3
Morley Street	A1-B1-B2-C2	Wakefield Road	E2-E1-F1	Greengate Road	B1	View Road	A3
Neal Street	B1-C1	Wapping Road	E5	Hanover Street	C2	Victoria Road	A1
Nelson Street	C2-C1-D1	Well Street	D3-E3	High Street	B2	Waterside Lane	B1
Northgate	C4-C5	Westgate	B4-C4-C3	Highfield Lane	A3-A2-B2	West Lane	A2-B2
North Parade	C4-C5	West Street	E3	Holker Street	B3	Woodville Road	A3-B3
North Wing	E4-E5	White Abbey Road	A5-B5-B4	Ivy Street	A3-B3	Worth Way	C1-C2
Otley New Road	F4-F5	Wigan Street	A4-B4	Kendal Street	C1		
Otley Road	E4-F4-F5	William Street	B1-C1	Kensington Street	A1-B1		
Peckover Street	E4-E3-F3	Wilton Street	B1-B2	Lawkholme Lane	B2-C2-C3		
Peel Street	E2-E3			Long Croft	B1-C1		
Pemberton Drive	A1	**Keighley**		Lord Street	B2		
Petergate	D3	Aireworth Street	A1-B1	Low Mill Lane	C2		
Piccadilly	C3-C4	Alice Street	B3-C3	Luton Street	A2-B2		
Portland Street	C1-D1	Alkincote Street	B1	Malsis Road	A1		
Priestley Street	E5	Beck Street	B1	Market Street	B1-B2		
Princes View	C1	Becks Road	A1-A2	Marlborough Street	C3		
Princes Way	C2	Belgrave Road	A2-A3	Marley Street	B1		
Quebec Street	B3-B2-C2	Berry Lane	B1	Marriner Road	B1		
Rawson Road	B4-C4	Bradford Road	C2-C3	Mayfield Road	A3-B3		
Rawson Square	C4	Bradford Street	C3	Mornington Street	A3-B3		
Richmond Road	A2	Caledonia Road	C3	North Street	B2-B3		
Salem Street	C5	Cark Road	B3	Oakworth Road	A1-B1-B2		
Sawrey Place	B1	Cartmel Road	A2-A3	Otley Street	B1		
School Street	C4-D4-D5	Cashmere Street	A2	Park Lane	C1		
Sharpe Street	C1	Castle Road	B3	Park Wood Street	C1-C2		
Smith Street	A3	Cavendish Street	B2-C2	Parker Street	B1		
Southgate	B3	Church Street	B1-B2	Parson Street	C3		
Stone Street	C5	Cliffe Street	A3-B3	Plover Street	C3		
Stott Hill	D4-E4	Coney Lane	C1-C2	Richmond Street	A3		
Sunbridge Road	A4-A3-B3-C3	Croft Street	A1	Russell Street	B2		
Swan Street	B1-C1	Damside	B1	Scott Street	B2-B3		

LEGEND

Town Plan

AA Recommended Route	
Other roads	
Restricted roads	
Buildings of interest	Market
Car parks	P
Parks and open spaces	
One Way Streets	←

Area Plan

A roads	
B roads	
Urban area	
Locations	Richmond O

BRADFORD

St George's, built with the profits of the wool trade, is one of Bradford's imposing Victorian buildings. It is once again being used for the purpose for which it was intended – a concert hall – and has exceptionally good acoustics.

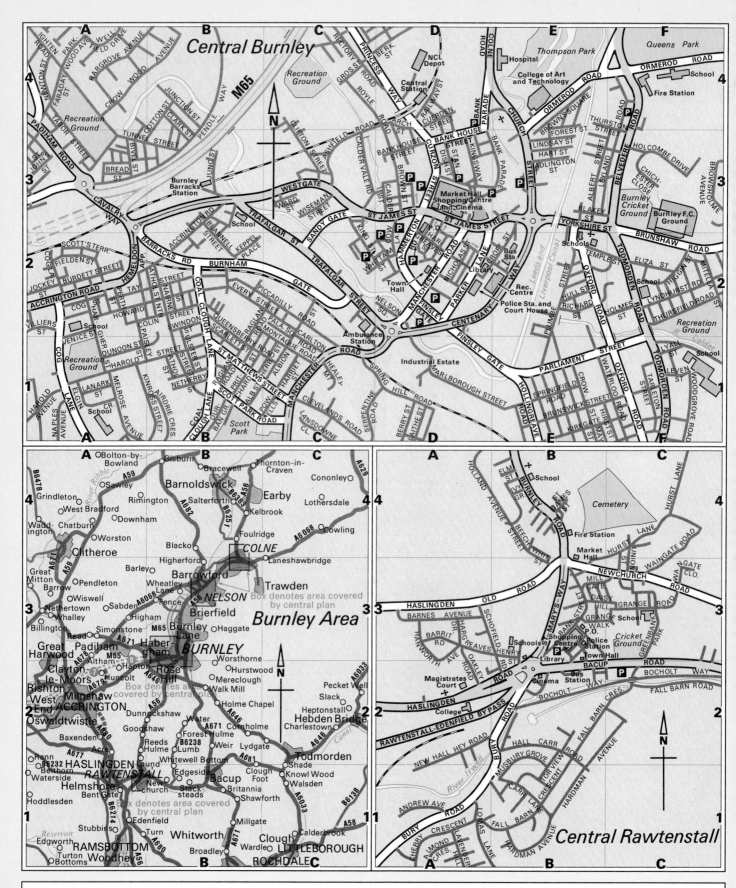

Burnley

International fame was brought to Burnley in the 1960s by its local football team, which can still be seen playing at Turf Moor. An old mill town lying in a bend of the Leeds and Liverpool Canal, Burnley's prosperity is reflected in the fine new developments it has seen, particularly since the opening of the M65. Half a mile south-east of the town stands Towneley Hall, a restored house dating back to the 14th century, which houses an art gallery and museum with an interesting local history collection.

Rawtenstall has made its name in the manufacture of felt, and now enjoys the luxury of an artificial ski-slope in Haslingden Old Road among its many good sports facilities.

Nelson was named after a pub, called Nelson's Inn (in honour of the hero of Trafalgar). It once stood alone here, but a burgeoning cotton town sprang up around it during the 19th century, and eventually took its name. Not far off looms the dark mass of Pendle Hill — the notorious haunt of Lancashire witches.

Colne's 18th-century wool trading prosperity is remembered in the fine Cloth Hall, which dates from this period. With a past traceable back to Roman times, Colne is also the site of the British in India Museum, which stands in Sun Street and can be visited at weekends in summer.

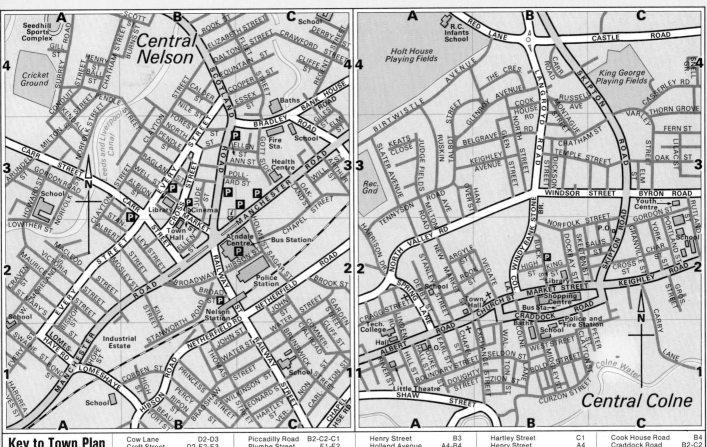

Key to Town Plan and Area Plan

Town Plan

AA Recommended roads ▬▬▬
Other roads ▬▬▬
Restricted roads ▭▭▭▭
Buildings of interest Mill ▬
One way street ←
Car Parks **P**
Parks and open spaces ▭

Area Plan

A roads ▬▬
B roads ▬▬
Locations Hawkshaw ○
Urban area ▭

STREET INDEX

BURNLEY

Accrington Road	A2-B2-B3
Adlington Street	E3
Airdrie Crescent	B1
Albert Street	E3-F3
Albion Street	B1-C1-C2
Arch Street	D4-D3
Ashfield Road	C3-C4-D4
Athol Street	B1
Athol Street North	B1
Bank House Road	D3-D4
Bank Parade	D4-D3-E3
Barracks Road	A3-A2-B2
Belvedere Road	F3-F4
Berkeley Street	C4-D4
Berry Street	D1
Bivel Street	A3
Blakey Street	E3-F3
Blannel Street	B2-B3
Bread Street	E3-E4
Brown's Square	E3-E4
Brown Street	D3
Brownsholme Avenue	F3
Brunshaw Road	F2-F3
Brunswick Street	E1-F1
Burdett Street	A2
Burnham Gate	B2-C2
Calder Street	D3
Calder Vale Road	C3
Carlton Road	C1-C2
Cavalry Way	A3
Centenary Way	D1-D2-E2-E3
Chichester Close	F3
Church Street	E3-E4
Clark Street	B3-B4
Clevelands Road	C1
Clifton Street	C3-C4
Coal Clough Lane	A1-A2
Cog Lane	A1-A2
Cog Street	A2
Colin Street	A2-B2
Colne Road	D4-E4
Cotton Street	A3-B3-B4
Cow Lane	D2-D3
Croft Street	D2-E2-E3
Crowther Street	E1
Crow Wood Avenue	A4-B4
Cuerden Street	D4
Curzon Street	D3
Dunoon Street	A1
Durban Grove	B1
Elgin Crescent	A1
Eliza Street	F2
Every Street	B2-C2
Faraday Street	A4
Fielden Street	B1
Finsley Gate	D2-D1-E1
Forest Street	E4
Grosvenor Street	C4
Hammerton Road	D2-D3
Hargher Street	A1-A2
Hargreaves Street	D2-D3
Hargrove Avenue	A4-B4
Harold Avenue	A1
Harold Street	A1-B1
Harriet Street	C1
Hart Street	E3
Healey Mount	C1
Hemeldon Approach	A2
Herbert Street	B1-C1
Higgin Street	F2
Hirst Street	E1-F1
Holcombe Drive	F3
Hollingreave Road	A1
Holmes Street	E2-F2
Howard Street	A2-B2
Hull Street	E2
Ighten Road	A4
Jockey Street	A2
Junction Street	B3, B4
Keppel Place	B2
King Street	C2-C3
Kingsway	D3
Kinross Street	A1-B1
Kirkgate	E1-F1
Laithe Street	D1
Lanark Street	A1
Lansdowne Close	C1
Leven Street	F1
Leyland Road	E3-F3-F4
Lindsay Street	F1
Lyall Street	F1
Lyndhurst Road	F2
Manchester Road	C1-D1-D2-D3
Marlborough Street	D1-E1
May Street	E1
Melrose Avenue	A1
Mitella Street	F2
Montague Road	B2-C2-C1
Nairne Street	B1-B2
Naples Avenue	A1
Nelson Square	D2
Netherby Street	B1
Newton Street	F1
Nicholas Street	D2
Ormerod Road	E3-E4-F4
Oxford Road	E2-F2-F1
Padiham Road	A3-A4
Paisley Street	A2-A1-B1
Palatine Square	A2
Parker Lane	D2-D3
Parkwood Road	A1-B2
Parliament Street	E1-F1-F2
Pendle Way	A3-B3-B4
Perth Street	A2

Piccadilly Road	B2-C2-C1
Plumbe Street	E1-E2
Powell Street	B1-C1
Princess Way	C4-D4
Pritchard Street	B1
Queensberry Road	B2-B1-C1
Raglan Road	B1-B2-C2
Railway Street	D4
Rectory Road	C4-D4
Richard Street	E2
Royle Road	C4-D4-D3
St James Street	C3-D3-E3
St John's Street	A3
St Matthews Street	B1-C1
Sandy Gate	C2-C3
Scarlett Street	B1-B2
Scott Park Road	B1-C1
Scott's Terrace	A2
Serpentine Road	C1-D1
Springfield Road	E1
Spring Hill Road	C1-D1
Standish Street	D3
Swindon Street	B2
Tabor Street	A3-A4
Tartleton Street	F1
Tay Street	A2-B2
Temple Street	E2-F2
Thursfield Road	F2
Thurston Street	E4-F4-F3
Todmorden Road	F1-F2
Trafalgar Street	B3-C3-C2-D2
Tunnel Street	A3-B3
Ulster Street	B1-B2
Venice Street	A1-A2
Villiers Street	A2
Ward Street	C3
Waterloo Road	E1-F1
Wellfield Drive	A4
Westgate	B3-C3
Whittam Street	C2-D2
Wiseman Street	C3
Woodgrove Road	F1
Yorkshire Street	E3

RAWTENSTALL

Almond Crescent	A1
Andrew Avenue	A1
Bacup Road	B2-C2
Bank Street	B3
Barnes Avenue	A3
Barrit Road	A3
Beech Street	B4
Bocholt Way	B2-C2
Burnley Road	B4
Bury Road	A1-B1-B2
Carr Lane	B1
Cherry Crescent	A1
Daisy Hill	B3-C3
Elm Street	B4
Fall Barn Crescent	A1-B1-B2-C2
Fallbarn Road	C2
Grange Road	A1
Grange Walk	B3-C3
Greenbank Park	C2
Hall Carr Road	B1-B2
Hanworth Avenue	A3
Hardman Avenue	B1-B2-C2
Hargreaves Drive	A3-B3
Haslingden Road	A2-B2
Haslingden Old Road	A3-B3

Henry Street	B3
Holland Avenue	A4-B4
Hurst Lane	B3-B4-C4
Ivy Grove	B4
Lavender Hill	A1
Lomas Lane	A1-B1
Mill Gate	B3-C3
Musbury Grove	B1-B2-B1
Newchurch Road	B3-C3
New Hall Hey Road	A1-A2
Oakley Road	A2-A3
Rawtenstall-Edenfield By-Pass	A2-B2
St James Street	B4
St Mary's Way	B4
Schofield Road	A3-B3-B2
Union Street	C3-C4
Waingate Close	C3
Waingate Road	C3-C4
Whittle Street	B3-B4

NELSON

Albert Street	A2-B2
Albion Street	B3
Ann Street	B3-C3
Arthur Street	C3
Arundel Street	A3
Ball Street	A4
Bank House Road	C4
Beaufort Street	B1
Bishop Street	A1-A2
Bond Street	A1
Bradley Road	B3-C3
Bradshaw Street	B1-C1
Broad Street	B2
Broadway	B2
Brook Street	C2
Brunswick Street	C1
Burns Street	B4
Calder Street	B4
Carlton Street	C1
Carr Street	A3-B3-B2
Chatham Street	A4-B4
Chapel House Road	C4
Chapel Street	C2-C3
Clayton Street	A2-A3-B3-B4
Cliffe Street	C4
Clifford Street	C1
Cobden Street	B1
Commercial Road	C1-C2
Conduit Street	A3-A4
Cooper Street	B4-C4
Craven Street	A2
Crawford Street	B4
Cross Street	B2-B3
Dalton Street	B4-C4
Derby Street	C4
Ellen Street	B2
Ellen Street	B3-C3
Elizabeth Street	B4-C4
Elm Street	C3
Essex Street	B4-C4
Every Street	A1-A2-B2-B3-B4
Fleet Street	B4-C4
Forest Street	B3-B4
Fountain Street	B4-C4
Garden Street	C1-C2
Giles Street	C3-C4
Gill Street	A4
Gordon Road	A3
Gott Side	C3
Hargreaves Street	A1

Hartley Street	C1
Henry Street	A4
Hibson Road	B1
Hibson Street	B2-C2
High Street	A1
Holme Street	C2-C3
Hope Street	B2
Howard Street	A3
John Street	B1-C1, C2
Jude Street	B2-B3
Kendall Street	A3-A4
Kiln Street	B1-B2
Leonard Street	C1
Lomeshaye	A1-B1
Lomeshaye Road	A1-B1
Lowther Street	A2-A3
Macleod Street	A2
Manchester Road	A1-A2-B2-C2-C3
Market Street	B2-B3
Maurice Street	A3
Milton Street	A3-A4
Mosley Street	A2-B2
Netherfield Road	B1-B2-C2
Nile Street	B3-B4
Norfolk Street	A2-A3-A4
North Street	B3
Oakland Street	C3
Pendle Street	A4-B4-B3
Percy Street	B1
Pollard Street	B3-C3
Princess Street	B1-C1
Raglan Street	B3
Railway Street	B2-C2-C1
Regent Street	C4
Ripon Street	B1
Rook Street	B4-C4
St Mary's Street	A1-A2
Sagar Street	C1
Scotland Road	B2-B3-B4
Scott Street	A4-B4
Stanley Street	A3-A2-B2
Stanworth Road	B1-B2
Surrey Road	A4
Swaine Street	A1
Thomas Street	B1-C1
Vernon Street	C1
Victoria Street	A1
Water Street	B1-C1-C2
Wellington Street	B3
West Moreland Street	A2
Wilkinson Street	B1-C1
William Street	C2

COLNE

Albert Road	A1-A2
Argyle Road	A2-B2
Belgrave Road	A3-B3
Birtwistle Avenue	A3-A4-B4
Bold Street	A1-B1
Boundary Road	B1
Buck Street	C3
Byron Road	C3
Carr Road	B4
Carry Lane	C1-C2
Casserley Road	C4
Castle Road	B4-C4
Chapel Street	A1
Charles Street	C2
Chatham Street	B3-C3
Church Street	B1
Clayton Street	B1
Colne Lane	B1-B2

Cook House Road	B4
Craddock Road	B2-C2
Cragg Street	A1-A2
Cross Street	C2
Curzon Street	B1-C1
Derby Street	A1-A2
Dickson Street	B3
Dockray Street	B2
Doughty Street	A1-B1
Duke Street	A1
Earl Street	A1
Elm Street	C3
Exchange Street	A1-B1
Fern Street	C3
Glenroy Avenue	A3-B3-B4
Glen Street	B3
Gordon Street	C3
Granville Street	C2
Grosvenor Street	C1-C2
Hall Street	A1
Hanover Street	A3-B3
Harrison Drive	A2
High Street	B2
Hill Street	A1
Ivegate	B2
Judge Fields	A3
Keats Close	A3
Keighley Avenue	A3-B3
Keighley Road	C2
King Street	B2
Langroyd Road	B3-B4
Lilac Street	C3
Linden Road	A1-A2
Market Street	B2-C2
Midgley Street	B1
Milton Road	A2-A3
Montague Street	B3-B4
New Market Street	A2
Norfolk Street	B2-C2
North Street	B3-B4
North Valley Road	A2
Oak Street	C3
Peter Street	C1
Portland Street	C2
Red Lane	A4-B4
River Street	A1
Rook Street	A2-B2
Ruskin Avenue	A2-A3-A4
Russell Avenue	B4-C4
Rutland Street	C2-C3
Salisbury Street	B2-C2
Seldon Street	B1
Shaw Street	A1-B1
Skelton Street	B1
Skipton Road	B4-C4-C3-C2
Slater Avenue	A3
Snell Grove	C4
Spring Lane	A1-A2
Stanley Street	A3
Stone Bridge	B2-B3
Talbot Street	A3-A4-B4
Temple Street	B3-C3
Tennyson Road	A2-A3
The Crescent	B4
Thorn Grove	C3
Varley Street	C3-C4
Walton Street	B1
West Street	B1
Windsor Street	B3-C3
Windy Bank	B2
York Street	C2
Zion Street	B1

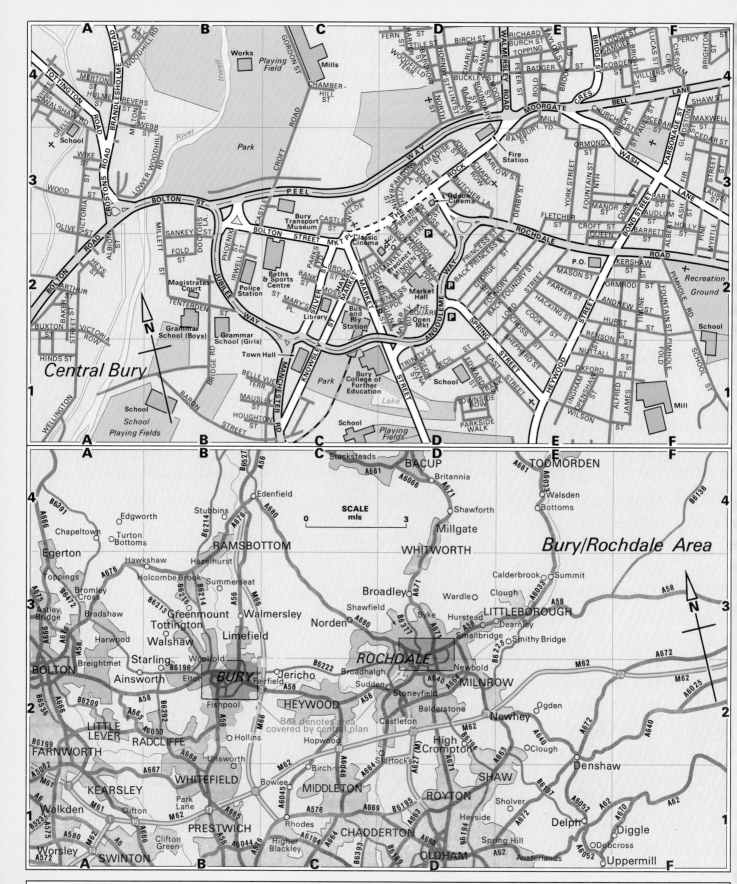

Bury / Rochdale

Bury has been celebrated for its black pudding for over a century, and this special delicacy is still an important attraction of Bury Market. The market has been chartered since 1440 and nearby is Bury's oldest building — the Two Tubs, said to have been built around two giant oak trees in the reign of Charles II. Celebrated sons of Bury include 'flying shuttle' inventor John Kay who was born here. His invention helped to transform 18th-century weaving, and the town remembers him by the John Kay Gardens, where his statue stands.

Rochdale Gracie Fields came from Rochdale — a town which saw dramatic changes in the early 19th century. This was when the textile mills arrived and brought with them a whole new lifestyle for local people. They rose to the challenge with innovations like the now worldwide co-operative movement, the brainchild of the 'Rochdale Pioneers' whose original shop has become a museum in the Toad Lane Conservation Area. More radical ideas came from Rochdale-born John Bright, campaigner for the repeal of the Corn Laws in 1846. His statue is one of many in the town, which also has the unusual Lancashire Dialect Writers Memorial. The town centre is dominated by a magnificent Victorian Gothic Town Hall, set in parks and gardens with the medieval Parish Church of St Chad nearby.

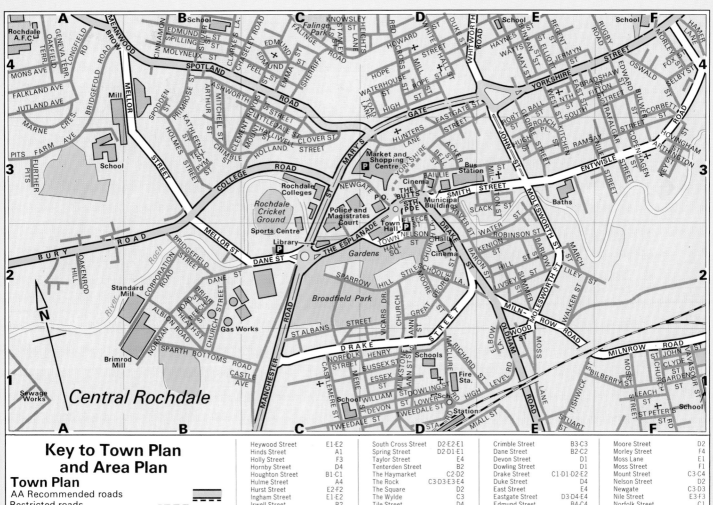

Central Rochdale

Key to Town Plan and Area Plan

Town Plan

AA Recommended roads
Restricted roads
Other roads
Buildings of interest — Hospital
Car parks — P
Churches — +
Parks and open spaces

Area Plan

A roads
B roads
Locations — Bottoms
Urban area

Street Index with Grid Reference

Bury

Albert Street	F2-F3
Albion Street	A2-A3
Alfred Street	E1-F1-F2
Andrew Street	E2-F2
Angouleme Way	D1-D2
Ash Street	F3
Arthur Street	A2
Audlum Street	F3
Back Foundry Street	D2-E2
Back Princess Street	D2-E2-E3
Badger Street	E4
Baker Street	A2
Bambury Street	E3-E4
Bank Street	C2
Barcroft Street	D4
Barlow Street	D3-E3
Baron Street	B1-C1
Barrett Street	F2-F3
Bazaar Street	D4
Bell Lane	E4-F4
Belle Vue Terrace	B1-C1
Benson Street	E2-E1-F1
Birch Street	D4
Bold Street	E4
Bolton Road	A2-A3
Bolton Street	A3-B3-C3-C2
Bond Street	F2-F3
Boundary Street	D4
Brandlesholme Road	A3-A4
Brick Street	E3-F3-F4
Bridge Road	B1-B2
Bridge Street	E4
Bright Street	E4
Brighton Street	F4
Broad Street	C2
Brook Street	E4
Buckley Street	D4-E4
Butcher Lane	D3
Buxton Street	A2
Castle Street	C3
Castle Croft Road	B3-C3-C4
Cecil Street	D1
Cedar Street	F3-F4
Chamberhill Street	C4
Chapel Row	D3
Charles Street	D4
Chesham Crescent	F4
Church Street	E4-F4-F3
Clerke Street	D2-D3
Cobden Street	E4-F4
Cook Street	E2
Cork Street	F3
Croft Street	E3-F3
Cross Street	D2-D3
Crostons Road	A3
Derby Street	E3
Doctors Lane	B2-B3
East Street	D1-E1
Eden Street	D3
Edward Street	D1
Ely Drive	A4
Fern Street	D4
Fletcher Street	E3
Flint Street	D4
Fir Street	F3
Fold Street	B2
Foundry Street	D2-E2
Fountain Street	F2
Fountain Street North	E3
Frank Street	D1-E1
Franklin Street	D4
George Street	D2-E2
Georgiana Street	C2-D2
Georgiana Street	D1
Gladstone Street	F3-F4
Gordon Street	C4
Hacking Street	E2
Harper Street	D4
Haymarket	C2
Heys Street	A2

Heywood Street	E1-E2
Hinds Street	A1
Holly Street	F3
Hornby Street	D4
Houghton Street	B1-C1
Hulme Street	A4
Hurst Street	E2-F2
Ingham Street	E1-E2
Irwell Street	B2
James Street	F1
John Street	D3
Jubilee Way	B3-B2-C2
Kershaw Street	F2
Knowsley Street	C1-C2
Laurel Street	F3
Lodge Street	E4-E4
Lord Street	D2-E2
Lower Woodhill Road	A3-B3
Lucas Street	F4
Manchester Road	C1
Manor Street	E3-F3
Market Parade	D2
Market Place	C2-C3
Market Street	C2-D2-D1
Mason Street	E2
Mausley Street	B1-C1
Maxwell Street	F4
Merton Street	A4
Mill Yard	E4
Millett Street	B2-B3
Milton Street	A4
Minden Parade	D2
Moor Street	D4
Moorgate Crescent	E4
Moss Street	C2
Murray Road	D2
Myrtle Street	F2-F3
North Street	D4
Nuttall Street	E1-F1
Olive Street	A2-A3
Openshaw Street	E1
Orell Street	A3-A4
Ormond Street	E3
Ormrod Street	E2-F2
Oxford Street	E1-F1
Paradise Street	D3
Parker Street	E2
Parks Yard	C2
Parkside Walk	F3-F4
Parsonage Street	F3-F4
Parsons Lane	D3
Peel Way	B3-C3-D3-D4-E4
Percy Street	E4
Peter Street	F4
Phoenix Street	B2-B3
Pimhole Fold	F1-F2
Pimhole Road	F2
Pine Street	F2-F3
Princess Parade	D2
Princess Street	D2-D3
Queen Street	E2
Raby Street	F3
Revers Street	A4
Richard Burch Street	E4
Rochdale Road	D3-E3-E2-F2
St Mary's Place	F3
St Pauls Street	F3-F4
Samuel Street	E4-F4
Sankey Street	B2
School Street	F1-F2
Shaw Street	E3
Shepherd Street	E1-E2
Silver Street	C2

South Cross Street	D2-E2-E1
Spring Street	D2-D1-E1
Taylor Street	E4
Tenterden Street	B2
The Haymarket	C2-D2
The Rock	C3-D3-E3-E4
The Square	D2
The Wylde	C3
Tile Street	D4
Tinune Street	F2
Tithe Barn Street	D3
Topping Street	E4
Tottington Road	A3-A4
Townside Row	D1
Trinity Street	D1
Union Arcade	D2
Union Street	D2-D3
Victoria Row	A1-A2
Victoria Street	A2-A3
Villiers Street	F4
Walmersley Road	F4
Walshaw Road	A3-A4
Wash Lane	E4-E3-F3
Webb Street	A3-B3
Wellington Street	A1-A2
White Street	A4
Wike Street	A3
Wilson Street	E1-F1
Wood Street	A3
Woodfield Terrace	D4
Woodhill Road	A4-B4
York Street	E3

Rochdale

Acker Street	D3
Albion Road	B1-B2
Ann Street	D1-D2
Arthington Street	F3
Arthur Street	B3-B4
Ashworth Street	B4-C4-C3
Baillie Street	D3-E3
Ball Street	E4
Barlow Street	E2
Baron Street	D2-E2
Beech Street	B2
Bell Street	D3
Bilberry Street	E1-F1
Bradshaw Street	E4-F4
Briar Street	B2
Bridgefield Street	B2
Bridgefold Road	A3-A4
Bulwer Street	F3-F4
Bunyan Street	E4
Bury Road	A2-B2-B3
Castle Avenue	B1-C1
Castlemere Street	C1
Chaseley Road	B4-C4
Church Lane	D2-D3
Church Road	F1
Church Stile	D1-D2
Church Street	B1-B2
Cinnamon Street	B4
Clarke's Lane	B4
Clement Royds Street	B3-C3-C4
Clover Street	C3
Clyde Street	F1
College Road	B3-C3
Copenhagen Street	F3
Corbett Street	F4
Corporation Road	A1-B1-B2

Crimble Street	B3-C3
Dane Street	B2-C2
Devon Street	D1
Dowling Street	D1
Drake Street	C1-D1-D2-E2
Duke Street	D4
East Street	E4
Eastgate Street	D3-D4-E4
Edmund Street	B4-C4
Edward Street	F4
Elbow Lane	E1-E2
Elliott Street	E4
Emma Street	C4
Entwisle Road	E3-F3-F4
Essex Street	D1
Falinge Road	C4
Falkland Avenue	A4
Fishwick Street	E1
Fitton Street	E4-F4
Fleece Street	D3
Fox Street	F4
Further Pits	A3
Garden Street	F1
Geneva Terrace	A4
George Street	E3-E4
Great George Street	D2
Halliwell Street	C3
Hamer Lane	F4
Haynes Street	F4
Heath Street	B1-B2
Heights Lane	C4
Henry Street	D1
High Street	D4
High Level Road	D1-E1
Hill Street	E2
Holland Street	C3
Holmes Street	B3
Hope Street	D4
Hovingham Street	F3
Howard Street	D1
Hugh Street	E3
Hunters Lane	D3
Jermyn Street	E4
John Street	E3
Jutland Avenue	A4
Kathleen Street	B3
Kenion Street	E2
Key Street	F3
Kitchen Street	E3
Knowsley Street	C4
Leach Street	F1
Liley Street	E2-F2
Littledale Street	C3-C4
Livsey Street	E2
Longfield Road	A4
Lower Tweedale Street	D1
Maclure Road	D1
Manchester Road	C1-C2
March Street	E2
Marne Crescent	A3-A4
May Street	E4
Meanwood Brow	B4
Mellor Street	C2-B2-B3-B4-A4
Mere Street	C1-D1
Miall Street	D1-E1
Milkstone Road	D1
Mill Street	D4
Milnrow Road	E2-E1-F1
Milton Street	E3
Mitchell Street	B3-B4
Molesworth Street	E2-E3
Molyneux Street	B4
Mons Avenue	A4

Moore Street	D2
Morley Street	F4
Moss Lane	E1
Moss Street	F1
Mount Street	C3-C4
Nelson Street	D2
Newgate	C3-D3
Nile Street	E3-F3
Norfolk Street	C1
Norman Road	B1-B2
North Street	E4
Oakenrod Hill	A2
Oakfield Terrace	A4
Oldham Road	E1-E2
Oswald Street	F4
Peel Street	D1
Pilling Street	B4
Pits Farm Avenue	A3
Primrose Street	B4
Pym Street	B3
Ramsay Street	E3-F3
Red Cross Street	D4
Regent Street	E4
Richard Street	D1-E1
River Street	D2-D3
Roach Place	E3
Robert Street	E3
Robinson Street	E2
Rope Street	D4
Rugby Road	E4-F4
St Albans Street	C1-C2-D2
St John Street	F1
St Mary's Gate	C2-C3-D3-D4
St Peter's Street	F1
School Lane	D2
Selby Street	F4
Sherriff Street	C4
Silver Street	B4
Slack Street	D3-E3
Smith Street	D3-E3
South Parade	D3
South Street	E3-E4-F4
Sparrow Hill	C2-D2
Sparth Bottoms Road	B1-C1
Spodden Street	B4
Spotland Road	B4-C4-C3-D3
Stanley Street	C4
Station Road	D1
Stuart Street	E1
Summer Street	E2
Sussex Street	C1-D1
Tell Street	B3
The Butts	D3
The Esplanade	C2-D2-D3
Toad Lane	D4
Town Hall Square	D2
Trafalgar Street	F3-F4
Tweedale Street	C1-D1
Vavasour Street	F1
Vicars Drive	D1-D2
Walker Street	E2
Water Street	D2-E2-E3
Waterhouse Street	D4
Watts Street	D4
West Street	E3-E4
Whitehall Street	D4
Whitworth Road	D4
William Street	C1-D1
Wood Street	E1-E2
Yorkshire Street	D3-E3-E4-F4

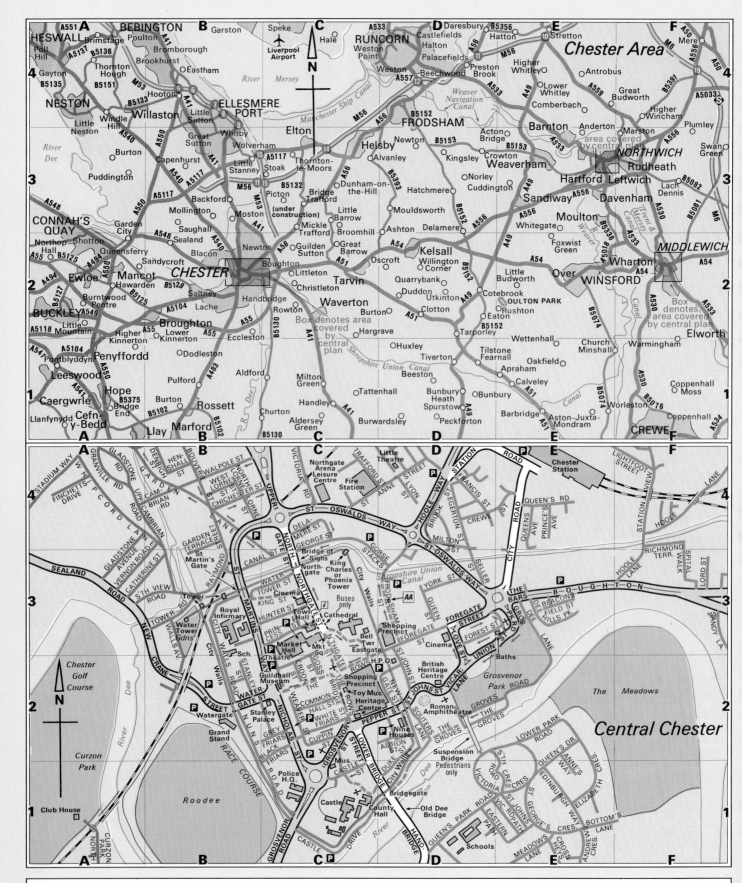

Chester

Chester is the only English city to have preserved the complete circuit of its Roman and medieval walls. On the west side, the top of the walls is now at pavement level, but on the other three sides the walk along the ramparts is remarkable. Two of the old watchtowers contain small museums: the Water Tower, built to protect the old river port, displays relics of medieval Chester; King Charles's Tower, from which Charles I watched the defeat of the Royalist army at the Battle of Rowton Moor in 1645, portrays Chester's role in the Civil War.

Looking down from the top of the Eastgate, crowned with the ornate and gaily-coloured Jubilee Clock erected in 1897, the view down the main street, the old Roman *Via Principalis*, reveals a dazzling display of the black-and-white timbered buildings for which Chester is famous. One of these, Providence House, bears the inscription 'God's Providence is Mine Inheritance', carved in thanks for sparing the survivors of the plague of 1647 that ravaged the city.

On either side of Eastgate, Watergate and Bridge Street are the Rows, a feature unique to Chester, and dating back at least to the 13th century. These covered galleries of shops, raised up at first-floor level, protected pedestrians from weather and traffic. Chester's magnificent cathedral has beautifully carved choir stalls.

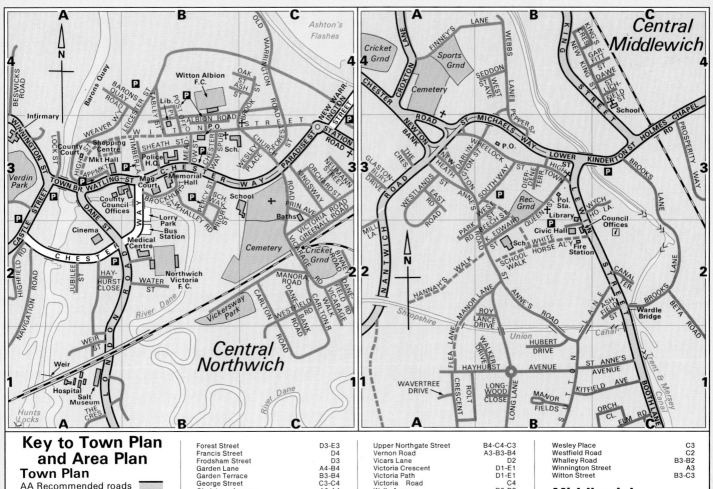

Central Northwich

Central Middlewich

Key to Town Plan and Area Plan

Town Plan
AA Recommended roads
Other roads
Restricted roads
Buildings of interest — College
One Way Streets
Car Parks — P
Parks and open spaces
Churches — +

Area Plan
A roads
B roads
Locations — DuddonO
Urban area

Street Index with Grid Reference

Chester

Albion Street	D2
Andrews Crescent	E1
Anne's Way	E2-E1
Beaconsfield Street	E3
Black Friars	C1-C2
Bottom's Lane	E1-F1
Boughton	E3-F3
Bouverie Street	B4
Bridge Street	C2
Brook Street	D4
Cambrian Road	A4-B4
Canal Street	B3-C3
Castle Drive	C1
Castle Street	C1
Catherine Street	A3-B3
Chichester Street	B4-C4
City Road	E3-E4
City Walls Road	B3-B2
Commonhall Street	C2
Crewe Street	D4-E4
Crook Street	C2
Cross Heys	E1
Cuppin Street	C2
Curzon Park North	A1
Dee Hills Park	E3
Dee Lane	E3
Delamere Street	C4
Denbigh Street	B4
Duke Street	D1-D2
Eastern Path	D1-E1
Edinburgh Way	E1
Egerton Street	D4
Elizabeth Crescent	E1-E2
Finchetts Drive	A4
Foregate Street	D3
Forest Street	D3-E3
Francis Street	D4
Frodsham Street	D3
Garden Lane	A4-B4
Garden Terrace	B3-B4
George Street	C3-C4
Gladstone Avenue	A3-A4
Gladstone Road	A4
Gorse Stacks	C4-C3-D3
Goss Street	C2
Granville Road	A4
Grey Friars	C2
Grosvenor Park Road	E3
Grosvenor Road	C1
Grosvenor Street	C1-C2
Groves Road	D2-E2
Handbridge	D1
Henshall Street	B4
Hoole Lane	F3-F4
Hoole Way	D4
Hunter Street	B3-C3
King Street	B3-C3
Lightfoot Street	E4-F4
Lord Street	F3
Lorne Street	B4
Lower Bridge Street	C2-C1-D1
Lower Park Road	D2-E2
Love Street	D3
Lyon Street	D4
Meadows Lane	E1
Milton Street	D4
New Crane Street	A3-B3-B2
Newgate Street	D2
Nicholas Street	C2-C1
Northgate Street	C3-C2
North Lorne Street	B4
Nuns Road	B2-B1-C1
Pepper Street	C2-D2
Princess Street	C3
Prince's Avenue	E4
Queens Avenue	E4
Queen's Drive	E1-E2
Queen's Park Road	D1-E1
Queen's Road	E4
Queen Street	D3
Raymond Street	B3-B4
Richmond Terrace	F4
St Anne Street	C4-D4
St George's Crescent	E1
St Johns Road	E1
St Johns Street	D2
St John Street	D3-D2
St Martins Way	B4-B3-C3-B2-C2
St Oswalds Way	C4-D4-D3
Sealand Road	A3
Seller Street	D3
Souters Lane	D2
South Crescent Road	D2-E2-E1
South View Road	A3-B3
Spital Walk	F4-F3
Stadium Way	A4
Stanley Street	B2
Station Road	D4-E4
Station View	F4
The Bars	E3
The Groves	D2-E2
The Rows	C2
Tower Road	B3
Trafford Street	C4-D4
Union Street	D2-D3-E3
Upper Cambrian Road	A4-B4-B3
Upper Northgate Street	B4-C4-C3
Vernon Road	A3-B3-B4
Vicars Lane	D2
Victoria Crescent	D1-E1
Victoria Path	D1-E1
Victoria Road	C4
Walls Avenue	B3-B2
Walpole Street	B4
Watergate Street	B2-C2
Water Tower Street	B3-C3
Weaver Street	C2
West Lorne Street	B4
White Friars	C2
Whipcord Lane	A4-B4
York Street	D3

Northwich

Albion Road	B3
Apple Market	A3
Ash Street	B4-C4
Barons Quay Road	A4-B4
Beswicks Road	A4
Binney Road	C2
Brockhurst Street	B3
Brook Street	B3-C3-C4
Carlton Road	C2-C1
Castle Street	A2-A3
Chester Way	A2-B2-B3-C3
Chester Way Spur	B3
Church Road	C3
Danebank Road	C2-C1
Danefield Road	C2
Dane Street	A3-A2
Forest Street	C3
Greenall Road	C2-C3
Hayhurst Close	A2
Highfield Road	A2
High Street	A3
Jubilee Street	A2
Kingsway	C3
Leicester Street	B3-B4
Lock Street	A3
London Road	A1-A2-B2
Manora Road	C2
Meadow Street	B3
Navigation Road	A1-A2
Neumann Street	C3
New Warrington Street	C3-C4
Oak Street	B4-C4
Old Warrington Road	C4-C3
Orchard Street	C3
Paradise Street	C3
Percy Street	B3
Post Office Place	B4-B3
Princes Avenue	C3
Priory Street	B2-B3
School Way	B3
Sheath Street	B3
Station Road	C3
The Crescent	A1
Tabley Street	B4-B3
Timber Lane	B3
Town Bridge	A3
Vicarage Road	C2
Vicarage Walk	C2
Victoria Road	C2-C3
Water Street	B2
Watling Street	A3-B3
Weaver Way	A3-B3-B4
Weir Street	A1
Wesley Place	C3
Westfield Road	C2
Whalley Road	B3-B2
Winnington Street	A3
Witton Street	B3-C3

Middlewich

Ashfield Street	C2
Beech Street	B2-B3
Beta Road	C2-C1
Booth Lane	C1
Brooks Lane	C3-C2
Canal Terrace	C2
Chester Road	A4-A3
Croxton Lane	A4
Darlington Street	A3-B3
Dawe Street	C4
Dierdene Terrace	B3
East Road	A3
Elm Road	C1
Finney's Lane	A4-B4
Flea Lane	A1
Garfitt Street	B4-C4
Glastonbury Drive	A3
Hannah's Walk	A2-B2
Hayhurst Avenue	A1-B1
High Town	B3
Holmes Chapel Road	C3-C4
Hubert Drive	B1
Kinderton Street	B3-C3
King Edward Street	B2
King's Crescent	B4-C4
King Street	B4-C4-C3
Kitfield Avenue	B1-C1
Lewin Street	B3-B2-C2-C1
Lichfield Street	C4
Long Lane	B1
Longwood Close	B2
Lower Street	B3
Manor Fields	B1
Manor Lane	A2-B2
Mill Lane	A2
Nantwich Road	A1-A2-A3
New King Street	B4-C4
Newton Bank	A4-A3
Newton Heath	A3
Orchard Close	C1
Park Road	A2-B2
Pepper Street	B4-B3
Prosperity Way	C3
Queen Street	B2-B3
Rolt Crescent	A1-B1
Roy Lance Drive	B2
St Anne's Avenue	B1-C1
St Anne's Road	A3-B3-B2-B1
St Michaels Way	A3-B3
School Walk	B4
Seddon Street	B4
Southway	B3
Sutton Lane	B1-B2-C2
The Crescent	A3
Walker Drive	B1
Wavertree Drive	A1
Webbs Lane	B4
West Avenue	B4
West Street	B3
Westlands Road	A3-A2
Wheelock Street	A3-B3
White Horse Alley	B2
Wych House Lane	B3-C3

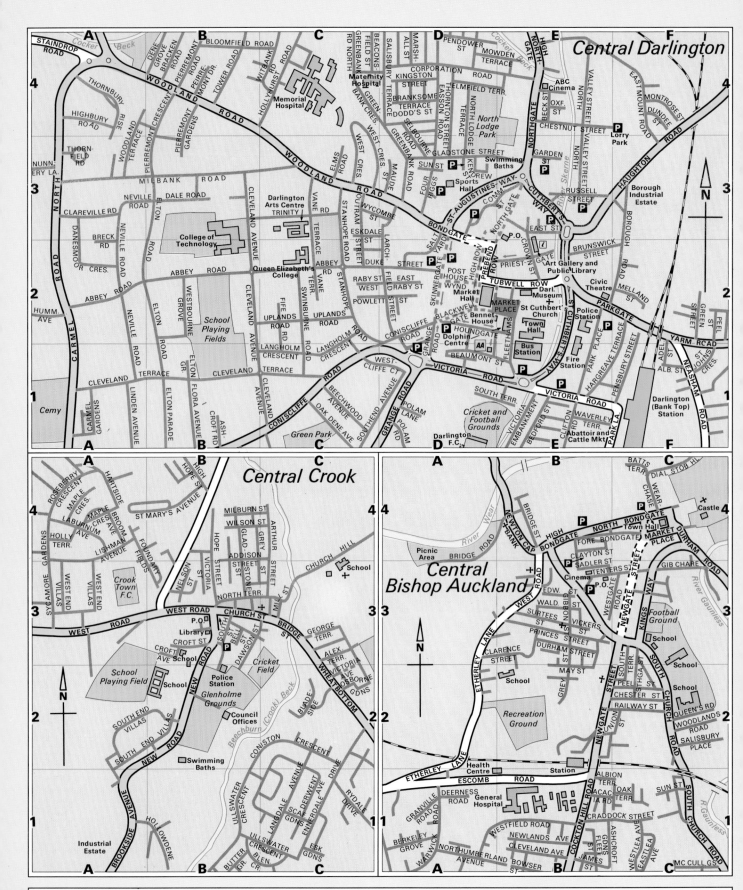

Darlington

Railways and Darlington have gone together since 1825, when George Stephenson's *Locomotion*, the world's first public steam train, passed through on its historic journey from Witton Park to Stockton-on-Tees. The *Locomotion* is now on show with other rolling stock at the Darlington Railway Museum. Appropriately, this is at North Road Station, which is one of the country's earliest.

The town became a major industrial centre during the industrial revolution, and a number of Georgian houses can be seen in the Market Square area. Bennet House, a former merchant's residence, is used side by side with community service organisations, and it stands side by side with the new Dolphin Centre, the most recent addition to the town's leisure facilities. The Parish Church of St Cuthbert is 12th-century, and the Edwardian style of the 1907 Civic Theatre has been carefully preserved.

Bishop Auckland's castle has been the seat of the Bishops of Durham since the 12th century, and stands in an extensive park which is now owned by the local council.

Crook lies between the twin peaks of Mount Pleasant and Dowfold Hill, and has the unusual feature of the 'Blue Stone' or 'Devil's Stone'. Preserved in the Market Place, the stone is thought to have come from Borrowdale in the Lake District, during the Ice Age.

22

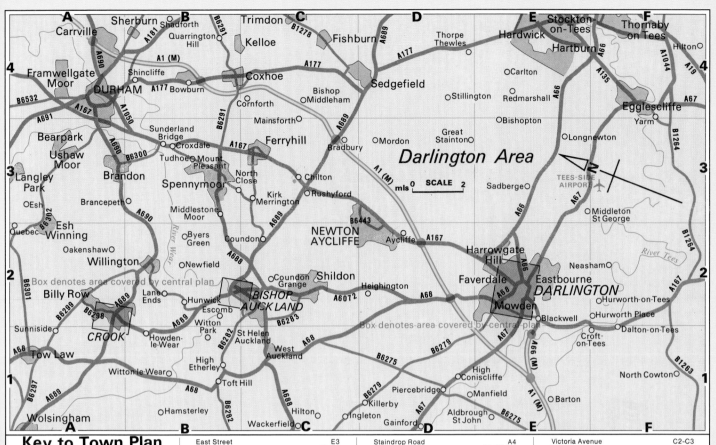

Key to Town Plan and Area Plan

Town Plan

AA Recommended roads
Restricted roads
Other roads
Buildings of interest   Town Hall
One Way Streets
Car Parks   P
Parks and open spaces
Churches   ✝

Area Plan

A roads
B roads
Locations   Mount Pleasant○
Urban area

Street Index with Grid Reference

Darlington

Abbey Road	A2-B2-C2
Adelaide Street	F1-F2
Albert Street	F1
Ashcroft Road	B1
Beaconsfield Street	C4
Beaumont Street	D1-E1
Beck Street	E4
Bedford Street	E1
Beechwood Avenue	C1
Blackwellgate	D2
Bloomfield Road	B4-C4
Bondgate	D2-D3
Borough Road	E2-F2-F3
Bracken Road	B4
Branksome Terrace	D4
Breck Road	A2
Brunswick Street	E2-F2
Carmel Gardens	A1
Carmel Road North	A1-A2-A3-A4
Chestnut Street	E4
Clareville Road	A3
Cleveland Avenue	B3-B2-B1-C1
Cleveland Terrace	A1-B1-C1
Clifton Road	E1
Commercial Street	D3-E3
Coniscliffe Road	B1-C1-D1-D2
Corporation Road	D4-E4
Crown Street	E2-E3
Cuthbert's Way	E3
Dale Road	B3
Danesmoor Crescent	A2-A3
Dene Grove	B4
Dodd's Street	D4
Duke Street	C2-D2
Dundee Street	F4
Easson Road	D3-D4
East Mount Street	E4-F4-F3
East Raby Street	D2
East Street	E3
Elmfield Terrace	D4-E4
Elms Road	C3
Elton Grove	B1
Elton Parade	B1
Elton Road	B1-B2-A2-B2-B3
Eskdale Street	C3-D3
Fife Road	C1-C2
Fleethams	E1-E2
Flora Avenue	B1
Four Riggs	D3
Garden Street	E3
Gladstone Street	D3-E3
Grange Road	C1-D1-D2
Greenbank Crescent	C4-D4
Greenbank Road	D3-D4
Greenbank Road North	C4
Green Street	F2
Hargreave Terrace	E1-F1-F2
Haughton Road	E3-F3-F4
Highbury Road	A4
High Northgate	E4
High Row	D2
Hollyhurst Road	B4-C4
Houndgate	D2-E2
Hummersknott Avenue	A2
Kendrew Street	D3
Kingston Street	D4
Langholm Crescent	B1-C1-C2
Larchfield Street	D2-D3
Linden Avenue	A1
Market Place	D2-E2
Marshall Street	D4
Maude Street	D3
Melland Street	F2
Milbank Road	A3-B3-C3
Montrose Street	F4
Mowden Terrace	D4-E4
Neasham Road	F1-F2
Neville Road	A1-A2-A3-B3
Northgate	D2-D3-E3-E4
North Lodge Terrace	D3-D4
Nunnery Lane	A3
Oak Dene Avenue	C1
Outram Street	C2-C3
Oxford Street	E4
Parkgate	E2-F2
Park Lane	E1-F1
Park Place	E1-E2
Peel Street	F2
Pendower Street	D4
Pensbury Street	F1-F2
Pierremont Crescent	B3-B4
Pierremont Drive	B4
Pierremont Gardens	B3-B4
Pierremont Road	B4
Polam Lane	D1
Polam Road	D1
Post House Wynd	D2
Powlett Street	C2-D2
Prebend Row	D2
Priestgate	D2-E2
Raby Street West	C2-D2
Russell Street	E3
St Augustines Way	D3-E3
St Cuthbert's Way	E1-E2
St Johns Crescent	F1
Salisbury Terrace	D4
Salt Yard	D2-D3
Selbourne Road	D3-D4
Skinnergate	D2-D3
Southend Avenue	C1-D1
South Terrace	D1-E1

Staindrop Road	A4
Stanhope Road	C3-C2-D2
Swinburne Road	C1-C2
Sun Street	D3
Thornbury Rise	A3-A4
Thornfield Road	A3
Thornton Street	D3-D4
Tower Road	B4
Trinity Road	B3-C3
Tubwell Row	D2-E2
Uplands Road	B2-C2
Valley Street North	E3-E4
Vane Terrace	C2-C3
Victoria Embankment	E1
Victoria Road	D1-E1
Waverley Terrace	E1
Westbourne Grove	B2
Westcliffe Court	C1-D1
West Crescent	C3-C4
Witbank Road	C4
Woodland Road	A4-B4-C4-C3-D3
Woodland Terrace	A3-A4
Wycombe Street	C3-D3
Yarm Road	F1-F2

Crook

Addison Street	B4-C4
Alexandra Terrace	C3
Arthur Street	C3-C4
Bell Street	B3
Bladeside	C2
Blencathra Crescent	B1-C1
Bridge Street	C3
Brookside Avenue	A1
Broom Avenue	A4
Buttermere Grove	B1
Church Hill	C3-C4
Church Street	B3-C3
Coniston Crescent	B1-B2-C2
Croft Avenue	B3
Croft Street	B3
Dawson Street	B2-B3-C3
Derwent Avenue	B1
Ennerdale Drive	C1-C2
Esk Gardens	C1
Foundary Fields	A4-A3-B3
George Terrace	C3
Gladstone Street	B3-B4
Grey Street	B3-B4
Hartside	A4
High Hope Street	B4
Hollowdene	A1-B1
Holly Terrace	A4
Hope Street	B3-B4
Laburnum Avenue	A4
Langdale Avenue	C1-C2
Lishman Avenue	A4
Maple Crescent	A4
Milburn Street	B4-C4
Mill Street	C3
Nelson Street	B3
New Road	A2-B2-B3
North Terrace	B3-C3
Osborne Gardens	A4
Roseberry Crescent	A4
Rydale Drive	C1
St Mary's Avenue	A4-B4
Scafell Gardens	C1
Southend Villas	A2-B2
South Street	B3
Sycamore Gardens	A3-A4
Ullswater Crescent	B1-C1

Victoria Avenue	C2-C3
Victoria Street	B3-B4
West End Villas	A3
West Road	A3-B3
Wheatbottom	C2-C3
Wilson Street	B4-C4

Bishop Auckland

Acacia Road	B1-C1
Albion Terrace	B1-C1
Ashcroft Gardens	B1
Batts Terrace	C4
Berkeley Grove	A1
Bowser Street	B4
Bridge Road	A3-A4-B4
Bridge Street	B4
Chester Street	B2-C2
Clarence Street	A3-B3
Clayton Street	B4
Cleveland Avenue	B1
Cockton Hill Road	B1-B2
Craddock Street	B1-C1
Deerness Road	A1
Dial Stob Hill	C4
Durham Road	C3-C4
Durham Street	B3
Eastlea Avenue	C1
Edward Street	B3
Escomb Road	A1-B1
Etherley Lane	A1-A2-A3-B3
Fleet Street	B1
Fore Bondgate	B4-C4
Gib Chare	C3
Gibbon Street	B3
Granville Road	A1
Grey Street	B2-B3
High Bondgate	B4
James Street	B1
Kings Way	C3
McCullogh Gardens	C1
Market Place	C4
May Street	B2-B3
Newgate Street	B2-C2-C3-C4
Newlands Avenue	B1
Newton Cap Bank	B4
North Bondgate	B4-C4
Northumberland Avenue	A1-B1
Oak Terrace	C1
Peel Street	C2
Princes Street	B3
Queen's Road	C2
Railway Street	B2-C2
Sadler Street	B3
Salisbury Place	C2
South Church Road	C1-C2-C3
Southgate Street	C2-C3
South Terrace	C2-C3
Sun Street	C1
Surtees Street	B3
Tenters Street	B3-C3
Union Street	B2-C2
Vickers Street	B3
Waldon Street	B3
Warwick Road	A1
Wearchase	C4
Westfield Road	A1-B1
Westgate Road	B3-C3
Westlea Avenue	C1
West Road	B3-B4
Woodlands Road	C2

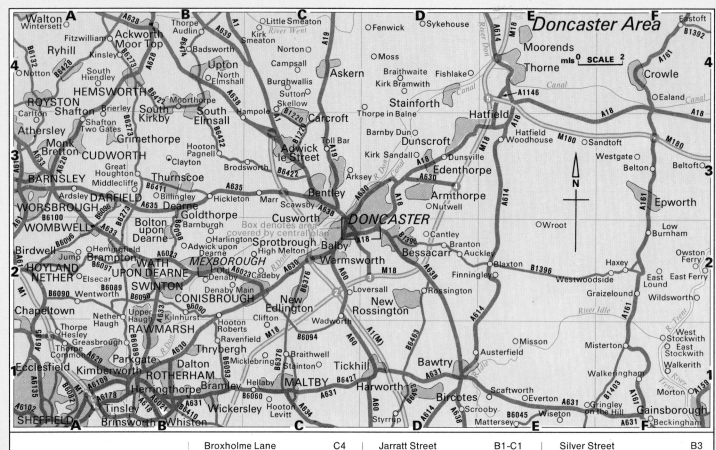

Key to Town Plan and Area Plan

Town Plan
- A A Recommended roads
- Other roads
- Restricted roads
- Buildings of interest   Hall
- Car Parks   P
- AA Service Centre   AA
- Parks and open spaces
- One way streets

Area Plan
- A roads
- B roads
- Locations   Ashton O
- Urban area

Street Index — with grid reference

Central Doncaster

Alderson Drive	D2-E2-E3
Apley Road	C2
Ardeen Road	E4-F4
Avondale Road	F3
Bawtry Road	F1-F2
Belle Vue Avenue	E1-F1-F2
Bennetthorpe	D2-E2
Broxholme Lane	C4
Buckingham Road	E4
Carr House Road	C1-D1-E1-E2
Chequer Avenue	C1-D1-E1
Chequer Road	C1-C2-C3
Christchurch Road	B4-C4-C3
Church View	A4-B4
Church Way	B4-C4
Cleveland Street	A1-A2-B2-B3
Clumber Road	E1
College Road	B2-C2
Copley Road	B4-C4
Craithie Road	E4-F4-F3
Cunningham Road	C1-C2
Danum Road	D1-E1-E2
Dockin Hill Road	B4-C4
Dublin Road	F4
Duke Street	A3-B3-B2
East Laithe Gate	B3-C3
Elmfield Road	C1-C2
Firbeck Road	D2-E2
Franklin Crescent	E2-E3
Glamis Road	F3
Glyn Avenue	C4
Goldsborough Road	E3-F3
Granby Crescent	E2
Greendyke Road	A1-B1
Grey Friar's Road	A4-B4
Hallgate	B3-C3
Hamilton Road	D1
Hampton Road	E3-E4
Harewood Road	F3
High Street	B3
Highfield Road	C4-D4
Holyrood Road	E4-E3-F3
Imperial Crescent	E4
Jarratt Street	B1-C1
King's Road	C4
Lakeen Road	F4
Lawn Avenue	C3-D3
Lawn Road	C3-D3
Leger Way	F2-F3
Leicester Avenue	F3
Limetree Avenue	D1-E1
Low Fisher Gate	B4
Manor Drive	E2-E3
Marlborough Road	E4
Milton Walk	B1-B2
Neterhall Road	B4-C4
North Bridge Road	A4
Osborne Road	E4
Oxford Street	B1
Palmer Street	C1
Park Road	C3-C4
Queens Road	C4-D4
Rainton Road	C1
Regent Square	C3
Roberts Road	A1
Roman Road	D1-D2
Rufford Road	E1
St Anne's Road	F1-F2
St Cecilia's Road	E1-F1
St Helen's Road	E1-F1
St Hilda's Road	E1-F1
St James Street	A1-A2-B2
St Mary's Road	D4
St Sepulchre Gate West	A1-A2
St Ursula's Road	F1
Sandy Lane	E1
Sandbeck Road	E1-E2
Sandringham Road	E3-F3-F4
Shaftesbury Avenue	F3
Silver Street	B3
South Parade	C3-C2-D2
South Street	C1
Stockil Road	D1
Theobald Avenue	D1
Thoresby Avenue	E1
Thorne Road	C3-C4-D4
Trafford Way	A3-A2-B2-B1-B3
Town Moor Avenue	D4-E4-E3-F3-F2
Tudor Road	F4
Waterdale	B2-B3-C3
Welbeck Road	D2-E2
Whitburn Road	C2
Windsor Road	D4-E4
Wood Street	B3
Zetland Road	E4-F4-F3

Mexborough

Adwick Road	C2-C3-C4-B4
Albert Road	B3-B4
Alexandra Road	B3-C3
Argyle Road	B3
Auckland Road	C3
Bank Street	B2-B1-C1
Carlyle Road	B2-B3
Cemetery Road	A4-B4
Church Street	C1
College Road	B2-C2
Cromwell Road	B3
Dolcliff Road	A2-A3-A2-B2
Garden Street	A2-B2
Genoa Street	C2-C3

Doncaster

Diana Rigg, Kevin Keegan and Freddie Trueman are just a few of the popular figures of fame who come from Doncaster, a busy commercial and industrial town which is set in a predominantly coalmining area and happens to be the birthplace of a good many celebrities. The town is also notable for its racecourse, which has been the site of the St Leger since the late 18th century, and it is well provided with professional football from Doncaster Rovers, who play in the Canon League.

Amongst the town's interesting older buildings, the 19th-century Church of St George was designed by Sir Gilbert Scott, and one of the few surviving Victorian Mansion Houses can also be seen here. The local Museum and Art Gallery offers displays of geology, natural history and the past of the Doncaster area. A museum of social history is housed in the attractive setting of Cusworth Hall, a fine 18th-century Palladian mansion which stands on the outskirts of the town.

Mexborough was a small village until the changes of the early 19th century fostered its expansion into an industrial town. The modern developments of streets and housing in more recent years have left Mexborough very little in the way of older buildings, but the Parish Church of St John the Baptist has retained vestiges of its Norman origins.

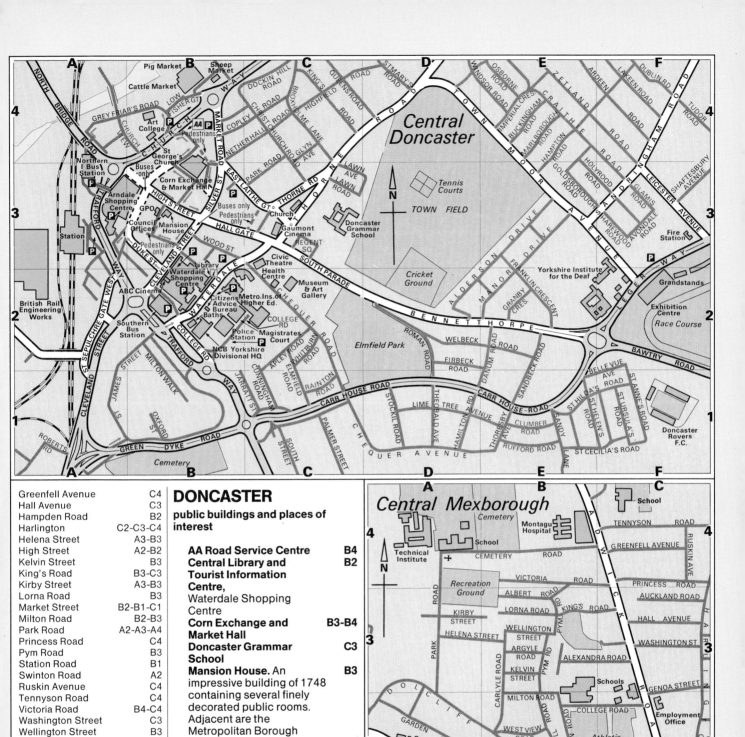

Central Doncaster

DONCASTER
public buildings and places of interest

AA Road Service Centre	B4
Central Library and Tourist Information Centre, Waterdale Shopping Centre	B2
Corn Exchange and Market Hall	B3-B4
Doncaster Grammar School	C3
Mansion House. An impressive building of 1748 containing several finely decorated public rooms. Adjacent are the Metropolitan Borough Council Offices	B3
Museum and Art Gallery*	C2
St George's Church Designed by Sir Gilbert Scott and completed in 1858, it stands on the site of a Norman church destroyed by fire in 1853. The pinnacled tower rises to 170 feet.	B4
Technical College	B2-C2

Central Mexborough

DONCASTER
Britain's oldest racecourse has long been a mecca for punters — amongst its better known visitors is Charles Dickens, who in 1875 watched the 110th St Leger from the ornate and still-used 18th-century grandstand.

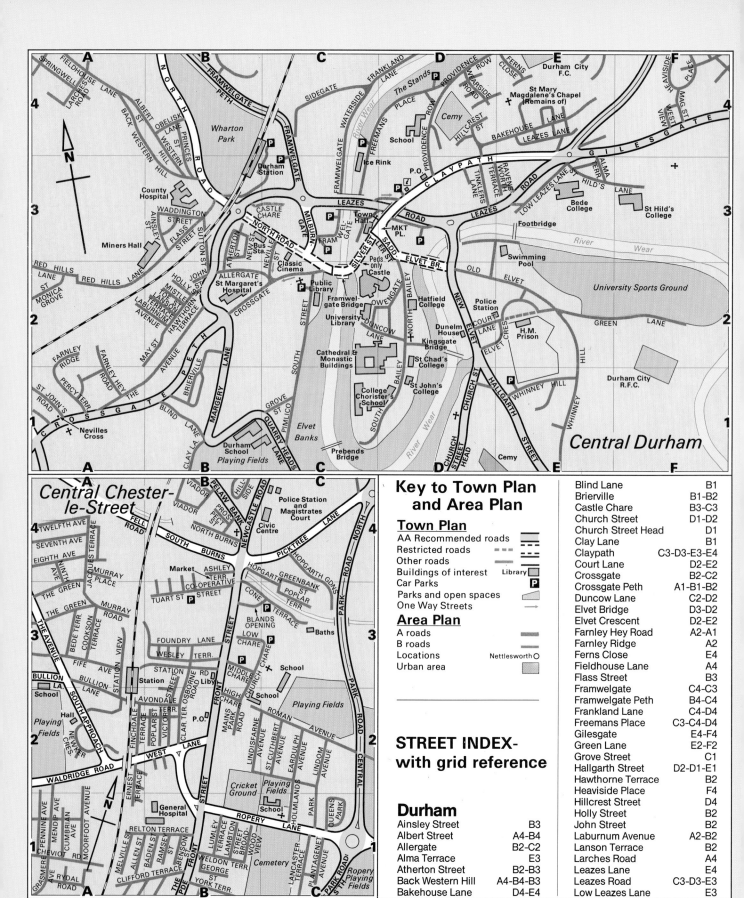

Central Durham

Central Chester-le-Street

Durham

The castle and the cathedral stand side by side high above the city like sentinels, dramatically symbolising the military and religious power Durham wielded in the past. Its origins date from about 995 when the remains of St Cuthbert arrived from Lindisfarne and his shrine was a popular centre of pilgrimage. Soon after that early fortifications were built, later replaced by a stone

castle which became the residence of the Prince-Bishops of Durham – powerful feudal rulers appointed by the King. Today the city's university, the oldest in England after Oxford and Cambridge, occupies the castle and most of the buildings around peaceful, secluded Palace Green. The splendid Norman cathedral, sited on the other side of the Green, is considered to be one of the finest in Europe. Its combination of strength and size, tempered with grace and beauty, is awe-inspiring.

Under the shadow of these giants the old city streets, known as vennels, ramble down the bluff past the 17th-century Bishop Cosin's House and the old grammar school, to the thickly-wooded banks of the Wear. Here three historic bridges link the city's heart with the pleasant Georgian suburbs on the other side of the river.

Although Durham is not an industrial city, it has become the venue for the North-East miners' annual Gala Day in July.

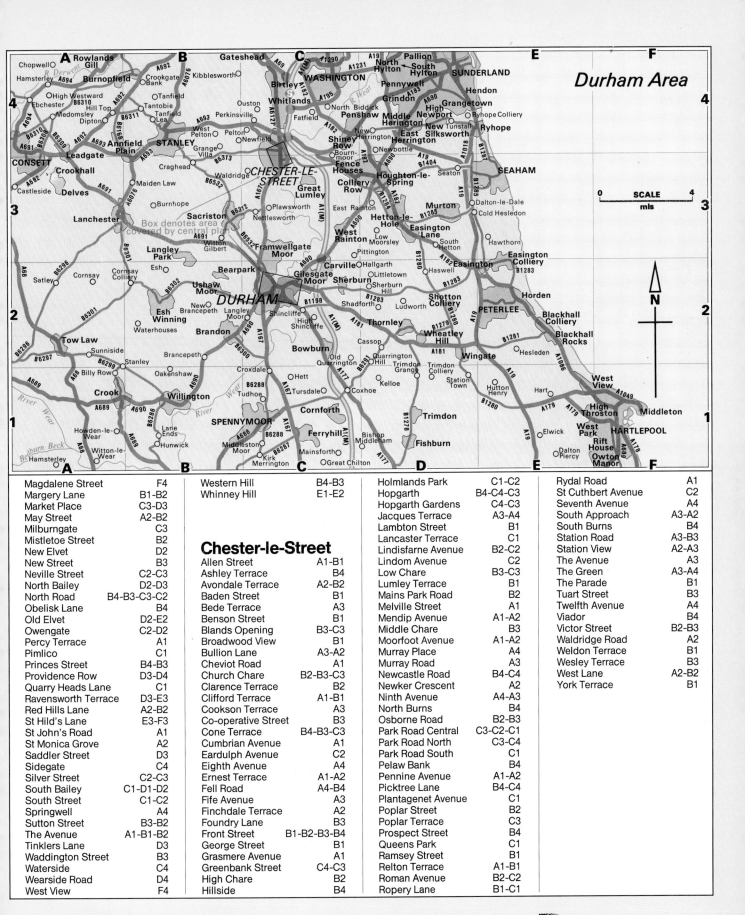

Durham Area

Magdalene Street	F4
Margery Lane	B1-B2
Market Place	C3-D3
May Street	A2-B2
Milburngate	C3
Mistletoe Street	B2
New Elvet	D2
New Street	B3
Neville Street	C2-C3
North Bailey	D2-D3
North Road	B4-B3-C3-C2
Obelisk Lane	B4
Old Elvet	D2-E2
Owengate	C2-D2
Percy Terrace	A1
Pimlico	C1
Princes Street	B4-B3
Providence Row	D3-D4
Quarry Heads Lane	C1
Ravensworth Terrace	D3-E3
Red Hills Lane	A2-B2
St Hild's Lane	E3-F3
St John's Road	A1
St Monica Grove	A2
Saddler Street	D3
Sidegate	C4
Silver Street	C2-C3
South Bailey	C1-D1-D2
South Street	C1-C2
Springwell	A4
Sutton Street	B3-B2
The Avenue	A1-B1-B2
Tinklers Lane	D3
Waddington Street	B3
Waterside	C4
Wearside Road	D4
West View	F4

Western Hill	B4-B3
Whinney Hill	E1-E2

Chester-le-Street

Allen Street	A1-B1
Ashley Terrace	B4
Avondale Terrace	A2-B2
Baden Street	B1
Bede Terrace	A3
Benson Street	B1
Blands Opening	B3-C3
Broadwood View	B1
Bullion Lane	A3-A2
Cheviot Road	A1
Church Chare	B2-B3-C3
Clarence Terrace	B2
Clifford Terrace	A1-B1
Cookson Terrace	A3
Co-operative Street	B3
Cone Terrace	B4-B3-C3
Cumbrian Avenue	A1
Eardulph Avenue	C2
Eighth Avenue	A4
Ernest Terrace	A1-A2
Fell Road	A4-B4
Fife Avenue	A3
Finchdale Terrace	A2
Foundry Lane	B3
Front Street	B1-B2-B3-B4
George Street	B1
Grasmere Avenue	A1
Greenbank Street	C4-C3
High Chare	B2
Hillside	B4

Holmlands Park	C1-C2
Hopgarth	B4-C4-C3
Hopgarth Gardens	C4-C3
Jacques Terrace	A3-A4
Lambton Street	B1
Lancaster Terrace	C1
Lindisfarne Avenue	B2-C2
Lindom Avenue	C2
Low Chare	B3-C3
Lumley Terrace	B1
Mains Park Road	B2
Melville Street	A1
Mendip Avenue	A1-A2
Middle Chare	B3
Moorfoot Avenue	A1-A2
Murray Place	A4
Murray Road	A3
Newcastle Road	B4-C4
Newker Crescent	A2
Ninth Avenue	A4-A3
North Burns	B4
Osborne Road	B2-B3
Park Road Central	C3-C2-C1
Park Road North	C3-C4
Park Road South	C1
Pelaw Bank	B4
Pennine Avenue	A1-A2
Picktree Lane	B4-C4
Plantagenet Avenue	C1
Poplar Street	B2
Poplar Terrace	C3
Prospect Street	B4
Queens Park	C1
Ramsey Street	B1
Relton Terrace	A1-B1
Roman Avenue	B2-C2
Ropery Lane	B1-C1

Rydal Road	A1
St Cuthbert Avenue	C2
Seventh Avenue	A4
South Approach	A3-A2
South Burns	B4
Station Road	A3-B3
Station View	A2-A3
The Avenue	A3
The Green	A3-A4
The Parade	B1
Tuart Street	B3
Twelfth Avenue	A4
Viador	B4
Victor Street	B2-B3
Waldridge Road	A2
Weldon Terrace	B1
Wesley Terrace	B3
West Lane	A2-B2
York Terrace	B1

DURHAM
High above the wooded banks of the River Wear, Durham's castle and cathedral crown the steep hill on which the city is built. They share the site with several of the university's attractive old buildings.

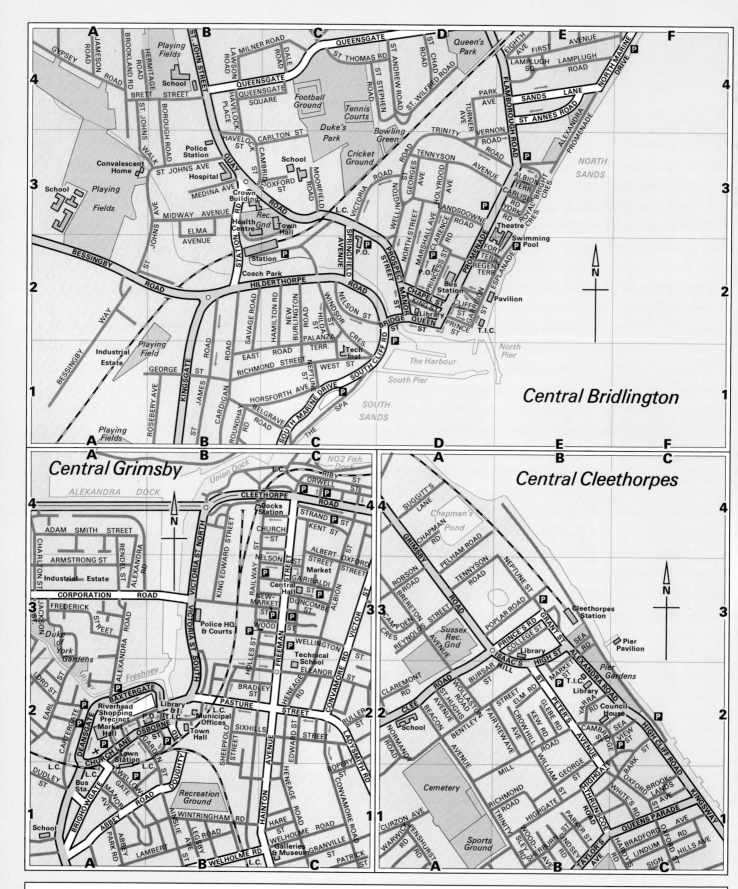

East coast towns

Scarborough is a classic seaside resort. It has good beaches and all the amusements required of a popular holiday destination, and it also shares in the grandeur of the impressive 12th-century castle ruins which stand on a headland between its two principal beaches.

Bridlington has thrived and flourished as a resort, with fine beaches sheltered by towering Flamborough Head. The older part of the town has several Georgian buildings, and the Bayle Gate (part of former priory) is now a museum. Nearby Sewerby Hall is a Georgian country house set in extensive parkland, and includes a small zoo.

Grimsby was little more than a village not so very long ago, but in the 19th century it rapidly expanded into a major River Humber port. The medieval Parish Church of St James still has some 14th-century features, and also worth seeing are the Welholme Galleries' museum and art gallery.

Cleethorpes has dealt effectively with the vagaries of tide and weather by installing an artificial beach and wave machine in its seafront Leisure Centre pool. Succulent oysters were the pride of the town in its fishing village days, but now visitors prefer to come for the sandy beaches and the entertainments which have made it such a popular resort. Sidney Park is noted for its aviaries and an arch made from a whale's jawbone.

LEGEND

Town Plan

AA Recommended roads
Other roads
Restricted roads
Buildings of interest **Hall**
Churches +
Car parks **P**
Parks and open spaces
One way streets →

Street Index with Grid Reference

Bridlington

Albion Terrace	E3
Alexandra Promenade	E3-E4
Belgrave Road	B1-C1
Bessingby Road	A2-B2
Bessingby Way	A1-A2
Borough Road	B4-B3
Brett Street	A4-B4
Bridge Street	D2
Bright Crescent	D3
Brookland Road	A4
Cambridge Street	B3-C3
Cardigan Road	B1-B2
Carlisle Road	E3
Carlton Street	B3-C3
Chapel Street	D2
Clarence Road	D2-D3
Cliff Street	D2
Dale Road	C4
East Road	B1-C1
Eighth Avenue	E4
Elma Avenue	B2-B3
Esplanade	D2-E2
First Avenue	E4
Flamborough Road	E4-E3
Fort Terrace	D2
Garrison Street	D2
George Street	B1
Gypsey Road	A4
Hamilton Road	C1-C2
Havelock Place	B4
Havelock Street	B3
Hermitage Road	A4-B4
Hilderthorpe Road	B2-C2
Holyrood Avenue	D3
Horsforth Avenue	B1-C1
Jameson Road	A4
Kingsgate	B1-B2
King Street	D2
Lamplugh Road	E4
Lamplugh Square	E4
Lansdowne Road	D3
Lawson Road	B4
Manor Street	D2
Marshall Avenue	D2-D3
Medina Avenue	B3
Midway Avenue	B3
Milner Road	B4-C4
Moorfield Road	C3
Nelson Street	C2
Neptune Street	C1
New Burlington Road	C2
North Marine Drive	E4-F4
North Street	D2-D3
Oxford Street	C3
Palanza Terrace	C1-C2
Park Avenue	D4
Prince Street	D2
Princess Street	D2
Promenade	D2-D3-E3
Prospect Street	D2
Quay Road	B3-C3
Queensgate	B4-C4
Queensgate Square	B4-C4
Queen Street	D2
Regent Terrace	D2
Richmond Street	B1-C1
Rosebery Avenue	B1
Roundhay Road	B1
Royal Crescent	D3
St Andrew Road	D4
St Annes Road	E4
St Chad Road	D4
St Georges Avenue	D3
St Hilda Street	C2
St James Road	B1-B2
St Johns Avenue	A2-B3
St John Street	B4
St Johns Walk	A4-A3-B3
St Stephen Road	C4-D4
St Thomas Road	C4-D4
St Wilfred Road	D4
Sands Lane	E4
Savage Road	B1-B2
South Cliff Road	C1-D1-D2
South Marine Drive	C1
Springfield Avenue	C3-C2
Station Road	B2-B3
Tennyson Avenue	D3
The Spa	C1
Trinity Road	D3-E3
Turner Avenue	D4
Vernon Road	D2-E3
Victoria Road	C3-D3

Wellington Road	D3
West Street	D3
Windsor Crescent	C2-C1
York Road	E3

Grimsby

Abbey Park Road	A1
Abbey Road	A1-B1
Adam Smith Street	A4
Ainsley Street	B1
Albert Street	C4-C3
Albion Street	C3-C4
Alexandra Road	A2-A3-A4
Armstrong Street	A3
Baxtergate	A2-B2
Bradley Street	B2-C2
Brighowgate	A1
Buller Street	C2
Cartergage	A2
Charlton Street	A4-A3
Church Lane	A1-A2
Church Street	B4-C4
Cleethorpes Road	B4-C4
Convamore Road	C1-C2-C3
Corporation Road	A3-B3
Deansgate	A2
Doughty Road	B1-B2
Dudley Street	A1
Duncombe Street	C1
Earl Street	A2
Edward Street	C2
Eleanor Street	C2
Frederick Street	C2
Freeman Street	C3-C4
Garden Street	B2-B1
Garibaldi Street	C3
Granville Street	C1
Hainton Avenue	C1-C2
Hare Street	C1
Heneage Road	C1-C2
Holles Street	B2-B3
Jackson Street	A3
Kent Street	A4
King Edward Street	B3-B4
Ladysmith Road	C1-C2
Lambert Road	A1-B1
Legsby Avenue	B1
Lord Street	A2
Manor Avenue	A1
Nelson Street	C3
Newmarket Street	B3-C3
Orwell Street	C4
Osborne Street	A2-B2
Oxford Street	C3
Pasture Street	B2-C2
Patrick Street	C1
Railway Street	B3-B4
Rendel Street	A4-A3
Riby Street	C4
Ropery Street	C1-C2
Sheepfold Street	B2
Sixhills Street	B2-C2
Strand Street	A4
Victor Street	C3
Victoria Street North	B3-B4
Victoria Street South	B3-B2
Welholme Road	B1-C1
Wellington Street	C3
Wellowgate	A1
Wintringham Road	B1
Wood Street	B3-C3

Cleethorpes

Alexandra Road	B3-B2-C2
Bark Street	C1-C2
Beacon Avenue	A2-A1
Bentley Street	A2-A3
Bradford Avenue	C1
Brereton Avenue	A3
Brooklands Avenue	C1
Bursar Street	A2
Cambridge Street	B2
Campden Crescent	A3
Chapman Road	A4
Claremont Road	A2
Clee Road	A2-A3
College Street	B3
Crowhill Avenue	B2
Curzon Avenue	A1
Elm Road	B2
Fairview Avenue	A2-B2
George Street	B1-B2
Glebe Road	B2
Grant Street	B3
Grimsby Road	A4-A3
Hardy's Lane	C1
High Cliff Road	C2-C1
Highgate	B1-B2
High Street	B2-B3
Isaac's Hill	B3-B2
Kew Road	B2
Kingsway	C1
Lindsey Road	B1
Lindum Road	C1
Market Street	B2
Mill Road	B1-B2
Neptune Street	B3
Normandy Road	A2
Oxford Street	C1
Parker Street	B1
Pelham Road	A3-A4
Penshurst Road	A1
Poplar Road	A3-B3
Prince's Road	B3
Queens Parade	C1
Reynolds Street	A3
Richmond Road	B1

Robson Road	A3
St Hughs Avenue	A2
St Peter's Avenue	B2
Sea Road	B3
Sea View Street	C2
Sherburn Street	B1
Sign Hills Avenue	C1
Suggitt's Lane	A4
Taylor's Avenue	B1
Tennyson Road	A3
Thrunscoe Road	B1
Trinity Road	B1
Warwick Road	A1
White's Road	C1
William Street	B2-B1
Wollaston Road	A2
Woodsley Avenue	B1
Yarra Road	B2

Scarborough

Aberdeen Walk	B3-C3
Albion Road	C2
Avenue Road	A2-B2
Avenue Victoria	C1-C2-D2-D1
Bar Street	C3
Bellevue Street	B3
Belvedere Place	C1-D1
Belvedere Road	C1-D1
Blenheim Terrace	B4-C4
Cambridge Street	B3
Candler Street	A2-A3-B3
Castlegate	D4
Castle Road	B3-B4-C4-D4
Columbus Ravine	A4-B4-B3-A3-B3
Commercial Street	A2-B2
Cromwell Road	B2
Cross Street	C3-C4
Crown Terrace	C2
Dean Road	A3-B3-B4
Durham Street	B4
Eastborough	C3-C4-D4
Esplanade	C2-D2-D1
Esplanade Gardens	C1-C2
Esplanade Road	C1-C2
Falsgrave Road	A2-B2
Filey Road	C2-C1-D1
Fore Shore Road	C3-C4-D4
Garfield Road	A3
Gladstone Road	A2-B2-B3
Glen Bridge	A3-A4
Gordon Street	A3
Hampton Road	A2
Hibernia Street	A2-A3
Highfield	A1-A2
Holbeck Avenue	D1
Holbeck Hill	D1
Holbeck Road	D1
Hope Street	B4
Hoxton Road	A3-B3
James Street	B3-B4
King Street	C3
Lonesborough Road	B2
Long Westgate	C4-D4
Lowdale Avenue	A4
Manor Road	A2-A3
Marine Drive	D4
Moorland Road	B4
Mountside	C1
Nares Street	A3
Nelson Street	B3
Newborough	C3
North Marine Road	B4-C4
North Street	B3-C3
Northstead Manor Drive	A4
Northway	B3
Oak Road	A1-A2
Oliver's Mount Road	B1-C1
Oriel Crescent	B1
Paradise	C4-D4
Park Avenue	A1-A2
Park Street	A2
Peasholm Drive	A3-A4
Princess Street	D4
Prince of Wales Terrace	C2
Prospect Road	A3-B3
Queen Margaret's Road	B1-C1
Queens Parade	B4
Queen Street	C3-C4
Raleigh Street	A3
Ramsey Street	A3
Ramshill Road	C2-C3
Roscoe Street	B2
Rosebery Avenue	A1
Rothbury Street	A3-B3
Royal Albert Drive	B4-C4
Royal Avenue	B2-C2
Ryndleside	A4
St Johns Road	A2
St Martins Avenue	C1
St Sepulchre Street	C4-D4
St Thomas Street	C3-C4
Sandside	D4
Scalby Road	A2
Sea Cliff Road	D1
Seamer Road	A2-A1-B1

Spring Bank	A1
Spring Hill Road	A1
Stepney Avenue	A2
Stepney Road	A2
The Garlands	B1-C1
The Glade	B1-C1
Tindall Street	B3
Tollergate	C4
Trafalgar Road	B4
Trafalgar Square	B4
Trinity Road	B1-C1
Valley Bridge	C2
Valley Bridge Road	B3-C3
Valey Road	A1-A2-B1-B2-C2-C3
Vernon Road	C3
Victoria Park Mount	A4
Victoria Road	B2-B3
Victoria Street	B3
Weaponness Drive	C1
Westborough	B2-B3-C3
Westbourne Grove	B1-B2-C2-C1
Westover Road	B2
West Street	C2-C1-D1
Westwood	B2
Westwood Road	B2
Wrea Lane	B3-B4
Wykeham Street	A2-B2
York Place	B3-C3

Central Scarborough

(map)

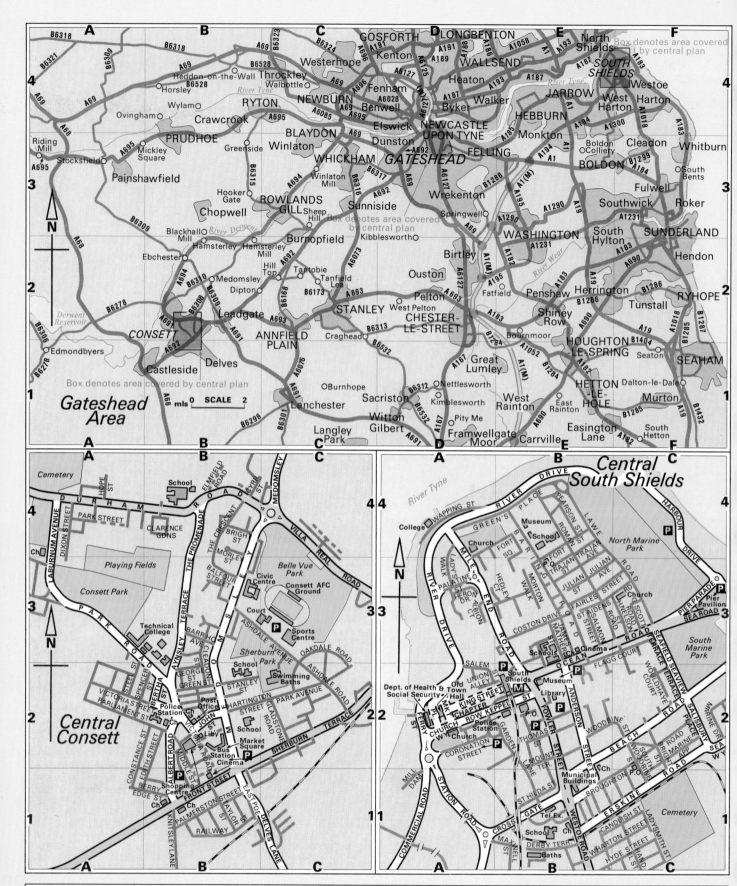

Gateshead

Seven bridges make the link across the Tyne to Newcastle from Gateshead, which is largely a modern town: a disastrous fire in the 19th century destroyed most of its older buildings. One notable escape from the fire was St Mary's Church, which has been heavily restored but still has some of its 12th-century features, and serves as a reminder that this is in fact an ancient Tyneside settlement. The town has suffered in this century too, with the decline of its dock area, but light engineering has come to take the place of its older industries, and the town has world renown today as a venue for national and international events at its celebrated athletics stadium.

South Shields has safe, sandy beaches and a good selection of entertainments and amusements for visitors, and another of its attractions is the South Tyneside Leisure and Gymnastics Centre, where the extensive swimming complex includes a wave machine. Overlooking the market square is the fine 18th-century Old Town Hall — irreverently known by locals as the Pepperpot. The Metal Arts Precinct features the work of local artists, and the Arbeia Roman Fort and Museum can be visited in Baring Street.

Consett was once a steel producing town, and has a pleasant Derwentside setting with a number of attractive parks.

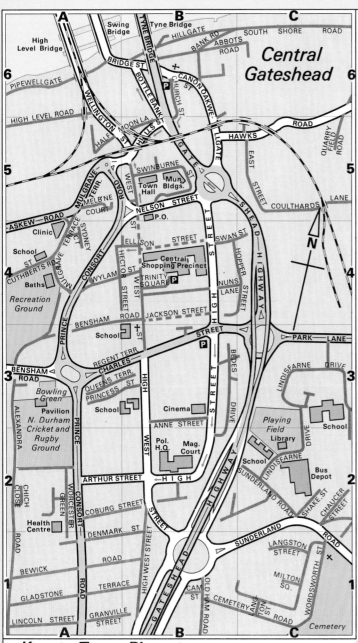

Central Gateshead

High West Street	B1-B2-B3	
Hillgate	B6	
Hills Street	B5	
Hopper Street	B4-C4-B4	
Jackson Street	B4	
Langton Street	C1	
Lincoln Street	A1	
Lindisfarne Drive	C2-C3	
Melbourne Court	A5	
Milton Square	C1	
Mulgrave Terrace	A4-A5	
Nelson Street	B5	
Nuns Lane	B4-C4	
Oakwell Gate	B5-B6	
Old Ham Road	B1	
Park Lane	C3	
Pipewell Gate	A6	
Prince Consort Road	A1-A2-A3-A4-A5-B5	
Princess Street	A3-B3	
Quarryfield Road	C5-C6	
Queens Terrace	A3-B3	
Regent Terrace	A3-B3	
St Cuthberts Road	A4	
Shakespeare Street	C2	
South Shore Road	B6-C6	
Sunderland Road	B1-C1-C2-C1	
Swan Street	B4-C4	
Swinburne Street	B5	
Trinity Square	B4	
Tyne Bridge	B6	
Wellington Street	A6-A5-B5	
West Street	B3-B4-B5	
Worcester Green	A1-A2	
Wordsworth Street	C1	
Wylam Street	A4-B4	

Consett

Albert Road	B1-B2
Ashdale Avenue	B3-C3
Ashdale Road	C2
Aynsley Terrace	B2-B3
Balfour Street	B3
Barr House Avenue	B3
Berry Edge Street	A1-B1
Bertha Street	B2
Bright Street	B4
Clarence Gardens	B4
Cleadon Street	B2-B3
Constance Road	A1-A2-B2
Cyril Street	B4-C4
Delves Lane	B1-C1
Dixon Street	A3-A4
Durham Road	A4-B4
East Parade	B1
Edith Street	A1-B1-B2
Elmfield Road	B4
Front Street	B1
George Street	B2
Gladstone Road	C2
Green Street	B2
Hartington Street	B2-C2
Hope Street	A4
John Street	B2
Knitsley Lane	B1
Laburnum Avenue	A3-A4
Medomsley	B2-B3-B4-C4
Middle Street	B1-B2
Morley Street	B4
Oakdale Road	C2-C3
Palmerston Street	B1
Park Avenue	C2
Park Road	A3-B3-B2-A2
Park Street	A4
Parliament Street	A2-B2
Railway Street	B1
Sherburn Terrace	B2-C2
Spencer Street	A2-B2
Stanley Street	B2
Steel Street	A2-A3
The Crescent	B4
The Promenade	B3-B4
Taylor Street	B1

Victoria Road	B1-B2
Victoria Street	A2-B2
Villa Real Road	C3-C4

South Shields

Albion Court	A3
Anderson Street	B1-B2
Baring Road	B3-B4
Beach Road	B1-B2-C2
Bright Street	C2
Broughton Road	B1-C1-C2
Candlish Street	B1-C1
Chapter Row	A2
Church Way	A2
Commercial Road	A1-A2
Coronation Street	A2
Coston Drive	B3
Crossgate	A1-B1
Derby Terrace	B1
Erskine Road	B1-C1-C2
Fairles Street	B3-C3
Ferry Street	A2
Flagg Court	B2-B3-C3
Fort Square	B3-B4
Fowler Street	B1-B2
Garden Lane	B1-B2
Greens Place	A4-B4
Handel Street	C1
Harbour Drive	C3-C4
Hedley Court	A3-B3
Henry Nelson Street	C3
Heron Drive	A3
Hyde Street	B1-C1
James Mather Street	B3
Julian Avenue	B3-C3
Julian Street	B3
Keppel Street	A2-B2
King Street	A2-B2
Lady's Walk	A3-A4
Ladysmith Street	C1
Lawe Road	B4-C4-C3
Market Place	A2
Marine Approach	C2
Marine Drive	C2
Maxwell Street	A1-B1
Mile End Road	A4-A3-B3-B2
Milldam	A1
Morton Walk	B3
Mount Terrace	B2
Ocean Road	B2-B3-C3
Palatine Street	A3
Pearsons Street	B4
Pier Parade	C3
River Drive	A2-A3-A4-B4-C4
Roman Road	B4-B3-C3
St Aidens Road	B3-C3
St Hilda Street	B1
Salem Street	A2
Salisbury Place	C2
Salmon Street	B3
Scott Road	C3
Sea Road	C3
Sea Way	C2
Seafield Terrace	C2-C3
Seaview Terrace	C2
South Woodbine Street	C1-C2
Station Road	A1-A2
Thomas Street	B2
Trajan Avenue	B4
Trajan Street	B3-B4
Union Alley	A2-B2
Wapping Street	A4
Westoe Road	B1
Wharton Street	B1-C1
Woodbine Street	B2-C2
Wouldhaye Court	C2

Key to Town Plan and Area Plan

Town Plan
AA Recommended roads
Other roads
Restricted roads
Buildings of interest — Cinema
One Way Streets
Parks and open spaces
Car Parks — P
Churches — †
Metro Stations — M

Area Plan
A roads
B roads
Locations — Ripley O
Urban area

Street Index with Grid Reference

Gateshead

Abbots Road	B6-C6
Alexandra Road	A1-A2-A3
Anne Street	B3
Arthur Street	A2-B2
Askew Road	A4-A5
Bank Road	B6
Bedes Drive	B2-B3
Bensham Road	A3-A4-B4
Bewick Road	A1-B1
Bottle Bank	B5-B6
Bridge Street	A6-B6
Camilla Street	B1
Canon Street	B6
Cemetery Road	B1-C1
Charles Street	A3-B3-C3
Chaucer Street	C2
Chichester Close	A2
Church Street	B5-B6
Coburg Street	A2-B2
Coulthards Lane	C5
Denmark Street	A1-B1-B2
East Street	C5
Ellison Street	A4-B4
Gateshead Highway	B1-B2-C2-C3-C4-C5-B5-B6
Gladstone Terrace	A1-B1
Granville Street	A1-B1
Half Moon Lane	A5-B5
Hawks Road	B5-C5-C6
Hector Street	A4-B4
High Level Road	A5-A6
High Street	B2-B3-B4-B5

31

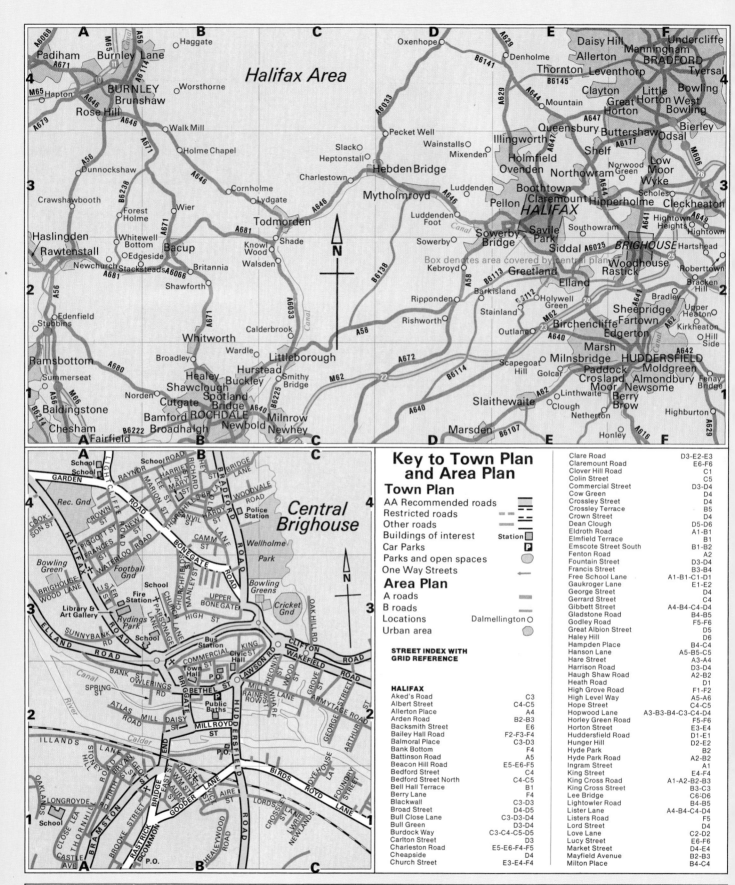

Key to Town Plan and Area Plan

Town Plan
AA Recommended roads
Restricted roads
Other roads
Buildings of interest — Station □
Car Parks — P
Parks and open spaces
One Way Streets

Area Plan
A roads
B roads
Locations — Dalmellington ○
Urban area

STREET INDEX WITH GRID REFERENCE

HALIFAX

Aked's Road	C3
Albert Street	C4-C5
Allerton Place	A4
Arden Road	B2-B3
Backsmith Street	E6
Bailey Hall Road	F2-F3-F4
Balmoral Place	C3-D3
Bank Bottom	F4
Battinson Road	A5
Beacon Hill Road	E5-E6-F5
Bedford Street	C4
Bedford Street North	C4-C5
Bell Hall Terrace	B1
Berry Lane	F4
Blackwall	C3-D3
Broad Street	D4-D5
Bull Close Lane	C3-D3-D4
Bull Green	D3-D4
Burdock Way	C3-C4-C5-D5
Carlton Street	D3
Charleston Road	E5-E6-F4-F5
Cheapside	D4
Church Street	E3-E4-F4
Clare Road	D3-E2-E3
Claremount Road	E6-F6
Clover Hill Road	C1
Colin Street	C5
Commercial Street	D3-D4
Cow Green	D4
Crossley Street	D4
Crossley Terrace	B5
Crown Street	D4
Dean Clough	D5-D6
Eldroth Road	A1-B1
Elmfield Terrace	B1
Emscote Street South	B1-B2
Fenton Road	A2
Fountain Street	D3-D4
Francis Street	B3-B4
Free School Lane	A1-B1-C1-D1
Gaukroger Lane	E1-E2
George Street	D4
Gerrard Street	C4
Gibbett Street	A4-B4-C4-D4
Gladstone Road	B4-B5
Godley Road	F5-F6
Great Albion Street	D5
Haley Hill	D6
Hampden Place	B4-C4
Hanson Lane	A5-B5-C5
Hare Street	A3-A4
Harrison Road	D3-D4
Haugh Shaw Road	A2-B2
Heath Road	D1
High Grove Road	F1-F2
High Level Way	A5-A6
Hope Street	C4-C5
Hopwood Lane	A3-B3-B4-C3-C4-D4
Horley Green Road	F5-F6
Horton Street	E3-E4
Huddersfield Road	D1-E1
Hunger Hill	D2-E2
Hyde Park	B2
Hyde Park Road	A2-B2
Ingram Street	A1
King Street	E4-F4
King Cross Road	A1-A2-B2-B3
King Cross Street	B3-C3
Lee Bridge	C6-D6
Lightowler Road	B4-B5
Lister Lane	A4-B4-C4-D4
Listers Road	F5
Lord Street	D4
Love Lane	C2-D2
Lucy Street	E6-F6
Market Street	D4-E4
Mayfield Avenue	B2-B3
Milton Place	B4-C4

Halifax

Rising up from the eastern edge of the Pennine Hills, this old industrial town occupies a magnificent setting and offers an unexpected wealth of fine buildings. Jewel in the crown is Piece Hall, a unique 18th-century cloth hall built around a quadrangle, which serves as a fitting testimony to the town's long history of textile manufacture. The Perpendicular style Parish Church is 15th-century; the Town Hall was designed by the same architect as the Houses of Parliament, and is thought by some to be one of the finest in the country. Most eccentric of the town's monuments must be Wainhouse Tower, designed as a chimney, but never used as such. It is now an ornamental tower and viewpoint. Halifax also has no less than three model villages: purpose-built to house textile workers these would have been ahead of their time when first constructed. Not content with the history to be seen in its buildings, the town also offers the insights into the past of Bankfield Museum and Shibbden Hall.

Brighouse is the reputed burial place of Robin Hood, who might have fared far worse than this friendly and welcoming town nestling in the valley of the River Calder. An industrial centre with a charming setting, it has several pleasant open spaces, and country walks can be enjoyed only a short distance from the town centre.

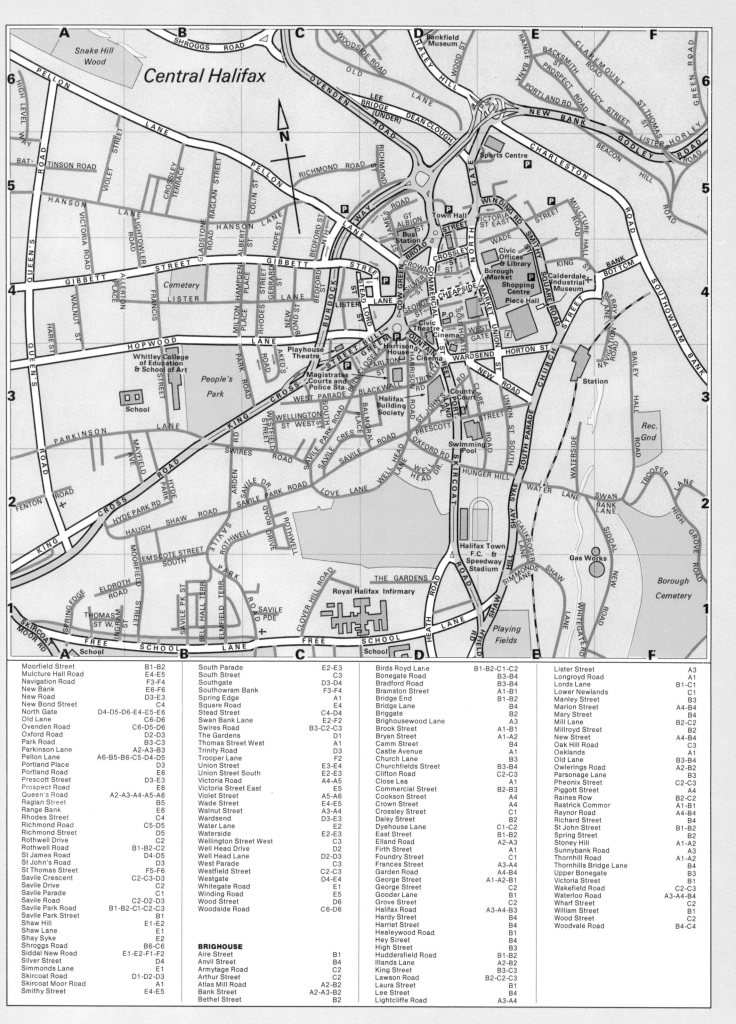

Central Halifax

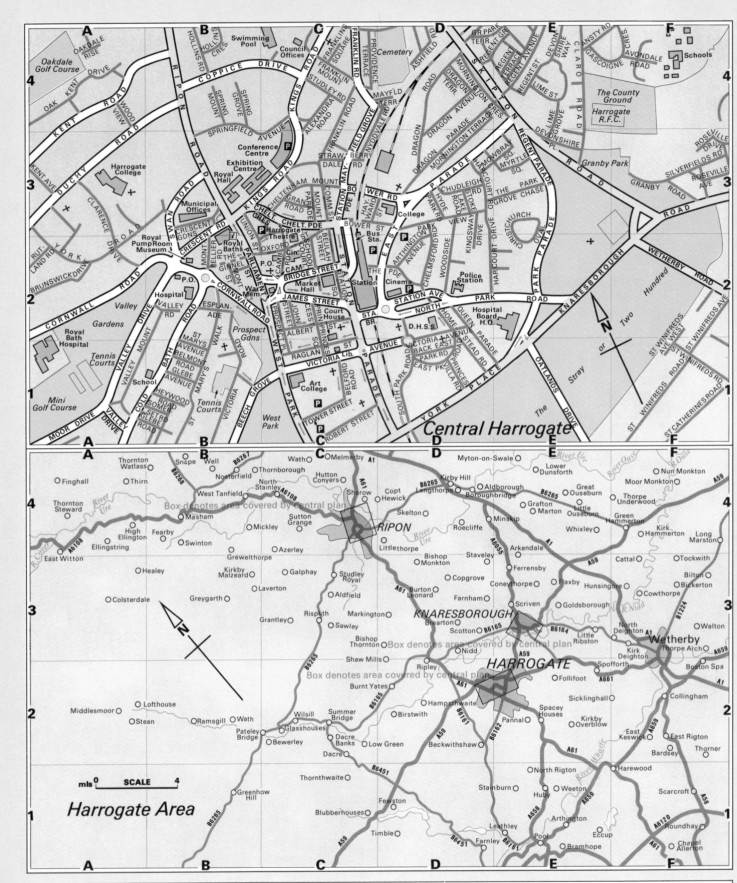

Harrogate

Dignified Victorian stone buildings and lovely gardens reflect Harrogate's 19th-century popularity as a spa town and its Royal Baths, opened in 1897, became one of the largest hydrotherapy establishments in the world. More recently the town has become a busy conference centre, the main venues being the Royal Hall and the elegant old Assembly Rooms. A glass-covered walkway in Valley Gardens leads to the Sun Pavilion and part of the lovely Harlow Car Gardens is used for experimental horticulture.

Ripon, known as the Gateway to the Dales, stands at the junction of three rivers; the Ure, the Skell and the Laver. Its small cathedral, a delightful 12th-century building occupying the site of an Anglo-Saxon church, has a small museum of church treasures in the original crypt. One corner of the town's rectangular market square is marked by the medieval Wakeman's house, now a local museum and tourist information centre.

Knaresborough Here buildings scramble higgledy-piggledy up a rocky outcrop from the banks of the River Nidd to the town's ruined 14th-century castle. The keep, two baileys and two gatehouses have survived, and there is a museum in the grounds. The town is able to claim two records; it has the oldest linen-mill and the oldest chemist's shop in England.

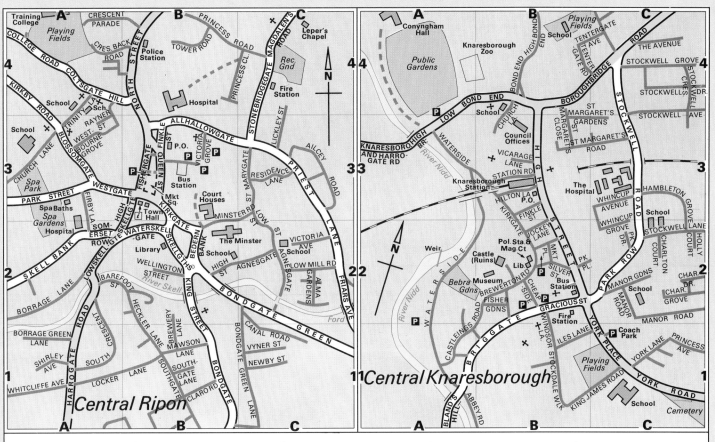

Central Ripon

Central Knaresborough

LEGEND

Town Plan

AA recommended route
Restricted roads
Other roads
Buildings of interest   Station ▣
Car parks   🅿
Parks and open spaces
One way streets ←

Area Plan

A roads
B roads
Locations   Nidd ○
Urban area

Street Index with Grid Reference

Harrogate

Albert Street	C2
Alexandra Road	C4
Ansty Road	E4-F4
Arthington Avenue	D2
Ashfield Road	D4
Avondale Road	F4
BackEast Park Road	D1
Beech Grove	B1-C1
Belford Road	C1
Belmont Road	B1
Beulah Street	C2
Bower Road	C3-D3
Bower Street	C3-D3
Brunswick Drive	A2
Cambridge Road	C2
Cambridge Street	C2
Chelmsford Road	D2-D3
Cheltenham Crescent	B3-C3
Cheltenham Mount	C3
Cheltenham Parade	C3
Christchurch Oval	E2-E3
Chudleigh Road	D3
Clarence Drive	A2-A3
Claro Road	E3-E4
Cold Bath Road	A1-B1-B2
Commercial Street	C3
Coppice Drive	B4-C4

Cornwall Road	A2-B2-C2
Crescent Gardens	B3
Crescent Road	B2-B3
Devonshire Place	E3
Devonshire Way	E4
Dragon Avenue	D3-D4
Dragon Parade	D3-D4
Dragon Road	D3-D4
Dragon Terrace	D4
Duchy Road	A3-A4-B4
East Parade	D2-D3-E3-E4
East Park Road	D1-D2
Esplanade	B2
Franklin Mount	C4
Franklin Road	C3-C4
Franklins Square	C4
Gascoigne Crescent	E4-F4
Glebe Avenue	B1
Glebe Road	A1-B1
Granby Road	F3
Granville Road	C3
Grove Park Terrace	D4-E4
Harcourt Drive	D2-D3
Harcourt Road	D3
Hayward Street	C3-D3
Heywood Road	B1
Hollins Crescent	B4
Hollins Road	B4
Homestead Road	D1-D2
Hyde Park Road	D3
James Street	C2
John Street	C2
Kent Avenue	A3
Kent Road	A3-A4-B4
King's Road	B3-C3-C4
Kingsway Drive	D2-D3
Knaresborough Road	E1-E2-F2-F3
Lime Grove	E3-E4
Lime Street	E4
Mayfield Grove	C3-C4
Mayfield Terrace	C4-D4
Montpellier Road	B2
Montpellier Street	B2
Moor Drive	A1
Mornington Crescent	D4-E4
Mornington Terrace	D3-D4
Mount Parade	C3
Mowbray Square	D3-E3
Myrtle Square	E3
North Park Road	D2-E2
Nyddvale Road	C3-C4-D4
Oakdale Rise	A4
Oak Kent Drive	A4
Oatlands Drive	E1
Oxford Street	B2-C2-C3
Park Chase	E3
Park Parade	E1-E2-E3
Park View	D3
Parliament Street	B3-B2-C2
Princes Square	C1-C2
Princes Street	C2
Princes Villa Road	D1
Prospect Place	C1-C2
Providence Terrace	C3
Queen Parade	D2-D1-E1
Raglan Street	C1-C2
Regent Avenue	E4
Regent Grove	D4-E4
Regent Parade	E3-E4
Regent Street	E4

Regent Terrace	E4
Ripon Road	B3-B4
Robert Street	C1
Roseville Avenue	F3
Roseville Drive	F3
Rutland Road	A2
St Catherine's Road	F1
St Marys Avenue	B1
St Mary's Walk	B1-B2
St Winifreds Avenue	F1-F2
St Winifreds Avenue West	F1-F2
St Winifreds Road	F1
School Court	C2
Silverfields Road	F3
Skipton Road	D4-E4-E3-F3
Somerset Road	A1-B1
South Park Road	D1
Springfield Avenue	B4-B3-C3-C4
Spring Grove	B4
Spring Mount	B4
Station Avenue	D2
Station Bridge	C2
Station Parade	C3-C2-C1-D1
Station Square	C2
Stoke Lake Road	D3
Strawberry Dale Road	C3
Studley Road	C4
Swan Road	B2-B3
The Ginnel	B2
The Grove	D3-E3
The Parade	C2-D2
Tower Street	C1
Union Street	B2-B3
Valley Drive	A1-A2-B2
Valley Mount	A1-B1-B2
Valley Road	B2
Victoria Avenue	C1-D1-D2
Victoria Road	B1-B2
West Park	C1-C2
Wetherby Road	F2
Woodside	D2-D3
Wood View	A4
York Place	D1-E1
York Road	A3-A2-A3-B3

Ripon

Agnesgate	B2-C2
Ailcey Road	C3
Allhallowgate	B3-C3
Alma Gardens	C2
Barefoot Street	A2-B2
Bedern Bank	B2
Blossomgate	A3
Bondgate	B1
Bondgate Green	B2-C2-C1
Bondgate Green Lane	C1-C2
Borrage Green Lane	A1
Borrage Lane	A2
Brewery Lane	B1-B2
Canal Road	C1-C2
Church Lane	A3
Claro Road	B1
College Road	A4
Coltsgate Hill	A4-B4
Crescent Back Road	A4-B4
Crescent Parade	A4-B4

Finkle Street	B3
Firby Lane	A2-A3
Fishergate	B3
Friars Avenue	C1-C2
Harrogate Road	A1-A2
Heckler Lane	B1-B2
High Skellgate	A3-A2-B2-B3
High Street	B2
King Street	B1-B2
Kirkby Road	A3-A4
Kirkgate	B2-B3
Lickley Street	C3-C4
Locker Lane	A1-B1
Low Mill Lane	C2
Lowskellgate	A2
Low Street	C2-C3
Magdalen's Road	C4
Mawson Lane	B1
Minster Road	B2-B3-C3
Newby Street	C1
North Street	B3-B4
Park Street	A3
Priest Lane	C2-C3
Princess Close	B4-C4
Princes Road	B4-C4
Queen Street	B3
Rayner Street	A3-A4
Residence Lane	C3
St Agnesgate	C2
St Marygate	C3
Shirley Avenue	A1
Skell Bank	A2
Skellgarths	B2
Somerset Row	A2
South Crescent	A1-A2
Southgate	B1
Southgate Lane	B1
Stonebridgegate	C3-C4
Tower Road	B4
Trinity Lane	A3-A4
Victoria Avenue	C2
Victoria Grove	B3
Vyner Street	C1
Waterskellgate	A2-B2
Wellington Street	B2
Westbourne Grove	A3
Westgate	A3-B3
Whitcliffe Avenue	A1

Knaresborough

Abbey Road	A1-B1
Bland's Hill	A1
Bond End	B4
Boroughbridge Road	B4-C4
Brewerton Road	B2
Briggate	A1-B1-B2
Castleings Road	A1-B1-B2
Charlton Court	C2
Charlton Drive	C2
Charlton Grove	C2
Cheapside	B2
Church Lane	B3-B4
Finkle Street	B3
Fisher Gardens	B2
Gracious Street	B2
Hambleton Grove	C2-C3

High Bond End	B4
High Bridge	A3
High Street	B2-B3-B4
Hilton Lane	B3
Holly Court	C2
Iles Lane	B1-C1
Jockey Lane	B2-B3
King James Road	B1-C1
Kirkgate	B2-B3
Knaresborough and Harrogate Road	A3
Low Bond End	A3-A4-B4
Manor Gardens	C2
Manor Road	C2
Market Place	B2
Park Drive	C2
Park Place	B2-C2
Park Row	C2
Princess Avenue	C1
St Margaret's Close	B3-B4
St Margaret's Gardens	B3-C3
St Margaret's Road	B3-C3
Silver Street	B2
Station Road	B3
Stockdale Walk	B1
Stockwell Avenue	C4
Stockwell Crescent	C4
Stockwell Drive	C4
Stockwell Grove	C4
Stockwell Lane	C2
Stockwell Road	C2-C3-C4
Tentergate Avenue	B4-C4
Tentergate Road	B4-C4
The Avenue	C4
Vicarage Lane	B3
Waterside	A1-A2-B2-B3-A3
Whincup Avenue	C3
Whincup Grove	C2-C3
Windsor Lane	B1-B2
York Lane	C1
York Place	B2-C2-C1
York Road	C1

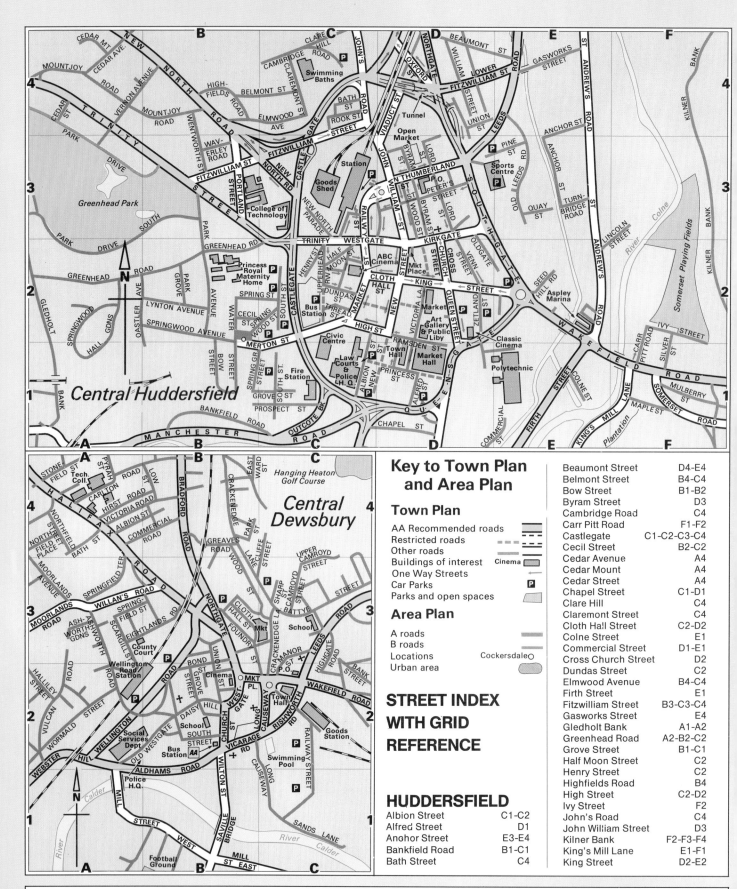

Key to Town Plan and Area Plan

Town Plan

AA Recommended roads	
Restricted roads	
Other roads	
Buildings of interest	Cinema
One Way Streets	
Car Parks	P
Parks and open spaces	

Area Plan

A roads	
B roads	
Locations	Cockersdale○
Urban area	

STREET INDEX
WITH GRID
REFERENCE

HUDDERSFIELD

Albion Street	C1-C2
Alfred Street	D1
Anchor Street	E3-E4
Bankfield Road	B1-C1
Bath Street	C4
Beaumont Street	D4-E4
Belmont Street	B4-C4
Bow Street	B1-B2
Byram Street	D3
Cambridge Road	C4
Carr Pitt Road	F1-F2
Castlegate	C1-C2-C3-C4
Cecil Street	B2-C2
Cedar Avenue	A4
Cedar Mount	A4
Cedar Street	A4
Chapel Street	C1-D1
Clare Hill	C4
Claremont Street	C4
Cloth Hall Street	C2-D2
Colne Street	E1
Commercial Street	D1-E1
Cross Church Street	D2
Dundas Street	C2
Elmwood Avenue	B4-C4
Firth Street	E1
Fitzwilliam Street	B3-C3-C4
Gasworks Street	E4
Gledholt Bank	A1-A2
Greenhead Road	A2-B2-C2
Grove Street	B1-C1
Half Moon Street	C2
Henry Street	C2
Highfields Road	B4
High Street	C2-D2
Ivy Street	F2
John's Road	C4
John William Street	D3
Kilner Bank	F2-F3-F4
King's Mill Lane	E1-F1
King Street	D2-E2

Huddersfield

With a long history of textile making and a more recent involvement in chemicals and engineering, Huddersfield has for many years been a busy industrial and commercial centre. But another aspect of the town is its fine old buildings: the best area for these is around St George's Square, where the railway station's mid-19th-century colonnaded facade is thought by some to be one of the finest in the country.

Yet another side to Huddersfield is its role as a venue for local choirs and bands, who regularly come here for performances at the Town Hall. A good collection of English watercolours can be seen in the art gallery in Princess Alexandra Walk, and the Tolson Memorial Museum in Ravensknowle Park deals with geology, natural history and the area's own rich past. Near the village of Almondsbury to the south stands Castle

Hill, an ancient hill fort topped with a 19th-century tower.

Dewsbury is one of the main towns of the West Yorkshire Heavy Woollen District, and is well known for its manufacture of blankets and carpets. Lying on the River Calder, this is a popular market and shopping centre, and has its own museum and art gallery. Places of interest include the parish church, which has retained some 12th-century features.

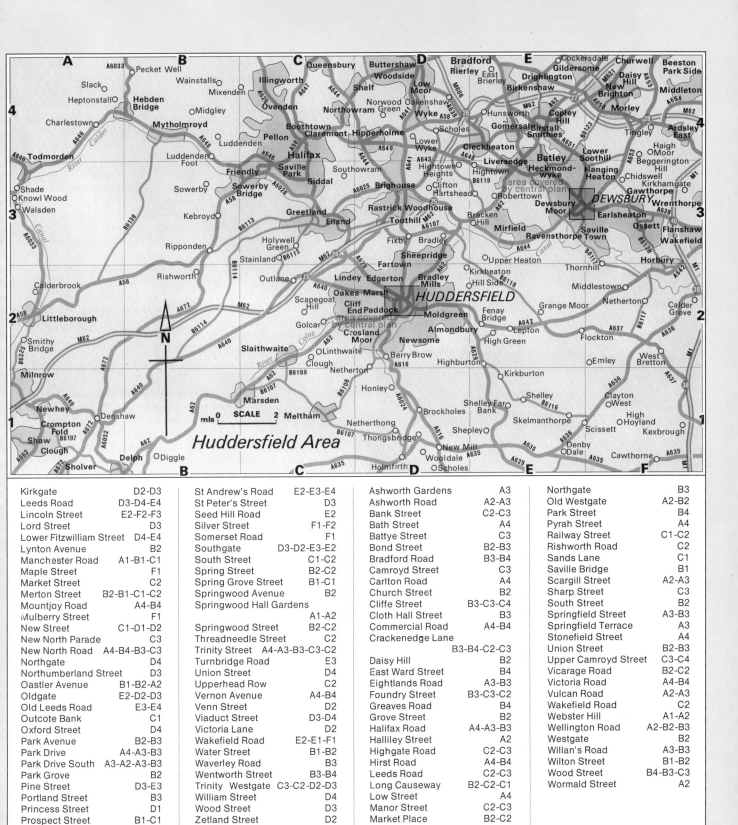

Huddersfield Area

SCALE mls 0 — 2

Kirkgate	D2-D3	St Andrew's Road	E2-E3-E4
Leeds Road	D3-D4-E4	St Peter's Street	D3
Lincoln Street	E2-F2-F3	Seed Hill Road	E2
Lord Street	D3	Silver Street	F1-F2
Lower Fitzwilliam Street	D4-E4	Somerset Road	F1
Lynton Avenue	B2	Southgate	D3-D2-E3-E2
Manchester Road	A1-B1-C1	South Street	C1-C2
Maple Street	F1	Spring Street	B2-C2
Market Street	C2	Spring Grove Street	B1-C1
Merton Street	B2-B1-C1-C2	Springwood Avenue	B2
Mountjoy Road	A4-B4	Springwood Hall Gardens	
Mulberry Street	F1		A1-A2
New Street	C1-D1-D2	Springwood Street	B2-C2
New North Parade	C3	Threadneedle Street	C2
New North Road	A4-B4-B3-C3	Trinity Street	A4-A3-B3-C3-C2
Northgate	D4	Turnbridge Road	E3
Northumberland Street	D3	Union Street	D4
Oastler Avenue	B1-B2-A2	Upperhead Row	C2
Oldgate	E2-D2-D3	Vernon Avenue	A4-B4
Old Leeds Road	E3-E4	Venn Street	D2
Outcote Bank	C1	Viaduct Street	D3-D4
Oxford Street	D4	Victoria Lane	D2
Park Avenue	B2-B3	Wakefield Road	E2-E1-F1
Park Drive	A4-A3-B3	Water Street	B1-B2
Park Drive South	A3-A2-A3-B3	Waverley Road	B3
Park Grove	B2	Wentworth Street	B3-B4
Pine Street	D3-E3	Trinity Westgate	C3-C2-D2-D3
Portland Street	B3	William Street	D4
Princess Street	D1	Wood Street	D3
Prospect Street	B1-C1	Zetland Street	D2
Quay Street	E3		
Queensgate	D1-D2-E2		
Queen Street	D1-D2	**DEWSBURY**	
Railway Street	C3		
Ramsden Street	D1-D2	Albion Street	A4-B4
Rook Street	C4	Aldhams Road	A2-A1-B1-B2

Ashworth Gardens	A3	Northgate	B3
Ashworth Road	A2-A3	Old Westgate	A2-B2
Bank Street	C2-C3	Park Street	B4
Bath Street	A4	Pyrah Street	A4
Battye Street	C3	Railway Street	C1-C2
Bond Street	B2-B3	Rishworth Road	C2
Bradford Road	B3-B4	Sands Lane	C1
Camroyd Street	C3	Saville Bridge	B1
Carlton Road	A4	Scargill Street	A2-A3
Church Street	B2	Sharp Street	C3
Cliffe Street	B3-C3-C4	South Street	B2
Cloth Hall Street	B3	Springfield Street	A3-B3
Commercial Road	A4-B4	Springfield Terrace	A3
Crackenedge Lane		Stonefield Street	A4
	B3-B4-C2-C3	Union Street	B2-B3
Daisy Hill	B2	Upper Camroyd Street	C3-C4
East Ward Street	B4	Vicarage Road	B2-C2
Eightlands Road	A3-B3	Victoria Road	A4-B4
Foundry Street	B3-C3-C2	Vulcan Road	A2-A3
Greaves Road	B4	Wakefield Road	C2
Grove Street	B2	Webster Hill	A1-A2
Halifax Road	A4-A3-B3	Wellington Road	A2-B2-B3
Halliley Street	A2	Westgate	B2
Highgate Road	C2-C3	Willan's Road	A3-B3
Hirst Road	A4-B4	Wilton Street	B1-B2
Leeds Road	C2-C3	Wood Street	B4-B3-C3
Long Causeway	B2-C2-C1	Wormald Street	A2
Low Street	A4		
Manor Street	C2-C3		
Market Place	B2-C2		
Mill Street East	B1-C1		
Mill Street West	A1-B1		
Moorlands Avenue	A3-A4		
Moorlands Road	A3		
Northfield Place	A4		
Northfield Street	A4		

HUDDERSFIELD
Designed by J. P. Pritchett and built in the 1840s, the splendid railway station is one of the earlier ones, but is quite outstanding with its Corinthian columns and pediment flanked by fine colonnades.

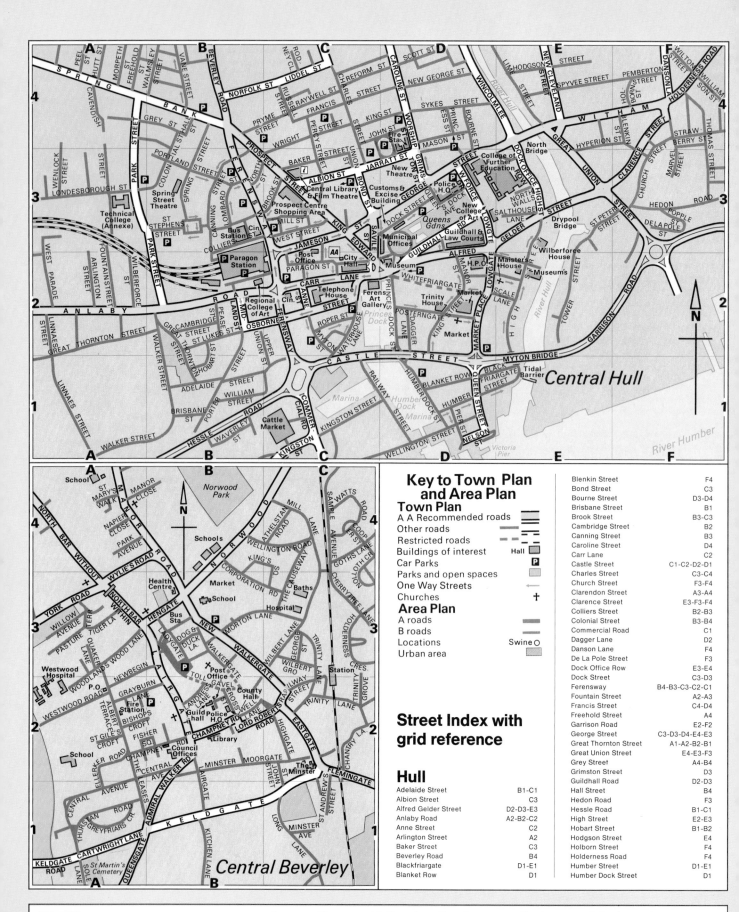

Key to Town Plan and Area Plan

Town Plan

A A Recommended roads	
Other roads	
Restricted roads	
Buildings of interest	Hall
Car Parks	P
Parks and open spaces	
One Way Streets	
Churches	+

Area Plan

A roads	
B roads	
Locations	Swine O
Urban area	

Street Index with grid reference

Hull

Adelaide Street	B1-C1
Albion Street	C3
Alfred Gelder Street	D2-D3-E3
Anlaby Road	A2-B2-C2
Anne Street	C2
Arlington Street	A2
Baker Street	C3
Beverley Road	B4
Blackfriargate	D1-E1
Blanket Row	D1

Blenkin Street	F4
Bond Street	C3
Bourne Street	D3-D4
Brisbane Street	B1
Brook Street	B3-C3
Cambridge Street	B2
Canning Street	B3
Caroline Street	D4
Carr Lane	C2
Castle Street	C1-C2-D2-D1
Charles Street	C3-C4
Church Street	F3-F4
Clarendon Street	A3-A4
Clarence Street	E3-F3-F4
Colliers Street	B2-B3
Colonial Street	B3-B4
Commercial Road	C1
Dagger Lane	D2
Danson Lane	F4
De La Pole Street	F3
Dock Office Row	E3-E4
Dock Street	C3-D3
Ferensway	B4-B3-C3-C2-C1
Fountain Street	A2-A3
Francis Street	C4-D4
Freehold Street	A4
Garrison Road	E2-F2
George Street	C3-D3-D4-E4-E3
Great Thornton Street	A1-A2-B2-B1
Great Union Street	E4-E3-F3
Grey Street	A4-B4
Grimston Street	D3
Guildhall Road	D2-D3
Hall Street	B4
Hedon Road	F3
Hessle Road	B1-C1
High Street	E2-E3
Hobart Street	B1-B2
Hodgson Street	E4
Holborn Street	F4
Holderness Road	F4
Humber Street	D1-E1
Humber Dock Street	D1

Hull

Officially Kingston-upon-Hull, this ancient port was specially laid out with new docks in 1293, on the decree of Edward I, and echoes of the town's past can be seen in the Town Docks Museum. The docks and the fishing industry are synonymous with Hull – it has Britain's busiest deep-sea fishing port – although flour-milling, vegetable oil extraction and petrochemical production are also important. The centre of Hull consists of broad streets and spacious squares and parks, such as Queen's Gardens, laid out on the site of what used to be Queen's Dock. The older part of the town which lies south-east of here between the docks and the River Hull is full of character, with a number of Georgian buildings and places of interest.

Beverley is one of England's most distinguished towns. Between its two principal buildings – the famous Minster and St Mary's Church – are medieval streets and pleasing market squares graced by redbrick Georgian houses built by the landed gentry of the East Riding during the town's heyday as a fashionable resort. The Minster's twin towers soar above the rooftops of the town as a constant reminder that here is one of the most beautiful pieces of Gothic architecture in Europe. The wealth of beauty and detail throughout is immense, but carving in both stone and wood is one of its most outstanding features.

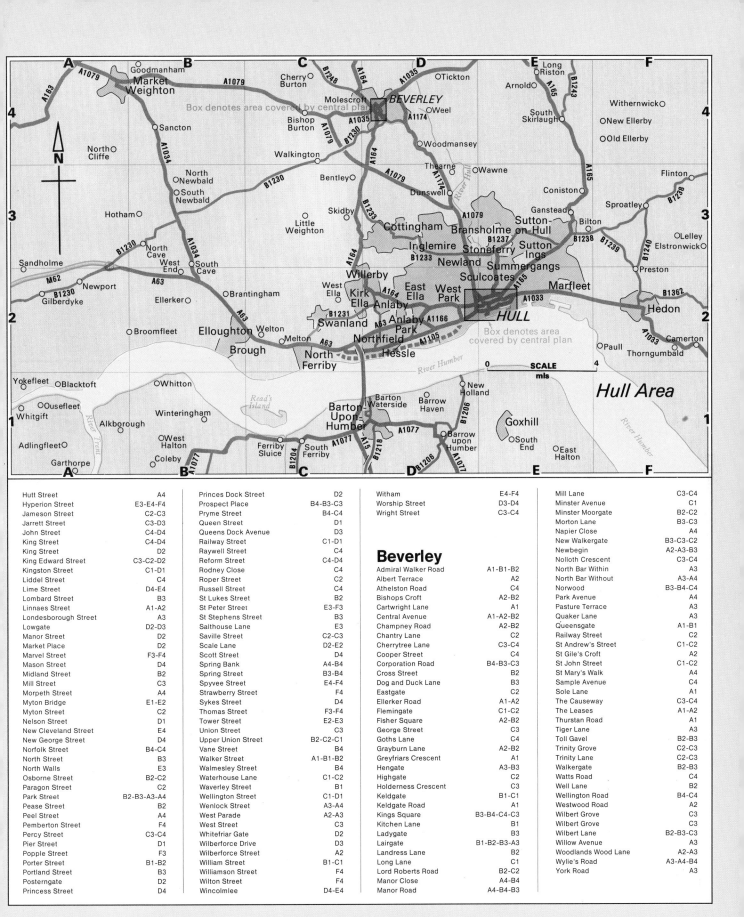

Hull Area

Hutt Street	A4	Princes Dock Street	D2
Hyperion Street	E3-E4-F4	Prospect Place	B4-B3-C3
Jameson Street	C2-C3	Pryme Street	B4-C4
Jarrett Street	C3-D3	Queen Street	D1
John Street	C4-D4	Queens Dock Avenue	D3
King Street	C4-D4	Railway Street	C1-D1
King Street	D2	Raywell Street	C4
King Edward Street	C3-C2-D2	Reform Street	C4-D4
Kingston Street	C1-D1	Rodney Close	C4
Liddel Street	C4	Roper Street	C2
Lime Street	D4-E4	Russell Street	C4
Lombard Street	B3	St Lukes Street	B2
Linnaes Street	A1-A2	St Peter Street	E3-F3
Londesborough Street	A3	St Stephens Street	B3
Lowgate	D2-D3	Salthouse Lane	E3
Manor Street	D2	Saville Street	C2-C3
Market Place	D2	Scale Lane	D2-E2
Marvel Street	F3-F4	Scott Street	D4
Mason Street	D4	Spring Bank	A4-B4
Midland Street	B2	Spring Street	B3-B4
Mill Street	C3	Spyvee Street	E4-F4
Morpeth Street	A4	Strawberry Street	F4
Myton Bridge	E1-E2	Sykes Street	D4
Myton Street	C2	Thomas Street	F3-F4
Nelson Street	D1	Tower Street	E2-E3
New Cleveland Street	E4	Union Street	C3
New George Street	D4	Upper Union Street	B2-C2-C1
Norfolk Street	B4-C4	Vane Street	B4
North Street	B3	Walker Street	A1-B1-B2
North Walls	E3	Walmesley Street	B4
Osborne Street	B2-C2	Waterhouse Lane	C1-C2
Paragon Street	C2	Waverley Street	B1
Park Street	B2-B3-A3-A4	Wellington Street	C1-D1
Pease Street	B2	Wenlock Street	A3-A4
Peel Street	A4	West Parade	A2-A3
Pemberton Street	F4	West Street	C3
Percy Street	C3-C4	Whitefriar Gate	D2
Pier Street	D1	Wilberforce Drive	D3
Popple Street	F3	Wilberforce Street	A2
Porter Street	B1-B2	William Street	B1-C1
Portland Street	B3	Williamson Street	F4
Posterngate	D2	Wilton Street	F4
Princess Street	D4	Wincolmlee	D4-E4

Witham	E4-F4	Mill Lane	C3-C4
Worship Street	D3-D4	Minster Avenue	C1
Wright Street	C3-C4	Minster Moorgate	B2-C2
		Morton Lane	B3-C3
		Napier Close	A4

Beverley

Admiral Walker Road	A1-B1-B2	New Walkergate	B3-C3-C2
Albert Terrace	A2	Newbegin	A2-A3-B3
Athelston Road	C4	Nolloth Crescent	C3-C4
Bishops Croft	A2-B2	North Bar Within	A3
Cartwright Lane	A1	North Bar Without	A3-A4
Central Avenue	A1-A2-B2	Norwood	B3-B4-C4
Champney Road	A2-B2	Park Avenue	A4
Chantry Lane	C2	Pasture Terrace	A3
Cherrytree Lane	C3-C4	Quaker Lane	A3
Cooper Street	C4	Queensgate	A1-B1
Corporation Road	B4-B3-C3	Railway Street	C2
Cross Street	B2	St Andrew's Street	C1-C2
Dog and Duck Lane	B3	St Gile's Croft	A2
Eastgate	C2	St John Street	C1-C2
Ellerker Road	A1-A2	St Mary's Walk	A4
Flemingate	C1-C2	Sample Avenue	C4
Fisher Square	A2-B2	Sole Lane	A1
George Street	C3	The Causeway	C3-C4
Goths Lane	C4	The Leases	A1-A2
Grayburn Lane	A2-B2	Thurstan Road	A1
Greyfriars Crescent	A1	Tiger Lane	A3
Hengate	A3-B3	Toll Gavel	B2-B3
Highgate	C2	Trinity Grove	C2-C3
Holderness Crescent	C3	Trinity Lane	C2-C3
Keldgate	B1-C1	Walkergate	B2-B3
Keldgate Road	A1	Watts Road	C4
Kings Square	B3-B4-C4-C3	Well Lane	B2
Kitchen Lane	B1	Wellington Road	B4-C4
Ladygate	B3	Westwood Road	A2
Lairgate	B1-B2-B3-A3	Wilbert Grove	C3
Landress Lane	B2	Wilbert Grove	C3
Long Lane	C1	Wilbert Lane	B2-B3-C3
Lord Roberts Road	B2-C2	Willow Avenue	A3
Manor Close	A4-B4	Woodlands Wood Lane	A2-A3
Manor Road	A4-B4-B3	Wylie's Road	A3-A4-B4
		York Road	A3

HULL
Schemes to cross the Humber estuary were first discussed over 100 years ago, but it was not until 1981 that the mammoth project was sucessfully completed. At 4626ft, the Humber Bridge has the longest main span in the world.

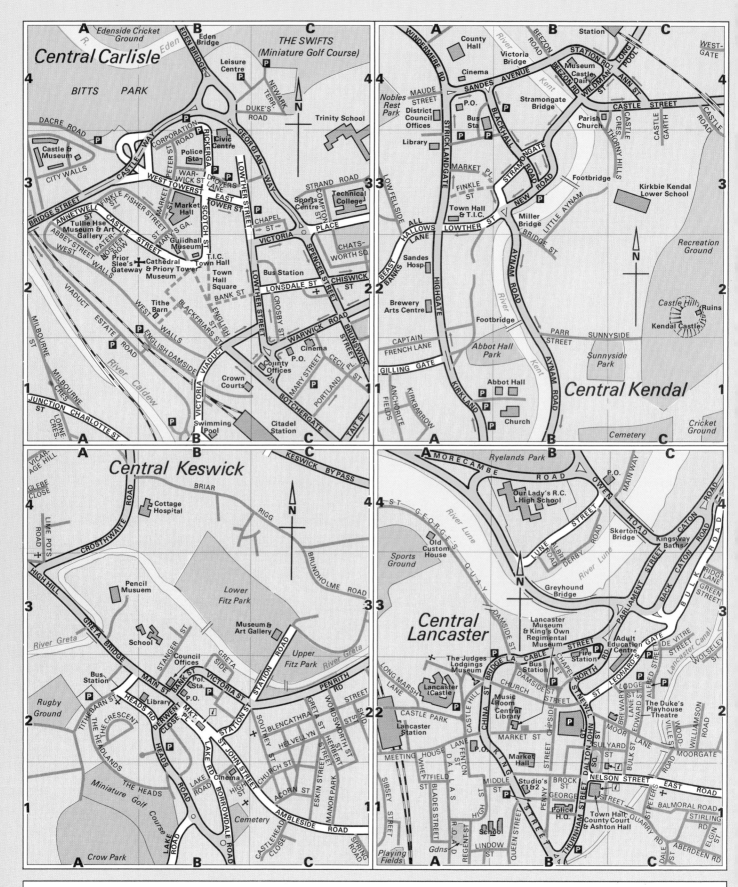

Lake District

Keswick With the River Greta running through it and Skiddaw looming above, this is a charming, quiet market town set amid beautiful scenery at the southern end of Derwentwater. The Fitz Park Museum and Art Gallery houses a collection of manuscripts by the numerous authors and poets who took their inspiration from the Lakeland.

Windermere has remained unspoiled despite the enormous popularity it has won as a holiday resort. Centred around its extensive lake, it stands in a setting which has been exalted by poets and artists for years. Windermere's architecture is mainly Victorian, as a result of the railway coming in the mid-19th century and bringing prosperity to the town. But conservationists campaigned to stop the railway going any further, and so the natural peace of the area was preserved.

Lancaster Dominating the city from its hilltop site, Lancaster Castle was once the headquarters of the Duchy and is still in use today — as a prison. Its late Georgian courtrooms and the beautiful Shire Hall are open to visitors. Close by stands the Priory, an architectural gem, and also of interest is the early 17th-century Judge's Lodgings house, which provided accommodation for assize judges for 150 years. The building now houses a display of dolls, with beautiful

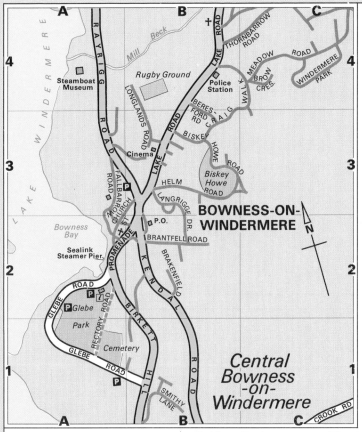

Central
Bowness
-on-
Windermere

LEGEND

AA Recommended roads
Restricted roads
Other roads
Buildings of interest   Library
Car Parks   P
Parks and open spaces
One Way Streets   ←
Churches   †

Street Index with Grid Reference

Carlisle

furniture from Gillows and other cabinet makers. *Kendal's* motto is "Wool Is My Bread" — a constant reminder that wool was the town's staple trade for over 600 years and brought it the prosperity which it still enjoys today. Flemish weavers started the industry when they settled here in the 14th century, and the town is now a centre for the production of such different products as turbines, carpets, shoes, socks and hornware — although its best known product must be

the sustaining Kendal Mint Cake. An interesting local feature are the numerous named and numbered yards which lie tucked away through Kendal's archways and down alleyways, and were once a focus of small industry.
Carlisle Bonnie Prince Charlie proclaimed his father King of England from the steps of Carlisle Cross before marching south to be taken prisoner by the Duke of Cumberland, and Carlisle Castle was the centre of turbulent scenes between English and

Scots from Norman times to the Jacobite rebellion. This is the 'Border City', capital of the Border area between England and Scotland. But as well as a past of conflict it can also claim to have some beautiful buildings. Finest of all perhaps is the cathedral; other places of interest are the Guildhall, which is 15th-century, Tullie House (a fine Jacobean building with Victorian extensions), and the city's museum and art gallery, which has a good collection of artefacts from its past.

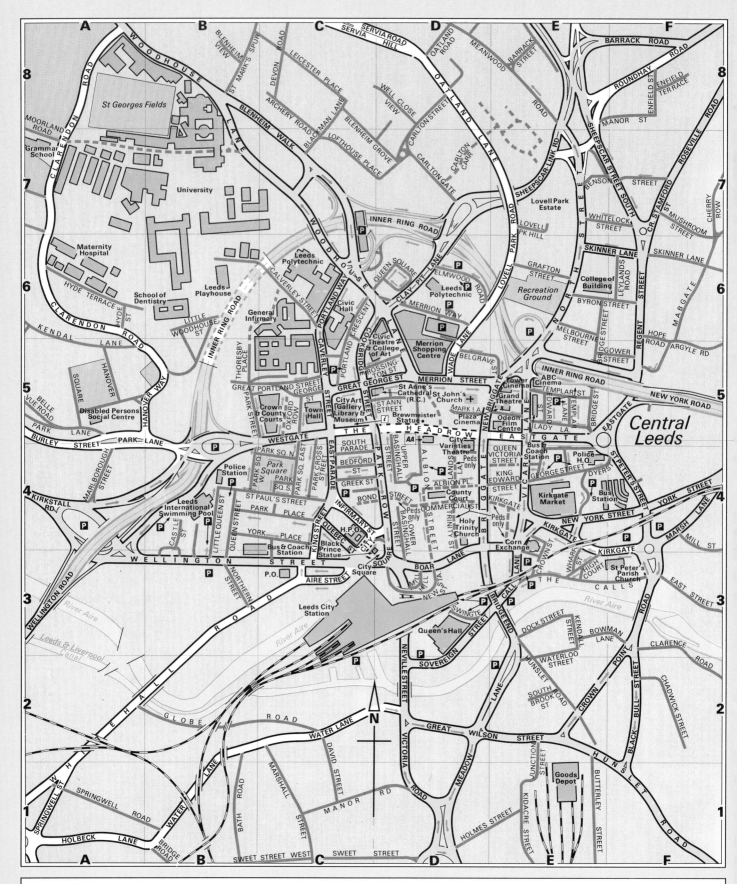

Leeds

In the centre of Leeds is its town hall – a monumental piece of architecture with a 225ft clock-tower. It was opened by Queen Victoria in 1858, and has been a kind of mascot for the city ever since. It exudes civic pride; such buildings could only have been created in the heyday of Victorian prosperity and confidence. Leeds' staple industry has always been the wool trade, but it only became a boom town towards the end of the 18th century, when textile mills were introduced. Today, the wool trade and ready-made clothing (Mr Hepworth and Mr Burton began their work here) are still important, though industries like paper, leather, furniture and electrical equipment are prominent.

Across Calverley Street from the town hall is the City Art Gallery, Library and Museum. Its collections include sculpture by Henry Moore, who was a student at Leeds School of Art. Nearby is the Headrow, Leeds' foremost shopping thoroughfare. On it is the City Varieties Theatre, venue for many years of the famous television programme 'The Good Old Days'. Off the Headrow are several shopping arcades, of which Leeds has many handsome examples. Leeds has a good number of interesting churches; perhaps the finest is St John's, unusual in that it dates from 1634, a time when few churches were built.

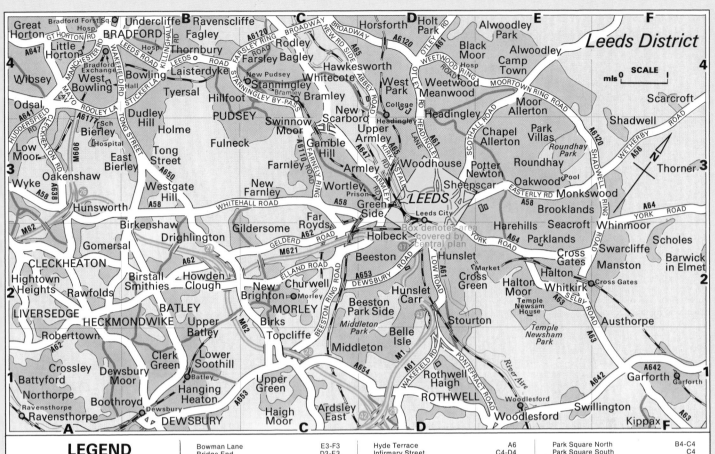

Leeds District

SCALE mls 0 | |

LEGEND

Town Plan

AA Recommended roads
Other roads
Restricted roads
Buildings of interset — Museum
AA Service Centre — AA
Parks and open spaces
Car Parks — P
Churches — +
One way streets

District Plan

A roads
B roads
Stations — Kirkgate
Urban area
Buildings of interest — Hospital

Street Index with Grid Reference

Leeds

Aire Street	C3
Albion Place	D4
Albion Street	D3-D4-D5
Archery Road	C7-C8
Argyle Road	F5
Barrack Road	E8-F8
Barrack Street	E8
Bath Road	B1-B2
Bedford Street	C4
Belgrave Street	D5-E5
Belle Vue Road	A5
Benson Street	E7-F7
Black Bull Street	F1-F2-F3
Blackman Lane	C7-C8
Blenheim Grove	C8-C7-D7
Blenheim View	B8
Blenheim Walk	B8-C8-C7
Boar Lane	D3-D4
Bond Street	C4-D4
Bowman Lane	E3-F3
Bridge End	D3-E3
Bridge Road	B1
Bridge Street	E5-E6
Briggate	D3-D4-D5
Burley Street	A4-A5
Butterley Street	E1-E2
Byron Street	E6-F6
Call Lane	E3
Calverley Street	C5-C6
Carlton Carr	D7
Carlton Gate	D7
Carlton Street	D7-D8
Castle Street	B3-B4
Chadwick Street	F2
Chapletown Road	E8
Cherry Row	F7
City Square	C3-C4-D4-D3
Clarence Road	F2-F3
Clarendon Road	A8-A7-A6-A5-B5
Clay Pit Lane	D6
Commercial Street	D4
Cookbridge Street	C5-C6-D6
Cross Stamford Street	F6-F7
Crown Street	E3-E4
Crown Point Road	E2-F2-F3
David Street	C1-C2
Devon Road	C8
Dock Street	E3
Dyer Street	E4-F4
East Parade	C4-C5
East Street	F3
Eastgate	E5-F5
Edward Street	E5
Elmwood Road	D6
Enfield Street	F8
Enfield Terrace	F8
George Street	C5
George Street	E4
Globe Road	A2-B2-C2
Gower Street	E5-F5
Grafton Street	E6
Great George Street	C5-D5
Great Portland Street	B5-C5-D5
Great Wilson Street	D2-E2
Greek Street	C4-D4
Hanover Square	A5
Hanover Way	A5-B5
High Court	E3
Holbeck Lane	A1-B1
Holmes Street	D1-E1
Hope Road	F5-F6
Hunslett Road	E3-E2-E1-F1-F2
Hyde Street	A6
Hyde Terrace	A6
Infirmary Street	C4-D4
Inner Ring Road	B5-B6-C6-C7-D7-D6-E6-E5-F5
Junction Street	E1-E2
Kendal Lane	A5-A6
Kendal Street	E3
Kidacre Street	E1
King Street	C3-C4
King Edward Street	D4-E4
Kirkgate	E4-E3-F3-F4
Kirkstall Road	A4
Lady Lane	E5
Lands Lane	D4-D5
Leicester Place	C8
Leylands Road	F6
Lisbon Street	B3-B4
Little Queen Street	B3-B4
Little Woodhouse Street	B6
Lofthouse Place	C7-D7
Lovell Park Hill	E7
Lovell Park Road	D6-E6-E7
Lower Basinghall Street	D3-D4
Mabgate	F6
Manor Road	C1-D1
Manor Street	E8-F8
Mark Lane	D5
Marlborough Street	A4
Marsh Lane	F4
Marshall Street	C1-C2
Meadow Lane	D1-D2-E2-E3
Meanwood Road	D8-E8
Melbourne Street	E6
Merrion Street	D5-E5
Merrion Way	D6
Mill Hill	D3
Mill Street	F4
Moorland Road	A7-A8
Mushroom Street	F6-F7
Neville Street	D2-D3
New Briggate	D5-E5
New Station Street	D3
New York Road	F5
New York Street	E4-F4
North Street	E5-E6-E7
Northern Street	B3
Oatland Lane	D8-D7-E7
Oatland Road	D8
Oxford Row	C5
Park Cross Street	C4-C5
Park Lane	A5-B5-B4
Park Place	B4-C4
Park Row	C4-C5-D5-D4
Park Square East	C4
Park Square North	B4-C4
Park Square South	C4
Park Square West	B4
Park Street	B5-C5
Portland Crescent	C5-C6
Portland Way	C6
Quebec Street	C3-C4
Queen Street	B3-B4
Queen Square	C6-D6
Queen Victoria Street	D4-E4
Regent Street	F5-F6
Roseville Road	F7-F8
Rossington Street	C5-D5
Roundhay Road	E8-F8
St Ann Street	C5-D5
St Mark's Spur	B8-C8
St Paul's Street	B4-C4
St Peter's Street	E4-F4
Servia Hill	C8-D8
Servia Road	C8-D8
Sheepscar Link Road	E7-E8
Sheepscar Street North	E8
Sheepscar Street South	E8-E7-F7
Skinner Lane	E6-F6
South Brook Street	E2
South Parade	C4
Sovereign Street	D2-D3-E3
Springwell Road	A1-B1
Springwell Street	A1
Sweet Street	C1-D1
Sweet Street West	B1-C1
Swinegate	D3
The Calls	E3-F3
The Headrow	C5-D5
Templar Lane	E5
Templar Street	E5
Thoresby Place	B5-B6
Trinity Street	D4
Upper Basinghall Street	D4-D5
Vicar Lane	E4-E5
Victoria Road	D1-D2
Wade Lane	D5-D6
Water Lane	B1-B2-C2-D2
Waterloo Street	E2-E3
Well Close View	D8
Wellington Road	A3
Wellington Street	A3-B3-C3
Westgate	B4-B5-C5-C4
Wharf Street	E3-E4
Whitehall Road	A1-A2-B2-B3-C3
Whitelock Street	E7-F7
Woodhouse Lane	A8-B8-B7-C7-C6-D6-D5
York Place	B4-C4
York Street	F4

LEEDS
Offices now occupy the handsome twin-towered Civic Hall which stands in Calverley Street in front of the new buildings of Leeds Polytechnic. This area of the city – the commercial centre – has been extensively redeveloped

Liverpool

Although its dock area has been much reduced, Liverpool was at one time second only to London in pre-eminence as a port. Formerly the centrepiece of the docks area are three monumental buildings – the Dock Board Offices, built in 1907 with a huge copper-covered dome; the Cunard Building, dating from 1912 and decorated with an abundance of ornamental carving; and best-known of all, the world-famous Royal Liver Building, with the two 'liver birds' crowning its twin cupolas.

Some of the city's best industrial buildings have fallen into disuse in recent years, and have been preserved as monuments of the industrial age. One has become a maritime museum housing full-sized craft and a workshop where maritime crafts are demonstrated. Other museums and galleries include the Walker Art Gallery, with excellent collections of European painting and sculpture; Liverpool City Libraries, one of the oldest and largest public libraries in Britain, with a vast collection of books and manuscripts; and Bluecoat Chambers, a Queen Anne building now used as a gallery and concert hall. Liverpool has two outstanding cathedrals: the Roman Catholic, completed in 1967 in an uncompromising controversial style; and the Protestant, constructed in the great tradition of Gothic architecture, but begun in 1904 and only recently completed.

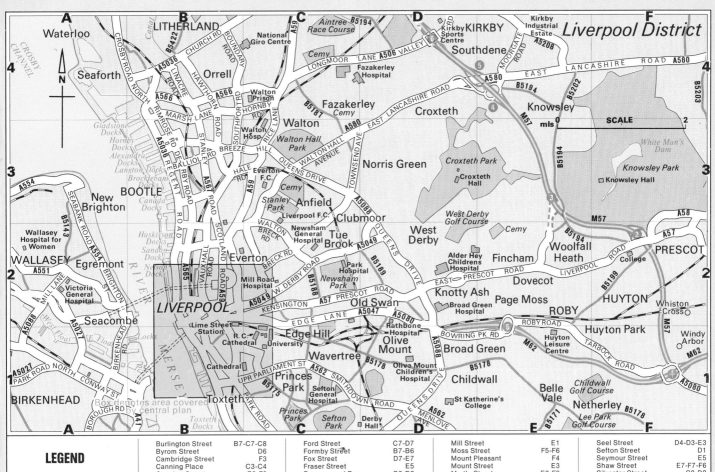

Liverpool District

(Map showing: Waterloo, Litherland, Kirkby, Southdene, Seaforth, Orrell, Walton, Fazakerley, Croxteth, Knowsley, Norris Green, Croxteth Park, Knowsley Park, Bootle, New Brighton, Anfield, Clubmoor, West Derby, Woolfall Heath, Prescot, Wallasey, Egremont, Everton, Tue Brook, Fincham, Dovecot, Huyton, Seacombe, Liverpool, Edge Hill, Old Swan, Knotty Ash, Page Moss, Roby, Huyton Park, Birkenhead, Wavertree, Olive Mount, Broad Green, Childwall, Belle Vale, Netherley, Toxteth, Princes Park, Sefton Park)

LEGEND

Town Plan

AA recommended route
Restricted roads
Other roads
Buildings of interest — Castle 🔲
Car parks — P
Parks and open spaces
One way streets ←

District Plan

A roads
B roads
Locations — Sefton ○

Street Index with Grid Reference

Liverpool

Street	Grid
Addison Street	C6-D6
Arrad Street	F3-F4-F3
Barton Street	B6
Bath Street	A6-B6-B5
Bedford Street South	F2-F3
Berry Street	E3
Birkett Street	D6-E6-E7
Blackburn Place	E3-F3
Blackstock Street	C7-D7
Blenheim Street	C8-D8
Blundell Street	C2-D2
Bold Street	D4-D3-E3
Breck Road	F8
Brick Street	D2
Brook Street	B5
Brownlow Hill	D4-E4-F4
Brow Side	E7-F7
Brunswick Road	F6
Brunswick Street	B4-C4
Burlington Street	B7-C7-C8
Byrom Street	D6
Cambridge Street	F3
Canning Place	C3-C4
Canning Street	E2-F2
Carlton Street	A8-B8-B7
Carter Street	F1
Carver Street	E6-F6
Caryl Street	D1
Castle Street	C4-C5
Catherine Street	F2-F3
Chadwick Street	B7
Chaloner Street	C2-C1-D1-D2
Chatham Street	F2
Chapel Street	B5
Cheapside	C5
Chisenhale Street	B7-C7
Christian Street	D6
Christian Street	D6-D7
Churchill Way North	C6-D6-D5
Church Street	C4-D4
Clarence Street	E4
Colquitt Street	D3-E3
Cook Street	C4
Cooper Street	D4
Copperas Hill	D4-E4-E5
Cornhill	C2-C3
Cotton Street	A8-B8
Cresswell Street	F7
Crown Street	F4-F5
Dale Street	C5
Daulby Street	F5
Dawson Street	D5-D4
Derby Square	C4
Devon Street	E6-F6
Dexter Street	E1
Dickson Street	A8-B8
Dryden Street	D8
Dublin Street	A8-B8
Duke Street	C3-D3-E3
Dundee Street	B6
Earle Street	B5
Eaton Street	B6-C6
Eldon Street	C7
Elliot Street	D4
Erskine Street	F6
Everton Brow	E7
Everton Road	F7-F8
Everton Terrace	E8-E7-F7
Exchange Street East	B5-C5
Falkner Street	F2-F3
Falkner Street	F2-F3
Fleet Street	D3-D4
Flint Street	D1
Fontenoy Street	D6
Ford Street	C7-D7
Formby Street	B7-B6
Fox Street	D7-E7
Fraser Street	E5
Freemasons' Row	C6-D6
Gascoyne Street	B6-C6
Gibson Street	F1
Gilbert Street	D3
Gill Street	E4-E5
Goree Piazza	B4
Grafton Street	D1
Great Crosshall Street	C6
Great George Street	E1-E2-E3
Great Homer Street	D7-D8
Great Howard Street	B6-B7-B8
Great Newton Street	E5-E4-F4
Greenland Street	D1
Green Street	C8-D8
Hampton Street	E1-F1
Hanover Street	C3-C4-D4
Hardman Street	E3
Hatton Garden	C5-C6
Henry Street	D3
Heyworth Street	F8
Hill Street	D1-E1
Hood Street	D5
Hope Street	E2-E3-F3-F4
Hurst Street	C2-C3
Huskisson Street	F2
Islington	E6-F6
Jamaica Street	D1-D2
James Street	B4-C4
Jordan Street	D1-D2
Juvenal Street	D7
Kempston Street	E5-F5-F6
Kent Street	D2-D3
Kepler Street	E8-F8
Kings Dock Street	C2-C2
King Edward Street	B5-B6
Kingsway (Tunnel)	A6-A7-B7-C7
Kitchen Street	C2-D2
Landseer Road	F8
Langsdale Street	E6-F6
Leece Street	E3
Leeds Street	B6-C6
Limekiln Lane	C7-D7-D8
Lime Street	D4-D5
London Road	D5-E5-F5
Lord Nelson Street	D5-E5
Lord Street	C4
Love Lane	B7-B8
Lydia Ann Street	D3
Mansfield Street	E6
Mann Island	B4
Mathews Street	C4
Mill Street	E1
Moss Street	F5-F6
Mount Pleasant	F4
Mount Street	E3
Myrtle Street	E3-F3
Naylor Street	C6-D6
Nelson Street	D2-D3-E3
Neptune Street	B6
Netherfield Road North	E8-E7
Netherfield Road South	E7-E8
New Bird Street	D1-D2
New Islington	E6-F6
New Quay	B5
North John Street	C4-C5
Norton Street	E5
Oil Street	A7-B7
Old Hall Street	B5-B6
Oriel Street	C6-C7-D7
Oxford Street	F3-F4
Pall Mall	B7-B6-C6-B5-C5
Paradise Street	C3-C4
Parker Street	D4
Park Lane	C3-D3-D2
Park Way	F1-F2
Parliament Street	D1-E1-E2
Paul Street	C7-D7
Pembroke Place	E5-F5
Percy Street	E2-F2
Porter Street	A7-B7
Prescot Street	F5-F6
Prince Edwin Street	E7-E8
Prince's Road	F1-F2
Queensway (Tunnel)	A3-A4-B4-C4-C5
Ranelagh Street	D4
Regent Street	A7-B7
Renshaw Street	D4-E4-E3
Richmond Row	D7-E7
Roberts Street	B6
Rodney Street	E3-E4
Roe Street	D5
Roscoe Street	E3-E4
Roscommon Street	D8-E8
Rose Place	D7-E7
Rose Vale	E8
Russell Street	E4-E5
St Anne Street	D7-D6-E6
St James's Place	E1
St James Road	E2-E1
St James's Street	D2-D1-E1
Salisbury Street	E7-E6-F6
Saltney Street	A8-B8
Sandon Street	F2
School Lane	C4-D4
Scotland Road	D6-D7-D8
Seel Street	D4-D3-E3
Sefton Street	D1
Seymour Street	E5
Shaw Street	E7-F7-F6
Silvester Street	C8-D8
Simpson Street	D1-D2
Slater Street	D3-D4
Soho Street	E6-E7
South John Street	C4
Sparling Street	C2-D2
Spencer Street	F7
Stanhope Street	D1-E1
Stone Street	B8
Strand Street	B4-C4-C3
Tabley Street	C2-C3-D3
Tatlock Street	C8
Titchfield Street	C7-C8
Tithebarn Street	B5-C5-C6
The Strand	B4
Upper Duke Street	E3
Upper Hampton Street	F2
Upper Hill Street	E1-F1
Upper Parliament Street	F2
Upper Pitt Street	D2
Upper Stanhope Street	E1
Upper Stanhope Street	E1-F1
Vauxhall Road	C6-C7-C8
Victoria Street	C4-C5-D5
Village Street	F7
Vine Street	F3
Vulcan Street	A7-A8
Wapping	C2-C3
Waterloo Road	A8-A7-B7-A6-B6
Water Street	B4-B5-C5
Whitechapel	C4-C5-D5
Wilbraham Street	D8
William Brown Street	D5
William Henry Street	E6-E7-F7
Windsor Street	E1-F1
Wood Street	D4-D3-E3
York Street	C3-D3

LIVERPOOL
The Metropolitan Cathedral of Christ the King is one of Liverpool's most striking landmarks. Crowning the conical roof is a tower of stained glass which throws a pool of coloured light on to the altar below.

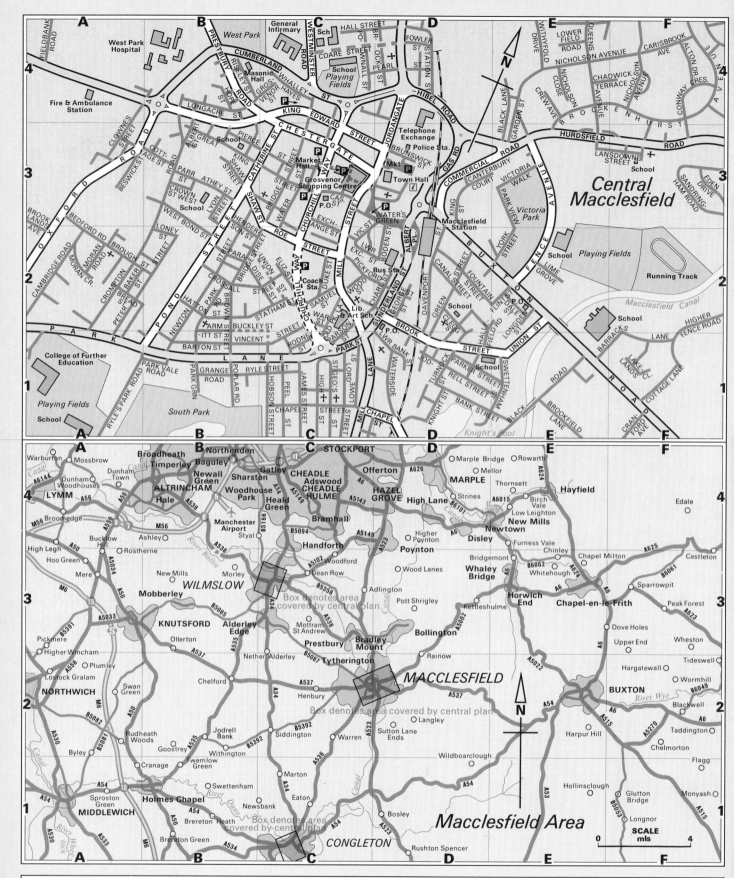

Macclesfield

One hundred and eight steps rise up to the Church of St Michael, which makes a striking and dramatic backdrop to the town that rises to meet it. The church can also be entered on the level from the market place, and its large monuments are amongst the best in Cheshire. The church is the finest reminder of the town's medieval origins, and other buildings of architectural interest include some

early mills and Georgian houses. Once the centre of the English silk industry, Macclesfield today concentrates on the production of man-made fibres, and still remains a pleasant market town. Amongst its open spaces, West Park is one of the oldest public parks in the country, and has at its entrance the Macclesfield Museum and Art Gallery, where a fine Egyptian collection can be seen.

Congleton Stone Age man is thought to have built the chambered tomb known as Bridestones

which stands on the road to Leek, so Congleton can claim to date from Neolithic times. The town's medieval street plan is still intact, and it has some fine Tudor buildings — a legacy to its prosperity at this time. Now an important cattle market and textile town, its focal point is the fine Venetian-Gothic style Victorian Town Hall.

Wilmslow nestles in the valleys of the Bollin and Dean. With one of the area's most picturesque positions, this is a pleasant dormitory town.

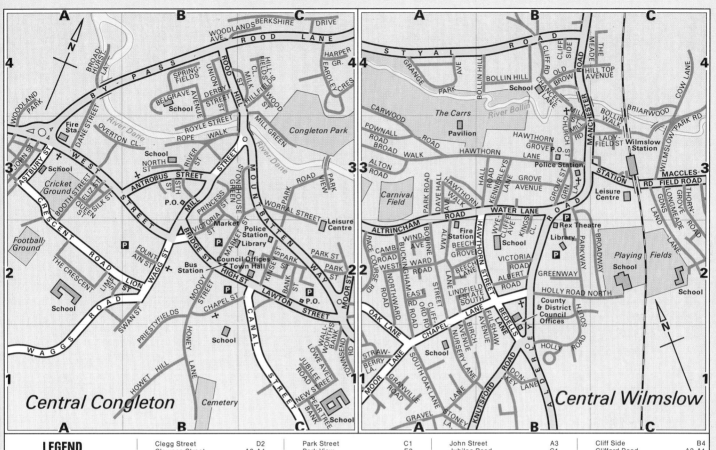

Central Congleton

Central Wilmslow

LEGEND

Town Plan

AA recommended route
Restricted roads
Other roads
Buildings of interest — Hall
Car parks — P
Parks and open spaces

Area Plan

A roads
B roads
Locations — Littleton○
Urban area

Street Index with Grid Reference

Macclesfield

Albert Place	D2-D3
Albert Street	B3-B4
Alton Drive	F4
Armitt Street	B2-B1
Athey Street	B3
Baker Street	A2
Bank Street	D1-E1
Barracks Lane	E1-F1-F2
Barton Street	B1
Bedford Road	A3-A2
Beswick Street	A3
Black Lane	E3-E4
Black Road	E1
Boden Street	D2-D3
Bread Street	C2
Bridge Street	B2-C2-C3
Brock Street	D4
Brockenhurst Avenue	E3-E4-F4
Brook Street	D2-D1-E1
Brookfield Lane	E1
Brooklands Avenue	A3-A2
Brough Street	A2-B2
Brown Street	B2-B1
Brunswick Street	D3
Buckley Street	B2-B1-C1-C2
Buxton Road	D3-D2-E2-E1-F1
Cambridge Road	A2
Canal Street	D2
Canterbury Court	D3
Carisbrook Avenue	F4
Castle Street	C3
Catherine Street	B3-C3
Chadwick Terrace	E4-F4
Chapel Street	C1-D1
Charlotte Street	D2
Chestergate	C4-C3
Churchill Way	C2-C3
Clegg Street	D2
Clownes Street	A3-A4
Coare Street	C4-D4
Commercial Road	D3-E3
Conway Crescent	F4
Cottage Lane	F1
Cottage Street	A3-B3
Cranford Avenue	F1
Crew Avenue	E4
Crompton Road	A2-B2-B3
Crossall Street	B2-C2
Crown Street West	B3
Cumberland Street	B4-C4
Dale Street	E2
Davenport Street	D1-D2-D3
Duke Street	C2
Eden Drive	F3
Elizabeth Street	C2
Exchange Street	C3-C2
Fence Avenue	E2-E3
Fieldbank Road	A4
Flint Street	E2
Fountain Street	D2
Fowler Street	D4
Garden Street	E3-E4
Gas Road	D3
George Street	D2
Grange Road	B1
Great King Street	B3-C3
Green Street	D1-D2
Grosvenor Street	B4-C4
Hallefield Road	D1-D2
Hall Street	C4-D4
Hatton Street	B2
Henderson Street	B3-B2
Hibel Road	D4-D3
High Street	C1
Higher Fence Road	F1-F2
Hobson Street	C1
Hope Street	B4
Hurdsfield Road	E3-F3
James Street	C1
Jodrell Street	D1-E1
Jordangate	D3-D4
King Street	D3
King Edward Street	C4-C3-D3
Knight Street	D1
Lakelands Close	F1
Lansdowne Street	E3-F3
Lime Grove	E2
Loney Street	B2
Longacre Street	B4
Longden Street	E2
Lord Street	C1
Lowe Street	C1
Lower Bank Street	D2-D1
Lower Exchange Street	C2-D2
Lower Field Road	E4
Lyon Street	B3
Mill Lane	C1
Mill Street	C2-C3
Moran Crescent	A2
Moran Road	A2
Newton Street	B1-B2
Nicholson Avenue	E4-F4
Nicholson Close	E4
Old Park Lane	C1-C2
Oxford Road	A2-A3-B3-B4
Paradise Street	B2-C2
Park Green	C1
Park Lane	A2-A1-B1-C1
Park Road	B2
Park Street	C1
Park View	E3
Parker Street	D1-E1
Park Vale Road	A1-B1
Parr Street	A2
Parsonage Street	C1-C2
Pearl Street	C4-D4
Peel Street	C1
Peter Street	A1-A2-B2
Pickford Street	C2-D2
Pierce Street	B3-C3
Pond Street	A1-B1-B2-B3
Poplar Road	B1
Pownall Street	C2
Prestbury Road	B4-C4
Queens Avenue	E4-E3
Riseley Street	B4
Rodney Street	C1
Roe Street	B3-C2
Ryle Street	B1-C1
Ryle's Park Road	A1
St George's Street	C1
Samuel Street	C2
Sandringham Road	F3
Shaw Street	B3-C3
Stratham Street	B2-C2
Station Street	D4
Sunderland Street	C1-C2-D2
Swettenham Street	E1
Turnock Street	D1
Union Street	B2-C2
Union Street	E1-E2
Victoria Street	C2-C3-D3
Victoria Walk	E3
Vincent Street	B1-C1-C2
Wardle Street	C2
Waterside	D1
Water Street	C2-C3
Water's Green	D3
West Bond Street	B3-B2
Westminster Road	C4
Whalley Hayes	C4
Withyfold Drive	E4
Wood Street	C2
York Street	E2

Congleton

Antrobus Street	B3
Astbury Street	A3
Bank Street	C2
Belgrave Avenue	B4-B3
Berkshire Drive	B4-C4
Booth Street	A2-A3
Bridge Street	B2
Broadhurst Lane	A4
By-Pass	A3-A4-B4
Canal Road	C2-C1
Chapel Street	B2-C2
Crescent Road	A3-A2
Dane Street	A3-A4
Derby Street	B4
Eardley Crescent	C4
Elizabeth Street	A3
Fountain Street	B2
Harper Grove	C4
High Street	B2-C2
Hillfields	C4
Hillfields Close	C4
Honey Lane	B2-B1
Howet Hill	A1-B1

Wilmslow

Albert Road	B2
Alderley Road	B1-B2-B3-C3
Alma Lane	A2
Alton Road	A3
Altrincham Road	A2-A3-B3
Bedells Lane	B2-B1
Beech Grove	A2
Beech Lane	A2
Birch Avenue	A2-A1
Bollin Hill	B4
Bollin Walk	C3
Bourne Street	A2
Briarwood	C4
Broad Walk	A3
Broadway	B3-B2-C2
Buckingham Road	A2-A1
Cambridge Road	A2
Carwood Road	A4-A3
Chancel Lane	B4
Chapel Lane	A1-A2-B2
Church Street	B3
Cliff Road	B4
John Street	A3
Jubilee Road	C1
Kinsey Street	C2
Lawton Street	C2
Lime Street	A2
Lion Street	A2-B2
Lowe Avenue	C1
Market Street	B2-C2-C3
Milk Street	B4-C4
Mill Green	C4-C3
Mill Street	B3-C3
Moody Street	B2
Moor Street	C2
Mountbatten Way	C3-C2
New Street	C1
North Street	B3
Overton Close	A3-B3
Park Road	C3
Park Street	C2
Park View	C3
Pear Tree Bank	C1
Priestyfields	B1-B2
Princess Street	B2-B3
Queen Street	A3
River Street	B3
Rood Hill	B4-C4
Rood Lane	B4-C4
Rope Walk	B3
Royle Street	B3-B4-C4
Silk Street	A3
South Street	B3
Springfields	B4
Stonehouse Green	C3
Swan Street	A1-A2-B2
The Crescent	A2
Townsend Road	C1
Union Street	B4
Victoria Street	B2-B3
Wagg Street	B2
Waggs Road	A1-A2-B2
Wallworths Bank	C1
West Street	A3-B3-B2
Wood Street	C4
Woodland Park	A3-A4
Woodlands Avenue	B4-C4
Worral Street	C3-C2

Cliff Side	B4
Clifford Road	A2-A1
Cow Lane	C4
Dave Hall Avenue	A3
Donkey Lane	B1
Eastwood Road	A2
Fulshaw Avenue	B2-B1
Grange Park Avenue	A4
Granville Road	A1
Gravel Lane	A1
Green Lane	B3
Greenway	B2
Grove Avenue	B3
Grove Street	B3
Hall Road	B3
Hawthorn Grove	B3
Hawthorn Lane	A3-B3
Hawthorn Street	A2-B2-B3
Hawthorn Walk	A3
Hill Top Avenue	B4-C4
Holly Road North	B2-C2
Holly Road South	B1-B2
Kennerleys Lane	B3
Kings Close	B2-B3
Knutsford Road	A1-B1
Ladyfield Street	C3
Land Lane	C3-C2
Lindfield Estate South	A2
Longmeade Gardens	C3-C2
Macclesfield Road	C3
Manchester Road	B3-C3-C4-B4
Mill Road	B3
Mill Street	B4-B3
Moor Lane	A1
Northward Road	A2-A1
Nursery Lane	A1-B1
Oak Lane	A2-A1
Old Brow	B4
Park Road	A3
Parkway	B3-B2
Pownall Road	A3
Race Course Road	A2
South Oak Lane	A1
Station Road	C3
Stoney Lane	A1
Strawberry Lane	A1
Styal Road	A4-B4
The Meade	C4
Thorngrove Road	C3-C2
Victoria Road	B2
Water Lane	B3
Westward Road	A2
Wilmslow Park Road	C3-C4
Windsor Avenue	A2
Wyecliffe Avenue	B2-B3

47

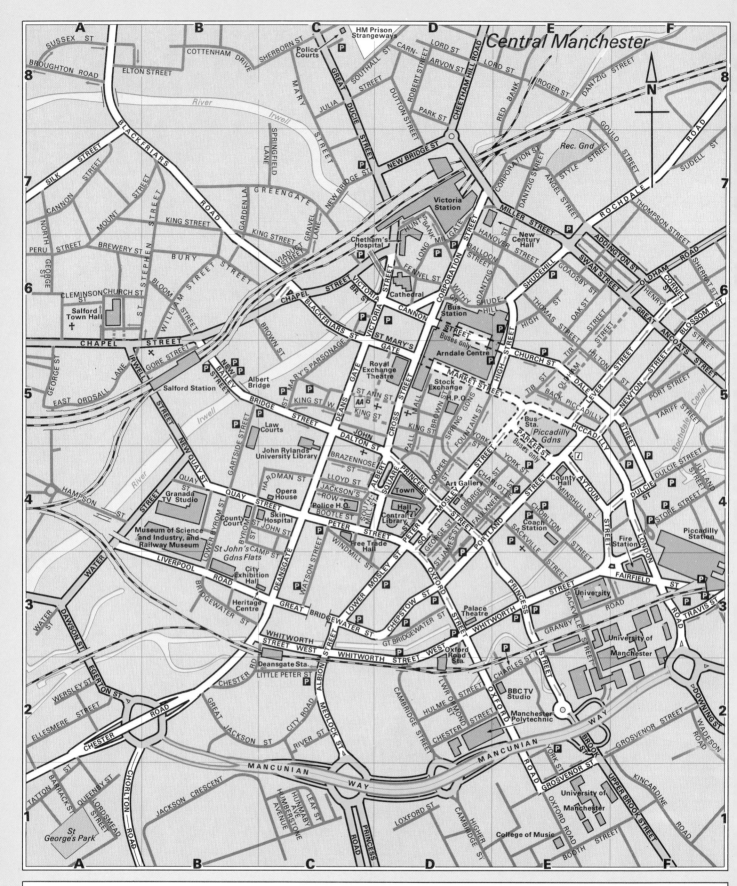

Manchester

The gigantic conurbation called Greater Manchester covers a staggering 60 square miles, reinforcing Manchester's claim to be Britain's second city. Commerce and industry are vital aspects of the city's character, but it is also an important cultural centre – the Halle Orchestra has its home at the Free Trade Hall (a venue for many concerts besides classical music), there are several theatres, a library (the John Rylands) which houses one of the most important collections of books in the world, and a number of museums and galleries, including the Whitworth Gallery with its lovely watercolours.

Like many great cities it suffered badly during the bombing raids of World War II, but some older buildings remain, including the town hall, a huge building designed in Gothic style by Alfred Waterhouse and opened in 1877. Manchester Cathedral dates mainly from the 15th century and is noted for its fine tower and outstanding carved woodwork. Nearby is Chetham's Hospital, also 15th-century and now housing a music school. Much new development has taken place, and more is planned. Shopping precincts cater for the vast population, and huge hotels have provided services up to international standards. On the edge of the city is the Belle Vue centre, a large entertainments complex including concert and exhibition facilities, and a speedway stadium.

Manchester District map showing areas including Pendlebury, Swinton, Salford, Eccles, Stretford, Manchester, Cheetham Hill, Harpurhey, Failsworth, Droylsden, Ashton-under-Lyne, Denton, Reddish, and others.

Key to Town Plan and Area Plan

Town Plan

AA Recommended roads	═══
Other roads	───
Restricted roads	▬▬▬
Buildings of interest	Baths ▢
Car parks	P
Parks and open spaces	▱
Churches	†
AA Centre	AA
One Way Streets	←

District Plan

A roads	───
B roads	▬▬▬

STREET INDEX
-with grid reference

Manchester

Addington Street	E7-E6-F6
Albert Square	C4-D4
Albion Street	C2-C3
Angel Street	E7
Aytoun Street	E4-F4-F3-E3
Back Piccadilly	E5-F5-F4
Balloon Street	D6-E6
Barrack Street	A1
Blackfriars Road	A8-A7-B7-B6-C6
Blackfriars Street	C5-C6
Bloom Street	B6
Blossom Street	F6
Booth Street	E1-F1
Bootle Street	C4
Brazennose Street	C4-D4
Brewery Street	A6-B6
Bridge Street	B5-C5
Bridgewater Street	B3
Brook Street	E2
Broughton Road	A8
Brown Street	B6-C6-C5
Brown Street	D4-D5
Bury Street	B6-C6
Byrom Street	B4
Cambridge Street	D2
Camp Street	B4-C4-C3
Cannon Street	A7
Cannon Street	D6-D5-E5
Carnarvon Street	D8
Chapel Street	A6-A5-B5-B6-C6-D6
Charles Street	E2
Charlotte Street	D4-E4
Cheetham Hill Road	D7-D8
Chepstow Street	D3
Chester Road	A1-A2-B2-C2-C3
Chester Street	D2-E2
Chorlton Road	B2-A2-A1-B1
Chorlton Street	E3-E4
Church Street	A6-B6
Church Street	E5
Cleminson Street	A6
City Road	C2
Cooper Street	D4
Cornel Street	F6
Corporation Street	D6-D7-E7
Cottenham Drive	B8
Cross Street	D4-D5-D6
Dale Street	E5-F5-F4
Dantzig Street	D6-E6-E7-E8-F8
Dawson Street	A3
Deansgate	C3-C4-C5
Downing Street	F2
Dulcie Street	F4
Dutton Street	D7-D8
East Ordsall Lane	A5
Egerton Street	A2
Ellesmere Street	A2
Elton Street	A8-B2
Fairfield Street	F3
Faulkner Street	D4-E4
Fennel Street	D6
Fountain Street	D4-D5
Garden Lane	B6-B7
Gartside Street	B4-B5
George Street	A5
George Street	D3-D4-E4
Goadsby Street	E6
Gore Street	B5
Gould Street	E8-E7-F7
Granby Road	E3-F3
Gravel Lane	C6-C7
Great Ancoats Street	F5-F6
Great Bridgewater Street	C3-D3
Great Ducie Street	C8-C7-D7
Great Jackson Street	B2-C2
Greengate	B7-C7
Grosvenor Street	E1-E2-F2
Hampson Street	A4
Hanover Street	D7-D6-E6
Hardman Street	C4
Henry Street	F5-F6
High Street	E5-E6
Higher Cambridge Street	D1
Hilton Street	E5-F5
Hulme Street	D2
Humberstone Avenue	C1
Hunmaby Avenue	C1
Hunt's Bank	D6-D7
Irwell Street	A5-B5
Jackson Crescent	B1-C1
Jackson's Row	C4
John Dalton Street	C5-C4-D4-D5
Julia Street	C8-D8
Jutland Street	F4
Kincardine Road	F1-F2
King Street	A7-B7-B6-C6
King Street	C5-D5
King St West	C5
Leaf Street	C1
Lever Street	E5-F5-F6
Little Peter Street	B2-C2
Liverpool Road	A4-A3-B4-B3-C3
Lloyd Street	C4
London Road	F3-F4
Long Millgate	D6-D7
Lord Street	D8-E8
Lordsmead Street	A1
Lower Byrom Street	B3-B4
Lower Mosley Street	C3-D3-D4
Lower Ormond Street	D2
Loxford Street	D1
Mancunian Way	B2-B1-C2-C1-D1-D2-E2-F2
Market Street	D5-E5
Mary Street	C7-C8
Medlock Street	C2
Miller Street	D7-E7-E6
Minshull Street	E4
Mosley Street	D4-D5-E4-E5
Mount Street	A6-A7-B7
Newton Street	F5
New Bailey Street	B5
New Bridge Street	C7-D7
North George Street	A6-A7
New Quay Street	B4-B5
Oak Street	E6
Oldham Road	E5-E6-F6
Oldham Street	D3-D3-E3
Oxford Road	D2-E2-E1
Oxford Street	D4-D3-D2
Pall Mall	D4-D5
Park Street	D8
Parker Street	E4-E5
Peru Street	A6
Peter Street	C4-D4
Piccadilly	E5-E4-F4
Port Street	F5
Portland Street	D3-D4-E4-E5
Princess Road	C1-D1
Princess Street	D4-E4-D3-E3-E2
Quay Street	B4-C4
Queenby Street	A1
Red Bank	E7-E8
River Street	C2
Robert Street	D8
Rochdale Road	E7-F7-F8
Roger Street	E8
St Ann Street	C5-D5
St Mary's Gate	C5-C6-D5-D6
St Mary's Parsonage	C5-C6
St James Street	D3-D4
St John Street	B4-C4
St Peter Square	D4
St Stephen Street	A6-B6-B7
Sackville Street	E2-E3-E4
Sherrat Street	F6
Sherborn Street	B8-C8
Shudehill	D6-E6
Silk Street	A7
Southall Street	C8-D8
Southmill Street	C4
Spring Gardens	D4-D5
Springfield Lane	C7-C8
Store Street	F4
Style Street	E7-E8
Sudell Street	F7-F8
Sussex Street	A8
Swan Street	E6-F6
Tatton Street	A1
Tariff Street	F5
Thomas Street	E5-E6
Thompson Street	F6-F7
Tib Street	E5-E6-E6-F6
Travis Street	F3
Upper Brook Street	E2-E1-F1
Viaduct Street	C6
Victoria Bridge Street	C6-D6
Victoria Street	C6-D6
Wadeson Road	F2
Water Street	A3-A4-B4
Watson Street	C3-C4
Wersley Street	A2
Whitworth Street	D3-E3
Whitworth Street West	B3-C3-C2-D2-D3
William Street	B6
Windmill Street	C4-C3-D3
Withy Green	D6
York Street	D5-D4-E4

MANCHESTER

The Barton Swing Bridge carries the Bridgewater Canal over the Manchester Ship Canal, which links Manchester with the sea nearly 40 miles away. Completed in 1894, the canal is navigable by vessels up to 15,000 tons.

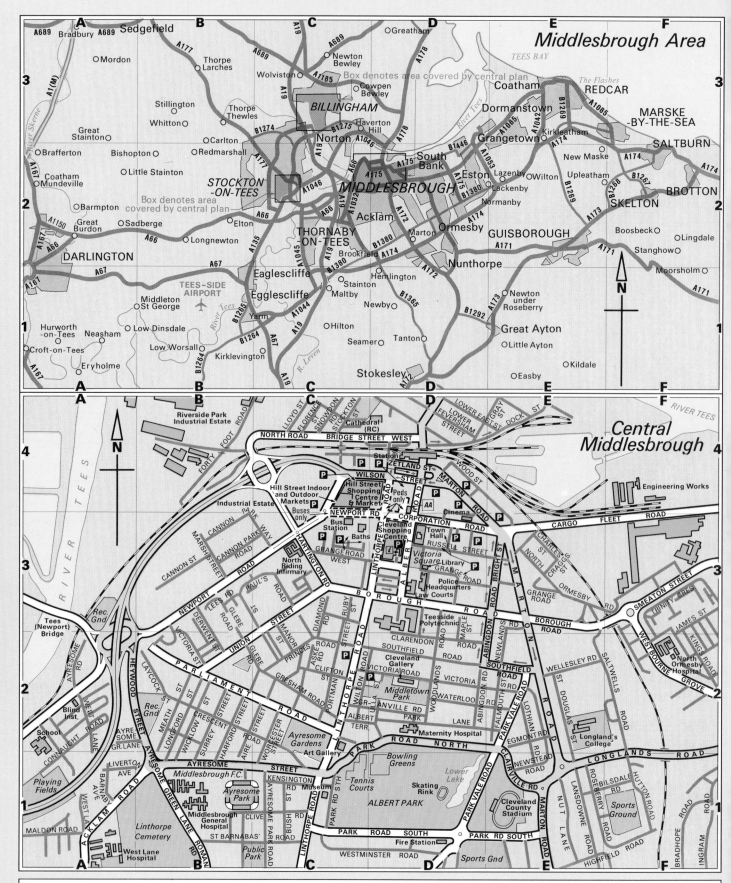

Middlesbrough

Heavy industry dominates Middlesbrough. It has been a centre of iron and steel manufacture since the 1840s although much of the steel-making has moved eastwards to a new works near Redcar. Its rise had begun ten years before, when the Stockton and Darlington Railway purchased land here and turned what had been a quiet riverside village into a busy coal exporting town. Middlesbrough's most notable structure is the Transporter Bridge, built across the Tees in 1911. It is one of only two bridges of its type left in Britain. The town centre is modern with spacious shopping areas and new public buildings. The Dorman Museum covers the region's history and there are two major art galleries.

Stockton has a place in transport history; it was here, on 27 September 1825, that the world's first steam passenger railway service began. The town, also situated on the River Tees, became an engineering and shipbuilding centre and is still an important industrial centre today. It has a town hall of 1763 standing in the middle of one of the widest main streets in England.

Billingham also stands on the Tees, and the river was one of the factors which encouraged various chemical industries to become established here. North Sea oil has given a boost to that industry, and the town centre has been completely rebuilt with every facility.

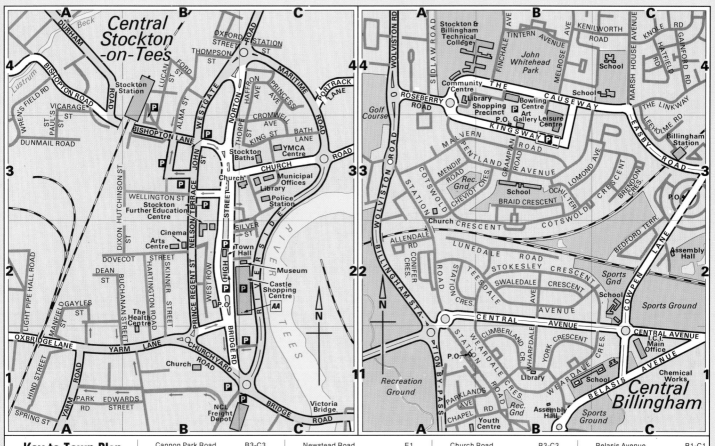

Central Stockton-on-Tees

Central Billingham

Key to Town Plan and Area Plan

Town Plan

AA Recommended roads
Other roads
Restricted roads
Buildings of interest
Car Parks   P
Parks and open spaces
One way street

Area Plan

A roads
B roads
Locations   Aycliffe ○
Urban area

Street Index with Grid Reference

Middlesbrough

Stockton-on-Tees

Billingham

MIDDLESBROUGH

In 1911 the Transporter Bridge was built to replace the river ferry between Port Clarence and Middlesbrough. It is still used today and a special viewing platform has been built to enable visitors to watch the bridge in operation.

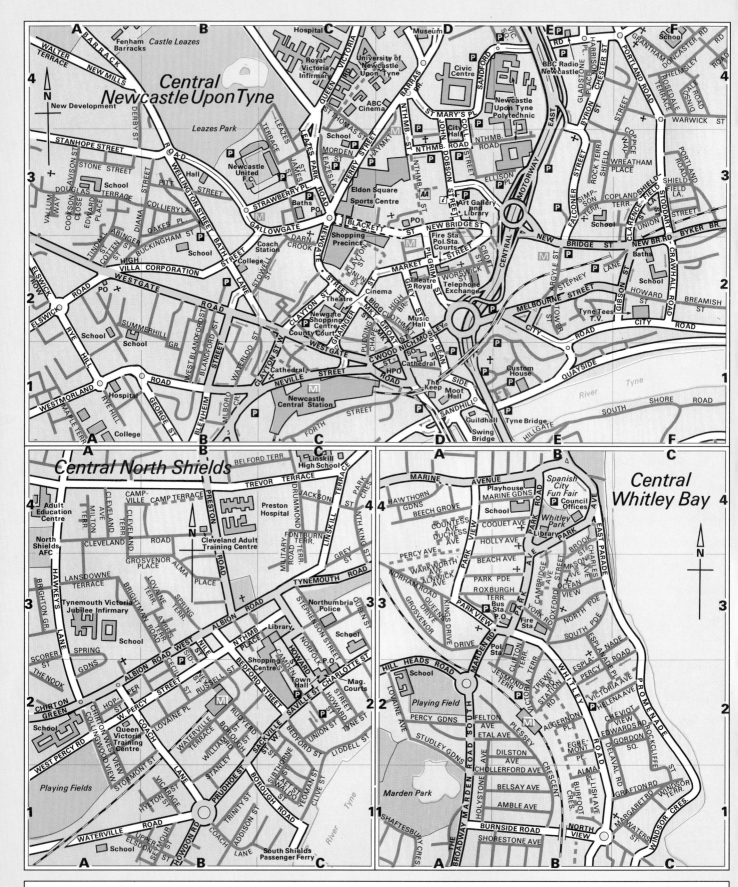

Newcastle

Six bridges span the Tyne at Newcastle; they all help to create a striking scene, but the most impressive is the High Level Bridge, built by Robert Stephenson in 1845-49 and consisting of two levels, one for the railway and one for the road. It is from the river that some of the best views of the city can be obtained. Grey Street is Newcastle's most handsome thoroughfare. It dates from the

time, between 1835 and 1840, when much of this part of the city was replanned and rebuilt. Elegant façades curve up to Grey's Monument. Close to the Monument is the Eldon Centre, combining sports facilities and shopping centre to form an integrated complex which is one of the largest of its kind in Europe. Newcastle has many museums. The industrial background of the city is traced in the Museum of Science and Engineering, while the Laing Art Gallery and Museum covers painting,

costumes and local domestic history. The Hancock Museum has an exceptional natural history collection and the John George Joicey Museum has period displays in a 17th-century almshouse. In Black Gate is one of Britain's most unusual museums – a collection of over 100 sets of bagpipes. Within the University precincts are three further museums. Of the city's open spaces, Town Moor is the largest. At nearly 1,000 acres it is big enough to feel genuinely wild.

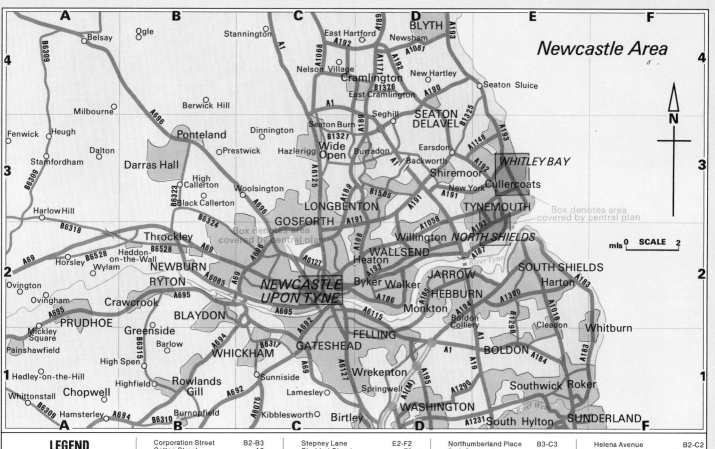

Newcastle Area

BLYTH
East Hartford
Newsham
Nelson Village
Cramlington
East Cramlington
New Hartley
Seaton Sluice
Seaton Burn
SEATON DELAVEL
Ogle
Stannington
Belsay
Berwick Hill
Dinnington
Seghill
Earsdon
WHITLEY BAY
Milbourne
Ponteland
Prestwick
Hazlerigg
Wide Open
Burradon
Backworth
Shiremoor
New York
Cullercoats
Fenwick
Heugh
Stamfordham
Darras Hall
High Callerton
Woolsington
LONGBENTON
TYNEMOUTH
Dalton
Black Callerton
GOSFORTH
Willington
NORTH SHIELDS
Harlow Hill
Throckley
Heddon-on-the-Wall
NEWBURN
WALLSEND
Heaton
Horsley
Wylam
RYTON
Byker
Walker
JARROW
SOUTH SHIELDS
Harton
Ovington
Crawcrook
BLAYDON
NEWCASTLE UPON TYNE
HEBBURN
Monkton
Boldon Colliery
Cleadon
Whitburn
Ovingham
PRUDHOE
Greenside
Barlow
WHICKHAM
GATESHEAD
FELLING
BOLDON
Mickley Square
Painshawfield
High Spen
Rowlands Gill
Sunniside
Wrekenton
Springwell
Southwick
Roker
Hedley-on-the-Hill
Chopwell
Highfield
Lamesley
WASHINGTON
Whittonstall
Hamsterley
Burnopfield
Kibblesworth
Birtley
South Hylton
SUNDERLAND

Box denotes area covered by central plan

N

mls 0 SCALE 2

River Tyne
River Wear

53

LEGEND

Town Plan

AA recommended route
Restricted roads
Other roads
Buildings of interest — Hall
Car parks — P
Parks and open spaces
Metro stations — M
One way streets

Area Plan

A roads
B roads
Locations — Craghead○
Urban area

Street Index with Grid Reference

Newcastle

Abinger Street	A2
Argyle Street	E2
Avison Street	A3
Barrack Road	A4-B4-B3
Barras Bridge	D4
Bath Lane	B2-C2
Bigg Market Street	C2-D2
Blackett Street	C3-D3-D2
Blandford Street	B1-B2
Blenheim Street	B1-B2
Breamish Street	F2
Buckingham Street	A2-B2-B3
Byker Bridge	F2-F3
Byran Street	E3-E4
Central Motorway	E1-D1-D2-E2-E3-E4
Chester Street	E4
City Road	E1-E2-F2
Clarence Street	F2-F3
Clayton Street	C2
Clayton Street West	B1-C1-C2
Clothmarket	D2
College Street	D3-D4
Colliery Lane	B3
Collingwood Street	C1-D1
Cookson Close	A3
Copland Terrace	E3-F3
Coppice Way	F3
Corporation Street	B2-B3
Cotten Street	A2
Crawhill Road	F2
Croft Street	D2
Darn Crook	C2-C3
Dean Street	D1-D2
Derby Street	A3-A4
Diana Street	A2-A3-B3
Dinsdale Road	F4
Doncaster Road	F4
Douglas Terrace	A3-B3
Edward Place	A3
Ellison Place	D3-E3
Elswick Road	A2
Elswick Row	A2
Falconer Street	E3
Forth Street	C1-D1
Gallowgate	B3-C3
George Street	A1-B1
Gibson Street	F2
Gladstone Place	F4
Grainger Street	C1-C2-D2
Grantham Road	F4
Grey Street	D2
Great Market	D1-D2
Harrison Place	E4
Haymarket	D3-D4
Helmsley Road	F4
High Bridge	D2
High Villa	A2
Hillgate	E1
Howard Street	F2
John Dobson Street	D3-D4
Leazes Lane	C3
Leazes Park Road	C3-C4
Leazes Terrace	C3-C4
Maple Terrace	A1
Market Street	D2
Marlborough Crescent	B1
Melbourne Street	E2-F2
Morden Street	C3
Moseley Street	D1-D2
Neville Street	C1
New Bridge Road	F2-F3
New Bridge Street	D3-E3-E2-F2
Newgate Street	C2-C3
New Mills	A4
Northumberland Street	D4-D3-E4
Nun Street	C2
Oakes Place	A2-B2-B3
Perry Street	C3-D3-D4
Pilgrim Street	D2
Pitt Street	B3
Portland Road	F3-F4
Pudding Chape	C1-C2
Quayside	D1-E1-F1-F2
Queen Victoria Road	C4
Rock Terrace	E3
Rosedale Terrace	F4
Rye Hill	A1-A2
St James Street	C3
St Mary's Place	D4
St Nicholas Square	D1-D2
St Thomas Street	C3-C4
Sandford Road	D4-E4
Sandhill	D1
Shield Street	E3-F3-F4
Sheildfield Lane	F3
Side	D1
Simpson Terrace	E3
South Shore Road	E1-F1
Stanhope Street	A3-B3
Stepney Lane	E2-F2
Stoddart Street	F3
Stone Street	A3
Stowell Street	B2-C2
Strawberry Place	B3-C3
Summerhill Grove	A2-B2-B1
Tindall Street	A2
Tower Street	E2
Union Street	F3
Vallum Way	A3
Victoria Square	E4
Walter Terrace	A4
Warwick Street	F4
Waterloo Street	B1-B2-C2
Wellington Street	B3
Westgate Road	A2-B2-C2-C1-D1
Westmorland Road	A1-B1
West Blandford Street	B1-B2
Worswick Street	D2
Wreatham Place	E3-F3

North Shields

Addison Street	B1
Albion Road	B3-C3
Albion Road West	A2-B2-B3
Alma Place	B3
Ayre's Terrace	B3
Bedford Street	B3-B2-C2
Belford Terrace	B4-C4
Borough Road	B2-B1-C1
Brightman Road	A3-B3
Brighton Grove	A3
Camden Street	C2-C3
Camp Terrace	B4
Campville	A4-B4
Cecil Street	B2
Charlotte Street	C2-C3
Chirton Green	A2
Chirton West View	A1-A2
Cleveland Avenue	A4
Cleveland Road	A4-B4
Cleveland Terrace	A3-A4
Clive Street	C1-C2
Coach Lane	A2-B2-B1
Collingwood View	A1-A2
Drummond Terrace	C3-C4
Fontbarn Terrace	C4
Grey Street	C3-C4
Grosvenor Place	A3-B3
Hawkey's Lane	A2-A3-A4
Hopper Street	A2
Howard Street	C2-C3
Howdon Road	B1
Hylton Street	A1-B1
Jackson Street	C4
Laet Street	C1
Lansdowne Terrace	A3
Liddell Street	C2
Linskill Terrace	C3-C4
Lovaine Place	B2
Lovaine Terrace	B3
Military Road	C3-C4
Milton Terrace	A4
Nile Street	B3
Norfolk Street	C2-C3
North King Street	C3-C4

Newcastle (cont.)

Northumberland Place	B3-C3
Park Crescent	C4
Preston Road	B3-B4
Prudhoe Street	B1-B2
Queen Street	C3
Rudyard Street	B2-C2-C1
Russell Street	B2
Sackville Street West	B2-C2
Saville Street	C2
Scorer Street	A2-A3
Seymour Street	B1
Sibthorne Street	C1-C2
Sidney Street	B2-B3
Spring Gardens	A2-A3
Spring Terrace	B3
Stanley Street	B1-B2
Stephenson Street	C2-C3
Stormont Street	A1-A2-B2
The Nook	A2
Trevor Terrace	B4-C4
Trinity Street	B1
Tyne Street	C2
Tynemouth Road	C3
Union Street	C2
Upper Elsdon Street	A1-B1
Vicarage Street	B1
Waldo Street	C1
Waterville Road	A1-B1
Waterville Terrace	B2
West Percy Road	A1-A2
West Percy Street	A2-B2-B3
William Street	B2-C2
Yeoman Street	C1-C2

Whitley Bay

Algernon Place	B2
Alma Place	B1
Alnwick Avenue	A3
Amble Avenue	A1-B1
Beach Avenue	A3-B3-B4
Beech Grove	A4
Belsay Avenue	A1-B1
Brook Street	B3-B4
Burfoot Crescent	B1
Burnside Road	A1-B1
Cambridge Avenue	B3-B4
Charles Avenue	B3-B4
Cheviot View	B2-C2
Chollerford Avenue	A1-B1
Clifton Terrace	B2-B3
Coquet Avenue	A4-B4
Countess Avenue	A4
Delaval Road	B2-C2-C1
Dilston Avenue	A2-B2
Duchess Avenue	A4
East Parade	B3-B4
Edwards Road	B2-C2
Egremont Place	B2
Esplanade	B2-B3-C3
Esplanade Place	B3-B2-C2
Etal Avenue	B2
Felton Avenue	A2-B2
Gordon Square	C2
Grafton Road	C1
Grosvenor Drive	A3
Hawthorne Gardens	A4
Helena Avenue	B2-C2
Hill Heads Road	A2-A3-A2
Holly Avenue	A4-B4
Holystone Avenue	A1-A2
Jesmond Terrace	A2-B2
Kings Drive	A3
Lish Avenue	B1
Lovaine Avenue	A4
Marden Road	A2-A3-B3
Marden Road South	A1-A2
Margaret Road	C1
Marine Avenue	A4-B4
Marine Gardens	A4-B4
Mason Avenue	B3
Norham Road	A3
North Parade	B3
North View	B1
Ocean View	B3
Oxford Street	B3-B4
Park Avenue	B3-B4
Park Parade	A3-B3
Park Road	B4
Park View	A3-A4
Percy Avenue	A3-A4
Percy Gardens	A2
Percy Road	B2-C2-C3
Plessey Crescent	A2-B2-B1
Promenade	C1-C2-C3
Queens Drive	A3
Rockcliffe Street	C1-C2
Roxburgh Terrace	A3-B3
Shaftesbury Crescent	A1
Shorestone Avenue	A1-B1
South Parade	B3
Station Road	B2
Studley Gardens	A1-A2
The Broadway	A1
Trewit Road	B3
Victoria Avenue	B2-C2
Victoria Terrace	B2-B3
Warkworth Avenue	A3
Waters Street	C1
Whitley Road	B1-B2-B3
Windsor Crescent	C1
Windsor Terrace	C1
York Road	B3

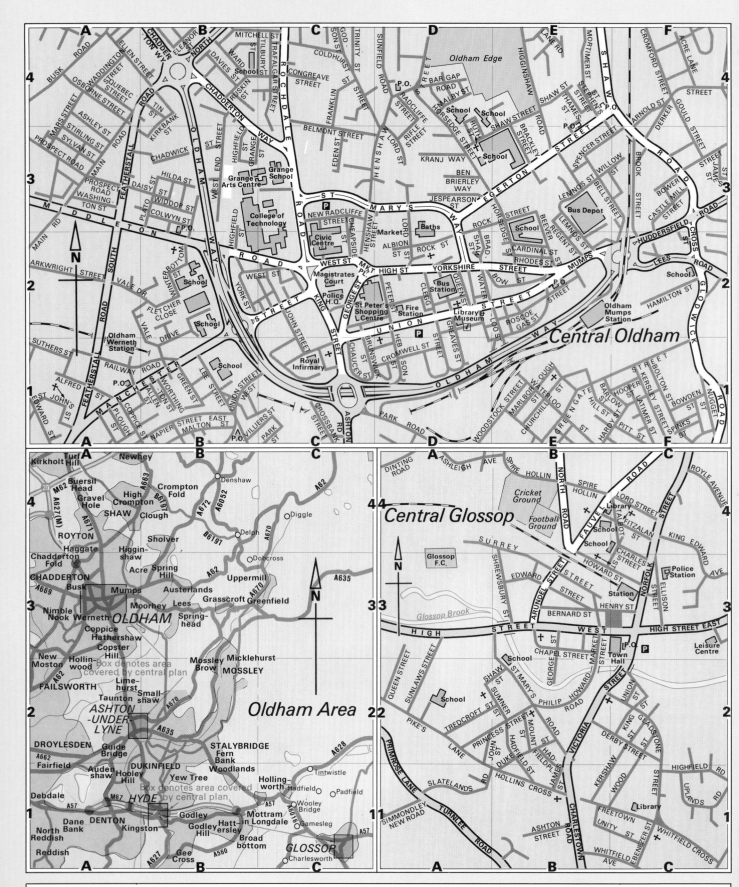

Oldham

Snooker championships are a feature of Oldham's Queen Elizabeth Hall, which is also in frequent use by the BBC for recording concerts. This ex-mill town has prospered with the coming of the M62, and as well as the Civic Centre, which is the site of the hall, it also has a fine modern Town Square Shopping Centre. In a pleasant combination of the old and new, it stands proudly alongside the old-established Tommyfield Market, said to be one of the country's largest permanent markets. The Local Interest Centre traces Oldham's past.

Ashton-under-Lyne Pride of Ashton-under-Lyne is the Parish Church of St Michael, noted for its fine 16th-century stained glass.

Glossop Cobbled streets, 17th-century stone houses and easy access to the Dark Peak moors are among the attractions of this High Peaks town. A popular touring centre, it also draws railway enthusiasts: nearby Dinting Railway Centre has a fine collection of steam locomotives offering rides most Sundays and Bank Holidays, while Manor Park is noted for its miniature steam railway. The park also draws the crowds for the annual local festival, which is held here each July.

Hyde lies in the Tame Valley and was once a centre for cotton manufacturing and for coal mining. Good shops and sports facilities can be found in the town.

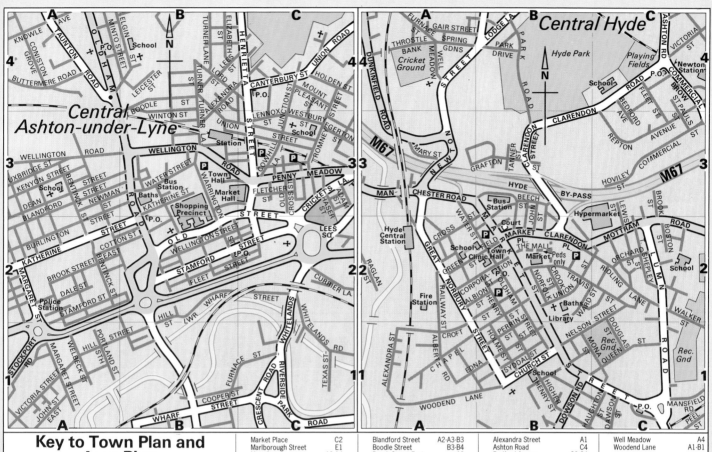

Central Ashton-under-Lyne

Central Hyde

Key to Town Plan and Area Plan

Town Plan

AA Recommended roads	
Restricted roads	
Other roads	
Buildings of interest	Theatre
Car Parks	P
Parks and open spaces	

Area Plan

A roads	
B roads	
Locations	Dobcross ○
Urban area	

STREET INDEX WITH GRID REFERENCE

OLDHAM

Acre Lane	F4
Albion Street	D2
Alfred Street	A1
Allen Street	B1
Arkwright Street	A2
Arnold Street	F4
Ashley Street	A3-A4
Ashton Road	C1
Bar Gap Road	D4
Barlow Street	E1-F1
Beever Street	E2-E3
Bell Street	E3-F3
Belmont Street	C4-C3-D3
Ben Brierley Way	D3
Bolton Street	F1
Bow Street	D2-E2
Bower Street	F3
Bowden Street	F1
Brackley Street	E3
Bradshaw Street	D2-D3
Brook Street	F2-F3
Brunswick Street	C1
Busk Road	A4
Cardinal Street	E2
Castle Mill Street	F3
Chadderton Way	B4-B3-C3
Chadwick Street	B3
Chaucer Street	C1
Cheapside Street	C2-C3
Churchill Street	E1
Clegg Street	D1-D2
Coldhurst Street	C4-D4-D3
Colwyn Street	B3
Congreave Street	C4
Coppice Street	A1-B1
Cromford Street	F4
Cromwell Street	C1-D1
Cross Street	F2-F3
Crossbank Street	C1
Daisy Street	A3-B3
Davies Street	B4
Derker Street	F3-F4
Eden Street	C3

Edward Street	A1
Egerton Street	D3-E3-E4
Eleanor Street	B4
Ellen Street	A4-B4
Featherstall Road North	
	A3-A4-B4
Featherstall Road South	
	A1-A2-A3
Fletcher Close	B2
Franklin Street	C4
Gas Street	E1-E2
George Street	C2
Glodwick Road	F1-F2
Godson Street	C4
Gould Street	F3-F4
Grange Street	B3-C3
Greaves Street	D1-D2
Green Street	B1
Greengate Street	E1-F1
Hamilton Street	F2
Hardy Street	E1-F1
Hebson Street	D1-D2
Henshaw Street	C2-C3-D3-D4
High Street	B2-B3
Highfield Street	B2-B3
Higginshaw Road	E3-E4
Hilda Street	B3
Hill Street	E1-F1
Hooper Street	F1
Horsedge Street	D4-D3-E3-E2
Huddersfield Road	F2-F3
Jespearson Street	D3
John Street	C1-C2
Kersley Street	F1
King Street	C1-C2
Kirkbank Street	B3-B4
Kranj Way	D3
Lane Road	E4
Latimer Street	F1
Lee Street	B1
Lees Road	F2
Lemnos Street	E2-E3
Lord Street	D2-D3
Main Road	A2-A3-A4
Malby Street	D4
Malton Street	B1
Manchester Street	
	A1-B1-B2-C2

Market Place	C2
Marlborough Street	E1
Mars Street	A3-A4
Middleton Road	A3-B3-B2-C2
Mitchell Street	B4-C4
Mortimer Street	E4
Mumps	E2
Napier Street East	A1-B1
New Radcliffe Street	C3
Nugget Street	F1
Oldham WayB4-B3-B2-B1-C1-D1-E1-E2-F2	
Osborne Street	A4
Park Road	C1-D1
Park Street	C1
Peter Street	D2
Pitt Street	F1
Plato Street	B3
Plough Street	A1
Prospect Road	A3
Quebec Street	A4
Queen Street	D2
Radcliffe Street	D4
Railway Road	A1-B1
Regent Street	E2-E3
Rhodes Street	E2
Rifle Street	D3-D4
Rochdale Road	C2-C3-C4
Rock Street	D2-D3-E3
Roscoe Street	E2
Ruskin Street	B4
Ruth Street	D3-D4
St Jame's Street	F3
St John's Street	A1
St Mary's Way	C3-D3-D2
St Stephen's Street	E4
Shaw Road	E4-F4-F3
Shaw Street	D3-E3-E4
Spencer Street	E3-F3
Spinks Street	F1
Stirling Street	A3
Sunfield Road	D4
Suthers Street	A1
Sylvan Street	A3
Thames Street	E4
Tilbury Street	B4-C4
Tin Street	B4
Trafalgar Street	C4
Trinity Street	C4
Union Street	C1-C2-D2-E2
Union Street West	B1-C1
Vale Drive	A2-B2-B1
Villiers Street	B1-C1
Waddington Street	A4
Ward Street	B4-C4
Washington Street	A3
Waterloo Street	D2-E2-E1
West Street	B2-C2
West End Street	B3-B4
Widdop Street	B3
Willow Road	B3
Willow Street	E3-F3
Winterbottom Street	B2
Woodstock Street	D1-E1
Worthington Street	B1
York Street	B2
Yorkshire Street	D2-E2

ASHTON-UNDER-LYNE

Adam Street	C3
Alexandra Road	B3-B4-C4
Bentinck Street	A2-A3

Blandford Street	A2-A3-B3
Boodle Street	B3-B4
Brook Street East	C3-C4
Burlington Street	A2-A3-B3
Buttermere Road	A4
Canterbury Street	C4
Coniston Grove	A4
Cooper Street	B1-C1
Cotton Street	A2-B2
Cowhill Lane	C3
Crescent Road	C1
Cricket's Lane	C3
Currier Lane	C2
Dale Street	A2
Dean Street	A2-A3-B3
Egerton Street	C3
Elgin Street	A4-B4
Elizabeth Street	B4
Fleet Street	B2-C2
Fletcher Street	C3
Furnace Street	B1-C1
Haser Street	C3
Henrietta Street	B4-C4-C3
Hill Street	A1-B1-B2
Holden Street	C4
John Street East	A1
Junction Street	C3-C4
Katherine Street	A2-B2-B3
Kenyon Street	A3
Knowle Avenue	A4
Lees Square	C2
Lees Street	B4
Leicester Street	B4
Lennox Street	C3
Lord Street	B4
Lower Wharf Street	B2-C2
Margaret Street	A1-A2
Minto Street	A4-B4
Mount Pleasant Street	C4
Newman Street	A3-B3
Old Street	B2-B3-C3-C2
Old Cross Street	C3
Oldham Road	A4-A3-B3-B2
Park Road	C1
Penny Meadow	C3
Portland Street South	A1
Riverside	C1
Romney Street	C3-C4
Stamford Street	A1-A2-B2-C2
Stockport Road	A1
Taunton Road	A4
Texas Street	C1
Turner Lane	B3-B4
Turner Street	B4
Union Road	C4
Union Street	B4-B3-C3
Uxbridge Street	A3
Victoria Street	A1
Warrington Street	B2-B3
Water Street	B3
Welbeck Street	A4
Wellington Road	A3-B3-C3
Wellington Street	B2-C2
Westbury Street	C3
Wharf Street	B1-C1
Whitelands	C1-C2
Whitelands Road	C1-C2
Winton Street	B3-B4

HYDE

Albert Road	A1
Albion Street	A2-B2

Alexandra Street	A1
Ashton Road	C4
Bedford Avenue	C3-C4
Beech Street	B3
Boston Street	C2
Brook Street	C3
Chapel Street	A1-B1-B2
Church Street	B1
Clarendon Place	A1
Clarendon Road	B3-B4-C4
Clarendon Street	B3
Commercial Brow	C3-C4
Commercial Street	C3
Corporation Street	A2-B2
Croft Street	A1-A2-B2
Crook Street	B2
Cross Street	A2-B2-B3
Dawson Street	C1
Douglas Street	C1-C2
Dowson Road	B1
Dunkinfield Road	A3-A4
Edna Street	A1-B1
Fleet Street	C3-C4
Furnace Street	A4
Gair Street	A4
Grafton Street	A3-B3
Great Norbury Street	
	A3-A2-A1-B1
Greenfield Street	A2-B2
Haughton Street	B1-C1
Henry Street	B1-B2
Higher Henry Street	B1
Holme Street	B1
Hoviley Street	C3
Hyde By-pass	A3-B3-C3
John Street	B2-B3
Lewis Street	C2-C3
Lodge Lane	B4
Lumn Road	C1-C2
Manchester Road	A3
Mansfield Road	C1
Market Place	B2
Market Street	B3-B2-B1-C1
Mary Street	A3
Mona Street	B1-C1
Mottram Road	C2
Nelson Street	B1-C1-C2
Newton Street	A3-A4
Norfolk Street	B2
Oldham Street	B1-B2
Orchard Street	C2
Park Drive	B4
Park Road	B3-B4
Peel Street	C1
Perrin Street	B1-B2
Queen Street	C1
Raglan Street	A2
Railway Street	A1-A2
Ridling Lane	B2-C2
Repton Avenue	C3-C4
St Pauls Street	C3-C4
Spring Gardens	A4
Syddal Street	B1
Tanner Street	B3
The Mall	B2
Throstle Bank	A4
Tom Shepley Street	C2
Travis Street	B2-C2
Union Street	B2-C2
Victoria Street	C4
Walker Street	C1-C2
Ward Street	B2-C2
Water Street	A3-A2-B2

Well Meadow	A4
Woodend Lane	A1-B1

GLOSSOP

Arundel Street	B3
Ashleigh Avenue	A4-B4
Ashton Street	B1
Bernard Street	B3
Chapel Street	B3
Charles Street	C3-C4
Charlestown Road	B1
Derby Street	B2-C2
Dinting Road	A4
Duke Street	B1-B2
Ebenezer Street	C1
Edward Street	B3
Ellison Street	C3
Fauvel Road	B4-C4
Fitzalan Street	C4
Freetown	B1-C1
George Street	B2-B3
Gladstone Street	B2-C2-C1
Hadfield Place	B1-B2
Hadfield Street	B1-B2
Henry Street	B3-C3
High Street East	C3
High Street West	A3-B3-C3
Highfield Road	C1
Hollins Cross	A1-B1
Howard Street	B4-B3-C3
James Street	B1
John Street	A2
Kershaw Street	B1-C1-C2
King Street	C2
King Edward Avenue	C3-C4
Lord Street	C4
Market Street	B2-B3
Mount Street	B2
Norfolk Street	C3-C4
North Road	B4
Philip Howard Road	B2
Pike's Lane	A1-A2
Primrose Lane	A1-A2
Princess Street	A2-B2
Queen Street	A2-A3
Royle Avenue	C4
St Mary's Road	B2-B3
Shaw Street	A2-B2
Simmondley New Road	A1
Slatelands Road	A1
Shrewsbury Street	B3-B4
Spire Hollin	B4
Sumner Street	A2-B2
Sunlaws Street	A2-A3
Surrey Street	A4-B4-B3
Talbot Street	B3-C3-C4
Tredcroft Street	A2-B2
Turnlee Road	A1-B1
Union Street	C2
Unity Street	B1-C1
Uplands Road	C1
Victoria Street	B2-C2-C3
Whitfield Avenue	B1-C1
Whitfield Cross	C1
Wood Street	B1-C1-C2

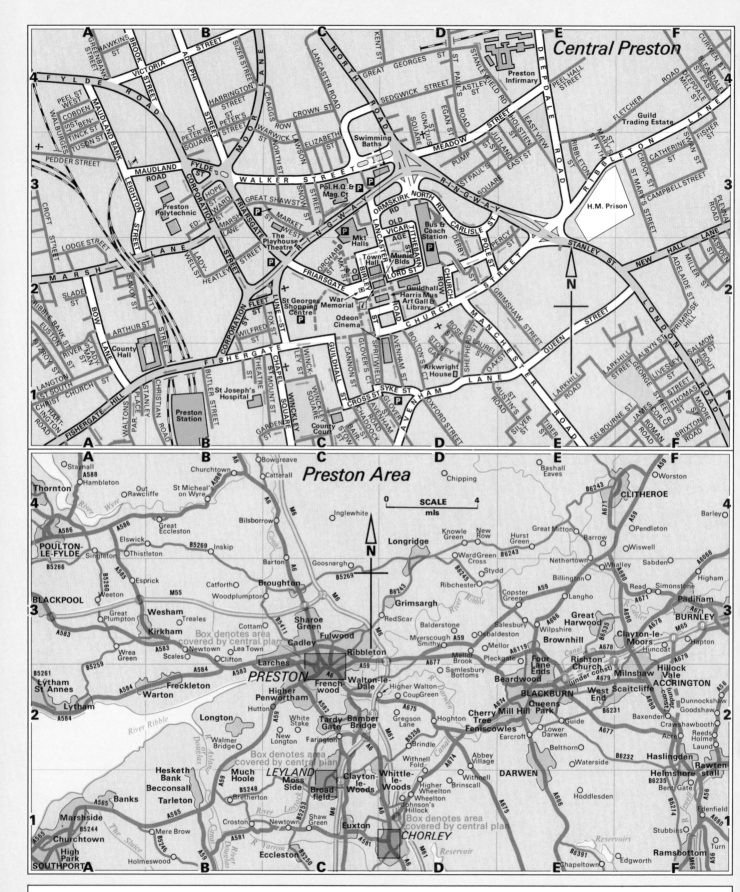

Preston

The decline of the cotton trade after World War I hit Preston badly: this was one of the most important centres in the 19th century.
But today the town is once again an important industrial centre, and one which is well-served by the motorway network.

By way of contrast, Preston also offers a generous number of parks and open spaces, and the River Ribble offers pleasant riverside walks. It has an impressive Market Square, where the neo-classical Harris Museum and Art Gallery houses an extensive collection of decorative and fine art, and displays on social history and archaeology can also be seen here.

Leyland was transformed by the setting up in 1892 of Leyland Motors, which later became Leyland Vehicles. Less well known is the town's restored 16th-century grammar school, now the home of the Museum and Exhibition Centre. Another attractive feature is Worden Park, which offers 160 acres of natural beauty and is also the venue of the Leyland Festival.

Chorley Fast expanding Chorley was once a major cotton centre and it's still a flourishing industrial town, although now its interests are more widely based. Close to the centre the wooded park and 16th-century house of Astley Hall are situated.

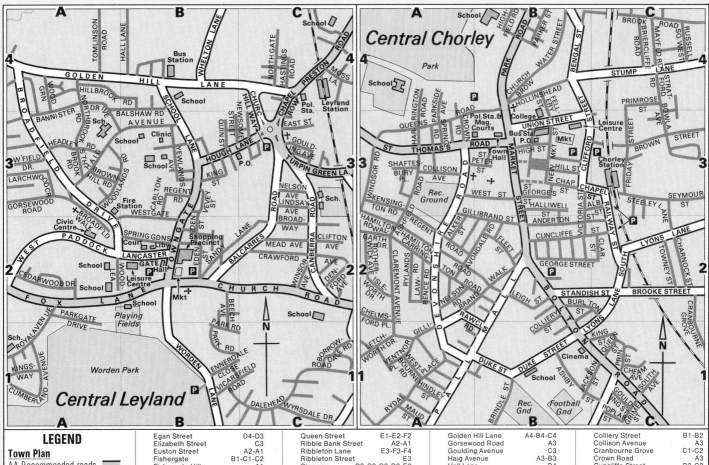

Central Chorley

Central Leyland

LEGEND

Town Plan

AA Recommended roads	
Other roads	
Restricted roads	
Buildings of interest	Station ▣
Churches	†
Car parks	Ⓟ
Parks and open spaces	
One way streets	→

Area Plan

A roads	
B roads	
Locations	Warehorne ○
Urban area	

STREET INDEX

Preston

Adelaide Street	F2
Adelphi Street	B4-B3
Albyn Street	F1-F2
Arthur Street	A2-B2
Aspden Street	F3-F2
Astley Street	D4
Avenham Lane	D1-E1
Avenham Road	C1-D1
Avenham Street	D2-D1
Bairstow Street	C1
Bentinck Street	A3-A4
Birley Street	C2-D2
Bleasdale Street East	F4
Bolton's Court	D2-D1
Bow Lane	A2-A1
Brixton Road	F1
Brook Street	A4-B4
Butler Street	B1
Campbell Street	F3
Cannon Street	C2-C1
Carlisle Street	D3
Catherine Street	F3
Chaddock Street	C1
Chapel Street	C1
Christ Church Street	A1
Christian Road	B1
Church Row	D2
Church Street	D2-E2
Cobden Street	A4
Coronation Crescent	F1
Corporation Street	B3-B2-B1
Cragg's Row	C4
Croft Street	A3-A2
Crook Street	F3
Cross Street	C1-D1
Crown Street	C4
Curwen Street	F4
Deepdale Mill Street	F4
Deepdale Road	E4-E3
Derby Street	D3-D2
East Street	D3-E3
East View	E4-E3
Edward Street	B2-B3
Egan Street	D4-D3
Elizabeth Street	C3
Euston Street	A2-A1
Fishergate	B1-C1-C2
Fishergate Hill	A1
Fisher Street	F3-F4
Fitzroy Street	A2-A1
Fleet Street	B2-C2
Fletcher Road	E3-E4-F4
Fox Street	C2-C1
Friargate	B3-B2-C2-C3
Fylde Road	A4-B4
Fylde Street	B3
Garden Street	B1-C1
George Street	F1
Glover's Court	C2-C1
Glover Street	D1
Great Georges Street	C4-D4
Great Shaw Street	B3-C3
Greenbank Street	A4
Grimshaw Street	D2-E2-E1
Guildhall Street	C2-C1
Harrington Street	B4
Hartington Road	A1
Hawkins Street	A4
Heatley Street	B2
Holstien Street	E4-E3
Hope Street	B3
James Street	F1
Jutland Street	D3-E3
Kent Street	D4
Ladyman Street	A2-A1
Ladywell Street	B2
Lancaster Road	C4-C3-C2-D2-D3
Langton Street South	A1
Larkhill Road	E1
Larkhill Street	E1-F1
Laurel Street	D2-D1
Lawson Street	C4-C3
Leighton Street	A3-A2
Livesley Street	F1
Lodge Street	A2
London Road	F2-F1
Lord Street	D2
Lune Street	C2
Manchester Road	D2-E2-E1
Market Street	C2
Market Street West	C2
Marsh Lane	A2-B2-B3
Maudland Bank	A4-A3
Maudland Road	A3-B3
Meadow Street	D3-D4-E4
Miller Street	F2
Moor Lane	B3-B4-C4
Moore Street	F1
Mount Street	C1
New Hall Lane	F2-F3
North Road	C4-D4-D3
North Street	C3
Oak Street	D1-E1
Old Vicarage	D3
Orchard Street	C2
Ormskirk Road	C3-D3
Oxford Street	D1
Peel Hall Street	E4
Peel Street West	A4
Pedder Street	A3
Percy Street	D2-E2-E3
Pitt Street	A2-B2-B1
Plevna Road	F3
Pole Street	D3-D2
Primrose Hill	F2
Pump Street	D3
Queen Street	E1-E2-F2
Ribble Bank Street	A2-A1
Ribbleton Lane	E3-F3-F4
Ribbleton Street	E3
Ringway	B2-C2-C3-D3-E3
River Street	A1-A2
Roman Road	F1
Rose Street	D2
St Austin's Road	D1-E1
St Ignatius Square	D4-D3
St Mary's Street	F3-F2
St Mary's Street North	E3
St Paul's Road	D4-D3
St Paul's Square	D3-E3
St Peter's Square	B3
St Peter's Street	B4
Salmon Street	F1-F2
Savoy Street	A2
Sedgwick Street	C4-D4
Selbourne Street	E1-F1
Shepherd Street	D1-D2
Silver Street	E1
Sizer Street	B4
Slade Street	A2
Snow Street	C3
Spritwield	C2-D2-C1-D1
Stanleyfield Road	D4-E4
Stanley Place	A1
Stanley Street	E2-F2
Stoney Gate	D2-D1
Syke Street	C1-D1
Swan Street	F4-F3
Theatre Street	B1
Thomas Street	F1
Tiber Street	E1
Tithebarn Street	D3-D2
Trout Street	F1
Tuson Street	A3-A4
Victoria Street	A4-B4
Walburges	A4-A3
Walker Street	B3-C3
Waltons Parade	A1
Warwick Street	B4-B3-C3
Wilfred Street	B2-C2
Winkley Square	C1
Winkley Street	C1

Leyland

Balcarres Road	B2-C2-C3
Balshaw Road	A4-B4
Bannister Drive	A3-A4
Beech Avenue	B1-B2
Borrowdale Road	C1
Broadfield Drive	B2-A2-A3-A4
Broadfield Walk	A2-A3
Broadway	C2
Brownhill Road	A3
Canberra Road	C2-C3
Carlton Road	B3
Cedarwood Drive	A2
Chapel Row	C3-C4
Churchill Way	C3-C4
Church Road	B2-C2
Clifton Avenue	C2
Crawford Avenue	C2
Cumberland Avenue	A1
Dalehead Road	B1-C1
Denford Avenue	C2
East Street	C2
Eden Street	B2-B3
Ennerdale Close	B1-C1
Fox Lane	A2-B2

Leyland (continued)

Golden Hill Lane	A4-B4-C4
Gorsewood Road	A3
Goulding Avenue	C3
Haig Avenue	A3-B3
Hall Lane	B4
Hastings Road	C4
Headley Road	A3
Hillbrook Road	A4-B4
Hough Lane	B3-C3
King Street	B3
Kingsway	A1
Lancaster Gate	B2
Larchwood Crescent	A3
Lindsey Avenue	C3
Mead Avenue	C2
Moss Lane	C4
Nelson Avenue	C3
Newsome Street	B3
Northbrook Road	A3-A4
Northgate	C4
Parkgate Drive	A1-A2
Park Road	B1
Preston Road	C4
Quin Street	B3
Regent Road	B3
Royal Avenue	A1-A2
Sandy Lane	B2-C2
School Lane	B3-B4
Southbrook Road	A3
Spring Gardens	B2
Tomlinson Road	A4
Towngate	B1-B2-B3
Turpin Green Lane	C3
Vevey Street	B3
Vicarsfield Road	B1-C1
Westfield Drive	A3
Westgate	B2-B3
West Paddock	A2
Whelton Lane	B4
Winsor Avenue	C2
Wood Green	A4
Woodlands Road	A3-B3
Woodlea	A2
Worden Lane	B1
Wyrsdale Drive	C1
Yewlands Avenue	B3

Chorley

Albert Street	B3-C3
Alker Street	A2
Anderton Street	B2-C2
Ashby Street	B1-C1
Ashfield Road	A2-A3
Avondale Road	A2-B2
Bengal Street	B4
Bolton Road	B2-B1-C1
Bowland Avenue	C3-C4
Briercliffe Road	C3-C4
Brindle Street	B1
Brooke Street	C2
Brook Road	B4-C4
Brown Street	C3
Burlington Street	B2-C2
Carrington Road	A2-B2
Chapel Street	B3-C3
Charnock Street	C2
Cheam Avenue	C1
Chelmsford Place	A2
Church Brow	B4
Claremont Avenue	A1-A2
Clarence Street	C2
Clifford Street	B4-B3-C3
Colliery Street	B1-B2
Collison Avenue	A3
Cranbourne Grove	C1-C2
Crown Road	A3
Cuncliffe Street	B2-C2
Devonshire Road	A1-A2-A3
Duke Street	B1
Fellery Street	B3-B4
Fleet Street	B2
Friday Street	C3-C4
George Street	B2-C2
Gillibrand Street	A3-A2-B2
Gillibrand Walk	A1-A2-B2
Goulding Street	C1
Grime Street	C1
Halliwell Street	B3
Hamilton Road	A3-A2-B2
Harington Road	A3-A4
Highfield Road	B4
High Street	B3
Hill Street	B3
Hindley Street	A1
Hollinshead	B4
Isleworth Drive	A2
Jackson Street	B1-C1
Kensington Road	A3
King Street	B1-C1
Lawrence Road	A2
Leigh Street	B2
Letchworth Drive	A1
Lyons Lane	C2
Lyons Lane South	B1-C1-C2
Market Street	B2-B3
Maud Street	A1
Mayfield Road	C4
Nelson Road	A2
New Market Street	B3
Pall Mall	A1-B1-B2
Parker Street	B4
Park Road	B4
Parkside Avenue	A3-A4
Poplar Street	C1
Primrose Street	C4
Princess Street	C1
Queens Road	A3-B3-B4
Queen Street	C1
Railway Street	C2-C3
Rawcliffe Road	A1-A2-B2-B1
Regent Road	A2-A3
Rotherwick Avenue	A2
Russell Square West	C4
Rydal Place	A1
Rylands Road	A2
St George's Street	B3
St Peter Street	A3-B3
St Thomas's Road	A3-B3
Seymour Street	A3
Shaftesbury Place	A3
South Avenue	C1
Spring Road	A3
Standish Street	B2-C2
Steeley Lane	C2-C3
Stratford Road	C4
Stump Lane	B4-C4
Towney Street	C2
Union Street	B3
Ventnor Place	A1
Victoria Street	B2-B3
Walgarth Drive	A2
Water Street	B4
Westbourne Road	A1
West Street	A3-B3
Windsor Road	A3

57

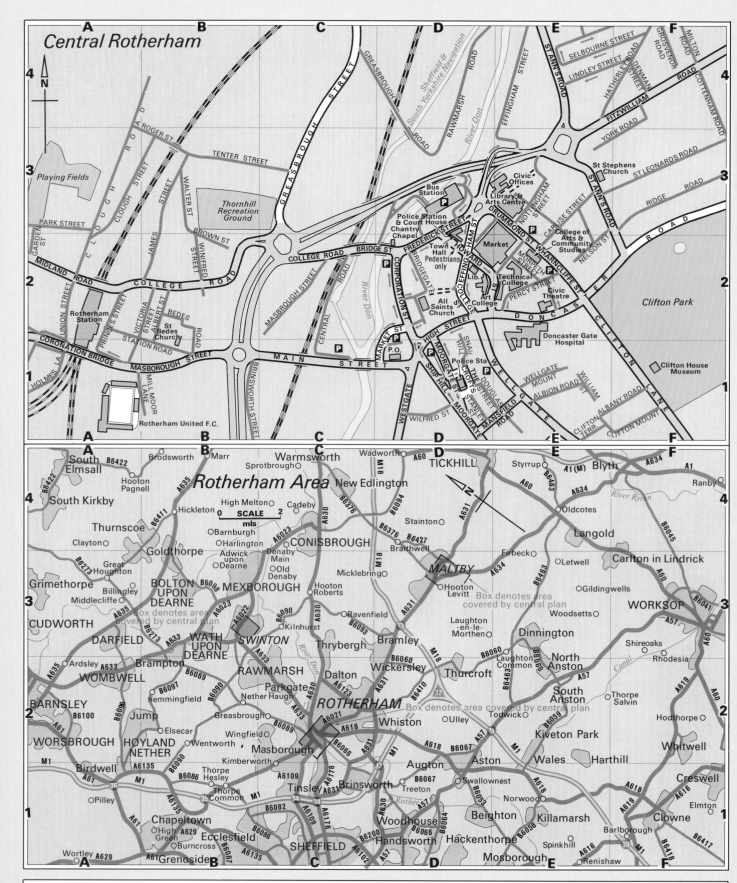

Rotherham

Evidence of Rotherham's industry goes back at least as far as the Romans, whose ironworking artefacts have been found here. They were followed by a group of 12th-century monks who established a mining site, and in the 18th century came the beginnings of Rotherham as a major industrial centre with iron smelting on a large scale. Today this is a pleasant town with broad, largely 19th- and 20th-century streets, and offering a pleasant blend of architectural styles. Outstanding in both senses is the large, Norman Perpendicular Church of All Saints with its majestic spire and interior, and another cause for pride is the medieval chapel on Rotherham Bridge. Typical of its time, this is now one of only three perfect examples surviving in the country.

Swinton Rich coal seams beneath the town are chiefly responsible for modern Swinton, but its name is more widely associated with Rockingham pottery which is much sought-after today. Just one kiln from the original pottery remains, and can be seen off the A633 Swinton to High Haugh road.

Maltby's coalfields only began to be worked about half a century ago, and more recent developments give it the feel of a bright modern town. But a pre-coal, pre-industrial Maltby still exists, and can be reached by steps and steep slopes from the main centre.

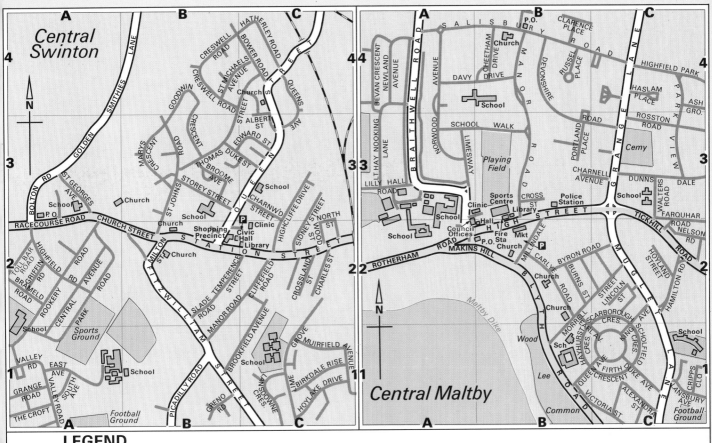

Central Swinton

4

N

3

2

1

A · B · C

Creswell Road · Hatherley Road · Bower Road · Queens Ave · St Michaels Avenue · Albert St · Edward St · Thomas Duke St · Broome Ave · Storey Street · Charnw'd Street · Highcliffe Drive · Sidney Street · North St · Crossland St · Charles St · Muirfield Avenue · Birkdale Rise · Hoylake Drive · Lansdowne Cres · Greno Rd · Grove · Brookfield Avenue · Manor Road · Slade · Temperence · Cliffefield Road · Goodwin · Creswell Crescent · Road · Marys Crescent · St Johns · St Georges Ave · Golden Smithies Lane · Bolton Rd · Racecourse Road · Church Street · Milton St · Fitzwilliam · Street · Picadilly Road · Greno Rd · Station Street · Toll Bar Road · Highfield · Griffin Rd · Bramled Road · Rookery Rd · Central · Park Avenue · Road · Sports Ground · School · Valley Rd · East Ave · South · Valley Rd · Grange Road · The Croft · Football Ground · Church · School · Church · Shopping Precinct · P · Clinic · Civic Hall · Library · Church

Central Maltby

4

3

2

1

N

A · B · C

Salisbury Road · Clarence Place · P.O. · Russell Place · Highfield Park · Bevan Crescent · Newland Avenue · Cheetham Drive · Church · Manor Road · Devonshire · Portland Place · Haslam Place · Ash Gro. · Norwood Avenue · Davy Drive · School · School Walk · Charnell Avenue · Rosston Road · Park View · Haslam Place · Dunns Dale · Little Hay Nooking Lane · Limesway · Lilly Hall Road · Playing Field · Sports Centre · Clinic · Library · Cross · Police Station · School · Walters Road · Dale · School · Grange Road · Lilly Hall · School · Council Offices · Hall · High Street · Mkt · Farquhar Road · Nelson Rd · Rotherham Road · Fire Sta · P.O. · Makins Hill · Church · Millndale · Carlyle Road · Byron Road · Hoyland Street · Hamilton Rd · Maltby Dike · Morrell St · Church · Church · Lincoln St · Scarborough Cres. · Burns St · King Ave · Scholfield · School · Wood · Lee · Sch · Hayhurst Cres. · Earl Av. · Firth Crescent · Duke Ave · Queen Crescent · Alexandra · Lansbury Ave · Cripps Clo. · School · Common · Victoria St. · Queens Ave · Football Ground

LEGEND

Town Plan

One Way Streets	
A A Recommended roads	
Other roads	
Restricted roads	
Buildings of interest	Theatre
Car Parks	P
Parks and open spaces	

Area Plan

A roads	
B roads	
Locations	Nutwell ○
Urban area	

Central Rotherham

Albany Road	E1-F1
Albert Street	B1-B2
Albion Road	E1
Bedes Road	B1-B2
Bridge Street	C2-D2
Bridgegate	D2
Brinsworth Street	B1
Brown Street	B2-B3
Carlisle Street	E2-E3
Central Road	C1-C2
Clifton Lane	E2-F2-F1
Clifton Mount	E1-F1
Clifton Terrace	E1
Clough Road	A2-A3-A4-B4
Clough Street	A2-A3-B3
College Road	A2-B2-C2
College Street	D2
Coronation Bridge	A1-A2
Corporation Street	D1-D2
Cottenham Road	F3-F4
Denman Street	F4
Doncaster Road	D2-E2-F2-F3
Douglas Street	D1-E1
Drummond Street	D3-E3-E2
Effingham Street	D2-D3, E3-E4
Fitzwilliam Road	E3-E4-F4
Frederick Street	D2-D3
Garden Street	A2-A3
Greasbrough Road	C4-D4-D3
Greasbrough Street	C3-C4
Grosvenor Road	F4
Hatherley Road	E4-F4
High Street	D1-D2
Holmes Lane	A1
Howard Street	D2-E2-D2
James Street	B2-B3
Lindley Street	E4-F4
Main Street	B1-C1-D1
Mansfield Road	D1-E1
Market Street	D1-D2
Masbrough Street	C2
Masborough Street	A1-B1, C2
Midland Road	A2
Mill Moor Lane	A1-B1
Milton Road	F4
Moorgate	D1
Moorgate Street	D1-D2
Morpeth Street	E2
Nelson Street	E2-E3
Nottingham Street	E3
Park Street	A3
Percy Street	E2
Princes Street	A1-A2
Rawmarsh Road	D3-D4
Ridge Road	F3
Roger Street	A4-A3-B3
St Ann's Road	E4-E3-F3-F2
St Leonards Road	E3-F3
Selbourne Street	E4-F4
Ship Hill	D1
Snail Hill	D1-D2
Stanley Street	D1
Station Road	A2-A1-B1
Tenter Street	B3-C3
The Crofts	D1
Union Street	A1-A2
Victoria Street	A2-B2
Walter Street	B3
Wellgate	D2-D1-E1
Wellgate Mount	E1
Westgate	D1
Wharncliffe Street	E2
Wilfred Street	D1
William Street	E1
Winifred Street	B2
York Road	E3-F3-F4

Central Maltby

Alexandra Street	C1
Ash Grove	C4
Bevan Crescent	A4
Blyth Road	B2-B1-C1
Braithwell Road	A3-A4
Burns Street	B2
Byron Road	B2-C2
Carlyle Road	B2
Charnell Avenue	B3-C3
Cheetham Drive	B4
Clarence Place	B4-C4
Cripps Close	C1
Cross Street	B3
Davy Drive	A4-B4
Devonshire Road	B4-B3-C3
Duke Avenue	C1
Dunns Dale	C3
Earl Avenue	B2-B1-C1
Farquhar Road	C2-C3
Firth Crescent	B1-C1
Grange Lane	C3-C4
Hamilton Road	C2
Haslam Place	C4
Hayhurst Crescent	B1
High Street	A2-B2-B3-C3
Highfield Park	C4
Hoyland Street	C2
King Avenue	C1-C2
Lansbury Avenue	C1
Limesway	A3
Lilly Hall Road	A3
Lincoln Street	C2
Little Hay Nooking Lane	A3-A4
Makins Hill	A2-B2
Manor Road	B3-B4
Millndale	B2-B3
Morrell Street	B1-B2-C2
Muglet Lane	C1-C2-C3
Nelson Street	C2
Newland Avenue	A4
Norwood Avenue	A3-A4
Park View	C3-C4
Portland Place	B3
Queen Avenue	B1-C1
Rosston Road	C3
Rotherham Road	A2
Russel Place	B4
Salisbury Road	A4-B4-C4
Scarborough Crescent	B1-B2-C2
Scholfield Crescent	C1
School Walk	A3-B3
Tickhill Road	C2-C3
Victoria Street	B1-C1
Walters Road	C3

Central Swinton

Albert Street	C3-C4
Birkdale Rise	C1
Bolton Road	A3
Bower Road	B4-C4
Brameld Road	A2
Brookfield Avenue	B1-C1-C2
Broome Avenue	B3
Central Avenue	A1-A2
Charles Street	C2
Charnwood Street	C3
Church Street	A3-A2-B2
Cliffefield Road	C2
Creswell Road	B4
Crossland Street	C2
Duke Street	B3-C3
East Avenue	A1
Edward Street	B3-C3
Fitzwilliam Street	B2-B1-C1
Golden Smithies Lane	A3-A4-B4
Goodwin Crescent	B3-B4
Grange Road	A1
Greno Road	B1
Griffin Road	A2
Hatherley Road	B4-C4
Highcliffe Drive	C2-C3
Highfield Road	A2
Hoylake Drive	C1
Landsdowne Crescent	C1
Lime Grove	C1-C2
Manor Road	B1-B2-C2
Marys Crescent	B3
Milton Street	B2
Muirfield Avenue	C1
North Street	C2-C3
Park Road	B1
Picadilly Road	B2-B3-C3-C4
Queen Street	C3-C4
Queens Avenue	A2-A3
Racecourse Road	A1-A2
Rookery Road	A3
St Georges Avenue	B2-B3
St Johns Road	B4-C4
St Michaels Avenue	C2-C3
Sidney Street	B2
Slade Road	A1
South Avenue	B2-C2
Station Street	B3
Storey Street	B2-C2
Temperence Street	A1
The Croft	B3-B4-C4
Thomas Street	A2
Toll Bar Road	A1
Valley Road	C2
Wood Street	

ROTHERHAM
Begun in 1483 and used after the Reformation as an almshouse, town prison, plague isolation hospital and tobacconist's shop, the Chapel of Our Lady on Chantry Bridge was restored and rededicated in 1924.

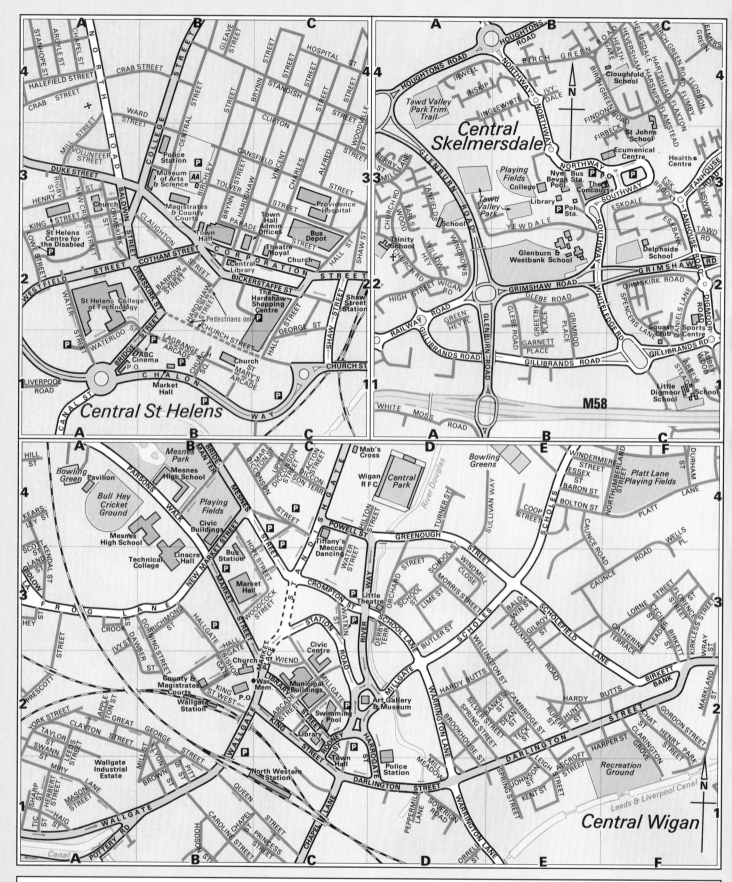

Central St Helens

Central Skelmersdale

Central Wigan

St Helens

Pilkington Glass have been manufacturing glassware here for over 150 years, and today there is a fascinating museum attached to the company's Prescot Road works. A town of fine sporting facilities, St Helens also offers the attractions of its noted Rugby League team and of horse racing at Haydock Park Racecourse, which lies to the north-east of the town.

Wigan is known to millions through George Orwell's book *The Road to Wigan Pier*, but has seen radical changes in recent years. Not least of these has been the development of the area around the Leeds and Liverpool Canal, where the original pier, or wharf, is being turned into a Leisure and Recreation Centre. Several old warehouses have been renovated and a working mill engine is on display, while providing visitors with food and drink is a new pub — the Orwell.

Skelmersdale's once-important coal mining has declined in recent years, but the establishment in the 1960s of a New Town offering all the appropriate facilities has helped to attract new industries. A history dating back to the Romans can be traced here.

Leigh stands on the Leeds and Liverpool Canal. Familiar to Rugby enthusiasts for its Rugby League team, it's also popular with anglers and sailors for 1,000-acre Pennington Flash Country Park.

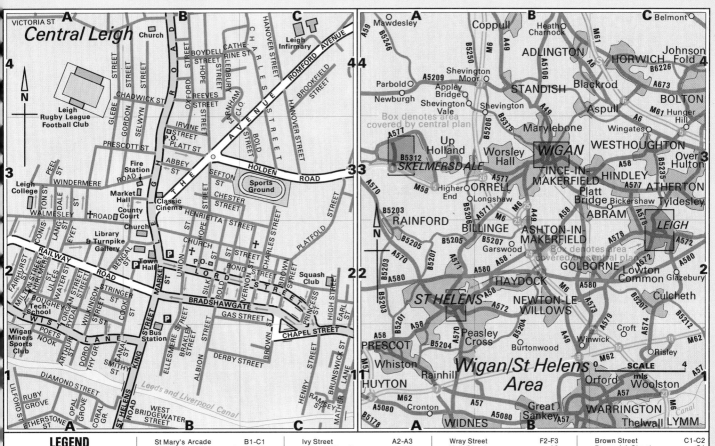

LEGEND

Town Plan

AA recommended route
Restricted roads
Other roads
Buildings of interest — Station ▣
Car parks — 🅿
Parks and open spaces — ▢
One way streets — ←

Area Plan

A roads
B roads
Locations — West Toppings ○
Urban area — ▢

Street index with Grid Reference

St Helens

Alfred Street	C3-C4
Argyle Street	A4
Baldwin Street	A2-A3
Barrow Street	B2
Bickerstaffe Street	B2-C2
Birchley Street	B2-B3-B4
Bridge Street	A1-B1-B2
Brynn Street	B3-B4-C4
Canal Street	A1
Cansfield Street	B3-C3
Central Street	B3-B4
Chalon Way	A1-B1-C1
Chapel Street	A4
Charles Street	C2-C3-C4
Church Square	B1
Church Street	B2-B1-C1
Claughton Street	A3-B3-B2
Clifton Street	B4-C4-C3
College Street	A3-B3-B4
Corporation Street	B2-C2
Cotham Street	B2
Crab Street	A4-B4
Duke Street	A3-B3
George Street	C1-C2
Gleave Street	B4
Halefield Street	A4
Hall Street	C1-C2-C3
Hardshaw Street	B2-B3-C3-C4
Henry Street	A3
Hospital Street	C4
King Street	A2-A3
Lagrange Arcade	B1
Liverpool Road	A1
Mill Street	A3-A4
New Cross Street	A2-A3
North Road	A3-A4
Ormskirk Street	A3-A2-B2
Parade Street	B3-B2-C2
Rigby Street	A3
St Mary's Arcade	B1-C1
Shaw Street	C1-C2-C3
Standish Street	C4
Stanhope Street	A4
Tolver Street	B3-C3-C2
Vincent Street	B2-C2-C3-C4
Volunteer Street	A3
Ward Street	A4-B4-B3
Waterloo Street	A1-A2-B2
Water Street	A1-B1
Westfield Street	A2
Woodville Street	C3-C4

Wigan

Acton Street	C4
Appleton Street	A2
Arcade Street	C2
Ascroft Street	E1-E2
Baldwin Street	E3
Bankes Street	D2-E2
Baron Street	E4
Birkett Bank	F2
Birkett Street	F2-F3
Bishop Gate	B2
Bolton Street	E4
Brideman Terrace	B4
Brookhouse Street	D1-D2
Brown Street	B1-B2
Butler Street	D3
Cambridge Street	E2
Caroline Street	B1
Catherine Terrace	B4
Caunce Road	E4-E3-F3-F4
Cecil Street	F3
Chapel Lane	C1
Chapel Street	B1-C1
Chat Street	F2
Clarington Grove	F1-F2
Clayton Street	A2-B2
Coop Street	E4
Crompton Street	C3
Crook Street	A3
Darlington Street	C1-D1-E1-E2-F2
Dawber Street	A3-A2-B2
Dean Street	E2
Derby Terrace	D3
Dicconson Street	B4-C4
Dicconson Terrace	C4
Dorning Street	B2-B3
Durham Street	F4
Essex Street	E4
Florence Street	F3
Frog Lane	A3-A4
Gidlow Lane	A3
Gilroy Street	E3
Gordon Street	F2
Great George Street	A2-B2-B1
Greenough Street	D4-D3-E3
Haig Street	A1
Hallgate	B2-B3
Hardy Butts	D2-E2-F2
Harper Street	E2-F2
Harrogate Street	C2-D2-D1
Henry Park Street	F1-F2
Herbert Street	A1
Hey Street	A3
Hill Street	A4
Hilton Street	C4-D4
Hodson Street	B1
Hope Street	B4-B3-C3
Hunt Street	E2
Ivy Street	A2-A3
Johnson Street	E1
Kearsley Street	A4
Kendal Street	A3-A4
Kent Street	E1
King Street	C1-C2
King Street West	B2
Kirkless Street	F2-F3
Land Street	A3
Leader Street	F3
Leeds Street	A1-A2
Leigh Street	E1-E2
Library Street	C2
Lime Street	D3
Lorne Street	E3-F3
Lyon Street	B1-B2
Market Place	C2-C3
Market Street	B3-C3-C2
Markland Street	F2
Marton Street	C4
Mason Street	A1
Mesnes Street	B4-C4-C3
Millgate	C2-D2
Mill Meadow	D1-D2
Mill Street	B1-B2
Miry Lane	A1
Morris Street	C2
New Market Street	B3-B4
Northumberland Street	F4
Orchard Street	D3
Orrell Street	D1
Parsons Walk	A4-B4-B3
Peppermill Lane	D1
Pitt Street	B1
Platt Lane	A1
Prescott Street	A2-A3
Princess Street	B1-C1
Pottery Road	A1-B1
Powell Street	C4
Queen Street	B1-C1
Richmond Street	B3
River Way	D2-C2-C3-C4-D4
Rodney Street	C2
Rupert Street	E2
Scholes	D2-D3-E3-E4
Scholefield Lane	E3-E2-F2
School Lane	D2-D3
School Street	D3-D4
Scott Street	A3-A4
Sharp Street	A1
Silver Street	D2-E2
Soverign Road	D1
Spring Street	D2-E2-E1
Standishgate	C3-C4
Station Road	C2-C3
Sullivan Way	D4-E4
Swann Street	A1-A2
Taylor Street	A2
Teck Street	E2
Tic Street	A1
Turner Street	D4
Upper Dicconson Street	C4
Vauxhall Road	E2-E3
Wallgate	A1-B1-B2-C2
Warrington Lane	D2-D1-E1
Water Street	C3-C4
Watkin Street	C3
Wellington Street	D3-D2-E2
Wells Place	F4
Wiend	C2
Windermere Street	E4-F4
Windmill Close	D3
Woodcock Street	B3-C3
Wray Street	F2-F3
York Street	A2

Skelmersdale

Abbeystead	C1
Abbeywood	C1
Berry Street	A3
Birch Green Road	B4-C4
Church Road	A2-A3
Daniels Lane	C1-C2
Digmoor Road	C2
Elmers Green	C4
Elswick	C3
Eskbrook	C3
Eskbank	C2-C3
Eskdale	C2-C3
Findon	B4-C4
Firbeck	B3-C3-C4
Flamstead	C3-C4
Flaxton	C4
Flimby	C4
Flordon	C4
Garnett Place	A2
Gillibrands Road	A2-A1-B1-C1
Glebe Road	B1-B2
Glenburn Road	A1-B1-B2-A2-A3-A4
Greenhey Place	A2
Greetby Place	B1-B2
Grimrod Place	B1-B2
Grimshaw Road	B2-C2
Harsnips	C4
Hartshead	C4
Heathbrook	B4-C4
Helmsdale	C4
Heversham	C4
High Street	A2
Houghtons Road	A4-B4
Inglewhite	A4-B4
Inskip	A4-B4
Irwell	A4-B4
Ivydale	B4
Mill Lane	A3
Northway	B4-B3-C3
Ormskirk Road	C2
Railway Road	A1-A2
Southway	B2-B3-C3
Spencers Lane	C1-C2
Tanfields	A3
Tanhouse Road	C2-C3
Tarlswood	A2-A3
Tawd Road	A2
White Ledge Road	B2-C2-C1
White Moss Road	A1
Wigan Road	A2
Willow Hey	A2
Windrows	A2
Yewdale	A3-A2-B2-B3

Leigh

Abbey Street	B3
Albion Street	B1-B2
Arthur Street	A1
Bengal Street	A2-B2
Bold Street	B2-C2-C3
Bond Street	B2-C2
Boughey Street	A2
Boydell Street	B4
Bradshawgate	B2-C2
Brakley Street	B1
Brookfield Street	C4
Brown Street	C1-C2
Brunswick Street	C1
Canal Street	A1
Catherine Street	B4-C4
Chadwick Street	A4-B4
Chapel Street	C1
Charles Street	C2-C3-C4
Chester Street	B3-C3
Church Street	B2-C2
Coniston Street	A2-A3
Cook Street	A1-B1-B2
Coral Grove	A1
Derby Street	B1-C1
Diamond Street	A1
Dorothy Grove	A1
Earl Street	C1-C2
Ellesmere Street	B1-B2
Etherstone	A1
Eyet Street	A2-A3
Fairhurst Street	A2
Farnham Close	B3-B4-C4-B4
Gas Streets	B2-C2-C1
Glebe Street	A3-A4
Gordon Street	A3-B3-B4
Hanover Street	C3-C4
Henrietta Street	B3-C3-C2
Henry Street	C1
High Street	C1-C2
Holden Road	B3-C3
Hope Street	B2-B3-B4
Irvine Street	B3
King Street	B1-B2
Langdale Street	A2-A3
Ledbury Street	B4
Leigh Road	B2-B3-B4
Lilford Street	A1
Lord Street	B2-C2
Market Street	B2
Mather Lane	C1
Milton Street	A2
Opal Grove	A1
Organ Street	A2
Oxford Street	B3-B4
Peel Street	A3
Platfold Street	C2-C3
Platt Street	B3
Poets Nook	A1
Prescott Street	A3-B3
Princess Street	C2
Railway Road	A2-B2
Ramsey Street	C1
Reeves Street	B4
Romford Avenue	C4
Ruby Grove	A1
Rydal Street	A1-A2
St Helens Road	A1-B1
Sefton Street	B3
Selwyn Street	B3-B4
Silk Street	B2
Smithy Street	A1-B1
Stringer Street	A1
The Avenue	B3-C3-C4
Thirlmere Street	A1
Twist Lane	A2-A1-B1
Ulleswater Street	A2
Union Street	B2-B3
Vernon Street	B2-C2
Victoria Street	A4
Walmesley Road	A3-A2-B2
West Bridgewater Street	A1-B1
Wilkinson Street	A1-A2
Windermere Road	A3-B3

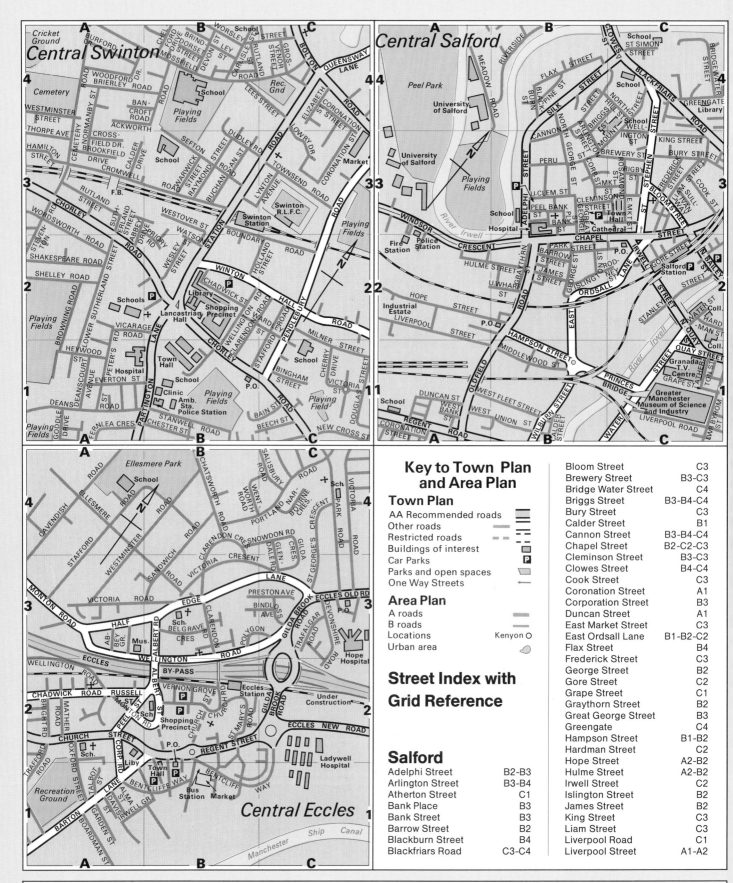

Key to Town Plan and Area Plan

Town Plan

AA Recommended roads
Other roads
Restricted roads
Buildings of interest
Car Parks
Parks and open spaces
One Way Streets

Area Plan

A roads
B roads
Locations   Kenyon ○
Urban area

Street Index with Grid Reference

Salford

Adelphi Street	B2-B3
Arlington Street	B3-B4
Atherton Street	C1
Bank Place	B3
Bank Street	B3
Barrow Street	B2
Blackburn Street	B4
Blackfriars Road	C3-C4
Bloom Street	C3
Brewery Street	B3-C3
Bridge Water Street	C4
Briggs Street	B3-B4-C4
Bury Street	C3
Calder Street	B1
Cannon Street	B3-B4-C4
Chapel Street	B2-C2-C3
Cleminson Street	B3-C3
Clowes Street	B4-C4
Cook Street	C3
Coronation Street	A1
Corporation Street	B3
Duncan Street	A1
East Market Street	C3
East Ordsall Lane	B1-B2-C2
Flax Street	B4
Frederick Street	C3
George Street	B2
Gore Street	C2
Grape Street	C1
Graythorn Street	B2
Great George Street	B3
Greengate	C4
Hampson Street	B1-B2
Hardman Street	C2
Hope Street	A2-B2
Hulme Street	A2-B2
Irwell Street	C2
Islington Street	B2
James Street	B2
King Street	C3
Liam Street	C3
Liverpool Road	C1
Liverpool Street	A1-A2

Salford

Salford exploded into phenomenal growth with the Industrial Revolution — it was one of the fastest expanding places in the country, with vast areas of mills and poor quality housing. Much of this old Salford has disappeared, and the city now offers an interesting and lively blend of the industrial, commercial, rural and even maritime. It also boasts a fine university, and has been recorded for posterity in the paintings of L. S. Lowry, who knew it well. The Museum and Art Gallery has a collection of his work, and also of interest here is a Victorian street reconstruction. The Museum of Mining has two reproduction coalmines, and recalling a far older Salford is timber-framed Ordsall Hall's museum.

Swinton is said to owe its name to the unglamourous occupation of rearing pigs, but its more recent background is coal. An industrial area and residential district of Manchester, it has its own Civic Centre and a shopping precinct flanked by the attractive Victorian church of St Peter.

Eccles cakes first came from a shop in Church Street, where they are still being made to the original recipe. A busy area squeezed between the Manchester Ship Canal and the M62, this was once a group of medieval villages. Monk's Hall is Tudor and houses a museum. The Church of St Mary the Virgin dates from the 12th century.

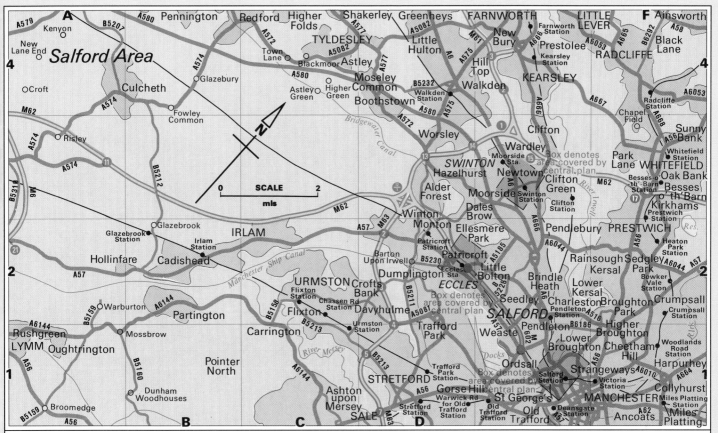

Lower Byrom Street	C1	Brindley Street	B4	Shakespeare Road	A2	Eccles New Road	C2
Market Street	B3-C3	Brookfield Drive	A3	Shelley Road	A2	Eccles Old Road	C3
Meadow Road	A4-B4	Browning Road	A1-A2	Stafford Road	B1-C1-C2	Ellesmere Road	A4-A3-B3
Middlewood Street	B1	Buchanan Street	B3	Stanwell Road	B1	Garden Street	A1
Mount Street	B3-C3-C4	Burford Drive	A4	Station Road	B2-B3-C3-C4	Gilda Brook Road	C2-C3
North Bailey Street	C2	Calder Street	A3	Steventon Road	A2-A3	Gilda Crescent	C3-C4
North George Street	B3-B4	Carlisle Street	B4	Sutherland Street	A3	Glendale Road	C3-C4
North Hill Street	B4-C4	Cemetery Road	A3-A4	Thorpe Avenue	A3	Half Edge Lane	A3-B3-C3
North Quay Street	C1-C2	Chadwick Street	B2	Townsend Road	C3	Irwell Grove	A1-B1
Oldfield Road	A1-B1-B2	Chelford Drive	B4	Vicarage Road	A2-B2	Mather Road	A2
Park Street	B2-C2	Cherry Drive	C1	Victoria Road	C1	Monton Road	A3
Peel Street	B3	Chester Street	B1	Wardley Street	B2-C2	Monton Road	A2-B2
Peru Street	B3	Chorley Road	A3-A2-B2-B1-C1	Warwick Street	B3	Narbourne Crescent	C4
Pine Street	B4	Clarendon Road	B1-B2-C2	Watson Street	B2	Oxford Street	A1-A2
Princes Bridge	B1-C1	Coronation Street	C3-C4	Wellington Road	B1-B2	Park Road	C3-C4
Quay Street	C1	Cromwell Road	A3-B3	Wesley Street	B2	Peel Street	A2
Regent Road	A1-B1	Crossfield Drive	A3	Westminster Street	A4	Polygon	B3-C3
Rigby Street	C3	Deanscourt Avenue	A1	Westover Street	B2-B3	Portland Road	B4-C4
Riverside	B4	Deans Road	A1	Winton Hall Road	B2-C2	Preston Avenue	B3-C3
Rodney Street	B2-C2	Devon Street	B4	Woodford Drive	A4	Regent Street	B2
Rosamond Street	C3	Dorset Street	B4	Wordsworth Road	A2-A3	Russel Street	A2
St Simon Street	C4	Douglas Street	C1	Worsley Street	B4-C4	St George's Crescent	C3-C4
St Stephen Street	C3-C4	Dudley Road	B4-B3-C3			St Mary's Road	B2
Silk Street	B4-C4	Elizabeth Street	C4			Salisbury Road	C4
Stanley Street	C2	Everton Street	A1-B1	**Eccles**		Sandwich Road	B3-B4
Sullivan Way	C3	Fernlea Crescent	A1	Abbey Grove	A3	Snowdon Road	B4-C4
Upper Cleminson Street	B3	Goddle Drive	A1	Albert Road	B3	Stafford Road	A3-A4-B4
Upper Wharf Street	B2	Grosvenor Street	C4	Albert Street	B2	Talbot Street	A1
Water Street	B1-C1-C2	Hamilton Street	A3	Alma Street	A1	Trafalgar Road	C3
Wellington Street	C3-C4	Heywood Street	A1	Barton Lane	A1-A2-B2	Trafford Road	A1-A2
West Bank Street	A1	Holland Street	B2-C2	Belgrave Crescent	B3	Vernon Grove	B2
West Fleet Street	A1-B1	Lees Street	B4-C4	Bentcliffe Way		Victoria Crescent	B3-C3
West Union Street	A1-B1	Lower Sutherland Street	A1-A2		A1-B1-B2-B1-C1-C2	Victoria Road	A3-B3
Wilburn Street	B1	Lowry Drive	C3-C4	Bindloss Avenue	B3-C3	Victoria Road	C3-C4
Windsor Crescent	A3-A2-B2	Lynton Avenue	B3-C3	Boardman Street	A1	Wellington Road	A2-A3
		Milner Street	C1-C2	Bright Road	A2	Wellington Road	
		Mossfield Road	A4-B4-C4	Cavendish Road	A3-A4		A3-A2-B2-B3-C3
Swinton		New Cross Street	C1	Chadwick Road	A2	Wentworth Road	B4-C4
Abbey Drive	A2-A3-B3	Normanby Street	A3-A4	Chatsworth Road	B4	Westminster Road	A3-A4-B4
Ackworth Road	A4-B4	Partington Lane	A1-B1-B2	Church Road	B2		
Bain Street	B1-C1	Pendlebury Road	C1-C2-C3	Church Street	A2-B2		
Bancroft Road	A4-B4	Priory Road	A3-B3-B2	Clarendon Crescent	B3-B4-B3		
Beech Street	B1-C1	Queensway Lane	C4	Clarendon Road	B3		
Bingham Street	C1	Raymond Street	B3	Corporation Road	A1-A2		
Bolton Road	C4	Rutland Street	B4-C4	Davis Street	A1		
Boundary Road	B3-B2-C2	Rutland Street	A3	Devonshire Road	C2-C3		
Brierley Road	A4-B4	St Peter's Road	A1-A2	Eccles By-pass	A3-A2-B2-C2		
		Sefton Road	B3-B4				

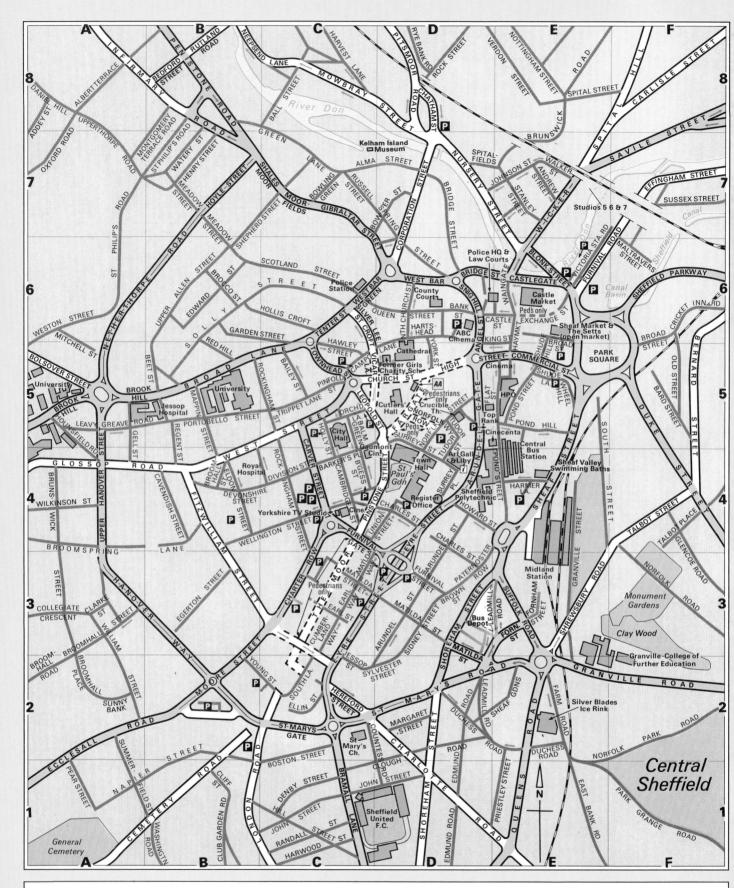

Sheffield

Cutlery – which has made the name of Sheffield famous throughout the world – has been manufactured here since at least as early as the time of Chaucer. The god of blacksmiths, Vulcan, is the symbol of the city's industry, and he crowns the town hall, which was opened in 1897 by Queen Victoria. At the centre of the industry, however, is Cutlers' Hall, the headquarters of the Company of Cutlers. This society was founded in 1624 and has the right to grant trade marks to articles of a sufficiently high standard. In the hall is the company's collection of silver, with examples of craftsmanship dating back every year to 1773. A really large collection of cutlery is kept in the city museum. Steel production, a vital component of the industry, was greatly improved when the crucible process was invented here in 1740. At Abbeydale Industrial Hamlet, 3½ miles south-west of the city centre, is a complete restored site open as a museum and showing 18th-century methods of steel production. Sheffield's centre, transformed since World War II, is one of the finest and most modern in Europe. There are no soot-grimed industrial eyesores here, for the city has stringent pollution controls and its buildings are carefully planned and set within excellent landscaping projects. Many parks are set in and around the city, and the Pennines are within easy reach.

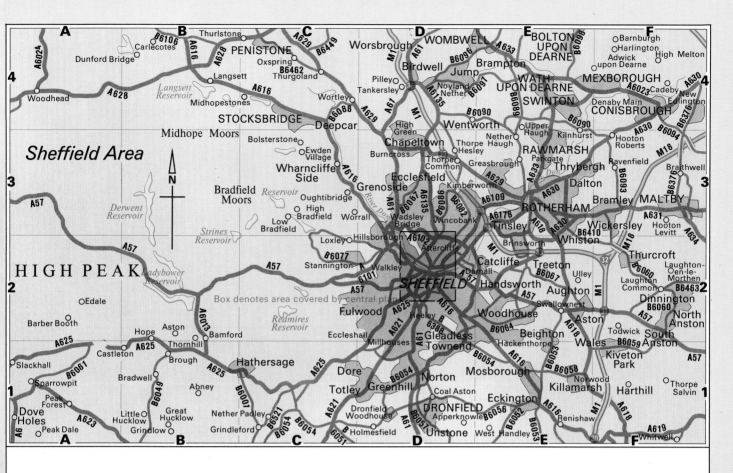

LEGEND

Town Plan

AA Recommended roads
Other roads
Restricted roads
Buildings of interest
One Way Streets
Car Parks   P
Parks and open spaces

Area Plan

A roads
B roads
Locations   Oakworth ○
Urban area

Street Index with grid reference

Sheffield

Addey Street	A7-A8
Albert Terrace	A8
Alma Street	C7-D7
Andrew Street	E7
Angel Street	D5-D6
Arundel Gate	D4-D5
Arundel Street	C2-D2-D3-D4
Bailey Street	C5
Ball Street	C8
Balm Green	C4-C5
Bank Street	D6
Bard Street	F5
Barker's Pool	C4-C5-D5
Bedford Street	B8
Beet Street	B5
Bernard Street	F4-F5-F6
Blonk Street	E6
Bolsover Street	A5
Boston Street	C1-C2
Bower Street	C7-D7
Bowling Green	C7
Bramall Lane	C1-C2
Bridge Street	D7-D6-E6
Broad Lane	B5-C5-C6
Broad Street	E6.F5-F6
Brocco Street	B6
Brook Hill	A5-B5
Broomhall Place	A2
Broomhall Road	A2
Broomhall Street	A2-A3,B4
Broomspring Lane	A4-B4
Brown Street	D3

Brunswick Street	A3-A4
Brunswick Road	E7-E8
Burgess Street	C4
Cambridge Street	C4
Campo Lane	C5-D5-D6
Carlisle Street	F8
Carver Street	C4-C5
Castle Street	D6-E6
Castlegate	E6
Cavendish Street	B4
Cemetery Road	A1-B1-B2
Charles Street	D3-D4
Charlotte Road	C2-D2-D1-E1
Charter Row	C3-C4
Chatham Street	D7-D8
Church Street	C5-D5
Clarke Street	A3
Cliff Street	B1
Clough Road	C1-D1-D2
Club Garden Road	B1
Collegiate Crescent	A3
Commercial Street	E5
Corporation Street	D6-D7
Countess Road	C2-D2-D1
Cricket Inn Road	F6
Cumberland Way	C3
Daniel Hill	A8
Denby Street	C1
Devonshire Street	B4-C4
Division Street	C4
Duchess Road	D2-E2
Duke Street	F4-F5
Earl Street	C3
Earl Way	C3
East Bank Road	E1-E2
Ecclesall Road	A1-A2-B2
Edmund Road	D1-D2
Edward Street	B6
Effingham Street	F7
Egerton Street	B3
Eldon Street	B4
Ellin Street	C2
Eyre Street	C2-C3-D3-D4
Exchange Street	E6
Fargate	D5
Farm Road	E2
Fitzwilliam Street	B4-B3-C3
Flat Street	E5
Fornham Street	E3
Furnival Gate	C3-C4-D3-D4
Furnival Road	E6-F6-F7
Furnival Street	D3
Garden Street	B6-C6-C5
Gell Street	A4-A5
Gibraltar Street	C7-C6-D6
Glencoe Road	F3-F4
Glossop Road	A4-B4
Granville Road	E2-F2
Granville Street	E3-E4
Green Lane	B8-C8-C7
Hanover Way	A3-B3-B2
Harmer Lane	E4
Hartshead	D6
Harwood Street	C1
Harvest Lane	C8

Hawley Street	C5
Haymarket	E5-E6
Henry Street	B7
Hereford Street	C2
High Street	D5-E5
Hill Street	B1-C1
Hollis Croft	B6-C6
Holly Street	C4-C5
Hounsfield Road	A4-A5
Howard Street	D4-E4
Hoyle Street	B7
Infirmary Road	A8-B8 B7
Jessop Street	C2
John Street	C1-D1
Johnson Street	D7-E7
King Street	D5-E5-E6
Leadmill Road	D2-D3-E3
Leavy Greave Road	A5-B5
Lee Croft	C5-C6
Leopold Street	C4-D5
London Road	C1-B1-B2-C2
Maltravers Street	F6
Mappin Street	B4-B5
Margaret Street	D2
Matilda Street	C3-D3-D2
Matilda Way	C3
Meadow Street	B6-B7
Mitchell Street	A5-A6
Montgomery Terrace Road	A7-B7-B8
Moorfields	C7
Moore Street	B2-B3-C3
Mowbray Street	C8-D8-D7
Napier Street	A1-B1-B2
Neepsend Lane	B8-C8
Netherthorpe Road	A5-A6-B6-B7
Norfolk Park Road	E1-E2-F2
Norfolk Road	F3-F4
Norfolk Row	D5
Norfolk Street	D4-D5
North Church Street	D6
Nottingham Street	C2
Nursery Street	D7-E7-E6
Old Street	F5-F6
Orchard Lane	C5
Oxford Road	A7-A8
Park Grange Road	E1-F1
Park Square	E5-E6-F6-F5
Paternoster Row	D3-D4-E4
Pear Street	A1
Penistone Road	B7-B8
Pinfold Street	C5
Pinstone Street	C4-D4-D5
Pitsmoor Road	D8
Pond Hill	E5
Pond Street	E4-E5
Portobello Street	B5-C5
Priestley Street	D1-E1-E2
Queen Street	C6-D6
Queen's Road	E1-E2
Randall Street	C1
Red Hill	B5-B6
Regent Street	B4-B5
Rock Street	D8
Rockingham Street	B5-C5-C4

Russell Street	C7
Rutland Road	B8
Rye Bank Road	D8
St Mary's Gate	C2
St Mary's Road	C2-D2-E2-E3
St Philip's Road	A6-A7-B7-B8
Savile Street	E7-F7-F8
Scotland Street	B6-C6
Shales Moor	B7-C7
Sheaf Gardens	D2-E2
Sheaf Street	E4-E5
Sheffield Parkway	F6
Shepherd Street	B6-B7-C7
Shoreham Street	D1-D2-D3-E3
Shrewsbury Road	E3-E4-F3-F4
Shude Lane	E5
Shude Hill	E5-E6
Sidney Street	D3
Silver Street	C6
Snig Hill	D6
Solly Street	B5-B6-C6
South Lane	C2
South Street	E4-E5
Spital Hill	E7-E8-F8
Spital Street	E8-F8
Spitalfields	D7-E7
Spring Street	D6-D7
Stanley Street	E7
Suffolk Road	E3
Summerfield Street	A2-A1-B1
Sunny Bank	A2
Surrey Place	D4
Surrey Street	D4-D5
Sussex Street	F7
Sylvester Street	C2-D2
Talbot Place	F4
Talbot Street	F4
Tenter Street	C6
The Moor	C3-C4
Townhead Street	C5
Trippet Lane	C5
Tudor Street	D4-D5
Tudor Way	D5
Union Street	C4-D4
Upper Allen Street	B6
Upper Hanover Street	A3-A4-A5
Upperthorpe Road	A7-A8
Verdon Street	D8-E8
Vicar Lane	C5-D5
Victoria Station Road	E6-E7-F7
Waingate	E6
Walker Street	E7
Washington Road	B1
Watery Street	B7-B8
Wellington Street	B4-C4
West Bar	D6
West Bar Green	D6
West Street	B4-B5-C5
Weston Street	A5-A6
Wheel Hill	E5
Wicker	E6-E7
Wilkinson Street	A4
William Street	A2-A3
York Street	D5-D6
Young Street	B2-C2

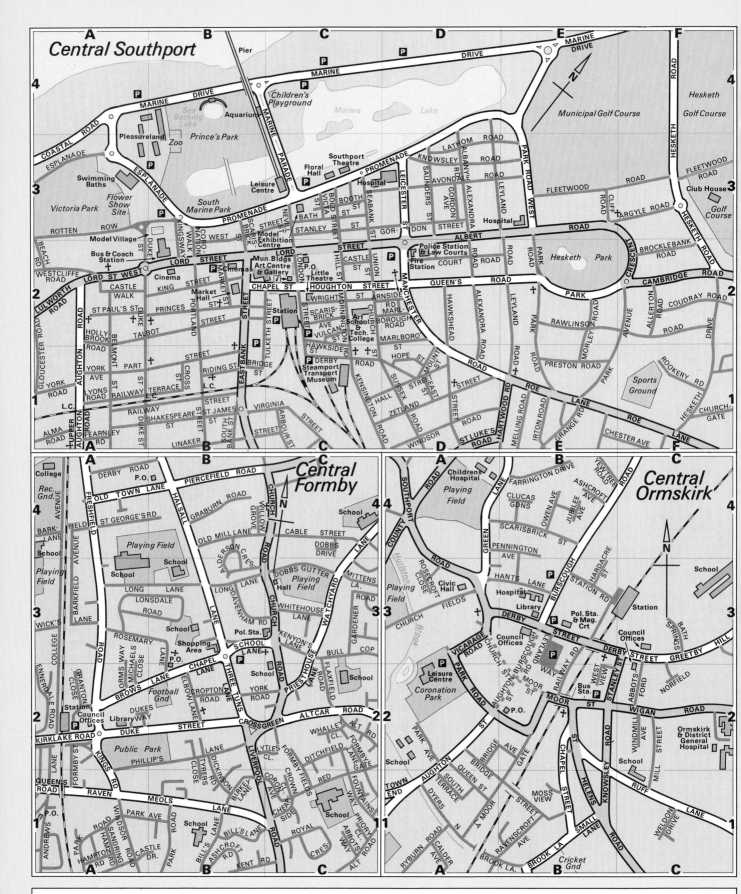

Southport

Seven miles of firm beaches and a ¾-mile long pier are just two of the attractions of Southport, which has been a popular resort since the 18th century. The elegant Victorian buildings of Lord Street run parallel with the Promenade, designated a conservation area, and in Lord Street itself, Atkinson Gallery houses a collection of 19th- and 20th-century art. The town also enjoys the distinction of having its own Botanic Gardens, and here the exhibits of the Botanic Gardens Museum include a collection of 18th- and 19th-century china. By way of contrast, Southport also offers the delights of such different areas of interest as the Steam Transport Museum, a model village and a model railway. Also to be seen are the birds and animals of Southport Zoo, which stretches over 1½ acres of land.

Formby people were farmers and seafarers right up until the 19th century. Unsuccessful attempts were made then to turn the town into a resort, and the National Trust now controls some 400 acres of the foreshore and sand dunes that lie to the west.

Ormskirk Granted a Royal Charter in 1670, Ormskirk's market has been the focal point of the town ever since. Standing at the junction of two trunk roads, this is still very much a market town, even though it has seen expansion in its industries and its residential areas.

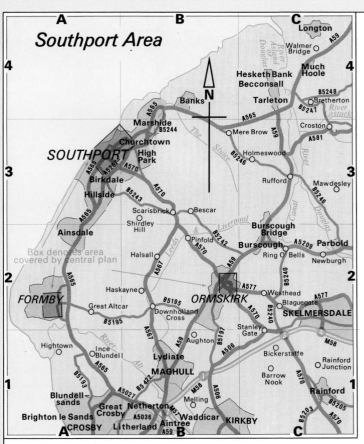

Southport Area

Box denotes area covered by central plan

Key to Town Plan and Area Plan

Town Plan
AA Recommended roads
Other roads
Restricted roads
Buildings of interest
Car Parks
Parks and open spaces
One Way Streets

Area Plan
A roads
B roads
Locations   Brasted ○
Urban area

Street Index with Grid Reference

Southport

Albany Road	D3-D4
Albert Road	D2-D3-E3
Alexandra Road	D1-D2-D3
Allerton Road	F2
Alma Road	A1
Arbour Street	C1
Argyle Road	E3-F3
Arnside Road	C2-D2
Aughton Road	A1-A2
Avondale Road	D3-E3
Bath Street	C3
Beach Road	A2-A3
Belmont Street	A1-A2
Bold Street	C2-C3
Booth Street	C3
Bridge Street	B1
Brocklebank Road	F2
Cambridge Road	F2
Castle Street	C2
Castle Walk	A2
Chapel Street	B2-C2
Chester Avenue	E1-F1
Churchgate	F1
Church Street	C1-C2
Cliff Road	E3
Coastal Road	A3-A4
Coronation Walk	B2-B3
Coudray Road	F2
Court Road	D2-E2
Cross Street	B1
Derby Road	C1
Duke Street	A1-A2-A3
East Street	D1
Eastbank Street	B1-B2
Esplanade	A3-B3
Fearnley Road	A1
Fleetwood Road	E3-F3
Gloucester Road	A1-A2
Gordon Avenue	D3
Gordon Street	C3-D3
Grange Road	E1
Hall Street	C1-D1
Hartwood Road	D1-E1
Hawkshead Street	D1-D2
Hawkside Street	C1-C2
Hesketh Drive	F1-F2
Hesketh Road	F2-F3-F4
Hill Street	C2
Hollybrook Road	A2
Hope Street	D1
Houghton Street	C2-D2
Irton Road	E1
Kensington Road	C1-D1
King Street	A2-B2
Kingsway	B2-B3
Knowsley Road	D3-E3
Lathom Road	D3-E3
Leicester Street	D3
Leyland Road	D4-D3-E3-E2-E1
Linaker Street	B1-C1
London Street	C1-C2
Lord Street	B2-C2-D2
Lord Street West	A2
Lulworth Road	A2
Lyons Road	A1
Manchester Road	D2-D1-E1
Marine Drive	A4-B4-C4-D4-E4-F4
Marine Parade	B4-C4-C3
Market Street	B2
Marlborough Road	C2-D2
Marlborough Street	C2-D2
Melling Road	E1
Morley Road	E1-E2
Mornington Road	C1-C2
Mount Street	D1
Nevill Street	C2-C3
Park Avenue	E1-E2-F2
Park Crescent	E2-F2-F3-E3
Park Road	E1-E2-E3
Park Road West	E3-E4
Part Street	A1-B1
Portland Street	B1-B2
Preston Road	E1
Princes Street	A2-B2
Promenade	B3-C3-D3-D4-E4
Queen's Road	D2-E2
Railway Street	A1-B1
Railway Terrace	A1-B1
Rawlinson Road	E2-F2
Riding Street	B1
Roe Lane	E1-F1
Rookery Road	F1
Rotten Row	A3
St James Street	B1
St Luke's Road	D1
St Paul's Street	A2
Saunders Street	D3
Scarisbrick Avenue	C2
Scarisbrick Street	B2-B3
Seabank Street	C2-C3
Shakespeare Street	A1-B1
South Bank Street	B1
Stanley Street	C3
Sussex Street	C1-D1
Talbot Street	A2-B2
Tulketh Street	B1-B2-C2
Union Street	C3
Upper Aughton Road	A1
Victa Street	C3
Virginia Street	B1-C1
Vulcan Street	C2
Westcliffe Road	A2
West Street	B2-B3-C3
Windsor Road	D1
Wright Street	C2
York Avenue	A1
York Road	A1
Zetland Street	C1-D1

Formby

Abbots Way	C1
Alderson Crescent	B3-B4
Alt Road	C1-C2
Altcar Road	C2
Andrews Lane	A1-A2
Ashcroft Road	B1
Barkfield Avenue	A3-A4
Barkfield Lane	A4
Bill's Lane	B1-C1
Birkey Lane	B1
Brows Lane	A2-B2
Bull Cop	C3
Cable Street	C4
Castle Drive	A1-B1
Chapel Lane	B2-B3
Cheapside	C1
Church Road	C2-C3-B3-B4-C4
College Avenue	A2-A3-A4
Coron Avenue	B1-C1
Cropton Road	B2
Crossgreen	B2-C2
Crown Close	C1
Davenham Road	B3-C3
Derby Road	A4-B4
Dickinson Road	B1-B2
Ditchfield	C2
Dobbs Drive	C4
Dobbs Gutter	C3
Duke Street	A2-B2
Dukes Way	A2
Elbow Lane	B2
Ennerdale Road	A2
Flaxfield Road	C2-C3
Formby Fields	C1-C2
Formby Lane	C2
Formby Street	A1-A2
Fountains Way	C1
Freshfield Road	A2-A3-A4
Gardener Road	C3
Graburn Road	B4
Granton Close	A2
Halsall Lane	B3-B4
Hampton Road	A1
Kent Road	B1-C1
Kenyon's Lane	C3
Kings Road	A1-A2
Kirklake Road	A2
Liverpool Road	B2-B1-C1
Long Lane	A3-B3
Lonsdale Road	A3-B3
Lytles Close	B2-C2
Michaels Close	A2-A3
Mittens Lane	C3
Old Mill Lane	B4
Old Town Lane	A4-B4
Orms Way	A2-A3
Park Avenue	A1-B1

Park Road	A1-B1
Phillip's Lane	A1-A2-B2
Piercefield Road	B4
Priesthouse Lane	C2-C3
Priory Close	C1
Queen's Road	A1
Raven Meols Lane	A1-B1-C1
Red Gate	C1-C2
Rosemary Lane	A3-B3-B2
Royal Crescent	C1
St George's Road	A4-B4
Sandringham Road	A1
School Lane	B3-C3
Three Tuns Lane	B2-B3
Tyrers Close	B1-B2
Watchyard Lane	C3-C4
Whalley Close	C3
Whitehouse Lane	C3
Wick's Lane	A3
Willow Grove	B4
Windsor Road	A1
York Road	B2-C2

Ormskirk

Abbotsford	C2-C3
Ashcroft Avenue	B4
Aughton Street	A1-A2-B2
Bath Springs	C3
Bridge Avenue	A2-B2
Bridge Street	A2-A1-B1
Brook Lane	A1-B1
Burscough Road	B4-C4
Burscough Street	B2-B3-B4
Calder Avenue	A1
Chapel Street	B1-B2
Church Fields	A3
Church Street	A3-B3-B2
Clucas Gardens	B4
County Road	A3-A4
Derby Street	A3-B3-C3
Dyers Lane	A1
Farrington Drive	B4
Green Lane	A3-A4-B4
Greetby Hill	C3
Hants Lane	A3-B3
Hardacre Street	B3
Jubilee Avenue	B4
Knowsley Road	B1-B2
Leyland Way	B2-B3
Mill Street	C1-C2
Moor Gate	A1-B1-B2
Moor Street	B2
Moss View	B1
Norfield	C2-C3
Owen Avenue	B4
Park Avenue	A2
Park Road	A2-A3
Pennington Avenue	A4-B4
Queen Street	A1-A2
Railway Road	B2-B3
Ravenscroft Avenue	B1
Rosecroft Close	A3
Ruff Lane	B2-B1-C1
Ryburn Road	A1
St Helens Road	B2-B1-C1
Scarisbrick Street	A4-B4
Small Lane	B1
Southport Road	A3-A4
South Terrace	A1
Stanley Street	B2-C2-C3
Station Road	B3
Town End	A1
Vicarage Road	A3
Weldon Drive	C1
West View	B2
Wigan Road	B2-C2
Windmill Avenue	C2
Yew Tree Road	B4-C4

SOUTHPORT
Retreating seas and a growing expanse of sands inspired the creation in the late 19th century of the 86-acre Marine Lake — a boating lake spanned by Princes Park Bridge and flanked by attractive gardens.

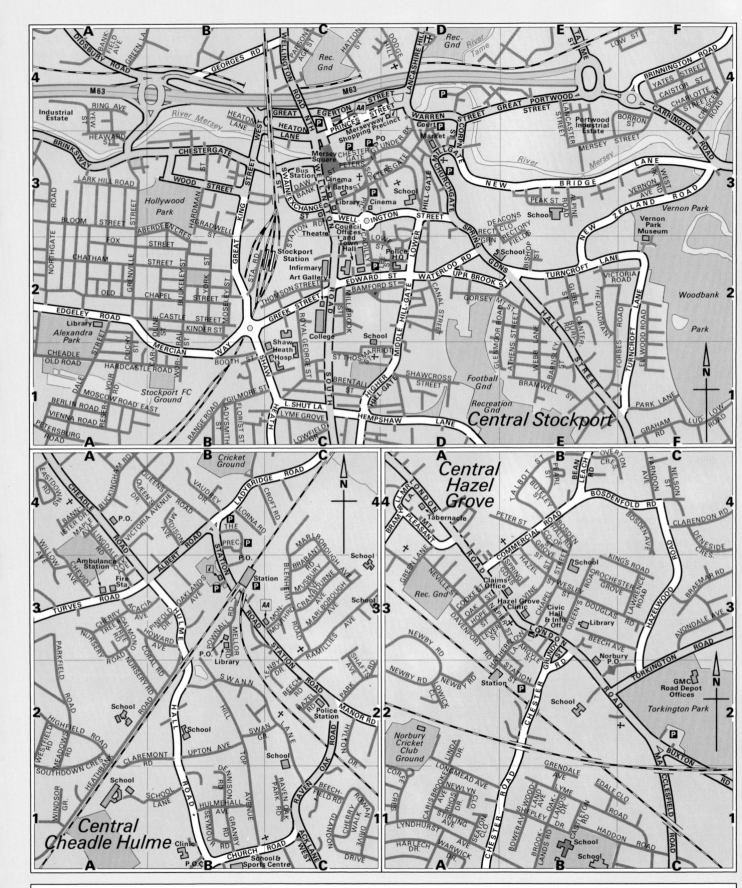

Stockport

The cafes, bandstand and open air travelators of the Merseyway Shopping Precinct stand in direct contrast with the narrow cobbled streets that run close to Stockport's old established traditional market, and the lively mixture must have contributed to making the town the popular destination for shoppers that it is today. Standing on the River Mersey, this was once a textile town, and today its good road and rail connections with the rest of the country have helped to keep it busy in its new role as commercial and industrial centre. It has a museum at Vernon Park and professional football is provided by Stockport County, currently in the Fourth Division of the Canon League.

Cheadle Hulme has become a popular place to live, with its good facilities for shopping and for recreation. It can also boast the lovely Bramhall Hall among its places of interest: this black and white half-timbered mansion dates from the 14th century and lies to the south-east in a pleasantly landscaped park.

Hazel Grove is a relatively new name for this settlement. In its old days as a village, it was called simply Bullock Smithy, and only switched to the less earthy Hazel Grove in the mid-19th century. Today it can offer a wide variety of water sports at extensive Torkington Park.

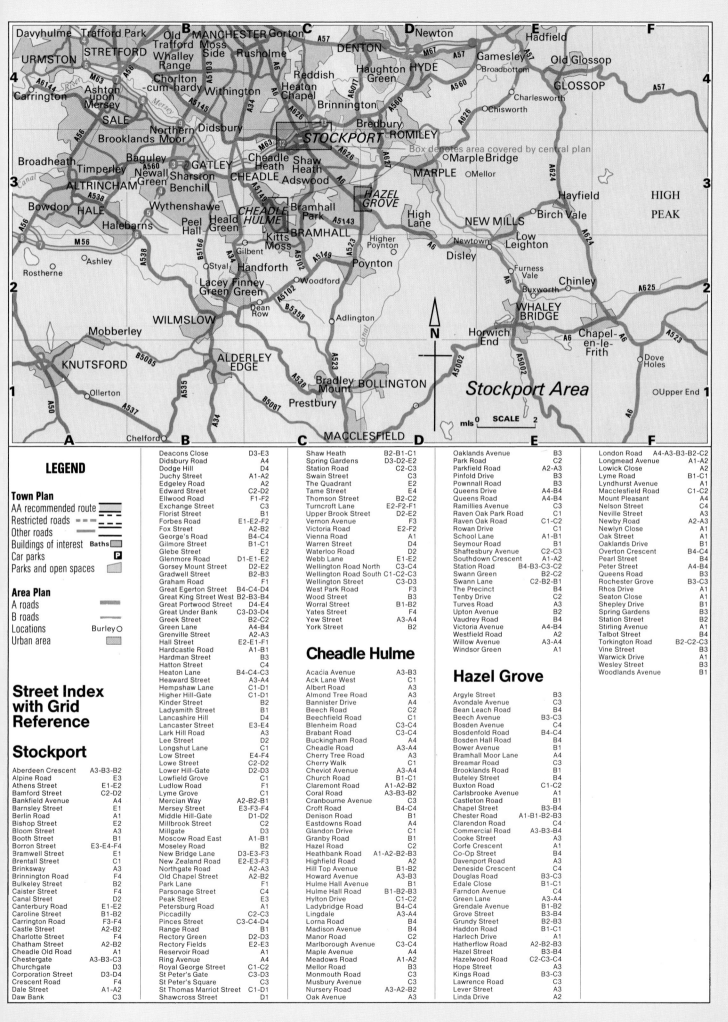

LEGEND

Town Plan

AA recommended route
Restricted roads
Other roads
Buildings of interest — Baths
Car parks — P
Parks and open spaces

Area Plan

A roads
B roads
Locations — Burley ○
Urban area

Street Index with Grid Reference

Stockport

Aberdeen Crescent	A3-B3-B2
Alpine Road	E3
Athens Street	E1-E2
Bamford Street	C2-D2
Bankfield Avenue	A4
Barnsley Street	E1
Berlin Road	A1
Bishop Street	E2
Bloom Street	A3
Booth Street	B1
Borron Street	E3-E4-F4
Bramwell Street	E1
Brentall Street	C1
Brinksway	A3
Brinnington Road	F4
Bulkeley Street	B2
Caister Street	F4
Canal Street	D2
Canterbury Road	E1-E2
Caroline Street	B1-B2
Carrington Road	F3-F4
Castle Street	A2-B2
Charlotte Street	F4
Chatham Street	A2-B2
Cheadle Old Road	A1
Chestergate	A3-B3-C3
Churchgate	D3
Corporation Street	D3-D4
Crescent Road	F4
Dale Street	A1-A2
Daw Bank	C3

Deacons Close	D3-E3
Didsbury Road	A4
Dodge Hill	D4
Duchy Street	A1-A2
Edgeley Road	A2
Edward Street	C2-D2
Ellwood Road	F1-F2
Exchange Street	C3
Florist Street	B1
Forbes Road	E1-E2-F2
Fox Street	A2-B2
George's Road	B4-C4
Gilmore Street	B1-C1
Glebe Street	E2
Glenmore Road	D1-E1-E2
Gorsey Mount Street	D2-E2
Gradwell Street	B2-B3
Graham Road	F1
Great Egerton Street	B4-C4-D4
Great King Street West	B2-B3-B4
Great Portwood Street	D4-E4
Great Under Bank	C3-D3-D4
Greek Street	B2-C2
Green Lane	A4-B4
Grenville Street	A2-A3
Hall Street	E2-E1-F1
Hardcastle Road	A1-B1
Hardman Street	B3
Hatton Street	C4
Heaton Lane	B4-C4-C3
Heaward Street	A3-A4
Hempshaw Lane	C1-D1
Higher Hill-Gate	C1-D1
Kinder Street	B2
Ladysmith Street	B1
Lancashire Hill	D4
Lancaster Street	E3-E4
Lark Hill Road	A3
Lee Street	D2
Longshut Lane	C1
Low Street	E4-F4
Lowe Street	C2-D2
Lower Hill-Gate	D2-D3
Lowfield Grove	C1
Ludlow Road	F1
Lyme Grove	C1
Mercian Way	A2-B2-B1
Mersey Street	E3-F3-F4
Middle Hill-Gate	D1-D2
Millbrook Street	B1
Millgate	D3
Moscow Road East	A1-B1
Moseley Road	B2
New Bridge Lane	D3-E3-F3
New Zealand Road	E2-E3-F3
Northgate Road	A2-A3
Old Chapel Street	A2-B2
Park Lane	F1
Parsonage Street	C4
Peak Street	E3
Petersburg Road	A1
Piccadilly	C2-C3
Pinces Street	C3-C4-D4
Range Road	B1
Rectory Green	D2-D3
Rectory Fields	E2-E3
Reservoir Road	A1
Ring Avenue	A4
Royal George Street	C1-C2
St Peter's Gate	C3-D3
St Peter's Square	C3
St Thomas Marriot Street	C1-D1
Shawcross Street	D1

Shaw Heath	B2-B1-C1
Spring Gardens	D3-D2-E2
Station Road	C2-C3
Swain Street	C3
The Quadrant	E2
Tame Street	E4
Thomson Street	B2-C2
Turncroft Lane	E2-F2-F1
Upper Brook Street	D2-E2
Vernon Avenue	F3
Victoria Road	E2-F2
Vienna Road	A1
Warren Street	D4
Waterloo Road	D2
Webb Lane	E1-E2
Wellington Road North	C3-C4
Wellington Road South	C1-C2-C3
Wellington Street	C3-D3
West Park Road	F3
Wood Street	B3
Worral Street	B1-B2
Yates Street	F4
Yew Street	A3-A4
York Street	B2

Cheadle Hulme

Acacia Avenue	A3-B3
Ack Lane West	C1
Albert Road	A3
Almond Tree Road	A3
Bannister Drive	A4
Beech Road	C2
Beechfield Road	C1
Blenheim Road	C3-C4
Brabant Road	C3-C4
Buckingham Road	A4
Cheadle Road	A3-A4
Cherry Tree Road	A3
Cherry Walk	C1
Cheviot Avenue	A3-A4
Church Road	B1-C1
Claremont Road	A1-A2-B2
Coral Road	A3-B3-B2
Croft Road	B4-C4
Denison Road	B1
Eastdowns Road	A4
Glandon Drive	C1
Granby Road	B1
Hazel Road	C2
Heathbank Road	A1-A2-B2-B3
Highfield Road	A2
Hill Top Avenue	B1-B2
Howard Avenue	A3-B3
Hulme Hall Avenue	B1
Hulme Hall Road	B1-B2-B3
Hylton Drive	C1-C2
Ladybridge Road	B4-C4
Lingdale	A3-A4
Lorna Road	B4
Madison Avenue	B4
Manor Road	C2
Marlborough Avenue	C3-C4
Maple Avenue	A4
Meadows Road	A1-A2
Mellor Road	B3
Monmouth Road	C3
Musbury Avenue	C3
Nursery Road	A3-A2-B2
Oak Avenue	A3

Oaklands Avenue	B3
Park Road	C2
Parkfield Road	A2-A3
Pinfold Drive	B3
Pownall Road	B3
Queens Drive	A4-B4
Queens Road	A4-B4
Ramillies Avenue	C3
Raven Oak Park Road	C1
Raven Oak Road	C1-C2
Rowan Drive	C1
School Lane	A1-B1
Seymour Road	B1
Shaftesbury Avenue	C2-C3
Southdown Crescent	A1-A2
Station Road	B4-B3-C3-C2
Swann Green	B2-C2
Swann Lane	C2-B2-B1
The Precinct	B4
Tenby Drive	C2
Turves Road	A3
Upton Avenue	B2
Vaudrey Road	B4
Victoria Avenue	A4-B4
Westfield Road	A2
Willow Avenue	A3-A4
Windsor Green	A1

Hazel Grove

Argyle Street	B3
Avondale Avenue	C3
Bean Leach Road	B4
Beech Avenue	B3-C3
Bosden Avenue	C4
Bosdenfold Road	B4-C4
Bosden Hall Road	B4
Bower Avenue	B1
Bramhall Moor Lane	A4
Breamar Road	C3
Brooklands Road	B1
Buteley Street	B4
Buxton Road	C1-C2
Carlsbrooke Avenue	A1
Castleton Road	B1
Chapel Street	B3-B4
Chester Road	A1-B1-B2-B3
Clarendon Road	C4
Commercial Road	A3-B3-B4
Cooke Street	A3
Corfe Crescent	A1
Co-Op Street	B4
Davenport Road	A3
Deneside Crescent	C4
Douglas Road	B3-C3
Edale Close	B1-C1
Farndon Avenue	C4
Green Lane	A3-A4
Grendale Avenue	B1-B2
Grove Street	B3-B4
Grundy Street	B2-B3
Haddon Road	B1-C1
Harlech Drive	A1
Hatherflow Road	A2-B2-B3
Hazel Street	B3-B4
Hazelwood Road	C2-C3-C4
Hope Street	A3
Kings Road	B3-C3
Lawrence Road	C3
Lever Street	A3
Linda Drive	A2

London Road	A4-A3-B3-B2-C2
Longmead Avenue	A1-A2
Lowick Close	A2
Lyme Road	B1-C1
Lyndhurst Avenue	A1
Macclesfield Road	C1-C2
Mount Pleasant	A4
Nelson Street	C4
Neville Street	A3
Newby Road	A2-A3
Newlyn Close	A1
Oak Street	A1
Oaklands Drive	B1
Overton Crescent	B4-C4
Pearl Street	B4
Peter Street	A4-B4
Queens Road	B3
Rochester Grove	B3-C3
Rhos Drive	A1
Seaton Close	A1
Shepley Drive	B1
Spring Gardens	B3
Station Street	B2
Stirling Avenue	A1
Talbot Street	B4
Torkington Road	B2-C2-C3
Vine Street	B3
Warwick Drive	A1
Wesley Street	B3
Woodlands Avenue	B1

69

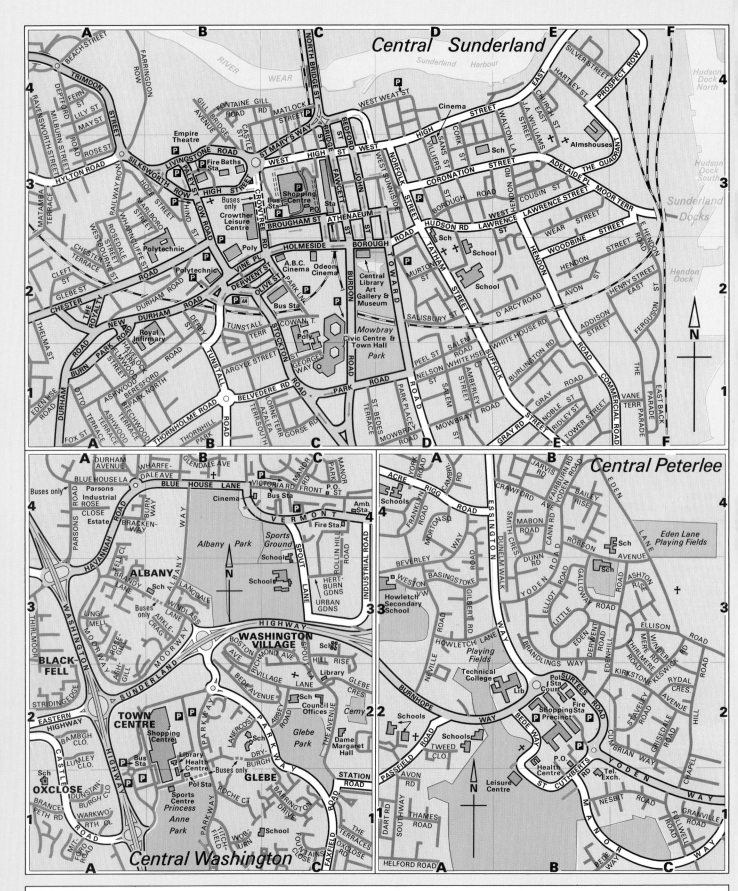

Sunderland

Renowned for its shipbuilding industry, Sunderland is also an important coal port. Its name is derived from the fact that it was 'sundered' from a monastery founded on the far bank of the River Wear in 674. Wearmouth Bridge, originally built in 1796, but replaced in 1929, was one of the first cast-iron bridges in the country. A modern Civic Centre and three museums feature among the town's amenities. Nearby are the fine beaches of Roker and Seaburn.

Peterlee, built to attract industry in the 1950s, is one of Durham's most successful New Towns. It is named after Peter Lee, who started work down the mines at the age of ten, and rose to become president of the Miners' Union. An unexpected but welcome feature of the town is Castle Eden Dene – a three-mile stretch of natural woodland kept as a nature reserve.

Washington is another New Town burgeoning in this industrial corner of north-east England. In the original village stands 17th-century Washington Old Hall, the former home of George Washington's ancestors. Now in the care of the National Trust, it has been fully restored in period style. Another far cry from industry is the Wildfowl Trust's 103-acre park on the north bank of the Wear, where visitors can observe a comprehensive collection of the world's waterfowl in landscaped surroundings.

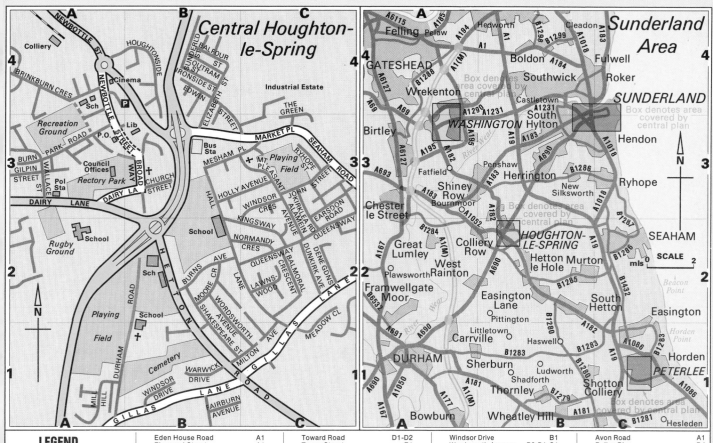

Central Houghton-le-Spring

Sunderland Area

LEGEND

Town Plan

AA recommended route
Restricted roads
Other roads
Buildings of interest — Cinema
Car parks — P
Parks and open spaces
One way streets

Area Plan

A roads
B roads
Locations — Haswell ○
Urban area

Street Index with Grid Reference

Sunderland

Addison Street	E2-F2
Adelaide Place	E3
Amberley Street	D1
Argyle Street	B1-C1
Ashwood Road	A1-B1-B2
Ashwood Terrace	A1
Athenaeum	C3-D3
Avon Street	E2
Azalea Terrace South	B1-C1
Beach Street	A4
Beechwood Terrace	A1-B1
Bedford Street	C3-C4
Belvedere Road	B1-C1
Beresford Park North	A1-B1
Borough Road	C2-D2-D3-E3
Bridge Street	C3-C4
Brougham Street	C3
Burdon Road	C1-C2
Burlington Road	E1
Burn Park Road	A1-A2
Castle Street	B3-B4
Chester Road	A2-B2
Chester Terrace	A2
Church Street East	E3-E4
Cleft Street	A2
Commercial Road	E1-F1
Cork Street	D3-D4
Coronation Street	D3-E3
Cousin Street	E3
Cowan Terrace	C2
Crowtree Road	B3-C3-C2
D'Arcy Road	D2-E2
Deptford Road	A3-A4
Derby Street	B2
Derwent Street	B2-C2
Durham Road	A1-A2-B2
East Back Parade	F1
East Hendon Road	F2-F3
Eden House Road	A1
Elmwood Street	A1
Farringdon Row	A3-A4-B4
Fawcett Street	C2-C3
Ferguson Street	F2
Fern Street	A4
Fontaine Road	B4
Fox Street	A1
Gill Bridge Avenue	B3-B4
Gill Road	B4-C4
Glebe Street	A2
Gorse Road	C1
Gray Road	D1-E1
Hartley Street	E4
Havelock Terrace	A2-A1-B1
Hendon Road	E1-E2-E3
Hendon Street	E2-F2
Henry Street East	F2
High Street East	D3-D4-E4
High Street West	B3-C3-D3
Hind Street	B2-B3
Holmeside	C2
Hope Street	A3-B3
Hudson Road	D3
Hylton Road	A3
J. A. Williams Street	E3-E4
John Street	C2-C3
Lawrence Street	E3
Lily Street	A4
Livingstone Road	B3
Lorne Terrace	C1
Low Road	B2-B3
Matamba Terrace	A3
Marlborough Street	A3-B3
Matlock Street	C4
May Street	A3-A4
Milburn Street	A3-A4
Moor Terrace	E3-F3
Mowbray Road	D1-E1
Murton Street	D2
Nelson Street	D1
New Durham Road	A2-B2
Noble Street	E1
Norfolk Street	D3
North Bridge Street	C4
Olive Street	B2-C2
Otto Terrace	A1
Paley Street	B3
Park Lane	C2
Park Road	C1-D1
Park Place	D1
Peel Street	D1
Prospect Row	E4-F4
Railway Row	A3
Ravensworth Street	A3-A4
Ridley Street	E1
Rosedale Street	A2-A3
Rose Street	A3
St Bedes Terrace	C1-D1
St George's Way	C1
St Mary's Way	C3-C4
Salisbury Street	D2
Sans Street	D3-D4
Salem Road	D1-D2
Salem Street	D1
Silksworth Row	A3-B3
Silver Street	E4-F4
Stockton Road	B2-C2-C1
Suffolk Street	D1-E1
Tatham Street	D2-D3
Thelma Street	A1-A2
Thornhill Park	B1
Thornholme Road	B1
Toward Road	D1-D2
Tower Street	E1
Trimdon Street	A3-A4
Tunstall Road	B1
Tunstall Terrace	B2-C2
The Parade	F1
The Royalty	A2
The Quadrant	E3-F3-F4-E4
Vane Terrace	F1
Villiers Street	D3
Vine Place	B2-C2
Walton Lane	E3-E4
Wear Street	E3
Westbourne Street	A2-A3
West Lawrence Street	D3-E3
West Sunniside	C2
West Weat Street	C4-D4
Wharncliffe Street	A2-A3
White House Court	D1
White House Road	D1-E1-E2
Woodbine Street	E2-E3-F3

Houghton-le-Spring

Alamein Avenue	C2-C3
Balfour Street	B4
Balmoral Crescent	C2
Brinkburn Crescent	A4
Broadway	B3
Burn Park Road	A3
Burns Avenue	B2
Church Street	B3
Dairy Lane	A3-B3
Dene Gardens	C2
Dunkirk Avenue	C2
Durham Road	A1-B1-B2
Earsdon Road	C3
Edwin Street	B4-B3-C3
Elizabeth Street	B3-B4
Fairburn Avenue	B1
Gillas Lane	A1-B1-C1-C2
Gilpin Street	A3
Hall Lane	B3-B2-C2
Hetton Road	B2-B1-C1
Holly Avenue	B3-C3
Houghtonside	A4-B4
Ironside Street	B4
John Street	C3
Kingsway	B2-C2
Kirklea Road	C2-C3
Lawnswood	C2
Market Place	C2
Meadow Close	C1-C2
Mesham Place	B3-C3
Mill Hill	A1
Milton Avenue	B1-C1
Moore Lane	B2
Mount Pleasant	C3
Newbottle Street	A4-A3-B3
Normandy Crescent	B2-C2
Outram Street	B4
Queensway	B2-C2-C3
Ryhope Street	C3
Seaham Road	C3
Shakespeare Street	B1-B2
Sunderland Street	B4
The Green	C3-C4
Wallace Street	A3
Warwick Drive	B1
Windsor Crescent	C3
Windsor Drive	B1
Wordsworth Avenue	B2-B1-C1

Washington

Abbey Road	C2
Albany Way	B3-B4
Arklecrag	B3
Ashgill	A2
Bamborough Close	A2
Barrington Drive	C1
Bede Avenue	B3-B2-C2
Blue House Lane	A4-B4
Boston Avenue	B2-B3
Bracken Way	A4
Brancepeth Road	A1
Brandy Lane	A3
Burn Way	A4-B4
Castle Road	A1-A2
Dryburgh	B2-C2
Dunstanburgh Close	A1
Durham Avenue	A4
Eastern Highway	A2
Faxfield Road	C1
Fell Close	A3-A4
Fountains Close	C1
Front Street	C4
Glebe Crescent	C2
Glendale Avenue	B4
Havannah Road	A3-A4
Hertburn Gardens	C3
Hill Rise	C3
Industrial Road	C3-C4
Lanercost	B2
Langdale	B3
Lingmell	A3
Lumley Close	A2
Manor Park	C4
Manor Road	C4
Mitford Road	A1
Moorway	A3-A2-B2-B3
Oxclose Road	C1
Parkway	B1-B2-C2-C1
Parsons Road	A3-A4
Richmond Avenue	B2-B3-C3
Roche Court	B1
Rollin Hill Road	C3-C4
Rose Close	A4
Rosegill	A3
Spout Lane	C2-C3-C4
Station Road	C1
Stridingedge	A2
Sunderland Highway	A2-B2-B3-C3
The Avenue	C1-C2
The Terraces	C1
Thirlmoor	A3
Titchfield	B1
Urban Gardens	C3
Vermont	B4-C4
Victoria Road	B4-C4
Village Lane	B2-C2
Warkworth Close	A4
Washington Highway	A1-A2-A3-A4
Wharfedale Avenue	A4-B4
Windlass Lane	B3
Woburn	B1

Peterlee

Acre Rigg Road	A4
Ashton Rise	C3
Avon Road	A1
Bailey Rise	B4
Basingstoke Road	A3-A4
Bede Way	B2, B1-C1
Beverley Way	A3-A4
Brandlings Way	B3
Burnhope Way	A2-A3-B2
Cambridge Road	A4
Cann Road	B4
Chapel Hill Road	C1-C2-C3
Crawford Avenue	B4
Cumbrian Way	B2-C2-C1
Dart Road	A1
Derwent Road	B3
Dunelm Walk	B3-B4
Dunn Road	B2
Edenhill Road	C2-C3
Eden Lane	B4-C4-C3
Elliot Road	B3
Ellison Road	C3
Essington Way	A4-B4-A3-B3-B2
Fairburn Road	B4
Franklyn Road	A4
Fullwell Road	C1
Galloway Road	B4-B3-C3
Gilbert Road	A3
Granville Road	C1
Grisedale Road	C2
Helford Road	B2
Howletch Lane	A3-B3
Jarvis Road	B4
Keswick Road	C2-C3
Kirkstone Avenue	C2
Little Eden	B3
Mabon Road	B4
Manor Way	B1-C1
Morton Square	A4
Nesbit Road	B1-C1
Neville Road	A2-A3
Passfield Road	A1-A2
Robson Avenue	B4-B3-C3
Rydal Crescent	C2
St Cuthberts Road	B1-B2
Smith Crescent	B4
Southway	A1
Staveley Road	C2
Surtees Road	B2
Thames Road	A1
Thirlmere Road	C2-C3
Tweed Close	A2
Weston View	A3
Windermere Road	C3
Yoden Road	B3-B4
Yoden Way	B2-C2-C1
York Road	A4

71

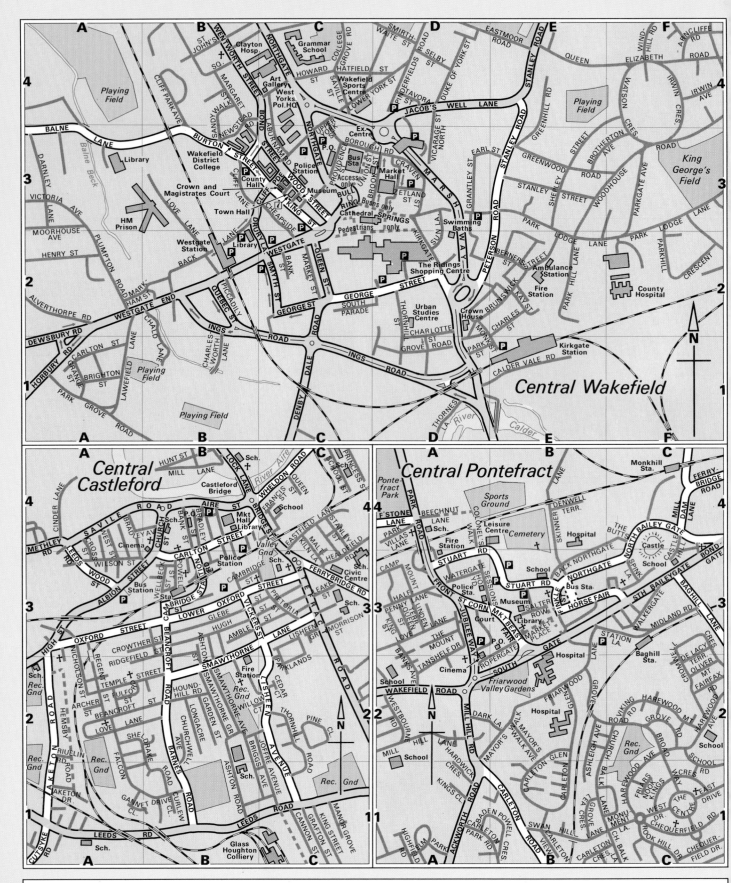

Wakefield

Towers and turrets unfolding over the hillsides greet the visitor to Wakefield, and the 247-ft spire of the Cathedral Church of All Saints has been a landmark for over 500 years. Today the spire looms over the Bull Ring pedestrian precinct which is part of a town centre development, and even older is the stone-built, nine-arched Old Bridge, site of the 14th-century Chapel of St Mary. This was among the finest of the bridge chapels — perhaps because even in the 13th century, Wakefield was an important weaving and dyeing centre (coal mining and a growing reputation as an international industrial centre are more important today). The excellent art gallery has an enterprising collection of modern sculpture and paintings.

Castleford Birthplace of Henry Moore in 1898, this mining and bottlemaking town is on the site of a Roman station. The Castleford Library Museum Room shows late 18th-century Castleford pottery.

Pontefract has been making Pontefract cakes for over 200 years, although today imported, not home-grown, liquorice is used. Its castle was one of the strongest in the north in medieval times and a bloody place of execution in the Wars of the Roses; of Pontefract's 18th- and 19th-century buildings, the Town Hall has the plaster casts used for the panel's at Nelson's Column's base.

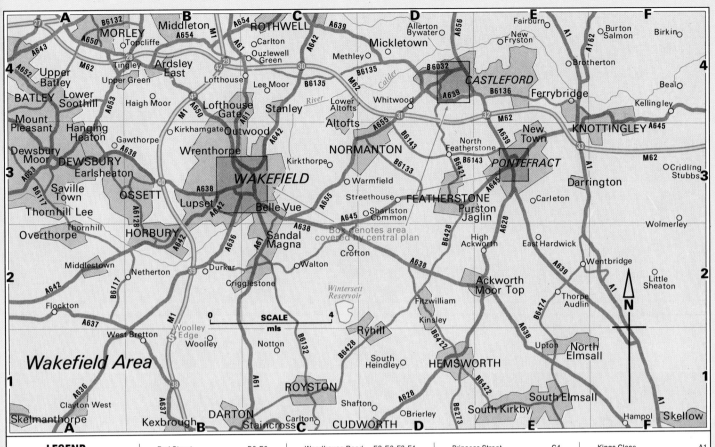

LEGEND

Town Plan
AA Recommended route
Restricted roads
Other roads
Buildings of interest
Car parks ⓟ
Parks and open spaces
One way streets →

Area Plan
A roads
B roads
Locations ○
Urban area

Street Index with grid Reference

Wakefield

Almshouse Lane	D2
Alvethorne Road	A2
Arncliffe Road	F4
Back Lane	B2-B3
Balne Lane	A4-A3-B3
Bank Street	C2
Berners Street	E2
Bond Street	C3-C4
Borough Road	C3-D3
Brighton Street	A1
Brook Street	D3
Brotherton Avenue	E3-F3
Brunswick Street	D2-E2
Bull Ring	C3
Burton Street	B3-C3
Calder Vale Road	D1-E1
Carlton Street	A1
Chald Lane	B1-B2
Charles Street	E2
Charlesworth Lane	B1-B2
Charlotte Street	D1-D2
Cheapside	C2-C3
Cliff Lane	B3
Cliff Parade	B3-C3
Cliff Park Avenue	B4
College Grove Road	C4
Craven Street	D3
Darnley Lane	A3
Denby Dale Road	C1-C2
Dewsbury Road	A1-A2
Drury Lane	B2-B3-C3-C2
Duke of York Street	D4
Earl Street	D3-E3
Eastmoor Road	D4-E4
George Street	C2-D2
Grange Street	A1
Grantley Street	D3
Greenhill Road	E3-E4
Greenwood Road	E3-F3
Grove Road	D1
Grove Street	D1
Hatfield Street	C4-D4
Henry Street	A2
Horbury Road	A1
Howard Street	C4
Ings Road	B2-C2-C1-D1
Irwin Avenue	F4
Irwin Crescent	F3-F4
Jacob's Well Lane	D4-E4
Kay Street	E2
King Street	C3
Kirkgate	D2-D3
Laburnham Road	C3-C4
Lawefield Lane	A1-A2
Love Lane	B2-B3
Lower York Street	C4-D4
Margaret Street	B4
Market Street	C2
Markham Street	A2-B2
Marsh Way	D2-D3
Monk Street	D2-E2-E1
Moorhouse Avenue	A3
Newstead Road	B3-B4
Northgate	C3-C4
Park Street	D1-E1
Parkgate Avenue	F2-F3
Park Grove Road	A1-B1
Parkhill Crescent	F2-F3
Park Hill Lane	E2
Park Lodge Lane	D3-E3-E2-F2-F3
Peterson Road	D2-E2-E3
Piccadilly	B2
Pinderfields Road	D4
Plumpton Road	A2-A3
Providence Street	C3
Quebec Street	B2
Queen Street	C2
Queen Elizabeth Road	E4-F4
St John's Square	B4
Sandy Walk	B3-B4
Saville Street	C4
Selby Street	D4
Shepley Street	E3-E4-F3
Smirthwaite Street	D4
Smyth Street	C2
South Parade	C2-D2
Springs	D3
Stanley Road	E3-E4
Stanley Street	E3
Sun Lane	D2-D3
Tavora Street	D4
Thornes Lane	D1
Thornhill Street	D1-D2
Union Street	C3
Upper York Street	C3-C4
Vicarage Street North	D3-D4
Victoria Avenue	A3
Watson Crescent	F3-F4
Wentworth Street	D4
Westgate	C2-C3
Westgate End	A1-A2-B2
Windhill Road	F4
Wood Street	C3
Woodhouse Road	E2-E3-F3-F4
Zetland Street	D3

Castleford

Aire Street	B4
Aketon Drive	A1
Aketon Road	A1-A2-A3
Albion Street	A3-B3
Amble Street	B3-C3
Archer Street	A2
Ashton Road	B1-B2
Ashton Street	B2-B3
Bank Street	B4
Barnes Road	B1-B2
Beancroft Road	B2-B3
Beancroft Street	A2-B2
Bradley Avenue	A4-B4
Bradley Street	B4
Bridge Street	B4-C4
Briggs Avenue	B2-B1-C1
Cambridge Street	B3-C3
Cannon Street	C1
Carlton Street	B3-B4
Cedar Court	C2
Church Street	B4
Churchwell Avenue	B1-B2
Cinder Lane	A4
Cross Street	A3-A4
Crowther Street	A3-B3
Curlew Close	B1
Cutsyke Road	A1
Eastfield Lane	C4
Falcon Drive	A2-A1-B1
Ferrybridge Road	C3
Francis Street	C4
Fulford Street	A2
Gannet Close	A1-B1
Garden Street	B2
Glebe Street	B3-C3
Grafton Street	C1
Healdfield Road	C3-C4
Hemsby Road	A1-A2
High Street	A2-A3
Houndhill Road	B2
Hugh Street	B3-C3
Hunt Street	B4
Joffre Avenue	B2-C2-C1
King Street	C1
Leake Street	C3
Leeds Road	A3-A4
Leeds Road	A1-B1-C1
Lisheen Avenue	C1-C2-C3
Lisheen Grove	C3
Lock Lane	B4
Longacre	B2
Love Lane	A2-B2
Lower Oxford Street	B3-C3
Maltkiln Lane	C3-C4
Manor Grove	C1
Methley Road	A3-A4
Mill Lane	B4
Morrison Street	C3
Nicholson Street	A2-A3
Oxford Street	A3-B3
Parklands	C2-C3
Pine Close	C2
Pontefract Road	C2-C3-C4
Powell Street	B3
Pretoria Street	C3
Princess Street	C4
Queen Street	C4
Regent Street	A2-A3
Ridgefield Street	A2-B2-B3
Riuelin Road	A2
Savile Road	A4-B4
School Street	C4
Sheldrake Road	A2-B2-B1
Smawthorne Avenue	B2
Smawthorne Grove	B2
Smawthorne Lane	B2-B3-C3
Stanley Street	B3
Station Road	B3
Temple Street	A2-B2
Thornhill Road	C1-C2
Vickers Street	B3-C3
Wellbeck Street	B3
West Street	A3-A4
Wheldon Road	B4-C4
Willow Court	B2-C2
Wilson Street	A3
Wood Street	A3

Pontefract

Ackworth Road	A1
Ashleigh Avenue	B1-B2
Back Northgate	B3-B4-C4
Baden Powell Crescent	A1-B1
Baghill Lane	C3
Banks Avenue	A2-A3
Beast Fair	B3
Beechnut Lane	A4
Bandgate	C3-C4
Broad Way	C1-C2
Camp Mount	A3
Carleton Crescent	B1-C1
Carleton Glen	B1-B2
Carleton Road	A1-B1
Carleton View	B1
Carleton Park Road	A1-B1
Castle Hill	C3-C4
Chequerfield Drive	C1
Chequerfield Road	C1
Church Balk Lane	B1-B2-C1-C2
Colonel's Walk	A4
Corn Market	A3-B3
Cromwell Crescent	C2-C3
Dark Lane	A2-B2
De Lacy Terrace	C2-C3
Denwell Terrace	B4
East Drive	C1
Elm Park	A1
Fairfax Road	C2
Featherstone Lane	A4
Ferrybridge Road	C4
Finkel Street	B3
Friars Nook	C1
Friarwood Lane	B2-B3
Front Street	A3
Grove Road	B2-C2
Grove Lea Crescent	C1
Half Penny Lane	A3
Hardwick Crescent	A1
Harewood Avenue	C1-C2
Harewood Mount	C2
Highfield Road	A1
Horse Fair	B3-C3
Jubilee Way	A2-A3
King Street	A3
Kings Close	A1
Kings Crescent	C1
Linden Terrace	A3
Love Lane	A3
Market Place	B3
Mayor's Walk	A2-B2
Mayor's Walk Avenue	B2
Midland Road	C3
Mill Dam Lane	C4
Mill Hill Lane	A2
Mill Hill Road	A1-A2
Monument Lane	C1
North Bailey Gate	C3-C4
Northgate	B3-C3
Oliver Mount	C2
Park Road	A3-A4
Park Villas Lane	A4
Queen Street	A3
Rook Hill Drive	C1
Ropergate	A2-A3-B3
Salter Row	B3
School Road	C1-C2
Sessions House Yard	A3
Skinner Lane	B3-B4
South Baileygate	C3
South Gate	A2-B2-B3
Spink Lane	A3
Station Lane	B3-C3
Stuart Road	A3-A4-B3-B4
Swan Hill Lane	B1
Tanshelf Drive	A2-A3
The Butts	C4
The Centre	C1
The Mount	A3
Viking Road	C2
Wakefield Road	A2
Walkergate	C3
Watergate	A3
West Drive	C1
Westbourne Road	A2

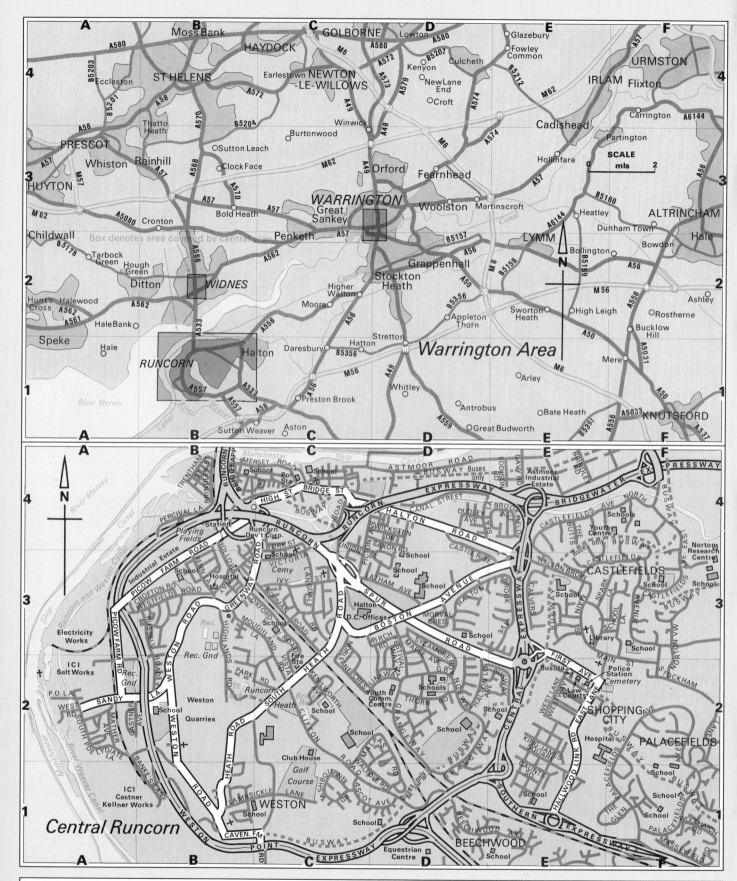

Warrington

This industrial town, situated near the Manchester Ship Canal, has been designated a New Town and is therefore expanding rapidly. Its traditional industry was clock-making, but in recent years this has given way to light industry, chemical production, metal casting and engineering. A few old houses can still be seen in the town, including the half-timbered Barley Mow inn.

Runcorn, on the River Mersey, is another industrial centre and has extensive petrochemical works. However, Norton Priory on the eastern edge of the town is of particular interest. Set in seven acres of landscaped woodland, the remains of the priory include a 12th-century undercroft notable for its beautiful carved passage. Excavation of the site in 1978 won the National Archaeological Award and the museum here, as well as containing various finds from the priory, has one of the best

exhibitions on medieval monastic life in Britain.

Widnes was just a collection of scattered villages before the Runcorn Gap and St Helen's Railway Company built the world's first railway, canal and dock complex here in the mid-19th century. Chemical and alkali works began to develop and the area rapidly grew into an industrial town with large housing estates. Today Widnes is linked to Runcorn by the railway bridge of 1868 and a road bridge which was built in 1961.

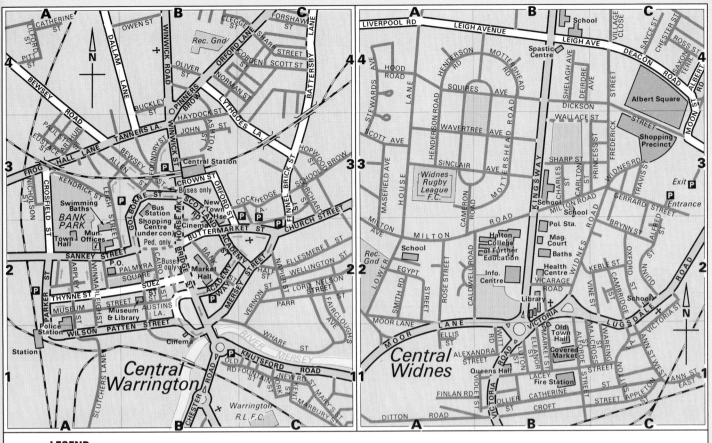

LEGEND

Town Plan

AA recommended route
Restricted roads
Other roads
Buildings of interest   Club
Car parks   P
Parks and open spaces
One way streets

Area Plan

A roads
B roads
Locations   Grittleton ○
Urban area

Street Index with Grid Reference

Warrington

Academy Street	B2-C2
Academy Way	B2
Allen Street	A3-B3
Arpley Street	A1-A2
Arthur Street	A3
Ashton Street	B3
Austins Lane	B2
Bank Street	B2
Battersby Lane	C3-C4
Bewsey Road	A3-A4
Bewsey Street	A3-B3
Brick Street	C3
Bridge Street	B2
Buckley Street	B4
Buttermarket Street	B2-C2
Cairo Street	B2
Catherine Street	A4
Chester Road	B1
Church Street	C2-C3
Clegge Street	B4-C4
Cobden Street	B4-C4
Cockhedge Lane	B3-C3
Crossfield Street	A2-A3
Crown Street	B3
Dallem Lane	A4-B4-B3
Ellesmere Street	C2
Eustace Street	A3
Fairclough's Avenue	C1-C2
Fennel Street	C2-C3
Forshaw Street	C4
Foundry Street	B3
Fountain Street	C1
Froghall Lane	A3
Golborne Street	B2-B3
Half Street	C2
Haydock Street	B3-B4
Horse Market	B2-B3
Hopwood Street	C3
John Street	B3
Kendrick Street	A3
Kent Street	C1
Knutsford Road	B1-C1
Leigh Street	A3-A2-B2
Lilford Street	A4
Lord Nelson Street	C2
Lythgoes Lane	B4-B3-C3
Marbury Street	C1
Mersey Street	B1-B2-C2
Museum Street	B2-B3
Napier Street	C2
New Road	C1
Nicholson Street	A3
Norman Street	B4-C4
Old Road	B1
Oliver Street	B4
Orford Lane	B4-C4
Orford Street	B2-B3
Owen Street	A4-B4
Palmyra Square	A2-B2
Parker Street	A1-A2
Parr Street	C2
Paul Street	A3
Pinners Brow	B4
Pitt Street	A4
Richard Street	C3
St Mary's Street	C1
Sankey Street	A2-B2
School Brow	C3
Scotland Road	B2-B3
Scott Street	C4
Sharp Street	C4
Slutchers Lane	A1
Suez Street	B2
Tanners Lane	A3-B3
Thynne Street	A2
Vernon Street	C1-C2
Wellington Street	C2
Wharf Street	B1-B2-C2-C1
Wilson Patten Street	A1-B1-B2
Winmarleigh Street	A1-A2
Winwick Road	B4
Winwick Street	B3
York Street	C1

Runcorn

Ascot Avenue	C1-D1
Ashbourne Road	C1
Astmoor Road	C4-D4-E4
Banke's Lane	A2-A1-B1
Beechwood Avenue	D1-E1
Birch Road	C3-D3
Boston Avenue	C3-D3-E3
Bridge Street	C4
Bridgewater Expressway	E4-F4
Brindley Road	E4
Brindley Street	B4
Brookfield Avenue	E3
Calvers	E4
Canal Street	C4-D4
Castner Avenue	A2
Castle Rise	D4-D3-E3
Castlefields Avenue	E3-F3
Castlefields Avenue East	F3-F4
Castlefields Avenue North	E3-E4-F4
Cavendish Farm Road	B1-C1
Central Expressway	E1-E2-E3-E4
Clifton Road	C2-C1-D1
Crofton Road	B3
Davy Road	E4
Dudley Avenue	D4
East Lane	E2
Eddison Road	E4
Festival Way	D2-D3
First Avenue	E2-E3
Gaunts Square	E1-E2
Grangeway	D1-D2
Greenway Road	B3-C3-C4
Hallwood Link Road	E1-E2
Halton Brook Avenue	D3-E3
Halton Brow	E3
Halton Lodge Avenue	D2
Halton Road	C4-D4-E4
Heath Road	C2-C3-C4
Heath Road South	B1-B2-C2
High Street	B4-C4
Highlands Road	B2-B3
Hollow Way	B3-B4
Ivy Street	C3
Kenilworth Avenue	C2
King James Square	E2
Lambsickle Lane	B1-C1
Langdale Road	C3
Latham Avenue	C3-D3
Linkway	D2
Lydiate Lane	A2-B2
Main Street	E3-F3-F2
Malpas Road	C1-C2-D2-D1
Maple Avenue	D2-D3
Masseyfield Road	F1
Mather Avenue	A2
Mersey Road	B4-C4
Morval Crescent	D3
Moughland Lane	B3-C3
Norleane Crescent	C2-C3
Norman Road	C3
Norton View	F2-F3
Oxford Road	B3-C3-C2
Palacefields Avenue	F1-F2
Park Road	B2-C2
Penn Lane	B3
Percival Lane	B4
Picow Farm Road	A2-A3-B3-B4
Picton Avenue	C3-C4-B4
Post Office Lane	A2
Runcorn Bridge Approach	B4
Runcorn Expressway	C4-D4-E4
Runcorn Spur Road	B4-C4-C3-D3-E3-E2
Russell Road	B2-B3
Sandy Lane	A2-B2
Saxon Road	C4-D4
School Lane	E3-F3
Sea Lane	D4
South Parade	A2
Southern Expressway	E1-F1
Spark Lane	E3-F3
Stockham Lane	F2-F3
Sycamore Road	D2-D3
The Butts	E4
The Glen	E1-F1
Thorn Road	D2
Trentham Street	B4
Union Street	C4-D4-D3
Victoria Road	C3-C4
Vista Road	C2-C3
Walpole Road	C2-C1-D1
West Lane	E2
West Road	A2
Westfield Road	A3-B3
Weston Road	B1-B2-B3
Weston Point Expressway	B4-B3-A3-B3-B2-B1-C1-D1
Westway	E2
Wicksten Drive	C4-D4
Woodhatch Road	F1
York Street	C3-C4

Widnes

Albert Road	C4
Alexandra Street	A1-B1
Alforde Street	B1-B2
Alfred Street	C2
Ann Street East	C1
Ann Street West	C1
Appleton Street	C1
Brynn Street	C2
Caldwell Road	A2-B2
Cambridge Street	C2
Cameron Road	A2-A3
Carlton Street	B3
Catherine Street	B1-C1
Charles Street	B3
Chester Street	C4
Croft Street	B1-C1
Deacon Road	C4
Deidre Avenue	B4
Dickson Street	B4-C4-C3
Ditton Road	A1-B1
Egypt Street	B1
Eleanor Street	B1
Ellis Street	A1
Finlan Road	A1-B1
Frederick Street	C3-C4
Gerrard Street	C3
Henderson Road	A3-A4-B4
Hood Road	A4
Keble Street	B2-C2
Kingsway	B2-B3-B4
Lacey Street	B1-C1
Leigh Avenue	A4-B4-C4
Liverpool Road	A4
Lower House Lane	A2-A3-A4
Lugsdale Road	B2-C2-C1-C2
Luton Street	B1
Major Cross Street	B2-B1-C1
Market Street	B1-B2
Masefield Avenue	A2-A3
Milton Avenue	A2
Milton Road	A2-B2-B3-C3
Moor Lane	A1-A2-B2-B1
Moon Street	C3-C4
Mottershead Road	A3-B3-B4
Ollier Street	B1
Oxford Street	C2
Princess Street	C3
Quinn Street	C2
Rose Street	A2
Ross Street	C4
Saxon Terrace	C4
Sayce Street	C4
Scott Avenue	A3
Sharp Street	B3-C3
Shelagh Avenue	B4
Sinclair Avenue	A3-B3
Smith Road	A2
Squires Avenue	A4-B4
Stewards Avenue	A3-A4
Sutton Lane	C1
Travis Street	C3
Vicarage Road	B2
Victoria Road	B1
Victoria Square	B1-B2
Victoria Street	C1-C2
Village Close	C4
Vine Street	C2
Violet Road	B1
Wallace Street	B3-C3
Wavertree Avenue	A3-B3
Widnes Road	B2-C2-C3
Witt Road	B1

75

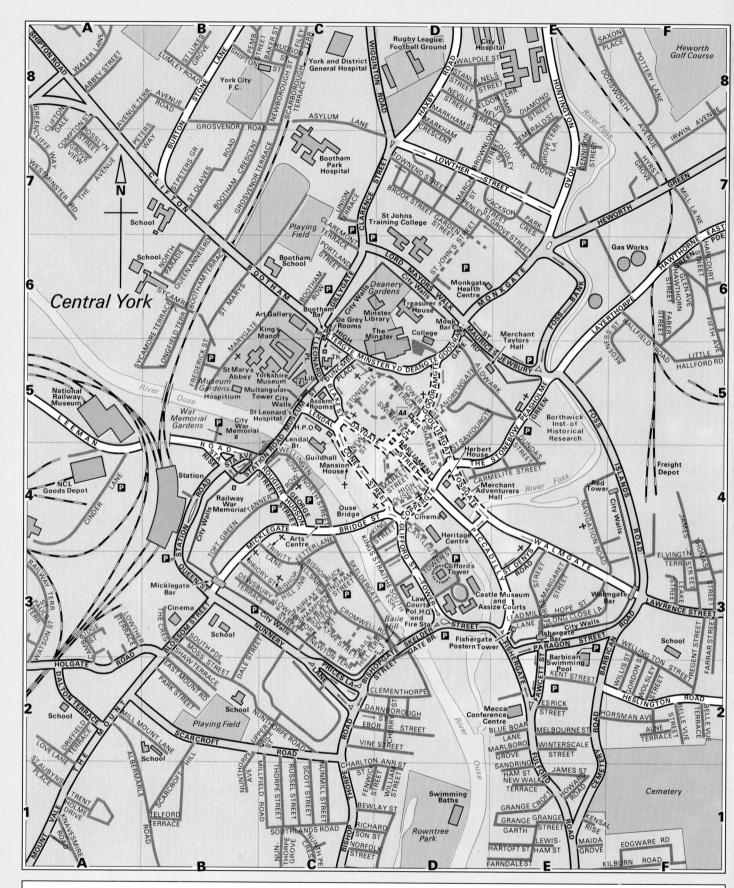

York

York Minster, unquestionably the city's outstanding glory, is considered to be one of the greatest cathedral churches in Europe. It is especially famous for its lovely windows which contain more than half the medieval stained glass in England.

Great medieval walls enclose the historic city centre and their three-mile circuit offers magnificent views of the Minster, York's numerous fine buildings, churches and the River Ouse. The ancient streets consist of a maze of alleys and lanes, some of them so narrow that the overhanging upper storeys of the houses almost touch. The most famous of these picturesque streets is The Shambles, formerly the butchers' quarter of the city, but now colonised by antique and tourist shops. York flourished throughout Tudor, Georgian and Victorian times and handsome buildings from these periods also feature throughout the city.

The Castle Museum gives a fascinating picture of York as it used to be and the Heritage Centre interprets the social and architectural history of the city. Other places of exceptional note in this city of riches include the Merchant Adventurer's Hall; the Treasurer's House, now owned by the National Trust and filled with fine paintings and furniture; the Jorvik Viking Centre, where there is an exciting restoration of the original Viking settlement at York, and the National Railway Museum.

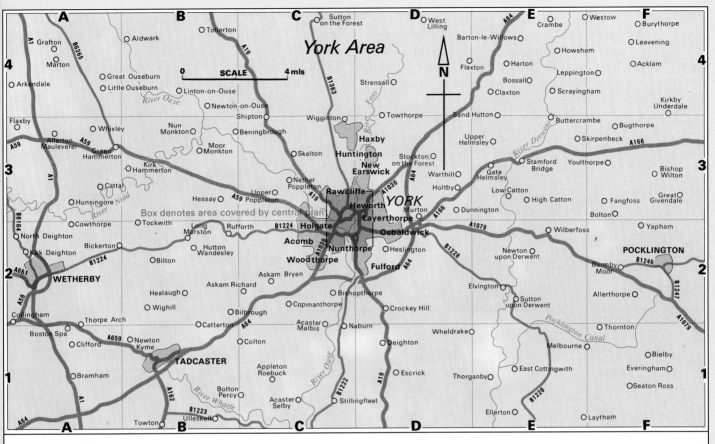

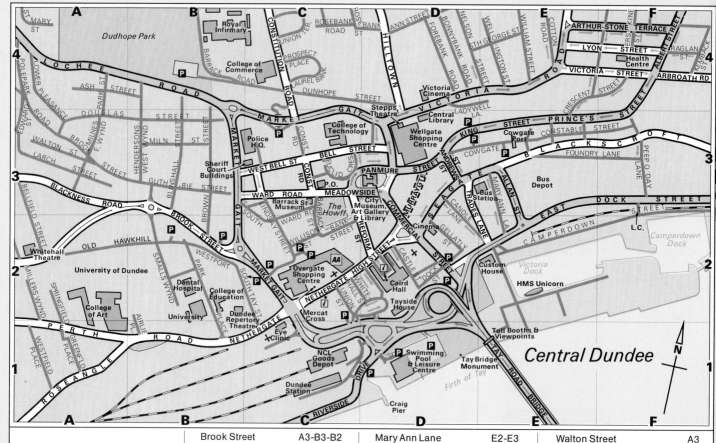

LEGEND

Town Plan

AA Recommended roads	
Restricted roads	
Other roads	
Buildings of interest	Hospital
Car Parks	P
Parks and open spaces	
One Way Streets	→
Churches	†

STREET INDEX-
with grid reference

Dundee Third largest city of Scotland and capital of Tayside, Dundee is a major port with a long and colourful maritime history, and it was also central to the 19th-century textile boom. But with its setting of moors, lochs and mountains, Dundee has become a centre for tourists. The city has a fine landmark in St Mary Tower, also known as Old Steeple, and the Mills Observatory has a refracting telescope and other displays dealing with astronomy and space exploration. Two top-flight football teams are based in the city and complement its fine sports facilities.

Inverness has long been called the 'Capital of the Highlands' and stands at the eastern end of the Great Glen, on the banks of the River Ness. Amongst the many places of interest that draw visitors to the town, Aberstaff House dates from the 16th century and has a rare, good example of an old turnpike stair. St Andrew's Cathedral has fine carved columns.

Perth Sir Walter Scott's 'Fair Maid of Perth' lived in a 14th-century house which still stands in this historic old Tayside town. St John's Kirk is a magnificent example of 16th-century Gothic architecture and notable as the scene of John Knox's fiery sermon against church idolatry in 1599 — a sermon which is now regarded as one of the major milestones of the Reformation. Also of interest are the Caithness Glass Factory (open to visitors) and the Perth Museum and Art Gallery.

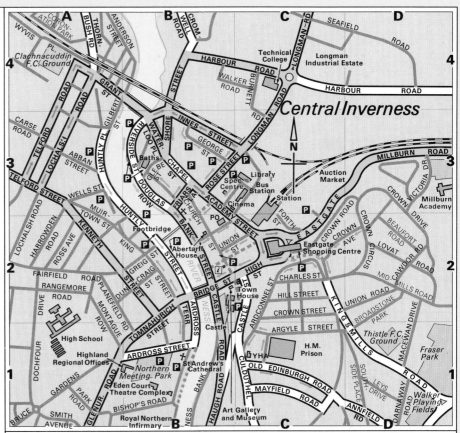

Central Inverness

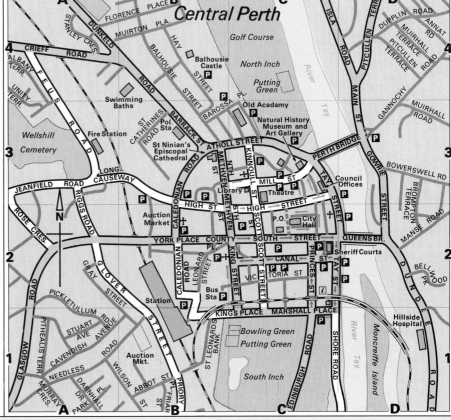

Central Perth

INVERNESS
Crowding the skyline with its battlements and towers, Inverness Castle commands an imposing site above the town — but was only built in the last century.

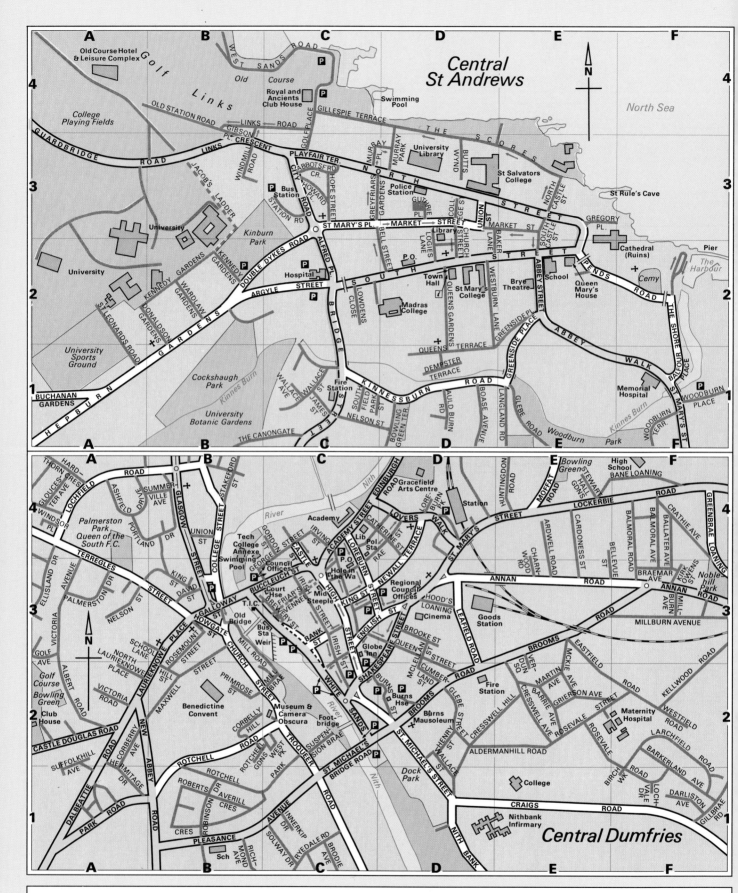

Central St Andrews

North Sea

Central Dumfries

St Andrews is synonymous with golf. There are no less than 15 golf courses in the vicinity, and the Royal and Ancient Golf Club, founded in the 18th century, has come to be regarded as the international headquarters of the game. But the town's links with the past go back even further: it has a distinguished university which was founded in 1411, its castle is 13th-century and the cathedral dates from the 12th century.

Stirling lies just north of Bannockburn, where

Robert the Bruce inflicted a swingeing defeat on the armies of England in 1314, and twelve years later he held his first parliament in the town's Cambuskenneth Abbey, which can still be seen. The castle dates back to the 13th century and its Landmark Centre provides an exciting audio-visual display. The Wallace Memorial offers fine views.

Oban has been a popular desination for tourists since the 19th century, not least because of its ferry links with the Hebrides. Visitors

can see paperweights being made at the local glassworks, and other attractions are the fine views of the town and its surroundings to be seen from McCaig's Tower and Pulpit Hill.

Dumfries is Walter Scott's 'Queen of the South': a fine country town and market centre of old sandstone and spacious parks. Robert Burns spent the last years of his life here, and Burns House, where he died in 1796, is now a museum. His Mausoleum stands in St Michael's Churchyard.

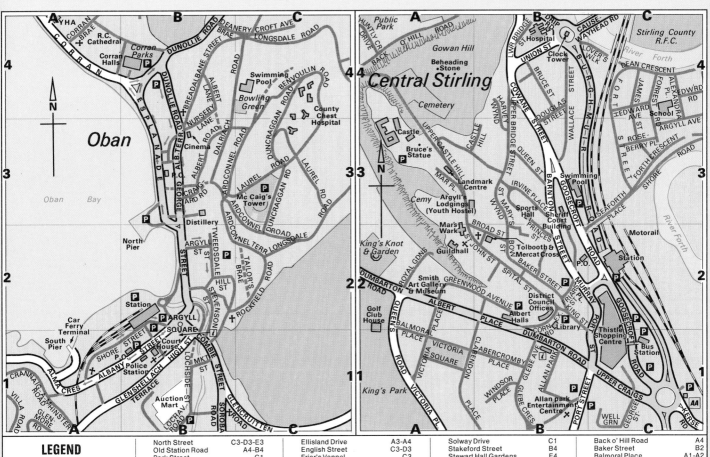

LEGEND

Town Plan

- AA Recommended roads
- Other roads
- Restricted roads
- Buildings of interest — Station ▪
- Churches — ✝
- Car parks — P
- Parks and open spaces
- One way streets — →

Street Index with Grid Reference

St Andrews

Abbey Street	E2
Abbey Walk	E2-E1-F1
Abbotsford Crescent	C3
Alfred Place	C2-C3
Argyle Street	B2-C2
Auld Burn Road	D1
Baker Lane	D2-D3
Balfour Place	F1
Bell Street	C3-C2-D2
Boase Avenue	D1
Bowling Green Terrace	D1
Bridge Street	C1-C2
Buchanan Gardens	A1
Butts Wynd	D3
Church Street	D2-D3
City Road	C3
College Street	D3
Dempster Terrace	D1
Donaldson Gardens	B2-C2
Double Dykes Road	B2-C2-C3
Gibson Place	B3-B4
Gillespie Terrace	C4-D4
Glebe Road	E1
Golf Place	C3-C4
Greenside Place	D1-D2-E2-E1
Gregory Place	E3
Greyfriars Gardens	C3
Guardbridge Road	A4-A3-B3
Guthrie Place	D3
Hepburn Gardens	A1-B1-B2
Hope Street	C3
Howard Place	C3
Jacob's Ladder	B3
James Street	C1
Kennedy Gardens	A2-B2
Kinnessburn Road	C1-D1-E1
Langland Road	E1
Links Crescent	B3-C3
Links Road	B4-C4
Logies Lane	D2-D3
Lowdens Close	C2
Market Street	D3-E3
Murray Park	D3-D4
Murray Place	C3-D3
Nelson Street	C1-D1
North Castle Street	E3
North Street	C3-D3-E3
Old Station Road	A4-B4
Park Street	C1
Pends Road	E2-F2
Playfair Terrace	C3
Queens Gardens	D1-D2
Queens Terrace	D1
St Leonards Road	A1-A2
St Mary's Place	C3
St Mary's Street	F1
South Castle Street	E2-E3
South Field	C1
South Street	C2-D2-E2
Station Road	C3
The Canongate	B1-C1
The Scores	D4-D3-E3
The Shore	F1-F2
Union Street	D3
Wallace Avenue	C1
Wallace Street	C1
Wardlaw Gardens	B2
Westburn Lane	D1-D2
West Sands Road	B4-C4
Windmill Road	B3
Woodburn Place	F1
Woodburn Terrace	F1

Dumfries

Academy Street	C3-C4
Albert Road	A2-A3
Aldermanhill Road	D2-E2
Annan Road	D3-E3-F3
Ardwell Road	E3-E4
Ashfield Drive	A4
Averill Crescent	B1
Ballater Avenue	F3-F4
Balmoral Avenue	F3-F4
Balmoral Road	F3-F4
Ban Loaning	E4-F4
Bank Street	C3
Barkerland Avenue	F1-F2
Barrie Avenue	E2
Bellevue Street	E3-E4
Birch Walk	F1
Braemar Avenue	F3
Brewery Street	B3-C3
Brodie Avenue	C1
Brooke Street	D3
Brooms Road	D2-D3-E3-F3
Buccleuch Street	B3-C3
Burns Street	C2-D2
Cardoness Street	E3-E4
Castle Douglas Road	A2
Castle Street	C3-C4
Catherine Street	C4-D4
Charnwood Road	D1-D2
Chuch Street	B3-B2-C2
College Street	B3-B4
Corbelly Hill	B2
Corberry Avenue	A1-A2
Craigs Road	D1-E1-F1
Crathie Avenue	F4
Cresswell Avenue	E2
Cresswell Hill	D2-E2
Cumberland Street	D2
Dalbeattie Road	A1-A2
Darliston Avenue	F1
David Street	B3
Eastfield Road	E3-E2-F2
Edinburgh Road	C4-D4
Ellisland Drive	A3-A4
English Street	C3-D3
Friar's Vennel	C3
Galloway Street	B3
George Street	B3-C3-C4
Gillbrae Road	F1
Glasgow Street	B3-B4
Glebe Street	D2
Gloucester Avenue	A4
Golf Avenue	A3
Gordon Street	C4
Greenbrae Loaning	F3-F4
Grierson Avenue	E2
Hardthorn Crescent	A4
Henry Street	D2
Hermitage Drive	A1-A2
High Street	C2-C3
Hill Street	B2
Hood's Loaning	D3
Howgate Street	B3
Huntingdon Road	E4
Innerkip Drive	C1
Irish Street	C2-C3
Irving Street	C4
Kellwood Road	F2-F3
King Street	B3
King Street	C3
Kirkowens Street	F3
Larchfield Road	F1-F2
Laurieknowe Place	A2-B2-B3
Leafield Road	D3
Lochfield Road	A4-B4
Lochvale Drive	F1
Lockerbie Road	E4-F4
Loreburn Park	D4
Loreburn Street	C4-C3-D3
Lovers Walk	C4-D4
Martin Avenue	E2
Maxwell Street	A2-B2-B3
McLellan Street	D2-D3
Mickie Avenue	E2-E3
Mill Brae	C2
Millburn Avenue	E3-F3
Mill Road	B3-C3-C2
Moffat Road	E4
Nelson Street	A3
New Abbey Road	A2-B2-B1
Newall Terrace	C3-D3-D4
North Bank	D1
North Laurieknowe Place	A2
Palmerston Drive	A3
Park Road	A1
Pleasance Avenue	B1-C1
Portland Drive	A4-B4
Primrose Street	B2
Queen Street	D2-D3
Rae Street	C3-C4-D4
Richmond Avenue	B1
Roberts Crescent	B1
Robinson Drive	B1
Rosemount Street	B2-B3
Rosevale Road	E2-F2-F1
Rosevale Street	E2-F2
Rotchell Gardens	B2-C2
Rotchell Park	B1-C1-C2
Rotchell Road	B1-B2-C2
Ryedale Road	C1
St Michael's Bridge Road	C1-C2-D2
St Michael's Street	D1-D2
St Mary's Street	D3-D4-E4
School Lane	A3-B3
Shakespeare Street	C2-D2-D3
Solway Drive	C1
Stakeford Street	B4
Stewart Hall Gardens	E4
Suffolkhill Avenue	A1-A2
Summerville Avenue	A4-B4
Suspension Brae	C2
Terregles Street	A4-A3-B3
Troqueer Road	C1-C2
Union Street	B4
Verdun Square	E2-E3
Victoria Avenue	A3
Victoria Road	A2
Wallace Street	D1-D2
Westfield Road	F2
West Park	C2
White Sands	C2
Windsor Place	A4

Oban

Albany Street	A1-B1-B2
Albert Lane	B4
Albert Road	B3
Albert Terrace	B3
Alma Crescent	B4
Ardconnel Road	C3-B3-C3-C2
Ardconnel Terrace	B3-B2-C2
Argyll Square	B1-B2
Argyll Street	B2
Benvoulin Road	C3-C4
Breadalbane Street	B3-B4-C4
Combie Street	B1
Corran Brae	A4
Corran Esplanade	A4-B4-B3
Craigard Road	B3
Crannaig-a-Mhinster Road	A1
Croft Avenue	C4
Dalriach Road	B3-B4-C4
Deanery Brae	B4-C4
Duncraggan Road	C2-C3-C4
Dunolie Road	B3-B4
George Street	B2-B3
Glencruitten Road	B1-C1
Glenmore Road	A1
Glenshellach Terrace	A1-B1
High Street	B2
Hill Street	B2
Laurel Road	B3-C3
Lochavillin Road	B1
Lochside Street	B1
Longsdale Road	C2-C3
Longsdale Road	C4
Market Street	B1
Nursery Lane	B3-B4
Rockfield Road	B2-C2
Shore Street	A1-B1-B2
Soroba Road	B1
Stevenson Street	B1-B2
Tailor's Brae	C2
Tweedsdale Street	B2
Villa Road	A1

Stirling

Abercromy Place	A1-B1
Albert Place	A2-B2
Alexandra Place	C4
Allan Park	B1
Argyll Avenue	C3-C4
Back o' Hill Road	A4
Baker Street	B2
Balmoral Place	A1-A2
Barnton Street	B2-B3
Bow Street	B2
Broad Street	A2-B2
Bruce Street	B4
Burghmuir Road	B4-C4-C3-B3-C3-C2
Castle Hill	A3-B3
Causewayhead Road	B4-C4
Clarendon Place	B2-B1-A1-B1
Corn Exchange Road	B2
Cowane Street	B3-B4
Dean Crescent	C4
Douglas Street	B3-B4
Drip Road	B4
Dumberton Road	A2, B2-B1
Edward Avenue	C4
Edward Road	C4
Forrest Road	C3-C4
Forth Crescent	C3
Forth Street	C3-C4
Friar's Street	B2
George Street	C1
Glebe Avenue	B1
Glebe Crescent	B1
Goosecroft Road	B3-B2-C2-C1
Greenwood Avenue	A2-B2
Harvey Wynd	B3-B4
Huntley Crescent Drive	A4
Irvine Place	B3
James Street	C3-C4
Kerse Road	C1
King Street	B2
Lover's Walk	B4-C4
Lower Bridge Street	B4
Mar Place	A3
Murray Place	B2-C2
Port Street	B1-C1-C2
Princes Street	B2-B3
Queen's Road	A1-A2
Queen Street	B3
Roseberry Place	C3
Royal Gardens	A2
St John Street	A2-B2
St Mary's Wynd	B2-B3
Seaforth Place	B2-C2-C3
Shore Road	C3
Spital Street	B2
Union Street	B4
Upper Bridge Street	B3-B4
Upper Castle Hill	A3-A4
Upper Craigs	C1
Victoria Place	A1-A2
Victoria Square	A1
Wallace Street	B3-B4
Well Green	C1
Windsor Place	B1

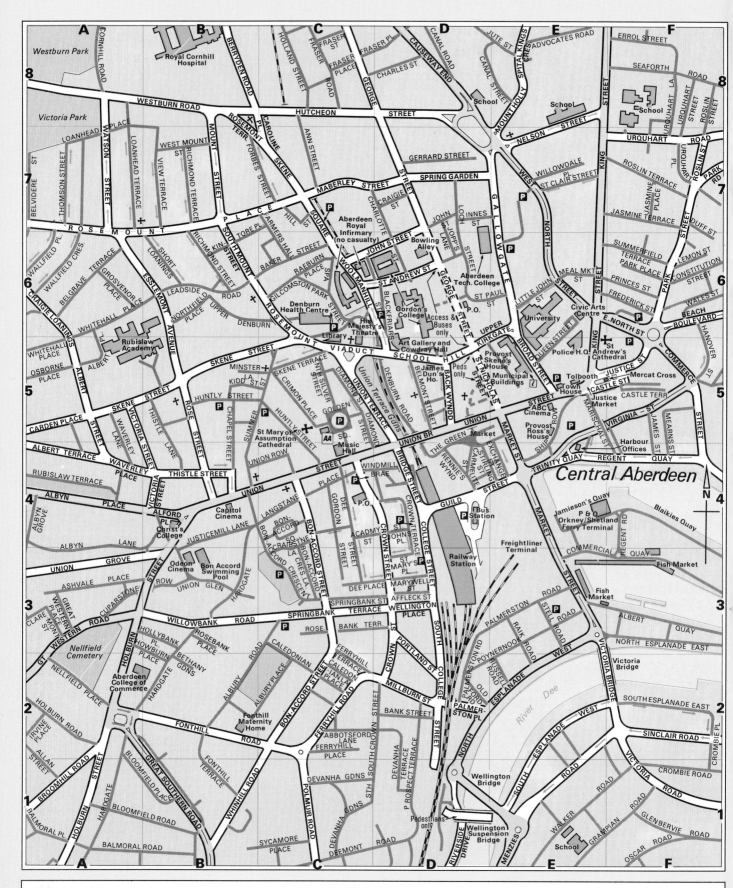

Aberdeen

Granite gives Aberdeen its especial character; but this is not to say that the city is a grim or a grey place, the granites used are of many hues – white, blue, pink and grey. Although the most imposing buildings date from the 19th century, granite has been used to dramatic effect since at least as early as the 15th century. From that time dates St Machar's Cathedral, originally founded in AD580, but rebuilt several times, especially after a devasting fire started on the orders of Edward III of England in 1336. St Machar's is in Old Aberdeen, traditionally the ecclesiastical and educational hub of the city, while 'New' Aberdeen (actually no newer) has always been the commercial centre. Even that definition is deceptive, for although Old Aberdeen has King's College, founded in 1494, New Aberdeen has Marischal College, founded almost exactly a century later (but rebuilt in 1844) and every bit as distinguished as a seat of learning. Both establishments functioned as independent universities until they were merged in 1860 to form Aberdeen University. The North Sea oil boom has brought many changes to the city, some of which threatened its character. But even though high-rise buildings are now common, the stately façades, towers and pillars of granite still reign supreme and Union Street remains one of the best thoroughfares in Britain.

82

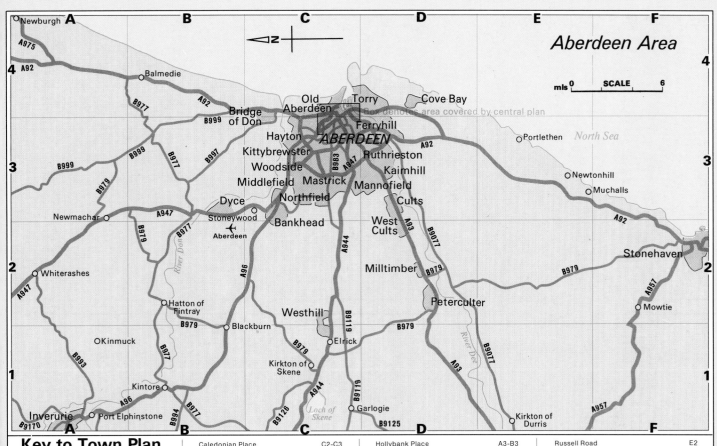

Aberdeen Area

North Sea

Key to Town Plan and Area Plan

Town Plan

A A Recommended roads
Other roads
Restricted roads
Buildings of interest   Cinema
Car Parks
Parks and open spaces
A A Centre
One Way Streets

Area Plan

A roads
B roads
Locations   Hattoncrook ○
Urban area

Street Index with Grid Reference

Aberdeen

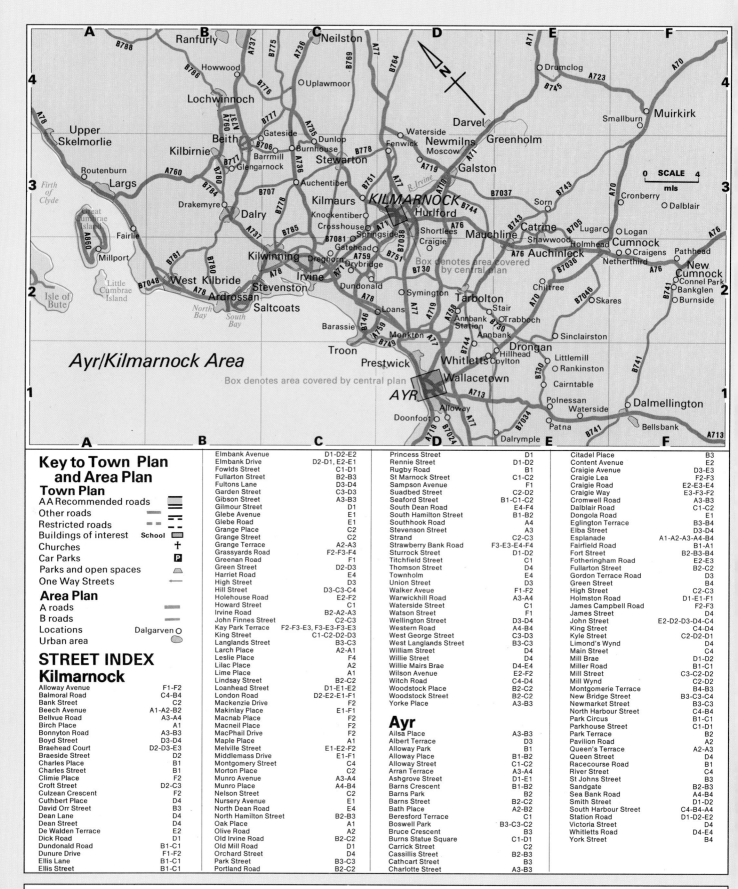

Ayr/Kilmarnock Area

Box denotes area covered by central plan

Key to Town Plan and Area Plan

Town Plan

AA Recommended roads
Other roads
Restricted roads
Buildings of interest — School
Churches — †
Car Parks — P
Parks and open spaces
One Way Streets

Area Plan

A roads
B roads
Locations — Dalgarven
Urban area

STREET INDEX
Kilmarnock

Alloway Avenue	F1-F2
Balmoral Road	C4-B4
Bank Street	C2
Beech Avenue	A1-A2-B2
Bellvue Road	A3-A4
Birch Place	A1
Bonnyton Road	A3-B3
Boyd Street	D3-D4
Braehead Court	D2-D3-E3
Braeside Street	D2
Charles Place	B1
Charles Street	B1
Climie Place	F2
Croft Street	D2-C3
Culzean Crescent	F2
Cuthbert Place	D4
David Orr Street	B3
Dean Lane	D4
Dean Street	D4
De Walden Terrace	E2
Dick Road	D1
Dundonald Road	B1-C1
Dunure Drive	F1-F2
Ellis Lane	B1-C1
Ellis Street	B1-C1
Elmbank Avenue	D1-D2-E2
Elmbank Drive	D2-D1, E2-E1
Fowlds Street	C1-D1
Fullarton Street	B2-B3
Fultons Lane	D3-D4
Garden Street	C3-D3
Gibson Street	A3-B3
Gilmour Street	D1
Glebe Avenue	E1
Glebe Road	E1
Grange Place	C2
Grange Street	C2
Grange Terrace	A2-A3
Grassyards Road	F2-F3-F4
Greenan Road	F1
Green Street	D2-D3
Harriet Road	E4
High Street	D3
Hill Street	D3-C3-C4
Holehouse Road	E2-F2
Howard Street	C1
Irvine Road	B2-A2-A3
John Finnes Street	C2-C3
Kay Park Terrace	F2-F3-E3, F3-E3-F3-E3
King Street	C1-C2-D2-D3
Langlands Street	B3-C3
Larch Place	A2-A1
Leslie Place	F4
Lilac Place	A2
Lime Place	A1
Lindsay Street	B2-C2
Loanhead Street	D1-E1-E2
London Street	D2-E2-E1-F1
Mackenzie Drive	F2
Makinlay Place	E1-F1
Macnab Place	F2
Macneil Place	F2
MacPhail Drive	F2
Maple Place	A1
Melville Street	E1-E2-F2
Middlemass Drive	E1-F1
Montgomery Street	C4
Morton Place	C2
Munro Avenue	A3-A4
Munro Place	A4-B4
Nelson Street	C2
North Dean Road	E4
North Hamilton Street	B2-B3
Oak Place	A1
Olive Road	A2
Old Irvine Road	B2-C2
Old Mill Road	D1
Orchard Street	D4
Park Street	B3-C3
Portland Road	B2-C2
Princess Street	D1
Rennie Street	D1-D2
Rugby Road	B1
St Marnock Street	C1-C2
Sampson Avenue	F1
Suadbed Street	C2-D2
Seaford Street	B1-C1-C2
South Dean Road	E4-F4
South Hamilton Street	B1-B2
Southhook Road	A4
Stevenson Street	A3
Strand	C2-C3
Strawberry Bank Road	F3-E3-E4-F4
Sturrock Street	D1-D2
Titchfield Street	C1
Thomson Street	D4
Townhill	E4
Union Street	D3
Walker Aveue	F1-F2
Warwickhill Road	A3-A4
Waterside Street	C1
Watson Street	F1
Wellington Street	D3-D4
Western Road	A4-B4
West George Street	C3-D3
West Langlands Street	B3-C3
William Street	D4
Willie Street	D4
Willie Mairs Brae	D4-E4
Wilson Avenue	E2-F2
Witch Road	C4-D4
Woodstock Place	B2-C2
Woodstock Street	B2-C2
Yorke Place	A3-B3

Ayr

Ailsa Place	A3-B3
Albert Terrace	D3
Alloway Park	B1
Alloway Place	B1-B2
Alloway Street	C1-C2
Arran Terrace	A3-A4
Ashgrove Street	D1-E1
Barns Crescent	B1-B2
Barns Park	B2
Barns Street	B2-C2
Bath Place	A2-B2
Beresford Terrace	C1
Boswell Park	B3-C3-C2
Bruce Crescent	B3
Burns Statue Square	C1-D1
Carrick Street	C2
Cassillis Street	B2-B3
Cathcart Street	B3
Charlotte Street	A3-B3
Citadel Place	B3
Content Avenue	E2
Craigie Avenue	D3-E3
Craigie Lea	F2-F3
Craigie Road	E2-E3-E4
Craigie Way	E3-F3-F2
Cromwell Road	A3-B3
Dalblair Road	C1-C2
Dongola Road	E1
Eglington Terrace	B3-B4
Elba Street	D3-D4
Esplanade	A1-A2-A3-A4-B4
Fairfield Road	B1-A1
Fort Street	B2-B3-B4
Fotheringham Road	E2-E3
Fullarton Street	B2-C2
Gordon Terrace Road	D3
Green Street	B4
High Street	C2-C3
Holmston Road	D1-E1-F1
James Campbell Road	F2-F3
James Street	C4
John Street	E2-D2-D3-D4-C4
King Street	C4-D4
Kyle Street	C2-D2-D1
Limond's Wynd	D4
Main Street	C4
Mill Brae	D1-D2
Miller Road	B1-C1
Mill Street	C3-C2-D2
Mill Wynd	C2-D2
Montgomerie Terrace	B4-B3
New Bridge Street	B3-C3-C4
Newmarket Street	B3-C3
North Harbour Street	C4-B4
Park Circus	B1-C1
Parkhouse Street	C1-D1
Park Terrace	B2
Pavilion Road	A2
Queen's Terrace	A2-A3
Queen Street	D4
Racecourse Road	B1
River Street	C4
St Johns Street	B3
Sandgate	B2-B3
Sea Bank Road	A4-B4
Smith Street	D1-D2
South Harbour Street	C4-B4-A4
Station Road	D1-D2-E2
Victoria Street	D4
Whitletts Road	D4-E4
York Street	B4

Ayr

Set on the lovely coastline of the Firth of Clyde, Ayr enjoys a well-deserved reputation as one of Scotland's most attractive seaside resorts. Its fine natural assets of sandy beaches and pastoral river scenery have been augmented by extensive parks and gardens, as well as a host of leisure amenities.

However, some of Ayr's visitors are drawn to the town by its associations with Scotland's beloved national poet – Robert Burns. He was born at the nearby village of Alloway and many of the places immortalised in his poems can be seen in Ayr. These include the medieval Auld Brig, one of the famour 'twa brigs' that span the River Ayr. The thatched Tam O'Shanter Inn in the High Street, now a museum devoted to Burns, and an imposing statue, are further reminders that this was 'Rabbie's' town.

Ayr has been a prosperous fishing port for centuries and its harbour provides a particularly charming focal point to the town. Surprisingly, few buildings pre-date the 19th century, but one exception is Loudon Hall – a fine 16th-century town house now open to the public. Several handsome Georgian edifaces surround Wellington Square, overlooked by the soaring steeple of the Town Buildings. A statue here commemorates another son of Ayr, John Macadam, who invented the road surface that bears his name.

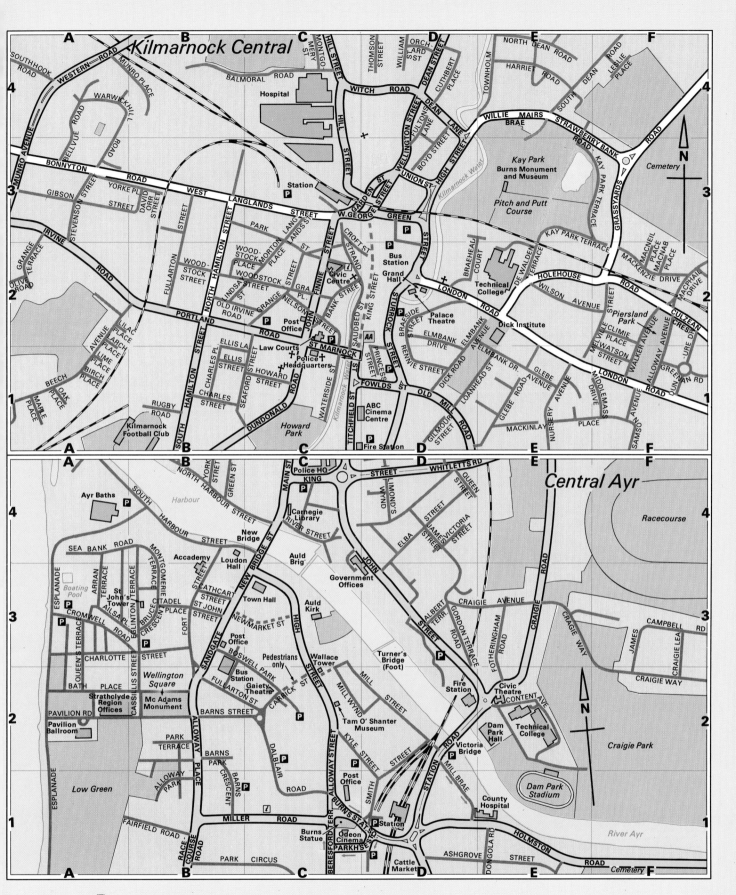

Kilmarnock Central

A · B · C · D · E · F

SOUTHHOOK ROAD
WESTERN ROAD
MUNRO PLACE
WARWICKHILL
BELLVUE ROAD
MUNRO AVENUE
BONNYTON ROAD
GIBSON STREET
STEVENSON STREET
YORKE PL.
DAVID ORR STREET
WEST LANGLANDS STREET
Station
BALMORAL ROAD
WITCH ROAD
Hospital
THOMSON STREET
WILLIAM ST
DEAN STREET
CUTHBERT PLACE
NORTH DEAN ROAD
DEAN ROAD
HARRIET ROAD
TOWNHOLM
SOUTH DEAN ROAD
LESLIE PLACE
WILLIE MAIRS BRAE
STRAWBERRY BANK
Cemetery
N
Kay Park Burns Monument and Museum
Pitch and Putt Course
KAY PARK TERRACE
GRASSYARDS ROAD
MACNEIL PLACE
MACNAB PLACE
MACKENZIE DRIVE
MAGPHAIL DRIVE
CULZEAN CRES.
GRANGE TERRACE
OLIVE ROAD
IRVINE ROAD
FULLARTON STREET
NORTH HAMILTON STREET
PARK
MORTON PLACE
LANG ST.
WOODSTOCK PLACE
WOODSTOCK STREET
LINDSAY ST.
GRANGE STREET
NELSON STREET
FINNIE STREET
BANK STREET
STRAND
CROFT ST.
W.GEORGE ST
GARDEN STREET
UNION ST
WELLINGTON STREET
FULTON ST
BOYD STREET
HIGH STREET
GREEN STREET
STURROCK STREET
Bus Station
Grand Hall
Civic Centre
BRAEHEAD COURT
DE WALDEN TERRACE
KAY PARK TERRACE
HOLEHOUSE ROAD
WILSON AVENUE
Technical College
PIERSLAND PARK
MELVILLE STREET
CLIMIE STREET
WATSON STREET
WALKER AVENUE
ALLOWAY AVENUE
GREENAN RD
LURE DR.
PORTLAND STREET
OLD IRVINE ROAD
Post Office
ST MARNOCK
AA
Law Courts
Police Headquarters
ELLIS LA.
ELLIS STREET
HOWARD STREET
SEAFORD STREET
CHARLES PL.
CHARLES STREET
LILAC PLACE
LARCH PLACE
LIME PLACE
BIRCH PLACE
AVENUE
BEECH PLACE
OAK PLACE
MAPLE PLACE
SOUTH HAMILTON STREET
DUNDONALD ROAD
RUGBY ROAD
Kilmarnock Football Club
Howard Park
WATERSIDE ST
TITCHFIELD ST
FOWLDS STREET
JOHN STREET
KING STREET
SAUDBED ST
PRINCES ST
RENNIE STREET
Palace Theatre
Braeside Street
ELMBANK DRIVE
DICK ROAD
LOANHEAD ST
LONDON ROAD
ELMBANK AVENUE
Dick Institute
ELMBANK DR.
GLEBE ROAD
GLEBE AVENUE
MIDDLEMASS DRIVE
NURSERY AVENUE
SAMSON AVENUE
ABC Cinema Centre
Fire Station
GILMOUR STREET
OLD MILL ROAD
MACKINLAY PLACE
LONDON ROAD

Central Ayr

A · B · C · D · E · F

Ayr Baths
Harbour
SOUTH HARBOUR STREET
NORTH HARBOUR STREET
YORK STREET
GREEN ST
MAIN ST
Police HQ
KING STREET
WHITLETTS RD
LIMOND'S WYND
QUEEN STREET
Racecourse
SEA BANK ROAD
Esplanade
Boating Pool
ARRAN TERRACE
MONTGOMERIE TERRACE
Accademy
Loudon Hall
Carnegie Library
RIVER STREET
New Bridge
Auld Brig'
ELBA STREET
JAMES STREET
VICTORIA STREET
JOHN STREET
St John's Tower
CITADEL
EGLINTON TERRACE
BRUCE CRESCENT
ST JOHN STREET
FORT STREET
Town Hall
NEWMARKET ST
HIGH STREET
Auld Kirk
Government Offices
CROMWELL ROAD
CHARLOTTE STREET
CASSILLIS STREET
SANDGATE
Post Office
BOSWELL PARK
Bus Station
Gaiety Theatre
CARRICK ST
Wallace Tower
Turner's Bridge (Foot)
ALBERT TERR.
GORDON TERRACE
CRAIGIE AVENUE
FOTHERINGHAM ROAD
CRAIGIE ROAD
CRAIGIE WAY
JAMES STREET
CAMPBELL RD
CRAIGIE LEA
CRAIGIE WAY
QUEEN'S TERRACE
BATH PLACE
Wellington Square
Mc Adams Monument
FULLARTON ST
BARNS STREET
DALBLAIR ROAD
MILL WYND
Tam O' Shanter Museum
KYLE STREET
MILL STREET
Fire Station
Civic Theatre
CONTENT AVE.
Technical College
Dam Park Hall
N
Craigie Park
Pavilion RD
Strathclyde Region Offices
Pavilion Ballroom
PARK TERRACE
ALLOWAY PLACE
BARNS PARK
BARNS CRESCENT
ALLOWAY STREET
BERESFORD TERR.
BURNS STATUE SQ
STATION ROAD
SMITH STREET
MILL BRAE
Victoria Bridge
Dam Park Stadium
County Hospital
Low Green
ESPLANADE
FAIRFIELD ROAD
RACECOURSE ROAD
MILLER ROAD
PARK CIRCUS
Burns Statue
Odeon Cinema
PARKH'S
Post Office
Station
Cattle Market
ASHGROVE STREET
DONGOLA RD
HOLMSTON ROAD
River Ayr
Cemetery

AYR
The town has been an important fishing port on the Firth of Clyde for several hundred years. Today, Ayr is a major seaside resort and tourist centre and the harbour is as busy as ever, with yachts and leisure craft.

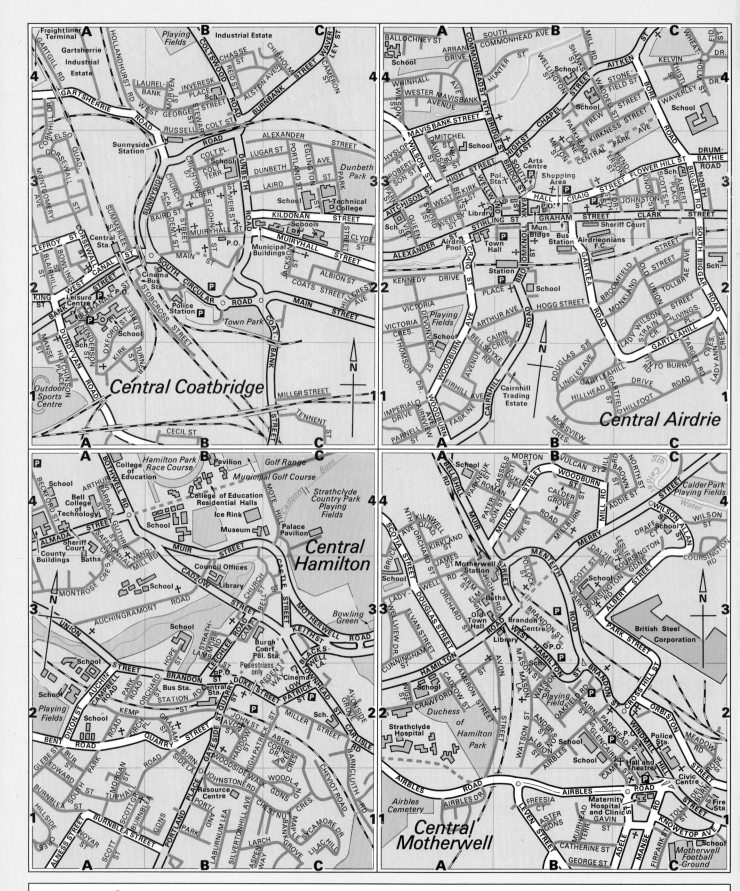

Coatbridge

Six villages went into the making of Coatbridge, a town whose iron and coal mining made it the centre of the Scottish iron industry. Scotland's first railway was here, but today Coatbridge achieves industrial prominence via its waterway, which gives it the largest inland port in Britain and is part of a major project to revitalise the entire town. Drumpellier Country Park nearby stands in fine wood and loch surroundings.

Airdrie Few industrial towns make such a pleasant first impression on the visitor as Airdrie, which, for all its industrial past, still has the air of a country market centre.

Motherwell Heartland of Scottish steelmaking, the place where the metal for the hulls of the *Queen Mary* and *Queen Elizabeth* was forged, Motherwell is a town where industry is heard and felt. But the town's name has gentler origins: it comes from a well — or pool — dedicated to the Virgin Mary, the site of which is marked by a plaque in Ladywell Road.

Hamilton's most notable landmark is the beautiful dome construction of Hamilton Mausoleum, noted for the six-second echo it produces. An industrial centre set in attractive surroundings, the town also enjoys a race course and an ice-rink, and in Strathclyde Park, it has excellent land and water sports facilities.

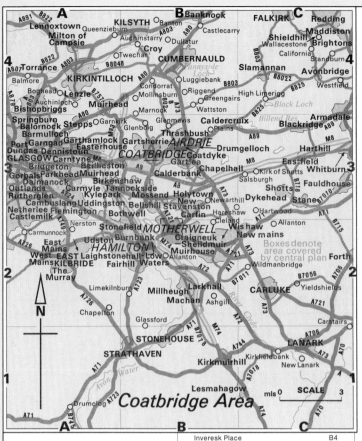

Coatbridge Area

SCALE
mls 0   3

Key to Town Plan and Area Plan

Town Plan

A A Recommended roads
Other roads
Restricted roads
Buildings of interest   Mill
Car Parks   P
Parks and open spaces

Area Plan

A roads
B roads
Locations   Banton O
Urban Area

Street Index with Grid Reference

Coatbridge

Academy Street	B2-B3
Albert Street	B3
Albion Street	C2
Alexander Street	B3-C3
Alston Avenue	B4-C4
Baird Street	B3
Bank Street	A2
Blairhill Street	A2
Bowling Street	A2
Buchanan Street	A2
Burnbank Street	B4-C4
Cameron Street	C4
Cecil Street	B1
Chassels Street	B4
Chisholm Street	C4
Church Street	B2-B3
Clyde Street	C2
Coatbank Street	C1-C2
Coats Street	C2
Colt Place	B3
Colt Terrace	B3
Coltswood Road	B4
Cornhill Drive	A3-A4
Corsewall Street	A2-A3
Crichton Street	B3
Dunbeth Avenue	B3-C3
Dunbeth Road	B2-B3
Dundyvan Road	A1-A2
Eglinton Street	C3
Gartgill Road	A4
Gartsherrie Road	A4-B3-B4
Henderson Street	A1-A2
Hillcrest Avenue	C2
Hollandhurst Road	A4
Hutchinson Place	A1
Inveresk Place	B4
Jackson Street	C2
Kelso Quadrant	A3
Kildonan Street	C3
King Street	A2
Kirk Street	A1-A2
Laird Street	B3-C3
Laurelbank	A4-B4
Lefroy Street	A2
Lugar Street	B3-C3
Main Street	B2-C2
Manse Street	A1-A2
Miller Street	C1
Montgomery Avenue	A3
Morton Street	B4
Muiryhall Street	B2-B3-C2-C3
Oxford Street	A1-A2
Park Street	C2-C3
Portland Street	C3
Reid Street	B4
Russel Colt Street	B3-B4
St John Street	B2-B3
South Circular Road	B2
Stewart Street	B3-B4
Stobcross Street	A2-B1-B2
Summerlee Street	A2-A3
Sunnyside Road	A3-B3
Tennent Street	C1
Turner Street	A1
Waverley Street	C4
Weir Street	B3
West Canal Street	A2
West George Street	A4-B4

Airdrie

Aitchison Street	A3
Aitken Street	B4-C4
Albert Place	C3
Alexander Street	A2-A3
Arran Drive	A4
Arthur Avenue	A2-B2
Ballochney Street	A4
Bank Street	B3
Bell Street	A3
Bellsdyke Road	A1-A2-B1
Broomfield Street	B2-C2
Broomknoll Street	B2-B3
Bore Road	C3-C4
Burnbank Street	A3
Burns Crescent	C1-C2
Cairnhill Crescent	A1-B2
Cairnhill Road	A1-B1-B2
Cairnview	A1
Central Park Avenue	B3-C3-C4
Chapel Street	B4
Clark Street	C3
Commonhead Street	A4
Craig Street	A2
Davidson Street	A3
Devonview Street	A1-A2
Douglas Street	B1-B2
Drumbathie Road	C3
Faskine Avenue	A1
Firhill Avenue	A1
Flowerhill Street	C3
Forsyth Street	C3
Frew Street	B4-C4
Gartfield Street	B1
Gartlea Road	B1-B2-B3
Gartleahill	B1-C1-C2
Graham Street	B3
Hallcraig Street	B3-C3

Hamilton

Henderson Street	C3
High Street	A3
High Street East	B3
Hillfoot Road	C1
Hillhead Drive	B1-C1
Hogg Street	B2
Hunter Street	A4-B4
Hyslop Street	A3
Imperial Drive	A1
Johnston Street	C3
Kelvin Drive	C4
Kennedy Drive	A2
Kirkness Street	B3-B4-C4
Knox Street	C3
Lady Ann Crescent	C1-C2
Lady Wilson Street	C2
Lingley Avenue	B1
Livingstone Place	C2
Mavis Bank Street	A3-A4
Mill Road	B4
Milton Street	B3
Mitchel Street	A3
Monkland Street	B2-C2
Mossview Crescent	B1
North Biggar Road	C3
North Bridge Street	A3-A4-B3
Old Union Street	C2
Park Street	A3
Parkhead Lane	B3
Parnell Street	A1
Queen Victoria Street	A3
Reid Street	C4
Robertson Street	A3
Scotts Place	C3
Shanks Street	B4
South Biggar Road	C2-C3
South Bridge Street	B3
South Commmonhead Avenue	A4-B4
Stirling Street	A3-B3
Stonefield Street	B4-C4
Strain Street	C2
Sword Street	A3
Target Road	C1-C2
Thomson Drive	A1-A2
Thistle Street	C4
Tinto Road	C1
Tollbrae Avenue	C2
Victoria Crescent	A2
Victoria Place	A2-B2
Waddell Street	B4-C4
Waverley Drive	C4
Wellington Street	B4
Wellwynd	A3-B3
Wesley Street	A3
West Kirk Street	A3
Western Mavisbank Avenue	A4
Wheatholm Street	C4
Whinhall Avenue	A4
Wilson Street	A3-A4
Woodburn Avenue	A1-A2

Hamilton

Abercorn Crescent	C2
Abercorn Drive	C1
Almada Street	A4
Alness Street	A1
Arthur Street	A4
Aspen Way	B1
Auchincampbell Road	A2
Auchingramont Road	A3-B3
Avon Street	B2
Avonside Grove	C2
Barncluith Road	C1-C2
Barrack Street	A4
Beckford Street	A4
Bent Road	A2
Blackswell Lane	C3
Bothwell Road	A4
Brandon Street	B2
Burnblea Gardens	A1-B1
Burnblea Street	A1-B1
Burns Street	A1-A2
Burnside Lane	B2
Cadzow Street	B3-C3
Campbell Street	B3-C3
Carlisle Road	C2
Castle Street	C3
Chestnut Crescent	B1-C1
Cheviot Road	C1-C2
Church Street	B3-C3
Duke Street	B2-C2
Dixon Street	A2
Edward Street	A1
Gateside Street	B2
Glebe Street	A1-A2
Graham Street	A4
Guthrie Street	A4
Haddow Street	B2
High Patrick Street	B2-C2
Hillside Crescent	A1
Hope Street	B2-B3
John Street	B2
Johnstone Road	B1
Keith Street	C3
Kemp Street	A2-B2
Laburnum Lea	B1
Lamb Street	B2-B3
Larch Grove	B1-C1
Leechlee Road	B2-B3
Lilac Hill	C1
Low Patrick Street	C2
Maple Bank	C1
Miller Street	C2
Montrose Crescent	A3
Morgan Street	A1
Mote Hill	C4
Motherwell Road	C3
Muir Street	B4-C4
Noyar Street	A1
Orchard Place	A2
Orchard Street	B2
Park Road	A2
Portland Park	B1
Portland Place	B1
Quarry Street	A2-B2
Regent Way	C2
Saffronhall Crescent	A3-A4
Scott Grove	A1

Motherwell

Scott Street	A1
Silvertonhill Avenue	B1
Station Road	B2
Strathmore Road	B3
South Park Road	A1-A2
Sycamore Drive	C1
Townhead Street	C2
Tuphall Road	A1-B2
Union Street	A2-A3
Windmill Road	A3-B4
Woodland Gardens	C1
Woodside Walk	B1-B2

Motherwell

Addie Street	B4-C4
Adele Street	C1
Airbles Drive	A1
Airbles Road	A1-B1-C1
Airbles Street	B2
Albert Street	B3-C3
Albion Street	B2
Allan Street	C4
Anderson Street	B2
Aster Gardens	B1
Avon Street	A1-A2-B2-B3-A3
Bellshill Road	A4
Brandon Street	B2-B3-C2
Brown Street	B4-C4
Bruce Avenue	A3-A4
Cadzow Street	A2
Cairn Street	B2
Calder Grove	B4
Cameron Street	A2
Camp Street	B1-B2-C2
Cassels Street	B4
Catherine Street	B1
Coursington Gardens	C3
Coursington Road	B3-C3-C4
Crawford Street	A2
Cross Hill Street	C2
Cunningham Street	A2-A3
Dalziel Street	B3-B4
Dellburn Street	C1
Douglas Street	A3
Draffen Court	C4
Duke Street	B4
Elm Street	A3
Elvan Street	A3
Farm Street	A3
Firpark Street	C1
Freesia Court	B1
Gavin Street	B1-C1
George Street	B1
Glencairn Street	B2-C2-C1
Hamilton Road	A2-A3-B3
High Road	A3-B3
James Street	A3-A4
Kilnwell Quad	A4
Kirk Street	B4
Kirkland Street	A4
Knowetop Avenue	C1
Ladywell Road	A3
Leslie Street	C3-C4
Leven Street	B1
Manse Street	C1
Mason Lane	B2
Mason Street	B2-B3
Meadow Road	C2
Menteith Road	B3-B4
Merry Street	B4-C4
Mill Road	B4
Millburn Street	B4
Milton Street	A4-B4
Morton Street	B4
Muir Street	A4-B3
Muirhead Terrace	B1
Nigel Street	A2
North Street	C4
North Orchard Street	A3-A4
Oakfield Road	B2
Orbiston Street	C1-C2
Orchard Street	A3
Park Street	B3-C3
Parkhead Street	B2-C2
Parkneuk Street	A4
Paterson Street	A4-B4
Pollock Street	B3
Roman road	A4-B4
Rose Street	C2
Scotia Street	A3-A4
Scott Street	B3
Toll Street	C1
Vulcan Street	B4
Watson Street	B2
Wellview Drive	A3
West Hamilton Street	B2-B3
Wilson Street	C4
Windmill Hill Street	C1-C2
Woodburn Street	B4

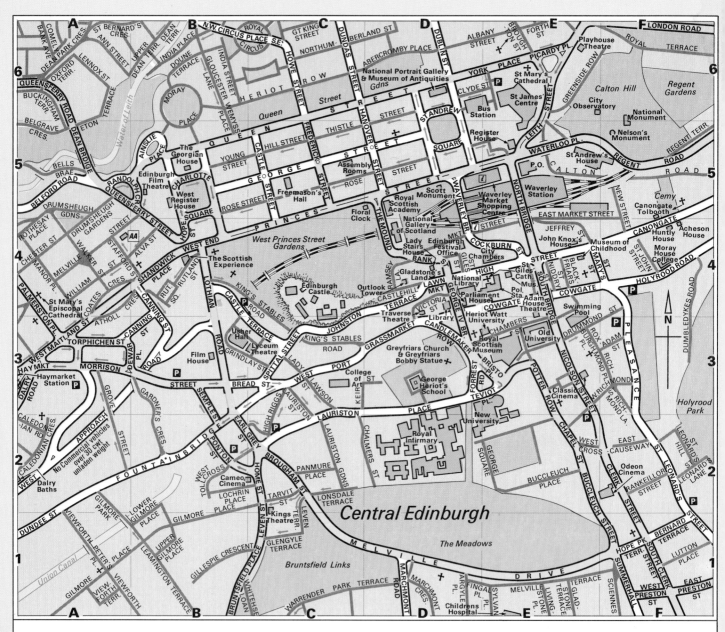

Key to Town Plan and Area Plan

Town Plan
A A Recommended roads
Other roads
Restricted roads
Buildings of intrest   Gallery
Car Parks   P
Parks and open spaces
One Way Streets
Churches   ✝

Area Plan
A roads
B roads
Locations   Newcraighall ○
Urban area

Street Index with Grid Reference

Edinburgh

Abercromby Place	C6-D6
Adam Street	F3
Ainslie Place	B5
Albany Street	D6-E6
Alva Street	A4-B4
Ann Street	A6
Argyle Place	D1
Athol Crescent	A3-A4-B4
Bank Street	D4
Belford Road	A5
Belgrave Crescent	A5
Bells Brae	A5
Bernard Terrace	F1
Blackfriars Street	E4

Bread Street	B3-C3
Bristo Place	D3-E3
Brougham Street	C2
Broughton Street	E6
Bruntsfield Place	B1-C1
Buccleuch Place	E2
Buccleauch Street	E2-F2-F1
Buckingham Terrace	A5-A6
Caledonian Crescent	A2
Caledonian Road	A2
Calton Road	E5-F5
Candlemaker Row	D3
Canning Street	A3-B3-B4
Canongate	E4-F4-F5
Castle Hill	D4
Castle Street	C5
Castle Terrace	B4-B3-C3
Chalmers Street	C2-D2
Chambers Street	D3-E3
Charlotte Square	B4-B5

Chapel Street	E2
Chester Street	A4
Clerk Street	F1-F2
Clyde Street	D6-E6
Coates Crescent	A4-B4
Cockburn Street	D4-E4
Comely Bank Avenue	A6
Cowgate	D4-E4-F4
Dalry Road	A3
Dean Bridge	A5
Dean Park Crescent	A6
Dean Terrace	B6
Dewar Place	A3-B3
Doune Terrace	B6
Drummond Street	E3-F3-F4
Drumsheugh Gardens	A4-A5
Dublin Street	D6
Dumbiedykes Road	F3-F4
Dundas Street	C6
Dundee Street	A1-A2

Edinburgh

Scotland's ancient capital, dubbed the "Athens of the North", is one of the most splendid cities in the whole of Europe. Its buildings, its history and its cultural life give it an international importance which is celebrated every year in its world-famous festival. The whole city is overshadowed by the craggy castle which seems to grow out of the rock itself. There has been a fortress here since the 7th century and most of the great figures of Scottish history have been associated with it. The old town grew up around the base of Castle Rock within the boundaries of the defensive King's Wall and, unable to spread outwards, grew upwards in a maze of tenements. However, during the 18th century new prosperity from the shipping trade resulted in the building of the New Town and the regular, spacious layout of the Georgian development makes a striking contrast with the old hotch-potch of streets. Princes Street is the main east-west thoroughfare with excellent shops on one side and Princes Street Gardens with their famous floral clock on the south side.

As befits such a splendid capital city there are numerous museums and art galleries packed with priceless treasures. Among these are the famous picture gallery in 16th-century Holyroodhouse, the present Royal Palace, and the fascinating and unusual Museum of Childhood.

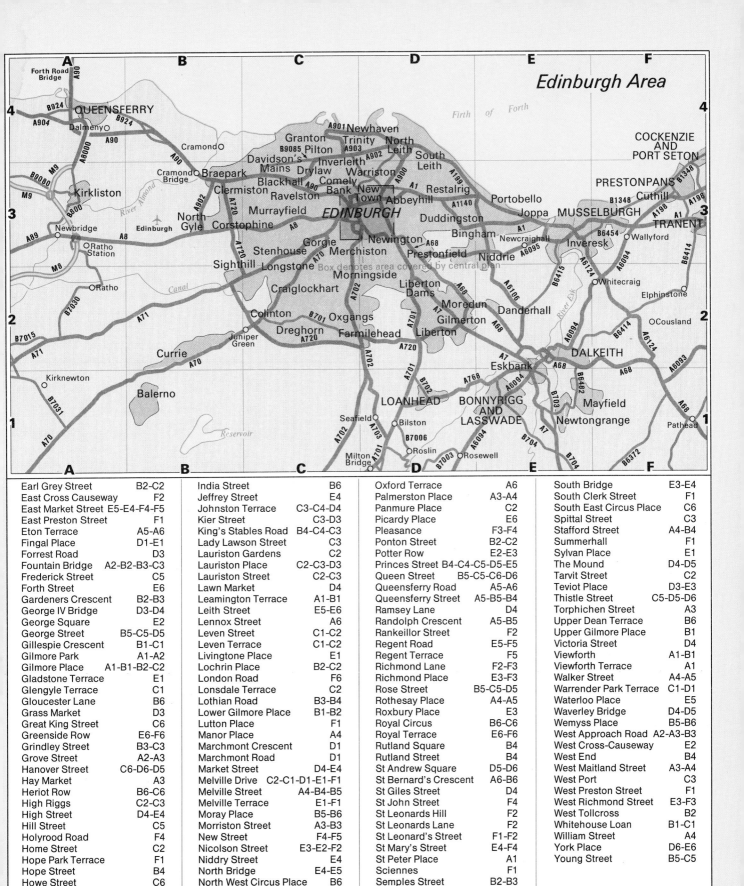

Edinburgh Area

EDINBURGH
Holyrood Palace orginated as a guest house for the Abbey of Holyrood in the 16th century, but most of the present building was built for Charles II. Mary Queen of Scots was one of its most famous inhabitants.

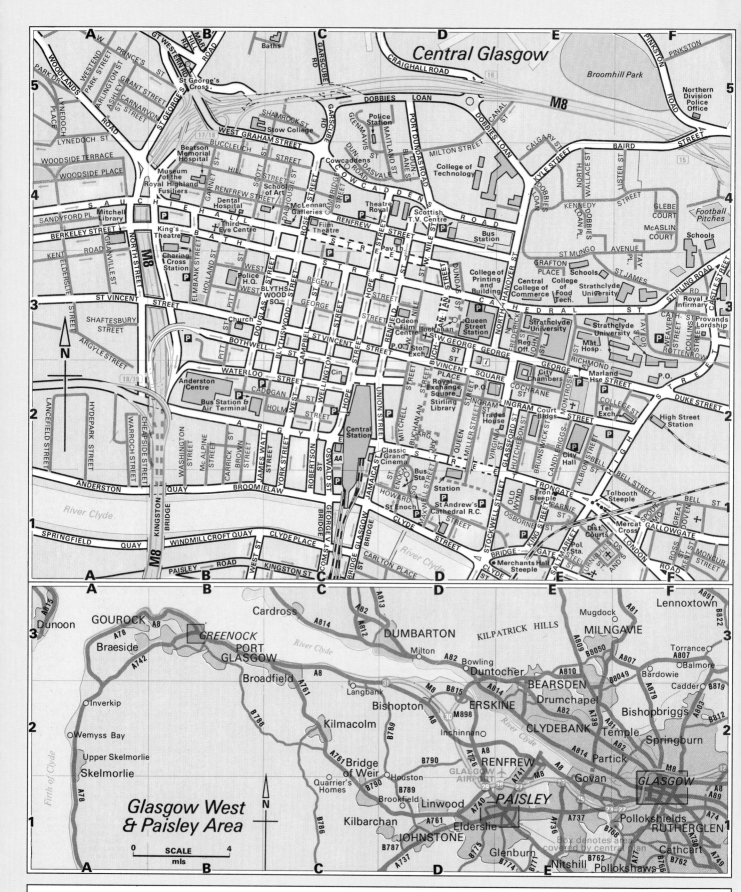

Glasgow

Although much of Glasgow is distinctly Victorian in character, its roots go back very many centuries. Best link with the past is the cathedral; founded in the 6th century, it has features from many succeeding centuries, including an exceptional 13th- century crypt. Nearby is Provand's Lordship, the city's oldest house. It dates from 1471 and is now a museum. Two much larger museums are to

be found a little out of the centre – the Art Gallery and Museum contains one of the finest collections of paintings in Britain, while the Hunterian Museum, attached to the University, covers geology, archaeology, ethnography and more general subjects. On Glasgow Green is People's Palace – a museum of city life. Most imposing of the Victorian buildings are the City Chambers and City Hall which was built in 1841 as a concert hall but now houses the Scottish National Orchestra.

Paisley is famous for the lovely fabric pattern to which it gives its name. It was taken from fabrics brought from the Near East in the early 19th century, and its manufacture, along with the production of thread, is still important.

Greenock has been an important port and shipbuilding centre since as early as the 16th century. Its most famous son is James Watt, the inventor of steam power, born here in 1736. The town has numerous memorials to the great man.

90

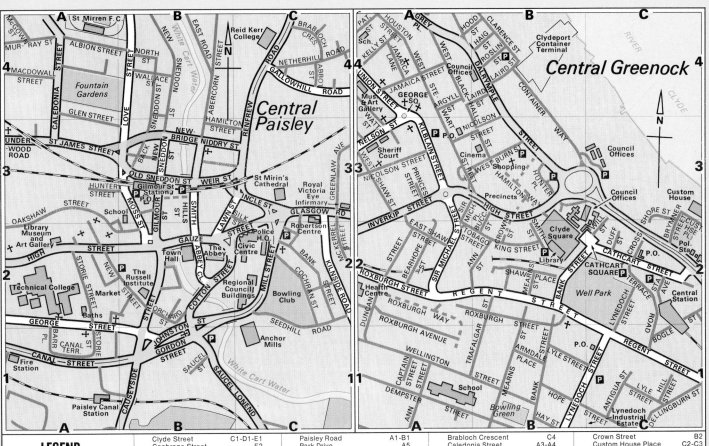

Central Paisley / Central Greenock

LEGEND

Town Plan
AA recommended route
Restricted roads
Other roads
Buildings of interest   Station ▣
Car parks   ℗
Parks and open spaces
One way streets

Area Plan
A roads
B roads
Locations   Garvock ○
Urban area

Street Index with grid reference

Glasgow

Albion Street	E1-E2
Anderston Quay	A2-A1-B1
Argyle Arcade	D2
Argyle Street	A3-A2-B2-C2-D2-D1-E1
Arlington Street	A5
Ashley Street	A5
Baird Street	E4-E5-F5-F4
Bath Street	B4-C4-C3-D3
Bell Street	E2-E1-F1
Berkeley Street	A4
Blythswood Square	B3-C3
Blythswood Street	C2-C3
Bothwell Street	B3-C3-C2
Bridgegate	D1-E1
Bridge Street	C1
Broomielaw	B1-C1
Brown Street	B1-B2
Brunswick Street	E2
Buccleuch Street	B4-C4
Buchanan Street	D3-D4
Cadogan Street	B2-C2
Calgary Street	E4-E5-E4
Canal Street	D5-E5
Candleriggs	E1-E2
Cambridge Street	C4
Carlton Place	C1-D1
Carnarvon Street	A5-B5
Carrick Street	B1-B2
Castle Street	F3
Cathedral Street	D3-E3-F3
Cheapside Street	A1-A2
Clyde Place	B1-C1
Clyde Street	C1-D1-E1
Cochrane Street	E2
College Street	E2-F2
Collins Street	F3
Commerce Street	C1
Cowcaddens Road	C4-D4-E4
Craighall Road	C5-D5
Dalhousie Street	C4
Dobbies Loan	C5-D5-E5-E4-A5
Dobbies Loan Place	E4
Douglas Street	B3-C3
Duke Street	F2
Dunblane Street	D4-D5
Dundas Street	D3
Dundasvale Road	C4-D4
Elderslie Street	A3-A4
Elmbank Street	B3-B4
Gallowgate	E1-F1
Garscube Road	C4-C5
Garnet Street	F4
George V Bridge	C1
George Square	D3-E3-E2-D2
George Street	E3-E2-F2
Glasgow Bridge	C1
Glassford Street	E2
Glebe Court	F4
Glenmavis Street	C5-C4-D4
Grafton Place	E3
Grant Street	A5-B5
Granville Street	A3-A4
Great Dovenhill	F1
Great Western Road	A5-B5
High Street	E1-E2-F2-F3
Hill Street	B4-C4
Holland Street	B3-B4
Holm Street	C2
Hope Street	C2-C3-C4-D4
Howard Street	C1-D1
Hutcheson Street	E1-E2
Hyde Park Street	A1-A2
Ingram Street	D2-E2-F2
Jamaica Street	C1-C2-D2
James Watt Street	B1-B2-C2
John Street	E3
Kennedy Street	E4-F4
Kent Road	A3-A4
Kent Street	F1
King Street	E1
Kingston Bridge	B1
Kingston Street	B1-C1
Kyle Street	E4
Lancefield Street	A1-A2
Lister Street	F4
London Road	E1-F1
Lyndoch Place	A5
Lyndoch Street	A4-A5
McAlpine Street	B1-B2
McAslin Court	F4
Maitland Street	C5-D5-D4
Maryhill Road	B5
Maxwell Street	D1-D2
Miller Street	D2
Milton Street	D4-D5
Mitchell Street	D2
Moncur Street	F1
Montrose Street	E2-E3
North Street	A3-A4
North Frederick Street	E3
North Hannover Street	D3-E3-E4
North Wallace Street	E4
Old Wynd	E1
Osborne Street	E1
Oswald Street	C1-C2

Paisley Road	A1-B1
Park Drive	A5
Parnie Street	E1
Pinkston Drive	F5
Pinkston Road	F5
Pitt Street	B2-B3-B4
Port Dundas Road	D4-D5
Queen Street	D2
Renfield Street	D4-D3-C3-C2-D2
Renfrew Street	B4-C4-D4
Richmond Street	E3-E2-F2
Robertson Street	C1-C2
Rose Street	C3-C4
Ross Street	F1
Rottenrow	F3
St Andrew's Square	E1-F1
St Enoch Square	D1-D2
St George's Road	A4-B4-B5
St James Road	E3-F3
St Mungo Avenue	E3-E4-F4
St Vincent Place	D2-D3
St Vincent Street	A3-B3-C3-D3-D2
Saltmarket	E1
Sandyford Place	A4
Sauchiehall Street	A4-B4-C4-C3-D3
Scott Street	B4-C4
Shaftesbury Street	A3
Shamrock Street	B5-C5-C4
Spoutmouth	F1
Springfield Quay	A1
Steel Street	E1
Stirling Road	F3
Stockwell Street	D1-E1
Taylor Place	F4
Taylor Street	F3
Trongate	E1
Turnbull Street	E1
Union Street	C2-D2
Virginia Street	D2-E2
Warroch Street	A1-A2
Washington Street	B1-B2
Waterloo Street	B2-C2
Weaver Street	F3
Wellington Street	C2-C3
West Street	B1
West Campbell Street	C2-C3
West George Street	B3-C3-D3
West Graham Street	B5-C5-C4
West Nile Street	D3-D4
West Prince's Street	A5-B5
West Regent Street	B3-C3-D3
Westend Park Street	A4
Windmill Croft Quay	B1
Woodlands Road	A4-A5
Woodside Place	A4
Woodside Terrace	A4
York Street	C1-C2

Paisley

Abbey Close	B2
Abbot Street	C4
Abercorn Street	B3-B4
Albion Street	A4-B4
Back Sneddon Street	B3-B4
Bank Street	C2
Barr Place	A1
Brabloch Crescent	C4
Caledonia Street	A3-A4
Canal Street	A1-B1
Canal Terrace	A1
Causeyside Street	A1-B1-B2
Cochran Street	C2
Cotton Street	B2
East Road	B4
Gallowhill Road	C4
Gauze Street	B2-C2-C3
George Street	A1-B1-B2-A2
Gilmour Street	B2-B3
Glasgow Road	C3
Glen Street	A4-A3-B3
Gordon Street	B1
Greenlaw Avenue	C3
Hamilton Street	B3-C3
High Street	A2-B2
Hunter Street	A3-B3
Incle Street	C3
Johnston Street	B1-B2
Kilnside Road	C2-C3
Lawn Street	B2-B3-C3
Love Street	B3-B4
Macdowall Street	A4
McGown Street	A4
McKerrel Street	C2-C3
Mill Street	C2
Moss Street	B2-B3
Murray Street	A4
Netherhill Road	C4
Newbridge	B3
New Sneddon Street	B3-B4
New Street	A2-B2
Niddry Street	B3-C3
North Street	B4
Oakshaw Street	A2-A3-B2
Old Sneddon Street	B3
Orchard Street	B2
Renfrew Road	C3-C4
St James Street	A3
Saucel Lonend	B1-C1
Saucel Street	B1
Seedhill Road	C1-C2
Silk Street	B3-C3-C2
Smith Hills Street	B2-B3
Storie Street	A1-A2
Underwood Road	A3
Wallace Street	B4
Weir Street	B3-C3

Crown Street	B2
Custom House Place	C2-C3
Dalrymple Street	A4-B4-B3
Dellingburn Street	C1
Dempster Street	A1-B1
Duff Street	C2
Duncan Street	A1-A2
East Shaw Street	A2-A3
George Square	A3-A4
Grey Place	A4
Haig Street	B4
Hamilton Way	B3
Hay Street	B1
High Street	A3-B3-B2
Hill Street	C1
Hood Street	A4-B4
Hope Street	B1-C1
Houston Street	A4
Hunter Place	B3
Inverkip Street	A2-A3
Jamaica Lane	A4
Jamaica Street	A4
Kelly Street	A4
Kilblain Street	A3
King Street	B2
Laird Street	A4-B4
Lyle Street	B1-C1
Lynedoch Street	B1-C1-C2
Mearns Street	B1-B2
Nelson Street	A3
Nicolson Street	A3-B3
Patrick Street	A4
Princes Street	A3
Regent Street	A2-B2-C2-C1
Roslin Street	B4
Roxburgh Avenue	A1-A2
Roxburgh Street	A2-B2-B1
Roxburgh Way	A1-A2
Shaw Place	B2
Sir Michael Place	A2-A3
Sir Michael Street	A2-A3
Smith Street	B2
Station Avenue	C2
Terrace Road	C1-C2
Tobago Street	A2-B2
Trafalgar Street	A1-B1-B2
Union Street	A3-A4
Watt Street	A3-A4
Wellington Street	A1-B1
West Blackhall Street	A4-A3-B3
West Burn Street	A3-B3
West Shaw Street	A3
West Stewart Street	A4-A3-B3
William Street	C2-C3

Greenock

Ann Street	A1
Ann Street	A2-B2
Antigua Street	C1
Argyll Street	A4
Armdale Place	B1
Bank Street	B1-B2-C2
Bearhope Street	A2
Bogle Street	C1-C2
Brymner Street	C2-C3
Buccleugh	B2-B3
Captain Street	A1
Cathcart Square	B2-C2
Cathcart Street	C2
Clarence Street	B4
Container Way	B1
Cross Shore Street	C2-C3

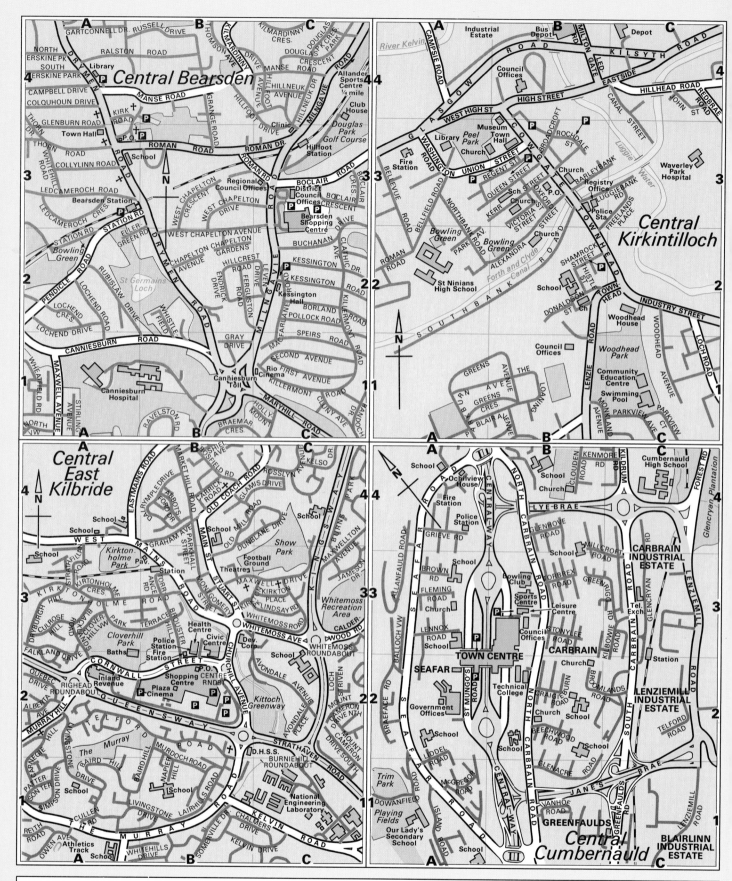

Glasgow environs

Cumbernauld is a New Town — built during the 1950s and '60s, it was specially designed to provide easy access for both motorists and pedestrians. A multi-level shopping area, a sports centre and a thriving local theatre are some of the amenities it enjoys, and amongst the many parks and open spaces in the area, Palacerigg Country Park (1½ miles to the south-east) covers over 600 acres.

Bearsden is noted for its public parks and woodland areas. It became established as a residential area in the 19th century, but a number of Georgian buildings are used by the community: Kilmardinny House, for instance, is an Arts Centre with a small theatre.

East Kilbride was well-known for its shoemaking and weaving in the 18th century. Its designation as a New Town shortly after the end of World War I boosted its expansion, and today, it is noted for

the good integration of new buildings with old. Popular attractions among the modern buildings are the arcaded shopping precinct and the Dollan Swimming Pool, lying beneath an unusually deep roof within the town's central park.

Kirkintilloch Once a station on the old Roman wall, Kirkintilloch in recent years has suffered from the decline of a good many local industries. The former Parish Church of St Mary has been converted into a local history museum.

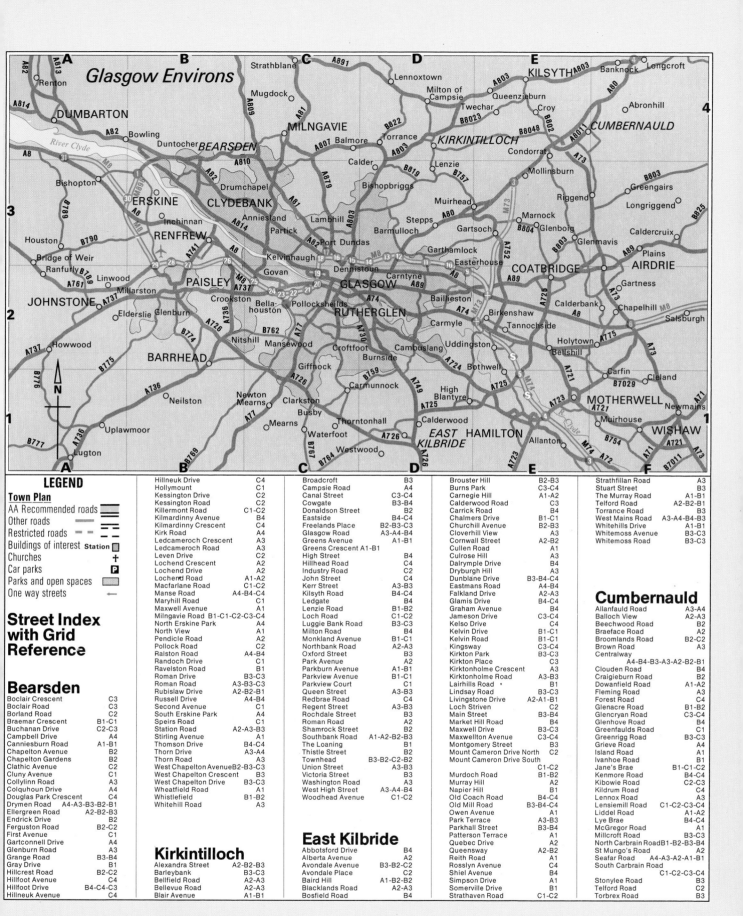

Glasgow Environs

LEGEND

Town Plan
- AA Recommended roads
- Other roads
- Restricted roads
- Buildings of interest — Station
- Churches — †
- Car parks — P
- Parks and open spaces
- One way streets ←

Street Index with Grid Reference

Bearsden

Boclair Crescent	C3
Boclair Road	C3
Borland Road	C2
Braemar Crescent	B1-C1
Buchanan Drive	C2-C3
Campbell Avenue	A4
Canniesburn Road	A1-B1
Chapelton Avenue	B2
Chapelton Gardens	B2
Clathic Avenue	C2
Cluny Avenue	C1
Collylinn Road	A3
Colquhoun Drive	A4
Douglas Park Crescent	C4
Drymen Road	A4-A3-B3-B2-B1
Ellergreen Road	A2-B2-B3
Endrick Drive	B2
Ferguston Road	B2-C2
First Avenue	C1
Gartconnell Drive	A4
Glenburn Road	A3
Grange Road	B3-B4
Gray Drive	B1
Hillcrest Road	B2-C2
Hillfoot Avenue	C4
Hillfoot Drive	B4-C4-C3
Hillneuk Avenue	C4
Hillneuk Drive	C4
Hollymount	C1
Kessington Drive	C2
Kessington Road	C2
Killermont Road	C1-C2
Kilmardinny Avenue	B4
Kilmardinny Crescent	C4
Kirk Road	A4
Ledcameroch Crescent	A3
Ledcameroch Road	A3
Leven Drive	C2
Lochend Crescent	A2
Lochend Drive	A2
Lochend Road	A1-A2
Macfarlane Road	C1-C2
Manse Road	A4-B4-C4
Maryhill Road	C1
Maxwell Avenue	A1
Milngavie Road	B1-C1-C2-C3-C4
North Erskine Park	A4
North View	A1
Pendicle Road	A2
Pollock Road	C2
Ralston Road	A4-B4
Randoch Drive	C1
Ravelston Road	B1
Roman Drive	B3-C3
Roman Road	A3-B3-C3
Rubislaw Drive	A2-B2-B1
Russell Drive	A4-B4
Second Avenue	C1
South Erskine Park	A4
Speirs Road	C1
Station Road	A2-A3-B3
Stirling Avenue	A1
Thomson Drive	B4-C4
Thorn Drive	A3-A4
Thorn Road	A3
West Chapelton Avenue	B2-B3-C3
West Chapelton Crescent	B3
West Chapelton Drive	B3-C3
Wheatfield Road	A1
Whistlefield	B1-B2
Whitehill Road	A3

Kirkintilloch

Alexandra Street	A2-B2-B3
Barleybank	B3-C3
Bellfield Road	A2-A3
Bellevue Road	A2-A3
Blair Avenue	A1-B1
Broadcroft	B3
Campsie Road	A4
Canal Street	C3-C4
Cowgate	B3-B4
Donaldson Street	B2
Eastside	B4-C4
Freelands Place	B2-B3-C3
Glasgow Road	A3-A4-B4
Greens Avenue	A1-B1
Greens Crescent	A1-B1
High Street	B4
Hillhead Road	C4
Industry Road	C2
John Street	C2
Kerr Street	A3-B3
Kilsyth Road	B4-C4
Ledgate	B4
Lenzie Road	B1-B2
Loch Road	C1-C2
Luggie Bank Road	B3-C3
Milton Road	B4
Monkland Avenue	B1-C1
Northbank Road	A2-A3
Oxford Street	B3
Park Avenue	A2
Parkburn Avenue	A1-B1
Parkview Avenue	B1-C1
Parkview Court	C1
Queen Street	A3-B3
Redbrae Road	C4
Regent Street	A3-B3
Rochdale Street	B3
Roman Road	A2
Shamrock Street	B2
Southbank Road	A1-A2-B2-B3
The Loaning	B1
Thistle Street	B2
Townhead	B3-B2-C2-B2
Union Street	A3-B3
Victoria Street	B3
Washington Road	A3
West High Street	A3-A4-B4
Woodhead Avenue	C1-C2

East Kilbride

Abbotsford Drive	B4
Alberta Avenue	A2
Avondale Avenue	B3-B2-C2
Avondale Place	A2
Baird Hill	A1-B2-B2
Blacklands Road	A2-A3
Bosfield Road	B4
Brouster Hill	B2-B3
Burns Park	C3-C4
Carnegie Hill	A1-A2
Calderwood Road	C3
Carrick Road	B4
Chalmers Drive	B1-C1
Churchill Avenue	B2-B3
Cloverhill View	A3
Cornwall Street	A2-B2
Cullen Road	A1
Culrose Hill	A3
Dalrymple Drive	B4
Dryburgh Hill	A3
Dunblane Road	B3-B4-C4
Eastmans Road	A4-B4
Falkland Drive	A2-A3
Glamis Drive	B4-C4
Graham Avenue	B4
Jameson Drive	C3-C4
Kelso Drive	C4
Kelvin Drive	B1-C1
Kelvin Road	B1-C1
Kingsway	C3-C4
Kirkton Park	B3-C3
Kirkton Place	C3
Kirktonholme Crescent	A3
Kirktonholme Road	A3-B3
Lairhills Road	B1
Lindsay Road	B3-C3
Livingstone Drive	A2-A1-B1
Loch Striven	C2
Main Street	B3-B4
Market Hill Road	B4
Maxwell Drive	B3-C3
Maxwellton Avenue	C3-C4
Montgomery Street	B3
Mount Cameron Drive North	C2
Mount Cameron Drive South	C1-C2
Murdoch Road	B1-B2
Murray Hill	A2
Napier Hill	B1
Old Coach Road	B4-C4
Old Mill Road	B3-B4-C4
Owen Avenue	A1
Park Terrace	A3-B3
Parkhall Street	B3-B4
Patterson Terrace	A1
Quebec Drive	A2
Queensway	A2-B2
Reith Road	A1
Rosslyn Avenue	C4
Shiel Avenue	B4
Simpson Drive	A1
Somerville Drive	B1
Strathaven Road	C1-C2
Strathfillan Road	A3
Stuart Street	B3
The Murray Road	A1-B1
Telford Road	A2-B2-B1
Torrance Road	B3
West Mains Road	A3-A4-B4-B3
Whitehills Drive	A1-B1
Whitemoss Avenue	B3-C3
Whitemoss Road	B3-C3

Cumbernauld

Allanfauld Road	A3-A4
Balloch View	A2-A3
Beechwood Road	B2
Braeface Road	A2
Broomlands Road	B2-C2
Brown Road	A3
Centralway	A4-B4-B3-A3-A2-B2-B1
Clouden Road	B4
Craigieburn Road	B2
Dowanfield Road	A1-A2
Fleming Road	A3
Forest Road	C4
Glenacre Road	B1-B2
Glencryan Road	C3-C4
Glenhove Road	B4
Greenfaulds Road	C1
Greenrigg Road	B3-C3
Grieve Road	A4
Island Road	A1
Ivanhoe Road	B1
Jane's Brae	B1-C1-C2
Kenmore Road	B4-C4
Kibowie Road	C2-C3
Kildrum Road	C4
Lennox Road	A3
Lensiemill Road	C1-C2-C3-C4
Liddel Road	A1-A2
Lye Brae	B4-C4
McGregor Road	A1
Millcroft Road	B3-C3
North Carbrain Road	B1-B2-B3-B4
St Mungo's Road	A2
Seafar Road	A4-A3-A2-A1-B1
South Carbrain Road	C1-C2-C3-C4
Stonylee Road	B3
Telford Road	C2
Torbrex Road	B3

EAST KILBRIDE
A fine modern Civic Centre symbolises the forward-looking approach of East Kilbride — an agricultural town of just 2,400 people in 1946, but now one of Britain's biggest new towns.

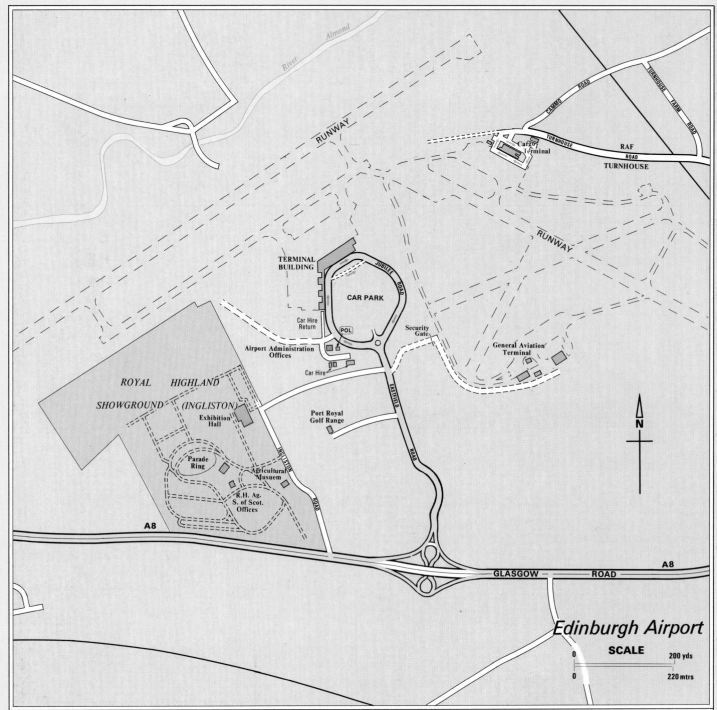

Edinburgh Airport

Charter flights to international holiday destinations such as Spain, Italy, Corsica and Portugal, business flights to Paris, Amsterdam and Frankfurt and commuter links with the Leeds, Humberside, East Midlands and Norwich Airports are among the services offered by Edinburgh Airport.

Originally known as Turnhouse Aerodrome, it was used by the Royal Flying Corps in World War I, because its closeness to the railway allowed for the delivery of aircraft by rail. The airport remained under military control and in World War II was a fighter station — a period commemorated by the vintage Spitfire which is on display near the cargo terminal.

Next came the very different years of redevelopment, and the British Airports Authority took control in 1971. A new runway and terminal building had been added by 1977, the year in which HM the Queen honoured Edinburgh Airport by coming here to open the new building.

Available for the convenience of passengers and other visitors to the airport today is the

Aerogrill on the first floor. Refreshments are also supplied by the buffet on the ground floor. Alongside each of these is a bar, and to complement the service they provide, the International Departure Lounge also offers the facilities of a bar and buffet.

Ready to deal with any enquiries or problems that arise is the Airport Information Desk, which is situated on the main concourse of the Terminal, and is open from 7am to 11pm.

For those wishing to watch the aeroplanes and the airport at work, a spectators' viewing terrace has been provided. This is accessible by lift and is open to visitors during daylight hours. The terrace runs along the northern side of the second floor of the Terminal.

The airport can be reached by car via the A8 from Edinburgh, and open air car parking is available for 1,025 vehicles. A regular coach service operates between Edinburgh (Waverley Bridge) and the airport, and the journey takes 25 minutes. There is also a coach service to link it with Glasgow Airport, with a pick-up point on the A8 outside the airport.

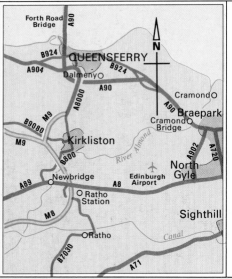

Glasgow Airport

Crucial as the fast link between Scotland's business community and the financial centre of London, this is Scotland's busiest international airport. Business flights have been calculated to make up approximately 40 per cent of Glasgow Airport's traffic, but it is also popular with other travellers — both scheduled and holiday flights are operated from here and go to a wide variety of destinations around the world.

The original site was known as Abbotsinch, and was used as an aerodrome by 602 Squadron of the Royal Auxiliary Air Force. During World War II it was converted into an RAF station, and was an important base at this time for the Fleet Air Arm. With the coming of peace and up until 1963, the airport became essentially a centre for repairs and for the fitting and testing of new aircraft.

By the early 1960s, however, it had been decided that the runway facilities at nearby Renfrew Airport were inadequate. Abbotsinch was selected as a more suitable site, and over the next three years the old aerodrome was to see a period of

major redevelopment. Finally, it was renamed Glasgow Airport, and was officially opened as such by HM the Queen in 1966. Military connections of the past were remembered by the hanging in the main terminal of the crest and ship's bell of *HMS Sanderling,* which had operated from here during the war years.

In 1975, the ownership of the airport passed to the British Airports Authority. For car drivers, it lies eight miles west of Glasgow off the M8 at Junction 28. The airport is also accessible from the A8 west of Renfrew. Two car parks provide parking spaces under cover for 712 vehicles, and open air parking is provided for a further 1,164.

There are regular coach services direct from Central Glasgow, and coach services also operate between the airport and Edinburgh. Local buses run from Renfrew and Paisley.

For travellers and other visitors to the airport coming by British Rail, the nearest station is Paisley (Gilmour Street), which stands approximately one mile from the airport. Train connections are available to Ayrshire, Gourock, Glasgow and Wemyss Bay.

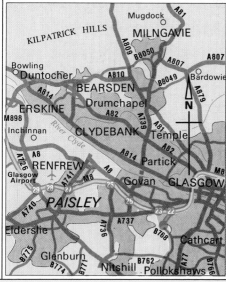

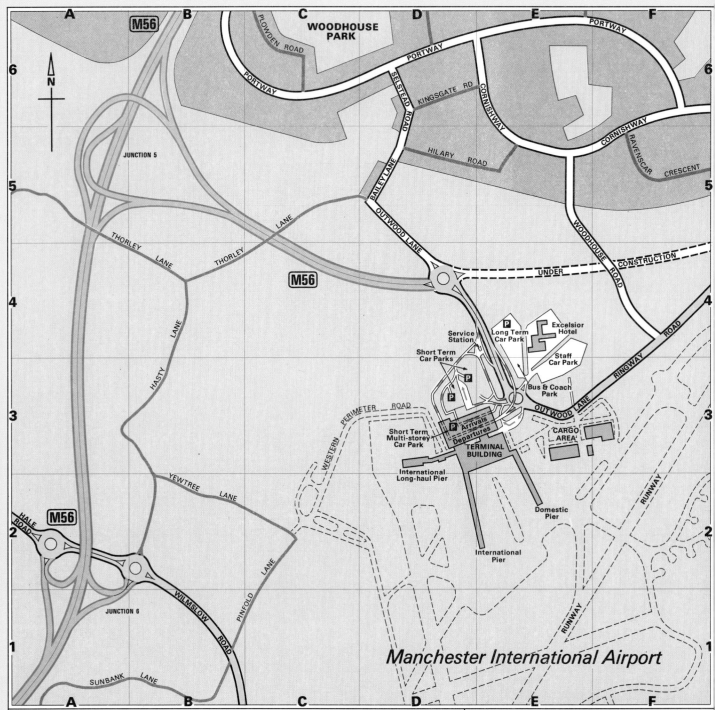

Manchester International Airport

Manchester International Airport

Nine miles south of the city of Manchester lies Manchester International Airport, operating flights to and from the Midlands, the north west, north east, Yorkshire and Wales. As well as flights within Britain, there are regular scheduled services operating to all the major business centres in Europe, the Far East and Australia. Charter and inclusive tour flights also operate from here to destinations world-wide.

The airport has been in use since just before World War II, and enjoys the distinction that its main buildings were opened by HRH Prince Philip. This was not until 1962, when the Prince became the first pilot to park an aircraft alongside the arrivals pier, and the first passenger to use the airport's facilities.

Today Manchester International has a spacious concourse area on the first floor of the terminal.

A bank, post office, bookstall, tobacconist and pharmacy are situated here. At the apron end of the concourse (and lying adjacent to the observation windows) is the Concourse Cafe, a self-service restaurant and bar. Also offering refreshments for travellers and other visitors to the airport is the 200-seat Lancaster restaurant and cocktail lounge, which overlooks International Pier B, and within just two minutes walk the Excelsior Hotel offers 300 bedrooms, a restaurant, a coffee shop and a bar.

The airport is well placed for passengers coming here by both road and rail. It offers easy access to the M56 and to the national motorway network. Greater Manchester Transport buses link the airport to Manchester and to Stockport all the year round, and also make a link to most towns in Greater Manchester during the summer months. Coach services also run to Birmingham, Liverpool, Lancaster, Leeds and Sheffield.

For railway travellers, the nearest station to the airport is Heald Green, which is about two miles away and has two bus services. Frequent trains go to Manchester (Piccadilly) and to Crewe.

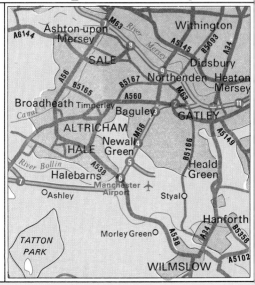